THE VECTOR ANALYSIS PROBLEM SOLVER®

REGISTERED TRADEMARK

Staff of Research and Education Association
Dr. Emil G. Milewski, Chief Editor

Research and Education Association
61 Ethel Road West
Piscataway, New Jersey 08854

THE VECTOR ANALYSIS
PROBLEM SOLVER ®

Printed in the United States of America

Library of Congress Catalog Card Number 94-67820

International Standard Book Number 0-87891-554-0

PROBLEM SOLVER is a registered trademark of
Research and Education Association, Piscataway, New Jersey

WHAT THIS BOOK IS FOR

Students have found vector analysis a difficult subject to understand and learn. Despite the publication of hundreds of textbooks in this field, each one intended to provide an improvement over previous textbooks, students continue to remain perplexed as a result of the numerous conditions that must often be remembered and correlated in solving a problem. Various possible interpretations of terms used in vector analysis have also contributed to much of the difficulties experienced by students.

In a study of the problem, REA found the following basic reasons underlying students' difficulties with vector analysis taught in schools:

(a) No systematic rules of analysis have been developed which students may follow in a step-by-step manner to solve the usual problems encountered. This results from the fact that the numerous different conditions and principles which may be involved in a problem, lead to many possible different methods of solution. To prescribe a set of rules to be followed for each of the possible variations, would involve an enormous number of rules and steps to be searched through by students, and this task would perhaps be more burdensome than solving the problem directly with some accompanying trial and error to find the correct solution route.

(b) Textbooks currently available will usually explain a given principle in a few pages written by a professional who has an insight in the subject matter that is not shared by students. The explanations are often written in an abstract manner which leaves the students confused as to the application of the principle. The explanations given are not sufficiently detailed and extensive to make the student aware of the wide range of applications and different aspects of the principle being studied. The numerous possible variations of principles and their applications are usually not discussed, and it is left for the students to discover these for themselves while doing exercises. Accordingly, the average student is expected to rediscover that which has been long known and practiced, but not published or explained extensively.

(c) The examples usually following the explanation of a topic are too few in number and too simple to enable the student to obtain a thorough grasp of the principles involved. The explanations do not provide sufficient basis to enable a student to solve problems that may be subsequently assigned for homework or given on examinations.

The examples are presented in abbreviated form which leaves out much material between steps, and requires that students derive the omitted material themselves. As a result, students find the examples difficult to understand--contrary to the purpose of the examples.

Examples are, furthermore, often worded in a confusing manner. They do not state the problem and then present the solution. Instead, they pass through a general discussion, never revealing what is to be solved for.

Examples, also, do not always include diagrams/graphs, wherever appropriate, and students do not obtain the training to draw diagrams or graphs to simplify and organize their thinking.

(d) Students can learn the subject only by doing the exercises themselves and reviewing them in class, to obtain experience in applying the principles with their different ramifications.

In doing the exercises by themselves, students find that they are required to devote considerably more time to vector analysis than to other subjects of comparable credits, because they are uncertain with regard to the selection and application of the theorems and principles involved. It is also often necessary for students to discover those "tricks" not revealed in their texts (or review books), that make it possible to solve problems easily. Students must usually resort to methods of trial-and-error to discover these "tricks", and as a result they find that they may sometimes spend several hours in solving a single problem.

(e) When reviewing the exercises in classrooms, instructors usually request students to take turns in writing solutions on the boards and explaining them to the class. Students often find it difficult to explain in a manner that holds the interest of the class, and enables the remaining students to follow the material written on the boards. The remaining students seated in the class are, furthermore, too occupied with copying the material from the boards, to listen to the oral explanations and concentrate on the methods of solution.

This book is intended to aid students in vector analysis in overcoming the difficulties described, by supplying detailed illustrations of the solution methods which are usually not apparent to students. The solution methods are illustrated by problems selected from those that are most often assigned for class work and given on examinations. The problems are arranged in order of complexity to enable students to learn and understand a particular topic by reviewing the problems in sequence. The problems are illustrated with detailed step-by-step explanations, to save students the large amount of time that is often needed to fill in the gaps that are usually found between steps of illustrations in textbooks or review/outline books.

The staff of REA considers vector analysis a subject that is best learned by allowing students to view the methods of analysis and solution techniques themselves. This approach to learning the subject matter is similar to that practiced in various scientific laboratories, particularly in the medical fields.

In using this book, students may review and study the illustrated problems at their own pace; they are not limited to the time allowed for explaining problems on the board in class.

When students want to look up a particular type of problem and solution, they can readily locate it in the book by referring to the index which has been extensively prepared. It is also possible to locate a particular type of problem by glancing at just the material within the boxed portions. To facilitate rapid scanning of the problems, each problem has a heavy border around it. Furthermore, each problem is identified with a number immediately above the problem at the right-hand margin.

To obtain maximum benefit from the book, students should familiarize themselves with the section, "How To Use This Book," located in the front pages.

To meet the objectives of this book, problems were selected on the basis of what is usually encountered in assignments and examinations. Each problem was solved meticulously to illustrate the steps which are usually difficult for students to comprehend. Gratitude for his work in this area is due to Dr. Emil G. Milewski, Chief Editor. Orlando Perez deserves special praise for his conscientious efforts and often imaginative contributions which resulted in a comprehensive and clearly understandable manuscript.

Gratitude is also expressed to the many persons involved in the difficult task of typing the manuscript with its endless changes, and to the REA art staff who prepared the numerous detailed illustrations together with the layout and physical features of the book.

The difficult task of coordinating the efforts of all persons was carried out by Carl Fuchs. His conscientious work deserves much appreciation. He also trained and supervised art and production personnel in the preparation of the book for printing.

Finally, special thanks are due to Helen Kaufmann for her unique talents to render those difficult border-line decisions and constructive suggestions related to the design and organization of the book.

Max Fogiel, Ph.D.
Program Director

HOW TO USE THIS BOOK

This book can be an invaluable aid to students in vector anaylsis as a supplement to their textbooks. The book is subdivided into 23 chapters, each dealing with a separate topic. The subject matter is developed beginning with vectors and scalars, linear dependence, derivatives of vectors, differential geometry and calculus, gradient, divergence and extending through linear algebra, tensor notation, applications in physics, ordinary, double, surface, and volume integrals. Also included are problems in cylindrical, spherical, and curvilinear coordinates, theorems of Green and Stokes, and divergence theorem. An extensive number of applications have been included, since these appear to be more troublesome to students.

TO LEARN AND UNDERSTAND A TOPIC THOROUGHLY

1. Refer to your class text and read the section pertaining to the topic. You should become acquainted with the principles discussed there. These principles, however, may not be clear to you at that time.

2. Then locate the topic you are looking for by referring to the "Table of Contents" in front of this book, "The Vector Analysis Problem Solver."

3. Turn to the page where the topic begins and review the problems under each topic, in the order given. For each topic, the problems are arranged in order of complexity, from the simplest to the more difficult. Some problems may appear similar to others, but each problem has been selected to illustrate a different point or solution method.

To learn and understand a topic thoroughly and retain its contents, it will be generally necessary for students to review the problems several times. Repeated review is essential in order to gain experience in recognizing the principles that should be applied, and in selecting the best solution technique.

TO FIND A PARTICULAR PROBLEM

To locate one or more problems related to a particular subject matter, refer to the index. In using the index, be certain to note that the numbers given there refer to problem numbers, not page numbers. This arrangement of the index is intended to facilitate finding a problem more rapidily, since two or more problems may appear on a page.

If a particular type of problem cannot be found readily, it is recommended that the student refer to the "Table of Contents" in the front pages, and then turn to the chapter which is applicable to the problem being sought. By scanning or glancing at the material that is boxed, it will generally be possible to find problems related to the one being sought, without consuming considerable time. After the problems have been located, the solutions can be reviewed and studied in detail. For this purpose of locating problems rapidly, students should acquaint themselves with the organization of the book as found in the "Table of Contents".

In preparing for an exam, locate the topics to be covered on the exam in the "Table of Contents," and then review the problems under those topics several times. This should equip the student with what might be needed for the exam.

This "Problem Solver" book in vector analysis can be used as a textbook without any other instructional aid. The book has been written and organized to include all the definitions and theorems that are necessary for complete courses in vector analysis. After studying basic algebra and calculus, a student can learn vector analysis from this book alone.

CONTENTS

Chapter No.   **Page No.**

1 VECTORS AND SCALARS   1

  Basic Definitions; Graphical and Component
  Representation of Vectors   2
  Graphical Operations and Scalar Multiplication   10
  Analytical Operations on Vectors   21
  Applications in Geometry and Physics   26

**2 MAGNITUDE, LINEAR DEPENDENCE AND
BASE VECTORS**   34

  Magnitude of a Vector   36
  Applications in Geometry and Physics   42
  Linear Combination, Linear Dependence of
  Vectors   46
  Representation of Vectors in Terms of Base
  Vectors   55

**3 THE SCALAR PRODUCT AND THE VECTOR
PRODUCT**   64

  Definitions and Properties of the Scalar Product   66
  Applications in Geometry and Physics   71

ix

Geometrical Definition of Vector Product   81
Component Definition of Vector Product   85
Scalar Triple Product and Vector Triple Product   92
Identities and Reciprocal Vectors   97
Vectors Equations of Lines, Planes, Spheres and the
Moment of a Vector   102

4   ORDINARY DERIVATIVES OF VECTORS   112

Vector Functions and Parametric Equations of a
Curve   113
Limits, Continuity and the Derivative of a Vector
Function   121
Graphical Representation of the Derivative, Tangent
Vector and Basic Properties   132
Vector Solutions to Differential Equations   141

5   APPLICATIONS OF ORDINARY DERIVATIVES OF VECTORS IN DIFFERENTIAL GEOMETRY AND MECHANICS   146

Space Curves, Frenet Formulas, Characteristic
Vectors and Plane Curves   147
Identities Involving Characteristic Vectors   171
Position Vector, Velocity, Angular Velocity and
Acceleration   177
Tangential and Normal Components of
Acceleration   188
Newton's Laws, Moment Vector, Angular Momentum
and Center of Mass   195
Trajectories and Collisions of Particles   205
Rigid Body Mechanics, Coordinate Systems and
Inertial Systems   210

6   DIFFERENTIAL CALCULUS OF FUNCTIONS OF SEVERAL VARIABLES   220

Continuous Functions, Partial Derivatives and Total
Differential   222
Derivatives and Differentials of Composite Functions,
Scalar Fields and Vector Fields   233

Gradient of a Scalar Field   244
Properties of the Gradient Operator   247
Tangent Plane, Directional Derivative and Laplacian
Operator   252

7 PARTIAL DIFFERENTIATION OF VECTORS, GRADIENT AND DIVERGENCE   268

Partial Differentiation of Vectors   269
Gradient of a Scalar Field and Functionally Related
Functions   282
The Divergence and Laplacian Operators   290
Identities Involving Gradient and Divergence,
Solenoidal Vectors   297

8 CURL OF A VECTOR FIELD   308

Definition, Properties and Identities of the Curl
Operator   309
Irrotational (Conservative) Vector Fields, Solenoidal
Vector Fields   319
Laplacian Operator and Combined Operations   326
Complex Indentities Involving Curl, Divergence, and
Gradient Operators   332
Scalar Potential, Other Differential Operators and
Dyadics   341

9 ELEMENTS OF LINEAR ALGEBRA   356

Mappings, Binary Operations, Groves, Rings and
Fields   358
Vector Spaces and Span Sets   364
Position Vectors, Transformations, Invariants,
Linear Combinations and Rotation   373
Linear Transformations   385
Linearly Independent Vectors and The Fundamental
Theorem of Linear Algebra   401
Transformation of Cartesian Coordinate Systems,
Determinants and Inverse Transformations   405

10 TENSOR NOTATION   413

Systems of Order Zero, One, Two ....., Kronecker
Delta and Summation Convention   415
Basic Operations and Contraction of Systems,
Symmetric and Sken-Symmetric Systems,
e-System   420
Determinants, Cofactors, Systems of Linear Equations
and Quadratic Forms   428
Scalar and Vector Product, Differentiation, Gradient,
Divergence, Rotation and The Laplacian in Tensor
Notation   435

11 APPLICATIONS OF GRADIENT, DIVERGENCE AND CURL IN PHYSICS   445

Graphical Representation of Vector Fields   445
Gravitation, Harmonic Functions, Reflection of Light,
Ridgid Body Rotation, Surface Tension and
Elasticity   450
Concepts in Fluid Dynamics   461
Concepts in Heat Flow   481
Concepts in Electromagnetics, Maxwell's
Equations   485

12 ORDINARY INTEGRALS OF VECTORS AND LINE INTEGRALS   504

Ordinary Vector Integration, Integral of Scalar and
Vector Product of Vectors   506
Kinematics, Central Force, Angular Momentum,
Aerial Velocity and Kepler's Laws   512
Parametric Representation, Orientation and Length
of Curves   520
Line Integrals, Work Done in a Force Field   527
Integration of Tangential and Normal Components of
a Vector, Kinetic and Potential Energy, Regions and
Domains   546
Conservative Vector Fields, Scalar Potential   554
Curl of a Conservative Field   562
Exact Differentials, Particle in the Conservative
Field and Vector Potential   572

13 DOUBLE INTEGRALS   582

Smooth Surfaces, Orientation and Vectors Normal to
a Surface   583
Definition of Double Integral, Iterated Integrals   593
Double Integrals Representing Area   606
Double Integrals Representing Volume   612
Center of Mass and Moments of Inertia   616
Transformation of Coordinates   628

14 SURFACE INTEGRALS OF VECTORS, FLUX   635

Surfaces, Unit Normal Vector, and Parametric
Representation of a Surface   636
Surfaces Given by $Z=f(x,y)$ 645
Flux of a Vector Field   657
Special Cases of Vector Integration, Cartesian Form
of Surface Integrals   675

15 SURFACE INTEGRALS AND FLUX
IN PHYSICAL APPLICATIONS   683

Flux of a Fluid Flow   683
Heat Flow   687
Electric Field, Gauss' Law and Electrostatic
Potential   694

16 VOLUME INTEGRALS   704

Definition of Triple Integral, Riemann Sums, Iterated
Integrals   705
Volume of a Region   716
Triple Integration in Cylindrical and Spherical
Coordinates   723
Multiple Integrals, Mass and Density, Center of
Gravity   732
Moment of Inertia   737
Volume Integrals of Vectors, Surface and Volume
Integral Relationship, Gauss' Law and Electrostatic
Potential   746

17 GREEN'S THEOREM IN THE PLANE 758

Green's Theorem, Applications and Verification of
Green's Theorem   759
Area Bounded by a Closed Curve, Polar
Coordinates   777
Green's Theorem (Extended Version)   786
Green's Theorem for Multiply-Connected Regions and
its Applications   790
Green's Theorem in Vector Notation   802
Applications in Physics-Force Field, Flow,
Circulation and Gauss' Theorem   806
Cauchy-Riemann Equations, Line Integrals
Independent of Path   815
Transformation of Coordinates   825

18 CONSERVATIVE VECTOR FIELDS 828

19 DIVERGENCE THEOREM 854

Divergence Theorem, Basic Applications   855
Verification of the Divergence Theorem   869
Basic Applications of the Divergence Theorem   876
Basic Identities, Green's First and Second
Identities   883
Applications of Green's Identities, Harmonic
Functions   888
Further Applications of the Divergence Theorem   895
Definition of Divergence, Gradient and Rotation   899
Gauss' Theorem, Solid Angle, Divergence of
n-dimensional Space   904

20 STOKES' THEOREM 945

Del Operator, Rotation of a Vector Function   946
Stokes' Theorem, Proof of Stokes' Theorem   949
Applications of Stokes' Theorem   965
Basic Identities Involving Stokes' Theorem, Further
Applications   979
Stokes' Theorem for Surfaces Given in Parametric
Form   992
Another Definition of Rotation, Further

Applications   996
Applications in Electromagnetics   1003
Irrotational Fields   1006
Solenidal Fields   1011

21 CYLINDRICAL AND SPHERICAL COORDINATES 1015

Polar Coordinates   1016
Coordinate Surfaces and Curves, Orthogonal
Systems   1020
The Unit Tangent Vectors of the Cylindrical
Coordinate System   1026
Element of Arc Length, Volume Element and Scale
Factors of the Cylindrical and Spherical Coordinate
Systems   1031
The Unit Tangent Vectors of the Spherical
Coordinate System   1040
Volume Element in Spherical, Cylindrical and
Curvilinear Coordinates   1048
The Gradient, Divergence, Curl, Laplacian and
Jacobian in Cylindrical and Spherical
Coordinates   1057

22 CURVILINEAR COORDINATES 1088

Coordinate Surfaces, Coordinate Curves, Orthogonal
Coordinate Systems   1089
Unit Tangent Vectors and Scale Factors   1093
Element of Arc Length, Volume Element   1099
The Gradient Divergence, Curl and Laplacian in
Orthogonal Coordinates   1102
Some Types of Orthogonal Coordinate Systems   1110
Transformation of Coordinates-Orthogonal
Coordinate Systems   1116
Contravariant and Covariant Components of a
Vector, Metric Coefficients and the Jacobian of a
Transformation   1127

23 ADVANCED TOPICS 1142

MATRIX METHODS IN VECTOR ANALYSIS 1142

LINEAR ORTHOGONAL TRANSFORMATIONS   1179

Transformation Matrix, Rotation, Orthogonal
Transformation   1179
Transformation of Scalar and Vector Fields,
Transformation of grad f, div $\bar{F}$ and Properties
of curl $\bar{F}$ 1184

TRANSPORT THEOREM   1191

Flux Through a Moving Surface   1191
Flux Transport Theorem   1193
Reynold's Transport Theorem, Euler's Expansion
Formula   1203

DIFFERENTIAL FORMS   1207

Differential One-form, Exterior Product   1207
Differential Two-form, Differential p-forms, Addition
and Multiplication of Forms   1211
Properties of p-forms, Integrals of One-forms and
p-forms   1219

EXTERIOR DERIVATIVE   1228

Exterior Differentiation, Basic Identities,
Conservative and Solenoidal Fields   1228
Green's Theorem, Stokes' Theorem, Divergence
Theorem, Exact Differential Forms   1236

APPENDIX   1242

INDEX   1252

CHAPTER 1

VECTORS AND SCALARS

INTRODUCTION

The definitions and basic properties of vectors and scalars are introduced in this chapter. It is of the utmost importance for the student to visualize and clearly understand the difference between a scalar quantity and a vector quantity.

When we discuss temperature, time, length, or energy, one number gives us all the information necessary. "The temperature is now 85F" is a statement which depicts precisely how hot the day is at the moment. These quantities which can be fully described by one number are called scalars.

The situation becomes more difficult when we discuss velocity, acceleration, or force. "The wind is blowing at 50 mph" is an insufficient statement. It is necessary to know not only the strength of the wind, but the direction as well. For instance, the statement "The wind is blowing north-easterly at 50 mph" contains all the necessary information needed to describe the wind. These quantities which have magnitude and direction are called vectors.

With a few exceptions, the right hand cartesian coordinate system will be employed throughout the book. Its advantages will be discussed in the future; the component and graphical representation of vectors is also introduced in this chapter. They both yield equivalent expressions. Using these two representations of vectors, basic operations such as addition, subtraction and multiplication of vectors by scalars are introduced. The fundamental laws of addition and subtraction are proven for both the graphical and component representation of vectors.

Certain problems at the end of the chapter concern the applications of vector calculus to physics and geometry. Throughout the book we will attempt to show how the use of vector analysis simplifies and clarifies otherwise complicated problems in physics and mathematics.

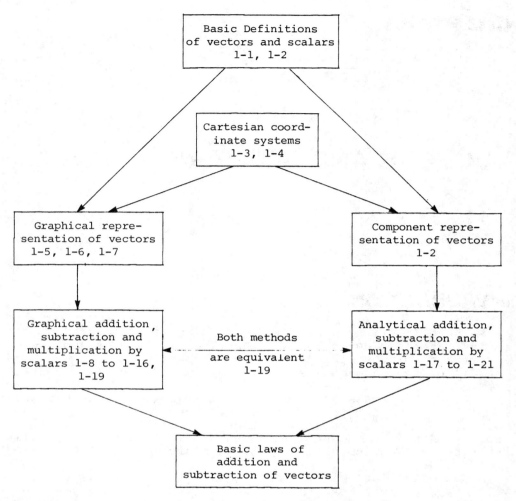

This chart is provided to facilitate rapid understanding of the inter-
relationships of the topics and subject matter in this chapter. Also
shown are the problem numbers associated with the subject matter.

BASIC DEFINITIONS, GRAPHICAL AND COMPONENT REPRESENTATION OF VECTORS

● **PROBLEM** 1-1

1) Give three examples of a scalar quantity and a vector
   quantity.

2) Which of the following are scalars and which are vectors?

   a) time   e) entropy
   b) magnetic field intensity   f) acceleration
   c) force   g) gravitational coefficient
   d) volume

Solution: 1) A scalar is a quantity which has magnitude only and no direction. Common examples of scalars are mass, temperature and area. A scalar may be sufficiently represented by any real number with an appropriate sign (this number indicates the magnitude, in some convenient scale, of the quantity). For example, mass may be denoted by

5 grams, 2 pounds, 3 kilograms, and temperature by

$27\,^0C$, $-15\,^0F$, $4125K$,

where C, F and K represent the Celcius, Fahrenheit, and Kelvin scales respectively.

Unlike a scalar quantity, a vector quantity possesses both magnitude and direction. Common examples of vectors are:

Electric field intensity, velocity and momentum.

A vector in one-, two- or three-dimensional space can be represented by an arrow; the length of the arrow indicates the magnitude of the vector while the direction indicates the direction of the vector.

2) By virtue of the above definitions, we conclude that:

time is a scalar
magnetic field intensity is a vector
force is a vector
volume is a scalar
entropy is a scalar
acceleration is a vector
gravitational coefficient is a scalar

Note that the quantity speed is a scalar, while velocity is a vector. Indeed, when we speak of the speed of a particle, say

$15\,\frac{m}{sec}$, we are solely concerned with the numerical value

(15 m/sec) and not with the direction of the motion. On the other hand, when considering the velocity of a particle, it is necessary to give both the speed and direction of the motion (eg. 15 m/sec, northeast).

● PROBLEM 1-2

Determine the dimension of the following vectors:

$\bar{a} = (1,\ 2)$

$\bar{b} = (0,\ 4)$

$\bar{c} = (1,\ 5,\ -6,\ \sqrt{2},\ 4)$

$\bar{d} = (3,\ 7,\ 4+\alpha)$

<u>Solution</u>: In this book, vectors will be indicated by a letter with a bar over it, as in $\bar{a}$. We will often denote a vector with a letter indicating its orig<u>in</u> followed by a letter indicating its terminal point, as in $\overline{AB}$.

You may find in other books other notations commonly used, such as bold faced type, or component notation, as in (a_i) or (x_α), where i and α indicate the dimension of the vector. The last notation is often used in elasticity and special and general theory of relativity; in the former the vectors are three-dimensional while in the latter they are four-dimensional.

The dimension of a vector is equal to the number of its components. Thus,

Vector $\bar{a}$ = (1,2) has two components and is two-dimensional.

Vector $\bar{b}$ = (0,4) is two-dimensional.

Vector $\bar{c}$ has five components and is therefore five-dimensional.

Vector $\bar{d}$ is three-dimensional.

● **PROBLEM 1-3**

Describe the relationship between the three-dimensional Euclidean space (or one- or two-dimensional subspace) and a coordinate system. How does one construct a rectangular cartesian coordinate system?

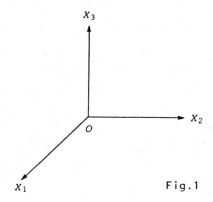

Fig.1

<u>Solution</u>: We will use the concepts of point, line, plane, and space without definition. These concepts are based on our everyday life experience. David Hilbert described this axiomatic approach to geometry in his <u>Grundlagen der Geometrie</u>, <u>1900</u>.

The fact that we live in a three-dimensional Euclidean space is an axiom and we don't have to prove it. A coordinate system establishes one-to-one correspondence between the triples of real numbers and the points of a three-dimensional

Euclidean space. It is possible to establish many different (as a matter of fact, infinitely many) coordinate systems. The most common and the simplest is the rectangular cartesian coordinate system, shown in Fig. 1.

A rectangular cartesian coordinate system consists of three concurrent and mutually perpendicular lines called axes, which are denoted x_1, x_2, x_3. The points of each axis correspond to the elements of the set of all real numbers. This is called a one-to-one correspondence. To each point of the three-dimensional space there corresponds an ordered triple of real numbers (x_1, x_2, x_3), and conversely, for every ordered triple of real numbers there exists a point. The numbers are often denoted by (x,y,z).

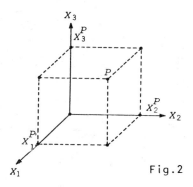

Fig.2

As shown in Fig. 2, to point P there corresponds a triple (x_1^P, x_2^P, x_3^P) of real numbers called coordinates of P. Conversely, to the triple of real numbers (x_1^P, x_2^P, x_3^P) there corresponds point P, which is uniquely defined by this triple.

The coordinate system enables us to establish the "geography" of the space.

● PROBLEM 1-4

Figure 1 shows four rectangular Cartesian coordinate systems. Determine which ones are right-handed and which are left-handed.

Solution: Consider a triangle determined by the points
A:(1,0,0)   B:(0,1,0)   C:(0,0,1)

as shown in Figure 2. If, as observed from the origin (0,0,0) the triangle orientation A→B→C is clockwise, then the associated rectangular cartesian coordinate system is right-handed. If the orientation A→B→C is counterclockwise, the coordinate system is left-handed. Throughout this book we will be using the right-handed coordinate system.

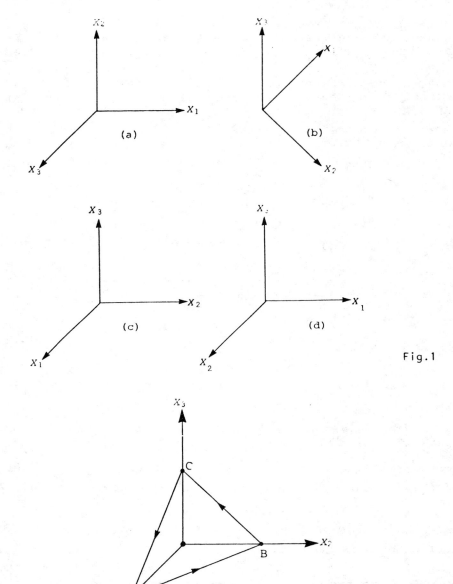

(a)

(b)

(c)

(d)

Fig.1

Fig. 2

We can now determine the orientation of the systems:
a) right-handed
b) left-handed
c) right-handed
c) left-handed

Represent graphically the following vectors

$\bar{a} = (2, 1)$

$\bar{b} = (0, 6)$

$\bar{c} = (-2, -4)$

$\bar{d} = (3, 2, 7)$

$\bar{e} = (2, -4, 3)$

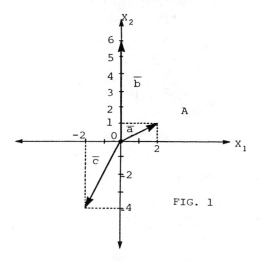

FIG. 1

Solution: The first three vectors are two-dimensional. They can be represented in the two-dimensional cartesian coordinate system.

Vector $\bar{a}$ has two coordinates, the first is equal to 2, $x_1 = 2$, the second is equal to 1, $x_2 = 1$. In the system shown in Fig. 1, mark point 2 on the x_1 axis and point 1 on the x_2 axis.

Next, draw a rectangle, whose diagonal $\overline{OA}$ represents vector $\bar{a}$. In the same manner, find the graphic representation of vectors $\bar{b}$ and $\bar{c}$. Note that the x_1 component of vector $\bar{b}$ is zero, thus $\bar{b}$ is located on the x_2 axis.

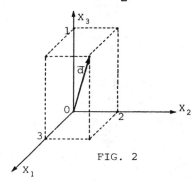

FIG. 2

Vectors $\bar{d}$ and $\bar{e}$ are three-dimensional. To represent them graphically, use the three-dimensional right-handed rectangular cartesian coordinate system shown in Fig. 2.

The components of vector $\bar{d}=(3,2,7)$ are 3, 2 and 7. Mark point 3 on the x_1-axis, point 2 on the x_2-axis and point 7 on the x_3-axis. Then build a rectangular parallelepiped whose edges have lengths 3, 2 and 7 respectively. The diagonal of this parallelepiped represents vector $\bar{d}$.

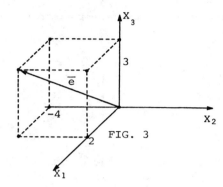

FIG. 3

Fig. 3 shows the graphical representation of vector $\bar{e}$.

Note that vectors which are one-, two- and three-dimensional can be represented graphically. Vectors of dimension four, five or higher, cannot be represented graphically in the manner shown above.

● **PROBLEM 1-6**

Represent graphically

1)   a car travelling 20 $\frac{km}{h}$ in a direction 20° east of north

2)   a speedboat moving 150 $\frac{km}{h}$ in a direction 30° east of south

3)   a force of 15 kg in the west direction

4)   a force of 25 kg in a direction 15° north of east.

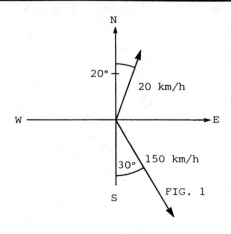

FIG. 1

Solution: A rectangular system of coordinates, as shown in Fig. 1, will be used. The directions north, east, south, and west are as indicated.

In examples 1 and 2, a unit of length represents 10 $\frac{km}{h}$.

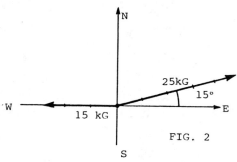

FIG. 2

In examples 3 and 4, a unit of length represents 5kg. Both vectors are shown in Fig. 2.

● **PROBLEM 1-7**

A car travels 5 miles due north, then 7 miles due northwest. Represent both displacements graphically. Determine the final position of the car

1) graphically
2) analytically

Assume that the car starts its journey from the origin of the system.

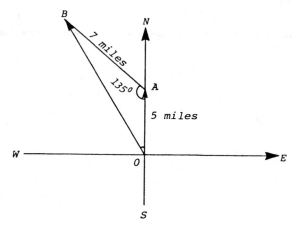

Solution: First represent both displacements graphically as shown in the figure. Vector $\overline{OA}$ represents displacement of 5 miles north. One unit of length is equal to 1 mile. After this part of the trip, the car is located at point A.

Vector $\overline{AB}$ represents a displacement of 7 miles northwest,

9

point B. The vector OB represents the total displacement of the car, therefore

$$\overline{OB} = \overline{OA} + \overline{AB} \qquad (1)$$

This equation represents the triangle law of vector addition.

1) Since each unit of the diagram represents 1 mile, the magnitude of OB is approximately 11 miles.

   The angle ∢ AOB is found to be approximately 26^0

2) To determine analytically the position of the car, apply the law of cosines to the triangle OAB.

$$OB^2 = OA^2 + AB^2 - 2 \cdot OA \cdot AB \ \cos \ ∢ \ OAB \qquad (2)$$

Substituting numerical values

$$OA = 5, \quad AB = 7, \quad ∢OAB = 135^0 \qquad (3)$$

then

$$OB = \sqrt{5^2 + 7^2 - 2 \cdot 5 \cdot 7 \cdot \cos \ 135^0} = 11.11 \ miles \qquad (4)$$

To find the direction, apply the law of sines

$$\frac{AB}{\sin \ ∢AOB} = \frac{OB}{\sin \ 135^0} \qquad (5)$$

thus

$$\sin \ ∢AOB = \frac{AB}{OB} \ \sin \ 135^0 = \frac{7}{11.11} \cdot 0.707 = 0.4455 \qquad (6)$$

$$∢AOB = 26.45^0 \qquad (7)$$

Thus vector $\overline{OB}$ has magnitude 11.11 miles and direction 26.45^0 west of north.

GRAPHICAL OPERATIONS AND SCALAR MULTIPLICATION

● PROBLEM 1-8

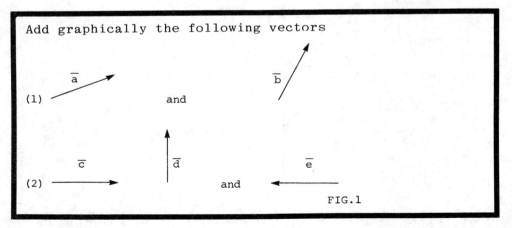

Add graphically the following vectors

(1) $\overline{a}$ and $\overline{b}$

(2) $\overline{c}$ and $\overline{d}$ and $\overline{e}$

FIG.1

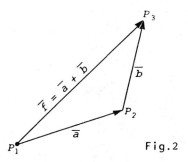

Fig.2

Solution: 1) To find the sum of the vectors $\overline{a}$ and $\overline{b}$, use the following construction. Choose an initial point P_1 and construct $\overline{P_1P_2} = \overline{a}$ and $\overline{P_2P_3} = \overline{b}$. Note that the terminal point of $\overline{a}$ is the initial point of $\overline{b}$. The sum of the vectors $\overline{a}$ and $\overline{b}$ is vector $\overline{c} = \overline{P_1P_3}$ shown in Fig. 2.

Then, $\overline{a} + \overline{b} = \overline{f}$

or $\quad \overline{P_1P_2} + \overline{P_2P_3} = \overline{P_1P_3}$ $\hspace{3cm}$ (1)

It should be noted that the addition of $\overline{a} + \overline{b}$ as defined above is independent of the choice of the initial point P_1.

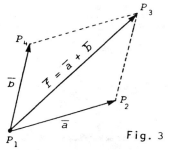

Fig. 3

Another method of finding the sum $\overline{a} + \overline{b}$ is the parallelogram method. Choose an initial point P_1 and construct $\overline{P_1P_2} = \overline{a}$ and $\overline{P_1P_4} = \overline{b}$ as shown in Fig. 3.

Next, construct the parallelogram $P_1P_2P_3P_4$, whose diagonal $\overline{P_1P_3}$ is the sum of vectors $\overline{a}$ and $\overline{b}$. Therefore

$$\overline{a} + \overline{b} = \overline{f}$$
$$\overline{P_1P_2} + \overline{P_1P_4} = \overline{P_1P_3}$$ $\hspace{3cm}$ (2)

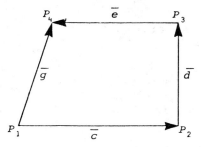

Fig. 4

2) Choose the initial point P_1 and construct $\overline{c} = \overline{P_1P_2}$, then $\overline{d} = \overline{P_2P_3}$ and $\overline{e} = \overline{P_3P_4}$. The sum of the vectors $\overline{c}$, $\overline{d}$, and $\overline{e}$ is vector $\overline{g} = \overline{P_1P_4}$, shown in Fig. 4.

Then, $\overline{g} = \overline{c} + \overline{d} + \overline{e}$ (3)

or $\overline{P_1P_4} = \overline{P_1P_2} + \overline{P_2P_3} + \overline{P_3P_4}$ (4)

$$\overline{a} \qquad \overline{b} \qquad \overline{a} = \overline{b}$$

FIG. 5

One should remember that two vectors $\overline{a}$ and $\overline{b}$ are equal ($\overline{a} = \overline{b}$) if they have the same magnitude (length) and direction regardless of the position of their initial points. The vectors $\overline{a}$ and $\overline{b}$ in Fig. 5 are equal.

● **PROBLEM 1-9**

Construct graphically the following vectors:

1) $\overline{a} - \overline{b}$

2) $\overline{d} + \overline{e} - \overline{f}$

where vectors $\overline{a}$, $\overline{b}$, $\overline{d}$, $\overline{e}$, $\overline{f}$ are

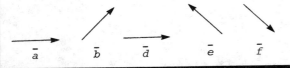

$\overline{a}$ $\overline{b}$ $\overline{d}$ $\overline{e}$ $\overline{f}$

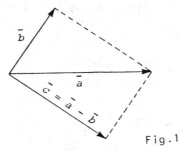

Fig.1

Solution: 1) To find vector $\overline{c}$ such that $\overline{c} = \overline{a} - \overline{b}$ use the following construction. First draw vectors $\overline{a}$ and $\overline{b}$ as shown in Fig. 1.

Since $\overline{c} = \overline{a} - \overline{b}$, then $\overline{c} + \overline{b} = \overline{a}$. In Fig.1, $\overline{a}$ is the sum of the two vectors $\overline{b}$ and $\overline{c}$. Constructing the parallelogram whose diagonal is $\overline{a}$ and one of the edges is $\overline{b}$, find the other edge $\overline{c}$ such that

$$\overline{c} = \overline{a} - \overline{b}$$

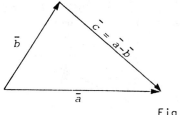

Fig.2

A shorter method is to draw the vectors $\bar{a}$ and $\bar{b}$ as shown in Fig. 2.

Then draw a vector $\bar{c}$ from the terminal point of $\bar{b}$ to the terminal point of $\bar{a}$, then

$$\bar{c} = \bar{a} - \bar{b}$$

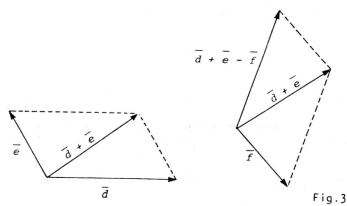

Fig.3

2) The construction of vector $\bar{d} + \bar{e} - \bar{f}$ is shown in Fig. 3. First, find the sum of vectors $\bar{d}$ and $\bar{e}$, then having vectors $\bar{d} + \bar{e}$ and $\bar{f}$, construct the vector $\bar{d} + \bar{e} - \bar{f}$.

Consider vector $\bar{a}$ as shown.

Multiplying $\bar{a}$ by the following scalars $\alpha = 2$, $\beta = \frac{1}{2}$ and $\gamma = -3$, gives

$$\alpha\bar{a} = 2\bar{a}$$
$$\beta\bar{a} = \tfrac{1}{2}\bar{a}$$
$$\gamma\bar{a} = -3\bar{a}$$

It is desired to sketch each of these three vectors $2\bar{a}$, $\frac{1}{2}\bar{a}$ and $-3\bar{a}$. To draw the vector $2\bar{a}$, draw a vector which has the same direction as $\bar{a}$, is parallel to $\bar{a}$ and has twice the length of $\bar{a}$.

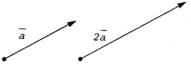

The vector $\beta\bar{a} = \frac{1}{2}\bar{a}$ is drawn in the same manner. It is parallel to $\bar{a}$ and has the same direction as $\bar{a}$. The length of $\beta\bar{a}$ is half the length of $\bar{a}$.

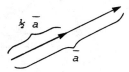

Finally, the vector $\gamma\bar{a} = -3\bar{a}$, is parallel to $\bar{a}$, but in the opposite direction, since $\gamma = -3$ is a negative number. The length of $-3\bar{a}$ is three times the length of $\bar{a}$.

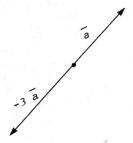

● **PROBLEM** 1-10

Prove the following laws of addition and subtraction of vectors:

1) $\bar{a} + \bar{b} = \bar{b} + \bar{a}$ commutative law
2) $\bar{a}+(\bar{b}+\bar{c}) = (\bar{a}+\bar{b})+\bar{c}$ associative law
3) $\bar{a} + \bar{b} = \bar{c}$ if and only if $\bar{b} = \bar{c} - \bar{a}$
4) $\bar{a} + \bar{0} = \bar{a}$, $\bar{a} - \bar{a} = \bar{0}$

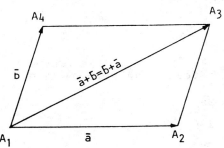

Fig. 1

Solution: 1) Construct the parallelogram $A_1A_2A_3A_4$ where $\overline{A_1A_2} = \bar{a}$ and $\overline{A_1A_4} = \bar{b}$ as shown in Fig. 1.

Since $\overline{A_1A_2} = \overline{A_4A_3} = \bar{a}$ $\qquad\qquad\qquad\qquad\qquad$ (1)

and $\overline{A_1A_4} = \overline{A_2A_3} = \bar{b}$ $\qquad\qquad\qquad\qquad\qquad$ (2)

14

it follows immediately from Fig. 1 that

$$\bar{a} + \bar{b} = \bar{b} + \bar{a} \qquad (3)$$

2) Choose any three vectors $\bar{a}$, $\bar{b}$, and $\bar{c}$ and construct the diagram shown in Fig. 2

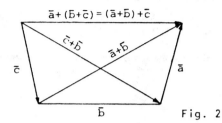

Fig. 2

It is clear that the order in which the vectors are grouped does not change the final result. The associative law can be extended to any number of vectors.

The sum of any number of vectors can always be interpreted as a line segment from the initial point of the first vector to the terminal point of the last vector. Fig. 3 shows the sum of five vectors,

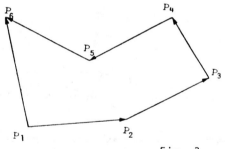

Fig. 3

$$\overline{P_1P_2} + \overline{P_2P_3} + \overline{P_3P_4} + \overline{P_4P_5} + \overline{P_5P_6} = \overline{P_1P_6} \qquad (4)$$

Reversing the direction of the last vector,

$$\overline{P_1P_2} + \overline{P_2P_3} + \overline{P_3P_4} + \overline{P_4P_5} + \overline{P_5P_6} + \overline{P_6P_1} = \bar{0} \qquad (5)$$

In general the sum of vectors which are represented by the consistently directed sides of a closed polygon is always $\bar{0}$.

3) This is basically the definition of subtraction. It also states that the difference of two vectors is uniquely defined. That is, for any two vectors $\bar{a}$ and $\bar{b}$, there exists one and only one vector $\bar{c}$ such that $\bar{c} = \bar{a} - \bar{b}$.

4) Here $\bar{0}$ represents the zero vector. It can be represented by a degenerate line segment $\overline{AA}$, which is nothing more than a single point.

A parallelogram construction would show that

$$\bar{a} + \bar{0} = \bar{a} \qquad\qquad (6)$$

or using the results of 3),

$$\bar{a} - \bar{a} = \bar{0} \qquad\qquad (7)$$

● **PROBLEM 1-11**

Forces of 2 pounds and 4 pounds act at an angle of 135^0 on an object. Determine graphically what force is necessary to balance them.

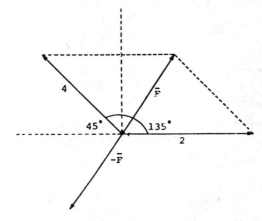

Solution: Draw both forces of 2 and 4 pounds. Note that $135^0 = 90^0 + 45^0$. Since force $\bar{F}$ is the sum of both forces, to balance force $\bar{F}$ we have to apply the object force $-\bar{F}$ of the same magnitude but in opposite direction to $\bar{F}$.

● **PROBLEM 1-12**

Five forces $\bar{F}_1$, $\bar{F}_2$, $\bar{F}_3$, $\bar{F}_4$, $\bar{F}_5$ act on a point P, as shown in Fig. 1. Find the force $\bar{F}_6$, that if applied to point P, would prevent it from moving.

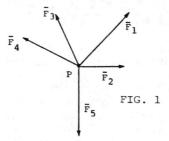

FIG. 1

Solution: The sum $\bar{F}$ of the forces $\bar{F}_1$, $\bar{F}_2$, $\bar{F}_3$, $\bar{F}_4$ and $\bar{F}_5$ must be found before proceeding. The method described in Problem 1-10 will be used. Fig. 2 shows the construction of $\bar{F}$.

$$\bar{F}_1 + \bar{F}_2 + \bar{F}_3 + \bar{F}_4 + \bar{F}_5 = \bar{F} \qquad\qquad (1)$$

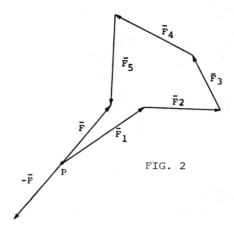

FIG. 2

This equation means that all the forces $\overline{F}_1$, $\overline{F}_2$, $\overline{F}_3$, $\overline{F}_4$, $\overline{F}_5$

can be replaced by a single force $\overline{F}$. To prevent P from moving, apply force $-\overline{F}$ to p. In such case, the sum of the forces

$$\overline{F} + (-\overline{F}) = \overline{0} \qquad (2)$$

is equal to zero and the system is in equilibrium.

Strictly speaking, such a system is either at rest or moves with constant velocity.

● **PROBLEM** 1-13

Points O, A, B, C, in the $x_1 x_2$ plane, have the following coordinates

O:(0,0), A:(3,2), B:(4,5), C:($\frac{1}{2}$,8)

Let $\overline{a} = \overline{OA}$, $\overline{b} = \overline{OB}$, and $\overline{c} = \overline{BC}$,

construct graphically the vectors

$\overline{a} + \overline{c}$ and $\overline{a} + \overline{b} + \overline{c}$.

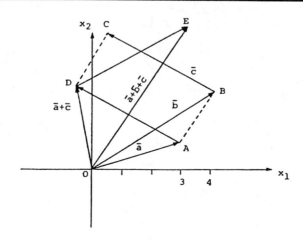

Solution: The rectangular system of coordinates will be used to indicate points O, A, B, C as shown in the figure. Next, draw vectors $\bar{a}$, $\bar{b}$, and $\bar{c}$. To find $\bar{a}+\bar{c}$ move rigidly vector $\bar{c}$ to the new position (i.e. the old vector and the new vector are parallel) parallel to, and having the same direction as, the original vector.

The initial point of the "moved" vector $\bar{c}$ is now A. Note that AD is parallel to BC. Vector $\overline{OD}$ is the sum of vectors $\bar{a}$ and $\bar{c}$

$$\overline{OD} = \bar{a} + \bar{c} \qquad (1)$$

To find $\bar{a}+\bar{b}+\bar{c} = (\bar{a}+\bar{c})+\bar{b}$, move vector $\bar{b}$ rigidly in such a way that its initial point is the terminal point of vector $\overline{OD}$. Note that OB is parallel to DE. The sum of vectors $\bar{a}$, $\bar{b}$, and $\bar{c}$ is represented by vector $\overline{OE}$, therefore

$$\overline{OE} = \bar{a} + \bar{b} + \bar{c} \qquad (2)$$

● **PROBLEM 1-14**

Vectors $\bar{a}$ and $\bar{b}$ are non-collinear (not parallel to the same line). Let $\bar{r}$ be any vector lying in the plane determined by $\bar{a}$ and $\bar{b}$. Express $\bar{r}$ in terms of $\bar{a}$ and $\bar{b}$.

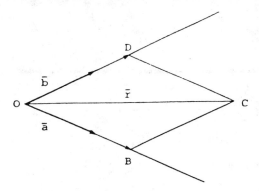

Solution: Since vectors $\bar{a}$ and $\bar{b}$ are non-collinear, move rigidly vectors $\bar{a}$, $\bar{b}$, and $\bar{r}$ in such a way that their initial points will coincide, as shown in the figure.

Let O be the initial point of the vectors $\bar{a}$, $\bar{b}$, and $\bar{r}$. Construct the parallelogram OBCD. From the terminal point C of vector $\bar{r}$ draw lines parallel to the vectors $\bar{a}$ and $\bar{b}$ and obtain points B and D. These points define vectors $\overline{OB}$ and $\overline{OD}$. Then

$$\overline{OC} = \overline{OB} + \overline{OD} \qquad (1)$$

Since the vectors $\bar{a}$ and $\overline{OB}$ are collinear, then

$$\overline{OB} = \alpha\bar{a} \qquad (2)$$

Again, vectors $\bar{b}$ and $\overline{OD}$ are collinear, thus

$$\overline{OD} = \beta\bar{b} \qquad (3)$$

Parameters α and β are scalars. Substituting eqs.(2) and (3) into eq.(1),obtain

$$\overline{OC} = \overline{r} = \overline{OB} + \overline{OD} = \alpha\overline{a} + \beta\overline{b}$$
or
$$\overline{r} = \alpha\overline{a} + \beta\overline{b} \tag{4}$$

Later on in the book, this same problem will be solved analytically, that is without geometrical constructions. Vectors $\overline{a}$ and $\overline{b}$ are called base vectors and vectors $\alpha\overline{a}$ and $\beta\overline{b}$ are called component vectors of $\overline{r}$ in the directions $\overline{a}$ and $\overline{b}$ respectively.

● **PROBLEM** 1-15

Let $\overline{a}$, $\overline{b}$, $\overline{c}$ be three non-coplanar vectors; that is vectors which are not located on one plane. Furthermore, let $\overline{r}$ be any given vector. Express vector $\overline{r}$ in terms of vectors $\overline{a}$, $\overline{b}$, and $\overline{c}$.

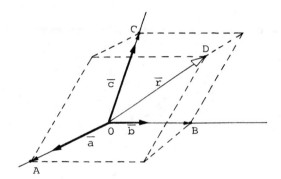

Solution: Since the vectors $\overline{a}$, $\overline{b}$, and $\overline{c}$ are non-coplanar, they are not parallel to the same plane.

Move rigidly vectors $\overline{a}$, $\overline{b}$, $\overline{c}$ and $\overline{r}$ in such a way that they will have the common initial point O, as shown in the figure.

Through the terminal point of $\overline{r}$ (point D in the figure) pass three planes-each of which is parallel to the planes determined by vectors $\overline{a}$ and $\overline{b}$; $\overline{a}$ and $\overline{c}$; and $\overline{b}$ and $\overline{c}$,respectively. Then obtain points A, B, and C, which define the vectors $\overline{OA}$, $\overline{OB}$ and $\overline{OC}$. It is quite simple to verify the equation

$$\overline{r} = \overline{OD} = \overline{OA}+\overline{OB}+\overline{OC} \tag{1}$$

Since the vectors $\overline{a}$ and $\overline{OA}$ are parallel, there exists a real number α such that

$$\overline{OA} = \alpha\overline{a} \tag{2}$$

For vectors $\overline{OB}$ and $\overline{OC}$,

$$\overline{OB} = \beta\overline{b} \tag{3}$$

19

$$\overline{OC} = \gamma\overline{c} \tag{4}$$

where β, γ are real numbers.

Substituting eqs.(2), (3), (4) into eq.(1),

$$\overline{r} = \alpha\overline{a} + \beta\overline{b} + \gamma\overline{c} \tag{5}$$

For a given set of vectors $\overline{a}$, $\overline{b}$, $\overline{c}$, and $\overline{r}$, the parameters α, β, γ are uniquely defined.

● **PROBLEM** 1-16

Points A, B, C are given with position vectors $\overline{a}$, $\overline{b}$, $\overline{c}$. Show that if the vector equation

$$\alpha\overline{a} + \beta\overline{b} + \gamma\overline{c} = 0 \tag{1}$$

holds with respect to the origin 0, then it will hold with respect to any other origin 0' if and only if

$$\alpha + \beta + \gamma = 0 \tag{2}$$

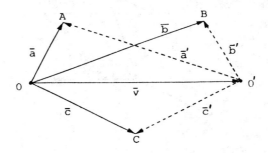

Solution: The points and their position vectors with respect to 0 and 0' are indicated in the figure.

Note that $\overline{a}'$, $\overline{b}'$, $\overline{c}'$ are the position vectors of A, B, C with respect to 0'. $\overline{v}$ is the position vector of 0' with respect to 0. From the figure,

$$\overline{a} = \overline{a}' + \overline{v}$$

$$\overline{b} = \overline{b}' + \overline{v} \tag{3}$$

$$\overline{c} = \overline{c}' + \overline{v}$$

Substituting eq.(3) into eq.(1), yields

$$\alpha(\overline{a}'+\overline{v}) + \beta(\overline{b}'+\overline{v}) + \gamma(\overline{c}'+\overline{v}) = 0 \tag{4}$$

or

$$(\alpha+\beta+\gamma)\overline{v} + \alpha\overline{a}'+\beta\overline{b}'+\gamma\overline{c}' = 0 \tag{5}$$

From eq.(5), one concludes that

$$\alpha\overline{a}' + \beta\overline{b}' + \gamma\overline{c}' = 0 \qquad (6)$$

if and only if

$$(\alpha+\beta+\gamma)\overline{v} = 0 \qquad (7)$$

Since eq.(7) is to be true for any vector $\overline{v} \neq 0$, then

$$\alpha + \beta + \gamma = 0 \qquad (8)$$

ANALYTICAL OPERATIONS ON VECTORS

● **PROBLEM** 1-17

The following vectors are given

$\overline{a} = (2,1)$ $\overline{b} = (-3,5)$

$\overline{c} = (2,4,1)$ $\overline{d} = (1,-2,3)$.

Find analytically, (i.e. without graphical constructions) the following vectors

1) $\overline{a} + \overline{b}$
2) $3\overline{a}$
3) $2\overline{a} + \frac{3}{4}\overline{b}$
4) $\overline{c} + \overline{d}$
5) $2\overline{c} - \overline{d}$
6) $3\overline{c} - 3\overline{d}$

Solution: Let the vectors $\overline{x}$ and $\overline{y}$ be n-dimensional vectors, such that

$$\overline{x} = (x_1, x_2, x_3, \ldots, x_n)$$
$$\overline{y} = (y_1, y_2, y_3, \ldots y_n) \qquad (1)$$

The sum of the vectors $\overline{x}$ and $\overline{y}$ is then

$$\overline{x} + \overline{y} = (x_1+y_1, x_2+y_2, \ldots, x_n+y_n) \qquad (2)$$

Let α be a real number, and define the vector $\alpha\overline{x}$ as a vector whose components are

$$\alpha\overline{x} = (\alpha x_1, \alpha x_2, \alpha x_3, \ldots \alpha x_n) \qquad (3)$$

Using definitions (2) and (3), solve the problems:

1) $\overline{a} + \overline{b} = (2,1) + (-3,5) = (-1,6)$

2) $3\overline{a} = 3(2,1) = (6,3)$

3) $2\bar{a} + \frac{3}{4}\bar{b} = 2(2,1) + \frac{3}{4}(-3,5) = (4,2) + \left(-\frac{9}{4},\frac{15}{4}\right) = \left(\frac{7}{4},\frac{23}{4}\right)$

4) $\bar{c} + \bar{d} = (2,4,1) + (1,-2,3) = (3,2,4)$

5) $2\bar{c} - \bar{d} = 2(2,4,1) - (1,-2,3) = (4,8,2) - (1,-2,3) = (3,10,-1)$

6) $3\bar{c} - 3\bar{d} = 3(2,4,1) - 3(1,-2,3) = (6,12,3) - (3,-6,9) = (3,18,-6)$

Note that addition and subtraction of vectors can be performed for vectors of the same magnitude only. The expression

$$(2,1) + (3,4,5)$$

does not make any sense.

● PROBLEM 1-18

Using the component representation of vectors, prove the following laws:

1) the commutative law
$$\bar{a} + \bar{b} = \bar{b} + \bar{a}$$

2) the associative law
$$\bar{a} + (\bar{b}+\bar{c}) = (\bar{a}+\bar{b}) + \bar{c}$$

3) $\bar{a} + \bar{b} = \bar{c}$ if and only if $\bar{b} = \bar{c} - \bar{a}$

4) $\bar{a} + \bar{0} = \bar{a}$; $\bar{a} - \bar{a} = \bar{0}$

Solution: In general, assume that the vectors are n-dimensional

$$\bar{a} = (a_1, a_2, \ldots, a_n)$$

$$\bar{b} = (b_1, b_2, \ldots, b_n)$$

$$\bar{c} = (c_1, c_2, \ldots, c_n)$$

1) $\bar{a} + \bar{b} = (a_1, a_2, \ldots, a_n) + (b_1, b_2, \ldots, b_n)$

$= (a_1+b_1, a_2+b_2, \ldots, a_n+b_n) = (b_1+a_1, b_2+a_2, \ldots, b_n+a_n)$

$= (b_1, b_2, \ldots, b_n) + (a_1, a_2, \ldots, a_n) = \bar{b} + \bar{a}$

Here we used the fact that real numbers are commutative.

2) $\bar{a}+(\bar{b}+\bar{c}) = (a_1,a_2,\ldots,a_n) + \left[(b_1,b_2,\ldots,b_n) + (c_1,c_2,\ldots,c_n)\right] =$

$= (a_1,a_2,\ldots,a_n) + (b_1+c_1, b_2+c_2, \ldots, b_n+c_n) =$

$$=(a_1+b_1+c_1,\ a_2+b_2+c_2,\ldots,\ a_n+b_n+c_n) =$$

$$=(a_1+b_1,a_2+b_2,\ldots,a_n+b_n)+(c_1,c_2,\ldots,c_n) = (\overline{a} + \overline{b}) + \overline{c}$$

Here we used the fact that real numbers are associative.

3) and 4) follow immediately from the properties of real numbers.

● **PROBLEM** 1-19

Show that in two- and three-dimensional space the graphical and analytical methods of

1) addition
2) subtraction

of vectors lead to the same results.

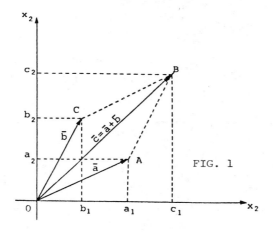

FIG. 1

Solution: 1) For simplicity use the two-dimensional space. The results can be easily extended to the three-dimensional space. Fig. 1 shows vectors $\overline{a}$ and $\overline{b}$, whose components are $\overline{a} = (a_1,\ a_2)$, $\overline{b} = (b_1,b_2)$ as indicated on the x_1- and x_2-axis. Using the parallelogram method, find vector $\overline{c} = \overline{a} + \overline{b}$, which is the diagonal of the parallelogram OABC.

Then denote the components of vector $\overline{c}$ as $(c_1,\ c_2)$. Since OC is parallel to AB and OA is parallel to CB, then

$$b_1 = a_1c_1 \quad \text{and} \quad a_2 = b_2c_2 \tag{1}$$

From Fig. 1,

$$c_1 = a_1 + a_1c_1$$

and

$$c_2 = b_2 + b_2c_2 \tag{2}$$

23

Substituting eq.(1) into eq.(2), gives

$$c_1 = a_1 + b_1$$

(3)

$$c_2 = a_2 + b_2$$

and

$$\bar{c} = \bar{a} + \bar{b} = (a_1 + b_1, \; a_2 + b_2)$$

(4)

Thus, the graphical and analytical methods are equivalent.

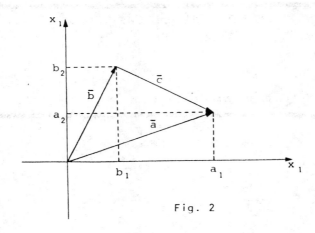

Fig. 2

2) Fig. 2 illustrates the construction of the vector

$$\bar{c} = \bar{a} - \bar{b}$$

(5)

Since

$$\bar{b} + \bar{c} = \bar{a}$$

(6)

then

$$(b_1, \; b_2) + (c_1, \; c_2) = (a_1, \; a_2)$$

From Fig. 2,

$$c_1 = b_1 a_1$$

$$c_2 = -a_2 b_2 \quad \text{(the second coordinate of } \bar{c}$$

is negative)

and

$$a_1 = b_1 + b_1 a_1 = b_1 + c_1$$

(8)

$$a_2 = b_2 - a_2 b_2 = b_2 + c_2$$

Then,

$$\bar{c} = (c_1, c_2) = (a_1 - b_1, \; a_2 - b_2) = \bar{a} - \bar{b}$$

(9)

Again, both methods, graphical and analytical, lead to the same results. Graphical representation of vectors is only possible in one-, two- and three-dimensional spaces. For higher dimensions, the graphical representation of vectors in the described manner is not possible. This is due to the fact that we live in, and thus are restricted to, a three-dimensional space.

24

Let $\bar{a}$ and $\bar{b}$ be given vectors, such that
$$\bar{a} = (a_1, a_2, a_3)$$
$$\bar{b} = (b_1, b_2, b_3)$$
Find vectors $\bar{x}$ and $\bar{y}$ which satisfy the following equations

$$3\bar{x} + \bar{y} = 2\bar{a} + \bar{b} \tag{1}$$

$$-2\bar{x} + 4\bar{y} = \bar{a} - 2\bar{b} \tag{2}$$

<u>Solution</u>: Solve equation (1) for $\bar{y}$; doing this

$$\bar{y} = 2\bar{a} + \bar{b} - 3\bar{x} \tag{3}$$

Multiplying eq.(3) by 4 and substituting into eq.(2), obtain

$$4\bar{y} = 8\bar{a} + 4\bar{b} - 12\bar{x}$$

and

$$-2\bar{x} + 8\bar{a} + 4\bar{b} - 12\bar{x} = \bar{a} - 2\bar{b}$$

$$-14\bar{x} = -7\bar{a} - 6\bar{b}$$

$$\bar{x} = \frac{1}{2}\bar{a} + \frac{3}{7}\bar{b} \tag{4}$$

Substituting eq.(4) into eq.(3), obtain

$$\bar{y} = 2\bar{a}+\bar{b} - 3(\frac{1}{2}\bar{a} + \frac{3}{7}\bar{b}) = 2\bar{a} - \frac{3}{2}\bar{a} + \bar{b} - \frac{9}{7}\bar{b}$$

$$= \frac{1}{2}\bar{a} - \frac{2}{7}\bar{b} \tag{5}$$

Vectors $\bar{x}$ and $\bar{y}$ are the solution to equations (1) and (2).

Let vectors $\bar{a}$, $\bar{b}$, $\bar{c}$ be given such that

$$\bar{a} = (2,4,1)$$
$$\bar{b} = (3,-2,1)$$
$$\bar{c} = (-1,-1,2)$$

Find the following vectors

1) $\bar{d} = \bar{a} + 2\bar{b}$

2) $\bar{e} = 2\bar{a} - \bar{b} + 2\bar{c}$

3) $\bar{f} = 100\bar{a} - \bar{b}$

4) $\bar{g} = \bar{a} + \bar{b} + \alpha\bar{c}$ where α is a scalar

5) $\bar{h} = \bar{a} + 2\bar{b} + 3\bar{c}$

Solution: 1) $\bar{d}$ = (2,4,1) + 2(3,-2,1) = (2,4,1) + (6,-4,2)

$\qquad\qquad$ = (8,0,3)

2) $\bar{e}$ = 2(2,4,1) - (3,-2,1) + 2(-1,-1,2)

$\qquad$ = (4,8,2) - (3,-2,1) + (-2,-2,4) = (-1,8,5)

3) $\bar{f}$ = 100(2,4,1) - (3,-2,1) = (200,400,100) - (3,-2,1)

$\qquad$ = (197,402,99)

4) $\bar{g}$ = (2,4,1) + (3,-2,1) + α(-1,-1,2)

$\qquad$ = (5-α, 2-α, 2+2α)

5) $\bar{h}$ = (2,4,1) + 2(3,-2,1) + 3(-1,-1,2)

$\qquad$ = (2,4,1) + (6,-4,2) + (-3,-3,6) = (5,-3,9)

APPLICATIONS IN GEOMETRY AND PHYSICS

● **PROBLEM** 1-22

A river is flowing at a speed of 20 $\frac{km}{h}$. A boat is crossing the river at a water speed of 20 $\frac{km}{h}$ as shown in Fig. 1. What is the direction and land speed of the boat? Is it possible for this boat to cross the river in the shortest way, i.e. from point A to point B?

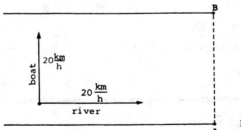

FIG. 1

Solution: Using the parallelogram method, find the speed of the boat as measured from the land. The diagonal of the square is equal to 20$\sqrt{2}$, thus the speed of the boat is 20$\sqrt{2}$ $\frac{km}{h}$ $\approx$ 28 $\frac{km}{h}$, at an angle of 45°. In answering the second question, notice that for the boat to cross the river from A to B, its speed as seen from the land has to be from A to B.

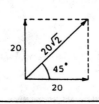

FIG. 2

26

Thus the boat has to steer more against the current.
Assume that the direction of the boat is 45° against the
current, see Fig. 3.

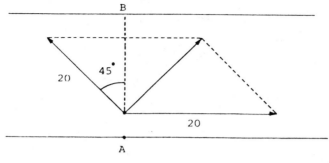

Fig. 3

The diagonal of the parallelogram is not directed from A to B.
Therefore the boat has to steer still more against the current.
Because the speed of the boat is equal to the speed of the
current, it is impossible for this boat to cross the river from
A to B.

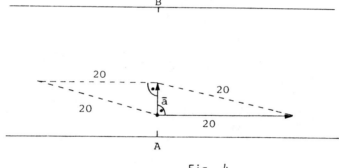

Fig. 4

The same conclusion can be reached using the parallelogram
method (see Fig. 4).

Vector $\bar{a}$ (which can be very small) indicates the speed of the
boat as seen from land. Using the parallelogram, obtain an
orthogonal triangle whose hypotenuse is equal to one of its
sides. This is a contradiction, thus the vector $\bar{a}$, which is a
diagonal of a parallelogram and is directed from A to B, is
equal to $\bar{0}$.

● PROBLEM 1-23

An airplane moves in a northwesterly direction at a speed of
250 $\frac{miles}{hr}$ relative to the ground. The wind, at 80 $\frac{miles}{hr}$
relative to the ground, is blowing from west to east. At what
speed and in what direction would the plane have traveled if
there were no wind?

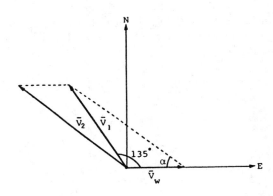

Solution: The problem is illustrated in the figure,

where

$\overline{V}_w$ is the wind velocity

$\overline{V}_1$ is the velocity of the plane relative to the ground while the wind is blowing, and $\overline{V}_2$ is the velocity of the plane without wind. Then

$$\overline{V}_1 = \overline{V}_2 + \overline{V}_w$$

By the law of cosines,

$$(V_2)^2 = (V_1)^2 + (V_w)^2 - 2V_1 V_w \cdot \cos 135^0$$

$$= 311.7 \frac{mi}{hr}$$

Using the law of sines,

$$\frac{V_2}{\sin 135^0} = \frac{V_1}{\sin \alpha}$$

or

$$\sin \alpha = \frac{V_1 \cdot \sin 135^0}{V_2} = 0.567$$

and

$$\alpha = 34.55^0$$

Thus, without wind, the plane would be moving at a speed of $311.7 \frac{mi}{hr}$, at a direction of 34.55^0 north of west.

● **PROBLEM** 1-24

Prove the following theorems:

1) the line segment joining the mid-points of two sides of a triangle is parallel to the third side and has half of its length.

2) the diagonals of a parallelogram bisect each other.

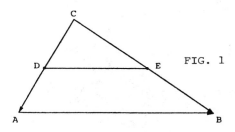

FIG. 1

Solution: Fig. 1 shows the triangle ABC, where D and E are mid-points. Form the following relations

$$\overline{CA} + \overline{AB} = \overline{CB} \qquad (1)$$

or

$$\overline{AB} = \overline{CB} - \overline{CA} \qquad (2)$$

and

$$\overline{DE} = \overline{CE} - \overline{CD} = \frac{1}{2}\,\overline{CB} - \frac{1}{2}\,\overline{CA} = \qquad (3)$$

$$= \frac{1}{2}\,(\overline{CB} - \overline{CA}) = \frac{1}{2}\,\overline{AB}$$

That completes the proof.

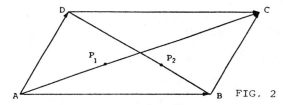

FIG. 2

2) Fig. 2 shows the parallelogram with two diagonals. Assume that they don't bisect each other and let P_1 be the mid-point of AC and P_2 the mid-point of BD.

One has the following relations

$$\overline{AP_2} = \overline{AB} + \overline{BP_2} = \overline{AB} + \frac{1}{2}\,\overline{BD} =$$

$$\overline{AB} + \frac{1}{2}\,(\overline{AD} - \overline{AB}) = \frac{1}{2}\,\overline{AB} + \frac{1}{2}\,\overline{AD} \qquad (4)$$

and

$$\overline{AP_1} = \frac{1}{2}\,\overline{AC} = \frac{1}{2}\,(\overline{AB} + \overline{BC}) = \frac{1}{2}\,(\overline{AB} + \overline{AD})$$

$$= \frac{1}{2}\,\overline{AB} + \frac{1}{2}\,\overline{AD} = \overline{AP_2} \qquad (5)$$

Therefore the points P_1 and P_2 coincide, and the diagonals AC and BD bisect each other.

● **PROBLEM 1-25**

Prove that:

The medians of a triangle meet in a single point which trisects each of these medians.

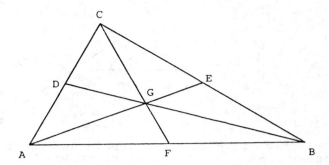

Solution: The points D, E, F are the middle points of the sides.

Point G lies on the median BD. There exists a scalar p such that

$$\overline{DG} = p\ \overline{DB}$$

and

$$\overline{AG} = \overline{AD} + \overline{DG} = \overline{AD} + p\ \overline{DB} \qquad (1)$$

Since G lies on the median CF,

$$\overline{AG} = \overline{AF} + s\ \overline{FC}, \text{ where} \qquad (2)$$

p and s are scalars. Equating eq.(1) and eq.(2), obtain

$$\overline{AD} + p\ \overline{DB} = \overline{AF} + s\ \overline{FC}. \qquad (3)$$

Then expressing all the vectors in eq.(3) in terms of vectors $\overline{AB}$ and $\overline{AC}$

$$\overline{AD} = \frac{1}{2}\ \overline{AC}$$

$$\overline{AF} = \frac{1}{2}\ \overline{AB}$$

$$\overline{DB} = -\frac{1}{2}\ \overline{AC} + \overline{AB} \qquad (4)$$

$$\overline{FC} = -\frac{1}{2}\ \overline{AB} + \overline{AC}$$

Substituting eq.(4) into eq.(3), obtain

$$\frac{1}{2}\ \overline{AC} + p(-\frac{1}{2}\ \overline{AC} + \overline{AB}) = \frac{1}{2}\ \overline{AB} + s(-\frac{1}{2}\ \overline{AB} + \overline{AC})$$

$$\overline{AB}(\frac{1}{2} - p - \frac{1}{2}s) = \overline{AC}(\frac{1}{2} - s - \frac{1}{2}p) \qquad (5)$$

Vectors $\overline{AB}$ and $\overline{AC}$ are not linearly dependent, therefore

$$\frac{1}{2} - p - \frac{1}{2}s = 0$$

$$\frac{1}{2} - s - \frac{1}{2}p = 0 \qquad (6)$$

Solving for s and p,

$$s = p = \frac{1}{3}$$

and

$$\overline{DG} = \frac{1}{3}\,\overline{DB}$$

$$\overline{FG} = \frac{1}{3}\,\overline{FC}$$

The same procedure is followed to prove

$$\overline{GE} = \frac{1}{3}\,\overline{AE}$$

● **PROBLEM** 1-26

Find point C, which divides the line segment AB in the ratio p:q.

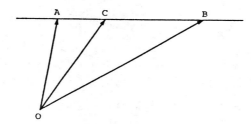

Solution: Let O be the origin of the system and vectors $\overline{OA}$, $\overline{OC}$, $\overline{OB}$ the position vectors of points A, C, and B respectively. Point C is located on the line segment AB in such a position that

$$\frac{\overline{AC}}{p} = \frac{\overline{CB}}{q} \qquad (1)$$

as shown in the figure. Then

$$\overline{AC} = \overline{OC} - \overline{OA}$$
$$\overline{CB} = \overline{OB} - \overline{OC} \qquad (2)$$

Substituting eq.(2) into eq.(1), obtain

$$\frac{\overline{OC} - \overline{OA}}{p} = \frac{\overline{OB} - \overline{OC}}{q} \qquad (3)$$

Solving for $\overline{OC}$, gives

$$q(\overline{OC} - \overline{OA}) = p(\overline{OB} - \overline{OC})$$

$$q\overline{OC} - q\overline{OA} = p\overline{OB} - p\overline{OC}$$

$$\overline{OC} = \frac{p\overline{OB} + q\overline{OA}}{p + q} \qquad (4)$$

Equation (4) gives the position vector $\overline{OC}$, which divides AB in the given ratio $\frac{p}{q}$.

● **PROBLEM** 1-27

Let ABCD be any quadrilateral and K, L, M, N be the mid-points of its sides. Show that connecting the mid-points of the consecutive sides forms a parallelogram.

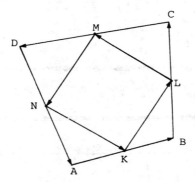

Solution: The quadrilateral and the mid-points K, L, M, N are shown in the figure.

It must be shown that KLMN is a parallelogram.

From the figure,

$$\overline{KL} = \frac{1}{2}\,\overline{AB} + \frac{1}{2}\,\overline{BC} = \frac{1}{2}\,(\overline{AB} + \overline{BC})$$

$$\overline{LM} = \frac{1}{2}\,(\overline{BC} + \overline{CD})$$

$$\overline{MN} = \frac{1}{2}\,(\overline{CD} + \overline{DA})$$ (1)

$$\overline{NK} = \frac{1}{2}\,(\overline{DA} + \overline{AB})$$

and

$$\overline{AB} + \overline{BC} + \overline{CD} + \overline{DA} = \overline{0}$$

or (2)

$$\overline{AB} + \overline{BC} = -(\overline{CD} + \overline{DA})$$

Combining eq.(2) and eq.(1), obtain

$$\overline{KL} = \frac{1}{2}\,(\overline{AB} + \overline{BC}) = -\frac{1}{2}\,(\overline{CD} + \overline{DA}) = -\overline{MN} = \overline{NM}$$

(3)

$$\overline{LM} = \frac{1}{2}\,(\overline{BC} + \overline{CD}) = -\frac{1}{2}\,(\overline{AB} + \overline{DA}) = -\overline{NK} = \overline{KN}$$

The opposite sides are equal and parallel, therefore KLMN is a parallelogram.

Points A, B, C, D, E, F, G, H are the vertices of the parallelepiped shown in the figure.

Express the vectors $\overline{AC}$, $\overline{AF}$, $\overline{AG}$, $\overline{AH}$, $\overline{FG}$, $\overline{EG}$ in terms of $\overline{b}$, $\overline{e}$,
and $\overline{d}$, where
$$\overline{AB} = \overline{b}, \quad \overline{AE} = \overline{e}, \quad \overline{AD} = \overline{d}.$$

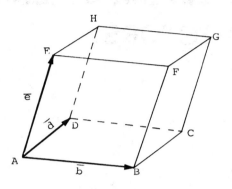

Solution: From the figure,

$$\overline{AC} = \overline{AB} + \overline{BC} = \overline{b} + \overline{d}$$

$$\overline{AF} = \overline{AB} + \overline{BF} = \overline{b} + \overline{e}$$

$$\overline{AG} = \overline{AC} + \overline{CG} = (\overline{AB} + \overline{BC}) + \overline{CG} = \overline{b} + \overline{d} + \overline{e}$$

$$\overline{AH} = \overline{AD} + \overline{DH} = \overline{d} + \overline{e}$$

$$\overline{FG} = \overline{AD} = \overline{d}$$

$$\overline{EG} = \overline{EF} + \overline{FG} = \overline{b} + \overline{d}$$

CHAPTER 2

MAGNITUDE, LINEAR DEPENDENCE AND BASE VECTORS

INTRODUCTION

Having established all the pertinent basic definitions of vector calculus, the book now moves one step further and discusses the concept of the magnitude of a vector. The magnitude of a vector is nothing more than the length of the arrow representing it. The properties as well as applications of the magnitude of a vector are also discussed.

The chapter then moves on to the notion of linear dependence of vectors. Certain theorems given in this chapter will allow us to determine if a given set of vectors is linearly dependent or independent. These theorems lead directly to the definition of the basis of a vector space, which is one of the most important concepts in vector analysis. In three dimensional space, a basis is formed by any three linearly independent vectors called base vectors. The chapter then goes on to prove that any vector in a given vector space can be represented as a linear combination of the base vectors. This enables us to analyze the relationships between vectors and their properties in terms of base vectors. Therefore a basis of a vector space can be regarded as some sort of common denominator for all the vectors of this given space.

Chapter 2 then goes on to study in detail the relationship between the graphical representation and component representation of vectors.

The concept of the basis will be returned to in the later chapters when discussing linear transformations of coordinate systems. The properties of these transformations establish the foundations of special and general relativity.

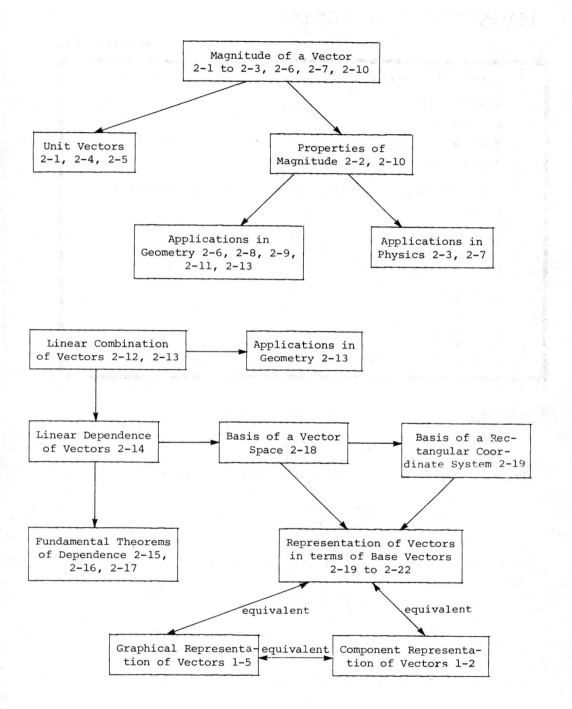

This chart is provided to facilitate rapid understanding of the inter-
relationships of the topics and subject matter in this chapter. Also
shown are the problem numbers associated with the subject matter.

MAGNITUDE OF A VECTOR

1) Find the magnitude of the following vectors:

$\overline{a}$ = (1, 4)

$\overline{b}$ = (4, 3, 0)

$\overline{c}$ = (0, -1, 1)

$\overline{d}$ = (6, 1, 0, -1, 2)

2) Which of the following vectors are unit vectors?

$\overline{a}$ = (1, 0)

$\overline{b}$ = $\left(1, \frac{1}{2}\right)$

$\overline{c}$ = (1, -1)

$\overline{d}$ = $\left(\frac{1}{\sqrt{2}}, -\frac{1}{\sqrt{2}}\right)$

$\overline{e}$ = $\left(\frac{1}{2}, 0, \frac{\sqrt{3}}{2}\right)$

$\overline{f}$ = (1, 0, 0, 0)

<u>Solution</u>: 1) Let $\overline{x}$ be an n-dimensional vector

$$\overline{x} = (x_1, x_2, \ldots x_n) \tag{1}$$

The magnitude of a vector $\overline{x}$, denoted by $|\overline{x}|$, is defined as

$$|\overline{x}| \equiv \sqrt{x_1^2 + x_2^2 + \ldots + x_n^2} \tag{2}$$

Using this definition, the magnitudes of vectors $\overline{a}$, $\overline{b}$, $\overline{c}$, $\overline{d}$ are:

$|\overline{a}| = |(1, 4)| = \sqrt{1^2 + 4^2} = \sqrt{17}$

$|\overline{b}| = |(4, 3, 0)| = \sqrt{4^2 + 3^2} = \sqrt{25} = 5$

$|\overline{c}| = |(0, -1, 1)| = \sqrt{1 + 1} = \sqrt{2}$

$|\overline{d}| = |(6, 1, 0, -1, 2)| = \sqrt{36+1+1+4} = \sqrt{42}$

2) A unit vector is a vector whose magnitude is equal to 1.

$|\overline{a}| = \sqrt{1} = 1$ is a unit vector

36

$|\bar{b}| = \sqrt{1 + \dfrac{1}{4}} \neq 1$ is not a unit vector

$|\bar{c}| = \sqrt{1 + 1} \neq 1$ is not a unit vector

$|\bar{d}| = \sqrt{\dfrac{1}{2} + \dfrac{1}{2}} = 1$ is a unit vector

$|\bar{e}| = \sqrt{\dfrac{1}{4} + \dfrac{3}{4}} = 1$ is a unit vector

$|\bar{f}| = \sqrt{1} = 1$ is a unit vector

● **PROBLEM** 2-2

Find the geometrical interpretation of the magnitude of a vector in two- and three-dimensional space.

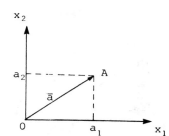

Fig. 1

Solution: Let $\bar{a}$ be any given two-dimensional vector

$$\bar{a} = (a_1, a_2)$$

Fig. 1 shows the graphical representation of vector $\bar{a}$.

By the Pythagorean theorem

$$(OA)^2 = a_1^2 + a_2^2 \tag{1}$$

On the other hand the magnitude of vector $\bar{a}$ is

$$|\bar{a}| = |\overline{OA}| = \sqrt{a_1^2 + a_2^2} \tag{2}$$

Thus in two-dimensional space the magnitude of a vector is simply its length.

Fig. 2 shows the graphical representation of

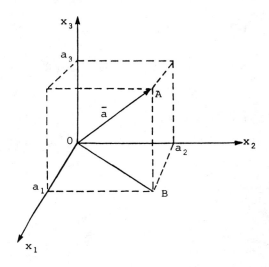

$$\bar{a} = (a_1, a_2, a_3) \tag{3}$$

in the three-dimensional space.

Using the Pythagorean theorem,

$$(OB)^2 = a_1^2 + a_2^2 \tag{4}$$

and

$$(OA)^2 = (OB)^2 + a_3^2 \tag{5}$$

Substituting eq. (4) into eq. (5),

$$(OA)^2 = a_1^2 + a_2^2 + a_3^2 \tag{6}$$

This shows that in three-dimensional space also, the magnitude of a vector is equal to its length,

$$|\bar{a}| = \sqrt{a_1^2 + a_2^2 + a_3^2} \tag{7}$$

● **PROBLEM 2-3**

A particle of mass m is suspended by two weightless strings as shown in the figure. The gravitational force acting on the particle is mg. Find the magnitude of tension $\bar{T}_1$ and $\bar{T}_2$ associated with the strings.

Solution: Since the system is in the state of equilibrium, the total force acting on the mass m is equal to $\bar{0}$, therefore

$$\bar{T}_1 + \bar{T}_2 + m\bar{g} = \bar{0}$$

The components of $\bar{T}_1$ are $|T_1| \cos \phi_1$, $|\bar{T}_1| \sin \phi_1$, and the components of $\bar{T}_2$ are $|\bar{T}_2| \cos \phi_2$ and $|\bar{T}_2| \sin \phi_2$.

Thus,

$$|\bar{T}_1| \cos \phi_1 + |\bar{T}_2| \cos \phi_2 = 0 \tag{1}$$

$$|\bar{T}_1| \sin \phi_1 + |\bar{T}_2| \sin \phi_2 - m|\bar{g}| = 0 \tag{2}$$

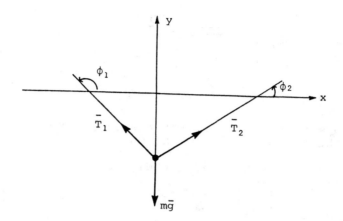

The first equation states that the sum of the x-components of all the forces acting on mass m is equal to zero. The second equation states that the total sum of the y-components of the forces acting on mass m is equal to zero. Solving the system of equations for $|\bar{T}_1|$ and $|\bar{T}_2|$,

$$|\bar{T}_1| = \frac{-m|\bar{g}|\cos\phi_2}{\sin(\phi_2 - \phi_1)} \qquad |\bar{T}_2| = \frac{m|\bar{g}|\cos\phi_1}{\sin(\phi_2-\phi_1)}$$

● **PROBLEM 2-4**

1) A three-dimensional vector $\bar{a}$ is given

$$\bar{a} = (a_1,\ a_2,\ a_3)$$

Find a unit vector that is parallel to $\bar{a}$.

2) For each of the following vectors find a parallel unit vector:

$$\bar{a} = (2,\ 4)$$
$$\bar{b} = (-1,\ 3)$$
$$\bar{c} = (2,\ 4,\ 1)$$
$$\bar{d} = (1,\ 5,\ 2,\ 1)$$
$$\bar{e} = (\alpha,\ 2\alpha,\ \alpha+1,\ 6)$$

Solution: 1) Let $\bar{u}$ be a unit vector parallel to $\bar{a}$. Since it is a unit vector

$$|\bar{u}| = \sqrt{u_1^2 + u_2^2 + u_3^2} = 1 \qquad (1)$$

Vectors $\bar{a}$ and $\bar{u}$ are parallel, thus

$$\bar{u} = \alpha\bar{a} \qquad (2)$$

where α is a scalar. Then

$$|\bar{u}| = |\alpha\bar{a}| = |(\alpha a_1,\ \alpha a_2,\ \alpha a_3)| \qquad (3)$$

or

$$1 = \sqrt{\alpha^2 a_1^2 + \alpha^2 a_2^2 + \alpha^2 a_3^2} \qquad (4)$$

Solving eq. (4) for α,

39

$$\alpha = \frac{1}{\sqrt{a_1^2 + a_2^2 + a_3^2}} = \frac{1}{|\overline{a}|} \qquad (5)$$

Eq. (2) becomes

$$\overline{u} = \frac{\overline{a}}{|\overline{a}|} \qquad (6)$$

Thus, to obtain a unit vector parallel to a given vector, divide the vector by its magnitude.

This holds for vectors of any dimension.

$$|\overline{u}| = \left| \frac{\overline{a}}{|\overline{a}|} \right| = \frac{|\overline{a}|}{|\overline{a}|} = 1 \qquad (7)$$

2)
$$\overline{u}_a = \frac{\overline{a}}{|\overline{a}|} = \frac{1}{\sqrt{4 + 16}} \overline{a} = \frac{1}{\sqrt{20}} \overline{a} = \left(\frac{2}{\sqrt{20}}, \frac{4}{\sqrt{20}} \right)$$

$$\overline{u}_b = \frac{1}{\sqrt{1 + 9}} \overline{b} = \frac{1}{\sqrt{10}} \overline{b} = \left(\frac{-1}{\sqrt{10}}, \frac{3}{\sqrt{10}} \right)$$

$$\overline{u}_c = \frac{1}{\sqrt{4 + 16 + 1}} \overline{c} = \frac{1}{\sqrt{21}} \overline{c} = \left(\frac{2}{\sqrt{21}}, \frac{4}{\sqrt{21}}, \frac{1}{\sqrt{21}} \right)$$

$$\overline{u}_d = \frac{1}{\sqrt{1 + 25 + 4 + 1}} \overline{d} = \frac{1}{\sqrt{31}} \overline{d} = \left(\frac{1}{\sqrt{31}}, \frac{5}{\sqrt{31}}, \frac{2}{\sqrt{31}}, \frac{1}{\sqrt{31}} \right)$$

$$\overline{u}_e = \frac{1}{\sqrt{\alpha^2 + 4\alpha^2 + \alpha^2 + 2\alpha + 1 + 36}} \overline{e} = \frac{1}{\sqrt{6\alpha^2 + 2\alpha + 37}} \overline{e}$$

● **PROBLEM 2-5**

Find a unit vector parallel to the sum of the vectors $\overline{a}$ and $\overline{b}$, where

$$\overline{a} = (3, 4, 2)$$
$$\overline{b} = (1, -3, -5) \qquad (1)$$

Solution: Compute the sum of the vectors $\overline{a}$ and $\overline{b}$

$$\overline{c} = \overline{a} + \overline{b} = (3, 4, 2) + (1, -3, -5) = (4, 1, -3) \qquad (2)$$

A unit vector parallel to $\overline{c}$ is given by

$$\overline{u} = \frac{\overline{c}}{|\overline{c}|} \qquad (3)$$

The magnitude of vector $\overline{c}$ is given by

$$|\overline{c}| = \sqrt{16 + 1 + 9} = \sqrt{26} \qquad (4)$$

Substituting eq. (4) and eq. (2) into eq. (3)

$$\overline{u} = \frac{\overline{c}}{|\overline{c}|} = \frac{1}{\sqrt{26}}(4, 1, -3) = \left(\frac{4}{\sqrt{26}}, \frac{1}{\sqrt{26}}, \frac{-3}{\sqrt{26}} \right) \qquad (5)$$

Then verify that $\bar{u}$ is a unit vector,

$$|\bar{u}| = \sqrt{\frac{16}{26} + \frac{1}{26} + \frac{9}{26}} = \sqrt{\frac{26}{26}} = 1 \qquad (6)$$

● **PROBLEM** 2-6

The initial point of a vector is P_1 (x_1, y_1, z_1) and the terminal point is P_2 (x_2, y_2, z_2), as shown in the figure. Determine the direction and magnitude of this vector.

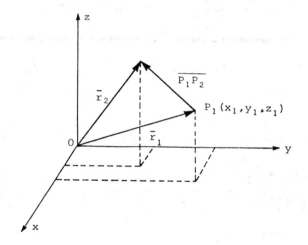

Solution: The position vector of P_1 is

$$\bar{r}_1 = (x_1, y_1, z_1) \qquad (1)$$

The position vector of P_2 is

$$\bar{r}_2 = (x_2, y_2, z_2) \qquad (2)$$

Vector $\bar{r}_2$ is the sum of vectors $\bar{r}_1$ and $\overline{P_1P_2}$

$$\bar{r}_2 = \bar{r}_1 + \overline{P_1P_2} \qquad (3)$$

$$\overline{P_1P_2} = \bar{r}_2 - \bar{r}_1 \qquad (4)$$

or

$$\overline{P_1P_2} = (x_2, y_2, z_2) - (x_1, y_1, z_1) = (x_2 - x_1, y_2 - y_1, z_2 - z_1)$$

The magnitude of vector $\overline{P_1P_2}$ is

$$\left|\overline{P_1P_2}\right| = \sqrt{(x_2 - x_1)^2 + (y_2 - y_1)^2 + (z_2 - z_1)^2}$$

and its direction is from point P_1 to point P_2. Note that the magnitude of vector $\overline{P_1P_2}$ is the distance between points P_1 and P_2.

APPLICATIONS IN GEOMETRY AND PHYSICS

Forces

$$\overline{F}_1 = (f_1^1, \ f_2^1, \ f_3^1)$$

$$\overline{F}_2 = (f_1^2, \ f_2^2, \ f_3^2)$$

$$\overline{F}_3 = (f_1^3, \ f_2^3, \ f_3^3) \tag{1}$$

$$\overline{F}_4 = (f_1^4, \ f_2^4, \ f_3^4)$$

are acting on an object. Find the magnitude of the resultant of these forces.

<u>Solution</u>: The resultant of the forces $\overline{F}_1$, $\overline{F}_2$, $\overline{F}_3$, $\overline{F}_4$ is given by

$$\overline{F} = \overline{F}_1 + \overline{F}_2 + \overline{F}_3 + \overline{F}_4 \tag{2}$$

Substituting eq. (1) into eq. (2), obtain $\overline{F}$. The magnitude of $\overline{F}$ is

$$|\overline{F}| = |\overline{F}_1 + \overline{F}_2 + \overline{F}_3 + \overline{F}_4| = \tag{3}$$

$$\sqrt{(f_1^1 + f_1^2 + f_1^3 + f_1^4)^2 + (f_2^1 + f_2^2 + f_2^3 + f_2^4)^2 + (f_3^1 + f_3^2 + f_3^3 + f_3^4)^2}$$

In general, when

$$\overline{F} = \sum_{i=1}^{K} \overline{F}_i \tag{4}$$

and

$$\overline{F}_i = (f_1^i, \ f_2^i, \ f_3^i)$$

then

$$|\overline{F}| = \left[\left(\sum_{i=1}^{K} f_1^i \right)^2 + \left(\sum_{i=1}^{K} f_2^i \right)^2 + \left(\sum_{i=1}^{K} f_3^i \right)^2 \right]^{\frac{1}{2}} \tag{5}$$

Let A be a fixed point in the $x_1 x_2$ plane and let B and C vary in the $x_1 x_2$ plane such that

$$|\overline{AB}| = 3 \quad \text{and} \quad |\overline{BC}| = 2.$$

1) Find the locus of C.

2) Find the locus of C if B varies in the $x_1 x_2$ plane such that $|\overline{AB}| = 3$ and C varies in the space while $|BC| = 2$.

3) Find the locus of C if B and C vary in the space.

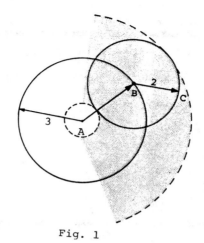

Fig. 1

<u>Solution</u>: 1) Since A is a fixed point and B varies so that $|\overline{AB}| = 3$, one obtains a circle of radius 3 as shown in Fig. 1.

For every possible location of point B, obtain a circle of radius 2 and center at B as all possible locations of point C. Thus the locus of C is the annulus between two circles of radii 5 and 1 and center at A (shaded area in Fig. 1).

2) Since B varies in the $x_1 x_2$ plane so that $|\overline{AB}| = 3$, one obtains a circle as all possible locations of B. But C varies in the space so that $|\overline{BC}| = 2$. Thus for every point B, one obtains a sphere of radius 2 and center at B.

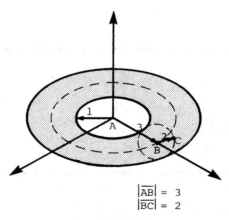

$|\overline{AB}| = 3$
$|\overline{BC}| = 2$

Fig. 2

In this case the locus of C is a solid torus, shown in Fig. 2.

3) Since both B and C vary in space, the locus of C is a shell of outer radius 5 and inner radius 1.

43

Let A and B be fixed points in space.

For each of the following cases find the locus of point C:

1) $|\overline{AC}| + |\overline{BC}| = |\overline{AB}|$
2) $|\overline{AB}| + |\overline{BC}| = |\overline{AC}|$
3) $|\overline{AC}|^2 + |\overline{BC}|^2 = |\overline{AB}|^2$
4) $|\overline{AC}| = |\overline{BC}|$
5) $|\overline{AC}| \geq |\overline{BC}|$
6) $|\overline{AC}| + |\overline{BC}| = 2|\overline{AB}|$

Solution: 1)   The locus of C is the line segment AB.

2)   The locus of C are all the points of

   line p, lying to the right of point B.

3)   The locus is a sphere with AB as diameter.

4)   The locus is a plane perpendicular to AB at its mid-point.

5)   The plane described in 4) divides the space into two sub-spaces.   The locus of C is the subspace containing point B.

6)   The locus is an ellipsoid.

Prove that
$$|\overline{a} + \overline{b}| \leq |\overline{a}| + |\overline{b}| \qquad (1)$$
for any vectors
$$\overline{a} = (a_1, a_2, a_3)$$
$$\overline{b} = (b_1, b_2, b_3) \qquad (2)$$

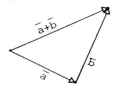

Solution: Represent vectors $\overline{a}$, $\overline{b}$ and $\overline{a} + \overline{b}$ graphically as shown in the figure.

For any triangle, the length of two sides is bigger than the length of the third side.

To prove eq. (1) analytically, start with the following inequality

$$0 \leq (a_1b_2 - a_2b_1)^2 + (a_1b_3 - a_3b_1)^2 + (a_2b_3 - a_3b_2)^2 \qquad (3)$$

or

$$2a_1b_2a_2b_1 + 2a_1b_3a_3b_1 + 2a_2b_3a_3b_2 \leq a_1^2b_2^2 + a_2^2b_1^2 + a_1^2b_3^2 + a_3^2b_1^2 + a_2^2b_3^2 + a_3^2b_2^2$$

Adding to both sides $(a_1^2b_2^2 + a_2^2b_2^2 + a_3^2b_3^2)$ after some basic operations,

$$(a_1b_1 + a_2b_2 + a_3b_3)^2 \leq (a_1^2 + a_2^2 + a_3^2)(b_1^2 + b_2^2 + b_3^2) \qquad (4)$$

Taking the square root of both sides and multiplying by 2,

$$2a_1b_1 + 2a_2b_2 + 2a_3b_3 \leq 2\sqrt{a_1^2 + a_2^2 + a_3^2}\sqrt{b_1^2 + b_2^2 + b_3^2} \qquad (5)$$

After adding $(a_1^2 + a_2^2 + a_3^2 + b_1^2 + b_2^2 + b_3^2)$ and transforming,

$$(a_1 + b_1)^2 + (a_2 + b_2)^2 + (a_3 + b_3)^2 \leq \left[\sqrt{a_1^2 + a_2^2 + a_3^2} + \sqrt{b_1^2 + b_2^2 + b_3^2}\right]^2 \qquad (6)$$

Taking the square root of both sides,

$$\sqrt{(a_1 + b_1)^2 + (a_2 + b_2)^2 + (a_3 + b_3)^2} \leq \sqrt{a_1^2 + a_2^2 + a_3^2} + \sqrt{b_1^2 + b_2^2 + b_3^2} \qquad (7)$$

or

$$|\overline{a} + \overline{b}| \leq |\overline{a}| + |\overline{b}| \qquad (8)$$

Note that the inequality (8) is true for any two vectors of any dimension.

● **PROBLEM 2-11**

The direction cosines of the vector $\overline{OA}$ are the numbers $\cos \alpha$, $\cos \beta$ and $\cos \rho$, where α, β, ρ are the angles which the vector $\overline{OA}$ makes with the positive directions of the coordinate axes. Show that

$$\cos^2\alpha + \cos^2\beta + \cos^2\rho = 1 \qquad (1)$$

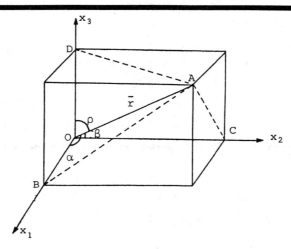

Solution: Vector $\overline{OA}$ and the angles α, β, ρ are shown in the figure. The coordinates of vector $\overline{OA}$ are (x_1, x_2, x_3).

Triangle OAB is a right triangle with right angle $\gtrless$ OBA, therefore

$$\cos \alpha = \frac{x_1}{|\overline{r}|} \qquad (2)$$

Triangle OAC is a right triangle with right angle $\gtrless$ ACO, therefore

$$\cos \beta = \frac{x_2}{|\overline{r}|} \qquad (3)$$

Triangle OAD is a right triangle with right angle $\gtrless$ ADO, then

$$\cos \rho = \frac{x_3}{|\overline{r}|} \qquad (4)$$

Also

$$|\overline{r}| = \sqrt{x_1^2 + x_2^2 + x_3^2}$$

and

$$\cos^2 \alpha + \cos^2 \beta + \cos^2 \rho = \frac{x_1^2}{|\overline{r}|^2} + \frac{x_2^2}{|\overline{r}|^2} + \frac{x_3^2}{|\overline{r}|^2} = \frac{x_1^2 + x_2^2 + x_3^2}{x_1^2 + x_2^2 + x_3^2} = 1 \qquad (5)$$

LINEAR COMBINATION, LINEAR DEPENDENCE OF VECTORS

● PROBLEM 2-12

1) Express the vector
$$\overline{a} = (2, 7)$$
as a linear combination of vectors:
a) $\overline{b}_1 = (2, 4) \qquad \overline{b}_2 = (-1, 3)$
b) $\overline{c}_1 = (4, 4) \qquad \overline{c}_2 = (5, 5)$

2) Express the vector
$$\overline{b} = (2, -1, 3)$$
as a linear combination of vectors:
a) $\overline{d}_1 = (2, 4, 1) \qquad \overline{d}_2 = (3, 7, 1)$
b) $\overline{e}_1 = (1, 0, 0) \qquad \overline{e}_2 = (0, 1, 0) \qquad \overline{e}_3 = (0, 0, 1)$
c) $\overline{f}_1 = (2, 4, 1) \qquad \overline{f}_2 = (3, 1, 7) \qquad \overline{f}_3 = (-1, 2, 2)$

Solution: Let $\overline{a}_1, \overline{a}_2, \ldots \overline{a}_n$ be any set of n-dimensional vectors. Vector $\overline{b}$, such that

$$\overline{b} = \alpha_1 \overline{a}_1 + \alpha_2 \overline{a}_2 + \ldots + \alpha_n \overline{a}_n \qquad (1)$$

where α_1, α_2,...α_n are scalars, is called a linear combination
of vectors

$$\bar{a}_1, \bar{a}_2,...\bar{a}_n \tag{2}$$

1) a) To express $\bar{a} = (2, 7)$ as a linear combination of $\bar{b}_1$
and $\bar{b}_2$, solve for α_1 and α_2, where

$$\bar{a} = \alpha_1 \bar{b}_1 + \alpha_2 \bar{b}_2 \tag{3}$$

or

$(2, 7) = \alpha_1(2, 4) + \alpha_2(-1, 3) = (2\alpha_1-\alpha_2, 4\alpha_1+3\alpha_2)$

and

$$2 = 2\alpha_1 - \alpha_2$$
$$7 = 4\alpha_1 + 3\alpha_2 \tag{4}$$

Solving system (4),

$$\alpha_1 = \frac{13}{10} \qquad \alpha_2 = \frac{3}{5}$$

Vector $\bar{a}$ can be expressed as

$$\bar{a} = \frac{13}{10}\bar{b}_1 + \frac{3}{5}\bar{b}_2 \tag{5}$$

b) $\bar{a} = \alpha_1 \bar{c}_1 + \alpha_2 \bar{c}_2 \tag{6}$

or

$(2, 7) = \alpha_1(4, 4) + \alpha_2(5, 5) \tag{7}$

and

$$2 = 4\alpha_1 + 5\alpha_2$$
$$7 = 4\alpha_1 + 5\alpha_2 \tag{8}$$

This system does not have any solution, therefore vector $\bar{a}$ can
not be expressed as a linear combination of $\bar{c}_1$ and $\bar{c}_2$.

2) a) To express $\bar{b}$ as a linear combination of $\bar{d}_1$ and $\bar{d}_2$,
follow the same procedure used in example 1.

Thus, $\bar{b} = \alpha_1\bar{d}_1 + \alpha_2\bar{d}_2 \tag{9}$

and $(2, -1, 3) = \alpha_1(2, 4, 1) + \alpha_2(3, 7, 1) \tag{10}$

$$2 = 2\alpha_1 + 3\alpha_2$$
$$-1 = 4\alpha_1 + 7\alpha_2 \tag{11}$$
$$3 = \alpha_1 + \alpha_2$$

This system does not have any solution, thus $\bar{b}$ can not be
expressed as a linear combination of $\bar{d}_1$ and $\bar{d}_2$.

b) $\bar{b} = \alpha_1\bar{e}_1 + \alpha_2\bar{e}_2 + \alpha_3\bar{e}_3 \tag{12}$

Comparing the components,

$$2 = \alpha_1$$
$$-1 = \alpha_2 \tag{13}$$
$$3 = \alpha_3$$

Thus $\qquad \bar{b} = 2\bar{e}_1 - \bar{e}_2 + 3\bar{e}_3$ $\qquad\qquad$ (14)

c) $\bar{b} = \alpha_1\bar{f}_1 + \alpha_2\bar{f}_2 + \alpha_3\bar{f}_3$ $\qquad\qquad\qquad$ (15)

or

$\qquad (2, -1, 3) = (2\alpha_1, 4\alpha_1, \alpha_1) + (3\alpha_2, \alpha_2, 7\alpha_2) + (-\alpha_3, 2\alpha_3, 2\alpha_3)$ $\quad$ (16)

$$2 = 2\alpha_1 + 3\alpha_2 - \alpha_3$$
$$-1 = 4\alpha_1 + \alpha_2 + 2\alpha_3 \qquad\qquad (17)$$
$$3 = \alpha_1 + 7\alpha_2 + 2\alpha_3$$

Solving system (17),

$$\alpha_1 = -\frac{10}{69} \qquad \alpha_2 = \frac{41}{69} \qquad \alpha_3 = \frac{-35}{69}$$

Thus
$$\bar{b} = -\frac{10}{69}\bar{f}_1 + \frac{41}{69}\bar{f}_2 - \frac{35}{69}\bar{f}_3 \qquad\qquad (18)$$

● **PROBLEM 2-13**

Let O, A, B be fixed points in space and

$$\overline{OC} = \frac{\alpha\ \overline{OA} + \beta\ \overline{OB}}{\alpha + \beta}, \qquad \alpha + \beta \neq 0 \qquad\qquad (1)$$

Find the locus of the point C if

1) $\alpha \geq 0, \quad \beta \geq 0$

2) α and β are any scalars

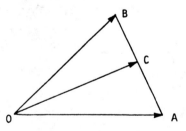

Solution: Write equation (1) in the form

$$\overline{OC} = \frac{\alpha}{\alpha+\beta}\ \overline{OA} + \frac{\beta}{\alpha+\beta}\ \overline{OB}$$

$$= \frac{\alpha}{\alpha+\beta}\ \overline{OA} + \frac{\beta}{\alpha+\beta}\ \overline{OA} - \frac{\beta}{\alpha+\beta}\ \overline{OA} + \frac{\beta}{\alpha+\beta}\ \overline{OB}$$

$$= \left(\frac{\alpha}{\alpha+\beta} + \frac{\beta}{\alpha+\beta}\right)\overline{OA} + \frac{\beta}{\alpha+\beta}(\overline{OB} - \overline{OA})$$

$$= \overline{OA} + \frac{\beta}{\alpha+\beta}(\overline{OB} - \overline{OA}) \qquad\qquad (2)$$

Since $\overline{OB} - \overline{OA} = \overline{AB}$, eq. (2) becomes

$$\overline{OC} = \overline{OA} + \frac{\beta}{\alpha+\beta}\ \overline{AB} \qquad\qquad (3)$$

1) For α and β nonnegative,

$$0 \leq \frac{\beta}{\alpha + \beta} \leq 1 \tag{4}$$

Thus, the locus of C is the line segment AB, as shown in the figure.

2) For any scalars α and β, the coefficient $\frac{\beta}{\alpha + \beta}$ can take any value and the locus of C is the straight line determined by A and B.

● PROBLEM 2-14

Determine which of the following sets of vectors are linearly dependent.

1) $\bar{a} = (1, 2)$ $\bar{b} = (3, 4)$

2) $\bar{c} = (2, 5)$ $\bar{d} = (4, 10)$

3) $\bar{e} = (1, 0)$ $\bar{f} = (2, 1)$ $\bar{g} = (3, 2)$

4) $\bar{h} = (1, 2, 1)$ $\bar{k} = (2, 3, 2)$

Solution: Use the following definition of the linear dependence of the vectors.

Definition: A set of vectors $\bar{a}_1$, $\bar{a}_2$,...$\bar{a}_\kappa$ is said to be linearly dependent if and only if there are κ real numbers α_1, α_2,...α_κ not all zero, such that

$$\alpha_1 \bar{a}_1 + \alpha_2 \bar{a}_2 + ... + \alpha_\kappa \bar{a}_\kappa = \bar{0} \tag{1}$$

A set of vectors is linearly independent if and only if it is. not a linearly dependent set.

1) Therefore

$$\alpha_1 \bar{a} + \alpha_2 \bar{b} = \alpha_1(1, 2) + \alpha_2(3, 4) = \bar{0}$$

$$(\alpha_1, 2\alpha_1) + (3\alpha_2, 4\alpha_2) = \bar{0} \tag{2}$$

and

$$\alpha_1 + 3\alpha_2 = 0$$
$$2\alpha_1 + 4\alpha_2 = 0 \tag{3}$$

The only solution to this system is

$$\alpha_1 = 0$$
$$\alpha_2 = 0 \tag{4}$$

Thus the vectors $\bar{a}$ and $\bar{b}$ are linearly independent.

2) $\alpha_1 \bar{c} + \alpha_2 \bar{d} = \alpha_1(2, 5) + \alpha_2(4, 10) =$

$$(2\alpha_1, 5\alpha_1) + (4\alpha_2, 10\alpha_2) = \bar{0} \tag{5}$$

In the component form,

$$2\alpha_1 + 4\alpha_2 = 0$$
$$5\alpha_1 + 10\alpha_2 = 0 \tag{6}$$

One of the possible solutions is

$$\alpha_1 = -2, \quad \alpha_2 = 1, \quad \text{thus the system is \textbf{linearly dependent}.}$$

3) $\alpha_1 \bar{e} + \alpha_2 \bar{f} + \alpha_3 \bar{g} = \bar{0}$

$$\alpha_1(1, 0) + \alpha_2(2, 1) + \alpha_3(3, 2) = \tag{7}$$

$$(\alpha_1, 0) + (2\alpha_2, \alpha_2) + (3\alpha_3, 2\alpha_3) = \bar{0}$$

In the component form

$$\alpha_1 + 2\alpha_2 + 3\alpha_3 = 0$$
$$\alpha_2 + 2\alpha_3 = 0 \tag{8}$$

One of the possible solutions is

$$\alpha_1 = 1, \quad \alpha_2 = -2, \quad \alpha_3 = 1 \tag{9}$$

thus the system is linearly dependent.

4) $\alpha_1 \bar{h} + \alpha_2 \bar{\kappa} = \bar{0}$ $\tag{10}$

$$\alpha_1(1, 2, 1) + \alpha_2(2, 3, 2) =$$

$$(\alpha_1, 2\alpha_1, \alpha_1) + (2\alpha_2, 3\alpha_2, 2\alpha_2) = 0$$

$$\alpha_1 + 2\alpha_2 = 0$$
$$2\alpha_1 + 3\alpha_2 = 0 \tag{11}$$
$$\alpha_1 + 2\alpha_2 = 0$$

The only solution to this system is $\alpha_1 = 0$, $\alpha_2 = 0$, thus the system is linearly independent.

● **PROBLEM 2-15**

1) Show that in two-dimensional space the vectors (0, 1) and (1, 0) are linearly independent.

2) Show that in three-dimensional space the vectors (1, 0, 0), (0, 1, 0), (0, 0, 1) are linearly independent.

3) Express vector $\bar{a} = (a_1, a_2)$ as a linear combination of vectors (1,0), (0,1).

4) Express vector $\bar{b} = (b_1, b_2, b_3)$ as a linear combination of vectors (1,0,0), (0,1,0), (0,0,1).

Solution: 1) The linear combination of vectors

(1,0) and (0,1) is

$$\alpha_1(1,0) + \alpha_2(0,1) = \overline{0} \tag{1}$$

$$\alpha_1 = 0$$
$$\alpha_2 = 0 \tag{2}$$

Thus the vectors are linearly independent.

2) For three-dimensional space

$$\alpha_1(1,0,0) + \alpha_2(0,1,0) + \alpha_3(0,0,1) = \overline{0} \tag{3}$$

Thus $\alpha_1 = 0$
$$\alpha_2 = 0 \tag{4}$$
$$\alpha_3 = 0$$

and the vectors are linearly independent.

3) $\overline{a} = \lambda_1(1,0) + \lambda_2(0,1) = (a_1, a_2)$ $\tag{5}$

thus $\lambda_1 = a_1$ and $\lambda_2 = a_2$

and therefore $\overline{a} = a_1(1,0) + a_2(0,1)$ $\tag{6}$

In two-dimensional space, vectors (1,0) and (0,1) form a base, that means that any vector in this space can be expressed as a linear combination of (1,0) and (0,1). These vectors are usually denoted by

$$\overline{i} = (1,0)$$
$$\overline{j} = (0,1) \tag{7}$$

4) In three-dimensional space,

$$\overline{b} = (b_1, b_2, b_3) = \lambda_1(1,0,0) + \lambda_2(0,1,0) + \lambda_3(0,0,1) \tag{8}$$

Thus

$$b_1 = \lambda_1$$
$$b_2 = \lambda_2 \tag{9}$$
$$b_3 = \lambda_3$$

and vector $\overline{b}$ can be expressed

$$\overline{b} = b_1(1,0,0) + b_2(0,1,0) + b_3(0,0,1) \tag{10}$$

In three-dimensional space, vectors (1,0,0), (0,1,0), (0,0,1) form a base. Any vector in this space can be represented as a linear combination of these vectors. They are denoted by

$$\overline{i} = (1,0,0)$$
$$\overline{j} = (0,1,0) \tag{11}$$
$$\overline{k} = (0,0,1)$$

1) Show that in a two-dimensional space any set of three vectors is linearly dependent.

2) Show that in a three-dimensional space any set of four vectors is linearly dependent.

Solution: 1) Let the vectors be $\overline{a} = (a_1, a_2)$; $\overline{b} = (b_1, b_2)$; $\overline{c} = (c_1, c_2)$. Form the linear combination

$$\lambda_1 \overline{a} + \lambda_2 \overline{b} + \lambda_3 \overline{c} = \overline{0}$$

$$\lambda_1(a_1, a_2) + \lambda_2(b_1, b_2) + \lambda_3(c_1, c_2)$$

$$= (\lambda_1 a_1, \lambda_1 a_2) + (\lambda_2 b_1, \lambda_2 b_2) + (\lambda_3 c_1, \lambda_3 c_2) = (0, 0)$$

This equation is equivalent to the set of linear equations

$$\lambda_1 a_1 + \lambda_2 b_1 + \lambda_3 c_1 = 0$$

$$\lambda_1 a_2 + \lambda_2 b_2 + \lambda_3 c_2 = 0$$

Now show that this set of equations have nontrivial solutions only. If $a_1 = b_1 = c_1 = 0$, then λ_1, λ_2 and λ_3 can be chosen to satisfy the second equation and the first equation will be satisfied automatically.

Assume that $c_1 \neq 0$, then from the first equation

$$\lambda_3 = -\frac{1}{c_1}(\lambda_1 a_1 + \lambda_2 b_1)$$

Substituting λ_3 into the second equation

$$\lambda_1 a_2 + \lambda_2 b_2 - \frac{c_2}{c_1}(\lambda_1 a_1 + \lambda_2 b_1) = 0$$

Multiplying by c_1

$$\lambda_1 a_2 c_1 + \lambda_2 b_2 c_1 - \lambda_1 a_1 c_2 - \lambda_2 b_1 c_2 = 0$$

or

$$\lambda_1(a_2 c_1 - a_1 c_2) + \lambda_2(b_2 c_1 - b_1 c_2) = 0$$

This equation has nontrivial solutions, arbitrarily choose λ_1,

$$\lambda_1 = 1$$

Then for λ_2 and λ_3,

$$\lambda_2 = \frac{a_1 c_2 - a_2 c_1}{b_2 c_1 - b_1 c_2}$$

$$\lambda_3 = -\frac{1}{c_1}\left[a_1 + b_1 \frac{a_1 c_2 - a_2 c_1}{b_2 c_1 - b_1 c_2}\right]$$

That proves that the system of three vectors in a two-dimensional space is linearly dependent.

2) Let the system of four vectors in a three-dimensional space be

$$\bar{a} = (a_1, a_2, a_3) \quad \bar{b} = (b_1, b_2, b_3)$$
$$\bar{c} = (c_1, c_2, c_3) \quad \bar{d} = (d_1, d_2, d_3)$$

The linear combination is

$$\lambda_1 \bar{a} + \lambda_2 \bar{b} + \lambda_3 \bar{c} + \lambda_4 \bar{d} = \bar{0}$$

which is equivalent to the set of linear equations

$$\lambda_1 a_1 + \lambda_2 b_1 + \lambda_3 c_1 + \lambda_4 d_1 = 0 \tag{1}$$
$$\lambda_1 a_2 + \lambda_2 b_2 + \lambda_3 c_2 + \lambda_4 d_2 = 0 \tag{2}$$
$$\lambda_1 a_3 + \lambda_2 b_3 + \lambda_3 c_3 + \lambda_4 d_3 = 0 \tag{3}$$

Show that this system has a nontrivial solution, if
$a_1 = b_1 = c_1 = d_1 = 0$, then solve the second and third
equations only. They have nontrivial solutions only (because
we are solving a system of two equations with four unknowns).
The first equation is satisfied automatically. Assume that
$d_1 \neq 0$, from eq. (1) obtain

$$\lambda_4 = - \frac{1}{d_1}(\lambda_1 a_1 + \lambda_2 b_1 + \lambda_3 c_1) \tag{4}$$

Substituting eq. (4) into eq. (2) and eq. (3),

$$\lambda_1(d_1 a_2 - d_2 a_1) + \lambda_2(d_1 b_2 - d_2 b_1) + \lambda_3(d_1 c_2 - d_2 c_1) = 0 \tag{5}$$
$$\lambda_1(d_1 a_3 - d_3 a_1) + \lambda_2(d_1 b_3 - d_3 b_1) + \lambda_3(d_1 c_3 - d_3 c_1) = 0 \tag{6}$$

If all the coefficients of eq. (5) are equal to zero, that is

$$d_1 a_2 - d_2 a_1 = 0$$
$$d_1 b_2 - d_2 b_1 = 0$$
$$d_1 c_2 - d_2 c_1 = 0$$

then eq. (6) has a nontrivial solution and eq. (5) is satisfied automatically.

Assume that $d_1 c_2 - d_2 c_1 \neq 0$.

From eq. (5) compute λ_3.

$$\lambda_3 = - \frac{1}{d_1 c_2 - d_2 c_1} \left[\lambda_1(d_1 a_2 - d_2 a_1) + \lambda_2(d_1 b_2 - d_2 b_1) \right] \tag{7}$$

Substituting eq. (7) into eq. (6)

$$\lambda_1(d_1 a_3 - d_3 a_1) + \lambda_2(d_1 b_3 - d_3 b_1) - \frac{d_1 c_3 - d_3 c_1}{d_1 c_2 - d_2 c_1} \left[\lambda_1(d_1 a_2 - d_2 a_1) \right.$$
$$\left. + \lambda_2(d_1 b_2 - d_2 b_1) \right] = 0 \tag{8}$$

53

Eq. (8) can be simplified to

$$\lambda_1 \left[(d_1a_3-d_3a_1)(d_1c_2-d_2c_1)-(d_1a_2-d_2a_1)(d_1c_3-d_3c_1)\right] +$$
$$+\lambda_2 \left[(d_1b_3-d_3b_1)(d_1c_2-d_2c_1)-(d_1b_2-d_2b_1)(d_1c_3-d_3c_1)\right] = 0 \qquad (9)$$

Then set $\lambda_1 = 1$. From eq. (9) compute λ_2

$$\lambda_2 = \frac{(d_1a_2-d_2a_1)(d_1c_3-d_3c_1)-(d_1a_3-d_3a_1)(d_1c_2-d_2c_1)}{(d_1b_3-d_3b_1)(d_1c_2-d_2c_1)-(d_1b_2-d_2b_1)(d_1c_3-d_3c_1)} \qquad (10)$$

Substituting $\lambda_1 = 1$ and eq. (10) into eq. (7) λ_3 is found.

Substituting λ_1, λ_2, λ_3 into eq. (4), λ_4 is found. A non-

trivial solution of eq. (1)-(3) was found, therefore any system of four vectors in a three-dimensional space is linearly dependent.

The above results are special cases of a general theorem. In an n-dimensional space any set of n + 1 vectors is linearly dependent. The maximum number of independent vectors in this space is n.

● **PROBLEM 2-17**

1) Show that in three-dimensional space a set of three vectors $\bar{a}$, $\bar{b}$, $\bar{c}$ is linearly dependent if and only if

$$\begin{vmatrix} a_1 & a_2 & a_3 \\ b_1 & b_2 & b_3 \\ c_1 & c_2 & c_3 \end{vmatrix} = 0 \qquad (1)$$

2) Determine if the vectors

$$\bar{r}_1 = (2,4,1)$$
$$\bar{r}_2 = (0,3,-1)$$
$$\bar{r}_3 = (2,1,1)$$

are linearly dependent.

Solution: 1) First prove that if the vectors $\bar{a}$, $\bar{b}$, $\bar{c}$ are linearly dependent, then the determinant of eq. (1) is equal to zero. By definition, when vectors $\bar{a}$, $\bar{b}$, $\bar{c}$ are linearly dependent, then

$$\alpha\bar{a} + \beta\bar{b} + \rho\bar{c} = 0 \qquad (2)$$

where α, β, ρ are not all zero.

Let us assume $\alpha \neq 0$, then

$$\bar{a} = -\frac{1}{\alpha}(\beta\bar{b}+\rho\bar{c}) \qquad (3)$$

or

$$a_1 = -\frac{1}{\alpha}(\beta b_1 + \rho c_1)$$

$$a_2 = -\frac{1}{\alpha}(\beta b_2 + \rho c_2) \tag{4}$$

$$a_3 = -\frac{1}{\alpha}(\beta b_3 + \rho c_3)$$

Considering eq. (1), eq. (4) expresses one row of the determinant of components as a linear combination of the other two rows. Therefore the determinant is equal to zero

$$\begin{vmatrix} a_1 & a_2 & a_3 \\ b_1 & b_2 & b_3 \\ c_1 & c_2 & c_3 \end{vmatrix} = 0 \tag{5}$$

To prove this in the opposite direction, assume that the determinant is equal to zero. Then eq. (2)

$$\alpha\bar{a} + \beta\bar{b} + \rho\bar{c} = 0$$

is satisfied by

$$\alpha = \begin{vmatrix} b_2 & b_3 \\ c_2 & c_3 \end{vmatrix} \qquad \beta = -\begin{vmatrix} a_2 & a_3 \\ c_2 & c_3 \end{vmatrix} \qquad \rho = \begin{vmatrix} a_2 & a_3 \\ b_2 & b_3 \end{vmatrix} \tag{6}$$

That proves the theorem.

Note that when all the determinants of eq. (6) are equal to zero, one may choose other determinants which are cofactors of

$$\begin{vmatrix} a_1 & a_2 & a_3 \\ b_1 & b_2 & b_3 \\ c_1 & c_2 & c_3 \end{vmatrix}$$

2) Check the value of the determinant

$$\begin{vmatrix} 2 & 4 & 1 \\ 0 & 3 & -1 \\ 2 & 1 & 1 \end{vmatrix} = 6-8-6+2 \neq 0$$

Thus the vectors $\bar{r}_1$, $\bar{r}_2$, $\bar{r}_3$ are linearly independent.

REPRESENTATION OF VECTORS IN TERMS OF BASE VECTORS

● PROBLEM 2-18

Show that the plane $x_1 x_2$ is a two-dimensional vector space and vectors $\bar{i}_1 = (1,0)$

(1)

$$\bar{i}_2 = (0,1)$$

are its basis.

Solution: A vector space V is said to be n-dimensional, written dim V = n, if there exist linearly independent vectors $\bar{i}_1, \bar{i}_2, \ldots \bar{i}_n$ such that any vector $\bar{a} \varepsilon V$ can be represented as a linear combination of vectors $\bar{i}_1, \bar{i}_2, \ldots \bar{i}_n$. Vectors $\bar{i}_1, \bar{i}_2, \ldots \bar{i}_n$ form a basis of V.

Vectors $\bar{i}_1 = (1,0)$ and $\bar{i}_2 = (0,1)$ are linearly independent, indeed

$$\alpha_1 \bar{i}_1 + \alpha_2 \bar{i}_2 = \bar{0} \tag{2}$$

$$\alpha_1 = 0 \quad \text{and} \quad \alpha_2 = 0$$

Any vector $\bar{a}$ can be represented as a linear combination of $\bar{i}_1$ and $\bar{i}_2$

$$\bar{a} = \alpha_1 \bar{i}_1 + \alpha_2 \bar{i}_2 \tag{3}$$

$$(a_1, a_2) = \alpha_1 (1,0) + \alpha_2 (0,1) = (\alpha_1, \alpha_2)$$

thus

$$\alpha_1 = a_1, \quad \alpha_2 = a_2$$

and

$$\bar{a} = a_1 \bar{i}_1 + a_2 \bar{i}_2 \tag{4}$$

In a similar fashion it can be shown that the space $x_1 x_2 x_3$ is a three-dimensional vector space.

● **PROBLEM 2-19**

1) For a rectangular right-handed coordinate system define the base vectors graphically and analytically.

2) Express vector $\bar{a} = (a_1, a_2, a_3)$ in terms of base vectors. Illustrate the construction graphically.

Solution: 1) Fig. 1 shows a right-handed rectangular coordinate system, where there are three unit vectors, having the directions of the positive x_1, x_2, x_3 axes of a three-dimensional rectangular coordinate system.

The vectors are denoted $\bar{i}_1, \bar{i}_2, \bar{i}_3$. It is desired to show that these vectors form a basis in the three-dimensional space (in other words, to prove that these vectors, $\bar{i}_1, \bar{i}_2, \bar{i}_3$ are linearly independent) and that any vector in the space can be represented as a linear combination of them.

Analytically these vectors can be expressed as

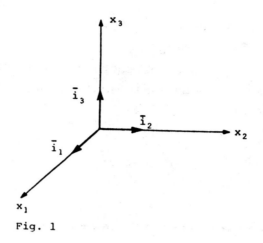

Fig. 1

$$\overline{i}_1 = (1,0,0)$$
$$\overline{i}_2 = (0,1,0)$$
$$\overline{i}_3 = (0,0,1)$$

$\overline{i}_1, \overline{i}_2, \overline{i}_3$ are linearly independent, indeed

$$\alpha_1 \overline{i}_1 + \alpha_2 \overline{i}_2 + \alpha_3 \overline{i}_3 = \overline{0}$$

which leads to $\alpha_1 = \alpha_2 = \alpha_3 = 0$.

Let $\quad \overline{a} = (a_1, a_2, a_3)$, then

$$\overline{a} = \beta_1 \overline{i}_1 + \beta_2 \overline{i}_2 + \beta_3 \overline{i}_3$$
$$= (\beta_1, 0, 0) + (0, \beta_2, 0) + (0, 0, \beta_3) = (a_1, a_2, a_3)$$

Thus $\qquad \beta_1 = a_1, \qquad \beta_2 = a_2, \qquad \beta_3 = a_3$
and
$$\overline{a} = a_1 \overline{i}_1 + a_2 \overline{i}_2 + a_3 \overline{i}_3$$

Scalars a_1, a_2 and a_3 are called the coordinates of vector $\overline{a}$.

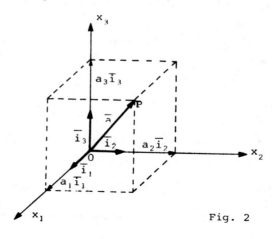

Fig. 2

2) Let $\bar{a}$ be any vector in space,
$$\bar{a} = (a_1, a_2, a_3)$$
Construct $\overline{OP} = \bar{a}$, then the coordinates of P are a_1, a_2, a_3 and O is the origin of the system, as shown in Fig. 2.

From Fig. 2,
$$\bar{a} = a_1\bar{i}_1 + a_2\bar{i}_2 + a_3\bar{i}_3$$
Thus vector $\bar{a}$ is represented graphically as the sum of vectors $a_1\bar{i}_1$, $a_2\bar{i}_2$, $a_3\bar{i}_3$.

● **PROBLEM 2-20**

Express the following vectors in terms of base vectors:
1) $\bar{b} = (1,3)$
2) $\bar{c} = (4,0)$
3) $\bar{d} = (1,5,7)$
4) $\bar{e} = (2,-3,4)$
5) $\bar{f} = (1,4,-1,2)$
6) $\bar{g} = (-1,0,4,2,\sin \alpha)$

Solution: 1) Vector $\bar{b} = (1,3)$ is two-dimensional. Two-dimensional space has two base vectors
$$\bar{i}_1 = (1,0)$$
$$\bar{i}_2 = (0,1)$$
$$\bar{b} = (1,3) = 1(1,0) + 3(0,1) = \bar{i}_1 + 3\bar{i}_2$$

2) $\bar{c} = (4,0) = 4(1,0) + 0(0,1) = 4\bar{i}_1$

3) $\bar{d} = (1,5,7)$
In this case, $\bar{d}$ is a three-dimensional vector. The base vectors are:
$$\bar{i}_1 = (1,0,0) \quad \bar{i}_2 = (0,1,0) \quad \bar{i}_3 = (0,0,1)$$
and
$$\bar{d} = \bar{i}_1 + 5\bar{i}_2 + 7\bar{i}_3$$

4) $\bar{e} = (2,-3,4) = 2\bar{i}_1 - 3\bar{i}_2 + 4\bar{i}_3$

5) $\bar{f}$ is a four-dimensional vector, the base vectors are
$$\bar{i}_1 = (1,0,0,0) \quad \bar{i}_2 = (0,1,0,0) \quad \bar{i}_3 = (0,0,1,0)$$
$$\bar{i}_4 = (0,0,0,1) \quad \bar{f} = (1,4,-1,2) = \bar{i}_1 + 4\bar{i}_2 - \bar{i}_3 + 2\bar{i}_4$$

6) $\bar{g}$ belongs to the five-dimensional vector space, thus

$$\overline{g} = (-1,0,4,2,\sin\ \alpha) = -\overline{i}_1 + 4\overline{i}_3 + 2\overline{i}_4 + \sin\alpha\overline{i}_5$$

where

$$\overline{i}_1 = (1,0,0,0,0) \quad \overline{i}_3 = (0,0,1,0,0) \quad \overline{i}_4 = (0,0,0,1,0)$$

$$\overline{i}_5 = (0,0,0,0,1)$$

● **PROBLEM** 2-21

Express vector $\overline{a} = (2,-5,3)$ as a linear combination of vectors

$$\overline{b}_1 = (1,-3,2)$$

$$\overline{b}_2 = (2,-4,-1) \tag{1}$$

$$\overline{b}_3 = (1,-5,7)$$

<u>Solution</u>: Find the scalars α_1, α_2, α_3 such that

$$\overline{a} = \alpha_1\overline{b}_1 + \alpha_2\overline{b}_2 + \alpha_3\overline{b}_3 \tag{2}$$

or

$$(2,-5,3) = \alpha_1(1,-3,2) + \alpha_2(2,-4,-1) + \alpha_3(1,-5,7) \tag{3}$$

Comparing the coordinates, obtain the following system of equations

$$\begin{aligned} 2 &= \alpha_1 + 2\alpha_2 + \alpha_3 \\ -5 &= -3\alpha_1 - 4\alpha_2 - 5\alpha_3 \\ 3 &= 2\alpha_1 - \alpha_2 + 7\alpha_3 \end{aligned} \tag{4}$$

Using elementary row operations, reduce this system to echelon form

$$\begin{aligned} \alpha_1 + 2\alpha_2 + \alpha_3 &= 2 \\ 2\alpha_2 - 2\alpha_3 &= 1 \\ 0 &= 3 \end{aligned} \tag{5}$$

The system is inconsistent and $\overline{a}$ cannot be expressed as a linear combination of $\overline{b}_1$, $\overline{b}_2$, $\overline{b}_3$. This is due to the fact that the vectors $\overline{b}_1$, $\overline{b}_2$, $\overline{b}_3$ are linearly dependent.

Let us repeat the criterion of dependence. In the three-dimensional space a set of three vectors $\overline{a}$, $\overline{b}$, $\overline{c}$ is linearly dependent if and only if

$$\begin{vmatrix} a_1 & a_2 & a_3 \\ b_1 & b_2 & b_3 \\ c_1 & c_2 & c_3 \end{vmatrix} = 0 \tag{6}$$

59

Substituting eq. (1) into the determinant, obtain:

$$\begin{vmatrix} 1 & -3 & 2 \\ 2 & -4 & -1 \\ 1 & -5 & 7 \end{vmatrix} = -28+3-20+8-5+42 = 0 \tag{7}$$

Thus the vectors $\bar{b}_1$, $\bar{b}_2$, $\bar{b}_3$ are linearly dependent.

● **PROBLEM** 2-22

Let $\bar{a}$ be a vector in a three-dimensional space, $\bar{a} = (1,-2,5)$. Express $\bar{a}$ as a linear combination of vectors:

1) $\bar{d}_1 = (2,1,3)$ $\bar{d}_2 = (1,1,2)$ $\bar{d}_3 = (2,3,1)$

2) $\bar{e}_1 = (1,1,1)$ $\bar{e}_2 = (1,2,3)$ $\bar{e}_3 = (2,-1,1)$

Solution: 1)   First check if the vectors $\bar{d}_1$, $\bar{d}_2$ and $\bar{d}_3$ are linearly independent and form a basis of the three-dimensional space.

$$\begin{vmatrix} \bar{d}_1 \\ \bar{d}_2 \\ \bar{d}_3 \end{vmatrix} = \begin{vmatrix} 2 & 1 & 3 \\ 1 & 1 & 2 \\ 2 & 3 & 1 \end{vmatrix} = 15-19 = -4 \neq 0 \tag{1}$$

Thus the vectors $\bar{d}_1$, $\bar{d}_2$, $\bar{d}_3$ are linearly independent and constitute a basis of the vector space.   To find the coordinates of $\bar{a}$ in this basis,

$$\bar{a} = \alpha_1 \bar{d}_1 + \alpha_2 \bar{d}_2 + \alpha_3 \bar{d}_3 \tag{2}$$

or

$$(1,-2,5) = \alpha_1(2,1,3)+\alpha_2(1,1,2)+\alpha_3(2,3,1)$$

and

$$1 = 2\alpha_1 + \alpha_2 + 2\alpha_3$$
$$-2 = \alpha_1 + \alpha_2 + 3\alpha_3 \tag{3}$$
$$5 = 3\alpha_1 + 2\alpha_2 + \alpha_3$$

Solving system (3),

$$\alpha_1 = \frac{3}{2}, \quad \alpha_2 = 1, \quad \alpha_3 = \frac{-3}{2} \tag{4}$$

Thus, vector $\bar{a}$ can be expressed as

$$\bar{a} = \frac{3}{2}\bar{d}_1 + \bar{d}_2 - \frac{3}{2}\bar{d}_3 \tag{5}$$

2)   Now check if the vectors $\bar{e}_1$, $\bar{e}_2$, $\bar{e}_3$ are linearly independent, doing this

$$\begin{vmatrix} \bar{e}_1 \\ \bar{e}_2 \\ \bar{e}_3 \end{vmatrix} = \begin{vmatrix} 1 & 1 & 1 \\ 1 & 2 & 3 \\ 2 & -1 & 1 \end{vmatrix} \neq 0 \tag{6}$$

Thus vectors $\bar{e}_1$, $\bar{e}_2$, $\bar{e}_3$ are linearly independent and they form a basis of the three-dimensional vector space.

Form the linear combination

$$\bar{a} = \beta_1 \bar{e}_1 + \beta_2 \bar{e}_2 + \beta_3 \bar{e}_3 \tag{7}$$

$$(1,-2,5) = \beta_1(1,1,1) + \beta_2(1,2,3) + \beta_3(2,-1,1)$$

Then obtain the following system of equations

$$1 = \beta_1 + \beta_2 + 2\beta_3$$
$$-2 = \beta_1 + 2\beta_2 - \beta_3 \tag{8}$$
$$5 = \beta_1 + 3\beta_2 + \beta_3$$

Solving (8)

$$\beta_1 = -6, \quad \beta_2 = 3, \quad \beta_3 = 2 \tag{9}$$

Substituting eq. (9) into eq. (7)

$$\bar{a} = -6\bar{e}_1 + 3\bar{e}_2 + 2\bar{e}_3 \tag{10}$$

In a vector space there are an infinite number of possible bases. Some of them, for instance

$$\bar{i}_1 = (1,0,0), \quad \bar{i}_2 = (0,1,0), \quad \bar{i}_3 = (0,0,1)$$

of the three-dimensional space, are used for their simplicity.

● **PROBLEM** 2-23

Consider a system of n electric charges e_1, e_2,...,e_n; let $\bar{r}_i$ be the position vector of e_i (i=1,2,...,n) with respect to the origin 0. The dipole moment of the system of charges is defined as

$$\bar{p} = \sum_{i=1}^{n} e_i \bar{r}_i \tag{1}$$

and the center of charge of the system is

$$\bar{R} = \frac{\bar{p}}{\sum\limits_{i=1}^{n} e_i} = \frac{\sum\limits_{i=1}^{n} e_i \bar{r}_i}{\sum\limits_{i=1}^{n} e_i} \tag{2}$$

where

$$\sum_{i=1}^{n} e_i \neq 0.$$

The system of charges is called neutral if

$$\sum_{i=1}^{n} e_i = 0 \tag{3}$$

1) Show that the dipole moment of a neutral system is independent of the origin 0.

2) Express this moment in terms of the centers of the systems of negative and positive charges making up the original system.

Solution: 1) Let the dipole moment with respect to an origin 0 be

$$\bar{p} = \sum_{i=1}^{n} e_i \bar{r}_i \tag{4}$$

and with respect to another origin 0' be

$$\bar{p}' = \sum_{i=1}^{n} e_i \bar{r}'_i \tag{5}$$

where

$$\overline{00'} = \bar{a} \tag{6}$$

Thus, the position vectors are

$$\bar{r}'_i = \bar{r}_i + \bar{a} \tag{7}$$

Substituting eq. (7) into eq. (5), obtain

$$\bar{p}' = \sum_{i=1}^{n} e_i \bar{r}'_i = \sum_{i=1}^{n} e_i (\bar{r}_i + \bar{a}) =$$

$$= \sum_{i=1}^{n} e_i \bar{r}_i + \sum_{i=1}^{n} e_i \bar{a} \tag{8}$$

But

$$\sum_{i=1}^{n} e_i = 0 \tag{9}$$

and

$$\sum_{i=1}^{n} e_i \bar{a} = \bar{a} \sum_{i=1}^{n} e_i = 0 \tag{10}$$

Thus

$$\bar{p}' = \bar{p} \tag{11}$$

2) The system consists of negative and positive charges, so that

$$\sum_{i=1}^{n} e_i = \sum e_j^- + \sum e_k^+ , \tag{12}$$

denote

$$\sum e_k^+ = -\sum e_j^- = Q \tag{13}$$

Thus, the centers of the systems of negative and positive charges are

$$\bar{R}^- = \frac{\sum e_j^- \bar{r}_j^-}{\sum e_j^-} \quad , \quad \bar{R}^+ = \frac{\sum e_k^+ \bar{r}_k^+}{\sum e_k^+} \tag{14}$$

Thus, the dipole moment of the original system is

$$\bar{p} = \sum_{i=1}^{n} e_i \bar{r}_i = \sum e_k^+ \bar{r}_k^+ + \sum e_j^- \bar{r}_j^- =$$

$$= \bar{R}^+ \sum e_k^+ + \bar{R}^- \sum e_j^- = Q(\bar{R}^+ - \bar{R}^-) \tag{15}$$

CHAPTER 3

THE SCALAR PRODUCT AND THE VECTOR PRODUCT

INTRODUCTION

Having considered addition and subtraction of vectors, the next step is to consider multiplication of vectors. Chapter 3 introduces both forms of vector multiplication - the scalar product (also called dot product) and the vector product (cross product). The first few problems of the chapter are completely devoted to the component and geo- metrical definition of the scalar product. Once familiar with the scalar product, the student is introduced to the vector product...to which the geometrical definition, for visualization purposes, is introduced before the component definition.

The chapter then proceeds to the application of the vector and scalar product to geometry, physics as well as their effect on perpendicular vectors and the base vectors.

The chapter then goes on to introduce the scalar triple product and vector triple product. Both of these products are used to prove a number of frequently used identities.

Lastly, the chapter discusses how the vector and scalar product, when applied to problems in analytic geometry, pro- vide us with relatively simple vector equations of lines, planes and spheres.

THE SCALAR PRODUCT

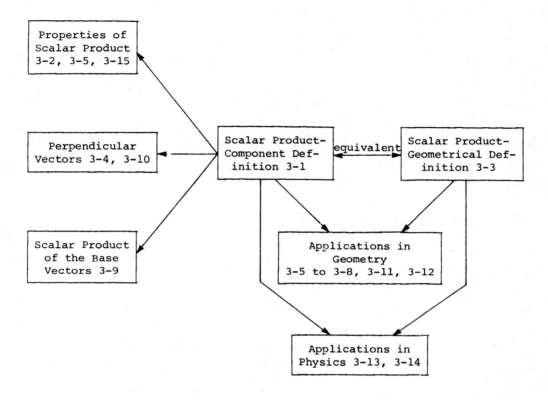

Properties of Scalar Product 3-2, 3-5, 3-15	
Perpendicular Vectors 3-4, 3-10	Scalar Product-Component Definition 3-1
Scalar Product of the Base Vectors 3-9	

Scalar Product-Component Definition 3-1 — equivalent — Scalar Product-Geometrical Definition 3-3

Applications in Geometry 3-5 to 3-8, 3-11, 3-12

Applications in Physics 3-13, 3-14

THE VECTOR PRODUCT

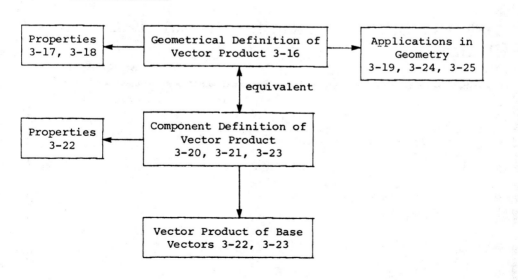

Properties 3-17, 3-18 ← Geometrical Definition of Vector Product 3-16 → Applications in Geometry 3-19, 3-24, 3-25

equivalent

Properties 3-22 ← Component Definition of Vector Product 3-20, 3-21, 3-23

Vector Product of Base Vectors 3-22, 3-23

SCALAR TRIPLE PRODUCT AND VECTOR TRIPLE PRODUCT

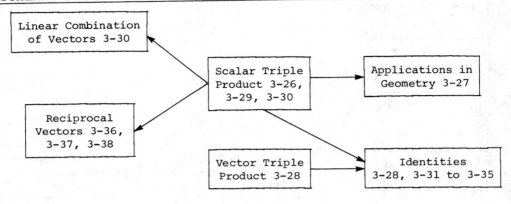

APPLICATIONS OF VECTORS IN GEOMETRY

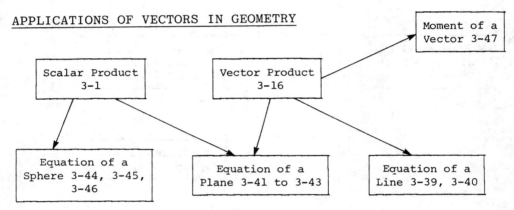

This chart is provided to facilitate rapid understanding of the inter-relationships of the topics and subject matter in this chapter. Also shown are the problem numbers associated with the subject matter.

DEFINITIONS AND PROPERTIES OF THE SCALAR PRODUCT

● PROBLEM 3-1

Find the scalar product (also called the dot product) of the following vectors:

1) $\bar{a} = (2,3)$ and $\bar{b} = (1,-1)$

2) $\bar{c} = (4,1)$ and $\bar{d} = (6,-5)$

3) $\bar{e} = (1,2,-3)$ and $\bar{f} = (-1,1,2)$

4) $\bar{g} = (2,4)$ and $\bar{h} = (1,5,3)$

5) $\bar{k} = (0,\sin\alpha,1,3)$ and $\bar{l} = (2,4,-2,1)$

6) $\bar{p} = (\sin\omega t,\cos\omega t)$ and $\bar{q} = (\sin\omega t,\cos\omega t)$

<u>Solution</u>: In general, the scalar product of two n-dimensional vectors

and
$$\bar{a} = (a_1, a_2, \ldots, a_n)$$
$$\bar{b} = (b_1, b_2, \ldots, b_n)$$

is defined as $\bar{a} \cdot \bar{b} \equiv a_1 b_1 + a_2 b_2 + \ldots + a_n b_n$ (1)

In two dimensions,

$$\bar{a} \cdot \bar{b} \equiv a_1 b_1 + a_2 b_2 \tag{2}$$

in three dimensions

$$\bar{a} \cdot \bar{b} \equiv a_1 b_1 + a_2 b_2 + a_3 b_3 \tag{3}$$

The scalar product of the given vectors using eq.(1), (2) and (3) are as follows

1) $\bar{a} \cdot \bar{b} = (2,3) \cdot (1,-1) = 2 \cdot 1 + 3 \cdot (-1) = -1$

2) $\bar{c} \cdot \bar{d} = (4,1) \cdot (6,-5) = 4 \cdot 6 + 1 \cdot (-5) = 24 - 5 = 19$

3) $\bar{e} \cdot \bar{f} = (1,2,-3) \cdot (-1,1,2) = -1+2-6 = -5$

4) $\bar{g} \cdot \bar{h}$

The scalar product of $\bar{g}$ **and** $\bar{h}$ cannot be computed because vector $\bar{g}$ is two-dimensional and vector $\bar{h}$ is three-dimensional. The scalar product is defined only for two vectors of the same dimension.

5) $\bar{k} \cdot \bar{l} = (0, \sin\alpha, 1, 3) \cdot (2, 4, -2, 1) =$

$$= 4\sin\alpha - 2 + 3 = 1 + 4\sin\alpha$$

6) $\bar{p} \cdot \bar{q} = (\sin\omega t, \cos\omega t) \cdot (\sin\omega t, \cos\omega t) =$

$$= \sin^2 \omega t + \cos^2 \omega t = 1$$

● **PROBLEM 3-2**

Prove that the scalar product is commutative, that is

$$\bar{a} \cdot \bar{b} = \bar{b} \cdot \bar{a} \tag{1}$$

for any two vectors

$$\bar{a} = (a_1, a_2, \ldots, a_n)$$

$$\bar{b} = (b_1, b_2, \ldots, b_n) \tag{2}$$

and distributive, that is

$$\bar{a} \cdot (\bar{b} + \bar{c}) = \bar{a} \cdot \bar{b} + \bar{a} \cdot \bar{c} \tag{3}$$

where

$$\bar{c} = (c_1, c_2, \ldots, c_n)$$

Solution: 1) By definition,

$$\overline{a} \cdot \overline{b} = a_1 b_1 + a_2 b_2 + \ldots + a_n b_n = b_1 a_1 + b_2 a_2 + \ldots + b_n a_n =$$

$$= \overline{b} \cdot \overline{a} \qquad (4)$$

That proves eq.(1). The property which states that for any two real numbers α and β

$$\alpha\beta = \beta\alpha$$

was used throughout this proof.

2) Here, again using the definition of the scalar product,

$$\overline{a} \cdot (\overline{b} + \overline{c}) = (a_1, a_2, \ldots, a_n) \cdot (b_1 + c_1, b_2 + c_2, \ldots, b_n + c_n) \qquad (5)$$

$$= a_1(b_1 + c_1) + a_2(b_2 + c_2) + \ldots + a_n(b_n + c_n) = a_1 b_1 + a_1 c_1 + a_2 b_2 + a_2 c_2$$

$$+ \ldots + a_n b_n + a_n c_n = (a_1 b_1 + a_2 b_2 + \ldots + a_n b_n) + (a_1 c_1 + a_2 c_2 + \ldots + a_n c_n)$$

$$= \overline{a} \cdot \overline{b} + \overline{a} \cdot \overline{c}$$

That proves eq.(3). The property that real numbers are distributive was used throughout this proof. The distributive property says that for any three real numbers α, β and ρ,

$$\alpha(\beta + \rho) = \alpha\beta + \alpha\rho$$

● **PROBLEM 3-3**

Show that in two- and three-dimensional space both of the following definitions of the scalar product are equivalent.

Definition I:

Let $\overline{a}$ and $\overline{b}$ be two vectors

$$\overline{a} = (a_1, a_2, a_3)$$

$$\overline{b} = (b_1, b_2, b_3) \qquad (1)$$

and α be the smallest nonnegative angle between $\overline{a}$ and $\overline{b}$ as shown in Fig. 1

$$0° \leq \alpha \leq 180°$$

The scalar product $\overline{a} \cdot \overline{b}$ is defined as

$$\overline{a} \cdot \overline{b} = |\overline{a}||\overline{b}| \cos \alpha \qquad (2)$$

where $|\overline{a}|$ and $|\overline{b}|$ are magnitudes of $\overline{a}$ and $\overline{b}$ respectively.

Definition II:

Let $\overline{a} = (a_1, a_2, a_3)$ and $\overline{b} = (b_1, b_2, b_3)$ the scalar product is defined as

$$\overline{a} \cdot \overline{b} = a_1 b_1 + a_2 b_2 + a_3 b_3 \qquad (3)$$

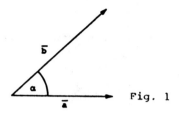

Fig. 1

Solution: Start with the first definition and denote $|\bar{a}| = a$, $|\bar{b}| = b$. Fig. 2 shows vectors $\bar{a}$ and $\bar{b}$.

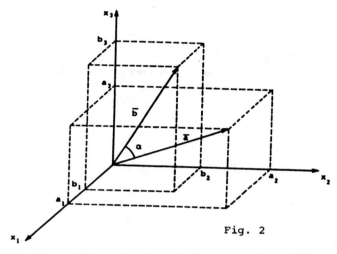

Fig. 2

From Fig. 2 the direction cosines of the vectors $\bar{a}$ and $\bar{b}$ are:

$\dfrac{a_1}{a}$ (between $\bar{a}$ and $\bar{x}_1$ axis) $\dfrac{a_2}{a}$ (between $\bar{a}$ and $\bar{x}_2$ axis)

$$\frac{a_3}{a} \quad \text{(between } \bar{a} \text{ and } \bar{x}_3 \text{ axis)} \tag{4}$$

For vector $\bar{b}$, the direction cosines are

$$\frac{b_1}{b}, \quad \frac{b_2}{b}, \quad \frac{b_3}{b}, \quad \text{for the } x_1, x_2, \text{ and } x_3\text{-axis} \tag{5}$$

respectively.

In analytic geometry there is a formula that can express angle α in terms of the direction cosines, namely

$$\cos \alpha = \frac{a_1}{a}\frac{b_1}{b} + \frac{a_2}{a}\frac{b_2}{b} + \frac{a_3}{a}\frac{b_3}{b} \tag{6}$$

or

$$ab \cos \alpha = a_1 b_1 + a_2 b_2 + a_3 b_3 \tag{7}$$

However, from Definition II,

$$a_1 b_1 + a_2 b_2 + a_3 b_3 = \bar{a} \cdot \bar{b}$$

Thus $\bar{a} \cdot \bar{b} = |\bar{a}||\bar{b}| \cos \alpha$ (8)

and therefore both definitions are equivalent.

69

Vector $\bar{a}$ is given such that

$$\bar{a} = (2,-3,1)$$

Which of these vectors

$$\bar{b} = (2,2,2)$$
$$\bar{c} = (4,-1,0)$$
$$\bar{d} = (-1,-2,-3)$$
$$\bar{e} = (2,-9,-31)$$

are perpendicular to $\bar{a}$?

Solution: Vectors $\bar{a}$ and $\bar{b}$ (none of which is a null vector) are perpendicular if

$$\bar{a} \cdot \bar{b} = 0 \qquad\qquad (1)$$

Using this definition, form a scalar product of two vectors and check if it is equal to zero.

1) $\bar{a} \cdot \bar{b} = (2,-3,1) \cdot (2,2,2) = 4-6+2 = 0$

Thus vectors $\bar{a}$ and $\bar{b}$ are perpendicular

2) $\bar{a} \cdot \bar{c} = (2,-3,1) \cdot (4,-1,0) = 8+3 = 11$

Vectors $\bar{a}$ and $\bar{c}$ are not perpendicular

3) $\bar{a} \cdot \bar{d} = (2,-3,1) \cdot (-1,-2,-3) = -2+6-3 = 1$

Vectors $\bar{a}$ and $\bar{d}$ are not perpendicular

4) $\bar{a} \cdot \bar{e} = (2,-3,1) \cdot (2,-9,-31) = 4+27-31 = 0$

Vectors $\bar{a}$ and $\bar{e}$ are perpendicular

● PROBLEM 3-5

1) Show that $|\bar{a}| = \sqrt{\bar{a} \cdot \bar{a}}$ for any vector $\bar{a} = (a_1,a_2,a_3)$.

2) If $\bar{a} \cdot \bar{b} = 0$ and $|\bar{a}| \neq 0$, $|\bar{b}| \neq 0$, show that $\bar{a}$ is perpendicular to $\bar{b}$.

3) Find the angle between the vectors

$$\bar{a} = (1,4,7) \quad \text{and} \quad \bar{b} = (2,3,1).$$

Solution: 1) From the definition of the magnitude of a vector and the scalar product,

$$|\overline{a}| = \sqrt{a_1^2 + a_2^2 + a_3^{2'}} = \sqrt{\overline{a} \cdot \overline{a}}$$

2) $\overline{a} \cdot \overline{b} = |\overline{a}||\overline{b}| \cos \alpha = 0$ and $|\overline{a}| \neq 0$ and $|\overline{b}| \neq 0$,

then $\cos \alpha = 0$

or $\alpha = 90^{\circ}$

Thus vectors $\overline{a}$ and $\overline{b}$ are perpendicular.

3) From the definition of the scalar product, obtain

$$\overline{a} \cdot \overline{b} = (1,4,7) \cdot (2,3,1) = 2+12+7 = 21$$

On the other hand the scalar product can be expressed as

$$\overline{a} \cdot \overline{b} = |\overline{a}||\overline{b}| \cos \alpha = \sqrt{1+16+49} \cdot \sqrt{4+9+1} \cos \alpha =$$

$$= \sqrt{66} \cdot \sqrt{14} \cos \alpha = 30.39 \cos \alpha = 21$$

Solving for $\cos \alpha$,

and
$$\cos \alpha = \frac{21}{30.39} = 0.69$$
$$\alpha = 46^{\circ}$$

APPLICATIONS IN GEOMETRY AND PHYSICS

● **PROBLEM 3-6**

1) Find the angles which the vector

$$\overline{a} = (2,4,-5)$$

makes with the coordinate axes.

2) Find the projection of the vector

$$\overline{a} = (2,5,1) \quad \text{on the vector} \quad \overline{b} = (1,1,3)$$

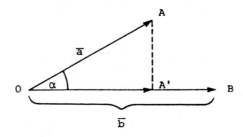

Solution: 1) Let α, β, ρ be the angles which $\overline{a}$ makes with the positive x_1, x_2, x_3 axes respectively and let $\overline{i}_1$, $\overline{i}_2$, $\overline{i}_3$ be the base vectors. Then

$$\overline{a} \cdot \overline{i}_1 = |a||i_1| \cos \alpha = \sqrt{4+16+25} \cos \alpha = \sqrt{45} \cos \alpha \qquad (1)$$

On the other hand

$$\overline{a} \cdot \overline{i}_1 = (2,4,-5) \cdot (1,0,0) = 2 \qquad (2)$$

Combining eqs.(1) and (2), and solving for α

$$\cos \alpha = \frac{2}{\sqrt{45}} = 0.298 \qquad (3)$$

$$\alpha = 73^o$$

In the same fashion

$$\overline{a} \cdot \overline{i}_2 = \sqrt{45} \cos \beta$$

and

$$\overline{a} \cdot \overline{i}_2 = 4$$

$$\therefore \cos \beta = \frac{4}{\sqrt{45}} = 0.596 \qquad (4)$$

$$\beta = 53^o$$

$$\overline{a} \cdot \overline{i}_3 = \sqrt{45} \cos \rho$$

$$\overline{a} \cdot \overline{i}_3 = -5$$

$$\cos \rho = \frac{-5}{\sqrt{45}} = -0.745 \qquad (5)$$

$$\rho = 138^o$$

2) The projection of a vector $\overline{a}$ on a vector $\overline{b}$ is illustrated in the figure.

The projection of vector $\overline{a}$ on vector $\overline{b}$ is in the direction of vector $\overline{b}$. Let us find the unit vector in the direction of $\overline{b}$, $\overline{u}_b$

$$\overline{u}_b = \frac{\overline{b}}{|\overline{b}|} = \frac{1}{\sqrt{11}} (1,1,3) \qquad (6)$$

The projection of vector $\overline{a}$ is then

$$(\overline{a} \cdot \overline{u}_b) \, \overline{u}_b = \left[(2,5,1) \cdot \left(\frac{1}{\sqrt{11}}, \frac{1}{\sqrt{11}}, \frac{3}{\sqrt{11}} \right) \right] \frac{1}{\sqrt{11}} (1,1,3) \qquad (7)$$

$$= \frac{1}{\sqrt{11}} (2+5+3) \frac{1}{\sqrt{11}} (1,1,3) = \frac{10}{11} (1,1,3)$$

Using the scalar product, prove the law of cosines for plane triangles.

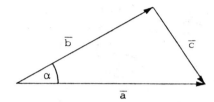

Solution: Consider a triangle as shown in the figure,

where
$$\overline{a} = \overline{b} + \overline{c}$$
or $$\overline{c} = \overline{a} - \overline{b}$$ (1)

Taking the scalar product,

$$\overline{c} \cdot \overline{c} = (\overline{a} - \overline{b}) \cdot (\overline{a} - \overline{b}) = \overline{a} \cdot \overline{a} - 2\overline{a} \cdot \overline{b} + \overline{b} \cdot \overline{b} =$$
$$= |\overline{a}|^2 + |\overline{b}|^2 - 2\overline{a} \cdot \overline{b}$$ (2)

The scalar product is defined as

$$\overline{a} \cdot \overline{b} = ab \cos \alpha$$ (3)

Substituting eq.(3) into eq.(2) we find

$$c^2 = a^2 + b^2 - 2ab \cos \alpha$$ (4)

where
$$|\overline{a}| = a \qquad |\overline{b}| = b \qquad |\overline{c}| = c$$

The vectors $\overline{a}$, $\overline{b}$, $\overline{c}$ are given such that

$$\overline{a} = (2,4,1) \quad \overline{b} = (3,-1,2) \quad \overline{c} = (5,3,3)$$

Show that these vectors form a triangle. Find the angles of the triangle and check if their sum is equal to $180°$.

Solution: Vectors $\overline{a}$, $\overline{b}$, $\overline{c}$ are shown in Figure 1.

It is found that
$$\overline{a} + \overline{b} = \overline{c}$$ (1)
because
$$(2,4,1)+(3,-1,2) = (5,3,3)$$

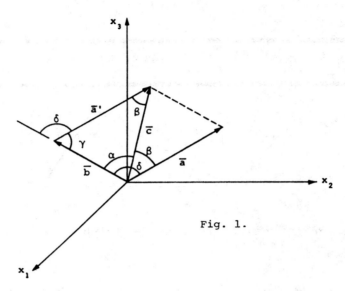

Fig. 1.

To form a triangle, rigidly move vector $\bar{a}$, without changing its direction, in such a way that the initial point of vector $\bar{a}$ and the terminal point of vector $\bar{b}$ coincide.

To find the angles of the triangle, form the scalar products of the vectors $\bar{a}$, $\bar{b}$, $\bar{c}$.

First compute the magnitudes of the vectors

$$a = |\bar{a}| = \sqrt{4+16+1} = \sqrt{21}$$

$$b = |\bar{b}| = \sqrt{9+1+4} = \sqrt{14} \qquad (2)$$

$$c = |\bar{c}| = \sqrt{25+9+9} = \sqrt{43}$$

then

$$\bar{b} \cdot \bar{c} = 15-3+6 = 18 = b\,c\,\cos\alpha = \sqrt{14} \cdot \sqrt{43}\,\cos\alpha$$

and

$$\cos\alpha = \frac{18}{\sqrt{602}} = 0.7336 \qquad (3)$$

$$\alpha = 42.8^{\circ}$$

$$\bar{a} \cdot \bar{c} = (2,4,1) \cdot (5,3,3) = 10+12+3 = 25 = ac\,\cos\beta$$

$$= \sqrt{21} \cdot \sqrt{43}\,\cos\beta$$

$$\cos\beta = \frac{25}{\sqrt{903}} = 0.8319 \qquad (4)$$

and

$$\beta = 33.7^{\circ}$$

To find the angle γ, note that using the scalar product of $\bar{a}$ and $\bar{b}$ gives the angle δ between vectors $\bar{a}$ and $\bar{b}$. From the figure it is seen that

$$\delta + \gamma = 180^{\circ} \qquad (5)$$

74

$$\bar{a} \cdot \bar{b} = 6-4+2 = 4 = a\ b\ \cos\ \delta = \sqrt{21} \cdot \sqrt{14}\ \cos\ \delta$$

$$\cos\ \delta = \frac{4}{\sqrt{294}} = 0.2332 \tag{6}$$

and $$\delta = 76.5^{\circ}$$

From eq.(5),

$$\gamma = 180^{\circ} - 76.5^{\circ} = 103.5^{\circ} \tag{7}$$

Thus
$$\alpha+\beta+\gamma = 42.8^{\circ}+33.7^{\circ}+103.5^{\circ} = 180^{\circ}$$

● **PROBLEM 3-9**

Find all possible scalar products of the base vectors

1) $\bar{i}_1 = (1,0)$ and $\bar{i}_2 = (0,1)$

2) $\bar{i}_1 = (1,0,0)$ $\bar{i}_2 = (0,1,0)$ $\bar{i}_3 = (0,0,1)$

<u>Solution</u>: 1) With two vectors $\bar{i}_1$ and $\bar{i}_2$ in the two-dimensional space, form the following scalar products

$$\bar{i}_1 \cdot \bar{i}_1 = (1,0) \cdot (1,0) = 1$$

$$\bar{i}_2 \cdot \bar{i}_2 = (0,1) \cdot (0,1) = 1 \tag{1}$$

$$\bar{i}_1 \cdot \bar{i}_2 = \bar{i}_2 \cdot \bar{i}_1 = (0,1) \cdot (1,0) = 0$$

2) In the three-dimensional space,

$$\bar{i}_1 \cdot \bar{i}_1 = (1,0,0) \cdot (1,0,0) = 1$$

$$\bar{i}_2 \cdot \bar{i}_2 = (0,1,0) \cdot (0,1,0) = 1$$

$$\bar{i}_3 \cdot \bar{i}_3 = (0,0,1) \cdot (0,0,1) = 1 \tag{2}$$

$$\bar{i}_1 \cdot \bar{i}_2 = \bar{i}_2 \cdot \bar{i}_1 = (1,0,0) \cdot (0,1,0) = 0$$

$$\bar{i}_1 \cdot \bar{i}_3 = \bar{i}_3 \cdot \bar{i}_1 = (1,0,0) \cdot (0,0,1) = 0$$

$$\bar{i}_2 \cdot \bar{i}_3 = \bar{i}_3 \cdot \bar{i}_2 = (0,1,0) \cdot (0,0,1) = 0$$

In the general case of an n-dimensional space, the base vectors are $\bar{i}_1$, $\bar{i}_2$,...,$\bar{i}_n$ and the scalar product is

$$\bar{i}_k \cdot \bar{i}_1 = \begin{cases} 1 & \text{for} \quad k=1 \\ 0 & \text{for} \quad k \neq 1 \end{cases} \tag{3}$$

This function is known as the Kronecker delta function

$$\delta_{ij} = \begin{cases} 1 & \text{for} \quad i=j \\ 0 & \text{for} \quad i \neq j \end{cases}$$

● **PROBLEM** 3-10

Determine the value of α such that vectors $\overline{a}$ and $\overline{b}$ are perpendicular and vectors $\overline{c}$ and $\overline{d}$ are perpendicular, where

1) $\overline{a} = 2\overline{i}_1 + 3\alpha\overline{i}_2 + \overline{i}_3$, $\quad \overline{b} = 4\overline{i}_1 + 2\overline{i}_2 + 4\alpha\overline{i}_3$

2) $\overline{c} = 2\alpha\overline{i}_1 + 4\overline{i}_2 + 3\overline{i}_3 + \overline{i}_4$, $\quad \overline{d} = \alpha\overline{i}_1 + 2\overline{i}_2 - \overline{i}_3 + 2\overline{i}_4$

Solution: 1) Form the scalar product of vectors $\overline{a}$ and $\overline{b}$

$$\overline{a} \cdot \overline{b} = (2\overline{i}_1 + 3\alpha\overline{i}_2 + \overline{i}_3) \cdot (4\overline{i}_1 + 2\overline{i}_2 + 4\alpha\overline{i}_3)$$

(1)

$$= 8 + 6\alpha + 4\alpha$$

$\overline{a}$ and $\overline{b}$ are to be perpendicular, therefore

$$\overline{a} \cdot \overline{b} = 8 + 10\alpha = 0$$

and

$$\alpha = -\frac{4}{5}$$

(2)

2) The scalar product of vectors $\overline{c}$ and $\overline{d}$ is

$$\overline{c} \cdot \overline{d} = (2\alpha\overline{i}_1 + 4\overline{i}_2 + 3\overline{i}_3 + \overline{i}_4) \cdot (\alpha\overline{i}_1 + 2\overline{i}_2 - \overline{i}_3 + 2\overline{i}_4)$$

(3)

$$= 2\alpha^2 + 8 - 3 + 2 = 2\alpha^2 + 7 = 0$$

It is seen that there is no real α such that $\overline{c} \cdot \overline{d} = 0$.

Using imaginary numbers,

$$\alpha_1 = i\sqrt{\frac{7}{2}} \qquad \alpha_2 = -i\sqrt{\frac{7}{2}}$$

(4)

In higher physics we frequently deal with vectors whose components are complex numbers.

● **PROBLEM** 3-11

Vectors $\overline{a}$ and $\overline{b}$ are given such that

$$\overline{a} = (-1, 2, 4)$$

$$\overline{b} = (3, 2, 7)$$

Find a unit vector $\overline{u}$ perpendicular to the plane determined by $\overline{a}$ and $\overline{b}$.

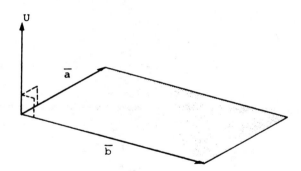

Solution: Since the unit vector $\bar{u}$ is perpendicular to the plane determined by $\bar{a}$ and $\bar{b}$ it is also perpendicular to both $\bar{a}$ and $\bar{b}$.

Let

$$\bar{u} = (u_1, u_2, u_3) \qquad (1)$$

then,

$$\bar{u} \cdot \bar{a} = 0$$

and

$$\bar{u} \cdot \bar{b} = 0 \qquad (2)$$

or

$$-u_1 + 2u_2 + 4u_3 = 0$$

$$3u_1 + 2u_2 + 7u_3 = 0 \qquad (3)$$

Solving for u_2 and u_3,

$$u_2 = \frac{19}{6} u_1, \qquad u_3 = -\frac{4}{3} u_1 \qquad (4)$$

Thus, $\bar{u}$ can be written as

$$\bar{u} = \left(u_1, \frac{19}{6} u_1, -\frac{4}{3} u_1 \right) \qquad (5)$$

Since $\bar{u}$ is a unit vector, then

and

$$|\bar{u}| = \sqrt{u_1^2 + u_1^2 \left(\frac{19}{6}\right)^2 + u_1^2 \left(\frac{4}{3}\right)^2} = |u_1| \cdot 3.578 = 1$$

$$u_1 = \frac{1}{3.578} = 0.279 \qquad (6)$$

Then obtain

$$\bar{u} = (0.279, \ 0.884, \ -0.372)$$

The unit vector is shown in the figure.

● **PROBLEM 3-12**

Let $\bar{u}_1$ and $\bar{u}_2$ be unit vectors in the $x_1 x_2$ plane, with α and β the angles between the positive x_1-axis, and $\bar{u}_1$ and $\bar{u}_2$ respectively. Using the scalar product of

77

$\bar{u}_1 \cdot \bar{u}_2$ prove the formulas

$$\cos(\beta-\alpha) = \cos\beta\cos\alpha + \sin\beta\sin\alpha \qquad (1)$$

$$\cos(\beta+\alpha) = \cos\beta\cos\alpha - \sin\beta\sin\alpha \qquad (2)$$

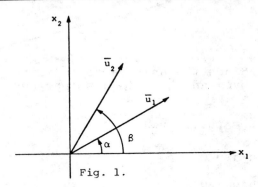

Fig. 1.

Solution: Express $\bar{u}_1$ and $\bar{u}_2$ in terms of the base vectors $\bar{i}_1$ and $\bar{i}_2$. From Fig. 1,

$$\bar{u}_1 = \cos\alpha\,\bar{i}_1 + \sin\alpha\,\bar{i}_2 \qquad (3)$$

$$\bar{u}_2 = \cos\beta\,\bar{i}_1 + \sin\beta\,\bar{i}_2 \qquad (4)$$

Since $\bar{u}_1$ and $\bar{u}_2$ are unit vectors, the scalar product is

$$\bar{u}_1 \cdot \bar{u}_2 = |\bar{u}_1||\bar{u}_2|\cos(\beta-\alpha) = (\cos\alpha\,\bar{i}_1 - \sin\alpha\,\bar{i}_2) \cdot (\cos\beta\,\bar{i}_1 + \sin\beta\,\bar{i}_2)$$

$$= \cos\beta\cos\alpha + \sin\beta\sin\alpha = \cos(\beta-\alpha) \qquad (5)$$

The angle between the vectors $\bar{u}_1$ and $\bar{u}_2$ is $\beta-\alpha$.

In solving for $\cos(\alpha+\beta)$, position the vector $\bar{u}_1$ as shown in Fig. 2.

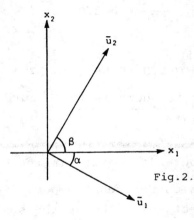

Fig.2.

78

Eqs.(3) and (4) now become

$$\bar{u}_1 = \cos\alpha\,\bar{i}_1 - \sin\alpha\,\bar{i}_2 \qquad (6)$$

$$\bar{u}_2 = \cos\beta\,\bar{i}_1 + \sin\beta\,\bar{i}_2 \qquad (7)$$

The angle between the vectors $\bar{u}_1$ and $\bar{u}_2$ is $\alpha+\beta$ and their scalar product is

$$\bar{u}_1 \cdot \bar{u}_2 = |\bar{u}_1||\bar{u}_2|\,\cos(\alpha+\beta) = (\cos\alpha\,\bar{i}_1 - \sin\alpha\,\bar{i}_2)\cdot(\cos\beta\,\bar{i}_1 + \sin\beta\,\bar{i}_2)$$

$$= \cos\alpha\cos\beta - \sin\alpha\sin\beta = \cos(\alpha+\beta)$$

● **PROBLEM 3-13**

Force $\bar{F}$ is applied to an object which moves along a vector $\bar{r}$. Find the work done by this force, when

$$\bar{F} = (2,3,1)$$

$$\bar{r} = (1,4,1)$$

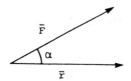

Solution: From mechanics the work W is equal to

$$W = Fs\cos\alpha \qquad (1)$$

where F = magnitude of force

s = distance

α = the angle between $\bar{F}$ and $\bar{r}$ as shown in the figure.

The right-hand side of equation (1) is equal to $\bar{F}\cdot\bar{r}$, (because $\bar{F}\cdot\bar{r} = |F||r|\cos\alpha$, and $|r| = s$) thus

$$W = Fs\cos\alpha = \bar{F}\cdot\bar{r} = (2,3,1)\cdot(1,4,1) =$$

$$= 2 + 12 + 1 = 15 \qquad (2)$$

● **PROBLEM 3-14**

Very often in physics we deal with a constant force field. In such a field the force acting on an object is always the same vector, regardless of the position of the object. A good approximation of a constant force field is the gravitational field of the earth. Show that the work done by a constant force field, while moving a particle from A to B, is the same for all broken lines joining A and B.

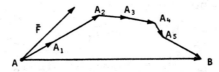

Solution: Since force $\overline{F}$ is the same in any given region of the space, the work done while moving a particle from A to B is given by $W = \overline{F} \cdot \overline{AB}$

Take any broken line consisting of segments AA_1, A_1A_2, ...$A_{n-1}A_n$, A_nB. Then represent segments as vectors $\overline{AA_1}$, $\overline{A_1A_2}$, ...$\overline{A_{n-1}A_n}$, $\overline{A_nB}$.

The work done along the segment line is

$$W' = \overline{F} \cdot \overline{AA_1} + \overline{F} \cdot \overline{A_1A_2} + \ldots + \overline{F} \cdot \overline{A_{n-1}A_n} + \overline{F} \cdot \overline{A_nB} = \qquad (2)$$

$$= \overline{F} \cdot (\overline{AA_1} + \overline{A_1A_2} + \ldots + \overline{A_{n-1}A_n} + \overline{A_nB})$$

The expression in the bracket is equal to $\overline{AB}$, thus

$$\overline{AA_1} + \overline{A_1A_2} + \ldots + \overline{A_{n-1}A_n} + \overline{A_nB} = \overline{AB} \qquad (3)$$

Substituting eq.(3) into eq.(2),

$$W' = \overline{F} \cdot \overline{AB} \qquad (4)$$

and $\qquad W' = W'$

This proves that in a constant force field the work done while moving an object from A to B does not depend on the path taken.

● **PROBLEM 3-15**

Let $\overline{a}$ and $\overline{b}$ be any vectors in the three-dimensional vector space

$$\overline{a} = (a_1, a_2, a_3)$$

$$\overline{b} = (b_1, b_2, b_3)$$

Prove the identity

$$\overline{a} \cdot \overline{b} = \frac{1}{2}(|\overline{a} + \overline{b}|^2 - |\overline{a}|^2 - |\overline{b}|^2) \qquad (1)$$

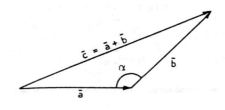

Solution: First, note that

$$|\overline{a}|^2 = (\sqrt{a_1^2+a_2^2+a_3^2})^2 = a_1^2+a_2^2+a_3^2 = \overline{a}\cdot\overline{a} \qquad (2)$$

Then transform the right side of eq.(1).

$$\frac{1}{2}(|\overline{a}+\overline{b}|^2 - |\overline{a}|^2 - |\overline{b}|^2)$$

$$= \frac{1}{2}\left[(\overline{a}+\overline{b})\cdot(\overline{a}+\overline{b}) - \overline{a}\cdot\overline{a} - \overline{b}\cdot\overline{b}\right] \qquad (3)$$

$$= \frac{1}{2}\left[\overline{a}\cdot\overline{a} + 2\overline{a}\cdot\overline{b} + \overline{b}\cdot\overline{b} - \overline{a}\cdot\overline{a} - \overline{b}\cdot\overline{b}\right]$$

$$= \overline{a}\cdot\overline{b}$$

That proves eq.(1).

Now prove eq.(1) using the geometrical representation of vectors and the law of cosines. The triangle is shown in the figure.

The law of cosines states that

$$c^2 = a^2 + b^2 - 2ab \cos \alpha \qquad (4)$$

Using eq.(2),

$$c^2 = |\overline{c}|^2 = |\overline{a}+\overline{b}|^2$$

$$a^2 = |\overline{a}|^2 \qquad (5)$$

$$b^2 = |\overline{b}|^2$$

The scalar product of $\overline{a}$ and $\overline{b}$ is given by

$$\overline{a}\cdot\overline{b} = ab \cos(180°- \alpha) \qquad (6)$$

Note that one has to take the smallest angle between $\overline{a}$ and $\overline{b}$, thus take $180° - \alpha$.

Substituting eq.(5) and eq.(6) into eq.(4) obtain

$$\frac{1}{2}(|\overline{a}+\overline{b}|^2 - |\overline{a}|^2 - |\overline{b}|^2) = \overline{a}\cdot\overline{b} \qquad (7)$$

GEOMETRICAL DEFINITION OF VECTOR PRODUCT

● PROBLEM 3-16

Find vector $\overline{c}$, such that

$$\overline{c} = \overline{a} \times \overline{b} \qquad (1)$$

81

where
$$\overline{a} = (0,2,5)$$
$$\overline{b} = (2,-4,0)$$
(2)

$\overline{a} \times \overline{b}$ denotes the vector product of vectors $\overline{a}$ and $\overline{b}$.

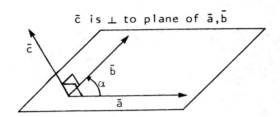

$\overline{c}$ is ⊥ to plane of $\overline{a},\overline{b}$

Solution: Start with the definition of the vector product of two vectors $\overline{a}$ and $\overline{b}$. Let $\overline{a}$ and $\overline{b}$ be two vectors and α the smallest non-negative angle between them, $0° \leq \alpha \leq 180°$ as shown in the figure. The vector product of $\overline{a}$ and $\overline{b}$ denoted by $\overline{a} \times \overline{b}$ is vector $\overline{c}$

$$\overline{c} = \overline{a} \times \overline{b}$$

such that

1) $\overline{c}$ is perpendicular to $\overline{a}$ and $\overline{b}$

2) the direction of $\overline{c}$ is such that $\overline{a}$, $\overline{b}$ and $\overline{c}$ form a right-handed system

3) $c = ab \sin \alpha$ (3)

First find the magnitudes of $\overline{a}$ and $\overline{b}$.

$$a = |\overline{a}| = \sqrt{4+25} = \sqrt{29}$$
$$b = |\overline{b}| = \sqrt{4+16} = \sqrt{20}$$
(4)

From the scalar product, find the angle α

$$\overline{a} \cdot \overline{b} = (0,2,5) \cdot (2,-4,0) = -8$$

Since

$$\overline{a} \cdot \overline{b} = ab \cos \alpha ,$$
(5)

$$\cos \alpha = \frac{\overline{a} \cdot \overline{b}}{ab} = \frac{-8}{\sqrt{29} \cdot \sqrt{20}} = -0.332$$
(6)

and
$$\alpha = 109°$$

The magnitude of $\overline{c}$ is

$$c = ab \sin \alpha = \sqrt{29} \cdot \sqrt{20} \sin 109° = 22.8$$
(7)

Vector $\overline{c}$ is perpendicular to $\overline{a}$ and $\overline{b}$ and the direction of $\overline{c}$ is such that $\overline{a}$, $\overline{b}$, $\overline{c}$ form a right-handed system.

Prove that

1) for any two vectors $\bar{a}$ and $\bar{b}$,   (1)

$\bar{a} \times \bar{b} = -\bar{b} \times \bar{a}$

2) If $\bar{a} \times \bar{b} = \bar{0}$ and $a \neq 0$ and $b \neq 0$ (2)

then $\bar{a}$ is parallel to $\bar{b}$.

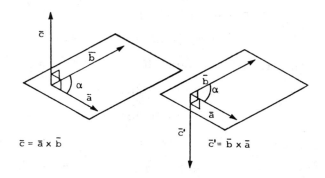

$\bar{c} = \bar{a} \times \bar{b}$ $\bar{c}' = \bar{b} \times \bar{a}$

Solution: Let $\bar{a} \times \bar{b} = \bar{c}$

and $\bar{b} \times \bar{a} = \bar{c}'$

The magnitude of vector $\bar{c}$ is

$$c = ab \sin \alpha$$

and of vector c'

$$c' = ba \sin \alpha$$

Therefore vectors $\bar{c}$ and $\bar{c}'$ have the same magnitude.

Vectors $\bar{a}$, $\bar{b}$, $\bar{c}$ form a right-handed system. Vectors $\bar{b}$, $\bar{a}$, $\bar{c}'$, form a right-handed system. Thus, as shown in the figure, vectors $\bar{c}$ and $\bar{c}'$ have opposite directions and the same magnitude, thus

$$\bar{c} = -\bar{c}'$$

therefore $\bar{a} \times \bar{b} = -\bar{b} \times \bar{a}$ (3)

2) Since $\bar{a} \times \bar{b} = \bar{0}$,   (4)

from the definition of the vector product,

$$\bar{a} \times \bar{b} = ab \sin \alpha = 0 \quad (5)$$

$a \neq 0$ and $b \neq 0$, therefore

$$\sin \alpha = 0$$

and

$$\alpha = 0^O \quad \text{or} \quad \alpha = 180^O$$

Thus the vectors $\bar{a}$ and $\bar{b}$ are parallel.

● **PROBLEM 3-18**

For any two vectors $\bar{a}$ and $\bar{b}$, prove the identity

$$|\bar{a} \times \bar{b}|^2 + |\bar{a} \cdot \bar{b}|^2 = |\bar{a}|^2|\bar{b}|^2 \qquad (1)$$

Solution: The magnitude of vector $\bar{c} = \bar{a} \times \bar{b}$ is

$$|\bar{c}| = |\bar{a} \times \bar{b}| = ab \sin \alpha \qquad (2)$$

where α is the angle between the vectors $\bar{a}$ and $\bar{b}$.

The magnitude of the scalar product is

$$|\bar{a} \cdot \bar{b}| = ab \cos \alpha \qquad (3)$$

Squaring eq.(2) and eq.(3) and adding the two together,

$$|\bar{a} \times \bar{b}|^2 + |\bar{a} \cdot \bar{b}|^2 = a^2b^2 \sin^2\alpha + a^2b^2 \cos^2\alpha$$

$$= a^2b^2(\sin^2\alpha + \cos^2\alpha) = a^2b^2 = |\bar{a}|^2 \, |\bar{b}|^2 \qquad (4)$$

which proves eq.(1).

● **PROBLEM 3-19**

Using vectors, prove the law of sines for a triangle

$$\frac{\sin \alpha}{a} = \frac{\sin \beta}{b} = \frac{\sin \gamma}{c} \qquad (1)$$

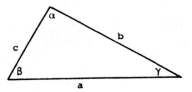

Solution: Use the following:

$$|\bar{a} \times \bar{b}| = \text{area of parallelogram with sides } \bar{a} \text{ and } \bar{b}$$

and

$$|\bar{a} \times \bar{b}| = ab \sin\phi, \text{ where} \phi \qquad (2)$$

is the angle between $\bar{a}$ and $\bar{b}$. Note that
the area of the parallelogram with sides $\bar{a}$ and $\bar{b}$

$=$ area of the parallelogram with sides $\bar{c}$ and $\bar{a}$

$=$ area of the parallelogram with sides $\bar{c}$ and $\bar{b}$

Denote this area by S. Then

$$|\bar{a} \times \bar{b}| = S = ab \sin \gamma \qquad (3)$$

$$|\bar{c} \times \bar{b}| = S = cb \sin \alpha \qquad (4)$$

$$|\bar{c} \times \bar{a}| = S = ca \sin \beta \qquad (5)$$

Comparing equations (3) and (4),

$$ab \sin \gamma = cb \sin \alpha$$

or

$$\frac{\sin \alpha}{a} = \frac{\sin \gamma}{c} \qquad (6)$$

Comparing eqs.(4) and (5), gives

$$cb \sin \alpha = ca \sin \beta$$

or

Thus

$$\frac{\sin \alpha}{a} = \frac{\sin \beta}{b} \qquad (7)$$

$$\frac{\sin \alpha}{a} = \frac{\sin \beta}{b} = \frac{\sin \gamma}{c} \qquad (8)$$

COMPONENT DEFINITION OF VECTOR PRODUCT

● **PROBLEM** 3-20

Determine the components of vector $\bar{c}$ in terms of the components of $\bar{a}$ and $\bar{b}$, where

$$\bar{c} = \bar{a} \times \bar{b} \qquad (1)$$

and

$$\bar{a} = (a_1, a_2, a_3)$$

$$\bar{b} = (b_1, b_2, b_3)$$

Solution: $\bar{c}$ is perpendicular to $\bar{a}$ and $\bar{b}$, thus

$$\bar{a} \cdot \bar{c} = 0$$

$$\bar{b} \cdot \bar{c} = 0 \qquad (2)$$

or

$$a_1 c_1 + a_2 c_2 + a_3 c_3 = 0$$

$$b_1 c_1 + b_2 c_2 + b_3 c_3 = 0$$

Solving eq.(2) for c_1 and c_2 in terms of c_3,

$$\frac{c_1}{a_2 b_3 - a_3 b_2} = \frac{c_2}{a_3 b_1 - a_1 b_3} = \frac{c_3}{a_1 b_2 - a_2 b_1} = A \qquad (3)$$

then

$$c_1 = A(a_2 b_3 - a_3 b_2)$$

$$c_2 = A(a_3b_1 - a_1b_3) \qquad (4)$$

$$c_3 = A(a_1b_2 - a_2b_1)$$

To find A, note that

$$c^2 = c_1^2 + c_2^2 + c_3^2$$

or

$$c^2 = A^2\left[(a_2b_3 - a_3b_2)^2 + (a_3b_1 - a_1b_3)^2 + (a_1b_2 - a_2b_1)^2\right] \qquad (5)$$

$$= A^2\left[a_1^2(b_2^2+b_3^2)+a_2^2(b_1^2+b_3^2)+a_3^2(b_1^2+b_2^2)-2(a_2b_2a_3b_3+a_3b_3a_1b_1+a_1b_1a_2b_2)\right]$$

and

$$a_1^2(b_2^2 + b_3^2) = a_1^2(b^2 - b_1^2)$$

$$a_2^2(b_1^2 + b_3^2) = a_2^2(b^2 - b_2^2) \qquad (6)$$

$$a_3^2(b_1^2 + b_2^2) = a_3^2(b^2 - b_3^2)$$

Substituting eq.(6) into eq.(5),

$$c^2 = A^2\left[(a_1^2+a_2^2+a_3^2)b^2-(a_1b_1+a_2b_2+a_3b_3)^2\right] \qquad (7)$$

$$= A^2\left[a^2b^2 - (ab\ \cos\alpha)^2\right] = A^2a^2b^2(1 - \cos^2\alpha)$$

$$= A^2a^2b^2\ \sin^2\alpha$$

But

$$c^2 = a^2b^2\ \sin^2\alpha \qquad (8)$$

and A must be such that

$$A^2 = 1 \qquad (9)$$

or

$$A = \pm 1$$

Accept the positive solution only, A = 1. For A = -1 eq.(4) does not produce the right-handed system. Then,

$$\overline{c} = \overline{a} \times \overline{b} = (a_2b_3 - a_3b_2,\ a_3b_1 - a_1b_3,\ a_1b_2 - a_2b_1) \qquad (10)$$

or in terms of the base vectors

$$\overline{c} = \overline{a} \times \overline{b} = (a_2b_3 - a_3b_2)\ \overline{i}_1 + (a_3b_1 - a_1b_3)\ \overline{i}_2 \qquad (11)$$

$$+ (a_1b_2 - a_2b_1)\overline{i}_3$$

● **PROBLEM 3-21**

Show that the vector product $\overline{c} = \overline{a} \times \overline{b}$
where

$$\overline{a} = (a_1, a_2, a_3)$$

$$\overline{b} = (b_1, b_2, b_3)$$

can be expressed in determinant form as

$$\bar{c} = \bar{a} \times \bar{b} = \begin{vmatrix} \bar{i}_1 & \bar{i}_2 & \bar{i}_3 \\ a_1 & a_2 & a_3 \\ b_1 & b_2 & b_3 \end{vmatrix} \tag{1}$$

<u>Solution</u>: From the definition of the determinant,

$$\begin{vmatrix} \bar{i}_1 & \bar{i}_2 & \bar{i}_3 \\ a_1 & a_2 & a_3 \\ b_1 & b_2 & b_3 \end{vmatrix} = \bar{i}_1 a_2 b_3 - \bar{i}_1 a_3 b_2 + \bar{i}_2 a_3 b_1 - \bar{i}_2 a_1 b_3 \\ + \bar{i}_3 a_1 b_2 - \bar{i}_3 a_2 b_1 \tag{2}$$

$$= (a_2 b_3 - a_3 b_2)\bar{i}_1 + (a_3 b_1 - a_1 b_3)\bar{i}_2 + (a_1 b_2 - a_2 b_1)\bar{i}_3$$

Thus
$$\bar{c} = \bar{a} \times \bar{b} = (a_2 b_3 - a_3 b_2, \ a_3 b_1 - a_1 b_3, \ a_1 b_2 - a_2 b_1) \tag{3}$$

and both forms are equivalent.

● **PROBLEM 3-22**

1) Prove that the vector product is distributive, that is

$$\bar{a} \times (\bar{b} + \bar{c}) = \bar{a} \times \bar{b} + \bar{a} \times \bar{c} \tag{1}$$

where

$$\bar{a} = (a_1, a_2, a_3)$$

$$\bar{b} = (b_1, b_2, b_3) \tag{2}$$

$$\bar{c} = (c_1, c_2, c_3)$$

2) Let $\bar{i}_1$, $\bar{i}_2$, $\bar{i}_3$ be the base vectors

$$\bar{i}_1 = (1,0,0)$$

$$\bar{i}_2 = (0,1,0) \tag{3}$$

$$\bar{i}_3 = (0,0,1)$$

Show that

$$\bar{i}_1 \times \bar{i}_1 = \bar{0} \qquad \bar{i}_1 \times \bar{i}_2 = \bar{i}_3$$

$$\overline{i}_2 \times \overline{i}_2 = \overline{0} \qquad \overline{i}_2 \times \overline{i}_3 = \overline{i}_1 \qquad\qquad (4)$$

$$\overline{i}_3 \times \overline{i}_3 = \overline{0} \qquad \overline{i}_3 \times \overline{i}_1 = \overline{i}_2$$

Solution: 1) Two vectors $\overline{k}$ and $\overline{l}$ are equal if and only if their components are equal, or

$$k_1 = l_1, \quad k_2 = l_2, \quad k_3 = l_3, \quad \text{we write } \overline{k} = \overline{l}$$

Denote

$$\overline{d} = \overline{a} \times (\overline{b} + \overline{c})$$
$$\overline{e} = \overline{a} \times \overline{b} + \overline{a} \times \overline{c} \qquad\qquad (5)$$

in the component form

$$(d_1, d_2, d_3) = (a_1, a_2, a_3) \times (b_1+c_1, \ b_2+c_2, \ b_3+c_3) \quad (6)$$

Using the definition of the vector product in the component form, obtain

$$\overline{d} = (d_1, d_2, d_3) = \Big[a_2(b_3+c_3)-a_3(b_2+c_2), \ a_3(b_1+c_1)-a_1(b_3+c_3),$$

$$\hspace{4cm} (7)$$

$$a_1(b_2+c_2)-a_2(b_1+c_1) \Big]$$

$$= (a_2b_3-a_3b_2+a_2c_3-a_3c_2, \ a_3b_1-a_1b_3+a_3c_1-a_1c_3, \ a_1b_2-a_2b_1+a_1c_2-a_2c_1)$$

$$= (a_2b_3-a_3b_2, \ a_3b_1-a_1b_3, \ a_1b_2-a_2b_1)$$

$$+ (a_2c_3-a_3c_2, \ a_3c_1-a_1c_3, \ a_1c_2-a_2c_1) = \overline{a} \times \overline{b} + \overline{a} \times \overline{c}$$

2) Proceed by showing that for any vector $\overline{a} = (a_1, a_2, a_3)$
$$\overline{a} \times \overline{a} = \overline{0}$$

Indeed $\quad \overline{a} \times \overline{a} = a \cdot a \sin\alpha = 0 \qquad\qquad (8)$

because $\alpha = 0$ and $\sin\alpha = 0$

That proves
$$\overline{i}_1 \times \overline{i}_1 = \overline{i}_2 \times \overline{i}_2 = \overline{i}_3 \times \overline{i}_3 = \overline{0} \qquad\qquad (9)$$

From the definition of the vector product, obtain

$$\overline{i}_1 \times \overline{i}_2 = (1,0,0) \times (0,1,0) = (0,0,1) = \overline{i}_3$$

$$\overline{i}_2 \times \overline{i}_3 = (0,1,0) \times (0,0,1) = (1,0,0) = \overline{i}_1 \qquad\qquad (10)$$

$$\overline{i}_3 \times \overline{i}_1 = (0,0,1) \times (1,0,0) = (0,1,0) = \overline{i}_2$$

Vectors $\bar{a}$ = (2,3,5) and $\bar{b}$ = (1,-3,2) are given. Find vector $\bar{c}$

where $\bar{c}$ = $\bar{a}$ x $\bar{b}$ (1)

using

1)   the component expression for the vector product

2)   the determinant expression for the vector product

3)   the coordinate expression for the vector product. Remember that for the base vectors

$$\bar{i}_1 \times \bar{i}_1 = \bar{i}_2 \times \bar{i}_2 = \bar{i}_3 \times \bar{i}_3 = \bar{0}$$

$$\bar{i}_1 \times \bar{i}_2 = \bar{i}_3 \qquad\qquad \bar{i}_k \times \bar{i}_1 = -\bar{i}_1 \times \bar{i}_k \qquad (2)$$

$$\bar{i}_2 \times \bar{i}_3 = \bar{i}_1$$

$$\bar{i}_3 \times \bar{i}_1 = \bar{i}_2$$

Solution: 1) In the component form vector $\bar{c}$

$$\bar{c} = \bar{a} \times \bar{b} \quad \text{is given by}$$

$$\bar{c} = (a_2 b_3 - a_3 b_2, \ a_3 b_1 - a_1 b_3, \ a_1 b_2 - a_2 b_1) \qquad (3)$$

Substituting $\bar{a}$ and $\bar{b}$, obtain

$$\bar{c} = (3\cdot2 + 5\cdot3, \ 5\cdot1 - 2\cdot2, \ -2\cdot3 - 3\cdot1)$$

$$= (21, 1, -9) \qquad (4)$$

2) In the determinant form, vector $\bar{c}$ can be expressed as

$$\bar{c} = \begin{vmatrix} \bar{i}_1 & \bar{i}_2 & \bar{i}_3 \\ a_1 & a_2 & a_3 \\ b_1 & b_2 & b_3 \end{vmatrix} \qquad (5)$$

Substituting $\bar{a}$ and $\bar{b}$ into eq.(5), obtain

$$\bar{c} = \begin{vmatrix} \bar{i}_1 & \bar{i}_2 & \bar{i}_3 \\ 2 & 3 & 5 \\ 1 & -3 & 2 \end{vmatrix} \qquad (6)$$

$$= \bar{i}_1 \ 3\cdot2 + \bar{i}_2 \ 5\cdot1 + \bar{i}_3 \ 2\cdot(-3) - \bar{i}_1(-3)\cdot5 - \bar{i}_2 \ 2\cdot2 - \bar{i}_3 \ 3\cdot1$$

$$= \bar{i}_1(6+15) + \bar{i}_2(5-4) + \bar{i}_3(-6-3)$$

$$= 21\,\bar{i}_1 + \bar{i}_2 - 9\bar{i}_3$$

3)   Vectors $\bar{a}$ and $\bar{b}$ can be represented as

$$\bar{a} = 2\bar{i}_1 + 3\bar{i}_2 + 5\bar{i}_3$$

$$\bar{b} = \bar{i}_1 - 3\bar{i}_2 + 2\bar{i}_3 \tag{7}$$

Substituting eq.(7) into

$$\bar{c} = \bar{a} \times \bar{b}$$

and using eq.(2), obtain

$$\bar{c} = \bar{a} \times \bar{b} \tag{8}$$

$$= (2\bar{i}_1+3\bar{i}_2+5\bar{i}_3) \times (\bar{i}_1-3\bar{i}_2+2\bar{i}_3)$$

$$= 2\bar{i}_1 \times \bar{i}_1-6\bar{i}_1 \times \bar{i}_2+4\bar{i}_1 \times \bar{i}_3+3\bar{i}_2 \times \bar{i}_1-9\bar{i}_2 \times \bar{i}_2+6\bar{i}_2 \times \bar{i}_3$$

$$+5\bar{i}_3 \times \bar{i}_1-15\bar{i}_3 \times \bar{i}_2+10\bar{i}_3 \times \bar{i}_3$$

$$= -6\bar{i}_1 \times \bar{i}_2-3\bar{i}_1 \times \bar{i}_2+6\bar{i}_2 \times \bar{i}_3+15\bar{i}_2 \times \bar{i}_3-4\bar{i}_3 \times \bar{i}_1+5\bar{i}_3 \times \bar{i}_1$$

$$= -9\bar{i}_1 \times \bar{i}_2+21\bar{i}_2 \times \bar{i}_3+\bar{i}_3 \times \bar{i}_1$$

$$= 21\bar{i}_1 + \bar{i}_2 - 9\bar{i}_3$$

● PROBLEM 3-24

1)   Prove that the area S of the parallelogram with the vectors $\bar{a}$ and $\bar{b}$ forming adjacent edges is

$$S = |\bar{a} \times \bar{b}| \tag{1}$$

2)   Find the area of the triangle having vertices at

$$A(2,1,4) \qquad B(3,-2,1) \qquad C(7,2,1) \tag{2}$$

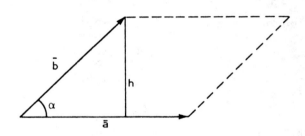

90

Solution: The parallelogram is shown in the figure.

The area of the parallelogram is given by

$$S = a h \tag{3}$$

but

$$h = b \sin \alpha$$

and

$$S = a h = ab \sin \alpha = |\bar{a} \times \bar{b}|. \tag{4}$$

2) Obtain vectors $\overline{AB}$ and $\overline{AC}$

$$\overline{AB} = (3-2)\bar{i}_1 + (-2-1)\bar{i}_2 + (1-4)\bar{i}_3 = \bar{i}_1 - 3\bar{i}_2 - 3\bar{i}_3$$

$$\overline{AC} = (7-2)\bar{i}_1 + (2-1)\bar{i}_2 + (1-4)\bar{i}_3 = 5\bar{i}_1 + \bar{i}_2 - 3\bar{i}_3 \tag{5}$$

The area of the triangle is

$$S = \frac{1}{2} \left| \overline{AB} \times \overline{AC} \right|$$

$$= \frac{1}{2} \begin{vmatrix} \bar{i}_1 & \bar{i}_2 & \bar{i}_3 \\ 1 & -3 & -3 \\ 5 & 1 & -3 \end{vmatrix} = \frac{1}{2} \left| 12\bar{i}_1 - 12\bar{i}_2 + 16\bar{i}_3 \right| \tag{6}$$

$$= \frac{1}{2} \sqrt{12^2 + 12^2 + 16^2} = 11.66$$

● **PROBLEM 3-25**

For a closed surface define the vector area as the vector whose magnitude is equal to the area and whose direction is perpendicular (outward) to the area.

Show that

$$\bar{S}_1 + \bar{S}_2 + \bar{S}_3 + \bar{S}_4 = 0 \tag{1}$$

where $\bar{S}_1$, $\bar{S}_2$, $\bar{S}_3$, $\bar{S}_4$ are the vector areas of a tetrahedron.

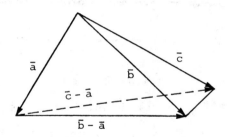

<u>Solution</u>: The tetrahedron is shown in the figure.
The area of the triangle with sides $\bar{a}$ and $\bar{b}$ is $\frac{1}{2}\left|\bar{a} \times \bar{b}\right|$.
The area vectors for each face of the tetrahedron are

$$\bar{V}_1 = \frac{1}{2} \bar{a} \times \bar{b} \quad ; \quad \bar{V}_2 = \frac{1}{2} \bar{b} \times \bar{c}$$

$$\bar{V}_3 = \frac{1}{2} \bar{c} \times \bar{a} \quad ; \quad \bar{V}_4 = \frac{1}{2} (\bar{c}-\bar{a}) \times (\bar{b}-\bar{a})$$

(2)

Note that $\bar{V}_3 = \frac{1}{2}(\bar{c} \times \bar{a})$ and not $\frac{1}{2}(\bar{a} \times \bar{c})$ because the vector area $\bar{V}_3$ has direction perpendicular to the face of the tetrahedron in the outward direction.

Thus
$$\bar{V}_1+\bar{V}_2+\bar{V}_3+\bar{V}_4 = \frac{1}{2}\left[\bar{a} \times \bar{b}+\bar{b} \times \bar{c}+\bar{c} \times \bar{a}+(\bar{c}-\bar{a})\times(\bar{b}-\bar{a})\right]$$

(3)

$$= \frac{1}{2}\left[\bar{a} \times \bar{b}+\bar{b} \times \bar{c}+\bar{c} \times \bar{a}+\bar{c} \times \bar{b}-\bar{c} \times \bar{a}-\bar{a} \times \bar{b}+\bar{a} \times \bar{a}\right] = \bar{0}$$

Therefore
$$\bar{V}_1 + \bar{V}_2 + \bar{V}_3 + \bar{V}_4 = \bar{0}$$

(4)

This result can be easily generalized to a closed polyhedron.

SCALAR TRIPLE PRODUCT AND VECTOR TRIPLE PRODUCT

● **PROBLEM 3-26**

1) Let $\bar{a}$, $\bar{b}$ and $\bar{c}$ be any three vectors. Express their scalar triple product, sometimes denoted $\begin{bmatrix} \bar{a} & \bar{b} & \bar{c} \end{bmatrix}$ in determinant form.

2) Prove the following theorem:

If the vectors in a scalar triple product are subjected to an even number of permutations, then the value of the product is not changed; however, if the number of permutations is odd, then the value of the product is changed only in sign.

<u>Solution</u>: 1) A scalar triple product of vectors $\bar{a}$, $\bar{b}$, $\bar{c}$ is defined as

$$\begin{bmatrix} \bar{a} & \bar{b} & \bar{c} \end{bmatrix} = \bar{a} \cdot (\bar{b} \times \bar{c})$$

(1)

To express (1) in determinant form, compute its value.

$$\bar{a} \cdot (\bar{b} \times \bar{c}) = (a_1, a_2, a_3) \cdot (b_2 c_3 - b_3 c_2, \; b_3 c_1 - b_1 c_3, \; b_1 c_2 - b_2 c_1)$$

92

$$= a_1(b_2c_3-b_3c_2) + a_2(b_3c_1-b_1c_3) + a_3(b_1c_2-b_2c_1)$$

$$= \begin{vmatrix} a_1 & a_2 & a_3 \\ b_1 & b_2 & b_3 \\ c_1 & c_2 & c_3 \end{vmatrix} \qquad (2)$$

2) To prove the theorem, use the determinant form of a scalar triple product

$$[\, \overline{a}\ \overline{b}\ \overline{c}\,] = \overline{a}\cdot(\overline{b}\ x\ \overline{c}) = \begin{vmatrix} a_1 & a_2 & a_3 \\ b_1 & b_2 & b_3 \\ c_1 & c_2 & c_3 \end{vmatrix} \qquad (3)$$

We see that a single permutation produces an interchange of two rows in the determinant. Such interchange of rows results in a change of sign.

Therefore,

$$\overline{a}\cdot(\overline{b}\ x\ \overline{c}) = -\overline{a}\cdot(\overline{c}\ x\ \overline{b}) = \overline{b}\cdot(\overline{c}\ x\ \overline{a}) = -\overline{b}\cdot(\overline{a}\ x\ \overline{c})$$
$$= \overline{c}\cdot(\overline{a}\ x\ \overline{b}) = -\overline{c}\cdot(\overline{b}\ x\ \overline{a}) \qquad (4)$$

● **PROBLEM 3-27**

Show that the volume V of the parallelepiped with the vectors $\overline{a}$, $\overline{b}$ and $\overline{c}$ forming adjacent edges as shown in the figure, is given by

$$V = |\overline{a}\cdot(\overline{b}\ x\ \overline{c})| \qquad (1)$$

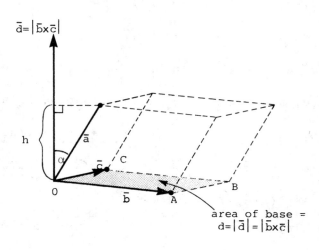

area of base = $d=|\overline{d}|=|\overline{b}x\overline{c}|$

Solution: Denote

$$\overline{d} = \overline{b} \text{ x } \overline{c}$$

and

$$d = |\overline{b} \text{ x } \overline{c}|$$

It was shown previously that d represents the area of the parallelogram OABC. Then

$$V = dh \qquad (2)$$

where h is the altitude of the parallelepiped. By definition, $\overline{d}$ is perpendicular to the base, thus

$$h = a|\cos \alpha| \qquad (3)$$

and

$$V = dh = ad |\cos \alpha| = |\overline{a} \cdot \overline{d}| = |\overline{a} \cdot (\overline{b} \text{ x } \overline{c})| \qquad (4)$$

● **PROBLEM 3-28**

The expression

$$\overline{a} \text{ x } (\overline{b} \text{ x } \overline{c})$$

is called the vector triple product.

Prove the following identities

$$\overline{a} \text{ x } (\overline{b} \text{ x } \overline{c}) = (\overline{a} \cdot \overline{c})\overline{b} - (\overline{a} \cdot \overline{b})\overline{c} \qquad (1)$$

$$(\overline{a} \text{ x } \overline{b}) \text{ x } \overline{c} = (\overline{c} \cdot \overline{a})\overline{b} - (\overline{c} \cdot \overline{b})\overline{a} \qquad (2)$$

Solution: To prove eq.(1) compute the components of both sides of eq.(1). From the definition of the vector product, obtain

$$\overline{a} \text{ x } (\overline{b} \text{ x } \overline{c}) = (a_1, a_2, a_3) \text{ x } (b_2 c_3 - b_3 c_2, \; b_3 c_1 - b_1 c_3, \; b_1 c_2 - b_2 c_1)$$

$$= \Big[a_2(b_1 c_2 - b_2 c_1) - a_3(b_3 c_1 - b_1 c_3), \; a_3(b_2 c_3 - b_3 c_2) - a_1(b_1 c_2 - b_2 c_1), $$
$$a_1(b_3 c_1 - b_1 c_3) - a_2(b_2 c_3 - b_3 c_2) \Big] \qquad (3)$$

$$= \Big[b_1(a_2 c_2 + a_3 c_3) - c_1(a_2 b_2 + a_3 b_3), $$
$$b_2(a_1 c_1 + a_3 c_3) - c_2(a_1 b_1 + a_3 b_3), \; b_3(a_1 c_1 + a_2 c_2) - c_3(a_1 b_1 + a_2 b_2) \Big]$$

$$= \Big[b_1(a_1 c_1 + a_2 c_2 + a_3 c_3) - c_1(a_1 b_1 + a_2 b_2 + a_3 b_3), \; b_2(a_1 c_1 + a_2 c_2 + a_3 c_3) $$
$$- c_2(a_1 b_1 + a_2 b_2 + a_3 b_3), \; b_3(a_1 c_1 + a_2 c_2 + a_3 c_3) - c_3(a_1 b_1 + a_2 b_2 + a_3 b_3) \Big]$$

$$= \Big[b_1(\overline{a} \cdot \overline{c}), \; b_2(\overline{a} \cdot \overline{c}), \; b_3(\overline{a} \cdot \overline{c}) \Big] - \Big[c_1(\overline{a} \cdot \overline{b}), \; c_2(\overline{a} \cdot \overline{b}), \; c_3(\overline{a} \cdot \overline{b}) \Big]$$

$$= (\overline{a} \cdot \overline{c}) \, \overline{b} - (\overline{a} \cdot \overline{b}) \, \overline{c}$$

That completes the proof. The same method can be used to prove eq.(2).

The shortest method, however, is to rewrite eq.(1) in the form

$$(\overline{b} \times \overline{c}) \times \overline{a} = (\overline{a} \cdot \overline{b})\, \overline{c} - (\overline{a} \cdot \overline{c})\, \overline{b} \qquad (4)$$

then replace

vector $\overline{b}$ by $\overline{a}$

$$\overline{b} \to \overline{a}$$

vector $\overline{c}$ by $\overline{b}$

$$\overline{c} \to \overline{b}$$

vector $\overline{a}$ by $\overline{c}$

$$\overline{a} \to \overline{c}$$

Then, obtain

$$(\overline{b} \times \overline{c}) \times \overline{a} = (\overline{a} \cdot \overline{b})\, \overline{c} - (\overline{a} \cdot \overline{c})\, \overline{b}$$
$$\downarrow \quad \downarrow \quad \downarrow \quad \downarrow\ \downarrow \quad \downarrow \quad \ \ \downarrow\ \downarrow \quad \downarrow \qquad (5)$$
$$(\overline{a} \times \overline{b}) \times \overline{c} = (\overline{c} \cdot \overline{a})\, \overline{b} - (\overline{c} \cdot \overline{b})\, \overline{a}$$

That proves identity (2).

● **PROBLEM 3-29**

Let $\overline{a}$ and $\overline{b}$ be given vectors and α be a given scalar.
Find all vectors $\overline{c}$ such that

$$\overline{a} \times \overline{c} = \overline{b} \qquad (1)$$
$$\overline{a} \cdot \overline{c} = \alpha \qquad (2)$$

Solution: Take eq.(1), multiply it by $\overline{a}$

$$\overline{a} \cdot (\overline{a} \times \overline{c}) = \overline{a} \cdot \overline{b} \qquad (3)$$

Since the left side is equal to zero, then

$$\overline{a} \cdot \overline{b} = 0 \qquad (4)$$

In the case where $\overline{a} \cdot \overline{b} \neq 0$, the system (1), (2) has no solution.
Assume that
$$\overline{a} \cdot \overline{b} = 0 \quad \text{and} \quad \overline{a} \neq \overline{0}$$

Then, use the identity

$$(\overline{a} \times \overline{c}) \times \overline{b} = (\overline{b} \cdot \overline{a})\overline{c} - (\overline{c} \cdot \overline{b})\overline{a} \qquad (5)$$

if $\overline{b} = \overline{a}$, then

$$(\overline{a} \times \overline{c}) \times \overline{a} = (\overline{a} \cdot \overline{a})\overline{c} - (\overline{a} \cdot \overline{c})\overline{a} \qquad (6)$$

From eq.(1),

$$\overline{a} \times \overline{c} = \overline{b}$$

from eq.(2)
$$\overline{a} \cdot \overline{c} = \alpha$$
Eq.(6) becomes
$$\overline{b} \times \overline{a} = a^2 \overline{c} - \alpha \overline{a} \tag{7}$$

Solving for $\overline{c}$
$$\overline{c} = \frac{1}{a^2}(\overline{b} \times \overline{a} + \alpha \overline{a}) \tag{8}$$

● **PROBLEM 3-30**

Let $\overline{a}$, $\overline{b}$, $\overline{c}$ be three given vectors not lying in the same plane. Show that any vector $\overline{d}$ can be expressed as a linear combination of the vectors $\overline{a}$, $\overline{b}$, $\overline{c}$.

<u>Solution</u>: To express the vector $\overline{d}$ in the form
$$\overline{d} = \alpha_a \overline{a} + \alpha_b \overline{b} + \alpha_c \overline{c} \tag{1}$$

vector multiply eq.(1) by $\overline{c}$, thus
$$\overline{d} \times \overline{c} = \alpha_a \, \overline{a} \times \overline{c} + \alpha_b \, \overline{b} \times \overline{c} \tag{2}$$

Note that
$$\alpha_c \, \overline{c} \times \overline{c} = \overline{0}$$

Then, scalar multiply eq.(2) by $\overline{b}$
$$\overline{b} \cdot \overline{d} \times \overline{c} = \alpha_a \, \overline{b} \cdot \overline{a} \times \overline{c} \tag{3}$$

Note that
$$\alpha_b \, \overline{b} \cdot \overline{b} \times \overline{c} = 0$$

Thus, solving eq.(3) for α_a,
$$\alpha_a = \frac{\overline{b} \cdot \overline{d} \times \overline{c}}{\overline{b} \cdot \overline{a} \times \overline{c}} = \frac{-\overline{d} \cdot \overline{b} \times \overline{c}}{-\overline{a} \cdot \overline{b} \times \overline{c}} = \frac{\overline{d} \cdot \overline{b} \times \overline{c}}{\overline{a} \cdot \overline{b} \times \overline{c}} \tag{4}$$

To find α_b scalar multiply eq. (2) by a, thus
$$\overline{a} \cdot \overline{d} \times \overline{c} = \alpha_b \, \overline{a} \cdot \overline{b} \times \overline{c} \tag{5}$$

Solving for α_b,
$$\alpha_b = \frac{\overline{a} \cdot \overline{d} \times \overline{c}}{\overline{a} \cdot \overline{b} \times \overline{c}} = \frac{\overline{d} \cdot \overline{a} \times \overline{c}}{\overline{b} \cdot \overline{a} \times \overline{c}} \tag{6}$$

To find α_c, vector multiply eq.(1) by $\overline{a}$, thus
$$\overline{d} \times \overline{a} = \alpha_b \, \overline{b} \times \overline{a} + \alpha_c \, \overline{c} \times \overline{a} \tag{7}$$

and scalar multiply eq.(7) by $\overline{b}$

96

$$\overline{b} \cdot \overline{d} \times \overline{a} = \alpha_c \ \overline{b} \cdot \overline{c} \times \overline{a} \qquad (8)$$

Solving for α_c

$$\alpha_c = \frac{\overline{b} \cdot \overline{d} \times \overline{a}}{\overline{b} \cdot \overline{c} \times \overline{a}} = \frac{\overline{d} \cdot \overline{b} \times \overline{a}}{\overline{c} \cdot \overline{b} \times \overline{a}} \qquad (9)$$

Substituting eqs.(4), (6) and (9) into eq.(1)

$$\overline{d} = \left(\frac{\overline{d} \cdot \overline{b} \times \overline{c}}{\overline{a} \cdot \overline{b} \times \overline{c}} \right) \overline{a} + \left(\frac{\overline{d} \cdot \overline{a} \times \overline{c}}{\overline{b} \cdot \overline{a} \times \overline{c}} \right) \overline{b} + \left(\frac{\overline{d} \cdot \overline{b} \times \overline{a}}{\overline{c} \cdot \overline{b} \times \overline{a}} \right) \overline{c} \qquad (10)$$

IDENTITIES AND RECIPROCAL VECTORS

● **PROBLEM 3-31**

Prove the identity

$$(\overline{a} + \overline{b}) \cdot (\overline{a} \times \overline{c}) \times (\overline{a} + \overline{b}) = 0 \qquad (1)$$

Solution: First prove the following property of the scalar triple product:

$\overline{a} \times \overline{b} \cdot \overline{c} = 0$ if and only if the vectors $\overline{a}$, $\overline{b}$, $\overline{c}$ are coplanar.

That can be easily seen from the fact that $|\overline{a} \times \overline{b} \cdot \overline{c}|$ is equal to the volume of a parallelepiped with sides $\overline{a}$, $\overline{b}$, $\overline{c}$. The volume is equal to zero only when the vectors are coplanar. In eq.(1) the vector $\overline{a} + \overline{b}$ appears twice. Thus all three vectors are coplanar, because two of them are equal.

Therefore their scalar triple product is equal to zero.

$$(\overline{a} + \overline{b}) \cdot (\overline{a} \times \overline{c}) \times (\overline{a} + \overline{b}) = 0 \qquad (2)$$

● **PROBLEM 3-32**

Show that

$$\overline{a} \times \left[\overline{a} \times (\overline{a} \times \overline{b}) \right] = (\overline{a} \cdot \overline{a}) \ (\overline{b} \times \overline{a}) \qquad (1)$$

Solution: Denote
$$\overline{c} = \overline{a} \times \overline{b} \qquad (2)$$

Using the equation (see Problem 3-28)

$$\overline{a} \times (\overline{b} \times \overline{c}) = (\overline{a} \cdot \overline{c}) \ \overline{b} - (\overline{a} \cdot \overline{b}) \ \overline{c} \qquad (3)$$

rewrite eq.(1) as

$$\bar{a} \times \left[\bar{a} \times (\bar{a} \times \bar{b})\right] = \bar{a} \times (\bar{a} \times \bar{c}) = (\bar{a}\cdot\bar{c})\bar{a} - (\bar{a}\cdot\bar{a})\bar{c}$$

$$= \left[\bar{a}\cdot(\bar{a} \times \bar{b})\right]\bar{a} - (\bar{a}\cdot\bar{a})(\bar{a} \times \bar{b}) \qquad (4)$$

The term $\bar{a}\cdot(\bar{a} \times \bar{b})$ is the scalar triple product of coplanar vectors, and therefore is equal to 0.

And we are left with

$$\bar{a} \times \left[\bar{a} \times (\bar{a} \times \bar{b})\right] = -(\bar{a}\cdot\bar{a})(\bar{a} \times \bar{b}) = (\bar{a}\cdot\bar{a})(\bar{b} \times \bar{a}) \qquad (5)$$

● **PROBLEM 3-33**

Prove the identities:

1) $(\bar{a} \times \bar{b}) \times (\bar{c} \times \bar{d}) = (\bar{a} \times \bar{b}\cdot\bar{d})\bar{c} - (\bar{a} \times \bar{b}\cdot\bar{c})\bar{d}$ (1)

2) $(\bar{a} \times \bar{b})\cdot(\bar{c} \times \bar{d}) = (\bar{a}\cdot\bar{c})(\bar{b}\cdot\bar{d}) - (\bar{a}\cdot\bar{d})(\bar{b}\cdot\bar{c})$ (2)

<u>Solution</u>: 1) Use the identity (see Problem 3-28)

$$\bar{a} \times (\bar{b} \times \bar{c}) = (\bar{a}\cdot\bar{c})\bar{b} - (\bar{a}\cdot\bar{b})\bar{c} \qquad (3)$$

In eq.(3) replace $\bar{a}$ by $\bar{a} \times \bar{b}$, $\bar{b}$ by $\bar{c}$ and $\bar{c}$ by $\bar{d}$ as indicated by the arrows

$$\bar{a} \times (\bar{b} \times \bar{c}) = (\bar{a} \cdot \bar{c})\bar{b} - (\bar{a} \cdot \bar{b})\bar{c}$$
$$\downarrow \quad \downarrow \quad \downarrow \qquad \downarrow \quad \downarrow\downarrow \qquad \downarrow \quad \downarrow$$
$$(\bar{a} \times \bar{b}) \times (\bar{c} \times \bar{d}) = (\bar{a} \times \bar{b}\cdot\bar{d})\bar{c} - (\bar{a} \times \bar{b}\cdot\bar{c})\bar{d} \qquad (4)$$

The proof is completed.

2) Use the identity

$$\bar{a}\cdot(\bar{b} \times \bar{c}) = \bar{b}\cdot(\bar{c} \times \bar{a}) \qquad (5)$$

(see problem 3-26).

In eq. (5) replace $\bar{a}$ by $\bar{a} \times \bar{b}$, $\bar{b}$ by $\bar{c}$ and $\bar{c}$ by $\bar{d}$ as indicated by the arrows. Doing this,

$$\bar{a} \cdot (\bar{b} \times \bar{c}) = \bar{b} \cdot(\bar{c} \times \bar{a}) \qquad (6)$$
$$\downarrow \quad \downarrow \quad \downarrow \quad \downarrow \quad \downarrow \quad \downarrow$$
$$(\bar{a} \times \bar{b})\cdot(\bar{c} \times \bar{d}) = \bar{c} \cdot \left[\bar{d} \times (\bar{a} \times \bar{b})\right] \qquad (7)$$

Using the identity

$$\bar{a} \times (\bar{b} \times \bar{c}) = (\bar{a}\cdot\bar{c})\bar{b} - (\bar{a}\cdot\bar{b})\bar{c} \qquad (8)$$

Obtain

$$\bar{c} \cdot \left[\bar{d} \times (\bar{a} \times \bar{b})\right] = \bar{c}\cdot\left[(\bar{d}\cdot\bar{b})\bar{a} - (\bar{d}\cdot\bar{a})\bar{b}\right]$$
$$= (\bar{a}\cdot\bar{c})(\bar{b}\cdot\bar{d}) - (\bar{a}\cdot\bar{d})(\bar{b}\cdot\bar{c}) \qquad (9)$$

98

Combining eq.(7) and eq.(9), obtain

$$(\overline{a} \times \overline{b}) \cdot (\overline{c} \times \overline{d}) = (\overline{a} \cdot \overline{c})(\overline{b} \cdot \overline{d}) - (\overline{a} \cdot \overline{d})(\overline{b} \cdot \overline{c}) \qquad (10)$$

This is known as the identity of Lagrange.

● **PROBLEM 3-34**

Prove the identity:

$$\begin{vmatrix} \overline{a} \cdot \overline{a} & \overline{a} \cdot \overline{b} \\ \overline{a} \cdot \overline{b} & \overline{b} \cdot \overline{b} \end{vmatrix} = |\overline{a} \times \overline{b}|^2 \qquad (1)$$

Solution: From the definition of the determinant, obtain

$$\begin{vmatrix} \overline{a} \cdot \overline{a} & \overline{a} \cdot \overline{b} \\ \overline{a} \cdot \overline{b} & \overline{b} \cdot \overline{b} \end{vmatrix} = (\overline{a} \cdot \overline{a})(\overline{b} \cdot \overline{b}) - (\overline{a} \cdot \overline{b})(\overline{a} \cdot \overline{b}) \qquad (2)$$

Use the identity

$$(\overline{a} \times \overline{b}) \cdot (\overline{c} \times \overline{d}) = (\overline{a} \cdot \overline{c})(\overline{b} \cdot \overline{d}) - (\overline{a} \cdot \overline{d})(\overline{b} \cdot \overline{c}) \qquad (3)$$

(see Problem 3-33).

Put $\overline{c} = \overline{a}$ and $\overline{d} = \overline{b}$ in eq.(3), thus

$$(\overline{a} \times \overline{b}) \cdot (\overline{a} \times \overline{b}) = (\overline{a} \cdot \overline{a})(\overline{b} \cdot \overline{b}) - (\overline{a} \cdot \overline{b})(\overline{a} \cdot \overline{b}) \qquad (4)$$

Combining eqs.(2) and (4),

$$\begin{vmatrix} \overline{a} \cdot \overline{a} & \overline{a} \cdot \overline{b} \\ \overline{a} \cdot \overline{b} & \overline{b} \cdot \overline{b} \end{vmatrix} = (\overline{a} \times \overline{b}) \cdot (\overline{a} \times \overline{b}) = |\overline{a} \times \overline{b}|^2 \qquad (5)$$

● **PROBLEM 3-35**

Prove the identity:

$$\overline{a} \times (\overline{b} \times \overline{c}) + \overline{b} \times (\overline{c} \times \overline{a}) + \overline{c} \times (\overline{a} \times \overline{b}) = \overline{0} \qquad (1)$$

Solution: Use the identity

$$\overline{a} \times (\overline{b} \times \overline{c}) = (\overline{a} \cdot \overline{c})\overline{b} - (\overline{a} \cdot \overline{b})\overline{c} \qquad (2)$$

(see Problem 3-28)

For the second term of eq.(1),

$$\overline{b} \times (\overline{c} \times \overline{a}) = (\overline{b} \cdot \overline{a})\overline{c} - (\overline{b} \cdot \overline{c})\overline{a} \qquad (3)$$

and for the third term

$$\overline{c} \times (\overline{a} \times \overline{b}) = (\overline{c} \cdot \overline{b})\overline{a} - (\overline{c} \cdot \overline{a})\overline{b} \qquad (4)$$

Adding eqs.(2), (3) and (4), gives

$$\bar{a} \times (\bar{b} \times \bar{c}) + \bar{b} \times (\bar{c} \times \bar{a}) + \bar{c} \times (\bar{a} \times \bar{b}) \qquad (5)$$

$$= (\bar{a} \cdot \bar{c})\bar{b} - (\bar{a} \cdot \bar{b})\bar{c} + (\bar{a} \cdot \bar{b})\bar{c} - (\bar{b} \cdot \bar{c})\bar{a} + (\bar{b} \cdot \bar{c})\bar{a} - (\bar{a} \cdot \bar{c})\bar{b}$$

$$= \bar{0}$$

That proves the identity.

● **PROBLEM 3-36**

Prove that two sets of vectors $\bar{a}$, $\bar{b}$, $\bar{c}$ and $\bar{a}'$, $\bar{b}'$, $\bar{c}'$ are reciprocal sets of vectors if and only if

$$\bar{a}' = \frac{\bar{b} \times \bar{c}}{\bar{a} \cdot \bar{b} \times \bar{c}}, \qquad \bar{b}' = \frac{\bar{c} \times \bar{a}}{\bar{a} \cdot \bar{b} \times \bar{c}}, \qquad \bar{c}' = \frac{\bar{a} \times \bar{b}}{\bar{a} \cdot \bar{b} \times \bar{c}} \qquad (1)$$

Solution: Two sets of vectors $\bar{a}$, $\bar{b}$, $\bar{c}$, such that $\bar{a} \cdot \bar{b} \times \bar{c} \neq 0$, and $\bar{a}'$, $\bar{b}'$, $\bar{c}'$ are called reciprocal sets of vectors if

$$\bar{a} \cdot \bar{a}' = \bar{b} \cdot \bar{b}' = \bar{c} \cdot \bar{c}' = 1 \qquad \text{and} \qquad (2)$$

$$\bar{a}' \cdot \bar{b} = \bar{a}' \cdot \bar{c} = \bar{b}' \cdot \bar{a} = \bar{b}' \cdot \bar{c} = \bar{c}' \cdot \bar{a} = \bar{c}' \cdot \bar{b} = 0 \qquad (3)$$

Now show that if the sets of vectors $\bar{a}$, $\bar{b}$, $\bar{c}$ and $\bar{a}'$, $\bar{b}'$, $\bar{c}'$ are reciprocal then eq.(1) holds.

From eq.(3), one concludes that $\bar{a}'$ is orthogonal to $\bar{b}$ and to $\bar{c}$, thus it has the direction of $\bar{b} \times \bar{c}$. Therefore the vector $\bar{a}'$ can be expressed as

$$\bar{a}' = \alpha \, \bar{b} \times \bar{c} \qquad (4)$$

where α is a scalar.

From eq.(2), $\bar{a} \cdot \bar{a}' = 1$, thus scalar multiplying eq.(4) by $\bar{a}$,

$$\bar{a} \cdot \bar{a}' = \alpha \, \bar{a} \cdot \bar{b} \times \bar{c} = 1 \qquad (5)$$

Solving for α,

$$\alpha = \frac{1}{\bar{a} \cdot \bar{b} \times \bar{c}} \qquad (6)$$

Thus

$$\bar{a}' = \frac{\bar{b} \times \bar{c}}{\bar{a} \cdot \bar{b} \times \bar{c}} \qquad (7)$$

In the same manner

$$\bar{b}' = \beta \, \bar{c} \times \bar{a} \qquad (8)$$

$$\beta = \frac{1}{\bar{a} \cdot \bar{b} \times \bar{c}}$$

and

$$\bar{b}' = \frac{\bar{c} \times \bar{a}}{\bar{a} \cdot \bar{b} \times \bar{c}} \qquad (9)$$

and

$$\bar{c}' = \frac{\bar{a} \times \bar{b}}{\bar{a} \cdot \bar{b} \times \bar{c}}$$

That completes the first part of the proof. Next, show that if the vectors $\bar{a}'$, $\bar{b}'$, $\bar{c}'$ are given by eq.(1), then the sets $\bar{a}$, $\bar{b}$, $\bar{c}$ and $\bar{a}'$, $\bar{b}'$, $\bar{c}'$ are reciprocal sets.

Doing this

$$\bar{a} \cdot \bar{a}' = \bar{a} \cdot \frac{\bar{b} \times \bar{c}}{\bar{a} \cdot \bar{b} \times \bar{c}} = \frac{\bar{a} \cdot \bar{b} \times \bar{c}}{\bar{a} \cdot \bar{b} \times \bar{c}} = 1 \qquad (10)$$

$$\bar{b} \cdot \bar{b}' = \bar{b} \cdot \frac{\bar{c} \times \bar{a}}{\bar{a} \cdot \bar{b} \times \bar{c}} = \frac{\bar{b} \cdot \bar{c} \times \bar{a}}{\bar{a} \cdot \bar{b} \times \bar{c}} = \frac{\bar{a} \cdot \bar{b} \times \bar{c}}{\bar{a} \cdot \bar{b} \times \bar{c}} = 1 \qquad (11)$$

$$\bar{c} \cdot \bar{c}' = \bar{c} \cdot \frac{\bar{a} \times \bar{b}}{\bar{a} \cdot \bar{b} \times \bar{c}} = \frac{\bar{c} \cdot \bar{a} \times \bar{b}}{\bar{a} \cdot \bar{b} \times \bar{c}} = \frac{\bar{a} \cdot \bar{b} \times \bar{c}}{\bar{a} \cdot \bar{b} \times \bar{c}} = 1 \qquad (12)$$

$$\bar{a}' \cdot \bar{b} = \frac{\bar{b} \times \bar{c}}{\bar{a} \cdot \bar{b} \times \bar{c}} \cdot \bar{b} = 0 \qquad (13)$$

In the same way, it can be shown that

$$\bar{a}' \cdot \bar{c} = \bar{b}' \cdot \bar{a} = \bar{b}' \cdot \bar{c} = \bar{c}' \cdot \bar{a} = \bar{c}' \cdot \bar{b} = 0$$

● **PROBLEM 3-37**

The set of vectors $\bar{a}$, $\bar{b}$, $\bar{c}$ and $\bar{a}'$, $\bar{b}'$, $\bar{c}'$ are reciprocal sets. Show that if

$$\bar{a} \cdot \bar{b} \times \bar{c} = V \qquad (1)$$

then

$$\bar{a}' \cdot \bar{b}' \times \bar{c}' = \frac{1}{V} \qquad (2)$$

Solution: Since $\bar{a}$, $\bar{b}$, $\bar{c}$ and $\bar{a}'$, $\bar{b}'$, $\bar{c}'$ are reciprocal sets,

$$\bar{a}' = \frac{\bar{b} \times \bar{c}}{\bar{a} \cdot \bar{b} \times \bar{c}}, \qquad \bar{b}' = \frac{\bar{c} \times \bar{a}}{\bar{a} \cdot \bar{b} \times \bar{c}}, \qquad \bar{c}' = \frac{\bar{a} \times \bar{b}}{\bar{a} \cdot \bar{b} \times \bar{c}} \qquad (3)$$

Substituting eq.(1) into eq.(3),

$$\bar{a}' = \frac{\bar{b} \times \bar{c}}{V}, \qquad \bar{b}' = \frac{\bar{c} \times \bar{a}}{V}, \qquad \bar{c}' = \frac{\bar{a} \times \bar{b}}{V} \qquad (4)$$

Then

$$\bar{a}' \cdot \bar{b}' \times \bar{c}' = \frac{(\bar{b} \times \bar{c}) \cdot (\bar{c} \times \bar{a}) \times (\bar{a} \times \bar{b})}{V^3}$$

$$= \frac{(\overline{a} \times \overline{b}) \cdot (\overline{b} \times \overline{c}) \times (\overline{c} \times \overline{a})}{V^3} \qquad (5)$$

Then using the identity
$$(\overline{a} \times \overline{b}) \cdot (\overline{b} \times \overline{c}) \times (\overline{c} \times \overline{a}) = (\overline{a} \cdot \overline{b} \times \overline{c})^2, \qquad (6)$$

Eq.(5) becomes
$$\overline{a}' \cdot \overline{b}' \times \overline{c}' = \frac{(\overline{a} \cdot \overline{b} \times \overline{c})^2}{V^3} = \frac{V^2}{V^3} = \frac{1}{V} \qquad (7)$$

● **PROBLEM 3-38**

Show that any vector $\overline{d}$ can be expressed in terms of the reciprocal vectors.

<u>Solution</u>: To solve this problem, use the identity:

$$(\overline{a} \times \overline{b}) \times (\overline{c} \times \overline{d}) = \overline{b}(\overline{a} \cdot \overline{c} \times \overline{d}) - \overline{a}(\overline{b} \cdot \overline{c} \times \overline{d}) = \overline{c}(\overline{a} \cdot \overline{b} \times \overline{d}) - \overline{d}(\overline{a} \cdot \overline{b} \times \overline{c}) \qquad (1)$$

(see Problem 3-33).

Solving eq.(1) for $\overline{d}$,

$$\overline{d} = \frac{\overline{a}(\overline{b} \cdot \overline{c} \times \overline{d}) + \overline{c}(\overline{a} \cdot \overline{b} \times \overline{d}) - \overline{b}(\overline{a} \cdot \overline{c} \times \overline{d})}{\overline{a} \cdot \overline{b} \times \overline{c}} \qquad (2)$$

or

$$\overline{d} = \frac{\overline{d} \cdot \overline{b} \times \overline{c}}{\overline{a} \cdot \overline{b} \times \overline{c}} \overline{a} + \frac{\overline{d} \cdot \overline{c} \times \overline{a}}{\overline{a} \cdot \overline{b} \times \overline{c}} \overline{b} + \frac{\overline{d} \cdot \overline{a} \times \overline{b}}{\overline{a} \cdot \overline{b} \times \overline{c}} \overline{c} \qquad (3)$$

$$= \overline{d} \cdot \frac{\overline{b} \times \overline{c}}{\overline{a} \cdot \overline{b} \times \overline{c}} \overline{a} + \overline{d} \cdot \frac{\overline{c} \times \overline{a}}{\overline{a} \cdot \overline{b} \times \overline{c}} \overline{b} + \overline{d} \cdot \frac{\overline{a} \times \overline{b}}{\overline{a} \cdot \overline{b} \times \overline{c}} \overline{c}$$

Since the vectors $\overline{a}$, $\overline{b}$, $\overline{c}$ and $\overline{a}'$, $\overline{b}'$, $\overline{c}'$ are reciprocal,

$$\overline{a}' = \frac{\overline{b} \times \overline{c}}{\overline{a} \cdot \overline{b} \times \overline{c}}, \qquad \overline{b}' = \frac{\overline{c} \times \overline{a}}{\overline{a} \cdot \overline{b} \times \overline{c}}, \qquad \overline{c}' = \frac{\overline{a} \times \overline{b}}{\overline{a} \cdot \overline{b} \times \overline{c}} \qquad (4)$$

(see Problem 3-36).
Substituting eq.(4) into eq.(3), gives

$$\overline{d} = (\overline{d} \cdot \overline{a}') \overline{a} + (\overline{d} \cdot \overline{b}') \overline{b} + (\overline{d} \cdot \overline{c}') \overline{c} \qquad (5)$$

VECTOR EQUATIONS OF LINES, PLANES, SPHERES AND THE MOMENT OF A VECTOR

● **PROBLEM 3-39**

A line in space can be defined in several ways. The equation which must be satisfied by the position-vector $\overline{x}$ of every point X on the line is called the equation of the line.

Find the equation of the line through a given point and parallel to a given vector.

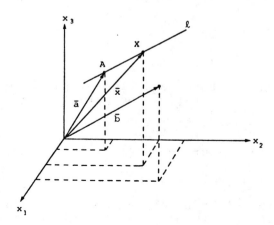

Solution: Let A be the given point, with position vector $\bar{a}$ and let $\bar{b}$ be the given vector, as shown in the figure. Further, let X be a general point on ℓ, whose position vector is $\bar{x}$.

By definition, $\overline{AX}$ is parallel to $\bar{b}$, thus

$$\overline{AX} \times \bar{b} = \bar{0} \tag{1}$$

Also

$$\bar{a} + \overline{AX} = \bar{x}$$

or

$$\overline{AX} = \bar{x} - \bar{a} \tag{2}$$

Substituting eq.(2) into eq.(1), obtain the line equation

$$(\bar{x} - \bar{a}) \times \bar{b} = \bar{0} \tag{3}$$

● PROBLEM 3-40

Find the equation of the line

1) through two given points A and B

2) through a given point A and perpendicular to the plane through three given points B, C and D.

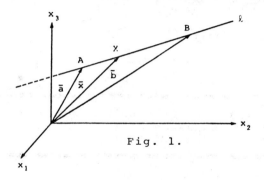

Fig. 1.

Solution: 1) Let $\bar{a}$ and $\bar{b}$ be position-vectors of the given points A and B respectively. Let $\bar{x}$ be the position vector of any point X on the line as shown in Fig. 1.

From Fig. 1,

$$\bar{a} + \overline{AB} = \bar{b} \tag{1}$$

or

$$\overline{AB} = \bar{b} - \bar{a}$$

Using the result that the equation of the line through a point F whose position vector is $\bar{f}$ and parallel to $\bar{g}$ is

$$(\bar{x} - \bar{f}) \times \bar{g} = 0, \tag{2}$$

obtain (after substituting eq.(1) into eq.(2))

$$(\bar{x} - \bar{a}) \times (\bar{b} - \bar{a}) = \bar{0} \tag{3}$$

2) Let A be the given point on the line ℓ and let B, C and D be the given points defining the plane, as shown in Fig. 2.

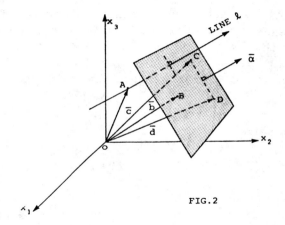

FIG.2

Let $\bar{a}$, $\bar{b}$, $\bar{c}$ and $\bar{d}$ be the position vectors of A, B, C and D. Define vector $\bar{\alpha}$ such that

$$\bar{\alpha} = \bar{b} \times \bar{c} + \bar{c} \times \bar{d} + \bar{d} \times \bar{b} \tag{4}$$

$\bar{\alpha}$ is perpendicular to the plane S. Thus, the equation of the line through a given point A and parallel to $\bar{\alpha}$ is

$$(\bar{x} - \bar{a}) \times \bar{\alpha} = 0 \tag{5}$$

where $\bar{\alpha}$ is given by eq.(4).

● **PROBLEM 3-41**

Let A, B and C be three given points, which do not lie on one line. Find the equation of the plane S containing these three points.

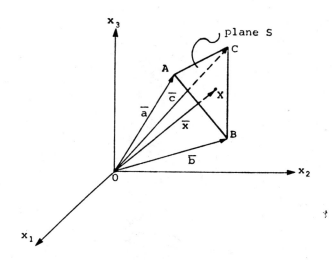

Solution: The figure illustrates the problem.

Let $\bar{a}$, $\bar{b}$ and $\bar{c}$ denote the position vectors of the points A, B and C, respectively. Let X be a general point on the plane S, whose position vector is $\bar{x}$. Introduce vector $\bar{\alpha}$ such that

$$\bar{\alpha} = \bar{a} \times \bar{b} + \bar{b} \times \bar{c} + \bar{c} \times \bar{a} \tag{1}$$

It can be shown that $\bar{\alpha}$ is perpendicular to the plane S.

If $A:(a_1,a_2,a_3)$ is a point on the plane and $\bar{\alpha}$ is a vector perpendicular to the plane, then the equation of the plane is

$$(\bar{x} - \bar{a}) \cdot \bar{\alpha} = 0 \tag{2}$$

and therefore

$$\bar{a} \cdot \bar{\alpha} = \bar{a} \cdot (\bar{a} \times \bar{b} + \bar{b} \times \bar{c} + \bar{c} \times \bar{a}) = \bar{a} \cdot (\bar{b} \times \bar{c}) \tag{3}$$

Thus
$$(\bar{x} - \bar{a}) \cdot \bar{\alpha} = \bar{x} \cdot \bar{\alpha} - \bar{a} \cdot \bar{\alpha} = 0 \tag{4}$$

Substituting eq.(3) into eq.(4),

$$\bar{x} \cdot \bar{\alpha} = \bar{a} \cdot (\bar{b} \times \bar{c}) \tag{5}$$

where $\bar{\alpha} = \bar{a} \times \bar{b} + \bar{b} \times \bar{c} + \bar{c} \times \bar{a}$

● **PROBLEM 3-42**

1) Find the equation of the plane through a given point P and perpendicular to a given vector $\bar{a}$, where $P:(p_1,p_2,p_3)$ and $\bar{a} = (a_1,a_2,a_3)$.

2) Find the equation of the plane that passes through $\underline{A} = (1,6,2)$ and is perpendicular to the vector $\bar{a} = (2,4,1)$.

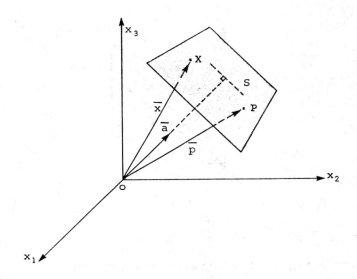

<u>Solution</u>: 1) Vector $\bar{a}$ and point P are shown in the figure.

Let X be any point on S and let $\bar{x}$ and $\bar{p}$ denote the position-vectors of X and P respectively. Vector $\overline{PX}$ is perpendicular to $\bar{a}$, thus

$$\overline{PX} \cdot \bar{a} = 0 \tag{1}$$

and

$$\overline{PX} = \bar{x} - \bar{p} \tag{2}$$

thus

$$(\bar{x} - \bar{p}) \cdot \bar{a} = 0 \tag{3}$$

or in the component form

$$(x_1-p_1,\ x_2-p_2,\ x_3-p_3) \cdot (a_1, a_2, a_3) = 0 \tag{4}$$

2) Vector $\bar{a}$ is given by

$$\bar{a} = (2,4,1)$$

and point A is (1,6,2). (A is equivalent to pt. P.)

Substituting these values into eq.(4)

$$(x_1-1,\ x_2-6,\ x_3-2) \cdot (2,4,1)$$

$$= 2(x_1-1) + 4(x_2-6) + (x_3-2) = 0 \tag{5}$$

Thus,

$$x_3 = -2(x_1-1) - 4(x_2-6) + 2$$

Points of the plane can be represented in the form

$$(x_1,\ x_2,\ -2(x_1-1) - 4(x_2-6) +2)$$

where x_1 and x_2 are any real parameters.

Let A be the given point and $\bar{b}$ the given vector. Find the vector $\bar{d}$, originating from a point C, which is perpendicular to a plane S, where S passes through the given point A and is perpendicular to the given vector $\bar{b}$.

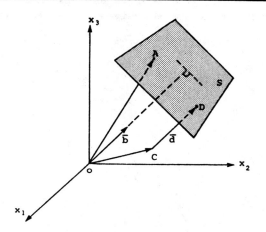

Solution: The problem is illustrated in the figure.
Begin by finding the vector $\bar{d}$ which is perpendicular to the plane S. Since both vectors $\bar{d}$ and $\bar{b}$ are perpendicular to the plane S,

$$\bar{d} = \alpha\bar{b} \tag{1}$$

where α is a scalar constant.

From the figure, obtain

$$\overline{OC} + \overline{CD} + \overline{DA} + \overline{AO} = \bar{0} \tag{2}$$

or

$$\overline{OC} + \alpha\bar{b} + \overline{DA} - \overline{OA} = 0 \tag{3}$$

$\bar{b}$ is perpendicular to $\overline{DA}$, hence

$$\bar{b}\cdot\overline{DA} = 0 \tag{4}$$

Multiplying both sides of eq.(3) by $\bar{b}$ obtain

$$(\overline{OC} - \overline{OA})\cdot\bar{b} + \alpha b^2 = 0 \tag{5}$$

Solving eq.(5) for α, gives

$$\alpha = \frac{-(\overline{OC}-\overline{OA})\cdot\bar{b}}{b^2} \tag{6}$$

Substitution for α in eq.(1) yields

$$\bar{d} = \frac{(\overline{OA}-\overline{OC})\cdot\bar{b}}{b^2}\,\bar{b} \tag{7}$$

Denoting $\overline{OA} = \bar{a}$ and $\overline{OC} = \bar{c}$, then

$$\bar{d} = \frac{(\bar{a}-\bar{c})\cdot\bar{b}}{b^2}\,\bar{b} \tag{8}$$

Let S be a sphere of radius r and center at a point A.

Find the equation of the plane P which is tangent to the sphere at a point B, as shown in the figure.

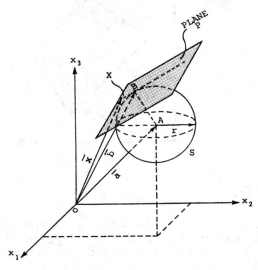

Solution: Let X be any point on the plane P. Vectors $\bar{a}$, $\bar{b}$, $\bar{x}$ are position vectors of points A, B and X respectively. From the figure it follows that

$$\overline{AX} = \overline{AB} + \overline{BX} \qquad (1)$$

and,
$$\overline{AX} = \bar{x} - \bar{a} \qquad (2)$$

therefore
$$\bar{x} - \bar{a} = \overline{AB} + \overline{BX} \qquad (3)$$

Multiply eq.(3) scalarly by $\overline{AB}$

$$\overline{AB} \cdot (\bar{x} - \bar{a}) = \overline{AB} \cdot \overline{AB} + \overline{AB} \cdot \overline{BX} \qquad (4)$$

$$\overline{AB} \cdot \overline{AB} = r^2 \qquad (5)$$

and
$$\overline{AB} \cdot \overline{BX} = 0 \qquad (\overline{AB} \text{ is perpendicular to } \overline{BX})$$

also,
$$\overline{AB} = \bar{b} - \bar{a} \qquad (6)$$

Substituting eq.(6) and eq.(5) into eq.(4), get

$$(\bar{b} - \bar{a}) \cdot (\bar{x} - \bar{a}) = r^2 \qquad (7)$$

● **PROBLEM** 3-45

Find the equation of a sphere of radius r and center at a point A.

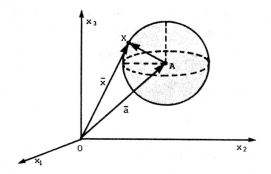

Solution: Let $\bar{a}$ be the position vector of point A and $\bar{x}$ the position vector of any point X on the sphere as shown in the figure.

Since the radius of the sphere is r,

$$\overline{AX} \cdot \overline{AX} = |\overline{AX}|^2 = r^2 \tag{1}$$

From the figure,

$$\bar{a} + \overline{AX} = \overline{OX} = \bar{x}$$

or

$$\overline{AX} = \bar{x} - \bar{a} \tag{2}$$

Substituting eq.(2) into eq.(1),

$$(\bar{x} - \bar{a}) \cdot (\bar{x} - \bar{a}) = r^2$$

● **PROBLEM 3-46**

Prove the following property of a sphere:

the angle at the surface of a sphere subtended by a diameter of the sphere is a right angle (denoted α in the figure).

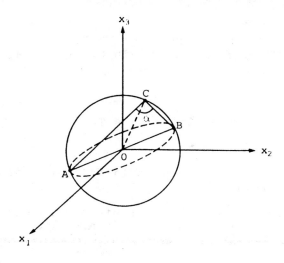

Solution: Assume for convenience that the center of the sphere is located at the origin of the system as shown in the figure.

AB is a diameter of the sphere and C any point on the sphere. From the figure,

$$\overline{BC} = \overline{OC} - \overline{OB} \tag{1}$$

and

$$\overline{AC} = \overline{OC} - \overline{OA}$$

Thus

$$\overline{BC} \cdot \overline{AC} = (\overline{OC} - \overline{OB}) \cdot (\overline{OC} - \overline{OA}) \tag{2}$$

$$= \overline{OC} \cdot \overline{OC} - \overline{OC} \cdot \overline{OA} - \overline{OB} \cdot \overline{OC} + \overline{OB} \cdot \overline{OA}$$

$$= \overline{OC} \cdot \overline{OC} - \overline{OC} \cdot (\overline{OA} + \overline{OB}) + \overline{OB} \cdot \overline{OA}$$

Then,

$$\overline{OA} + \overline{OB} = 0 \tag{3}$$

$$\overline{OB} \cdot \overline{OA} = -r^2 \qquad (\text{because } \overline{OB} = -\overline{OA})$$

where r is the radius of the sphere.

Eq.(2) can be written as

$$\overline{BC} \cdot \overline{AC} = \overline{OC} \cdot \overline{OC} + \overline{OB} \cdot \overline{OA} = r^2 - r^2 = 0 \tag{4}$$

Thus $\overline{BC}$ and $\overline{AC}$ are perpendicular and

$$\alpha = 90^\circ \tag{5}$$

● **PROBLEM 3-47**

The moment of vector $\overline{a}$ about the point O is the vector $\overline{M}$ defined as

$$\overline{M} = \overline{r} \times \overline{a} \tag{1}$$

where $\overline{r}$ is a vector with origin at O and whose terminal point coincides with the origin of vector $\overline{a}$, as shown in Fig. 1.

Show that:

1) if $\overline{M}$ is the moment of $\overline{a}$ about the point O, then

$$M = ma \tag{2}$$

where m is the perpendicular distance from O to the line of action of $\overline{a}$.

2) The moments about a point of any two equal vectors with the same line of action are equal.

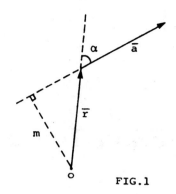

FIG.1

Solution: 1)   Since $\overline{M} = \overline{r} \times \overline{a}$,   (3)

But $M = ra \sin \alpha$ (4)

                       $\sin \alpha = \dfrac{m}{r}$ (5)

hence

                       $M = ra \sin \alpha = ra \dfrac{m}{r} = ma$ (6)

2)   Fig. 2 shows two equal vectors with the same line of action.

Both moments are defined as

                       $\overline{M} = \overline{r} \times \overline{a}$

                       $\overline{M}' = \overline{r}' \times \overline{a}$ (7)

They have equal magnitudes

                       $M = ma$

                       $M' = ma$ (8)

$\overline{M}$ and $\overline{M}'$ have the same direction, because vectors $\overline{r}$, $\overline{r}'$ and $\overline{a}$ are coplanar.

Thus $\overline{M} = \overline{M}'$ (9)

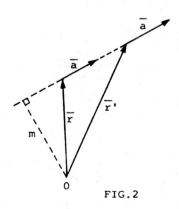

FIG.2

111

CHAPTER 4

ORDINARY DERIVATIVES OF VECTORS

INTRODUCTION

Chapter 4 introduces a fundamental concept in vector analysis - the concept of the vector function. In the most general case, a vector function can be a function of n vectors ($\bar{r}_n$) and k scalars (t_k).

$$\bar{a} = \bar{a}(\bar{r}_1, \bar{r}_2, \bar{r}_3, \ldots, \bar{r}_n, t_1, t_2, t_3, \ldots, t_k)$$

In physical applications however, vector functions are usually reduced to functions of a position vector $\bar{r}$ and time t.

$$\bar{a} = \bar{a}(\bar{r}, t)$$

For now, this book will consider the simplest case of a vector function - that of a scalar argument.

$$\bar{a} = \bar{a}(t)$$

More complicated vector functions will be dealt with later in the book.

In defining the derivative of a vector function (of a scalar argument), $\bar{a} = \bar{a}(t)$, the student will find that the analysis varies only slightly from ordinary mathematical analysis. The reason for this is that a vector function can be considered as an ordered number of ordinary functions.

$$\bar{a}(t) = \left[a_1(t), a_2(t), a_3(t), \ldots, a_n(t) \right]$$

The number of ordinary functions are equal to the dimension of the vector space. For instance, in three-dimensional space, a vector $\bar{a} = \bar{a}(t)$ can be expressed as

$$\bar{a}(t) = \left[a_1(t), a_2(t), a_3(t) \right]$$

where $a_1(t), a_2(t),$ and $a_3(t),$ which are the components of $\bar{a},$ are ordinary functions. Since there are three ordinary functions, the dimension of this vector space is equal to three.

This chapter also introduces parametric equations of a curve in space, as well as the definition of the tangent vector, which allows us to obtain a clear geometrical interpretation of a vector function and its derivative. In the future, vector functions and derivatives of vector functions will be applied to geometry and physics problems.

The last few problems of the chapter discuss the similarities between differential equations of vector functions and ordinary differential equations.

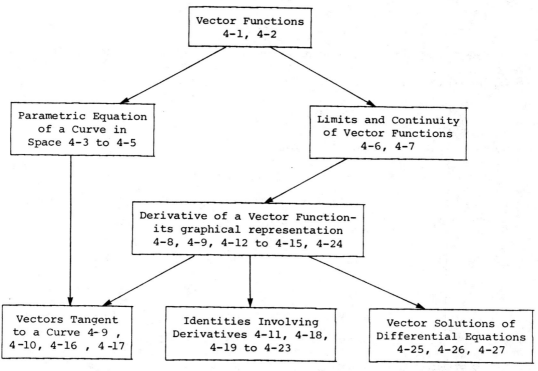

This chart is provided to facilitate rapid understanding of the interrelationships of the topics and subject matter in this chapter. Also shown are the problem numbers associated with the subject matter.

VECTOR FUNCTIONS AND PARAMETRIC EQUATIONS OF A CURVE

● **PROBLEM** 4-1

Let $\bar{r}(t)$ be a vector function given by

$$\bar{r}(t) = t\bar{a} + (1-t)\bar{b}, \qquad 0 \leq t \leq 1 \qquad (1)$$

where
$$\bar{a} = (a_1, a_2, a_3)$$
$$\bar{b} = (b_1, b_2, b_3) \tag{2}$$

are two given vectors.

Express $\bar{r}(t)$

    1) in the component form
    2) in terms of the base vectors.

Solution: 1) In the n-dimensional vector space, a vector $\bar{a}$ is expressed in the component form when all of its components $a_1, a_2, \ldots, a_n$ are given. That is,

$$\bar{a} = (a_1, a_2, \ldots, a_n)$$

The maximum number of components of a vector in the n-dimensional space is n. To express vector $\bar{r}(t)$ in the component form, we have to find $r_1(t)$, $r_2(t)$, $r_3(t)$ such that

$$\bar{r}(t) = \left[r_1(t), r_2(t), r_3(t) \right]$$

Substituting eq.(2) into eq.(1),

$$\bar{r}(t) = t\bar{a} + (1-t)\bar{b} = t(a_1, a_2, a_3) + (1-t)(b_1, b_2, b_3) \tag{3}$$

Multiplying and adding the corresponding components in eq.(3),

$$\bar{r}(t) = (ta_1, ta_2, ta_3) + \left[(1-t)b_1, (1-t)b_2, (1-t)b_3 \right]$$
$$= \left[ta_1 + (1-t)b_1, ta_2 + (1-t)b_2, ta_3 + (1-t)b_3 \right] \tag{4}$$

Eq.(4) expresses the vector $\bar{r}(t)$ in terms of its components.

2) Let $\bar{a}$ be any vector in the n-dimensional vector space and $\bar{i}_1, \bar{i}_2, \ldots, \bar{i}_n$ be the base vectors of this space. Note that an n-dimensional vector space has n base vectors. Vector $\bar{a}$ can be expressed uniquely as a linear combination of the base vectors; that is

$$\bar{a} = a_1 \bar{i}_1 + a_2 \bar{i}_2 + \ldots + a_n \bar{i}_n.$$

In this case, the vector space is three-dimensional, therefore it is necessary to find three base vectors. The simplest choice is

$$\bar{i} = (1, 0, 0)$$
$$\bar{j} = (0, 1, 0) \tag{5}$$
$$\bar{k} = (0, 0, 1)$$

Now, express vectors $\bar{a}$ and $\bar{b}$ in terms of these base vectors,

$$\bar{a} = a_1\bar{i} + a_2\bar{j} + a_3\bar{k}$$

$$\bar{b} = b_1\bar{i} + b_2\bar{j} + b_3\bar{k} \tag{6}$$

Substituting eq.(6) into eq.(1),

$$\bar{r}(t) = t\bar{a} + (1-t)\bar{b} = t(a_1\bar{i}+a_2\bar{j}+a_3\bar{k}) + (1-t)(b_1\bar{i}+b_2\bar{j}+b_3\bar{k})$$

$$= \left[ta_1+(1-t)b_1\right]\bar{i} + \left[ta_2+(1-t)b_2\right]\bar{j} + \left[ta_3+(1-t)b_3\right]\bar{k} \tag{7}$$

Eq.(7) expresses vector $\bar{r}(t)$ as a linear combination of the base vectors $\bar{i}$, $\bar{j}$, $\bar{k}$.

● **PROBLEM 4-2**

1)   Express the vector function

$$\bar{a}(t) = t^2\bar{i} + 3t\bar{j} + 4t\bar{k} \tag{1}$$

in component form.

2)   Express the vector function

$$\bar{r}(u) = u^2\bar{a} + e^u\bar{b} \tag{2}$$

in the component form and in terms of the base vectors.

$\bar{a}$ and $\bar{b}$ are given vectors such that

$$\bar{a} = (a_1, a_2, a_3)$$

$$\bar{b} = (b_1, b_2, b_3) \tag{3}$$

Solution: 1)   It is desired to find the three components of the vector $\bar{a}(t)$. Since in eq.(1) there are three base vectors $\bar{i}$, $\bar{j}$, $\bar{k}$, we assume that the vector space is three-dimensional.

The base vectors are

$$\bar{i} = (1,0,0)$$

$$\bar{j} = (0,1,0) \tag{4}$$

$$\bar{k} = (0,0,1)$$

Substituting eq.(4) into eq.(1),

$$\bar{a}(t) = t^2(1,0,0) + 3t(0,1,0) + 4t(0,0,1)$$

$$= (t^2,0,0) + (0,3t,0) + (0,C,4t) \tag{5}$$

$$= (t^2, 3t, 4t).$$

Vector $\bar{a}(t)$ is a vector function of variable t only. The components of $\bar{a}(t)$ are also functions of t. Assuming that the coordinate axes are fixed and do not depend on t, then a vector function $\bar{a}(t)$ is determined by three scalar functions which are the components of $\bar{a}(t)$.

2) To express $\bar{r}(u)$ in the component form, determine all of its components. Vectors $\bar{a}$ and $\bar{b}$ are given by eq.(3) where

$$\bar{a} = (a_1, a_2, a_3)$$

$$\bar{b} = (b_1, b_2, b_3) \tag{6}$$

are already in the component form.

Substituting eq.(6) into eq.(2),

$$\bar{r}(u) = u^2\bar{a} + e^u\bar{b} = u^2(a_1, a_2, a_3) + e^u(b_1, b_2, b_3)$$

$$= (u^2a_1, u^2a_2, u^2a_3) + (e^ub_1, e^ub_2, e^ub_3) \tag{7}$$

$$= (u^2a_1 + e^ub_1, \ u^2a_2 + e^ub_2, \ u^2a_3 + e^ub_3)$$

To express $\bar{r}(u)$ in terms of the base vectors, write $\bar{r}(u)$ as a linear combination of the base vectors. In the three-dimensional space, the base vectors are

$$\bar{i} = (1,0,0)$$

$$\bar{j} = (0,1,0) \tag{8}$$

$$\bar{k} = (0,0,1)$$

Now express vectors a and b, as given by eq.(3), in terms of the base vectors.

Doing this,

$$\bar{a} = (a_1, a_2, a_3) = (a_1, 0, 0) + (0, a_2, 0) + (0, 0, a_3) =$$

$$= a_1(1,0,0) + a_2(0,1,0) + a_3(0,0,1) =$$

$$= a_1\bar{i} + a_2\bar{j} + a_3\bar{k} \tag{9}$$

also,
$$\bar{b} = b_1\bar{i} + b_2\bar{j} + b_3\bar{k}$$

To find the representation of $\bar{r}(u)$ in terms of the base vectors, substitute eq.(9) into eq.(2) and obtain

$$\bar{r}(u) = u^2\bar{a} + e^u\bar{b} = u^2(a_1\bar{i} + a_2\bar{j} + a_3\bar{k}) + e^u(b_1\bar{i} + b_2\bar{j} + b_3\bar{k})$$

$$= (u^2a_1 + e^ub_1)\ \bar{i} + (u^2a_2 + e^ub_2)\ \bar{j} + (u^2a_3 + e^ub_3)\ \bar{k} \tag{10}$$

Eq.(10) gives the representation of $\bar{r}(u)$ in terms of the base vectors; that is, as a linear combination of the base vectors.

The vector function $\bar{r} = \bar{r}(t)$ can be represented graphically as a curve in the three-dimensional Euclidean space as shown in Fig. 1.

For every value of the parameter t, point P is determined such that

$$\bar{r}(t) = \overline{OP} \qquad (1)$$

As the value of the parameter t varies, point P will trace out a curve in space. The equation

$$\bar{r}(t) = \left[x_1(t), \ x_2(t), \ x_3(t)\right] \qquad (2)$$

is a parametric equation of the curve traced by point P. P.

For the vector function

$$\bar{r}(t) = (t, \ 3t, \ t^2+1) \qquad (3)$$

find the values of $\bar{r}(t)$ for

$$t = 0, \quad t = 1, \quad t = 2, \quad t = 3$$

Sketch the curve represented by eq.(1).

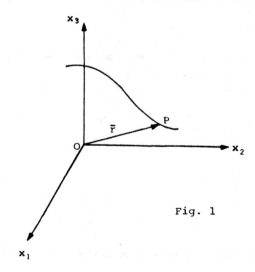

Fig. 1

Solution: First, find $\bar{r}(t)$ for the given values of the parameter t

$$\bar{r}(t) = (t, \ 3t, \ t^2+1)$$

for t = 0 $\bar{r}(0) = (0,0,1)$

for t = 1 $\bar{r}(1) = (1,3,2)$ (4)

for t = 2 $\bar{r}(2) = (2,6,5)$

for t = 3 $\bar{r}(3) = (3,9,10)$

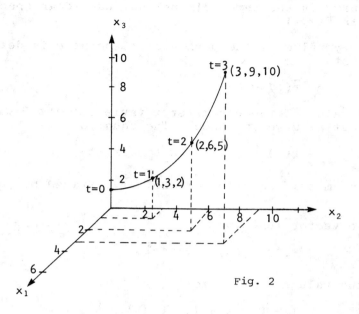

Fig. 2

The curve $\bar{r}(t) = (t, 3t, t^2+1)$ is shown in Fig. 2.

Since all the components of $\bar{r}(t)$ are continuous functions of t, the curve is continuous.

● **PROBLEM 4-4**

In the three-dimensional Euclidean space, a particle A moves along a curve whose parametric equation is

$$\bar{r}_A(t) = (e^t+2, \ t^2, \ t+1) \qquad (1)$$

where the parameter t is time.

Particle B moves along a curve given by

$$\bar{r}_B(t) = (2t+3, \ \tfrac{3}{2}t^2, \ 3t+1) \qquad (2)$$

Determine if particles A and B will collide in space.

Solution: Particles A and B will collide if both of them will have the same position in space at the same time. That is, at

t = t', then

$$\bar{r}_A(t') = \bar{r}_B(t') \qquad (3)$$

118

Substituting eq.(1) and eq.(2) into eq.(3) yields

$$(e^t+2,\ t^2,\ t+1) = \left(2t+3,\ \tfrac{3}{2}t^2,\ 3t+1\right) \tag{4}$$

Eq.(4) is equivalent to the set of three equations

$$e^t+2 = 2t+3$$

$$t^2 = \frac{3}{2}\ t^2 \tag{5}$$

$$t+1 = 3t+1$$

The only solution to this system is t = 0. Therefore, particles A and B will collide at time t = 0, or

$$\bar{r}_A(0)\ =\ \bar{r}_B(0)\ =\ (3,0,1) \tag{6}$$

Both particles at the time t=0 will be located at the point (3,0,1).

● **PROBLEM 4-5**

1) Sketch the curve whose parametric equations are

$$x_1 = 3 \sin t$$

$$x_2 = 3 \cos t \tag{1}$$

$$x_3 = 5$$

2) Sketch the curve whose parametric equations are

$$x_1 = a \cos t$$

$$x_2 = b \sin t \tag{2}$$

$$x_3 = 0$$

3) Find the parametric equations representing a circular helix (see Fig. 1.).

Solution: 1) First, consider the equations

$$x_1 = 3 \sin t$$

$$x_2 = 3 \cos t \tag{3}$$

To find the shape of the curve, determine the distance between

119

a point on the curve and the x_3-axis. Doing this,

$$r = \sqrt{x_1^2 + x_2^2} = \sqrt{9\sin^2 t + 9\cos^2 t} = 3 \qquad (4)$$

Equation (4) represents a circle of radius 3. Since $x_3 = 5$, this circle is located on the plane $x_3 = 5$ as shown in Fig. 2.

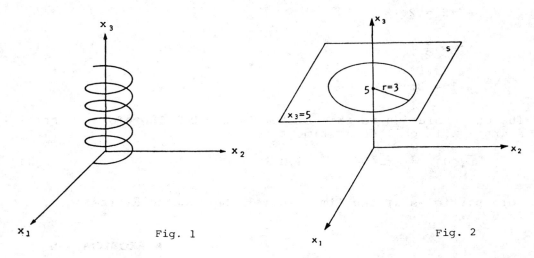

Fig. 1   Fig. 2

In this case, the expression $x_1^2 + x_2^2$ was obtained by squaring the $\sin t$ and $\cos t$ terms. In general, whenever $\sin t$ and $\cos t$ terms appear in an equation, it makes sense to get rid of them using the identity

$$\sin^2 t + \cos^2 t = 1.$$

2) From geometry, we should realize that these parametric equations represent an ellipse in the plane $x_3 = 0$. The center of the ellipse is at the origin as shown in Fig. 3.

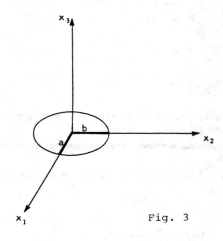

Fig. 3

3) Viewing Fig. 1 from the top, that is from the x_3 direction, we see a circle of radius r whose parametric equations are

120

$$x_1 = r \cos t$$

$$x_2 = r \sin t \qquad (5)$$

as shown in Fig. 4.

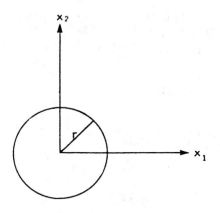

Fig. 4

From Fig. 1 we see that x_3 increases proportionally to t; in other words, we can express x_3 as a constant times t, therefore,

$$x_1 = r \cos t$$

$$x_2 = r \sin t \qquad (5)$$

$$x_3 = \alpha t$$

LIMITS, CONTINUITY AND THE DERIVATIVE OF A VECTOR FUNCTION

● **PROBLEM** 4-6

Find the limits of the following vector functions

1) $\bar{r}(t) = (3, t, 2t)$ for $t \to 5$

2) $\bar{r}(t) = (t^2 + 1, \ 2t, \ \sin t)$ for $t \to 0$

3) $\bar{r}(t) = (2t^2, \ t^3 + 1, \ \alpha t)$ for $t \to 1$

4) $\bar{r}(t) = \left(\dfrac{\sin t}{t}, \ t^2, \ t \right)$ for $t \to 0$

Solution: A vector function $\bar{r}(t)$ is said to have a limit $\bar{u}$, denoted by $\lim\limits_{t \to t_o} \bar{r}(t)$ as t approaches t_o

121

$$\lim_{t \to t_o} \bar{r}(t) = \bar{u} \tag{1}$$

if

$$\lim_{t \to t_o} |\bar{r}(t) - \bar{u}| = 0 \tag{2}$$

This means that the difference between $\bar{r}(t)$ and $\bar{u}$ can be made arbitrarily small for t sufficiently close to t_o. Note that $|\bar{r}(t) - \bar{u}|$ is the magnitude of the vector $\bar{r}(t) - \bar{u}$.

1) $$\lim_{t \to 5} \bar{r}(t) = (3,5,10) \tag{3}$$

To verify that the magnitude of the vector $\bar{r}(t) - \bar{u}$ can be made arbitrarily small,

$$\bar{r}(t) - \bar{u} = (3,t,2t) - (3,5,10) = (0,t-5,2t-10)$$

The magnitude is given by

$$|\bar{r}(t) - \bar{u}| = \sqrt{(t-5)^2+(2t-10)^2} \tag{4}$$

For $t \to 5$,

$$\sqrt{(t-5)^2+(2t-10)^2} \to 0$$

and indeed the magnitude of $\bar{r}(t) - \bar{u}$ can be made arbitrarily small.

2) $$\lim_{t \to 0} \bar{r}(t) = \lim_{t \to 0}(t^2+1,\ 2t,\ \sin t) = (1,0,0) \tag{5}$$

3) $$\lim_{t \to 1} \bar{r}(t) = \lim_{t \to 1}(2t^2,\ t^3+1,\ \alpha t) = (2,2,\alpha) \tag{6}$$

4) $$\lim_{t \to 0} \bar{r}(t) = \lim_{t \to 0}\left(\frac{\sin t}{t}, t^2, t\right) = (1,0,0) \tag{7}$$

Here, the fact that

$$\lim_{t \to 0} \frac{\sin t}{t} = 1 \quad \text{was used.}$$

In all of the above calculations the fact that

$$\lim_{t \to t_o} \bar{r}(t) = \left[\lim_{t \to t_o} r_1(t),\ \lim_{t \to t_o} r_2(t), \ldots, \lim_{t \to t_o} r_n(t)\right] \tag{8}$$

was also used.

Eq.(8) states that to find the limit of a vector function, one must find the limits of its components first.

Determine if the following vector functions are continuous.

1) $\bar{r}(t) = (t^2, e^t, 2t+1)$

2) $\bar{r}(t) = (t, t+1, f(t))$

where $\qquad f(t) = \begin{cases} 0 & \text{for } t \leq 0 \\ 1 & \text{for } t > 0 \end{cases}$

3) $\bar{r}(t) = (\sin t + \cos t, t-2, |t|)$

Solution: The function $\bar{r} = \bar{r}(t)$ is said to be continuous at $t = t_o$ if

$$\lim_{t \to t_o} \bar{r}(t) = \bar{r}(t_o) \qquad (1)$$

Also, $\bar{r}(t)$ is continuous at $t = t_o$ if and only if its components $x_1(t)$, $x_2(t)$, $x_3(t)$ are continuous at $t = t_o$.

The function $\bar{r}(t)$ is continuous over an interval $t_1 \leq t \leq t_2$ if it is continuous for every t in this interval.

1) $\bar{r}(t) = \left(x_1(t), x_2(t), x_3(t)\right) = (t^2, e^t, 2t+1) \qquad (2)$

All the functions

$$x_1(t) = t^2$$
$$x_2(t) = e^t$$
$$x_3(t) = 2t + 1$$

are continuous for $t \in R'$, therefore $\bar{r}(t)$ is continuous.

2) In this case,

$$x_1(t) = t$$
$$x_2(t) = t + 1 \qquad (3)$$
$$x_3(t) = f(t), \quad \text{where}$$

function f(t) is not continuous for t = 0. Thus $\bar{r}(t)$ is not continuous in the neighborhood of t = 0.

3) $\qquad x_1(t) = \sin t + \cos t$

$$x_2(t) = t - 2 \qquad (4)$$

$$x_3(t) = |t|$$

where
$$|t| = \begin{cases} t & \text{for } t \geq 0 \\ -t & \text{for } t < 0 \end{cases} \tag{5}$$

Function $x_3(t) = |x|$ is continuous. Since all the functions $x_1(t)$, $x_2(t)$, $x_3(t)$ are continuous, the vector function $\bar{r}(t)$ is also continuous.

● **PROBLEM** 4-8

Using the definition of the derivative of a vector function, find

1) $\dfrac{d\bar{r}}{dt}$ where $\bar{r}(t) = (2, t, t^2)$

2) $\dfrac{d\bar{r}}{dt}$ where $\bar{r}(t) = (t, 2t, t+1)$

3) $\dfrac{d\bar{u}}{dt}$ where $\bar{u}(t) = (t, e^t, t^2)$

Solution: The derivative of a vector function $\bar{r}(t)$ is defined as the limit:

$$\frac{d\bar{r}}{dt} = \lim_{\Delta t \to 0} \frac{\bar{r}(t+\Delta t) - \bar{r}(t)}{\Delta t} = \lim_{\Delta t \to 0} \frac{\Delta \bar{r}}{\Delta t} \tag{1}$$

(assume that such a limit exists).

1) To find the derivative of $\bar{r}(t) = (2, t, t^2)$ apply the definition of the derivative given by eq.(1). This direct method of finding the derivative is seldom used in practical calculations, where one deals with functions that are more complicated.

Substituting $\bar{r}(t) = (2, t, t^2)$ into eq.(1), obtain

$$\frac{d\bar{r}}{dt} = \lim_{\Delta t \to 0} \frac{\bar{r}(t+\Delta t)-\bar{r}(t)}{\Delta t} = \lim_{\Delta t \to 0} \frac{\left[2, t+\Delta t, (t+\Delta t)^2\right]-(2,t,t^2)}{\Delta t}$$

$$= \lim_{\Delta t \to 0} \frac{(0, \Delta t, 2t\Delta t+(\Delta t)^2)}{\Delta t} = \lim_{\Delta t \to 0} \ 0, \left(\frac{\Delta t}{\Delta t}, \ \frac{2t\Delta t+(\Delta t)^2}{\Delta t}\right)$$

$$= (0, 1, 2t) \tag{2}$$

2) Here again substitute $\bar{r}(t) = (t, 2t, t+1)$ into eq.(1) and obtain

$$\frac{d\bar{r}}{dt} = \lim_{\Delta t \to 0} \frac{\left[t+\Delta t, 2(t+\Delta t), t+\Delta t+1\right]- (t, 2t, t+1)}{\Delta t}$$

$$= \lim_{\Delta t \to 0} \frac{(\Delta t, \ 2\Delta t, \ \Delta t)}{\Delta t} = (1,2,1) \tag{3}$$

3) Substituting $\bar{u}(t) = (t, \ e^t, \ t^2)$ into eq.(1), gives

$$\frac{d\bar{u}}{dt} = \lim_{\Delta t \to 0} \frac{\left[t+\Delta t, e^{t+\Delta t}, (t+\Delta t)^2 \right] - (t, \ e^t, \ t^2)}{\Delta t}$$

$$= \lim_{\Delta t \to 0} \left[\frac{\Delta t}{\Delta t}, \ \frac{e^{t+\Delta t} - e^t}{\Delta t}, \ \frac{2t\Delta t + (\Delta t)^2}{\Delta t} \right] \tag{4}$$

$$= (1, \ e^t, \ 2t)$$

● **PROBLEM** 4-9

1) Express the derivative of the vector function $\bar{r}(t)$ in terms of the derivatives of the components of $\bar{r}(t)$.

2) Illustrate graphically the concept of $\frac{d\bar{r}}{dt}$.

Solution: The derivative of a vector function $\bar{r}(t)$ is defined as

$$\frac{d\bar{r}}{dt} = \lim_{\Delta t \to 0} \frac{\bar{r}(t+\Delta t) - \bar{r}(t)}{\Delta t} \tag{1}$$

Since the vector $\bar{r}(t)$ is a function of t, each of its components is also a function of t, thus

$$\bar{r}(t) = (x_1(t), \ x_2(t), \ x_3(t)) \tag{2}$$

For $\bar{r}(t+\Delta t)$, obtain

$$\bar{r}(t+\Delta t) = (x_1(t+\Delta t), \ x_2(t+\Delta t), \ x_3(t+\Delta t)) \tag{3}$$

Substituting eq.(2) and eq.(3) into eq.(1) yields

$$\frac{d\bar{r}}{dt} = \lim_{\Delta t \to 0} \frac{\bar{r}(t+\Delta t) - \bar{r}(t)}{\Delta t} \tag{4}$$

$$= \lim_{\Delta t \to 0} \frac{(x_1(t+\Delta t), \ x_2(t+\Delta t), \ x_3(t+\Delta t)) - (x_1(t), x_2(t), x_3(t))}{\Delta t}$$

$$= \lim_{\Delta t \to 0} \frac{(x_1(t+\Delta t) - x_1(t), x_2(t+\Delta t) - x_2(t), x_3(t+\Delta t) - x_3(t))}{\Delta t}$$

$$= \left(\frac{dx_1}{dt}, \ \frac{dx_2}{dt}, \ \frac{dx_3}{dt} \right)$$

The definition of the derivative of an ordinary function, that is

125

$$\lim_{\Delta t \to 0} \frac{x_1(t+\Delta t) - x_1(t)}{\Delta t} = \frac{dx_1}{dt} \tag{5}$$

was used in eq.(4). One can write the same equation for $x_2(t)$ and $x_3(t)$.

From eq.(4) we conclude that to differentiate a vector function, one has to differentiate each component separately. In general, when

$$\bar{r}(t) = (x_1(t), x_2(t), \ldots, x_n(t)) \tag{6}$$

is an n-dimensional vector, its derivative is given by

$$\frac{d\bar{r}}{dt} = \left(\frac{dx_1}{dt}, \frac{dx_2}{dt}, \ldots, \frac{dx_n}{dt}\right) \tag{7}$$

2) The construction of $\frac{d\bar{r}}{dt}$ is shown in the figure. Vector $\overline{OP}$, with o fixed, represents $\bar{r}(t)$, while vector $\overline{OP'}$ represents $\bar{r}(t') = \bar{r}(t + \Delta t)$.

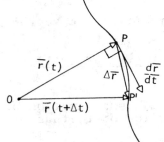

From the figure,

$$\bar{r}(t) + \Delta\bar{r} = \bar{r}(t + \Delta t) \tag{8}$$

or

$$\Delta\bar{r} = \bar{r}(t + \Delta t) - \bar{r}(t) \tag{9}$$

$\Delta\bar{r}$ represents vector $\overline{PP'}$ which is the displacement of the moving point P in the interval t to $(t + \Delta t)$. Of course $\Delta\bar{r}$ is a vector and $\frac{\Delta\bar{r}}{\Delta t}$ is a vector (because it is a vector $\Delta\bar{r}$ multiplied by a scalar $\frac{1}{\Delta t}$). The limit $\lim_{\Delta t \to 0} \frac{\Delta\bar{r}}{\Delta t} = \frac{d\bar{r}}{dt}$ is also a vector. When $\frac{d\bar{r}}{dt} \neq \bar{0}$, the vector $\frac{d\bar{r}}{dt}$ represents the tangent to the curve at the point P. The tangent is defined as the limiting position (if the limit exists) of a secant.

● PROBLEM 4-10

Find the unit vector tangent to the curve

$$\bar{r}(t) = (3t^2+2, \sin t + t^2, 5t+1) \tag{1}$$

Solution: A vector tangent to the curve $\overline{r}(t)$ is given by $\dfrac{d\overline{r}}{dt}$. Differentiate $\overline{r}(t)$ and obtain

$$\frac{d\overline{r}}{dt} = \frac{d}{dt}\,(3t^2+2,\ \sin t +t^2,\ 5t+1)$$

$$= (6t,\ \cos t + 2t,\ 5) \tag{2}$$

Vector $\dfrac{d\overline{r}}{dt}$ is tangent to $\overline{r}(t)$ but is not a unit vector. The magnitude of $\dfrac{d\overline{r}}{dt}$ is

$$\left|\frac{d\overline{r}}{dt}\right| = \sqrt{(6t)^2+(\cos t +2t)^2+5^2} \tag{3}$$

In order to obtain a unit vector from any vector, one has to divide the vector by its magnitude. Thus, a unit vector tangent to

$$\overline{r}(t) = (3t^2+2,\ \sin t +t^2,\ 5t+1) \text{ is}$$

$$T = \frac{\dfrac{d\overline{r}}{dt}}{\left|\dfrac{d\overline{r}}{dt}\right|} = \frac{(6t,\ \cos t +2t,\ 5)}{\sqrt{(6t)^2+(\cos t +2t)^2+5^2}} \tag{4}$$

● **PROBLEM** 4-11

Prove the following properties of the derivative

1) $\dfrac{d}{dt}\,(\overline{u} + \overline{v}) = \dfrac{d\overline{u}}{dt} + \dfrac{d\overline{v}}{dt}$

2) $\dfrac{d}{dt}\,(\overline{u} \cdot \overline{v}) = \overline{u}\cdot\dfrac{d\overline{v}}{dt} + \dfrac{d\overline{u}}{dt}\cdot\overline{v}$

3) $\dfrac{d}{dt}\,(\overline{u} \times \overline{v}) = \overline{u} \times \dfrac{d\overline{v}}{dt} + \dfrac{d\overline{u}}{dt} \times \overline{v}$

4) $\dfrac{d}{dt}\,(g\overline{u}) = g\,\dfrac{d\overline{u}}{dt} + \dfrac{dg}{dt}\,\overline{u}$

    where $g = g(t)$ is a scalar function of t.

5) If $\dfrac{d\overline{a}}{dt} = \overline{0}$, then $\overline{a}$ is a constant vector.

Solution: To prove the above properties, use the component representation of the vectors, which are ordinary functions of a single scalar variable t. Then apply the well-known properties of the differentiation of ordinary functions.

1) In the component form, vectors $\overline{u}$ and $\overline{v}$ are

$$\bar{u}(t) = (u_1(t),\ u_2(t),\ u_3(t))$$

$$\bar{v}(t) = (v_1(t),\ v_2(t),\ v_3(t)) \tag{1}$$

Thus

$$\frac{d}{dt}(\bar{u}+\bar{v}) = \frac{d}{dt}\left[(u_1,\ u_2,\ u_3) + (v_1,\ v_2,\ v_3)\right]$$

$$= \frac{d}{dt}\left[u_1+v_1,\ u_2+v_2,\ u_3+v_3\right] = \left[\frac{d}{dt}(u_1+v_1),\frac{d}{dt}(u_2+v_2),\frac{d}{dt}(u_3+v_3)\right]$$

$$= \left(\frac{du_1}{dt}+\frac{dv_1}{dt},\ \frac{du_2}{dt}+\frac{dv_2}{dt},\ \frac{du_3}{dt}+\frac{dv_3}{dt}\right) \tag{2}$$

$$= \left(\frac{du_1}{dt},\ \frac{du_2}{dt},\ \frac{du_3}{dt}\right) + \left(\frac{dv_1}{dt},\ \frac{dv_2}{dt},\ \frac{dv_3}{dt}\right)$$

$$= \frac{d\bar{u}}{dt} + \frac{d\bar{v}}{dt}$$

Here the property which states that for ordinary functions, f = f(t) and g = g(t),

$$\frac{d}{dt}(f + g) = \frac{df}{dt} + \frac{dg}{dt}$$

was used.

2) $\quad \frac{d}{dt}(\bar{u}\cdot\bar{v}) = \frac{d}{dt}(u_1v_1 + u_2v_2 + u_3v_3)$

$$= \frac{d}{dt}(u_1v_1) + \frac{d}{dt}(u_2v_2) + \frac{d}{dt}(u_3v_3) \tag{3}$$

$$= \frac{du_1}{dt}v_1 + \frac{dv_1}{dt}u_1 + \frac{du_2}{dt}v_2 + \frac{dv_2}{dt}u_2 + \frac{du_3}{dt}v_3 + \frac{dv_3}{dt}u_3$$

$$= \frac{d\bar{u}}{dt}\cdot\bar{v} + \frac{d\bar{v}}{dt}\cdot\bar{u}$$

Here the following property was used

$$\frac{d}{dt}(fg) = \frac{df}{dt}g + f\frac{dg}{dt} \tag{4}$$

along with the definition of the scalar product,

$$\bar{u}\cdot\bar{v} = u_1v_1 + u_2v_2 + u_3v_3$$

3) Define $\bar{w}$ such that $\bar{w} = \bar{u} \times \bar{v}$, then, $\tag{5}$

$$\Delta\bar{w} = (\bar{u} + \Delta\bar{u}) \times (\bar{v} \times \Delta\bar{v}) - (\bar{u} \times \bar{v}) \tag{6}$$

and

$$\frac{\Delta\bar{w}}{\Delta t} = \frac{\Delta\bar{u} \times \bar{v} + \bar{u} \times \Delta\bar{v} + \Delta\bar{u} \times \Delta\bar{v}}{\Delta t}$$

$$\tag{7}$$

$$= \frac{\Delta\bar{u}}{\Delta t} \times v + \bar{u} \times \frac{\Delta\bar{v}}{\Delta t} + \frac{\Delta\bar{u}}{\Delta t} \times \Delta\bar{v}$$

Note that

$$\lim_{\Delta t \to 0} \frac{\Delta \overline{u}}{\Delta t} \times \Delta \overline{v} = \frac{d\overline{u}}{dt} \times \overline{0} = \overline{0}, \qquad (8)$$

since

$$\lim_{\Delta t \to 0} \Delta \overline{v} = \overline{0}$$

Taking the lim on both sides of eq.(7),
$$\Delta t \to 0$$

$$\lim_{\Delta t \to 0} \frac{\Delta \overline{w}}{\Delta t} = \frac{d\overline{w}}{dt} = \frac{d}{dt}(\overline{u} \times \overline{v})$$

$$= \lim_{\Delta t \to 0} \frac{\Delta \overline{u} \times \overline{v} + \overline{u} \times \Delta \overline{v} + \Delta \overline{u} \times \Delta \overline{v}}{\Delta t} = \frac{d\overline{u}}{dt} \times \overline{v} + \overline{u} \times \frac{d\overline{v}}{dt} \quad (9)$$

4) $\frac{d}{dt}(g\overline{u}) = \frac{d}{dt}(gu_1, gu_2, gu_3)$

$$= \left(g\frac{du_1}{dt} + u_1\frac{dg}{dt}, \; g\frac{du_2}{dt} + u_2\frac{dg}{dt}, \; g\frac{du_3}{dt} + u_3\frac{dg}{dt}\right) \qquad (10)$$

$$= g\frac{d\overline{u}}{dt} + \frac{dg}{dt}\overline{u}$$

In the component form, vector $\overline{a}$ is

$$\overline{a} = (a_1, \; a_2, \; a_3)$$

Then

$$\frac{d\overline{a}}{dt} = \left(\frac{da_1}{dt}, \; \frac{da_2}{dt}, \; \frac{da_3}{dt}\right) = \overline{0} \qquad (11)$$

Thus all the components a_1, a_2, a_3 are constants and consequently vector $\overline{a}$ is a constant vector.

● **PROBLEM 4-12**

Differentiate the following vector functions:

1) $\overline{r}(t) = (2t, \; t^2+t, \; \sin t)$

2) $\overline{r}(t) = (e^t, \; 3e^t, \; t^4-t^3)$

3) $\overline{r}(t) = (\sin^2 t, \; t^2, \; t-1)$

Solution: 1) In differentiating a vector function, we must differentiate each component separately. Thus,

$$\frac{d\overline{r}}{dt} = \left(\frac{d}{dt}(2t), \; \frac{d}{dt}(t^2+t), \; \frac{d}{dt}(\sin t)\right) \qquad (1)$$

$$= (2, \; 2t+1, \; \cos t)$$

2) $\frac{d\overline{r}}{dt} = \left(\frac{d}{dt}(e^t), \; \frac{d}{dt}(3e^t), \; \frac{d}{dt}(t^4-t^3)\right)$

$$= (e^t, 3e^t, 4t^3 - 3t^2)$$

3) $\dfrac{d\bar{r}}{dt} = \left(\dfrac{d}{dt} (\sin^2 t), \dfrac{d}{dt} (t^2), \dfrac{d}{dt} (t-1) \right)$

$$= (2 \sin t \cos t, 2t, 1) \tag{3}$$

This chapter deals mainly with three-dimensional vectors. The same rules however, do apply to vectors of other dimensions.

● **PROBLEM 4-13**

Given $\bar{r}(t) = \sin t \, \bar{i} + \cos t \, \bar{j} + 2t\bar{k}$, find   (1)

1) $\dfrac{d\bar{r}}{dt}$.   2) $\left| \dfrac{d\bar{r}}{dt} \right|$.   3) $\dfrac{d^2\bar{r}}{dt^2}$.   4) $\left| \dfrac{d^2\bar{r}}{dt^2} \right|$.

Solution: 1) Differentiate each component separately, remembering that the base vectors $\bar{i}$, $\bar{j}$, $\bar{k}$ are constant.

$$\dfrac{d\bar{r}}{dt} = \dfrac{d}{dt} (\sin t)\bar{i} + \dfrac{d}{dt} (\cos t)\bar{j} + \dfrac{d}{dt} (2t)\bar{k}$$

$$= \cos t \, \bar{i} - \sin t \, \bar{j} + 2\bar{k} \tag{2}$$

2) The magnitude of a vector $\bar{r}$ is defined as

$$|\bar{r}| = \sqrt{ x_1^2 + x_2^2 + x_3^2 } \tag{3}$$

where x_1, x_2, x_3 are components of $\bar{r}$. Thus

$$\left| \dfrac{d\bar{r}}{dt} \right| = \sqrt{\cos^2 t + \sin^2 t + 4} = \sqrt{5} \tag{4}$$

3) The second derivative of a vector $\bar{r} = \bar{r}(t)$ is defined as

$$\dfrac{d^2\bar{r}}{dt^2} = \dfrac{d}{dt} \left(\dfrac{d\bar{r}}{dt} \right) \tag{5}$$

In the same manner one defines any higher derivative of $\bar{r}$ as

$$\dfrac{d^n\bar{r}}{dt^n} = \dfrac{d}{dt} \left(\dfrac{d^{n-1}\bar{r}}{dt^{n-1}} \right) \tag{6}$$

Substituting eq.(2) into eq.(5) yields

$$\dfrac{d^2\bar{r}}{dt^2} = \dfrac{d}{dt} \left(\dfrac{d\bar{r}}{dt} \right) = \dfrac{d}{dt} (\cos t \, \bar{i} - \sin t \, \bar{j} + 2\bar{k})$$

$$= -\sin t \, \bar{i} - \cos t \, \bar{j} \tag{7}$$

4) The magnitude of $\dfrac{d^2\bar{r}}{dt^2}$ is

$$\left| \dfrac{d^2\bar{r}}{dt^2} \right| = \sqrt{\sin^2 t + \cos^2 t} = 1 \tag{8}$$

For $\bar{r}(t) = \left[\ln(t^3+1),\ e^{-2t},\ t^2\right]$ find

1) $\dfrac{d\bar{r}}{dt}$ 2) $\left|\dfrac{d\bar{r}}{dt}\right|$ 3) $\dfrac{d^2\bar{r}}{dt^2}$ 4) $\left|\dfrac{d^2\bar{r}}{dt^2}\right|$

at $t = 0$.

<u>Solution</u>: 1) Differentiate each component separately and obtain

$$\frac{d\bar{r}}{dt} = \frac{d}{dt}\left[\ln(t^3+1),\ e^{-2t},\ t^2\right]$$

$$= \left[\frac{d}{dt}\ln(t^3+1),\ \frac{d}{dt}e^{-2t},\ \frac{d}{dt}t^2\right] \tag{1}$$

$$= \left[\frac{3t^2}{t^3+1},\ -2e^{-2t},\ 2t\right]$$

At $t = 0$ eq.(1) becomes

$$\left.\frac{d\bar{r}}{dt}\right|_{t=0} = \left[0,\ -2,\ 0\right] \tag{2}$$

2) The magnitude of $\dfrac{d\bar{r}}{dt}$ at $t = 0$ is

$$\left.\left|\frac{d\bar{r}}{dt}\right|\right|_{t=0} = \sqrt{4} = 2 \tag{3}$$

3) Using the definition of the second derivative

$$\frac{d^2\bar{r}}{dt^2} = \frac{d}{dt}\left(\frac{d\bar{r}}{dt}\right)$$

and eq.(1), obtain

$$\frac{d^2\bar{r}}{dt^2} = \frac{d}{dt}\left(\frac{3t^2}{t^3+1},\ -2e^{-2t},\ 2t\right) \tag{4}$$

$$= \left(\frac{-3t^4+6t}{(t^3+1)^2},\ 4e^{-2t},\ 2\right)$$

$$\therefore\ \left.\frac{d^2\bar{r}}{dt^2}\right|_{t=0} = (0,\ 4,\ 2) \tag{5}$$

4) At $t = 0$ the magnitude of $\dfrac{d^2\bar{r}}{dt^2}$ is

$$\left.\left|\frac{d^2\bar{r}}{dt^2}\right|\right|_{t=0} = \sqrt{16+4} = \sqrt{20} \tag{6}$$

GRAPHICAL REPRESENTATION OF THE DERIVATIVE, TANGENT VECTOR AND BASIC PROPERTIES

Let $\bar{r}(t)$ and $\bar{u}(t)$ be given by

$$\bar{r}(t) = (\sin t, \ t^2, \ 3)$$
$$\bar{u}(t) = (t+1, \ \sin t, \ e^t) \tag{1}$$

evaluate

1) $\dfrac{d}{dt} (\bar{r} + \bar{u})$

2) $\dfrac{d}{dt} (\bar{r} \cdot \bar{u})$

3) $\dfrac{d}{dt} (\bar{r} \cdot \bar{r})$

4) $\dfrac{d}{dt} (\bar{r} \times \bar{u})$

<u>Solution</u>: First evaluate

$$\frac{d\bar{r}}{dt} \quad \text{and} \quad \frac{d\bar{u}}{dt}$$

$$\frac{d\bar{r}}{dt} = (\cos t, \ 2t, \ 0)$$
$$\frac{d\bar{u}}{dt} = (1, \ \cos t, \ e^t) \tag{2}$$

1) $\dfrac{d}{dt} (\bar{r}+\bar{u}) = \dfrac{d\bar{r}}{dt} + \dfrac{d\bar{u}}{dt} = (\cos t, \ 2t, \ 0) + (1, \ \cos t, \ e^t)$

$$= (\cos t + 1, \ 2t+\cos t, \ e^t) \tag{3}$$

2) $\dfrac{d}{dt} (\bar{r} \cdot \bar{u}) = \bar{r} \cdot \dfrac{d\bar{u}}{dt} + \bar{u} \cdot \dfrac{d\bar{r}}{dt} = (\sin t, \ t^2, \ 3) \cdot (1, \ \cos t, \ e^t)$

$$+ \ (t+1, \ \sin t, \ e^t) \cdot (\cos t, \ 2t, \ 0) \tag{4}$$

$$= \sin t + t^2 \cos t + 3e^t + (t+1)\cos t + 2t \sin t$$

3) $\dfrac{d}{dt} (\bar{r} \cdot \bar{r}) = \bar{r} \cdot \dfrac{d\bar{r}}{dt} + \bar{r} \cdot \dfrac{d\bar{r}}{dt} = 2\bar{r} \cdot \dfrac{d\bar{r}}{dt}$

$$= 2(\sin t, \ t^2, \ 3) \cdot (\cos t, \ 2t, \ 0) = 2(\sin t \cos t + 2t^3) \tag{5}$$

4) $\dfrac{d}{dt} (\bar{r} \times \bar{u}) = \bar{r} \times \dfrac{d\bar{u}}{dt} + \dfrac{d\bar{r}}{dt} \times \bar{u}$

$$= (\sin t,\ t^2,\ 3) \times (1,\ \cos t,\ e^t) + (\cos t,\ 2t,\ 0) \times (t+1,\ \sin t,\ e^t)$$

$$= (t^2\ e^t - 3\cos t,\ 3 - e^t\sin t,\ \sin t \cos t - t^2)$$

$$+ (2te^t,\ -e^t\cos t,\ \sin t \cos t - 2t^2 - 2t) \tag{6}$$

$$= (t^2 e^t - 3\cos t + 2te^t,\ 3 - e^t\sin t - e^t\cos t,\ 2\sin t \cos t - 3t^2 - 2t).$$

Note: The results of problem 4-11 were used in parts 1, 2 and 4 of this problem.

● **PROBLEM** 4-16

A curve is described by the parametric equations

$$x_1 = x_1(s)$$

$$x_2 = x_2(s) \tag{1}$$

$$x_3 = x_3(s)$$

where s, measured from a fixed point on the curve, represents the arc length of the curve. Show that if

$$\bar{r} = \bar{r}(s)$$

is the position vector of any point on the curve, then

$$\frac{d\bar{r}}{ds}$$

is a unit vector tangent to the curve.

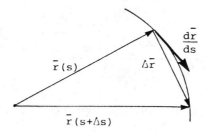

Solution: The tangent to a curve is defined as the limiting position of a secant. From the definition

$$\frac{d\bar{r}}{ds} = \lim_{\Delta s \to 0} \frac{\Delta \bar{r}}{\Delta s} \tag{2}$$

and the figure, one concludes that $\frac{d\bar{r}}{ds}$ is tangent to the curve. Note, that when $\Delta s \to 0$, then $\bar{r}(s+\Delta s) \to \bar{r}(s)$ and $\Delta \bar{r}$ and $\frac{d\bar{r}}{ds}$ is given by

$$\left| \frac{d\overline{r}}{ds} \right| = \sqrt{\left(\frac{dx_1}{ds}\right)^2 + \left(\frac{dx_2}{ds}\right)^2 + \left(\frac{dx_3}{ds}\right)^2} \qquad (3)$$

Since s is the arc length of the curve,

$$ds^2 = (dx_1)^2 + (dx_2)^2 + (dx_3)^2 \qquad (4)$$

and

$$1 = \frac{(dx_1)^2 + (dx_2)^2 + (dx_3^2)}{ds^2} = \left(\frac{dx_1}{ds}\right)^2 + \left(\frac{dx_2}{ds}\right)^2 + \left(\frac{dx_3}{ds}\right)^2 \qquad (5)$$

Substituting eq.(5) into eq.(3), gives

$$\left| \frac{d\overline{r}}{ds} \right| = \sqrt{\left(\frac{dx_1}{ds}\right)^2 + \left(\frac{dx_2}{ds}\right)^2 + \left(\frac{dx_3}{ds}\right)^2} = 1 \qquad (6)$$

Thus $\frac{d\overline{r}}{ds}$ is a unit vector tangent to the curve $\overline{r} = \overline{r}(s)$.

● **PROBLEM 4-17**

Let $\overline{r}(t)$ be the position vector of a point moving along a curve. Show that if s is the distance traversed by this point from time t_o to time t, then

$$\frac{ds}{dt} = \sqrt{\left(\frac{dx_1}{dt}\right)^2 + \left(\frac{dx_2}{dt}\right)^2 + \left(\frac{dx_3}{dt}\right)^2} \qquad (1)$$

Find the velocity vector $\overline{v}$ of the moving point.

Solution: Let ds be the distance traversed by the point from t to t + dt. $d\overline{s}$ is a vector whose components are

$$d\overline{s} = (dx_1, dx_2, dx_3). \qquad (2)$$

The magnitude of $d\overline{s}$ is $ds = |d\overline{s}| = \sqrt{d\overline{s} \cdot d\overline{s}} = \sqrt{(dx_1)^2 + (dx_2)^2 + (dx_3)^2}$ (3)

Thus

$$\frac{ds}{dt} = \sqrt{\left(\frac{dx_1}{dt}\right)^2 + \left(\frac{dx_2}{dt}\right)^2 + \left(\frac{dx_3}{dt}\right)^2} \qquad (4)$$

Let $\overline{r}(t) = \overline{OP}$ be the position vector of the moving point. And

let $\qquad \overline{v} = \frac{d\overline{r}}{dt} \qquad (5)$

It is required to show that $\overline{v}$ is the velocity vector of the moving point. Note that $\overline{v}$ is tangent to the curve traced by the point, and thus points in the direction of motion.

The magnitude of $\overline{v}$ is

$$|\overline{v}| = \left| \frac{d\overline{r}}{dt} \right| = \sqrt{\left(\frac{dx_1}{dt}\right)^2 + \left(\frac{dx_2}{dt}\right)^2 + \left(\frac{dx_3}{dt}\right)^2} = \frac{ds}{dt} \qquad (6)$$

Thus, the magnitude of $\overline{v}$ is equal to $\frac{ds}{dt}$ which is the speed of the point. Vector $\bar{v} = \frac{d\bar{r}}{dt}$ is therefore the velocity vector of the point.

If $|\bar{a}(t)| = $ const, show that $\bar{a}$ is perpendicular to $\frac{d\bar{a}}{dt}$.

Solution: Two vectors are perpendicular when their scalar product is equal to zero. For the magnitude of $\bar{a}(t)$,

$$|\bar{a}(t)| = \sqrt{\bar{a}(t) \cdot \bar{a}(t)} = \text{const.} \qquad (1)$$

and as a result of eq.(1)

$$\bar{a}(t) \cdot \bar{a}(t) = \text{const.} \qquad (2)$$

To find $\frac{d\bar{a}}{dt}$, differentiate eq.(2),

$$\bar{a}(t) \cdot \frac{d\bar{a}}{dt} + \bar{a}(t) \cdot \frac{d\bar{a}}{dt} = 0$$

and

$$\bar{a}(t) \cdot \frac{d\bar{a}}{dt} = 0 \qquad (3)$$

From eq.(3), one concludes that the vectors $\bar{a}(t)$ and $\frac{d\bar{a}}{dt}$ are perpendicular. This result is more clear when we find the physical interpretation of the problem. When $\bar{a}(t)$ is the position vector of a moving point, and

$$|\bar{a}(t)| = \text{const.}, \qquad (4)$$

then the trajectory of the point is a circle of radius

$$|\bar{a}(t)| = \sqrt{\bar{a}(t) \cdot \bar{a}(t)} \qquad (5)$$

The velocity vector is $\frac{d\bar{a}}{dt}$ and is perpendicular to $\bar{a}(t)$, since the trajectory of the point is a circle.

Show that if

$$\bar{u}(t) = \bar{a} \cos t + \bar{b} \sin t \qquad (1)$$

where $\bar{a}$ and $\bar{b}$ are constant vectors, then

$$\bar{u}(t) \cdot \left[\frac{d\bar{u}}{dt} \times \frac{d^2\bar{u}}{dt^2}\right] = 0 \qquad (2)$$

Solution: Since $\bar{a}$ and $\bar{b}$ are constant vectors,

$$\frac{d\bar{u}}{dt} = -\bar{a} \sin t + \bar{b} \cos t \qquad (3)$$

and

$$\frac{d^2\overline{u}}{dt^2} = -\overline{a}\cos t - \overline{b}\sin t \qquad (4)$$

Note that $\frac{d^2\overline{u}}{dt^2}$ is the second derivative of $\overline{u}(t)$, which is obtained by differentiating twice the vector function $\overline{u}(t)$, thus

$$\frac{d^2\overline{u}}{dt^2} = \frac{d}{dt}\left(\frac{d\overline{u}}{dt}\right) \qquad (5)$$

In the same manner one can define the derivatives of higher order as

$$\frac{d^n\overline{u}}{dt^n} = \frac{d}{dt}\left(\frac{d^{n-1}\overline{u}}{dt^{n-1}}\right) \qquad (6)$$

Substituting eqs.(3) and (4) into eq.(2), gives

$$(\overline{a}\cos t + \overline{b}\sin t)\cdot\left[(-\overline{a}\sin t + \overline{b}\cos t)\times(-\overline{a}\cos t - \overline{b}\sin t)\right] \overset{?}{=} 0 \quad (7)$$

The question mark indicates that eq.(7) still has to be proved. Using the identities

$$\overline{c}\times\overline{c} = \overline{0}$$

$$(\overline{c}+\overline{d})\times\overline{e} = \overline{c}\times\overline{e} + \overline{d}\times\overline{e} \qquad (8)$$

The expression in the square bracket can be simplified to

$$(-\overline{a}\sin t + \overline{b}\cos t)\times(-\overline{a}\cos t - \overline{b}\sin t)$$

$$= \sin^2 t\ \overline{a}\times\overline{b} - \cos^2 t\ \overline{b}\times\overline{a} = \sin^2 t\ \overline{a}\times\overline{b} + \cos^2 t\ \overline{a}\times\overline{b}$$

$$= (\sin^2 t + \cos^2 t)\ \overline{a}\times\overline{b} = \overline{a}\times\overline{b} \qquad (9)$$

Using eq.(9) eq.(7) can be written as

$$(\overline{a}\cos t + \overline{b}\sin t)\cdot(\overline{a}\times\overline{b}) \overset{?}{=} 0 \qquad (10)$$

or

$$\cos t\ \overline{a}\cdot(\overline{a}\times\overline{b}) + \sin t\ \overline{b}\cdot(\overline{a}\times\overline{b}) \overset{?}{=} 0 \qquad (11)$$

Denoting

$$\overline{a}\times\overline{b} = \overline{c}$$

it is obvious that

$$\overline{a}\cdot(\overline{a}\times\overline{b}) = 0 \qquad (12)$$

and

$$\overline{b}\cdot(\overline{a}\times\overline{b}) = 0$$

because vector $\overline{c}$ is perpendicular to vectors $\overline{a}$ and $\overline{b}$ by definition of the vector product. Thus eq.(11), as well as eq.(2), has been proved

$$\overline{u}(t)\cdot\left[\frac{d\overline{u}}{dt}\times\frac{d^2\overline{u}}{dt^2}\right] = 0 \qquad (13)$$

If $\bar{u} = \bar{u}(t)$ is a vector function of t, show that

$$\frac{d}{dt}\left[\bar{u}\cdot\left(\frac{d\bar{u}}{dt} \times \frac{d^2\bar{u}}{dt^2}\right)\right] = \frac{d^3\bar{u}}{dt^3}\cdot\left(\bar{u} \times \frac{d\bar{u}}{dt}\right) \qquad (1)$$

Solution: As a first step, simplify the left side of eq.(1). Do this by differentiating the left side of eq.(1) using the identities

$$\frac{d}{dt}(\bar{a}\cdot\bar{b}) = \bar{a}\cdot\frac{d\bar{b}}{dt} + \frac{d\bar{a}}{dt}\cdot\bar{b} \qquad (2)$$

$$\frac{d}{dt}(\bar{a} \times \bar{b}) = \bar{a} \times \frac{d\bar{b}}{dt} + \frac{d\bar{a}}{dt} \times \bar{b} \qquad (3)$$

where $\bar{a}(t)$ and $\bar{b}(t)$ are differentiable vector functions.

Transform the left side of eq.(1) as follows

$$\frac{d}{dt}\left[\bar{u}\cdot\left(\frac{d\bar{u}}{dt} \times \frac{d^2\bar{u}}{dt^2}\right)\right] = \bar{u}\cdot\frac{d}{dt}\left(\frac{d\bar{u}}{dt} \times \frac{d^2\bar{u}}{dt^2}\right) + \frac{d\bar{u}}{dt}\cdot\left(\frac{d\bar{u}}{dt} \times \frac{d^2\bar{u}}{dt^2}\right) \qquad (4)$$

Then, since

$$\frac{d\bar{u}}{dt}\cdot\left(\frac{d\bar{u}}{dt} \times \frac{d^2\bar{u}}{dt^2}\right) = 0 \qquad (5)$$

(because the vectors $\frac{d\bar{u}}{dt}$ and $\frac{d\bar{u}}{dt} \times \frac{d^2\bar{u}}{dt^2}$ are perpendicular),

eq.(4) can be written as

$$\frac{d}{dt}\left[\bar{u}\cdot\left(\frac{d\bar{u}}{dt} \times \frac{d^2\bar{u}}{dt^2}\right)\right] = \bar{u}\cdot\frac{d}{dt}\left(\frac{d\bar{u}}{dt} \times \frac{d^2\bar{u}}{dt^2}\right)$$

$$= \bar{u}\cdot\left[\left(\frac{d\bar{u}}{dt} \times \frac{d^3\bar{u}}{dt^3}\right)+\left(\frac{d^2\bar{u}}{dt^2} \times \frac{d^2\bar{u}}{dt^2}\right)\right] = \bar{u}\cdot\left(\frac{d\bar{u}}{dt} \times \frac{d^3\bar{u}}{dt^3}\right) \qquad (6)$$

Note that,

$$\frac{d^2\bar{u}}{dt^2} \times \frac{d^2\bar{u}}{dt^2} = \bar{0} \qquad (7)$$

Using the identity

$$\bar{a}\cdot(\bar{b} \times \bar{c}) = \bar{c}\cdot(\bar{a} \times \bar{b}), \qquad (8)$$

eq.(6) can be written in the form

$$\frac{d}{dt}\left[\bar{u}\cdot\left(\frac{d\bar{u}}{dt} \times \frac{d^2\bar{u}}{dt^2}\right)\right] = \bar{u}\cdot\left(\frac{d\bar{u}}{dt} \times \frac{d^3\bar{u}}{dt^3}\right)$$

$$= \frac{d^3\bar{u}}{dt^3}\cdot\left(\bar{u} \times \frac{d\bar{u}}{dt}\right) \qquad (9)$$

Show that for any two vectors $\bar{a}$ and $\bar{b}$

$$\bar{a} \times \frac{d^2\bar{b}}{dt^2} - \frac{d^2\bar{a}}{dt^2} \times \bar{b} = \frac{d}{dt}\left(\bar{a} \times \frac{d\bar{b}}{dt} - \frac{d\bar{a}}{dt} \times \bar{b}\right) \qquad (1)$$

Solution: As in most cases involving the proof of some identity, try to transform one side of the equation in order to make it equal to the other side.

Looking at eq.(1), the most obvious way to transform the equation is to get rid of $\frac{d}{dt}$ on the right hand side. Thus

$$\frac{d}{dt}\left(\bar{a} \times \frac{d\bar{b}}{dt} - \frac{d\bar{a}}{dt} \times \bar{b}\right) = \frac{d}{dt}\left(\bar{a} \times \frac{d\bar{b}}{dt}\right) - \frac{d}{dt}\left(\frac{d\bar{a}}{dt} \times \bar{b}\right)$$

$$= \bar{a} \times \frac{d^2\bar{b}}{dt^2} + \frac{d\bar{a}}{dt} \times \frac{d\bar{b}}{dt} - \frac{d\bar{a}}{dt} \times \frac{d\bar{b}}{dt} - \frac{d^2\bar{a}}{dt^2} \times \bar{b} \qquad (2)$$

$$= \bar{a} \times \frac{d^2\bar{b}}{dt^2} - \frac{d^2\bar{a}}{dt^2} \times \bar{b}$$

Show that for any vector function $\bar{a}(t)$

$$\bar{a} \cdot \frac{d\bar{a}}{dt} = a \frac{da}{dt} \qquad (1)$$

where $\qquad a = |\bar{a}|$

Solution: Since $a = |\bar{a}|$, then

$$\bar{a} \cdot \bar{a} = a^2 \qquad (2)$$

Try to prove eq.(1) by differentiating eq.(2). Thus

$$\frac{d}{dt}(\bar{a} \cdot \bar{a}) = \frac{d}{dt}(a^2) \qquad (3)$$

or

$$\bar{a} \cdot \frac{d\bar{a}}{dt} + \bar{a} \cdot \frac{d\bar{a}}{dt} = 2\bar{a} \cdot \frac{d\bar{a}}{dt} = 2a\frac{da}{dt} \qquad (4)$$

or

$$\bar{a} \cdot \frac{d\bar{a}}{dt} = a\frac{da}{dt} \qquad (5)$$

Another method of proving eq.(1) is to represent the vectors in component form, thus

$$\bar{a} = (a_1, a_2, a_3) \qquad (6)$$

and

$$a = \sqrt{a_1^2 + a_2^2 + a_3^2} \qquad (7)$$

Differentiating eq.(7),

$$\frac{da}{dt} = \frac{1}{2\sqrt{a_1^2+a_2^2+a_3^2}}\left(2a_1\frac{da_1}{dt} + 2a_2\frac{da_2}{dt} + 2a_3\frac{da_3}{dt}\right)$$

$$= \frac{a_1\frac{da_1}{dt} + a_2\frac{da_2}{dt} + a_3\frac{da_3}{dt}}{\sqrt{a_1^2+a_2^2+a_3^2}} = \frac{\bar{a}\cdot\frac{d\bar{a}}{dt}}{a} \qquad (8)$$

or $\qquad a\frac{da}{dt} = \bar{a}\cdot\frac{d\bar{a}}{dt}$

Both methods lead to the same result.

● **PROBLEM** 4-23

Find $\dfrac{d}{dt}\left(\bar{a}\cdot\dfrac{d\bar{b}}{dt} - \dfrac{d\bar{a}}{dt}\cdot\bar{b}\right)$ $\qquad (1)$

if $\bar{a}(t)$ and $\bar{b}(t)$ are differentiable vector functions of t such that

$$\bar{a} = (e^t, 5t^2, t+1)$$
$$\bar{b} = (\alpha t^2, \sin t, t^2) \qquad (2)$$

where α is a constant parameter.

Solution: To find the required expression, one can substitute directly $\bar{a}(t)$ and $\bar{b}(t)$ and perform all the operations. However, the faster method would be to first simplify eq.(1) and then substitute into eq.(2).

Thus

$$\frac{d}{dt}\left(\bar{a}\cdot\frac{d\bar{b}}{dt} - \frac{d\bar{a}}{dt}\cdot\bar{b}\right) = \bar{a}\cdot\frac{d^2\bar{b}}{dt^2} + \frac{d\bar{a}}{dt}\cdot\frac{d\bar{b}}{dt} - \frac{d\bar{a}}{dt}\cdot\frac{d\bar{b}}{dt} - \frac{d^2\bar{a}}{dt^2}\cdot\bar{b}$$

$$= \bar{a}\cdot\frac{d^2\bar{b}}{dt^2} - \frac{d^2\bar{a}}{dt^2}\cdot\bar{b} \qquad (3)$$

Next, find the first and second derivatives of $\bar{a}(t)$ and $\bar{b}(t)$.

$$\frac{d\bar{a}}{dt} = (e^t, 10t, 1)$$
$$\qquad (4)$$
$$\frac{d^2\bar{a}}{dt^2} = (e^t, 10, 0)$$

$$\frac{d\bar{b}}{dt} = (2\alpha t, \cos t, 2t)$$
$$\qquad (5)$$
$$\frac{d^2\bar{b}}{dt^2} = (2\alpha, -\sin t, 2)$$

139

Substituting eqs.(4) and (5) into eq.(3), gives

$$\frac{d}{dt}\left(\overline{a}\cdot\frac{d\overline{b}}{dt} - \frac{d\overline{a}}{dt}\cdot\overline{b}\right) = \overline{a}\cdot\frac{d^2\overline{b}}{dt^2} - \frac{d^2\overline{a}}{dt^2}\cdot\overline{b}$$

$$= (e^t,5t^2,t+1)\cdot(2\alpha,-\sin t, 2)-(e^t,10,0)\cdot(\alpha t^2,\sin t, t^2) \qquad (6)$$

$$= 2\alpha e^t - 5t^2\sin t + 2(t+1) - \alpha t^2 e^t - 10 \sin t$$

● **PROBLEM** 4-24

Let $\overline{a}$ and $\overline{b}$ be two vector functions such that

$$\overline{a}(t) = (t^5+1, 2\sin t, 0), \quad \text{and}$$

$$\overline{b}(t) = (e^t, t, 2t) \qquad\qquad (1)$$

Determine

$$\frac{d^2}{dt^2}(\overline{a} \times \overline{b}) \qquad\qquad (2)$$

Solution: First try to simplify eq.(2), as follows

$$\frac{d^2}{dt^2}(\overline{a} \times \overline{b}) = \frac{d}{dt}\left(\overline{a} \times \frac{d\overline{b}}{dt} + \frac{d\overline{a}}{dt} \times \overline{b}\right)$$

$$(3)$$

$$= \overline{a} \times \frac{d^2\overline{b}}{dt^2} + \frac{d\overline{a}}{dt} \times \frac{d\overline{b}}{dt} + \frac{d\overline{a}}{dt} \times \frac{d\overline{b}}{dt} + \frac{d^2\overline{a}}{dt^2} \times \overline{b}$$

$$= \overline{a} \times \frac{d^2\overline{b}}{dt^2} + 2 \frac{d\overline{a}}{dt} \times \frac{d\overline{b}}{dt} + \frac{d^2\overline{a}}{dt^2} \times \overline{b} \qquad (4)$$

In this case, eq.(4) is more complicated than eq.(2).

Therefore it is better to evaluate the original eq.(4). Find the vector $\overline{c}$ such that

$$\overline{c} = \overline{a} \times \overline{b} \qquad\qquad (5)$$

Substituting eq.(1) into eq.(5), gives

$$\overline{c} = (t^5+1, 2\sin t, 0) \times (e^t,t,2t)$$

$$(6)$$

$$=(2\sin t (2t), - (t^5+1)2t, (t^5+1)t - 2\sin t e^t)$$

The first derivative of $\overline{c}$ is

$$\frac{d\overline{c}}{dt} = (4t\cos t + 4\sin t, - 10t^5 - 2(t^5+1),$$

$$(7)$$

$$6t^5+1 - 2\cos t e^t - 2\sin t e^t)$$

and the second derivative is

$$\frac{d^2\overline{c}}{dt^2} = (-4t\sin t + 4\cos t +4\cos t, -60t^4, 30t^4+2\sin t e^t$$

$$- 2\cos t\, e^t - 2\cos t\, e^t - 2\sin t\, e^t)$$

$$= (-4t\sin t + 8\cos t,\ -60t^4,\ 30t^4 - 4e^t\cos t\ )$$

VECTOR SOLUTIONS TO DIFFERENTIAL EQUATIONS

Show that

$$\bar{r} = \bar{C}_1 e^{-t}\cos 2t + \bar{C}_2 e^{-t}\sin 2t, \tag{1}$$

where $\bar{C}_1$ and $\bar{C}_2$ are constant vectors, is a solution to the differential equation

$$\frac{d^2\bar{r}}{dt^2} + 2\frac{d\bar{r}}{dt} + 5\bar{r} = \bar{0} \tag{2}$$

<u>Solution</u>: First find $\dfrac{d\bar{r}}{dt}$ and $\dfrac{d^2\bar{r}}{dt^2}$.

$$\frac{d\bar{r}}{dt} = -\bar{C}_1 e^{-t}\cos 2t - 2\bar{C}_1 e^{-t}\sin 2t - \bar{C}_2 e^{-t}\sin 2t + 2\bar{C}_2 e^{-t}\cos 2t$$

$$= e^{-t}(-\bar{C}_1\cos 2t + 2\bar{C}_2\cos 2t - 2\bar{C}_1\sin 2t - \bar{C}_2\sin 2t) \tag{3}$$

$$= e^{-t}\left[(2\bar{C}_2 - \bar{C}_1)\cos 2t - (2\bar{C}_1 + \bar{C}_2)\sin 2t\right]$$

The second derivative of $\bar{r}$ is given by $\dfrac{d^2\bar{r}}{dt^2} = \dfrac{d}{dt}\left(\dfrac{d\bar{r}}{dt}\right)$

$$= \frac{d}{dt}\left\{ e^{-t}\left[(2\bar{C}_2 - \bar{C}_1)\cos 2t - (2\bar{C}_1 + \bar{C}_2)\sin 2t\right]\right\}$$

$$= -e^{-t}\left[(2\bar{C}_2 - \bar{C}_1)\cos 2t - (2\bar{C}_1 + \bar{C}_2)\sin 2t\right]$$

$$+ e^{-t}\left[-2(2\bar{C}_2 - \bar{C}_1)\sin 2t - 2(2\bar{C}_1 + \bar{C}_2)\cos 2t\right]. \tag{4}$$

Substituting eqs.(3), (4), and (1) into eq.(2), obtain

$$-e^{-t}\left[(2\bar{C}_2 - \bar{C}_1)\cos 2t - (2\bar{C}_1 + \bar{C}_2)\sin 2t\right] + e^{-t}\left[-2(2\bar{C}_2 - \bar{C}_1)\sin 2t\right.$$

$$\left. -2(2\bar{C}_1 + \bar{C}_2)\cos 2t\right] + 2e^{-t}\left[(2\bar{C}_2 - \bar{C}_1)\cos 2t - (2\bar{C}_1 + \bar{C}_2)\sin 2t\right]$$

$$+ 5\bar{C}_1 e^{-t}\cos 2t + 5\bar{C}_2 e^{-t}\sin 2t$$

$$= e^{-t}(2\bar{C}_2 - \bar{C}_1)\cos 2t - e^{-t}(2\bar{C}_1 + \bar{C}_2)\sin 2t$$

$$-2e^{-t}(2\bar{C}_2 - \bar{C}_1)\sin 2t - 2e^{-t}(2\bar{C}_1 + \bar{C}_2)\cos 2t + 5\bar{C}_1 e^{-t}\cos 2t$$

$$+5\overline{C}_1e^{-t}\cos 2t+5\overline{C}_2e^{-t}\sin 2t \tag{5}$$

$$=e^{-t}\left[\cos 2t(2\overline{C}_2-\overline{C}_1-4\overline{C}_1-2\overline{C}_2+5\overline{C}_1)+\sin 2t(-2\overline{C}_1-\overline{C}_2-4\overline{C}_2+2\overline{C}_1+5\overline{C}_2)\right]=0$$

Thus

$$\overline{r}=\overline{C}_1e^{-t}\cos 2t+\overline{C}_2e^{-t}\sin 2t \tag{6}$$

is a solution of eq.(2).

Note that eq.(2) can be written in the component form, that is as three differential equations for the scalar functions $r_1(t)$, $r_2(t)$, and $r_3(t)$. Each component of $\overline{r}(t)$ given by eq.(1) is thus a solution of the respective differential equation.

● **PROBLEM 4-26**

Find the general solution of the differential equation

$$\frac{d^2\overline{x}}{dt^2}-2\frac{d\overline{x}}{dt}-3\overline{x}=10\overline{a}\sin t+\overline{b}(2t+1) \tag{1}$$

where $\overline{a}$ and $\overline{b}$ are constant vectors.

Solution: Use the following theorem to solve the problem.

Theorem
The general solution of a linear vector differential equation

$$\left(f_n\frac{d^n}{dt^n}+f_{n-1}\frac{d^{n-1}}{dt^{n-1}}+\dots+f_1\frac{d}{dt}+f_0\right)\overline{x}=\overline{a}, \tag{2}$$

denoted $G[\overline{x}]=\overline{a}$,

where $\overline{a}$ and f_0, $f_1,\dots,f_n$ are given functions of the scalar t and $\overline{x}$ is an unknown vector, is given by

$$\overline{x}=\overline{Y}+\overline{A} \tag{3}$$

where $\overline{A}$ is a particular solution of the differential equation, and

$$\overline{Y}=\overline{c}_1y_1+\overline{c}_2y_2+\dots+\overline{c}_ny_n, \text{ where} \tag{4}$$

y_1, $y_2,\dots,y_n$ are n linearly independent solutions of the homogeneous scalar differential equation $G[y]=0$

and $\overline{c}_1$, $\overline{c}_2$, ..., $\overline{c}_n$ are arbitrary constant vectors.

To solve eq.(1), find two linearly independent solutions of

$$\frac{d^2y}{dt^2}-2\frac{dy}{dt}-3y=0 \tag{5}$$

The auxiliary equation is

$$m^2 - 2m - 3 = 0$$

with the roots -1, 3, therefore

$$\overline{Y} = \overline{c}_1 e^{-t} + \overline{c}_2 e^{3t} \qquad (6)$$

To find a particular solution $\overline{A}$ of eq.(1), use the method of undetermined coefficients. Since the function on the right-hand side of eq.(1) is

$$10\overline{a}\,\sin t + \overline{b}(2t+1) \qquad (7)$$

look for a particular solution $\overline{A}$ in the form

$$\overline{A} = \overline{c}\,\sin t + \overline{d}\,\cos t + \overline{e}t + \overline{f} \qquad (8)$$

where $\overline{c}$, $\overline{d}$, $\overline{e}$, $\overline{f}$ are constant vectors.

Then,

$$\frac{d\overline{A}}{dt} = \overline{c}\,\cos t - \overline{d}\,\sin t + \overline{e} \qquad (8a)$$

and

$$\frac{d^2\overline{A}}{dt^2} = -\overline{c}\,\sin t - \overline{d}\,\cos t \qquad (8b)$$

since $\overline{A}$ is the particular solution, substitute equations (8), (8a) and (8b) into eq.(1).

Doing this gives

$$-\overline{c}\,\sin t - \overline{d}\,\cos t + \overline{e} - 2\overline{c}\,\cos t + 2\overline{d}\,\sin t - 2\overline{e}$$

$$-3\overline{c}\,\sin t - 3\overline{d}\,\cos t - 3\overline{e}t - 3\overline{f}$$

$$= 10\overline{a}\,\sin t + \overline{b}(2t + 1)$$

or, after rearranging terms,

$$(-\overline{c} + 2\overline{d} - 3\overline{c})\sin t + (-2\overline{c} - \overline{d} - 3\overline{d})\cos t + (-3\overline{e})t$$
$$+(-2\overline{e} - 3\overline{f}) = (10\overline{a})\,\sin t + (2\overline{b})\,t + \overline{b} \qquad (8c)$$

Since both sides of equation (8c) are equal, the sum of all the coefficients of the t, sin t, and cos t terms, as well as the constant terms on the left side of the equation must equal the sum of all the respective coefficients on the right side of the equation.

With this in mind, it follows that

$$-\overline{c} + 2\overline{d} - 3\overline{c} = 10\overline{a}$$

$$-\overline{d} - 2\overline{c} - 3\overline{d} = \overline{0}$$

$$-3\overline{e} = 2\overline{b} \qquad (9)$$

$$-2\overline{e} - 3\overline{f} = \overline{b}$$

Solving system (9), we find

$$\bar{e} = -\frac{2}{3}\bar{b} \qquad \bar{c} = -2\bar{a}$$

$$\bar{f} = \frac{1}{9}\bar{b} \qquad \bar{d} = \bar{a} \tag{10}$$

Thus the solution of equation (1) is

$$\bar{x} = \bar{Y}+\bar{A} = \bar{c}_1 e^{-t}+\bar{c}_2 e^{3t}-2\bar{a}\sin t+\bar{a}\cos t-\frac{2}{3}\bar{b}t+\frac{1}{9}\bar{b}$$

$$= \bar{c}_1 e^{-t}+\bar{c}_2 e^{3t}+\bar{a}(\cos t - 2\sin t) + \bar{b}(-\frac{2}{3}t+\frac{1}{9})$$

● **PROBLEM 4-27**

Solve the following differential equations

$$1) \quad \frac{d^2\bar{r}}{dt^2} - \frac{d\bar{r}}{dt} - 6\bar{r} = \bar{0}$$

$$2) \quad \frac{d^2\bar{r}}{dt^2} + 4\frac{d\bar{r}}{dt} - 5\bar{r} = \bar{0}$$

<u>Solution</u>: 1) Find two linearly independent solutions of the equation

$$\frac{d^2y}{dt^2} - \frac{dy}{dt} - 6y = 0 \tag{1}$$

The auxiliary equation of this differential equation is

$$p^2 - p - 6 = 0 \tag{2}$$

The roots are

$$p_1 = 3 \qquad p_2 = -2$$

The solutions of eq.(1) are

$$e^{3t} \quad \text{and} \quad e^{-2t} \tag{4}$$

The required solution is the linear combination of (4), therefore

$$\bar{r}(t) = \bar{C}_1 e^{3t} + \bar{C}_2 e^{-2t} \tag{5}$$

2) As in the previous case, solve the equation

$$\frac{d^2y}{dt^2} + 4\frac{dy}{dt} - 5y = 0 \tag{6}$$

The auxiliary equation is

$$p^2 + 4p - 5 = 0 \tag{7}$$

the roots are $p_1 = 1$, $p_2 = -5$.

The solution is then given by

$$\bar{r}(t) = \bar{C}_1 e^t + \bar{C}_2 e^{-5t} \tag{8}$$

CHAPTER 5

APPLICATIONS OF ORDINARY DERIVATIVES OF VECTORS IN DIFFERENTIAL GEOMETRY AND MECHANICS

INTRODUCTION

Chapter 5 is completely devoted to the application of ordinary derivatives to Physics and Differential Geometry.

Part 1 of the chapter deals exclusively with differential geometry. The concept of the space curve, and its parametric representation is introduced. The highly important Frenet Formulas, which lead to the characteristic vectors of a space curve, namely the tangent, normal and binormal vectors as well as the curvature and torsion of a curve, are also introduced. Osculating, normal and rectifying planes, as well as the concept of the plane curve are then discussed.

The second part of Chapter 5 is concerned with the application of ordinary derivatives to Physics problems. Basic kinematic concepts, such as velocity, angular velocity and acceleration are discussed in terms of the position vector of a particle. The different coordinate systems used to describe the acceleration of a particle are then introduced. Lastly, the center of mass as well as the hodograph of motion are also discussed.

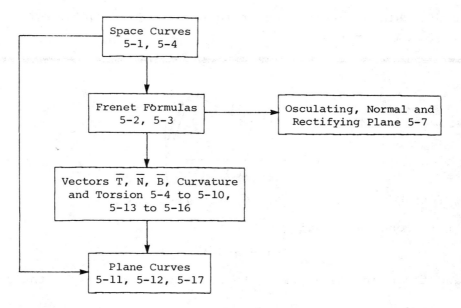

This chart is provided to facilitate rapid understanding of the inter-relationships of the topics and subject matter in this chapter. Also shown are the problem numbers associated with the subject matter.

SPACE CURVES, FRENET FORMULAS, CHARACTERISTIC VECTORS AND PLANE CURVES

● **PROBLEM** 5-1

A curve in space is given in the parametric form

$$\overline{r} = \overline{r}(t), \quad t_1 \leq t \leq t_2 \qquad (1)$$

where $\overline{r} = \overline{OA}$

such that point O is fixed.

1) Show that if $\dfrac{d\overline{r}}{dt} \equiv \overline{0}$ for $t_1 \leq t \leq t_2$,

then the curve degenerates into a single point.

2) Show that if

$$\frac{d\overline{r}}{dt} = \overline{0}, \quad \frac{d^2\overline{r}}{dt^2} = \overline{0}, \dots, \frac{d^n\overline{r}}{dt^n} = \overline{0}, \quad \frac{d^{n+1}\overline{r}}{dt^{n+1}} \neq 0 \qquad (2)$$

for $t = t_o$

then

$$\left. \frac{d^{n+1}\overline{r}}{dt^{n+1}} \right|_{t=t_o}$$

147

represents a tangent vector to the curve at the point A_O, where $\overline{OA}_O = \bar{r}(t_O)$.

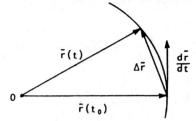

Solution: 1) Since $\frac{d\bar{r}}{dt} \equiv \bar{0}$ for all $t_1 \leq t \leq t_2$

it is concluded that

$$\bar{r}(t) = \text{const.} \tag{3}$$

and the curve degenerates to a single point A such that

$$\bar{r} = \overline{OA} \tag{4}$$

2) Consider the vector

$$\frac{\bar{r}(t) - \bar{r}(t_O)}{(t-t_O)^{n+1}} \tag{5}$$

which represents a secant to the curve, as shown in the figure.

Now, evaluate the limit of this vector as $t \to t_O$. De l'Hôpital's rule states that if the $\lim_{x \to a} f(x) = 0$ and $\lim_{x \to a} g(x) = 0$, then

$$\lim_{x \to a} \frac{f(x)}{g(x)} = \lim_{x \to a} \frac{f'(x)}{g'(x)} \tag{6}$$

provided the limit on the right-hand side exists. Applying eq.(6) to eq.(5),

$$\lim_{t \to t_O} \frac{\bar{r}(t) - \bar{r}(t_O)}{(t-t_O)^{n+1}} = \lim_{t \to t_O} \frac{\frac{d}{dt}\bar{r}(t)}{(n+1)(t-t_O)^n} \tag{7}$$

Here, we have a problem because both functions $\frac{d\bar{r}}{dt}$ and $(n+1)(t-t_O)^n$ approach 0 as $t \to t_O$.

From eq.(2), we see that De l'Hôpital's rule has to be applied n+1 times to obtain the (n+1) derivative, which is not 0. Doing this,

$$\lim_{t \to t_O} \frac{\bar{r}(t) - \bar{r}(t_O)}{(t-t_O)^{n+1}} = \lim_{t \to t_O} N \frac{d^{n+1}\bar{r}}{dt^{n+1}} = N \frac{d^{n+1}\bar{r}}{dt^{n+1}}\bigg|_{t=t_O} \tag{8}$$

where N is a constant obtained from differentiating $(t-t_O)^{n+1}$.

Since the tangent to a curve is the limiting position of a secant, from eq.(8) one concludes that

$$\frac{d^{n+1}\bar{r}}{dt^{n+1}}\bigg|_{t=t_o}$$

represents a tangent vector to the curve $\bar{r} = \bar{r}(t)$.

Prove the Frenet formulas:

$$\frac{d\bar{T}}{ds} = \frac{1}{\rho} \bar{N} \tag{1}$$

$$\frac{d\bar{B}}{ds} = -\tau\bar{N} \tag{2}$$

$$\frac{d\bar{N}}{ds} = -\frac{1}{\rho} \bar{T} + \tau\bar{B} \tag{3}$$

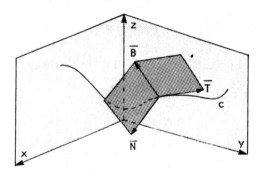

Solution: Eqs.(1)-(3) are the basic equations of differential geometry.

Let C be a curve in space described by

$$\bar{r} = \bar{r}(s) \tag{4}$$

as shown in the figure.

Define vector $\bar{T}$, called the unit tangent vector to the curve C, as

$$\bar{T} = \frac{d\bar{r}}{ds} \tag{5}$$

(see Problem 4-16). The rate at which $\bar{T}$ changes with respect to s is given by $\frac{d\bar{T}}{ds}$. Vector $\frac{d\bar{T}}{ds}$ is perpendicular to $\bar{T}$. That can be shown by differentiating $\bar{T}\cdot\bar{T} = 1$, indeed

$$\frac{d}{dt}(\bar{T}\cdot\bar{T}) = \bar{T}\cdot\frac{d\bar{T}}{ds} = \frac{d}{dt}(1) = 0 \tag{6}$$

Since the scalar product is equal to zero, vector $\overline{T}$ is perpendicular to $\frac{d\overline{T}}{ds}$. Now define vector $\overline{N}$, called the principal normal to the curve, as a unit vector in the direction of $\frac{d\overline{T}}{ds}$; thus,

$$\overline{N} = \rho \, \frac{d\overline{T}}{ds}$$

where ρ is a scalar called the radius of curvature.   (7)
Alternatively, the above equation can be written as

$$\frac{d\overline{T}}{ds} = \frac{1}{\rho} \, \overline{N}$$

The vector $\overline{B}$, called the binormal vector, is defined as:

$$\overline{B} = \overline{T} \times \overline{N}$$ (8)

Since $\overline{T}$ is perpendicular to $\overline{N}$,

$$|\overline{B}| = |\overline{T} \times \overline{N}| = |\overline{T}| \, |\overline{N}| \, \sin 90^{\circ} = 1$$

and thus $\overline{B}$ is a unit vector.

Differentiating eq.(8), we obtain

$$\frac{d\overline{B}}{ds} = \overline{T} \times \frac{d\overline{N}}{ds} + \frac{d\overline{T}}{ds} \times \overline{N} = \overline{T} \times \frac{d\overline{N}}{ds}$$ (9)

Since $\frac{d\overline{T}}{ds}$ and $\overline{N}$ are parallel, it follows that

$$\frac{d\overline{T}}{ds} \times \overline{N} = \overline{0}$$ (10)

From eq.(9), we obtain

$$\overline{T} \cdot \frac{d\overline{B}}{ds} = \overline{T} \cdot \overline{T} \times \frac{d\overline{N}}{ds} = 0$$ (11)

Here the identity

$$\overline{a} \cdot \overline{a} \times \overline{b} = 0 \quad \text{was used, this holds}$$

for any vectors $\overline{a}$ and $\overline{b}$.

From eq.(11), we conclude that $\overline{T}$ is perpendicular to $\frac{d\overline{B}}{ds}$.

Differentiating $\overline{B} \cdot \overline{B} = 1$, gives

$$\overline{B} \cdot \frac{d\overline{B}}{ds} = 0$$ (12)

thus $\frac{d\overline{B}}{ds}$ is perpendicular to $\overline{B}$.

Since $\frac{d\overline{B}}{ds}$ is perpendicular to $\overline{T}$ and $\overline{B}$, $\frac{d\overline{B}}{ds}$ must be parallel to $\overline{N}$, (note that $\overline{T}$ is perpendicular to $\overline{B}$) and

$$\frac{d\overline{B}}{ds} = -\tau \overline{N}$$ (13)

where τ is the torsion.

Since vectors $\overline{T}$, $\overline{N}$, $\overline{B}$ form a right-handed system, then $\overline{N}$, $\overline{B}$, $\overline{T}$ also form a right-handed system and

$$\overline{N} = \overline{B} \times \overline{T} \tag{14}$$

Differentiating eq.(14), gives

$$\frac{d\overline{N}}{ds} = \overline{B} \times \frac{d\overline{T}}{ds} + \frac{d\overline{B}}{ds} \times \overline{T} = \overline{B} \times \frac{1}{\rho} \overline{N} - \tau \overline{N} \times \overline{T}$$

$$= -\frac{1}{\rho} \overline{T} + \tau \overline{B} \tag{15}$$

which proves eq.(3).

The Frenet formulas are also written in the form

$$\frac{d\overline{T}}{ds} = k\overline{N}$$

$$\frac{d\overline{N}}{ds} = -k\overline{T} + \tau\overline{B}$$

$$\frac{d\overline{B}}{ds} = -\tau\overline{N}$$

where k is the curvature of C $(k = \frac{1}{\rho})$.

Note that the Frenet formulas refer to the rates of change of the three orthogonal unit vectors $\overline{T}$, $\overline{N}$, and $\overline{B}$.

● **PROBLEM** 5-3

Show that the Frenet formulas can be written in the form

$$\frac{d\overline{T}}{ds} = \overline{u} \times \overline{T} \tag{1}$$

$$\frac{d\overline{N}}{ds} = \overline{u} \times \overline{N} \tag{2}$$

$$\frac{d\overline{B}}{ds} = \overline{u} \times \overline{B} \tag{3}$$

and determine the vector $\overline{u}$.

Solution: Start with the original Frenet formulas

$$\frac{d\overline{T}}{ds} = \frac{1}{\rho} \overline{N} \tag{4}$$

$$\frac{d\overline{N}}{ds} = -\frac{1}{\rho} \overline{T} + \tau \overline{B} \tag{5}$$

$$\frac{d\overline{B}}{ds} = -\tau\overline{N} \tag{6}$$

151

where $\bar{B} = \bar{T} \times \bar{N}$.   (7)

Eqs.(2) and (5) yield

$$\frac{d\bar{N}}{ds} = \bar{u} \times \bar{N} = -\frac{1}{\rho}\bar{T} + \tau\bar{B} \quad (8)$$

From eq.(8), we will attempt to determine $\bar{u}$.
Substitute eq.(7) into eq.(8)

$$\bar{u} \times \bar{N} = -\frac{1}{\rho}\bar{T} + \tau\bar{T} \times \bar{N} \quad (9)$$

In the Frenet formulas eq.(5) involves all the vectors $\bar{T}$, $\bar{N}$, $\bar{B}$. It is for this reason that we compare this equation with equation (2), in determining the vector $\bar{u}$.

In the right-hand side of eq.(9) $(-\frac{1}{\rho}\bar{T} + \tau\bar{T} \times \bar{N})$, the first term $-\frac{1}{\rho}\bar{T}$ should be expressed as a vector product of some vector and $\bar{N}$.
In the following identity

$$\bar{a} \times (\bar{b} \times \bar{c}) = \bar{b}(\bar{a}\cdot\bar{c}) - \bar{c}(\bar{a}\cdot\bar{b}) \quad (10)$$

replace vectors $\bar{a}$, $\bar{b}$, $\bar{c}$ by the vectors $\bar{T}$ and $\bar{N}$. Try the combination

$$\bar{a} = \bar{N}, \quad \bar{b} = \bar{T}, \quad \bar{c} = \bar{N}$$

$$\bar{N} \times (\bar{T} \times \bar{N}) = \bar{T}(\bar{N}\cdot\bar{N}) - \bar{N}(\bar{N}\cdot\bar{T}) \quad (11)$$

Since the vector $\bar{N}$ is a unit vector,

$$\bar{N}\cdot\bar{N} = 1$$

The vectors $\bar{T}$ and $\bar{N}$ are perpendicular, thus

$$\bar{T}\cdot\bar{N} = 0$$

Eq.(11) becomes

$$\bar{N} \times (\bar{T} \times \bar{N}) = \bar{T} \quad (12)$$

or

$$-\bar{T} = (\bar{T} \times \bar{N}) \times \bar{N}$$

Since $\bar{T} \times \bar{N} = \bar{B}$,

$$-\bar{T} = \bar{B} \times \bar{N} \quad (13)$$

Substituting eq.(13) into eq.(9), obtain

$$\bar{u} \times \bar{N} = -\frac{1}{\rho}\bar{T} + \tau\bar{T} \times \bar{N} = \frac{1}{\rho}\bar{B} \times \bar{N} + \tau\bar{T} \times \bar{N}$$

$$= (\frac{1}{\rho}\bar{B} + \tau\bar{T}) \times \bar{N} \quad (14)$$

Thus

$$\bar{u} = \frac{1}{\rho}\bar{B} + \tau\bar{T} \quad (15)$$

Now, to verify eqs.(1)-(3), substitute eq.(15) into eq.(1) and obtain

$$\frac{d\overline{T}}{ds} = \overline{u} \times \overline{T} = (\frac{1}{\rho} \overline{B} + \tau\overline{T}) \times \overline{T} = \frac{1}{\rho} \overline{B} \times \overline{T}$$

$$= \frac{1}{\rho}(\overline{T} \times \overline{N}) \times \overline{T} \qquad (16)$$

The vectors $\overline{T}$ and $\overline{N}$ are perpendicular unit vectors. Keeping this in mind while using the vector properties,

$$(\overline{T} \times \overline{N}) \times \overline{T} = (\overline{T}\cdot\overline{T})\overline{N} - (\overline{T}\cdot\overline{N})\overline{T} = |\overline{T}|^2\overline{N} = \overline{N}$$

thus,

$$(\overline{T} \times \overline{N}) \times \overline{T} = \overline{N}$$

therefore equation (16), is reduced to

$$\frac{d\overline{T}}{ds} = \frac{1}{\rho}(\overline{T} \times \overline{N}) \times \overline{T} = \frac{1}{\rho} \overline{N} \qquad (16b)$$

Eq.(16b) is one of the Frenet formulas - eq.(4).

Substituting eq.(15) into eq.(2), obtain

$$\frac{d\overline{N}}{ds} = \overline{u} \times \overline{N} = (\frac{1}{\rho} \overline{B} + \tau\overline{T}) \times \overline{N} = (\frac{1}{\rho} \overline{T} \times \overline{N} + \tau\overline{T}) \times \overline{N}$$

$$= -\frac{1}{\rho} \overline{T} + \tau\overline{T} \times \overline{N} = -\frac{1}{\rho} \overline{T} + \tau\overline{B} \qquad (17)$$

which is eq.(5).

Substituting eq.(15) into eq.(3), gives

$$\frac{d\overline{B}}{ds} = \overline{u} \times \overline{B} = (\frac{1}{\rho} \overline{B} + \tau\overline{T}) \times \overline{B} = \tau\overline{T} \times \overline{B}$$

$$= \tau\overline{T} \times (\overline{T} \times \overline{N}) = -\tau\overline{N} \qquad (18)$$

which is eq.(6).

● **PROBLEM 5-4**

If a space curve is described by

$$x = 2 \cos t$$

$$y = 2 \sin t \qquad (1)$$

$$z = 5t,$$

sketch the space curve and find

1. the unit tangent vector $\overline{T}$,

2. the principal normal vector $\overline{N}$, the radius of curvature ρ and curvature k,

3. the binormal vector $\overline{B}$, torsion τ and radius of torsion σ.

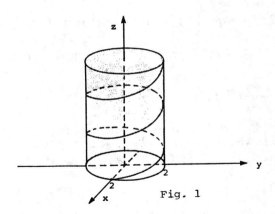

Fig. 1

Solution: Note that in eq.(1), x contains a linear cos t term and y a linear sin t term. Thus one should check $x^2 + y^2$ to see if the sin squared and cos squared terms drop out. This will leave us with a simpler expression to sketch. Doing this,

$$x^2 + y^2 = 4 \cos^2 t + 4 \sin^2 t = 4 \tag{2}$$

Since z = 5t and $x^2 + y^2 = 4$, the curve is a circular helix which lies on the cylinder $x^2 + y^2 = 4$ as shown in fig.1.

The position vector for any point on the curve is

$$\bar{r} = (2\cos t, \ 2 \sin t, \ 5t) \tag{3}$$

1. To find the unit tangent vector $\bar{T}$, differentiate $\bar{r}$, thus

$$\frac{d\bar{r}}{dt} = (-2\sin t, \ 2\cos t, \ 5) \tag{4}$$

$$\frac{ds}{dt} = \left| \frac{d\bar{r}}{dt} \right| = \sqrt{\frac{d\bar{r}}{dt} \cdot \frac{d\bar{r}}{dt}} = \sqrt{4\sin^2 t + 4\cos^2 t + 25} = \sqrt{29} \tag{5}$$

The unit tangent vector $\bar{T}$ is defined as

$$\bar{T} = \frac{d\bar{r}}{ds} \tag{6}$$

Substituting eq.(4) and eq.(5) into eq.(6), obtain

$$\bar{T} = \frac{d\bar{r}}{ds} = \frac{\frac{d\bar{r}}{dt}}{\frac{ds}{dt}} = \left(-\frac{2}{\sqrt{29}} \sin t, \frac{2}{\sqrt{29}} \cos t, \frac{5}{\sqrt{29}} \right) \tag{7}$$

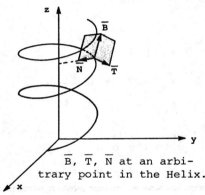

$\bar{B}, \ \bar{T}, \ \bar{N}$ at an arbitrary point in the Helix.

154

2. To find the vector $\bar{N}$ compute $\dfrac{d\bar{T}}{dt}$

$$\frac{d\bar{T}}{dt} = \frac{d}{dt}\left(-\frac{2}{\sqrt{29}}\sin t,\ \frac{2}{\sqrt{29}}\cos t,\ \frac{5}{\sqrt{29}}\right) = \left(-\frac{2}{\sqrt{29}}\cos t,\ -\frac{2}{\sqrt{29}}\sin t,\ 0\right) \qquad (8)$$

$$\frac{d\bar{T}}{ds} = \frac{d\bar{T}}{dt}\cdot\frac{dt}{ds} = \frac{d\bar{T}}{dt}\cdot\frac{1}{\dfrac{ds}{dt}} = \frac{\dfrac{d\bar{T}}{dt}}{\dfrac{ds}{dt}}$$

$$= \left(-\frac{2}{29}\cos t,\ -\frac{2}{29}\sin t,\ 0\right) \qquad (9)$$

Since $\qquad \dfrac{d\bar{T}}{ds} = \dfrac{1}{\rho}\bar{N} = k\bar{N},\qquad$ where $\bar{N}$ is a unit vector,

$$\left|\frac{d\bar{T}}{ds}\right| = |k|\ |\bar{N}| = k \qquad \text{since } k \geq 0 \qquad (10)$$

Substituting eq.(9) into eq.(10), gives

$$k = \left|\frac{d\bar{T}}{ds}\right| = \sqrt{\frac{d\bar{T}}{ds}\cdot\frac{d\bar{T}}{ds}} = \sqrt{\frac{4}{29^2}\cos^2 t + \frac{4}{29^2}\sin^2 t} = \frac{2}{29} \qquad (11)$$

and $\rho = \dfrac{1}{k} = \dfrac{29}{2}$

$$\qquad (12)$$

From $\qquad \dfrac{d\bar{T}}{ds} = k\bar{N},\qquad$ arrive at

$$\bar{N} = \frac{1}{k}\frac{d\bar{T}}{ds} = \rho\frac{d\bar{T}}{ds} \qquad (13)$$

Substituting eq.(12) and eq.(9) into eq.(13), obtain

$$\bar{N} = \frac{29}{2}\left(-\frac{2}{29}\cos t,\ -\frac{2}{29}\sin t,\ 0\right) = (-\cos t,\ -\sin t,\ 0) \qquad (14)$$

3. The binormal vector $\bar{B}$ is defined as

$$\bar{B} = \bar{T} \times \bar{N} \qquad (15)$$

Substituting eqs.(7) and (14) into eq.(15), gives

$$\bar{B} = \begin{vmatrix} \bar{i} & \bar{j} & \bar{k} \\[2mm] -\dfrac{2}{\sqrt{29}}\sin t & \dfrac{2}{\sqrt{29}}\cos t & \dfrac{5}{\sqrt{29}} \\[2mm] -\cos t & -\sin t & 0 \end{vmatrix} \qquad (16)$$

$$= \frac{5}{\sqrt{29}}\sin t\ \bar{i} - \frac{5}{\sqrt{29}}\cos t\ \bar{j} + \frac{2}{\sqrt{29}}\bar{k} = \left(\frac{5}{\sqrt{29}}\sin t,\ -\frac{5}{\sqrt{29}}\cos t,\ \frac{2}{\sqrt{29}}\right)$$

Now verify that $\bar{B}$ is a unit vector:

$$|\bar{B}| = \sqrt{\frac{25}{29}\sin^2 t + \frac{25}{29}\cos^2 t + \frac{4}{29}} = \sqrt{\frac{29}{29}} = 1 \qquad (17)$$

$$\frac{d\bar{B}}{dt} = \left(\frac{5}{\sqrt{29}} \cos t, \frac{5}{\sqrt{29}} \sin t, 0\right) \qquad (18)$$

and

$$\frac{d\bar{B}}{ds} = \frac{\frac{d\bar{B}}{dt}}{\frac{ds}{dt}} = \left(\frac{5}{29} \cos t, \frac{5}{29} \sin t, 0\right) \qquad (19)$$

From the equation

$$\frac{d\bar{B}}{ds} = -\tau\bar{N}, \qquad (20)$$

substituting eqs.(19) and (14), we arrive at

$$\left(\frac{5}{29} \cos t, \frac{5}{29} \sin t, 0\right) = -\tau(-\cos t, -\sin t, 0) \qquad (21)$$

and thus

$$\tau = \frac{5}{29} \qquad (22)$$

and

$$\sigma = \frac{1}{\tau} = \frac{29}{5} \qquad (23)$$

● **PROBLEM 5-5**

A space curve is given by

$$x = t$$
$$y = t^2 \qquad (1)$$
$$z = t^3$$

Find

1. the curvature k

2. the torsion τ

Solution: 1. The position vector is
$$\bar{r}(t) = (t, t^2, t^3) \qquad (2)$$

Then

$$\dot{\bar{r}} = \frac{d\bar{r}}{dt} = (1, 2t, 3t^2) \qquad (3)$$

From eq.(3), find $\dot{s}$.

$$\dot{s} = |\dot{\bar{r}}| = \sqrt{1+4t^2+9t^4} \qquad (4)$$

The unit tangent vector is,

$$\bar{T} = \frac{d\bar{r}}{ds} = \frac{\frac{d\bar{r}}{dt}}{\frac{ds}{dt}} = \frac{\dot{\bar{r}}}{\dot{s}} \qquad (4)$$

Thus

$$\overline{T} = \left(\frac{1}{\sqrt{1+4t^2+9t^4}}, \quad \frac{2t}{\sqrt{1+4t^2+9t^4}}, \quad \frac{3t^2}{\sqrt{1+4t^2+9t^4}} \right) \quad (6)$$

Since

$$k = \left| \frac{d\overline{T}}{ds} \right| \quad (7)$$

and $\overline{T} = \overline{T}(t)$, compute

$$\frac{d\overline{T}}{ds} = \frac{\dot{\overline{T}}}{\dot{s}}$$

Differentiating eq.(6),

$$\dot{\overline{T}} = \left[\frac{-4t - 18t^3}{(1 + 4t^2+9t^4)^{3/2}}, \quad \frac{2 - 18t^4}{(1 + 4t^2+9t^4)^{3/2}}, \quad \frac{6t + 12t^3}{(1 + 4t^2+9t^4)^{3/2}} \right] \quad (8)$$

Thus $\dfrac{\dot{\overline{T}}}{\dot{s}}$ can be written

$$\frac{\dot{\overline{T}}}{\dot{s}} = \frac{d\overline{T}}{ds} = \left[\frac{-4t - 18t^3}{(1 + 4t^2+9t^4)^2}, \quad \frac{2 - 18t^4}{(1 + 4t^2+9t^4)^2}, \quad \frac{6t + 12t^3}{(1 + 4t^2+9t^4)^2} \right] \quad (9)$$

From eq.(7),

$$k = \left| \frac{d\overline{T}}{ds} \right| = \sqrt{\frac{(4t + 18t^3)^2 + (2 - 18t^4)^2 + (6t + 12t^3)^2}{(1 + 4t^2+9t^4)^4}} \quad (10)$$

$$= \frac{2\sqrt{1 + 9t^2+9t^4}}{(1 + 4t^2+9t^4)^{3/2}}$$

2. The normal vector $\overline{N}$ is given by

$$\overline{N} = \frac{1}{k} \frac{d\overline{T}}{ds} \quad (11)$$

Substituting eqs.(10) and (9) into eq.(11), gives

$$\overline{N} = \frac{(1+4t^2+9t^4)^{\frac{3}{2}}}{2\sqrt{1+9t^2+9t^4}} \left(\frac{-4t-18t^3}{(1+4t^2+9t^4)^2}, \quad \frac{2-18t^4}{(1+4t^2+9t^4)^2}, \quad \frac{6t+12t^3}{(1+4t^2+9t^4)^2} \right)$$

$$= \frac{1}{\sqrt{1+9t^2+9t^4} \cdot \sqrt{1+4t^2+9t^4}} (-2t-9t^3, \ 1-9t^4, \ 3t+6t^3) \quad (12)$$

From the Frenet formula

$$\frac{d\overline{B}}{ds} = -\tau\overline{N} \quad \text{then} \quad \tau = \left| \frac{d\overline{B}}{ds} \right| \quad (13)$$

The binormal vector $\overline{B}$ is given by

$$\overline{B} = \overline{T} \times \overline{N} \quad (14)$$

Substituting eq.(6) and eq.(12) into eq.(14), gives

157

$$\bar{B} = \frac{1}{\sqrt{1+4t^2+9t^4}} (1, 2t, 3t^2) \times \frac{(-2t - 9t^3, 1 - 9t^4, 3t + 6t^3)}{\sqrt{1+9t^2+9t^4}\ \sqrt{1+4t^2+9t^4}}$$

$$= \frac{(27t^6+12t^4+3t^2, -27t^5-12t^3-3t, 9t^4+4t^2+1)}{(1+4t^2+9t^4)\ \sqrt{1+9t^2+9t^4}} \qquad (15)$$

Then

$$\tau = \left| \frac{d\bar{B}}{ds} \right| = \left| \frac{\dot{\bar{B}}}{\dot{s}} \right| \qquad (16)$$

Differentiating $\bar{B}$ and substituting $\dot{\bar{B}}$ and eq.(4) into eq.(16), we obtain

$$\tau = \frac{1}{\sqrt{1+4t^2+9t^4}} \left[\frac{d}{dt} \frac{(27t^6+12t^4+3t^2, -27t^5-12t^3-3t, 9t^4+4t^2+1)}{(1+4t^2+9t^4)\ \sqrt{1+9t^2+9t^4}} \right]$$

$$= \frac{3}{1+9t^2+9t^4}$$

● **PROBLEM 5-6**

Using the results of Problem 5-5, find the equations, in vector and rectangular (component) form, for the

1. tangent

2. principal normal

3. binormal

to the curve

$$x = t, \quad y = t^2, \quad z = t^3 \qquad (1)$$

at the point where t=1.

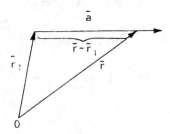

Solution: For t = 1, eq.(6) of problem 5-5 becomes

$$\bar{T}_1 = \left(\frac{1}{\sqrt{14}}, \frac{2}{\sqrt{14}}, \frac{3}{\sqrt{14}} \right) \qquad (2)$$

Eq. (12) of problem 5-5 becomes

158

$$\overline{N}_1 = \left(\frac{-11}{\sqrt{19 \cdot 14}}, \frac{-8}{\sqrt{19 \cdot 14}}, \frac{9}{\sqrt{19 \cdot 14}} \right) \qquad (3)$$

$$= \left(\frac{-11}{\sqrt{266}}, \frac{-8}{\sqrt{266}}, \frac{9}{\sqrt{266}} \right)$$

From eq.(15) of the same problem, we obtain

$$\overline{B}_1 = \left(\frac{3}{\sqrt{19}}, \frac{-3}{\sqrt{19}}, \frac{1}{\sqrt{19}} \right) \qquad (4)$$

Note that if $\overline{a}$ denotes any given vector and $\overline{r}_1$ and $\overline{r}$ are the position vectors of the initial point of $\overline{a}$ and an arbitrary point of $\overline{a}$ respectively, then $\overline{r}-\overline{r}_1$ is parallel to $\overline{a}$ and the equation of $\overline{a}$ becomes

$$\overline{a} \times (\overline{r}-\overline{r}_1) = \overline{0} \qquad (5)$$

as shown in the figure.

From this, the equation of the tangent vector can be written as

$$\overline{T}_1 \times (\overline{r}-\overline{r}_1) = \overline{0} \qquad (6)$$

Likewise, the equation of the principal normal is

$$\overline{N}_1 \times (\overline{r}-\overline{r}_1) = \overline{0}, \text{ and} \qquad (7)$$

the equation of the binormal is

$$\overline{B}_1 \times (\overline{r}-\overline{r}_1) = \overline{0} \qquad (8)$$

In rectangular form,

$$\overline{r} = (x, y, z) \qquad (9)$$

$$\overline{r}_1 = (1, 1, 1)$$

and

$$\overline{r}-\overline{r}_1 = (x-1, y-1, z-1) \qquad (10)$$

Substituting eq.(2) and (10) into eq.(6), yields

$$\left(\frac{1}{\sqrt{14}}, \frac{2}{\sqrt{14}}, \frac{3}{\sqrt{14}} \right) \times (x-1, y-1, z-1) = \overline{0}$$

or

$$\left(\frac{2}{\sqrt{14}} (z-1) - \frac{3}{\sqrt{14}} (y-1), \frac{3}{\sqrt{14}} (x-1) - \frac{1}{\sqrt{14}} (z-1), \right.$$

$$\left. \frac{1}{\sqrt{14}} (y-1) - \frac{2}{\sqrt{14}} (x-1) \right) = \overline{0} \equiv (0,0,0)$$

since the respective components on both sides of the equation are equal, then

159

$$\frac{2}{\sqrt{14}} (z-1) - \frac{3}{\sqrt{14}} (y-1) = 0$$

$$\frac{3}{\sqrt{14}} (x-1) - \frac{1}{\sqrt{14}} (z-1) = 0$$

$$\frac{1}{\sqrt{14}} (y-1) - \frac{2}{\sqrt{14}} (x-1) = 0$$

the first two equations yield,

$$(z-1) = \frac{3}{2} (y-1)$$

and

$$3(x-1) = (z-1)$$

or equivalently,

$$z-1 = \frac{3}{2} (y-1) = 3(x-1) \tag{11}$$

this is the equation of the tangent vector $\overline{T}$ in rectangular form.

Next, for the equation of the normal vector, we follow the same procedure we followed for the tangent vector, that is, we substitute eq.(3) and (10) into eq.(7), doing this,

$$\left(\frac{-11}{\sqrt{266}}, \frac{-8}{\sqrt{266}}, \frac{9}{\sqrt{266}} \right) \times (x-1, y-1, z-1) = \overline{0}$$

after going through the cross multiplication, and equating the components, obtain

$$\frac{-(z-1)}{9} = \frac{y-1}{8} = \frac{x-1}{11} \tag{12}$$

for the binormal, we will once again follow the same procedure; that is we will substitute eq.(4) and (10) into eq.(8), after going through the same process we went through for the $\overline{T}$ and $\overline{N}$ vectors, the rectangular equation for the binormal $\overline{B}$ becomes

$$x-1 = -(y-1) = 3(z-1) \tag{13}$$

● PROBLEM 5-7

For the curve described in problem 5-5, that is,

$$x = t, \quad y = t^2, \quad z = t^3,$$

find the equations for the

1. osculating plane

2. normal plane

3. rectifying plane

to the curve at the point where $t = 1$. First find the equations in vector form, then in rectangular form.

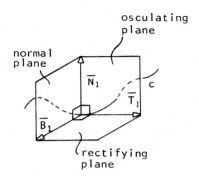

normal plane · osculating plane · $\overline{N}_1$ · $\overline{T}_1$ · c · $\overline{B}_1$ · rectifying plane

Solution: 1. The osculating plane is the plane which contains the tangent vector and the principal normal vector. Refer to Fig. 1. Let $\overline{r}$ be the position vector of any point in the plane and $\overline{r}_1$ the position vector of the point for which $t = 1$. The vector $\overline{r} - \overline{r}_1$ is perpendicular to $\overline{B}_1$, the binormal at the point $t = 1$. Thus

$$\overline{B}_1 \cdot (\overline{r} - \overline{r}_1) = 0 \tag{1}$$

From problem 5-6, eq.(4),

$$\overline{B}_1 = \left(\frac{3}{\sqrt{19}}, \frac{-3}{\sqrt{19}}, \frac{1}{\sqrt{19}} \right) \tag{2}$$

Since $\overline{r}_1 = (1, 1, 1)$ eq.(1) becomes

$$\left(\frac{3}{\sqrt{19}}, \frac{-3}{\sqrt{19}}, \frac{1}{\sqrt{19}} \right) \cdot (x-1, y-1, z-1) = \frac{3(x-1)}{\sqrt{19}} - \frac{3(y-1)}{\sqrt{19}} + \frac{z-1}{\sqrt{19}} = 0$$

or

$$3(x-1) - 3(y-1) + z-1 = 0 \tag{3}$$

This is the rectangular form of equation (1), which in turn is the equation of the osculating plane.

The normal plane is defined as the plane which contains the normal and binormal vectors, and therefore is perpendicular to the tangent vector at the given point. Thus

$$\overline{T}_1 \cdot (\overline{r} - \overline{r}_1) = 0 \tag{4}$$

From Problem 5-6

$$\overline{T}_1 = \left(\frac{1}{\sqrt{14}}, \frac{2}{\sqrt{14}}, \frac{3}{\sqrt{14}} \right)$$

In the rectangular form, eq.(4) becomes

$$\left(\frac{1}{\sqrt{14}}, \frac{2}{\sqrt{14}}, \frac{3}{\sqrt{14}} \right) \cdot (x-1, y-1, z-1)$$

$$= \frac{x-1}{\sqrt{14}} + \frac{2(y-1)}{\sqrt{14}} + \frac{3(z-1)}{\sqrt{14}} = 0$$

or

$$x-1 + 2(y-1) + 3(z-1) = 0 \tag{5}$$

3. The rectifying plane is defined as the plane which contains the tangent and binormal vectors, and therefore is perpendicular to the principal normal at the given point.

Thus

$$\bar{N}_1 \cdot (\bar{r} - \bar{r}_1) = 0 \tag{6}$$

Since

$$\bar{N}_1 = \left(\frac{-11}{\sqrt{19 \cdot 14}}, \frac{-8}{\sqrt{19 \cdot 14}}, \frac{9}{\sqrt{19 \cdot 14}} \right) \tag{7}$$

(see Problem 5-6), eq.(6) in the rectangular form becomes

$$-11(x-1) - 8(y-1) + 9(z-1) = 0 \tag{8}$$

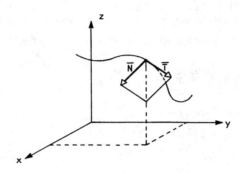

The normal, osculating and rectifying planes to the curve C at the point P are shown in the figure.

● **PROBLEM 5-8**

Find the curvature for the circular helix described by

$$\bar{r}(t) = (a \cos t, a \sin t, bt) \tag{1}$$

Solution: From the Frenet formula

$$\frac{d\bar{T}}{ds} = k\bar{N} \tag{2}$$

Solving for k

$$k = \left| \frac{d\bar{T}}{ds} \right| \tag{3}$$

($\bar{N}$ is a unit vector.) The curve in eq.(1) is given as a function of t, thus

$$\frac{d\bar{T}}{ds} = \frac{d\bar{T}}{dt} \cdot \frac{dt}{ds} = \frac{\frac{d\bar{T}}{dt}}{\frac{ds}{dt}} \tag{4}$$

where $\bar{T} = \dfrac{d\bar{r}}{ds}$ (5)

and

$$\frac{ds}{dt} = \left| \frac{d\overline{r}}{dt} \right| \tag{6}$$

Substituting eqs.(4),(5),(6) into eq.(3), gives

$$k = \left| \frac{d\overline{T}}{ds} \right| = \frac{\left| \frac{d\overline{T}}{dt} \right|}{\left| \frac{ds}{dt} \right|} = \frac{\left| \frac{d\overline{T}}{dt} \right|}{\left| \frac{d\overline{r}}{dt} \right|} \tag{7}$$

From eq.(1),

$$\frac{d\overline{r}}{dt} = (-a \sin t, \ a \cos t, \ b) \tag{8}$$

and

$$\frac{ds}{dt} = \sqrt{\frac{d\overline{r}}{dt} \cdot \frac{d\overline{r}}{dt}} = \sqrt{a^2 \sin^2 t + a^2 \cos^2 t + b^2} = \sqrt{a^2 + b^2} \tag{9}$$

$$\overline{T} = \frac{d\overline{r}}{ds} = \frac{\frac{d\overline{r}}{dt}}{\frac{ds}{dt}} = \left(\frac{-a}{\sqrt{a^2+b^2}} \sin t, \ \frac{a}{\sqrt{a^2+b^2}} \cos t, \ \frac{b}{\sqrt{a^2+b^2}} \right) \tag{10}$$

Differentiating eq.(10) with respect to t, results in

$$\frac{d\overline{T}}{dt} = \left(\frac{-a}{\sqrt{a^2+b^2}} \cos t, \ \frac{-a}{\sqrt{a^2+b^2}} \sin t, \ 0 \right) \tag{11}$$

From eq.(7),

$$k = \frac{\left| \frac{d\overline{T}}{dt} \right|}{\left| \frac{d\overline{r}}{dt} \right|} = \frac{\sqrt{\frac{a^2}{a^2+b^2}(\cos^2 t + \sin^2 t)}}{\sqrt{a^2+b^2}} = \frac{a}{a^2+b^2} \tag{12}$$

The curvature of a circular helix is a constant for all values of t.

● **PROBLEM 5-9**

A space curve is given in the parametric form

$$x = t + \frac{t^3}{3}$$

$$y = t - \frac{t^3}{3} \tag{1}$$

$$z = t^2$$

Determine

1. the unit tangent vector $\overline{T}$

2. the curvature k

3. the principal normal $\overline{N}$

163

4. the binormal vector $\overline{B}$

5. the torsion τ

Solution: 1. The position vector for any point on the curve is

$$\overline{r}(t) = \left(t + \frac{t^3}{3},\ t - \frac{t^3}{3},\ t^2 \right) \tag{2}$$

The unit tangent vector $\overline{T}$ is given by

$$\overline{T} = \frac{d\overline{r}}{ds} \tag{3}$$

Since $\overline{r} = \overline{r}(t)$, then

$$\overline{T} = \frac{d\overline{r}}{ds} = \frac{\frac{d\overline{r}}{dt}}{\frac{ds}{dt}} = \frac{\dot{\overline{r}}}{\dot{s}} \tag{4}$$

(a dot appearing above a vector denotes the first derivative of that vector with respect to time, two dots denotes the second derivative, three dots the third derivative, and so on. Therefore

$$\frac{d\overline{r}}{dt} = \dot{\overline{r}}, \quad \frac{d^2\overline{r}}{dt^2} = \ddot{\overline{r}}, \cdots)$$

Differentiating eq.(2), gives

$$\dot{\overline{r}}(t) = (1 + t^2,\ 1 - t^2,\ 2t) \tag{5}$$

Since $\dot{s} = |\dot{\overline{r}}|$, from eq.(5) $\tag{6}$

$$\dot{s} = \sqrt{(1+t^2)^2+(1-t^2)^2+4t^2} = \sqrt{2+4t^2+2t^4} = \sqrt{2}(1+t^2) \tag{7}$$

Substituting eqs.(5) and (7) into eq.(4), obtain

$$\overline{T} = \left(\frac{1+t^2}{\sqrt{2}(1+t^2)},\ \frac{1-t^2}{\sqrt{2}(1+t^2)},\ \frac{2t}{\sqrt{2}(1+t^2)} \right)$$
$$= \left(\frac{1}{\sqrt{2}},\ \frac{1-t^2}{\sqrt{2}(1+t^2)},\ \frac{\sqrt{2}t}{1+t^2} \right) \tag{8}$$

2. From the Frenet formula

$$\frac{d\overline{T}}{ds} = k\overline{N}$$

where $\overline{N}$ is a unit vector, obtain

$$k = \left| \frac{d\overline{T}}{ds} \right| \tag{9}$$

where

$$\frac{d\overline{T}}{ds} = \frac{\frac{d\overline{T}}{dt}}{\frac{ds}{dt}} = \frac{\dot{\overline{T}}}{\dot{s}} \tag{10}$$

From eq.(8) find the time derivative of $\overline{T}$,

$$\dot{\overline{T}} = \frac{d}{dt}\left(\frac{1}{\sqrt{2}}, \frac{1-t^2}{\sqrt{2}(1+t^2)}, \frac{\sqrt{2}t}{1+t^2}\right) \tag{11}$$

$$= \left(0, \frac{-4\sqrt{2}t}{2(1+t^2)^2}, \frac{\sqrt{2}(1-t^2)}{(1+t^2)^2}\right)$$

Substituting eqs.(11), (10) and (7) into eq.(9), obtain

$$k = \left|\frac{d\overline{T}}{ds}\right| = \frac{\left|\dot{\overline{T}}\right|}{\dot{s}} = \left|\left(0, \frac{-4t}{2(1+t^2)^3}, \frac{1-t^2}{(1+t^2)^3}\right)\right|$$

$$= \sqrt{\frac{4t^2+1-2t^2+t^4}{(1+t^2)^6}} = \frac{\sqrt{(1+t^2)^2}}{(1+t^2)^3} = \frac{1}{(1+t^2)^2} \tag{12}$$

3. From

$$\frac{d\overline{T}}{ds} = k\overline{N}$$

solve for $\overline{N}$

$$\overline{N} = \frac{1}{k}\frac{d\overline{T}}{ds} = \frac{1}{k}\frac{\dot{\overline{T}}}{\dot{s}} \tag{13}$$

Substituting eq.(11), eq.(7), and eq.(12) into eq.(13), gives

$$\overline{N} = (1+t^2)^2 \cdot \frac{1}{\sqrt{2}(1+t^2)} \cdot \left(0, \frac{-2\sqrt{2}t}{(1+t^2)^2}, \frac{\sqrt{2}(1-t^2)}{(1+t^2)^2}\right)$$

$$= \left(0, \frac{-2t}{1+t^2}, \frac{1-t^2}{1+t^2}\right) \tag{14}$$

4. The binormal vector $\overline{B}$ is given by

$$\overline{B} = \overline{T} \times \overline{N} \tag{15}$$

Substituting eq.(8) into eq. (15), gives

$$\overline{B} = \left(\frac{1}{\sqrt{2}}, \frac{1-t^2}{\sqrt{2}(1+t^2)}, \frac{\sqrt{2}t}{1+t^2}\right) \times \left(0, \frac{-2t}{1+t^2}, \frac{1-t^2}{1+t^2}\right)$$

$$= \left(\frac{1}{\sqrt{2}}, -\frac{1-t^2}{\sqrt{2}(1+t^2)}, \frac{-\sqrt{2}t}{1+t^2}\right) \tag{16}$$

5. From the Frenet formula

$$\frac{d\overline{B}}{ds} = -\tau\overline{N}$$

where $\overline{N}$ is a unit vector,

$$\tau = \left|\frac{d\overline{B}}{ds}\right| \tag{17}$$

Note that

$$\frac{d\overline{B}}{ds} = \frac{\frac{d\overline{B}}{dt}}{\frac{ds}{dt}} = \frac{\dot{\overline{B}}}{\dot{s}} \tag{18}$$

From eq.(16), obtain $\dot{\overline{B}}$

$$\dot{\overline{B}} = \frac{d}{dt} \left(\frac{1}{\sqrt{2}}, \; -\frac{1-t^2}{\sqrt{2}(1+t^2)}, \; \frac{-\sqrt{2}t}{1+t^2} \right)$$

$$= \left(0, \; \frac{2\sqrt{2}t}{(1+t^2)^2}, \; \frac{-\sqrt{2}(1-t^2)}{(1+t^2)^2} \right) \tag{19}$$

Substituting eqs.(7), (18), (19) into eq.(17), obtain

$$\tau = \left| \frac{\dot{\overline{B}}}{\dot{s}} \right| = \left| \left(0, \; \frac{2t}{(1+t^2)^3}, \; \frac{-(1-t^2)}{(1+t^2)^3} \right) \right|$$

$$= \sqrt{\frac{4t^2+(1-t^2)^2}{(1+t^2)^6}} = \frac{1}{(1+t^2)^2} \tag{20}$$

Note that for the curve given in eq.(1), $k = \tau$. $\tag{21}$

● **PROBLEM 5-10**

If the parametric equations of a curve are

$$\overline{r}(s) = (x(s), \; y(s), \; z(s)), \tag{1}$$

show that the radius of curvature of the curve is given by

$$\rho = \left[\left(\frac{d^2x}{ds^2} \right)^2 + \left(\frac{d^2y}{ds^2} \right)^2 + \left(\frac{d^2z}{ds^2} \right)^2 \right]^{-\frac{1}{2}} \tag{2}$$

Solution: To prove eq.(2) use the Frenet formula - the simplest one involving

$$\frac{d\overline{T}}{ds} = \frac{1}{\rho}\overline{N} \tag{3}$$

Note that $\overline{N}$ is a unit vector. From eq.(3), obtain

$$\left| \frac{d\overline{T}}{ds} \right| = \frac{1}{|\rho|} |\overline{N}| = \frac{1}{\rho} \tag{4}$$

$$\rho = \left| \frac{d\overline{T}}{ds} \right|^{-1} \tag{5}$$

The unit tangent vector $\overline{T}$ is defined by

$$\overline{T} = \frac{d\overline{r}}{ds} \tag{6}$$

Substituting eq.(1) into eq.(6), gives

$$\overline{T} = \frac{d\overline{r}}{ds} = \left[\frac{dx}{ds}, \; \frac{dy}{ds}, \; \frac{dz}{ds} \right] \tag{7}$$

To obtain $\frac{d\overline{T}}{ds}$, differentiate eq.(7) and obtain

$$\frac{d\overline{T}}{ds} = \left[\frac{d^2x}{ds^2}, \frac{d^2y}{ds^2}, \frac{d^2z}{ds^2}\right] \tag{8}$$

Combining eqs.(5) and (8), obtain

$$\rho = \left|\frac{d\overline{T}}{ds}\right|^{-1} = \left[\sqrt{\frac{d\overline{T}}{ds}\frac{d\overline{T}}{ds}}\right]^{-1} = \left[\frac{d\overline{T}}{ds}\frac{d\overline{T}}{ds}\right]^{-\frac{1}{2}}$$

$$= \left[\left(\frac{d^2x}{ds^2}\right)^2 + \left(\frac{d^2y}{ds^2}\right)^2 + \left(\frac{d^2z}{ds^2}\right)^2\right]^{-\frac{1}{2}} \tag{9}$$

● **PROBLEM 5-11**

Show that for a plane curve the torsion $\tau = 0$.

<u>Solution</u>: Denote the position vector of a point P on the curve by

$$\overline{r}(s) = (x, y, 0) \tag{1}$$

The third component is zero since the curve is plane.

From eq.(1) compute the unit tangent vector

$$\overline{T} = \frac{d\overline{r}}{ds} = \left(\frac{dx}{ds}, \frac{dy}{ds}, 0\right) \tag{2}$$

The third component of $\overline{T}$ is equal to zero.

$$\overline{T} = (T_1, T_2, 0) \tag{3}$$

From the Frenet formula

$$\frac{d\overline{T}}{ds} = k\overline{N} \tag{4}$$

and eq.(3), obtain

$$\left(\frac{dT_1}{ds}, \frac{dT_2}{ds}, 0\right) = k(N_1, N_2, N_3) \tag{5}$$

Thus $N_3 = 0$.

$$\overline{N} = (N_1, N_2, 0) \tag{6}$$

The vector $\overline{B}$ is defined as

$$\overline{B} = \overline{T} \times \overline{N} \tag{7}$$

Substituting eq.(3) and eq.(6) into eq.(7), obtain

$$\overline{B} = (T_2N_3 - T_3N_2, \ T_3N_1 - T_1N_3, \ T_1N_2 - T_2N_1) \tag{8}$$

$$= (0, 0, B_3)$$

From the Frenet formula

$$\frac{d\overline{B}}{ds} = -\tau\overline{N} \tag{9}$$

and from eqs.(6) and (8),

$$\left(0, 0, \frac{d\overline{B}_3}{ds}\right) = -\tau(N_1, N_2, 0) \tag{10}$$

Comparing the coordinates of both sides of eq.(10), it is clear that

$$0 = -\tau N_1$$
$$\tag{11}$$
$$0 = -\tau N_2$$

Thus $\tau = 0$ for the plane curve.

● **PROBLEM** 5-12

1. Consider a plane curve in the xy plane. Find the radius of curvature of a curve whose equation is $y = y(x)$, $z = 0$.

2. Find the radius of curvature, at $x = 0$, of the curve whose equation is $y = x^2$.

<u>Solution</u>: 1. The curve is described by the equations

$$y = y(x); \quad z = 0 \tag{1}$$

The position vector of any point P on the curve is

$$\overline{OP} = \overline{r} = (x, y(x), 0) \tag{2}$$

To find the tangent vector to the curve, differentiate eq.(2)

$$\frac{d\overline{r}}{dx} = \left(1, \frac{dy}{dx}, 0\right) \tag{3}$$

Then

$$\frac{ds}{dx} = \sqrt{\frac{d\overline{r}}{dx} \cdot \frac{d\overline{r}}{dx}} = \sqrt{1 + \left(\frac{dy}{dx}\right)^2} \tag{4}$$

Denote

$$\frac{dy}{dx} \text{ as } y' \text{ and } \frac{d^2y}{dx^2} \text{ as } y'' \tag{5}$$

The unit tangent vector to the curve is given by

$$\overline{T} = \frac{\frac{d\overline{r}}{dx}}{\frac{ds}{dx}} = \left(\frac{1}{\sqrt{1+y'^2}}, \frac{y'}{\sqrt{1+y'^2}}, 0\right) \tag{6}$$

168

The radius of curvature of the curve can be calculated from the Frenet formula

$$\frac{d\overline{T}}{ds} = k\overline{N} = \frac{1}{\rho}\,\overline{N} \tag{7}$$

Taking the magnitude of both sides of eq.(7), obtain

$$\left|\frac{d\overline{T}}{ds}\right| = \frac{1}{\rho}\,|\overline{N}| = \frac{1}{\rho}$$

Thus

$$\rho = \frac{1}{\left|\dfrac{d\overline{T}}{ds}\right|} \tag{8}$$

To find $\dfrac{d\overline{T}}{ds}$ differentiate eq.(6)

$$\frac{d\overline{T}}{dx} = \left(-\frac{y'y''}{\sqrt{1+y'^2}\,(1+y'^2)},\ \frac{y''\,(1+y'^2)-y'^2\,y''}{\sqrt{1+y'^2}\,\sqrt{1+y'^2}},\ 0\right) \tag{9}$$

From eqs.(4) and (9),

$$\frac{d\overline{T}}{ds} = \left(\frac{-y'y''}{(1+y'^2)^2},\ \frac{y''}{(1+y'^2)^2},\ 0\right) \tag{10}$$

Substituting eq.(10) into eq.(8), gives

$$\rho = \frac{1}{\left(\dfrac{y'^2\cdot y''^2 + y''^2}{(1+y'^2)^4}\right)^{1/2}} = \frac{(1+y'^2)^{\frac{3}{2}}}{|y''|} \tag{11}$$

2. The equation of the curve is

$$y = x^2 \tag{12}$$

Thus

$$y' = \frac{dy}{dx} = 2x, \qquad y'' = \frac{d^2y}{dx^2} = 2 \tag{13}$$

Substituting eq.(13) into eq.(11), gives

$$\rho = \frac{(1+4x^2)^{\frac{3}{2}}}{2} \tag{14}$$

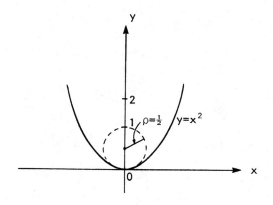

At x = 0, the radius of curvature is

$$\rho \Big|_{x=0} = \frac{1}{2}$$

as shown in the figure.

● **PROBLEM** 5-13

Find the curvature k for the space curve given by

$$x = 1 + \cos\theta$$

$$y = \theta + \sin\theta \qquad\qquad (1)$$

$$z = 4\cos\frac{\theta}{2}$$

Solution: To find K, we will use the Frenet formulas. The position vector for any point on the curve is

$$\bar{r}(\theta) = (1 + \cos\theta,\ \theta + \sin\theta,\ 4\cos\frac{\theta}{2}) \qquad (2)$$

Differentiating eq.(2) with respect to θ yields

$$\frac{d\bar{r}}{d\theta} = (-\sin\theta,\ 1 + \cos\theta,\ -2\sin\frac{\theta}{2}) \qquad (3)$$

From the equation

$$\frac{ds}{d\theta} = \left|\frac{d\bar{r}}{d\theta}\right| = \sqrt{\frac{d\bar{r}}{d\theta} \cdot \frac{d\bar{r}}{d\theta}} \qquad (4)$$

find $\frac{ds}{d\theta}$;   doing this, we get

$$\frac{ds}{d\theta} = \sqrt{\sin^2\theta + 1 + 2\cos\theta + \cos^2\theta + 4\sin^2\frac{\theta}{2}}$$

$$= \sqrt{\sin^2\theta + \cos^2\theta + 1 + 2\cos\theta + 2 - 2\cos\theta} = 2 \qquad (5)$$

In eq.(5) the identity

$$\sin^2\frac{\theta}{2} = \frac{1 - \cos\theta}{2} \qquad \text{was used.} \qquad (6)$$

The unit tangent vector $\bar{T}$ to the curve is given by

$$\bar{T} = \frac{d\bar{r}}{ds} = \frac{\frac{d\bar{r}}{d\theta}}{\frac{ds}{d\theta}} = \left(-\frac{\sin\theta}{2},\ \frac{1+\cos\theta}{2},\ -\sin\frac{\theta}{2}\right) \qquad (7)$$

differentiating $\bar{T}$, yields

$$\frac{d\bar{T}}{d\theta} = \left(-\frac{\cos\theta}{2},\ -\frac{\sin\theta}{2},\ -\frac{1}{2}\cos\frac{\theta}{2}\right) \qquad (8)$$

From eqs.(5) and (8), obtain

$$\frac{d\overline{T}}{ds} = \frac{\frac{d\overline{T}}{d\Theta}}{\frac{ds}{d\Theta}} = \left(-\frac{\cos\Theta}{4}, \ -\frac{\sin\Theta}{4}, \ -\frac{1}{4}\cos\frac{\Theta}{2} \right) \qquad (9)$$

Now, from the Frenet formula

$$\frac{d\overline{T}}{ds} = k\overline{N}, \qquad (10)$$

take the magnitude of both sides and solve for k; doing this

$$\left| \frac{d\overline{T}}{ds} \right| = k \ |\overline{N}|$$

and

$$k = \left| \frac{d\overline{T}}{ds} \right| \qquad (11)$$

($\overline{N}$ is a unit vector).

Substituting eq.(9) into eq.(11) yields

$$k = \sqrt{\frac{\cos^2\Theta + \sin^2\Theta + \cos^2\frac{\Theta}{2}}{16}} = \frac{1}{4}\sqrt{1 + \cos^2\frac{\Theta}{2}} \qquad (12)$$

IDENTITIES INVOLVING CHARACTERISTIC VECTORS

Show that

$$\frac{\tau}{\rho^2} = \frac{d\overline{r}}{ds} \cdot \left[\frac{d^2\overline{r}}{ds^2} \times \frac{d^3\overline{r}}{ds^3} \right] \qquad (1)$$

Solution: To prove eq.(1), use the Frenet formulas. Vector $\overline{T}$ is defined as

$$\overline{T} = \frac{d\overline{r}}{ds} \qquad (2)$$

Differentiating eq.(2) and using the Frenet formula

$$\frac{d\overline{T}}{ds} = k\,\overline{N}, \text{ obtain}$$

$$\frac{d^2\overline{r}}{ds^2} = \frac{d\overline{T}}{ds} = k\,\overline{N} \qquad (3)$$

Differentiating eq.(3) and using the Frenet formula

$$\frac{d\overline{N}}{ds} = \tau\overline{B} - k\overline{T}, \quad \text{obtain}$$

$$\frac{d^3\overline{r}}{ds^3} = k\,\frac{d\overline{N}}{ds} + \frac{dk}{ds}\,\overline{N} = k(\tau\overline{B} - k\overline{T}) + \frac{dk}{ds}\,\overline{N} \qquad (4)$$

171

$$= k\tau\overline{B} - k^2\overline{T} + \frac{dk}{ds}\overline{N}$$

Substituting expressions (2), (3), (4) into

$$\frac{d\overline{r}}{ds} \cdot \frac{d^2\overline{r}}{ds^2} \times \frac{d^3\overline{r}}{ds^3}, \text{ obtain}$$

$$\frac{d\overline{r}}{ds} \cdot \frac{d^2\overline{r}}{ds^2} \times \frac{d^3\overline{r}}{ds^3} = \overline{T} \cdot k\overline{N} \times (k\tau\overline{B} - k^2\overline{T} + \frac{dk}{ds}\overline{N})$$

$$= \overline{T} \cdot (k^2\tau\overline{N}x\overline{B} - k^3\overline{N}x\overline{T} + k\frac{dk}{ds}\overline{N}x\overline{N}) \qquad (5)$$

$$= \overline{T} \cdot (k^2\tau\overline{T} + k^3\overline{B}) = k^2\tau = \frac{\tau}{\rho^2}$$

The definition of the vector $\overline{B}$ ($\overline{B} = \overline{T} \times \overline{N}$), was used in eq.(5).

● **PROBLEM 5-15**

A curve in space is given by

$$\overline{r} = \overline{r}(t) \qquad (1)$$

Show that if
$$|\dot{\overline{r}}(t)| \neq 0 \qquad (2)$$

then the curvature K is equal to

$$K = \frac{|\dot{\overline{r}}(t) \times \ddot{\overline{r}}(t)|}{|\dot{\overline{r}}(t)|^3} \qquad (3)$$

Solution: Express the first and second derivative of $\overline{r}(t)$ in terms of the unit tangent vector $\overline{T}$.

$$\dot{\overline{r}}(t) = \frac{d\overline{r}}{dt} = \frac{ds}{dt}\overline{T} \qquad (4)$$

where

$$\overline{T} = \frac{d\overline{r}}{ds}$$

$$\ddot{\overline{r}}(t) = \frac{d^2\overline{r}}{dt^2} = \frac{ds}{dt}\dot{\overline{T}} + \frac{d^2s}{dt^2}\overline{T} \qquad (5)$$

Thus
$$\dot{\overline{r}}(t) \times \ddot{\overline{r}}(t) = \frac{ds}{dt}\overline{T} \times \left[\frac{ds}{dt}\dot{\overline{T}} + \frac{d^2s}{dt^2}\overline{T}\right]$$

$$= \frac{ds}{dt}\frac{ds}{dt}\left(\overline{T} \times \dot{\overline{T}}\right) \qquad (6)$$

The second term,
$$\frac{ds}{dt}\frac{d^2s}{dt^2}\left(\overline{T} \times \overline{T}\right) \text{ is equal to } \overline{0}.$$

Therefore

$$\dot{\overline{T}}(t) = \frac{d\overline{T}}{dt} = \frac{ds}{dt}\frac{d\overline{T}}{ds} \qquad (7)$$

Substituting eq.(8) into eq.(7), gives

$$\dot{\bar{r}} \times \ddot{\bar{r}} = \left(\frac{ds}{dt}\right)^2 \bar{T} \times \dot{\bar{T}} = \left(\frac{ds}{dt}\right)^3 \bar{T} \times \frac{d\bar{T}}{ds}$$

$$= \left(\frac{ds}{dt}\right)^3 \bar{T} \times K\bar{N} \qquad (8)$$

In eq.(9) the Frenet formula

$$\frac{d\bar{T}}{ds} = K\bar{N} \quad \text{was used.}$$

The binormal vector $\bar{B}$ is defined as

$$\bar{B} = \bar{T} \times \bar{N} \qquad (9)$$

and $|\bar{B}| = 1$ since $\bar{T}$ and $\bar{N}$ are unit orthogonal vectors.

Eq.(9) can be written in the form

$$\dot{\bar{r}} \times \ddot{\bar{r}} = \left(\frac{ds}{dt}\right)^3 K\bar{B} \qquad (10)$$

Taking the magnitude of both sides of the equation,

$$|\dot{\bar{r}}(t) \times \ddot{\bar{r}}(t)| = \left|\left(\frac{ds}{dt}\right)^3 K\bar{B}\right| = \left|\left(\frac{ds}{dt}\right)^3\right| K \qquad (11)$$

and

$$K = \frac{|\dot{\bar{r}}(t) \times \ddot{\bar{r}}(t)|}{\left|\left(\frac{ds}{dt}\right)^3\right|}, \qquad (12)$$

Note that

$$\frac{ds}{dt} = |\dot{\bar{r}}(t)|, \text{ and} \qquad (13)$$

eq.(13) then becomes

$$K = \frac{|\dot{\bar{r}}(t) \times \ddot{\bar{r}}(t)|}{|\dot{\bar{r}}(t)|^3} \qquad (14)$$

● PROBLEM 5-16

A curve in space is given by

$$\bar{r} = \bar{r}(t) \qquad (1)$$

Show that the torsion of the curve is

$$\tau = \frac{\dot{\bar{r}} \cdot \ddot{\bar{r}} \times \dddot{\bar{r}}}{|\dot{\bar{r}} \times \ddot{\bar{r}}|^2} \qquad (2)$$

<u>Solution</u>: To prove eq.(2), use the results of Problem 5-14.

Notice that eq.(1) of Problem 5-14 and eq.(2) of this problem resemble each other.

Since $\bar{r} = \bar{r}(t)$, and

$$\dot{\bar{r}} = \frac{d\bar{r}}{ds} \cdot \frac{ds}{dt} \tag{3}$$

differentiating eq.(3) with respect to time, gives

$$\ddot{\bar{r}} = \frac{d}{dt}\left(\frac{d\bar{r}}{ds}\frac{ds}{dt}\right) = \frac{d\bar{r}}{ds}\frac{d^2s}{dt^2} + \left(\frac{ds}{dt}\right)^2\frac{d^2\bar{r}}{ds^2} \tag{4}$$

For the third derivative of $\bar{r}(t)$, from eq.(4), obtain

$$\dddot{\bar{r}} = \frac{d\bar{r}}{ds}\frac{d^3s}{dt^3} + \frac{d^2\bar{r}}{ds^2}\frac{d^2s}{dt^2}\frac{ds}{dt} + 2\frac{d^2\bar{r}}{ds^2}\frac{d^2s}{dt^2}\frac{ds}{dt} + \frac{d^3\bar{r}}{ds^3}\left(\frac{ds}{dt}\right)^3 \tag{5}$$

The next step is to find an expression for $\dot{\bar{r}}\cdot\ddot{\bar{r}} \times \dddot{\bar{r}}$.

Notice that it is not necessary to keep the parentheses around the $(\ddot{\bar{r}} \times \dddot{\bar{r}})$ term; indeed, it is understood that the expression $\dot{\bar{r}}\cdot\ddot{\bar{r}} \times \dddot{\bar{r}}$ refers to the dot-product of vector $\dot{\bar{r}}$ and vector $(\ddot{\bar{r}} \times \dddot{\bar{r}})$; not the dot-product $(\dot{\bar{r}}\cdot\ddot{\bar{r}})$ crossed with $\dddot{\bar{r}}$ (the expression $(\dot{\bar{r}}\cdot\ddot{\bar{r}}) \times \dddot{\bar{r}}$ does not make sense, since the cross-product is defined for two vectors only, and $\dot{\bar{r}}\cdot\ddot{\bar{r}}$ is a scalar).

   Now, proceed with the problem by substituting eqs.(3), (4) and (5) to obtain

$$\dot{\bar{r}}\cdot\ddot{\bar{r}} \times \dddot{\bar{r}} = \left(\frac{ds}{dt}\right)^6 \frac{d\bar{r}}{ds} \cdot \frac{d^2\bar{r}}{ds^2} \times \frac{d^3\bar{r}}{ds^3} \tag{6}$$

Substituting eq.(1) of Problem 5-14 into eq.(6), we obtain

$$\dot{\bar{r}}\cdot\ddot{\bar{r}} \times \dddot{\bar{r}} = \left(\frac{ds}{dt}\right)^6 \frac{d\bar{r}}{ds}\cdot\frac{d^2\bar{r}}{ds^2} \times \frac{d^3\bar{r}}{ds^3} = \frac{\tau}{\rho^2}\left(\frac{ds}{dt}\right)^6 \tag{7}$$

and

$$\frac{ds}{dt} = \left|\frac{d\bar{r}}{dt}\right| = |\dot{\bar{r}}| \tag{8}$$

We obtain, from eqs.(7) and (8),

$$\tau = \frac{\dot{\bar{r}}\cdot\ddot{\bar{r}} \times \dddot{\bar{r}}}{|\dot{\bar{r}}|^6}\rho^2 = \frac{\dot{\bar{r}}\cdot\ddot{\bar{r}} \times \dddot{\bar{r}}}{|\dot{\bar{r}}|^6 K^2} \tag{9}$$

since $\rho = \dfrac{1}{K}$

From Problem 5-15,

$$K = \frac{|\dot{\bar{r}} \times \ddot{\bar{r}}|}{|\dot{\bar{r}}|^3} \tag{10}$$

Substituting eq.(10) into eq.(9), gives

174

$$\tau = \frac{\dot{\overline{r}} \cdot \ddot{\overline{r}} \times \dddot{\overline{r}} \; |\dot{\overline{r}}|^6}{|\dot{\overline{r}}|^6 |\dot{\overline{r}} \times \ddot{\overline{r}}|^2} = \frac{\dot{\overline{r}} \cdot \ddot{\overline{r}} \times \dddot{\overline{r}}}{|\dot{\overline{r}} \times \ddot{\overline{r}}|^2} \qquad (11)$$

A curve is given in the parametric form

$$x = \frac{2t-1}{t+1}, \quad y = \frac{t^2}{t+1}, \quad z = t+2 \qquad (1)$$

Find the torsion of the curve.

Solution: Since the curve is given in the form $\overline{r} = \overline{r}(t)$ use the results of Problem 5-16 to compute the torsion of the curve. Thus for τ,

$$\tau = \frac{\dot{\overline{r}} \cdot (\ddot{\overline{r}} \times \dddot{\overline{r}})}{|\dot{\overline{r}} \times \ddot{\overline{r}}|^2} \qquad (2)$$

From eq.(1) the position vector of any point on the curve is

$$\overline{r}(t) = \left(\frac{2t-1}{t+1}, \frac{t^2}{t+1}, t+2 \right) \qquad (3)$$

and

$$\dot{\overline{r}}(t) = \frac{d\overline{r}}{dt}, \; \ddot{\overline{r}}(t) = \frac{d^2\overline{r}}{dt^2}, \text{ etc.} \qquad (4)$$

Taking the time derivative of eq.(3),obtain

$$\dot{\overline{r}}(t) = \left(\frac{3}{(t+1)^2}, \frac{t^2+2t}{(t+1)^2}, 1 \right) \qquad (5)$$

Differentiating again, gives

$$\ddot{\overline{r}}(t) = \left(\frac{-6}{(t+1)^3}, \frac{2}{(t+1)^3}, 0 \right) \qquad (6)$$

To find $\dddot{\overline{r}}$ differentiate eq.(6) and obtain

$$\dddot{\overline{r}}(t) = \left(\frac{18}{(t+1)^4}, \frac{-6}{(t+1)^4}, 0 \right) \qquad (7)$$

The next step is to substitute the proper derivatives in eq.(2) to find τ.

First, find $\ddot{\overline{r}} \times \dddot{\overline{r}}$

Substituting eq.(6) and eq.(7) gives

$$\ddot{\overline{r}} \times \dddot{\overline{r}} = \left(0, \; 0, \; \frac{-6}{(t+1)^3} \cdot \frac{-6}{(t+1)^4} - \frac{2}{(t+1)^3} \cdot \frac{18}{(t+1)^4} \right)$$

$$= (0, 0, 0) \qquad (8)$$

Thus from eq.(8), one concludes that $\tau = 0$.

Recall from problem 5-11 that the torsion τ is equal to zero for a plane curve. Thus this problem could be solved by proving that the curve which has the parametric form of eq.(1) is a plane curve. To prove this, begin with the general equation of a plane and solve for the coefficients A, B, C, and D.

$$Ax + By + Cz - D = 0 \qquad (9a)$$

If the coefficients A, B, C are real and not equal to zero, then the parametric equations given by eq.(1) form a plane. If any of the coefficients A, B, or C equal zero, then eq.(1) does not describe a plane and the torsion τ would not equal zero.

Since there are four unknowns (A, B, C, D), four equations must be formed that contain these unknowns. To find these 4 equations, find the intersection of the plane with each of the coordinate planes (yz plane, xz plane, xy plane). For the yz plane, the x coordinate is equal to zero. For the xz and xy planes, y = 0 and z = 0 respectively. Therefore, for these three intersections one obtains the following equations from eq.(9a).

$$yB + zC - D = 0 \qquad \text{for } x=0 \qquad (9b)$$

$$xA + zC - D = 0 \qquad \text{for } y=0 \qquad (9c)$$

$$xA + yB - D = 0 \qquad \text{for } z=0 \qquad (9d)$$

(Note that the values of x, y, z can be determined for each eq.) If one considers the line y = z, then equation (9a) becomes

$$xA + yB + Cy - D = 0 \quad \text{or} \qquad (9e)$$

$$xA + y(B+C) - D = 0 \quad \text{which gives us our fourth}$$

equation.

To evaluate the x, y, z values for each of the four equations, proceed as follows:

For eq.(9b), x = 0, since $x = \frac{2t-1}{t+1}$, t must equal $\frac{1}{2}$. Since

$t = \frac{1}{2}$, $z = \frac{5}{2}$ and $y = \frac{1}{6}$ (because z=t+2 and $y = \frac{t^2}{t+1}$).

For eq.(9c), y = 0, since $y = \frac{t^2}{t+1}$, then t = 0. At t = 0, z=2, and x = -1 (because z=t+2 and $x = \frac{2t-1}{t+1}$).

For eq.(9d), z = 0, therefore t = -2 (because z=t+2) and

$y = -4$ ($y = \frac{t^2}{t+1}$) and x = 5 ($x = \frac{2t-1}{t+1}$)

For eq. (9e), y = z, or $\frac{t^2}{t+1} = t+2$ or 3t+2 = 0 and $t = \frac{-2}{3}$.

For $t = \frac{-2}{3}$, x = -7, $z = \frac{4}{3}$ and $y = \frac{4}{3}$.

Substituting these values of x, y, and z into equations (9a),

(9b), (9c) and (9d) respectively, obtain

$$\frac{1}{6} B + \frac{5}{2} C - D = 0$$

$$-A + 2C - D = 0$$

$$5A - 4B - D = 0$$

$$-7A + \frac{4}{3}(B+C) - D = 0$$

Solving this system of four equations, one obtains

$$A = 1 \quad B = 3 \quad C = -3 \quad D = -7$$

Therefore eq.(1) is a curve that lies on the plane

$$x + 3y - 3z = -7$$

and the torsion is thus zero.

POSITION VECTOR, VELOCITY, ANGULAR VELOCITY AND ACCELERATION

● **PROBLEM** 5-18

The position vector of a point P is given by

$$\overline{u} = (A+\alpha t, \ B+\beta t, \ C+\gamma t) \tag{1}$$

where t is the time and A, B, C, α, β, γ are constants. Find the trajectory of point P as well as its velocity vector and its speed.

<u>Solution</u>:. From eq.(1), we conclude that point P travels according to the equations

$$x_1 = A + \alpha t$$

$$x_2 = B + \beta t \tag{2}$$

$$x_3 = C + \gamma t$$

Eqs.(2) are parametric equations of a straight line in space through the point (A, B, C) and with direction numbers α, β, γ.

The trajectory of the point P is thus a straight line.

The velocity of a point is defined as the first derivative of the position vector with respect to time

$$\overline{V} = \frac{d\overline{u}}{dt} \tag{3}$$

From eq.(1), obtain

$$\overline{V} = \frac{d\overline{u}}{dt} = (\alpha, \beta, \gamma) \tag{4}$$

The speed of the point is defined as the magnitude of its velocity vector.

$$v = |\overline{V}| = \frac{ds}{dt} \tag{5}$$

Substituting eq.(4) into eq.(5), obtain

$$v = |\overline{V}| = \sqrt{\alpha^2 + \beta^2 + \gamma^2} \tag{6}$$

Next investigate the special case where the velocity vector is a unit vector, $|\overline{V}| = 1$. From eq.(6),

$$v = |\overline{V}| = \sqrt{\alpha^2 + \beta^2 + \gamma^2} = 1 \tag{7}$$

where α, β, γ are direction cosines, due to the condition

$$\sqrt{\alpha^2 + \beta^2 + \gamma^2} = 1 \tag{8}$$

Let s be the distance traversed by the point from time t_o to time t. Then (see Problem 4-17)

$$\frac{ds}{dt} = \sqrt{\left(\frac{dx_1}{dt}\right)^2 + \left(\frac{dx_2}{dt}\right)^2 + \left(\frac{dx_3}{dt}\right)^2}$$

and $\tag{9}$

$$v = |\overline{V}| = \frac{ds}{dt}$$

For $|\overline{V}| = 1$ eq.(9) gives $\frac{ds}{dt} = 1$ $\tag{10}$

and both parameters can be identified within the accuracy of an additive constant f, thus

$$s = t + f \tag{11}$$

If s is measured from the position t = 0 and in the direction of increasing t, then

$$s = t \tag{12}$$

Eqs.(2) then become

$$x_1 = A + \alpha s$$

$$x_2 = B + \beta s \tag{13}$$

$$x_3 = C + \gamma s$$

which are the parametric equations of the straight line in terms of the parameter s.

● **PROBLEM** 5-19

A particle moves according to the equations

$$x = \sin 2t$$

178

$$y = \cos 2t \tag{1}$$

$$z = e^{-t}$$

where t is time.

1) Determine the velocity of the particle.

2) Determine the acceleration of the particle.

3) Find the magnitude of the velocity and acceleration at t = 0.

Solution: Eqs.(1) are parametric equations of the curve along which this particle travels. The position vector $\bar{r}$ of the particle is

$$\bar{r} = \bar{r}(t) = (\sin 2t, \cos 2t, e^{-t}) \tag{2}$$

1) The velocity vector is

$$\bar{v} = \frac{d\bar{r}}{dt} \tag{3}$$

Substituting $\bar{r}(t)$ from eq.(2) into eq.(3), obtain

$$\bar{v} = \frac{d\bar{r}}{dt} = (2\cos 2t, -2\sin 2t, -e^{-t}) \tag{4}$$

2) The acceleration of the particle is given by

$$\bar{a} = \frac{d^2\bar{r}}{dt^2} = \frac{d\bar{v}}{dt} \tag{5}$$

Again, substituting eq.(4) into eq.(5), gives

$$\bar{a} = \frac{d\bar{v}}{dt} = (-4\sin 2t, -4\cos 2t, e^{-t}) \tag{6}$$

Eq.(6) gives the acceleration of the particle as a function of time.

3) From eq.(4), at t = 0 the velocity is

$$\bar{v}\Big|_{t=0} = (2, 0, -1) \tag{7}$$

and its magnitude

$$\left|\bar{v}\Big|_{t=0}\right| = \sqrt{4+1} = \sqrt{5} \tag{8}$$

Note that eq.(8) gives the speed of the particle at t = 0.

Next compute the acceleration of the particle at t = 0 from eq.(6)

$$\bar{a}\Big|_{t=0} = (0, -4, 1) \tag{9}$$

The magnitude of $\bar{a}$ at t = 0 is

$$\left. \left| \bar{a} \right| \right|_{t=0} = \sqrt{16+1} = \sqrt{17} \tag{10}$$

A particle moves along a curve whose parametric equations are

$$x_1 = 2 \sin 2t$$

$$x_2 = \cos t \tag{1}$$

$$x_3 = e^t$$

1) Find the velocity and acceleration vector of the particle.

2) Compute the magnitude of the velocity and acceleration at t = 0.

<u>Solution</u>: 1) The position vector of the particle is given by

$$\bar{r}(t) = (2 \sin 2t, \cos t, e^t) \tag{2}$$

Then the velocity vector is

$$\bar{v} = \frac{d\bar{r}}{dt} = \left(\frac{d}{dt}(2\sin 2t), \frac{d}{dt}(\cos t), \frac{d}{dt}(e^t) \right)$$

$$= (4 \cos 2t, -\sin t, e^t) \tag{3}$$

The acceleration vector of a particle is defined as

$$\bar{a} = \frac{d\bar{v}}{dt} = \frac{d^2\bar{r}}{dt^2} \tag{4}$$

Then,

$$\bar{a} = \frac{d}{dt} (4 \cos 2t, -\sin t, e^t)$$

$$= (-8 \sin 2t, -\cos t, e^t) \tag{5}$$

2) The magnitude of the velocity vector at t = 0 is given by

$$|\bar{v}| = \sqrt{(4\cos 0)^2+(\sin 0)^2+(e^0)^2} = \sqrt{16+1} = \sqrt{17} \tag{6}$$

and the magnitude of the acceleration vector at t = 0 is

$$|\bar{a}| = \sqrt{1 + 1} = \sqrt{2} \tag{7}$$

A particle moves along the curve

$$\bar{r}(t) = (2t, t^2+1, t-1) \tag{1}$$

Find the components of the velocity and acceleration vectors in the direction of $\bar{b}$, where

$$\bar{b} = (1, -2, -2) \tag{2}$$

Solution: The velocity vector of the particle is given by

$$\bar{v} = \frac{d\bar{r}}{dt} = \frac{d}{dt} (2t, \ t^2+1, \ t-1)$$
$$= (2, \ 2t, \ 1) \tag{3}$$

The unit vector in the direction of $\bar{b}$ is

$$\frac{\bar{b}}{|\bar{b}|} = \frac{(1,-2,-2)}{\sqrt{1+4+4}} = \frac{1}{\sqrt{9}} (1,-2,-2) = \left(\frac{1}{3}, \ \frac{-2}{3}, \ \frac{-2}{3}\right) \tag{4}$$

To find the components of the velocity $\bar{v}$ in the direction $\bar{b} = (1,-2,-2)$, scalar multiply vector $\bar{v}$ and the unit vector in the direction of $\bar{b}$. From eq.(3) and eq.(4),

$$\bar{v} \cdot \frac{\bar{b}}{|\bar{b}|} = (2,2t,1) \cdot \left(\frac{1}{3}, \frac{-2}{3}, \frac{-2}{3}\right) = \frac{2}{3} - \frac{4t}{3} - \frac{2}{3} \tag{5}$$
$$= -\frac{4}{3} t$$

This component is a function of time. The acceleration of the particle is given by

$$\bar{a} = \frac{d\bar{v}}{dt} \ . \tag{6}$$

Thus

$$\bar{a} = \frac{d}{dt} (2, \ 2t, \ 1) = (0, \ 2, \ 0) \tag{7}$$

Since the acceleration is not a function of time, the particle moves with constant acceleration.

The component of the acceleration in the given direction is

$$\frac{d\bar{v}}{dt} \cdot \frac{\bar{b}}{|\bar{b}|} = (0,2,0) \cdot \left(\frac{1}{3}, \ -\frac{2}{3}, \ -\frac{2}{3}\right) = -\frac{4}{3} \tag{8}$$

● **PROBLEM** 5-22

The position vector of a point is given by

$$r(t) = (r \cos\omega t, \ r \sin\omega t) \tag{1}$$

where $\omega \geq 0$.

Find the trajectory of the point, its angular velocity, the velocity vector, and the speed.

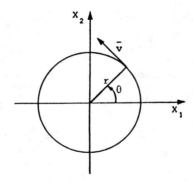

Solution: Since the coordinates of the point contain $\cos\omega t$ and $\sin\omega t$ in the linear form, that is

$$x_1 = r\cos\omega t$$

$$x_2 = r\sin\omega t, \tag{2}$$

the trajectory is a circle. To verify it, compute $x_1^2 + x_2^2$, thus

$$x_1^2 + x_2^2 = r^2\cos^2\omega t + r^2\sin^2\omega t = r^2 \tag{3}$$

Therefore the trajectory is a circle with the center at 0 and radius r. At any time t, the polar angle θ is

$$\theta = \omega t \tag{4}$$

as shown in the figure.

The angular velocity is given by

$$\frac{d\theta}{dt} = \omega \tag{5}$$

The velocity vector is defined as

$$\bar{v} = \frac{d\bar{r}}{dt} = \left(\frac{dx_1}{dt}, \frac{dx_2}{dt}\right) \tag{6}$$

Substituting eq.(1) into eq.(6), obtain

$$\bar{v} = \frac{d\bar{r}}{dt} = (-r\omega\sin\omega t, r\omega\cos\omega t) \tag{7}$$

Note that $\bar{v}$ is perpendicular to $\bar{r}$. Indeed, from eqs.(1) and (7),

$$\bar{v}\cdot\bar{r} = (-r\omega\sin\omega t, r\omega\cos\omega t)\cdot(r\cos\omega t, r\sin\omega t)$$

$$= -r^2\omega\sin\omega t\cos\omega t + r^2\omega\sin\omega t\cos\omega t = 0 \tag{8}$$

The speed of the point is then given by

$$v = |\bar{v}| = \sqrt{r^2\omega^2\sin^2\omega t + r^2\omega^2\cos^2\omega t} = r\omega \tag{9}$$

Point P moves in the xy plane and has polar coordinates
(r, θ). Find the components of the velocity vector $\bar{v}$ along
the r direction and along the θ direction. Find the speed
of the point P.

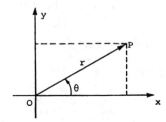

FIG. 1

Solution: Point P is moving in the xy plane. Its polar
coordinates (r, θ) are functions of time

$$r = r(t)$$
$$\theta = \theta(t)$$
$\qquad (1)$

Let $\overline{OP}$ be the position vector of the point P, as shown in
Fig. 1. Then,

$$\overline{OP} = (r \cos\theta, \ r \sin\theta) \qquad (2)$$

or, in terms of the base vectors,

$$\overline{OP} = r \cos\theta \bar{i} + r \sin\theta \bar{j} \qquad (3)$$

Let $\bar{k}$ be a unit vector such that

$$\bar{k} = \cos\theta \bar{i} + \sin\theta \bar{j} \qquad (4)$$

Eq.(3) can be written in the form

$$\overline{OP} = r(\cos\theta \bar{i} + \sin\theta \bar{j}) = r\bar{k} \qquad (5)$$

Substituting eq.(5) into the definition of the velocity vector,
obtain

$$\bar{v} = \frac{d}{dt} \overline{OP} = \frac{d}{dt} (r\bar{k}) = r \frac{d\bar{k}}{dt} + \frac{dr}{dt} \bar{k} \qquad (6)$$

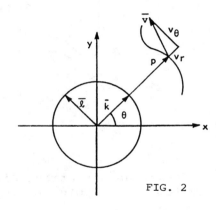

FIG. 2

183

Vector $\overline{k}$ has the same direction as $\overline{OP}$, (see Fig. 2) and

$$\frac{d\overline{k}}{dt} = \frac{d}{dt} (\cos\theta\overline{i} + \sin\theta\overline{j}) = -\sin\theta \frac{d\theta}{dt} \overline{i} + \cos\theta \frac{d\theta}{dt} \overline{j}$$

$$= \frac{d\theta}{dt} (-\sin\theta\overline{i} + \cos\theta\overline{j}) \qquad (7)$$

Note that $\frac{d\overline{k}}{dt}$ is perpendicular to $\overline{OP}$.

Denote
$$\overline{\ell} = -\sin\theta\overline{i} + \cos\theta\overline{j} \qquad (8)$$

Eq.(6) can be written in the form

$$\overline{v} = r \frac{d\overline{k}}{dt} + \frac{dr}{dt} \overline{k} = \frac{dr}{dt} \overline{k} + r \frac{d\theta}{dt} \overline{\ell} \qquad (9)$$

Then denote
$$v_r = \frac{dr}{dt} \qquad v_\theta = \frac{d\theta}{dt} r \qquad (10)$$

Eq.(9) can be written in the form

$$\overline{v} = v_r \overline{k} + v_\theta \overline{\ell} \qquad (11)$$

The speed of point P is given by

$$v = \sqrt{v_r^2 + v_\theta^2} = \sqrt{\left(\frac{dr}{dt}\right)^2 + r^2\left(\frac{d\theta}{dt}\right)^2} \qquad (12)$$

● **PROBLEM 5-24**

Find the components of the velocity and acceleration in
the directions of the parametric lines of the cylindrical
coordinates, r, θ, z.

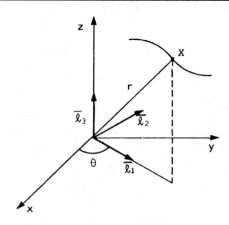

Solution: Note that the directions of the parametric lines of
a coordinate system at any point X are those directions in

184

which one of the coordinates increases and the other two coordinates remain constant.

The cylindrical coordinates of a point X are r, θ, z, as shown in the figure. The base vectors of the coordinate system xyz are $\bar{i}$, $\bar{j}$, $\bar{k}$.

Let $\bar{l}_1$, $\bar{l}_2$, $\bar{l}_3$ be unit vectors at O such that $\bar{l}_1$ points toward the projection of X on the xy plane, $\bar{l}_3$ is equal to $\bar{k}$ and $\bar{l}_2$ is such that the triad $\bar{l}_1$, $\bar{l}_2$, $\bar{l}_3$ point in the directions of the parametric lines of the cylindrical coordinates r, θ, z of X.

The vectors $\bar{l}_1$, $\bar{l}_2$, $\bar{l}_3$ and $\bar{i}$, $\bar{j}$, $\bar{k}$ are related by

$$\bar{l}_1 = \bar{i} \cos\theta + \bar{j} \sin\theta$$

$$\bar{l}_2 = -\bar{i} \sin\theta + \bar{j} \cos\theta \tag{1}$$

$$\bar{l}_3 = \bar{k}$$

Differentiating eq.(1) with respect to t, gives

$$\frac{d\bar{l}_1}{dt} = \frac{d\bar{l}_1}{d\theta}\frac{d\theta}{dt} = (-\bar{i}\sin\theta + \bar{j}\cos\theta)\dot{\theta} = \bar{l}_2\,\dot{\theta}$$

$$\frac{d\bar{l}_2}{dt} = \frac{d\bar{l}_2}{d\theta}\frac{d\theta}{dt} = (-\bar{i}\cos\theta - \bar{j}\sin\theta)\dot{\theta} = -\bar{l}_1\dot{\theta} \tag{2}$$

$$\frac{d\bar{l}_3}{dt} = \bar{0}$$

Where

$$\frac{d\theta}{dt} = \dot{\theta}$$

From the figure it follows that the position vector $\bar{r}$ of the particle is

$$\bar{r} = r\bar{l}_1 + z\bar{k} \tag{3}$$

Thus

$$\bar{v} = \frac{d\bar{r}}{dt} = \dot{r}\bar{l}_1 + r\frac{d\bar{l}_1}{dt} + \dot{z}\bar{k} + z\dot{\bar{k}} \tag{4}$$

Applying eq.(2) to eq.(4), results in

$$\bar{v} = \dot{r}\bar{l}_1 + r\dot{\theta}\bar{l}_2 + \dot{z}\bar{l}_3 \tag{5}$$

The components of $\bar{v}$ are

$$\bar{v} = (\dot{r}, r\dot{\theta}, \dot{z}) \tag{6}$$

To obtain the acceleration of the particle differentiate eq.(5) thus

$$\bar{a} = \frac{d\bar{v}}{dt} = \ddot{r}\bar{l}_1 + (\dot{r}\dot{\theta}+r\ddot{\theta})\bar{l}_2 + \ddot{z}\bar{l}_3 + \dot{r}\frac{d\bar{l}_1}{dt} + r\dot{\theta}\frac{d\bar{l}_2}{dt} + \dot{z}\frac{d\bar{l}_3}{dt} \tag{7}$$

185

Substituting eq.(2) into eq.(7),

$$\bar{a} = (\ddot{r} - r\dot{\theta}^2)\bar{I}_1 + (2\dot{r}\dot{\theta}+r\ddot{\theta})\bar{I}_2 + \ddot{z}\bar{I}_3 \qquad (8)$$

The components of $\bar{a}$ are

$$\bar{a} = (\ddot{r} - r\dot{\theta}^2, \; 2\dot{r}\dot{\theta} + r\ddot{\theta}, \; \ddot{z}) \qquad (9)$$

● **PROBLEM 5-25**

Point P is moving in the xy plane according to the equations

$$x = 4 - 3t$$
$$y = 2 + 3t \qquad (1)$$

Find the r and θ velocity components v_r, v_θ.
Draw the trajectory and verify graphically the decomposition obtained for t = 0.

<u>Solution</u>: The radius r is given by

$$r = \sqrt{x^2+y^2} \qquad (2)$$

Substituting eq.(1) into eq.(2),

$$r = \sqrt{(4-3t)^2+(2+3t)^2} = \sqrt{18t^2-12t+20} \qquad (3)$$

The components v_r and v_θ are defined as

$$v_r = \frac{dr}{dt} \qquad (4)$$

and $\qquad v_\theta = r\frac{d\theta}{dt} \qquad (5)$

Substituting eq.(3) into eq.(4), obtain

$$v_r = \frac{d}{dt}(\sqrt{18t^2-12t+20}) = \frac{36t-12}{2\sqrt{18t^2-12t+20}} \qquad (6)$$

$$= \frac{18t-6}{\sqrt{18t^2-12t+20}}$$

To find v_θ, notice that

$$\tan\theta = \frac{y}{x} \qquad (7)$$

or $\qquad \theta = \arctan\frac{y}{x} \qquad (8)$

Substituting eq.(8) into eq.(5), gives

$$v_\theta = r\frac{d}{dt}\left(\arctan\frac{y}{x}\right) = r\cdot\frac{1}{1+\left(\frac{y}{x}\right)^2}\frac{d}{dt}\left(\frac{y}{x}\right)$$

$$= \frac{r}{1+\left(\frac{y}{x}\right)^2} \quad \left[-yx^{-2}\frac{dx}{dt} + \frac{\frac{dy}{dt}}{x} \right] \qquad (9)$$

where from eq.(1)

$$\frac{dx}{dt} = -3 \quad \text{and} \quad \frac{dy}{dt} = 3$$

then, noting that $r = x^2+y^2$, it follows that

$$v_\theta = \frac{x^2}{\sqrt{x^2+y^2}} \left[\frac{-y(-3)}{x^2} + \frac{3x}{x^2} \right]$$

$$= \frac{x^2}{\sqrt{x^2+y^2}} \cdot \frac{3(4-3t)+3(2+3t)}{x^2} = \frac{1}{\sqrt{x^2+y^2}} \cdot (12-9t+6+9t)$$

$$= \frac{18}{\sqrt{18t^2-12t+20}}$$

The trajectory of the point is shown in the figure.

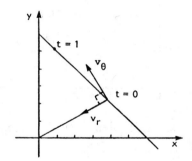

The velocity vector is

$$\bar{v} = \left(\frac{dx}{dt}, \frac{dy}{dt} \right) = (-3,\ 3) \qquad (10)$$

For $t = 0$, eq.(6) becomes

$$v_r \Big|_{t=0} = \frac{-6}{\sqrt{20}} \qquad (11)$$

and

$$v_\theta \Big|_{t=0} = \frac{18}{\sqrt{20}} \qquad (12)$$

Also

$$v = |\bar{v}| = \sqrt{9+9} = \sqrt{18} \qquad (13)$$

is equal to

$$\sqrt{v_r^2 + v_\theta^2} = \sqrt{\frac{18^2}{20} + \frac{6^2}{20}} = \sqrt{18} \qquad (14)$$

and thus

$$v = |\bar{v}| = \sqrt{v_r^2 + v_\theta^2} \qquad (15)$$

187

TANGENTIAL AND NORMAL COMPONENTS OF ACCELERATION

A particle moves along a curve in the xy plane with velocity $\bar{v}$. Show that the acceleration of the particle is given by

$$\bar{a} = \frac{dv}{dt}\bar{T} + \frac{v^2}{\rho}\bar{N} \qquad (1)$$

where $\bar{T}$ is the unit tangent vector to the space curve, $\bar{N}$ the unit normal vector, ρ the radius of curvature, and $v = |\bar{v}|$.

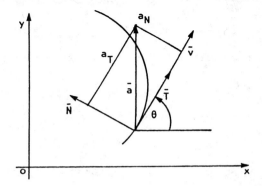

Solution: Define a unit tangent vector in the direction of motion as

$$T = \frac{\bar{v}}{v} \qquad (2)$$

$\bar{T}$ can be written as

$$\bar{T} = \cos\theta\bar{i} + \sin\theta\bar{j} \qquad (3)$$

as shown in the figure.

Then

$$\frac{d\bar{v}}{dt} = \frac{d}{dt}(v\bar{T}) = v\frac{d\bar{T}}{dt} + \frac{dv}{dt}\bar{T} \qquad (4)$$

Differentiating eq.(3), gives

$$\frac{d\bar{T}}{dt} = \frac{d\theta}{dt}(-\sin\theta\bar{i} + \cos\theta\bar{j}) = \bar{n} \qquad (5)$$

Vector $\bar{n}$ is perpendicular to $\bar{T}$ and has magnitude $\left|\frac{d\theta}{dt}\right|$

Vector $\bar{n}$ can be expressed as

$$\bar{n} = \left|\frac{d\theta}{dt}\right|\bar{N} \qquad (6)$$

188

where $\overline{N}$ is a unit normal vector.

If $\theta = \theta(s)$, then

$$\left|\frac{d\theta}{dt}\right| = \left|\frac{d\theta}{ds}\right| \frac{ds}{dt} = \frac{1}{\rho} v \tag{7}$$

where $\qquad \rho = \left|\frac{ds}{d\theta}\right| \quad$ is the radius of curvature of the path.

Eq.(6) can be written in the form

$$\overline{n} = \frac{v}{\rho} \overline{N} \tag{8}$$

Combining eq.(8), eq.(4) and (5), results in

$$\overline{a} = \frac{d\overline{v}}{dt} = \frac{v^2}{\rho} \overline{N} + \frac{dv}{dt} \overline{T} \tag{9}$$

Thus vector $\overline{a}$ is represented in its normal and tangential components.

● **PROBLEM 5-27**

A point is moving according to the equations

$$x = r \cos\omega t$$
$$y = r \sin\omega t \tag{1}$$

Find the tangential and normal components of acceleration.

Solution: The acceleration $\overline{a}$ of a point can be expressed by its normal and tangential components as:

$$\overline{a} = \frac{v^2}{\rho} \overline{N} + \frac{dv}{dt} \overline{T} \tag{2}$$

The velocity vector of the point is

$$\overline{v} = \left(\frac{dx}{dt}, \frac{dy}{dt}\right) = (-r\omega \sin\omega t, r\omega \cos\omega t) \tag{3}$$

its magnitude is

$$v = |\overline{v}| = \sqrt{r^2\omega^2\sin^2\omega t + r^2\omega^2\cos^2\omega t} = r\omega \tag{4}$$

Since r and ω are constant,

$$\frac{dv}{dt} = \frac{d}{dt}(r\omega) = 0 \tag{5}$$

The tangential component is equal to 0.

$$a_T = 0 \tag{6}$$

The normal component is

$$a_N = \frac{v^2}{\rho} \qquad (7)$$

where

$$\rho = \left|\frac{ds}{d\theta}\right| = r \qquad (8)$$

Substituting eq.(4), and eq.(8) into eq.(7), gives

$$a_N = \frac{r^2\omega^2}{r} = r\omega^2$$

● **PROBLEM** 5-28

A particle rotates around the unit circle according to the equation

$$x = \cos(e^t)$$
$$y = \sin(e^t) \qquad (1)$$

Find the normal acceleration and the tangential acceleration of the particle.

Solution: The position vector of the particle is

$$\overline{r} = \cos(e^t)\overline{i} + \sin(e^t)\overline{j} \qquad (2)$$

The velocity is

$$\overline{v} = \frac{d\overline{r}}{dt} = -e^t\sin(e^t)\overline{i} + e^t\cos(e^t)\overline{j} \qquad (3)$$

Differentiating eq.(3) with respect to time, the acceleration of the particle is then

$$\frac{d^2r}{dt^2} = \overline{a} = e^t\left[-\sin(e^t)\overline{i} + \cos(e^t)\overline{j}\right] - e^{2t}\left[\cos(e^t)\overline{i} + \sin(e^t)\overline{j}\right] \quad (4)$$

The tangential component of the acceleration is given by $e^t \overline{T}$ where

$$\overline{T} = -\sin(e^t)\overline{i} + \cos(e^t)\overline{j} \ ; \ |\overline{T}| = 1 \qquad (5)$$

and the normal component is

$$e^{2t} \overline{N}$$

where

$$\overline{N} = -\cos(e^t)\overline{i} - \sin(e^t)\overline{j} \qquad (6)$$

is the unit normal vector.

Therefore,

$$\overline{a} = e^t \overline{T} + e^{2t} \overline{N} \qquad (7)$$

and

$$\frac{ds}{dt} = \left|\frac{d\overline{r}}{dt}\right| = \sqrt{(e^t)^2\sin^2(e^t) + (e^t)^2\cos^2(e^t)} = \sqrt{e^{2t}} = e^t \quad (8)$$

Thus
$$s = e^t \tag{9}$$

and the curvature of the unit circle is 1.

A particle moves according to the equations

$$x = t - 1$$
$$y = 2t - t^2 \tag{1}$$

Find the acceleration of the particle, its speed, the curvature of the path of motion and the tangential and normal components a_T and a_N.

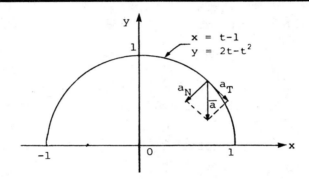

Solution: From eq.(1) solve for y in terms of x.

Since $x = t - 1$,   then $t = x + 1$

substituting x+1 for t in equation (1), obtain

$$y = 2(x+1) - (x+1)^2 = 1 - x^2$$

therefore, the particle moves along the parabola

$$y = 1 - x^2 \tag{2}$$

The position vector of the particle is

$$\bar{r} = (t-1)\bar{i} + (2t-t^2)\bar{j} \tag{3}$$

The velocity is given by

$$\frac{d\bar{r}}{dt} = \bar{i} + 2(1-t)\bar{j} \tag{4}$$

Differentiating eq.(4), the acceleration of the particle is then

$$\frac{d^2\bar{r}}{dt^2} = 0\bar{i} - 2\bar{j} \tag{5}$$

191

The particle has a downward vertical acceleration of constant magnitude. The speed is given by

$$\left|\frac{d\overline{r}}{dt}\right| = \sqrt{1 + 4(1-t)^2} = \frac{ds}{dt} \tag{6}$$

The trajectory of the particle is shown in the figure. The tangent vector to the path of the particle is

$$\overline{T} = \left(\sqrt{1+4(1-t)^2}\right)^{-1}\left[\overline{i} + 2(1-t)\overline{j}\right]$$

$$= \frac{\overline{i}+2(1-t)j}{\sqrt{1 + 4(1-t)^2}} \tag{7}$$

Differentiating with respect to time, gives

$$\frac{d\overline{T}}{dt} = \frac{2}{[1+4(1-t)^2]^{3/2}}\left[2(1-t)\overline{i} - \overline{j}\right] \tag{8}$$

The normal vector to the path is

$$\overline{N} = \frac{1}{\sqrt{1+4(1-t)^2}}\left[2(1-t)\overline{i} - \overline{j}\right] \tag{9}$$

Also,

$$\frac{d\overline{T}}{ds} = \frac{\dfrac{d\overline{T}}{dt}}{\dfrac{ds}{dt}} = \frac{2}{[1+4(1-t)^2]^2}\left[2(1-t)\overline{i} - \overline{j}\right] \tag{10}$$

$$= \frac{2}{[1+4(1-t)^2]^{\frac{3}{2}}}\,\overline{N}$$

Thus the curvature of the trajectory of the particle is

$$k = \frac{2}{[1 + 4(1-t)^2]^{3/2}} \tag{11}$$

and

$$a_T = \frac{d^2s}{dt^2} = -\frac{4(1-t)}{\sqrt{1+4(1-t)^2}} \tag{12}$$

$$a_N = \left(\frac{ds}{dt}\right)^2 k = \frac{2}{\sqrt{1 + 4(1-t)^2}}$$

● **PROBLEM 5-30**

Point P moves in the xy plane with velocity $\overline{v}$ and acceleration $\overline{a}$. Show that

$$1)\ \left|\overline{v} \times \overline{a}\right| = \frac{v^3}{\rho} \tag{1}$$

$$2)\ \rho = \frac{\left[\left(\dfrac{dx}{dt}\right)^2 + \left(\dfrac{dy}{dt}\right)^2\right]^{\frac{3}{2}}}{\left|\dfrac{dx}{dt}\dfrac{d^2y}{dt^2} - \dfrac{dy}{dt}\dfrac{d^2x}{dt^2}\right|} \tag{2}$$

where ρ is the radius of curvature.

Solution: 1) The acceleration vector $\bar{a}$ can be expressed in terms of its normal and tangential components as follows

$$\bar{a} = \frac{d\bar{v}}{dt} = \frac{dv}{dt}\,\bar{T} + \frac{v^2}{\rho}\,\bar{N} \tag{3}$$

where $\bar{T}$ is a unit tangent vector in the direction of motion and $\bar{N}$ is a unit normal vector perpendicular to $\bar{T}$.

Let us evaluate $\left|\bar{v} \times \bar{a}\right|$

$$\left|\bar{v} \times \bar{a}\right| = \left|\bar{v} \times \left(\frac{dv}{dt}\,\bar{T} + \frac{v^2}{\rho}\,\bar{N}\right)\right| = \left|\frac{dv}{dt}\,\bar{v} \times \bar{T} + \frac{v^2}{\rho}\,\bar{v} \times \bar{N}\right| \tag{4}$$

Since the vectors $\bar{v}$ and $\bar{T}$ are parallel, their vector product is equal to $\bar{0}$. Eq.(4) becomes

$$\left|\bar{v} \times \bar{a}\right| = \left|\frac{v^2}{\rho}\,\bar{v} \times \bar{N}\right| \tag{5}$$

Since $\bar{N}$ is a unit vector perpendicular to $\bar{v}$, then

$$\left|\bar{v} \times \bar{N}\right| = \left|\bar{v}\right|\,\left|\bar{N}\right|\,\sin(\bar{v},\,\bar{N}) = v \tag{6}$$

Substituting eq.(6) into eq.(5), obtain

$$\left|\bar{v} \times \bar{a}\right| = \frac{v^2}{\rho}\left|\bar{v} \times \bar{N}\right| = \frac{v^3}{\rho} \tag{7}$$

2) Compute ρ from eq.(7)

$$\rho = \frac{v^3}{\left|\bar{v} \times \bar{a}\right|}$$

The point moves in the xy plane, thus

$$\bar{v} = \left(\frac{dx}{dt},\,\frac{dy}{dt}\right) \tag{8}$$

$$\bar{a} = \left(\frac{d^2x}{dt^2},\,\frac{d^2y}{dt^2}\right) \tag{9}$$

From eq.(8),

$$v^3 = \left[\sqrt{\left(\frac{dx}{dt}\right)^2 + \left(\frac{dy}{dt}\right)^2}\,\right]^3 = \left[\left(\frac{dx}{dt}\right)^2 + \left(\frac{dy}{dt}\right)^2\right]^{\frac{3}{2}} \tag{10}$$

From eq.(8) and eq.(9), obtain

$$\left|\bar{v} \times \bar{a}\right| = \left|\left(\frac{dx}{dt},\frac{dy}{dt}\right) \times \left(\frac{d^2x}{dt^2},\frac{d^2y}{dt^2}\right)\right| = \left|\frac{dx}{dt}\frac{d^2y}{dt^2} - \frac{dy}{dt}\frac{d^2x}{dt^2}\right| \tag{11}$$

Thus

$$\rho = \frac{v^3}{\left|\bar{v} \times \bar{a}\right|} = \frac{\left[\left(\frac{dx}{dt}\right)^2 + \left(\frac{dy}{dt}\right)^2\right]^{\frac{3}{2}}}{\left|\frac{dx}{dt}\frac{d^2y}{dt^2} - \frac{dy}{dt}\frac{d^2x}{dt^2}\right|} \tag{12}$$

Show that in the absence of a force, a particle moves in a straight line with constant velocity.

Solution: One of the postulates of classical mechanics is that the axes in space can be chosen so that Newton's equations are valid. Let us choose the fixed axes in space with origin at O and corresponding unit vectors $\bar{i}$, $\bar{j}$, $\bar{k}$. The basic vectors describing the motion of a particle P of mass m are:

$$\bar{r} = \overline{OP} = x\bar{i} + y\bar{j} + z\bar{k} \tag{1}$$

where $\bar{r}$ is the position vector

$$\bar{v} = \frac{d\bar{r}}{dt} = \frac{dx}{dt}\bar{i} + \frac{dy}{dt}\bar{j} + \frac{dz}{dt}\bar{k} \tag{2}$$

Differentiation with respect to time is often denoted by the dot as in

$$\frac{dg(t)}{dt} = \dot{g}(t)$$

Thus eq.(2) can be written in the form

$$\bar{v} = \dot{\bar{r}} = \dot{x}\bar{i} + \dot{y}\bar{j} + \dot{z}\bar{k} \qquad \text{where}$$

$\bar{v}$ is the velocity vector and

$$\bar{a} = \frac{d\bar{v}}{dt} = \frac{d^2x}{dt^2}\bar{i} + \frac{d^2y}{dt^2}\bar{j} + \frac{d^2z}{dt^2}\bar{k} = \ddot{x}\bar{i} + \ddot{y}\bar{j} + \ddot{z}\bar{k} \quad \text{where} \tag{3}$$

$\bar{a}$ is the acceleration vector.

$$\bar{F} = X\bar{i} + Y\bar{j} + Z\bar{k} \qquad \text{where} \tag{4}$$

$\bar{F}$ is the force vector.

The motion of P is described by Newton's Second Law, namely

$$\bar{F} = m\bar{a} \tag{5}$$

If no force is acting, then

$$\bar{F} = \bar{0} \tag{6}$$

and eq.(5) becomes

$$m\bar{a} = \bar{0} \tag{7}$$

Eq.(7) is equivalent to

$$\frac{d^2x}{dt^2} = 0, \quad \frac{d^2y}{dt^2} = 0, \quad \frac{d^2z}{dt^2} = 0 \tag{8}$$

Solving eq.(8), gives
$$x = A + \alpha t$$

$$y = B + \beta t \qquad (9)$$

$$z = C + \gamma t$$

where A, B, C, α, β, γ are arbitrary constants. Eq.(9) can be written in vector form as

$$\overline{r} = \overline{a} + \overline{b}t \qquad (10)$$

where
$$\overline{a} = (A, B, C) \qquad (11)$$

$$\overline{b} = (\alpha, \beta, \gamma)$$

Eq.(10) describes a straight line. The velocity of the particle is equal to $\overline{b}$ and is constant.

NEWTON'S LAWS, MOMENT VECTOR, ANGULAR MOMENTUM AND CENTER OF MASS

● **PROBLEM** 5-32

A particle P of mass m moves in space subject to a force

$$\overline{F} = X\overline{i} + Y\overline{j} + Z\overline{k} \qquad (1)$$

which is constant.

1. Express the position vector of the particle in terms of time t.

2. Assume that the axes in space are chosen so that $\overline{F}$ is parallel to the z axis. Determine the position vector $\overline{r} = \overline{r}(t)$ for this case.

   Show that in this case the trajectory of the particle is a parabola.

Solution: 1. Newton's Second Law states that

$$\overline{F} = m\overline{a} \qquad (2)$$

where
$$\overline{a} = \frac{d^2x}{dt^2}\,\overline{i} + \frac{d^2y}{dt^2}\,\overline{j} + \frac{d^2z}{dt^2}\,\overline{k} \qquad (3)$$

Combining eqs.(1), (2), and (3), gives

$$X\overline{i} + Y\overline{j} + Z\overline{k} = m\frac{d^2x}{dt^2}\,\overline{i} + m\frac{d^2y}{dt^2}\,\overline{j} + m\frac{d^2z}{dt^2}\,\overline{k} \qquad (4)$$

or
$$X = m\frac{d^2x}{dt^2}$$

$$Y = m\frac{d^2y}{dt^2} \qquad (5)$$

$$Z = m\frac{d^2z}{dt^2}$$

Integrating the first expression of eq.(5), gives

$$\frac{X}{m} t + a_1 = \frac{dx}{dt}$$

integrating again

$$\frac{X}{m} t^2 + a_1 t + a_2 = x$$

or

$$x = \frac{1}{2m} X t^2 + a_1 t + a_2 \tag{6}$$

In the same manner, we find that

$$y = \frac{1}{2m} Y t^2 + b_1 t + b_2$$

$$z = \frac{1}{2m} Z t^2 + c_1 t + c_2$$

where a_1, a_2, b_1, b_2, c_1, c_2 are constants which can be determined from additional conditions – for example the initial position and initial velocity of the particle or the position of the particle at $t = t_1$ and $t = t_2$.

2. Since $\bar{F}$ is parallel to the z-axis, the x and y components of this vector are equal to zero, thus

$$X = 0$$
$$Y = 0 \tag{7}$$

Substituting eq.(7) into eq.(6), gives

$$x = a_1 t + a_2$$

$$y = b_1 t + b_2 \tag{8}$$

$$z = \frac{1}{2m} Z t^2 + c_1 t + c_2$$

To show that the trajectory of a particle whose motion is described by eq.(8) is a parabola, assume that at $t = 0$ the particle is located at the origin of the system, thus eq.(8) for $t = 0$ becomes

$$x = a_2$$
$$y = b_2 \tag{9}$$
$$z = c_2$$

For the origin, $x = y = z = 0$, therefore $a_2 = b_2 = c_2 = 0$. Eq.(8) then, becomes

$$x = a_1 t$$

$$y = b_1 t \tag{10}$$

$$z = \frac{1}{2m} Z t^2 + c_1 t$$

From the first equation, $t = \frac{x}{a_1}$, substituting $t = \frac{x}{a_1}$ into the second and third equation, results in

$$y = \frac{b_1}{a_1} x$$

$$z = \frac{1}{2m} Z \frac{x^2}{a_1^2} + \frac{c_1}{a_1} x \tag{11}$$

or

$$z = \frac{Z}{2ma_1^2} x^2 + \frac{c_1}{a_1} x \tag{12}$$

Then denote

$$\frac{Z}{2ma_1^2} = p \quad , \quad \frac{c_1}{a_1} = q \tag{13}$$

Eq.(12) can then be written in the form

$$z = px^2 + qx = px^2 + qx + \frac{q^2}{4p} - \frac{q^2}{4p}$$

$$= p\left(x + \frac{q}{2p}\right)^2 - \frac{q^2}{4p} \tag{14}$$

or

$$z + \frac{q^2}{4p} = p\left(x + \frac{q}{2p}\right)^2 \tag{15}$$

Now transform the coordinates; doing this

$$z' = z + \frac{q^2}{4p}$$

$$x' = x + \frac{q}{2p} \tag{16}$$

Eq.(15) now becomes

$$z' = px'^2 \tag{17}$$

which is the equation of a parabola.

● **PROBLEM 5-33**

Show that the moment of a force is equal to the rate of change of angular momentum. Let $\bar{r}$ be the position vector of a particle of mass m and $\bar{F}$ be the vector sum of all forces acting on the particle.

Solution: Newton's Second Law describes the motion of a particle as

$$\overline{F} = m\overline{a} \qquad (1)$$

Since
$$\overline{a} = \frac{d\overline{v}}{dt} \qquad (2)$$

equation (1) can be written in the form

$$\overline{F} = \frac{d}{dt}(m\overline{v}) \qquad (3)$$

where $m\overline{v}$ is the linear momentum of the particle.

The angular momentum of the particle about O (the origin of the system) is defined as

$$\overline{r} \times m\overline{v} \qquad (4)$$

and the moment of the force $\overline{F}$ is defined as

$$\overline{r} \times \overline{F} \qquad (5)$$

From eq.(3),
$$\overline{r} \times \overline{F} = \overline{r} \times \frac{d}{dt}(m\overline{v}) = m\overline{r} \times \frac{d\overline{v}}{dt} \qquad (6)$$

Note that

$$\frac{d}{dt}(\overline{r} \times \overline{v}) = \overline{r} \times \frac{d\overline{v}}{dt} + \frac{d\overline{r}}{dt} \times \overline{v} = \overline{r} \times \frac{d\overline{v}}{dt} + \overline{v} \times \overline{v} = \overline{r} \times \frac{d\overline{v}}{dt} \qquad (7)$$

Substituting eq.(7) into eq.(6), obtain

$$\overline{r} \times \overline{F} = \frac{d}{dt}(\overline{r} \times m\overline{v}) \qquad (8)$$

$\overline{r} \times m\overline{v}$ is called the angular momentum of a particle about an origin 0.

● **PROBLEM 5-34**

Consider the motion of a system of particles P_1, P_2,...P_n.

Show that if there are no external forces, the center of mass of the system moves with constant velocity along a straight line.

Solution: Let the position vectors of the particles P_1, P_2,...P_n be $\overline{r}_1 = \overline{OP_1}$, $\overline{r}_2 = \overline{OP_2}$,...$\overline{r}_n = \overline{OP_n}$. The equations of motion for the i-th particle are
$$\overline{F}_i = m_i\overline{a}_i \qquad (i = 1, 2,...n) \qquad (1)$$

Expand equation (1)

$$\overline{F}_1 + \overline{F}_2 + ... + \overline{F}_n = m_1\overline{a}_1 + m_2\overline{a}_2 + ... + m_n\overline{a}_n \qquad (2)$$

The position vector of the center of mass of a system is

$$\bar{r}_c = \overline{OP}_c \tag{3}$$

where P_c is the center of mass, and

$$M\bar{r}_c = m_1\bar{r}_1 + m_2\bar{r}_2 + \ldots + m_n\bar{r}_n \tag{4}$$

where $\quad M = m_1 + m_2 + \ldots + m_n$

Thus

$$\bar{r}_c = \frac{m_1\bar{r}_1 + m_2\bar{r}_2 + \ldots + m_n\bar{r}_n}{m_1 + m_2 + \ldots + m_n} \tag{5}$$

M is the total mass of the system. The center of mass has velocity

$$\bar{V}_c = \frac{d\bar{r}_c}{dt} \tag{6}$$

and acceleration

$$\bar{a}_c = \frac{d\bar{V}_c}{dt} = \frac{d^2\bar{r}_c}{dt^2} \tag{7}$$

Let

$$\bar{F} = \bar{F}_1 + \bar{F}_2 + \ldots + \bar{F}_n \tag{8}$$

Eq.(2) can be written in the form

$$\bar{F} = M\bar{a}_c \tag{9}$$

where $\bar{F}$ is the resultant of all the forces applied. Each force $\bar{F}_i$ can be expressed as a sum of the internal and external forces

$$\bar{F}_i = \bar{F}_i^{int} + \bar{F}_i^{ext} \tag{10}$$

The internal force $\bar{F}_i^{int}$ is a sum of all forces due to the interactions between the particle P_i and the other particles, thus

$$\bar{F}_i^{int} = \sum_{\substack{j=1 \\ j \neq i}}^{j=n} \bar{F}_{i,j}^{int} \tag{11}$$

where $F_{i,j}^{int}$ is the interaction of the particle P_j on the particle P_i.

Newton's Third Law states that P_i and P_j exert equal and opposite forces on each other, both along the line P_iP_j.

Thus

$$\bar{F}_{i,j}^{int} = -\bar{F}_{j,i}^{int} \tag{12}$$

From eq.(12), one concludes that the sum of all the internal forces is equal to $\bar{0}$.

$$\sum_{i=1}^{i=n} \bar{F}_i^{int} = \sum_{i=1}^{i=n} \sum_{\substack{j=1 \\ j \neq i}}^{j=n} \bar{F}_{i,j}^{int} = \bar{0} \qquad (13)$$

If there are no external forces eq.(8) becomes

$$\bar{F} = \sum_{i=1}^{i=n} \bar{F}_i = \sum_{i=1}^{i=n} \bar{F}_i^{int} + \sum_{i=1}^{i=n} \bar{F}_i^{ext} = \bar{0} \qquad (14)$$

For $\bar{F} = \bar{0}$ eq.(9) is

$$M\bar{a}_c = \bar{0} \qquad (15)$$

or

$$M \frac{d^2\bar{r}_c}{dt^2} = \bar{0}$$

and

$$\bar{r}_c = \bar{e}t + \bar{g} \qquad (16)$$

where $\bar{e}$ and $\bar{g}$ are constant vectors. The vector $\bar{r} = \bar{e}t + \bar{g}$ describes a motion with constant velocity along a straight line. (see problem 5-31).

● **PROBLEM 5-35**

A particle P moves in the xy plane. Express its angular momentum about the origin in terms of polar coordinates.

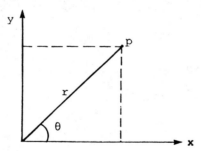

Solution: The angular momentum of a particle is defined as

$$\bar{r} \times m\bar{v} \qquad (1)$$

where $\bar{r}$ is the position vector of the particle and $\bar{v}$ its velocity. Since the particle moves in the xy plane, then

$$\bar{r} = (x, y, 0)$$
$$\bar{v} = (\dot{x}, \dot{y}, 0) \qquad (2)$$

Substituting eq.(2) into eq.(1), gives

$$\bar{r} \times m\bar{v} = m(x, y, 0) \times (\dot{x}, \dot{y}, 0) =$$
$$= m(0, 0, x\dot{y} - y\dot{x}) \qquad (3)$$

200

x and y can be expressed in terms of the polar coordinates

$$x = r \cos \theta$$
$$y = r \sin \theta \qquad (4)$$

as shown in the figure.

Differentiating eq.(4) with respect to time, gives

$$\dot{x} = \dot{r} \cos \theta - r \sin \theta \dot{\theta}$$
$$\dot{y} = \dot{r} \sin \theta + r \cos \theta \dot{\theta} \qquad (5)$$

Substituting eq.(5) and eq.(4) into eq.(3),

$$m(0, 0, x\dot{y} - y\dot{x})$$
$$= m\left[0,0,r\cos\theta(\dot{r}\sin\theta+r\cos\theta\dot{\theta})-r\sin\theta(\dot{r}\cos\theta-r\sin\theta\dot{\theta})\right]$$
$$= m\left[0,0,r^2\cos^2\theta\dot{\theta}+r^2\sin^2\theta\dot{\theta}\right] = (0,\ 0,\ mr^2\dot{\theta}) \qquad (6)$$

● **PROBLEM 5-36**

1. Show that in the absence of external forces, the total angular momentum of a system of particles $P_1, \ldots P_n$ remains constant for any motion of the system.

2. Give the conditions for the static equilibrium of a rigid body.

Solution: 1. Let the position vectors of the particles $P_1, \ldots P_n$ be $\overline{r}_i = \overline{OP}_i$ for $i = 1, \ldots n$ and the velocity vectors be $\overline{V}_i = \dfrac{d\overline{r}_i}{dt}$.

The equations of motion are, from Newton's second law,

$$\frac{d}{dt}(m_i\overline{v}_i) = \overline{F}_i \qquad \text{for } i = 1, \ldots n \qquad (1)$$

Multiplying vectorially by $\overline{r}_i$ and adding, we obtain

$$\frac{d}{dt}(\overline{r}_1 \times m_1\overline{v}_1 + \overline{r}_2 \times m_2\overline{v}_2 + \ldots + \overline{r}_n \times m_n\overline{v}_n)$$
$$= \overline{r}_1 \times \overline{F}_1 + \ldots + \overline{r}_n \times \overline{F}_n \qquad (2)$$

where

$$\frac{d}{dt}(\overline{r} \times \overline{v}) = \overline{r} \times \frac{d\overline{v}}{dt} + \frac{d\overline{r}}{dt} \times \overline{v} = \overline{r} \times \frac{d\overline{v}}{dt} + \overline{v} \times \overline{v} = \overline{r} \times \frac{d\overline{v}}{dt}$$

The left-hand side of eq.(2) represents the rate of change of the total angular momentum of the system of particles.

From Newton's Third Law of motion, we conclude that the moments of internal forces cancel.

Indeed, let $\overline{F}_{i,j}^{int}$ be the force exerted by P_j on P_i and $\overline{F}_{j,i}^{int}$ be the force exerted by P_i on P_j, then

$$\overline{F}_{i,j}^{int} = -\overline{F}_{j,i}^{int} \tag{3}$$

The moment of these forces is equal to

$$\overline{OP}_i \times \overline{F}_{i,j}^{int} + \overline{OP}_j \times \overline{F}_{j,i}^{int}$$

$$= (\overline{OP}_j + \overline{P_jP_i}) \times \overline{F}_{i,j}^{int} + \overline{OP}_j(-\overline{F}_{i,j}^{int}) \tag{4}$$

$$= \overline{P_jP_i} \times \overline{F}_{i,j}^{int} = \overline{0}$$

Note that $\overline{F}_{i,j}^{int}$ acts along the line P_jP_i. Thus the total moment in eq.(2) comes from the external forces. If there are no external forces the right-hand side of eq.(2) is equal to $\overline{0}$ and we conclude that the total angular momentum is constant.

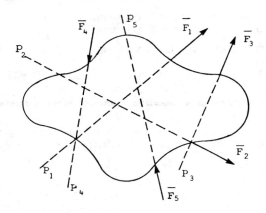

2. Denote the forces acting on a rigid body by $\overline{F}_1$, $\overline{F}_2$,...$\overline{F}_n$. They are applied at the points P_1, P_2,...P_n. Each force has a line of action p_i as shown in the figure.

Sliding the force $\overline{F}_i$ along the line p_i has no effect on

$$\overline{F} = \overline{F}_1 + \overline{F}_2 + ...+ \overline{F}_n \tag{5}$$

and it does not change the total moment about 0.

$$\overline{r}_1 \times \overline{F}_1 + \overline{r}_2 \times \overline{F}_2 + ...+ \overline{r}_n \times \overline{F}_n \tag{6}$$

The rigid body is in equilibrium when

$$\overline{F}_1 + \overline{F}_2 + \overline{F}_3 + ...+ \overline{F}_n = \overline{0} \tag{7}$$

and

$$\bar{r}_1 \times \bar{F}_1 + \bar{r}_2 \times \bar{F}_2 + \ldots + \bar{r}_n \times \bar{F}_n = \bar{0} \qquad (8)$$

● **PROBLEM** 5-37

Point P moves in space with velocity $\bar{v} = \overline{OF}$. $\qquad (1)$

Point F defined by eq.(1) traces the curve called the hodograph of the motion of the point P.

Find the hodograph for the following motions

1. $\overline{OP} = (5t,\ 2t+1,\ 3t)$

2. $\overline{OP} = (r\cos\omega t,\ r\sin\omega t,\ 0)$

3. $\overline{OP} = (3t^2,\ 4t^2-2,\ 2t^2)$

4. $\overline{OP} = (\cos t,\ \sin t,\ 2t)$

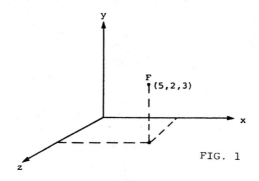

FIG. 1

Solution: 1. Differentiating $\overline{OP}$, results in

$$\bar{v} = \frac{d}{dt}\ \overline{OP} = \frac{d}{dt}\ (5t,\ 2t+1,\ 3t) = (5,\ 2,\ 3) \qquad (2)$$

Thus the hodograph is a single point with coordinates given by eq.(2) (see Fig.1).

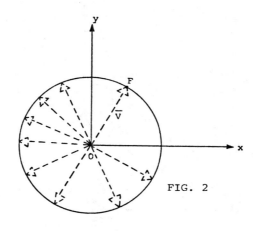

FIG. 2

2. $\bar{v} = \frac{d}{dt} \overline{OP} = \frac{d}{dt} (r\cos\omega t, r\sin\omega t, 0) = (-r\omega\sin\omega t, r\omega\cos\omega t, 0)$ (3)

The magnitude of $\bar{v} = \overline{OF}$ is given by

$$\sqrt{v_x^2 + v_y^2 + v_z^2} = \sqrt{r^2\omega^2\sin^2\omega t + r^2\omega^2\cos^2\omega t} = r\omega \qquad (4)$$

Since the velocity vector $\bar{v} = \overline{OF}$ has a constant magnitude, it represents a rotating vector lying in the x-y plane. Thus, the hodograph is a circle with radius $r\omega$ and center at O, as shown in Fig.2.

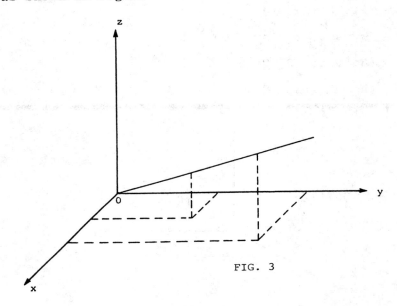

FIG. 3

3. $\bar{v} = \frac{d}{dt} \overline{OP} = \frac{d}{dt} (3t^2, 4t^2-2, 2t^2)$ (5)

   $= (6t, 8t, 4t)$

The hodograph is a straight line (see Fig.3).

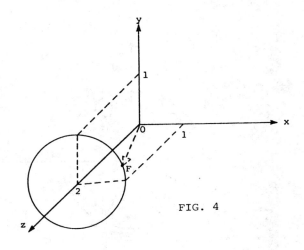

FIG. 4

4. $\overline{v} = \dfrac{d}{dt}\ \overline{OP} = \dfrac{d}{dt}\ (\cos t,\ \sin t,\ 2t) = (-\sin t,\ \cos t,\ 2)$ (6)

The hodograph is a circle of radius 1 and center at $(0,0,2)$, as shown in Fig.4.

TRAJECTORIES AND COLLISIONS OF PARTICLES

Show that if a force $\overline{F}$ acting on a moving particle is always directed along the tangent to the trajectory, then the trajectory is a straight line.

<u>Solution</u>: The force acting on a particle is

$$\overline{F} = m\overline{a} = m\ \frac{d^2\overline{r}}{dt^2}$$ (1)

Since $\overline{F}$ is directed along the tangent, then

$$\overline{F} = m\overline{a} = \alpha\ \frac{d\overline{r}}{dt}$$ (2)

where α is a constant and

$$\overline{V} = \frac{d\overline{r}}{dt}$$ (3)

is tangent to the trajectory.
Combining eqs.(1), (2), and (3), obtain

$$\frac{d^2\overline{r}}{dt^2} - \frac{\alpha}{m}\ \frac{d\overline{r}}{dt} = \overline{0}$$ (4)

Integrating eq.(4), then

$$\frac{d\overline{r}}{dt} - \frac{\alpha}{m}\ \overline{r} = \overline{b}$$ (5)

where $\overline{b}$ is a constant vector.
Integrating eq.(5), gives

$$\overline{r} = \overline{c}\ f(t) - \frac{m\overline{b}}{\alpha}$$ (6)

where $\overline{c}$ is a constant vector and $f(t)$ satisfies the differential equation

$$\dot{f}(t) - \frac{\alpha}{m}\ f(t) = 0$$ (7)

Recalling the vector form of a straight line ($\overline{r} = \overline{a} + \overline{b}t$), eq.(6) clearly represents a straight line. The trajectory of the moving particle subject to the given force is therefore a straight line.

• **PROBLEM** 5-39

The trajectory of a moving particle is such that

$$\frac{d\overline{r}}{dt} \cdot \left(\frac{d^2\overline{r}}{dt^2} \times \frac{d^3\overline{r}}{dt^3}\right) = 0 \qquad (1)$$

Show that $\overline{r} = \overline{r}(t)$ is a plane curve.

Solution: From eq.(1) one concludes that $\frac{d^3\overline{r}}{dt^3}$ is a linear combination of vectors $\frac{d^2\overline{r}}{dt^2}$ and $\frac{d\overline{r}}{dt}$, thus

$$\frac{d^3\overline{r}}{dt^3} = \alpha \frac{d^2\overline{r}}{dt^2} + \beta \frac{d\overline{r}}{dt} \qquad (2)$$

where α and β are constants. Integrating eq.(2), we obtain

$$\frac{d^2\overline{r}}{dt^2} = \alpha \frac{d\overline{r}}{dt} + \beta \overline{r} + \overline{b} \qquad (3)$$

where $\overline{b}$ is a constant vector.

The solution of eq.(3) can be written in the form

$$\overline{r} = -\frac{1}{\beta} \overline{b} + f_1(t)\overline{d}_1 + f_2(t)\overline{d}_2 \qquad (4)$$

where $\overline{d}_1$ and $\overline{d}_2$ are constant vectors and $f_1(t)$ and $f_2(t)$ are two independent solutions of the differential equation

$$\ddot{f}(t) = \alpha\dot{f}(t) + \beta f(t) \qquad (5)$$

• **PROBLEM** 5-40

A particle is moving under the influence of a gravitational force. Show that its trajectory is a conic section.

Solution: Start with the equation of motion of the particle

$$\frac{d\overline{v}}{dt} = -k\frac{\overline{r}}{r^3} = -k\frac{\overline{r}_o}{r^2} \qquad (1)$$

where k is a constant and

$$\overline{v} = \frac{d\overline{r}}{dt} \qquad (2)$$

$$\overline{r}_o = \frac{\overline{r}}{r} \qquad (3)$$

Taking the vector product of eq.(1) with $\overline{r}$, gives

$$\overline{r} \times \frac{d\overline{v}}{dt} = -k\overline{r} \times \frac{\overline{r}}{r^3} = \overline{0} \qquad (4)$$

206

Thus

$$\frac{d}{dt} (\bar{r} \times \bar{v}) = \bar{v} \times \bar{v} + \bar{r} \times \frac{d\bar{v}}{dt} = \bar{0} \tag{5}$$

and

$$\bar{r} \times \bar{v} = \bar{d} = \overline{const}. \tag{6}$$

The vector $\bar{d}$ can be written in the form

$$\bar{d} = \bar{r} \times \bar{v} = \bar{r} \times \frac{d\bar{r}}{dt} = r\bar{r}_0 \times \frac{d}{dt} (r\bar{r}_0)$$

$$= r\bar{r}_0 \times \left(\frac{dr}{dt}\bar{r}_0 + r \frac{d\bar{r}_0}{dt} \right) \tag{7}$$

Applying the identity

$$\bar{a} \times (\bar{b} \times \bar{c}) = \bar{b}(\bar{a}\cdot\bar{c}) - \bar{c}(\bar{a}\cdot\bar{b}) \tag{8}$$

obtain

$$\frac{d\bar{v}}{dt} \times \bar{d} = - \frac{k\bar{r}_0 \times \bar{d}}{r^2} = k \frac{d\bar{r}_0}{dt} \tag{9}$$

Note that

$$\bar{r}_0 \cdot \frac{d\bar{r}_0}{dt} = \frac{1}{2} \frac{d}{dt} (\bar{r}_0\cdot\bar{r}_0) = 0 \tag{10}$$

Since $\bar{d} = \overline{const}$, then

$$\frac{d}{dt} (\bar{v} \times \bar{d}) = k \frac{d\bar{r}_0}{dt} \tag{11}$$

Integrating eq.(11), obtain

$$\bar{v} \times \bar{d} = k\bar{r}_0 + \bar{P} \tag{12}$$

where $\bar{P}$ is a constant vector.

Thus

$$(\bar{v} \times \bar{d})\cdot\bar{r} = kr + \bar{r}\cdot\bar{P} = kr + rP\cos\alpha \tag{13}$$

where α is the angle between $\bar{r}$ and $\bar{P}$.
Using the identity

$$(\bar{a} \times \bar{b})\cdot\bar{c} = (\bar{b} \times \bar{c})\cdot\bar{a} = (\bar{c} \times \bar{a})\cdot\bar{b} \tag{14}$$

obtain

$$(\bar{v} \times \bar{d})\cdot\bar{r} = \bar{d}\cdot(\bar{r} \times \bar{v}) = \bar{d}\cdot\bar{d} = d^2 \tag{15}$$

Thus

$$d^2 = kr + rP \cos\alpha \tag{16}$$

or

$$r = \frac{\dfrac{d^2}{k}}{1 + \dfrac{P}{k} \cos\alpha} \tag{17}$$

Eq.(17) is the equation of a conic section - a hyperbola,
parabola, or ellipse in polar coordinates.

207

Consider the collision of two identical particles. Their velocities are $\overline{v}_1$ and $\overline{v}_2$ before the collision, and $\overline{w}_1$ and $\overline{w}_2$ after the collision. Assuming that momentum and kinetic energy are conserved, then

$$\overline{v}_1 + \overline{v}_2 = \overline{w}_1 + \overline{w}_2 \tag{1}$$

and

$$\frac{mv_1^2}{2} + \frac{mv_2^2}{2} = \frac{mw_1^2}{2} + \frac{mw_2^2}{2} , \tag{2}$$

or

$$v_1{}^2 + v_2{}^2 = w_1{}^2 + w_2{}^2 \tag{3}$$

1) Express $\overline{w}_1$ and $\overline{w}_2$ in terms of $\overline{v}_1$ and $\overline{v}_2$.

2) Show that the relative velocities

$$\overline{u} = \overline{v}_2 - \overline{v}_1 \tag{4}$$

$$\overline{u}' = \overline{w}_2 - \overline{w}_1 \tag{5}$$

have the same magnitude before and after the collision.

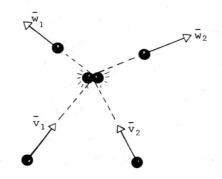

Solution: 1) Eqs.(1) and (3) make up a system of four scalar equations with the six components of $\overline{w}_1$ and $\overline{w}_2$. To solve the system, introduce two additional parameters describing the geometry of the collision, that is the position of the plane of the trajectories. Proceed by defining a unit vector $\overline{k}$, ($|\overline{k}| = 1$) such that

$$\overline{w}_1 - \overline{v}_1 = \alpha\overline{k} \tag{6}$$

From eq.(1),

$$\overline{w}_2 - \overline{v}_2 = -\alpha\overline{k} \tag{7}$$

Next, find the parameter α. From eq.(3)

$$v_1^2 + v_2^2 = w_1^2 + w_2^2 = (\overline{v}_1 + \alpha\overline{k})^2 + (\overline{v}_2 - \alpha\overline{k})^2$$
$$= v_1^2 + 2\alpha(\overline{v}_1 \cdot \overline{k}) + \alpha^2 + v_2^2 - 2\alpha(\overline{v}_2 \cdot \overline{k}) + \alpha^2 \tag{8}$$

Thus

$$\alpha = \overline{k} \cdot (\overline{v}_2 - \overline{v}_1) = \overline{k} \cdot \overline{u} \tag{9}$$

Substituting eq.(9) into eqs.(6) and (7), gives

$$\overline{w}_1 = \overline{v}_1 + \overline{k}(\overline{k} \cdot \overline{u}) \tag{10}$$

$$\overline{w}_2 = \overline{v}_2 - \overline{k}(\overline{k} \cdot \overline{u}) \tag{11}$$

2) To prove that $|\overline{u}| = |\overline{u}'|$ subtract eq.(5) from eq.(4) and apply eqs.(10) and (11). Then,

$$\overline{u} - \overline{u}' = \overline{v}_2 - \overline{w}_2 - \overline{v}_1 + \overline{w}_1 = \overline{k}(\overline{k} \cdot \overline{u}) + \overline{k}(\overline{k} \cdot \overline{u}) \tag{12}$$

or

$$\overline{u}' = \overline{u} - 2\overline{k}(\overline{k} \cdot \overline{u}) \tag{13}$$

where $\overline{k}$ is a unit vector.

Squaring eq.(13), results in

$$u'^2 = u^2 - 4(\overline{k} \cdot \overline{u})^2 + 4k^2(\overline{k} \cdot \overline{u})^2 = u^2 \tag{14}$$

Thus

$$|\overline{u}| = |\overline{u}'| \tag{15}$$

• PROBLEM 5-42

Consider the collision of two particles of mass m_1 and m_2. Show that the relative velocity is preserved under the collision.

Solution: Let the velocities of the particles before the collision be $\overline{v}_1$, $\overline{v}_2$ and after the collision $\overline{w}_1$, $\overline{w}_2$. The law of conservation of momentum states that

$$\overline{p}_1 + \overline{p}_2 = \overline{p}_1' + \overline{p}_2' \tag{1}$$

where

$$\overline{p}_1 = m_1\overline{v}_1 , \qquad \overline{p}_2 = m_2\overline{v}_2 \tag{2}$$

and

$$\overline{p}_1' = m_1\overline{w}_1 , \qquad \overline{p}_2' = m_2\overline{w}_2 \tag{3}$$

The kinetic energy is conserved, thus

$$p_1^2 + Mp_2^2 = p_1'^2 + Mp_2'^2 \tag{4}$$

where

$$M = \frac{m_1}{m_2}$$

Define the unit vector $\overline{k}$

$$\overline{p}_1' - \overline{p}_1 = \alpha\overline{k} \tag{5}$$

$$\overline{p}_2' - \overline{p}_2 = -\alpha\overline{k} \tag{6}$$

From eqs.(4), (5), and (6), compute α

$$\alpha = \frac{2}{1+M} \, \overline{k} \cdot (M\overline{p}_2 - \overline{p}_1) = \frac{2m_1}{1+M} \, (\overline{k} \cdot \overline{u}) \qquad (7)$$

Substituting eq.(7) into eqs.(5) and (6), obtain

$$\overline{p}_1' = \overline{p}_1 + \frac{2}{1+M} \, \overline{k} \left[\overline{k} \cdot (M\overline{p}_2 - \overline{p}_1) \right] = \overline{p}_1 + \frac{2m_1}{1+M} \, \overline{k}(\overline{k} \cdot \overline{u}) \qquad (8)$$

$$\overline{p}_2' = \overline{p}_2 - \frac{2}{1+M} \, \overline{k} \left[\overline{k} \cdot (M\overline{p}_2 - \overline{p}_1) \right] = \overline{p}_2 - \frac{2m_1}{1+M} \, \overline{k}(\overline{k} \cdot \overline{u}) \qquad (9)$$

Thus

$$M\overline{p}_2' - \overline{p}_1' = M\overline{p}_2 - \overline{p}_1 - 2\overline{k} \left[\overline{k} \cdot (M\overline{p}_2 - \overline{p}_1) \right] \qquad (10)$$

or

$$\overline{u}' = \overline{u} - 2\overline{k}(\overline{k} \cdot \overline{u}) \qquad (11)$$

where

$$\overline{u}' = \overline{w}_2 - \overline{w}_1 \qquad (12)$$

Squaring eq.(11),

$$u'^2 = u^2 \qquad (13)$$

thus proving that the relative velocities remain equal under a collision.

RIGID BODY MECHANICS, COORDINATE SYSTEMS AND INERTIAL SYSTEMS

● **PROBLEM** 5-43

Consider a rigid body rotating about the z axis (see Fig.1). Show that the velocity vector of any point P of the body can be expressed as

$$\overline{v} = \overline{\omega} \times \overline{OP} \qquad (1)$$

where $\overline{\omega}$ is the angular velocity vector and $\overline{OP}$ is the position vector of point P. Also, show that

$$\frac{d\overline{v}}{dt} = (\overline{\omega} \cdot \overline{OP})\overline{\omega} - \omega^2 \overline{OP} + \overline{\alpha} \times \overline{OP} \qquad (2)$$

where $\overline{\alpha}$ is the angular acceleration vector.

Solution: Since the body rotates about the z-axis, each point P of the body describes a circle

$$x = r \cos\theta, \quad y = r \sin\theta, \quad z = z \qquad (3)$$

The velocity vector of P is given by

$$\overline{v} = \frac{d}{dt} \, \overline{OP}$$

where $\overline{OP} = r\cos\theta\,\overline{i} + r\sin\theta\,\overline{j} + z\overline{k}$. Therefore,

$$\overline{v} = -r\sin\theta\,\frac{d\theta}{dt}\,\overline{i} + r\cos\theta\,\frac{d\theta}{dt}\,\overline{j} \tag{4}$$

Note that since r is constant, $\frac{dr}{dt} = 0$.

One defines the angular velocity vector as

$$\overline{\omega} = \frac{d\theta}{dt}\,\overline{k} \tag{5}$$

Compute the vector product $\overline{\omega} \times \overline{OP}$ using eqs.(4) and (5), doing this

$$\overline{\omega} \times \overline{OP} = \left(\frac{d\theta}{dt}\,\overline{k}\right) \times (r\cos\theta\,\overline{i} + r\sin\theta\,\overline{j} + z\overline{k}) \tag{6}$$

$$= \frac{d\theta}{dt}\,r\cos\theta(\overline{k} \times \overline{i}) + \frac{d\theta}{dt}\,r\sin\theta(\overline{k} \times \overline{j}) + \frac{d\theta}{dt}\,z(\overline{k} \times \overline{k})$$

$$= \frac{d\theta}{dt}\,r\cos\theta\,\overline{j} - \frac{d\theta}{dt}\,r\sin\theta\,\overline{i}$$

Here the following identities were used

$$\overline{k} \times \overline{i} = \overline{j}$$
$$\overline{k} \times \overline{j} = -\overline{i} \tag{7}$$
$$\overline{k} \times \overline{k} = \overline{0}$$

Substituting eq.(4) into eq.(6), obtain

$$\overline{\omega} \times \overline{OP} = \overline{v} \tag{8}$$

To find the acceleration of the point P, differentiate eq.(8)

$$\frac{d\overline{v}}{dt} = \frac{d}{dt}\,(\overline{\omega} \times \overline{OP}) = \overline{\omega} \times \frac{d\,\overline{OP}}{dt} + \frac{d\overline{\omega}}{dt} \times \overline{OP}$$

$$= \overline{\omega} \times \overline{v} + \frac{d\overline{\omega}}{dt} \times \overline{OP} \tag{9}$$

The angular acceleration vector $\overline{\alpha}$ is given by

$$\overline{\alpha} = \frac{d\overline{\omega}}{dt} = \frac{d^2\theta}{dt^2}\,\overline{k} \tag{10}$$

Using eq.(10),write eq.(9) in the form

$$\frac{d\overline{v}}{dt} = \overline{\omega} \times (\overline{\omega} \times \overline{OP}) + \overline{\alpha} \times \overline{OP} = (\overline{\omega} \cdot \overline{OP})\overline{\omega} - \omega^2\overline{OP} + \overline{\alpha} \times \overline{OP} \tag{11}$$

● **PROBLEM 5-44**

A rigid body rotates with constant angular speed ω, the axis of rotation is $x = \frac{y}{3} = \frac{z}{2}$. Find the speed of a point of the body as it passes through the point (3,4,5).

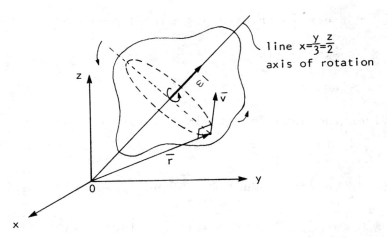

line $x = \frac{y}{3} = \frac{z}{2}$
axis of rotation

Solution: Since the axis of rotation is $x = \frac{y}{3} = \frac{z}{2}$, the origin O is located on this axis as shown in the figure.

The velocity of the point is given by

$$\bar{v} = \bar{\omega} \times \bar{r} \tag{1}$$

where $\bar{\omega}$ is the angular velocity and $\bar{r}$ the position vector of the point.

The vector $\quad \bar{a} = \bar{i} + 3\bar{j} + 2\bar{k} \tag{2}$

is parallel to the axis

$$x = \frac{y}{3} = \frac{z}{2}$$

Since the angular velocity vector $\bar{\omega}$ has magnitude ω and is parallel to the axis of rotation, then

$$\bar{\omega} = \omega\bar{u} \tag{3}$$

where $\bar{u}$ is a unit vector in the direction of $\bar{a}$. In other words,

$$\bar{u} = \frac{\bar{a}}{|\bar{a}|}$$

$$= \frac{1}{\sqrt{14}} (\bar{i} + 3\bar{j} + 2\bar{k}) = \frac{1}{\sqrt{14}} \bar{i} + \frac{3}{\sqrt{14}} \bar{j} + \frac{2}{\sqrt{14}} \bar{k} \tag{4}$$

Substituting eq.(4) into eq.(3), gives

$$\bar{\omega} = \pm\omega\left(\frac{1}{\sqrt{14}} \bar{i} + \frac{3}{\sqrt{14}} \bar{j} + \frac{2}{\sqrt{14}} \bar{k}\right) \tag{5}$$

The position vector of the point is

$$\bar{r} = 3\bar{i} + 4\bar{j} + 5\bar{k} \tag{6}$$

Substituting eq.(5) and eq.(6), into eq.(1), we obtain

$$\bar{v} = \bar{\omega} \times \bar{r} = \pm\omega \begin{vmatrix} \bar{i} & \bar{j} & \bar{k} \\ \dfrac{1}{\sqrt{14}} & \dfrac{3}{\sqrt{14}} & \dfrac{2}{\sqrt{14}} \\ 3 & 4 & 5 \end{vmatrix} = \pm\left(\dfrac{7}{\sqrt{14}}\,\bar{i} + \dfrac{1}{\sqrt{14}}\,\bar{j} - \dfrac{5}{\sqrt{14}}\,\bar{k} \right)\omega$$

The speed of the point is therefore

$$|\bar{v}| = \omega\sqrt{\dfrac{49 + 1 + 25}{14}} = \omega\sqrt{\dfrac{75}{14}} \tag{8}$$

● **PROBLEM 5-45**

Consider the planar motion of a rigid body, where each point of the rigid body moves in a plane parallel to a fixed plane. If we consider the x-y plane to be a cross-section of the body, and if this cross section is parallel to the plane of motion, then for a point A in this cross-section, show that for any point B(see figure) there exist vectors $\bar{\omega}$ and $\bar{\alpha}$ such that

$$\bar{V}_B = \bar{V}_A + \bar{\omega} \times \overline{AB} \tag{1}$$

$$\bar{a}_B = \bar{a}_A + \bar{\alpha} \times \overline{AB} - \omega^2\overline{AB} \tag{2}$$

where $\bar{V}_A, \bar{a}_A$ and $\bar{V}_B, \bar{a}_B$ are the velocity and acceleration vectors of points A and B respectively.

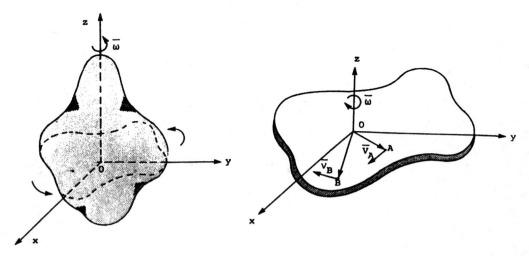

(a) plane motion of a rigid body; dotted line represents x-y plane cross section.

(b) more detailed look at cross-section lying in x-y plane with points A and B and their corresponding velocities.

<u>Solution</u>: From the figure,

$$\overline{OB} = \overline{OA} + \overline{AB} \tag{3}$$

The vector $\overline{AB}$ can be represented as

$$\overline{AB} = r \cos\theta \overline{i} + r \sin\theta \overline{j} \tag{4}$$

where r is constant.

Substituting eq.(4) into eq.(3), obtain

$$\overline{OB} = \overline{OA} + r \cos\theta \overline{i} + r \sin\theta \overline{j} \tag{5}$$

Since $\overline{OB}$ and $\overline{OA}$ are the position vectors of the points B and A, differentiation with respect to time t will give the velocity vectors. Differentiating eq.(5) with respect to t gives

$$\frac{d}{dt} \overline{OB} = \frac{d}{dt} \overline{OA} - r \sin\theta \frac{d\theta}{dt} \overline{i} + r \cos\theta \frac{d\theta}{dt} \overline{j}. \tag{6}$$

Since r is constant, $\frac{d}{dt} r = 0$

and,

$$\frac{d}{dt} \overline{OB} = \overline{v}_B$$
$$\frac{d}{dt} \overline{OA} = \overline{v}_A \tag{7}$$

Then denote

$$\overline{\omega} = \frac{d\theta}{dt} \overline{k} \tag{8}$$

Substituting eqs.(7), (8) into eq.(6) and using the identities

$$\overline{i} = -\overline{k} \times \overline{j}$$
$$\overline{j} = \overline{k} \times \overline{i}$$

obtain

$$\overline{v}_B = \overline{v}_A - r \sin\theta \frac{d\theta}{dt} \overline{i} + r \cos\theta \frac{d\theta}{dt} \overline{j}$$
$$= \overline{v}_A + r \sin\theta \frac{d\theta}{dt} \overline{k} \times \overline{j} + r \cos\theta \frac{d\theta}{dt} \overline{k} \times \overline{i} \tag{9}$$
$$= \overline{v}_A + \overline{\omega} \times (r \cos\theta \overline{i} + r \sin\theta \overline{j}) = \overline{v}_A + \overline{\omega} \times \overline{AB}$$

Since differentiating the velocity vector $\overline{v}$ with respect to t gives the acceleration vector $\overline{a}$, differentiating eq.(9) yields

$$\frac{d}{dt} \overline{v}_B = \frac{d}{dt} \overline{v}_A + \frac{d}{dt} (\overline{\omega} \times \overline{AB})$$

or

$$\overline{a}_B = \overline{a}_A + \frac{d\overline{\omega}}{dt} \times \overline{AB} + \overline{\omega} \times \frac{d\overline{AB}}{dt} \tag{10}$$

Denote

$$\frac{d\overline{\omega}}{dt} = \frac{d^2\theta}{dt^2} \overline{k} = \overline{\alpha} \tag{11}$$

Substituting eq.(11) into eq.(10), yields

$$\bar{a}_B = \bar{a}_A + \bar{\alpha} \times \overline{AB} + \frac{d\theta}{dt} \bar{k} \times (-r\sin\theta \frac{d\theta}{dt} \bar{i} + r\cos\theta \frac{d\theta}{dt} \bar{j})$$

$$= \bar{a}_A \times \bar{\alpha} \times \overline{AB} - \left(\frac{d\theta}{dt}\right)^2 r \sin\theta\bar{j} - \left(\frac{d\theta}{dt}\right)^2 r \cos\theta\bar{i} \qquad (12)$$

$$= \bar{a}_A + \bar{\alpha} \times \overline{AB} - \omega^2\overline{AB}$$

● PROBLEM 5-46

Let X,Y,Z, be a coordinate system fixed in space and having origin at O. If x,y,z represents a coordinate system having the same origin O which rotates with respect to X,Y,Z, then given any vector $\bar{A}$ (see fig.1), we denote

$$\frac{d\bar{A}}{dt}\bigg|_{X,Y,Z} \quad \text{and} \quad \frac{d\bar{A}}{dt}\bigg|_{x,y,z} \qquad (1)$$

as the time derivative of $\bar{A}$ with respect to the fixed X,Y,Z system and the rotating x,y,z system respectively.

1) Show that there exists a vector $\bar{\omega}$ such that

$$\frac{d\bar{A}}{dt}\bigg|_{X,Y,Z} = \frac{d\bar{A}}{dt}\bigg|_{x,y,z} + \bar{\omega} \times \bar{A} \qquad (2)$$

2) If $D_{X,Y,Z}$ and $D_{x,y,z}$ denotes the time derivative operator in the fixed and rotating systems respectively, then show that

$$D_{X,Y,Z} \bar{u}(t) = D_{x,y,z} \bar{u}(t) + \bar{\omega} \times \bar{u}(t) \qquad (3)$$

where $\bar{u}(t)$ is any given vector.

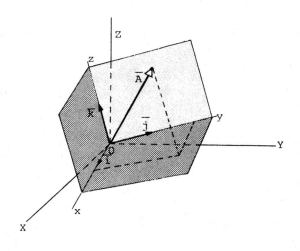

Solution: Let $\bar{i}$, $\bar{j}$, $\bar{k}$ be the unit base vectors in the xyz system. As observed from the XYZ fixed system the vectors $\bar{i}$, $\bar{j}$, $\bar{k}$ change with respect to time. The vector $\bar{A}$ can be expressed in terms of the $\bar{i}$, $\bar{j}$, $\bar{k}$ vectors as follows

$$\bar{A} = A_1 \bar{i} + A_2 \bar{j} + A_3 \bar{k} \tag{4}$$

Differentiating in the XYZ system,

$$\left.\frac{d\bar{A}}{dt}\right|_{XYZ} = \frac{dA_1}{dt}\bar{i} + \frac{dA_2}{dt}\bar{j} + \frac{dA_3}{dt}\bar{k} + A_1\frac{d\bar{i}}{dt} + A_2\frac{d\bar{j}}{dt} + A_3\frac{d\bar{k}}{dt} \tag{5}$$

Since

$$\left.\frac{d\bar{A}}{dt}\right|_{xyz} = \frac{dA_1}{dt}\bar{i} + \frac{dA_2}{dt}\bar{j} + \frac{dA_3}{dt}\bar{k} \tag{6}$$

one can write eq.(5) in the form

$$\left.\frac{d\bar{A}}{dt}\right|_{XYZ} = \left.\frac{d\bar{A}}{dt}\right|_{xyz} + A_1\frac{d\bar{i}}{dt} + A_2\frac{d\bar{j}}{dt} + A_3\frac{d\bar{k}}{dt} \tag{7}$$

Remembering that $\bar{i}$ is a unit vector, differentiate the equation

$$\bar{i} \cdot \bar{i} = 1$$

Then

$$\frac{d\bar{i}}{dt} \cdot \bar{i} = 0$$

Thus the vectors $\frac{d\bar{i}}{dt}$ and $\bar{i}$ are perpendicular.

Vector $\frac{d\bar{i}}{dt}$ perpendicular to $\bar{i}$ lies on the plane of $\bar{j}$ and $\bar{k}$.

Similarly $\frac{d\bar{j}}{dt}$ lies on the plane of $\bar{i}$ and $\bar{k}$ and $\frac{d\bar{k}}{dt}$ lies on the plane of $\bar{i}$ and $\bar{j}$. Therefore,

$$\frac{d\bar{i}}{dt} = p_1\bar{j} + p_2\bar{k}$$

$$\frac{d\bar{j}}{dt} = p_3\bar{i} + p_4\bar{k} \tag{8}$$

$$\frac{d\bar{k}}{dt} = p_5\bar{i} + p_6\bar{j}$$

Differentiating $\bar{i} \cdot \bar{j} = 0$, yields

$$\bar{i} \cdot \frac{d\bar{j}}{dt} + \bar{j} \cdot \frac{d\bar{i}}{dt} = 0$$

From eq.(8)

$$\bar{i} \cdot \frac{d\bar{j}}{dt} = p_3 \quad \text{and} \quad \bar{j} \cdot \frac{d\bar{i}}{dt} = p_1$$

Thus $\quad\quad p_1 = -p_3 \tag{9}$

From $\bar{i} \cdot \bar{k} = 0$ one has $\bar{k} \cdot \frac{d\bar{i}}{dt} + \bar{i} \cdot \frac{d\bar{k}}{dt} = 0$

and $\quad p_5 = -p_2$ $\hfill (10)$

From $\overline{j} \cdot \overline{k} = 0$ one has $\overline{j} \cdot \dfrac{d\overline{k}}{dt} + \overline{k} \cdot \dfrac{d\overline{j}}{dt} = 0$

and $\quad p_6 = -p_4$ $\hfill (11)$

Substituting eqs.(9), (10), and (11) into eq.(8), yields

$$\frac{d\overline{i}}{dt} = p_1\overline{j} + p_2\overline{k}$$

$$\frac{d\overline{j}}{dt} = p_1\overline{i} + p_4\overline{k} \qquad (12)$$

$$\frac{d\overline{k}}{dt} = -p_2\overline{i} - p_4\overline{j}$$

Denote $\qquad p_1 = \omega_3, \quad p_2 = -\omega_2, \quad p_4 = \omega_1$

System (12) can be written in the form

$$\frac{d\overline{i}}{dt} = \omega_3\overline{j} - \omega_2\overline{k}$$

$$\frac{d\overline{j}}{dt} = -\omega_3\overline{i} + \omega_1\overline{k} \qquad (13)$$

$$\frac{d\overline{k}}{dt} = \omega_2\overline{i} - \omega_1\overline{j}$$

Therefore
$$A_1\frac{d\overline{i}}{dt} + A_2\frac{d\overline{j}}{dt} + A_3\frac{d\overline{k}}{dt} = (A_3\omega_2 - A_2\omega_3)\overline{i}$$

$$+ (A_1\omega_3 - A_3\omega_1)\overline{j} + (A_2\omega_1 - A_1\omega_2)\overline{k}$$

$$= \begin{vmatrix} \overline{i} & \overline{j} & \overline{k} \\ \omega_1 & \omega_2 & \omega_3 \\ A_1 & A_2 & A_3 \end{vmatrix} = \overline{\omega} \times A \qquad (14)$$

That proves eq.(1).

Note that $\overline{\omega} = \omega_1\overline{i} + \omega_2\overline{j} + \omega_3\overline{k}$ is the angular velocity vector of the moving system with respect to the fixed system.

2. $\qquad D_{XYZ}\,\overline{A} = \left.\dfrac{d\overline{A}}{dt}\right|_{XYZ}$ $\hfill (15)$

$$D_{xyz}\,\overline{A} = \left.\frac{d\overline{A}}{dt}\right|_{xyz}$$

where the first equation is the derivative of the fixed system and the second the derivative of the moving x, y, z system. From eq.(1),

217

$$D_{XYZ} \overline{A} = D_{xyz} \overline{A} + \overline{\omega} \times \overline{A} \tag{16}$$

Eq. (16) can be written in the operator form as

$$D_{XYZ} \equiv D_{xyz} + \overline{\omega} \times \tag{17}$$

● **PROBLEM 5-47**

Let XYZ be a coordinate system fixed in space whose origin
is O; and xyz be a coordinate system rotating with respect
to XYZ whose origin is also O.   Determine

1.   the velocity

2.   the acceleration

of a moving particle as seen by the observer in the XYZ
system and by the observer in the xyz system.

Solution: 1.   One has the following operator equivalence

$$D_{XYZ} \equiv D_{xyz} + \overline{\omega} \times \tag{1}$$

Let $\overline{r}$ be the position vector of the particle. Using eq.(1),

$$D_{XYZ} \overline{r} = D_{xyz} \overline{r} + \overline{\omega} \times \overline{r} \tag{2}$$

Since D_{XYZ} is the time derivative operator in the fixed system

$D_{XYZ} \overline{r} = \overline{V}_{XYZ}$ represents the velocity of a particle relative to
the fixed system.

Similarly $D_{xyz} \overline{r} = \overline{V}_{xyz}$ represents the velocity of the particle relative to the moving system.

Finally $\overline{\omega} \times \overline{r} = \overline{v}$ represents the velocity of the moving system
relative to the fixed system.

Eq.(2) can be written in the form

$$\overline{V}_{XYZ} = \overline{v}_{xyz} + \overline{v} \tag{3}$$

Note that the roles of the fixed and moving systems can be
interchanged.   That is, one can consider xyz to be the fixed
system and XYZ the system rotating with respect to xyz.

For this purpose one must interchange XYZ and xyz and replace
ω by $-\overline{\omega}$ since the relative rotation is reversed.

Eq.(3) becomes

$$\overline{V}_{xyz} = \overline{V}_{XYZ} - \overline{\omega} \times \overline{r}$$

or

$$\bar{V}_{xyz} + \bar{\omega} \times \bar{r} = \bar{V}_{XYZ} \tag{4}$$

2. To determine the acceleration of the particle in the fixed system,

$$D^2_{XYZ} \bar{r} = D_{XYZ}(D_{XYZ} \bar{r}) \tag{5}$$

differentiate eq.(2)

$$D_{XYZ}(D_{XYZ} \bar{r}) = D_{XYZ}(D_{xyz} \bar{r} + \bar{\omega} \times \bar{r})$$

$$= (D_{xyz} + \bar{\omega}x)(D_{xyz} \bar{r} + \bar{\omega} \times \bar{r}) = D_{xyz}(D_{xyz} \bar{r} + \bar{\omega} \times \bar{r})$$

$$+ \bar{\omega} \times (D_{xyz} \bar{r} + \bar{\omega} \times \bar{r}) = D^2_{xyz} \bar{r} + D_{xyz}(\bar{\omega} \times \bar{r}) + \bar{\omega} \times (\bar{\omega} \times \bar{r}) \tag{6}$$

$$= D^2_{xyz} \bar{r} + 2\bar{\omega} \times D_{xyz} \bar{r} + (D_{xyz}\bar{\omega}) \times \bar{r} + \bar{\omega} \times (\bar{\omega} \times \bar{r})$$

Let
$$\bar{a}_{XYZ} = D^2_{XYZ} \bar{r}$$ be the acceleration of a particle relative to the fixed system and $$\bar{a}_{xyz} = D^2_{xyz} \bar{r}$$ be the acceleration of a particle relative to the moving system.

$$\bar{a} = 2\bar{\omega} \times D_{xyz} \bar{r} + (D_{xyz}\bar{\omega}) \times \bar{r} + \bar{\omega} \times (\bar{\omega} \times \bar{r}) \tag{7}$$

is the acceleration of the moving system relative to the fixed system.

$$\bar{a}_{XYZ} = \bar{a}_{xyz} + \bar{a} \tag{8}$$

If $\bar{\omega}$ is a constant vector then $D_{xyz}\bar{\omega} = \bar{0}$ and

$$\bar{a} = 2\bar{\omega} \times D_{xyz} \bar{r} + \bar{\omega} \times (\bar{\omega} \times \bar{r}). \tag{9}$$

In eq.(9) $2\bar{\omega} \times D_{xyz} \bar{r}$ is called the Coriolis acceleration and $\bar{\omega} \times (\bar{\omega} \times \bar{r})$ is called the centripetal acceleration.

CHAPTER 6

DIFFERENTIAL CALCULUS OF FUNCTIONS OF SEVERAL VARIABLES

INTRODUCTION

Chapter 6 introduces the differential calculus of functions of several variables. The differential calculus of functions of several variables is nothing more than an extension of the differential calculus of a single variable function (discussed in Chapter 5). Thus, with only slight modifications, we are able to derive the definition of the partial derivative by applying the definition of the ordinary derivative. Before this definition can be derived however, the student should be familiar with the concept of the partial derivative. The partial derivative of a function is described as the derivative of this function with respect to one particular variable while holding all other variables fixed (constant).

For instance, if z is a function of two variables x and y, then there are two partial derivatives (higher order and mixed partial derivatives will be avoided for now), the partial derivative of z with respect to x, denoted by $\frac{\partial z}{\partial x}$, in which case y is being held constant, and the partial of z with respect to y, denoted by $\frac{\partial z}{\partial y}$, in which case x is being held fixed.

After discussing continuity of a function of several variables, Chapter 6 proceeds to the mathematical definition of the partial derivative and how its actually derived from ordinary derivatives.

Recall that Chapter 5 discussed the derivative of a function with respect to a single independent variable, usually called x, where $y = f(x)$. Chapter VI introduces the case where the variable x is no longer an independent variable but is rather a function of some other variable (usually t). The derivative of y with respect to t, such that $y = y(x)$ and $x = x(t)$, is a slightly more complex concept that will be discussed in this chapter.

Chapter 6 then proceeds to the definition of the most

fundamental differential operator in vector analysis -- The Operator Nabla (also called Gradient), symbolyzed by "∇" (read "DEL").

From the operator nabla one derives the concept of another differential operator -- the Laplacian, denoted by "∇²". The Laplacian operator leads to a very important class of vector functions, namely, the harmonic and biharmonic vector functions.

The chapter closes with the definition of the directional derivative and its application to geometry and physics.

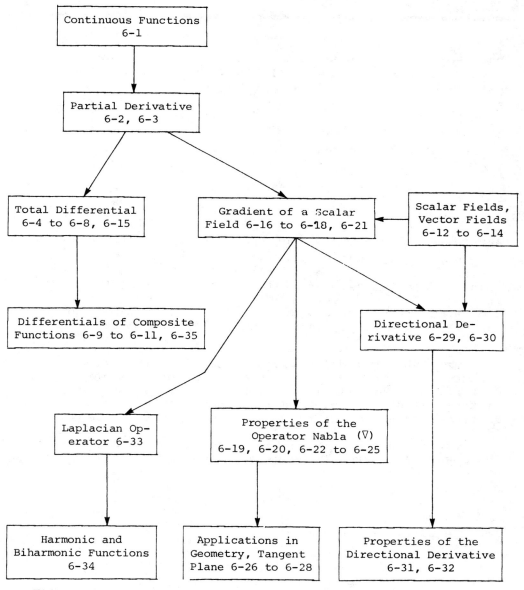

This chart is provided to facilitate rapid understanding of the inter-relationships of the topics and subject matter in this chapter. Also shown are the problem numbers associated with the subject matter.

CONTINUOUS FUNCTIONS, PARTIAL DERIVATIVES AND TOTAL DIFFERENTIAL

Determine if the function

$$f(x, y) = \frac{x^2 - y^2}{x^2 + y^2} \tag{1}$$

is continuous at the origin.

Solution: Start with the definition of continuity. For this purpose, here are some basic concepts on the theory of sets. The set of points in the xy plane refers to any collection of points, finite or infinite in number.

The neighborhood of a point (x_0, y_0) is the set of points inside a circle having center (x_0, y_0) and radius ε. Each point in the neighborhood of (x_0, y_0) must satisfy the inequality

$$\sqrt{(x - x_0)^2 + (y - y_0)^2} < \varepsilon \tag{2}$$

A set is called open if every point (x_1, y_1) of the set has a neighborhood which lies within the set. Thus, the interior of a circle is open, while the interval [0,1] is not open, since point 0 does not have any neighborhood lying wholly within the interval [0,1]. A set is called a connected open set or a domain, if it is open and any two points A and B of the set can be joined by a broken line lying wholly within the set.

From the last definition, we conclude that the interior of a circle is a domain. The region is a set consisting of a domain and some or all of its boundary points. A boundary point of a set is a point every neighborhood of which contains at least one point not in the set and one point in the set.

For an interval [2 3] the boundary points are 2 and 3. The boundary points of the circular domain

$$x^2 + y^2 < 1$$

are the points for which

$$x^2 + y^2 = 1$$

Let f(x,y) be a function over the domain D and let (x_0, y_0) be a point of D or a boundary point of D. The equation

$$\lim_{\substack{x \to x_0 \\ y \to y_0}} f(x,y) = a \tag{3}$$

means that for any $\varepsilon > 0$ there exists a $\delta > 0$ such that for every (x,y) of the neighborhood of (x_0, y_0) of radius δ,

$$|f(x,y) - a| < \varepsilon \tag{4}$$

If the point (x_0, y_0) is in D and

$$\lim_{\substack{x \to x_0 \\ y \to y_0}} f(x,y) = f(x_0, y_0) \tag{5}$$

then $f(x,y)$ is said to be continuous at (x_0, y_0).

We can show that the function defined in eq.(1)

$$f(x,y) = \frac{x^2 - y^2}{x^2 + y^2}$$

is not continuous at $(0,0)$. To find the limit

$$\lim_{\substack{x \to o \\ y \to o}} \frac{x^2 - y^2}{x^2 + y^2} , \tag{6}$$

assume that the points (x,y) approach $(0,0)$ on the line $x=y$; then

$$\lim_{\substack{x \to o \\ y \to o \\ x = y}} \frac{x^2 - y^2}{x^2 + y^2} = 0 \tag{7}$$

If the points (x,y) approach $(0,0)$ on the y axis, then,

$$\lim_{\substack{x = o \\ y \to o}} \frac{x^2 - y^2}{x^2 + y^2} = -1 \tag{8}$$

From eqs.(7) and (8), we conclude that the function $f(x,y) = \frac{x^2 - y^2}{x^2 + y^2}$ has no limiting value at $(0,0)$ and is not continuous at $(0,0)$.

All of the above basic theorems on limits and continuity hold without change for functions of two or more variables.

Using the definition of the partial derivative, find

$$\frac{\partial f}{\partial x}, \quad \frac{\partial f}{\partial y} \quad \text{where}$$

1. $f(x,y) = x^2 - y^2$ (1)

2. $x^2 + y^2 = f^2(x,y) + 1$

                                                   (2)

3. Give the geometrical interpretation of the partial derivative.

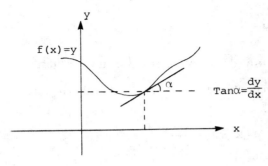

Fig. 1

Solution: 1. Let $f(x,y)$ be a function defined over a domain D in the xy plane and let (x_0, y_0) be a point in D. The function $f(x, y_0)$ depends on x alone and is defined over an interval containing x_0. The partial derivative of $f(x,y)$ with respect to x at (x_0, y_0) is defined as

$$\frac{\partial f}{\partial x}(x_0, y_0) = \lim_{\Delta x \to 0} \frac{f(x_0 + \Delta x, y_0) - f(x_0, y_0)}{\Delta x} \qquad (3)$$

In similar fashion, the partial derivative of $f(x,y)$ with respect to y at (x_0, y_0) is

$$\frac{\partial f}{\partial y}(x_0, y_0) = \lim_{\Delta y \to 0} \frac{f(x_0, y_0 + \Delta y) - f(x_0, y_0)}{\Delta y} \qquad (4)$$

These partial derivatives may be denoted by

$$\frac{\partial f}{\partial x}\bigg|_{(x_0, y_0)}, \quad \frac{\partial f}{\partial y}\bigg|_{(x_0, y_0)}$$

Thus for the function

$$f(x,y) = x^2 - y^2,$$

we have

$$\frac{\partial f}{\partial x} = \lim_{\Delta x \to 0} \frac{f(x+\Delta x, y) - f(x,y)}{\Delta x}$$

$$= \lim_{\Delta x \to 0} \frac{(x+\Delta x)^2 - y^2 - x^2 + y^2}{\Delta x} = \lim_{\Delta x \to 0} \frac{2x\Delta x + (\Delta x)^2}{\Delta x} = 2x \quad (5)$$

and

$$\frac{\partial f}{\partial y} = \lim_{\Delta y \to 0} \frac{f(x, y+\Delta y) - f(x,y)}{\Delta y} = \lim_{\Delta y \to 0} \frac{x^2 - (y+\Delta y)^2 - x^2 + y^2}{\Delta y}$$

$$\quad (6)$$

$$= \lim_{\Delta y \to 0} \frac{-2y\Delta y - (\Delta y)^2}{\Delta y} = -2y$$

Note that one can define the partial derivatives of functions of more than two variables in the same manner as above.

2. Differentiate eq.(2) with respect to x

$$2x = 2f \frac{\partial f}{\partial x} \quad (7)$$

and with respect to y

$$2y = 2f \frac{\partial f}{\partial y} \quad (8)$$

Thus

$$\frac{\partial f}{\partial x} = \frac{x}{f}$$

and $\quad\quad\quad\quad\quad\quad\quad\quad (f \neq 0) \quad\quad\quad\quad\quad\quad (9)$

$$\frac{\partial f}{\partial y} = \frac{y}{f}$$

3. In the case of a real-valued function f(x) = y of a single real variable, the value of the derivative $\frac{dy}{dx}$ at a point is the slope of the tangent line to the graph of the function at that point, as shown in Fig. 1.

Without losing generality, one can consider a function z = f(x,y). Its graph is the set of points (x,y, f(x,y)) in R^3, as shown in Fig. 2(a). Assume that x and y are in the domain of f.

Intersect the surface f with the vertical plane y = b. Points A, B, C, D are located on this plane. The intersection of the surface with this plane is a curve

$$z = f(x,y) = f(x,b), \quad \text{since } y = b. \quad (10)$$

The slope of the curve f(x,b) at x = a is

$$\frac{\partial f}{\partial x} (a,b) \quad (11)$$

At y = b the slope of the curve f(a,y) is equal to

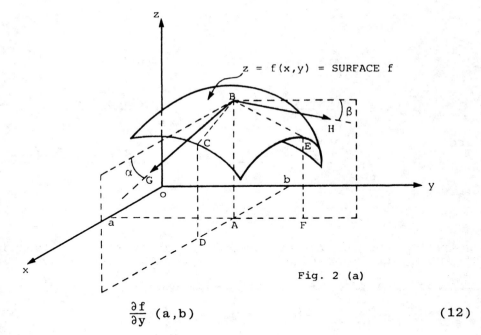

z = f(x,y) = SURFACE f

Fig. 2 (a)

$$\frac{\partial f}{\partial y} (a,b) \tag{12}$$

then

$$\tan \alpha = \frac{\partial f}{\partial x} (a,b)$$

$$\tag{13}$$

$$\tan \beta = \frac{\partial f}{\partial y} (a,b)$$

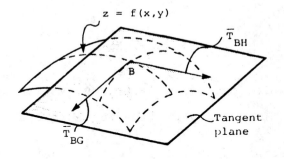

Fig. 2 (b)

The angles α, β are shown in Fig. 2(a). The values of tan α and tan β are the slopes of the tangent vectors to the two curves located on the graph of the function f. These two tangent vectors $\overline{T}_{BG}$ and $\overline{T}_{BH}$ determine a tangent plane to the graph of f as shown in Fig. 2(b). The plane containing both tangent lines is given by the equation

$$z = f(a,b) + (x-a) \frac{\partial f}{\partial x} (a,b) + (y-b) \frac{\partial f}{\partial y} (a,b) \tag{14}$$

This is the equation of a plane tangent to the surface f at the point (a,b, f(a,b)).

226

1. Evaluate $\dfrac{\partial f}{\partial x_1}$ and $\dfrac{\partial f}{\partial x_2}$ for

$$f = x_1^2 + x_2^2 \tag{1}$$

$$f = \frac{x_1}{x_1^2 + x_2^2} \tag{2}$$

$$x_1^3 + x_1 x_2^2 - x_1^2 f + f^3 - 4 = 0 \tag{3}$$

$$f = \sqrt{e^{x_1 + x_2} - x_2^2} \tag{4}$$

2. The function $f(x,y,z)$ is given by:

$$f(x,y,z) = x^2 + xy^2 + xyz + z^2 \tag{5}$$

Evaluate the following derivatives

$$\frac{\partial f}{\partial x}, \quad \frac{\partial f}{\partial y}, \quad \frac{\partial f}{\partial z} \tag{6}$$

$$\frac{\partial^2 f}{\partial x \partial y}, \quad \frac{\partial^2 f}{\partial y \partial x}, \quad \frac{\partial^2 f}{\partial x \partial z}, \quad \frac{\partial^2 f}{\partial z \partial x} \tag{7}$$

$$\frac{\partial^3 f}{\partial x \partial y \partial z} \tag{8}$$

Solution: 1. For $f = x_1^2 + x_2^2$,

$$\frac{\partial f}{\partial x_1} = 2x_1 \; ; \quad \frac{\partial f}{\partial x_2} = 2x_2 \tag{9}$$

For $f = \dfrac{x_1}{x_1^2 + x_2^2}$

$$\frac{\partial f}{\partial x_1} = \frac{-x_1^2 + x_2^2}{(x_1^2 + x_2^2)^2} \; ; \quad \frac{\partial f}{\partial x_2} = \frac{-2x_1 x_2}{(x_1^2 + x_2^2)^2} \tag{10}$$

For the function

$$x_1^3 + x_1 x_2^2 - x_1^2 f + f^3 - 4 = 0$$

differentiating with respect to x_1, gives

$$3x_1^2 + x_2^2 - 2x_1 f - x_1^2 \frac{\partial f}{\partial x_1} + 3f^2 \frac{\partial f}{\partial x_1} = 0 \tag{11}$$

Solving eq.(11) for $\dfrac{\partial f}{\partial x_1}$,

$$\frac{\partial f}{\partial x_1} = \frac{3x_1^2 + x_2^2 - 2x_1 f}{x_1^2 - 3f^2} \tag{12}$$

Differentiating eq.(3) with respect to x_2, gives

$$2x_1 x_2 - x_1^2 \frac{\partial f}{\partial x_2} + 3f^2 \frac{\partial f}{\partial x_2} = 0 \tag{13}$$

227

Solving eq.(13) for $\frac{\partial f}{\partial x_2}$,

$$\frac{\partial f}{\partial x_2} = \frac{2x_1 x_2}{x_1^2 - 3f^2} \tag{14}$$

For $f = \sqrt{e^{x_1 + x_2} - x_2^2}$

$$\frac{\partial f}{\partial x_1} = \frac{1}{2\sqrt{e^{x_1 + x_2} - x_2^2}} \; e^{(x_1 + x_2)} \tag{15}$$

$$\frac{\partial f}{\partial x_2} = \frac{1}{2\sqrt{e^{x_1 + x_2} - x_2^2}} \left(e^{(x_1 + x_2)} - 2x_2 \right)$$

2. Differentiating eq.(5), obtain

$$\frac{\partial f}{\partial x} = 2x + y^2 + yz \tag{16}$$

$$\frac{\partial f}{\partial y} = 2xy + xz \tag{17}$$

$$\frac{\partial f}{\partial z} = xy + 2z \tag{18}$$

To find $\frac{\partial^2 f}{\partial x \partial y}$, differentiate eq.(17) to obtain

$$\frac{\partial^2 f}{\partial x \partial y} = \frac{\partial}{\partial x}\left(\frac{\partial f}{\partial y}\right) = \frac{\partial}{\partial x} (2xy + xz) = 2y + z \tag{19}$$

To find $\frac{\partial^2 f}{\partial y \partial x}$ differentiate eq.(16), thus

$$\frac{\partial^2 f}{\partial y \partial x} = \frac{\partial}{\partial y} (2x + y^2 + yz) = 2y + z \tag{20}$$

It is not coincidental that both partial derivatives (eq.(19) and eq.(20)) are equal. The following theorem plays an important part in the differential calculus.

Theorem:

If in the domain of a function, all the derivatives are continuous, then

$$\frac{\partial^2 f}{\partial x \partial y} = \frac{\partial^2 f}{\partial y \partial x} \tag{21}$$

It can be shown that this theorem is true for any higher order derivative and for functions of any number of independent variables.
As an example, from eq.(18)

$$\frac{\partial^2 f}{\partial x \partial z} = \frac{\partial}{\partial x} (xy + 2z) = y \tag{22}$$

228

Based on the above theorem, we can conclude that

$$\frac{\partial^2 f}{\partial z \partial x} = \frac{\partial^2 f}{\partial x \partial z} = y \tag{23}$$

Finally, we can also write

$$\frac{\partial^3 f}{\partial x \partial y \partial z} = \frac{\partial^3 f}{\partial y \partial x \partial z} = \frac{\partial}{\partial y}\left(\frac{\partial^2 f}{\partial x \partial z}\right) = \frac{\partial}{\partial y}(y) = 1 \tag{24}$$

(Here we substituted eq.(23) into eq.(24).)

● **PROBLEM** 6-4

Find the total differential of the following functions

1. $z(x,y) = x^2 - y^2 + 2xy$

2. $f(x,y,z,t) = xt + xy + zt^2$

Solution: If a function $f(x,y)$ has continuous first partial derivatives in some domain D, then f has a differential

$$df = \frac{\partial f}{\partial x} dx + \frac{\partial f}{\partial y} dy \tag{1}$$

at every point (x,y) of D.

The above definition is called the "fundamental lemma", or more simply, the "total differential". The above definition holds true for any function of any number of variables. For example, for $f(x,y,z)$, we have

$$df = \frac{\partial f}{\partial x} dx + \frac{\partial f}{\partial y} dy + \frac{\partial f}{\partial z} dz \tag{2}$$

1. The function $z(x,y)$ is defined over the plane xy. Its partial derivatives are

$$\frac{\partial z}{\partial x} = 2x + 2y$$

$$\frac{\partial z}{\partial y} = -2y + 2x \tag{3}$$

Both partial derivatives are continuous over the xy plane. Thus one can apply the Fundamental Lemma and obtain

$$dz = \frac{\partial z}{\partial x} dx + \frac{\partial z}{\partial y} dy \tag{4}$$

Substituting eq.(3) into eq.(4), gives

$$dz = (2x + 2y) dx + (-2y + 2x) dy \tag{5}$$

2. Since the function $f(x,y,z,t)$ is a polynomial, all of its partial derivatives are continuous. From the Fundamental Lemma,

$$df = \frac{\partial f}{\partial x} dx + \frac{\partial f}{\partial y} dy + \frac{\partial f}{\partial z} dz + \frac{\partial f}{\partial t} dt$$

$$= (t+y)dx + xdy + t^2dz + (x+2zt) \, dt \tag{6}$$

● **PROBLEM** 6-5

A function $f(x,y)$ has the value $f(2,5) = 7$ and the derivatives $f_x(2,5) = 3$, $f_y(2,5) = 1$. Using the definition of the total differential, estimate the values of

$$f(2.2, \; 5.1) \quad \text{and} \quad f(1.9, \; 5.2)$$

Solution: For a function with continuous first partial derivatives,

$$df = \frac{\partial f}{\partial x} dx + \frac{\partial f}{\partial y} dy \tag{1}$$

Note that the notation f_x and f_y is the same as

$$\frac{\partial f}{\partial x} = f_x \qquad \frac{\partial f}{\partial y} = f_y$$

For $f(2.2, \; 5.1)$, we have $dx = 0.2$ because the value of the function is given at $x = 2$. For dy, we have $dy = 0.1$.

Substituting dx, dy, and the values of the partial derivatives into eq. (1), obtain

$$df = \frac{\partial f}{\partial x} dx + \frac{\partial f}{\partial y} dy = 3 \cdot 0.2 + 1 \cdot 0.1 = 0.6 + 0.1 = 0.7 \tag{2}$$

Since $df = f(x+dx, \; y+dy) - f(x,y)$, then

$$f(x+dx, \; y+dy) = f(x,y) + df, \text{ and} \tag{3}$$

$$f(2.2, \; 5.1) = f(2, \; 5) + 0.7 = 7.7 \tag{4}$$

Accordingly, for $f(1.9, \; 5.2)$,

$$dx = -0.1 \quad \text{and} \quad dy = 0.2$$

Substituting into eq.(1),

$$df = \frac{\partial f}{\partial x} dx + \frac{\partial f}{\partial y} dy = 3 \cdot (-0.1) + 1 \cdot (0.2)$$

$$= -0.3 + 0.2 = -0.1 \tag{5}$$

Thus

$$f(1.9, \; 5.2) = 6.9 \tag{6}$$

Using the fundamental lemma, find the total differential of the functions

1) $f(x_1, x_2, x_3) = x_1^2 - x_2^2 + x_3^3$

2) $f(x_1, x_2, x_3) = 2x_1 x_2 + \sin x_2 + x_3^2$

Solution: The fundamental lemma states that if $f = f(x_1, x_2, x_3)$ has continuous first partial derivatives in the region D, then f has a differential

$$df = \frac{\partial f}{\partial x_1} dx_1 + \frac{\partial f}{\partial x_2} dx_2 + \frac{\partial f}{\partial x_3} dx_3 \qquad (1)$$

at every point (x_1, x_2, x_3) of D.

1) Find $\frac{\partial f}{\partial x_1}$, $\frac{\partial f}{\partial x_2}$ and $\frac{\partial f}{\partial x_3}$

$$\frac{\partial f}{\partial x_1} = 2x_1$$

$$\frac{\partial f}{\partial x_2} = -2x_2 \qquad (2)$$

$$\frac{\partial f}{\partial x_3} = 3x_3^2$$

All the partial derivatives are continuous, therefore to find df, apply eq.(1).

$$df = \frac{\partial f}{\partial x_1} dx_1 + \frac{\partial f}{\partial x_2} dx_2 + \frac{\partial f}{\partial x_3} dx_3$$

$$= 2x_1 dx_1 - 2x_2 dx_2 + 3x_3^2 dx_3 \qquad (3)$$

2) The partial derivatives are

$$\frac{\partial f}{\partial x_1} = 2x_2$$

$$\frac{\partial f}{\partial x_2} = 2x_1 + \cos x_2$$

$$\frac{\partial f}{\partial x_3} = 3x_3^2$$

all of them are continuous, thus

$$df = \frac{\partial f}{\partial x_1} dx_1 + \frac{\partial f}{\partial x_2} dx_2 + \frac{\partial f}{\partial x_3} dx_3 \qquad (4)$$

$$= 2x_2 dx_1 + (2x_1 + \cos x_2) dx_2 + 3x_3^2 dx_3$$

Describe the Pfaff problem.

Solution: Consider a differential of the form

$$dU = \sum_{i=1}^{n} X_i dx_i \qquad (1)$$

where X_1, X_2,...,X_n are functions of independent variables and dU is the total differential. Eq.(1) is called a Pfaff expression. Expression (1) is an inexact differential, because in general, the value of U depends upon the path of integration. When the value of U does not depend on the path of integration, the expression is an exact or perfect differential, and then eq.(1) is integrable.

Pfaff's problem deals with the cases when eq.(1) is not integrable. If it contains 2n or (2n-1) variables it is equivalent to not more than n algebraic equations.

Pfaff's problem is encountered in advanced theories of mechanics and thermodynamics.

Find the differentials of the following functions:

1) $f = \dfrac{x_1}{x_2}$

2) $f = \sqrt{x_1^2 + x_2^2 + x_3^2}$

3) $f = \log \sqrt{x_1^2 + x_2^2}$

4) $f = \dfrac{1}{\sqrt{x_1^2 + x_2^2 + x_3^2}}$

Solution: 1) The differential is given by

$$df = \frac{\partial f}{\partial x_1} dx_1 + \frac{\partial f}{\partial x_2} dx_2 \qquad (1)$$

Note that in this case, function f does not depend on x_3.

$$df = \frac{1}{x_1} dx_1 - \frac{x_1}{x_2^2} dx_2 = \frac{x_2 dx_1 - x_1 dx_2}{x_2^2} \qquad (2)$$

2) $df = \dfrac{\partial f}{\partial x_1} dx_1 + \dfrac{\partial f}{\partial x_2} dx_2 + \dfrac{\partial f}{\partial x_3} dx_3 \qquad (3)$

where

$$\frac{\partial f}{\partial x_1} = \frac{2x_1}{2\sqrt{x_1^2 + x_2^2 + x_3^2}} = \frac{x_1}{\sqrt{x_1^2 + x_2^2 + x_3^2}}$$

$$\frac{\partial f}{\partial x_2} = \frac{x_2}{\sqrt{x_1^2 + x_2^2 + x_3^2}} \qquad (4)$$

$$\frac{\partial f}{\partial x_3} = \frac{x_3}{\sqrt{x_1^2 + x_2^2 + x_3^2}}$$

Substituting eq.(4) into eq.(3), obtain

$$df = \frac{x_1 dx_1 + x_2 dx_2 + x_3 dx_3}{\sqrt{x_1^2 + x_2^2 + x_3^2}} \qquad (5)$$

3) $\frac{\partial f}{\partial x_1} = \frac{\partial}{\partial x_1} \left(\log \sqrt{x_1^2 + x_2^2} \right) = \frac{1}{\sqrt{x_1^2 + x_2^2}} \cdot \frac{2x_1}{2\sqrt{x_1^2 + x_2^2}} = \frac{x_1}{x_1^2 + x_2^2}$

$$\qquad (6)$$

$$\frac{\partial f}{\partial x_2} = \frac{x_2}{x_1^2 + x_2^2}$$

For the differential,

$$df = \frac{x_1 dx_1 + x_2 dx_2}{x_1^2 + x_2^2} \qquad (7)$$

4) $\frac{\partial f}{\partial x_1} = \frac{-1}{2(x_1^2 + x_2^2 + x_3^2)^{3/2}} \cdot 2x_1 = \frac{-x_1}{(x_1^2 + x_2^2 + x_3^2)^{3/2}}$

$$\qquad (8)$$

$$\frac{\partial f}{\partial x_2} = \frac{-x_2}{(x_1^2 + x_2^2 + x_3^2)^{3/2}}$$

$$\frac{\partial f}{\partial x_3} = \frac{-x_3}{(x_1^2 + x_2^2 + x_3^2)^{3/2}}$$

Substituting eq.(8) into the general formula,

$$df = \frac{-x_1 dx_1 - x_2 dx_2 - x_3 dx_3}{(x_1^2 + x_2^2 + x_3^2)^{3/2}} \qquad (9)$$

DERIVATIVES AND DIFFERENTIALS OF COMPOSITE FUNCTIONS, SCALAR FIELDS AND VECTOR FIELDS

● PROBLEM 6-9

1. Find $\frac{df}{dt}$, if $f = x^y$ where $\qquad (1)$

x and y are functions of t, i.e.

233

$$x = x(t), \quad y = y(t)$$

2. Show that for f(x,y), where

$$x = r\cos\theta, \quad y = r\sin\theta$$

the following identity holds

$$\left(\frac{\partial f}{\partial r}\right)^2 + \frac{1}{r^2}\left(\frac{\partial f}{\partial \theta}\right)^2 = \left(\frac{\partial f}{\partial x}\right)^2 + \left(\frac{\partial f}{\partial y}\right)^2 \qquad (2)$$

Solution: In both parts 1 and 2, one deals with the different-- ials of functions of functions, and therefore we must apply the following theorem:

Theorem:

Let   f = f(x,y)   and   x = x(t),   y = y(t)   then

$$\frac{df}{dt} = \frac{\partial f}{\partial x}\frac{dx}{dt} + \frac{\partial f}{\partial y}\frac{dy}{dt} \qquad (3)$$

In general, if   f = f(x,y,t,...)   and

$$x = x(u,v,w,\ldots), \quad y = y(u,v,w,\ldots), \quad t = t(u,v,w,\ldots)$$

then

$$\frac{\partial f}{\partial u} = \frac{\partial f}{\partial x}\frac{\partial x}{\partial u} + \frac{\partial f}{\partial y}\frac{\partial y}{\partial u} + \frac{\partial f}{\partial t}\frac{\partial t}{\partial u} + \ldots,$$

$$\frac{\partial f}{\partial v} = \frac{\partial f}{\partial x}\frac{\partial x}{\partial v} + \frac{\partial f}{\partial y}\frac{\partial y}{\partial v} + \frac{\partial f}{\partial t}\frac{\partial t}{\partial v} + \ldots \qquad (4)$$

The above rules are called "chain rules", they are essential in the differential calculus of composite functions.

1. The function f is a function of x and y, and both functions x and y are functions of t. We can apply eq.(3), doing this

$$\frac{df}{dt} = \frac{\partial f}{\partial x}\frac{dx}{dt} + \frac{\partial f}{\partial y}\frac{dy}{dt} \qquad (5)$$

where $f = x^y$.

The partial derivatives are

$$\frac{\partial f}{\partial x} = y\,x^{y-1} \quad \text{and} \qquad (6)$$

$$\frac{\partial f}{\partial y} = x^y \ln x \qquad (7)$$

Substituting eqs.(6) and (7) into eq.(5),

$$\frac{df}{dt} = y\,x^{y-1}\frac{dx}{dt} + x^y \ln x \frac{dy}{dt} \qquad (8)$$

2. The partial derivatives $\frac{\partial f}{\partial r}$ and $\frac{\partial f}{\partial \theta}$ can be written as follows:

$$\frac{\partial f}{\partial r} = \frac{\partial f}{\partial x}\frac{\partial x}{\partial r} + \frac{\partial f}{\partial y}\frac{\partial y}{\partial r}$$

$$\frac{\partial f}{\partial \theta} = \frac{\partial f}{\partial x}\frac{\partial x}{\partial \theta} + \frac{\partial f}{\partial y}\frac{\partial y}{\partial \theta}$$

(9)

From $x = r \cos \theta$ and $y = r \sin \theta$,

$$\frac{\partial x}{\partial r} = \cos \theta \qquad \frac{\partial y}{\partial r} = \sin \theta$$

$$\frac{\partial x}{\partial \theta} = -r \sin \theta \quad \frac{\partial y}{\partial \theta} = r \cos \theta$$

(10)

Substituting eqs.(10) into eq.(9), obtain

$$\frac{\partial f}{\partial r} = \cos \theta \frac{\partial f}{\partial x} + \sin \theta \frac{\partial f}{\partial y}$$

$$\frac{\partial f}{\partial \theta} = -r \sin \theta \frac{\partial f}{\partial x} + r \cos \theta \frac{\partial f}{\partial y}$$

(11)

Substituting eq.(11) into the left hand side of eq.(2), obtain

$$\left(\frac{\partial f}{\partial r}\right)^2 + \frac{1}{r^2}\left(\frac{\partial f}{\partial \theta}\right)^2 = \left(\cos \theta \frac{\partial f}{\partial x} + \sin \theta \frac{\partial f}{\partial y}\right)^2$$

$$+ \frac{1}{r^2}\left(-r \sin \theta \frac{\partial f}{\partial x} + r \cos \theta \frac{\partial f}{\partial y}\right)^2 = \left(\frac{\partial f}{\partial x}\right)^2 + \left(\frac{\partial f}{\partial y}\right)^2$$

(12)

● **PROBLEM 6-10**

1. Find the partial derivatives

$$\frac{\partial f}{\partial x} \quad \text{and} \quad \frac{\partial f}{\partial y} \quad \text{where}$$

$$f = \frac{x^3 + 1}{y}$$

(1)

2. Find the partial derivatives

$$\frac{\partial r}{\partial x} \quad \text{and} \quad \frac{\partial r}{\partial y} \quad \text{where}$$

$$r^2 = x^2 + y^2$$

(2)

Solution: Use the following theorem to solve this problem.

Theorem:
If the differential formula

$$df = \frac{\partial f}{\partial x} dx + \frac{\partial f}{\partial y} dy + \frac{\partial f}{\partial z} dz + \ldots$$

(3)

holds for $f = f(x,y,z,...)$ and $dx = \Delta x$, $dy = \Delta y$, $dz = \Delta z...$, then this remains true when x, y, z,... are all functions of other independent variables and dx, dy, dz,... are the corresponding differentials. From this theorem one concludes immediately that any equation in differentials which is true for one choice of independent and dependent variables is also true for any other choice of independent and dependent variables. In practice this means that in order to compute partial derivatives, one can compute differentials assuming that all variables are functions of one hypothetical variable. In doing so one can apply all the rules of ordinary differential calculus.

1. $dF = \dfrac{\partial f}{\partial x}\,dx + \dfrac{\partial f}{\partial y}\,dy$ (4)

from eq.(1)

$$\frac{\partial f}{\partial x} = \frac{1}{y}(3x^2) \quad \text{and} \quad \frac{\partial f}{\partial y} = \frac{-(x^3 + 1)}{y^2}$$ (5)

Substituting back into eq.(4)

$$dF = \frac{3x^2}{y}\,dx - \frac{x^3 + 1}{y^2}\,dy$$ (6)

2. Differentiating eq.(2)

$$r\,dr = x\,dx + y\,dy$$ (7)

or

$$dr = \frac{x}{r}\,dx + \frac{y}{r}\,dy$$ (8)

Since r is a function of x and y

$$dr = \frac{\partial r}{\partial x}\,dx + \frac{\partial r}{\partial y}\,dy$$ (9)

and

$$\frac{\partial r}{\partial x} = \frac{x}{r} \qquad \frac{\partial r}{\partial y} = \frac{y}{r}$$

● **PROBLEM 6-11**

In thermodynamics the state of a substance is described by the parameters: V-volume, T-temperature, p-pressure, and U-internal energy.
These four parameters are related by two equations.
Therefore, one can choose any two parameters as independent variables, the other two being dependent variables.

The second law of thermodynamics can be written as follows:

$$\frac{\partial U}{\partial V} - T\frac{\partial p}{\partial T} + p = 0$$ (1)

where V, T are independent.

Show that eq.(1) can be written in the following equivalent forms:

$$\frac{\partial T}{\partial V} + T\frac{\partial p}{\partial U} - p\frac{\partial T}{\partial U} = 0 \qquad \text{(V, U independent)}$$ (2)

$$\frac{\partial U}{\partial p} + T \frac{\partial V}{\partial T} + p \frac{\partial V}{\partial p} = 0 \qquad \text{(p, T independent)} \qquad (3)$$

$$T \frac{\partial (p,V)}{\partial (T,U)} - p \frac{\partial V}{\partial U} - 1 = 0 \qquad \text{(T, U independent)} \qquad (4)$$

$$\frac{\partial T}{\partial p} - T \frac{\partial V}{\partial U} + p \frac{\partial (V,T)}{\partial (U,p)} = 0 \qquad \text{(U, p independent)} \qquad (5)$$

$$T - p \frac{\partial T}{\partial p} + \frac{\partial (T,U)}{\partial (V,p)} = 0 \qquad \text{(V, p independent)} \qquad (6)$$

Solution: First consider eq.(1). Here U and p are functions of V and T

$$U = U(V,T)$$
$$p = p(V,T) \qquad\qquad\qquad\qquad (7)$$

Thus
$$dU = A \, dV + B \, dT$$
$$dp = C \, dV + D \, dT \qquad\qquad\qquad (8)$$

where
$$A = \frac{\partial U}{\partial V}, \qquad B = \frac{\partial U}{\partial T}$$
$$C = \frac{\partial p}{\partial V}, \qquad D = \frac{\partial p}{\partial T} \qquad\qquad (9)$$

Eq.(1) can be written in the form

$$A - TD + p = 0 \qquad\qquad\qquad\qquad (10)$$

To prove eq.(2) note that V and U are independent variables and T and p are functions of V and U.

$$T = T(V,U)$$
$$p = p(V,U) \qquad\qquad\qquad\qquad (11)$$

From eq.(11) one can write the differentials

$$dT = \alpha \, dV + \beta \, dU$$
$$dp = \gamma \, dV + \delta \, dU \qquad\qquad\qquad (12)$$

or
$$dU = \frac{1}{\beta} dT - \frac{\alpha}{\beta} dV$$
$$dp = (\gamma - \frac{\alpha\delta}{\beta}) \, dV + \frac{\delta}{\beta} dT \qquad (13)$$

Comparing the coefficients of eq.(8) and eq.(13)

$$A = -\frac{\alpha}{\beta} \qquad D = \frac{\delta}{\beta} \qquad\qquad\qquad (14)$$

Eq.(10) can be written in terms of the coefficients α, β, δ, as

$$-\frac{\alpha}{\beta} - T \frac{\delta}{\beta} + p = 0 \qquad\qquad\qquad (15)$$

Since $\alpha = \frac{\partial T}{\partial V}$, eq.(15) becomes

$$\alpha + T\delta - p\beta = 0$$

or

$$\frac{\partial T}{\partial V} + T \frac{\partial p}{\partial U} - p \frac{\partial T}{\partial U} = 0 \tag{16}$$

Equation (3) can be proved in the same manner. To prove eq.(4) note that T and U are independent, thus

$$p = p(T,U) \qquad V = V(T,U)$$

The differentials are

$$dp = \alpha\,dT + \beta\,dU$$
$$dV = \gamma\,dT + \delta\,dU \tag{17}$$

Solving eq.(17) for dp and dU

$$dp = \frac{\beta}{\delta}\,dV + \left(\alpha - \frac{\beta\gamma}{\delta}\right) dT$$
$$dU = \frac{1}{\delta}\,dV - \frac{\gamma}{\delta}\,dT \tag{18}$$

Comparing eqs.(8) and (18), obtain

$$A = \frac{1}{\delta} \qquad D = \alpha - \frac{\beta\gamma}{\delta} \tag{19}$$

Substituting eq.(19) into eq.(10), yields

$$\frac{1}{\delta} - T\left(\alpha - \frac{\beta\gamma}{\delta}\right) + p = 0$$

or

$$T(\alpha\delta - \beta\gamma) - p\delta - 1 = 0 \tag{20}$$

where

$$\delta = \frac{\partial V}{\partial U}$$

then

$$\alpha\delta - \beta\gamma = \frac{\partial p}{\partial T}\frac{\partial V}{\partial U} - \frac{\partial p}{\partial U}\frac{\partial V}{\partial T} = \begin{vmatrix} \dfrac{\partial p}{\partial T} & \dfrac{\partial p}{\partial U} \\[2ex] \dfrac{\partial V}{\partial T} & \dfrac{\partial V}{\partial U} \end{vmatrix}$$

$$= \frac{\partial(p,V)}{\partial(T,U)} \tag{21}$$

Here $\frac{\partial(p,V)}{\partial(T,U)}$ is the Jacobian of p, V with respect to T, U. Eq.(20) can be written in the form

$$T \frac{\partial(p,V)}{\partial(T,U)} - p \frac{\partial V}{\partial U} - 1 = 0 \tag{22}$$

In a similar manner, one can prove eqs.(5) and (6). The Jacobian determinants are frequently used in the differential calculus of several variables. For example if

$$f = f(x,y,z)$$

$$g = g(x,y,z)$$

$$h = h(x,y,z)$$

then

$$\frac{\partial(f,g,h)}{\partial(x,y,z)} = \begin{vmatrix} \dfrac{\partial f}{\partial x} & \dfrac{\partial f}{\partial y} & \dfrac{\partial f}{\partial z} \\[2mm] \dfrac{\partial g}{\partial x} & \dfrac{\partial g}{\partial y} & \dfrac{\partial g}{\partial z} \\[2mm] \dfrac{\partial h}{\partial x} & \dfrac{\partial h}{\partial y} & \dfrac{\partial h}{\partial z} \end{vmatrix}$$

is the Jacobian of f, g, h with respect to x, y, z.

● **PROBLEM** 6-12

1. Define a scalar field and give two examples of a scalar field.

2. Define a vector field and give two examples of a vector field.

Solution: 1. Let V denote a region in space and let X be a general point in V. In most cases one deals with a three-dimensional cartesian space. But the definition of a scalar field is general and can be applied to any space.

Furthermore let x_1, x_2, x_3 be the rectangular cartesian coordinate system. Thus the position vector of a point X can be written in the form

$$\bar{x} = (x_1, x_2, x_3) = x_1\bar{i}_1 + x_2\bar{i}_2 + x_3\bar{i}_3 \tag{1}$$

where $\bar{i}_1$, $\bar{i}_2$, $\bar{i}_3$ are the base vectors of the coordinate system. If with each point in the region V there corresponds a scalar f such that

$$V \ni \bar{x} = (x_1, x_2, x_3) \rightarrow f(\bar{x}) = f(x_1, x_2, x_3) \tag{2}$$

then the values of f associated with all the points in V define a scalar field over V. The expression $V \ni \bar{x}$ means $\bar{x}$ belongs to V.

Examples of scalar fields:

Let V be the three-dimensional cartesian space, then f such that
$$f(x_1, x_2, x_3) = x_1^2 + 2x_1x_2x_3 + x_3^4 \tag{3}$$

defines a scalar field over R^3.

Let
$$f(x_1, x_2, x_3) = \frac{1}{x_1} + \frac{1}{x_2} + \frac{1}{x_3}, \tag{4}$$

then f defines a scalar field for all the points in R^3 except those for which $x_1 = 0$ or $x_2 = 0$ or $x_3 = 0$.

2. If with each point of V a value of a vector $\bar{f}$ is associated such that

$$V \ni \bar{x} = (x_1, x_2, x_3) \rightarrow \bar{f}(x_1, x_2, x_3) \qquad (5)$$

then $\bar{f}$ defines a vector field over V.

Examples of vector fields:

Let V be the three-dimensional cartesian space and let

$$\bar{f}(x_1, x_2, x_3) = (x_1+x_2, x_2+x_3, x_3^2) \qquad (6)$$

then $\bar{f}$ defines a vector field over R^3. Let V be the xy plane and let

$$\bar{f}(x, y) = (xy, x + y, y^2) \qquad (7)$$

then $\bar{f}$ defines a vector field over the xy plane.

Very often it is necessary to consider scalar and vector fields which vary with a parameter, for example time t. In this case, a scalar field and a vector field may be represented by

$$f = f(\bar{x},t) = f(x_1, x_2, x_3, t)$$

$$\bar{f} = \bar{f}(\bar{x},t) = \bar{f}(x_1, x_2, x_3, t) \qquad (8)$$

In many physical applications of vector calculus, the scalar and vector fields play a crucial role. Examples of scalar and vector fields in physics will be given later in this book.

● **PROBLEM 6-13**

A scalar field f is defined by

$$f(x_1, x_2, x_3) = 2x_1^2 x_2 - x_2 + 3x_2 x_3 \qquad (1)$$

A vector field $\bar{g}$ is defined by

$$\bar{g}(x_1, x_2, x_3) = (x_1+x_2, x_1 x_2, x_3) \qquad (2)$$

Find f and $\bar{g}$ at the points

1. (0,0,0)

2. (-1,2,3)

3. (1,1,1)

4. (2,-1,1)

5. (0,0,1)

Solution: For the scalar field f, substituting the appropriate values of x_1, x_2, x_3 into eq.(1), obtain

1. $f(0,0,0) = 0$

2. $f(-1,2,3) = 2 \cdot (-1)^2 \cdot 2 - 2 + 3 \cdot 2 \cdot 3 = 20$

3. $f(1,1,1) = 2 \cdot 1 \cdot 1 - 1 + 3 \cdot 1 \cdot 1 = 2 - 1 + 3 = 4$

4. $f(2,-1,1) = 2 \cdot 4 \cdot (-1) + 1 + 3 \cdot (-1) \cdot 1 = -10$

5. $f(0,0,1) = 0 - 0 + 3 \cdot 0 = 0$

For the vector field $\bar{g}$ substitute the values of x , x , x into eq.(2)

1. $\bar{g}(0,0,0) = (0,0,0)$

2. $\bar{g}(-1,2,3) = (-1+2, -1 \cdot 2, 3) = (1,-2,3)$

3. $\bar{g}(1,1,1) = (2,1,1)$

4. $\bar{g}(2,-1,1) = (1,-2,1)$

5. $\bar{g}(0,0,1) = (0,0,1)$

● **PROBLEM** 6-14

Sketch the vector fields defined by

1) $\bar{f}(x_1, x_2) = (x_1, x_2)$

2) $\bar{f}(x_1, x_2) = (2x_1, x_2)$

3) $\bar{f}(x_1, x_2, x_3) = (x_1, x_2, x_3)$

Solution: 1) For each point (x_1, x_2) of the $x_1 x_2$ plane there is defined a unique vector $x_1 \bar{i}_1 + x_2 \bar{i}_2$ of magnitude $\sqrt{x_1^2 + x_2^2}$. The direction of the vector is outward from the origin. All vectors associated with points on the circles $x_1^2 + x_2^2 = a^2$ have the same magnitude a, as shown in Fig. 1.

2) The vector field is given by

$$\bar{f}(x_1, x_2) = (2x_1, x_2)$$

The magnitude of the vector is $\sqrt{4x_1^2 + x_2^2}$. The vectors of the same magnitude a, such that

$$a = \sqrt{4x_1^2 + x_2^2}$$

are located on the ellipse, as shown in Fig. 2.

241

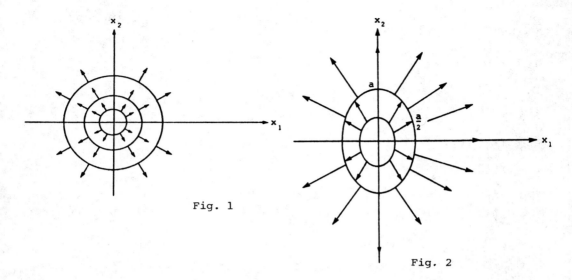

Fig. 1

Fig. 2

The vectors are directed outward from the origin.

3) The magnitude of each vector

$$\overline{f}(x_1 , x_2 , x_3) = (x_1 , x_2 , x_3)$$

is

$$|\overline{f}| = \sqrt{x_1^2 + x_2^2 + x_3^2}$$

thus all points on the sphere $a = \sqrt{x_1^2 + x_2^2 + x_3^2}$ have vectors of the same magnitude. This vector field resembles that of a fluid emerging from source 0 and flowing in all directions in space.

Very often in physics one deals with vector fields. One of the most important is the gravitational field. If $\overline{F}$ is the gravitational force exerted on a particle of mass m at the point (x,y,z) by a mass M located at the origin of the system, then Newton's law of gravitation can be written in the form

$$\overline{F} = -k \ \frac{Mm}{r^2} \ \frac{\overline{r}}{r}$$

where $\overline{r}$ is the vector from the origin to the mass m and k a gravitational constant. Since $\frac{\overline{r}}{r}$ is a unit vector the magnitude of $\overline{F}$ is $F = \frac{kMm}{r^2}$

As a second example, consider the field $\overline{F}$ described by

$$\overline{F} = \frac{1}{[(x+1)^2+y^2] [(x-1)^2+y^2]} \left[2(x^2-y^2-1), \ 4xy \right]$$

This field is shown in the figure.

242

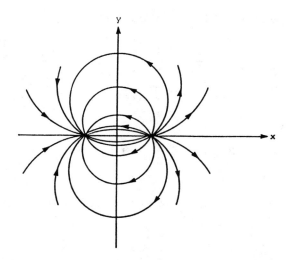

The vector $\overline{F}$ represents the electric force field due to two
infinite straight wires, perpendicular to the xy plane at (1,0)
and (-1,0), and oppositely charged with electricity.

● **PROBLEM 6-15**

A certain scalar field $f(x_1, x_2, x_3)$ has the value

   $f(2,1,3) = 5.$ (1)

The partial derivatives'are

   $\frac{\partial f}{\partial x_1}$ (2,1,3) = 2

                                                                      (2)

   $\frac{\partial f}{\partial x_2}$ (2,1,3) = -2

   $\frac{\partial f}{\partial x_3}$ (2,1,3) = 3

Estimate the value of the scalar field for the points

1) f(2.1, 0.8, 3.1)

2) f(1.9, 0.9, 3)

Solution: Since the scalar field is a function of x_1, x_2, x_3
one can write the differential of f in the form

$$\Delta f = \frac{\partial f}{\partial x_1} \Delta x_1 + \frac{\partial f}{\partial x_2} \Delta x_2 + \frac{\partial f}{\partial x_3} \Delta x_3 \qquad (3)$$

1) It is required to estimate the value of f(2.1, 0.8, 3.1),
    where the value of f(2,1,3) is given, thus

   $\Delta x_1 = 0.1, \quad \Delta x_2 = -0.2, \quad \Delta x_3 = 0.1$ (4)

243

Substituting values (4) into eq.(3),

$$\Lambda f = \frac{\partial f}{\partial x_1}\bigg|_{(2,1,3)} \cdot \Delta x_1 + \frac{\partial f}{\partial x_2}\bigg|_{(2,1,3)} \cdot \Delta x_2 + \frac{\partial f}{\partial x_3}\bigg|_{(2,1,3)} \cdot \Delta x_3$$

$$= 2 \cdot 0.1 + (-2) \cdot (-0.2) + 3 \cdot (0.1) = 0.2 + 0.4 + 0.3 = 0.9 \tag{5}$$

Thus the value of f is

$$f(2.1, \ 0.8, \ 3.1) = 5 + 0.9 = 5.9 \tag{6}$$

2) For the point (1.9, 0.9, 3),

$$\Delta x_1 = -0.1, \qquad \Delta x_2 = -0.1, \qquad \Delta x_3 = 0$$

and for Δf,

$$\Delta f = 2 \cdot (-0.1) + (-2) \cdot (-0.1) + 3.0 = -0.2 + 0.2 = 0$$

Therefore

$$f(1.9, \ 0.9, \ 3) = 5$$

GRADIENT OF A SCALAR FIELD

● **PROBLEM** 6-16

If $f(x_1, \ x_2, \ x_3) = 2x_1^2 x_2 - x_1 x_3$,

find ∇f (grad f)
at the point (2, -1,1).

Solution: Operator ∇(read del, also called nabla) is defined
as

$$\nabla \equiv \frac{\partial}{\partial x_1}\bar{i}_1 + \frac{\partial}{\partial x_2}\bar{i}_2 + \frac{\partial}{\partial x_3}\bar{i}_3 \tag{1}$$

If $f(x_1, \ x_2, \ x_3)$ is a differentiable scalar field, then one defines the vector field ∇f, such that

$$\nabla f = \left(\frac{\partial}{\partial x_1}\bar{i}_1 + \frac{\partial}{\partial x_2}\bar{i}_2 + \frac{\partial}{\partial x_3}\bar{i}_3\right) f = \frac{\partial f}{\partial x_1}\bar{i}_1 + \frac{\partial f}{\partial x_2}\bar{i}_2 + \frac{\partial f}{\partial x_3}\bar{i}_3 \tag{2}$$

or in the component notation

$$\nabla f = \left(\frac{\partial f}{\partial x_1}, \ \frac{\partial f}{\partial x_2}, \ \frac{\partial f}{\partial x_3}\right) \tag{3}$$

In our case,

$$\nabla f = \left[\frac{\partial}{\partial x_1}\left(2x_1^2 x_2 - x_1 x_3\right), \ \frac{\partial}{\partial x_2}\left(2x_1^2 x_2 - x_1 x_3\right), \ \frac{\partial}{\partial x_3}\left(2x_1^2 x_2 - x_1 x_3\right)\right]$$

$$= (4x_1x_2 - x_3, \; 2x_1^2, \; -x_1) \tag{4}$$

Note that the notation grad f is often used, since

$$\nabla f \equiv \text{grad } f.$$

Evaluate ∇f at the point (2,3,5). The scalar field f is given by

$$f(x_1, \; x_2, \; x_3) = 2\sin x_1 - x_1^2 x_2 x_3 + x_1 e^{x_2} \tag{1}$$

Solution: By definition ∇f is equal to

$$\nabla f \equiv \left(\frac{\partial f}{\partial x_1}, \; \frac{\partial f}{\partial x_2}, \; \frac{\partial f}{\partial x_3} \right) \tag{2}$$

Compute the partial derivatives of f,

$$\frac{\partial f}{\partial x_1} = 2\cos x_1 - 2x_1 x_2 x_3 + e^{x_2}$$

$$\frac{\partial f}{\partial x_2} = -x_1^2 x_3 + x_1 e^{x_2} \tag{3}$$

$$\frac{\partial f}{\partial x_3} = -x_1^2 x_2$$

Then
$$\nabla f = \left(2\cos x_1 - 2x_1 x_2 x_3 + e^{x_2}, \; -x_1^2 x_3 + x_1 e^{x_2}, \; -x_1^2 x_2 \right) \tag{4}$$

The value of ∇f at the point (2,3,5) is

$$\nabla f = (2\cos 2 - 2 \cdot 3 \cdot 2 \cdot 5 + e^3, \; -4 \cdot 5 + 2e^3, \; -4 \cdot 3)$$

$$= (-40.74, \; 20.17, \; -12)$$

If $\quad f(x_1, \; x_2, \; x_3) = 4x_1^2 x_3 - x_2^2 x_3 \tag{1}$

find ∇f at the point (1,-1,2).

Express ∇f in terms of the base vectors.

Solution: Operator gradient, denoted ∇ can be written in the form

$$\nabla \equiv \frac{\partial}{\partial x_1} \bar{i}_1 + \frac{\partial}{\partial x_2} \bar{i}_2 + \frac{\partial}{\partial x_3} \bar{i}_3 \tag{2}$$

Thus $\qquad \nabla f \equiv \left(\frac{\partial}{\partial x_1} \bar{i}_1 + \frac{\partial}{\partial x_2} \bar{i}_2 + \frac{\partial}{\partial x_3} \bar{i}_3 \right) f \tag{3}$

Substituting eq.(1) into eq.(3) yields

$$\nabla f = \left(\frac{\partial}{\partial x_1} \, \overline{i}_1 + \frac{\partial}{\partial x_2} \, \overline{i}_2 + \frac{\partial}{\partial x_3} \, \overline{i}_3 \right) \left(4x_1^2 x_3 - x_2^2 x_3 \right)$$

$$= \overline{i}_1 \, \frac{\partial}{\partial x_1} (4x_1^2 x_3 - x_2^2 x_3) + \overline{i}_2 \, \frac{\partial}{\partial x_2} (4x_1^2 x_3 - x_2^2 x_3) \qquad (4)$$

$$+ \overline{i}_3 \, \frac{\partial}{\partial x_3} (4x_1^2 x_3 - x_2^2 x_3)$$

$$= \overline{i}_1 \left(8x_1 x_3 \right) + \overline{i}_2 \left(-2x_2 x_3 \right) + \overline{i}_3 (4x_1^2 - x_2^2)$$

At the point $(1,-1,2)$, eq.(4) becomes

$$\nabla f = 16\overline{i}_1 + 4\overline{i}_2 + 3\overline{i}_3 \qquad (5)$$

or in the component form

$$\nabla f = (16, \ 4, \ 3) \qquad (6)$$

● **PROBLEM 6-19**

Let f and g be differentiable scalar functions

$$f = f\left(x_1, \ x_2, \ x_3 \right)$$
$$g = g\left(x_1, \ x_2, \ x_3 \right) \qquad (1)$$

Prove that

1) $\nabla(f + g) = \nabla f + \nabla g$

2) $\nabla(fg) = f\nabla g + g\nabla f$

Solution: 1)   Use operator nabla expressed in terms of the base vectors, thus

$$\nabla(f+g) = \left(\frac{\partial}{\partial x_1} \, \overline{i}_1 + \frac{\partial}{\partial x_2} \, \overline{i}_2 + \frac{\partial}{\partial x_3} \, \overline{i}_3 \right) (f+g)$$

$$= \overline{i}_1 \, \frac{\partial}{\partial x_1}(f+g) + \overline{i}_2 \, \frac{\partial}{\partial x_2}(f+g) + \overline{i}_3 \, \frac{\partial}{\partial x_3}(f+g) \qquad (2)$$

$$= \overline{i}_1 \, \frac{\partial f}{\partial x_1} + \overline{i}_1 \, \frac{\partial g}{\partial x_1} + \overline{i}_2 \, \frac{\partial f}{\partial x_2} + \overline{i}_2 \, \frac{\partial g}{\partial x_2} + \overline{i}_3 \, \frac{\partial f}{\partial x_3} + \overline{i}_3 \, \frac{\partial g}{\partial x_3}$$

$$= \left(\overline{i}_1 \, \frac{\partial}{\partial x_1} + \overline{i}_2 \, \frac{\partial}{\partial x_2} + \overline{i}_3 \, \frac{\partial}{\partial x_3} \right) f + \left(\overline{i}_1 \, \frac{\partial}{\partial x_1} + \overline{i}_2 \, \frac{\partial}{\partial x_2} + \overline{i}_3 \, \frac{\partial}{\partial x_3} \right) g$$

$$= \nabla f + \nabla g$$

2) $\nabla(fg) = \left(\overline{i}_1 \, \frac{\partial}{\partial x_1} + \overline{i}_2 \, \frac{\partial}{\partial x_2} + \overline{i}_3 \, \frac{\partial}{\partial x_3} \right) (fg)$

$$= \bar{i}_1 \frac{\partial}{\partial x_1}(fg) + \bar{i}_2 \frac{\partial}{\partial x_2}(fg) + \bar{i}_3 \frac{\partial}{\partial x_3}(fg) \qquad (3)$$

$$= \bar{i}_1 \left(f \frac{\partial g}{\partial x_1} + g \frac{\partial f}{\partial x_1} \right) + \bar{i}_2 \left(f \frac{\partial g}{\partial x_2} + g \frac{\partial f}{\partial x_2} \right) + \bar{i}_3 \left(f \frac{\partial g}{\partial x_3} + g \frac{\partial f}{\partial x_3} \right)$$

$$= f \left(\bar{i}_1 \frac{\partial g}{\partial x_1} + \bar{i}_2 \frac{\partial g}{\partial x_2} + \bar{i}_3 \frac{\partial g}{\partial x_3} \right) + g \left(\bar{i}_1 \frac{\partial f}{\partial x_1} + \bar{i}_2 \frac{\partial f}{\partial x_2} + \bar{i}_3 \frac{\partial f}{\partial x_3} \right)$$

$$= f \nabla g + g \nabla f$$

Throughout the proof the equation

$$\frac{\partial}{\partial x_k}(fg) = f \frac{\partial g}{\partial x_k} + g \frac{\partial f}{\partial x_k} \qquad (4)$$

was used.

PROPERTIES OF THE GRADIENT OPERATOR

• **PROBLEM** 6-20

Two scalar fields are given such that

$$f(x_1, x_2, x_3) = x_1^2 x_2 + e^{x_2 x_3}$$
$$g(x_1, x_2, x_3) = \sin x_2 + x_1 x_3^2 \qquad (1)$$

Find

1) $\nabla(f + g)$

2) $\nabla(fg)$

at the point $(-1,1,2)$.

Solution: 1) Use the following property of the gradient

$$\nabla(f+g) = \nabla f + \nabla g \qquad (2)$$

Evaluating both gradients, obtain

$$\nabla f = \left[\frac{\partial}{\partial x_1} \left(x_1^2 x_2 + e^{x_2 x_3} \right), \frac{\partial}{\partial x_2} \left(x_1^2 x_2 + e^{x_2 x_3} \right), \frac{\partial}{\partial x_3} \left(x_1^2 x_2 + e^{x_2 x_3} \right) \right]$$

$$= \left[2x_1 x_2, x_1^2 + x_3 e^{x_2 x_3}, x_2 e^{x_2 x_3} \right] \qquad (3)$$

$$\nabla g = \left[\frac{\partial}{\partial x_1}(\sin x_2 + x_1 x_3^2), \frac{\partial}{\partial x_2}(\sin x_2 + x_1 x_3^2), \frac{\partial}{\partial x_3}(\sin x_2 + x_1 x_3^2) \right]$$

$$= \left[x_3^2, \cos x_2, 2x_1 x_3 \right] \qquad (4)$$

Substituting eq.(3) and eq.(4) into eq.(2),

$$\nabla(f+g) = \left(2x_1x_2+x_3^2, \ x_1^2+\cos x_2+x_3 e^{x_2x_3}, \ x_2 e^{x_2x_3}+2x_1x_3\right) \qquad (5)$$

At the point $(-1,1,2)$, obtain

$$\nabla(f+g)\bigg|_{(-1,1,2)} = (-2+8, \ 1+\cos 1+2e^2, \ e^2-2\cdot 2)$$

$$= (6, \ 16.32, \ 3.39) \qquad (6)$$

2) From the formula,

$$\nabla(fg) = f\,\nabla g + g\,\nabla f \qquad (7)$$

Substituting eqs.(1), (3), (4) into eq.(7),

$$\nabla(fg) = \left(x_1^2 x_2 + e^{x_2x_3}\right)\left[x_3^2, \ \cos x_2, \ 2x_1x_3\right]$$

$$+ (\sin x_2 + x_1 x_3^2)\left[2x_1x_2, \ x_1^2 + x_3 e^{x_2x_3}, \ x_2 e^{x_2x_3}\right] \qquad (8)$$

At the point $(-1,1,2)$,

$$\nabla(fg)\bigg|_{(-1,1,2)} = (1 + e^2)\left[4, \ \cos 1, \ -4\right]$$

$$+ (\sin 1 - 4)\left[-2, \ 1 + 2e^2, \ e^2\right]$$

$$= 8.39\left[4, \ 0.54, \ -4\right] + (-3.16)\left[-2, \ 15.78, \ 7.39\right]$$

$$= (39.88, \ -45.33, \ -56.91) \qquad (9)$$

● **PROBLEM 6-21**

Find ∇f for

1) $f = \ln |\bar{r}|$

2) $f = \dfrac{1}{r}$

Solution: 1) $\bar{r} = \left(x_1, \ x_2, \ x_3\right)$ $\qquad (1)$

and

$$|\bar{r}| = \sqrt{x_1^2 + x_2^2 + x_3^2} \qquad (2)$$

The function f can be written as

$$f = \ln|\bar{r}| = \ln \sqrt{x_1^2 + x_2^2 + x_3^2} = \frac{1}{2}\ln(x_1^2 + x_2^2 + x_3^2) \qquad (3)$$

The gradient of f is given by

$$\nabla f = \frac{1}{2}\nabla\ln(x_1^2 + x_2^2 + x_3^2)$$

$$= \frac{1}{2}\left[\frac{\partial}{\partial x_1}\ln(x_1^2+x_2^2+x_3^2), \ \frac{\partial}{\partial x_2}\ln(x_1^2+x_2^2+x_3^2), \ \frac{\partial}{\partial x_3}\ln(x_1^2+x_2^2+x_3^2)\right] \qquad (4)$$

$$= \frac{1}{2}\left[\frac{2x_1}{x_1^2+x_2^2+x_3^2}, \frac{2x_2}{x_1^2+x_2^2+x_3^2}, \frac{2x_3}{x_1^2+x_2^2+x_3^2}\right] = \frac{1}{x_1^2+x_2^2+x_3^2}(x_1, x_2, x_3)$$

$$= \frac{\overline{r}}{r^2}$$

2) $\quad f = \frac{1}{r} = \frac{1}{\sqrt{x_1^2+x_2^2+x_3^2}}$ $\qquad\qquad (5)$

The gradient of f is

$$\nabla f = \nabla\left(\frac{1}{\sqrt{x_1^2+x_2^2+x_3^2}}\right)$$

$$= \left(\frac{\partial}{\partial x_1}\left(\frac{1}{\sqrt{x_1^2+x_2^2+x_3^2}}\right), \frac{\partial}{\partial x_2}\left(\frac{1}{\sqrt{x_1^2+x_2^2+x_3^2}}\right), \frac{\partial}{\partial x_3}\left(\frac{1}{\sqrt{x_1^2+x_2^2+x_3^2}}\right)\right)$$

$$= \left(\frac{-2x_1}{2(x_1^2+x_2^2+x_3^2)^{3/2}}, \frac{-2x_2}{2(x_1^2+x_2^2+x_3^2)^{3/2}}, \frac{-2x_3}{2(x_1^2+x_2^2+x_3^2)^{3/2}}\right)$$

$$\frac{-1}{(x_1^2+x_2^2+x_3^2)^{3/2}}(x_1, x_2, x_3) = \frac{-\overline{r}}{r^3} \qquad\qquad (6)$$

● **PROBLEM 6-22**

Prove the following relation

$$\nabla r^n = nr^{n-2}\,\overline{r} \qquad\qquad (1)$$

<u>Solution</u>: Since $\overline{r} = \left(x_1, x_2, x_3\right)$

then, $\qquad\qquad r = |\overline{r}| = \sqrt{x_1^2+x_2^2+x_3^2}$ $\qquad\qquad (2)$

and,

$$\nabla r^n = \nabla\left(\sqrt{x_1^2+x_2^2+x_3^2}\right)^n = \nabla\left(x_1^2+x_2^2+x_3^2\right)^{\frac{n}{2}}$$

$$= \left[\frac{\partial}{\partial x_1}\left(x_1^2+x_2^2+x_3^2\right)^{\frac{n}{2}}, \frac{\partial}{\partial x_2}\left(x_1^2+x_2^2+x_3^2\right)^{\frac{n}{2}}, \frac{\partial}{\partial x_3}\left(x_1^2+x_2^2+x_3^2\right)^{\frac{n}{2}}\right] \qquad (3)$$

$$= \left[\frac{n}{2}\left(x_1^2+x_2^2+x_3^2\right)^{\frac{n}{2}-1}\cdot 2x_1, \frac{n}{2}\left(x_1^2+x_2^2+x_3^2\right)^{\frac{n}{2}-1}\cdot 2x_2, \frac{n}{2}\left(x_1^2+x_2^2+x_3^2\right)^{\frac{n}{2}-1}\cdot 2x_3\right]$$

$$= \left(x_1^2+x_2^2+x_3^2\right)^{\frac{n}{2}-1} n\left[x_1, x_2, x_3\right]$$

$$= \left(x_1^2+x_2^2+x_3^2\right)^{\frac{n-2}{2}} n\left(x_1, x_2, x_3\right) = nr^{n-2}\,\overline{r}$$

Let f be a function of r

$$f = f(r)$$

Prove that

$$\nabla f(r) = \frac{df}{dr} \frac{\bar{r}}{r} \qquad (1)$$

<u>Solution</u>: From the definition of the gradient,

$$\nabla f(r) = \left(\frac{\partial}{\partial x_1} f(r), \frac{\partial}{\partial x_2} f(r), \frac{\partial}{\partial x_3} f(r) \right) \qquad (2)$$

where

$$r = r(x_1, x_2, x_3)$$

and

$$\frac{\partial}{\partial x_1} f(r) = \frac{\partial f}{\partial r} \frac{\partial r}{\partial x_1}$$

$$\frac{\partial}{\partial x_2} f(r) = \frac{\partial f}{\partial r} \frac{\partial r}{\partial x_2} \qquad (3)$$

$$\frac{\partial}{\partial x_3} f(r) = \frac{\partial f}{\partial r} \frac{\partial r}{\partial x_3}$$

Substituting eq.(3) into eq.(2),

$$\nabla f(r) = \left(\frac{\partial f}{\partial r} \frac{\partial r}{\partial x_1}, \frac{\partial f}{\partial r} \frac{\partial r}{\partial x_2}, \frac{\partial f}{\partial r} \frac{\partial r}{\partial x_3} \right) \qquad (4)$$

$$= \frac{\partial f}{\partial r} \nabla r$$

In general,

$$\nabla r^n = n r^{n-2} \bar{r}$$

thus

$$\nabla r = r^{-1} \bar{r} \qquad (5)$$

Substituting eq.(5) into eq.(4), obtain

$$\nabla f(r) = \frac{\partial f}{\partial r} \frac{\bar{r}}{r} \qquad (6)$$

Since $\frac{\partial f}{\partial r} = \frac{df}{dr}$ because $f = f(r)$, eq.(6) can be equivalently written as

$$\nabla f(r) = \frac{df}{dr} \frac{\bar{r}}{r} \qquad (7)$$

Evaluate $\nabla f(r)$ where

$$f(r) = \sin r + 5r - 2r^4 - 3r^6 - \frac{1}{\sqrt[3]{r}} \qquad (1)$$

Solution: To evaluate $\nabla f(r)$ use the definition of ∇ and perform all three partial differentiations

$$\frac{\partial}{\partial x_1}, \quad \frac{\partial}{\partial x_2}, \quad \text{and} \quad \frac{\partial}{\partial x_3} \ .$$

The easier method will be to use the following formula

$$\nabla f(r) = \frac{df}{dr} \frac{\bar{r}}{r} \tag{2}$$

which holds for any differentiable function $f(r)$.

Substituting eq.(1) into eq.(2),

$$\nabla f(r) = \frac{\bar{r}}{r} \frac{d}{dr} \left(\sin r + 5r - 2r^4 - 3r^6 - \frac{1}{\sqrt[3]{r}} \right)$$

$$= \frac{\bar{r}}{r} \left[\cos r + 5 - 8r^3 - 18r^5 + \frac{1}{3} r^{-\frac{4}{3}} \right] \tag{3}$$

$$= \left[\frac{\cos r}{r} + \frac{5}{r} - 8r^2 - 18r^4 + \frac{1}{3} r^{-\frac{7}{3}} \right] \bar{r}$$

● **PROBLEM** 6-25

1) Find $\psi(r)$ such that

$$\nabla \psi = 3r^5 \bar{r}$$

2) If $\nabla \phi = \dfrac{\bar{r}}{r^3}$ and $\phi(2) = 1$ find $\phi = \phi(r)$.

Solution: Use the following equation to solve both problems

$$\nabla f(r) = \frac{df}{dr} \frac{\bar{r}}{r} \tag{1}$$

where $f(r)$ is any differentiable function of r.

1) $\quad \nabla \psi = 3r^5 \bar{r} = \dfrac{d\psi}{dr} \dfrac{\bar{r}}{r} \tag{2}$

Solving for $\dfrac{d\psi}{dr}$,

$$\frac{d\psi}{dr} = 3r^6 \tag{3}$$

and integrating, obtain

$$\psi(r) = \frac{3}{7} r^7 + \text{const} \tag{4}$$

2) $\quad \nabla \phi = \dfrac{\bar{r}}{r^3}$

By virtue of eq.(1),

$$\nabla \phi = \frac{d\phi}{dr} \frac{\bar{r}}{r} = \frac{\bar{r}}{r^3} \tag{5}$$

251

Solving for $\dfrac{d\phi}{dr}$

$$\frac{d\phi}{dr} = \frac{1}{r^2} \tag{6}$$

Integrating eq.(6)

$$\phi(r) = -r^{-1} + const \tag{7}$$

From the condition $\phi(2) = 1$

$$\phi(2) = 1 = -\frac{1}{2} + const$$

$$const = \frac{3}{2}$$

therefore,

$$\phi(r) = -\frac{1}{r} + \frac{3}{2} \tag{8}$$

TANGENT PLANE, DIRECTIONAL DERIVATIVE AND LAPLACIAN OPERATOR

● **PROBLEM 6-26**

The surface is given by the equation

$$x^3 + y^3 + x^2 y - z^3 = -3 \tag{1}$$

Find the tangent plane and normal line to the surface at the point (2,2,3).

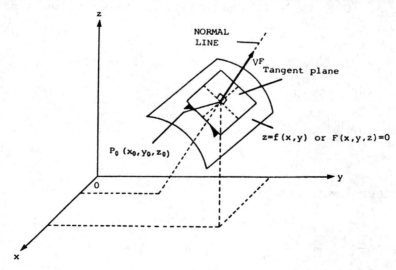

Solution: First consider the general case of a surface given by the equation

$$F(x,y,z) = 0 \tag{2}$$

252

and let (x_1, y_1, z_1) be a point on this surface. It is required
to find the equation of the plane which is tangent to the surface $F(x,y,z) = 0$ at the point (x_1, y_1, z_1).

Let $x = x(t)$, $y = y(t)$, $z = z(t)$ be a curve on the surface
passing through (x_1, y_1, z_1) at $t = t_1$.   Then

$$F\left[x(t), y(t), z(t)\right] = 0 \qquad (3)$$

Differentiating eq.(3) yiels

$$\frac{\partial F}{\partial x} dx + \frac{\partial F}{\partial y} dy + \frac{\partial F}{\partial z} dz = 0 \qquad (4)$$

where the partial derivatives are evaluated at (x_1, y_1, z_1).
Let (x,y,z) be a point on the tangent to the given curve at
(x_1, y_1, z_1).   The differentials in eq.(4) can be replaced by

$$dx = x - x_1, \quad dy = y - y_1, \quad dz = z - z_1 \qquad (5)$$

Substituting eq.(5) into eq.(4), and evaluating the partial
derivatives at the point (x_1, y_1, z_1) gives

$$(x - x_1) \frac{\partial F}{\partial x} + (y - y_1) \frac{\partial F}{\partial y} + (z - z_1) \frac{\partial F}{\partial z} = 0 \qquad (6)$$

Eq.(6) is the equation of a plane tangent to the surface
$F(x,y,z) = 0$ at the point (x_1, y_1, z_1).   Eq.(4) can be
written in the vector form as

$$\nabla F \cdot d\bar{r} = 0 \qquad (7)$$

or

$$grad\ F \cdot d\bar{r} = 0$$

where $d\bar{r} = (dx, dy, dz)$

From eq.(6) one concludes that the vector

$$\nabla F = \left(\frac{\partial F}{\partial x}, \frac{\partial F}{\partial y}, \frac{\partial F}{\partial z}\right) \equiv \frac{\partial F}{\partial x} \bar{i} + \frac{\partial F}{\partial y} \bar{j} + \frac{\partial F}{\partial z} \bar{k} \qquad (8)$$

is normal to the tangent plane at (x_1, y_1, z_1).   Vector ∇F is
called the gradient vector of the function $F(x,y,z)$, and is
shown in the figure.

To solve the problem one has to verify that the point $(2,2,3)$
is on the surface $x^3 + y^3 + x^2 y - z^3 = -3$.

Indeed,

$$x^3 + y^3 + x^2 y - z^3 = 2^3 + 2^3 + 2^2 2 - 3^3 = 24 - 27 = -3$$

thus the point is on the surface.

To use eq.(6), compute the partial derivatives at (2, 2, 3)

$$\left.\frac{\partial F}{\partial x}\right|_{(2,2,3)} = 3x^2 + 2xy \left.\right|_{(2,2,3)} = 20 \tag{9}$$

$$\left.\frac{\partial F}{\partial y}\right|_{(2,2,3)} = 3y^2 + x^2 \left.\right|_{(2,2,3)} = 16 \tag{10}$$

$$\left.\frac{\partial F}{\partial z}\right|_{(2,2,3)} = -3z^2 \left.\right|_{(2,2,3)} = -27 \tag{11}$$

Substituting eqs.(9), (10), and (11) into eq.(6) and remembering that $(x_1, y_1, z_1) = (2,2,3)$, obtain

$$20(x-2) + 16(y-2) - 27(z-3) = 0$$

or

$$20x + 16y - 27z + 9 = 0 \tag{12}$$

The plane $20x + 16y - 27z + 9 = 0$ is tangent to the surface $x^3 + y^3 + x^2y - z^3 = -3$ at the point (2,2,3).

To find the normal line, note that $\left.\nabla F\right|_{(x_1,y_1,z_1)}$ is normal to the tangent plane at (x_1, y_1, z_1) and

$$\left.\nabla F\right|_{(2,2,3)} = (20, 16, -27) \tag{13}$$

To find the line passing through the point (2,2,3) and parallel to the vector $\left.\nabla F\right|_{(2,2,3)}$, let $\overline{r}$ be the position vector of the general point of this line. From geometry one concludes that the equation of this line is,

$$\left[\overline{r} - \overline{a}\right] \times \overline{b} = \overline{0} \tag{14}$$

where $\overline{a}$ is the position vector of the given point, in our case (2,2,3) and $\overline{b}$ is the vector, in our case (20,16,-27).

Substituting into eq.(14)

$$(x-2, y-2, z-3) \times (20, 16, -27) = \overline{0}$$

or

$$x-2 = \frac{5(y-2)}{4} = \frac{-20(z-3)}{27} \tag{15}$$

Consider two intersecting surfaces

$$x^2 + y^2 - z^2 = -7$$

$$3x^2 + y^2 + z^2 = 13 \qquad (1)$$

The intersection of the surfaces determines a curve. Find the equation of the tangent line to the curve at the point $(1,1,3)$.

<u>Solution</u>: First consider the general case of a curve determined by two intersecting surfaces

$$f(x,y,z) = 0$$

$$g(x,y,z) = 0 \qquad (2)$$

Differentiating eq.(2) yields

$$\frac{\partial f}{\partial x}\, dx + \frac{\partial f}{\partial y}\, dy + \frac{\partial f}{\partial z}\, dz = 0$$

$$\frac{\partial g}{\partial x}\, dx + \frac{\partial g}{\partial y}\, dy + \frac{\partial g}{\partial z}\, dz = 0 \qquad (3)$$

where the partial derivatives are evaluated at (x_1,y_1,z_1).
Eq.(3) represents two intersecting tangent planes at the point (x_1,y_1,z_1). Replace the differentials dx, dy, dz by $x-x_1$, $y-y_1$, $z-z_1$. Therefore eq.(3) can be written in the vector form

$$\nabla f \cdot d\bar{r} = 0$$

$$\nabla g \cdot d\bar{r} = 0 \qquad (4)$$

From eq.(4) one concludes that $d\bar{r}$ is perpendicular to both ∇f and ∇g, thus,

$$d\bar{r} \times (\nabla f \times \nabla g) = \bar{0} \qquad (5)$$

Replacing the differentials, one can write in the component form

$$\frac{x - x_1}{\begin{vmatrix} \frac{\partial f}{\partial y} & \frac{\partial f}{\partial z} \\ \frac{\partial g}{\partial y} & \frac{\partial g}{\partial z} \end{vmatrix}} = \frac{y - y_1}{\begin{vmatrix} \frac{\partial f}{\partial z} & \frac{\partial f}{\partial x} \\ \frac{\partial g}{\partial z} & \frac{\partial g}{\partial x} \end{vmatrix}} = \frac{z - z_1}{\begin{vmatrix} \frac{\partial f}{\partial x} & \frac{\partial f}{\partial y} \\ \frac{\partial g}{\partial x} & \frac{\partial g}{\partial y} \end{vmatrix}} \qquad (6)$$

In terms of Jacobians, eq.(6) can be written in the form

$$\frac{x - x_1}{\frac{\partial(f,g)}{\partial(y,z)}} = \frac{y - y_1}{\frac{\partial(f,g)}{\partial(z,x)}} = \frac{z - z_1}{\frac{\partial(f,g)}{\partial(x,y)}} \qquad (7)$$

One could easily verify that point (1,1,3) is on the curve determined by the intersection of the surfaces

$$f(x,y,z) = x^2 + y^2 - z^2 = -7$$

$$g(x,y,z) = 3x^2 + y^2 + z^2 = 13$$

Indeed $\quad x^2 + y^2 - z^2 = 1^2 + 1^2 - 3^2 = -7$

and $\quad 3x^2 + y^2 + z^2 = 3 + 1 + 9 = 13$

Next, evaluate all the partial derivatives

$$\left.\frac{\partial f}{\partial x}\right|_{(1,1,3)} = 2x = 2; \qquad \left.\frac{\partial g}{\partial x}\right|_{(1,1,3)} = 6x = 6$$

$$\left.\frac{\partial f}{\partial y}\right|_{(1,1,3)} = 2y = 2; \qquad \left.\frac{\partial g}{\partial y}\right|_{(1,1,3)} = 2y = 2 \qquad (8)$$

$$\left.\frac{\partial f}{\partial z}\right|_{(1,1,3)} = -2z = -6; \qquad \left.\frac{\partial g}{\partial z}\right|_{(1,1,3)} = 2z = 6$$

Substituting eq.(8) into eq.(6) and taking $x_1 = 1$, $y_1 = 1$, $z_1 = 3$,

$$\frac{x - 1}{\begin{vmatrix} 2 & -6 \\ 2 & 6 \end{vmatrix}} = \frac{y - 1}{\begin{vmatrix} -6 & 2 \\ 6 & 6 \end{vmatrix}} = \frac{z - 3}{\begin{vmatrix} 2 & 2 \\ 6 & 2 \end{vmatrix}}$$

or

$$-\frac{x-1}{3} = \frac{y-1}{6} = z-3 \qquad (9)$$

● **PROBLEM 6-28**

Consider the two surfaces

$$f(x,y,z) = 0, \qquad g(x,y,z) = 0 \qquad (1)$$

whose intersection determines a curve. Find the equation of the plane normal to the curve at the point (x_1,y_1,z_1). Write this equation in the vector and rectangular form.

Solution: Since the point (x_1,y_1,z_1) is on the curve it is also on both surfaces f and g. Compute the gradient of f at (x_1,y_1,z_1)

$$\left.\nabla f\right|_{(x_1,y_1,z_1)} = \left.\left(\frac{\partial f}{\partial x}, \frac{\partial f}{\partial y}, \frac{\partial f}{\partial z}\right)\right|_{(x_1,y_1,z_1)} \qquad (2)$$

The vector $\left.\nabla f\right|_{(x_1,y_1,z_1)}$ is normal to the surface f at the point (x_1,y_1,z_1). Since the plane is normal to the curve at

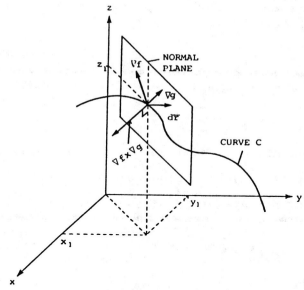

the point (x_1, y_1, z_1), the vector $\nabla f \Big|_{(x_1, y_1, z_1)}$ lies on this plane.

In the same manner, the vector $\nabla g \Big|_{(x_1, y_1, z_1)}$ is also on the plane.

Therefore the vector product of the vectors $\nabla f \times \nabla g$ is normal to the plane.

Then if a vector $d\bar{r}$ is located on the plane, it follows that

$$d\bar{r} \cdot \nabla f \times \nabla g = 0 \quad \left(\text{refer to the figure}\right) \qquad (3)$$

To write this equation in rectangular coordinates, note that

$$\nabla f = \left(\frac{\partial f}{\partial x}, \frac{\partial f}{\partial y}, \frac{\partial f}{\partial z} \right)$$

$$\nabla g = \left(\frac{\partial g}{\partial x}, \frac{\partial g}{\partial y}, \frac{\partial g}{\partial z} \right) \qquad (4)$$

The next step is to replace the differentials dx, dy, dz by

$$dx = x = x_1, \quad dy = y - y_1, \quad dz = z - z_1 \qquad (5)$$

Substituting eqs.(4) and (5) into eq.(3), obtain

$$\begin{vmatrix} x - x_1 & y - y_1 & z - z_1 \\ \dfrac{\partial f}{\partial x} & \dfrac{\partial f}{\partial y} & \dfrac{\partial f}{\partial z} \\ \dfrac{\partial g}{\partial x} & \dfrac{\partial g}{\partial y} & \dfrac{\partial g}{\partial z} \end{vmatrix} = 0 \qquad (6)$$

Eq.(6) is the equation of the plane normal to the curve at the point (x_1, y_1, z_1).

Compute the directional derivatives of the following functions

1. $f(x,y,z) = x^2 + 2y^2 - z^2$ at $(2,1,2)$ in the   (1)

   direction of the line from $(0,1,2)$ to $(3,4,5)$.

2. $f(x,y) = 4x - 2y$ at $(2,4)$ along the curve   (2)

   $y = x^2$ in the direction of increasing x.

Solution: The directional derivative of a function $f(x,y,z)$ in the direction of $\bar{v}$ at the point (x,y,z) is denoted by

$$\nabla_v \, f(x,y,z) \quad \text{or} \quad \nabla_v \, f \tag{3}$$

It is defined as

$$\nabla_v \, f = \lim_{\nabla s \to o} \frac{\Delta f}{\Delta s} \tag{4}$$

where Δf is the change in f and Δs is the distance in the direction of $\bar{v}$. A displacement from (x,y,z) in the direction of $\bar{v}$ can be written as

$$\Delta \bar{r} = (\Delta x, \Delta y, \Delta z) = (pv_x, \, pv_y, \, pv_z) \tag{5}$$

The directional derivative can be expressed as

$$\nabla_v \, f = \lim_{p \to o} \frac{f(x+pv_x, \, y+pv_y, \, z+pv_z) - f(x,y,z)}{p|\bar{v}|} \tag{6}$$

where $\Delta s = p|\bar{v}|$ and s is a positive scalar.

Eq.(6) can be written in the form

$$\nabla_v \, f = \frac{\partial f}{\partial x} \frac{v_x}{|\bar{v}|} + \frac{\partial f}{\partial y} \frac{v_y}{|\bar{v}|} + \frac{\partial f}{\partial z} \frac{v_z}{|\bar{v}|}$$

$$= \nabla f \cdot \frac{\bar{v}}{|\bar{v}|} \tag{7}$$

Note that $\dfrac{\bar{v}}{|\bar{v}|}$ is a unit vector $\bar{u}$ in the direction of $\bar{v}$. Using the direction cosines of $\bar{v}$,

$$\bar{u} = \frac{\bar{v}}{|\bar{v}|} = (\cos \alpha, \, \cos \beta, \, \cos \gamma) \tag{8}$$

Thus, the directional derivative of a function $f(x,y,z)$ is given by

$$\nabla_v f = \frac{\partial f}{\partial x} \cos \alpha + \frac{\partial f}{\partial y} \cos \beta + \frac{\partial f}{\partial z} \cos \gamma \qquad (9)$$

where α, β, γ are the direction angles of $\overline{v}$.

1. Find ∇f of the function

$$f(x,y,z) = x^2 + 2y^2 - z^2 \quad \text{at} \quad (2,1,2)$$

$$\nabla f \Big|_{(2,1,2)} = (2x,\ 4y,\ -2z) \Big|_{(2,1,2)} = (4,\ 4,\ -4) \qquad (10)$$

The vector $\overline{v}$ is the vector from the point $(0,1,2)$ to the point $(3,4,5)$, thus

$$\overline{v} = (3,4,5) - (0,1,2) = (3,3,3) \qquad (11)$$

Substituting eqs.(10) and (11) into eq.(7), yields

$$\nabla_v f = \nabla f \cdot \frac{\overline{v}}{|\overline{v}|} = (4,4,-4) \cdot \frac{(3,3,3)}{\sqrt{9+9+9}}$$

$$= \frac{12+12-12}{\sqrt{27}} = \frac{12}{\sqrt{27}} = \frac{4}{\sqrt{3}} \qquad (12)$$

2. As in the previous problem, first find ∇f. Since f is a function of x and y only,

$$\nabla f \Big|_{(2,4)} = \left(\frac{\partial f}{\partial x}, \frac{\partial f}{\partial y} \right) \Big|_{(2,4)} = (4,\ -2) \qquad (13)$$

It is required to evaluate the directional derivative of $f(x,y)$ in the direction of a vector which is tangent to the curve

$y = x^2$ at the point $(2,4)$. The tangent vector $\overline{v}$ can be written in the form

$$\overline{v} = \left(1, \frac{dy}{dx} \right) \Big|_{(2,4)} = (1,\ 2x) \Big|_{(2,4)} = (1,\ 4) \qquad (14)$$

The directional derivative is then given by

$$\nabla_v f = \nabla f \cdot \frac{\overline{v}}{|\overline{v}|} = (4,-2) \cdot \frac{(1,4)}{\sqrt{1+16}} = \frac{-4}{\sqrt{17}} \qquad (15)$$

● **PROBLEM 6-30**

1. Evaluate $\frac{\partial f}{\partial n}$, where $\overline{n}$ is a unit outer normal vector to the surface

$$x^2 + y^2 + z^2 = 9 \qquad (1)$$

The function f is $\quad f(x,y,z) = xyz \qquad (2)$

2) Find the directional derivative of ϕ in the direction

$\bar{a} = \left(\frac{1}{4}, \frac{1}{2}, \frac{\sqrt{11}}{4} \right)$, where ϕ is

$$\phi(x_1, x_2, x_3) = x_1^2 x_2 + x_2^2 x_3 + x_3^2 x_1$$

Solution: 1. Note that $\frac{\partial f}{\partial n}$ indicates the directional derivative of f at a point (x,y,z) of a surface S in the direction normal to S. The vector $\bar{n}$ is a unit normal vector; thus

$$\frac{\partial f}{\partial n} = \nabla_n f = \nabla f \cdot \bar{n} \tag{3}$$

For ∇f, obtain

$$\nabla f = \left(\frac{\partial f}{\partial x}, \frac{\partial f}{\partial y}, \frac{\partial f}{\partial z} \right) = (yz, \ xz, \ xy) \tag{4}$$

where the partial derivatives are taken at the general point (x,y,z).

The equation of the surface is

$$F(x,y,z) = x^2 + y^2 + z^2 - 9 = 0 \tag{5}$$

The vector ∇F is normal to the surface, thus

$$\nabla F = \left(\frac{\partial F}{\partial x}, \frac{\partial F}{\partial y}, \frac{\partial F}{\partial z} \right) = (2x, \ 2y, \ 2z) \tag{6}$$

The normal vector $\bar{n}$ is given by

$$\bar{n} = \frac{\nabla F}{|\nabla F|} = \frac{(2x,2y,2z)}{\sqrt{4x^2+4y^2+4z^2}} = \frac{(x,y,z)}{\sqrt{x^2+y^2+z^2}} \tag{7}$$

Substituting eq.(4) and eq.(7) into eq.(3),

$$\frac{\partial f}{\partial n} = \nabla f \cdot \bar{n} = (yz,xz,xy) \cdot \frac{(x,y,z)}{\sqrt{x^2+y^2+z^2}}$$

$$\tag{8}$$

$$= \frac{xyz+xyz+xyz}{\sqrt{x^2+y^2+z^2}} = \frac{3xyz}{\sqrt{x^2+y^2+z^2}}$$

2. The directional derivative of ϕ in the direction $\bar{n}$, where $\bar{n}$ is a unit vector, is given by

$$\bar{n} \cdot \nabla \phi \tag{9}$$

It represents the rate of change of ϕ at (x_1,x_2,x_3) in the direction $\bar{n}$

Indeed,

$$\bar{n} \cdot \nabla \phi = |\bar{n}||\nabla \phi| \cos \alpha = |\nabla \phi| \cos \alpha \tag{10}$$

For the gradient of ϕ obtain

260

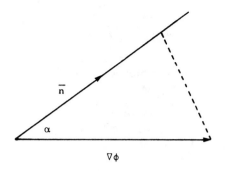

$$\nabla\phi = \left(\frac{\partial\phi}{\partial x_1}, \ \frac{\partial\phi}{\partial x_2}, \ \frac{\partial\phi}{\partial x_3} \right) = (2x_1 x_2 + x_3^2, \ x_1^2 + 2x_2 x_3, \ x_2^2 + 2x_3 x_1) \qquad (11)$$

The directional derivative is given by

$$\bar{a} \cdot \nabla\phi = \left(\frac{1}{4}, \ \frac{1}{2}, \ \frac{\sqrt{11}}{4} \right) \cdot (2x_1 x_2 + x_3^2, \ x_1^2 + 2x_2 x_3, \ x_2^2 + 2x_1 x_3)$$

$$\qquad (12)$$

$$= \frac{x_1 x_2}{2} + \frac{x_3^2}{4} + \frac{x_1^2}{2} + x_2^2 x_3 + \frac{\sqrt{11} \, x_2^2}{4} + \frac{\sqrt{11} \, x_1 x_3}{2}$$

● **PROBLEM 6-31**

Prove the following theorems:

<u>Theorem 1</u>:

The component of ∇f in the direction of a unit vector $\bar{v}$ is equal to the directional derivative of f in that direction.

<u>Theorem 2</u>:

The gradient vector ∇f points in the direction in which f increases most rapidly. The maximum value of $\frac{df}{ds}$ is equal to $|\nabla f|$.

<u>Theorem 3</u>:

The vector field ∇f is normal to the surfaces f = const.

<u>Solution</u>: <u>Theorem 1</u> – The component of vector $\bar{b}$ in the direction of $\bar{a}$ is

$$\text{comp}_{\bar{a}} \ \bar{b} = \bar{b} \cdot \frac{\bar{a}}{|\bar{a}|} \qquad (1)$$

Thus, the component of ∇f in the direction of a unit vector $\bar{v}$ is

$$|\nabla f| \ \cos\theta \qquad (2)$$

where θ is the angle between the vectors ∇f and $\bar{v}$. Since $\bar{v}$ is a unit vector,

261

$$|\nabla f| \cos \theta = \nabla f \cdot \bar{v} = \nabla_v f \qquad (3)$$

The right-hand side of eq.(3) is the directional derivative of f in the direction $\bar{v}$.

Theorem 2 - To prove this theorem, note that

$$\frac{df}{ds} = \frac{\partial f}{\partial x}\frac{dx}{ds} + \frac{\partial f}{\partial y}\frac{dy}{ds} + \frac{\partial f}{\partial z}\frac{dz}{ds} = \nabla f \cdot \frac{d\bar{r}}{ds} = \nabla f \cdot \bar{v} \qquad (4)$$

where $\bar{v} = \dfrac{d\bar{r}}{ds}$ is a unit vector.

Comparing eqs.(4) and (3), yields

$$\frac{df}{ds} = \nabla f \cdot \bar{v} = |\nabla f| \cos \theta \qquad (5)$$

Thus, $\dfrac{df}{ds}$ attains its maximum value

$$\frac{df}{ds}_{max} = |\nabla f| \qquad (6)$$

when $\theta = 0$.

Theorem 3 - Let X be a point on the surface f = const, and $\bar{v}$ be a unit tangent vector to this surface at the point X. The value of $\dfrac{df}{ds}$ at X, corresponding to the direction of $\bar{v}$ is equal to zero. Therefore,

$$\nabla f \cdot \bar{v} = 0 \qquad (7)$$

Thus ∇f is perpendicular to all vectors at X tangent to the surface f = const.

● **PROBLEM 6-32**

Using the theorems of Problem 6-31 and the definition of the directional derivative, solve the following problems:

1. For the function $f(x,y,z) = 2x^2+y^2-z^2$ find $\dfrac{df}{ds}$ in the direction of the vector $\bar{v} = (3,2,1)$ at the point (1,4,1).

2. A fly is sitting on a lamp located at the point (2,1,4). The temperature of the room is given by

   $f(x,y,z) = x^3 + y^2 + z$. In what direction should the fly go to get cool as soon as possible?

3. If $f(x,y,z) = e^x + y^2 + z^2$, what is the maximum value of $\dfrac{df}{ds}$ at the point (2,1,1)?

4. Find a unit vector normal to the surface
   $$x^2+2y^2-3z^2 = -1$$
   at the point (3,1,2).

Solution: 1. First evaluate the value of ∇f at the point (1,4,1). Doing this

$$\nabla f \Big|_{(1,4,1)} = \nabla(2x^2+y^2-z^2) \Big|_{(1,4,1)}$$

$$= (4x,2y,-2z) \Big|_{(1,4,1)}$$

$$= (4,\ 8,\ -2)$$

From equation (4) of Problem 6-31

$$\frac{df}{ds} = \nabla f \cdot \frac{\bar{v}}{|\bar{v}|} \tag{2}$$

where $\frac{\bar{v}}{|\bar{v}|}$ is a unit vector in the direction of the vector $\bar{v}$.

Substituting eq.(1) and the value of $\bar{v} = (3,2,1)$ into eq.(2),

$$\frac{df}{ds} = \nabla f \cdot \frac{\bar{v}}{|\bar{v}|} = (4,8,-2) \cdot \frac{(3,2,1)}{\sqrt{3^2+2^2+1^2}} \tag{3}$$

$$= \frac{26}{\sqrt{14}}$$

2. Grad f indicates the direction of maximum increase of the function f. Thus, in our case (or the case of the fly) the vector grad f computed at the point (2,1,4) indicates the direction of maximum increase of temperature. Correspondingly the vector -grad f points in the direction of maximum decrease of temperature. Therefore,

$$-\text{grad } f \Big|_{(2,1,4)} = -\nabla(x^3+y^2+z) \Big|_{(2,1,4)}$$

$$= -(3x^2,\ 2y,\ 1) \Big|_{(2,1,4)} \tag{4}$$

$$= (-12,\ -2,\ -1)$$

3. From Theorem 2 of Problem 6-31, the maximum value of $\frac{df}{ds}$ is $|\nabla f|$. Thus

$$\max\left(\frac{df}{ds}\right) = |\nabla f| = \left|\nabla(e^x+y^2+z^2)\right|_{(2,1,1)}\Big|$$

$$= \left|(e^x,\ 2y,\ 2z)\right|_{(2,1,1)}\Big| = \left|(e^2,\ 2,\ 2)\right| \tag{5}$$

$$= \sqrt{e^4 + 8}$$

4. For ∇f at the point (3,1,2), obtain

$$\nabla f \Big|_{(3,1,2)} = \nabla(x^2+2y^2-3z^2) \Big|_{(3,1,2)}$$

$$= (2x,\ 4y,\ -6z) \Big|_{(3,1,2)} = (6,\ 4,\ -12) \tag{6}$$

Note that $x^2+2y^2-3z^2 = -1$ is an isotimic surface for the function $f(x,y,z) = x^2+2y^2-3z^2$. Thus the unit normal vector is

$$\bar{n}_1 = \frac{(6,4,-12)}{\sqrt{6^2+4^2+12^2}} = \frac{(6,4,-12)}{14} = \left(\frac{3}{7}, \frac{2}{7}, \frac{-6}{7}\right) \qquad (7)$$

or

$$\bar{n}_2 = -\bar{n}_1 = \frac{(-6,-4,12)}{\sqrt{6^2+4^2+12^2}} = \left(-\frac{3}{7}, -\frac{2}{7}, \frac{6}{7}\right) \qquad (8)$$

Both vectors $\bar{n}_1$ and $\bar{n}_2$ are unit vectors normal to the surface at the point (3,1,2).

● **PROBLEM 6-33**

1. Find the Laplacian of

$$f(x,y) = e^x \sin y \qquad (1)$$

2. Find the Laplacian of

$$f(x,y,z) = x^2 + xy^2 + 2z^3 \qquad (2)$$

Solution: The operator ∇ can be written in the form

$$\nabla \equiv \frac{\partial}{\partial x}\,\bar{i} + \frac{\partial}{\partial y}\,\bar{j} + \frac{\partial}{\partial z}\,\bar{k} \qquad (3)$$

Thus

$$\nabla^2 = \nabla\cdot\nabla = \frac{\partial^2}{\partial x^2} + \frac{\partial^2}{\partial y^2} + \frac{\partial^2}{\partial z^2} \qquad (4)$$

If $f = f(x,y,z)$, then the Laplacian of f, denoted by Δf or by $\nabla^2 f$, is

$$\nabla^2 f = \frac{\partial^2 f}{\partial x^2} + \frac{\partial^2 f}{\partial y^2} + \frac{\partial^2 f}{\partial z^2} \qquad (5)$$

In the case of a function of two independent variables $f(x,y)$ the Laplacian of f is

$$\nabla^2 f = \frac{\partial^2 f}{\partial x^2} + \frac{\partial^2 f}{\partial y^2} \qquad (6)$$

Substituting eq.(1) into eq.(6), obtain

$$\nabla^2 f = \frac{\partial^2}{\partial x^2}(e^x \sin y) + \frac{\partial^2}{\partial y^2}(e^x \sin y)$$

$$= e^x \sin y - e^x \sin y = 0 \qquad (7)$$

From eq.(7), it is evident that $e^x \sin y$ is a harmonic function (see Problem 6-34).

2. In this case, f is a function of three independent variables. Substituting eq.(2) into eq.(5), gives

$$\nabla^2 f = \frac{\partial^2 f}{\partial x^2} + \frac{\partial^2 f}{\partial y^2} + \frac{\partial^2 f}{\partial z^2} = 2 + 2x + 12z \qquad (8)$$

In the same manner, one can also define the Laplacian of a function of more than three independent variables.

Let $f = f(x_1, x_2, \ldots, x_n)$ be a function of n independent variables. The Laplacian of f is defined as

$$\nabla^2 f \equiv \frac{\partial^2 f}{\partial x_1^2} + \frac{\partial^2 f}{\partial x_2^2} + \ldots + \frac{\partial^2 f}{\partial x_n^2} \qquad (9)$$

● **PROBLEM 6-34**

1. Show that the following functions are harmonic in x and y.

   $$f(x,y) = \log \sqrt{x^2+y^2} \qquad (1)$$

   $$g(x,y) = x^2 - y^2 \qquad (2)$$

2. Show that the function

   $$f(x,y,z) = x^2 + y^2 - 2z^2 \qquad (3)$$

   is harmonic in x, y, and z.

3. Show that every harmonic function is biharmonic.

Solution: 1. If $f = f(x,y)$ has continuous second derivatives in a domain D and
$$\nabla^2 f = 0 \qquad (4)$$
in D, then f is said to be harmonic in D.

Substituting eq.(1) into eq.(4), we obtain

$$\nabla^2 f = \frac{\partial^2}{\partial x^2}(\log \sqrt{x^2+y^2}) + \frac{\partial^2}{\partial y^2}(\log \sqrt{x^2+y^2})$$

$$= \frac{\partial}{\partial x}\left(\frac{x}{x^2+y^2}\right) + \frac{\partial}{\partial y}\left(\frac{y}{x^2+y^2}\right) = \frac{x^2+y^2-2x^2}{(x^2+y^2)^2} + \frac{x^2+y^2-2y^2}{(x^2+y^2)^2} = 0 \qquad (5)$$

Thus, $\log \sqrt{x^2+y^2}$ is a harmonic function.

For $g(x,y) = x^2 - y^2$,

$$\nabla^2 g = \frac{\partial^2}{\partial x^2}(x^2-y^2) + \frac{\partial^2}{\partial y^2}(x^2-y^2) = 2 - 2 = 0 \qquad (6)$$

$g(x,y) = x^2 - y^2$ is a harmonic function. Note that in both cases the second derivative of the functions are continuous.

2. The function $f(x,y,z)$ is harmonic in x, y, z if it has continuous second derivatives in the domain D and

$$\nabla^2 f = 0. \qquad (7)$$

265

Substituting eq.(3) into eq.(7),

$$\nabla^2 f = \frac{\partial^2 f}{\partial x^2} + \frac{\partial^2 f}{\partial y^2} + \frac{\partial^2 f}{\partial z^2} = 2 + 2 - 4 = 0 \qquad (8)$$

The second derivatives of the function f are continuous, thus from eq.(8) one concludes that f is a harmonic function.

3. The fact that every harmonic function is biharmonic can be easily derived from the definition of the biharmonic function.   If

$$\nabla^4 f = \nabla^2 (\nabla^2 f) = 0 \qquad (9)$$

then f is a biharmonic function.

For a function of two variables f(x,y),   eq.(9) becomes

$$\nabla^4 f = \nabla^2 (\nabla^2 f) = \frac{\partial^4 f}{\partial x^4} + 2 \frac{\partial^4 f}{\partial^2 x \partial^2 y} + \frac{\partial^4 f}{\partial y^4} = 0 \qquad (10)$$

If the function f is harmonic, that is if $\nabla^2 f = 0$,   then

$$\nabla^4 f = \nabla^2 (\nabla^2 f) = 0 \qquad (11)$$

and the function is biharmonic.

Very often one deals with biharmonic equations in the theory of elasticity. Not every biharmonic function is harmonic, for example

$$f(x,y) = xy^2$$

$$\nabla^4 f = \nabla^4 (xy^2) = 0 \qquad (12)$$

but

$$\nabla^2 f = \frac{\partial^2}{\partial x^2} (xy^2) + \frac{\partial^2}{\partial y^2} (xy^2) = 2x \qquad (13)$$

● **PROBLEM 6-35**

Let f = f(x,y) and x = x(t), y = y(t).

Derive expressions for $\frac{df}{dt}$ and $\frac{d^2 f}{dt^2}$.

Solution: Applying the chain rule, obtain

$$\frac{df}{dt} = \frac{\partial f}{\partial x} \frac{dx}{dt} + \frac{\partial f}{\partial y} \frac{dy}{dt} \qquad (1)$$

To find $\frac{d^2 f}{dt^2}$ differentiate eq.(1) and use the product rule.

$$\frac{d^2 f}{dt^2} = \frac{d}{dt}\left(\frac{df}{dt}\right) = \frac{\partial f}{\partial x} \frac{d^2 x}{dt^2} + \frac{dx}{dt} \frac{d}{dt}\left(\frac{\partial f}{\partial x}\right) + \frac{\partial f}{\partial y} \frac{d^2 y}{dt^2} + \frac{dy}{dt} \frac{d}{dt}\left(\frac{\partial f}{\partial y}\right) \qquad (2)$$

Then evaluate the expressions $\frac{d}{dt}\left(\frac{\partial f}{\partial x}\right)$ and $\frac{d}{dt}\left(\frac{\partial f}{\partial y}\right)$.

For this purpose apply eq.(1) to $\left(\frac{\partial f}{\partial x}\right)$ and $\left(\frac{\partial f}{\partial y}\right)$ and obtain

$$\frac{d}{dt}\left(\frac{\partial f}{\partial x}\right) = \frac{\partial^2 f}{\partial x^2}\frac{dx}{dt} + \frac{\partial^2 f}{\partial x \partial y}\frac{dy}{dt} \tag{3}$$

$$\frac{d}{dt}\left(\frac{\partial f}{\partial y}\right) = \frac{\partial^2 f}{\partial x \partial y}\frac{dx}{dt} + \frac{\partial^2 f}{\partial y^2}\frac{dy}{dt} \tag{4}$$

Substituting eqs.(3) and (4) into eq.(2)

$$\frac{d^2 f}{dt^2} = \frac{\partial f}{\partial x}\frac{d^2 x}{dt^2} + \frac{\partial^2 f}{\partial x^2}\left(\frac{dx}{dt}\right)^2 + 2\frac{\partial^2 f}{\partial x \partial y}\frac{dx}{dt}\frac{dy}{dt}$$
$$+ \frac{\partial^2 f}{\partial y^2}\left(\frac{dy}{dt}\right)^2 + \frac{\partial f}{\partial y}\frac{d^2 y}{dt^2} \tag{5}$$

In a similar manner, one can also find higher derivatives of f such as
$$\frac{d^3 f}{dt^3}, \quad \frac{d^4 f}{dt^4} \quad \text{etc.}$$

CHAPTER 7

PARTIAL DIFFERENTIATION OF VECTORS, GRADIENT AND DIVERGENCE

INTRODUCTION

Chapter 7 is devoted to the partial differentiation of vector functions. Since a vector function is nothing more than an ordered sequence of scalar (ordinary) functions, all of the theorems and formulas discussed in the previous chapter on ordinary differentiation are applicable to vector differentiation.

After discussing curvilinear coordinates and the concept of functional dependence, the definition of the gradient of a scalar field is then repeated in order to introduce another highly important differential operator - the divergence of a vector field. Though there are many identities involving the gradient and divergence, this chapter will be concerned with the most frequently used identities only. Before moving on to the next chapter, the student is strongly advised to become well acquainted with both the gradient and divergence operators.

The divergence, in particular, will lead to a very important class of vectors, namely, the solenoidal vectors. Solenoidal vectors are frequently encountered in physics.

Finally, before starting Chapter 7, it is important for the student to keep in mind that the gradient acts upon a scalar field and produces a vector field in return; while the divergence acts upon a vector field and yields a scalar field.

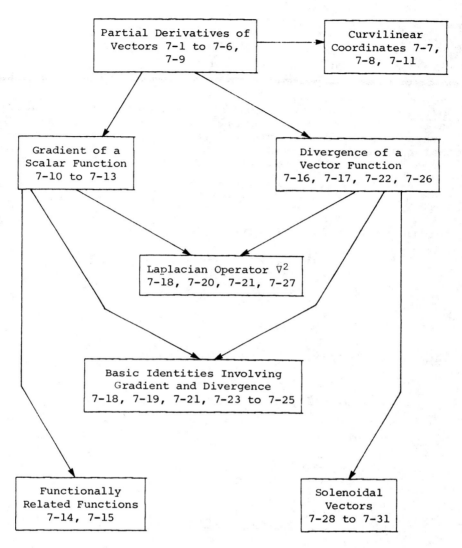

This chart is provided to facilitate rapid understanding of the inter-relationships of the topics and subject matter in this chapter. Also shown are the problem numbers associated with the subject matter.

PARTIAL DIFFERENTIATION OF VECTORS

● **PROBLEM** 7-1

Using the definition of the partial derivative of a vector, find

1. $\dfrac{\partial \bar{a}}{\partial u}$

2. $\dfrac{\partial \bar{a}}{\partial v}$

3. $\dfrac{\partial^2 \overline{a}}{\partial u \partial v}$

where $\qquad \overline{a} = (u^2 v,\ u + e^v,\ u + v^2)$ $\hfill$ (1)

Solution: The partial derivatives of a vector are defined in the same manner as partial derivatives of functions of several independent variables (see Chapter VI). Assume that $\overline{b}$ is a vector whose components are functions of the three independent variables x, y, z:

$$\overline{b} = (b_1,\ b_2,\ b_3) \hfill (2)$$

(or in compact form $\overline{b} = \overline{b}(x,y,z)$) where

$$b_1 = b_1(x,y,z)$$

$$b_2 = b_2(x,y,z) \hfill (3)$$

$$b_3 = b_3(x,y,z)$$

The partial derivatives of $\overline{b}$ are defined as

$$\frac{\partial \overline{b}}{\partial x} = \lim_{\Delta x \to o} \frac{\overline{b}(x+\Delta x,y,z) - \overline{b}(x,y,z)}{\Delta x} \hfill (4)$$

$$\frac{\partial \overline{b}}{\partial y} = \lim_{\Delta y \to o} \frac{\overline{b}(x,y+\Delta y,z) - \overline{b}(x,y,z)}{\Delta y} \hfill (5)$$

$$\frac{\partial \overline{b}}{\partial z} = \lim_{\Delta z \to o} \frac{\overline{b}(x,y,z+\Delta z) - \overline{b}(x,y,z)}{\Delta z} \hfill (6)$$

if the limits exist.

1. Using the definition of the partial derivative, we obtain

$$\frac{\partial \overline{a}}{\partial u} = \lim_{\Delta u \to o} \frac{\overline{a}(u+\Delta u,v) - \overline{a}(u,v)}{\Delta u}$$

$$= \lim_{\Delta u \to o} \frac{((u+\Delta u)^2 v,\ u+\Delta u+e^v,\ u+\Delta u+v^2) - (u^2 v,\ u+e^v,\ u+v^2))}{\Delta u}$$

$$= \lim_{\Delta u \to o} \frac{(2u\Delta u v + (\Delta u)^2 v,\ \Delta u,\ \Delta u)}{\Delta u}$$

$$= \lim_{\Delta u \to o} \; (2uv + v\Delta u, \; 1, \; 1) = (2uv, \; 1, \; 1) \tag{7}$$

2. Here again, from the definition of the partial derivative,

$$\frac{\partial \overline{a}}{\partial v} = \lim_{\Delta v \to o} \frac{(u^2(v+\Delta v), \; u+e^{v+\Delta v}, \; u + (v+\Delta v)^2) - (u^2 v, \; u+e^v, \; u+v^2)}{\Delta v}$$

$$= \lim_{\Delta v \to o} \frac{(u^2 \Delta v, \; e^v \cdot e^{\Delta v} - e^v, \; 2v\Delta v + (\Delta v)^2)}{\Delta v} \tag{8}$$

$$= \lim_{\Delta v \to o} \; \left(u^2, \; e^v \cdot \frac{e^{\Delta v} - 1}{\Delta v}, \; 2v + \Delta v \right) = (u^2, \; e^v, \; 2v)$$

To compute the limit

$$\lim_{\Delta v \to o} \; \frac{e^{\Delta v} - 1}{\Delta v} \tag{9}$$

apply de l'Hôpital's rule, which states that if

$$\lim_{x \to a} f(x) = 0 \quad \text{and} \quad \lim_{x \to a} g(x) = 0, \quad \text{then}$$

$$\lim_{x \to a} \frac{f(x)}{g(x)} = \lim_{x \to a} \frac{f'(x)}{g'(x)}$$

provided the limit on the right side exists.

Therefore,

$$\lim_{\Delta v \to o} \; \frac{e^{\Delta v} - 1}{\Delta v} = \lim_{\Delta v \to o} \; e^{\Delta v} = 1 \tag{10}$$

3. Note that

$$\frac{\partial^2 \overline{a}}{\partial u \partial v} = \frac{\partial}{\partial u} \left(\frac{\partial \overline{a}}{\partial v} \right) \tag{11}$$

Substituting eq.(8) into eq.(11), we find

$$\frac{\partial}{\partial u} \left(\frac{\partial \overline{a}}{\partial v} \right) = \frac{\partial}{\partial u} \; (u^2, \; e^v, \; 2v)$$

$$= \lim_{\Delta u \to o} \frac{((u+\Delta u)^2, e^V, 2v) - (u^2, e^V, 2v)}{\Delta u} \qquad (12)$$

$$= \lim_{\Delta u \to o} \frac{((2u\Delta u+(\Delta u)^2, 0, 0)}{\Delta u} = (2u, 0, 0)$$

If $\bar{a}$ has continuous partial derivatives of the second order, then

$$\frac{\partial^2 \bar{a}}{\partial u \partial v} = \frac{\partial^2 \bar{a}}{\partial v \partial u} \qquad (13)$$

In other words, the order of differentiation does not matter.

● **PROBLEM 7-2**

If
$$\bar{a}(x_1, x_2, x_3, x_4) = (x_1 x_4, \ x_3 x_2^2, \ x_3, \ 5x_2, \ 6x_1^2 + \cos x_2) \quad (1)$$
find

1. $\dfrac{\partial \bar{a}}{\partial x_1}$, $\dfrac{\partial \bar{a}}{\partial x_2}$, $\dfrac{\partial \bar{a}}{\partial x_3}$, $\dfrac{\partial \bar{a}}{\partial x_4}$

2. $\dfrac{\partial^2 \bar{a}}{\partial x_1 \partial x_2}$, $\dfrac{\partial^2 \bar{a}}{\partial x_2 \partial x_3}$, $\dfrac{\partial^2 \bar{a}}{\partial x_1 \partial x_3}$

3. $\dfrac{\partial^3 \bar{a}}{\partial x_1 \partial x_2 \partial x_3}$, $\dfrac{\partial^3 \bar{a}}{\partial x_2^2 \partial x_3}$, $\dfrac{\partial^3 \bar{a}}{\partial x_2 \partial x_1^2}$

<u>Solution</u>: The partial derivatives of vectors are calculated in the same manner as the partial derivatives of scalar functions. Below are given some basic rules for partial differentiation of vectors.

Let $\bar{a} = \bar{a}(x,y,z)$ and $\bar{b} = \bar{b}(x,y,z)$, then

$$\frac{\partial}{\partial x}(\bar{a} \cdot \bar{b}) = \bar{a} \cdot \frac{\partial \bar{b}}{\partial x} + \frac{\partial \bar{a}}{\partial x} \cdot \bar{b} \qquad (2)$$

$$\frac{\partial}{\partial x}(\bar{a} \times \bar{b}) = \bar{a} \times \frac{\partial \bar{b}}{\partial x} + \frac{\partial \bar{a}}{\partial x} \times \bar{b} \qquad (3)$$

$$\frac{\partial^2}{\partial x \partial y}(\bar{a} \cdot \bar{b}) = \frac{\partial}{\partial x}\left[\frac{\partial}{\partial y}(\bar{a} \cdot \bar{b})\right] = \frac{\partial}{\partial x}\left[\bar{a} \cdot \frac{\partial \bar{b}}{\partial y} + \frac{\partial \bar{a}}{\partial y} \cdot \bar{b}\right]$$

$$\qquad (4)$$

$$= \bar{a} \cdot \frac{\partial^2 \bar{b}}{\partial x \partial y} + \frac{\partial \bar{a}}{\partial x} \cdot \frac{\partial \bar{b}}{\partial y} + \frac{\partial \bar{a}}{\partial y} \cdot \frac{\partial \bar{b}}{\partial x} + \frac{\partial^2 \bar{a}}{\partial x \partial y} \cdot \bar{b}$$

1. For first order partial derivatives,

$$\frac{\partial \overline{a}}{\partial x_1} = \frac{\partial}{\partial x_1} (x_1 x_4, \ x_3 x_2^2, \ x_3, \ 5x_2, \ 6x_1^2 + \cos x_2)$$

$$= (x_4, \ 0, \ 0, \ 0, \ 12x_1) \tag{5}$$

$$\frac{\partial \overline{a}}{\partial x_2} = \frac{\partial}{\partial x_2} (x_1 x_4, \ x_3 x_2^2, \ x_3, \ 5x_2, \ 6x_1^2 + \cos x_2)$$

$$= (0, \ 2x_3 x_2, \ 0, \ 5, \ -\sin x_2) \tag{6}$$

$$\frac{\partial \overline{a}}{\partial x_3} = \frac{\partial}{\partial x_3} (x_1 x_4, \ x_3 x_2^2, \ x_3, \ 5x_2, \ 6x_1^2 + \cos x_2)$$

$$= (0, \ x_2^2, \ 1, \ 0, \ 0) \tag{7}$$

$$\frac{\partial \overline{a}}{\partial x_4} = \frac{\partial}{\partial x_4} (x_1 x_4, \ x_3 x_2^2, \ x_3, \ 5x_2, \ 6x_1^2 + \cos x_2)$$

$$= (x_1, \ 0, \ 0, \ 0, \ 0) \tag{8}$$

2. Taking the partial derivative of eq.(6) with respect to x_1,

$$\frac{\partial^2 \overline{a}}{\partial x_1 \partial x_2} = \frac{\partial}{\partial x_1} (0, \ 2x_3 x_2, \ 0, \ 5, \ -\sin x_2) = (0,0,0,0,0) \tag{9}$$

From eq.(7),

$$\frac{\partial^2 \overline{a}}{\partial x_2 \partial x_3} = \frac{\partial}{\partial x_2} (0, \ x_2^2, \ 1, \ 0, \ 0) = (0, \ 2x_2, \ 0, \ 0, \ 0) \tag{10}$$

From eq.(7),

$$\frac{\partial^2 \overline{a}}{\partial x_1 \partial x_3} = \frac{\partial}{\partial x_1} (0, \ x_2^2, \ 1, \ 0, \ 0) = (0, \ 0, \ 0, \ 0, \ 0) \tag{11}$$

3. From eq.(11),

$$\frac{\partial^3 \overline{a}}{\partial x_1 \partial x_2 \partial x_3} = \frac{\partial^3 \overline{a}}{\partial x_2 \partial x_1 \partial x_3} = \frac{\partial}{\partial x_2} (0,0,0,0,0) = (0,0,0,0,0) \tag{12}$$

From eq.(10),

$$\frac{\partial^3 \overline{a}}{\partial x_2^2 \partial x_3} = \frac{\partial}{\partial x_2} \left(\frac{\partial^2 \overline{a}}{\partial x_2 \partial x_3} \right) = \frac{\partial}{\partial x_2} (0, \ 2x_2, \ 0, \ 0, \ 0)$$

$$= (0, \ 2, \ 0, \ 0, \ 0) \tag{13}$$

From eq.(9),

$$\frac{\partial^3 \overline{a}}{\partial x_2 \partial x_1^2} = \frac{\partial}{\partial x_1} \left(\frac{\partial^2 \overline{a}}{\partial x_1 \partial x_2} \right) = \frac{\partial}{\partial x_1} (0, \ 0, \ 0, \ 0, \ 0)$$

$$= (0, \ 0, \ 0, \ 0, \ 0) \tag{14}$$

273

If
$$\bar{a} = x_1^2\bar{i} + x_1 x_2\bar{j} + (2x_3+4)\bar{k} , \tag{1}$$
find
$$\frac{\partial\bar{a}}{\partial x_1}, \quad \frac{\partial\bar{a}}{\partial x_2}, \quad \frac{\partial\bar{a}}{\partial x_3}, \quad \frac{\partial^2\bar{a}}{\partial x_1\,\partial x_2}, \quad \frac{\partial^2\bar{a}}{\partial x_2\,\partial x_1}$$

Solution: Every vector can be written in the component form, that is
$$\bar{a} = (a_1,\ a_2,\ a_3)$$

or as a linear combination of the base vectors, as in
$$\bar{a} = a_1\bar{i} + a_2\bar{j} + a_3\bar{k}$$

Both forms are equivalent.

Eq.(1) can be written
$$\bar{a} = (x_1^2,\ x_1 x_2,\ 2x_3 + 4) \tag{2}$$

The partial derivatives of $\bar{a}$ are:

$$\frac{\partial\bar{a}}{\partial x_1} = \frac{\partial}{\partial x_1}(x_1^2,\ x_1 x_2,\ 2x_3 + 4)$$
$$= (2x_1,\ x_2,\ 0) \tag{3}$$

$$\frac{\partial\bar{a}}{\partial x_2} = \frac{\partial}{\partial x_2}(x_1^2,\ x_1 x_2,\ 2x_3 + 4)$$
$$= (0,\ x_1,\ 0) \tag{4}$$

$$\frac{\partial\bar{a}}{\partial x_3} = \frac{\partial}{\partial x_3}(x_1^2,\ x_1 x_2,\ 2x_3 + 4)$$
$$= (0,\ 0,\ 2) \tag{5}$$

The higher partial derivatives are defined as follows

$$\frac{\partial^2\bar{a}}{\partial x_1^2} = \frac{\partial}{\partial x_1}\left(\frac{\partial\bar{a}}{\partial x_1}\right) \tag{6}$$

$$\frac{\partial^2\bar{a}}{\partial x_1\,\partial x_2} = \frac{\partial}{\partial x_1}\left(\frac{\partial\bar{a}}{\partial x_2}\right) \tag{7}$$

Any higher partial derivative can be defined in this manner,

$$\frac{\partial^4 f}{\partial x_1\,\partial x_3\,\partial x_4\,\partial x_5} = \frac{\partial}{\partial x_1}\left\{\frac{\partial}{\partial x_3}\left[\frac{\partial}{\partial x_4}\left(\frac{\partial f}{\partial x_5}\right)\right]\right\} \tag{8}$$

Substituting eq.(4) into eq.(7),

$$\frac{\partial^2 \bar{a}}{\partial x_1 \partial x_2} = \frac{\partial}{\partial x_1} \left(\frac{\partial \bar{a}}{\partial x_2} \right) = \frac{\partial}{\partial x_1} (0, x_1, 0) = (0, 1, 0) \qquad (9)$$

Since the second partial derivatives of $\bar{a}$ are continuous, the order of differentiation does not matter and we can write

$$\frac{\partial^2 \bar{a}}{\partial x_2 \partial x_1} = \frac{\partial^2 \bar{a}}{\partial x_1 \partial x_2} = (0, 1, 0) \qquad (10)$$

● **PROBLEM 7-4**

Vector $\bar{a}$ is a function of three independent variables x_1, x_2, x_3 such that

$$\bar{a} = (x_1^2 + 2x_2)\bar{i} + \sin x_2 \bar{j} + e^{x_1 x_3}\bar{k} \qquad (1)$$

Find

$$\frac{\partial \bar{a}}{\partial x_1}, \quad \frac{\partial \bar{a}}{\partial x_2}, \quad \frac{\partial \bar{a}}{\partial x_3}, \quad \frac{\partial^2 \bar{a}}{\partial x_1 \partial x_2}, \quad \frac{\partial^2 \bar{a}}{\partial x_1 \partial x_3}, \quad \frac{\partial^2 \bar{a}}{\partial x_2^2}.$$

Solution: Using the definition of the partial derivatives and the basic rules for partial differentiation of vectors, we find

$$\frac{\partial \bar{a}}{\partial x_1} = \frac{\partial}{\partial x_1} \left[(x_1^2 + 2x_2)\bar{i} + \sin x_2 \bar{j} + e^{x_1 x_3}\bar{k} \right]$$
$$= 2x_1 \bar{i} + x_3 e^{x_1 x_3}\bar{k} \qquad (2)$$

or

$$\frac{\partial \bar{a}}{\partial x_1} = (2x_1, 0, x_3 e^{x_1 x_3})$$

$$\frac{\partial \bar{a}}{\partial x_2} = \frac{\partial}{\partial x_2} \left[(x_1^2 + 2x_2)\bar{i} + \sin x_2 \bar{j} + e^{x_1 x_3}\bar{k} \right]$$
$$= 2\bar{i} + \cos x_2 \bar{j} = (2, \cos x_2, 0) \qquad (3)$$

$$\frac{\partial \bar{a}}{\partial x_3} = \frac{\partial}{\partial x_3} \left[(x_1^2 + 2x_2)\bar{i} + \sin x_2 \bar{j} + e^{x_1 x_3}\bar{k} \right] \qquad (4)$$
$$= x_1 e^{x_1 x_3}\bar{k} = (0, 0, x_1 e^{x_1 x_3})$$

$$\frac{\partial^2 \bar{a}}{\partial x_1 \partial x_2} = \frac{\partial}{\partial x_1} \left(\frac{\partial \bar{a}}{\partial x_2} \right) \qquad (5)$$

Substituting eq.(3) into eq.(5), we obtain

$$\frac{\partial^2 \bar{a}}{\partial x_1 \partial x_2} = \frac{\partial}{\partial x_1} \left[2\bar{i} + \cos x_2 \bar{j} \right] = (0, 0, 0) \qquad (6)$$

In the same manner,   (7)

$$\frac{\partial^2 \bar{a}}{\partial x_1 \partial x_3} = \frac{\partial}{\partial x_1}\left[x_1 e^{x_1 x_3}\bar{k}\right] = (0,\ 0,\ e^{x_1 x_3} + x_1 x_3 e^{x_1 x_3})$$

$$\frac{\partial^2 \bar{a}}{\partial x_2^2} = \frac{\partial}{\partial x_2}\left[2\bar{i} + \cos x_2\,\bar{j}\right] = (0,\ -\sin x_2, 0)\qquad (8)$$

● **PROBLEM** 7-5

If
$$f(x_1,\ x_2,\ x_3) = x_1^2 x_2 x_3$$
and   (1)
$$\bar{a} = (x_1,\ x_1 x_2,\ x_1 x_2 x_3)$$
find
$$\frac{\partial^3}{\partial x_1 \partial x_2^2}(f\bar{a})\qquad \text{at the point } (-1,\ 1,\ 2)\qquad (2)$$

Solution: First find $f\bar{a}$,

$$f\bar{a} = x_1^2 x_2 x_3(x_1,\ x_1 x_2,\ x_1 x_2 x_3) = (x_1^3 x_2 x_3,\ x_1^3 x_2^2 x_3,\ x_1^3 x_2^2 x_3^2)\quad (3)$$

For $\frac{\partial}{\partial x_2}(f\bar{a})$, obtain

$$\frac{\partial}{\partial x_2}(f\bar{a}) = \frac{\partial}{\partial x_2}(x_1^3 x_2 x_3,\ x_1^3 x_2^2 x_3,\ x_1^3 x_2^2 x_3^2)$$

$$= (x_1^3 x_3,\ 2x_1^3 x_3 x_2,\ 2x_1^3 x_3^2 x_2)$$ (4)

and

$$\frac{\partial^2}{\partial x_2^2}(f\bar{a}) = \frac{\partial}{\partial x_2}(x_1^3 x_3,\ 2x_1^3 x_3 x_2,\ 2x_1^3 x_3^2 x_2)$$

$$= (0,\ 2x_1^3 x_3,\ 2x_1^3 x_3^2)$$ (5)

Finally for $\frac{\partial^3}{\partial x_1 \partial x_2^2}(f\bar{a})$, we obtain

$$\frac{\partial^3}{\partial x_1 \partial x_2^2}(f\bar{a}) = \frac{\partial}{\partial x_1}\left[\frac{\partial^2}{\partial x_2^2}(f\bar{a})\right] = \frac{\partial}{\partial x_1}(0,\ 2x_1^3 x_3,\ 2x_1^3 x_3^2)$$

$$= (0,\ 6x_1^2 x_3,\ 6x_1^2 x_3^2)$$ (6)

At the point $(-1,\ 1,\ 2)$ we obtain

$$\frac{\partial^3}{\partial x_1 \partial x_2^2}(f\bar{a})\ \bigg|_{(-1,1,2)}$$

$$= (0,\ 6\cdot 2,\ 6\cdot 4) = (0,\ 12,\ 24)$$ (7)

If
$$\overline{a} = (2x_1^3 x_2 + x_3^2, \ x_2 e^{\alpha}, \ x_3^2 + \cos x_1),$$
find
$$\frac{\partial \overline{a}}{\partial x_1}, \ \frac{\partial \overline{a}}{\partial x_2}, \ \frac{\partial \overline{a}}{\partial x_3}, \ \frac{\partial^2 \overline{a}}{\partial x_1^2}, \ \frac{\partial^2 \overline{a}}{\partial x_2^2}, \ \frac{\partial^2 \overline{a}}{\partial x_3^2}, \ \frac{\partial^2 \overline{a}}{\partial x_1 \partial x_2}, \ \frac{\partial^2 \overline{a}}{\partial x_2 \partial x_1}, \ \frac{\partial^3 \overline{a}}{\partial x_1^3}$$

at the point (1, 2, -1).

Solution:

$$\frac{\partial \overline{a}}{\partial x_1} = \frac{\partial}{\partial x_1}\left[2x_1^3 x_2 + x_3^2, \ x_2 e^{\alpha}, \ x_3^2 + \cos x_1 \right]$$

$$= (6x_1^2 x_2, \ 0, \ -\sin x_1) \tag{1}$$

At the point (1, 2, -1)

$$\frac{\partial \overline{a}}{\partial x_1}\bigg|_{(1,2,-1)} = (6x_1^2 x_2, \ 0, \ -\sin x_1)\bigg|_{(1,2,-1)}$$

$$= (12, \ 0, \ -\sin 1) \tag{2}$$

$$\frac{\partial^2 \overline{a}}{\partial x_1^2}\bigg|_{(1,2,-1)} = \frac{\partial}{\partial x_1}(6x_1^2 x_2, \ 0, \ -\sin x_1)\bigg|_{(1,2,-1)}$$

$$= (12x_1 x_2, \ 0, \ -\cos x_1)\bigg|_{(1,2,-1)}$$

$$= (24, \ 0, \ -\cos 1) \tag{3}$$

$$\frac{\partial^3 \overline{a}}{\partial x_1^3}\bigg|_{(1,2,-1)} = \frac{\partial}{\partial x_1}(12x_1 x_2, \ 0, \ -\cos x_1)\bigg|_{(1,2,-1)}$$

$$= (12x_2, \ 0, \ \sin x_1)\bigg|_{(1,2,-1)}$$

$$= (24, \ 0, \ \sin 1)$$

$$\frac{\partial \overline{a}}{\partial x_2} = \frac{\partial}{\partial x_2}(2x_1^3 x_2 + x_3^2, \ x_2 e^{\alpha}, \ x_3^2 + \cos x)$$

$$= (2x_1^3, \ e^{\alpha}, \ 0) \tag{4}$$

At (1, 2, -1),

$$\frac{\partial \overline{a}}{\partial x_2}\bigg|_{(1,2,-1)} = (2, \ e^{\alpha}, \ 0) \tag{5}$$

$$\frac{\partial^2 \overline{a}}{\partial x_2^2} = \frac{\partial}{\partial x_2}(2x_1^3, \ e^{\alpha}, \ 0) = (0, \ 0, \ 0)$$

277

Note that $\dfrac{\partial^2 \overline{a}}{\partial x_2^2} = (0, 0, 0)$ for the whole space

$$\frac{\partial \overline{a}}{\partial x_3} = \frac{\partial}{\partial x_3} (2x_1^3 x_2 + x_3^2, \; x_2 e^\alpha, \; x_3^2 + \cos x_1) = (2x_3, \; 0, \; 2x_3) \quad (6)$$

For $(1, 2, -1)$

$$\left. \frac{\partial \overline{a}}{\partial x_3} \right|_{(1,2,-1)} = (-2, \; 0, \; -2)$$

$$\frac{\partial^2 \overline{a}}{\partial x_3^2} = \frac{\partial}{\partial x_3} (2x_3, \; 0, \; 2x_3) = (2, \; 0, \; 2) \quad (7)$$

$$\frac{\partial^2 \overline{a}}{\partial x_1 \partial x_2} = \frac{\partial}{\partial x_1} (2x_1^3, \; e^\alpha, \; 0) = (6x_1^2, \; 0, \; 0) \quad (8)$$

Since $\overline{a}$ has continuous second order derivatives,

$$\frac{\partial^2 \overline{a}}{\partial x_2 \partial x_1} = \frac{\partial^2 \overline{a}}{\partial x_1 \partial x_2} \quad (9)$$

Thus

$$\left. \frac{\partial^2 \overline{a}}{\partial x_1 \partial x_2} \right|_{(1,2,-1)} = \left. \frac{\partial^2 \overline{a}}{\partial x_2 \partial x_1} \right|_{(1,2,-1)} = (6, \; 0, \; 0) \quad (10)$$

● **PROBLEM 7-7**

1. A surface is given by the equation
    $$\overline{r} = \overline{r}(\alpha, \beta) \quad (1)$$
    Show that the vector $\overline{N}$, where
    $$\overline{N} = \frac{\partial \overline{r}}{\partial \alpha} \times \frac{\partial \overline{r}}{\partial \beta} \quad (2)$$
    is a vector normal to the surface.

2. Find a unit vector normal to the surface
    $$\overline{r} = \alpha^2 \overline{i} + \alpha \beta \overline{j} + \sin \beta \, \overline{k} \quad (3)$$

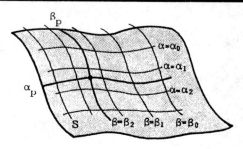

Fig.1

278

<u>Solution</u>: Consider eq.(1), where the vector $\bar{r}$ is a function of two independent variables α and β.

Let α be fixed and equal to α_0, $\alpha = \alpha_0$, then the equation $\bar{r} = \bar{r}(\alpha_0, \beta)$ represents a curve in space which we will denote by $\alpha = \alpha_0$. When α changes, taking fixed values α_1, α_2, α_3, we obtain a family of curves $\bar{r} = \bar{r}(\alpha_1, \beta)$, $\bar{r} = \bar{r}(\alpha_2, \beta)$ etc. Therefore, as α varies, $\bar{r} = \bar{r}(\alpha, \beta)$ represents a curve which moves in space and generates a surface S, as shown in Fig. (1). In the same fashion, we can change β and obtain a family of curves

$$\bar{r} = \bar{r}(\alpha, \beta_0), \quad \bar{r} = \bar{r}(\alpha, \beta_1), \quad \bar{r} = \bar{r}(\alpha, \beta_2) \text{ etc.}$$

Each value of α represents a curve on the surface S and each value of β represents a curve on the surface S. Taking definite values of α and β we obtain a point on the surface S.

The curves $\alpha = \alpha_p$ and $\beta = \beta_p$ intersect and define the point (α_p, β_p) on the surface. The numbers (α, β) define the curvilinear coordinates on the surface. When all the curves α and β are perpendicular at each point of intersection, the curvilinear coordinate system is said to be orthogonal.

1. The surface is described by the equation

$$\bar{r} = \bar{r}(\alpha, \beta)$$

The point P on the surface has coordinates (α_p, β_p), as shown in Fig. 2.

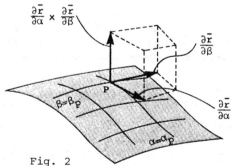

Fig. 2

Differentiating $\bar{r}$ with respect to α, obtain $\frac{\partial \bar{r}}{\partial \alpha}$. At the point P, $\beta = \beta_0$ and $\left.\frac{\partial \bar{r}}{\partial \alpha}\right|_{(\alpha_0, \beta_0)}$ is a vector tangent to the curve $\beta = \beta_0$ at P.

Similarly, $\frac{\partial \bar{r}}{\partial \beta}$ at P is tangent to the curve $\alpha = \alpha_0$.

Thus, vectors $\frac{\partial \bar{r}}{\partial \alpha}$ and $\frac{\partial \bar{r}}{\partial \beta}$ are vectors at P tangent to the curves which lie on the surface S. It follows that these vectors are tangent to the surface at P. From the definition of the vector product,

$\frac{\partial \overline{r}}{\partial \alpha} \times \frac{\partial \overline{r}}{\partial \beta}$ is a vector normal to S at P.

2. First, find the vectors $\frac{\partial \overline{r}}{\partial \alpha}$ and $\frac{\partial \overline{r}}{\partial \beta}$. Differentiating

eq.(3), we obtain $\qquad \frac{\partial \overline{r}}{\partial \alpha} = (2\alpha, \beta, 0)$ $\qquad\qquad$ (4)

$$\frac{\partial \overline{r}}{\partial \beta} = (0, \alpha, \cos\beta) \qquad\qquad (5)$$

The normal vector is given by

$$\overline{N} = \frac{\partial \overline{r}}{\partial \alpha} \times \frac{\partial \overline{r}}{\partial \beta} = (\beta\cos\beta, -2\alpha\cos\beta, 2\alpha^2) \qquad (6)$$

The unit normal vector is

$$\overline{n} = \frac{\overline{N}}{|\overline{N}|} = \frac{1}{\sqrt{\beta^2\cos^2\beta + 4\alpha^2\cos^2\beta + 4\alpha^4}} (\beta\cos\beta, -2\alpha\cos\beta, 2\alpha^2) \quad (7)$$

There are two unit vectors normal to the surface; $\overline{n}$ and $-\overline{n}$.

● **PROBLEM 7-8**

Derive the formula for the differential of the arc length of the surface

$$\overline{r} = \overline{r}(\alpha, \beta) \qquad\qquad (1)$$

Find the necessary and sufficient condition for the α, β curvilinear coordinate system to be orthogonal.

Solution: The differential of the arc length is given by the equation

$$ds^2 = d\overline{r} \cdot d\overline{r} \qquad\qquad (2)$$

Here, $\overline{r}$ is a function of the variables α and β. The differential of $\overline{r}$ is given by

$$d\overline{r} = \frac{\partial \overline{r}}{\partial \alpha} d\alpha + \frac{\partial \overline{r}}{\partial \beta} d\beta \qquad\qquad (3)$$

Substituting eq.(3) into eq.(2), obtain

$$ds^2 = d\overline{r} \cdot d\overline{r} = \left(\frac{\partial \overline{r}}{\partial \alpha} d\alpha + \frac{\partial \overline{r}}{\partial \beta} d\beta \right) \cdot \left(\frac{\partial \overline{r}}{\partial \alpha} d\alpha + \frac{\partial \overline{r}}{\partial \beta} d\beta \right)$$

$$\qquad\qquad\qquad\qquad\qquad\qquad\qquad\qquad (4)$$

$$= \frac{\partial \overline{r}}{\partial \alpha} \cdot \frac{\partial \overline{r}}{\partial \alpha} d\alpha^2 + 2 \frac{\partial \overline{r}}{\partial \alpha} \cdot \frac{\partial \overline{r}}{\partial \beta} d\alpha d\beta + \frac{\partial \overline{r}}{\partial \beta} \cdot \frac{\partial \overline{r}}{\partial \beta} d\beta^2$$

Now, let

$$A = \frac{\partial \overline{r}}{\partial \alpha} \cdot \frac{\partial \overline{r}}{\partial \alpha} \qquad (5)$$

$$B = \frac{\partial \overline{r}}{\partial \alpha} \cdot \frac{\partial \overline{r}}{\partial \beta} \qquad (6)$$

$$C = \frac{\partial \overline{r}}{\partial \beta} \cdot \frac{\partial \overline{r}}{\partial \beta} \qquad (7)$$

Equation (4) can be rewritten in the form

$$ds^2 = Ad\alpha^2 + 2Bd\alpha d\beta + Cd\beta^2 \qquad (8)$$

If the curvilinear coordinate system is to be orthogonal, then all the curves α = const and β = const are perpendicular at each point of intersection. In such a case the vectors $\frac{\partial \overline{r}}{\partial \alpha}$ and $\frac{\partial \overline{r}}{\partial \beta}$ are perpendicular and consequently $\frac{\partial \overline{r}}{\partial \alpha} \cdot \frac{\partial \overline{r}}{\partial \beta} = 0$.

We therefore conclude that the necessary and sufficient condition for the curvilinear system to be orthogonal is

$$B = \frac{\partial \overline{r}}{\partial \alpha} \cdot \frac{\partial \overline{r}}{\partial \beta} = 0 \qquad (9)$$

● **PROBLEM 7-9**

If $\overline{F} = \overline{F}(x_1, x_2, x_3, t)$ (1)

where $x_1 = x_1(t)$

$x_2 = x_2(t)$

$x_3 = x_3(t)$

prove that

$$\frac{d\overline{F}}{dt} = \frac{\partial \overline{F}}{\partial t} + \frac{\partial \overline{F}}{\partial x_1}\frac{dx_1}{dt} + \frac{\partial \overline{F}}{\partial x_2}\frac{dx_2}{dt} + \frac{\partial \overline{F}}{\partial x_3}\frac{dx_3}{dt} \qquad (2)$$

Assume differentiability of all the functions.

Solution: Express $\overline{F}$ as a combination of the base vectors $\overline{i}_1$, $\overline{i}_2$ and $\overline{i}_3$.

$$\overline{F} = F_1\overline{i}_1 + F_2\overline{i}_2 + F_3\overline{i}_3 \qquad (3)$$

Then

$$d\overline{F} = dF_1\overline{i}_1 + dF_2\overline{i}_2 + dF_3\overline{i}_3$$

$$= \left[\frac{\partial F_1}{\partial t} \, dt + \frac{\partial F_1}{\partial x_1} \, dx_1 + \frac{\partial F_1}{\partial x_2} \, dx_2 + \frac{\partial F_1}{\partial x_3} \, dx_3 \right] \bar{i}_1 \qquad (4)$$

$$+ \left[\frac{\partial F_2}{\partial t} \, dt + \frac{\partial F_2}{\partial x_1} \, dx_1 + \frac{\partial F_2}{\partial x_2} \, dx_2 + \frac{\partial F_2}{\partial x_3} \, dx_3 \right] \bar{i}_2$$

$$+ \left[\frac{\partial F_3}{\partial t} \, dt + \frac{\partial F_3}{\partial x_1} \, dx_1 + \frac{\partial F_3}{\partial x_2} \, dx_2 + \frac{\partial F_3}{\partial x_3} \, dx_3 \right] \bar{i}_3$$

Rewrite eq.(4) in the form

$$d\bar{F} = \left(\frac{\partial F_1}{\partial t} \, \bar{i}_1 + \frac{\partial F_2}{\partial t} \, \bar{i}_2 + \frac{\partial F_3}{\partial t} \, \bar{i}_3 \right) dt$$

$$+ \left(\frac{\partial F_1}{\partial x_1} \, \bar{i}_1 + \frac{\partial F_2}{\partial x_1} \, \bar{i}_2 + \frac{\partial F_3}{\partial x_1} \, \bar{i}_3 \right) dx_1 \qquad (5)$$

$$+ \left(\frac{\partial F_1}{\partial x_2} \, \bar{i}_1 + \frac{\partial F_2}{\partial x_2} \, \bar{i}_2 + \frac{\partial F_3}{\partial x_2} \, \bar{i}_3 \right) dx_2 + \left(\frac{\partial F_1}{\partial x_3} \, \bar{i}_1 + \frac{\partial F_2}{\partial x_3} \, \bar{i}_2 + \frac{\partial F_3}{\partial x_3} \, \bar{i}_3 \right) dx_3$$

$$= \frac{\partial \bar{F}}{\partial t} \, dt + \frac{\partial \bar{F}}{\partial x_1} \, dx_1 + \frac{\partial \bar{F}}{\partial x_2} \, dx_2 + \frac{\partial \bar{F}}{\partial x_3} \, dx_3$$

or

$$\frac{d\bar{F}}{dt} = \frac{\partial \bar{F}}{\partial t} + \frac{\partial \bar{F}}{\partial x_1} \frac{dx_1}{dt} + \frac{\partial \bar{F}}{\partial x_2} \frac{dx_2}{dt} + \frac{\partial \bar{F}}{\partial x_3} \frac{dx_3}{dt} \qquad (6)$$

Eq.(6) is often used in physics.

GRADIENT OF A SCALAR FIELD AND FUNCTIONALLY RELATED FUNCTIONS

● **PROBLEM** 7-10

1. Evaluate grad f, if

$$f(x,y,z) = x^2 + xy \sin y + xz^3 \qquad (1)$$

2. If f and g are scalar fields, prove that

$$\nabla \left(\frac{f}{g} \right) = g^{-2} (g \nabla f - f \nabla g) \qquad (2)$$

Solution: The nabla operator – ∇ was defined in Problem 6-16. Some properties of the gradient were discussed in Problems 6-17 to 6-25. The definition of the gradient will now be repeated.

Let (x,y,z) be the coordinate system in space and let f = f(x,y,z) be a scalar field defined in a certain domain of space. If the first partial derivatives of f exist in this domain, then we define the vector field ∇f as

$$\nabla f = \left(\frac{\partial f}{\partial x}, \frac{\partial f}{\partial y}, \frac{\partial f}{\partial z}\right) \tag{3}$$

The operator ∇ is defined as

$$\nabla \equiv \left(\frac{\partial}{\partial x}, \frac{\partial}{\partial y}, \frac{\partial}{\partial z}\right) \tag{4}$$

or equivalently as

$$\nabla \equiv \bar{i}\,\frac{\partial}{\partial x} + \bar{j}\,\frac{\partial}{\partial y} + \bar{k}\,\frac{\partial}{\partial z} \tag{5}$$

Often the term grad is used rather than ∇, thus

$$\nabla \equiv \text{grad} \tag{6}$$

and

$$\text{grad } f = \left(\frac{\partial f}{\partial x}, \frac{\partial f}{\partial y}, \frac{\partial f}{\partial z}\right) = \frac{\partial f}{\partial x}\bar{i} + \frac{\partial f}{\partial y}\bar{j} + \frac{\partial f}{\partial z}\bar{k} \tag{7}$$

1. Substituting eq.(1) into definition (3) yields

$$\nabla f = \left[\frac{\partial}{\partial x}(x^2+xy \sin y + xz^2), \ \frac{\partial}{\partial y}(x^2+xy \sin y + xz^2), \ \frac{\partial}{\partial z}(x^2+xy \sin y + xz^2)\right] \tag{8}$$

$$= (2x + y \sin y + z^2, \ x \sin y + xy \cos y, \ 2xz)$$

Note that in applying operator ∇ to a scalar field, we obtain a vector field.

2. The following identity holds for partial derivatives

$$\frac{\partial}{\partial x}\left(\frac{f}{g}\right) = \frac{g\,\frac{\partial f}{\partial x} - f\,\frac{\partial g}{\partial x}}{g^2} \tag{9}$$

For the partial derivatives with respect to y and z, we obtain

$$\frac{\partial}{\partial y}\left(\frac{f}{g}\right) = \frac{g\,\frac{\partial f}{\partial y} - f\,\frac{\partial g}{\partial y}}{g^2} \tag{10}$$

$$\frac{\partial}{\partial z}\left(\frac{f}{g}\right) = \frac{g\,\frac{\partial f}{\partial z} - f\,\frac{\partial g}{\partial z}}{g^2} \tag{11}$$

From the definition of $\nabla\left(\frac{f}{g}\right)$ and eqs.(9), (10) and (11),

$$\nabla\left(\frac{f}{g}\right) = \left[\frac{\partial}{\partial x}\left(\frac{f}{g}\right), \ \frac{\partial}{\partial y}\left(\frac{f}{g}\right), \ \frac{\partial}{\partial z}\left(\frac{f}{g}\right)\right]$$

$$= \left[\frac{g\frac{\partial f}{\partial x} - f\frac{\partial g}{\partial x}}{g^2}, \ \frac{g\frac{\partial f}{\partial y} - f\frac{\partial g}{\partial y}}{g^2}, \ \frac{g\frac{\partial f}{\partial z} - f\frac{\partial g}{\partial z}}{g^2}\right]$$

$$= \frac{1}{g^2}\left(g\frac{\partial f}{\partial x}, \ g\frac{\partial f}{\partial y}, \ g\frac{\partial f}{\partial z}\right) - \frac{1}{g^2}\left(f\frac{\partial g}{\partial x}, \ f\frac{\partial g}{\partial y}, \ f\frac{\partial g}{\partial z}\right) \tag{12}$$

$$= g^{-2}\left[g\nabla f - f\nabla g\right]$$

1. Show that ∇f is a vector perpendicular to the
   surface   f(x,y,z) = const.   (1)

2. Find a unit normal vector to the surface
   $x^2z + yz^2 = 3$ at the point (-1, 1, 2).

Solution: 1. The position vector of any point on the surface is $\bar{r}$ = (x,y,z).

The vector $d\bar{r} = dx\,\bar{i} + dy\,\bar{j} + dz\,\bar{k}$ lies on the plane tangent
to the surface at P.

Also, we have

$$df = \frac{\partial f}{\partial x}\,dx + \frac{\partial f}{\partial y}\,dy + \frac{\partial f}{\partial z}\,dz = 0 \qquad (2)$$

Eq.(2) can be written in the form

$$\left(\frac{\partial f}{\partial x}\,\bar{i} + \frac{\partial f}{\partial y}\,\bar{j} + \frac{\partial f}{\partial z}\,\bar{k}\right) \cdot (dx\,\bar{i} + dy\,\bar{j} + dz\,\bar{k}) = 0 \qquad (3)$$

Since $\bar{i}, \bar{j}, \bar{k}$ are mutually orthogonal unit vectors

$$\bar{i}\cdot\bar{i} = \bar{j}\cdot\bar{j} = \bar{k}\cdot\bar{k} = 1$$
$$\bar{i}\cdot\bar{j} = \bar{j}\cdot\bar{k} = \bar{i}\cdot\bar{k} = 0 \qquad (4)$$

From eq.(3), we have

$$\nabla f \cdot d\bar{r} = 0 \qquad (5)$$

Thus ∇f is perpendicular to $d\bar{r}$ and to the surface.

2. The gradient is given by

$$\nabla(x^2z + yz^2) = (2xz, z^2, x^2 + 2yz) \qquad (6)$$

At the point (-1, 1, 2), we obtain

$$\nabla(x^2z + yz^2)\Big|_{(-1,1,2)} = (-4, 4, 5) \qquad (7)$$

The vector $\bar{N}$ = (-4, 4, 5) is normal to the surface. The
unit vector in the same direction is given by

$$\bar{n} = \frac{\bar{N}}{|\bar{N}|} = \frac{(-4,4,5)}{\sqrt{16+16+25}} = \left(-\frac{4}{\sqrt{57}}, \frac{4}{\sqrt{57}}, \frac{5}{\sqrt{57}}\right) \qquad (8)$$

The position vector of a fixed point in space is

$$\bar{r}_1 = (x_1, y_1, z_1) \qquad\qquad (1)$$

Let $\qquad\qquad \bar{r}_2 = (x_2, y_2, z_2) \qquad\qquad (2)$

be the position vector of any point in space, and R be the distance between the points (x_1, y_1, z_1) and (x_2, y_2, z_2).

Show that ∇R is a unit vector in the direction of R (which points from point (x_1, y_1, z_1) to point (x_2, y_2, z_2)).

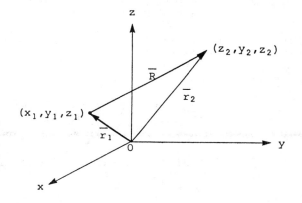

Solution: From the figure

$$\bar{R} = \bar{r}_2 - \bar{r}_1 \qquad\qquad (3)$$

Then

$$\bar{R} = (x_2, y_2, z_2) - (x_1, y_1, z_1)$$
$$= (x_2-x_1, y_2-y_1, z_2-z_1) \qquad\qquad (4)$$

The distance between the two points is the magnitude of the vector $\bar{R}$ given by eq.(4). Thus

$$R = \sqrt{(x_2-x_1)^2 + (y_2-y_1)^2 + (z_2-z_1)^2} \qquad\qquad (5)$$

Taking the gradient of R,

$$\nabla R = \nabla\left(\sqrt{(x_2-x_1)^2 + (y_2-y_1)^2 + (z_2-z_1)^2}\right) \qquad\qquad (6)$$

$$= \frac{1}{\sqrt{(x_2-x_1)^2+(y_2-y_1)^2+(z_2-z_1)^2}} (x_2-x_1, y_2-y_1, z_2-z_1)$$

$$= \frac{\bar{R}}{|\bar{R}|} = \frac{\bar{R}}{R}$$

In differentiating eq.(6) remember that (x_1, y_1, z_1) is fixed. From eq.(6) one concludes that ∇R is a unit vector in the direction of $\overline{R}$.

● **PROBLEM** 7-13

1. Let F be a differentiable function of x, y, z.

$$F = F(x, y, z) \tag{1}$$

Show that

$$dF = \nabla F \cdot d\overline{r} \tag{2}$$

2. Let G be a differentiable function of x, y, z, t

$$G = G(x, y, z, t) \tag{3}$$

where $x = x(t)$, $y = y(t)$, $z = z(t)$ are differentiable functions of t.

Prove that

$$\frac{dG}{dt} = \frac{\partial G}{\partial t} + \nabla G \cdot \frac{d\overline{r}}{dt} \tag{4}$$

<u>Solution</u>: 1. The differential of F (see Problem 6-4) is

$$dF = \frac{\partial F}{\partial x} dx + \frac{\partial F}{\partial y} dy + \frac{\partial F}{\partial z} dz \tag{5}$$

The right-hand side of eq.(5) can be written in the form

$$\frac{\partial F}{\partial x} dx + \frac{\partial F}{\partial y} dy + \frac{\partial F}{\partial z} dz = \left(\frac{\partial F}{\partial x}, \frac{\partial F}{\partial y}, \frac{\partial F}{\partial z}\right) \cdot (dx, dy, dz)$$

$$= \nabla F \cdot d\overline{r} \tag{6}$$

Thus

$$dF = \nabla F \cdot d\overline{r} \tag{7}$$

2. Since $G = G(x, y, z, t)$ the differential of G is given by

$$dG = \frac{\partial G}{\partial x} dx + \frac{\partial G}{\partial y} dy + \frac{\partial G}{\partial z} dz + \frac{\partial G}{\partial t} dt \tag{8}$$

Hence

$$\frac{dG}{dt} = \frac{\partial G}{\partial t} + \frac{\partial G}{\partial x}\frac{dx}{dt} + \frac{\partial G}{\partial y}\frac{dy}{dt} + \frac{\partial G}{\partial z}\frac{dz}{dt} \tag{9}$$

Eq. (9) can be written in the form

$$\frac{dG}{dt} = \frac{\partial G}{\partial t} + \left(\frac{\partial G}{\partial x}, \frac{\partial G}{\partial y}, \frac{\partial G}{\partial z}\right) \cdot \left(\frac{dx}{dt}, \frac{dy}{dt}, \frac{dz}{dt}\right)$$

$$= \frac{\partial G}{\partial t} + \nabla G \cdot \frac{d\overline{r}}{dt} \tag{10}$$

1. Show that a necessary and sufficient condition for the functions $f = f(x,y)$ and $g = g(x,y)$ to be functionally related by the equation

$$F(f,g) = 0 \qquad\qquad (1)$$

is

$$\nabla f \times \nabla g = \bar{0} \qquad\qquad (2)$$

2. Determine whether the functions

$$f(x,y) = e^{xy} + 5$$
$$\qquad\qquad (3)$$
$$g(x,y) = e^{2xy} + 10e^{xy}$$

are functionally related.

Solution: 1. First show that condition (2) is necessary. Assume that the functions f and g are functionally related by

$$F(f,g) = 0$$
or $\qquad\qquad (4)$
$$F\left[f(x,y),\ g(x,y)\right] = 0$$

Using the chain rule, differentiate eq.(4) with respect to x and y.

$$\frac{\partial F}{\partial f} \frac{\partial f}{\partial x} + \frac{\partial F}{\partial g} \frac{\partial g}{\partial x} = 0 \qquad\qquad (5)$$

$$\frac{\partial F}{\partial f} \frac{\partial f}{\partial y} + \frac{\partial F}{\partial g} \frac{\partial g}{\partial y} = 0 \qquad\qquad (6)$$

Since $\frac{\partial F}{\partial f}$ and $\frac{\partial F}{\partial g}$ are not both zero, eqs.(5) and (6) are consistent only if the determinant of the coefficients is zero. Thus

$$\begin{vmatrix} \frac{\partial f}{\partial x} & \frac{\partial g}{\partial x} \\ \frac{\partial f}{\partial y} & \frac{\partial g}{\partial y} \end{vmatrix} = \frac{\partial(f,g)}{\partial(x,y)} = 0 \qquad\qquad (7)$$

Eq.(2) can be written in the form

$$\nabla f \times \nabla g = \begin{vmatrix} \bar{i} & \bar{j} & \bar{k} \\ \frac{\partial f}{\partial x} & \frac{\partial f}{\partial y} & 0 \\ \frac{\partial g}{\partial x} & \frac{\partial g}{\partial y} & 0 \end{vmatrix} = \bar{k}\, \frac{\partial(f,g)}{\partial(x,y)} \qquad\qquad (8)$$

That proves that condition (2) is necessary. To show that

it is sufficient, assume that eq.(2) holds. Thus f and g have the same level curves. The equations

$$h = f(x,y)$$
$$k = g(x,y) \tag{9}$$

define a transformation from the xy plane to the hk plane. This transformation is degenerate because along each level curve of f and g the values of h and k are constant. Thus the level curve maps into a single point in the hk plane. Let (x_0, y_0) be a point in the domain of f and g. Since $\nabla f \neq 0$, f must either decrease or increase when moving from this point in a direction normal to the level curve. The same holds for g.

Eq.(9) maps a sufficiently small neighborhood in the xy plane on a curve in the hk plane. Thus,

$$h = F'(k) \tag{10}$$

or $$k = F'(h)$$

Substituting eq.(9) into eq.(10) obtain

$$f(x,y) - F'\left[g(x,y)\right] = 0 \tag{11}$$

Thus the conditions $F(f,g) = 0$ and $\nabla f \times \nabla g = \bar{0}$ for $f = f(x,y)$ and $g = g(x,y)$ are equivalent.

2. Two functions are functionally related if and only if

$$\nabla f \times \nabla g = \bar{0}. \tag{12}$$

Substituting eq.(3) into eq.(12),

$$\nabla f \times \nabla g = \nabla(e^{xy} + 5) \times \nabla(e^{2xy} + 10e^{xy})$$

$$= (ye^{xy}, xe^{xy}, 0) \times (2ye^{2xy} + 10\ ye^{xy}, 2xe^{2xy} + 10xe^{xy}, 0)$$

$$= \left[0,\ 0,\ ye^{xy}(2xe^{2xy}+10xe^{xy}) - xe^{xy}(2ye^{2xy}+10ye^{xy})\right]$$
$$= (0,\ 0,\ 0). \tag{13}$$

Thus, functions f and g are functionally related, indeed

$$f^2 - g - 25 = 0 \tag{14}$$

● **PROBLEM 7-15**

Determine whether the functions

$$f(x,y,z) = x + y + z$$

$$g(x,y,z) = x^2 + y + z \tag{1}$$

288

$$h(x,y,z) = x^3 + y + z$$

are functionally related.

<u>Solution</u>: Consider n functions of m variables

$$f_1(x_1, x_2, \ldots x_m), \ldots f_n(x_1, x_2, \ldots x_m) \tag{2}$$

For $n \leq m$, the condition of functional dependence

$$F\left[f_1(x_1, \ldots x_m), \ldots f_n(x_1, \ldots x_m)\right] \equiv 0 \tag{3}$$

is equivalent to the condition

$$\frac{\partial(f_1, \ldots f_n)}{\partial(x_{i_1}, \ldots x_{i_n})} \equiv 0 \tag{4}$$

for all choices of the n distinct indices $i_1, \ldots, i_n$ among the m numbers $1, 2, \ldots m$.

The proof of this theorem is similar to that of Problem 7-14. For example, let $f(x,y,z)$ and $g(x,y,z)$ be any two functions. The possible choices of the two independent variables are (x,y), (y,z), (x,z).

Eq.(4) becomes

$$\frac{\partial(f,g)}{\partial(x,y)} \equiv 0, \quad \frac{\partial(f,g)}{\partial(y,z)} \equiv 0, \quad \frac{\partial(f,g)}{\partial(x,z)} \equiv 0 \tag{5}$$

Thus for eq.(1), one obtains

$$\frac{\partial(f,g,h)}{\partial(x,y,z)} \equiv 0 \tag{6}$$

as a condition of functional dependence. Eq.(6) can be written in the form

$$\frac{\partial(f,g,h)}{\partial(x,y,z)} = \begin{vmatrix} \frac{\partial f}{\partial x} & \frac{\partial g}{\partial x} & \frac{\partial h}{\partial x} \\[6pt] \frac{\partial f}{\partial y} & \frac{\partial g}{\partial y} & \frac{\partial h}{\partial y} \\[6pt] \frac{\partial f}{\partial z} & \frac{\partial g}{\partial z} & \frac{\partial h}{\partial z} \end{vmatrix}$$

$$= \frac{\partial f}{\partial x}\frac{\partial g}{\partial y}\frac{\partial h}{\partial z} + \frac{\partial f}{\partial z}\frac{\partial h}{\partial y}\frac{\partial g}{\partial x} + \frac{\partial h}{\partial x}\frac{\partial f}{\partial y}\frac{\partial g}{\partial z}$$

$$- \frac{\partial f}{\partial z}\frac{\partial g}{\partial y}\frac{\partial h}{\partial x} - \frac{\partial g}{\partial z}\frac{\partial h}{\partial y}\frac{\partial f}{\partial x} - \frac{\partial h}{\partial z}\frac{\partial f}{\partial y}\frac{\partial g}{\partial x} \tag{7}$$

$$= \frac{\partial f}{\partial x}\left(\frac{\partial g}{\partial y}\frac{\partial h}{\partial z} - \frac{\partial g}{\partial z}\frac{\partial h}{\partial y}\right) + \frac{\partial f}{\partial y}\left(\frac{\partial g}{\partial z}\frac{\partial h}{\partial x} - \frac{\partial g}{\partial x}\frac{\partial h}{\partial z}\right) + \frac{\partial f}{\partial z}\left(\frac{\partial g}{\partial x}\frac{\partial h}{\partial y} - \frac{\partial g}{\partial y}\frac{\partial h}{\partial x}\right)$$

$$= \nabla f \cdot \nabla g \times \nabla h \equiv 0$$

Now compute ∇f, ∇g, ∇h of the functions f, g, h given by eq.(1)

$$\nabla f = \nabla(x+y+z) = (1, 1, 1)$$

$$\nabla g = \nabla(x^2+y+z) = (2x, 1, 1) \qquad\qquad (8)$$

$$\nabla h = \nabla(x^3+y+z) = (3x^2, 1, 1)$$

Substituting eq.(8) into eq.(7),

$$\nabla f \cdot \nabla g \times \nabla h = (1,1,1) \cdot \left[(2x, 1, 1) \times (3x^2, 1, 1)\right] =$$

$$= (1,1,1) \cdot (0,3x^2-2x, 2x-3x^2) = 3x^2-2x+2x-3x^2 = 0$$

Thus f, g, h are functionally related.

THE DIVERGENCE AND LAPLACIAN OPERATORS

● **PROBLEM 7-16**

Evaluate div $\bar{a}$, if

$$\bar{a} = x^2\bar{i} + 2xy\,\bar{j} - xyz\,\bar{k} \qquad\qquad (1)$$

<u>Solution</u>: Begin with the definition of the divergence of $\bar{a}$.

Let $\bar{a}$ be a vector field in a domain D in space. Its coordinates are scalar functions of x, y, z. Thus

$$\bar{a} = a_x\bar{i} + a_y\bar{j} + a_z\bar{k} \qquad\qquad (2)$$

and

$$a_x = a_x(x, y, z)$$

$$a_y = a_y(x, y, z) \qquad\qquad (3)$$

$$a_z = a_z(x, y, z)$$

If a_x, a_y, a_z have first partial derivatives, we can arrange them to form a square array

$$\begin{matrix} \dfrac{\partial a_x}{\partial x} & \dfrac{\partial a_x}{\partial y} & \dfrac{\partial a_x}{\partial z} \\[2mm] \dfrac{\partial a_y}{\partial x} & \dfrac{\partial a_y}{\partial y} & \dfrac{\partial a_y}{\partial z} \\[2mm] \dfrac{\partial a_z}{\partial x} & \dfrac{\partial a_z}{\partial y} & \dfrac{\partial a_z}{\partial z} \end{matrix} \qquad\qquad (4)$$

Taking the derivatives along the diagonal, construct the div $\bar{a}$ such that

$$\text{div } \bar{a} \equiv \frac{\partial a_x}{\partial x} + \frac{\partial a_y}{\partial y} + \frac{\partial a_z}{\partial z} \qquad (5)$$

Note that the divergence of a vector is not a vector. Substituting eq.(1) into eq.(5),

$$\text{div } \bar{a} = \frac{\partial}{\partial x}(x^2) + \frac{\partial}{\partial y}(2xy) + \frac{\partial}{\partial z}(-xyz) \qquad (6)$$

$$= 2x + 2x - xy = 4x - xy$$

Using the operator nabla - ∇, express eq.(5) in the form

$$\text{div } \bar{a} \equiv \frac{\partial a_x}{\partial x} + \frac{\partial a_y}{\partial y} + \frac{\partial a_z}{\partial z} = \left(\frac{\partial}{\partial x}, \frac{\partial}{\partial y}, \frac{\partial}{\partial z}\right) \cdot (a_x, a_y, a_z)$$

$$= \nabla \cdot \bar{a} \qquad (7)$$

The divergence of a vector is an important notion in fluid mechanics, where

$$\text{div}\rho\bar{v} + \frac{\partial \rho}{\partial t} = 0 \qquad (8)$$

is the equation of continuity, and in electromagnetic theory where

$$\text{div } \bar{E} = \frac{\rho}{\varepsilon_0} \qquad (9)$$

is one of Maxwell's equations.

● **PROBLEM 7-17**

Evaluate div $\bar{u}$ at the point (-1, 1, 2) for

$$\bar{u} = x^2 \bar{i} + e^{xy}\bar{j} + xyz\ \bar{k} \qquad (1)$$

Solution: From the definition of the divergence,

$$\text{div } \bar{u} = \left(\frac{\partial}{\partial x}\bar{i} + \frac{\partial}{\partial y}\bar{j} + \frac{\partial}{\partial z}\bar{k}\right) \cdot (x^2\bar{i} + e^{xy}\bar{j} + xyz\ \bar{k}) \qquad (2)$$

$$= \frac{\partial}{\partial x}(x^2) + \frac{\partial}{\partial y}(e^{xy}) + \frac{\partial}{\partial z}(xyz) = 2x + xe^{xy} + xy$$

At the point (-1, 1, 2), obtain

$$\text{div } \bar{u}\ \Big|_{(-1,1,2)} = 2x + xe^{xy} + xy\ \Big|_{(-1,1,2)} \qquad (3)$$

$$= -2 - e^{-1} - 1 = -3 - e^{-1}$$

Here div $\bar{u}$ was calculated directly from the definition of the divergence.

1.   Show that

$$\text{div grad } \phi = \nabla^2 \phi \qquad (1)$$

where ∇^2 is the Laplacian operator.

2.   Evaluate div grad f for

$$f(x,y,z) = \sin x + x^2yz \qquad (2)$$

<u>Solution</u>:   1.   By definition grad ϕ is given by

$$\text{grad } \phi = \left(\frac{\partial\phi}{\partial x}, \frac{\partial\phi}{\partial y}, \frac{\partial\phi}{\partial z}\right) \qquad (3)$$

Applying the definition of the divergence to eq.(3),

$$\text{div grad } \phi = \text{div}\left(\frac{\partial\phi}{\partial x}, \frac{\partial\phi}{\partial y}, \frac{\partial\phi}{\partial z}\right)$$

$$= \frac{\partial^2\phi}{\partial x^2} + \frac{\partial^2\phi}{\partial y^2} + \frac{\partial^2\phi}{\partial z^2} = \nabla^2\phi \qquad (4)$$

where ∇^2 is the Laplacian operator

$$\nabla^2 \equiv \frac{\partial^2}{\partial x^2} + \frac{\partial^2}{\partial y^2} + \frac{\partial^2}{\partial z^2} \qquad (5)$$

2.   From eq.(1), we conclude that

$$\text{div grad } f = \nabla^2 f \qquad (6)$$

Substituting eq.(2) into eq.(6),

$$\text{div grad } f = \nabla^2 f = \frac{\partial^2}{\partial x^2}(\sin x + x^2yz)$$

$$+ \frac{\partial^2}{\partial y^2}(\sin x + x^2yz) + \frac{\partial^2}{\partial z^2}(\sin x + x^2yz) \qquad (7)$$

$$= \frac{\partial}{\partial x}(\cos x + 2xyz) + \frac{\partial}{\partial y}(x^2z) + \frac{\partial}{\partial z}(x^2y)$$

$$= -\sin x + 2yz$$

Prove the following properties of the divergence

1. $\text{div}(\bar{a} + \bar{b}) = \text{div } \bar{a} + \text{div } \bar{b}$ \qquad (1)

2. $\text{div }(\phi\bar{a}) = (\text{grad } \phi)\cdot\bar{a} + \phi \text{ div } \bar{a}$ \qquad (2)

Assume that both vectors $\bar{a}$ and $\bar{b}$ have first partial derivatives and that the function ϕ is differentiable.

Solution: 1. Let

$$\bar{a} = a_1\bar{i} + a_2\bar{j} + a_3\bar{k} \qquad (3)$$

and $$\bar{b} = b_1\bar{i} + b_2\bar{j} + b_3\bar{k} \qquad (4)$$

The left side of eq.(1) is equal to

$$\text{div}(\bar{a} + \bar{b}) =$$

$$\left(\frac{\partial}{\partial x}\bar{i} + \frac{\partial}{\partial y}\bar{j} + \frac{\partial}{\partial z}\bar{k}\right) \cdot ((a_1+b_1)\bar{i} + (a_2 + b_2)\bar{j} + (a_3 + b_3)\bar{k})$$
$$\qquad (5)$$

$$= \frac{\partial}{\partial x}(a_1 + b_1) + \frac{\partial}{\partial y}(a_2 + b_2) + \frac{\partial}{\partial z}(a_3 + b_3)$$

$$= \frac{\partial a_1}{\partial x} + \frac{\partial a_2}{\partial y} + \frac{\partial a_3}{\partial z} + \frac{\partial b_1}{\partial x} + \frac{\partial b_2}{\partial y} + \frac{\partial b_3}{\partial z}$$

$$= \text{div } \bar{a} + \text{div } \bar{b}$$

2. To prove eq.(2), transform the left side of eq.(2). Doing this,

$$\text{div}(\phi\bar{a}) = \left(\frac{\partial}{\partial x}\bar{i} + \frac{\partial}{\partial y}\bar{j} + \frac{\partial}{\partial z}\bar{k}\right) \cdot \left[(\phi a_1)\bar{i} + (\phi a_2)\bar{j} + (\phi a_3)\bar{k}\right]$$

$$= \frac{\partial}{\partial x}(\phi a_1) + \frac{\partial}{\partial y}(\phi a_2) + \frac{\partial}{\partial z}(\phi a_3)$$

$$= \frac{\partial \phi}{\partial x}a_1 + \phi\frac{\partial a_1}{\partial x} + \frac{\partial \phi}{\partial y}a_2 + \phi\frac{\partial a_2}{\partial y} + \frac{\partial \phi}{\partial z}a_3 + \phi\frac{\partial a_3}{\partial z} \qquad (7)$$

$$= \left(\frac{\partial \phi}{\partial x}a_1 + \frac{\partial \phi}{\partial y}a_2 + \frac{\partial \phi}{\partial z}a_3\right) + \left(\phi\frac{\partial a_1}{\partial x} + \phi\frac{\partial a_2}{\partial y} + \phi\frac{\partial a_3}{\partial z}\right)$$

$$= (\text{grad } \phi) \cdot \bar{a} + \phi \text{ div } \bar{a}$$

Throughout this proof the following property was used

$$\frac{\partial}{\partial x}(fg) = f\frac{\partial g}{\partial x} + g\frac{\partial f}{\partial x} \qquad (8)$$

● PROBLEM 7-20

1. Show that $f = \frac{1}{r}$ is a solution to Laplace's (1) equation

$$\nabla^2 f = 0 \qquad (2)$$

2. Prove the following:

$$\nabla \cdot \left(\frac{\bar{r}}{r^3}\right) = 0 \qquad (3)$$

Solution: 1. This equation appears very often in physics. To prove it, substitute $f = \frac{1}{r}$ into eq.(2) and use the definition of ∇^2. Since

$$\nabla \equiv \left(\frac{\partial}{\partial x}, \frac{\partial}{\partial y}, \frac{\partial}{\partial z} \right) \tag{4}$$

then

$$\nabla^2 = \nabla \cdot \nabla = \left(\frac{\partial}{\partial x}, \frac{\partial}{\partial y}, \frac{\partial}{\partial z} \right) \cdot \left(\frac{\partial}{\partial x}, \frac{\partial}{\partial y}, \frac{\partial}{\partial z} \right) = \frac{\partial^2}{\partial x^2} + \frac{\partial^2}{\partial y^2} + \frac{\partial^2}{\partial z^2} \tag{5}$$

and $r^2 = x^2 + y^2 + z^2$ (6)

Eq.(2) becomes

$$\nabla^2 \left(\frac{1}{r} \right) = \left(\frac{\partial^2}{\partial x^2} + \frac{\partial^2}{\partial y^2} + \frac{\partial^2}{\partial z^2} \right) \left(\frac{1}{\sqrt{x^2+y^2+z^2}} \right) \tag{7}$$

The consecutive partial derivatives are

$$\frac{\partial}{\partial x} \left(\frac{1}{\sqrt{x^2+y^2+z^2}} \right) = \frac{\partial}{\partial x} (x^2+y^2+z^2)^{-\frac{1}{2}} = - \frac{x}{(x^2+y^2+z^2)^{3/2}} \tag{8}$$

$$\frac{\partial^2}{\partial x^2} = \frac{\partial}{\partial x} \left[\frac{-x}{(x^2+y^2+z^2)^{3/2}} \right] = 3x^2 (x^2+y^2+z^2)^{-\frac{5}{2}} - (x^2+y^2+z^2)^{-\frac{3}{2}}$$

$$= \frac{2x^2-y^2-z^2}{(x^2+y^2+z^2)^{5/2}} \tag{9}$$

In the same manner, we obtain

$$\frac{\partial^2}{\partial y^2} \left(\frac{1}{\sqrt{x^2+y^2+z^2}} \right) = \frac{2y^2-x^2-z^2}{(x^2+y^2+z^2)^{5/2}} \tag{10}$$

and

$$\frac{\partial^2}{\partial z^2} \left(\frac{1}{\sqrt{x^2+y^2+z^2}} \right) = \frac{2z^2-x^2-y^2}{(x^2+y^2+z^2)^{5/2}} \tag{11}$$

Substituting eqs.(9), (10) and (11) into eq.(7),

$$\nabla^2 \left(\frac{1}{r} \right) = \left(\frac{\partial^2}{\partial x^2} + \frac{\partial^2}{\partial y^2} + \frac{\partial^2}{\partial z^2} \right) \left(\frac{1}{\sqrt{x^2+y^2+z^2}} \right)$$

$$= \frac{2x^2-y^2-z^2+2y^2-x^2-z^2+2z^2-x^2-y^2}{(x^2+y^2+z^2)^{5/2}} = 0 \tag{12}$$

2. To prove eq.(3), use the results of Problem 7-19, part 2.

$$\text{div}(\phi \overline{a}) = (\text{grad } \phi) \cdot \overline{a} + \phi \text{ div } \overline{a} \tag{13}$$

Let $\phi = r^{-3}$ and $\overline{a} = \overline{r}$,

substituting into eq.(13), we find

$$\text{div } (r^{-3} \overline{r}) = (\text{grad } r^{-3}) \cdot \overline{r} + r^{-3} \text{div } \overline{r} \tag{14}$$

Note that

$$\text{div } \bar{r} = \frac{\partial x}{\partial x} + \frac{\partial y}{\partial y} + \frac{\partial z}{\partial z} = 3 \tag{15}$$

and

$$\text{grad } r^{-3} = \left(\frac{-3x}{r^5}, \frac{-3y}{r^5}, \frac{-3z}{r^5} \right) = -3(x,y,z)\frac{1}{r^5} = -3r^{-5}\bar{r} \tag{16}$$

Substituting eqs.(15) and (16) into eq.(14),

$$\text{div}(r^{-3}\bar{r}) = \nabla \cdot \left(\frac{\bar{r}}{r^3} \right) = -3r^{-5}\bar{r} \cdot \bar{r} + 3r^{-3} = -3r^{-5}(r^2) + 3r^{-3} = 0,$$

which completes the proof of eq.(3).

● **PROBLEM** 7-21

1. Prove

$$\nabla^2 r^n = n(n + 1)r^{n-2} \tag{1}$$

where n is a constant.

2. Evaluate

$$\nabla^2(\ln r) \tag{2}$$

Solution: 1. r is given by

$$r = \sqrt{x^2+y^2+z^2} \tag{3}$$

The operator ∇^2 is

$$\nabla^2 \equiv \frac{\partial^2}{\partial x^2} + \frac{\partial^2}{\partial y^2} + \frac{\partial^2}{\partial z^2} \tag{4}$$

Compute the consecutive partial derivatives of r^n.

$$\frac{\partial}{\partial x} r^n = \frac{\partial}{\partial x}(x^2+y^2+z^2)^{\frac{n}{2}} = nx(x^2+y^2+z^2)^{\frac{n-2}{2}} \tag{5}$$

$$\frac{\partial^2}{\partial x^2} r^n = \frac{\partial}{\partial x}\left[nx(x^2+y^2+z^2)^{\frac{n-2}{2}} \right]$$

$$= n(x^2+y^2+z^2)^{\frac{n-2}{2}} + nx^2(n-2)(x^2+y^2+z^2)^{\frac{n-4}{4}} \tag{6}$$

$$\frac{\partial^2}{\partial y^2} r^n = n(x^2+y^2+z^2)^{\frac{n-2}{2}} + ny^2(n-2)(x^2+y^2+z^2)^{\frac{n-4}{2}} \tag{7}$$

$$\frac{\partial^2}{\partial z^2} r^n = n(x^2+y^2+z^2)^{\frac{n-2}{2}} + nz^2(n-2)(x^2+y^2+z^2)^{\frac{n-4}{2}} \tag{8}$$

Adding eqs.(6), (7) and (8), we obtain

$$\nabla^2 r^n = \frac{\partial^2 r^n}{\partial x^2} + \frac{\partial^2 r^n}{\partial y^2} + \frac{\partial^2 r^n}{\partial z^2} = 3nr^{n-2} + n(n-2)r^{n-4}r^2$$

$$= r^{n-2}(3n + n^2 - 2n) = n(n + 1) r^{n-2} \tag{9}$$

2. Here again evaluate the partial derivatives of ln r.

$$\frac{\partial}{\partial x} (\ln r) = \frac{\partial}{\partial x} (\ln(x^2+y^2+z^2)^{\frac{1}{2}}) = \frac{\partial}{\partial x} (\tfrac{1}{2}\ln(x^2+y^2+z^2)) \qquad (10)$$

$$= \frac{x}{x^2+y^2+z^2}$$

$$\frac{\partial^2}{\partial x^2} (\ln r) = \frac{\partial}{\partial x} \left(\frac{x}{x^2+y^2+z^2}\right) = \frac{-x^2+y^2+z^2}{(x^2+y^2+z^2)^2} \qquad (11)$$

The second partial derivatives with respect to y and z are

$$\frac{\partial^2}{\partial y^2} (\ln r) = \frac{x^2-y^2+z^2}{(x^2+y^2+z^2)^2} \qquad (12)$$

$$\frac{\partial^2}{\partial z^2} (\ln r) = \frac{x^2+y^2-z^2}{(x^2+y^2+z^2)^2} \qquad (13)$$

Adding eqs.(11), (12) and (13),

$$\nabla^2(\ln r) = \frac{\partial^2}{\partial x^2} (\ln r) + \frac{\partial^2}{\partial y^2} (\ln r) + \frac{\partial^2}{\partial z^2} (\ln r) \qquad (14)$$

$$= \frac{-x^2+y^2+z^2+x^2-y^2+z^2+x^2+y^2-z^2}{(x^2+y^2+z^2)^2} = \frac{x^2+y^2+z^2}{(x^2+y^2+z^2)^2}$$

$$= \frac{1}{x^2+y^2+z^2} = \frac{1}{r^2}$$

● **PROBLEM** 7-22

Evaluate $\nabla(\nabla \cdot \bar{a})$ at the point (-1, 2, 1) for

$$\bar{a} = (x^2y-z)\bar{i} + (xy^3+y)\bar{j} - 3xyz^2\bar{k} \qquad (1)$$

Solution: The operator ∇ is defined as

$$\nabla \equiv \left(\frac{\partial}{\partial x}, \frac{\partial}{\partial y}, \frac{\partial}{\partial z}\right) \qquad (2)$$

The vector $\bar{a}$ can be written in the form

$$\bar{a} = (x^2y-z, \ xy^3+y, \ -3xyz^2) \qquad (3)$$

Substituting eqs.(3) and (2) into the expression $\nabla(\nabla \cdot \bar{a})$, gives

$$\nabla(\nabla \cdot \bar{a}) = \nabla\left[\left(\frac{\partial}{\partial x}, \frac{\partial}{\partial y}, \frac{\partial}{\partial z}\right) \cdot (x^2y-z, \ xy^3+y, \ -3xyz^2)\right]$$

$$= \nabla\left[\frac{\partial}{\partial x} (x^2y-z) + \frac{\partial}{\partial y} (xy^3+y) + \frac{\partial}{\partial z} (-3xyz^2)\right]$$

$$= \nabla\left[2xy + 3xy^2+1 - 6xyz\right]$$

$$= \left(\frac{\partial}{\partial x}, \frac{\partial}{\partial y}, \frac{\partial}{\partial z}\right) (2xy + 3xy^2+1 - 6xyz) \qquad (4)$$

$$= (2y + 3y^2 - 6yz, \ 2x + 6xy - 6xz, \ -6xy)$$

At the point $(-1,2,1)$

$$\nabla(\nabla \cdot \overline{a}) \Big|_{(-1,2,1)} = (2y+3y^2-6yz, \ 2x+6xy-6xz, \ -6xy) \Big|_{(-1,2,1)} \quad (5)$$

$$= (4, \ -8, \ 12)$$

IDENTITIES INVOLVING GRADIENT AND DIVERGENCE, SOLENOIDAL VECTORS

● **PROBLEM** 7-23

1. Prove that if $\overline{\omega}$ is a constant vector and $\overline{v} = \overline{\omega} \times \overline{r}$,   (1)

   then   div $\overline{v} = 0$ (2)

2. Prove that for any two differentiable scalar functions

$$\phi = \phi(x,y,z)$$
$$\psi = \psi(x,y,z) \quad (3)$$

   the following identity holds

$$\nabla^2(\phi\psi) = \phi \, \nabla^2 \psi + \psi \, \nabla^2 \phi + 2\nabla\phi \cdot \nabla\psi \quad (4)$$

Solution: 1.   In component form, the vectors $\overline{\omega}$ and $\overline{r}$ are

$$\overline{\omega} = (\omega_1, \ \omega_2, \ \omega_3)$$
$$\overline{r} = (x, \ y, \ z) \quad (5)$$

By definition the vector product of $\overline{\omega}$ and $\overline{r}$ is equal to

$$\overline{v} = \overline{\omega} \times \overline{r} = (\omega_1, \ \omega_2, \ \omega_3) \times (x, \ y, \ z)$$
$$= (\omega_2 z - \omega_3 y, \ \omega_3 x - \omega_1 z, \ \omega_1 y - \omega_2 x) \quad (6)$$

Taking the divergence of $\overline{v}$,

$$\text{div } \overline{v} = \frac{\partial v_1}{\partial x} + \frac{\partial v_2}{\partial y} + \frac{\partial v_3}{\partial z}$$

$$= \frac{\partial}{\partial x}(\omega_2 z - \omega_3 y) + \frac{\partial}{\partial y}(\omega_3 x - \omega_1 z) + \frac{\partial}{\partial z}(\omega_1 y - \omega_2 x) = 0 \quad (7)$$

Note that $\overline{\omega}$ is a constant vector and thus

$$\frac{\partial \omega_1}{\partial x} = \frac{\partial \omega_1}{\partial y} = \frac{\partial \omega_1}{\partial z} = 0$$

$$\frac{\partial \omega_2}{\partial x} = \frac{\partial \omega_2}{\partial y} = \frac{\partial \omega_2}{\partial z} = 0 \qquad (8)$$

$$\frac{\partial \omega_3}{\partial x} = \frac{\partial \omega_3}{\partial y} = \frac{\partial \omega_3}{\partial z} = 0$$

Vectors whose divergence is equal to zero are called solenoidal vectors. In this problem, vector $\bar{v}$ is solenoidal.

2. To prove eq.(4) we will use the following property

$$\frac{\partial}{\partial x} (\phi \psi) = \phi \frac{\partial \psi}{\partial x} + \psi \frac{\partial \phi}{\partial x} \qquad (9)$$

(the same holds for the partial derivatives with respect to y and z).

Using the definition of ∇^2

$$\nabla^2 = \frac{\partial^2}{\partial x^2} + \frac{\partial^2}{\partial y^2} + \frac{\partial^2}{\partial z^2} \qquad (10)$$

and eq.(9), we obtain

$$\nabla^2(\phi\psi) = \frac{\partial^2}{\partial x^2}(\phi\psi) + \frac{\partial^2}{\partial y^2}(\phi\psi) + \frac{\partial^2}{\partial z^2}(\phi\psi)$$

$$= \frac{\partial}{\partial x}\left[\frac{\partial}{\partial x}(\phi\psi)\right] + \frac{\partial}{\partial y}\left[\frac{\partial}{\partial y}(\phi\psi)\right] + \frac{\partial}{\partial z}\left[\frac{\partial}{\partial z}(\phi\psi)\right]$$

$$= \frac{\partial}{\partial x}\left[\phi\frac{\partial\psi}{\partial x} + \psi\frac{\partial\phi}{\partial x}\right] + \frac{\partial}{\partial y}\left[\phi\frac{\partial\psi}{\partial y} + \psi\frac{\partial\phi}{\partial y}\right] + \frac{\partial}{\partial z}\left[\phi\frac{\partial\psi}{\partial z} + \psi\frac{\partial\phi}{\partial z}\right]$$

$$= \phi\frac{\partial^2\psi}{\partial x^2} + 2\frac{\partial\phi}{\partial x}\frac{\partial\psi}{\partial x} + \psi\frac{\partial^2\phi}{\partial x^2} + \phi\frac{\partial^2\psi}{\partial y^2} + 2\frac{\partial\phi}{\partial y}\frac{\partial\psi}{\partial y} + \psi\frac{\partial^2\phi}{\partial y^2}$$

$$+ \phi\frac{\partial^2\psi}{\partial z^2} + 2\frac{\partial\phi}{\partial z}\frac{\partial\psi}{\partial z} + \psi\frac{\partial^2\phi}{\partial z^2} \qquad (11)$$

$$= \phi\left(\frac{\partial^2\psi}{\partial x^2} + \frac{\partial^2\psi}{\partial y^2} + \frac{\partial^2\psi}{\partial z^2}\right) + \psi\left(\frac{\partial^2\phi}{\partial x^2} + \frac{\partial^2\phi}{\partial y^2} + \frac{\partial^2\phi}{\partial z^2}\right)$$

$$+ 2\frac{\partial\phi}{\partial x}\frac{\partial\psi}{\partial x} + 2\frac{\partial\phi}{\partial y}\frac{\partial\psi}{\partial y} + 2\frac{\partial\phi}{\partial z}\frac{\partial\psi}{\partial z}$$

$$= \phi \nabla^2\psi + \psi \nabla^2\phi + 2 \nabla\phi \cdot \nabla\psi$$

where

$$\nabla\phi = \left(\frac{\partial\phi}{\partial x}, \frac{\partial\phi}{\partial y}, \frac{\partial\phi}{\partial z}\right)$$

and

$$\nabla\psi = \left(\frac{\partial\psi}{\partial x}, \frac{\partial\psi}{\partial y}, \frac{\partial\psi}{\partial z}\right) \qquad (12)$$

● **PROBLEM 7-24**

Let f and g be any differentiable functions

$$f = f(x,y,z)$$

$$g = g(x,y,z) \qquad (1)$$

Prove:

$$\text{div}(f \text{ grad } g - g \text{ grad } f) = f\nabla^2 g - g\nabla^2 f \qquad (2)$$

Solution: Apply the definitions of the gradient and divergence and transform the left side of eq.(2). Doing this

$$\text{div}\left[f \text{ grad } g - g \text{ grad } f \right]$$

$$= \text{div}\left[f\left(\frac{\partial g}{\partial x}, \frac{\partial g}{\partial y}, \frac{\partial g}{\partial z}\right) - g\left(\frac{\partial f}{\partial x}, \frac{\partial f}{\partial y}, \frac{\partial f}{\partial z}\right)\right]$$

$$= \text{div}\left[f\frac{\partial g}{\partial x} - g\frac{\partial f}{\partial x}, \; f\frac{\partial g}{\partial y} - g\frac{\partial f}{\partial y}, \; f\frac{\partial g}{\partial z} - g\frac{\partial f}{\partial z}\right]$$

$$= \frac{\partial}{\partial x}\left[f\frac{\partial g}{\partial x} - g\frac{\partial f}{\partial x}\right] + \frac{\partial}{\partial y}\left[f\frac{\partial g}{\partial y} - g\frac{\partial f}{\partial y}\right] + \frac{\partial}{\partial z}\left[f\frac{\partial g}{\partial z} - g\frac{\partial f}{\partial z}\right]$$

$$= f\frac{\partial^2 g}{\partial x^2} - g\frac{\partial^2 f}{\partial x^2} + f\frac{\partial^2 g}{\partial y^2} - g\frac{\partial^2 f}{\partial y^2} + f\frac{\partial^2 g}{\partial z^2} - g\frac{\partial^2 f}{\partial z^2} \qquad (3)$$

$$= f\nabla^2 g - g\nabla^2 f$$

That completes the proof.

We can also prove eq.(2) by using the results of Problem 7-19, namely,

$$\text{div }(\phi\overline{a}) = (\text{grad }\phi)\cdot\overline{a} + \phi \text{ div } \overline{a} \qquad (4)$$

Then substitute

$$\phi = f \quad \text{and} \quad \overline{a} = \text{grad } g \qquad (5)$$

into eq.(4), resulting in

$$\text{div }(f \text{ grad } g) = (\text{grad } f)\cdot(\text{grad } g) + f \text{ div grad } g \qquad (6)$$

Interchanging the functions f and g in eq.(6), we obtain

$$\text{div }(g \text{ grad } f) = (\text{grad } g)\cdot(\text{grad } f) + g \text{ div grad } f \qquad (7)$$

Subtracting eq.(7) from eq.(6) results in

div (f grad g) - div (g grad f) = div (f grad g-g grad f)

$$= (\text{grad } f)\cdot(\text{grad } g) + f \text{ div grad } g - (\text{grad } f)\cdot(\text{grad } g)$$

$$- g \text{ div grad } f$$

$$= f \text{ div grad } g - g \text{ div grad } f$$

$$= f\nabla^2 g - g\nabla^2 f \qquad (8)$$

The following identity was used in eq.(8)

$$\text{div grad } f = \text{div}\left(\frac{\partial f}{\partial x}, \frac{\partial f}{\partial y}, \frac{\partial f}{\partial z}\right) = \frac{\partial^2 f}{\partial x^2} + \frac{\partial^2 f}{\partial y^2} + \frac{\partial^2 f}{\partial z^2} = \nabla^2 f \qquad (9)$$

Prove the identity

$$\nabla \cdot \left[r\nabla\left(\frac{1}{r^3}\right)\right] - \nabla^2 \left[\nabla\cdot\left(\frac{\overline{r}}{r^2}\right)\right] = r^{-4} \tag{1}$$

<u>Solution</u>: Let

$$\alpha = \nabla \cdot \left[r \nabla \left(\frac{1}{r^3}\right)\right] \tag{2}$$

and

$$\beta = \nabla^2 \left[\nabla\cdot\left(\frac{\overline{r}}{r^2}\right)\right] \tag{3}$$

Now, to prove eq.(1), calculate α and β.

We have

$$\nabla\left(\frac{1}{r^3}\right) = \left[\frac{\partial}{\partial x}\left(\frac{1}{r^3}\right), \frac{\partial}{\partial y}\left(\frac{1}{r^3}\right), \frac{\partial}{\partial z}\left(\frac{1}{r^3}\right)\right] \tag{4}$$

and

$$\frac{\partial}{\partial x}\left(\frac{1}{r^3}\right) = \frac{\partial}{\partial x}\left[(x^2+y^2+z^2)^{-\frac{3}{2}}\right] = -3x(x^2+y^2+z^2)^{-\frac{5}{2}} \tag{5}$$

$$\frac{\partial}{\partial y}\left(\frac{1}{r^3}\right) = -3y(x^2+y^2+z^2)^{-\frac{5}{2}} \tag{6}$$

$$\frac{\partial}{\partial z}\left(\frac{1}{r^3}\right) = -3z(x^2+y^2+z^2)^{-\frac{5}{2}} \tag{7}$$

Substituting eqs.(5), (6) and (7) into eq.(4),

$$\nabla\left(\frac{1}{r^3}\right) = -3(x^2+y^2+z^2)^{-\frac{5}{2}}(x, y, z) \tag{8}$$

Multiplying eq.(8) by r,

$$r\nabla\left(\frac{1}{r^3}\right) = -3(x^2+y^2+z^2)^{-\frac{5}{2}}(x^2+y^2+z^2)^{\frac{1}{2}}(x, y, z) \tag{9}$$

$$= -3(x^2+y^2+z^2)^{-2}(x, y, z)$$

Substituting eq.(9) into eq.(2),

$$\alpha = \nabla\cdot\left[r\nabla\left(\frac{1}{r^3}\right)\right] = div\left[\frac{-3x}{(x^2+y^2+z^2)^2}, \frac{-3y}{(x^2+y^2+z^2)^2}, \frac{-3z}{(x^2+y^2+z^2)^2}\right]$$

$$= -3\frac{\partial}{\partial x}\left[\frac{x}{(x^2+y^2+z^2)^2}\right] - 3\frac{\partial}{\partial y}\left[\frac{y}{(x^2+y^2+z^2)^2}\right] - 3\frac{\partial}{\partial z}\left[\frac{z}{(x^2+y^2+z^2)^2}\right]$$

$$= \frac{3}{(x^2+y^2+z^2)^2} = 3r^{-4} \tag{10}$$

To evaluate β, first evaluate

$$\nabla\cdot\left(\frac{\overline{r}}{r^2}\right) = \frac{\partial}{\partial x}\left(\frac{x}{x^2+y^2+z^2}\right) + \frac{\partial}{\partial y}\left(\frac{y}{x^2+y^2+z^2}\right) + \frac{\partial}{\partial z}\left(\frac{z}{x^2+y^2+z^2}\right)$$

$$= \frac{3(x^2+y^2+z^2)-2x^2-2y^2-2z^2}{(x^2+y^2+z^2)^2} = \frac{1}{x^2+y^2+z^2} = \frac{1}{r^2} \quad (11)$$

Substituting eq.(11) into eq.(3),

$$\beta = \nabla^2 \left[\nabla \cdot \left(\frac{\bar{r}}{r^2} \right) \right] = \nabla^2 \left(\frac{1}{r^2} \right) \quad (12)$$

From Problem 7-21, part 1, we have

$$\nabla^2 r^n = n(n+1)r^{n-2} \quad (13)$$

In eq.(12), n = -2, thus

$$\beta = \nabla^2 \left(\frac{1}{r^2} \right) = -2(-2+1)r^{-2-2} = 2r^{-4} \quad (14)$$

Equation (1) can be written in the form

$$\alpha - \beta = r^{-4} \quad (15)$$

Substituting eqs.(10) and (14),

$$\alpha - \beta = 3r^{-4} - 2r^{-4} = r^{-4}, \quad (16)$$

which proves eq.(1).

● **PROBLEM 7-26**

Evaluate

$$\text{grad div } \bar{u} \quad (1)$$

for

$$\bar{u} = \frac{\bar{r}}{r} \quad (2)$$

where

$$r = \sqrt{x_1^2 + x_2^2 + x_3^2}$$

Solution: First, find div $\bar{u}$ for $\bar{u} = \frac{\bar{r}}{r}$

$$\text{div } \bar{u} = \text{div } \frac{\bar{r}}{r}$$

$$= \frac{\partial}{\partial x}\left[\frac{x}{(x^2+y^2+z^2)^{1/2}} \right] + \frac{\partial}{\partial y}\left[\frac{y}{(x^2+y^2+z^2)^{1/2}} \right] + \frac{\partial}{\partial z}\left[\frac{z}{(x^2+y^2+z^2)^{1/2}} \right]$$

$$= \frac{3(x^2+y^2+z^2)^{\frac{1}{2}}-x^2(x^2+y^2+z^2)^{-\frac{1}{2}}-y^2(x^2+y^2+z^2)^{-\frac{1}{2}}-z^2(x^2+y^2+z^2)^{-\frac{1}{2}}}{x^2+y^2+z^2}$$

$$\quad (3)$$

$$= \frac{3(x^2+y^2+z^2)^{\frac{1}{2}}-(x^2+y^2+z^2)^{\frac{1}{2}}}{x^2+y^2+z^2} = \frac{2}{(x^2+y^2+z^2)^{1/2}} = \frac{2}{r}$$

Taking the gradient of eq.(3),

$$\text{grad div } \bar{u} = \text{grad div } \frac{\bar{r}}{r} = \text{grad } \frac{2}{(x^2+y^2+z^2)^{1/2}}$$

$$= \left[\frac{\partial}{\partial x} \frac{2}{(x^2+y^2+z^2)^{1/2}}, \quad \frac{\partial}{\partial y} \frac{2}{(x^2+y^2+z^2)^{1/2}}, \quad \frac{\partial}{\partial z} \frac{2}{(x^2+y^2+z^2)^{1/2}}\right] \qquad (4)$$

$$= \left[-2x(x^2+y^2+z^2)^{-\frac{3}{2}}, \quad -2y(x^2+y^2+z^2)^{-\frac{3}{2}}, \quad -2z(x^2+y^2+z^2)^{-\frac{3}{2}}\right]$$

$$= -\frac{2}{r^3}(x,y,z) = -\frac{2\bar{r}}{r^3}$$

● **PROBLEM** 7-27

If $f = f(r)$, show that

$$\nabla^2 f(r) = \frac{d^2 f}{dr^2} + \frac{2}{r}\frac{df}{dr} \qquad (1)$$

Also, if $f(r)$ is given by

$$\nabla^2 f(r) = \alpha + \beta r^{-1}, \qquad (2)$$

show that $\qquad \nabla^2 f(r) = 0 \qquad (3)$

Solution: From the definition of ∇^2,

$$\nabla^2 f(r) = \frac{\partial^2}{\partial x^2} f(r) + \frac{\partial^2}{\partial y^2} f(r) + \frac{\partial^2}{\partial z^2} f(r) \qquad (4)$$

Evaluating the partial derivatives,

$$\frac{\partial f(r)}{\partial x} = \frac{df}{dr}\frac{\partial r}{\partial x} = \frac{df}{dr}\frac{\partial}{\partial x}(x^2+y^2+z^2)^{\frac{1}{2}} = \frac{df}{dr}\frac{x}{(x^2+y^2+z^2)^{\frac{1}{2}}} \qquad (5)$$

$$\frac{\partial^2 f(r)}{\partial x^2} = \frac{\partial}{\partial x}\left[\left(\frac{df}{dr}\right)\frac{x}{(x^2+y^2+z^2)^{\frac{1}{2}}}\right] + \frac{df}{dr}\frac{\partial}{\partial x}\left[\frac{x}{(x^2+y^2+z^2)^{\frac{1}{2}}}\right]$$

$$= \frac{d^2 f}{dr^2}\frac{x^2}{x^2+y^2+z^2} + \frac{df}{dr}\frac{(x^2+y^2+z^2)^{\frac{1}{2}}-x^2(x^2+y^2+z^2)^{-\frac{1}{2}}}{x^2+y^2+z^2} \quad (6)$$

In the same manner,

$$\frac{\partial^2 f(r)}{\partial y^2} = \frac{d^2 f}{dr^2}\frac{y^2}{x^2+y^2+z^2} + \frac{df}{dr}\frac{(x^2+y^2+z^2)^{\frac{1}{2}}-y^2(x^2+y^2+z^2)^{-\frac{1}{2}}}{x^2+y^2+z^2} \quad (7)$$

$$\frac{\partial^2 f(r)}{\partial z^2} = \frac{d^2 f}{dr^2}\frac{z^2}{x^2+y^2+z^2} + \frac{df}{dr}\frac{(x^2+y^2+z^2)^{\frac{1}{2}}-z^2(x^2+y^2+z^2)^{-\frac{1}{2}}}{x^2+y^2+z^2} \quad (8)$$

Adding eqs.(6), (7) and (8) yields

$$\nabla^2 f(r) = \frac{d^2 f}{dr^2}\frac{x^2+y^2+z^2}{x^2+y^2+z^2} + \frac{df}{dr}\frac{3(x^2+y^2+z^2)^{\frac{1}{2}}-(x^2+y^2+z^2)(x^2+y^2+z^2)^{-\frac{1}{2}}}{x^2+y^2+z^2}$$

$$\qquad (9)$$

$$= \frac{d^2 f}{dr^2} + \frac{df}{dr}\frac{2}{(x^2+y^2+z^2)^{\frac{1}{2}}} = \frac{d^2 f}{dr^2} + \frac{2}{r}\frac{df}{dr}$$

Substituting eq.(2) into eq.(3) leads to

$$\nabla^2 f(r) = \nabla^2(\alpha + \beta r^{-1}) \qquad (10)$$

Applying eq.(1) to eq.(10),

$$\nabla^2(\alpha + \beta r^{-1}) = \frac{d^2}{dr^2}(\alpha + \beta r^{-1}) + \frac{2}{r}\frac{d}{dr}(\alpha + \beta r^{-1})$$

$$= 2\beta r^{-3} - \frac{2\beta}{r}r^{-2} = 0 \tag{11}$$

● **PROBLEM 7-28**

1. Show that the vector

   $$\bar{a} = (x^2+y^2)\bar{i} + y\sin z\,\bar{j} + (-2xz + \cos z)\bar{k} \tag{1}$$

   is solenoidal.

2. If $\bar{b}$ is a solenoidal vector whose two components are

   $$\tag{2}$$

   $$b_1 = x^2y \text{ and } b_2 = e^x y + y^2,$$

   determine the third component, b_3.

Solution: 1. A solenoidal vector is a vector whose divergence is zero.

To show that $\bar{a}$ is a solenoidal vector, we have to compute div $\bar{a}$.

$$\text{div } \bar{a} = \frac{\partial}{\partial x}(x^2+y^2) + \frac{\partial}{\partial y}(y\sin z) + \frac{\partial}{\partial z}(-2xz + \cos z)$$

$$= 2x + \sin z - 2x - \sin z = 0 \tag{3}$$

Thus vector $\bar{a}$ is solenoidal.

2. Using eq.(2) write $\bar{b}$ in the form

$$\bar{b} = (b_1, b_2, b_3) = (x^2y, e^x y + y^2, b_3) \tag{4}$$

Since $\bar{b}$ is a solenoidal vector, div $\bar{b} = 0$. $\tag{5}$

Substituting eq.(4) into eq.(5),

$$\text{div } \bar{b} = \frac{\partial b_1}{\partial x} + \frac{\partial b_2}{\partial y} + \frac{\partial b_3}{\partial z}$$

$$= \frac{\partial}{\partial x}(x^2y) + \frac{\partial}{\partial y}(e^x y + y^2) + \frac{\partial b_3}{\partial z} \tag{6}$$

$$= 2xy + e^x + 2y + \frac{\partial b_3}{\partial z} = 0$$

From eq.(6), we obtain

$$\frac{\partial b_3}{\partial z} = -2xy - e^x - 2y \tag{7}$$

Thus b_3 is equal to

$$b_3 = -2xyz - e^x z - 2yz \qquad (8)$$

Since b_3 was integrated with respect to z, it can contain any function of x and y. Thus,

$$b_3 = -2xyz - e^x z - 2yz + f(x,y) \qquad (9)$$

The vector $\bar{b}$, whose components b_1, b_2, b_3 are given by eqs.(2) and (9), is solenoidal.

● **PROBLEM** 7-29

Let $f = f(x,y,z)$ and $g = g(x,y,z)$ be two differentiable scalar fields.

Prove that

$$\text{grad } f \times \text{grad } g \qquad (1)$$

is solenoidal.

Solution: By definition the gradient of a scalar is equal to

$$\text{grad } f = \left(\frac{\partial f}{\partial x}, \frac{\partial f}{\partial y}, \frac{\partial f}{\partial z} \right) \qquad (2)$$

$$\text{grad } g = \left(\frac{\partial g}{\partial x}, \frac{\partial g}{\partial y}, \frac{\partial g}{\partial z} \right) \qquad (3)$$

Using the definition of the vector product and substituting eqs.(2) and (3) into expression (1), we obtain

$$\text{grad } f \times \text{grad } g = \left(\frac{\partial f}{\partial x}, \frac{\partial f}{\partial y}, \frac{\partial f}{\partial z} \right) \times \left(\frac{\partial g}{\partial x}, \frac{\partial g}{\partial y}, \frac{\partial g}{\partial z} \right)$$

$$= \left(\frac{\partial f}{\partial y} \frac{\partial g}{\partial z} - \frac{\partial f}{\partial z} \frac{\partial g}{\partial y}, \frac{\partial f}{\partial z} \frac{\partial g}{\partial x} - \frac{\partial f}{\partial x} \frac{\partial g}{\partial z}, \frac{\partial f}{\partial x} \frac{\partial g}{\partial y} - \frac{\partial f}{\partial y} \frac{\partial g}{\partial x} \right) \qquad (4)$$

To prove that the vector $\text{grad } f \times \text{grad } g$ is solenoidal, we must evaluate its divergence. From eq.(4),

$$\text{div} \left[\text{grad } f \times \text{grad } g \right] =$$

$$\frac{\partial}{\partial x} \left(\frac{\partial f}{\partial y} \frac{\partial g}{\partial z} - \frac{\partial f}{\partial z} \frac{\partial g}{\partial y} \right) + \frac{\partial}{\partial y} \left(\frac{\partial f}{\partial z} \frac{\partial g}{\partial x} - \frac{\partial f}{\partial x} \frac{\partial g}{\partial z} \right) + \frac{\partial}{\partial z} \left(\frac{\partial f}{\partial x} \frac{\partial g}{\partial y} - \frac{\partial f}{\partial y} \frac{\partial g}{\partial x} \right)$$

$$= \frac{\partial^2 f}{\partial x \partial y} \frac{\partial g}{\partial z} + \frac{\partial f}{\partial y} \frac{\partial^2 g}{\partial x \partial z} - \frac{\partial^2 f}{\partial x \partial z} \frac{\partial g}{\partial y} - \frac{\partial^2 g}{\partial x \partial y} \frac{\partial f}{\partial z} + \frac{\partial^2 f}{\partial y \partial z} \frac{\partial g}{\partial x}$$

$$+ \frac{\partial f}{\partial z} \frac{\partial^2 g}{\partial y \partial x} - \frac{\partial^2 f}{\partial y \partial x} \frac{\partial g}{\partial z} - \frac{\partial f}{\partial x} \frac{\partial^2 g}{\partial y \partial z} + \frac{\partial^2 f}{\partial z \partial x} \frac{\partial g}{\partial y}$$

$$+ \frac{\partial f}{\partial x} \frac{\partial^2 g}{\partial z \partial y} - \frac{\partial^2 f}{\partial z \partial y} \frac{\partial g}{\partial x} - \frac{\partial f}{\partial y} \frac{\partial^2 g}{\partial z \partial x} = 0 \qquad (5)$$

From eq.(5) one concludes that the vector grad f x grad g is solenoidal.

● **PROBLEM** 7-30

Show that the vector

$$\bar{a} = (x^4y + 2x^2y^3 + xy^2z)\bar{i} + 4x^2y^3z^3\bar{j} + (-3x^3yz - 2xy^3z - 2x^2y^2z^4)\bar{k} \quad (1)$$

is not solenoidal.

Also show that vector $\bar{b}$, given by

$$\bar{b} = \frac{1}{xy}\,\bar{a} \qquad (2)$$

is solenoidal.

Solution: The vector $\bar{a}$ is solenoidal if

$$\text{div } \bar{a} = 0 \qquad (3)$$

Therefore to verify that $\bar{a}$ is not solenoidal, one must first evaluate div $\bar{a}$.

$$\text{div } \bar{a} = \frac{\partial}{\partial x}\left[x^4y + 2x^2y^3 + xy^2z\right] + \frac{\partial}{\partial y}\left[4x^2y^3x^3\right]$$

$$+ \frac{\partial}{\partial z}\left[-3x^3yz - 2xy^3z - 2x^2y^2z^4\right]$$

$$= 4x^3y + 4xy^3 + y^2z + 12x^2y^2z^3 - 3x^3y - 2xy^3 - 8x^2y^2z^3 \qquad (4)$$

$$= x^3y + 2xy^3 + y^2z + 4x^2y^2z^3$$

Therefore, vector $\bar{a}$, as given by eq.(1), is not solenoidal.

Next, evaluate the components of vector $\bar{b} = \frac{1}{xy}\,\bar{a}$; doing this,

$$\bar{b} = (x^3 + 2xy^2 + yz)\bar{i} + 4xy^2z^3\bar{j} + (-3x^2z - 2y^2z - 2xyz^4)\bar{k} \quad (5)$$

$$\text{div } \bar{b} = \frac{\partial}{\partial x}(x^3 + 2xy^2 + yz) + \frac{\partial}{\partial y}(4xy^2z^3)$$

$$+ \frac{\partial}{\partial z}(-3x^2z - 2y^2z - 2xyz^4)$$

$$= 3x^2 + 2y^2 + 8xyz^3 - 3x^2 - 2y^2 - 8xyz^3$$

$$= 0$$

Thus, $\bar{b}$ is a solenoidal vector, since div $\bar{b}$ = 0.

Find the most general differentiable function $f(r)$ such that

$$\left| \text{grad } f(r) \right| \Big|_{(-1,1,0)} = 5 \qquad (1)$$

That is, whose gradient at the point $x = -1$, $y = 1$, $z = 0$ is equal to 5. Assume that the function $\bar{r}f(r)$ is solenoidal.

Solution: From the second condition, that $\bar{r} f(r)$ is solenoidal, we obtain that

$$\text{div} \left[\bar{r} \, f(r) \right] = 0 \qquad (2)$$

Evaluating the divergence of $\bar{r} \, f(r)$ leads to

$$\text{div} \left[\bar{r} \, f(r) \right] = \frac{\partial}{\partial x} \left[x \, f(r) \right] + \frac{\partial}{\partial y} \left[y \, f(r) \right] + \frac{\partial}{\partial z} \left[z \, f(r) \right]$$

$$= f(r) + x \frac{\partial}{\partial x} f(r) + f(r) + y \frac{\partial}{\partial y} f(r) + f(r) + z \frac{\partial}{\partial z} f(r)$$

$$= 3f(r) + x \frac{df}{dr} \frac{\partial r}{\partial x} + y \frac{df}{dr} \frac{\partial r}{\partial y} + z \frac{df}{dr} \frac{\partial r}{\partial z} \qquad (3)$$

$$= 3f(r) + \frac{df}{dr} \left[x \frac{\partial r}{\partial x} + y \frac{\partial r}{\partial y} + z \frac{\partial r}{\partial z} \right]$$

$$= 3f(r) + \frac{df}{dr} \left[\frac{x^2 + y^2 + z^2}{\sqrt{x^2 + y^2 + z^2}} \right] = 3f(r) + \frac{df}{dr} r = 0$$

This results in the following differential equation

$$3f(r) + r \frac{df}{dr} = 0 \qquad (4)$$

or

$$3 \frac{1}{r} \, dr + \frac{1}{f(r)} \, df = 0 \qquad (5)$$

Integrating eq.(5), obtain

$$3 \ln r + \ln f(r) + A = 0 \qquad (6)$$

or

$$\ln r^{-3} + \ln \alpha = \ln f(r) = \ln(\alpha r^{-3})$$

Here A is constant, and α is constant such that

$$\ln \alpha = A$$

From eq.(6), obtain

$$f(r) = \alpha r^{-3} \qquad (7)$$

To determine the value of α, use the condition expressed in eq.(1). In Chapter VI, we introduced the equation

$$\text{grad } r^n = nr^{n-2}\,\bar{r} \tag{8}$$

Substituting eq.(7) into eq.(8), obtain

$$\text{grad } f(r) = \text{grad } \alpha r^{-3} = -3\alpha r^{-5}\bar{r} \tag{9}$$

Substituting eq.(9) into eq.(1),

$$\Big|\text{grad } f(r)\Big|\;\Big|_{(-1,1,0)} = \Big|-3\alpha r^{-5}\bar{r}\Big|\;\Big|_{(-1,1,0)}$$

$$= \frac{3\,|\alpha|}{(x^2+y^2+z^2)^{\frac{5}{2}}}\,|\bar{r}|\;\Big|_{(-1,1,0)} = \frac{3\,|\alpha|}{(x^2+y^2+z^2)^2}\;\Big|_{(-1,1,0)} \tag{10}$$

$$= \frac{3\,|\alpha|}{4} = 5$$

Thus
$$|\alpha| = \frac{20}{3} \tag{11}$$
or

$$\alpha = \pm\,\frac{20}{3}$$

Two functions meet the requirements of the problem

$$f(r) = \frac{20}{3}\,r^{-3} \tag{12}$$

and
$$f(r) = \frac{-20}{3}\,r^{-3} \tag{13}$$

CHAPTER 8

CURL OF A VECTOR FIELD

INTRODUCTION

Chapter 8 deals almost exclusively sith the rotation of a vector field. The rotation, also called "curl" of a vector is the last of the three fundamental differential operators; the others being the gradient and the divergence. To avoid confusion in the future, the student should recognize that the notations rot $\bar{a}$, curl $\bar{a}$ and $\nabla \times \bar{a}$ all refer to the rotation of a vector (in this case vector $\bar{a}$). One distinct characteristic of the rotation is that unlike the divergence (which acts on a vector and produces a scalar), the rotation, or curl, acts upon a vector and produces another vector in return. Since the curl of a vector is such an important and frequently used operator, the student is strongly advised to memorize each of its components. To simplify the memorization, the student should keep in mind that the rotation of a given vector $\bar{a}$ is the vector product of the gradient operator (∇) with the given vector $\bar{a}$. Thus,

$$\text{rot } \bar{a} \equiv \text{curl } \bar{a} \equiv \nabla \times \bar{a} = \left(\frac{\partial}{\partial x}, \frac{\partial}{\partial y}, \frac{\partial}{\partial z} \right) \times (a_x, a_y, a_z)$$

$$\text{or} \quad \text{curl } \bar{a} = \left(\frac{\partial a_z}{\partial y} - \frac{\partial a_y}{\partial z}, \frac{\partial a_x}{\partial z} - \frac{\partial a_z}{\partial x}, \frac{\partial a_y}{\partial x} - \frac{\partial a_x}{\partial y} \right)$$

Once becoming familiar with the curl, the student is then introduced to an important class of vector fields, namely, the irrotational (also called conservative) field. The characteristic property of this field is that it contains a so called "scalar potential", which will be later defined. As a result of this scalar potential, the student is able to derive a simple, uncomplicated mathematical description for an irrotational, or conservative, field. There are many physical fields which are conservative; one of which is the gravitational field.

Another class of vector fields considered in this chapter are solenoidal fields. Their mathematical properties, as well as their relation to irrotational fields, is discussed.

Laplace's equation, one of the most important equations in physics, is also discussed in this chapter.

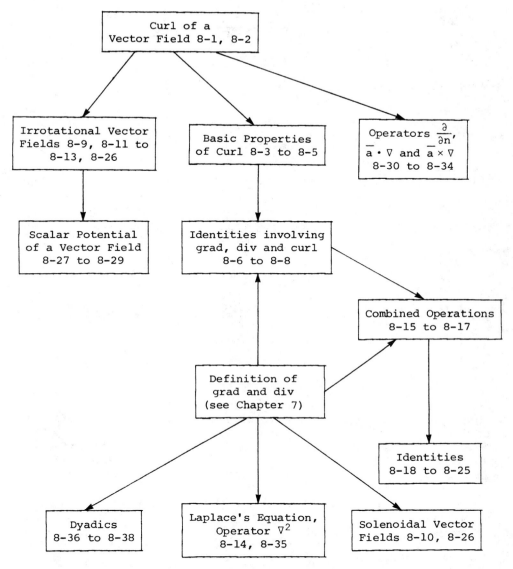

This chart is provided to facilitate rapid understanding of the inter-relationships of the topics and subject matter in this chapter. Also shown are the problem numbers associated with the subject matter.

DEFINITION, PROPERTIES AND IDENTITIES OF THE CURL OPERATORS

● **PROBLEM** 8-1

Find curl $\overline{a}$ at the point $(1,-2,1)$ for

$$\overline{a} = x^2 y^2 \overline{i} + 2xyz\,\overline{j} + z^2\,\overline{k} \qquad (1)$$

Solution: The curl of a vector field $\bar{a}$ is defined as

$$\text{curl } \bar{a} = \left(\frac{\partial a_z}{\partial y} - \frac{\partial a_y}{\partial z}\right)\bar{i} + \left(\frac{\partial a_x}{\partial z} - \frac{\partial a_z}{\partial x}\right)\bar{j} + \left(\frac{\partial a_y}{\partial x} - \frac{\partial a_x}{\partial y}\right)\bar{k} \quad (2)$$

Since the gradient operator is defined as

$$\nabla \equiv \frac{\partial}{\partial x}\bar{i} + \frac{\partial}{\partial y}\bar{j} + \frac{\partial}{\partial z}\bar{k},$$

definition (2) can be written in the form

$$\text{curl } \bar{a} = \text{rot } \bar{a} \equiv \nabla \times \bar{a} = \left(\frac{\partial}{\partial x}\bar{i} + \frac{\partial}{\partial y}\bar{j} + \frac{\partial}{\partial z}\bar{k}\right) \times (a_x\bar{i} + a_y\bar{j} + a_z\bar{k}) \quad (3)$$

$$= \begin{vmatrix} \bar{i} & \bar{j} & \bar{k} \\ \frac{\partial}{\partial x} & \frac{\partial}{\partial y} & \frac{\partial}{\partial z} \\ a_x & a_y & a_z \end{vmatrix} = \left(\frac{\partial a_z}{\partial y} - \frac{\partial a_y}{\partial z}, \frac{\partial a_x}{\partial z} - \frac{\partial a_z}{\partial x}, \frac{\partial a_y}{\partial x} - \frac{\partial a_x}{\partial y}\right) \quad (4)$$

Note that the notations curl $\bar{a}$, rot $\bar{a}$ and $\nabla \times \bar{a}$ are all equivalent and will be used interchangeably throughout this book. The curl or rotation of a vector plays a very important role in vector differential calculus. It is frequently used in electromagnetism, elasticity and hydrodynamics.

Substituting eq.(1) into eq.(2), we find

$$\text{curl } \bar{a} = \left[\frac{\partial a_z}{\partial y} - \frac{\partial a_y}{\partial z}\right]\bar{i} + \left[\frac{\partial a_x}{\partial z} - \frac{\partial a_z}{\partial x}\right]\bar{j} + \left[\frac{\partial a_y}{\partial x} - \frac{\partial a_x}{\partial y}\right]\bar{k}$$

$$= \left[\frac{\partial}{\partial y}(z^2) - \frac{\partial}{\partial z}(2xyz)\right]\bar{i} + \left[\frac{\partial}{\partial z}(x^2y^2) - \frac{\partial}{\partial x}(z^2)\right]\bar{j} + \quad (6)$$

$$\left[\frac{\partial}{\partial x}(2xyz) - \frac{\partial}{\partial y}(x^2y^2)\right]\bar{k}$$

$$= -2xy\bar{i} + (2yz - 2x^2y)\bar{k}$$

At the point (1,-2,1) curl $\bar{a}$ is equal to

$$\text{curl }\bar{a}\Big|_{(1,-2,1)} = \Big(-2xy\bar{i} + (2yz - 2x^2y)\bar{k}\Big)\Big|_{(1,-2,1)}$$

$$= 4\bar{i} \qquad\qquad (7)$$

Thus

$$\text{curl }\bar{a}\Big|_{(1,-2,1)} = 4\bar{i} = (4,0,0) \qquad\qquad (8)$$

● PROBLEM 8-2

If vector field $\bar{a}$ is given by

$$\bar{a} = x^2y^2\bar{i} + y^2z^2\bar{j} + x^2z^2\bar{k}, \qquad\qquad (1)$$

find

1. rot $\bar{a}$

2. rot rot $\bar{a}$

3. rot rot rot $\bar{a}$

<u>Solution</u>: 1. From the definition of the rotation,

$$\text{rot }\bar{a} = \left(\frac{\partial a_z}{\partial y} - \frac{\partial a_y}{\partial z}, \frac{\partial a_x}{\partial z} - \frac{\partial a_z}{\partial x}, \frac{\partial a_y}{\partial x} - \frac{\partial a_x}{\partial y}\right) \qquad (2)$$

The components of vector $\bar{a}$, given by eq.(1) are

$$a_x = x^2y^2$$

$$a_y = y^2z^2 \qquad\qquad (3)$$

$$a_z = x^2z^2$$

Substituting eq.(3) into eq.(2),

$$\text{rot }\bar{a} = (-2y^2z, -2xz^2, -2x^2y) \qquad\qquad (4)$$

2. The vector field rot rot $\bar{a}$ is defined as follows

$$\text{rot rot }\bar{a} = \text{rot}(\text{rot }\bar{a}) \qquad\qquad (5)$$

311

Substituting eq.(4) into eq.(5), we obtain

$$\text{rot rot } \bar{a} = \text{rot}(-2y^2z, -2xz^2, -2x^2y) \qquad (6)$$

From the definition of the rotation of a vector,

$$\text{rot rot } \bar{a} = \left[\frac{\partial}{\partial y}(-2x^2y) - \frac{\partial}{\partial z}(-2xz^2), \frac{\partial}{\partial z}(-2y^2z) - \frac{\partial}{\partial x}(-2x^2y),\right.$$

$$\left. \frac{\partial}{\partial x}(-2xz^2) - \frac{\partial}{\partial y}(-2y^2z)\right] = (-2x^2+4xz, -2y^2+4xy, -2z^2+4yz) \qquad (7)$$

3. To find rot rot rot $\bar{a}$, note that

$$\text{rot rot rot } \bar{a} = \text{rot}\left[\text{rot(rot } \bar{a})\right] \qquad (8)$$

Substituting eq.(7) into eq.(8) leads to

$$\text{rot rot rot } a = \text{rot}(-2x^2+4xz, -2y^2+4xy, -2z^2+4yz)$$

$$= \left[\frac{\partial}{\partial y}(-2z^2+4yz) - \frac{\partial}{\partial z}(-2y^2+4xy), \frac{\partial}{\partial z}(-2x^2+4xz) - \frac{\partial}{\partial x}(-2z^2+4yz),\right.$$

$$\left. \frac{\partial}{\partial x}(-2y^2+4xy) - \frac{\partial}{\partial y}(-2x^2+4xz)\right] \qquad (9)$$

$$= (4z, 4x, 4y) = 4(z, x, y)$$

$$= 4(z, x, y)$$

or
$$\text{rot rot rot } \bar{a} = 4z\bar{i} + 4x\bar{j} + 4y\bar{k}$$

● **PROBLEM 8-3**

Show that the curl satisfies the equations:

$$\text{curl } (\bar{a} + \bar{b}) = \text{curl } \bar{a} + \text{curl } \bar{b} \qquad (1)$$

$$\text{curl } (f\bar{a}) = f \text{ curl } \bar{a} + \text{grad } f \times \bar{a} \qquad (2)$$

Solution: To prove both equations, use the definition of the curl and some basic properties of partial derivatives. Let

$$\bar{a} = (a_1, a_2, a_3)$$

$$\bar{b} = (b_1, b_2, b_3) \qquad (3)$$

Then,

$$\text{curl}(\bar{a} + \bar{b}) = \nabla \times (\bar{a} \times \bar{b})$$

$$= \left(\frac{\partial}{\partial x}, \frac{\partial}{\partial y}, \frac{\partial}{\partial z}\right) \times (a_1+b_1, \ a_2+b_2, \ a_3+b_3)$$

$$= \left[\frac{\partial}{\partial y}(a_3+b_3) - \frac{\partial}{\partial z}(a_2+b_2), \ \frac{\partial}{\partial z}(a_1+b_1) - \frac{\partial}{\partial x}(a_3+b_3),\right.$$

$$\left. \frac{\partial}{\partial x}(a_2+b_2) - \frac{\partial}{\partial y}(a_1+b_1)\right]$$

$$= \left[\frac{\partial a_3}{\partial y} - \frac{\partial a_2}{\partial z}, \ \frac{\partial a_1}{\partial z} - \frac{\partial a_3}{\partial x}, \ \frac{\partial a_2}{\partial x} - \frac{\partial a_1}{\partial y}\right]$$

$$+ \left[\frac{\partial b_3}{\partial y} - \frac{\partial b_2}{\partial z}, \ \frac{\partial b_1}{\partial z} - \frac{\partial b_3}{\partial x}, \ \frac{\partial b_2}{\partial x} - \frac{\partial b_1}{\partial y}\right] \qquad (4)$$

$$= \text{curl } \bar{a} + \text{curl } \bar{b}$$

For equation (2),

$$\text{curl}(f\bar{a}) = \text{curl}(fa_1, \ fa_2, \ fa_3)$$

$$= \left[\frac{\partial}{\partial y}(fa_3) - \frac{\partial}{\partial z}(fa_2), \ \frac{\partial}{\partial z}(fa_1) - \frac{\partial}{\partial x}(fa_3), \ \frac{\partial}{\partial x}(fa_2) - \frac{\partial}{\partial y}(fa_1)\right]$$

$$\left[\left(f\frac{\partial a_3}{\partial y} + a_3\frac{\partial f}{\partial y} - f\frac{\partial a_2}{\partial z} - a_2\frac{\partial f}{\partial z}\right), \left(f\frac{\partial a_1}{\partial z} + a_1\frac{\partial f}{\partial z} - f\frac{\partial a_3}{\partial x} - a_3\frac{\partial f}{\partial x}\right),\right.$$

$$\left. \left(f\frac{\partial a_2}{\partial x} + a_2\frac{\partial f}{\partial x} - f\frac{\partial a_1}{\partial y} - a_1\frac{\partial f}{\partial y}\right)\right] \qquad (5)$$

$$= f\left[\frac{\partial a_3}{\partial y} - \frac{\partial a_2}{\partial z} \quad \frac{\partial a_1}{\partial z} - \frac{\partial a_3}{\partial x} \quad \frac{\partial a_2}{\partial x} - \frac{\partial a_1}{\partial y}\right]$$

$$+ \left[a_3\frac{\partial f}{\partial y} - a_2\frac{\partial f}{\partial z}, \ a_1\frac{\partial f}{\partial z} - a_3\frac{\partial f}{\partial x}, \ a_2\frac{\partial f}{\partial x} - a_1\frac{\partial f}{\partial y}\right] \qquad (6)$$

Since $\text{grad } f = \left(\frac{\partial f}{\partial x}, \frac{\partial f}{\partial y}, \frac{\partial f}{\partial z}\right)$, then

$$\text{grad } f \times \bar{a} = \left(\frac{\partial f}{\partial x}, \frac{\partial f}{\partial y}, \frac{\partial f}{\partial z}\right) \times (a_1, \ a_2, \ a_3)$$

$$= \left(a_3\frac{\partial f}{\partial y} - a_2\frac{\partial f}{\partial z}, \ a_1\frac{\partial f}{\partial z} - a_3\frac{\partial f}{\partial x}, \ a_2\frac{\partial f}{\partial x} - a_1\frac{\partial f}{\partial y}\right)$$

recognizing that eq.(7) is in eq.(6), eq.(6) can be written in the form
$$\text{curl}(f\bar{a}) = f \text{ curl } \bar{a} + \text{grad } f \times \bar{a}$$

● **PROBLEM** 8-4

Find

1. rot $\bar{a}$ + rot $\bar{b}$ (1)

    for the vectors

    $\bar{a} = (x^2y - e^{xyz}, \ z + x^2, \ xy)$

$$\overline{b} = (2x^2y + e^{xyz}, -x^2, xyz) \qquad (2)$$

2. $\text{rot }(f\overline{a})$ $\qquad (3)$

    for $f = x^2 + y^2$

    and $\overline{a} = (\ln y, xyz, y^2 + z^2)$ $\qquad (4)$

<u>Solution</u>: 1. From eq.(1) of Problem 8-3, we have

$$\text{rot }\overline{a} + \text{rot }\overline{b} = \text{rot}(\overline{a} + \overline{b}) \qquad (5)$$

where

$$\overline{a} + \overline{b} = (3x^2y, z, xy + xyz) \qquad (6)$$

Substituting eq.(6) into eq.(5) yields

$$\text{rot}(\overline{a} + \overline{b}) = \text{rot}(3x^2y, z, xy + xyz) =$$

$$\left[\frac{\partial}{\partial y}(xy+xyz) - \frac{\partial}{\partial z}(z), \ \frac{\partial}{\partial z}(3x^2y) - \frac{\partial}{\partial x}(xy+xyz), \right.$$

$$\left. \frac{\partial}{\partial x}(z) - \frac{\partial}{\partial y}(3x^2y) \right]$$

$$= \left[x + zx - 1, -y - yz, -3x^2 \right] = \text{rot }\overline{a} + \text{rot }\overline{b} \qquad (7)$$

2. Use the following identity

$$\text{rot}(f\overline{a}) = f \text{ rot }\overline{a} + \text{grad } f \times \overline{a} \qquad (8)$$

(See eq.(2) of Problem 8-3)
where

$$\text{grad } f = (2x, 2y, 0) \qquad (9)$$

and

$$\text{rot }\overline{a} = \left[\frac{\partial}{\partial y}(y^2+z^2) - \frac{\partial}{\partial z}(xyz), \ \frac{\partial}{\partial z}\ln y - \frac{\partial}{\partial x}(y^2+z^2), \right.$$

$$\left. \frac{\partial}{\partial x}(xyz) - \frac{\partial}{\partial y}\ln y \right] \qquad (10)$$

$$= \left(2y - xy, 0, yz - \frac{1}{y} \right)$$

Substituting eqs.(9) and (10) into eq.(8),

$$\text{rot}(fa) = (x^2+y^2)\left[2y-xy, 0, yz - \frac{1}{y} \right]$$

$$+ \left[2x, 2y, 0 \right] \times \left[\ln y, xyz, y^2+z^2 \right]$$

$$= \left[(x^2+y^2)(2y-xy), 0, (x^2+y^2)\left(yz-\frac{1}{y} \right) \right]$$

$$+ \left[2y(y^2+z^2), -2x(y^2+z^2), 2x^2yz - 2y\ln y \right] \qquad (11)$$

$$= \left[(x^2+y^2)(2y-xy)+2y(y^2+z^2), -2x(y^2+z^2), \right.$$

$$\left. (x^2+y^2)\left(yz-\frac{1}{y} \right) + 2x^2yz-2y\ln y \right]$$

1. Determine the constants α and β such that

$$\text{rot } \bar{a} = \bar{0} \tag{1}$$

for the vector

$$\bar{a} = (x + \alpha y, \, y + \beta x, \, z) \tag{2}$$

2. Show that

$$\text{rot } \frac{\bar{r}}{r^2} = \bar{0} \tag{3}$$

where $\bar{r} = (x, \, y, \, z)$

<u>Solution</u>: 1. Proceed by evaluating the rotation of vector $\bar{a}$

$$\text{rot } \bar{a} = \left[\frac{\partial}{\partial y} z - \frac{\partial}{\partial z}(y+\beta x), \, \frac{\partial}{\partial z}(x+\alpha y) - \frac{\partial}{\partial z} z, \, \frac{\partial}{\partial x}(y+\beta x) - \frac{\partial}{\partial y}(x+\alpha y) \right]$$

$$= (0, \, 0, \, \beta - \alpha) \tag{4}$$

Since it is required that rot $\bar{a} = \bar{0}$, $\alpha = \beta$
For any number α, the rotation of
$$\bar{a} = (x + \alpha y, \, y + \alpha x, \, z) \tag{5}$$

is equal to $\bar{0}$.

2. Find the rotation of the vector $\frac{\bar{r}}{r^2}$, where

$$\frac{\bar{r}}{r^2} = \left(\frac{x}{x^2+y^2+z^2}, \, \frac{y}{x^2+y^2+z^2}, \, \frac{z}{x^2+y^2+z^2} \right) \tag{6}$$

Substituting eq.(6) into the definition of rotation,

$$\text{rot } \frac{\bar{r}}{r^2} = \left(\frac{\partial}{\partial y} \frac{z}{x^2+y^2+z^2} - \frac{\partial}{\partial z} \frac{y}{x^2+y^2+z^2}, \right.$$

$$\left. \frac{\partial}{\partial z} \frac{x}{x^2+y^2+z^2} - \frac{\partial}{\partial x} \frac{z}{x^2+y^2+z^2}, \, \frac{\partial}{\partial x} \frac{y}{x^2+y^2+z^2} - \frac{\partial}{\partial y} \frac{x}{x^2+y^2+z^2} \right) \tag{7}$$

Next compute the partial derivatives appearing in eq.(7).

$$\frac{\partial}{\partial y} \frac{z}{x^2+y^2+z^2} = \frac{-2zy}{(x^2+y^2+z^2)^2}$$

$$\frac{\partial}{\partial z} \frac{y}{x^2+y^2+z^2} = \frac{-2yz}{(x^2+y^2+z^2)^2}$$

$$\frac{\partial}{\partial z} \frac{x}{x^2+y^2+z^2} = \frac{-2xz}{(x^2+y^2+z^2)^2} \tag{8}$$

$$\frac{\partial}{\partial x} \frac{z}{x^2+y^2+z^2} = \frac{-2xz}{(x^2+y^2+z^2)^2}$$

$$\frac{\partial}{\partial x} \frac{y}{x^2+y^2+z^2} = \frac{-2xy}{(x^2+y^2+z^2)^2}$$

$$\frac{\partial}{\partial y} \frac{x}{x^2+y^2+z^2} = \frac{-2xy}{(x^2+y^2+z^2)^2}$$

Substituting eq.(8) into eq.(7) results in

$$\text{rot } \frac{\bar{r}}{r^2} = \bar{0} \tag{9}$$

● **PROBLEM** 8-6

1.   Prove the identity

$$\nabla \cdot (\bar{a} \times \bar{r}) = \bar{r} \cdot (\nabla \times \bar{a}) \tag{1}$$

2.   Find

$$\nabla \cdot (\bar{a} \times \bar{r}) \tag{2}$$

   where

$$\bar{a} = (x^2+1, \ y^2+2, \ z^2+3) \tag{3}$$

Solution: 1.   To prove identity (1) use the definition of the divergence and the definition of rotation. Then, express   the vectors $\bar{a}$ and $\bar{r}$ in the component form

$$\bar{a} = (a_1, \ a_2, \ a_3)$$

$$\bar{r} = (x, \ y, \ z) \tag{4}$$

Evaluating the cross-product of $\bar{a}$ and $\bar{r}$,

$$\bar{a} \times \bar{r} = (za_2 - ya_3, \ xa_3 - za_1, \ ya_1 - xa_2) \tag{5}$$

Since the operator ∇ is defined as

$$\nabla \equiv \left(\frac{\partial}{\partial x}, \ \frac{\partial}{\partial y}, \ \frac{\partial}{\partial z} \right) \tag{6}$$

the scalar product of ∇ and $\bar{a} \times \bar{r}$ is

$$\nabla \cdot (\bar{a} \times \bar{r}) = \left(\frac{\partial}{\partial x}, \ \frac{\partial}{\partial y}, \ \frac{\partial}{\partial z} \right) \cdot (za_2 - ya_3, \ xa_3 - za_1, \ ya_1 - xa_2)$$

$$= z \frac{\partial a_2}{\partial x} - y \frac{\partial a_3}{\partial x} + x \frac{\partial a_3}{\partial y} - z \frac{\partial a_1}{\partial y} + y \frac{\partial a_1}{\partial z} - x \frac{\partial a_2}{\partial z}$$

$$= x \left(\frac{\partial a_3}{\partial y} - \frac{\partial a_2}{\partial z} \right) + y \left(\frac{\partial a_1}{\partial z} - \frac{\partial a_3}{\partial x} \right) + z \left(\frac{\partial a_2}{\partial x} - \frac{\partial a_1}{\partial y} \right) \tag{7}$$

$$= \bar{r} \cdot \text{rot } \bar{a} = \bar{r} \cdot (\nabla \times \bar{a})$$

Thus

$$\nabla \cdot (\bar{a} \times \bar{r}) = \bar{r} \cdot (\nabla \times \bar{a}) \tag{8}$$

2.   To obtain $\nabla \cdot (\bar{a} \times \bar{r})$ for

316

$$\bar{a} = (x^2+1,\ y^2+2,\ z^2+3), \tag{9}$$

use the identity

$$\nabla \cdot (\bar{a} \times \bar{r}) = \bar{r} \cdot (\nabla \times \bar{a}) \tag{10}$$

First, find $\nabla \times \bar{a}$

$$\nabla \times (x^2+1,\ y^2+2,\ z^2+3)$$

$$=\left(\frac{\partial}{\partial y}(z^2+3)-\frac{\partial}{\partial z}(y^2+2),\frac{\partial}{\partial z}(x^2+1)-\frac{\partial}{\partial x}(z^2+3),\frac{\partial}{\partial x}(y^2+2)-\frac{\partial}{\partial y}(x^2+1)\right)$$

$$= (0,0,0)$$

Thus

$$\nabla \times \bar{a} = \bar{0} \quad \text{and since} \quad \bar{r}\cdot(\nabla \times \bar{a}) = \bar{r}\cdot\bar{0} = 0, \tag{11}$$

then

$$\nabla \cdot (\bar{a} \times \bar{r}) = 0 \tag{12}$$

● **PROBLEM 8-7**

Show that for any scalar function f = f(x,y,z) with continuous partial derivatives, the following identity holds

$$\text{rot}(f\ \text{grad}\ f) = \bar{0} \tag{1}$$

Solution: The gradient of f is defined as

$$\text{grad}\ f = \left(\frac{\partial f}{\partial x},\ \frac{\partial f}{\partial y},\ \frac{\partial f}{\partial z}\right) \tag{2}$$

To evaluate the rotation of the vector, first find f grad f

$$f\ \text{grad}\ f = \left(f\frac{\partial f}{\partial x},\ f\frac{\partial f}{\partial y},\ f\frac{\partial f}{\partial z}\right) \tag{3}$$

From the definition of the rotation, obtain

rot(f grad f) =

$$\begin{aligned}
&= \left[\frac{\partial}{\partial y}\left(f\frac{\partial f}{\partial z}\right)-\frac{\partial}{\partial z}\left(f\frac{\partial f}{\partial y}\right),\ \frac{\partial}{\partial z}\left(f\frac{\partial f}{\partial x}\right)-\frac{\partial}{\partial x}\left(f\frac{\partial f}{\partial z}\right), \right. \\
&\qquad\qquad\qquad \left. \frac{\partial}{\partial x}\left(f\frac{\partial f}{\partial y}\right)-\frac{\partial}{\partial y}\left(f\frac{\partial f}{\partial x}\right)\right]
\end{aligned} \tag{4}$$

Since the second derivatives of f are continuous, the order of differentiation is arbitrary. Hence,

$$\begin{aligned}
&= \left(\frac{\partial f}{\partial y}\frac{\partial f}{\partial z}+f\frac{\partial^2 f}{\partial y\partial z}-\frac{\partial f}{\partial z}\frac{\partial f}{\partial y}-f\frac{\partial^2 f}{\partial z\partial y},\ \frac{\partial f}{\partial z}\frac{\partial f}{\partial x}+f\frac{\partial^2 f}{\partial z\partial x}-\frac{\partial f}{\partial x}\frac{\partial f}{\partial z}\right. \\
&\qquad \left. -f\frac{\partial^2 f}{\partial x\partial z},\ \frac{\partial f}{\partial x}\frac{\partial f}{\partial y}+f\frac{\partial^2 f}{\partial x\partial y}-\frac{\partial f}{\partial y}\frac{\partial f}{\partial x}-f\frac{\partial^2 f}{\partial y\partial x}\right)
\end{aligned} \tag{5}$$

317

= (0, 0, 0)

Therefore,

$$\text{rot}(f\ \text{grad}\ f) = \overline{0} \qquad\qquad (6)$$

● **PROBLEM** 8-8

Prove the following identities:

$$\text{curl grad}\ f = \overline{0} \qquad\qquad (1)$$

$$\text{div curl}\ \overline{a} = 0 \qquad\qquad (2)$$

Solution: To prove eq.(1), assume that f has continuous second partial derivatives. Then

$$\text{curl grad}\ f = \nabla \times (\nabla f) = \left(\frac{\partial}{\partial x},\ \frac{\partial}{\partial y},\ \frac{\partial}{\partial z}\right) \times \left(\frac{\partial f}{\partial x},\ \frac{\partial f}{\partial y},\ \frac{\partial f}{\partial z}\right)$$

$$= \left[\frac{\partial^2 f}{\partial y \partial z} - \frac{\partial^2 f}{\partial z \partial y},\ \frac{\partial^2 f}{\partial z \partial x} - \frac{\partial^2 f}{\partial x \partial z},\ \frac{\partial^2 f}{\partial x \partial y} - \frac{\partial^2 f}{\partial y \partial x}\right] \qquad (3)$$

Since the second partial derivatives are continuous, the order of differentiation is inconsequential. Therefore, equation (3) reduces to

$$(0,\ 0,\ 0) = \overline{0} = \text{curl grad}\ f$$

To prove eq.(2), assume that $\overline{a}$ has continuous second partial derivatives.

$$\text{div curl}\ \overline{a} = \nabla \cdot (\nabla \times \overline{a})$$

$$= \left(\frac{\partial}{\partial x},\ \frac{\partial}{\partial y},\ \frac{\partial}{\partial z}\right) \cdot \left[\left(\frac{\partial}{\partial x},\ \frac{\partial}{\partial y},\ \frac{\partial}{\partial z}\right) \times (a_1,\ a_2,\ a_3)\right]$$

$$= \left(\frac{\partial}{\partial x},\ \frac{\partial}{\partial y},\ \frac{\partial}{\partial z}\right) \cdot \left(\frac{\partial a_3}{\partial y} - \frac{\partial a_2}{\partial z},\ \frac{\partial a_1}{\partial z} - \frac{\partial a_3}{\partial x},\ \frac{\partial a_2}{\partial x} - \frac{\partial a_1}{\partial y}\right) \qquad (4)$$

$$= \frac{\partial}{\partial x}\left(\frac{\partial a_3}{\partial y} - \frac{\partial a_2}{\partial z}\right) + \frac{\partial}{\partial y}\left(\frac{\partial a_1}{\partial z} - \frac{\partial a_3}{\partial x}\right) + \frac{\partial}{\partial z}\left(\frac{\partial a_2}{\partial x} - \frac{\partial a_1}{\partial y}\right)$$

$$= \frac{\partial^2 a_3}{\partial x \partial y} - \frac{\partial^2 a_2}{\partial x \partial z} + \frac{\partial^2 a_1}{\partial y \partial z} - \frac{\partial^2 a_3}{\partial y \partial x} + \frac{\partial^2 a_2}{\partial z \partial x} - \frac{\partial^2 a_1}{\partial z \partial y}$$

$$= 0.$$

Both identities, curl grad $f = \overline{0}$ and div curl $\overline{a} = 0$, are highly important and are frequently used. The student is strongly advised to memorize them.

IRROTATIONAL (CONSERVATIVE) VECTOR FIELDS, SOLENOIDAL VECTOR FIELDS

1. Given the vector field,

$$\bar{a} = (y^2 + ze^{xz}, \; 2xy, \; xe^{xz}) \tag{1}$$

verify that

$$\text{curl } \bar{a} = \bar{0} \tag{2}$$

Find the function f such that

$$\bar{a} = \text{grad } f \tag{3}$$

__Solution__: From eq.(1) of Problem 8-8, we know that curl grad f = $\bar{0}$ for any scalar function f having continuous second partial derivatives.

From the above identity, we conclude that for a vector function $\bar{a}$, such that curl $\bar{a}$ = 0, there exists a scalar function f, such that $\bar{a}$ = grad f.

There are some further assumptions concerning this rule that will be investigated in the next chapter.

To verify eq.(2)

$$\text{curl } \bar{a} = \nabla \times \bar{a} = \left(\frac{\partial}{\partial x}, \; \frac{\partial}{\partial y}, \; \frac{\partial}{\partial z} \right) \times (y^2 + ze^{xz}, \; 2xy, \; xe^{xz})$$

$$= (0, \; e^{xz} + zx \, e^{xz} - e^{xz} - xze^{xz}, \; 2y - 2y) = \bar{0} \tag{4}$$

Since curl $\bar{a}$ = $\bar{0}$, there exists a function f such that

$$\bar{a} = \text{grad } f \tag{5}$$

Substituting eq.(1) into eq.(5),

$$(y^2 + ze^{xz}, \; 2xy, \; xe^{xz}) = \left(\frac{\partial f}{\partial x}, \; \frac{\partial f}{\partial y}, \; \frac{\partial f}{\partial z} \right) \tag{6}$$

Eq.(6) is equivalent to the following three equations

$$\frac{\partial f}{\partial x} = y^2 + ze^{xz} \tag{7}$$

$$\frac{\partial f}{\partial y} = 2xy \tag{8}$$

$$\frac{\partial f}{\partial z} = xe^{xz} \tag{9}$$

From eq.(7), we have

$$f(x, \; y, \; z) = xy^2 + e^{xz} + g(y, z) \tag{10}$$

where g(y,z) is any arbitrary function of y and z.

Substituting eq.(10) into eq.(8),

$$\frac{\partial f}{\partial y} = 2xy + \frac{\partial g}{\partial y} = 2xy \qquad (11)$$

Therefore,

$$\frac{\partial g}{\partial y} = 0 \quad \text{and} \quad g = g(z).$$

From eq.(9),

$$\frac{\partial f}{\partial z} = xe^{xz} + \frac{dg(z)}{dz} = xe^{xz} \qquad (12)$$

therefore $\frac{dg(z)}{dz} = 0$ and thus g = constant.

The function f is then

$$f(x,\ y,\ z) = xy^2 + e^{xz} + \text{const} \qquad (13)$$

● **PROBLEM** 8-10

Given the vector field

$$\overline{a} = (3x,\ 2y,\ -5z) \qquad (1)$$

verify that

$$\text{div } \overline{a} = 0. \qquad (2)$$

Also, find all vectors $\overline{b}$ such that

$$\text{curl } \overline{b} = \overline{a} \qquad (3)$$

Solution: Use eq.(2) of Problem 8-8, which states that for any vector $\overline{b}$,

$$\text{div curl } \overline{b} = 0 \qquad (4)$$

With some restrictions, which will be discussed later, it is safe to say that if there exists a vector $\overline{a}$ such that div $\overline{a} = 0$, then there exists a vector $\overline{b}$ such that $\overline{a} = \text{curl } \overline{b}$.

For the divergence of vector $\overline{a}$ given by eq.(1), obtain

$$\text{div } \overline{a} = \frac{\partial}{\partial x}(3x) + \frac{\partial}{\partial y}(2y) + \frac{\partial}{\partial z}(-5z) = 0 \qquad (5)$$

Now it is required to find $\overline{b}$ such that

$$\text{curl } \overline{b} = \overline{a} \qquad (6)$$

From eq.(4) one concludes that all solutions of eq.(6) are given by

$$\overline{b} = \overline{b}_o + \text{grad } f \qquad (7)$$

320

where $f = f(x,y,z)$ is an arbitrary scalar and $\bar{b}_o$ is any vector such that

$$\text{curl } \bar{b}_o = \bar{a} \tag{8}$$

(because if $\bar{b} = \bar{b}_o + \text{grad } f$, then curl $\bar{b} = \text{curl } (\bar{b}_o + \text{grad } f)$
$= \text{curl } \bar{b}_o + \text{curl grad } f = \text{curl } \bar{b}_o = \bar{a})$

Since $\bar{b}_o$ is any vector, one can arbitrarily choose

$$\bar{b}_o = (b_1, b_2, 0) \tag{9}$$

Substituting eq.(9) and eq.(1) into eq.(8)

$$\nabla \times \bar{b}_o = \bar{a}$$

or $\left(\dfrac{\partial}{\partial x}, \dfrac{\partial}{\partial y}, \dfrac{\partial}{\partial z}\right) \times (b_1, b_2, 0) = (3x, 2y, -5z) \tag{10}$

$$\left(-\dfrac{\partial b_2}{\partial z}, \dfrac{\partial b_1}{\partial z}, \dfrac{\partial b_2}{\partial x} - \dfrac{\partial b_1}{\partial y}\right) = (3x, 2y, -5z) \tag{11}$$

Eq.(11) is equivalent to the system of equations

$$\dfrac{\partial b_2}{\partial z} = -3x \tag{12}$$

$$\dfrac{\partial b_1}{\partial z} = 2y \tag{13}$$

$$\dfrac{\partial b_2}{\partial x} - \dfrac{\partial b_1}{\partial y} = -5z \tag{14}$$

From eq.(12)

$$b_2 = -3xz + g(x,y) \tag{15}$$

From eq.(13),

$$b_1 = 2yz + h(x,y) \tag{16}$$

Substituting eqs.(15) and (16) into eq.(14) yields

$$\dfrac{\partial b_2}{\partial x} - \dfrac{\partial b_1}{\partial y} = -3z + \dfrac{\partial g}{\partial x} - 2z - \dfrac{\partial h}{\partial y} = -5z \tag{17}$$

One can assume that $g(x,y) = h(x,y) = 0$, and for $\bar{b}_o$ obtain,

$$\bar{b}_o = (2yz, -3xz, 0) \tag{18}$$

Thus for $\bar{b}$, obtain

$$\bar{b} = (2yz, -3xz, 0) + \left(\dfrac{\partial f}{\partial x}, \dfrac{\partial f}{\partial y}, \dfrac{\partial f}{\partial z}\right) \tag{19}$$

where f is an arbitrary scalar function.

Vector $\bar{a}$, such that

$$\text{div } \bar{a} = 0 \qquad (20)$$

is called a solenoidal vector.

● **PROBLEM 8-11**

Find constants α, β, γ so that

$$\bar{a} = (3x-2y+\alpha z)\bar{i} + (\beta x+3y+5z)\bar{j} + (2x+\gamma y-z)\bar{k} \qquad (1)$$

is irrotational.

Also, find a scalar function f such that

$$\bar{a} = \text{grad } f \qquad (2)$$

Solution: Vector $\bar{a}$ is irrotational when

$$\text{curl } \bar{a} = \bar{0} \qquad (3)$$

Substituting eq.(1) into eq.(3),

$$\text{curl } \bar{a} = \nabla \times \bar{a} \qquad (4)$$

$$= \left(\frac{\partial}{\partial x}, \frac{\partial}{\partial y}, \frac{\partial}{\partial z} \right) \times (3x - 2y + \alpha z, \beta x + 3y + 5z, 2x + \gamma y - z)$$

$$= (\gamma - 5, \alpha - 2, \beta + 2)$$

From the condition curl $\bar{a} = \bar{0}$, we obtain

$$(\gamma - 5, \alpha - 2, \beta + 2) = (0, 0, 0) \qquad (5)$$

Thus $\gamma = 5$, $\alpha = 2$ and $\beta = -2$.

Substituting the values of the constants into eq.(1) yields

$$\bar{a} = (3x - 2y + 2z, -2x + 3y + 5z, 2x + 5y - z) \qquad (6)$$

From eq.(2), assume that

$$\bar{a} = \text{grad } f \qquad (7)$$

Substituting eq.(6) into eq.(7),

$$(3x - 2y + 2z, -2x + 3y + 5z, 2x + 5y - z) = \left(\frac{\partial f}{\partial x}, \frac{\partial f}{\partial y}, \frac{\partial f}{\partial z} \right) \qquad (8)$$

or

$$\frac{\partial f}{\partial x} = 3x - 2y + 2z \qquad (9)$$

$$\frac{\partial f}{\partial y} = -2x + 3y + 5z \qquad (10)$$

$$\frac{\partial f}{\partial z} = 2x + 5y - z \qquad (11)$$

Integrating eqs.(9), (10) and (11),

$$f = \frac{3}{2} x^2 - 2xy + 2xz + F(y,z) \qquad (12)$$

$$f = -2xy + \frac{3}{2} y^2 + 5yz + G(x,z) \qquad (13)$$

$$f = 2xz + 5yz - \frac{z^2}{2} + H(x,y) \qquad (14)$$

Since eqs.(12), (13) and (14) have to represent the same function f, comparing eq.(12) with eq.(13), eq.(12) with eq.(14) and eq.(13) with eq.(14) gives

$$f = \frac{3}{2} x^2 - 2xy + 2xz + \frac{3}{2} y^2 + 5yz - \frac{z^2}{2} \qquad (15)$$

Any constant can be added to f. One could easily verify that

$$\bar{a} = \text{grad } f \qquad (16)$$

Since curl $\bar{a} = \bar{0}$, the vector field $\bar{a}$ can be derived from the scalar field f, where $\bar{a} = \text{grad } f$. Vector $\bar{a}$ is called a conservative vector field and f is called the scalar potential of this field.

● **PROBLEM 8-12**

Determine whether the vector field $\bar{a}$

$$\bar{a} . = (e^x + y^2)\bar{i} + (2xy + z^3)\bar{j} + (3yz^2 + 2z)\bar{k} \qquad (1)$$

is conservative. Use the following two methods:

1. by computing curl $\bar{a}$

2. by finding the scalar potential of $\bar{a}$.

Solution: 1. A vector field is called conservative when its curl is equal to zero. Therefore, to determine if $\bar{a}$ is conservative, evaluate curl $\bar{a}$. Doing this,

$$\text{curl } \bar{a} = \nabla \times \bar{a} = \left(\frac{\partial}{\partial x}, \frac{\partial}{\partial y}, \frac{\partial}{\partial z} \right) \times (e^x + y^2, 2xy + z^3, 3yz^2 + 2z) =$$

$$= \left(\frac{\partial}{\partial y}(3yz^2 + 2z) - \frac{\partial}{\partial z}(2xy + z^3), \frac{\partial}{\partial z}(e^x + y^2) - \frac{\partial}{\partial x}(3yz^2 + 2z), \right.$$

$$\left. \frac{\partial}{\partial x}(2xy + z^3) - \frac{\partial}{\partial y}(e^x + y^2) \right)$$

$$= (3z^2 - 3z^2, 0, 2y - 2y) = (0, 0, 0) = \bar{0} \qquad (2)$$

Since curl $\bar{a} = \bar{0}$, the vector field $\bar{a}$ is conservative.

2. Assume that the scalar potential f of the vector field $\bar{a}$

exists, such that

$$\text{grad } f = \bar{a} \qquad (3)$$

Substituting eq.(1) into eq.(3) obtain three partial differential equations

$$\frac{\partial f}{\partial x} = e^x + y^2 \qquad (4)$$

$$\frac{\partial f}{\partial y} = 2xy + z^3 \qquad (5)$$

$$\frac{\partial f}{\partial z} = 3yz^2 + 2z \qquad (6)$$

To find the function f, integrate eq.(4) with respect to x while holding y and z constant. Thus

$$f = e^x + xy^2 + g(y,z) \qquad (7)$$

Here g(y,z) is any scalar function of y and z. Now differentiate eq.(7) with respect to y.

$$\frac{\partial f}{\partial y} = 2xy + \frac{\partial g}{\partial y} \qquad (8)$$

Comparing eqs.(5) and (8) we obtain

$$2xy + \frac{\partial g}{\partial y} = 2xy + z^3$$

or

$$\frac{\partial g}{\partial y} = z^3 \qquad (9)$$

Integrating eq.(9) with respect to y, we obtain

$$g(y,z) = z^3 y + h(z) \qquad (10)$$

Then differentiate eqs.(7) and (10) with respect to z.

$$\frac{\partial f}{\partial z} = \frac{\partial g}{\partial z} \qquad (11)$$

$$\frac{\partial g}{\partial z} = 3yz^2 + \frac{\partial h}{\partial z} \qquad (12)$$

Substituting eq.(12) into eq.(11),

$$\frac{\partial f}{\partial z} = 3yz^2 + \frac{\partial h}{\partial z} \qquad (13)$$

and comparing with eq.(6)

$$\frac{\partial f}{\partial z} = 3yz^2 + 2z = 3yz^2 + \frac{\partial h}{\partial z} \qquad (14)$$

Thus,

$$\frac{\partial h}{\partial z} = 2z \qquad (15)$$

and $h(z) = z^2 + C$ $\qquad$ (16)

where C is any constant.

From eqs.(16), (10) and (7),we obtain

$$f(x,y,z) = e^x + xy^2 + z^3y + z^2 + C \qquad (17)$$

● **PROBLEM 8-13**

Without computing curl $\bar{a}$, show that the vector field $\bar{a}$ as given below

$$\bar{a} = x^3y\,\bar{i} + yx^2\,\bar{j} + xz\,\bar{k} \qquad (1)$$

is not conservative.

Solution: If one were to assume that the vector field $\bar{a}$ is conservative, then there would exist a scalar field $f = f(x,y,z)$ such that
$$\text{grad } f = \bar{a} \qquad (2)$$

Substituting eq.(1) into eq.(2) and comparing the components, results in three differential equations of the form

$$\frac{\partial f}{\partial x} = F_1(x,y,z) \qquad \frac{\partial f}{\partial z} = F_3(x,y,z) \qquad (3)$$

$$\frac{\partial f}{\partial y} = F_2(x,y,z)$$

Or, since

$$\left(\frac{\partial f}{\partial x}, \frac{\partial f}{\partial y}, \frac{\partial f}{\partial z} \right) = (x^3y, \; yx^2, \; xz)$$

$$\frac{\partial f}{\partial x} = x^3y \qquad (4)$$

$$\frac{\partial f}{\partial y} = yx^2 \qquad (5)$$

$$\frac{\partial f}{\partial z} = xz \qquad (6)$$

If there is a scalar function f that satisfies eq.(4), (5) and (6), then f would be a scalar potential and vector field $\bar{a}$ would be conservative. This scalar function f would have to have continuous second partial derivatives in order to exist. A function has continuous second partial derivatives when

$$\frac{\partial f}{\partial x \partial y} = \frac{\partial f}{\partial y \partial x}$$

Differentiating eq.(4) with respect to y gives

$$\frac{\partial^2 f}{\partial y \partial x} = x^3 \qquad (7)$$

Differentiating eq.(5) with respect to x gives

$$\frac{\partial^2 f}{\partial x \partial y} = 2xy \qquad (8)$$

Since eq.(7) does not equal eq.(8), that is

$$\frac{\partial^2 f}{\partial y \partial x} \neq \frac{\partial^2 f}{\partial x \partial y},$$

then the second partial derivatives are not continuous, and therefore the scalar function f, such that grad f = $\bar{a}$ (where $\bar{a}$ is given by eq.(1)), does not exist.

Thus $\bar{a}$ is not a conservative vector field.

Note that this procedure is effective only as a negative proof that f does not exist.

If the mixed second derivatives of f were equal, it would not have necessarily meant that the vector field $\bar{a}$ is conservative.

For example, if

$$\bar{a} = (0, 0, y) \qquad (11)$$

then the second derivatives of f are all continuous and equal to zero, however

$$\text{curl } \bar{a} = (1, 0, 0)$$

is not equal to zero. Thus, even though the second derivatives of f are continuous, the vector field $\bar{a} = (0, 0, y)$ is not conservative.

LAPLACIAN OPERATOR AND COMBINED OPERATIONS

● **PROBLEM** 8-14

Let f(x,y,z) be any solution of Laplace's equation

$$\nabla^2 f = 0 \qquad (1)$$

Show that the vector ∇f is both solenoidal and irrotational.

Solution: The operator ∇^2 is defined as the scalar product of two gradient operators, thus

$$\nabla^2 \equiv \nabla \cdot \nabla = \left(\frac{\partial}{\partial x}, \frac{\partial}{\partial y}, \frac{\partial}{\partial z} \right) \cdot \left(\frac{\partial}{\partial x}, \frac{\partial}{\partial y}, \frac{\partial}{\partial z} \right)$$

$$= \frac{\partial^2}{\partial x^2} + \frac{\partial^2}{\partial y^2} + \frac{\partial^2}{\partial z^2} \qquad (2)$$

A vector $\bar{a}$ is called solenoidal when its divergence is zero, div $\bar{a} = 0$.
Compute the divergence of ∇f(grad f)   (3)

$$\text{div grad } f = \nabla \cdot \nabla f = \left(\frac{\partial}{\partial x}, \frac{\partial}{\partial y}, \frac{\partial}{\partial z} \right) \cdot \left(\frac{\partial f}{\partial x}, \frac{\partial f}{\partial y}, \frac{\partial f}{\partial z} \right)$$

(4)

$$= \frac{\partial^2 f}{\partial x^2} + \frac{\partial^2 f}{\partial y^2} + \frac{\partial^2 f}{\partial z^2} = \nabla^2 f$$

Since f is a solution of Laplace's equation

$$\nabla^2 f = 0,$$

then, from eq.(4)

$$\text{div grad } f = 0 \qquad (5)$$

and therefore ∇f is a solenoidal vector.
A vector $\bar{a}$ is called irrotational if

$$\text{curl } \bar{a} = \bar{0} \qquad (6)$$

From Problem 8-8, one obtains the following identity, which is true for any differentiable scalar f

$$\text{curl grad } f = \bar{0} \qquad (7)$$

Thus for any scalar $f = f(x,y,z)$, grad f is an irrotational vector.
In our case, since $f(x,y,z)$ is differentiable, ∇f is also an irrotational vector.

● **PROBLEM 8-15**

Given the vectors

$$\bar{a} = 3x^2y \ \bar{i} + 2x \ \bar{j} + yz \ \bar{k} \qquad (1)$$

$$\bar{b} = yz^2 \ \bar{i} + xy \ \bar{j} + z^2 \ \bar{k} \qquad (2)$$

and the scalar function

$$f = x^2 + yz \qquad (3)$$

find

1. $\bar{a} \cdot (\nabla f)$

2. $(\bar{a} \cdot \nabla) f$

3. $(\bar{a} \cdot \nabla) \bar{b}$

4. $\bar{a} \times (\nabla f)$

5. $(\bar{a} \times \nabla) f$

6. $(\bar{a} \times \nabla) \times \bar{b}$

Compare the results of parts 1 and 2, and 4 and 5.

327

Solution: 1. $\bar{a} \cdot (\nabla f) = (3x^2y,\ 2x,\ yz) \cdot \left(\dfrac{\partial f}{\partial x},\ \dfrac{\partial f}{\partial y},\ \dfrac{\partial f}{\partial z} \right)$ (4)

The gradient of the function f is given by

$$\nabla f = \left(\dfrac{\partial f}{\partial x},\ \dfrac{\partial f}{\partial y},\ \dfrac{\partial f}{\partial z} \right) = (2x,\ z,\ y)$$ (5)

Substituting eq.(5) into eq.(4),

$$\bar{a} \cdot (\nabla f) = (3x^2y,\ 2x,\ yz) \cdot (2x,\ z,\ y)$$ (6)

$$= 6x^3y + 2xz + y^2z$$

2. $(\bar{a} \cdot \nabla)f = \left[(3x^2y,\ 2x,\ yz) \cdot \left(\dfrac{\partial}{\partial x},\ \dfrac{\partial}{\partial y},\ \dfrac{\partial}{\partial z} \right) \right] (x^2 + yz)$

$$= \left(3x^2y\ \dfrac{\partial}{\partial x} + 2x\ \dfrac{\partial}{\partial y} + yz\ \dfrac{\partial}{\partial z} \right) (x^2 + yz)$$

$$= \left(3x^2y\ \dfrac{\partial}{\partial x}\ (x^2+yz) + 2x\ \dfrac{\partial}{\partial y}\ (x^2+yz) + yz\ \dfrac{\partial}{\partial z}\ (x^2+yz) \right)$$ (7)

$$= 3x^2y\ 2x + 2xz + yzy = 6x^3y + 2xz + y^2z$$

Since the results of 1 and 2 are equal, presume there exists an identity such that

$$\bar{a} \cdot (\nabla f) = (\bar{a} \cdot \nabla)f$$ (8)

To prove this, find $\bar{a} \cdot (\nabla f)$.

$$\bar{a} \cdot (\nabla f) = (a_1,\ a_2,\ a_3) \cdot \left(\dfrac{\partial f}{\partial x},\ \dfrac{\partial f}{\partial y},\ \dfrac{\partial f}{\partial z} \right)$$

$$= a_1\ \dfrac{\partial f}{\partial x} + a_2\ \dfrac{\partial f}{\partial y} + a_3\ \dfrac{\partial f}{\partial z} = \left(a_1\ \dfrac{\partial}{\partial x} + a_2\ \dfrac{\partial}{\partial y} + a_3\ \dfrac{\partial}{\partial z} \right) f$$

    (9)

$$= (a_1,\ a_2,\ a_3) \cdot \left(\dfrac{\partial}{\partial x},\ \dfrac{\partial}{\partial y},\ \dfrac{\partial}{\partial z} \right) f = (\bar{a} \cdot \nabla)f$$

Thus,

$$\bar{a} \cdot (\nabla f) = (\bar{a} \cdot \nabla)f$$ (10)

3. $(\bar{a} \cdot \nabla)\bar{b} = \left[(a_1,\ a_2,\ a_3) \cdot \left(\dfrac{\partial}{\partial x},\ \dfrac{\partial}{\partial y},\ \dfrac{\partial}{\partial z} \right) \right] (b_1,\ b_2,\ b_3)$

$$= \left[(3x^2y,\ 2x,\ yz) \cdot \left(\dfrac{\partial}{\partial x},\ \dfrac{\partial}{\partial y},\ \dfrac{\partial}{\partial z} \right) \right] (yz^2,\ xy,\ z^2)$$

    (11)

$$= \left(3x^2y\ \dfrac{\partial}{\partial x} + 2x\ \dfrac{\partial}{\partial y} + yz\ \dfrac{\partial}{\partial z} \right) (yz^2,\ xy,\ z^2)$$

Now denote by Λ the operator

$$3x^2y\ \dfrac{\partial}{\partial x} + 2x\ \dfrac{\partial}{\partial y} + yz\ \dfrac{\partial}{\partial z} \equiv \Lambda$$ (12)

Eq.(11) can be written in the form

$$(\bar{a} \cdot \nabla)\bar{b} = \Lambda(yz^2, \ xy, \ z^2) \qquad (13)$$

$$= (\Lambda yz^2, \ \Lambda xy, \ \Lambda z^2)$$

The operator Λ acts on each component, therefore

$$\Lambda \ yz^2 = \left(3x^2y \ \frac{\partial}{\partial x} + 2x \ \frac{\partial}{\partial y} + yz \ \frac{\partial}{\partial z}\right)yz^2$$

$$= \left(3x^2y \ \frac{\partial}{\partial x}(yz^2) + 2x \ \frac{\partial}{\partial y}(yz^2) + yz \ \frac{\partial}{\partial z}(yz^2)\right) \qquad (14)$$

$$= 2xz^2 + yz\left(2yz\right) = 2xz^2 + 2y^2z^2$$

$$\Lambda \ xy = \left(3x^2y \ \frac{\partial}{\partial x} + 2x \ \frac{\partial}{\partial y} + yz \ \frac{\partial}{\partial z}\right) xy = 3x^2y^2 + 2x^2 \qquad (15)$$

$$\Lambda \ z^2 = 2yz^2 \qquad (16)$$

Substituting eqs.(14), (15) and (16) into eq.(13), obtain

$$(\bar{a} \cdot \nabla)\bar{b} = (2xz^2 + 2y^2z^2, \ 3x^2y^2 + 2x^2, \ 2yz^2) \qquad (17)$$

4. $\quad \bar{a} \times (\nabla f) = (3x^2y, \ 2x, \ yz) \times (2x, \ z, \ y)$

$$= (2xy-yz^2, \ 2xyz-3x^2y^2, \ 3x^2yz-4x^2) \qquad (18)$$

5. $\quad (\bar{a} \times \nabla)f = \left[(3x^2y, \ 2x, \ yz) \times \left(\frac{\partial}{\partial x}, \ \frac{\partial}{\partial y}, \ \frac{\partial}{\partial z}\right)\right] (x^2 + yz)$

$$= \left(2x \ \frac{\partial}{\partial z} - yz \ \frac{\partial}{\partial y}, \ yz \ \frac{\partial}{\partial x} - 3x^2y \ \frac{\partial}{\partial z}, \ 3x^2y \ \frac{\partial}{\partial y} - 2x \ \frac{\partial}{\partial x}\right)(x^2+yz)$$

$$\qquad (19)$$

$$= (2xy - yz^2, \ 2xyz - 3x^2y^2, \ 3x^2yz - 4x^2)$$

Once again, since the results of 4 and 5 are equal, presume there exists an identity such that

$$\bar{a} \times (\nabla f) = (\bar{a} \times \nabla)f \qquad (20)$$

Proving this,

$$\bar{a} \times (\nabla f) = (a_1, \ a_2, \ a_3) \times \left(\frac{\partial f}{\partial x}, \ \frac{\partial f}{\partial y}, \ \frac{\partial f}{\partial z}\right)$$

$$= \left(a_2 \ \frac{\partial f}{\partial z} - a_3 \ \frac{\partial f}{\partial y}, \ a_3 \ \frac{\partial f}{\partial x} - a_1 \ \frac{\partial f}{\partial z}, \ a_1 \ \frac{\partial f}{\partial y} - a_2 \ \frac{\partial f}{\partial x}\right)$$

$$= \left(a_2 \ \frac{\partial}{\partial z} - a_3 \ \frac{\partial}{\partial y}, \ a_3 \ \frac{\partial}{\partial x} - a_1 \ \frac{\partial}{\partial z}, \ a_1 \ \frac{\partial}{\partial y} - a_2 \ \frac{\partial}{\partial x}\right)f \qquad (21)$$

$$= \left[(a_1, \ a_2, \ a_3) \times \left(\frac{\partial}{\partial x}, \ \frac{\partial}{\partial y}, \ \frac{\partial}{\partial z}\right)\right]f = (\bar{a} \times \nabla)f$$

6. $\quad (\bar{a} \times \nabla) \times \bar{b}$

$$= \left[(3x^2y, \ 2x, \ yz) \times \left(\frac{\partial}{\partial x}, \ \frac{\partial}{\partial y}, \ \frac{\partial}{\partial z}\right)\right] \times (yz^2, \ xy, \ z^2)$$

$$= \left(2x \frac{\partial}{\partial z} - yz \frac{\partial}{\partial y}, \; yz \frac{\partial}{\partial x} - 3x^2 y \frac{\partial}{\partial z}, \right.$$

$$\left. 3x^2 y \frac{\partial}{\partial y} - 2x \frac{\partial}{\partial x} \right) \times (yz^2, \; xy, \; z^2) \qquad (22)$$

$$= (-6x^2 yz - 3x^3 y + 2xy, \; 3x^2 yz^2 - 4xz, \; -xyz + 6x^2 y^2 z)$$

● **PROBLEM** 8-16

If $\quad \bar{a} = (x^2, \; xy, \; e^x + z)$ $\qquad\qquad$ (1)

$\quad \bar{b} = (y, \; 2x, \; xyz)$ $\qquad\qquad$ (2)

and $\quad f = y^2 + \sin x,$ $\qquad\qquad$ (3)

find

1. $\bar{a} \cdot \text{grad } f$

2. $(\text{rot } \bar{a}) \times (\text{grad } f)$

3. $(\text{div } \bar{a}) \bar{b}$

4. $\text{rot grad } f$

Solution: 1. The gradient of the function f given by eq.(3) is

$$\text{grad } f = \left[\frac{\partial}{\partial x}(y^2 + \sin x), \; \frac{\partial}{\partial y}(y^2 + \sin x), \; \frac{\partial}{\partial z}(y^2 + \sin x) \right]$$

$$= (\cos x, \; 2y, \; 0) \qquad (4)$$

Substituting eq.(1) and eq.(4) into the expression $\bar{a} \cdot \text{grad } f$, obtain

$$\bar{a} \cdot \text{grad } f = (x^2, \; xy, \; e^x + z) \cdot (\cos x, \; 2y, \; 0)$$

$$= x^2 \cos x + 2xy^2 \qquad (5)$$

2. For rot $\bar{a}$, obtain

$$\text{rot } \bar{a} = \left(\frac{\partial}{\partial x}, \; \frac{\partial}{\partial y}, \; \frac{\partial}{\partial z} \right) \times (x^2, \; xy, \; e^x + z)$$

$$= \left[\frac{\partial}{\partial y}(e^x + z) - \frac{\partial}{\partial z}(xy), \; \frac{\partial}{\partial z}(x^2) - \frac{\partial}{\partial x}(e^x + z), \; \frac{\partial}{\partial x}(xy) - \frac{\partial}{\partial y}(x^2) \right]$$

$$= (0, \; -e^x, \; y) \qquad (6)$$

Substituting eq.(6) and eq.(4) into the expression $(\text{rot } \bar{a}) \times (\text{grad } f)$, we obtain

$$(\text{rot } \bar{a}) \times (\text{grad } f) = (0, \; -e^x, \; y) \times (\cos x, \; 2y, \; 0)$$

$$= (-2y^2, \; y \cos x, \; e^x \cos x) \qquad (7)$$

3. The divergence of $\bar{a}$ is

$$\text{div } \bar{a} = \left(\frac{\partial}{\partial x}, \frac{\partial}{\partial y}, \frac{\partial}{\partial z} \right) \cdot (x^2, \ xy, \ e^x + z)$$

$$= 2x + x + 1 = 3x + 1 \tag{8}$$

Thus

$$(\text{div } \bar{a})\bar{b} = (3x + 1)(y, \ 2x, \ xyz) \tag{9}$$

$$= (3xy + y, \ 6x^2 + 2x, \ 3x^2yz + xyz)$$

4. There is an identity which states that if f is a differentiable scalar function with continuous second partial
derivatives, then

$$\text{rot grad } f = \bar{0} \quad \text{(see Problem 8-8)}$$

To verify that f, given by eq.(3) has continuous second
partial derivatives, obtain

$$\frac{\partial^2 f}{\partial x^2} = -\sin x \qquad \frac{\partial^2 f}{\partial y^2} = 2 \qquad \frac{\partial^2 f}{\partial y \partial x} = 0 \qquad \frac{\partial^2 f}{\partial x \partial y} = 0$$

Thus

$$\text{rot grad } (y^2 + \sin x) = \bar{0}$$

● **PROBLEM 8-17**

Evaluate $\text{rot} \left[\bar{r} \ f(r) \right]$, where $f = f(r)$ is a differentiable scalar function.

Solution: Applying the definition of the rotation, we
obtain

$$\text{rot} \left[\bar{r} \ f(r) \right] = \left(\frac{\partial}{\partial x}, \frac{\partial}{\partial y}, \frac{\partial}{\partial z} \right) \times (xf(r), \ yf(r), \ zf(r)) \tag{1}$$

$$= \left[\frac{\partial}{\partial y}(zf(r)) - \frac{\partial}{\partial z}(yf(r)), \ \frac{\partial}{\partial z}(xf(r)) - \frac{\partial}{\partial x}(zf(r)), \right.$$

$$\left. \frac{\partial}{\partial x}(yf(r)) - \frac{\partial}{\partial y}(xf(r)) \right]$$

$$= \left[z \frac{\partial f}{\partial y} - y \frac{\partial f}{\partial z}, \ x \frac{\partial f}{\partial z} - z \frac{\partial f}{\partial x}, \ y \frac{\partial f}{\partial x} - x \frac{\partial f}{\partial y} \right]$$

The partial derivatives of f are evaluated as follows

$$\frac{\partial f}{\partial x} = \frac{\partial}{\partial x} f(r) = \frac{df}{dr} \frac{\partial r}{\partial x} = \frac{df}{dr} \frac{\partial}{\partial x} \sqrt{x^2 + y^2 + z^2}$$

$$= \frac{df}{dr} \frac{x}{\sqrt{x^2 + y^2 + z^2}} = \frac{df}{dr} \frac{x}{r} \tag{2}$$

Similarly,

$$\frac{\partial f}{\partial y} = \frac{df}{dr} \frac{y}{r} \tag{3}$$

331

$$\frac{\partial f}{\partial z} = \frac{df}{dr}\,\frac{z}{r} \qquad\qquad\qquad (4)$$

Substituting eqs.(2), (3) and (4) into eq.(1), obtain

$$\text{rot}\left[\,\overline{r}\ f(r)\,\right] = z\,\frac{df}{dr}\,\frac{y}{r} - y\,\frac{df}{dr}\,\frac{z}{r}, \quad x\,\frac{df}{dr}\,\frac{z}{r} - z\,\frac{df}{dr}\,\frac{x}{r},$$

$$y\,\frac{df}{dr}\,\frac{x}{r} - x\,\frac{df}{dr}\,\frac{y}{r}\,\right]$$

$$\qquad\qquad\qquad\qquad (5)$$

$$= (0,\ 0,\ 0) = \overline{0}$$

COMPLEX IDENTITIES INVOLVING CURL, DIVERGENCE AND GRADIENT OPERATORS

● **PROBLEM** 8-18

Show that for any two vectors $\overline{a}$ and $\overline{b}$ the following identity is true

$$\text{div}\ (\overline{a} \times \overline{b}) = \overline{b}\cdot\text{curl}\ \overline{a} - \overline{a}\cdot\text{curl}\ \overline{b} \qquad (1)$$

Solution: Using the basic definitions of the divergence and curl, transform the right-hand side of equation (1).

$\overline{b}\cdot\text{curl}\ \overline{a} - \overline{a}\cdot\text{curl}\ \overline{b}$

$= \overline{b}\cdot(\nabla\times\overline{a}) - \overline{a}\cdot(\nabla\times\overline{b})$

$= (b_1,\ b_2,\ b_3)\cdot\left[\left(\dfrac{\partial}{\partial x},\ \dfrac{\partial}{\partial y},\ \dfrac{\partial}{\partial z}\right)\times(a_1,\ a_2,\ a_3)\right]$

$\qquad - (a_1,\ a_2,\ a_3)\cdot\left[\left(\dfrac{\partial}{\partial x},\ \dfrac{\partial}{\partial y},\ \dfrac{\partial}{\partial z}\right)\times(b_1,\ b_2,\ b_3)\right]$

$= (b_1,\ b_2,\ b_3)\cdot\left(\dfrac{\partial a_3}{\partial y} - \dfrac{\partial a_2}{\partial z},\ \dfrac{\partial a_1}{\partial z} - \dfrac{\partial a_3}{\partial x},\ \dfrac{\partial a_2}{\partial x} - \dfrac{\partial a_1}{\partial y}\right)$

$\qquad - (a_1,\ a_2,\ a_3)\cdot\left(\dfrac{\partial b_3}{\partial y} - \dfrac{\partial b_2}{\partial z},\ \dfrac{\partial b_1}{\partial z} - \dfrac{\partial b_3}{\partial x},\ \dfrac{\partial b_2}{\partial x} - \dfrac{\partial b_1}{\partial y}\right)$

$= b_1\left(\dfrac{\partial a_3}{\partial y} - \dfrac{\partial a_2}{\partial z}\right) + b_2\left(\dfrac{\partial a_1}{\partial z} - \dfrac{\partial a_3}{\partial x}\right) + b_3\left(\dfrac{\partial a_2}{\partial x} - \dfrac{\partial a_1}{\partial y}\right)$

$\qquad - a_1\left(\dfrac{\partial b_3}{\partial y} - \dfrac{\partial b_2}{\partial z}\right) - a_2\left(\dfrac{\partial b_1}{\partial z} - \dfrac{\partial b_3}{\partial x}\right) - a_3\left(\dfrac{\partial b_2}{\partial x} - \dfrac{\partial b_1}{\partial y}\right)$

$= b_3\dfrac{\partial a_2}{\partial x} + a_2\dfrac{\partial b_3}{\partial x} - b_2\dfrac{\partial a_3}{\partial x} - a_3\dfrac{\partial b_2}{\partial x}$

$\qquad + b_1\dfrac{\partial a_3}{\partial y} + a_3\dfrac{\partial b_1}{\partial y} - b_3\dfrac{\partial a_1}{\partial y} - a_1\dfrac{\partial b_3}{\partial y}$

$\qquad + b_2\dfrac{\partial a_1}{\partial z} + a_1\dfrac{\partial b_2}{\partial z} - b_1\dfrac{\partial a_2}{\partial z} - a_2\dfrac{\partial b_1}{\partial z} \qquad (2)$

$$= \frac{\partial}{\partial x} \left[a_2 b_3 - b_2 a_3 \right] + \frac{\partial}{\partial y} \left[a_3 b_1 - a_1 b_3 \right] + \frac{\partial}{\partial z} \left[a_1 b_2 - a_2 b_1 \right]$$

$$= \text{div} \ (a_2 b_3 - b_2 a_3, \ a_3 b_1 - a_1 b_3, \ a_1 b_2 - a_2 b_1)$$

$$= \text{div} \ (\bar{a} \times \bar{b})$$

which proves eq.(1).

● **PROBLEM** 8-19

Show that in general

$$\bar{a} \times (\nabla \times \bar{b}) \neq (\bar{a} \times \nabla) \times \bar{b} \qquad (1)$$

where $\bar{a}$ and $\bar{b}$ are two vectors.

Solution: Though an example cannot prove a theorem, or an identity, an example can disprove an identity or theorem.

Therefore, in order to show that

$$\bar{a} \times (\nabla \times \bar{b}) \neq (\bar{a} \times \nabla) \times \bar{b}$$

one must disprove the identity

$$\bar{a} \times (\nabla \times \bar{b}) = (\bar{a} \times \nabla) \times \bar{b} \qquad (2)$$

To do this, form an example by arbitrarily choosing a vector $\bar{a}$ and a vector $\bar{b}$. Take for instance,

$$\bar{a} = (xy, \ xz, \ 0)$$
$$\bar{b} = (y, \ -x, \ z) \qquad (3)$$

The left-hand side of eq.(2) is then equal to

$$\bar{a} \times (\nabla \times \bar{b}) = (xy, \ xz, \ 0) \times \left[\left(\frac{\partial}{\partial x}, \ \frac{\partial}{\partial y}, \ \frac{\partial}{\partial z} \right) \times (y, \ -x, \ z) \right] \qquad (4)$$

$$= (xy, \ xz, \ 0) \times (0, \ 0, \ -2) = (-2xz, \ 2xy, \ 0)$$

For the right-hand side of eq.(1),

$$(\bar{a} \times \nabla) \times \bar{b} = \left[(xy, \ xz, \ 0) \times \left(\frac{\partial}{\partial x}, \ \frac{\partial}{\partial y}, \ \frac{\partial}{\partial z} \right) \right] \times (y, \ -x, \ z) \qquad (5)$$

$$= \left(xz \ \frac{\partial}{\partial z}, \ -xy \ \frac{\partial}{\partial z}, \ xy \ \frac{\partial}{\partial y} - xz \ \frac{\partial}{\partial x} \right) \times (y, \ -x, \ z)$$

$$= (-xy - xz, \ xy - xz, \ 0)$$

Thus the identity is false and therefore

$$\bar{a} \times (\nabla \times \bar{b}) \neq (\bar{a} \times \nabla) \times \bar{b}$$

333

Prove the identity

$$\text{curl curl } \bar{a} = \text{grad div } \bar{a} - \nabla^2 \bar{a} \tag{1}$$

where

$$\nabla^2 \bar{a} = \left(\frac{\partial^2}{\partial x^2} + \frac{\partial^2}{\partial y^2} + \frac{\partial^2}{\partial z^2} \right) (a_1 \bar{i} + a_2 \bar{j} + a_3 \bar{k}) \tag{2}$$

<u>Solution</u>: Start with

$$\text{curl curl } \bar{a} \equiv \nabla \times (\nabla \times \bar{a}) \tag{3}$$

Then express $\nabla \times \bar{a}$ in terms of the base vectors

$$\nabla \times \bar{a} = \left(\frac{\partial a_3}{\partial y} - \frac{\partial a_2}{\partial z} \right) \bar{i} + \left(\frac{\partial a_1}{\partial z} - \frac{\partial a_3}{\partial x} \right) \bar{j} + \left(\frac{\partial a_2}{\partial x} - \frac{\partial a_1}{\partial y} \right) \bar{k} \tag{4}$$

Substituting eq.(4) into expression (3) obtain

$$\nabla \times (\nabla \times \bar{a}) =$$

$$\left[\frac{\partial}{\partial x} \bar{i} + \frac{\partial}{\partial y} \bar{j} + \frac{\partial}{\partial z} \bar{k} \right] \times \left[\left(\frac{\partial a_3}{\partial y} - \frac{\partial a_2}{\partial z} \right) \bar{i} + \left(\frac{\partial a_1}{\partial z} - \frac{\partial a_3}{\partial x} \right) \bar{j} + \left(\frac{\partial a_2}{\partial x} - \frac{\partial a_1}{\partial y} \right) \bar{k} \right]$$

$$= \left[\frac{\partial}{\partial y} \left(\frac{\partial a_2}{\partial x} - \frac{\partial a_1}{\partial y} \right) - \frac{\partial}{\partial z} \left(\frac{\partial a_1}{\partial z} - \frac{\partial a_3}{\partial x} \right) \right] \bar{i}$$

$$+ \left[\frac{\partial}{\partial z} \left(\frac{\partial a_3}{\partial y} - \frac{\partial a_2}{\partial z} \right) - \frac{\partial}{\partial x} \left(\frac{\partial a_2}{\partial x} - \frac{\partial a_1}{\partial y} \right) \right] \bar{j}$$

$$+ \left[\frac{\partial}{\partial x} \left(\frac{\partial a_1}{\partial z} - \frac{\partial a_3}{\partial x} \right) - \frac{\partial}{\partial y} \left(\frac{\partial a_3}{\partial y} - \frac{\partial a_2}{\partial z} \right) \right] \bar{k} \tag{5}$$

$$= \left(-\frac{\partial^2 a_1}{\partial y^2} - \frac{\partial^2 a_1}{\partial z^2} \right) \bar{i} + \left(-\frac{\partial^2 a_2}{\partial z^2} - \frac{\partial^2 a_2}{\partial x^2} \right) \bar{j} + \left(-\frac{\partial^2 a_3}{\partial x^2} - \frac{\partial^2 a_3}{\partial y^2} \right) \bar{k}$$

$$+ \left(\frac{\partial^2 a_2}{\partial y \partial x} + \frac{\partial^2 a_3}{\partial z \partial x} \right) \bar{i} + \left(\frac{\partial^2 a_3}{\partial z \partial y} + \frac{\partial^2 a_1}{\partial x \partial y} \right) \bar{j} + \left(\frac{\partial^2 a_1}{\partial x \partial z} + \frac{\partial^2 a_2}{\partial y \partial z} \right) \bar{k}$$

$$= \left(-\frac{\partial^2 a_1}{\partial x^2} - \frac{\partial^2 a_1}{\partial y^2} - \frac{\partial^2 a_1}{\partial z^2} \right) \bar{i} + \left(-\frac{\partial^2 a_2}{\partial x^2} - \frac{\partial^2 a_2}{\partial y^2} - \frac{\partial^2 a_2}{\partial z^2} \right) \bar{j}$$

$$+ \left(-\frac{\partial^2 a_3}{\partial x^2} - \frac{\partial^2 a_3}{\partial y^2} - \frac{\partial^2 a_3}{\partial z^2} \right) \bar{k} + \left(\frac{\partial^2 a_1}{\partial x^2} + \frac{\partial^2 a_2}{\partial y \partial x} + \frac{\partial^2 a_3}{\partial z \partial x} \right) \bar{i}$$

$$+ \left(\frac{\partial^2 a_1}{\partial x \partial y} + \frac{\partial^2 a_2}{\partial y^2} + \frac{\partial^2 a_3}{\partial y \partial z} \right) \bar{j} + \left(\frac{\partial^2 a_1}{\partial x \partial z} + \frac{\partial^2 a_2}{\partial y \partial} + \frac{\partial^2 a_3}{\partial z^2} \right) \bar{k}$$

$$= - \left(\frac{\partial^2}{\partial x^2} + \frac{\partial^2}{\partial y^2} + \frac{\partial^2}{\partial z^2} \right) (a_1 \bar{i} + a_2 \bar{j} + a_3 \bar{k})$$

$$+ \bar{i} \frac{\partial}{\partial x} \left(\frac{\partial a_1}{\partial x} + \frac{\partial a_2}{\partial y} + \frac{\partial a_3}{\partial z} \right) + \bar{j} \frac{\partial}{\partial y} \left(\frac{\partial a_1}{\partial x} + \frac{\partial a_2}{\partial y} + \frac{\partial a}{\partial z} \right)$$

$$+ \bar{k} \frac{\partial}{\partial z} \left(\frac{\partial a_1}{\partial x} + \frac{\partial a_2}{\partial y} + \frac{\partial a_3}{\partial z} \right)$$

$$= -\nabla^2 \overline{a} + \nabla(\nabla \cdot \overline{a})$$

Thus,

$$\nabla \times (\nabla \times \overline{a}) = -\nabla^2 \overline{a} + \nabla(\nabla \cdot \overline{a}) \qquad (6)$$

or

$$\text{curl curl } \overline{a} = \text{grad div } \overline{a} - \nabla^2 \overline{a}$$

● PROBLEM 8-21

Prove the following identities:

1. $\text{div}\left[\overline{a} \times (\overline{b} \times \overline{c})\right] = (\overline{a} \cdot \overline{c})\text{div } \overline{b} - (\overline{a} \cdot \overline{b})\text{div } \overline{c}$

$$+ \text{grad}(\overline{a} \cdot \overline{c}) \cdot \overline{b} - \text{grad}(\overline{a} \cdot \overline{b}) \cdot \overline{c} \qquad (1)$$

2. $\nabla^2 f = \text{div}(\text{curl } \overline{a} + \text{grad } f) \qquad (2)$

<u>Solution</u>: 1. Any identity involving the operators curl, div, grad can be proved applying the definition of the operators and the basic arithmetic tranformations.

Very often, the calculations become highly cumbersome, causing the student to make mistakes during the proof. At certain times however, it is possible to simplify lengthy identities by using other identities. Such is the case with eq.(1). Eq.(1) could be proved by performing the necessary lengthy calculations. The shorter method however, is to use the identity

$$\overline{a} \times (\overline{b} \times \overline{c}) = (\overline{a} \cdot \overline{c})\overline{b} - (\overline{a} \cdot \overline{b})\overline{c} \qquad (3)$$

Substituting eq.(3) into the left-hand side of eq.(1),

$$\text{div}\left[\overline{a} \times (\overline{b} \times \overline{c})\right] = \text{div}\left[(\overline{a} \cdot \overline{c})\overline{b} - (\overline{a} \cdot \overline{b})\overline{c}\right] \qquad (4)$$

since

$$\text{div}(\overline{u} + \overline{v}) = \text{div } \overline{u} + \text{div } \overline{v} \qquad (5)$$

Then,

$$\text{div}\left[(\overline{a} \cdot \overline{c})\overline{b} - (\overline{a} \cdot \overline{b})\overline{c}\right] = \text{div}\left[(\overline{a} \cdot \overline{c})\overline{b}\right] - \text{div}\left[(\overline{a} \cdot \overline{b})\overline{c}\right] \qquad (6)$$

Furthermore, since

$$\text{div}(\phi \overline{a}) = \phi \text{div } \overline{a} + \overline{a} \cdot \text{grad } \phi \qquad (7)$$

Applying eq.(7) to eq.(6),

$$\text{div}\left[(\overline{a} \cdot \overline{c})\overline{b}\right] - \text{div}\left[(\overline{a} \cdot \overline{b})\overline{c}\right]$$

$$= (\overline{a} \cdot \overline{c})\text{div } \overline{b} + \overline{b} \cdot \text{grad}(\overline{a} \cdot \overline{c}) - (\overline{a} \cdot \overline{b})\text{div } \overline{c} - \overline{c} \cdot \text{grad}(\overline{a} \cdot \overline{b}) \qquad (8)$$

That proves identity (1), since

$$\overline{a} \cdot \overline{b} = \overline{b} \cdot \overline{a} \qquad (9)$$

2. Consider the right-hand side of eq.(2),

$$\text{div}(\text{curl } \bar{a} + \text{grad } f) = \text{div curl } \bar{a} + \text{div grad } f \qquad (10)$$

From Problem 8-8, if $\bar{a}$ is any differentiable vector, then

$$\text{div curl } \bar{a} = 0 \qquad (11)$$

Thus eq.(10) reduces to

$$\text{div}(\text{curl } \bar{a} + \text{grad } f) = \text{div grad } f =$$

$$\nabla \cdot (\nabla f) = \left(\frac{\partial}{\partial x}, \frac{\partial}{\partial y}, \frac{\partial}{\partial z} \right) \cdot \left(\frac{\partial}{\partial x}, \frac{\partial}{\partial y}, \frac{\partial}{\partial z} \right) f$$

$$= \left(\frac{\partial^2}{\partial x^2} + \frac{\partial^2}{\partial y^2} + \frac{\partial^2}{\partial z^2} \right) f = \nabla^2 f \qquad (12)$$

● **PROBLEM 8-22**

Prove the following identities

1. $\text{div}(\text{grad } f \times f \text{ grad } g) = 0$ (1)

2. $\text{curl}(\text{curl } \bar{v} + \text{grad } f) = \text{curl curl } \bar{v}$ (2)

<u>Solution</u>: 1. The left-hand side of eq.(1) is the divergence of a vector product. Thus, the following identity can be used

$$\text{div}(\bar{a} \times \bar{b}) = \bar{b} \cdot \text{curl } \bar{a} - \bar{a} \cdot \text{curl } \bar{b} \qquad (3)$$

(see Problem 8-18). The left-hand side of eq.(1) can be transformed as follows

$$\text{div}(\text{grad } f \times f \text{ grad } g) = \qquad (4)$$

$$(f \text{ grad } g) \cdot \text{curl grad } f - \text{grad } f \cdot \text{curl}(f \text{ grad } g)$$

$$= -\text{grad } f \cdot \text{curl}(f \text{ grad } g)$$

Note that

$$\text{curl grad } f = \bar{0} \qquad (5)$$

Using the identity

$$\text{curl}(f\bar{a}) = f \text{ curl } \bar{a} + \text{grad } f \times \bar{a} \qquad (6)$$

from Problem 8-3, obtain

$$\text{div}(\text{grad } f \times f \text{ grad } g) = -\text{grad } f \cdot \text{curl}(f \text{ grad } g)$$

$$= -\text{grad } f \cdot \left[f \text{ curl grad } g + \text{grad } f \times \text{grad } g \right] \qquad (7)$$

$$= -\text{grad } f \cdot \text{grad } f \times \text{grad } g$$

Using the identity

336

$$\overline{a} \cdot \overline{a} \times \overline{b} = \overline{0} \qquad (8)$$

eq.(7) becomes identically zero.   Therefore

div(grad f × f grad g) = -grad f·grad f × grad g = 0

2.   Since

$$\text{curl}(\overline{a} + \overline{b}) = \text{curl } \overline{a} + \text{curl } \overline{b} \qquad (9)$$

transform the left-hand side of eq.(2),

$$\text{curl}(\text{curl } \overline{v} + \text{grad } f) = \text{curl curl } \overline{v} + \text{curl grad } f$$
$$= \text{curl curl } \overline{v} \qquad (10)$$

Note that

$$\text{curl grad } f = \overline{0} \qquad (11)$$

for any differentiable scalar field f.

Prove the identity

$$(\overline{a} \cdot \nabla)\overline{a} = \frac{1}{2} \nabla a^2 - \overline{a} \times (\nabla \times \overline{a}) \qquad (1)$$

Solution: The left-hand side of eq.(1) represents a vector, the right-hand side is also a vector. It is sufficient to perform the calculations for the first component and show that the first component of the vector on the left-hand side of the equation is equal to the first component of the vector on the right-hand side of the equation.   The other components can be obtained from symmetry.
The first component of the left-hand side vector is equal to

$$\left[(\overline{a} \cdot \nabla)\overline{a}\right]_1 = \left(a_1\frac{\partial}{\partial x} + a_2\frac{\partial}{\partial y} + a_3\frac{\partial}{\partial z}\right) a_1$$
$$= a_1\frac{\partial a_1}{\partial x} + a_2\frac{\partial a_1}{\partial y} + a_3\frac{\partial a_1}{\partial z} \qquad (2)$$

Here $\left[..\right]_1$ indicates the first component of the vector in the bracket.

For example

$$\left[\overline{b}\right]_2 = b_2; \quad \left[\overline{a} \times \overline{c}\right]_3 = a_1 c_2 - a_2 c_1 \qquad (3)$$

The first component of the vector on the right-hand side is equal to

$$\left[\frac{1}{2} \nabla a^2 - \overline{a} \times (\nabla \times \overline{a})\right]_1$$

$$= \frac{1}{2} \frac{\partial}{\partial x}(a^2) - \left[\overline{a} \times (\nabla \times \overline{a})\right]_1$$

$$= \frac{1}{2} \frac{\partial}{\partial x}(a_1^2 + a_2^2 + a_3^2) - \left(a_2 \left[\nabla \times \overline{a}\right]_3 - a_3 \left[\nabla \times \overline{a}\right]_2\right)$$

$$= \frac{1}{2} \frac{\partial}{\partial x}(a_1^2 + a_2^2 + a_3^2) - \left[a_2 \left(\frac{\partial a_2}{\partial x} - \frac{\partial a_1}{\partial y}\right) - a_3 \left(\frac{\partial a_1}{\partial z} - \frac{\partial a_3}{\partial x}\right)\right]$$

$$= a_1 \frac{\partial a_1}{\partial x} + a_2 \frac{\partial a_2}{\partial x} + a_3 \frac{\partial a_3}{\partial x} - a_2 \frac{\partial a_2}{\partial x} + a_2 \frac{\partial a_1}{\partial y} + a_3 \frac{\partial a_1}{\partial z} - a_3 \frac{\partial a_3}{\partial x}$$

$$= a_1 \frac{\partial a_1}{\partial x} + a_2 \frac{\partial a_1}{\partial y} + a_3 \frac{\partial a_1}{\partial z}$$

(4)

From eq.(2) and eq.(4), we conclude that the first components are equal.

It follows immediately that the second and the third components are also equal.

● **PROBLEM 8-24**

Prove the identity   (1)

$$\mathrm{grad}(\overline{a} \cdot \overline{b}) = (\overline{a} \cdot \nabla)\overline{b} + (\overline{b} \cdot \nabla)\overline{a} + (\overline{a} \times \mathrm{curl}\ \overline{b}) + (\overline{b} \times \mathrm{curl}\ \overline{a})$$

Solution: Since both sides of equation (1) are vectors, one can perform the calculations for the first component and then by symmetry obtain the equations for the other components. According to the notation used in Problem 8-23, we have

$$\left[\overline{a}\right]_1 = a_1, \quad \left[\overline{b}\right]_2 = b_2$$

The first component of the vector on the left-hand side of the equation is

$$\left[\mathrm{grad}(\overline{a} \cdot \overline{b})\right]_1 = \frac{\partial}{\partial x}(\overline{a} \cdot \overline{b})$$

(2)

$$= \frac{\partial}{\partial x}(a_1 b_1 + a_2 b_2 + a_3 b_3)$$

$$= a_1 \frac{\partial b_1}{\partial x} + b_1 \frac{\partial a_1}{\partial x} + a_2 \frac{\partial b_2}{\partial x} + b_2 \frac{\partial a_2}{\partial x} + a_3 \frac{\partial b_3}{\partial x} + b_3 \frac{\partial a_3}{\partial x}$$

The first component of the vector on the right-hand side of equation (1) is

$$\left[(\overline{a} \cdot \nabla)\overline{b} + (\overline{b} \cdot \nabla)\overline{a} + (\overline{a} \times \mathrm{curl}\ \overline{b}) + (\overline{b} \times \mathrm{curl}\ \overline{a})\right]_1$$

$$= (\overline{a} \cdot \nabla)b_1 + (\overline{b} \cdot \nabla)a_1 + a_2 \left[\mathrm{curl}\ \overline{b}\right]_3 - a_3 \left[\mathrm{curl}\ \overline{b}\right]_2$$

$$+ b_2 \left[\mathrm{curl}\ \overline{a}\right]_3 - b_3 \left[\mathrm{curl}\ \overline{a}\right]_2$$

$$= \left(a_1\frac{\partial}{\partial x} + a_2\frac{\partial}{\partial y} + a_3\frac{\partial}{\partial z}\right)b_1 + \left(b_1\frac{\partial}{\partial x} + b_2\frac{\partial}{\partial y} + b_3\frac{\partial}{\partial z}\right)a_1$$

$$+ a_2\left(\frac{\partial b_2}{\partial x} - \frac{\partial b_1}{\partial y}\right) - a_3\left(\frac{\partial b_1}{\partial z} - \frac{\partial b_3}{\partial x}\right) + b_2\left(\frac{\partial a_2}{\partial x} - \frac{\partial a_1}{\partial y}\right)$$

$$- b_3\left(\frac{\partial a_1}{\partial z} - \frac{\partial a_3}{\partial x}\right)$$

$$= a_1\frac{\partial b_1}{\partial x} + a_2\frac{\partial b_1}{\partial y} + a_3\frac{\partial b_1}{\partial z} + b_1\frac{\partial a_1}{\partial x} + b_2\frac{\partial a_1}{\partial y} + b_3\frac{\partial a_1}{\partial z}$$

$$+ a_2\frac{\partial b_2}{\partial x} - a_2\frac{\partial b_1}{\partial y} - a_3\frac{\partial b_1}{\partial z} + a_3\frac{\partial b_3}{\partial x} + b_2\frac{\partial a_2}{\partial x} - b_2\frac{\partial a_1}{\partial y}$$

$$- b_3\frac{\partial a_1}{\partial z} + b_3\frac{\partial a_3}{\partial x}$$

$$= a_1\frac{\partial b_1}{\partial x} + b_1\frac{\partial a_1}{\partial x} + a_2\frac{\partial b_2}{\partial x} + b_2\frac{\partial a_2}{\partial x} + a_3\frac{\partial b_3}{\partial x} + b_3\frac{\partial a_3}{\partial x}$$

Since eqs.(2) and (3) are equal, the first components of the vectors on the right-hand side of eq.(1) are equal to the first components of the vectors on the left-hand side of eq. (1). Through symmetry, it could be easily verified that the second and third components are also equal.

Note that the expression $\nabla \cdot \overline{a}$ is a scalar, since

$$\nabla \cdot \overline{a} = \left(\frac{\partial}{\partial x}, \frac{\partial}{\partial y}, \frac{\partial}{\partial z}\right) \cdot (a_1, a_2, a_3) = \frac{\partial a_1}{\partial x} + \frac{\partial a_2}{\partial y} + \frac{\partial a_3}{\partial z} \quad (4)$$

while $\overline{a} \cdot \nabla$ is an operator, since

$$\overline{a} \cdot \nabla = (a_1, a_2, a_3) \cdot \left(\frac{\partial}{\partial x}, \frac{\partial}{\partial y}, \frac{\partial}{\partial z}\right) = a_1\frac{\partial}{\partial x} + a_2\frac{\partial}{\partial y} + a_3\frac{\partial}{\partial z} \quad (5)$$

● **PROBLEM 8-25**

Prove the identity

$$\text{curl}(\overline{a} \times \overline{b}) = \overline{a}\ \text{div}\ \overline{b} - \overline{b}\ \text{div}\ \overline{a} + (\overline{b}\cdot\nabla)\overline{a} - (\overline{a}\cdot\nabla)\overline{b} \quad (1)$$

Solution: Here, again it will be proved that the first component of the vector on the left-hand side of eq.(1) is equal to the first component of the vector on the right-hand side. By symmetry, all the calculations can be rewritten for the second and third component. We have

$$\left[\text{curl}(\overline{a} \times \overline{b})\right]_1 = \frac{\partial}{\partial y}\left[\overline{a} \times \overline{b}\right]_3 - \frac{\partial}{\partial z}\left[\overline{a} \times \overline{b}\right]_2$$

$$\quad (2)$$

$$= \frac{\partial}{\partial y}(a_1 b_2 - a_2 b_1) - \frac{\partial}{\partial z}(a_3 b_1 - a_1 b_3)$$

The first component of the vector on the right-hand side of eq.(1) is equal to

$$\left[\bar{a}\ \text{div}\ \bar{b} - \bar{b}\ \text{div}\ \bar{a} + (\bar{b}\cdot\nabla)\bar{a} - (\bar{a}\cdot\nabla)\bar{b}\right]_1$$

$$= a_1\ \text{div}\ \bar{b} - b_1\ \text{div}\ \bar{a} + (\bar{b}\cdot\nabla)a_1 - (\bar{a}\cdot\nabla)b_1$$

$$= a_1\left(\frac{\partial b_1}{\partial x} + \frac{\partial b_2}{\partial y} + \frac{\partial b_3}{\partial z}\right) - b_1\left(\frac{\partial a_1}{\partial x} + \frac{\partial a_2}{\partial y} + \frac{\partial a_3}{\partial z}\right)$$

$$+ \left(b_1\frac{\partial}{\partial x} + b_2\frac{\partial}{\partial y} + b_3\frac{\partial}{\partial z}\right)a_1 - \left(a_1\frac{\partial}{\partial x} + a_2\frac{\partial}{\partial y} + a_3\frac{\partial}{\partial z}\right)b_1$$

$$= a_1\frac{\partial b_1}{\partial x} + a_1\frac{\partial b_2}{\partial y} + a_1\frac{\partial b_3}{\partial z} - b_1\frac{\partial a_1}{\partial x} - b_1\frac{\partial a_2}{\partial y} - b_1\frac{\partial a_3}{\partial z}$$

$$+ b_1\frac{\partial a_1}{\partial x} + b_2\frac{\partial a_1}{\partial y} + b_3\frac{\partial a_1}{\partial z} - a_1\frac{\partial b_1}{\partial x} - a_2\frac{\partial b_1}{\partial y} - a_3\frac{\partial b_1}{\partial z}$$

$$= a_1\frac{\partial b_2}{\partial y} + b_2\frac{\partial a_1}{\partial y} - a_2\frac{\partial b_1}{\partial y} - b_1\frac{\partial a_2}{\partial y} + a_1\frac{\partial b_3}{\partial z} + b_3\frac{\partial a_1}{\partial z}$$

$$- b_1\frac{\partial a_3}{\partial z} - a_3\frac{\partial b_1}{\partial z}$$

$$= \frac{\partial}{\partial y}(a_1 b_2) - \frac{\partial}{\partial y}(a_2 b_1) + \frac{\partial}{\partial z}(a_1 b_3) - \frac{\partial}{\partial z}(b_1 a_3)$$

$$= \frac{\partial}{\partial y}(a_1 b_2 - a_2 b_1) - \frac{\partial}{\partial z}(a_3 b_1 - a_1 b_3)$$

Thus, the first components are equal.

In the same manner, it can be shown that the second and third components are also equal.

● PROBLEM 8-26

Given two vectors $\bar{a}$ and $\bar{b}$ which are irrotational, prove that $\bar{a} \times \bar{b}$ is solenoidal.

Solution: A vector $\bar{d}$ is called solenoidal, if

$$\text{div}\ \bar{d} = 0 \tag{1}$$

To prove that $\bar{a} \times \bar{b}$ is solenoidal, it must be shown that

$$\text{div}\ \bar{a} \times \bar{b} = 0 \tag{2}$$

The divergence of a vector product has to be expressed in simpler terms in order to proceed. From Problem 8-18, obtain

$$\text{div}\ \bar{a} \times \bar{b} = \bar{b}\cdot\text{curl}\ \bar{a} - \bar{a}\cdot\text{curl}\ \bar{b} \tag{3}$$

Both vectors $\bar{a}$ and $\bar{b}$ are irrotational, therefore,

$$\text{curl}\ \bar{a} = \bar{0}$$

$$\text{curl}\ \bar{b} = \bar{0} \tag{4}$$

Substituting eq.(4) into eq.(3) we obtain

$$\text{div } \bar{a} \times \bar{b} = \bar{b} \cdot \bar{0} - \bar{a} \cdot \bar{0} = 0 \tag{5}$$

That proves that $\bar{a} \times \bar{b}$, where $\bar{a}$ and $\bar{b}$ are irrotational, is a solenoidal vector.

SCALAR POTENTIAL, OTHER DIFFERENTIAL OPERATORS AND DYADICS

● **PROBLEM** 8-27

Show that the vector $\bar{E} = \dfrac{\bar{r}}{r^2}$ is irrotational and find its scalar potential.

<u>Solution</u>: First, it must be shown that

$$\text{curl } \bar{E} = \bar{0} \tag{1}$$

From Problem 8-17, for any differentiable function $f(r)$,

$$\text{curl } \left[\bar{r} \; f(r) \right] = \bar{0} \tag{2}$$

In our case, $f(r) = \dfrac{1}{r^2}$ and

$$\text{curl } \bar{E} = \text{curl } \dfrac{\bar{r}}{r^2} = \bar{0} \tag{3}$$

Thus, $\bar{E}$ is irrotational.

The scalar potential of $\bar{E}$ is a scalar function f such that

$$\bar{E} = -\text{grad } f \tag{4}$$

Eq.(4) is equivalent to three partial differential equations

$$\frac{x}{x^2+y^2+z^2} = - \frac{\partial f}{\partial x} \tag{5}$$

$$\frac{y}{x^2+y^2+z^2} = - \frac{\partial f}{\partial y} \tag{6}$$

$$\frac{z}{x^2+y^2+z^2} = - \frac{\partial f}{\partial z} \tag{7}$$

Integrating eq.(5), obtain

$$f(x,y,z) = - \int \frac{x}{x^2+y^2+z^2} \, dx + g(y,z) \tag{8}$$

or

$$f(x,y,z) = \ln \frac{1}{\sqrt{x^2+y^2+z^2}} + \text{const} + g(y,z)$$

or equivalently, bringing the constant inside yields

$$f(x,y,z) = \ln \frac{\alpha}{\sqrt{x^2+y^2+z^2}} + g(y,z)$$

where α is some constant. (9)

Differentiate eq.(9) with respect to y

$$\frac{\partial f}{\partial y} = - \frac{y}{x^2+y^2+z^2} + \frac{\partial g}{\partial y} \qquad (10)$$

From eq.(10) and (6), obtain

$$\frac{\partial g}{\partial y} = 0 \qquad (11)$$

Thus $\qquad g = g(z)$ (12)

and eq.(9) becomes

$$f(x,y,z) = \ln \frac{\alpha}{\sqrt{x^2+y^2+z^2}} + g(z) \qquad (13)$$

Differentiating eq.(13) with respect to z, obtain

$$\frac{\partial f}{\partial z} = - \frac{z}{x^2+y^2+z^2} + \frac{dg}{dz} \qquad (14)$$

Comparing eqs.(7) and (14),

$$\frac{dg}{dz} = 0 \qquad (15)$$

Thus g = const. This constant g can be included in the constant α. Therefore

$$f(x,y,z) = \ln \frac{\alpha}{r} \qquad (16)$$

● **PROBLEM 8-28**

If $\bar{v}$ is a differentiable vector function, is the following relationship

$$\text{curl } \bar{v} = \bar{r} \qquad (1)$$

where $\bar{r} = (x,y,z)$, possible?

Solution: First assume that a function $\bar{v}$ such that curl $\bar{v} = \bar{r}$ does indeed exist. Eq.(1) is equivalent to three differential equations. Using the definition of the curl,

curl $\bar{v} = \nabla \times \bar{v}$

$$= \left(\frac{\partial v_z}{\partial y} - \frac{\partial v_y}{\partial z} \right)\bar{i} + \left(\frac{\partial v_x}{\partial z} - \frac{\partial v_z}{\partial x} \right)\bar{j} + \left(\frac{\partial v_y}{\partial x} - \frac{\partial v_x}{\partial y} \right)\bar{k} \qquad (2)$$

$$= \bar{r} = x\bar{i} + y\bar{j} + z\bar{k}$$

Comparing the components of the left-hand side and the right-hand side of eq.(2), obtain

$$\frac{\partial v_z}{\partial y} - \frac{\partial v_y}{\partial z} = x \tag{3}$$

$$\frac{\partial v_x}{\partial z} - \frac{\partial v_z}{\partial x} = y \tag{4}$$

$$\frac{\partial v_y}{\partial x} - \frac{\partial v_x}{\partial y} = z \tag{5}$$

Differentiating eq.(3) with respect to x, eq.(4) with respect to y and eq.(5) with respect to z, gives

$$\frac{\partial^2 v_z}{\partial x \partial y} - \frac{\partial^2 v_y}{\partial x \partial z} = 1 \tag{6}$$

$$\frac{\partial^2 v_x}{\partial y \partial z} - \frac{\partial^2 v_z}{\partial y \partial x} = 1 \tag{7}$$

$$\frac{\partial^2 v_y}{\partial z \partial x} - \frac{\partial^2 v_x}{\partial z \partial y} = 1 \tag{8}$$

Adding the left-hand and right-hand sides of eqs. (6), (7) and (8) yields

$$0 = 3 \tag{9}$$

Therefore our assumption that a vector function $\bar{v}$, such that curl $\bar{v} = \bar{r}$ exists, was wrong.

The same conclusion can be reached by using the identity

$$\text{div curl } \bar{v} = 0 \tag{10}$$

Taking div of both sides of eq.(1),

$$\text{div curl } \bar{v} = \text{div } \bar{r} \tag{11}$$

The left-hand side of eq.(11) is identical to eq.(10), which is equal to zero, while the right-hand side of eq.(11) is

$$\frac{\partial x}{\partial x} + \frac{\partial y}{\partial y} + \frac{\partial z}{\partial z} = 1 + 1 + 1 = 3$$

Therefore there is no vector $\bar{v}$ such that curl $\bar{v} = \bar{r}$.

● **PROBLEM** 8-29

Find a differentiable function $\bar{v}$ such that

$$\text{curl } \bar{v} = \bar{a} \tag{1}$$

where

$$\bar{a} = (\alpha, \beta, \gamma) \tag{2}$$

Solution: Assume that the components of $\bar{v}$ are linear polynomials. That is,

$$v_x = a_1 x + a_2 y + a_3 z \tag{3}$$

$$v_y = b_1 x + b_2 y + b_3 z \tag{4}$$

$$v_z = c_1 x + c_2 y + c_3 z \tag{5}$$

Eq.(1) can be written as a system of three equations.

$$\frac{\partial v_z}{\partial y} - \frac{\partial v_y}{\partial z} = \alpha \tag{6}$$

$$\frac{\partial v_x}{\partial z} - \frac{\partial v_z}{\partial x} = \beta \tag{7}$$

$$\frac{\partial v_y}{\partial x} - \frac{\partial v_x}{\partial y} = \gamma \tag{8}$$

Substituting eqs.(3), (4), (5) into eqs.(6), (7) and (8) yields

$$c_2 - b_3 = \alpha \tag{9}$$

$$a_3 - c_1 = \beta \tag{10}$$

$$b_1 - a_2 = \gamma \tag{11}$$

Eqs.(3), (4), (5) can be written in the form

$$v_x = a_1 x + a_2 y + a_3 z \tag{12}$$

$$v_y = (a_2 + \gamma)x + b_2 y + b_3 z \tag{13}$$

$$v_z = (a_3 - \beta)x + (\alpha + b_3)y + c_3 z \tag{14}$$

Here a_1, a_2, a_3, b_2, b_3, c_3 are any real numbers.

Note that since
$$\text{curl grad } f = \bar{0} \tag{15}$$

for any differentiable function f, one can add grad f to any solution $\bar{v}'$ of eq.(1).

That is, if curl $\bar{v}' = \bar{a}$ then

$$\text{curl}(\bar{v}' + \text{grad } f) = \bar{a} \tag{16}$$

Evaluate $\frac{\partial}{\partial n}$ (div $\bar{u}$)   at the point $(3,4,5)$ where

$$\bar{u} = x^2\bar{i} - 2y^2\bar{j} + z^2\bar{k}$$

and $\bar{n}$ is the unit outer normal vector to the sphere

$$x^2 + y^2 + z^2 = 4.$$

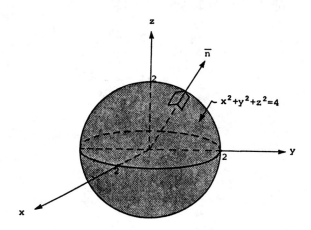

Solution: First compute div $\bar{u}$.

$$\text{div } \bar{u} = \left[\frac{\partial}{\partial x}\bar{i} + \frac{\partial}{\partial y}\bar{j} + \frac{\partial}{\partial z}\bar{k}\right] \cdot \left[x^2\bar{i} - 2y^2\bar{j} + z^2\bar{k}\right] =$$

$$= 2x - 4y + 2z \qquad (1)$$

Since   div $\bar{u}$ is a scalar function, let

$$f = \text{div } \bar{u} = 2x - 4y + 2z$$

The partial derivative of div $\bar{u}$, or f, with respect to the unit vector $\bar{n}$ is nothing more than the directional derivative of f in the $\bar{n}$ direction, therefore

$$\frac{\partial}{\partial n}(\text{div } \bar{u}) = \frac{\partial f}{\partial n} \equiv \nabla_n f = \nabla f \cdot \bar{n} \qquad (2)$$

Substituting eq.(1) into eq.(2), we obtain

$$\frac{\partial}{\partial n}(\text{div } \bar{u}) = \frac{\partial f}{\partial n} = \nabla(2x-4y+2z)\cdot\bar{n} = (2,-4,2)\cdot\bar{n} \qquad (3)$$

where $\bar{n}$ is a unit outer vector normal to the sphere

$$x^2 + y^2 + z^2 = 4.$$

Recall that if a surface is given by a function

$$\phi(x,y,z) = \text{const.},$$

then the gradient of ϕ, $\nabla\phi$, is an outer normal vector to the surface.

Therefore, for $\phi(x,y,z) = x^2+y^2+z^2 = 4 = $ const., we obtain

$$\nabla(x^2+y^2+z^2) = (2x, \ 2y, \ 2z) \tag{4}$$

Thus the unit outer normal vector is

$$\bar{n} = \frac{(2x, \ 2y, \ 2z)}{\sqrt{4x^2+4y^2+4z^2}} = \frac{(x, \ y, \ z)}{\sqrt{x^2+y^2+z^2}} \tag{5}$$

Substituting eq.(5) into eq.(3), obtain

$$\left.\frac{\partial}{\partial n} (\mathrm{div} \ \bar{u})\right|_{(3,4,5)} = \left.(2, \ -4, \ 2)\cdot\bar{n}\right|_{(3,4,5)}$$

$$= \left.\frac{(2,-4,2)\cdot(x,y,z)}{\sqrt{x^2+y^2+z^2}}\right|_{(3,4,5)} \tag{6}$$

$$= \left.\frac{2x - 4y + 2z}{\sqrt{x^2+y^2+z^2}}\right|_{(3 \ 4,5)}$$

$$= \frac{6 - 16 + 10}{\sqrt{9 + 16 + 25}} = 0$$

● **PROBLEM** 8-31

1. Show that if $\bar{n}$ is a unit vector, then

$$(\bar{n}\cdot\nabla)f = \nabla_n f. \tag{1}$$

2. Also, evaluate the following expression

$$\left[(x^2\bar{i}+2xy\bar{j}+e^z\bar{k})\cdot\nabla\right](x\bar{i} + 2y\bar{j} + z\bar{k}) \tag{2}$$

Solution: For any vector $\bar{v}$, the scalar product $\bar{v}\cdot\nabla$ is defined as the operator

$$\bar{v}\cdot\nabla = (v_x, \ v_y, \ v_z)\cdot\left(\frac{\partial}{\partial x}, \ \frac{\partial}{\partial y}, \ \frac{\partial}{\partial z}\right) \tag{3}$$

$$= v_x \frac{\partial}{\partial x} + v_y \frac{\partial}{\partial y} + v_z \frac{\partial}{\partial z}$$

Note that the scalar product involving ∇ is not commutative, that is $\nabla\cdot\bar{v} \neq \bar{v}\cdot\nabla$, indeed

$$\nabla\cdot\bar{v} = \frac{\partial v_x}{\partial x} + \frac{\partial v_y}{\partial y} + \frac{\partial v_z}{\partial z} \neq v_x \frac{\partial}{\partial x} + v_y \frac{\partial}{\partial y} + v_z \frac{\partial}{\partial z}$$

The above operator can be applied to a scalar function f:

$$(\overline{v} \cdot \nabla)f = v_x \frac{\partial f}{\partial x} + v_y \frac{\partial f}{\partial y} + v_z \frac{\partial f}{\partial z} \tag{4}$$

It can also be applied to a vector $\overline{a}$:

$$(\overline{v} \cdot \nabla)\overline{a} = v_x \frac{\partial \overline{a}}{\partial x} + v_y \frac{\partial \overline{a}}{\partial y} + v_z \frac{\partial \overline{a}}{\partial z} . \tag{5}$$

In this case, vector $\overline{n}$ takes the place of $\overline{v}$ above (eq.(4)). To prove eq.(1), we should note that from the definition of the directional derivative

$$\nabla_n f = \nabla f \cdot \overline{n} \tag{6}$$

The left-hand side of eq.(1) is

$$(\overline{n} \cdot \nabla)f = \left(n_x \frac{\partial}{\partial x} + n_y \frac{\partial}{\partial y} + n_z \frac{\partial}{\partial z} \right) f$$

$$= n_x \frac{\partial f}{\partial x} + n_y \frac{\partial f}{\partial y} + n_z \frac{\partial f}{\partial z}$$

$$= \overline{n} \cdot \nabla f = \nabla f \cdot \overline{n} = \nabla_n f \tag{7}$$

2. Using the component representation of vectors, we will perform all the necessary operations of eq.(2). Doing this,

$$\left[(x^2 \overline{i} + 2xy\overline{j} + e^z \overline{k}) \cdot \nabla \right] (x\overline{i} + 2y\overline{j} + z\overline{k})$$

$$= \left[(x^2, 2xy, e^z) \cdot \left(\frac{\partial}{\partial x}, \frac{\partial}{\partial y}, \frac{\partial}{\partial z} \right) \right] (x, 2y, z)$$

$$= \left(x^2 \frac{\partial}{\partial x} + 2xy \frac{\partial}{\partial y} + e^z \frac{\partial}{\partial z} \right) (x, 2y, z)$$

$$= \left(x^2 \frac{\partial x}{\partial x}, 2xy \frac{\partial (2y)}{\partial y}, e^z \frac{\partial z}{\partial z} \right)$$

$$= (x^2, 4xy, e^z)$$

● **PROBLEM** 8-32

Define the operator

$$\overline{a} \times \nabla \tag{1}$$

and show that the following identity holds

$$(\overline{a} \times \nabla) \cdot \overline{b} = \overline{a} \cdot (\nabla \times \overline{b}) \tag{2}$$

Solution: Denote the components of $\overline{a}$ as

$$\overline{a} = (a_1, a_2, a_3) \tag{3}$$

Define the vector product $\overline{a} \times \nabla$ as

$$\overline{a} \times \nabla \equiv (a_1, a_2, a_3) \times \left(\frac{\partial}{\partial x}, \frac{\partial}{\partial y}, \frac{\partial}{\partial z} \right)$$

$$= \left(a_2 \frac{\partial}{\partial z} - a_3 \frac{\partial}{\partial y}, \ a_3 \frac{\partial}{\partial x} - a_1 \frac{\partial}{\partial z}, \ a_1 \frac{\partial}{\partial y} - a_2 \frac{\partial}{\partial x} \right) \quad (4)$$

From eq.(4) we conclude that $\overline{a} \times \nabla$ is a vector operator. To prove identity (2), transform the left-hand side of eq.(2). From eq.(4), we have

$$(a \times \nabla) \cdot \overline{b} =$$

$$= \left(a_2 \frac{\partial}{\partial z} - a_3 \frac{\partial}{\partial y}, \ a_3 \frac{\partial}{\partial x} - a_1 \frac{\partial}{\partial z}, \ a_1 \frac{\partial}{\partial y} - a_2 \frac{\partial}{\partial x} \right) \cdot (b_1, b_2, b_3)$$

$$= \left(a_2 \frac{\partial}{\partial z} - a_3 \frac{\partial}{\partial y} \right) b_1 + \left(a_3 \frac{\partial}{\partial x} - a_1 \frac{\partial}{\partial z} \right) b_2 + \left(a_1 \frac{\partial}{\partial y} - a_2 \frac{\partial}{\partial x} \right) b_3$$

$$= a_1 \frac{\partial b_3}{\partial y} - a_1 \frac{\partial b_2}{\partial z} + a_2 \frac{\partial b_1}{\partial z} - a_2 \frac{\partial b_3}{\partial x} + a_3 \frac{\partial b_2}{\partial x} - a_3 \frac{\partial b_1}{\partial y}$$

$$= a_1 \left(\frac{\partial b_3}{\partial y} - \frac{\partial b_2}{\partial z} \right) + a_2 \left(\frac{\partial b_1}{\partial z} - \frac{\partial b_3}{\partial x} \right) + a_3 \left(\frac{\partial b_2}{\partial x} - \frac{\partial b_1}{\partial y} \right)$$

$$= (a_1, a_2, a_3) \cdot \left(\frac{\partial b_3}{\partial y} - \frac{\partial b_2}{\partial z}, \ \frac{\partial b_1}{\partial z} - \frac{\partial b_3}{\partial x}, \ \frac{\partial b_2}{\partial x} - \frac{\partial b_1}{\partial y} \right) \quad (5)$$

$$= \overline{a} \cdot \mathrm{curl} \ \overline{b} = \overline{a} \cdot (\nabla \times \overline{b})$$

When the operator ∇ is combined with the vector and scalar products, we can create an infinite number of different operators. However, it is important to keep in mind which entities an operator can act on.

For example, the operator $(\overline{a} \times \nabla)$ can act on a vector and yield a scalar

$$(\overline{a} \times \nabla) \cdot \overline{b} = \mathrm{scalar}$$

It can also act upon a vector and yield a vector,

$$(\overline{a} \times \nabla) \times \overline{b} = \mathrm{vector}$$

Lastly, it can act on a scalar and produce a vector

$$(\overline{a} \times \nabla)f = \mathrm{vector}$$

● **PROBLEM 8-33**

Prove the identity

$$\overline{a} \times (\nabla \times \overline{b}) - (\overline{a} \times \nabla) \times \overline{b} = \overline{a}(\nabla \cdot \overline{b}) - (\overline{a} \cdot \nabla)\overline{b} \quad (1)$$

where $\overline{a}$ and $\overline{b}$ are differentiable vectors.

Solution: Since eq.(1) is a vector identity, it must be shown that the components of the left-hand side, which is a vector, are equal to the corresponding components of the right-hand side. It will be sufficient to perform all the necessary calculations for the first component only. The expressions for the second and third components can be obtained easily from the first component.

As noted in earlier problems, the expression $\left[\bar{a}\right]_n$ indicates the nth component of a vector $\bar{a}$.

For example, if $\bar{a} = (a_1, a_2, a_3)$, then $\left[\bar{a}\right]_1 = a_1$

The first component of the left-hand side of eq.(1) is

$$\left[\bar{a} \times (\nabla \times \bar{b}) - (\bar{a} \times \nabla) \times \bar{b}\right]_1 = \left[\bar{a} \times (\nabla \times \bar{b})\right]_1 - \left[(\bar{a} \times \nabla) \times \bar{b}\right]_1$$

$$= a_2 \left[\nabla \times \bar{b}\right]_3 - a_3 \left[\nabla \times \bar{b}\right]_3 - \left[\bar{a} \times \nabla\right]_2 b_3 + \left[\bar{a} \times \nabla\right]_3 b_2$$

$$\tag{4}$$

$$= a_2\left(\frac{\partial b_2}{\partial x} - \frac{\partial b_1}{\partial y}\right) - a_3\left(\frac{\partial b_1}{\partial z} - \frac{\partial b_3}{\partial x}\right) - \left(a_3\frac{\partial}{\partial x} - a_1\frac{\partial}{\partial z}\right) b_3$$

$$+ \left(a_1\frac{\partial}{\partial y} - a_2\frac{\partial}{\partial x}\right) b_2$$

$$= a_1\left(\frac{\partial b_2}{\partial y} + \frac{\partial b_3}{\partial z}\right) - \left(a_2\frac{\partial b_1}{\partial y} + a_3\frac{\partial b_1}{\partial x}\right)$$

$$= a_1\left(\frac{\partial b_1}{\partial x} + \frac{\partial b_2}{\partial y} + \frac{\partial b_3}{\partial z}\right) - \left(a_1\frac{\partial b_1}{\partial x} + a_2\frac{\partial b_1}{\partial y} + a_3\frac{\partial b_1}{\partial z}\right)$$

$$= a_1(\nabla \cdot \bar{b}) - (\bar{a} \cdot \nabla)b_1 = \left[\bar{a}(\nabla \cdot \bar{b})\right]_1 - \left[(\bar{a} \cdot \nabla)\bar{b}\right]_1$$

$$= \left[\bar{a}(\nabla \cdot \bar{b}) - (\bar{a} \cdot \nabla)\bar{b}\right]_1$$

In the same manner, through symmetry, it can be shown that the second and third components are also equal.

● **PROBLEM 8-34**

Show that if f(x,y,z) is a homogeneous polynomial of degree n, then

$$(\bar{r} \cdot \nabla)f = nf \tag{1}$$

Solution: If f(x,y,z) satisfies the identity

$$f(\alpha x, \alpha y, \alpha z) = \alpha^n f(x,y,z) \tag{2}$$

then f is called a homogeneous function of order n.

To derive Euler's theorem on homogeneous functions, differentiate eq.(2) with respect to α, thus

$$\frac{\partial f}{\partial(\alpha x)}\frac{\partial(\alpha x)}{\partial\alpha} + \frac{\partial f}{\partial(\alpha y)}\frac{\partial(\alpha y)}{\partial\alpha} + \frac{\partial f}{\partial(\alpha z)}\frac{\partial(\alpha z)}{\partial\alpha} = n\alpha^{n-1}f(x,y,z)$$

$$\tag{3}$$

Now set $\alpha = 1$ in order to get rid of the parameter α in eq.(3).

$$\frac{\partial f}{\partial x} x + \frac{\partial f}{\partial y} y + \frac{\partial f}{\partial z} z = n\ f(x,y,z) \tag{4}$$

Eq.(4) can be written in the form

$$x\frac{\partial f}{\partial x} + y\frac{\partial f}{\partial y} + z\frac{\partial f}{\partial z} = \left(x\frac{\partial}{\partial x} + y\frac{\partial}{\partial y} + z\frac{\partial}{\partial z}\right)f \tag{5}$$

$$= (\overline{r}\cdot\nabla)f = nf$$

● **PROBLEM 8-35**

If $f\overline{a}$ satisfies Laplace's equation

$$\nabla^2(f\overline{a}) = \overline{0} \tag{1}$$

and

$$\mathrm{curl}(\mathrm{curl}\ f\overline{a}) = \overline{0} \tag{2}$$

show that

$$\nabla\left[(\nabla f)\cdot\overline{a} + f\nabla\cdot\overline{a}\right] = \overline{0} \tag{3}$$

Use only the identities proved in this chapter along with the one concerning divergence, namely

$$\nabla\cdot(f\overline{a}) = (\nabla f)\cdot\overline{a} + f\left(\nabla\cdot\overline{a}\right) \tag{4}$$

Solution: The fastest way to prove identity (3) is to find an identity involving both expressions $\nabla^2(f\overline{a})$ and $\mathrm{curl}\left[\mathrm{curl}(f\overline{a})\right]$. From Problem 8-20, obtain

$$\mathrm{curl\ curl}\ \overline{a} = \mathrm{grad\ div}\ \overline{a} - \nabla^2\overline{a} \tag{5}$$

Replace $\overline{a}$ by $f\overline{a}$ in eq.(5), thus

$$\mathrm{curl}(\mathrm{curl}\ f\overline{a}) = \nabla\left[\nabla\cdot(f\overline{a})\right] - \nabla^2(f\overline{a}) \tag{6}$$

Both expressions in eq.(1) and eq.(2) are equal to zero. Eq.(6) then becomes

$$\nabla\left[\nabla\cdot(f\overline{a})\right] = \overline{0} \tag{7}$$

Using eq.(4), the divergence of $f\overline{a}$ can be written in the form

$$\nabla\left[(\nabla f)\cdot\overline{a} + f\left(\nabla\cdot\overline{a}\right)\right] = \overline{0} \tag{8}$$

● **PROBLEM 8-36**

The operator nabla is defined as follows

$$\nabla \equiv \left(\frac{\partial}{\partial x},\ \frac{\partial}{\partial y},\ \frac{\partial}{\partial z}\right) = \frac{\partial}{\partial x}\overline{i} + \frac{\partial}{\partial y}\overline{j} + \frac{\partial}{\partial z}\overline{k} \tag{1}$$

The gradient of a scalar function f is defined as

$$\text{grad } f \equiv \nabla f = \left(\frac{\partial f}{\partial x}, \frac{\partial f}{\partial y}, \frac{\partial f}{\partial z}\right) = \frac{\partial f}{\partial x}\,\bar{i} + \frac{\partial f}{\partial y}\,\bar{j} + \frac{\partial f}{\partial z}\,\bar{k} \qquad (2)$$

Define grad $\bar{a}$, where $\bar{a}$ is a differentiable vector

$$\bar{a} = a_1\bar{i} + a_2\bar{j} + a_3\bar{k} \qquad (3)$$

Solution: Using the definition of the operator nabla,

$$\text{grad } \bar{a} = \nabla\bar{a} = \left(\frac{\partial}{\partial x}\,\bar{i} + \frac{\partial}{\partial y}\,\bar{j} + \frac{\partial}{\partial z}\,\bar{k}\right)(a_1\bar{i} + a_2\bar{j} + a_3\bar{k})$$

$$= \frac{\partial a_1}{\partial x}\,\bar{i}\,\bar{i} + \frac{\partial a_2}{\partial x}\,\bar{i}\,\bar{j} + \frac{\partial a_3}{\partial x}\,\bar{i}\,\bar{k}$$

$$+ \frac{\partial a_1}{\partial y}\,\bar{j}\,\bar{i} + \frac{\partial a_2}{\partial y}\,\bar{j}\,\bar{j} + \frac{\partial a_3}{\partial y}\,\bar{j}\,\bar{k} \qquad (4)$$

$$+ \frac{\partial a_1}{\partial z}\,\bar{k}\,\bar{i} + \frac{\partial a_2}{\partial z}\,\bar{k}\,\bar{j} + \frac{\partial a_3}{\partial z}\,\bar{k}\,\bar{k}$$

The quantities $\bar{i}\,\bar{i}$, $\bar{j}\,\bar{k}$, $\bar{k}\,\bar{k}$ etc. appearing in eq.(4) are called unit dyads. The expression

$$b_{11}\bar{i}\,\bar{i} + b_{12}\bar{i}\,\bar{j} + b_{13}\bar{i}\,\bar{k} + b_{21}\bar{j}\,\bar{i} + b_{22}\bar{j}\,\bar{j} + b_{23}\bar{j}\,\bar{k}$$

$$+ b_{31}\bar{k}\,\bar{i} + b_{32}\bar{k}\,\bar{j} + b_{33}\bar{k}\,\bar{k} \qquad (5)$$

is called a dyadic. The coefficients b_{11}, b_{12}, b_{13},...are the components of the dyadic.

Note that a dyadic is a generalization of a vector. While a vector has three components, a dyadic has 3^2 or 9 components and a triadic has 3^3 or 27 components. The notions of dyadic and triadic and their transformation properties play an important role in stress analysis.

● PROBLEM 8-37

Assuming the distributive law to hold, what is the meaning of the expression

$$\bar{a} \cdot \bar{\Lambda} \qquad (1)$$

where $\bar{a}$ is a vector and $\bar{\Lambda}$ is a dyadic.

Solution: First express the vector $\bar{a}$ as a linear combination of the base vectors,

$$\bar{a} = a_1\bar{i} + a_2\bar{j} + a_3\bar{k} \qquad (2)$$

Expressing $\bar{\Lambda}$ as a linear combination of the unit dyads, we have

$$\bar{\Lambda} = a_{11}\bar{i}\,\bar{i} + a_{12}\bar{i}\,\bar{j} + a_{13}\bar{i}\,\bar{k} + a_{21}\bar{j}\,\bar{i} + a_{22}\bar{j}\,\bar{j}$$

$$+ a_{23}\overline{j}\,\overline{k} + a_{31}\overline{k}\,\overline{i} + a_{32}\overline{k}\,\overline{j} + a_{33}\overline{k}\,\overline{k} \qquad (3)$$

Since the distributive law holds, we can write

$$\overline{a}\cdot\overline{\Lambda} = (a_1\overline{i} + a_2\overline{j} + a_3\overline{k})\cdot\overline{\Lambda}$$

$$= a_1\overline{i}\cdot\overline{\Lambda} + a_2\overline{j}\cdot\overline{\Lambda} + a_3\overline{k}\cdot\overline{\Lambda} \qquad (4)$$

Consider the first element $a_1\overline{i}\cdot\overline{\Lambda}$, of eq.(4). Temporarily neglect the coefficient a_1. The scalar product $\overline{i}\cdot\overline{\Lambda}$ is formed by taking the scalar product of $\overline{i}$ with each term of $\overline{\Lambda}$ and adding the results.

Therefore

$$\overline{i}\cdot a_{11}\overline{i}\,\overline{i} = a_{11}\overline{i}\cdot\overline{i}\,\overline{i} = a_{11}(\overline{i}\cdot\overline{i})\overline{i} = a_{11}\overline{i} \qquad (5)$$

$$\text{since } \overline{i}\cdot\overline{i} = 1$$

$$\overline{i}\cdot a_{12}\overline{i}\,\overline{j} = a_{12}(\overline{i}\cdot\overline{i})\overline{j} = a_{12}\overline{j} \qquad (6)$$

$$\overline{i}\cdot a_{13}\overline{i}\,\overline{k} = a_{13}(\overline{i}\cdot\overline{i})\overline{k} = a_{13}\overline{k} \qquad (7)$$

$$\overline{i}\cdot a_{21}\overline{j}\,\overline{i} = a_{21}(\overline{i}\cdot\overline{j})\overline{i} = \overline{0} \text{ since } \overline{i}\cdot\overline{j} = 0 \qquad (8)$$

$$\overline{i}\cdot a_{32}\overline{k}\,\overline{j} = a_{32}(\overline{i}\cdot\overline{k})\overline{j} = \overline{0} \text{ since } \overline{i}\cdot\overline{k} = 0 \qquad (9)$$

In the same manner, one can obtain all of the other terms. Taking the sum of all the terms

$$\overline{a}\cdot\overline{\Lambda} = a_1(a_{11}\overline{i} + a_{12}\overline{j} + a_{13}\overline{k}) + a_2(a_{21}\overline{i} + a_{22}\overline{j} + a_{23}\overline{k})$$

$$+ a_3(a_{31}\overline{i} + a_{32}\overline{j} + a_{33}\overline{k}) \qquad (10)$$

$$= (a_1a_{11} + a_2a_{21} + a_3a_{31})\overline{i} + (a_1a_{12} + a_2a_{22} + a_3a_{32})\overline{j}$$

$$+ (a_1a_{13} + a_2a_{23} + a_3a_{33})\,\overline{k}$$

From eq.(10) we conclude that the scalar product of a vector and a dyadic is a vector.

● **PROBLEM** 8-38

The dyadic $\overline{\Lambda}$ is defined as

$$\overline{\Lambda} = \overline{i}\,\overline{i} + \overline{j}\,\overline{j} + \overline{k}\,\overline{k} \qquad (1)$$

Find the geometrical representation of

$$\overline{r}\cdot\overline{\Lambda}\cdot\overline{r} = 4 \qquad (2)$$

Solution: There are two ways of computing $\overline{r}\cdot\overline{\overline{\Lambda}}\cdot\overline{r}$. One way is to take the dot product of $\overline{r}$ with $(\overline{\overline{\Lambda}}\cdot\overline{r})$, that is

$$\overline{r}\cdot(\overline{\overline{\Lambda}}\cdot\overline{r})$$

The other way is to take the dot product of $(\overline{r}\cdot\overline{\overline{\Lambda}})$ with $\overline{r}$,

$$(\overline{r}\cdot\overline{\overline{\Lambda}})\ \overline{r}$$

To compute the first expression $(\overline{r}\cdot(\overline{\overline{\Lambda}}\cdot\overline{r}))$, express the position vector $\overline{r}$ as

$$\overline{r} = x\overline{i} + y\overline{j} + z\overline{k} \tag{3}$$

Then,

$$\overline{r}\cdot(\overline{\overline{\Lambda}}\cdot\overline{r}) = (x\overline{i} + y\overline{j} + z\overline{k})\cdot\left[(\overline{i}\,\overline{i} + \overline{j}\,\overline{j} + \overline{k}\,\overline{k})\cdot(x\overline{i} + y\overline{j} + z\overline{k})\right] \tag{4}$$

where

$$\overline{i}\,\overline{i}\cdot(x\overline{i}) = x\overline{i}(\overline{i}\cdot\overline{i}) = x\overline{i} \tag{5}$$

$$\overline{j}\,\overline{j}\cdot(y\overline{j}) = y\overline{j}(\overline{j}\cdot\overline{j}) = y\overline{j} \tag{6}$$

$$\overline{k}\,\overline{k}\cdot(z\overline{k}) = z\overline{k}(\overline{k}\cdot\overline{k}) = z\overline{k} \tag{7}$$

All of the other terms are equal to zero because

$$\overline{i}\,\overline{i}\cdot(y\overline{j}) = y\overline{i}(\overline{i}\cdot\overline{j}) = y\overline{i}\cdot 0 = 0 \tag{8}$$

Substituting eqs.(5), (6), (7) into eq.(4), obtain

$$\overline{r}\cdot(\overline{\overline{\Lambda}}\cdot\overline{r}) = (x\overline{i} + y\overline{j} + z\overline{k})\cdot(x\overline{i} + y\overline{j} + z\overline{k})$$
$$= x^2 + y^2 + z^2 \tag{9}$$

Next, compute $(\overline{r}\cdot\overline{\overline{\Lambda}})\cdot\overline{r}$. Doing this, obtain

$$(\overline{r}\cdot\overline{\overline{\Lambda}})\cdot\overline{r} = \left[(x\overline{i} + y\overline{j} + z\overline{k})\cdot(\overline{i}\,\overline{i} + \overline{j}\,\overline{j} + \overline{k}\,\overline{k})\right]\cdot(x\overline{i} + y\overline{j} + z\overline{k}) \tag{10}$$
$$= (x\overline{i} + y\overline{j} + z\overline{k})\cdot(x\overline{i} + y\overline{j} + z\overline{k}) = x^2 + y^2 + z^2$$

Both expressions are equal, thus

$$\overline{r}\cdot(\overline{\overline{\Lambda}}\cdot\overline{r}) = (\overline{r}\cdot\overline{\overline{\Lambda}})\cdot\overline{r} = \overline{r}\cdot\overline{\overline{\Lambda}}\cdot\overline{r} = x^2 + y^2 + z^2 \tag{11}$$

The geometrical representation of

$$\overline{r}\cdot\overline{\overline{\Lambda}}\cdot\overline{r} = x^2 + y^2 + z^2 = 4 \tag{12}$$

is a sphere of radius 2 with center at the origin.

● **PROBLEM 8-39**

For both, the scalar and vector fields, define the basic algebraic operations as well as the basic differential operators. Also, list all fundamental identities.

Solution: Denote the scalar fields by f and g and the vector fields by $\overline{a}$ and $\overline{b}$. The basic operations are shown in the table.

Scalars	Vectors	Scalars and Vectors	Operations	
$f+g$.ᵗ¹	$\bar{a}+\bar{b}$ ²		Addition	*Algebraic Operations*
fg ³	$\bar{a}\cdot\bar{b}$ scalar product ⁴ $\bar{a}x\bar{b}$ vector product	$f\bar{a}$ ⁵	Multiplication	
$\dfrac{df}{dx}$ ⁶	$\dfrac{d\bar{a}}{dt}$ ⁷	$\dfrac{d}{dt}(f\bar{a})$ ⁸	Derivatives	*Differential Operations*
$\dfrac{\partial f}{\partial x}$ ⁹	$\dfrac{\partial \bar{a}}{\partial x}$ ¹⁰	$\dfrac{\partial}{\partial x}(f\bar{a})$ ¹¹	Partial Derivatives	
$\nabla f \equiv \text{grad } f$ ¹²	$\nabla\cdot\bar{a}\equiv\text{div }\bar{a}$ ¹³ $\nabla x\bar{a}\equiv\text{curl }\bar{a}$	$\nabla\cdot(f\bar{a})$ ¹⁴ $\nabla x(f\bar{a})$	$\nabla\equiv\left(\dfrac{\partial}{\partial x},\dfrac{\partial}{\partial y},\dfrac{\partial}{\partial z}\right)$	
∇^2 ¹⁵ $\bar{a}\cdot\nabla$	$\nabla x\nabla$ $\bar{a}x\nabla$	$\bar{a}\cdot\nabla$	Operators	

The basic properties of the operations given in the table are listed below (refer to the number on the top right-hand side of each box in the table).

1. $f + g = g + f$

$f + (g + h) = (f + g) + h$

2. $\bar{a} + \bar{b} = \bar{b} + \bar{a}$

$\bar{a} + (\bar{b} + \bar{c}) = (\bar{a} + \bar{b}) + \bar{c}$

$\bar{a} + \bar{0} = \bar{a}$

3. $fg = gf$

$f(gh) = (fg)h$

4. $\bar{a}\cdot\bar{b} = \bar{b}\cdot\bar{a}$

$\bar{a}\cdot(\bar{b} + \bar{c}) = \bar{a}\cdot\bar{b} + \bar{a}\cdot\bar{c}$

$\bar{a} \times \bar{b} = -\bar{b} \times \bar{a}$

$\bar{a} \times (\bar{b} + \bar{c}) = \bar{a} \times \bar{b} + \bar{a} \times \bar{c}$

$\bar{a} \times \bar{a} = \bar{0}$

5. $(f + g)\bar{a} = f\bar{a} + g\bar{a}$

$f(\bar{a} + \bar{b}) = f\bar{a} + f\bar{b}$

6. $\dfrac{d}{dx}(f + g) = \dfrac{df}{dx} + \dfrac{dg}{dx}$

$\dfrac{d}{dx}(fg) = f\dfrac{dg}{dx} + g\dfrac{df}{dx}$

354

7.
$$\frac{d}{dt}(\bar{a} + \bar{b}) = \frac{d\bar{a}}{dt} + \frac{d\bar{b}}{dt}$$

$$\frac{d}{dt}(\bar{a}\cdot\bar{b}) = \bar{a}\cdot\frac{d\bar{b}}{dt} + \frac{d\bar{a}}{dt}\cdot\bar{b}$$

$$\frac{d}{dt}(\bar{a}\times\bar{b}) = \bar{a}\times\frac{d\bar{b}}{dt} + \frac{d\bar{a}}{dt}\times\bar{b}$$

8.
$$\frac{d}{dt}(f\bar{a}) = f\frac{d\bar{a}}{dt} + \frac{df}{dt}\bar{a}$$

9.
$$\frac{\partial}{\partial x}(f + g) = \frac{\partial f}{\partial x} + \frac{\partial g}{\partial x}$$

$$\frac{\partial}{\partial x}(fg) = f\frac{\partial g}{\partial x} + g\frac{\partial f}{\partial x}$$

10.
$$\frac{\partial}{\partial x}(\bar{a} + \bar{b}) = \frac{\partial\bar{a}}{\partial x} + \frac{\partial\bar{b}}{\partial x}$$

$$\frac{\partial}{\partial x}(\bar{a}\cdot\bar{b}) = \bar{a}\cdot\frac{\partial\bar{b}}{\partial x} + \frac{\partial\bar{a}}{\partial x}\cdot\bar{b}$$

$$\frac{\partial}{\partial x}(\bar{a}\times\bar{b}) = \bar{a}\times\frac{\partial\bar{b}}{\partial x} + \frac{\partial\bar{a}}{\partial x}\times\bar{b}$$

11.
$$\frac{\partial}{\partial x}(f\bar{a}) = \bar{a}\frac{\partial f}{\partial x} + f\frac{\partial\bar{a}}{\partial x}$$

12.
$$\nabla(f + g) = \nabla f + \nabla g$$

$$\nabla(fg) = f\nabla g + g\nabla f$$

13.
$$\text{div}(\bar{a} + \bar{b}) = \text{div}\,\bar{a} + \text{div}\,\bar{b}$$

$$\text{div grad } f = \nabla^2 f$$

$$\text{curl}(\bar{a} + \bar{b}) = \text{curl}\,\bar{a} + \text{curl}\,\bar{b}$$

$$\text{curl grad } f = \bar{0}$$

$$\text{div curl }\bar{a} = 0$$

14.
$$\text{div}(f\bar{a}) = (\text{grad } f)\cdot\bar{a} + f\,\text{div}\,\bar{a}$$

$$\text{curl}(f\bar{a}) = f\,\text{curl}\,\bar{a} + \text{grad } f\times\bar{a}$$

15.
$$\nabla^2 \equiv \nabla\cdot\nabla \equiv \text{div grad}$$

$$\nabla^2 f = \text{div}(\text{curl}\,\bar{a} + \text{grad } f)$$

CHAPTER 9

ELEMENTS OF LINEAR ALGEBRA

INTRODUCTION

This chapter deals almost exclusively with the principles of linear algebra. After introducing binary operations, the chapter gradually moves on to such notions as groups, rings, fields and the concept of a vector space.

The regular cartesian spaces, R^2, R^3, or in general R^n, are then shown to be vector spaces; at which point, vector analysis and linear algebra meet. Many of the definitions and theorems of linear algebra are then directly applied to vector analysis.

The concept of a linear transformation and its matrix representation is also discussed in this chapter. The properties of transformations will play an important role in tensor analysis (Chapter 10).

After discussing transformations, the fundamental theorem of linear algebra, its significance and applications - is then introduced.

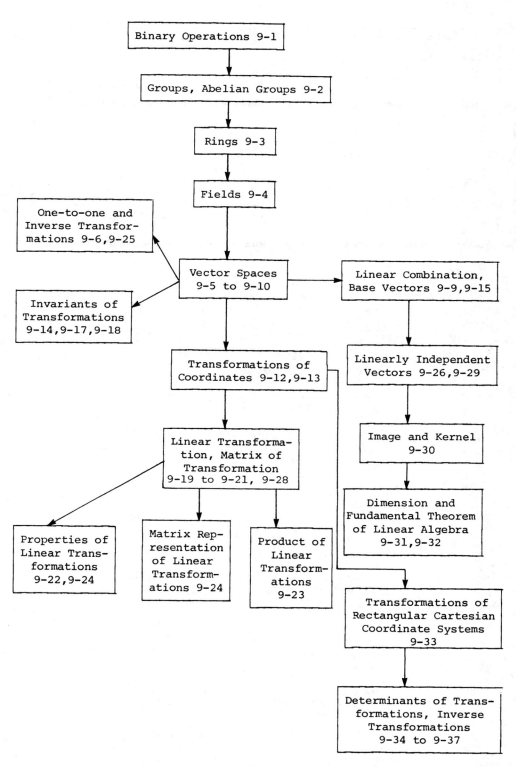

Binary Operations 9-1

Groups, Abelian Groups 9-2

Rings 9-3

Fields 9-4

One-to-one and Inverse Transformations 9-6,9-25

Invariants of Transformations 9-14,9-17,9-18

Vector Spaces 9-5 to 9-10

Linear Combination, Base Vectors 9-9,9-15

Transformations of Coordinates 9-12,9-13

Linearly Independent Vectors 9-26,9-29

Linear Transformation, Matrix of Transformation 9-19 to 9-21, 9-28

Image and Kernel 9-30

Properties of Linear Transformations 9-22,9-24

Matrix Representation of Linear Transformations 9-24

Product of Linear Transformations 9-23

Dimension and Fundamental Theorem of Linear Algebra 9-31,9-32

Transformations of Rectangular Cartesian Coordinate Systems 9-33

Determinants of Transformations, Inverse Transformations 9-34 to 9-37

This chart is provided to facilitate rapid understanding of the inter-relationships of the topics and subject matter in this chapter. Also shown are the problem numbers associated with the subject matter.

MAPPINGS, BINARY OPERATIONS, GROUPS, RINGS AND FIELDS

Let A and B be two sets such that

$$A = \left\{7, \ d, \ 24, \ -3\right\} \qquad (1)$$
$$B = \left\{2, \ 3, \ 1\right\}$$

Define and give an example of a mapping of set A into set B. Define and give an example of a binary operation on set A.

Solution: A mapping of a set A into a set B is a correspondence which assigns to every element p, such that pεA, a unique element q, such that qεB (see Figure 1). Often, instead of "mapping", the term "function" is used. In a many-to-one mapping, more than one element of a set A is assigned to only one unique element of a set B. Given any two sets, there are many possible many-to-one and one-to-one mappings.

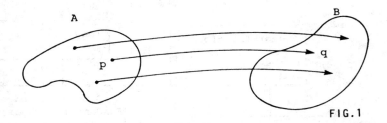

FIG.1

Fig. 2 gives an example of a many-to-one mapping of set A into set B. A binary operation on a set A is a mapping from A x A into A.

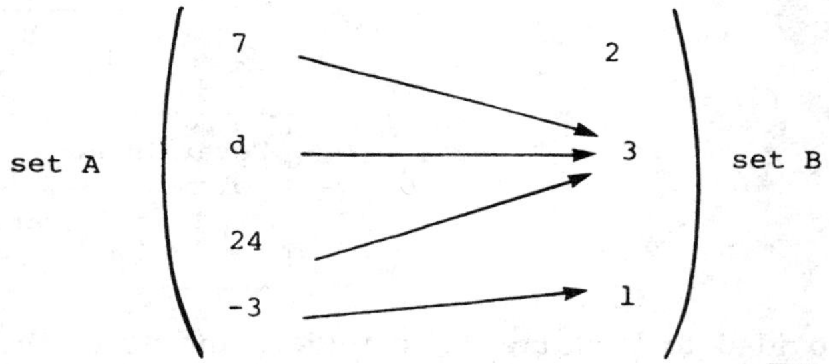

set A
7   2
d   3
24
-3   1
set B

FIG.2

The mapping of A x A into A is such that to every ordered pair (α,β) it assigns the first element of the pair

$$(\alpha, \beta) \to \alpha \qquad (4)$$

where α,β∈A.

This mapping is a binary operation. For A, as defined in eq.(1), one obtains

$$(7, 7) \to 7$$

$$(7, d) \to 7$$

$$(24, -3) \to 24 \qquad (5)$$

$$(d, 7) \to d$$

and so on.

If R is the set of real numbers, then the sum of a∈R and b∈R

$$a + b \in R,$$

and the product

$$a \cdot b \in R,$$

are binary operations.

● **PROBLEM** 9-2

Define a group and give an example of a finite group and an infinite group. Define an abelian (sometimes called commutative) group.

Solution: A group G is a system consisting of a set of elements, a binary operation *, and the following postulates:

1. G is closed under *. That means for all a∈G and b∈G also a*b∈G.

2. The operation * is associative. That is for all a, b, c ∈G

$$a*b*c = a*(b*c) = (a*b)*c \qquad (1)$$

3. The operation * has an identity element e∈G, such that for all a∈G

$$a*e = e*a = a \tag{2}$$

4. For every element aεG there exists an inverse element
   $a^{-1}\varepsilon$G such that

$$a*a^{-1} = a^{-1}*a = e \tag{3}$$

It is desired to show that the set of integers
$I = \{0, \pm1, \pm2, \pm3,...\}$ is a group under the operation of
addition.

   I is closed under addition since the sum of two integers is an integer. Addition is associative. Zero is an identity element.

$$a + 0 = 0 + a = a \tag{4}$$

An inverse element to a is -a, since

$$a +(-a) = (-a)+ a = 0. \tag{5}$$

Thus, the set of integers forms a group under the operation of addition. This is an infinite group. It is usually denoted by (I, +).

The set of real numbers (R, +) also forms a group.

   The following is an example of a finite group. Let C be the set of six congruences of an equilateral triangle.

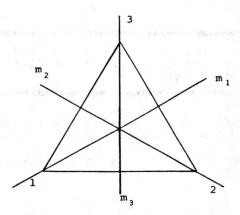

A congruence is any rigid motion of the equilateral triangle into itself. The elements of C are

   0 - no motion

  120° - rotation through 120°

  240° - rotation through 240°   (6)

m_1 - reflection in median m_1

m_2 - reflection in median m_2

m_3 - reflection in median m_3

Let the operation $*$ be such that $a*b$ means congruence a followed by congruence b. For example, $120^0 * 120^0 = 240^0$ or $240^0 * 120^0 = 0$. The results of the operation $*$ are gathered in the following table

a*b

	0	120^0	240^0	m_1	m_2	m_3	$= b$
0	0	120^0	240^0	m_1	m_2	m_3	
120^0	120^0	240^0	0	m_3	m_1	m_2	
240^0	240^0	0	120^0	m_2	m_3	m_1	(7)
m_1	m_1	m_2	m_3	0	120^0	240^0	
m_2	m_2	m_3	m_1	240^0	0	120^0	
m_3	m_3	m_1	m_2	120^0	240^0	0	

a = { (rows above) }

From the table, one concludes that

$C = \{0, 120^0, 240^0, m_1, m_2, m_3\}$ is closed under the op-

eration $*$ and that the associative law holds. The identity element is 0. The inverse elements are

$$0^{-1} = 0, \left(120^0\right)^{-1} = 240^0, \left(240^0\right)^{-1} = 120^0$$
$$m_1^{-1} = m_1, m_2^{-1} = m_2, m_3^{-1} = m_3$$

(8)

Thus $(C,*)$ is a group.

A group $(G,*)$ such that the operation $*$ is commutative is called an abelian or commutative group.

An operation $*$ is commutative if for every a, b∈G

$$a*b = b*a$$

(9)

The set of integers $(I,+)$ with the operation of addition is an abelian group, because

$$a + b = b + a \quad \text{for all a, b∈I.}$$

The group of congruences $(C,*)$ is not an abelian group, because

$$120^0 * m_1 = m_3$$

$$m_1 * 120^0 = m_2 \tag{10}$$

Thus,

$$120^0 * m_1 \neq m_1 \ 120^0 \tag{11}$$

● **PROBLEM** 9-3

Determine if the set of integers with the operations of addition and multiplication forms a commutative ring.

<u>Solution</u>: A ring is a mathematical system with two operations; denoted by $(R, *, \alpha)$.

<u>Definition</u>: A ring R is a set of elements with two operations $*$ and α such that:

1. R is an abelian group under the operation $*$

2. The operation α is associative in R

$$a \, \alpha \, (b \, \alpha \, c) = (a \, \alpha \, b) \, \alpha \, c \tag{1}$$

3. For any a, b, c εR, then

$$a \, \alpha \, (b * c) = (a \, \alpha \, b) * (a \, \alpha \, c) \tag{2}$$

$$(b * c) \, \alpha \, a = (b \, \alpha \, a) * (c \, \alpha \, a)$$

That is the operation α is left and right distributive with respect to the operation $*$.

If the operation α is commutative, then R is a commutative ring.

Consider the set of integers $(I, +, \cdot)$ with the operation of addition and multiplication.

Under the operation $+$, I is an abelian group,

$$a + b = b + a, \quad a, b \varepsilon I \tag{4}$$

The operation $\cdot$ is associative in I

$$a \cdot (b \cdot c) = (a \cdot b) \cdot c \tag{5}$$

For any a, b, c εI, then

$$a \cdot (b + c) = (a \cdot b) + (a \cdot c) \tag{6}$$

and

$$(b + c) \cdot a = (b \cdot a) + (c \cdot a) \tag{7}$$

Thus $(I, +, \cdot)$ is a ring.

Since the operation $\cdot$ is commutative $a \cdot b = b \cdot a$, $(I, +, \cdot)$ is a commutative ring.

If R contains an identity element for the operation α, then R is a ring with unity.

● **PROBLEM 9-4**

Define a field and give an example of an infinite field and a finite field.

Solution: A field, like a ring, is a mathematical system with two operations.

Definition: A field F, denoted $(F,*,\alpha)$ is a system which is a commutative ring with unity in which every element except the identity element for the operation $*$ has an inverse with respect to the operation α.

Consider the set of integers with the operation of addition and multiplication $(I,+,\cdot)$. From Problem 9-3, one knows that $(I,+,\cdot)$ forms a commutative ring with unity. But this set does not form a field since there are no multiplicative inverses in this set except for the element 1.

The set of rationals, that is the numbers that can be represented as $\frac{p}{q}$ where p and q are integers, $q \neq 0$, form a field under the operations of addition and multiplication. It will not be shown that the set of real numbers R with the operations of multiplication and addition forms a field. The set is closed with respect to addition and multiplication.

$$a + (b + c) = (a + b) + c$$
$$\text{and} \quad (a \cdot b) \cdot c = a \cdot (b \cdot c) \tag{1}$$

$$a + b = b + a, \quad a \cdot b = b \cdot a \tag{2}$$

$R(+,\cdot)$ is a commutative ring with unity. Each $a \varepsilon R$ has its additive inverse $-a$ and a multiplicative inverse $\frac{1}{a}$, where $a \neq 0$. Zero is the identity element for addition.

Thus, the set of real numbers $(R,+,\cdot)$ with the operations $+$ and $\cdot$ forms an infinite field.

Now, for an example of a finite field, define the operation modulus such that

$$a \equiv b(\text{mod } c) \tag{3}$$

which means that b is the remainder when a is divided by c. For example

$$10 \equiv 0(\text{mod } 5), \quad 5 \equiv 2(\text{mod } 3)$$

Choose $c = 5$ and construct a field from the integers mod 5. The operation mod 5 partitions the set of integers into five mutually disjoint classes. Indeed

$$0 \equiv 0(\text{mod } 5) \quad 5 \equiv 0(\text{mod } 5) \quad 10 \equiv 0(\text{mod } 5)$$

$$1 \equiv 1(\bmod\ 5) \qquad 6 \equiv 1(\bmod\ 5)$$
$$2 \equiv 2(\bmod\ 5) \qquad 7 \equiv 2(\bmod\ 5) \qquad (4)$$
$$3 \equiv 3(\bmod\ 5) \qquad 8 \equiv 3(\bmod\ 5)$$
$$4 \equiv 4(\bmod\ 5) \qquad 9 \equiv 4(\bmod\ 5)$$

which indicates that every integer is 0, 1, 2, 3 or 4. The addition and multiplication can be defined as follows

$$a(\bmod\ 5) + b(\bmod\ 5) = (a + b)(\bmod\ 5) \qquad (5)$$

$$a(\bmod\ 5) \cdot b(\bmod\ 5) = a \cdot b(\bmod\ 5) \qquad (6)$$

The set of classes with the addition and multiplication defined above forms a finite field. The laws of commutativity, associativity and distribution are fulfilled because a and b are integers. The identities for addition and multiplication are 0 and 1 respectively. The table below shows the additive inverses.

+	0	1	2	3	4	
0	0	1	2	3	4	
1	1	2	3	4	0	(7)
2	2	3	4	0	1	
3	3	4	0	1	2	
4	4	0	1	2	3	

This table indicates that every element has its additive inverse.

From the multiplication table

·	0	1	2	3	4	
0	0	0	0	0	0	
1	0	1	2	3	4	(8)
2	0	2	4	1	3	
3	0	3	1	4	2	
4	0	4	3	2	1	

We see that every element has its multiplicative inverse (except for 0). Thus the set of classes with the operations + and · forms a finite group.

VECTOR SPACES AND SPAN SETS

● **PROBLEM 9-5**

Show that the space R^n of n-triples of real numbers is a vector space over the field R. Define the operations.

Solution: The elements of R^n are

$$(x_1, \ldots, x_n) \in R^n \tag{1}$$

The operation of addition is defined as

$$(x_1, \ldots, x_n) + (y_1, \ldots, y_n) = (x_1+y_1, \ldots, x_n+y_n) \tag{2}$$

and the multiplication by a scalar $\alpha \in R$

$$\alpha(x_1, \ldots, x_n) = (\alpha x_1, \ldots, \alpha x_n) \tag{3}$$

Definition: A vector space is a set V, over a field F, which, together with the operations of scalar multiplication and addition, satisfies the eleven properties listed below.

The space R^n is defined over the field of real numbers R. It will be shown that R^n satisfies the vector space axioms.

1. R^n is closed under addition.

For $(x_1, \ldots, x_n) \in R^n$ and $(y_1, \ldots, y_n) \in R^n$,

$$(x_1, \ldots, x_n) + (y_1, \ldots y_n) = (x_1+y_1, \ldots, x_n+y_n) \tag{4}$$

All the sums x_1+y_1, x_2+y_2, $\ldots$, x_n+y_n are real numbers, thus

$$(x_1+y_1, \ldots, x_n+y_n) \in R^n \tag{5}$$

2. Addition is commutative. Indeed

$$(x_1, \ldots, x_n) + (y_1, \ldots, y_n) = (x_1+y_1, \ldots, x_n+y_n) \tag{6}$$

$$= (y_1+x_1, \ldots, y_n+x_n) = (y_1, \ldots, y_n) + (x_1, \ldots, x_n)$$

Here the fact that the addition of real numbers are commutative was used.

3. Addition is associative. Here again, utilize the fact that addition of real numbers is associative. That is for any α, β, $\gamma \in R$,

$$(\alpha+\beta) + \gamma = \alpha + (\beta+\gamma) \tag{7}$$

Then

$$\left[(x_1, \ldots, x_n) + (y_1, \ldots, y_n)\right] + (z_1, \ldots, z_n)$$

$$= (x_1+y_1, \ldots, x_n+y_n) + (z_1, \ldots, z_n) \tag{8}$$

$$= (x_1+y_1+z_1, \ldots, x_n+y_n+z_n)$$

$$= (x_1, \ldots, x_n) + (y_1+z_1, \ldots, y_n+z_n)$$

365

$$= (x_1, \ldots, x_n) + \left[(y_1, \ldots, y_n) + (z_1, \ldots, z_n) \right]$$

4. There exists a zero vector, such that

$$(x_1, \ldots, x_n) + (0, \ldots, 0) = (x_1, \ldots x_n) \qquad (9)$$

5. For each vector $(x_1, \ldots, x_n)$ there exists an additive inverse

$$-(x_1, \ldots, x_n) = (-x_1, \ldots, -x_n) \qquad (10)$$

and

$$(x_1, \ldots, x_n) + (-x_1, \ldots, -x_n) = (x_1 - x_1, \ldots, x_n - x_n)$$
$$= (0, \ldots, 0) \qquad (11)$$

6. R^n is closed under multiplication by a scalar. Let

$$(x_1, \ldots, x_n) \epsilon R^n \quad \text{and} \quad \alpha \epsilon R$$

then

$$\alpha(x_1, \ldots, x_n) = (\alpha x_1, \ldots, \alpha x_n) \epsilon R^n \qquad (12)$$

7. The first distributive law. Let

$$\overline{x}, \ \overline{y} \epsilon R^n \quad \text{and} \quad \alpha \epsilon R$$

It must be shown that

$$\alpha(\overline{x} + \overline{y}) = \alpha\overline{x} + \alpha\overline{y} \qquad (13)$$

$$\alpha \left[(x_1, \ldots, x_n) + (y_1, \ldots, y_n) \right]$$
$$\qquad (14)$$
$$= \alpha(x_1 + y_1, \ldots, x_n + y_n) = (\alpha(x_1 + y_1), \ldots, \alpha(x_n + y_n))$$
$$= (\alpha x_1 + \alpha y_1, \ldots, \alpha x_n + \alpha y_n) = \alpha(x_1, \ldots, x_n) + \alpha(y_1, \ldots, y_n)$$

8. The second distributive law: show that

$$(\alpha + \beta)\overline{x} = \alpha\overline{x} + \beta\overline{x}, \quad \alpha, \beta \epsilon R, \quad \overline{x} \epsilon R^n \qquad (15)$$

We have

$$(\alpha + \beta)(x_1, \ldots, x_n) = ((\alpha + \beta)x_1, \ldots, (\alpha + \beta)x_n)$$

$$= (\alpha x_1 + \beta x_1, \ldots, \alpha x_n + \beta x_n)$$
$$\qquad (16)$$
$$= (\alpha x_1, \ldots, \alpha x_n) + (\beta x_1, \ldots \beta x_n)$$

$$= \alpha(x_1, \ldots, x_n) + \beta(x_1, \ldots, x_n)$$

9. Associativity of scalar multiplication.
$$(\alpha\beta)\overline{x} = \alpha(\beta\overline{x}) \qquad (17)$$

$$(\alpha\beta)(x_1,\ldots,x_n) = (\alpha\beta x_1,\ldots,\alpha\beta x_n)$$
$$= \alpha(\beta x_1,\ldots,\beta x_n) \tag{18}$$

10. The existence of a unit element 1 from the field,

$$1(x_1,\ldots,x_n) = (x_1,\ldots,x_n) \tag{19}$$

"One" is a unit element.

11. One can prove the relationship

$$0(x_1,\ldots,x_n) = (0,\ldots,0). \tag{20}$$

Thus R^n is a vector space; with the operations of addition and multiplication by scalar

● **PROBLEM** 9-6

Consider the set of semi-magic squares of order 3 x 3. Define addition and multiplication by scalars and show that this set is a vector space over the field of real numbers.

Solution: A square array of numbers, such that every row and every column has the same total is called a semi-magic square. If the two diagonals also have the same total, then the square is called a magic square.

The matrix

$$\begin{bmatrix} 1 & 8 & 6 \\ 9 & 4 & 2 \\ 5 & 3 & 7 \end{bmatrix} \tag{1}$$

is a semi-magic square. Every row and column has a total of 15. This is not a magic square however, since one of the diagonals has a total of 12. Let M be the set of all 3 x 3 semi-magic squares and let

$$A = \begin{bmatrix} a_{ij} \end{bmatrix} \varepsilon\, M$$
$$B = \begin{bmatrix} b_{ij} \end{bmatrix} \varepsilon\, M \tag{2}$$

The addition operation is defined as

$$a_{ij} + b_{ij} = (a + b)_{ij} \qquad i,j = 1,\, 2,\, 3 \tag{3}$$

One concludes, from eq.(3), that the sum of two semi-magic squares is a semi-magic square. Thus, M is closed under addition. Since the real numbers are commutative and assoc-

iative with respect to addition, the addition defined in M
is also commutative and associative.

$$A + B = B + A$$
$$(A + B) + C = A + (B + C) \tag{4}$$

The matrix, whose elements are all zero, $0 = [0]$ is a
zero element of M.

$$A + 0 = A \tag{5}$$

An additive inverse of

$$A = \left[a_{ij}\right] \tag{6}$$

is

$$-A = \left[-a_{ij}\right] \tag{7}$$

Note that since A is a semi-magic square, -A is also a semi-
magic square and

$$A + (-A) = 0 \tag{8}$$

Multiplication by a real number is defined as

$$\alpha A = \left[\alpha a_{ij}\right] \text{ , where}$$

M is closed under the multiplication

$$(A \varepsilon M, \ \alpha \varepsilon R) \Longrightarrow (\alpha A \varepsilon M). \tag{10}$$

If A is a semi-magic square and α is a real number, then
αA is a semi-magic square. From the properties of real numbers, we obtain

$$(\alpha\beta)A = \alpha(\beta A) \tag{11}$$

$$(\alpha+\beta)A = \alpha A + \beta A$$

$$\alpha(A+B) = \alpha A + \alpha B$$

where A, $B \varepsilon M$ and $\alpha, \beta \varepsilon R$.

Thus M is a vector space.

● **PROBLEM 9-7**

Let T be the set of all functions of a non-empty set A
into the field of real numbers R.

$$f \varepsilon T; \quad f : A \to R \tag{1}$$

Show that T is a vector space under the following operations:

$$(f + g)(a) = f(a) + g(a) \tag{2}$$

where f, $g \varepsilon T$ and $a \varepsilon A$

and

$$(\alpha f)(a) = \alpha f(a) \tag{3}$$

where $f \varepsilon T$ and $\alpha \varepsilon R$.

Solution: The sum of two functions of A into R, as defined by eq.(2), is also a function of A into R. Hence, T is closed under addition. Addition is commutative because f(a) and g(a) are real numbers.

$$(f + g)(a) = f(a) + g(a) = g(a) + f(a) = (g + f)(a) \quad (4)$$

Since addition in R is associative

$$f(a) + \left[g(a) + h(a)\right] = \left[f(a) + g(a)\right] + h(a) \quad (5)$$

A zero vector is a function 0 such that

$$0(a) = 0 \quad \text{for all } a \varepsilon A \quad (6)$$

One has, for all $f \varepsilon T$,

$$f + 0 = f \quad (7)$$

The inverse of f is defined as

$$(-f)(a) = -f(a) \quad (8)$$

Thus

$$f(a) + (-f)(a) = 0 \quad (9)$$

Note that T is closed under multiplication by scalars. Indeed

$$\begin{pmatrix} f \varepsilon T \\ \alpha \varepsilon R \end{pmatrix} => (\alpha f \varepsilon T) \quad (10)$$

Since multiplication in R is associative,

$$(\alpha\beta) f(a) = \alpha(\beta f)(a) \quad (11)$$

where $\alpha, \beta \varepsilon R$.

Using the properties of the real numbers, one can prove the two distributive laws.

$$\alpha(f + g)(a) = \alpha f(a) + \alpha g(a) \quad (12)$$

$$(\alpha+\beta) f(a) = \alpha f(a) + \beta f(a) \quad (13)$$

For $1 \varepsilon R$, we obtain

$$1 f(a) = f(a) \quad (14)$$

Thus, it has been proven that T, under the operations of addition and multiplication as defined by eq.(2) and eq.(3), is a vector space.

T is often called a function space.

Show that the space V of potential functions of the nth degree is a vector space over the field of real numbers. Addition and scalar multiplication is defined below

$$f(x,y) + g(x,y) = (f + g)(x,y) \tag{1}$$

$$\alpha\left[f(x,y)\right] = \alpha f(x,y) \tag{2}$$

where f, $g \epsilon V$ and $\alpha \epsilon R$.

Find the dimension of this given space.

Solution: A function $f(x,y)$ is called a potential function if it is twice differentiable and satisfies the second-order partial differential equation

$$\frac{\partial^2 f}{\partial x^2} + \frac{\partial^2 f}{\partial y^2} = 0 \tag{3}$$

For example $f(x,y) = x$, $g(x,y) = xy$ satisfy eq.(2).

If $f(x,y)$ and $g(x,y)$ are potential functions then $f + g$ is a potential function

$$\frac{\partial^2(f+g)}{\partial x^2} + \frac{\partial^2(f+g)}{\partial y^2} = \frac{\partial^2 f}{\partial x^2} + \frac{\partial^2 f}{\partial y^2} + \frac{\partial^2 g}{\partial x^2} + \frac{\partial^2 g}{\partial y^2} = 0 \tag{4}$$

Thus, V is closed under addition as well as scalar multiplication.

$$\frac{\partial^2(\alpha f)}{\partial x^2} + \frac{\partial^2(\alpha f)}{\partial y^2} = \alpha\left[\frac{\partial^2 f}{\partial x^2} + \frac{\partial^2 f}{\partial y^2}\right] = 0 \tag{5}$$

In Problem 9-7 it was shown that the set of all real valued functions T is a vector space. The set of potential functions V is a subset of T, V⊂T. Since V is closed under addition and multiplication by scalars, and since it is a subset of a vector space, then V is a vector space.

The nth degree potential function $f(x,y)$ can be written in the form

$$f(x,y) = a_0 x^n + a_1 x^{n-1}y + \ldots + a_{n-1}xy^{n-1} + a_n y^n \tag{6}$$

Substituting eq.(6) into

$$\frac{\partial^2 f}{\partial x^2} + \frac{\partial^2 f}{\partial y^2} = 0, \tag{7}$$

one obtains

$$x^{n-2}\left[a_0(n-1)n+2a_2\right] + x^{n-3}y\left[a_1(n-1)(n-2) + 3\cdot 2a_3\right]$$
$$+ x^{n-4}y^2\left[a_2(n-2)(n-3) + 4\cdot 3a_4\right] +$$

370

$$\ldots + xy^{n-3}\left[a_{n-1}(n-1)(n-2) + 3\cdot 2a_{n-3}\right] \tag{8}$$
$$+ y^{n-2}\left[a_n n(n-1) + 2a_{n-2}\right] = 0$$

Eq.(8) should hold for all values of x and y. Thus all the coefficients in eq.(8) should be equal to zero.

$$a_2 = \frac{-n(n-1)}{2}\, a_0 \qquad a_3 = \frac{-(n-1)(n-2)}{3\cdot 2}\, a_1 \tag{9}$$

In general for a_i,

$$a_i = \frac{-[n-(i-1)][n-(i-2)]}{i(i-1)}\, a_{i-2} \tag{10}$$

Having coefficients a_0 and a_1 one can evaluate all the coefficients in eq.(6).

Thus, every potential function of degree n can be expressed as a linear combination of two potential functions of degree n. One with the coefficients evaluated from a_0 and the second with the coefficients evaluated from a_1.

The potential functions of degree n form a vector space of dimension 2.

● **PROBLEM** 9-9

Can the matrix A, given by

$$A = \begin{bmatrix} 3 & 4 \\ 7 & 1 \end{bmatrix} \tag{1}$$

be expressed as a linear combination of the matrices E_1, E_2, E_3 and E_4 shown below?

$$E_1 = \begin{bmatrix} 2 & 1 \\ 0 & 1 \end{bmatrix} \qquad E_2 = \begin{bmatrix} 1 & 0 \\ 1 & 0 \end{bmatrix}$$

$$E_3 = \begin{bmatrix} 1 & -1 \\ -1 & 0 \end{bmatrix} \qquad E_4 = \begin{bmatrix} -2 & 1 \\ 3 & 0 \end{bmatrix} \tag{2}$$

Solution: Matrix A can be expressed as a linear combination of E_1, E_2, E_3 and E_4 if an only if A can be expressed as

$$A = \alpha_1 E_1 + \alpha_2 E_2 + \alpha_3 E_3 + \alpha_4 E_4. \tag{3}$$

Therefore, one way of solving this problem is to determine the constants α_1 through α_4 shown above. The other method for solving this problem is much shorter however and will now be employed. First, note that the space of 2 × 2 matrices is a 4-dimensional space and thus any set of four linearly independent matrices can serve as its basis.

Thus, if we could show that the set of four matrices E_1, E_2, E_3 and E_4 are linearly independent, then this would be sufficient to show that matrix A could be expressed as a linear combination of these matrices (notice that this method does not consider the values of the constants α_1 through α_4 in eq.(3)).

To prove that matrices E_1 through E_4 are linearly independent, note that any set of matrices is linearly independent if

$$\beta_1 E_1 + \beta_2 E_2 + \beta_3 E_3 + \beta_4 E_4 = 0. \tag{4}$$

Or, in matrix form (by substituting eq.(2) into eq.(4)),

$$\begin{bmatrix} 2\beta_1 & \beta_1 \\ 0 & \beta_1 \end{bmatrix} + \begin{bmatrix} \beta_2 & 0 \\ \beta_2 & 0 \end{bmatrix} + \begin{bmatrix} \beta_3 & -\beta_3 \\ -\beta_3 & 0 \end{bmatrix} + \begin{bmatrix} -2\beta_4 & \beta_4 \\ 3\beta_4 & 0 \end{bmatrix} = \begin{bmatrix} 0 & 0 \\ 0 & 0 \end{bmatrix} \tag{5}$$

Eq.(5) is equivalent to the four equations:

$$2\beta_1 + \beta_2 + \beta_3 - 2\beta_4 = 0$$

$$\beta_1 - \beta_3 + \beta_4 = 0$$

$$\beta_2 - \beta_3 + 3\beta_4 = 0 \tag{6}$$

$$\beta_1 = 0$$

Solving the above system yields

$$\beta_1 = \beta_2 = \beta_3 = \beta_4 = 0,$$

and thus matrices E_1, E_2, E_3 and E_4 are linearly independent and form a basis of the vector space of 2 × 2 matrices. Therefore, in conclusion, matrix A can be expressed as a linear combination of E_1, E_2, E_3 and E_4.

● **PROBLEM 9-10**

Consider the three-dimensional vector space R^3. Let T be a subset of R^3,

$$T = \left\{ (1,0,1), (0,1,0) \right\} \tag{1}$$

Find the span of T.

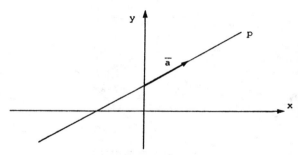

Solution: The set of all linear combinations of the vectors of T is called the span set of T and is denoted by SpT.

For example let the vector space be R^2 and T be the set consisting of one vector, vector $\bar{a}$, as shown in the figure.

$$T = \{\bar{a}\} \tag{2}$$

Then the span set of $\{\bar{a}\}$ is the set of all the vectors located on the line p. One can write

$$Sp\{\bar{a}\} = \{\bar{b}: \ \bar{b} = \alpha\bar{a}, \ \alpha\epsilon R\} . \tag{3}$$

That is, the span set of $\{\bar{a}\}$ is the set of all vectors $\bar{b}$ such that $\bar{b} = \alpha\bar{a}$ where $\alpha\epsilon R$.

The span set of the set T in eq.(1) is the set of all the linear combinations of (1,0,1) and (0,1,0). Thus,

$$\alpha(1,0,1) + \beta(0,1,0) = (\alpha,\beta,\alpha) \tag{4}$$

Note that SpT forms a vector space — indeed $(0,0,0)\epsilon$SpT.

If $(\alpha',\beta',\alpha')\epsilon$ SpT and $(\alpha'',\beta'',\alpha'')\epsilon$ SpT, then

$(\alpha',\beta',\alpha') + (\alpha'',\beta'',\alpha'') = (\alpha'+\alpha'',\beta'+\beta'',\alpha'+\alpha'')\epsilon$SpT $\tag{5}$

Thus SpT is closed under addition.

If $(\alpha,\beta,\alpha)\epsilon$ SpT and $p\epsilon R'$, then

$$p(\alpha,\beta,\alpha) = (p\alpha,p\beta,p\alpha) \ \epsilon \ SpT. \tag{6}$$

POSITION VECTORS, TRANSFORMATIONS, INVARIANTS, LINEAR COMBINATIONS AND ROTATION

● PROBLEM 9-11

1) Which of the vectors shown in the figure are position vectors?

2) Sketch vectors $\bar{a}$ = (2,1,4) and $\bar{b}$ = (3,-3,2); assuming that they are position vectors.

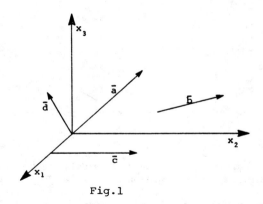

Fig.1

Solution: A vector is called a position vector if and only if the initial point is fixed at the origin of the coordinate system in question. Position vectors are usually denoted by $\bar{r}$, $\bar{r}_0$, $\bar{r}_1$ etc. From the Fig 1, one concludes that vectors $\bar{a}$ and $\bar{d}$ are position vectors while vectors $\bar{c}$ and $\bar{b}$ are not (their initial points do not coincide with the origin of the system).

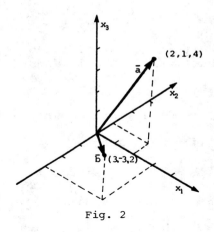

Fig. 2

2) Since vectors $\bar{a}$ and $\bar{d}$ are position vectors, their initial points coincide with the origin of the system - as shown in Fig 2.

● **PROBLEM 9-12**

1) Determine the transformation equations for two rectangular cartesian coordinate systems whose respective axes are parallel.

2) Determine the equation of a sphere of radius 4 whose center is at the point (1,3,5) with respect to the (x_1, x_2, x_3) system. Also, transform the (x_1, x_2, x_3) system into an (x_1', x_2', x_3') system. The origin of the (x_1', x_2', x_3') system is at the center of the sphere.

374

Lastly, write the algebraic equation of the sphere
in the new (primed) system.

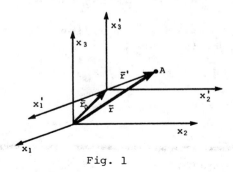

Fig. 1

Solution: 1) Let (x_1, x_2, x_3) and (x_1', x_2', x_3') represent the
two rectangular cartesian coordinate systems, whose respective axes are parallel, as shown in the figure.
If A is any point in space, then from the figure, we have

$$\bar{r} = \bar{r}_0 + \bar{r}'$$

or   (1)

$$\bar{r}' = \bar{r} - \bar{r}_0$$

Vector $\bar{r}'$ has the following coordinates in the $\bar{x}'$ system:

$$\bar{r}' = (x_1', x_2', x_3')$$ (2)

Thus, one has the following transformation equation

$$(x_1', x_2', x_3') = (x_1, x_2, x_3) - (x_1^0, x_2^0, x_3^0),$$ (3)

where (x_1^0, x_2^0, x_3^0) are the coordinates of the origin of the
primed system. In general, we can write

$$x_i = x_i' - x_i^0$$ (4)

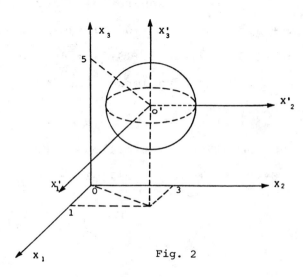

Fig. 2

375

at $(1,3,5)$ is represented by

$$(x_1-1)^2 + (x_2-3)^2 + (x_3-5)^2 = 16 \qquad (5)$$

Now, introduce a second rectangular system, denoted by "primes", such that

$$x_1' = x_1-1, \quad x_2' = x_2-3, \quad x_3' = x_3-5. \qquad (6)$$

In the primed system the equation of the sphere becomes (by substituting eq.(6) in eq.(5))

$$(x_1')^2 + (x_2')^2 + (x_3')^2 = 16 \qquad (7)$$

The sphere is shown in Fig. 2.

● **PROBLEM** 9-13

Consider the equation

$$9x^2 + 54x + 4y^2 - 8y + 49 = 0 \qquad (1)$$

Using a translation of axes, show that eq.(1) represents an ellipse.

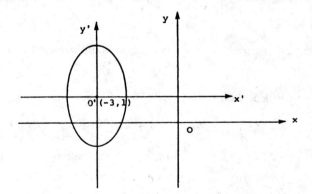

Solution: Complete the squares of x and y, and obtain

$$9x^2 + 54x + 4y^2 - 8y + 49 = 9(x^2+6x) + 4(y^2-2y) + 49$$
$$= 9[(x^2+6x+9)-9] + 4[(y^2-2y+1)-1] + 49 = 0 \qquad (2)$$

Now try to obtain an equation of the form

$$\frac{x^2}{a^2} + \frac{y^2}{b^2} = 1 \qquad (3)$$

which is the equation of an ellipse. From eq.(2), obtain

$$9[(x^2+6x+9)-9] + 4[(y^2-2y+1)-1] + 49$$

$$= 9(x^2+6x+9)-81 + 4(y^2-2y+1)-4 + 49 \qquad (4)$$

$$= \frac{x^2+6x+9}{4} + \frac{y^2-2y+1}{9} - 1 = 0$$

or

$$\frac{(x+3)^2}{4} + \frac{(y-1)^2}{9} = 1 \qquad (5)$$

Now, let

$$x' = x + 3$$
$$y' = y - 1 \qquad (6)$$

Eq.(5) becomes

$$\frac{x'^2}{4} + \frac{y'^2}{9} = 1 \qquad (7)$$

which is an equation of an ellipse as shown in the figure.

Here, O is the origin of the xy system and O' is the origin of the x'y' system. Note that eq.(6) describes a transformation of the coordinate system - such a transformation is called translation.

● **PROBLEM 9-14**

Show that, under the translation of axes, the distances are invariant

1. in three-dimensional space

2. in any general n-dimensional space.

<u>Solution</u>: 1. Consider a three-dimensional vector space R^3. Let A and B be two points in this space, such that

$$A\left(x_1^A,\ x_2^A,\ x_3^A\right)$$
$$B\left(x_1^B,\ x_2^B,\ x_3^B\right) \qquad (1)$$

The distance between A and B is

$$d\left(x^A, x^B\right) = \sqrt{\left(x_1^B-x_1^A\right)^2+\left(x_2^B-x_2^A\right)^2+\left(x_3^B-x_3^A\right)^2} \qquad (2)$$

Let T be the translation of axes such that

$$T:(x_1,x_2,x_3) \rightarrow (x_1',x_2',x_3') \qquad (3)$$

and

$$x_1' = x_1 + \alpha_1$$
$$x_2' = x_2 + \alpha_2 \qquad (4)$$
$$x_3' = x_3 + \alpha_3,$$

or using vector notation
$$\overline{r}' = \overline{r} + \overline{\alpha} \tag{5}$$

Points A and B are transformed into

$$T: A \to A'\left(x_1^{A'}, x_2^{A'}, x_3^{A'}\right)$$

$$T: B \to B'\left(x_1^{B'}, x_2^{B'}, x_3^{B'}\right) \tag{6}$$

From eq.(4) and (6), obtain

$$x_1^{A'} = x_1^{A} + \alpha_1 \qquad x_1^{B'} = x_1^{B} + \alpha_1$$

$$x_2^{A'} = x_2^{A} + \alpha_2 \qquad x_2^{B'} = x_2^{B} + \alpha_2 \tag{7}$$

$$x_3^{A'} = x_3^{A} + \alpha_3 \qquad x_3^{B'} = x_3^{B} + \alpha_3$$

The distance between A' and B' is defined as

$$d'\left(x^{A'}, x^{B'}\right) = \sqrt{\left(x_1^{B'} - x_1^{A'}\right)^2 + \left(x_2^{B'} - x_2^{A'}\right)^2 + \left(x_3^{B'} - x_3^{A'}\right)^2} \tag{8}$$

From eq.(7), we see that

$$x_1^{B'} - x_1^{A'} = \left(x_1^{B} + \alpha_1\right) - \left(x_1^{A} + \alpha_1\right) = x_1^{B} - x_1^{A}$$

$$x_2^{B'} - x_2^{A'} = x_2^{B} - x_2^{A} \tag{9}$$

$$x_3^{B'} - x_3^{A'} = x_3^{B} - x_3^{A}$$

Substituting eq.(9) into eq.(8), obtain

$$d'\left(x^{A'}, x^{B'}\right) = \sqrt{\left(x_1^{B} - x_1^{A}\right)^2 + \left(x_2^{B} - x_2^{A}\right)^2 + \left(x_3^{B} - x_3^{A}\right)^2}$$

$$= d\left(x^{A}, x^{B}\right) \tag{10}$$

Since $d'\left(x^{A'}, x^{B'}\right) = d\left(x^{A}, x^{A}\right)$, we conclude that distance is invariant, under translation.

2. For n-dimensional space R^n,

$$A(x_1, x_2 \ldots, x_n)$$

$$B(y_1, y_2, \ldots, y_n) \tag{11}$$

Let the transformation T be

$$T: \overline{x} \to \overline{x}'$$

$$\overline{x}' = \overline{x} + \overline{\alpha} \tag{12}$$

The distance between the points A and B is

$$d(x,y) = \sqrt{(y_1-x_1)^2 + (y_2-x_2)^2 + \ldots + (y_n-x_n)^2}$$

$$= \sqrt{\sum_{i=1}^{n} (y_i-x_i)^2} \qquad (13)$$

The transformation T transforms the points A and B into

$$T: \ A \to A' \qquad\qquad (14)$$

$$T: \ B \to B',$$

and

$$\bar{x}' = \bar{x} + \bar{\alpha} \qquad\qquad (15)$$

$$\bar{y}' = \bar{y} + \bar{\alpha}$$

Thus

$$y_i' - x_i' = (y_i+\alpha_i) - (x_i+\alpha_i) = y_i - x_i \qquad (16)$$

The distance between the points A' and B' is

$$d'(x',y') = \sqrt{(y_1'-x_1')^2 + (y_2'-x_2')^2 + \ldots + (y_n'-x_n')^2}$$

$$= \sqrt{\sum_{i=1}^{n} (y'-x')^2} = \sqrt{\sum_{i=1}^{n} (y_i-x_i)^2} = d(x,y)$$

Thus, the translation of axes is a transformation under which distances are invariant.

● **PROBLEM 9-15**

Express vector $\bar{a}$, given by

$$\bar{a} = (2, \ -1, \ 3), \qquad\qquad (1)$$

as a linear combination of the vectors:

$$\bar{e}_1 = (1, \ 0, \ 1)$$

$$\bar{e}_2 = (-1, \ 0, \ 2) \qquad\qquad (2)$$

$$\bar{e}_3 = (2, \ 1, \ -1)$$

Solution: Each vector can be represented uniquely as a linear combination of the basis vectors. Thus

$$\bar{a} = 2\bar{i} - \bar{j} + 3\bar{k} \qquad\qquad (3)$$

where $\bar{i}$, $\bar{j}$, $\bar{k}$ are basis vectors. Assume that the three vectors $\bar{e}_1$, $\bar{e}_2$ and $\bar{e}_3$ are linearly independent. Vector $\bar{a}$ can then be represented as a linear combination of $\bar{e}_1, \bar{e}_2, \bar{e}_3$ (the basis vectors) as

$$\bar{a} = \alpha_1 \bar{e}_1 + \alpha_2 \bar{e}_2 + \alpha_3 \bar{e}_3 \qquad (4)$$

Eq.(4) can be written in the following matrix form

$$\begin{bmatrix} 2 \\ -1 \\ 3 \end{bmatrix} = \begin{bmatrix} \alpha_1 - \alpha_2 + 2\alpha_3 \\ \alpha_3 \\ \alpha_1 + 2\alpha_2 - \alpha_3 \end{bmatrix} = \begin{bmatrix} 1 & -1 & 2 \\ 0 & 0 & 1 \\ 1 & 2 & -1 \end{bmatrix} \begin{bmatrix} \alpha_1 \\ \alpha_2 \\ \alpha_3 \end{bmatrix} \qquad (5)$$

Note that the columns of the matrix in eq.(5) are the vectors $\bar{e}_1, \bar{e}_2, \bar{e}_3$. From eq.(5), obtain the three equations

$$2 = \alpha_1 - \alpha_2 + 2\alpha_3$$

$$-1 = \alpha_3 \qquad (6)$$

$$3 = \alpha_1 + 2\alpha_2 - \alpha_3$$

Solving eq.(6) yields

$$\alpha_1 = \frac{10}{3} \qquad \alpha_2 = -\frac{2}{3} \qquad \alpha_3 = -1 \qquad (7)$$

Thus,

$$\bar{a} = \frac{10}{3} \bar{e}_1 - \frac{2}{3} \bar{e}_2 - \bar{e}_3 \qquad (8)$$

Eq.(8) represents vector $\bar{a}$ as a linear combination of the basis vectors.

● **PROBLEM 9-16**

Problem 9-15 transformed vector $\bar{a}$ from one set of basis vectors $\bar{i}, \bar{j}, \bar{k}$ to another set of basis vectors $\bar{e}_1, \bar{e}_2$ and $\bar{e}_3$ where

$$\bar{e}_1 = (1, 0, 1)$$

$$\bar{e}_2 = (-1, 0, 2) \qquad (1)$$

$$\bar{e}_3 = (2, 1, -1)$$

Under this transformation, vector $\bar{r} = (x,y,z)$ transforms into $\bar{r}' = (x',y',z')$. Find the new coordinates x',y',z'. Find the inverse transformation.

Solution: Denote the transformation by T. Thus

$$T: \bar{r} \to \bar{r}' \qquad (2)$$

where

$$\bar{r} = x'\bar{e}_1 + y'\bar{e}_2 + z'\bar{e}_3 \qquad (3)$$

or in the matrix form

$$
\begin{bmatrix} x \\ y \\ z \end{bmatrix} = \begin{bmatrix} 1 & -1 & 2 \\ 0 & 0 & 1 \\ 1 & 2 & -1 \end{bmatrix} \begin{bmatrix} x' \\ y' \\ z' \end{bmatrix} \tag{4}
$$

The columns of the matrix in eq.(4) are the vectors $\bar{e}_1$, $\bar{e}_2$
and $\bar{e}_3$. Eq.(4) represents a system of equations

$$x = x' - y' + 2z'$$

$$y = z' \tag{5}$$

$$z = x' + 2y' - z'$$

Solving for x', y', z' gives

$$x' = \frac{2}{3} x - y + \frac{1}{3} z$$

$$y' = y - \frac{1}{3} x + \frac{1}{3} z \tag{6}$$

$$z' = y$$

Substituting eq.(6) into eq.(3) yields

$$\bar{r} = \left(\frac{2}{3} x - y + \frac{1}{3} z \right) \bar{e}_1 + \left(y - \frac{1}{3} x + \frac{1}{3} z \right) \bar{e}_2 + y\, \bar{e}_3 \tag{7}$$

Eq.(4) represents the transformation from the xyz coordinates
to the x'y'z' coordinates. Eq.(6) can be written in the matrix form as

$$
\begin{bmatrix} x' \\ y' \\ z' \end{bmatrix} = \begin{bmatrix} \frac{2}{3} & -1 & \frac{1}{3} \\ -\frac{1}{3} & 1 & \frac{1}{3} \\ 0 & 1 & 0 \end{bmatrix} \begin{bmatrix} x \\ y \\ z \end{bmatrix} \tag{8}
$$

Eq.(8) represents the inverse transformation from the x'y'z'
coordinates to the xyz coordinates. The matrix in eq.(8) is
the inverse of the matrix in eq.(4). Indeed

$$
\begin{bmatrix} \frac{2}{3} & -1 & \frac{1}{3} \\ -\frac{1}{3} & 1 & \frac{1}{3} \\ 0 & 1 & 0 \end{bmatrix} \begin{bmatrix} 1 & -1 & 2 \\ 0 & 0 & 1 \\ 1 & 2 & -1 \end{bmatrix} = \begin{bmatrix} 1 & 0 & 0 \\ 0 & 1 & 0 \\ 0 & 0 & 1 \end{bmatrix} = I \tag{9}
$$

● **PROBLEM 9-17**

1. Consider the transformation defined in Problem 9-15
    Does this transformation leave distances invariant?

2. What are the conditions for the invariance of dist-
    ances in the plane and in the space?

Solution: 1. Take two points A and B, whose coordinates in the xyz system are

$$A(x_1, y_1, z_1)$$

$$B(x_2, y_2, z_2)$$
(1)

The distance between the points is

$$d(A,B) = \sqrt{(x_2-x_1)^2 + (y_2-y_1)^2 + (z_2-z_1)^2}$$
(2)

Under the transformation described in Problem 9-15, the points A and B are transformed to A' and B'. For simplicity, assume that point B is the origin of the xyz system. Eq.(2) can be written in the form

$$d(A,0) = \sqrt{x^2+y^2+z^2},$$
(3)

where index 1 is omitted.

From eq.(8) of Problem 9-16, one concludes that the origin (0,0,0) of the system xyz transforms into the origin (0,0,0) of the system x'y'z'. Also,

$$d'(A',0) = \sqrt{x'^2+y'^2+z'^2}$$
(4)

From eq.(8) of Problem 9-16,

$$x' = \frac{2}{3} x - y + \frac{1}{3} z$$

$$y' = y - \frac{1}{3} x + \frac{1}{3} z$$
(5)

$$z' = y$$

Substituting eq.(5) into eq.(4), obtain

$$d'(A',0) = \sqrt{\left(\frac{2}{3} x-y + \frac{1}{3} z\right)^2 + \left(y - \frac{1}{3} x + \frac{1}{3} z\right)^2 + y^2}$$
(6)

Obviously $d \neq d'$; thus under the transformation defined in Problem 9-15 the distances are not invariant.

2. Consider the transformation from the xy plane to the x'y' plane, where $\bar{i}$, $\bar{j}$ are the basis vectors of xy and $\bar{e}_1, \bar{e}_2$ are the basis vectors of x'y'. It is required to find the conditions under which this transformation will preserve distances. Start with an arbitrary vector

$$\bar{r} = x\bar{i} + y\bar{j}$$
(7)

In terms of the $\bar{e}_1$ and $\bar{e}_2$ vectors, $\bar{r}$ can be written as

$$\bar{r} = x'\bar{e}_1 + y'\bar{e}_2$$
(8)

The magnitude of $\bar{r}$ is

$$|\bar{r}| = \sqrt{\bar{r}\cdot\bar{r}} = \sqrt{x^2+y^2} \tag{9}$$

and in terms of $\bar{e}_1$ and $\bar{e}_2$

$$|\bar{r}| = \sqrt{\bar{r}\cdot\bar{r}} = \sqrt{x'^2\bar{e}_1\cdot\bar{e}_1+2x'y'\bar{e}_1\cdot\bar{e}_2+y'^2\bar{e}_2\cdot\bar{e}_2} \tag{10}$$

If $\bar{e}_1$ and $\bar{e}_2$ are orthogonal (perpendicular), then $\bar{e}_1\cdot\bar{e}_2 = 0$ and eq.(10) becomes

$$|\bar{r}| = \sqrt{x'^2\bar{e}_1\cdot\bar{e}_1+y'^2\bar{e}_2\cdot\bar{e}_2} \tag{11}$$

If $\bar{e}_1$ and $\bar{e}_2$ are unit vectors, then

$$|\bar{r}| = \sqrt{x'^2 + y'^2} \tag{12}$$

This is the same form of magnitude as in eq.(9). Thus, to insure invariance, the x'y' system to which the xy system has been transformed, must have a set of mutually perpendicular unit base vectors. That is,

$$\bar{e}_1\cdot\bar{e}_2 = 0, \quad \bar{e}_1\cdot\bar{e}_1 = 1, \quad \bar{e}_2\cdot\bar{e}_2 = 1.$$

A set of basis vectors which are orthogonal and of unit length is called an orthonormal set. In three-dimensional space, an orthonormal set $\bar{e}_1$, $\bar{e}_2$, $\bar{e}_3$ of basis vectors is such that

$$\bar{e}_1\cdot\bar{e}_1 = \bar{e}_2\cdot\bar{e}_2 = \bar{e}_3\cdot\bar{e}_3 = 1 \tag{13}$$

and

$$\bar{e}_1\cdot\bar{e}_2 = \bar{e}_1\cdot\bar{e}_3 = \bar{e}_2\cdot\bar{e}_3 = 0.$$

● **PROBLEM** 9-18

Write the equations for the rotation of axes in the xy plane. Determine if this transformation leaves distances invariant.

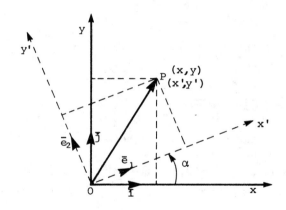

383

Solution: Consider a rotation of the xy coordinate system in its own plane. The angle of rotation with respect to the original system is α.

The rotation is shown in the figure. Vector $\overline{OP}$ can be represented in terms of the base vectors $\overline{i}$ and $\overline{j}$ as

$$\overline{OP} = x\overline{i} + y\overline{j} \tag{1}$$

or in terms of the base vectors $\overline{e}_1$ and $\overline{e}_2$,

$$\overline{OP} = x'\overline{e}_1 + y'\overline{e}_2 \tag{2}$$

From the figure, one can express the unit basis vectors, $\overline{e}_1$ and $\overline{e}_2$ as

$$\overline{e}_1 = \cos\alpha\,\overline{i} + \sin\alpha\,\overline{j} \tag{3}$$

$$\overline{e}_2 = \cos\left(\alpha + \frac{\pi}{2}\right)\overline{i} + \sin\left(\alpha + \frac{\pi}{2}\right)\overline{j} = -\sin\alpha\,\overline{i} + \cos\alpha\,\overline{j} \tag{4}$$

Thus, eq.(2) becomes

$$\overline{OP} = x\overline{i} + y\overline{j} = x'\overline{e}_1 + y'\overline{e}_2$$

$$= x'(\cos\alpha\,\overline{i} + \sin\alpha\,\overline{j}) + y'(-\sin\alpha\,\overline{i} + \cos\alpha\,\overline{j})$$

$$= (x'\cos\alpha - y'\sin\alpha)\overline{i} + (x'\sin\alpha + y'\cos\alpha)\overline{j} \tag{5}$$

Comparing eq.(5) with eq.(1), one obtains

$$x = x'\cos\alpha - y'\sin\alpha$$
$$y = x'\sin\alpha + y'\cos\alpha \tag{6}$$

Eq.(6) can be written in the matrix form

$$\begin{bmatrix} x \\ y \end{bmatrix} = \begin{bmatrix} \cos\alpha & -\sin\alpha \\ \sin\alpha & \cos\alpha \end{bmatrix} \begin{bmatrix} x' \\ y' \end{bmatrix} \tag{7}$$

From eq.(3) and eq.(4), one obtains

$$|\overline{e}_1| = \sqrt{\cos^2\alpha + \sin^2\alpha} = 1$$

$$|\overline{e}_2| = \sqrt{\sin^2\alpha + \cos^2\alpha} = 1 \tag{8}$$

$$\overline{e}_1 \cdot \overline{e}_2 = (\cos\alpha\,\overline{i} + \sin\alpha\,\overline{j}) \cdot (-\sin\alpha\,\overline{i} + \cos\alpha\,\overline{j}) = 0$$

Thus, since the basis vectors $\overline{e}_1$ and $\overline{e}_2$ are orthogonal unit vectors the rotation of axes leaves the distances invariant.

LINEAR TRANSFORMATIONS

Consider a transformation from the x'y' system to the xy system described by the equations

$$x = a_{11}x' + a_{12}y'$$
$$y = a_{21}x' + a_{22}y'$$

(1)

For any ordered pair (x',y') eq.(1) determines the corresponding pair (x,y). If this correspondence is unique, determine the transformation matrix. Determine if the transformation defined by eq.(1) is a linear transformation.

<u>Solution</u>: Eq.(1) can be written in the matrix form

$$\begin{bmatrix} x \\ y \end{bmatrix} = \begin{bmatrix} a_{11} & a_{12} \\ a_{21} & a_{22} \end{bmatrix} \begin{bmatrix} x' \\ y' \end{bmatrix}$$

(2)

or $\qquad\qquad \overline{x} = T\overline{x}'$ (3)

where

$$T = \begin{bmatrix} a_{11} & a_{12} \\ a_{21} & a_{22} \end{bmatrix}$$

(4)

is the transformation matrix. A linear transformation is defined as follows:

<u>Definition</u>: If V and U are vector spaces, a transformation

$$T: \ V \rightarrow U$$

is called a linear transformation of V into U if for any $\overline{x}, \overline{y} \epsilon V$ and any two scalars a, b

$$T(a\overline{x} + b\overline{y}) = aT(\overline{x}) + bT(\overline{y})$$

(5)

Let

$$\overline{x} = \begin{bmatrix} x_1 \\ x_2 \end{bmatrix}, \quad \overline{y} = \begin{bmatrix} y_1 \\ y_2 \end{bmatrix}$$

(6)

and a, b be any two scalars. From eq.(2), one obtains

$$T\begin{bmatrix} a\overline{x} + b\overline{y} \end{bmatrix} = \begin{bmatrix} a_{11} & a_{12} \\ a_{21} & a_{22} \end{bmatrix} \begin{bmatrix} ax_1 + by_1 \\ ax_2 + by_2 \end{bmatrix}$$

$$= \begin{bmatrix} a_{11}(ax_1+by_1) + a_{12}(ax_2+by_2) \\ a_{21}(ax_1+by_1) + a_{22}(ax_2+by_2) \end{bmatrix} \qquad (7)$$

$$= a \begin{bmatrix} a_{11} & a_{12} \\ a_{21} & a_{22} \end{bmatrix} \begin{bmatrix} x_1 \\ x_2 \end{bmatrix} + b \begin{bmatrix} a_{11} & a_{12} \\ a_{21} & a_{22} \end{bmatrix} \begin{bmatrix} y_1 \\ y_2 \end{bmatrix}$$

$$= a\,T\,\overline{x} + b\,T\,\overline{y}$$

Thus, the transformation given by eq.(1) is linear.

● **PROBLEM** 9-20

Which of the following transformations is linear?

1. the zero transformation

2. the identity transformation

3. a linear system of the form

$$x_i' = \sum_{k=1}^{n} a_{ik} x_k \qquad i = 1, \ldots n$$

4. T: $(x,y) \rightarrow (x+1, y+1)$ (1)

Solution: 1. Let T be the zero transformation; that is

$$T\,\overline{x} = \overline{0} \qquad (2)$$

for any vector $\overline{x}$. The zero transformation is linear if

$$T(a\overline{x} + b\overline{y}) = a\,T(\overline{x}) + b\,T(\overline{y}).$$

Since $T(a\overline{x} + b\overline{y}) = \overline{0}$

and $a\,T(\overline{x}) = \overline{0}$, $b\,T(\overline{y}) = \overline{0}$,

then $T(a\overline{x} + b\overline{y}) = a\,T(\overline{x}) + b\,T(\overline{y}) = \overline{0}$.

Thus the zero transformation is linear.

2. The transformation associating every vector $\overline{x}$ with itself is called the identity (or unit) transformation, denoted by E

$$E\overline{x} = \overline{x} \qquad (3)$$

Also $E(a\overline{x} + b\overline{y}) = a\overline{x} + b\overline{y} = a\,E(\overline{x}) + b\,E(\overline{y})$

Thus the identity transformation is a linear transformation.

3. Let $\overline{x}$ and $\overline{y}$ be two vectors

$$\overline{x} = (x_1, x_2, \ldots, x_n)$$

$$\overline{y} = (y_1, y_2, \ldots, y_n)$$ (4)

Then

$$T(a\overline{x} + b\overline{y}) = T(ax_1+by_1, \ ax_2+by_2, \ldots, ax_n+by_n)$$

$$= \begin{bmatrix} a_{11} & a_{12} \cdots a_{1n} \\ a_{21} & a_{22} \cdots a_{2n} \\ \cdot & \cdot \\ \cdot & \cdot \\ \cdot & \cdot \\ a_{n1} & a_{n2} \cdots a_{nn} \end{bmatrix} \begin{bmatrix} ax_1 + by_1 \\ ax_2 + by_2 \\ \cdot \\ \cdot \\ \cdot \\ ax_n + by_n \end{bmatrix}$$ (5)

$$= a \begin{bmatrix} a_{11} & a_{12} \cdots a_{1n} \\ a_{21} & a_{22} \cdots a_{2n} \\ \cdot & \cdot & \cdot \\ \cdot & \cdot & \cdot \\ \cdot & \cdot & \cdot \\ a_{n1} & a_{n2} \cdots a_{nn} \end{bmatrix} \begin{bmatrix} x_1 \\ x_2 \\ \cdot \\ \cdot \\ \cdot \\ x_n \end{bmatrix} + b \begin{bmatrix} a_{11} & a_{12} \cdots a_{1n} \\ a_{21} & a_{22} \cdots a_{2n} \\ \cdot & \cdot & \cdot \\ \cdot & \cdot & \cdot \\ \cdot & \cdot & \cdot \\ a_{n1} & a_{n2} \cdots a_{nn} \end{bmatrix} \begin{bmatrix} y_1 \\ y_2 \\ \cdot \\ \cdot \\ \cdot \\ y_n \end{bmatrix}$$

$$= a \ T\overline{x} + b \ T\overline{y}$$

Thus, this transformation is also linear.

4. From eq.(1)

$$T\left[a(x,y) + b(s,t)\right] = T(ax + bs, \ ay + bt)$$

$$= T(ax + bs + 1, \ ay + bt + 1)$$ (6)

and

$$a \ T(x,y) + b \ T(s,t) = a(x+1, \ y+1) + b(s+1, \ t+1)$$

$$= (ax+a \ , \ ay+a) + (bs+b, \ bt+b)$$

$$= (ax + bs + a + b, \ ay + bt + a + b)$$ (7)

Thus $\qquad T(a\overline{x} + b\overline{y}) \neq a \ T(\overline{x}) + b \ T(\overline{y})$

and the transformation is not linear.

● **PROBLEM 9-21**

1. Is the transformation

$$\overline{u} = A\overline{x} = \overline{a} \times \overline{x}$$ (1)

linear?

2. Explain why the transformation

$$T(x,y) = (x+y, \ x-y) \qquad (2)$$

is linear.

3. Explain why the transformation

$$T(x,y) = (x+2, \ y+1) \qquad (3)$$

is not linear.

Solution: 1. Let $\overline{x}$ and $\overline{y}$ be arbitrary vectors and α and β arbitrary scalars. To show that the transformation given by eq.(1) is linear, one has to prove that

$$A(\alpha\overline{x} + \beta\overline{y}) = \alpha A\overline{x} + \beta A\overline{y} \qquad (4)$$

Applying the properties of the vector product, one obtains

$$
\begin{aligned}
A(\alpha\overline{x} + \beta\overline{y}) &= \overline{a} \times \left[\alpha\overline{x} + \beta\overline{y} \right] \\
&= \overline{a} \times (\alpha\overline{x}) + \overline{a} \times (\beta\overline{y}) \\
&= \alpha\, \overline{a} \times \overline{x} + \beta\, \overline{a} \times \overline{y} \\
&= \alpha\, A\overline{x} + \beta\, A\overline{y}
\end{aligned}
\qquad (5)
$$

Therefore the transformation is linear.

2. The transformation given by eq.(2) can be written in matrix form as

$$T \begin{bmatrix} x \\ y \end{bmatrix} = \begin{bmatrix} x + y \\ x - y \end{bmatrix} \qquad (6)$$

From eq.(6), one obtains matrix T

$$\begin{bmatrix} 1 & 1 \\ 1 & -1 \end{bmatrix} \begin{bmatrix} x \\ y \end{bmatrix} = \begin{bmatrix} x + y \\ x - y \end{bmatrix} \qquad (7)$$

This system is linear, therefore the transformation defined by eq.(2) is linear.

3. For the transformation given by eq.(3) to be linear, matrix T must exist such that

$$T \begin{bmatrix} x \\ y \end{bmatrix} = \begin{bmatrix} x + 2 \\ y + 1 \end{bmatrix} \qquad (8)$$

Such a matrix does not exist and therefore the transformation is not linear.

1. Show that if T_1 and T_2 are linear transformations, then
    $T_1 + T_2$ and aT_1, where a is some scalar, are also linear transformations.

2. Let T_1 be given by

    $$x = 3x' + 2y'$$

    $$y = 2x' - y'$$

    (1)

    with domain (x',y') and values (x,y). Let T_2 be given by

    $$x'' = 3x - y$$

    $$y'' = 2x + 5y$$

    (2)

    with domain (x,y) and values (x'',y''). Find

    $T_2 T_1 \begin{bmatrix} 3 \\ -1 \end{bmatrix}$. Is the transformation $T_2 T_1$ linear?

Solution: 1. Let $\bar{x}$ and $\bar{y}$ be two arbitrary vectors and α and β two scalars. Since T_1 and T_2 are linear transformations, obtain

$$(T_1 + T_2)(\alpha\bar{x} + \beta\bar{y}) = T_1(\alpha\bar{x} + \beta\bar{y}) + T_2(\alpha\bar{x} + \beta\bar{y})$$

$$= \alpha T_1(\bar{x}) + \beta T_1(\bar{y}) + \alpha T_2(\bar{x}) + \beta T_2(\bar{y})$$

$$= \alpha\left[T_1(\bar{x}) + T_2(\bar{x})\right] + \beta\left[T_1(\bar{y}) + T_2(\bar{y})\right]$$

(3)

$$= \alpha(T_1 + T_2)(\bar{x}) + \beta(T_1 + T_2)(\bar{y})$$

Hence, $T_1 + T_2$ is a linear transformation. To show that aT_1 is a linear transformation, obtain

$$aT_1(\alpha\bar{x} + \beta\bar{y}) = a\left[\alpha T_1(\bar{x}) + \beta T_1(\bar{y})\right]$$

$$= \alpha\, aT_1(\bar{x}) + \beta\, aT_1(\bar{y})$$

(4)

Hence, aT_1 is a linear transformation.

2. To find $T_2 T_1 \begin{bmatrix} 3 \\ -1 \end{bmatrix}$, first find matrices T_1 and T_2. From eq.(1),

$$T_1 = \begin{bmatrix} 3 & 2 \\ 2 & -1 \end{bmatrix} \qquad (5)$$

where

$$\begin{bmatrix} x \\ y \end{bmatrix} = \begin{bmatrix} 3 & 2 \\ 2 & -1 \end{bmatrix} \begin{bmatrix} x' \\ y' \end{bmatrix} \qquad (6)$$

From eq.(2),

$$T_2 = \begin{bmatrix} 3 & -1 \\ 2 & 5 \end{bmatrix} \qquad (7)$$

where

$$\begin{bmatrix} x'' \\ y'' \end{bmatrix} = \begin{bmatrix} 3 & -1 \\ 2 & 5 \end{bmatrix} \begin{bmatrix} x \\ y \end{bmatrix} \qquad (8)$$

$$T_2 T_1 \begin{bmatrix} 3 \\ -1 \end{bmatrix} = T_2 \begin{bmatrix} 3 & 2 \\ 2 & -1 \end{bmatrix} \begin{bmatrix} 3 \\ -1 \end{bmatrix}$$

$$= T_2 \begin{bmatrix} 7 \\ 7 \end{bmatrix} = \begin{bmatrix} 3 & -1 \\ 2 & 5 \end{bmatrix} \begin{bmatrix} 7 \\ 7 \end{bmatrix} = \begin{bmatrix} 14 \\ 49 \end{bmatrix} \qquad (9)$$

Now compute $T_2 T_1$:

$$T_2 T_1 = \begin{bmatrix} 3 & -1 \\ 2 & 5 \end{bmatrix} \begin{bmatrix} 3 & 2 \\ 2 & -1 \end{bmatrix} = \begin{bmatrix} 7 & 7 \\ 16 & -1 \end{bmatrix} \qquad (10)$$

To find $T_2 T_1 \begin{bmatrix} 3 \\ -1 \end{bmatrix}$, use the matrix from eq.(10). Doing this,

$$T_2 T_1 \begin{bmatrix} 3 \\ -1 \end{bmatrix} = \begin{bmatrix} 7 & 7 \\ 16 & -1 \end{bmatrix} \begin{bmatrix} 3 \\ -1 \end{bmatrix} = \begin{bmatrix} 14 \\ 49 \end{bmatrix} \qquad (11)$$

Indeed, the results obtained in eq.(9) and eq.(11) are equivalent.

Thus, we conclude that the transformation $T_2 T_1$ is a linear transformation.

● **PROBLEM 9-23**

Define the product of two transformations and show that the product of two linear transformations is also a linear transformation.

Solution: Let T_1 be a transformation with domain U and values in V

$$T_1: U \to V \qquad (1)$$

and let T_2 be a transformation with domain V and values in W,

$$T_2: \ V \rightarrow W \tag{2}$$

The product transformation or composition

$$T_2T_1: \ U \rightarrow W \tag{3}$$

is defined as

$$T_2T_1(\overline{x}) = T_2\left[T_1(\overline{x})\right] \quad \text{for all } \overline{x}\varepsilon U \tag{4}$$

The product T_2T_1 is represented in the diagram.

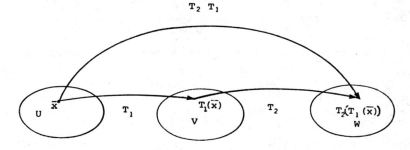

Now, take an arbitrary linear combination

$$\alpha\overline{x} + \beta\overline{y} \ \varepsilon \ U$$

Then

$$
\begin{aligned}
T_2T_1(\alpha\overline{x} + \beta\overline{y}) &= T_2\left[T_1(\alpha\overline{x} + \beta\overline{y})\right] \\
&= T_2\left[\alpha T_1(\overline{x}) + \beta T_1(\overline{y})\right] \\
&= \alpha\, T_2\left[T_1(\overline{x})\right] + \beta\, T_2\left[T_1(\overline{y})\right] \\
&= \alpha\, T_2T_1(\overline{x}) + \beta\, T_2T_1(\overline{y})
\end{aligned}
\tag{5}
$$

This proves that the product of two linear transformations is also a linear transformation.

● **PROBLEM 9-24**

Let V^3 be a vector space consisting of all spatial vectors; that is

$$\overline{x} \ \varepsilon \ V^3 \tag{1}$$

where $$\overline{x} = (x_1, \ x_2, \ x_3),$$

and let A be a transformation of V^3

$$A: \ V^3 \rightarrow V^3 \tag{2}$$

391

Show that there is a one-to-one correspondence between linear transformations of the vector space V^3 and square matrices of order three.

Solution: Let $\overline{x}$ be an arbitrary vector in V^3 such that
$$\overline{u} = A\,\overline{x} \qquad (3)$$
and let A be a square matrix of order three. From eq.(3), one concludes that this matrix defines a linear transformation. Hence, to every square matrix A of order three there corresponds a unique linear transformation. The converse of this statement is more difficult to prove. Assume that A is a linear transformation such that
$$\overline{u} = A\,\overline{x} \qquad (4)$$
The vectors of the orthonormal basis are $\overline{e}_1$, $\overline{e}_2$, $\overline{e}_3$. Hence,
$$\overline{x} = x_1\overline{e}_1 + x_2\overline{e}_2 + x_3\overline{e}_3 \qquad (5)$$
and for $\overline{u}$
$$\overline{u} = u_1\overline{e}_1 + u_2\overline{e}_2 + u_3\overline{e}_3 \qquad (6)$$
Since the transformation A is linear, one obtains
$$A\,\overline{x} = A(x_1\overline{e}_1 + x_2\overline{e}_2 + x_3\overline{e}_3)$$
$$= x_1 A\overline{e}_1 + x_2 A\overline{e}_2 + x_3 A\overline{e}_3 \qquad (7)$$

Each of the vectors $A\overline{e}_1$, $A\overline{e}_2$, $A\overline{e}_3$ can be represented as a linear combination of $\overline{e}_1$, $\overline{e}_2$, $\overline{e}_3$. Indeed,

$$A\overline{e}_1 = a_{11}\overline{e}_1 + a_{21}\overline{e}_2 + a_{31}\overline{e}_3$$
$$A\overline{e}_2 = a_{12}\overline{e}_1 + a_{22}\overline{e}_2 + a_{32}\overline{e}_3 \qquad (8)$$
$$A\overline{e}_3 = a_{13}\overline{e}_1 + a_{23}\overline{e}_2 + a_{33}\overline{e}_3$$

Substituting eq.(8) into eq.(7), one obtains
$$A\,\overline{x} = (a_{11}x_1 + a_{12}x_2 + a_{13}x_3)\overline{e}_1 + (a_{21}x_1 + a_{22}x_2 + a_{23}x_3)\overline{e}_2$$
$$+ (a_{31}x_1 + a_{32}x_2 + a_{33}x_3)\overline{e}_3 \qquad (9)$$
On the other hand $A\,\overline{x} = \overline{u}$, where
$$\overline{u} = u_1\overline{e}_1 + u_2\overline{e}_2 + u_3\overline{e}_3 \qquad (10)$$
Combining eqs.(9) and (10) yields
$$u_1 = a_{11}x_1 + a_{12}x_2 + a_{13}x_3$$
$$u_2 = a_{21}x_1 + a_{22}x_2 + a_{23}x_3 \qquad (11)$$
$$u_3 = a_{31}x_1 + a_{32}x_2 + a_{33}x_3$$

Eq.(11) can be written in the matrix form

$$\begin{bmatrix} u_1 \\ u_2 \\ u_3 \end{bmatrix} = \begin{bmatrix} a_{11} & a_{12} & a_{13} \\ a_{21} & a_{22} & a_{23} \\ a_{31} & a_{32} & a_{33} \end{bmatrix} \begin{bmatrix} x_1 \\ x_2 \\ x_3 \end{bmatrix} \qquad (12)$$

The matrix,

$$\begin{bmatrix} a_{11} & a_{12} & a_{13} \\ a_{21} & a_{22} & a_{23} \\ a_{31} & a_{32} & a_{33} \end{bmatrix},$$

is the matrix of the linear transformation A. Hence, it has been proved that to every linear transformation A of V^3 there corresponds a unique square matrix of order three.

The results of this problem can be easily generalized to any n-dimensional vector space.

Consider a linear transformation
$$\bar{u} = A\,\bar{x} \qquad (13)$$
of the n-dimensional vector space V^n. This transformation is described by a unique square matrix A

$$A = \begin{pmatrix} a_{11} & a_{12}\cdots a_{1n} \\ a_{21} & a_{22}\cdots a_{2n} \\ \vdots & \vdots \\ a_{n1} & a_{n2}\cdots a_{nn} \end{pmatrix} \qquad (14)$$

Note that the symbol A in eq.(13) denotes a transformation, and in eq.(14) denotes a matrix.

● **PROBLEM 9-25**

Which of the following transformations have inverse transformations?

1.
$$\begin{bmatrix} x' \\ y' \end{bmatrix} = \begin{bmatrix} 1 & -1 \\ 2 & 1 \end{bmatrix} \begin{bmatrix} x \\ y \end{bmatrix} \qquad (1)$$

2.
$$\begin{bmatrix} x' \\ y' \end{bmatrix} = \begin{bmatrix} 2 & 1 \\ 6 & 3 \end{bmatrix} \begin{bmatrix} x \\ y \end{bmatrix} \qquad (2)$$

Solution: To determine if the transformations have inverse transformations, apply the following theorem:

Theorem

An onto transformation

$$T: U \to V \tag{3}$$

has an inverse transformation

$$T^{-1}: V \to U \tag{4}$$

if and only if T is one-to-one; that is, if and only if

$$T\bar{x} = T\bar{y} \quad \text{implies} \quad \bar{x} = \bar{y} \quad \text{for all } \bar{x}, \bar{y} \in U.$$

1. Determine if the transformation defined by eq.(1) is one-to-one (obviously this transformation is an onto transformation). Let $T\bar{x} = T\bar{y}$, hence

$$\begin{bmatrix} 1 & -1 \\ 2 & 1 \end{bmatrix} \begin{bmatrix} x_1 \\ x_2 \end{bmatrix} = \begin{bmatrix} 1 & -1 \\ 2 & 1 \end{bmatrix} \begin{bmatrix} y_1 \\ y_2 \end{bmatrix} \tag{5}$$

or

$$x_1 - x_2 = y_1 - y_2 \tag{6}$$

$$2x_1 + x_2 = 2y_1 + y_2 \tag{7}$$

From eq.(6), we have

$$x_1 = x_2 + y_1 - y_2 \tag{8}$$

Substituting eq.(8) into eq.(7), one obtains

$$2x_2 + 2y_1 - 2y_2 + x_2 = 2y_1 + y_2 \tag{9}$$

or

$$x_2 = y_2$$

Eq.(8) leads to $x_1 = y_1$ and $\bar{x} = \bar{y}$.

Hence, this transformation is one-to-one and therefore has an inverse.

2. Taking arbitrary vectors $\bar{x}, \bar{y}$, we can write

$$\begin{bmatrix} 2 & 1 \\ 6 & 3 \end{bmatrix} \begin{bmatrix} x_1 \\ x_2 \end{bmatrix} = \begin{bmatrix} 2 & 1 \\ 6 & 3 \end{bmatrix} \begin{bmatrix} y_1 \\ y_2 \end{bmatrix} \tag{10}$$

or

$$2x_1 + x_2 = 2y_1 + y_2$$

$$6x_1 + 3x_2 = 6y_1 + 3y_2, \tag{11}$$

This system of equations reduces to one equation

$$2x_1 + x_2 = 2y_1 + y_2 \qquad (12)$$

which does not imply that $\overline{x} = \overline{y}$.

Hence, this transformation is not one-to-one and does not have an inverse transformation.

For those of you who don't remember the definitions of onto and one-to-one transformations, they will now be repeated.

A transformation $T: U \to V$ is called onto if for every $v \in V$ there exists $u \in U$ such that $T(u) = v$.

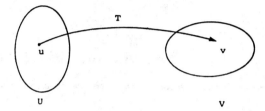

Using logical symbols, we can write: T is called onto if:

$$\forall \, v \in V \ni u \in U \mid T(u) = v$$

where "$\forall$" reads "for all" or "for every", "$\ni$" reads "there exists" and "$\mid$" indicates "such that".

A transformation $T: U \to V$ is called a one-to-one transformation if it is onto and satisfies the condition that $Tu_1 = Tu_2$ implies $u_1 = u_2$.

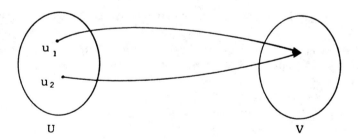

The transformation shown in the figure is not one-to-one. Using logical symbols, one can write T is called one-to-one if:

$$\forall \, u_1, \, u_2 \in U \ (Tu_1 = Tu_2) \Rightarrow (u_1 = u_2)$$

where $\Rightarrow$ reads "implies".

● **PROBLEM 9-26**

Let T be a one-to-one linear transformation in the three-dimensional vector space V^3;

$$T: V^3 \to V^3 \qquad (1)$$

where

$$T = \begin{bmatrix} 1 & -1 & 2 \\ 0 & 2 & 1 \\ 1 & 0 & 1 \end{bmatrix}$$ (2)

If three linearly independent vectors are given by

$$\bar{a} = [2, 0, 1]$$
$$\bar{b} = [1, 1, 0]$$ (3)
$$\bar{c} = [1, 1, 1] \ ,$$

determine if the vectors $T\bar{a}$, $T\bar{b}$, $T\bar{c}$ are linearly independent.

Solution: Recall that a set of $\{\bar{a}_1, \bar{a}_2, \ldots, \bar{a}_n\}$ vectors is said to be linearly dependent if there exist n real numbers $\alpha_1, \alpha_2, \ldots, \alpha_n$, not all of them zero, such that

$$\alpha_1\bar{a}_1 + \alpha_2\bar{a}_2 + \ldots + \alpha_n\bar{a}_n = \bar{0}$$ (4)

If relationship (4) holds only when

$$\alpha_1 = \alpha_2 = \ldots = \alpha_n = 0,$$ (5)

then the set of vectors is said to be linearly independent.

To determine if the vectors are linearly independent one can apply the following:

Theorem:

Vectors

$$\bar{a} = (a_1, a_2, a_3)$$
$$\bar{b} = (b_1, b_2, b_3)$$ (6)
$$\bar{c} = (c_1, c_2, c_3)$$

are linearly dependent if and only if

$$\begin{vmatrix} a_1 & a_2 & a_3 \\ b_1 & b_2 & b_3 \\ c_1 & c_2 & c_3 \end{vmatrix} = 0$$ (7)

and linearly independent if and only if

$$\begin{vmatrix} a_1 & a_2 & a_3 \\ b_1 & b_2 & b_3 \\ c_1 & c_2 & c_3 \end{vmatrix} \neq 0 \qquad (8)$$

Indeed, the three vectors $\overline{a}$, $\overline{b}$, $\overline{c}$ given in eq.(3) are

$$\begin{vmatrix} 2 & 0 & 1 \\ 1 & 1 & 0 \\ 1 & 1 & 1 \end{vmatrix} \neq 0 \qquad (9)$$

linearly independent.

From T, as given by eq.(2), we can compute $T\overline{a}$, $T\overline{b}$, $T\overline{c}$. Then, from the components of the vectors $T\overline{a}$, $T\overline{b}$, $T\overline{c}$, we can then obtain a determinant. If the value of this determinant is zero, the vectors are linearly dependent; if it is not zero, then they are linearly independent. There is, however, a shorter method for determining if the vectors $T\overline{a}$, $T\overline{b}$, $T\overline{c}$ are linearly independent. Consider the following theorem:

If T is a one-to-one and onto linear transformation, the image of a linearly independent set of vectors is linearly independent.

In our case, since T is a linear one-to-one and onto transformation, and the vectors $\overline{a}$, $\overline{b}$, $\overline{c}$ are linearly independent, their image $T\overline{a}$, $T\overline{b}$, $T\overline{c}$ are linearly independent vectors.

● **PROBLEM** 9-27

Prove the following theorems:

Theorem 1:

   If T is a linear transformation, then

$$T(\overline{0}) = \overline{0} \qquad (1)$$

Theorem 2:

   If T is a one-to-one linear transformation, then the image of a linearly dependent set of vectors is linearly dependent.

Theorem 3:

   If T is a one-to-one and onto linear transformation, the image of a linearly independent set of vectors is linearly independent.

Solution:

Theorem 1:

Note that
$$\bar{a} - \bar{a} = \bar{a} + (-1)\bar{a} = \bar{0} \qquad (2)$$

Since T is a linear transformation, then

$$T(\bar{0}) = T(\bar{a}-\bar{a}) = T\left[\bar{a} + (-1)\bar{a}\right]$$

$$= T(\bar{a}) - T(\bar{a}) = \bar{0} \qquad (3)$$

Thus, under a linear transformation, a zero is transformed into a zero.

Theorem 2:

Let $\{\bar{r}_1, \bar{r}_2, \ldots, r_n\}$ be any linearly dependent set of vectors. There exist scalars $\alpha_1, \alpha_2, \ldots, \alpha_n$ such that

$$\alpha_1\bar{r}_1 + \alpha_2\bar{r}_2 + \ldots + \alpha_n\bar{r}_n = \bar{0} \qquad (4)$$

where not all α's are zero. Since T is one-to-one, we can write

$$T(\bar{r}_1) = \bar{u}_1, \quad T(\bar{r}_2) = \bar{u}_2, \ldots, T(\bar{r}_n) = \bar{u}_n, \qquad (5)$$

thus,

$$T(\alpha_1\bar{r}_1 + \alpha_2\bar{r}_2 + \ldots + \alpha_n\bar{r}_n) = T(\bar{0}) = \bar{0} \qquad (6)$$

(see Theorem 1). On the other hand,

$$T(\alpha_1\bar{r}_1+\alpha_2\bar{r}_2+\ldots+\alpha_n\bar{r}_n) = \alpha_1 T(\bar{r}_1) + \alpha_2 T(\bar{r}_2)+\ldots+T(\bar{r}_n)$$

$$= \alpha_1\bar{u}_1 +\alpha_2\bar{u}_2 +\ldots+ \alpha_n\bar{u}_n = 0 \qquad (7)$$

Not all the coefficients are necessarily equal to zero, therefore the vectors $\bar{u}_1, \bar{u}_2, \ldots, \bar{u}_n$ are linearly dependent.

Theorem 3:

Let $\bar{r}_1, \bar{r}_2, \ldots, \bar{r}_n$ be a set of linearly independent vectors. Again, since T is one-to-one, each transformation can be represented as $T(\bar{r}_1) = \bar{u}_1, T(\bar{r}_2) = \bar{u}_2, \ldots, T(\bar{r}_n) = \bar{u}_n$. Now assume that the image set is linearly dependent. In which case there exist scalars $\alpha_1, \alpha_2, \ldots \alpha_n$ not all zero, such that

$$\alpha_1\bar{u}_1 + \alpha_2\bar{u}_2 + \ldots + \alpha_n\bar{u}_n = \bar{0}$$

Since T is linear, one has

$$T(\alpha_1\bar{r}_1+\alpha_2\bar{r}_2+\ldots+\alpha_n\bar{r}_n) = \alpha_1\bar{u}_1 + \alpha_2\bar{u}_2 +\ldots+ \alpha_n\bar{u}_n = \bar{0}$$

Since T is one-to-one and onto, one obtains

$$\alpha_1\bar{r}_1 + \alpha_2\bar{r}_2 +\ldots+ \alpha_n\bar{r}_n = \bar{0},$$

where, as stated before, not all $\alpha_1,\alpha_2,\ldots,\alpha_n$ are equal to zero (since our assumption of a linearly dependent image implies that $\alpha_1,\alpha_2,\ldots,\alpha_n$ are not all zero), and therefore, the set $\{\bar{r}_1,\bar{r}_2,\ldots,\bar{r}_n\}$ is linearly dependent. However, the problem states that the set of vectors $\{\bar{r}_1,\bar{r}_2,\ldots,\bar{r}_n\}$ are linearly independent, in which case one concludes that all α are equal to zero; thus proving the initial assumption wrong. Therefore the image set is not linearly dependent, as was initially assumed, but rather linearly independent.

From the above theorems, one concludes that if $\{\bar{e}_1,\bar{e}_2,\ldots,\bar{e}_n\}$ is a set of basis vectors of V and T is a linear transformation, such that

$$T: V \to U,$$

then $\{T(\bar{e}_1), T(\bar{e}_2),\ldots,T(\bar{e}_n)\}$ is a set of basis vectors for $T(V) = U$.

● **PROBLEM** 9-28

Show that the operations of differentiation and integration are linear transformations.

Solution: Consider the set of all bounded continuous functions defined on the interval [0,1] (or $0 \le x \le 1$). This interval can be denoted by the set C[0,1], which forms a vector space. Let M[0,1] be the subspace of C[0,1] consisting of all functions f such that both f and $\frac{df}{dx}$ are defined and continuous on [0,1].

Now, let T be a mapping of V into U

$$T: V \to U \qquad\qquad (1)$$

where V and U are vector spaces over the field R. T is a linear transformation if

$$T(V_1 + V_2) = T(V_1) + T(V_2) \qquad (2)$$

$$T(\alpha V_1) = \alpha T(V_1) \qquad (3)$$

for any V_1, V_2 ε V and any $\alpha \varepsilon$R. M[0,1] is a set of functions which have continuous derivatives on [0,1]. Hence, in this case

$$V = M[0,1]$$
$$\qquad (4)$$
$$U = C[0,1]$$

Let D denote the operation of differentiation

$$D: M[0,1] \rightarrow C[0,1] \qquad (5)$$

From the rules of differentiation, one obtains

$$D(f+g)(x) = \frac{d}{dx}(f+g)(x) = \frac{df}{dx} + \frac{dg}{dx}$$
$$\qquad (6)$$
$$= Df(x) + Dg(x)$$

$$D(\alpha f)(x) = \frac{d}{dx}(\alpha f)(x) = \alpha\frac{df}{dx} = \alpha Df(x) \qquad (7)$$

Thus D is a linear transformation of M[0,1] into C[0,1].

Denote the operation of integration by I. Thus

$$I\ f(x) = \int_0^x f(s)ds \qquad (8)$$

where the integral is defined for any continuous function, $f \varepsilon C[0,1]$. If f(x) is continuous, then $\int_0^x f(s)ds$ is also continuous.
Also,
$$I: C[0,1] \rightarrow C[0,1] \qquad (9)$$

By the rules of integration,

$$I[f(x) + g(x)] = \int_0^x [f(s) + g(s)]ds$$
$$\qquad (10)$$
$$= \int_0^x f(s)ds + \int_0^x g(s)ds = I\ f(x) + I\ g(x)$$

and

$$I[\alpha f(x)] = \int_0^x [\alpha f(s)]ds = \alpha\int_0^x f(s)ds$$
$$\qquad (11)$$
$$= \alpha I\ f(x).$$

Thus, I is a linear transformation of C[0,1] into itself.

LINEARLY INDEPENDENT VECTORS AND THE FUNDAMENTAL THEOREM OF LINEAR ALGEBRA

● **PROBLEM** 9-29

Three vectors

$$\bar{a}_1 = \begin{bmatrix} 3 \\ 2 \\ 1 \\ 0 \end{bmatrix} \quad \bar{a}_2 = \begin{bmatrix} 0 \\ 0 \\ 1 \\ 1 \end{bmatrix} \quad \bar{a}_3 = \begin{bmatrix} 1 \\ 1 \\ 0 \\ 0 \end{bmatrix} \tag{1}$$

are given in the four-dimensional space R^4. Find a vector $\bar{b}$ such that the set $\{\bar{a}_1, \bar{a}_2, \bar{a}_3, \bar{b}\}$ spans R^4.

Solution: If a set of four vectors spans R^4, then any vector in R^4 can be represented as a linear combination of the vectors from this set. Any set having this property forms a basis of R^4.

Before searching for vector $\bar{b}$, one should verify that vectors $\bar{a}_1, \bar{a}_2, \bar{a}_3$ are linearly independent. If they are not, then they cannot be used to form a basis.

Forming a linear combination of $\bar{a}_1, \bar{a}_2, \bar{a}_3$, one obtains

$$\alpha\bar{a}_1 + \beta\bar{a}_2 + \gamma\bar{a}_3 = \bar{0} \tag{2}$$

or

$$\alpha \begin{bmatrix} 3 \\ 2 \\ 1 \\ 0 \end{bmatrix} + \beta \begin{bmatrix} 0 \\ 0 \\ 1 \\ 1 \end{bmatrix} + \gamma \begin{bmatrix} 1 \\ 1 \\ 0 \\ 0 \end{bmatrix} = \begin{bmatrix} 0 \\ 0 \\ 0 \\ 0 \end{bmatrix} \tag{3}$$

Comparing the components leads to

$$\begin{aligned} 3\alpha + \gamma &= 0 \\ 2\alpha + \gamma &= 0 \\ \alpha + \beta &= 0 \\ \beta &= 0 \end{aligned} \tag{4}$$

Solving system (4), one obtains

$$\alpha = \beta = \gamma = 0 \tag{5}$$

Hence vectors $\bar{a}_1, \bar{a}_2, \bar{a}_3$ are linearly independent.

Now, to find a vector $\bar{b}$, such that the set of vectors $\{\bar{a}_1, \bar{a}_2, \bar{a}_3, \bar{b}\}$ would be a set of linearly independent vectors, develop the following expression

$$\alpha\bar{a}_1 + \beta\bar{a}_2 + \gamma\bar{a}_3 + \delta\bar{b} = \bar{0} \tag{6}$$

401

If the vectors are linearly independent, condition (6) implies

$$\alpha = \beta = \gamma = \delta = 0 \qquad (7)$$

Assume $\bar{b}$ to be

$$\bar{b} = \begin{bmatrix} b_1 \\ b_2 \\ b_3 \\ b_4 \end{bmatrix} \qquad (8)$$

Then, substitute eq.(8) into eq.(6) and solve the system of equations. Since it is required to find any vector $\bar{b}$ satisfying eqs.(6) and (7), choose the simplest form for $\bar{b}$, namely

$$\bar{b} = \begin{bmatrix} 1 \\ 0 \\ 0 \\ 0 \end{bmatrix} \qquad (9)$$

Substituting eq.(9) into eq.(6), we obtain

$$\alpha \begin{bmatrix} 3 \\ 2 \\ 1 \\ 0 \end{bmatrix} + \beta \begin{bmatrix} 0 \\ 0 \\ 1 \\ 1 \end{bmatrix} + \gamma \begin{bmatrix} 1 \\ 1 \\ 0 \\ 0 \end{bmatrix} + \delta \begin{bmatrix} 1 \\ 0 \\ 0 \\ 0 \end{bmatrix} = \begin{bmatrix} 0 \\ 0 \\ 0 \\ 0 \end{bmatrix} \qquad (10)$$

Eq.(10) is equivalent to the set of four equations

$$3\alpha + \gamma + \delta = 0$$

$$2\alpha + \gamma = 0$$

$$\alpha + \beta = 0 \qquad (11)$$

$$\beta = 0$$

Solving eq.(11) yields

$$\alpha = \beta = \gamma = \delta = 0 \qquad (12)$$

Thus, the vectors $\bar{a}_1, \bar{a}_2, \bar{a}_3$ and $\bar{b}$ are linearly independent and form a basis of the vector space R^4. These vectors, therefore, span R^4.

● **PROBLEM 9-30**

Let T be a linear transformation

$$T: R^4 \to R^3 \qquad (1)$$

such that

$$T(x_1, x_2, x_3, x_4) = (x_1 + x_2 - x_3 + 2x_4, \ 2x_1 - x_2 - 2x_3 + x_4, \ x_1 - x_3 + x_4) \qquad (2)$$

Find the corresponding basis and dimension of

1. Im T

2. ker(T)

Solution: Let P be a transformation
$$P: V \to U \qquad (3)$$
The image of P is a set of $u \varepsilon U$
$$\text{Im } P = \{u \varepsilon U: \forall v \varepsilon V \; P(v) = u\} \qquad (4)$$
That is, Im P is a set of all elements of U, such that for every $u \varepsilon$ Im P there exists $v \varepsilon V$ where $P(v) = u$.

First let us find what effect T has on a set of basis vectors in R^4. Choose the standard basis of R^4

$$\overline{e}_1 = (1,0,0,0) \qquad \overline{e}_2 = (0,1,0,0)$$
$$\overline{e}_3 = (0,0,1,0) \qquad \overline{e}_4 = (0,0,0,1) \qquad (5)$$
Thus
$$T(\overline{e}_1) = (1,2,1) \qquad T(\overline{e}_2) = (1,-1,0)$$
$$T(\overline{e}_3) = (-1,-2,-1) \qquad T(\overline{e}_4) = (2,1,1) \qquad (6)$$
Representing the rows of the transformation matrix by vectors $T(\overline{e}_1)$, $T(\overline{e}_2)$, $T(\overline{e}_3)$, $T(\overline{e}_4)$, one obtains

$$T = \begin{bmatrix} 1 & 2 & 1 \\ 1 & -1 & 0 \\ -1 & -2 & -1 \\ 2 & 1 & 1 \end{bmatrix} \qquad (7)$$

Note that the matrix in eq.(7) can be obtained directly from eq.(2). The columns are the coefficients of the right-hand side of eq.(2). Reducing matrix T to echelon form, one obtains

$$\begin{bmatrix} 1 & 2 & 1 \\ 1 & -1 & 0 \\ -1 & -2 & -1 \\ 2 & 1 & 1 \end{bmatrix} \to \begin{bmatrix} 1 & 2 & 1 \\ 1 & -1 & 0 \\ 0 & 0 & 0 \\ 0 & 0 & 0 \end{bmatrix} \qquad (8)$$

Thus, there are two independent vectors in T and the dimension of Im T is two. A basis of Im T is $(1,2,1)$ and $(1,-1,0)$.

The set of all elements in a vector space V that is transformed onto $0 \varepsilon U$ by a linear transformation $T: V \to U$ is called the null space or kernel of T.
$$\ker(T) = \{v \varepsilon V: T(v) = 0\} \qquad (9)$$
To find ker(T), we have to find all solutions of the system
$$x_1 + x_2 - x_3 + 2x_4 = 0$$
$$2x_1 - x_2 - 2x_3 + x_4 = 0 \qquad (10)$$

$$x_1 - x_3 + x_4 = 0$$

The matrix of coefficients of eq.(10) is

$$\begin{bmatrix} 1 & 1 & -1 & 2 \\ 2 & -1 & -2 & 1 \\ 1 & 0 & -1 & 1 \end{bmatrix} \tag{11}$$

Reducing it to echelon form, one obtains

$$\begin{bmatrix} 0 & 0 & 0 & 0 \\ 0 & -1 & 0 & -1 \\ 2 & 0 & -2 & 2 \end{bmatrix} \tag{12}$$

There are two independent rows in matrix (12), therefore

$$\dim \ker(T) = 2 \tag{13}$$

As a basis of ker(T), one can take any two independent solutions of eq.(10). For example,

$$\bar{b}_1 = (0,2,-2,-2) \quad \bar{b}_2 = (1,0,1,0), \tag{14}$$

satisfy eq.(10).

● **PROBLEM 9-31**

The linear transformation T: $R^4 \rightarrow R^4$ is given such that

$$T(x_1,x_2,x_3,x_4) = (x_1+x_4,\ 0,\ x_2,\ 0) \tag{1}$$

Find the dimensions of Im T and ker(T).

Solution: Let T be a linear transformation T: $V \rightarrow U$. The following theorem holds.

Theorem:

$$\dim V = \dim \text{Im } T + \dim \ker(T) \tag{2}$$

In our case $V = R^4$, thus

$$\dim V = 4 \tag{3}$$

It is now necessary to find either dim Im T or dim ker(T).

First, find dim Im T. Note that a linear transformation is fully described by the way it acts upon the basis vectors. Thus, taking the standard basis of R^4, one obtains the following from eq.(1)

$$T(\bar{e}_1) = (1,0,0,0) \qquad T(\bar{e}_2) = (0,0,1,0)$$

$$\tag{4}$$

$$T(\bar{e}_3) = (0,0,0,0) \qquad T(\bar{e}_4) = (1,0,0,0)$$

where

$$\bar{e}_1 = (1,0,0,0) \qquad \bar{e}_2 = (0,1,0,0).$$

$$\tag{5}$$

$$\bar{e}_3 = (0,0,1,0) \qquad \bar{e}_4 = (0,0,0,1)$$

The vectors $T(\bar{e}_1)$, $T(\bar{e}_2)$, $T(\bar{e}_3)$, $T(\bar{e}_4)$ span the set Im T. Therefore, dim Im T is the number of independent vectors $T(\bar{e}_i)$ i = 1,2,3,4. Note that $T(\bar{e}_1) = T(\bar{e}_4)$ and $T(\bar{e}_3) = \bar{0}$. Thus, there are only two independent vectors

$$(1,0,0,0) \quad \text{and} \quad (0,0,1,0) \tag{6}$$

and

$$\text{dim Im T} = 2.$$

Solving for dim ker(T) in eq.(2), one obtains

$$\text{dim ker(T)} = \text{dim V} - \text{dim Im T} =$$
$$= 4 - 2 = 2 \tag{7}$$

● **PROBLEM 9-32**

Let T be the linear transformation $T: R^3 \rightarrow R^3$ such that

$$T(x,y,z) = (0,y,z) \tag{1}$$

Find Im T and ker(T). Also, verify the fundamental theorem of linear algebra.

Solution: T transforms vectors in R^3 into vectors which have zero as their first coordinate. Thus, Im T is a two-dimensional subspace of R^3.

ker(T) contains all vectors in R^3 which are transformed into (0,0,0). From eq.(1) we see that

$$(\alpha,0,0) \rightarrow (0,0,0) \tag{2}$$

Thus ker(T) is a one-dimensional subspace of R^3, and therefore

$$\text{dim Im T} = 2$$
$$\text{dim ker(T)} = 1 \tag{3}$$

The fundamental theorem states that

$$\text{dim V} = \text{dim Im T} + \text{dim ker(T)} \tag{4}$$

In our case $V = R^3$. Thus

$$\text{dim } R^3 = 3 = 2 + 1, \tag{5}$$

which verifies eq (4).

TRANSFORMATION OF CARTESIAN COORDINATE SYSTEMS, DETERMINANTS AND INVERSE TRANSFORMATIONS

● **PROBLEM 9-33**

Write the transformation equations for two rectangular cartesian coordinate systems, having a common origin, such that there is no change of unit distance along the coordinate axes.

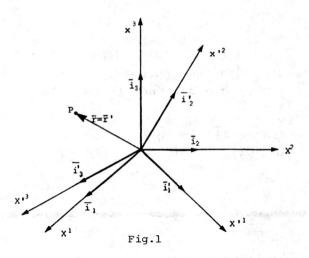

Fig.1

Solution: Before we proceed with the actual solution, con-sider the following notation:

When an index is repeated in a term, summation with re-spect to that index is understood over the appropriate range. For example

$$a_{ij}x^i \quad \text{stands for}$$

$$a_{1j}x^1 + a_{2j}x^2 + a_{3j}x^3$$

This convention is called the "summation convention". The Kronecker delta is defined as

$$\delta_{ij} = \delta^{ij} = \delta^i_j = \delta^j_i = \begin{cases} 0 & \text{if } i \neq j \\ 1 & \text{if } i = j. \end{cases}$$

For example,

$$\delta_{12} = 0, \quad \delta_{22} = 1 = \delta_{11}.$$

Both the summation convention and the Kronecker delta will be more thoroughly discussed in Chapter X.

Proceeding to the problem at hand, note that Fig. 1 illustrates the two coordinate systems being considered. Vectors $\bar{i}_1$, $\bar{i}_2$, $\bar{i}_3$ are the base vectors of the (x^1, x^2, x^3) system and $\bar{i}'_1$, $\bar{i}'_2$, $\bar{i}'_3$ are the base vectors of the (x'^1, x'^2, x'^3) system.

Note that vectors $\bar{i}'_1$, $\bar{i}'_2$, $\bar{i}'_3$ can be expressed in terms of $\bar{i}_1$, $\bar{i}_2$, $\bar{i}_3$; and vice versa.

Since there is no change in unit distance along the coordinate axes, we can write

$$\bar{r} = \bar{r}'$$

or

$$x^k \bar{i}_k = x'^k \bar{i}'_k$$

(1)

406

Now express $\bar{i}'_k$ in terms of $\bar{i}_j$. $\bar{i}'_1$ is a unit vector and its projections in the directions of $\bar{i}_1, \bar{i}_2, \bar{i}_3$ are the cosines of the angles made by $\bar{i}'_1$ with $\bar{i}_1, \bar{i}_2, \bar{i}_3$. Let the angles be $\alpha^1, \alpha^2, \alpha^3$ (see Fig. 2), and denote $\cos \alpha_1^k$ by

$$a_1^{\,k} = \cos \alpha_1^{\,k}. \qquad (2)$$

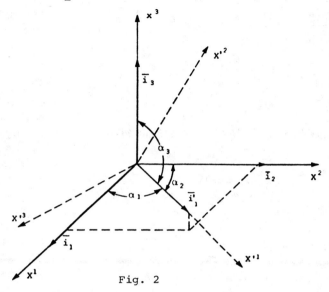

Fig. 2

Then one can write

$$\bar{i}'_1 = a_1^{\,1}\bar{i}_1 + a_1^{\,2}\bar{i}_2 + a_1^{\,3}\bar{i}_3 = a_1^{\,k}\bar{i}_k \qquad (3)$$

Now, denote $a_k^{\,j}$ by

$$a_k^{\,j} = \cos \alpha_k^{\,j} \qquad (4)$$

where $\alpha_k^{\,j}$ is the angle from $\bar{i}_j$ to $\bar{i}'_k$.
Then

$$\bar{i}'_n = a_n^{\,k}\bar{i}_k \qquad (5)$$

Substituting eq.(5) into eq.(1), one obtains

$$x^k \bar{i}_k = x'^{\,j} a_j^{\,n} \bar{i}_n \qquad (6)$$

or

$$x^n \bar{i}_n = x'^{\,j} a_j^{\,n} \bar{i}_n$$

$$(x^n - x'^{\,j} a_j^{\,n})\bar{i}_n = 0 \qquad (7)$$

Since the vectors $\bar{i}_n$ are linearly independent, we have

$$x^n = a_j^{\,n} x'^{\,j} \quad (\text{because } x^n - x'^{\,j} a_j^{\,n} = 0), \qquad (8)$$

which is the transformation formula.

The angle between two directions is given in terms of direction cosines

$$\cos \phi = \sum_{n=1}^{3} a_k{}^n a_\ell{}^n$$

Note that for $k = \ell$, vectors $\bar{i}'_k$ and $\bar{i}'_\ell$ coincide and $\cos 0 = 1$, for $k \neq \ell, \bar{i}'_k$ and $\bar{i}'_\ell$ are orthogonal and

$$\cos \frac{\pi}{2} = 0. \quad \text{Thus}$$

$$\sum_{n=1}^{3} a_k{}^n a_j{}^n = \delta_{kj}.$$

To summarize, the transformation is given by

$$x^n = a_j{}^n x'^j$$

with   (9)

$$\sum_{n=1}^{3} a_k{}^n a_\ell{}^n = \delta_{k\ell}$$

● **PROBLEM 9-34**

The transformation

$$x^j = a_k{}^j x'^k \tag{1}$$

where

$$\sum_{i=1}^{3} a_k{}^i a_\ell{}^i = \delta_{k\ell} \tag{2}$$

relates two right-handed rectangular cartesian coordinate systems.

1) Show that

$$\left[\det(a_i{}^j) \right]^2 = 1 \tag{3}$$

2) Find the inverse transformation of eq.(1).

Solution: 1) Using the determinant multiplication theorem, we can write eq.(2) as

$$\det \left(\sum_{i=1}^{3} a_k{}^i a_\ell{}^i \right) = \det(a_k{}^i) \cdot \det(a_\ell{}^i) \tag{4}$$

$$= \det(\delta_{k\ell})$$

It is known that

$$\det(\delta_{k\ell}) = 1 \tag{5}$$

Thus, substituting eq.(5) into eq.(4), one obtains

$$\left[\det(a_i{}^j)\right]^2 = 1 \tag{6}$$

Thus, there are two values for det $(a_i{}^j)$

$$\det(a_i{}^j) = 1 \quad \text{and} \quad \det(a_i{}^j) = -1 \tag{7}$$

It can be shown that for right-handed rectangular cartesian coordinate systems,

$$\det(a_i{}^j) = 1 \tag{8}$$

2) Let $A_\ell{}^n = \dfrac{\text{cofactor of } a_n{}^\ell \text{ in } \det(a_i{}^j)}{\det(a_i{}^j)}$

The transformation is given by

$$x^j = a_k{}^j \, x'{}^k \tag{9}$$

Multiply the three equations (9) by $A_1{}^\ell, A_2{}^\ell, A_3{}^\ell$ and add the results.

We then obtain

$$A_j{}^\ell \, x^j = A_j{}^\ell \, a_k{}^j \, x'{}^k, \tag{10}$$

and

$$A_j{}^\ell \, a_k{}^j = \delta_\ell^k$$

from which

$$A_j{}^\ell \, x^j = \delta_\ell^k \, x'{}^k = x'{}^\ell.$$

● **PROBLEM 9-35**

Show that the coefficients $A_i{}^j$ of the inverse transformation can be obtained from $a_k{}^\ell$ by interchanging rows and columns of the matrix; that is

$$A_i{}^j = a_j{}^i \tag{1}$$

Solution: $A_i{}^j$ is defined as

$$A_i{}^j = \frac{\text{cofactor of } a_j{}^i}{\det(a_i{}^j)} \quad \text{(see Problem 9-35)}, \tag{2}$$

also,

$$A_j{}^k \, a_k{}^\ell = \delta_i{}^\ell \tag{3}$$

409

Multiply eq.(3) by a_n^ℓ and sum from $\ell = 1$ to 3

$$\sum_{\ell=1}^{3} a_n^\ell \, A_j^k \, a_k^\ell = \sum_{\ell=1}^{3} \delta_j^\ell \, a_n^\ell \tag{4}$$

From Problem 9-33,

$$\sum_{\ell=1}^{3} a_n^\ell \, a_k^\ell = \delta_{nk} \tag{5}$$

Thus, substituting eq.(5) into eq.(4) yields

$$\delta_{nk} \, A_j^k = \sum_{\ell=1}^{3} \delta_j^\ell \, a_n^\ell$$

or

$$A_j^n = a_n^j \tag{6}$$

● **PROBLEM 9-36**

1) Show that the transformation described by

$$x^j = a_k^j \, x'^k \tag{1}$$

where

$$(a_i^j) = \begin{pmatrix} 0 & \dfrac{1}{2} & -\dfrac{\sqrt{3}}{2} \\[2mm] \dfrac{\sqrt{3}}{2} & \dfrac{\sqrt{3}}{4} & \dfrac{1}{4} \\[2mm] \dfrac{1}{2} & -\dfrac{3}{4} & -\dfrac{\sqrt{3}}{4} \end{pmatrix} \tag{2}$$

relates two right-handed rectangular cartesian coordinate systems. Assume that x^i is a right-handed system.

2) Find the inverse transformation to the transformation described by eqs.(1) and (2).

Solution: 1) We have to show that for matrix (2) the following relations hold

$$\sum_{n=1}^{3} a_k^n \, a_\ell^n = \delta_{k\ell} \tag{3}$$

and

$$\det(a_i^j) = 1 \tag{4}$$

Substituting eq.(2) into eq.(3), we obtain, for different combinations of k and ℓ,

$$a_1^1 a_1^1 + a_1^2 a_1^2 + a_1^3 a_1^3 = \frac{1}{2} \cdot \frac{1}{2} + \left(-\frac{\sqrt{3}}{2}\right) \cdot \left(-\frac{\sqrt{3}}{2}\right) = \frac{1}{4} + \frac{3}{4} = 1$$

$$a_2^1 a_2^1 + a_2^2 a_2^2 + a_2^3 a_2^3 = \frac{3}{4} + \frac{3}{16} + \frac{1}{16} = 1$$

$$a_3^1 a_3^1 + a_3^2 a_3^2 + a_3^3 a_3^3 = \frac{1}{4} + \frac{9}{16} + \frac{3}{16} = 1 \tag{5}$$

$$a_1^1 a_2^1 + a_1^2 a_2^2 + a_1^3 a_2^3 = \frac{\sqrt{3}}{8} - \frac{\sqrt{3}}{3} = 0$$

$$a_1^1 a_3^1 + a_1^2 a_3^2 + a_1^3 a_3^3 = -\frac{3}{8} + \frac{3}{8} = 0$$

$$a_2^1 a_3^1 + a_2^2 a_3^2 + a_2^3 a_3^3 = \frac{\sqrt{3}}{4} - \frac{3\sqrt{3}}{16} - \frac{\sqrt{3}}{16} = 0$$

Thus matrix $(a_i{}^j)$ satisfies condition (3).

Now check condition (4),

$$\det(a_i{}^j) = \begin{vmatrix} 0 & \frac{1}{2} & -\frac{\sqrt{3}}{2} \\ \frac{\sqrt{3}}{2} & \frac{\sqrt{3}}{4} & \frac{1}{4} \\ \frac{1}{2} & -\frac{3}{4} & -\frac{\sqrt{3}}{4} \end{vmatrix} = \frac{1}{4} \cdot \frac{1}{4} + \frac{3}{4} \cdot \frac{3}{4} + \frac{1}{2} \cdot \frac{3}{8} + \frac{3}{8} \cdot \frac{1}{2} = 1 \tag{6}$$

This completes the proof which states that the transformation described by (1) and (2) relates two right-handed rectangular cartesian coordinate systems.

2) Using the results of Problem 9-35, one concludes that the inverse transformation can be obtained from $a_i{}^j$ by interchanging rows and columns of the matrix, thus

$$\text{Inverse transformation coefficients} = \begin{pmatrix} 0 & \frac{\sqrt{3}}{2} & \frac{1}{2} \\ \frac{1}{2} & \frac{\sqrt{3}}{4} & -\frac{3}{4} \\ -\frac{\sqrt{3}}{2} & \frac{1}{4} & -\frac{\sqrt{3}}{4} \end{pmatrix} \tag{7}$$

● **PROBLEM** 9-37

Let $x^k = a_\ell{}^k x^{1\ell}$ (1)

be the transformation relating two cartesian rectangular systems. Show that the determinant of coefficients $a_i{}^j$ can be expressed in terms of partial derivatives as follows:

$$\left| \frac{\partial x^j}{\partial x^{1k}} \right| = \begin{vmatrix} \dfrac{\partial x^1}{\partial x^{11}} & \dfrac{\partial x^2}{\partial x^{11}} & \dfrac{\partial x^3}{\partial x^{11}} \\[3mm] \dfrac{\partial x^1}{\partial x^{12}} & \dfrac{\partial x^2}{\partial x^{12}} & \dfrac{\partial x^3}{\partial x^{12}} \\[3mm] \dfrac{\partial x^1}{\partial x^{13}} & \dfrac{\partial x^2}{\partial x^{13}} & \dfrac{\partial x^3}{\partial x^{13}} \end{vmatrix} \tag{2}$$

Solution: For k = 1, eq.(1) can be expressed as

$$x^1 = a_1^1 x^{11} + a_2^1 x^{12} + a_3^1 x^{13} \tag{3}$$

It is evident that x^1 is a linear function of x^{11}, x^{12} and x^{13}. Differentiating, one obtains

$$\frac{\partial x^1}{\partial x^{11}} = a_1^1$$

$$\frac{\partial x^1}{\partial x^{12}} = a_2^1 \tag{4}$$

$$\frac{\partial x^1}{\partial x^{13}} = a_3^1$$

In general, we can show that

$$\frac{\partial x^i}{\partial x^{1j}} = a_j^{\ i} \tag{5}$$

Thus

$$\left| a_j^{\ i} \right| = \left| \frac{\partial x^i}{\partial x^{1j}} \right| \tag{6}$$

CHAPTER 10

TENSOR NOTATION

INTRODUCTION

For those interested in studying tensor analysis, this chapter will serve as a brief introduction to the field. For those of you interested only in vector analysis, this chapter will reveal a new method of writing down everything that has been covered thus far. This method utilizes tensor notation.

Tensor notation is commonly used in the fields of elasticity, electromagnetism, the theory of relativity and in other branches of physics and mathematics.

Tensor notation utilizes such concepts as the Einstein convention, the Kronecker delta and the e-system -- all of which make often cumbersome calculations much more concise and clear.

Tensor notation is especially useful when dealing with components of vectors. For instance, consider the simple vector equation

$$\bar{a} = \bar{b}, \tag{1}$$

where $\bar{a}$ and $\bar{b}$ are three-dimensional vectors. Since any vector can be represented by its components, eq. (1) is a shorthand form for the three equations

$$a_1 = b_1, \quad a_2 = b_2, \quad a_3 = b_3 \tag{2}$$

However, in a more compact form, eq.(2) can be written as

$$a_i = b_i \qquad i = 1, 2, 3 \tag{3}$$

Notice that the fact that any statement about a vector is a statement about its respective components leads to the introduction of tensor notation. This might explain why tensor notation is often referred to as the "indical notation".

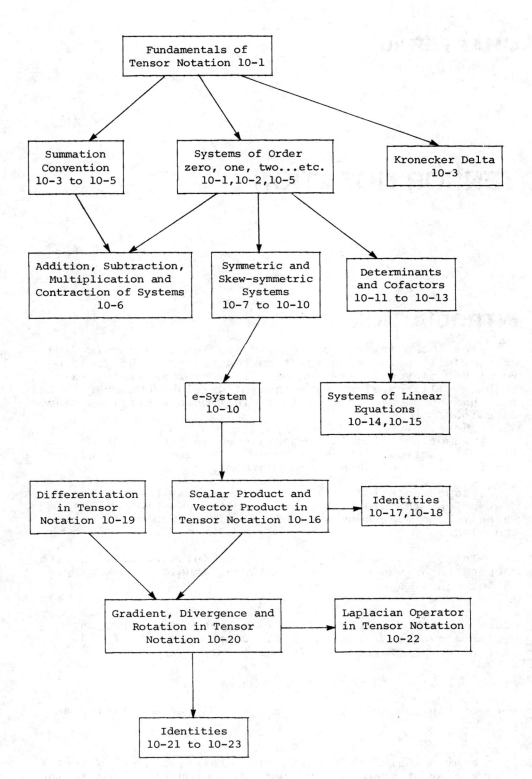

This chart is provided to facilitate rapid understanding of the inter-relationships of the topics and subject matter in this chapter. Also shown are the problem numbers associated with the subject matter.

SYSTEMS OF ORDER ZERO, ONE, TWO...., KRONECKER DELTA AND SUMMATION CONVENTION

● **PROBLEM** 10-1

1) Explain the indical notation in

$$x_k \quad (k = 1,2,3)$$

or

$$x^k \quad (k = 1,2,3)$$

2) Define a system of order zero, a system of the first order and a system of the second order.

3) Write out all the types of third order systems.

In each case the number of independent variables is three.

Solution: 1) Up to now, any set of three independent variables was represented by three different letters, as in x, y, z. However, in tensor calculus, any three independent variables are denoted by a single letter with an attached index. The index may be a subscript, as in x_i; or a superscript as in x^k (the superscript should not be interpreted as an exponent). The number of different values that any index may take is equal to the number of independent variables. Therefore, if there are three independent variables, then

$$k = 1, 2, 3.$$

Thus, $x_k \quad (k = 1,2,3)$

indicates x_1, x_2, x_3

and $x^k \quad (k = 1,2,3)$

indicates x^1, x^2, x^3

2) The order of a system is determined by the number of different indices. Systems with only one index are called first order systems. Examples of first order systems are

$$x_\ell, \quad b^k, \quad y^m$$

There are two types of first order systems; those in which the index is a subscript, as in x_i, and those in which the index is a superscript, as in x^ℓ.

Systems which depend on two indices are called second order systems. Both indices may either be subscripts or superscripts.

Three types of second order systems are

$$a_{ij}, \quad a^i_j, \quad a^{ij} \qquad (i,j = 1,2,3).$$

A single quantity, x, which has no indices is called a system of order zero.

4) A third order system is a system with three indices; thus, four types of third order systems are

$$a_{ijk}, \quad a^i_{jk}, \quad a^{ij}_k, \quad a^{ijk} \qquad (i,j,k = 1,2,3).$$

● **PROBLEM 10-2**

1) How many components are in a third order system if the number of independent variables is three?

2) How many components are in a third order system if the number of variables is four?

Solution: 1) First, denote a third order system by

$$a^{ijk}.$$

Since we are told that there are three variables, or "independent variables", then the indices i, j, k may take on any of the three numbers 1, 2 or 3. Or,

$$a^{ijk} \qquad i,j,k = 1,2,3$$

The number of components of any system is equal to the number of variables (the number of different values that an index may take) raised to a power equal to the order of the system.

In this case, the number of variables is 3 (each index may assume either of the values 1, 2 or 3) as well as the order is three (there are three different indices i, j, k).

Thus, the system

$$a^{ijk} \qquad i,j,k = 1,2,3$$

416

has 3^3, or 27 components.

Note that the number of variables is independent of (and not necessarily equal to) the order of a given system.

2) In this case, the given third order system is:

$$a^{ijk} \qquad i,j,k = 1,2,3,4.$$

Note that since the number of variables is four, any of the indices i, j or k may assume any of the values 1, 2, 3 or 4.

The number of components in this third order system is 4^3 or 64 components.

● PROBLEM 10-3

1) Describe the summation convention (also called the Einstein convention).

2) Using the summation convention express the following sums in compact form

$$x^1 \bar{i}_1 + x^2 \bar{i}_2 + x^3 \bar{i}_3$$

$$a^{11} p_1 + a^{12} p_2 + a^{13} p_3$$

$$\lambda^1{}_1 + \lambda^2{}_2 + \lambda^3{}_3 + \lambda^4{}_4$$

3) Define the Kronecker delta.

Solution: 1) The summation convention states that whenever the same index symbol appears in a term of an algebraic expression both as a superscript and a subscript, then the expression is to be summed over the range of that index. This index can be arbitrarily replaced by any other letter without changing the meaning of the expression -- such an index is called a dummy index.

2) Using the summation convention, obtain

$$x^1 \bar{i}_1 + x^2 \bar{i}_2 + x^3 \bar{i}_3 = x^k \bar{i}_k$$

where the range of k is 1, 2, 3;

$$a^{11} p_1 + a^{12} p_2 + a^{13} p_3 = a^{1i} p_i$$

where the range of i is 1, 2, 3; and

$$\lambda^1{}_1 + \lambda^2{}_2 + \lambda^3{}_3 + \lambda^4{}_4 = \lambda^\alpha{}_\alpha$$

where the range of α is 1, 2, 3, 4.

3) The Kronecker delta, denoted by $\delta_i{}^j$ is defined as

$$\delta_i{}^j = \begin{cases} 0 & i \neq j \\ 1 & i = j \end{cases}$$

The Kronecker delta may be equivalently denoted by

$$\delta^{ij} = \delta_{ij} = \delta^i{}_j$$

In the matrix form the Kronecker delta may be written as

$$\begin{pmatrix} \delta_1{}^1 & \delta_1{}^2 & \delta_1{}^3 \\ \delta_2{}^1 & \delta_2{}^2 & \delta_2{}^3 \\ \delta_3{}^1 & \delta_3{}^2 & \delta_3{}^3 \end{pmatrix} = \begin{pmatrix} 1 & 0 & 0 \\ 0 & 1 & 0 \\ 0 & 0 & 1 \end{pmatrix}$$

● **PROBLEM 10-4**

1) Find the value of $\delta_i{}^i$.

2) Write the following expression without using the Einstein convention

$$x^i = a^i{}_j x^{1j}$$

3) Find

$$a^{ij} b_{ij} \quad \text{for} \quad i,j = 1,2$$

$$a^{ij} b_{ij} \quad \text{for} \quad i,j = 1,2,3$$

4) Prove that

$$x^k = \delta^k{}_i x^i$$

Solution: 1) By definition,

$$\delta_i{}^i = \delta_1{}^1 + \delta_2{}^2 + \delta_3{}^3 = 3$$

2) If one assumes that the range of i and j is 1,2,3, then

$$x^1 = a^1{}_j x^{1j} = a^1{}_1 x^{11} + a^1{}_2 x^{12} + a^1{}_3 x^{13}$$

$$x^2 = a^2{}_j x^{1j} = a^2{}_1 x^{11} + a^2{}_2 x^{12} + a^2{}_3 x^{13}$$

$$x^3 = a^3{}_j x^{1j} = a^3{}_1 x^{11} + a^3{}_2 x^{12} + a^3{}_3 x^{13}$$

3) In the first case, where i,j = 1,2, we have

$$a^{ij} b_{ij} = a^{1j} b_{1j} + a^{2j} b_{2j} = a^{11} b_{11} + a^{12} b_{12} +$$

$$+ a^{21} b_{21} + b^{22} b_{22}$$

For i,j = 1,2,3, obtain

$$a^{ij} b_{ij} = a^{1j} b_{1j} + a^{2j} b_{2j} + a^{3j} b_{3j}$$

$$= a^{11} b_{11} + a^{12} b_{12} + a^{13} b_{13} + a^{21} b_{21} + a^{22} b_{22} + a^{23} b_{23}$$

$$+ a^{31} b_{31} + a^{32} b_{32} + a^{33} b_{33}.$$

4) For i = 1,2,3, we can write

$$x^k = \delta^k{}_i x^i = \delta^k{}_1 x^1 + \delta^k{}_2 x^2 + \delta^k{}_3 x^3$$

but all δ^k_i are equal to zero except for the case where i = k, in which case

$$\delta^k{}_i = \delta_i{}^i = 1$$

and

$$x^k = 1 \cdot x^k = x^k$$

● PROBLEM 10-5

1) Show that a^{ij}_j is a system of the first order and completely list its components.

2) What is the order of the sum

$$a_{jk\ell}\, x^j\, y^k\, z^\ell \qquad (j,k,\ell = 1,2,3)$$

and how many terms are there in this sum?

Solution: 1) According to the summation convention the expression a^{ij}_j is a system of the first order. The repeated index j is to be summed from 1 to 3, thus the system has only one actual index (j is the repeated "dummy" variable, not considered an index). The components of

$$a^{ij}_j \quad (i,j = 1,2,3) \quad \text{are}$$

$$a^{1j}_{j} = a^{11}_{1} + a^{12}_{2} + a^{13}_{3}$$

$$a^{2j}_{j} = a^{21}_{1} + a^{22}_{2} + a^{23}_{3}$$

$$a^{3j}_{j} = a^{31}_{1} + a^{32}_{2} + a^{33}_{3}$$

2) In the sum

$$a_{jk\ell} \, x^j \, y^k \, z^\ell$$

all the indices are repeated, therefore it is a system of order zero.

Since $j, k, \ell = 1, 2, 3$ there are 3 x 3 x 3 = 27 terms in this sum.

BASIC OPERATIONS AND CONTRACTION OF SYSTEMS, SYMMETRIC AND SKEW-SYMMETRIC SYSTEMS, E-SYSTEM

● PROBLEM 10-6

1) Add the following systems

    a) a^r and b^r

    b) c^i_j and b^k_ℓ

    c) x^r and b^{st}

    d) $a^{ijk}_{\ell m}$ and b^{rst}_{pq}

    where i, j, k, ℓ, s, t, m, p, q = 1, 2, 3.

2) Multiply the systems given by

    a) a^r and b^j

    b) c^{mn} and d^{st}_p

3) Given the fifth order system

$$a^{ij}_{k\ell m},$$

    contract indices j and m and determine the order of the resulting system.

Solution: Addition is defined for systems of the same order and type only. The sum of two such systems is obtained by adding each component of the first system to the corresponding component of the second system. The resulting system is of the same order and type as the original systems at hand.

a) $a^r + b^r$ = A first order system

b) $c^i_j + b^i_j$ = A second order system

c) Since addition is defined for systems of the same order only, x^r (a first order system) and b^{st} (a second order system) cannot be added.

d) $a^{ijk}_{\ell m} + b^{ijk}_{\ell m}$ = A fifth order system

2) Unlike addition, multiplication is defined for any two systems of any order or type. To find the product of any two given systems, one must multiply each component of the first system with each and every component of the second system.

The order of the product of two systems is equal to the sum of the orders of the two systems at hand.

Keeping this in mind, we conclude the following:

a) $a^r b^j$ is a second order system

b) $c^{mn} d^{st}_p$ is a fifth order system

3) To "contract" any two indices is nothing more than to equate these indices. Therefore, to contract the indices j and m in the fifth order system

$$a^{ij}_{k\ell m},$$

set m equal to j and obtain the new system

$$a^{ij}_{k\ell j}.$$

Now, since j is a repeated index, it must be summed from 1 to 3; thus

$$a^{ij}_{k\ell j} = a^{i1}_{k\ell 1} + a^{i2}_{k\ell 2} + a^{i3}_{k\ell 3}$$

Therefore, as a result of contracting indices j and m, a third order system was obtained.

Note that we can contract any two indices. For example, let $b^{ijk}_{\ell mnp}$ be a seventh order system. We can contract indices i and n to obtain

$$b^{ijk}_{\ell mip}$$

which is a fifth order system.

We can now contract indices j and ℓ to obtain

$$b^{ijk}_{jmip}, \text{ a third order system.}$$

How many distinct components are in

a) a general second order system

b) a symmetric second order system

c) a skew-symmetric second order system?

Solution: 1) Let a_{ij} represent any general second order system. For i,j = 1,2,3 (three independent variables), this second order system,

$$a_{ij} \qquad i,j = 1,2,3, \tag{1}$$

has $3^2 = 9$ components. This is obtained by recalling that the number of components in any system is equal to the number of different variables (in this case, since any of the two indices i or j may assume any of the values 1, 2 or 3, the number of variables is three) raised to a power equal to the order of the system (in this case, the order is two). The matrix representation of this general second order system is:

$$\begin{pmatrix} a_{11} & a_{12} & a_{13} \\ a_{21} & a_{22} & a_{23} \\ a_{31} & a_{32} & a_{33} \end{pmatrix} \tag{2}$$

2) A second order system is said to be symmetric when

$$a_{ij} = a_{ji}. \tag{3}$$

In general, a system is said to be symmetric in any two particular indices if the components of the system remain unaltered when these two indices are interchanged. Also, a system is said to be completely symmetric if the interchange of any two indices leaves the components unaltered.

Thus, for a second order symmetric system,

$$a_{ij} = a_{ji}$$

(4)

or $\quad a_{12} = a_{21}, \quad a_{13} = a_{31}, \quad a_{23} = a_{32}.$

Since three of the nine components are equal, a symmetric system of the second order has six distinct components

$$a_{11}, \ a_{22}, \ a_{33}, \ a_{12}, \ a_{13}, \ a_{23}.$$

(5)

The matrix representation of a symmetric second order system is

$$\begin{pmatrix} a_{11} & a_{12} & a_{13} \\ a_{12} & a_{22} & a_{23} \\ a_{13} & a_{23} & a_{33} \end{pmatrix}$$

(6)

3) A system is said to be skew-symmetric if the interchange of any two indices alters the sign of the component but not its numerical value. In other words,

$$a_{ij} = -a_{ji}$$

(7)

or

$$a_{11} = -a_{11}, \quad a_{12} = -a_{21}, \quad a_{13} = -a_{31}, \quad a_{23} = -a_{32} \quad \text{(8a)}$$

$$a_{11} = -a_{11}, \quad a_{22} = -a_{22}, \quad a_{33} = -a_{33} \quad \text{(8b)}$$

Note that the above equations (eq.8b) hold true only if

$$a_{11} = a_{22} = a_{33} = 0.$$

Therefore, the matrix representation of a skew-symmetric second order system is:

$$\begin{pmatrix} 0 & a_{12} & a_{13} \\ -a_{12} & 0 & a_{23} \\ -a_{13} & -a_{23} & 0 \end{pmatrix}$$

● **PROBLEM 10-8**

1) Show that any second order system a_{ij} can be represented by the sum

$$a_{ij} = b_{ij} + c_{ij}$$

(1)

where $b_{ij} = b_{ji}$ is a symmetric system and $c_{ij} = -c_{ji}$ is a skew-symmetric system.

2) Show that a completely skew-symmetric system of the third order has only one non-zero distinct component.

Solution: 1) Any second order system can be expressed as

$$a_{ij} = \tfrac{1}{2}(a_{ij} + a_{ji}) + \tfrac{1}{2}(a_{ij} - a_{ji}), \tag{2}$$

Indeed, expanding eq.(2) gives

$$a_{ij} = \tfrac{1}{2} a_{ij} + \tfrac{1}{2} a_{ij} + \tfrac{1}{2} a_{ji} - \tfrac{1}{2} a_{ji} = a_{ij}.$$

Now, if we express b_{ij} in terms of a_{ij} in the following manner:

$$b_{ij} = \tfrac{1}{2}(a_{ij} + a_{ji})$$

we notice that b_{ij} is, in fact, a symmetric system; indeed,

$$b_{ij} = \tfrac{1}{2}(a_{ij} + a_{ji}) = \tfrac{1}{2}(a_{ji} + a_{ij}) = b_{ji}$$

Now, if we let

$$c_{ij} = \tfrac{1}{2}(a_{ij} - a_{ji})$$

then c_{ij} is a skew-symmetric system; indeed,

$$c_{ij} = \tfrac{1}{2}(a_{ij} - a_{ji}) = -\tfrac{1}{2}(a_{ji} - a_{ij}) = -c_{ji}$$

Finally, to show that eq.(1) holds true, obtain

$$a_{ij} = b_{ij} + c_{ij}$$

$$= \tfrac{1}{2}(a_{ij} + a_{ji}) + \tfrac{1}{2}(a_{ij} - a_{ji})$$

$$= a_{ij} + \tfrac{1}{2} a_{ji} - \tfrac{1}{2} a_{ji}$$

$$= a_{ij}$$

2) Let a_{ijk} be a completely skew-symmetric third order system. Since it's a third order system, it has $3^3 = 27$ components. Now, notice that if we look at any of the components that have at least two of the same indices, such as

$$a_{221} \quad \text{or} \quad a_{332} \quad \text{or} \quad a_{111},$$

then, interchanging any of the two indices gives

$$a_{221} = -a_{122} = a_{212} = -a_{221}$$

$$a_{332} = -a_{233} = a_{323} = -a_{332}$$

424

$$a_{111} = -a_{111}$$

which indicates that

$$a_{221} = 0 = a_{332} = a_{111} = a_{133} = \ldots,$$

since the only possible way that any number can equal the negative of itself is if the number is, indentically zero.

From this, we conclude that the only possible distinct components are those which have no two indices equal. But, from component a_{123}, we can obtain all of the other non-zero components, indeed

$$a_{123} = -a_{132} = -a_{213} = a_{231} = -a_{321} = a_{312}$$

Therefore, there is only one distinct non-zero component in a third order skew-symmetric system.

● **PROBLEM** 10-9

1) Let a_{ij} be a second order system such that

$$\alpha a_{ij} + \beta a_{ji} = 0 \qquad (1)$$

Show that a_{ij} is skew-symmetric when $\alpha = \beta$ and symmetric when $\alpha = -\beta$.

2) Show that if a_{ij} is skew-symmetric, then

$$a_{ij} x^i x^j = 0. \qquad (2)$$

3) Show that if

$$a_{ij} x^i x^j = 0 \qquad (3)$$

for all values of x^i and x^j, then a_{ij} is skew-symmetric.

Solution: 1) Since i,j may assume any of the values 1,2,3, eq.(1) can be written in the form

$$\alpha a_{ji} + \beta a_{ij} = 0 \qquad (4)$$

Adding eqs.(1) and (4) gives

$$\alpha(a_{ij} + a_{ji}) + \beta(a_{ij} + a_{ji}) = (\alpha + \beta)(a_{ij} + a_{ji}) = 0 \qquad (5)$$

From eq.(5) we conclude that either $\alpha = \beta$, in which case a_{ij} is skew-symmetric; or $\alpha = -\beta$, in which case a_{ij} is symmetric.

2) We can write eq.(2) in the form

$$a_{ji} \ x^i x^j = 0 \tag{6}$$

Adding eqs.(3) and (6) gives

$$a_{ij} \ x^i x^j + a_{ji} \ x^i x^j = (a_{ij} + a_{ji}) x^i x^j = (a_{ij} - a_{ji}) x^i x^j = 0,$$

which proves eq.(2).

3) For all the values of x^i and x^j, we have

$$a_{ij} \ x^i x^j = 0 \tag{7}$$

Let $x^1 = 1, \quad x^2 = x^3 = 0$

Eq.(7) then becomes

$$a_{ij} \ x^i x^j = a_{11} \ x^1 x^1 = 0 \tag{8}$$

and thus $a_{11} = 0$.

Now take $x^1 = 1, \quad x^2 = 1, \quad x^3 = 0$, eq.(7) then becomes

$$a_{12} \ x^1 x^2 + a_{21} \ x^1 x^2 = 0$$

and thus $a_{12} = -a_{21}$

In the same manner we can show that

$$a_{22} = a_{33} = 0 \qquad a_{13} = -a_{31}, \qquad a_{23} = -a_{32}.$$

Thus $a_{ij} = -a_{ji}$ and therefore, a_{ij} is skew-symmetric.

● **PROBLEM 10-10**

1) If a_{ijk} is any skew-symmetric system of the third order, show that

$$a_{ijk} = a_{123} \ e_{ijk} \tag{1}$$

2) Prove that

$$\delta^{ijk}_{ijk} = 3! \tag{2}$$

$$\delta^{ijk}_{\ell jk} = 2\delta^{i}_{\ell} \tag{3}$$

Solution: 1) e_{ijk} is called the e-system and is defined as follows:

426

$$e^{ijk} = e_{ijk} = \begin{cases} 0 & \text{when any two of the indices are equal,} \\ 1 & \text{when } ijk \text{ is an even permutation of 123,} \\ -1 & \text{when } ijk \text{ is an odd permutation of 123.} \end{cases}$$

e_{ijk} is also called the "permutation symbol."

Note that in eq.(1) both sides are equal to zero when any two of the indices are equal. Therefore, eq.(1) can be replaced by

$$a_{123} = a_{123}\, e_{123} \tag{4}$$

Since a_{ijk} is skew-symmetric, any odd permutation of the indices 1,2,3 changes the sign of the left-hand side of eq.(1). By definition, for any odd permutation of 1,2,3, the value of e_{ijk} is equal to -1.

Using the same reasoning, one can show that for even permutations of 1,2,3, both sides of eq.(1) are equal.

2) By definition,

$$\delta^{ijk}_{\ell mn} \equiv e^{ijk}\, e_{\ell mn} \tag{5}$$

where

$$e^{ijk} = e_{ijk} \tag{6}$$

Contracting the indices k and n, one obtains

$$\delta^{ijk}_{\ell mk} = \delta^{ij1}_{\ell m1} + \delta^{ij2}_{\ell m2} + \delta^{ij3}_{\ell m3} \tag{7}$$

Contracting indices j and m, one obtains

$$\delta^{ijk}_{\ell jk} = \delta^{ij1}_{\ell j1} + \delta^{ij2}_{\ell j2} + \delta^{ij3}_{\ell j3} \tag{8}$$

Now contract the indices i and ℓ,

$$\delta^{ijk}_{ijk} = \delta^{ij1}_{ij1} + \delta^{ij2}_{ij2} + \delta^{ij3}_{ij3} \tag{9}$$

Each of the terms on the right-hand side of eq.(9) is equal to 2, indeed

$$\delta^{ij1}_{ij1} = \delta^{231}_{231} + \delta^{321}_{321} = 1 \cdot 1 + (-1)\cdot(-1) = 2 \tag{10}$$

Thus,

$$\delta^{ijk}_{ijk} = 3 \cdot 2 = 3!$$

3) Eq.(3) for $i = \ell$ becomes

$$\delta^{ijk}_{ijk} = 2\delta^i_i = 2(\delta^1_1 + \delta^2_2 + \delta^3_3) = 6 \tag{11}$$

which is eq.(2).

For $i \neq \ell$,

$$\delta_{\ell jk}^{ijk} = e^{ijk} e_{\ell jk} \qquad (12)$$

To show that the above sum is equal to zero, take

$$i = 1 \, , \quad \ell = 2, \quad \text{thus}$$

$$\delta_{2jk}^{1jk} = e^{1jk} e_{2jk}$$

All the terms with $j = 1$ or $j = 2$ are equal to zero. If $j = 3$, then for any k all the terms are equal to zero. Thus for $i \neq \ell$,

$$\delta_{\ell jk}^{ijk} = 0$$

which completes the proof.

$$\delta_{\ell jk}^{ijk} = 2\delta_{\ell}^{i}$$

It is easy to show that any other choice of the indices i and ℓ leads to the same results.

DETERMINANTS, COFACTORS, SYSTEMS OF LINEAR EQUATIONS AND QUADRATIC FORMS

● PROBLEM 10-11

1) Show that determinant A

$$A = \left| a_{mn} \right| = \begin{vmatrix} a_{11} & a_{12} & a_{13} \\ a_{21} & a_{22} & a_{23} \\ a_{31} & a_{32} & a_{33} \end{vmatrix} \qquad (1)$$

can be expressed in the form

$$A = e^{ijk} a_{i1} a_{j2} a_{k3} = e^{ijk} a_{1i} a_{2j} a_{3k} \qquad (2)$$

2) Show that

$$e^{ijk} a_{ir} a_{js} a_{kt} = e^{ijk} a_{ri} a_{sj} a_{tk} = Ae_{rst} \qquad (3)$$

Solution: 1) By definition, if the determinant is expanded in full by columns, then

$$A = \sum_{i,j,k=1}^{3} \pm\, a_{1i}\, a_{2j}\, a_{3k} \tag{4}$$

where i, j, k is a permutation of 1, 2, 3. The plus sign accounts for all even permutations, while the minus sign accounts for all odd permutations. Thus, using the permutation symbol e_{ijk} and the summation convention, we obtain

$$A = e^{ijk}\, a_{1i}\, a_{2j}\, a_{3k} \tag{5}$$

Fully expanding the determinant by rows gives

$$A = e^{ijk}\, a_{i1}\, a_{j2}\, a_{k3} \tag{6}$$

2) First, show that

$$e^{ijk}\, a_{ir}\, a_{js}\, a_{kt} \tag{7}$$

is completely skew-symmetric in r, s, t. Since i, j, k are dummy indices, substituting k for the dummy index i and substituting i for the dummy index k does not alter the sum. Thus

$$e^{ijk}\, a_{ir}\, a_{js}\, a_{kt} = e^{kji}\, a_{kr}\, a_{js}\, a_{it} = e^{kji}\, a_{it}\, a_{js}\, a_{kr} \tag{8}$$

$$= -e^{ijk}\, a_{it}\, a_{js}\, a_{kr}$$

Note that eq.(7) changes sign if r and t are interchanged. In the same manner, it can also be shown that (7) changes sign when any two of the indices r, s, t are interchanged.

Now, if a_{rst} is any skew-symmetric system of the third order, then

$$a_{rst} = a_{123}\, e_{rst} \quad \text{(see Problem 10-10)} \tag{9}$$

Since (7) is a skew-symmetric system of the third order, we can apply (9) to (7) to obtain

$$e^{ijk}\, a_{ir}\, a_{js}\, a_{kt} = e^{ijk}\, a_{i1}\, a_{j2}\, a_{k3}\, e_{rst} \tag{10}$$

From eq.(2).

$$A = e^{ijk}\, a_{i1}\, a_{j2}\, a_{k3} \tag{11}$$

Finally, substituting eq.(11) into eq.(10), obtain

$$e^{ijk}\, a_{ir}\, a_{js}\, a_{kt} = A\, e_{rst} \tag{12}$$

In the same manner, we can show that

$$e^{ijk}\, a_{ri}\, a_{sj}\, a_{tk} = A\, e_{rst} \tag{13}$$

429

1) Show that the cofactor A^{ir} of an element a_{ir} in a determinant is given by the formula

$$A^{ir} = \frac{1}{2!} e^{ijk} e^{rst} a_{js} a_{kt} \tag{1}$$

2) Show that the expansion of the determinant in terms of the elements of the r'th row is given by

$$a_{rk} A^{ik} = A \delta^i_r \tag{2}$$

and in terms of the rth column is

$$a_{kr} A^{ki} = A \delta^i_r \tag{3}$$

Solution: 1) Denote the determinant by

$$A = \begin{vmatrix} a_{11} & a_{12} & a_{13} \\ a_{21} & a_{22} & a_{23} \\ a_{31} & a_{32} & a_{33} \end{vmatrix} \tag{4}$$

When the determinant is fully expanded, any element, a_{ir}, appears once in each of a certain number of terms of the expansion. In this expression for the determinant, the coefficient of the element a_{ir} is equal to the cofactor of a_{ir}, called A^{ir}.

From the equation (refer to problem 10-11)

$$A = e^{ijk} a_{i1} a_{j2} a_{k3} = e^{ijk} a_{1i} a_{2j} a_{3k} \tag{5}$$

we conclude that the cofactor of a_{1i} is

$$e^{ijk} a_{2j} a_{3k} \tag{6}$$

Expression (6) can be written in the form

$$e^{ijk} a_{2j} a_{3k} = e^{123} e^{ijk} a_{2j} a_{3k}$$
$$= \frac{1}{2!} e^{1\ell m} e^{ijk} a_{ij} a_{mk} \tag{7}$$

To verify eq.(7), note that

$$\frac{1}{2!} \, e^{1 \ell m} \, e^{ijk} \, a_{\ell j} \, a_{mk} = \frac{1}{2}(e^{ijk} \, a_{2j} \, a_{3k} - e^{ijk} \, a_{3j} \, a_{2k})$$

(8)

$$= \frac{1}{2}(e^{ijk} \, a_{2j} \, a_{3k} - e^{ikj} \, a_{3k} \, a_{2j}) = \frac{1}{2} \cdot 2 e^{ijk} \, a_{2j} \, a_{3k}$$

Here the following identity was used

$$e^{ijk} \, a_{3j} \, a_{2k} = e^{ikj} \, a_{3k} \, a_{2j}.$$

Note that dummy indices can be replaced by any letter.

In the same manner, we can obtain the cofactors of elements a_{2j} and a_{3k}. Thus, the cofactor of an element a_{ir} is

$$A^{ir} = \frac{1}{2!} \, e^{ijk} \, e^{r\ell m} \, a_{j\ell} \, a_{km}.$$

(9)

2) The expansion of the determinant in terms of the rth row is

$$a_{rk} \, A^{ik}.$$

(10)

Substituting eq.(9) into eq.(10) yields

$$a_{rk} \, A^{ik} = a_{rk} \, \frac{1}{2!} \, e^{ijp} \, e^{ksm} \, a_{js} \, a_{pm} = \frac{1}{2!} \, e^{ijp} \, A \, e_{rjp}$$

(11)

$$= A \, \delta^i_r$$

In the same manner, one can prove that the expansion of the determinant in terms of the rth column is given by

$$a_{kr} \, A^{ki} = A \, \delta^i_r$$

(12)

● **PROBLEM 10-13**

1) Show that if a_{mn} is symmetric, then A^{mn} is also symmetric.

2) Show that if $A \neq 0$ and

$$\alpha^{ir} = \frac{A^{ir}}{A}$$

(1)

then

$$a_{kr} \, \alpha^{ki} = a_{rk} \, \alpha^{ik} = \delta^i_r$$

(2)

<u>Solution</u>: 1) Since a_{mn} is symmetric,

$$a_{mn} = a_{nm}.$$

(3)

A^{mn} is given by the formula

$$A^{mn} = \frac{1}{2!} e^{mjk} e^{nst} a_{js} a_{kt}$$

$$= \frac{1}{2!} e^{mjk} e^{nst} a_{sj} a_{tk} \tag{4}$$

$$= \frac{1}{2!} e^{nst} e^{mjk} a_{sj} a_{tk} = A^{nm}$$

Thus A^{mn} is symmetric.

2) Dividing equation

$$a_{rk} A^{ik} = A \; \delta^i_r \tag{5}$$

by A, gives

$$a_{rk} \frac{A^{ik}}{A} = a_{rk} \alpha^{ik} = \delta^i_r \tag{6}$$

Equation (6) is often used in tensor calculus.

In the same manner,

$$a_{kr} \alpha^{ki} = \delta^i_r. \tag{7}$$

● **PROBLEM 10-14**

Find the solution to the following system of three linear equations

$$a_{11}x^1 + a_{12}x^2 + a_{13}x^3 = b_1$$

$$a_{21}x^1 + a_{22}x^2 + a_{23}x^3 = b_2 \tag{1}$$

$$a_{31}x^1 + a_{32}x^2 + a_{33}x^3 = b_3$$

Solution: Using the summation convention one can write system (1) in the form

$$a_{ik}x^k = b_i \tag{2}$$

Assume that $A \neq 0$, where

$$A = \det \left[a_{ij} \right]$$

Multiply both sides of eq.(2) by $A^{i\ell}$ and sum i from 1 to 3.

$$A^{i\ell} a_{ik} x^k = A^{i\ell} b_i \tag{3}$$

or

$$A \; \delta^\ell_k \; x^k = A^{i\ell} b_i \tag{4}$$

But

$$\delta^{\ell}_{k} x^{k} = x^{\ell} \tag{5}$$

and dividing by A,

$$x^{\ell} = \frac{A^{i\ell} b_{i}}{A} \tag{6}$$

which is the solution to system (1). Note that it was assumed that $A \neq 0$. If $A = 0$ and all the cofactors $A^{i\ell}$ are not zero, then eq.(4) is inconsistent unless $A^{i\ell} b_{i} = 0$. In which case,

$$A^{i\ell}(a_{ik} x^{k} - b_{i}) = 0 \tag{7}$$

Thus, the three equations are linearly connected. Therefore it is sufficient to solve two of the three equations. The third equation will be automatically satisfied.

In analyzing the case where $b_{i} = 0$, the equations would have a unique solution, $x^{k} = 0$, if the determinant A is not equal to zero. If A does equal zero however, the equations have non-zero solutions x^{k}.

The condition $A = 0$ is necessary and sufficient for the system

$$a_{ij} x^{j} = 0 \tag{8}$$

to have a non-zero solution.

• **PROBLEM 10-15**

1) Define a positive definite quadratic form.

2) Show that if $a_{mn} x^{m} x^{n}$ is a positive definite quadratic form and a_{mn} and b_{mn} are two symmetric systems, then the roots of the determinantal equation

$$\left| \alpha a_{mn} - b_{mn} \right| = 0 \tag{1}$$

are all real.

Solution: 1) The quadratic form $a_{mn} x^{m} x^{n}$ is said to be positive definite if it vanishes only for $x^{k} = 0$ and is positive for all other real values of x^{k}.

2) Assume that eq.(1) has the solution

$$\alpha = \beta + i\gamma \tag{2}$$

433

then

$$\left| (\beta + i\gamma)a_{mn} - b_{mn} \right| = 0 \qquad (3)$$

Because the determinant in eq.(3) is equal to zero, one can write

$$\left[(\beta + i\gamma)a_{mn} - b_{mn} \right] \left[\lambda^n + i\mu^n \right] = 0 \qquad (4)$$

(see Problem 10-14).

Both the real and imaginary parts of eq.(4) are equal to zero.

$$\beta\, a_{mn}\, \lambda^n - \gamma\, a_{mn}\, \mu^n - b_{mn}\, \lambda^n = 0 \qquad (5)$$

$$\beta\, a_{mn}\, \mu^n + \gamma\, a_{mn}\, \lambda^n - b_{mn}\, \mu^n = 0 \qquad (6)$$

Now multiply eq.(5) by μ^m and eq.(6) by λ^m and obtain

$$\beta\, a_{mn}\, \lambda^n \mu^m - \gamma\, a_{mn}\, \mu^n \mu^m = b_{mn}\, \lambda^n \mu^m \qquad (7)$$

$$\beta\, a_{mn}\, \mu^n \lambda^m + \gamma\, a_{mn}\, \lambda^n \lambda^m = b_{mn}\, \mu^n \lambda^m \qquad (8)$$

Since a_{mn} is symmetric,

$$\beta\, a_{mn}\, \lambda^n \mu^m = \beta\, a_{nm}\, \lambda^n \mu^m = \beta\, a_{mn}\, \lambda^m \mu^n \qquad (9)$$

Subtracting eq.(7) from eq.(8), obtain

$$\gamma(a_{mn}\, \lambda^n \lambda^m + a_{mn}\, \mu^m \mu^n) = b_{mn}\, \mu^n \lambda^m - b_{mn}\, \lambda^n \mu^m \qquad (10)$$

Since b_{mn} is symmetric, one can write

$$b_{mn}\, \mu^n \lambda^m = b_{nm}\, \mu^n \lambda^m = b_{mn}\, \mu^m \lambda^n \qquad (11)$$

Note that a dummy index can be replaced by any other index. Eq.(10) becomes

$$\gamma(a_{mn}\, \lambda^n \lambda^m + a_{mn}\, \mu^m \mu^n) = 0 \qquad (12)$$

Since a_{mn} is positive definite and not all λ^n, μ^m are zero, one concludes that

$$\gamma = 0 \qquad (13)$$

and that the root, α, of eq.(1) is real.

SCALAR AND VECTOR PRODUCT, DIFFERENTIATION, GRADIENT, DIVERGENCE, ROTATION AND THE LAPLACIAN IN TENSOR NOTATION

● **PROBLEM** 10-16

Using the tensor notation write the expressions for the scalar product and vector product of two vectors.

Solution: In three-dimensional space, vectors $\bar{a}$ and $\bar{b}$ are denoted by a_i and b_j where $i,j = 1,2,3$. The scalar product of two vectors $\bar{a}$ and $\bar{b}$ is defined as

$$\bar{a} \cdot \bar{b} = a_1 b_1 + a_2 b_2 + a_3 b_3 \tag{1}$$

Using tensor notation eq.(1) can be written in the form

$$\bar{a} \cdot \bar{b} = a_i b_i \tag{2}$$

At times it is convenient to express the scalar product in the form

$$\bar{a} \cdot \bar{b} = \delta^{ij} a_i b_j \tag{3}$$

In order to define the vector product, it is helpful to recall the definition of the e-system

$$e^{ijk} = e_{ijk} = \begin{cases} 0 & \text{when any two of the indices are equal} \\ 1 & \text{when } i,j,k \text{ is an even permutation of } 1,2,3 \\ -1 & \text{when } i,j,k \text{ is an odd permutation of } 1,2,3. \end{cases} \tag{4}$$

Remember that the vector product of two vectors $\bar{a}$ and $\bar{b}$ is defined as

$$\bar{a} \times \bar{b} = (a_2 b_3 - a_3 b_2)\bar{i} + (a_3 b_1 - a_1 b_3)\bar{j} + (a_1 b_2 - a_2 b_1)\bar{k} \tag{5}$$

or in the determinant form

$$\bar{a} \times \bar{b} = \begin{vmatrix} \bar{i} & \bar{j} & \bar{k} \\ a_1 & a_2 & a_3 \\ b_1 & b_2 & b_3 \end{vmatrix} \tag{6}$$

Using the e-system, one can write the definition of the vector product in the form

$$\bar{a} \times \bar{b} = e^{ijk} a_j b_k = e_{ijk} a_j b_k \tag{7}$$

Remember that the terms are to be summed over all values of the repeated index.

To find the first component of $\bar{a} \times \bar{b}$, obtain

$$(\bar{a} \times \bar{b})_1 = e^{1jk} a_j b_k \tag{8}$$

Since all elements of e^{1jk} are zero except e^{123} and e^{132}, one has

$$(\bar{a} \times \bar{b})_1 = e^{1jk} a_j b_k \tag{9}$$

$$= e^{123} a_2 b_3 + e^{132} a_3 b_2 = a_2 b_3 - a_3 b_2$$

where
$$e^{123} = 1$$
$$e^{132} = -1 \tag{10}$$

● **PROBLEM** 10-17

1) Prove the identity

$$e_{ijk} e_{\ell mk} = \delta_{i\ell} \delta_{jm} - \delta_{im} \delta_{j\ell} \tag{1}$$

2) Simplify the expression

$$\bar{a} \times (\bar{b} \times \bar{c}) \tag{2}$$

Solution: 1) In eq.(1) k is a dummy index. The right-hand side of eq.(1) is zero unless it has the form 1-0 or 0-1. For the right side of eq.(1),

$$\delta_{i\ell} \delta_{jm} - \delta_{im} \delta_{j\ell} = \begin{cases} 1 & \text{if } i = \ell \text{ and } j = m \text{ but } i \neq m \\ & \qquad\qquad (\text{or } j \neq \ell) \\ -1 & \text{if } i = m \text{ and } j = \ell \text{ but } i \neq \ell \\ & \qquad\qquad \text{or } j \neq m \\ 0 & \text{in all other instances} \end{cases}$$

The left-hand side of eq.(1) is zero unless $i \neq j$ and $\ell \neq m$. Note that k is different from i,j,ℓ,m. In the sum, on the left-hand side of eq.(1) only one term is different from zero. The product is equal to +1 if ijk is a cyclic permutation of ℓmk, that is if $i = \ell$ and $j = m$. One obtains -1 for ijk having the opposite order to ℓmk, that is for $i = m$ and $j = \ell$. Thus, by comparing the conditions for the left- and right-hand side of eq.(1) to hold true, the identity has been proved.

2) Using tensor notation, one can write the ith component of $\bar{a} \times (\bar{b} \times \bar{c})$ as

$$\left[\bar{a} \times (\bar{b} \times \bar{c})\right]_i = e_{ijk} a_j \left[\bar{b} \times \bar{c}\right]_k$$

$$= e_{ijk} a_j e_{k\ell m} b_\ell c_m = e_{ijk} e_{k\ell m} a_j b_\ell c_m \tag{3}$$

436

Note that

$$e_{k\ell m} = -e_{\ell km} = e_{\ell mk} \tag{4}$$

One can apply eq.(1) to eq.(3) and obtain

$$\left[\overline{a} \times (\overline{b} \times \overline{c})\right]_i = e_{ijk}\, e_{\ell mk}\, a_j\, b_\ell\, c_m$$

$$= (\delta_{i\ell}\, \delta_{jm} - \delta_{im}\, \delta_{j\ell})a_j\, b_\ell\, c_m \tag{5}$$

$$= \delta_{i\ell}\, \delta_{jm}\, a_j\, b_\ell\, c_m - \delta_{im}\, \delta_{j\ell}\, a_j\, b_\ell\, c_m$$

$$= \delta_{jm}\, a_j\, b_i\, c_m - \delta_{j\ell}\, a_j\, b_\ell\, c_i$$

$$= b_i\, a_m\, c_m - c_i\, a_\ell\, b_\ell$$

Since $a_m c_m = \overline{a} \cdot \overline{c}$ and $a_\ell b_\ell = \overline{a} \cdot \overline{b}$, one has

$$b_i a_m c_m - c_i a_\ell b_\ell = \left[\overline{b}(\overline{a}\cdot\overline{c}) - \overline{c}(\overline{a}\cdot\overline{b})\right]_i \tag{6}$$

Thus proving the identity

$$\overline{a} \times (\overline{b} \times \overline{c}) = \overline{b}(\overline{a}\cdot\overline{c}) - \overline{c}(\overline{a}\cdot\overline{b}) \tag{7}$$

● **PROBLEM 10-18**

Using tensor notation

1) define the scalar triple product of vectors $\overline{a}$, $\overline{b}$ and $\overline{c}$

2) simplify the expression

$$(\overline{a} \times \overline{b}) \times (\overline{c} \times \overline{d}) \tag{1}$$

Solution: 1) Previously, the scalar triple product of three vectors $\overline{a}$, $\overline{b}$ and $\overline{c}$ was defined as

$$\overline{a} \cdot \overline{b} \times \overline{c} \tag{2}$$

In order to evaluate the scalar triple product, one must first find the vector product $\overline{b} \times \overline{c}$, (which is a vector) and then scalar multiply both vectors $\overline{a}$ and $\overline{b} \times \overline{c}$. Using tensor notation, we have

$$\overline{a} \cdot \overline{b} \times \overline{c} = a_i\, (\overline{b} \times \overline{c})_i$$

$$= a_i\, e_{ijk}\, b_j\, c_k = e_{ijk}\, a_i\, b_j\, c_k \tag{3}$$

In Problem 10-11, we proved that

$$\begin{vmatrix} a_1 & a_2 & a_3 \\ b_1 & b_2 & b_3 \\ c_1 & c_2 & c_3 \end{vmatrix} = e_{ijk}\, a_i\, b_j\, c_k \qquad (4)$$

Comparing eq.(3) and eq.(4) results in

$$\bar{a} \cdot \bar{b} \times \bar{c} = \begin{vmatrix} a_1 & a_2 & a_3 \\ b_1 & b_2 & b_3 \\ c_1 & c_2 & c_3 \end{vmatrix} \qquad (5)$$

2)   The ith component of expression (1) is

$$\left[(\bar{a} \times \bar{b}) \times (\bar{c} \times \bar{d})\right]_i = e_{ijk}(\bar{a} \times \bar{b})_j\, (\bar{c} \times \bar{d})_k$$

$$= e_{ijk}\, e_{jmn}\, a_m\, b_n\, e_{kpq}\, c_p\, d_q \qquad (6)$$

Let us first sum over j

$$e_{ijk}\, e_{jmn} = -e_{ikj}\, e_{mnj} = e_{kij}\, e_{mnj}$$

$$= \delta_{km}\, \delta_{in} - \delta_{kn}\, \delta_{im} \qquad (7)$$

Substituting eq.(7) into eq.(6), obtain

$$e_{ijk}\, e_{jmn}\, e_{kpq}\, a_m\, b_n\, c_p\, d_q$$

$$= (\delta_{km}\, \delta_{in} - \delta_{kn}\, \delta_{im})\, e_{kpq}\, a_m\, b_n\, c_p\, d_q \qquad (8)$$

$$= e_{kpq}\, a_k\, b_i\, c_p\, d_q - e_{kpq}\, a_i\, b_k\, c_p\, d_q$$

Applying eq.(3), one obtains

$$e_{kpq}\, a_k\, b_i\, c_p\, d_q - e_{kpq}\, a_i\, b_k\, c_p\, d_q$$

$$= \left[\bar{a} \cdot \bar{c} \times \bar{d}\right] b_i - \left[\bar{b} \cdot \bar{c} \times \bar{d}\right] a_i \qquad (9)$$

Thus, proving the identity

$$(\bar{a} \times \bar{b}) \times (\bar{c} \times \bar{d}) = \left[\bar{a} \cdot \bar{c} \times \bar{d}\right]\bar{b} - \left[\bar{b} \cdot \bar{c} \times \bar{d}\right]\bar{a} \qquad (10)$$

● **PROBLEM 10-19**

Using tensor notation, derive the rules for the derivative of the scalar product and the vector product.

Solution: In tensor notation the scalar product of two vectors is indicated by $\quad \bar{a} \cdot \bar{b} \equiv a_i b_i \qquad (1)$

438

Note that the differentiation of a vector function is carried out componentwise. That is, the kth component of $\frac{d\bar{a}}{dt}$ is the derivative of the kth component of $\bar{a}$,

$$\left(\frac{d\bar{a}}{dt}\right)_k \equiv \frac{da_k}{dt} \tag{2}$$

Differentiating eq.(1) with respect to t gives

$$\frac{d}{dt}(a_i b_i) = a_i \frac{db_i}{dt} + \frac{da_i}{dt} b_i \tag{3}$$

Thus proving the formula

$$\frac{d}{dt}(\bar{a} \cdot \bar{b}) = \bar{a} \cdot \frac{d\bar{b}}{dt} + \bar{b} \cdot \frac{d\bar{a}}{dt} \tag{4}$$

For the vector product one follows the same procedure. The vector product of $\bar{a}$ and $\bar{b}$ is

$$e_{ijk} a_j b_k \tag{5}$$

Differentiating (5), one obtains

$$\frac{d}{dt}(e_{ijk} a_j b_k) = e_{ijk} \frac{da_j}{dt} b_k + e_{ijk} a_j \frac{db_k}{dt} \tag{6}$$

Eq.(6) can be written in vector notation as

$$\frac{d}{dt}(\bar{a} \times \bar{b}) = \frac{d\bar{a}}{dt} \times \bar{b} + \bar{a} \times \frac{d\bar{b}}{dt} \tag{7}$$

● **PROBLEM** 10-20

Using tensor notation, define

1) the gradient of a scalar function ϕ

2) the divergence of a vector $\bar{a}$

3) the rotation of a vector $\bar{a}$.

Solution: 1) Let x_1, x_2, x_3 be three independent variables. They can be denoted by x_i, where i = 1, 2, 3. Let ϕ be a scalar function of x_1, x_2, x_3.

$$\phi = \phi(x_1, x_2, x_3) = \phi(x_i) \tag{1}$$

Introducing the notation

$$\frac{\partial \phi}{\partial x_k} \equiv \partial_k \phi \equiv \phi_{,k} \tag{2}$$

The gradient of ϕ can be denoted by

$$\partial_i \phi \quad \text{where } i = 1, 2, 3$$

or

$$\phi_{,i} \quad \text{where } i = 1, 2, 3.$$

2) The divergence of $\bar{a}$ is defined as

$$\text{div } \bar{a} \equiv \frac{\partial a_1}{\partial x_1} + \frac{\partial a_2}{\partial x_2} + \frac{\partial a_3}{\partial x_3}$$

(3)

$$= \frac{\partial a_i}{\partial x_i} = \partial_i a_i = a_{i,i}$$

Note that the expression is summed over the repeated index.

3) To derive the expression for the rotation of a vector in tensor notation, first note that

$$\text{curl } \bar{a} = \nabla \times \bar{a} \tag{4}$$

Operator del is defined as

$$\nabla \equiv \left(\frac{\partial}{\partial x}, \frac{\partial}{\partial y}, \frac{\partial}{\partial z} \right) \tag{5}$$

or in tensor notation

$$\nabla \equiv \frac{\partial}{\partial x_i} \equiv \partial_i \quad i = 1, 2, 3 \tag{6}$$

Treating curl $\bar{a}$ as a vector product of ∇ and $\bar{a}$, obtain

$$\text{curl } \bar{a} = \nabla \times \bar{a} = e_{ijk} \partial_j a_k$$

(7)

$$= e_{ijk} a_{k,j}$$

• **PROBLEM 10-21**

Using tensor notation, prove the following vector identities

1. $\nabla \cdot \phi \bar{a} = \phi \nabla \cdot \bar{a} + \bar{a} \cdot \nabla \phi$ (1)

2. $\nabla \times \phi \bar{a} = \phi \nabla \times \bar{a} + \nabla \phi \times \bar{a}$ (2)

3. $\nabla \times \bar{r} = \bar{0}$ (3)

4. $\nabla (\bar{a} \cdot \bar{r}) = \bar{a}$ where $\bar{a}$ is constant. (4)

Solution: 1. Using the results of Problem 10-20, the left-hand side of eq.(1) is equal to

$$\nabla \cdot \phi \bar{a} = \text{div}(\phi \bar{a}) = (\phi a_i)_{,i}$$

(5)

$$= \phi_{,i} \, a_i + \phi \, a_{i,i}$$

Also

$$\phi_{,i} = \left[\text{grad } \phi \right]_i = \left[\nabla \phi \right]_i \tag{6}$$

and

$$a_{i,i} = \text{div } \overline{a} = \nabla \cdot \overline{a} \tag{7}$$

Substituting eq.(6) and eq.(7) into eq.(5), obtain

$$\phi_{,i} \, a_i + \phi \, a_{i,i} = \overline{a} \cdot \nabla \phi + \phi (\nabla \cdot \overline{a}), \tag{8}$$

which proves eq.(1).

2. The ith component of the left-hand side of eq.(2) is

$$\left[\nabla \times \phi \overline{a} \right]_i = e_{ijk} \, (\phi a_k)_{,j} \tag{9}$$

Differentiating, one finds

$$e_{ijk} \, \phi_{,j} \, a_k + e_{ijk} \, \phi \, a_{k,j} \tag{10}$$

both terms can be expressed as

$$e_{ijk} \, \phi_{,j} \, a_k = \left[\nabla \phi \times \overline{a} \right]_i \tag{11}$$

$$e_{ijk} \, \phi \, a_{k,j} = \phi \left[\nabla \times \overline{a} \right]_i \tag{12}$$

Combining eqs.(9), (11) and (12), one obtains

$$\nabla \times \phi \overline{a} = \nabla \phi \times \overline{a} + \phi (\nabla \times \overline{a}) \tag{13}$$

3. Note that

$$\overline{r} = (x, y, z) = (x_1, x_2, x_3), \tag{14}$$

and the ith component of $\nabla \times \overline{r}$, denoted $(\nabla \times \overline{r})_i$, is

$$(\nabla \times \overline{r})_i = e_{ijk} \, \partial_j \, x_k \qquad \text{(see Problem 10-20)}$$

But

$$\partial_j \, x_k = \frac{\partial x_k}{\partial x_j}$$

is zero when $k \neq j$ and 1 when $k = j \left(\dfrac{\partial x_j}{\partial x_j} = 1 \right)$.

Recognizing that this is the equivalent of the Kronecker delta, δ_{kj}, eq.(3) becomes

$$(\nabla \times \overline{r})_i = e_{ijk} \, \delta_{kj} \tag{15}$$

Now, since δ_{kj} is zero when $k \neq j$, the only time $(\nabla \times \overline{r})_i$ can have a non-zero value is when $k = j$, and $\delta_{jj} = 1$. However, when $k = j$, e_{ijk} becomes e_{ijj}, which by definition is equal to zero (recall that when any two indices are equal, $e_{ijk} = 0$). Thus,

$$(\nabla \times \overline{r})_i = e_{ijk} \, \partial_j \, x_k = e_{ijk} \, \delta_{kj} = e_{ijj} = 0 \qquad (16)$$

4. Since $\overline{a}$ is a constant vector, one can find the ith component of $\nabla(\overline{a} \cdot \overline{r})$.

$$\left[\nabla(\overline{a} \cdot \overline{r})\right]_i = (\overline{a} \cdot \overline{r})_{,i} = (a_k r_k)_{,i}$$
$$= (a_k x_k)_{,i} = a_{k,i} \, x_k + a_k \, x_{k,i} \qquad (17)$$
$$= a_k \, \delta_{ki} = a_i = \left[\overline{a}\right]_i$$

which completes the proof of eq.(4).

● PROBLEM 10-22

Using tensor notation, define the Laplacian operator. Prove the following vector identities.

1. $\nabla \times (\nabla \times \overline{a}) = \nabla(\nabla \cdot \overline{a}) - \nabla^2 \overline{a}$ (1)

2. $\nabla \times (\nabla \phi) = \overline{0}$ (2)

3. $\nabla \cdot (\nabla \times \overline{a}) = 0$ (3)

Solution: The Laplacian of a scalar field ϕ is defined as div(grad ϕ) and denoted by ∇^2 or Δ. Thus,

$$\nabla^2 \phi \equiv \Delta \phi \equiv \text{div(grad } \phi) \qquad (4)$$

or

$$\nabla^2 \phi = \frac{\partial^2 \phi}{\partial x^2} + \frac{\partial^2 \phi}{\partial y^2} + \frac{\partial^2 \phi}{\partial z^2} \qquad (5)$$

Using tensor notation, one can write

$$\nabla^2 \equiv \partial_i \, \partial_i \qquad (6)$$

or

$$\nabla^2 \phi \equiv \partial_i \, \partial_i \phi \equiv \phi_{,ii} \qquad (7)$$

1. This problem will be using the notation $\partial_i \phi$ instead of $\phi_{,i}$. Both indicate differentiation with respect to x_i and both are commonly used in vector and tensor analysis. For the ith component of the left-hand side of eq.(1), one obtains

$$\left[\nabla \times (\nabla \times \overline{a})\right]_i = e_{ijk} \, \partial_j \left[\nabla \times \overline{a}\right]_k$$
$$= e_{ijk} \, \partial_j \left[e_{klm} \, \partial_l \, a_m\right] = e_{ijk} \, e_{klm} \, \partial_j \partial_l a_m \qquad (8)$$

From Problem 10-17,

$$e_{ijk}\, e_{\ell mk} = \delta_{i\ell}\, \delta_{jm} - \delta_{im}\, \delta_{j\ell} \tag{9}$$

Substituting eq.(9) into eq.(8) and noting that

$$e_{\ell mk} = e_{k\ell m} \tag{10}$$

one finds

$$e_{ijk}\, e_{k\ell m}\, \partial_j \partial_\ell\, a_m = (\delta_{i\ell}\, \delta_{jm} - \delta_{im}\, \delta_{j\ell}) \partial_j \partial_\ell\, a_m$$

$$= \partial_j \partial_i a_j - \partial_j \partial_j a_i = \partial_i \partial_j a_j - \partial_j \partial_j a_i \tag{11}$$

$$= \left[\nabla(\nabla \cdot \overline{a}) - \nabla^2 \overline{a} \right]_i$$

which proves eq.(1)

2. The ith component of the left-hand side of eq.(2) is

$$\left[\nabla \times (\nabla \phi) \right]_i = e_{ijk}\, \partial_j (\nabla \phi)_k$$

$$= e_{ijk}\, \partial_j \partial_k \phi \tag{12}$$

Since $\partial_j \partial_k \phi = \partial_k \partial_j \phi$ is symmetric and e_{ijk} is anti-symmetric, one concludes that

$$e_{ijk}\, \partial_j \partial_k \phi = 0 \tag{13}$$

Thus

$$\nabla \times (\nabla \phi) = \overline{0} \tag{14}$$

3. $$\nabla \cdot (\nabla \times \overline{a}) = \partial_i (\nabla \times \overline{a})_i$$

$$= \partial_i \left[e_{ijk}\, \partial_j\, a_{\underline{k}} \right] = e_{ijk}\, \partial_i \partial_j a_k = 0 \tag{15}$$

because $\partial_i \partial_j\, a_k = \partial_j \partial_i a_k$ is symmetric and e_{ijk} is anti-symmetric.

● **PROBLEM 10-23**

Using tensor notation, prove the following vector identities.

1. $\nabla \times (\overline{a} \times \overline{b}) = (\overline{b} \cdot \nabla)\overline{a} - (\overline{a} \cdot \nabla)\overline{b} + (\nabla \cdot \overline{b})\overline{a} - (\nabla \cdot \overline{a})\overline{b}$ (1)

2. $\nabla(\overline{a} \cdot \overline{b}) = (\overline{a} \cdot \nabla)\overline{b} + (\overline{b} \cdot \nabla)\overline{a} + \overline{a} \times (\nabla \times \overline{b}) + \overline{b} \times (\nabla \times \overline{a})$ (2)

Solution: 1. For the ith component of the left-hand side of eq.(1), one obtains

443

$$[\nabla \times (\bar{a} \times \bar{b})]_i = e_{ijk} \, \partial_j [\bar{a} \times \bar{b}]_k$$

$$= e_{ijk} \, \partial_j (e_{k\ell m} \, a_\ell \, b_m) \qquad (3)$$

$$= e_{ijk} \, e_{k\ell m} \, \partial_j (a_\ell \, b_m)$$

Using the identity

$$e_{ijk} \, e_{\ell m k} = \delta_{i\ell} \, \delta_{jm} - \delta_{im} \, \delta_{j\ell} \qquad (4)$$

obtain

$$e_{ijk} \, e_{\ell m k} \, \partial_j (a_\ell \, b_m)$$

$$= (\delta_{i\ell} \, \delta_{jm} - \delta_{im} \, \delta_{j\ell}) \, \partial_j (a_\ell \, b_m) \qquad (5)$$

$$= \partial_j (a_i \, b_j) - \partial_j (a_j \, b_i)$$

$$= a_i \partial_j b_j + b_j \partial_j a_i - a_j \partial_j b_i - b_i \partial_j a_j$$

$$= [(\bar{b} \cdot \nabla)\bar{a} - (\bar{a} \cdot \nabla)\bar{b} + (\nabla \cdot \bar{b})\bar{a} - (\nabla \cdot \bar{a})\bar{b}]_i$$

which completes the proof of eq.(1).

2. The proof of eq.(2) is slightly more complicated. In this case it is much simpler to work with the ith component of the right-hand side of eq.(2).

$$[(\bar{a} \cdot \nabla)\bar{b} + (\bar{b} \cdot \nabla)\bar{a} + \bar{a} \times (\nabla \times \bar{b}) + \bar{b} \times (\nabla \times \bar{a})]_i$$

$$= (a_j \partial_j) b_i + (b_j \, \partial_j) a_i + e_{ijk} \, a_j (\nabla \times \bar{b})_k + e_{ijk} b_j (\nabla \times \bar{a})_k$$

$$= a_j \partial_j b_i + b_j \partial_j a_i + e_{ijk} \, a_j \, e_{k\ell m} \, \partial_\ell b_m + e_{ijk} \, b_j \, e_{k\ell m} \, \partial_\ell a_m$$

$$= a_j \partial_j b_i + b_j \partial_j a_i + (\delta_{i\ell} \delta_{jm} - \delta_{im} \delta_{j\ell})(a_j \partial_\ell b_m + b_m \partial_\ell a_m) \qquad (6)$$

$$= a_j \partial_j b_i + b_j \partial_j a_i + a_j \partial_i b_j - a_j \partial_j b_i + b_j \partial_i a_j - b_j \partial_j a_i$$

$$= a_j \partial_i b_j + b_j \partial_i a_j = \partial_i (a_j b_j)$$

$$= \left[\nabla(\bar{a} \cdot \bar{b})\right]_i$$

CHAPTER 11

APPLICATIONS OF GRADIENT, DIVERGENCE AND CURL IN PHYSICS

INTRODUCTION

Throughout this book, whenever possible, various physics problems were given that attempted to illustrate the usefulness and significance of the mathematical theory covered.

This chapter is completely devoted to the applications of vector analysis to various branches of physics. Our attention focuses on the applications of the gradient, the divergence and rotation.

Often, vector analysis is just helpful in describing and explaining certain physical phenomena; in some cases however, as in the case of electromagnetism, vector analysis plays a crucial role. Indeed, without the use of some basic concepts and methods of vector analysis, one couldn't even attempt to sufficiently describe and explain the behavior of electromagnetic fields.

This chapter should indicate to the reader that vector analysis is not a form of "mathematics for itself" but is rather a highly useful instrument that has vast applications in such fields as mechanics, fluid dynamics and electromagnetics.

GRAPHICAL REPRESENTATION OF VECTOR FIELDS

● **PROBLEM 11-1**

Vector field $\bar{v}$, as shown in the figure, has no component in the z-direction. Determine whether the divergence of $\bar{v}$ at point A is positive or negative.

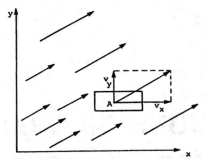

Solution: Since the third component of the vector field $\bar{v}$ is equal to zero, the divergence of $\bar{v}$ is given by

$$\text{div } \bar{v} = \frac{\partial v}{\partial x} + \frac{\partial v}{\partial y} \tag{1}$$

From the figure we see that the x component of vector $\bar{v}$ (v_x), increases in the direction of increasing x, thus

$$\frac{\partial v_x}{\partial x} > 0 \tag{2}$$

The figure also indicates that v_y increases in the direction of increasing y. Thus

$$\frac{\partial v_y}{\partial y} > 0 \tag{3}$$

From eqs.(1), (2) and (3), it is safe to conclude that at the point A the divergence of the vector field $\bar{v}$ is positive

$$\text{div } \bar{v} > 0. \tag{4}$$

The flux (amount of flow crossing the sides of the rectangle per unit time) increases in the positive y-direction and also increases in the positive x-direction. Thus the net flux through the sides of the rectangle around A is outward and the divergence is positive.

● **PROBLEM 11-2**

Consider a vector field $\bar{v}$ as shown in the figure.

If all the vectors $\bar{v}(x,y,z)$ are parallel to the x-y plane, determine whether the divergence of $\bar{v}$ at point A is positive or negative.

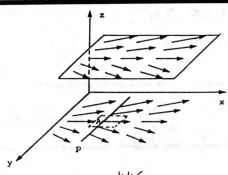

Solution: In general, any vector $\bar{v}$ can be written in the component form as

$$\bar{v} = (v_x, v_y, v_z) \tag{1}$$

Since all the vectors $\bar{v}$ are parallel to the x-y plane, the third component of $\bar{v}$ is equal to zero. Thus

$$\bar{v} = (v_x, v_y, 0) \tag{2}$$

Furthermore, the figure indicates that v_x is approximately constant. Thus, the divergence of $\bar{v}$ reduces to

$$\text{div } \bar{v} = \frac{\partial v_x}{\partial x} + \frac{\partial v_y}{\partial y} = \frac{\partial v_y}{\partial y} \tag{3}$$

To determine if $\frac{\partial v_y}{\partial y}$ is positive or negative, consider how the component v_y changes along the line p which passes through the point A. Notice that v_y is negative below A and positive above A. Thus

$$\frac{\partial v_y}{\partial y} > 0, \tag{4}$$

which indicates that div $\bar{v}$ is positive at point A.

Since v_x = const, the flux through the x faces of the parallelepiped at A will cancel. There is flux out of both of the y faces. Since the z component of $\bar{v}$ is zero, there is no flux in the z-direction and the divergence is therefore positive.

● **PROBLEM 11-3**

Consider the vector field $\bar{v}$ shown in the figure.

Determine the direction of curl $\bar{v}$.

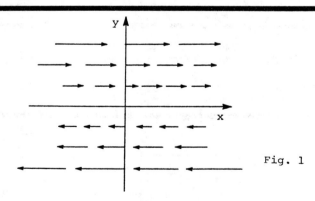

Fig. 1

Solution: The figure indicates that the y-component of the vector field is zero. Since the flow is in the x-y plane, it is assumed that the z-component is also zero. Close inspection of figure 1 also indicates that the magnitude (length) of the x-component (the only component in this case) is proportional to y. Therefore, $\bar{v}$ may be written as

$$\bar{v} = \alpha y \bar{i} + 0\bar{j} + 0\bar{k} = \alpha y \bar{i} \tag{1}$$

where α is some positive constant.

For curl $\overline{v}$, obtain

$$\text{curl } \overline{v} = \nabla \times \overline{v} = \left(\frac{\partial}{\partial x}, \frac{\partial}{\partial y}, \frac{\partial}{\partial z} \right) \times (\alpha y, 0, 0)$$

$$= (0, 0, -\alpha), \tag{2}$$

or curl $\overline{v} = -\alpha \overline{k}$. $\tag{3}$

Since α is a positive constant, curl $\overline{v}$ is directed in the negative z-direction, or into the page.

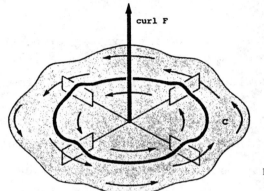

Fig. 2

   If vector field $\overline{v}$ were to represent the flow of a fluid, then a paddle wheel inserted into this flow would rotate most rapidly when its axis of rotation is placed parallel to the z-axis. Since curl $\overline{v}$ is perpendicular to the x-y plane and in the negative z-direction (into the page), the paddle wheel would rotate clockwise. If curl ∇ were directed in the positive z-direction, then it would rotate counter-clockwise as shown in figure 2.

● **PROBLEM 11-4**

Vector field $\overline{v}$, shown in the figure, is an approximate representation of the vortex (circular) flow of a fluid.

Determine the direction of curl $\overline{v}$ at the points A, B and C.

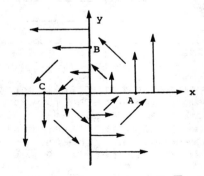

Solution: From the definition of curl $\overline{v}$,

448

$$\text{curl } \bar{v} = \left(\frac{\partial v_z}{\partial y} - \frac{\partial v_y}{\partial z}\right)\bar{i} + \left(\frac{\partial v_x}{\partial z} - \frac{\partial v_z}{\partial x}\right)\bar{j} + \left(\frac{\partial v_y}{\partial x} - \frac{\partial v_x}{\partial y}\right)\bar{k} \qquad (1)$$

Since it is assumed that the field $\bar{v}$ does not vary in the z-direction,

$$\frac{\partial v_y}{\partial z} = \frac{\partial v_x}{\partial z} = 0 \quad \text{and} \quad v_z = 0 \qquad (2)$$

Substituting (2) into eq. (1) yields

$$\text{curl } \bar{v} = 0\bar{i} + 0\bar{j} + \left(\frac{\partial v_y}{\partial x} - \frac{\partial v_x}{\partial y}\right)\bar{k}$$

$$= \left(\frac{\partial v_y}{\partial x} - \frac{\partial v_x}{\partial y}\right)\bar{k} \qquad (3)$$

From eq.(3), we can safely conclude that curl $\bar{v}$ points in the z-direction. It is now necessary to determine, from the figure, whether $\frac{\partial v_y}{\partial x} - \frac{\partial v_x}{\partial y}$ is positive or negative.

At point A, v_y is increasing in the x-direction, so that

$$\left.\frac{\partial v_y}{\partial x}\right|_A > 0 \qquad (4)$$

Since v_x is positive below point A and negative above point A, v_x decreases in the positive y-direction, and thus

$$\left.\frac{\partial v_x}{\partial y}\right|_A < 0 \qquad (5)$$

From eqs.(4) and (5) we conclude that

$$\left.\frac{\partial v_y}{\partial x}\right|_A - \left.\frac{\partial v_x}{\partial y}\right|_A > 0. \qquad (6)$$

Thus curl $\bar{v}$ points in the positive z-direction at the point A.

At the point B,

$$\left.\frac{\partial v_y}{\partial x}\right|_B > 0 \quad \text{and} \quad \left.\frac{\partial v_x}{\partial y}\right|_B < 0, \qquad (7)$$

so that

$$\left.\frac{\partial v_y}{\partial x}\right|_B - \left.\frac{\partial v_x}{\partial y}\right|_B > 0, \qquad (8)$$

which indicates that at point B curl $\bar{v}$ points in the positive z-direction.

At point C, v_y increases as we move in the positive x-direction, thus

$$\left.\frac{\partial v_y}{\partial x}\right|_C > 0. \qquad (9)$$

v_x is positive below point C and negative above point C; thus, through the point C, v_x decreases in the positive y-direction and therefore,

$$\left.\frac{\partial v_x}{\partial y}\right|_C < 0 \qquad (10)$$

and finally

$$\left.\frac{\partial v_y}{\partial x}\right|_C - \left.\frac{\partial v_x}{\partial y}\right|_C > 0. \qquad (11)$$

In conclusion, at all points A, B, and C, curl $\overline{v}$ points in the positive z-direction.

GRAVITATION, HARMONIC FUNCTIONS, REFLECTION OF LIGHT, RIGID BODY ROTATION, SURFACE TENSION AND ELASTICITY

● **PROBLEM** 11-5

Show that the gravitational field

$$\overline{F} = -k \frac{Mm}{r^2} \frac{\overline{r}}{r} \qquad (1)$$

is the gradient of the scalar field

$$f = \frac{kMm}{r} \qquad (2)$$

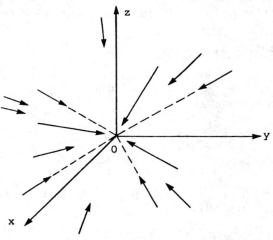

FIG. 1 INVERSE SQUARE FIELD

450

Solution: Recall that the gradient of a scalar field is given by

$$\text{grad } f = \frac{\partial f}{\partial x}\,\overline{i} + \frac{\partial f}{\partial y}\,\overline{j} + \frac{\partial f}{\partial z}\,\overline{k} \tag{3}$$

Eq.(3) may be written as

$$\text{grad } f = \left(\frac{\partial}{\partial x}\,\overline{i} + \frac{\partial}{\partial y}\,\overline{j} + \frac{\partial}{\partial z}\,\overline{k} \right) f,$$

or, since operator del is defined as

$$\nabla \equiv \frac{\partial}{\partial x}\,\overline{i} + \frac{\partial}{\partial y}\,\overline{j} + \frac{\partial}{\partial z}\,\overline{k},$$

eq.(3) may be written as

$$\text{grad } f = \nabla f.$$

To evaluate the gradient of the scalar field given by eq.(2), obtain

$$\text{grad } f = \text{grad } \frac{kMm}{r}, \tag{4}$$

where k, M and m are constants and r is the magnitude of the position vector $\overline{r}$. Since

$$\overline{r} = x\overline{i} + y\overline{j} + z\overline{k}, \tag{5}$$

the magnitude of $\overline{r}$ is given by

$$r = \sqrt{x^2 + y^2 + z^2} \tag{6}$$

Thus, $\text{grad } \dfrac{kMm}{r} = kMm\left[\dfrac{\partial}{\partial x}\left(\dfrac{1}{r} \right), \dfrac{\partial}{\partial y}\left(\dfrac{1}{r} \right), \dfrac{\partial}{\partial z}\left(\dfrac{1}{r} \right) \right]$

$$= kMm\left[\frac{\partial}{\partial x}\frac{1}{\sqrt{x^2+y^2+z^2}}, \frac{\partial}{\partial y}\frac{1}{\sqrt{x^2+y^2+z^2}}, \frac{\partial}{\partial z}\frac{1}{\sqrt{x^2+y^2+z^2}} \right] \tag{7}$$

$$= kMm\left[\frac{-x}{(x^2+y^2+z^2)^{\frac{3}{2}}}, \frac{-y}{(x^2+y^2+z^2)^{\frac{3}{2}}}, \frac{-z}{(x^2+y^2+z^2)^{\frac{3}{2}}} \right]$$

$$= \frac{-kMm}{x^2+y^2+z^2} \cdot \frac{1}{\sqrt{x^2+y^2+z^2}}\,(x,y,z) = -k\,\frac{Mm}{r^2}\,\frac{\overline{r}}{r},$$

which proves that

$$\overline{F} = \text{grad } f.$$

● **PROBLEM 11-6**

Verify that the function

$$f = \frac{1}{\sqrt{x^2+y^2+z^2}} \tag{1}$$

is harmonic everywhere but the origin.

Solution: Recall that a function f is said to be harmonic in a given domain if it has continuous second derivatives and

$$\frac{\partial^2 f}{\partial x^2} + \frac{\partial^2 f}{\partial y^2} + \frac{\partial^2 f}{\partial z^2} = 0. \tag{2}$$

Since the Laplacian operator is defined as

$$\Delta \equiv \nabla^2 = \frac{\partial^2}{\partial x^2} + \frac{\partial^2}{\partial y^2} + \frac{\partial^2}{\partial z^2},$$

eq.(2) may be rewritten as

$$\nabla^2 f = 0. \tag{3}$$

This indicates that we may alternatively define a harmonic function as a function which has continuous second derivatives and satisfies Laplace's equation in a given domain.

To verify that function f, given by

$$f = \frac{1}{\sqrt{x^2+y^2+z^2}} \tag{4}$$

is harmonic, obtain

$$\nabla^2\left(\frac{1}{\sqrt{x^2+y^2+z^2}}\right) = 0 \tag{5}$$

or

$$\left(\frac{\partial^2}{\partial x^2} + \frac{\partial^2}{\partial y^2} + \frac{\partial^2}{\partial z^2}\right) \frac{1}{(x^2+y^2+z^2)^{\frac{1}{2}}} = 0$$

where

$$\frac{\partial}{\partial x}\left(\frac{1}{(x^2+y^2+z^2)^{\frac{1}{2}}}\right) = \frac{-x}{(x^2+y^2+z^2)^{\frac{3}{2}}} \tag{6}$$

$$\frac{\partial}{\partial y}\left(\frac{1}{(x^2+y^2+z^2)^{\frac{1}{2}}}\right) = \frac{-y}{(x^2+y^2+z^2)^{\frac{3}{2}}} \tag{7}$$

$$\frac{\partial}{\partial z}\left(\frac{1}{(x^2+y^2+z^2)^{\frac{1}{2}}}\right) = \frac{-z}{(x^2+y^2+z^2)^{\frac{3}{2}}} \tag{8}$$

The second derivatives are then

$$\frac{\partial^2}{\partial x^2}\left(\frac{1}{\sqrt{x^2+y^2+z^2}}\right) = \frac{\partial}{\partial x}\left(\frac{-x}{(x^2+y^2+z^2)^{\frac{3}{2}}}\right) = \frac{2x^2-y^2-z^2}{(x^2+y^2+z^2)^{\frac{5}{2}}} \tag{9}$$

$$\frac{\partial^2}{\partial y^2}\left(\frac{1}{\sqrt{x^2+y^2+z^2}}\right) = \frac{2y^2-x^2-z^2}{(x^2+y^2+z^2)^{\frac{5}{2}}} \tag{10}$$

$$\frac{\partial^2}{\partial z^2}\left(\frac{1}{\sqrt{x^2+y^2+z^2}}\right) = \frac{2z^2-x^2-y^2}{(x^2+y^2+z^2)^{\frac{5}{2}}} \tag{11}$$

Before proceeding, notice that these second partial derivatives are discontinuous at the origin since they are undefined at the point (0,0,0). Since these second derivatives are not continuous at this point, the function f is not

harmonic at the origin. To verify that f is harmonic everywhere else, substitute eqs.(9), (10) and (11) into (5) and
obtain

$$\nabla^2 \left(\frac{1}{\sqrt{x^2+y^2+z^2}} \right) = \frac{2x^2+2y^2+2z^2-2x^2-2y^2-2z^2}{(x^2+y^2+z^2)^{\frac{5}{2}}}$$

$$= 0$$

Thus the function

$$f = \frac{1}{\sqrt{x^2+y^2+z^2}}$$

is harmonic everywhere but the origin. In physics, this
function f represents the electrostatic potential of a unit
charge located at the origin.

● **PROBLEM 11-7**

If the inner surface of an ellipse is a mirror, then
show that a ray of light emitting from focus F_1 will
be reflected from this inner surface to focus F_2.

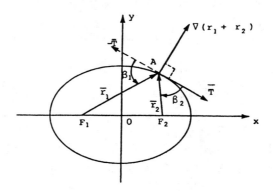

Solution: Let A be any point on the ellipse. The light
from F_1 will be reflected to F_2 when the line segments $F_1 A$
and $F_2 A$ make equal angles with the tangent to the ellipse at
A. In other words, the light will be reflected to F_2 when
$\beta_1 = \beta_2$. Line segments $F_1 A$ and $F_2 A$ can be represented, in
vector notation, as

$$\overline{r}_1 = \overline{F_1 A}$$
$$\overline{r}_2 = \overline{F_2 A} \tag{1}$$

An ellipse is the locus of all points P such that the sum of
distances from two fixed points F_1 and F_2 is a constant;
therefore

$$r_1 + r_2 = \text{const} \tag{2}$$

453

From Problem 7-11 part I, it was determined that

$$\nabla(r_1 + r_2)$$

is a normal to the ellipse, thus

$$\nabla(r_1 + r_2) \cdot \overline{T} = 0,$$

and therefore

$$(\nabla r_1) \cdot \overline{T} = -(\nabla r_2) \cdot \overline{T} = (\nabla r_2) \cdot (-\overline{T}) \qquad (3)$$

where $\overline{T}$ is a unit tangent to the ellipse, at point A, and ∇r_1, ∇r_2 are unit vectors in the direction of $\overline{r}_1$ and $\overline{r}_2$ respectively (See Problem 7-12). Note that the angle between ∇r_1 and $\overline{T}$ is equal to β_1 (vertical angles) and likewise, $(\not{}\nabla r_2, -\overline{T}) = \beta_2$.

Now, proceed by obtaining

$$(\nabla r_1) \cdot \overline{T} = |\nabla r_1| \, |\overline{T}| \, \cos(\not{}\nabla r_1, \overline{T})$$

$$= |\overline{T}| \cos(\not{}\nabla r_1, \overline{T}) = -(\nabla r_2) \cdot \overline{T} = (\nabla r_2) \cdot (-\overline{T}) \qquad (4)$$

$$= |\nabla r_2| \, |-\overline{T}| \cos(\not{}\nabla r_2, -\overline{T}) = |\overline{T}| \cos(\not{}\nabla r_2, -\overline{T})$$

Thus,

$$\cos(\not{}\nabla r_1, \overline{T}) = \cos(\not{}\nabla r_2, -\overline{T}), \qquad (5)$$

indicating that since the cosine of the angle between ∇r_1 and $\overline{T}$ is equal to the cosine of the angle between ∇r_2 and $-\overline{T}$, the angles themselves are equal.

In other words,

$$(\not{}\nabla r_1, \overline{T}) = \beta_1 = (\not{}\nabla r_2, -\overline{T}) = \beta_2$$

and therefore, the light from focus F_1 will be reflected from the ellipse to focus F_2.

● **PROBLEM 11-8**

If

$$\overline{v} = \overline{\omega} \times \overline{r}, \qquad (1)$$

where $\overline{\omega}$ is a constant vector, prove that

$$\overline{\omega} = \frac{1}{2} \, \text{curl} \, \overline{v} \qquad (2)$$

<u>Solution</u>: From the definition of the curl of a vector, obtain

$$\text{curl } \bar{v} = \nabla \times \bar{v} = \left(\frac{\partial}{\partial x}, \frac{\partial}{\partial y}, \frac{\partial}{\partial z} \right) \times \left[(\omega_1, \omega_2, \omega_3) \times (x,y,z) \right]$$

$$= \left(\frac{\partial}{\partial x}, \frac{\partial}{\partial y}, \frac{\partial}{\partial z} \right) \times (\omega_2 z - \omega_3 y, \ \omega_3 x - \omega_1 z, \ \omega_1 y - \omega_2 x)$$

$$= \left[\frac{\partial}{\partial y}(\omega_1 y - \omega_2 x) - \frac{\partial}{\partial z}(\omega_3 x - \omega_1 z), \ \frac{\partial}{\partial z}(\omega_2 z - \omega_3 y) - \frac{\partial}{\partial x}(\omega_1 y - \omega_2 x), \right.$$

$$\left. \frac{\partial}{\partial x}(\omega_3 x - \omega_1 z) - \frac{\partial}{\partial y}(\omega_2 z - \omega_3 y) \right] \qquad (3)$$

$$= (2\omega_1, \ 2\omega_2, \ 2\omega_3) = 2\bar{\omega}$$

or

$$\tfrac{1}{2} \text{ curl } \bar{v} = \bar{\omega} \qquad (4)$$

From this problem, it is evident that the curl of a vector field describes the rotational properties of the field. For example, if we consider the motion of a fluid, then in the regions where curl $\bar{v} \neq \bar{0}$ the fluid tends to rotate while in the regions where curl $\bar{v} = 0$ the fluid does not exhibit any rotation. A vector field without rotation is called an "irrotational field"; while a vector field with rotation is often referred to as a "vortex field".

● **PROBLEM 11-9**

Consider a rigid body rotating about an axis through the origin 0. If $\bar{v}$ is the velocity vector of a point P of the body, then evaluate

$$\text{div } \bar{v}$$

and

$$\text{curl } \bar{v}$$

assuming that the angular velocity vector $\bar{\omega}$ is constant.

<u>Solution</u>: Let $\bar{r} = x\bar{i} + y\bar{j} + z\bar{k}$ be the position vector of a point P of the body, as shown in the figure. The velocity vector $\bar{v}$ is given by

$$\bar{v} = \bar{\omega} \times \bar{r},$$

therefore,

$$\text{div } \bar{v} = \text{div } (\bar{\omega} \times \bar{r})$$

Notice that we now have to evaluate the divergence of a vector product. For this purpose, we will use the following identity. (See Problem 8-18.)

$$\text{div } (\bar{a} \times \bar{b}) = \bar{b} \cdot \text{curl } \bar{a} - \bar{a} \cdot \text{curl } \bar{b}$$

For $\bar{\omega}$ and $\bar{r}$ the above identity becomes

455

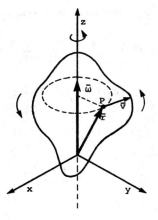

Fig. 1

$$\text{div } (\bar{\omega} \times \bar{r}) = \bar{r} \cdot \text{curl } \bar{\omega} - \bar{\omega} \cdot \text{curl } \bar{r}$$

Since we are told that $\bar{\omega}$ is a constant vector,

$$\text{curl } \bar{\omega} = \bar{0}$$

Also,

$$\text{curl } \bar{r} = \nabla \times \bar{r} = \left(\frac{\partial}{\partial y} z - \frac{\partial}{\partial z} y\right)\bar{i} + \left(\frac{\partial}{\partial z} x - \frac{\partial}{\partial x} z\right)\bar{j}$$

$$+ \left(\frac{\partial}{\partial x} y - \frac{\partial}{\partial y} x\right)\bar{k}$$

$$= \bar{0}$$

Therefore, we obtain that

$$\text{div } \bar{v} = \text{div } (\bar{\omega} \times \bar{r}) = 0$$

Now, to find curl $\bar{v}$, note that, as determined in Problem 11-8,

$$\bar{\omega} = \frac{1}{2} \text{curl } \bar{v}$$

and therefore

$$\text{curl } \bar{v} = 2\bar{\omega}$$

However, without using the results of Problem 11-8, we could alternatively determine curl $\bar{v}$ = curl $(\bar{\omega} \times \bar{r})$ by considering the following identity (see Problem 8-25)

$$\text{curl } (\bar{a} \times \bar{b}) = \bar{a} \text{ div } \bar{b} - \bar{b} \text{ div } \bar{a} + (\bar{b} \cdot \nabla)\bar{a} - (\bar{a} \cdot \nabla)\bar{b}$$

In our case, with $\bar{\omega} = \omega_1\bar{i} + \omega_2\bar{j} + \omega_3\bar{k}$, obtain

$$\text{curl } \bar{v} = \text{curl } (\bar{\omega} \times \bar{r})$$

$$= \bar{\omega} \text{ div } \bar{r} - \bar{r} \text{ div } \bar{\omega} + (\bar{r} \cdot \nabla)\bar{\omega} - (\bar{\omega} \cdot \nabla)\bar{r}$$

$$= \bar{\omega}\left(\frac{\partial x}{\partial x} + \frac{\partial y}{\partial y} + \frac{\partial z}{\partial z}\right) - \left(\omega_1 \frac{\partial}{\partial x} + \omega_2 \frac{\partial}{\partial y} + \omega_3 \frac{\partial}{\partial z}\right)\bar{r}$$

456

$$= 3\overline{\omega} - \overline{\omega}$$

$$= 2\overline{\omega}$$

which is exactly what we had determined before.

Consider a thin rubber membrane stretched out over the
x-y plane. The membrane is suddenly pushed up in a
certain spot, as shown in Fig. 1.

Derive an equation describing the shape of the surface.

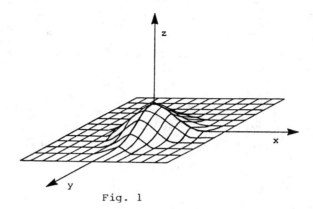

Fig. 1

<u>Solution</u>: Let τ denote the magnitude of the surface tension.
If a cut is made at any point in the body, the two sides of
the cut will tend to pull apart as a result of the surface
tension in the membrane. The magnitude of the surface
tension τ is the force per unit length which holds together
the two sides of the cut (see Fig. 2).

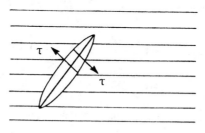

FIG.2

Proceed by establishing a system of coordinates such that
z = u is the vertical displacement of the membrane from the
unstretched position. Consider a little piece of the surface of the membrane whose length is Δx and whose width is
Δy. On this strip the forces are acting along each edge.
The cross section of the piece is shown in Fig. 3.

The force along edge 1 is $\tau_1 \Delta y$, directed tangent to the

457

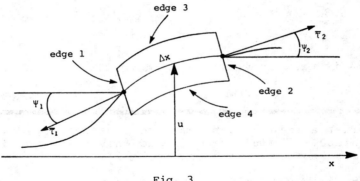

Fig. 3

surface at an angle ψ_1 with respect to the x-y plane. Along edge 2 the force is $\tau_2 \Delta y$ and the angle is ψ_2. For now, neglect for a moment the forces acting along edges 3 ($\tau_3 \Delta x$) and 4 ($\tau_4 \Delta x$). The total vertical force acting on 1 and 2 is

$$\Delta F = \tau_2 \Delta y \, \sin \psi_2 - \tau_1 \Delta y \, \sin \psi_1$$

$$= \left[\tau_2 \sin \psi_2 - \tau_1 \sin \psi_1 \right] \Delta y \tag{1}$$

For small distortions of the membrane, we have

$$\sin \psi = \tan \psi = \frac{\partial u}{\partial x} \tag{2}$$

Eq.(1) can be written in the form

$$\Delta F = \left[\tau_2 \left(\frac{\partial u}{\partial x} \right)_2 - \tau_1 \left(\frac{\partial u}{\partial x} \right)_1 \right] \Delta y \tag{3}$$

Also, for small Δx

$$\tau_2 \left(\frac{\partial u}{\partial x} \right)_2 - \tau_1 \left(\frac{\partial u}{\partial x} \right)_1 = \frac{\partial}{\partial x} \left(\tau \, \frac{\partial u}{\partial x} \right) \Delta x \tag{4}$$

Substituting eq.(4) into eq.(3) yields

$$\Delta F = \frac{\partial}{\partial x} \left(\tau \, \frac{\partial u}{\partial x} \right) \Delta x \Delta y \tag{5}$$

Now, the contribution from edges 3 and 4 is

$$\frac{\partial}{\partial y} \left(\tau \, \frac{\partial u}{\partial y} \right) \Delta y \Delta x \tag{6}$$

Thus, the total force is

$$\Delta F = \left[\frac{\partial}{\partial x} \left(\tau \, \frac{\partial u}{\partial x} \right) + \frac{\partial}{\partial y} \left(\tau \, \frac{\partial u}{\partial y} \right) \right] \Delta x \, \Delta y \tag{7}$$

Now, if the membrane is in equilibrium (the static case), then the external force f – the upward force per unit area,

458

is balanced by the internal force given by eq.(7). Therefore,

$$\Delta F = -f \ \Delta x \Delta y \tag{8}$$

for the static case.

Combining eqs.(7) and (8) gives

$$f = -\left[\frac{\partial}{\partial x}\left(\tau \ \frac{\partial u}{\partial x}\right) + \frac{\partial}{\partial y}\left(\tau \ \frac{\partial u}{\partial y}\right)\right]$$

or

$$f = -\nabla \cdot (\tau \nabla u) \tag{9}$$

where ∇ is the two-dimensional operator

$$\nabla \equiv \left(\frac{\partial}{\partial x}, \ \frac{\partial}{\partial y}\right) \tag{10}$$

If the tension τ is constant throughout the membrane, eq.(9) can be written as

$$\nabla^2 u = -\frac{f}{\tau} \tag{11}$$

● **PROBLEM 11-11**

Show that the equation of motion for an elastic-iso-tropic material is equivalent to two vector wave equations.

Solution: A material is said to be elastic if it returns to its original size and shape upon the removal of the forces which cause it to deform. In the theory of elasticity, the internal forces of a material are generally assumed to be sufficiently small so that the relative displacements, or deformations, can be considered proportional to the forces which cause them. Isotropic (non-crystalline), elastic materials have only two elastic constants.

To proceed with the problem, let

$$\bar{r} = (x, \ y, \ z)$$

and

$$\bar{r}' = (x', \ y', \ z')$$

be the position vectors of a point P (of the body) before and after deformation, respectively.

The displacement vector of point P is then

$$\bar{u} = \bar{r}' - \bar{r}. \tag{1}$$

If $\bar{f}$ is considered to be the force density, then the motion of an isotropic elastic material is described by

$$\bar{f} = (\lambda + \mu) \ \nabla(\nabla \cdot \bar{u}) + \mu\nabla^2\bar{u} \tag{2}$$

where λ and μ are constants related to the properties of the

459

elastic material.

Neglecting any body forces (such as gravity forces), the force density $\bar{f}$ may be expressed as

$$\bar{f} = \rho \frac{\partial^2 \bar{u}}{\partial t^2} \tag{3}$$

where ρ is the density of the material.

Substituting eq.(3) into eq.(2) yields

$$\rho \frac{\partial^2 \bar{u}}{\partial t^2} = (\lambda + \mu) \nabla(\nabla \cdot \bar{u}) + \mu \nabla^2 \bar{u} \tag{4}$$

Now, since any vector field can be expressed as the sum of a solenoidal field and an irrotational field, obtain

$$\bar{u} = \bar{u}_s + \bar{u}_{ir} \tag{5}$$

where

$$\nabla \cdot \bar{u}_s = 0 \tag{6}$$

and

$$\nabla \times \bar{u}_{ir} = \bar{0} \tag{7}$$

Since $\bar{u}_s$ is solenoidal and $\bar{u}_{ir}$ is irrotational. Substituting $\bar{u}_s + \bar{u}_{ir}$ for $\bar{u}$ in eq.(4) yields

$$\rho \frac{\partial^2}{\partial t^2}(\bar{u}_s + \bar{u}_{ir}) = (\lambda + \mu) \nabla(\nabla \cdot \bar{u}_{ir}) + \mu \nabla^2(\bar{u}_s + \bar{u}_{ir}) \tag{8}$$

Taking the divergence of eq.(8) gives

$$\text{div}\left(\rho \frac{\partial^2}{\partial t^2}(\bar{u}_s + \bar{u}_{ir})\right) = \text{div}\left[(\lambda + \mu) \nabla(\nabla \cdot \bar{u}_{ir}) + \mu \nabla^2(\bar{u}_s + \bar{u}_{ir})\right]$$

Since, by definition, the divergence of a vector is the dot product of the gradient operator with the vector itself, obtain

$$\rho \frac{\partial^2}{\partial t^2}(\nabla \cdot \bar{u}_s + \nabla \cdot \bar{u}_{ir}) = (\lambda + \mu) \nabla^2(\nabla \cdot \bar{u}_{ir}) + \mu \nabla \cdot \nabla^2 \bar{u}_{ir} \tag{9}$$

But, since $\nabla \cdot \bar{u}_s = 0$, eq.(9) can be simplified, after factoring out the operators ∇ and ∇^2, to obtain

$$\nabla \cdot \left\{ \rho \frac{\partial^2 \bar{u}_{ir}}{\partial t^2} - (\lambda + 2\mu) \nabla^2 \bar{u}_{ir} \right\} = 0 \tag{10}$$

Since $\nabla \times \bar{u}_{ir} = \bar{0}$, the curl of the bracketed expression must also equal zero. However, the only way that the divergence and curl of a given quantity can be zero is if that quantity is identically zero.

Therefore,

$$\rho \frac{\partial^2 \bar{u}_{ir}}{\partial t^2} = (\lambda + 2\mu) \nabla^2 \bar{u}_{ir} \tag{11}$$

or

$$\frac{\partial^2 \overline{u}_{ir}}{\partial t^2} = \frac{(\lambda + 2\mu)}{\rho} \nabla^2 \overline{u}_{ir} \qquad (12)$$

Since the general form of a vector wave equation is given by $\frac{\partial^2 \overline{U}}{\partial t^2} = c^2 \nabla^2 \overline{U}$, where $\overline{U}$ is the given vector and c is the speed of the travelling wave, we conclude that eq.(12) is a wave equation whose velocity is

$$c = \sqrt{\frac{\lambda + 2\mu}{\rho}} \qquad (13)$$

Now, taking the curl of eq.(8) leads to

$$\nabla \times \left[\rho \frac{\partial^2}{\partial t^2} (\overline{u}_s + \overline{u}_{ir}) \right] = \nabla \times \left[(\lambda + \mu) \nabla (\nabla \cdot \overline{u}_{ir}) + \mu \nabla^2 (\overline{u}_s + \overline{u}_{ir}) \right] \qquad (14)$$

or

$$\rho \frac{\partial^2}{\partial t^2} (\nabla \times \overline{u}_s + \nabla \times \overline{u}_{ir}) = (\lambda + \mu) \nabla \times \left[\nabla (\nabla \cdot \overline{u}_{ir}) \right]$$
$$+ \mu \nabla^2 \left[\nabla \times \overline{u}_s + \nabla \times \overline{u}_{ir} \right] \qquad (15)$$

But, again, $\nabla \times \overline{u}_{ir} = \overline{0}$, and since $\nabla \times \left[\nabla (\nabla \cdot \overline{u}_{ir}) \right] = \overline{0}$, eq.(15) simplifies to

$$\nabla \times \left(\rho \frac{\partial^2}{\partial t^2} \overline{u}_s \right) = \nabla \times \mu \nabla^2 \overline{u}_s \qquad (16)$$

or

$$\nabla \times \left(\rho \frac{\partial}{\partial t^2} \overline{u}_s - \mu \nabla^2 \overline{u}_s \right) = \overline{0} \qquad (17)$$

from which, we obtain

$$\rho \frac{\partial^2}{\partial t^2} \overline{u}_s = \mu \nabla^2 \overline{u}_s \qquad (18)$$

or

$$\frac{\partial^2}{\partial t^2} \overline{u}_s = \frac{\mu}{\rho} \nabla^2 \overline{u}_s \qquad (19)$$

We now recognize, from the general wave equation, that eq.(19) is a travelling wave whose speed is given by:

$$c_s = \sqrt{\frac{\mu}{\rho}}$$

CONCEPTS IN FLUID DYNAMICS

● **PROBLEM 11-12**

The motion of a fluid is described by the velocity field $\overline{v}(x,y,z)$.

Consider a small parallelepiped ABCDEFGH, having center at P(x,y,z), whose edges are parallel to the coordinate axes. Show that the loss of fluid per unit volume and per unit time is approximately given by div $\overline{v}$.

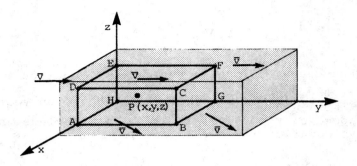

Solution: A parallelepiped with center at $P(x,y,z)$ is shown in the figure. The edges of the parallelepiped have magnitudes Δx, Δy, Δz respectively.

Consider the x component of the velocity $\bar{v}$. From the figure, we have

$$\text{x component of } \bar{v} \text{ at } P = v_1 \tag{1}$$

$$\text{x component of } \bar{v} \text{ at center of face ABCD} = v_1 + \frac{1}{2} \frac{\partial v_1}{\partial x} \Delta x \tag{2}$$

$$\text{x component of } \bar{v} \text{ at center of face EFGH} = v_1 - \frac{1}{2} \frac{\partial v_1}{\partial x} \Delta x \tag{3}$$

Note that eqs.(2) and (3) give only the approximate values of the x component of the vector $\bar{v}$. From eqs.(2) and (3), we have

$$\begin{matrix} \text{volume of fluid crossing} \\ \text{ABCD per unit time} \end{matrix} = \left(v_1 + \frac{1}{2} \frac{\partial v_1}{\partial x} \Delta x \right) \Delta y \Delta z \tag{4}$$

$$\begin{matrix} \text{volume of fluid crossing} \\ \text{EFGH per unit time} \end{matrix} = \left(v_1 - \frac{1}{2} \frac{\partial v_1}{\partial x} \Delta x \right) \Delta y \Delta z \tag{5}$$

Subtracting eq.(5) from eq.(4) gives

loss in volume in x direction per unit time is equal to

$$\left(v_1 + \frac{1}{2} \frac{\partial v_1}{\partial x} \Delta x \right) \Delta y \Delta z - \left(v_1 - \frac{1}{2} \frac{\partial v_1}{\partial x} \Delta x \right) \Delta y \Delta z \tag{6}$$

$$= \frac{\partial v_1}{\partial x} \Delta x \Delta y \Delta z$$

The loss in volume per unit time in the y and z directions are obtained in the same manner; and therefore

$$\begin{matrix} \text{loss in volume in y direction} \\ \text{per unit time} \end{matrix} = \frac{\partial v_2}{\partial y} \Delta x \Delta y \Delta z \tag{7}$$

$$\begin{matrix} \text{loss in volume in z direction} \\ \text{per unit time} \end{matrix} = \frac{\partial v_3}{\partial z} \Delta x \Delta y \Delta z \tag{8}$$

To obtain the total loss in volume per unit time, add eqs. (6), (7) and (8). Thus,

total loss in volume, per unit volume per unit time is

$$= \frac{\frac{\partial v_1}{\partial x} \Delta x \Delta y \Delta z + \frac{\partial v_2}{\partial y} \Delta x \Delta y \Delta z + \frac{\partial v_3}{\partial y} \Delta x \Delta y \Delta z}{\Delta x \Delta y \Delta z} = \frac{\partial v_1}{\partial x} + \frac{\partial v_2}{\partial y} + \frac{\partial v_3}{\partial z}$$

$$= \text{div } \bar{v} \tag{9}$$

Eq. (9) represents the exact loss in volume when $\Delta x \to 0$, $\Delta y \to 0$, $\Delta z \to 0$. If there is no loss of fluid anywhere, then

$$\text{div } \bar{v} = 0 \tag{10}$$

Vectors whose divergence is equal to zero are called solenoidal vectors. Eq.(10), div $\bar{v}$ = 0, is called the equation of continuity for an incompressible (constant density) fluid.

● **PROBLEM** 11-13

In fluid dynamics, the continuity equation for a fluid flow is given by

$$\frac{\partial \rho}{\partial t} + \text{div } (\rho \bar{v}) = 0, \tag{1}$$

where $\rho = \rho(x,y,z,t)$ is the density and $\bar{v} = \bar{v}(x,y,z,t)$ is the velocity of the given flow field. Show that the continuity equation can be alternatively written in the following forms:

$$\frac{\partial \rho}{\partial t} + (\text{grad } \rho) \cdot \bar{v} + \rho \text{ div } \bar{v} = 0 \tag{2}$$

and

$$\frac{D\rho}{Dt} + \rho \text{ div } \bar{v} = 0, \tag{3}$$

($\frac{D}{Dt}$ is called the Stokes derivative).

Solution: To derive eq.(2) from eq.(1), use eq.(2) of Problem 7-19:

$$\text{div } (\phi \bar{a}) = (\text{grad } \phi) \cdot \bar{a} + \phi \text{ div } \bar{a}$$

Substituting ρ for ϕ and $\bar{v}$ for $\bar{a}$ in the above identity, obtain

$$\text{div } (\rho \bar{v}) = (\text{grad } \rho) \cdot \bar{v} + \rho \text{ div } \bar{v} \tag{4}$$

Substituting eq.(4) into eq.(1) leads to

$$\frac{\partial \rho}{\partial t} + \text{div}(\rho \bar{v}) = \frac{\partial \rho}{\partial t} + (\text{grad } \rho) \cdot \bar{v} + \rho \text{ div } \bar{v} = 0,$$

which is eq.(2).

To obtain eq.(3) from eq.(1), note that the stokes derivative, $\frac{D}{Dt}$, is defined as:

$$\frac{D\rho}{Dt} \equiv \frac{\partial\rho}{\partial x}\frac{dx}{dt} + \frac{\partial\rho}{\partial y}\frac{dy}{dt} + \frac{\partial\rho}{\partial z}\frac{dz}{dt} + \frac{\partial\rho}{\partial t}$$

where
$$\rho = \rho(x,y,z,t)$$
and
$$x = x(t), \quad y = y(t), \quad z = z(t).$$

Since $\bar{v}$ is the velocity vector, it can be expressed as:

$$\bar{v} = \left(\frac{dx}{dt}, \frac{dy}{dt}, \frac{dz}{dt} \right)$$

Expanding eq.(2) gives

$$\frac{\partial\rho}{\partial t} + (grad\ \rho) \cdot \bar{v} + \rho\ div\ \bar{v}$$

$$= \frac{\partial\rho}{\partial t} + \left(\frac{\partial\rho}{\partial x}, \frac{\partial\rho}{\partial y}, \frac{\partial\rho}{\partial z} \right) \cdot \left(\frac{dx}{dt}, \frac{dy}{dt}, \frac{dz}{dt} \right) + \rho\ div\ \bar{v}$$

$$= \frac{\partial\rho}{\partial t} + \frac{\partial\rho}{\partial x}\frac{dx}{dt} + \frac{\partial\rho}{\partial y}\frac{dy}{dt} + \frac{\partial\rho}{\partial z}\frac{dz}{dt} + \rho\ div\ \bar{v}$$

$$= \frac{D\rho}{Dt} + \rho\ div\ \bar{v} = 0$$

Note that $\frac{D\rho}{Dt}$ is a measure of the rate of change of density at a point moving with the fluid.

● **PROBLEM 11-14**

Show that the vector field

$$\bar{v} = \left(\frac{-x}{r}, \frac{-y}{r}, \frac{-z}{r} \right) \qquad (1)$$

where

$$r = \sqrt{x^2+y^2+z^2} \qquad (2)$$

is a sink field.

Solution: In fluid dynamics, the basic equation describing the behavior of a fluid is given by the continuity equation,

$$\frac{\partial\rho}{\partial t} + div\ \rho\bar{v} = 0 \qquad (3)$$

where $\bar{v} = \bar{v}(x,y,z,t)$ is the velocity vector of the fluid and $\rho = \rho(x,y,z,t)$ is its density.

Since in most cases the fluid is neither destroyed nor created at any point, we say that it has no "sinks" or "sources". Mathematically, this can be expressed by the equation

$$div\ \rho\bar{v} = 0 \qquad (5)$$

464

To determine if the vector field $\bar{v}$ given by eq. (1) is a sink field (or source field), determine if div $\bar{v}$ is negative, positive, or zero. We have

$$\text{div } \bar{v} = \frac{\partial}{\partial x}\left(\frac{-x}{\sqrt{x^2+y^2+z^2}}\right) + \frac{\partial}{\partial y}\left(\frac{-y}{\sqrt{x^2+y^2+z^2}}\right) + \frac{\partial}{\partial z}\left(\frac{-z}{\sqrt{x^2+y^2+z^2}}\right)$$

$$= \frac{-(x^2+y^2+z^2) + x^2 - (x^2+y^2+z^2) + y^2 - (x^2+y^2+z^2) + z^2}{(x^2+y^2+z^2)\sqrt{x^2+y^2+z^2}}$$

$$= \frac{-2}{\sqrt{x^2+y^2+z^2}} \tag{6}$$

Thus for the whole space (x,y,z) we have

$$\text{div } \bar{v} < 0 \tag{7}$$

for $x,y,z \neq 0$.

This field is a sink field.

● **PROBLEM 11-15**

Consider the vortex flow of a fluid rotating with a constant angular velocity $\bar{\omega}$ about the z-axis. If the angular velocity vector $\bar{\omega}$ points in the positive z-direction, then determine the curl of the velocity vector, curl $\bar{v}$.

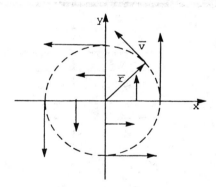

Solution: Since the angular velocity vector $\bar{\omega}$ is directed in the positive z-direction, it can be expressed as

$$\bar{\omega} = (0,0,\omega) \tag{1}$$

If vector $\bar{r}$ is expressed as

$$\bar{r} = (x,y,z) \tag{2}$$

then the velocity vector is given by

$$\bar{v} = \bar{\omega} \times \bar{r} \tag{3}$$

Substituting eq.(1) and eq.(2) into eq.(3) gives

$$\bar{v} = \bar{\omega} \times \bar{r}$$

$$= (0,0,\omega) \times (x,y,z) = (-\omega y, \omega x, 0)$$

The curl of $\bar{v}$ is then given by

$$\text{curl } \bar{v} = \nabla \times \bar{v} = \left(\frac{\partial}{\partial x}, \frac{\partial}{\partial y}, \frac{\partial}{\partial z} \right) \times (-\omega y, \omega x, 0)$$

$$= (0, 0, \omega+\omega) = (0, 0, 2\omega)$$

and thus

$$\text{curl } \bar{v} = 2\omega\bar{k}$$

Notice that since $\bar{\omega}$ is a constant, curl $\bar{v}$ is the same at every point in space.

● **PROBLEM 11-16**

The velocity of a steady fluid motion is

$$\bar{v} = (y, 0, 0) \qquad (1)$$

What are the trajectories of the moving points? Show that the flow is incompressible. What is the volume occupied at time t = 1 by the points which at time t = 0 fill the cube bounded by the planes x = 0, y = 0, z = 0, x = 1, y = 1 and z = 1?

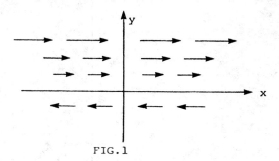

FIG.1

Solution: Let $\bar{v} = \bar{v}(x,y,z,t)$ denote the velocity vector and $\rho = \rho(x,y,z,t)$ denote the density. The continuity equation is given by

$$\frac{\partial \rho}{\partial t} + \text{div } \rho\bar{v} = 0 \qquad (2)$$

If the fluid is incompressible, eq.(2) becomes

$$\text{div } \bar{v} = 0 \qquad (3)$$

Taking the divergence of vector $\bar{v}$ as given by eq.(1) leads to

$$\text{div } \bar{v} = \left(\frac{\partial}{\partial x}, \frac{\partial}{\partial y}, \frac{\partial}{\partial z} \right) \cdot (y, 0, 0) = 0 \qquad (4)$$

And thus the flow is incompressible.

The vector field described by $\bar{v} = (y, 0, 0)$ is shown in Fig. 1.

Notice that all of the points of the fluid move in parallel straight paths. Now, the position of the points of interest at $t = 0$ and $t = 1$ is shown in Fig. 2.

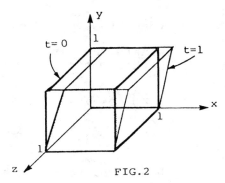

FIG.2

From Fig. 2, we see that the volume is the same at $t = 0$ and $t = 1$. Since $V_{t=0} = 1 \cdot 1 \cdot 1 = 1$, then

$$V_{t=1} = 1$$

Note that the bottom of the cube does not move. The motion of the points is parallel to the x-axis with $V_x = y$ and $V_y = V_z = 0$.

● **PROBLEM 11-17**

If the velocity field of a fluid is given by

$$\bar{v} = (x,0,0), \qquad (1)$$

sketch the velocities of the moving points of the fluid; show that the flow is not incompressible and determine the volume occupied, at time $t = 1$, by the points which at time $t = 0$ fill the cube $x = 0$, $y = 0$, $z = 0$, $x = 1$, $y = 1$ and $z = 1$.

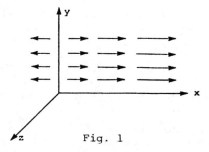

Fig. 1

<u>Solution</u>: The velocities (as given by vector field $\bar{v}$ of eq.(1)) are sketched in the manner shown in Fig. 1. Notice

467

that the points at x = 0 have zero velocity (they remain stationary), while all of the other points of the fluid have velocities which are parallel to the x-axis, and are proportional to x.

Now, since a flow is said to be incompressible if and only if

$$\text{div } \bar{v} = 0, \text{ (See Problem 11-16)}$$

it is necessary to evaluate the divergence of our given velocity field. Doing this, obtain

$$\text{div } \bar{v} = \left(\frac{\partial}{\partial x}, \frac{\partial}{\partial y}, \frac{\partial}{\partial z}\right) \cdot (x,0,0) = \frac{\partial x}{\partial x} = 1 \qquad (2)$$

Since div $\bar{v} \neq 0$, we conclude that the flow is not incompressible.

Next, since the position vector of a point (x,y,z) of the fluid is

$$\bar{r} = (x,y,z), \qquad (3)$$

the velocity of any point can be expressed as

$$\bar{v} = \frac{d\bar{r}}{dt} = \left(\frac{dx}{dt}, 0, 0\right) \qquad (4)$$

But, as given by eq.(1),

$$\bar{v} = (x,0,0)$$

and therefore, equating eqs.(1) and (4) results in

$$x = \frac{dx}{dt}$$

or, solving for dt and integrating,

$$dt = \frac{dx}{x} \qquad (5)$$

and

$$x = Ce^{t} \qquad (6)$$

where C is some constant. Note that eq.(6) gives us the displacement of any point of the fluid at any time t. Indeed,

$$\bar{r} = (Ce^{t}, 0, 0).$$

Now, to evaluate C, consider Fig. 2, which illustrates the motion of the initial cube of fluid.

At t = 0 the cube is ABCHLKOM (note that points ABOM do not move—they have zero velocity, since x = 0 at these points). At t = 1, the side CKLH will have moved to DEFG.

Since, as given by eq.(6),

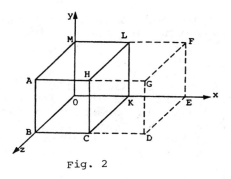

Fig. 2

$$x = Ce^t$$

and, since x = 1 at time t = 0, we obtain

$$1 = Ce^0 \quad \text{or} \quad C = 1. \tag{7}$$

At time t = 1,

$$x = e^t = e$$

and the points will occupy the volume enclosed by BDGAMOEF. Since x = e, the volume enclosed by the fluid at time t = 1 is V = e·1·1 = e units cubed.

● **PROBLEM 11-18**

Consider a small cube of fluid. Determine the total force resulting from the external pressure on the cube and derive the equation of equilibrium for the cube.

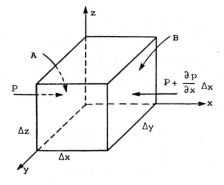

Solution: Before tackling the problem, certain principles concerning fluid statics, or hydrostatics should be discussed.

For one, we should note that when a fluid is at rest, there are no shear forces; therefore, the resulting stresses are always normal to any surface inside the fluid.

Also, it should be noted, again, due to the absense of shear forces, that the pressure, or "pressure stress", at any given point is the same in all directions.

Now, to proceed, note that the pressure is a function of position (not a function of time, since the fluid is at rest).

$$p = p(x,y,z) \tag{1}$$

Next, for purposes of simplicity, assume for a moment, that the pressure on the cube shown in the figure varies in the x-direction only. The pressure on face A is $p(x)$, while the pressure on face B is $p(x+\Delta x)$. If it is assumed that p is a differentiable function, then the pressure at $(x+\Delta x)$, or face B, is, according to Taylor's formula,

$$p(x+\Delta x) \approx p(x) + \frac{\partial p}{\partial x}\, \Delta x \tag{2}$$

(Note that the higher order terms of Taylor's expansion for the above function were neglected.)

Now, the force acting on side A is $p\Delta y \Delta z$, while the force on side B is

$$-\left[p + \frac{\partial p}{\partial x}\, \Delta x \right] \Delta y \Delta z \tag{3}$$

The total force in the x-direction, F_x, is then

$$F_x = p\Delta y \Delta z - \left[p + \frac{\partial p}{\partial x}\, \Delta x \right] \Delta y \Delta z$$

$$= - \frac{\partial p}{\partial x}\, \Delta x \Delta y \Delta z \tag{4}$$

Note that eq.(4) is the total force in the x-direction only. Now, if the pressure were to vary in the y and z directions as well, then following the same procedure would yield,

$$F_y = - \frac{\partial p}{\partial y}\, \Delta x \Delta y \Delta z$$

and $\qquad\qquad\qquad\qquad\qquad\qquad\qquad\qquad\qquad\qquad$ (5)

$$F_z = - \frac{\partial p}{\partial z}\, \Delta x \Delta y \Delta z$$

The total force on the cube is the sum of the forces on each face; therefore, in vector notation

$$\overline{F} = F_x \overline{i} + F_y \overline{j} + F_z \overline{k}$$

or, replacing the Δ's by differentials and factoring out gives

$$\overline{F} = -\left(\frac{\partial p}{\partial x}\, \overline{i} + \frac{\partial p}{\partial y}\, \overline{j} + \frac{\partial p}{\partial z}\, \overline{k} \right) dx\,dy\,dz$$

Now, for the force per unit volume, obtain (note that the bracketed expression is ∇p)

$$\frac{\overline{F}}{dx\,dy\,dz} = -\nabla p$$

The above force (per unit volume) is the force due to the external pressures; since the cube is in equilibrium, this force must be balanced by the internal or "body" forces (a typical body force is gravity). If these body forces are described by some general potential energy function, as is the case with gravitation, then the total force per unit mass due to these body forces may be given by

$$-\nabla\phi,$$

where ϕ represents the total potential energy, per unit mass, due to all the body forces. Now, since ρ is the density of the fluid, then the total force per unit volume of these body forces is

$$-\rho\nabla\phi$$

Therefore, the total force on the cube is the sum of the "pressure forces" and the body forces,

$$-\nabla p - \rho\nabla\phi = \overline{f}_{total},$$

and, since this cube is in equilibrium,

$$-\nabla p - \rho\nabla\phi = \overline{0} \tag{6}$$

or, if the density is constant (an incompressible fluid), eq.(6) reduces to

$$-\nabla p - \rho\nabla\phi = -\nabla p - \nabla(\rho\phi)$$

$$= -\nabla(p + \rho\phi) = \overline{0} \tag{7}$$

and, from eq.(7), we conclude that

$$p + \rho\phi = \text{const.}$$

● **PROBLEM 11-19**

Derive the equations of motion for an inviscid fluid. The final equations should be independent of pressure.

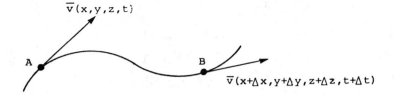

Solution: First, assume that the velocity of the fluid is significantly lower than the speed of sound in the fluid – this will lead us to conclude that the fluid is incompressible (of constant density)

$$\rho = \text{const.} \tag{1}$$

Next, recall that the continuity equation is expressed as,

$$\frac{\partial\rho}{\partial t} + \text{div}(\rho\overline{v}) = 0 \quad \text{(see Problem 11-13)} \tag{2}$$

Before proceeding, it should be noted that the continuity equation, also referred to as the "principle of conservation of matter", states that, in order to abide by the laws of nature, matter cannot appear or disappear from nowhere. Indeed, if matter flows away from a point, then there must be a decrease in the amount left behind.

Now, since we are dealing with an incompressible fluid the continuity equation becomes

$$\text{div } \bar{v} = 0$$

or

$$\nabla \cdot \bar{v} = 0 \tag{3}$$

Next, if we consider $\bar{f}$ to be the total force per unit volume (due to the acting pressure and body forces; note that since we are dealing with an inviscid fluid, there are no shear forces), then Newton's second law can be applied to the fluid to obtain

$$\rho \bar{a} = \bar{f} \tag{4}$$

where $\bar{a}$ is the acceleration of the fluid. Next, an expression for $\bar{f}$ is

$$\bar{f} = -\nabla p - \rho \nabla \phi \quad \text{(see Problem 11-18)} \tag{5}$$

where p is the pressure function and ϕ is a potential energy function describing the body forces of the fluid.

Substituting eq.(5) into eq.(4) gives

$$\rho \bar{a} = -\nabla p - \rho \nabla \phi \tag{6}$$

Now, we will attempt to obtain an expression for the acceleration of a fluid in terms of its velocity.

Consider the motion of any general particle from a point A with coordinates (x,y,z) to point B, coordinates (x+Δx, y+Δy, z+Δz).

The velocity is

$$\bar{v} = (v_x, v_y, v_z), \tag{7}$$

where

$$v_x = \frac{\Delta x}{\Delta t}$$

$$v_y = \frac{\Delta y}{\Delta t} \tag{8}$$

$$v_z = \frac{\Delta z}{\Delta t}$$

Now, assuming that $\bar{v}$ is a differentiable function and neglecting higher order terms, we obtain

$$\bar{v}(x+\Delta x, y+\Delta y, z+\Delta z, t+\Delta t)$$

$$= \overline{v}(x+v_x \Delta t, \ y+v_y \Delta t, \ z+v_z \Delta t, \ t+\Delta t)$$

$$= \overline{v}(x,y,z,t) + \frac{\partial \overline{v}}{\partial x} v_x \Delta t + \frac{\partial \overline{v}}{\partial y} v_y \Delta t$$

$$+ \frac{\partial \overline{v}}{\partial z} v_z \Delta t + \frac{\partial \overline{v}}{\partial t} \Delta t$$

$$= \overline{v}(x,y,z,t) + (\nabla \cdot \overline{v})\overline{v}\Delta t + \frac{\partial \overline{v}}{\partial t} \Delta t \qquad (9)$$

Now, since the acceleration is given by

$$\overline{a} = \frac{\overline{v}(x+\Delta x, \ y+\Delta y, \ z+\Delta z, \ t+\Delta t) - \overline{v}(x,y,z,t)}{\Delta t} \qquad (10)$$

obtain, after substituting eq.(9) into eq.(10),

$$\overline{a} = \frac{\overline{v}(x,y,z,t) + (\nabla \cdot \overline{v})\overline{v}\Delta t + \frac{\partial \overline{v}}{\partial t} \Delta t - \overline{v}(x,y,z,t)}{\Delta t}$$

$$\hspace{10cm} (11)$$

$$= (\nabla \cdot \overline{v})\overline{v} + \frac{\partial \overline{v}}{\partial t}$$

Next, substituting eq.(11) into eq.(6), gives

$$\frac{\partial \overline{v}}{\partial t} + (\nabla \cdot \overline{v})\overline{v} = - \frac{1}{\rho} \nabla p - \nabla \phi \qquad (12)$$

Now, we will define the vector field $\overline{\Omega}$, called the vorticity, as

$$\overline{\Omega} = \nabla \times \overline{v} \qquad (13)$$

Using the identity

$$(\overline{b} \cdot \nabla)\overline{b} = (\nabla \times \overline{b}) \times \overline{b} + \tfrac{1}{2}\nabla(\overline{b} \cdot \overline{b})$$

and eq.(13), eq.(12) can be rewritten in the form

$$\frac{\partial \overline{v}}{\partial t} + \overline{\Omega} \times \overline{v} + \tfrac{1}{2}\nabla v^2 = \frac{-1}{\rho} \nabla p - \nabla \phi \qquad (14)$$

which is the equation of motion of the fluid.

To eliminate pressure from eq.(14), note that for any general differentiable function, such as p,

$$\nabla \times (\nabla p) = \overline{0} \qquad (15)$$

Thus, taking the curl of eq.(14) and recalling that $\nabla \cdot \overline{v} = 0$, we obtain

$$\frac{\partial \overline{\Omega}}{\partial t} + \nabla \times (\overline{\Omega} \times \overline{v}) = \overline{0}, \qquad (16)$$

which, together with

$$\nabla \cdot \overline{v} = 0$$

and

$$\overline{\Omega} = \nabla \times \overline{v},$$

completely describe the velocity field $\bar{v}$ of the fluid.

It should now be noted that considering the motion of an inviscid fluid (no viscosity or shear forces within the flow) is an unrealistic, ideal consideration that is used only in obtaining approximate flow solutions to flows that have relatively low viscosity.

Indeed, it can be seen physically that in order for a fluid flow to exist, there must be corresponding shear-stresses (and consequently, some viscosity) within the flow.

● **PROBLEM** 11-20

Consider the motion of a fluid between two coaxial cylinders which are rotating at different angular velocities — as shown in Fig. 1. The inner cylinder, of radius r_1, is rotating with an angular velocity ω_1 while the outer cylinder, of radius r_2, is rotating with an angular velocity ω_2.

Obtain an expression for the velocity distribution of the enclosed fluid if the coefficient of viscosity is μ.

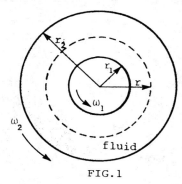

FIG.1

Solution: First, note that the coefficient of viscosity is nothing more than a proportionality constant relating the distance-rate of change of velocity to the corresponding shear stress. Thus, for a one-dimensional flow (say, in the x-direction), we obtain

$$\tau = \mu \, \frac{\partial v_x}{\partial y}$$

where τ represents the shear stress and μ is the coefficient of viscosity.

For a more complicated flow, such as a two-dimensional flow, where $\bar{v} = v_x \bar{i} + v_y \bar{j}$, we obtain

$$\tau_{xy} = \mu \, \frac{\partial \gamma_{xy}}{\partial t} \tag{1}$$

474

where τ_{xy} and γ_{xy} represent the shear stress and shear strain in the x-y plane respectively. The shear strain γ_{xy} is related to the velocity components by

$$\frac{\partial \gamma_{xy}}{\partial t} = \frac{\partial v_x}{\partial y} + \frac{\partial v_y}{\partial x} \qquad (2)$$

Substituting eq.(3) into eq.(2) gives

$$\tau_{xy} = \mu\left(\frac{\partial v_x}{\partial y} + \frac{\partial v_y}{\partial x}\right) \qquad (3)$$

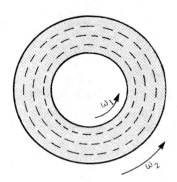

Fig. 2.

Dashed lines represent
constant shear-stress plots.

Now, for the fluid flow between the two concentric cylinders of Fig. 1, which is a two-dimensional flow problem, it should be noted that the velocity is a function of r,

$$v = v(r) \qquad (4)$$

For a fluid particle at some arbitrary radius r, we have

$$x = r \cos \omega t$$

and $\qquad (5)$

$$y = r \sin \omega t$$

where

$$v = \omega r$$

and ω is the angular velocity of the fluid at a distance r from the center.

Since

$$v_x = \frac{\partial x}{\partial t} \quad \text{and} \quad v_y = \frac{\partial y}{\partial t},$$

we obtain, from (5)

$$v_x = -r\omega \sin \omega t$$

$$= -\omega y \qquad (6)$$

and
$$v_y = r\omega \cos \omega t$$
$$= \omega x$$

From eq.(3), we have

$$\tau_{xy} = \mu\left[\frac{\partial}{\partial x}(\omega x) - \frac{\partial}{\partial y}(\omega y)\right]$$

Now, since ω is a function of x and y, carrying out the differentiation yields,

$$\tau_{xy} = \mu\left[\omega\,\frac{\partial}{\partial x}\,x + x\,\frac{\partial\omega}{\partial x} - \omega\,\frac{\partial}{\partial y}\,y - y\,\frac{\partial\omega}{\partial y}\right]$$

$$= \mu\left[x\,\frac{\partial\omega}{\partial x} - y\,\frac{\partial\omega}{\partial y}\right]$$

(7)

Now, if we investigate a fluid particle at the point y = 0, then

$$\frac{\partial\omega}{\partial y} = 0 \quad \text{and} \quad x\,\frac{\partial\omega}{\partial x} = r\,\frac{\partial\omega}{\partial r}$$

(8)

and eq.(7) then becomes

$$\tau_{xy}\bigg|_{y=0} = \mu x\,\frac{\partial\omega}{\partial x} = \mu r\,\frac{\partial\omega}{\partial r}$$

(9)

Though the above shear stress is evaluated at the point y = 0, it can be shown that for a given r, the shear stress is a constant for any point in the fluid flow. Indeed, at the point x = 0,

$$\tau_{xy}\bigg|_{x=0} = \mu y\,\frac{\partial\omega}{\partial y} = \mu r\,\frac{\partial\omega}{\partial r}$$

since

$$\frac{\partial\omega}{\partial x} = 0 \quad \text{and} \quad y\,\frac{\partial\omega}{\partial y} = r\,\frac{\partial\omega}{\partial r}$$

This means that constant shear-stress curves may be represented by concentric circles within the fluid flow, as shown in Fig. 2.

Now, to proceed in determining the velocity distribution, we will first derive an expression for the torque, T, acting across the cylindrical surface at some arbitrary radius r. Doing this, we obtain

$$T = \underbrace{(\text{shear stress})\cdot(\text{area})}_{\text{force}}\cdot(\text{moment arm})$$

$$= \left[\tau_{xy}\bigg|_{y=0}\right](2\pi r\ell)\,(r)$$

$$= 2\pi\mu\ell r^3\,\frac{d\omega}{dr}$$

(10)

But, since this is a steady flow, there is no angular accel-

476

eration and consequently the net torque acting between r and r + dr must be zero. Therefore, the torque given by eq.(10) must be independent of r, and thus

$$T = 2\pi\mu\ell r^3 \frac{d\omega}{dr} = 2\pi\mu\ell\alpha \qquad (11)$$

and

$$\alpha = r^3 \frac{d\omega}{dr}$$

or

$$d\omega = \frac{\alpha}{r^3} dr \qquad (12)$$

Integrating eq.(12) yields

$$\omega = \frac{-\alpha}{2r^2} + \beta \qquad (13)$$

Now, to determine the constants α and β, use the boundary conditions of the flow, namely at $r = r_1$, $\omega = \omega_1$ and at $r = r_2$, $\omega = \omega_2$.

Substituting the above boundary conditions into eq.(13) yields

$$\omega_1 = \frac{-\alpha}{2r_1^2} + \beta$$

$$\omega_2 = \frac{-\alpha}{2r_2^2} + \beta \qquad (14)$$

Solving for α and β gives

$$\alpha = \frac{2r_1^2 r_2^2}{r_2^2 - r_1^2}(\omega_2 - \omega_1)$$

$$\beta = \frac{r_2^2\omega_2 - r_1^2\omega_1}{r_2^2 - r_1^2} \qquad (15)$$

Eq.(13) gives the angular velocity of the fluid between the two rotating cylinders. The coefficients α and β are given by eq.(15).

Now, since

$$v = \omega r,$$

an expression for the velocity distribution as a function of r is

$$v = -\frac{\alpha}{2}\frac{1}{r} + \beta r$$

● **PROBLEM** 11-21

Derive the equations of motion for a fluid flow; include viscosity effects.

<u>Solution</u>: Since we are now going to consider the viscosity

477

of the fluid, we're simply going to add a viscous force, de-noted $\overline{f}_v$, to the solution of the inviscid fluid flow problem (as found in Problem 11-19). To do this, first obtain, from eq.(12) of Problem 11-19,

$$\rho\left[\frac{\partial\overline{v}}{\partial t} + (\overline{v}\cdot\nabla)\overline{v}\right] = -\nabla p - \rho\nabla\phi \qquad (1)$$

Now, to include the viscosity effects, we must add the force $\overline{f}_v$ to the right-hand side of eq.(1); doing this gives

$$\rho\left[\frac{\partial\overline{v}}{\partial t} + (\overline{v}\cdot\nabla)\overline{v}\right] = -\nabla p - \rho\nabla\phi + \overline{f}_v \qquad (2)$$

Now, note that the most general form of second-derivatives that can occur in a vector equation is a linear combination of the terms $\nabla^2\overline{v}$ and $\nabla(\nabla\cdot\overline{v})$. Therefore, selecting μ and $\mu + \mu'$ as the coefficients, the viscuous force $\overline{f}_v$ can be expressed (in terms of $\nabla^2\overline{v}$ and $\nabla(\nabla\cdot\overline{v})$), as

$$\overline{f}_v = \mu\nabla^2\overline{v} + (\mu+\mu')\nabla(\nabla\cdot\overline{v}) \qquad (3)$$

Combining eqs.(2) and (3), gives

$$\rho\left[\frac{\partial\overline{v}}{\partial t} + (\overline{v}\cdot\nabla)\overline{v}\right] = -\nabla p - \rho\nabla\phi + \mu\nabla^2\overline{v} + (\mu+\mu')\nabla(\nabla\cdot\overline{v}) \qquad (4)$$

Now, define the vorticity, $\overline{\Omega}$, as

$$\overline{\Omega} = \nabla \times \overline{v} \qquad (5)$$

Next, using the identity

$$(\overline{v}\cdot\nabla)v = (\nabla \times \overline{v}) \times \overline{v} + \tfrac{1}{2}\nabla(\overline{v}\cdot\overline{v}) \qquad (6)$$

and definition (5), eq.(4) can be written in the following form

$$\rho\left[\frac{\partial\overline{v}}{\partial t} + \overline{\Omega} \times \overline{v} + \tfrac{1}{2}\nabla v^2\right] = -\nabla p - \rho\nabla\phi + \mu\nabla^2\overline{v} + (\mu+\mu')\nabla(\nabla\cdot\overline{v}) \qquad (7)$$

Since we are dealing with an incompressible fluid,

$$\nabla\cdot\overline{v} = 0 \qquad (8)$$

and eq.(7) reduces to

$$\rho\left[\frac{\partial\overline{v}}{\partial t} + \overline{\Omega} \times \overline{v} + \tfrac{1}{2}\nabla v^2\right] = -\nabla p - \rho\nabla\phi + \mu\nabla^2\overline{v} \qquad (9)$$

Lastly, taking the curl of eq.(9) yields

$$\frac{\partial\overline{\Omega}}{\partial t} + \nabla \times (\overline{\Omega} \times \overline{v}) = \frac{\mu}{\rho}\nabla^2\overline{\Omega} \qquad (10)$$

Eq.(10) is the equation of motion for a viscous fluid.

Consider the flow of an incompressible viscous fluid
past a long cylinder of diameter d whose axis is normal
to the direction of flow. At large distances from the
cylinder, the velocity of flow is $\overline{w}$ = const, parallel
to the x-axis. At the surface of the cylinder, the velocity of the fluid is zero.

Show that

$$R = \frac{\rho}{\mu}\, wd,$$

called the "Reynolds number", can replace all four parameters ρ, μ, w, d.

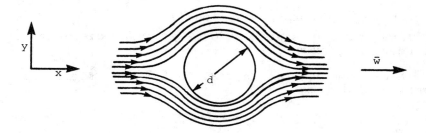

<u>Solution</u>: Begin by obtaining, from Problem 11-21, the
following equations of motion for an incompressible viscous
fluid

$$\overline{\Omega} = \nabla \times \overline{v} \tag{1}$$

and

$$\frac{\partial \overline{\Omega}}{\partial t} + \nabla \times (\overline{\Omega} \times \overline{v}) = \frac{\mu}{\rho}\, \nabla^2 \overline{\Omega} \tag{2}$$

For the surface of the cylinder, the following conditions
apply

$$v_x = v_y = v_z = 0$$

and

$$x^2 + y^2 = \frac{d^2}{4} \tag{3}$$

Note that we have four parameters μ, d, ρ, w at this point.
We will now attempt to replace these four parameters with
one parameter.

To proceed, note that the viscosity and density appear
in eq.(2) only as a ratio, and therefore, the ratio itself
can be considered as a parameter -- thus reducing the number
of parameters to three.

Next, if we introduce the new variables, x', y', z'
such that

$$x' = \frac{x}{d}, \quad y' = \frac{y}{d}, \quad \text{and} \quad z' = \frac{z}{d},$$

then eq.(3) can be written in the form

$$x^2 + y^2 = (x'd)^2 + (y'd)^2 = \frac{d^2}{4}$$

or

$$x'^2 + y'^2 = \frac{1}{4} \tag{5}$$

Since d is now eliminated from the equations, we are now left with only two parameters.

Introducing the variable v' as

$$v' = \frac{v}{w}, \tag{6}$$

we obtain, at large distances from the cylinder

$$v_x = \frac{w}{w} = 1, \quad v_y = v_z = 0 \tag{7}$$

Note that the second part of eq.(7), $v_y = v_z = 0$, is due to the fact that, as stated before, at large distances from the cylinder, $\overline{w}$ is parallel to the x-axis.

Now, from eqs.(4) and (6), obtain the following transformations of time

$$t' = \frac{x'}{v'} = \frac{\frac{x}{d}}{\frac{v}{w}} = \frac{x}{v}\frac{w}{d} = t\frac{w}{d} \tag{8}$$

In terms of the new variables, eq.(1) becomes

$$\overline{\Omega} = \nabla \times \overline{v} = \frac{w}{d} \nabla' \times v' = \frac{w}{d}\overline{\Omega}' \tag{9}$$

Note that since $x' = \frac{x}{d}$ and $\frac{\partial}{\partial x} = \frac{1}{d}\frac{\partial}{\partial x'}$, the "primed" del operator, ∇', is given by

$$\nabla' = \left(\frac{1}{d}\frac{\partial}{\partial x'}, \frac{1}{d}\frac{\partial}{\partial y'}, \frac{1}{d}\frac{\partial}{\partial z'}\right)$$

Eq.(2) can also be written as

$$\frac{\partial\overline{\Omega}'}{\partial t'} + \nabla' \times (\overline{\Omega} \times \overline{v}') = \frac{\mu}{\rho wd}\nabla'^2\overline{\Omega}' \tag{10}$$

Now, we can define a new constant

$$R = \frac{1}{\frac{\mu}{\rho wd}} = \frac{\rho}{\mu}wd \tag{11}$$

called the Reynolds number.

Omitting the primes, we can write the equation of motion for the flow as

$$\frac{\partial\overline{\Omega}}{\partial t} + \nabla \times (\overline{\Omega} \times \overline{v}) = \frac{1}{R}\nabla^2\overline{\Omega} \tag{12}$$

$$\overline{\Omega} = \nabla \times \overline{v}$$

480

where, for $x^2+y^2 = \frac{1}{4}$, $\bar{v} = 0$

and, for $x^2+y^2+z^2 \gg 1$ (i.e. at far distances from the cylinder), $v_x = 1$ and $v_y = v_z = 0$.

Note that in system (12) only one parameter appears.

The physical meaning of this is that we may have two different flows with the same Reynold's numbers,

$$R_1 = \frac{\rho_1}{\mu_1} w_1 d_1 = \frac{\rho_2}{\mu_2} w_2 d_2 = R_2 \qquad (13)$$

and the two flows will be similar.

The practical consequence of this similarity is that instead of investigating say, a life-size airplane, for example, we can more conveniently investigate a much smaller, geometrically similar model that, under a given velocity, has the same Reynold's number as the original specimen. Wind-tunnel experiments, for example, are based on this principle.

CONCEPTS IN HEAT FLOW

• **PROBLEM** 11-23

If the temperature is described as a function of the coordinates x, y, z,

$$T = T(x,y,z) \qquad (1)$$

then give the physical interpretation of the quantity

$$\frac{\Delta T}{\Delta s} = \frac{T(x+\Delta x, y+\Delta y, z+\Delta z) - T(x,y,z)}{\Delta s} \qquad (2)$$

and evaluate its limit as $\Delta s \to 0$.

Also, show that

$$\frac{dT}{ds} = \nabla T \cdot \frac{d\bar{r}}{ds} \qquad (3)$$

Solution: It should be noted here that the gradient operator plays an extremely important role in physics. The gradient operator enables us to obtain the vector fields from the corresponding scalar fields.

Most often, it is the vector field that is experimentally measured - therefore the numerical values for the vector field are directly obtainable.

However, it is mathematically more "elegant" to find

481

the scalar field corresponding to the vector field such that vector = grad (scalar). This mathematically obtained scalar field is, for the most part, a much more convenient tool and is much more "handy" as far as the necessary calculations are concerned.

Therefore, the logical structure that is followed is that we first start with an experimental procedure and measure the appropriate vector field which actually exists in the physical world. Then, through some mathematical procedures, we obtain the appropriate scalar field, which is of mathematical significance, that corresponds to the aforementioned vector field. We then perform certain mathematical calculations and subsequently transform the mathematical results back into the actual physical quantities (the experimentally - measurable quantities). This procedure is shown schematically in the figure.

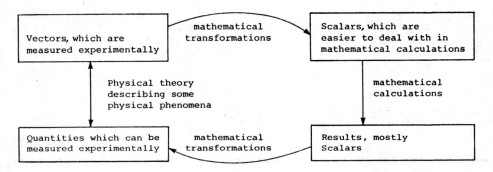

In eq.(2), $T(x,y,z)$ represents the temperature of the point (x,y,z) while $T(x+\Delta x, y+\Delta y, z+\Delta z)$ denotes the temperature of the point $(x+\Delta x, y+\Delta y, z+\Delta z)$. Also, ΔT and Δs represent the change in temperature and change in distance between the two points respectively. From this, we conclude that $\frac{\Delta T}{\Delta s}$ represents the average rate of change in temperature per unit distance in the direction from (x,y,z) to $(x+\Delta x, y+\Delta y, z+\Delta z)$. To find the limit of $\frac{\Delta T}{\Delta s}$, note that

$$\Delta T = \frac{\partial T}{\partial x} \Delta x + \frac{\partial T}{\partial y} \Delta y + \frac{\partial T}{\partial z} \Delta z \tag{5}$$

plus terms with $(\Delta x)^2$, $(\Delta y)^2$, $(\Delta z)^2$ and higher and, by definition,

$$\lim_{\Delta s \to o} \frac{\Delta T}{\Delta s} = \frac{dT}{ds} \tag{6}$$

Substituting eq.(5) into eq.(6), gives

$$\lim_{\Delta s \to o} \frac{\Delta T}{\Delta s} = \lim_{\Delta s \to o} \frac{\partial T}{\partial x} \frac{\Delta x}{\Delta s} + \frac{\partial T}{\partial y} \frac{\Delta y}{\Delta s} + \frac{\partial T}{\partial z} \frac{\Delta z}{\Delta s}$$
$$= \frac{\partial T}{\partial x} \frac{dx}{ds} + \frac{\partial T}{\partial y} \frac{dy}{ds} + \frac{\partial T}{\partial z} \frac{dz}{ds} = \frac{dT}{ds} \tag{7}$$

For explanation of the transformations in eq.(7) see Problem 6-4. Note that $\frac{dT}{ds}$ is the directional derivative of T.

From eq.(7), obtain

$$\frac{dT}{ds} = \frac{\partial T}{\partial x}\frac{dx}{ds} + \frac{\partial T}{\partial y}\frac{dy}{ds} + \frac{\partial T}{\partial z}\frac{dz}{ds}$$

$$= \left(\frac{\partial T}{\partial x}\,\bar{i} + \frac{\partial T}{\partial y}\,\bar{j} + \frac{\partial T}{\partial z}\,\bar{k}\right)\cdot\left(\frac{dx}{ds}\,\bar{i} + \frac{dy}{ds}\,\bar{j} + \frac{dz}{ds}\,\bar{k}\right) \qquad (8)$$

$$= \nabla T \cdot \frac{d\bar{r}}{ds}$$

where $\bar{r} = x\bar{i} + y\bar{j} + z\bar{k}$

● **PROBLEM** 11-24

Let T be the temperature of a material,

$$T = T(x,y,z) \qquad (1)$$

and let ϕ be the heat energy produced per unit volume per second by a source inside the material. Assuming the thermal conductivity K to be the function

$$K = K(x,y,z), \qquad (2)$$

derive the equation describing the flow of heat in the material.

Solution: Let $\bar{h}$ be the amount of heat energy which flows per unit time through a unit area perpendicular to the flow. The divergence of $\bar{h}$ represents the rate per unit volume at which heat is leaving the region.

$$\nabla \cdot \bar{h} = \text{loss of heat per unit volume} \qquad (3)$$

It is interesting to compare this result with the one obtained for a fluid (see Problem 11-12). Denoting the internal energy per unit volume as u, we obtain

$$\nabla \cdot \bar{h} = \phi - \frac{du}{dt} \qquad (4)$$

Now, if we consider steady state heat flow only, eq.(4) simplifies to

$$\nabla \cdot \bar{h} = \phi \qquad (5)$$

Next, if it is assumed that the heat current $\bar{h}$ is approximately proportional to the rate of change of temperature with respect to position, then one can write

$$\bar{h} = -K\nabla T \qquad (6)$$

where K is the constant of proportionality called the thermal conductivity.

Substituting eq.(6) into eq.(5) yields

$$\nabla \cdot (K\nabla T) = -\phi \qquad (7)$$

which is the equation of heat flow in the material.

Consider a cylinder of radius r_1 at temperature T_1. The cylinder is covered with a concentric sheath of insulating material, having thermal conductivity K, whose outside radius is r_2. The outside surface temperature is T_2. Determine the total amount of heat lost from a length L of the cylinder.

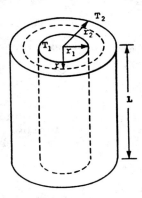

Solution: Since the cylinder is symmetrical, we can assume that h - the heat flow, depends only on the radial distance from the axial center

$$h = h(r) \tag{1}$$

Now, if we enclose the inner cylinder in an imaginary pipe of radius r and length L, then the total amount of heat H passing through this imaginary pipe is

$$H = (\text{area}) \cdot (\text{heat flow}) = 2\pi r L h$$

or

$$h = \frac{H}{2\pi r L} \tag{2}$$

But, the heat flow is also proportional to the gradient of temperature:

$$\overline{h} = -K\nabla T \quad \text{(see Problem 11-24)} \tag{3}$$

Since $h = h(r)$, we can write, from eq.(3),

$$h = -K\frac{dT}{dr} \tag{4}$$

Combining eqs.(2) and (4) results in

$$\frac{dT}{dr} = -\frac{H}{2\pi K L r} \tag{5}$$

Integrating from $r = r_1$ to $r = r_2$ yields

$$\int_{T_1}^{T_2} d\beta = \int_{r_1}^{r_2} -\frac{H}{2\pi K L r}\, d\alpha \tag{6}$$

(Note that β and α are dummy variables.)

$$T_2 - T_1 = -\left[\frac{H}{2\pi KL}\right] \ln\left(\frac{r_2}{r_1}\right) \qquad (7)$$

Solving eq.(7) for H yields

$$H = \frac{2\pi KL(T_1 - T_2)}{\ln\left(\frac{r_2}{r_1}\right)} \qquad (8)$$

CONCEPTS IN ELECTROMAGNETICS, MAXWELL'S EQUATIONS

● **PROBLEM** 11-26

In the theory of electromagnetic waves, we deal with the following differential equation

$$\frac{\partial^2 \overline{A}}{\partial r^2} + \frac{2}{r}\frac{\partial \overline{A}}{\partial r} = \frac{1}{c^2}\frac{\partial^2 \overline{A}}{\partial t^2} \qquad (1)$$

Show that

$$\overline{A} = \frac{\overline{b}_0 e^{i\omega\left(t - \frac{r}{c}\right)}}{r} \qquad (2)$$

where $\overline{b}_0$ is a constant vector and ω and c are constant scalars, satisfies the above differential equation.

Solution: Begin by finding all the necessary partial derivatives in eq.(1) using vector $\overline{A}$ as given by eq.(2). Differentiating eq.(2) with respect to time gives (note that r will not be held constant)

$$\frac{\partial \overline{A}}{\partial t} = \frac{i\omega\, \overline{b}_0 e^{i\omega\left(t - \frac{r}{c}\right)}}{r} = i\omega\overline{A} \qquad (3)$$

and

$$\frac{\partial^2 \overline{A}}{\partial t^2} = \frac{i^2\omega^2\overline{b}_0 e^{i\omega\left(t - \frac{r}{c}\right)}}{r} = \frac{-\omega^2\overline{b}_0 e^{i\omega\left(t - \frac{r}{c}\right)}}{r} = -\omega^2\overline{A}, \qquad (4)$$

since $i^2 = -1$.

Now, differentiating eq.(2) with respect to r gives

$$\frac{\partial \overline{A}}{\partial r} = \overline{b}_0\left[(-r^{-2})e^{i\omega\left(t - \frac{r}{c}\right)} + r^{-1}e^{i\omega\left(t - \frac{r}{c}\right)}\left(-\frac{i\omega}{c}\right)\right]$$

$$= \overline{b}_0 e^{i\omega\left(t - \frac{r}{c}\right)}\left[\frac{-i\omega}{cr} - \frac{1}{r^2}\right] = \overline{b}_0\frac{e^{i\omega\left(t - \frac{r}{c}\right)}}{r}\left(\frac{-i\omega}{c} - \frac{1}{r}\right) \qquad (5)$$

$$= \overline{A}\left(-\frac{i\omega}{c} - \frac{1}{r}\right)$$

and

$$\frac{\partial^2 \overline{A}}{\partial r^2} = \frac{\partial}{\partial r}\left[\overline{A}\left(-\frac{i\omega}{c} - \frac{1}{r}\right)\right] = \frac{\partial \overline{A}}{\partial r}\left(-\frac{i\omega}{c} - \frac{1}{r}\right) + \overline{A}\frac{\partial}{\partial r}\left(\frac{-i\omega}{c} - \frac{1}{r}\right)$$

$$= \overline{A}\left(\frac{-i\omega}{c} - \frac{1}{r}\right)^2 + \overline{A}\frac{1}{r^2} \tag{6}$$

Substituting eqs.(4), (5) and (6) into eq.(1) results in

$$\overline{A}\left(-\frac{i\omega}{c} - \frac{1}{r}\right)^2 + \overline{A}\frac{1}{r^2} + \frac{2}{r}\overline{A}\left(-\frac{i\omega}{c} - \frac{1}{r}\right) \tag{7}$$

$$= \overline{A}\frac{\omega^2}{c^2} + \overline{A}\frac{2i\omega}{cr} + \overline{A}\frac{1}{r^2} + \overline{A}\frac{1}{r^2} - \overline{A}\frac{2i\omega}{rc} - \overline{A}\frac{2}{r^2}$$

$$= -\overline{A}\frac{\omega^2}{c^2} = \frac{1}{c^2}(-\omega^2\overline{A}) = \frac{1}{c^2}\frac{\partial^2 \overline{A}}{\partial t^2}$$

which proves that $\overline{A}$, as given by eq.(2), satisfies eq.(1).

● **PROBLEM 11-27**

In electromagnetic theory, Maxwell's equations may be given by

$$\text{div } \overline{E} = 0 \tag{1}$$

$$\text{div } \overline{H} = 0 \tag{2}$$

$$\text{curl } \overline{E} = -\mu\frac{\partial \overline{H}}{\partial t} \tag{3}$$

$$\text{curl } \overline{H} = \varepsilon\frac{\partial \overline{E}}{\partial t} \tag{4}$$

Show that both vectors $\overline{E}$ and $\overline{H}$ satisfy the general wave equation.

<u>Solution</u>: Let $f = f(x,y,z,t)$ be any differentiable function. The wave equation is the second order partial differential equation

$$\frac{\partial^2 f}{\partial x^2} + \frac{\partial^2 f}{\partial y^2} + \frac{\partial^2 f}{\partial z^2} = c^2\frac{\partial^2 f}{\partial t^2} \tag{5}$$

where c represents the speed of light. For simplicity purposes, set $c = 1$ and $\mu = \varepsilon = 1$; (this will not affect the final results). Now, write eqs.(1)-(4) in the more convenient form

$$\nabla \cdot \overline{E} = 0 \tag{6}$$

$$\nabla \cdot \overline{H} = 0 \tag{7}$$

$$\nabla \times \overline{E} = -\frac{\partial \overline{H}}{\partial t} \tag{8}$$

$$\nabla \times \overline{H} = \frac{\partial \overline{E}}{\partial t} \tag{9}$$

Next, take the curl of both sides of eq.(8)

$$\nabla \times (\nabla \times \overline{E}) = \nabla \times \left(-\frac{\partial \overline{H}}{\partial t}\right) = -\frac{\partial}{\partial t}(\nabla \times \overline{H}) = -\frac{\partial}{\partial t}\left(\frac{\partial \overline{E}}{\partial t}\right)$$

(10)

$$= -\frac{\partial^2 \overline{E}}{\partial t^2}$$

From Problem 8-20, eq.(1), obtain the following identity

$$\nabla \times (\nabla \times \overline{a}) = \nabla(\nabla \cdot \overline{a}) - \nabla^2 \overline{a} \qquad (11)$$

Applying eq.(11) to eq.(10) yields

$$\nabla \times (\nabla \times \overline{E}) = \nabla(\nabla \cdot \overline{E}) - \nabla^2 \overline{E} = -\nabla^2 \overline{E} \qquad (12)$$

(since $\nabla \cdot \overline{E} = 0$)

Combining eqs.(10) and (12) results in

$$\nabla^2 \overline{E} = \frac{\partial^2 \overline{E}}{\partial t^2} \qquad (13)$$

which is the wave equation for vector $\overline{E}$. In the same manner, we find

$$\nabla \times (\nabla \times \overline{H}) = \nabla \times \left(\frac{\partial \overline{E}}{\partial t}\right) = \frac{\partial}{\partial t}(\nabla \times \overline{E}) = \frac{\partial}{\partial t}\left(-\frac{\partial \overline{H}}{\partial t}\right)$$

(14)

$$= -\frac{\partial^2 \overline{H}}{\partial t^2}$$

On the other hand,

$$\nabla \times (\nabla \times \overline{H}) = \nabla(\nabla \cdot \overline{H}) - \nabla^2 \overline{H} = -\nabla^2 \overline{H} \qquad (15)$$

Combining eqs.(14) and (15) gives

$$\nabla^2 \overline{H} = \frac{\partial^2 \overline{H}}{\partial t^2} \qquad (16)$$

which verifies that $\overline{H}$ also satisfies the wave equation.

● **PROBLEM 11-28**

From the general system of Maxwell's equations, derive the equations of electrostatics and magnetostatics and discuss the results.

Solution: In the most general case, Maxwell's equations are given by

$$\nabla \cdot \overline{E} = \frac{\rho}{\varepsilon} \qquad (1)$$

$$\nabla \times \overline{E} = -\mu \frac{\partial \overline{H}}{\partial t} \qquad (2)$$

$$\nabla \cdot \overline{H} = 0 \qquad (3)$$

$$\nabla \times \overline{H} = \varepsilon \frac{\partial \overline{E}}{\partial t} + \overline{J} \tag{4}$$

where $\overline{E}$ is the electric intensity, $\overline{H}$ is the magnetic intensity and $\overline{J}$ is the current density.

Constants ε and μ are called the permittivity and permeability respectively. The permittivity ε and the permeability μ are quantities that are determined by the material or medium considered and they are related by the expression

$$\varepsilon \mu = \frac{1}{c^2},$$

where c is the speed of light (3×10^8 m/sec). If the medium in consideration is free space, then ε becomes ε_0 (the permittivity of free space) and μ becomes μ_0 (the permeability of free space).

The numerical values of ε_0 and μ_0 are

$$\varepsilon_0 = \frac{1}{36\pi} \times 10^{-9} \text{ farad/meter}$$
$$\mu_0 = 4\pi \times 10^{-7} \text{ henry/meter} \tag{5}$$

In the static case, vectors $\overline{E}$ and $\overline{H}$ are constant and therefore

$$\frac{\partial \overline{E}}{\partial t} = \frac{\partial \overline{H}}{\partial t} = \overline{0} \tag{6}$$

Eqs.(1)-(4) become, for the static case,

$$\left. \begin{array}{l} \nabla \cdot \overline{E} = \frac{\rho}{\varepsilon} \\ \nabla \times \overline{E} = \overline{0} \end{array} \right\} \quad \text{Electrostatics} \tag{7}$$

$$\left. \begin{array}{l} \nabla \cdot \overline{H} = 0 \\ \nabla \times \overline{H} = \overline{J} \end{array} \right\} \quad \text{Magnetostatics} \tag{8}$$

Eqs.(7) and (8) represent the electrostatics and magnetostatics branch of electromagnetics respectively. It should be noted for this static case, that from the original four equations we obtain two distinct pairs of equations - leading us to conclude that vectors $\overline{E}$ and $\overline{H}$ are not related or interconnected. This tells us, for the static case, that electricity and magnetism in general are separate, distinct phenomena. Also, note that in this static case, vector $\overline{E}$ is irrotational (since $\nabla \times \overline{E} = \overline{0}$) while vector $\overline{H}$ is solenoidal (since $\nabla \cdot \overline{H} = 0$).

Lastly, note that if we were not considering the static case but rather the general case, then vectors $\overline{E}$ and $\overline{H}$ would be interconnected (as indicated by eqs.(2) and (4)).

1. From Maxwell's equations for electrostatics, derive Poisson's equation for the electrostatic potential.

2. Using Coulomb's law, find the electrostatic potential of a single charge located at the origin of a coordinate system.

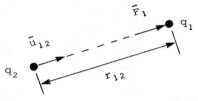

Fig. 1

Solution: 1. Obtain the following equations for electrostatics from Problem 11-28.

$$\nabla \cdot \overline{E} = \frac{\rho}{\varepsilon} \tag{1}$$

$$\nabla \times \overline{E} = \overline{0} \tag{2}$$

From eq.(2), it is concluded that the electric intensity vector $\overline{E}$ can be described as the gradient of some scalar potential ϕ,

$$\overline{E} = -\nabla\phi \tag{3}$$

Substituting eq.(3) into eq.(1) yields

$$\nabla \cdot \overline{E} = \nabla \cdot (-\nabla\phi) = -\nabla^2\phi = \frac{\rho}{\varepsilon}$$

or

$$\nabla^2\phi = -\frac{\rho}{\varepsilon} \tag{4}$$

Eq.(4) is a form of the general Poisson equation:

$$\nabla^2 f = \alpha.$$

Note that Laplace's equation, $\nabla^2 f = 0$, is a special case of Poisson's equation.

2. First, assume that we have two electric charges q_1 and q_2. The force on q_1 due to the charge q_2 is

$$\overline{F}_1 = \frac{1}{4\pi\varepsilon} \frac{q_1 q_2}{r_{12}^2} \overline{u}_{12} \tag{5}$$

where r_{12} is the distance between the charges and $\overline{u}_{12}$ is the unit vector in the direction from q_2 to q_1, as shown in Fig.1.

489

Eq.(5) is Coulomb's law. In most cases, Coulomb's law is applied together with the principle of superposition, which states that given any system of charges, the force on any charge is the vector sum of all the corresponding Coulomb forces resulting from each of the other charges.

Concepts of electrostatics are based on Coulomb's law and the principle of superposition. Both notions are expressed exactly by Maxwell's equations through a mathematically different form.

Results are shown in the table.

Maxwell equations	Electrostatics	Coulomb's Law
$\nabla \cdot \overline{E} = \dfrac{\rho}{\varepsilon}$	equivalent $\xleftrightarrow{\hspace{2cm}}$	$\overline{F}_1 = \dfrac{1}{4\pi\varepsilon} \dfrac{q_1 q_2}{r_{12}^2} \overline{u}_{12}$
$\nabla \times \overline{E} = \overline{0}$		Principle of Super-position

Now, from Coulomb's law, define the electric field vector as

$$\overline{E}_1 = \frac{\overline{F}_1}{q_1} = \frac{1}{4\pi\varepsilon} \frac{q_2}{r_{12}^2} \overline{u}_{12} \qquad (6)$$

If we place the charge q_2 at the origin of the coordinate system, then eq.(6) becomes

$$\overline{E} = \frac{1}{4\pi\varepsilon} \frac{q}{r^2} \overline{u} \qquad (7)$$

(indices 1 and 2 were omitted for purposes of simplicity).

From eq.(3), we have

$$-\text{grad } \phi = \overline{E} = \frac{1}{4\pi\varepsilon} \frac{q}{r^2} \overline{u} \qquad (8)$$

or

$$\left(\frac{\partial\phi}{\partial x}, \frac{\partial\phi}{\partial y}, \frac{\partial\phi}{\partial z}\right) = \frac{-1}{4\pi\varepsilon} \frac{q}{r^2} \left(\frac{x}{\sqrt{x^2+y^2+z^2}}, \frac{y}{\sqrt{x^2+y^2+z^2}}, \frac{z}{\sqrt{x^2+y^2+z^2}}\right)$$

Now, since $r = \sqrt{x^2+y^2+z^2}$, bringing the r^2 term inside and equating components results in

$$\frac{\partial\phi}{\partial x} = \frac{-q}{4\pi\varepsilon} \frac{x}{(x^2+y^2+z^2)^{\frac{3}{2}}} \qquad (9a)$$

$$\frac{\partial\phi}{\partial y} = \frac{-q}{4\pi\varepsilon} \frac{y}{(x^2+y^2+z^2)^{\frac{3}{2}}} \qquad (9b)$$

$$\frac{\partial\phi}{\partial z} = \frac{-q}{4\pi\varepsilon} \frac{z}{(x^2+y^2+z^2)^{\frac{3}{2}}} \qquad (9c)$$

Next, integrating eqs.(9a), (9b) and (9c) yields, respectively

$$\phi(x,y,z) = \frac{q}{4\pi\varepsilon} \frac{1}{(x^2+y^2+z^2)^{\frac{1}{2}}} + h(y,z)$$

$$\phi(x,y,z) = \frac{q}{4\pi\varepsilon} \frac{1}{(x^2+y^2+z^2)^{\frac{1}{2}}} + g(x,z)$$

$$\phi(x,y,z) = \frac{q}{4\pi\varepsilon} \frac{1}{(x^2+y^2+z^2)^{\frac{1}{2}}} + f(x,y)$$

Comparing the above three equations results in

$$h(y,z) = g(x,z) = f(x,y) = 0$$

and therefore

$$\phi(x,y,z) = \frac{q}{4\pi\varepsilon} \frac{1}{(x^2+y^2+z^2)^{\frac{1}{2}}}$$

$$= \frac{q}{4\pi\varepsilon} \frac{1}{r} \qquad (10)$$

The choice of the integrating constant will be discussed later. Eq.(10) gives the scalar potential of a single charge located at the origin of a system.

● **PROBLEM 11-30**

Find the scalar potential and the electric field of a dipole.

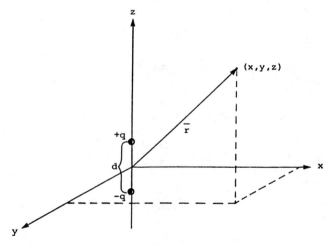

Fig.1 – dipole formed by two charges a
distance d apart

Solution: Two point charges +q and -q separated by the dis-tance d are located on the z-axis as shown in Fig. 1.

Using eq.(10) of Problem 11-29 for the scalar potential of a single charge, and the principle of superposition, obtain

$$\phi(x,y,z) = \frac{1}{4\pi\varepsilon}\left[\frac{q}{\sqrt{\left(z-\frac{d}{2}\right)^2+x^2+y^2}} + \frac{-q}{\sqrt{\left(z+\frac{d}{2}\right)^2+x^2+y^2}} \right] (1)$$

491

Eq.(1) is an exact formula for the scalar potential of two charges separated by a distance d. Now, note that taking the gradient of eq.(1) yields vector $\bar{E}$.

Next, note that the distance d is small in comparison with the distances at which we will measure the electric field. Using the binomial expansion and keeping only the first order terms in d, yields

$$\left(z - \frac{d}{2}\right)^2 \approx z^2 - zd \tag{2}$$

$$\left(z - \frac{d}{2}\right)^2 + x^2 + y^2 \approx x^2 + y^2 + z^2 - zd = r^2 - zd \tag{3}$$

$$= r^2\left(1 - \frac{zd}{r^2}\right)$$

and

$$\frac{1}{\sqrt{\left(z - \frac{d}{2}\right)^2 + x^2 + y^2}} \approx \frac{1}{\sqrt{r^2\left(1 - \frac{zd}{r^2}\right)}} = \frac{1}{r}\left(1 - \frac{zd}{r^2}\right)^{-\frac{1}{2}} \tag{4}$$

For the term $\left(1 - \frac{zd}{r^2}\right)^{-\frac{1}{2}}$, use the binomial expansion and drop the terms with d^2, d^3 etc.; doing this gives

$$\left(1 - \frac{zd}{r^2}\right)^{-\frac{1}{2}} \approx 1 + \frac{1}{2}\frac{zd}{r^2} \tag{5}$$

Substituting eq.(5) into eq.(4) yields

$$\frac{1}{\sqrt{\left(z - \frac{d}{2}\right)^2 + x^2 + y^2}} \approx \frac{1}{r}\left(1 + \frac{1}{2}\frac{zd}{r^2}\right) \tag{6}$$

In the same manner, we obtain

$$\frac{1}{\sqrt{\left(z + \frac{d}{2}\right)^2 + x^2 + y^2}} \approx \frac{1}{r}\left(1 - \frac{1}{2}\frac{zd}{r^2}\right) \tag{7}$$

Substituting the approximate eqs.(6) and (7) into eq.(1) results in

$$\phi(x,y,z) = \frac{1}{4\pi\varepsilon}\left[\frac{q}{r}\left(1 + \frac{1}{2}\frac{zd}{r^2}\right) - \frac{q}{r}\left(1 - \frac{1}{2}\frac{zd}{r^2}\right)\right] \tag{8}$$

$$= \left(\frac{1}{4\pi\varepsilon}\right)\frac{z}{r^3}qd$$

Now, we define the dipole moment as

$$p = qd \tag{9}$$

Since $\cos\theta = \frac{z}{r}$, eq.(8) can be written in the form

$$\phi(x,y,z) = \frac{1}{4\pi\varepsilon}\frac{p\cos\theta}{r^2} \tag{10}$$

Next, we define $\bar{p}$ as a vector whose magnitude is given by

$$|\bar{p}| = qd$$

and whose direction is along the axis of the dipole pointing from $-q$ toward $+q$, then

$$\bar{p} \cdot \bar{r} = rp \cos \theta$$

or

$$\frac{\bar{p} \cdot \bar{r}}{r} = p \cos \theta \qquad (11)$$

Since the $p \cos \theta$ appears in eq.(10), it can be written as

$$\phi(x,y,z) = \frac{1}{4\pi\varepsilon} \frac{\bar{p} \cdot \bar{r}}{r^3} \qquad (12)$$

Taking the gradient of ϕ gives us

$$E_x = -\frac{\partial\phi}{\partial x} = \frac{p}{4\pi\varepsilon} \frac{3zx}{r^5} \qquad (13)$$

$$E_y = -\frac{\partial\phi}{\partial y} = \frac{p}{4\pi\varepsilon} \frac{3zy}{r^5} \qquad (14)$$

$$E_z = -\frac{\partial\phi}{\partial z} = -\frac{p}{4\pi\varepsilon} \left(\frac{1}{r^3} - \frac{3z^2}{r^5} \right) \qquad (15)$$

and

$$\bar{E} = \frac{p}{4\pi\varepsilon} \left(\frac{3zx}{r^5}, \ \frac{3zy}{r^5}, \ \frac{3z^2}{r^5} - \frac{1}{r^3} \right)$$

● **PROBLEM 11-31**

The electromagnetic force on a charge q, called the Lorentz force, is given by the equation

$$\bar{F} = q(\bar{E} + \bar{v} \times \bar{H}) \qquad (1)$$

Evaluate div $\bar{F}$ in free space.

Solution: Taking the divergence of both sides of eq.(1) yields

$$\nabla \cdot \bar{F} = q \ \nabla \cdot \bar{E} + \ \nabla \cdot (\bar{v} \times \bar{H}) \qquad (2)$$

Now, use the following identity

$$\nabla \cdot (\bar{a} \times \bar{b}) = \bar{b} \cdot (\nabla \times \bar{a}) - \bar{a} \cdot (\nabla \times \bar{b}) \qquad (3)$$

to transform eq.(2). Doing this, obtain

$$\nabla \cdot \bar{F} = q \ \nabla \cdot \bar{E} + \bar{H} \cdot (\nabla \times \bar{v}) - \bar{v} \cdot (\nabla \times \bar{H}) \qquad (4)$$

From Maxwell's equations (see Problem 11-28), we have

$$\nabla \cdot \bar{E} = \frac{\rho}{\varepsilon} \qquad (5)$$

$$\nabla \times \overline{H} = \varepsilon \frac{\partial \overline{E}}{\partial t} + \overline{J} \qquad (6)$$

In free space $\rho = 0$, $\varepsilon = \varepsilon_0$ and $\overline{J} = \overline{0}$; thus eqs.(5) and (6) become

$$\nabla \cdot \overline{E} = 0 \qquad (7)$$

$$\nabla \times \overline{H} = \varepsilon_0 \frac{\partial \overline{E}}{\partial t} \qquad (8)$$

Substituting eqs.(7) and (8) into eq.(4) gives

$$\nabla \cdot \overline{F} = \overline{H} \cdot (\nabla \times \overline{v}) - \overline{v} \cdot \left(\varepsilon_0 \frac{\partial \overline{E}}{\partial t} \right) \qquad (9)$$

Note that if the electic field were static, that is $\frac{\partial \overline{E}}{\partial t} = \overline{0}$, and the velocity field irrotational, that is $\nabla \times \overline{v} = 0$, then force $\overline{F}$ would be solenoidal.

● PROBLEM 11-32

From Maxwell's equations of magnetostatics, derive the equation for the vector potential of a magnetic field.

Solution: From Problem 11-28, eq.(8), obtain the following set of equations

$$\nabla \cdot \overline{H} = 0 \qquad (1)$$

$$\nabla \times \overline{H} = \overline{J} \qquad (2)$$

Note that these equations are valid only for constant electric charge density vectors ($\overline{J}$ = const.) and for steady current flow, since in the static case neither vector $\overline{E}$ or vector $\overline{H}$ vary with time $\frac{\partial \overline{E}}{\partial t} = \overline{0} = \frac{\partial \overline{H}}{\partial t}$

Now, since $\nabla \cdot \overline{H} = 0$, vector $\overline{H}$ can be represented as the curl of some other vector field:

$$\overline{H} = \nabla \times \overline{A} \qquad (3)$$

For this representation of $\overline{H}$, eq.(1) is satisfied automatically; indeed

$$\nabla \cdot (\nabla \times \overline{A}) = 0 \qquad (4)$$

for any vector $\overline{A}$.

Vector field $\overline{A}$ is called the "vector potential". Two different vector potentials, say $\overline{A}$ and $\overline{A}'$, can lead to the same magnetic field $\overline{H}$:

$$\overline{H} = \nabla \times \overline{A} = \nabla \times \overline{A}' \qquad (5)$$

or

$$\nabla \times \overline{A} - \nabla \times \overline{A}' = \nabla \times (\overline{A} - \overline{A}') = \overline{0}$$

Recall that any vector whose curl is zero (an irrotational vector) can be expressed by the gradient of some scalar field. Therefore, for vector $(\overline{A} - \overline{A}')$, obtain

$$\overline{A} - \overline{A}' = \text{grad } \psi \tag{6}$$

or

$$\overline{A} = \overline{A}' + \text{grad } \psi$$

where ψ is some scalar function. Taking the divergence of both sides of eq.(6) leads to

$$\nabla \cdot \overline{A} = \nabla \cdot \overline{A}' + \nabla^2 \psi \tag{7}$$

Now, ψ may be chosen so that

$$\nabla \cdot \overline{A} = 0 \tag{8}$$

Thus, in magnetostatics, the vector potential $\overline{A}$ is defined such that

$$\overline{H} = \nabla \times \overline{A}$$

where

$$\nabla \cdot \overline{A} = 0 \tag{9}$$

Note that eq.(9) does not uniquely determine vector $\overline{A}$.

Now, substituting eq.(3) into eq.(2) yields

$$\nabla \times (\nabla \times \overline{A}) = \overline{J} \tag{10}$$

Using the vector identity

$$\nabla \times (\nabla \times \overline{A}) = \nabla(\nabla \cdot \overline{A}) - \nabla^2 \overline{A} \tag{11}$$

and eq.(8), obtain

$$\nabla^2 \overline{A} = -\overline{J} \tag{12}$$

Notice that eq.(12) is Poisson's equation.

Lastly, note that vector field $\overline{A}$ is not just a mere mathematical notion - it does, as a matter of fact, have much physical significance, particularly in the field of quantum mechanics.

● **PROBLEM 11-33**

From Maxwell's equations, derive the continuity equation for an electric charge.

Solution: The continuity equation states that an electric charge cannot be created or destroyed.

Now, if we consider a closed surface, the flux of current through this surface, given by $\nabla \cdot \overline{J}$, where $\overline{J}$ is the current density, represents the decrease of charge inside the surface, given by $-\frac{\partial \rho}{\partial t}$, where ρ denotes the charge density.

The equation of continuity is thus given by

$$\nabla \cdot \overline{J} = -\frac{\partial \rho}{\partial t} \tag{1}$$

Now, to derive eq.(1), take Maxwell's equation involving $\overline{J}$,

$$\nabla \times \overline{H} = \varepsilon \frac{\partial \overline{E}}{\partial t} + \overline{J} \tag{2}$$

and take its divergence. Doing this yields

$$\nabla \cdot (\nabla \times \overline{H}) = \varepsilon \nabla \cdot \left(\frac{\partial \overline{E}}{\partial t}\right) + \nabla \cdot \overline{J} \tag{3}$$

Note that the left-hand side of eq.(3) is zero, since the divergence of curl is always, identically, zero.

Now, assuming that $\overline{E}$ has continuous derivatives, obtain

$$\nabla \cdot \left(\frac{\partial \overline{E}}{\partial t}\right) = \frac{\partial}{\partial t}(\nabla \cdot \overline{E}) \tag{4}$$

Eq.(3) becomes

$$\nabla \cdot \overline{J} + \varepsilon \frac{\partial}{\partial t}(\nabla \cdot \overline{E}) = 0 \tag{5}$$

Next, note that from another of Maxwell's equations, we obtain

$$\nabla \cdot \overline{E} = \frac{\rho}{\varepsilon} \tag{6}$$

Substituting eq.(6) into eq.(5) leads to

$$\nabla \cdot \overline{J} = -\varepsilon \frac{\partial}{\partial t}(\nabla \cdot \overline{E}) = -\varepsilon \frac{\partial}{\partial t}\left(\frac{\rho}{\varepsilon}\right) = -\frac{\partial \rho}{\partial t} \tag{7}$$

Eq.(7) is the continuity equation - which states that electric charge is conserved. The time derivative of charge density with the minus sign represents the change in charge per unit time. This change of charge is a direct consequence of the flow of charge and it is mathematically equal to $\nabla \cdot \overline{J}$. Div $\overline{J}$ (or $\nabla \cdot \overline{J}$), represents the loss of charge per unit volume per unit time.

The continuity equation for electric charge can be written in the form

$$\frac{\partial \rho}{\partial t} + \nabla \cdot \overline{J} = 0$$

It is interesting to note the similarities between the above equation and the continuity equation for a fluid flow, given by

$$\frac{\partial \rho}{\partial t} + \nabla \cdot (\rho \overline{v}) = 0 \quad \text{(See Problem 11-13)}$$

496

Express Maxwell's equations in terms of the scalar potential ϕ (see Problem 11-29) and the vector potential $\overline{A}$ (see Problem 11-32).

<u>Solution</u>: The Maxwell equations are given by

$$\nabla \cdot \overline{E} = \frac{\rho}{\varepsilon} \tag{1}$$

$$\nabla \times \overline{E} = -\mu \frac{\partial \overline{H}}{\partial t} \tag{2}$$

$$\nabla \cdot \overline{H} = 0 \tag{3}$$

$$\nabla \times \overline{H} = \varepsilon \frac{\partial \overline{E}}{\partial t} + \overline{J} \tag{4}$$

Now, since $\overline{H}$ is a solenoidal vector (since $\nabla \cdot \overline{H} = 0$), it can be expressed as the curl of some vector $\overline{A}$:

$$\overline{H} = \nabla \times \overline{A} \tag{5}$$

since indeed

$$\nabla \cdot (\nabla \times \overline{A}) = \overline{0}$$

Vector $\overline{A}$ is called the vector potential (see Problem 11-32).

Substituting eq.(5) into eq.(2) results in

$$\nabla \times \overline{E} = -\frac{\partial}{\partial t} (\nabla \times \overline{A}) \tag{6}$$

and

$$\nabla \times \overline{E} + \frac{\partial}{\partial t}(\nabla \times \overline{A}) = 0$$

or, bringing the $\frac{\partial}{\partial t}$ term inside and factoring out the ∇ operator yields

$$\nabla \times \left(\overline{E} + \frac{\partial \overline{A}}{\partial t} \right) = \overline{0} \tag{7}$$

Now, since the curl of $\overline{E} + \frac{\partial \overline{A}}{\partial t}$ is zero, this vector can be expressed as the gradient of some scalar function ϕ,

$$\overline{E} + \frac{\partial \overline{A}}{\partial t} = -\nabla \phi \tag{8}$$

or

$$\overline{E} = -\nabla \phi - \frac{\partial \overline{A}}{\partial t} \tag{9}$$

From eqs.(5) and (9) we conclude that we need a vector function $\overline{A}$ and a scalar function ϕ to describe the electric and magnetic fields.

Now, notice that if vector $\overline{A}$ and scalar function ϕ are transformed in the following manner:

$$\overline{A}' = \overline{A} + \nabla\psi \tag{10}$$

$$\phi' = \phi - \frac{\partial\psi}{\partial t}$$

then the electric field and magnetic field defined by eqs. (5) and (9) will be the same for $(\overline{A},\phi)$ and $(\overline{A}', \phi')$.

Now, substitute eq.(9) into eq.(1) to obtain

$$\nabla \cdot \left(-\nabla\phi - \frac{\partial\overline{A}}{\partial t}\right) = \frac{\rho}{\varepsilon}$$

or

$$-\nabla^2\phi - \frac{\partial}{\partial t}\left(\nabla \cdot \overline{A}\right) = \frac{\rho}{\varepsilon} \tag{11}$$

Next, substitute eqs.(5) and (9) into eq.(4) to obtain

$$\nabla \times (\nabla \times \overline{A}) - \varepsilon \frac{\partial}{\partial t}\left(-\nabla\phi - \frac{\partial\overline{A}}{\partial t}\right) = \overline{J} \tag{12}$$

or

$$\nabla \times (\nabla \times \overline{A}) - \varepsilon \frac{\partial}{\partial t}\left(-\nabla\phi - \frac{\partial\overline{A}}{\partial t}\right) = \overline{J} \tag{13}$$

Now, using the identity

$$\nabla \times (\nabla \times \overline{A}) = \nabla(\nabla \cdot \overline{A}) - \check{\nabla}^2\overline{A},$$

and bringing in the $\frac{\partial}{\partial t}$ term, rewrite eq.(13) as

$$\nabla(\nabla \cdot \overline{A}) - \nabla^2\overline{A} + \varepsilon \frac{\partial}{\partial t} \nabla\phi + \varepsilon \frac{\partial^2\overline{A}}{\partial t^2} = \overline{J} \tag{14}$$

Next, since the divergence of $\overline{A}$ can be arbitrarily defined, let

$$\nabla \cdot \overline{A} = -\varepsilon \frac{\partial\phi}{\partial t} \tag{15}$$

Substituting eq.(15) into eq.(14) yields

$$\nabla\left(-\varepsilon \frac{\partial\phi}{\partial t}\right) - \nabla^2\overline{A} + \varepsilon \frac{\partial}{\partial t} \nabla\phi + \varepsilon \frac{\partial^2\overline{A}}{\partial t^2} = \overline{J} \tag{16}$$

Or, since $\nabla\left(-\varepsilon \frac{\partial\phi}{\partial t}\right) = -\varepsilon \frac{\partial}{\partial t}\nabla\phi$, eq.(16) reduces to

$$\nabla^2\overline{A} - \varepsilon \frac{\partial^2\overline{A}}{\partial t^2} = -\overline{J} \tag{17}$$

Now, substitute eq.(15) into eq.(11) to obtain

$$-\nabla^2\phi - \frac{\partial}{\partial t}\left(-\varepsilon \frac{\partial\phi}{\partial t}\right) = \frac{\rho}{\varepsilon}$$

or

$$\nabla^2\phi - \varepsilon \frac{\partial^2\phi}{\partial t^2} = \frac{-\rho}{\varepsilon} \tag{18}$$

Eqs.(11), (15), (16) and (18) represent Maxwell's equations expressed in terms of the vector potential $\overline{A}$ and the scalar potential ϕ.

The conservation of energy for an electromagnetic field can be expressed as

$$- \frac{\partial u}{\partial t} = \nabla \cdot \overline{S} + \overline{E} \cdot \overline{J} \tag{1}$$

where u denotes the energy density of the electromagnetic field and $\overline{S}$ is the energy flux, that is, the flow of energy per unit time across a unit area perpendicular to the flow.

Express quantities u and $\overline{S}$ in terms of the electric field $\overline{E}$ and the magnetic field $\overline{H}$.

Solution: First, notice that eq.(1), except for the $\overline{E} \cdot \overline{J}$ term, resembles some "continuity" or "conservation" equation.

The term $\overline{E} \cdot \overline{J}$ is of physical significance. For example, consider the Lorentz force (the electromagnetic force on a particle), given by

$$\overline{F} = q(\overline{E} + \overline{v} \times \overline{H})$$

The rate of work is $\overline{F} \cdot \overline{v}$; thus

$$\overline{F} \cdot \overline{v} = q(\overline{E} \cdot \overline{v}) + (\overline{v} \times \overline{H}) \cdot \overline{v}$$

$$= q(\overline{E} \cdot \overline{v}) \quad (\text{since } \overline{v} \cdot (\overline{v} \times \overline{H}) \equiv 0)$$

If there are n-particles per unit volume, then the rate of work is $nq \, \overline{E} \cdot \overline{v}$. Since $\overline{J} = nq \, \overline{v}$, the above equation can be written as

$$n(\overline{F} \cdot \overline{v}) = nq(\overline{E} \cdot \overline{v}) = \overline{E} \cdot \overline{J} \tag{2}$$

The quantity $\overline{E} \cdot \overline{J}$ represents the loss of energy per unit time per unit volume of the electromagnetic field.

Now, to express n and $\overline{S}$ in terms of $\overline{E}$ and $\overline{H}$, rewrite eq.(1) in the form

$$\overline{E} \cdot \overline{J} = - \frac{\partial u}{\partial t} - \nabla \cdot \overline{S} \tag{3}$$

Now, we will attempt to express $\overline{E} \cdot \overline{J}$ as a sum of two terms

$$\overline{E} \cdot \overline{J} = \frac{\partial}{\partial t} (\text{something}) + \nabla \cdot (\text{something}) \tag{4}$$

in hope to determine u and $\overline{S}$.

Take the Maxwell equation involving $\overline{J}$,

$$\nabla \times \overline{H} = \varepsilon \frac{\partial \overline{E}}{\partial t} + \overline{J} \tag{5}$$

Solving for $\overline{J}$, we obtain

$$\overline{J} = \nabla \times \overline{H} - \varepsilon \frac{\partial \overline{E}}{\partial t} \tag{6}$$

Substituting eq.(6) into eq.(3) leads to

$$\overline{E} \cdot \overline{J} = \overline{E} \cdot (\nabla \times \overline{H}) - \varepsilon \, \overline{E} \cdot \frac{\partial \overline{E}}{\partial t} \tag{7}$$

The last term can be written as

$$\varepsilon \, \overline{E} \cdot \frac{\partial \overline{E}}{\partial t} = \varepsilon \frac{1}{2} \left(\overline{E} \cdot \frac{\partial \overline{E}}{\partial t} + \frac{\partial \overline{E}}{\partial t} \cdot \overline{E} \right)$$

$$= \frac{1}{2} \varepsilon \frac{\partial}{\partial t} (\overline{E} \cdot \overline{E})$$

$$= \frac{\partial}{\partial t} \left(\frac{1}{2} \varepsilon \, \overline{E} \cdot \overline{E} \right) \tag{8}$$

Substituting eq.(8) into eq.(7), we obtain

$$\overline{E} \cdot \overline{J} = \overline{E} \cdot (\nabla \times \overline{H}) - \frac{\partial}{\partial t} \left(\frac{1}{2} \varepsilon \overline{E} \cdot \overline{E} \right) \tag{9}$$

Now, we will attempt to express the term $\overline{E} \cdot (\nabla \times \overline{H})$ in the form

$$\overline{E} \cdot (\nabla \times \overline{H}) = \nabla \cdot (\text{something})$$

by using the following identity

$$\nabla \cdot (\overline{a} \times \overline{b}) = \overline{b} \cdot (\nabla \times \overline{a}) - \overline{a} (\nabla \times \overline{b}) \tag{10}$$

Substituting $\overline{H}$ for $\overline{a}$ and $\overline{E}$ for $\overline{b}$ in eq.(10) yields

$$\nabla \cdot (\overline{H} \times \overline{E}) = \overline{E} \cdot (\nabla \times \overline{H}) - \overline{H} \cdot (\nabla \times \overline{E})$$

Or, solving for $\overline{E} \cdot (\nabla \times \overline{H})$ yields

$$\overline{E} \cdot (\nabla \times \overline{H}) = \nabla \cdot (\overline{H} \times \overline{E}) + \overline{H} \cdot (\nabla \times \overline{E}) \tag{11}$$

Now, substituting eq.(11) into eq.(9) yields

$$\overline{E} \cdot \overline{J} = \nabla \cdot (\overline{H} \times \overline{E}) + \overline{H} \cdot (\nabla \times \overline{E}) - \frac{\partial}{\partial t} (\tfrac{1}{2} \varepsilon \overline{E} \cdot \overline{E}) \tag{12}$$

Next, from the Maxwell equations, we have

$$\nabla \times \overline{E} = - \frac{\partial \overline{H}}{\partial t} \tag{13}$$

Therefore, the term $\overline{H} \cdot (\nabla \times \overline{E})$ can be written as

$$\overline{H} \cdot (\nabla \times \overline{E}) = \overline{H} \cdot \left(-\frac{\partial \overline{H}}{\partial t} \right) = \frac{\partial}{\partial t} (\tfrac{1}{2} \overline{H} \cdot \overline{H}) \tag{14}$$

Next, substituting eq.(14) into eq.(12) yields

$$\overline{E} \cdot \overline{J} = \nabla \cdot (\overline{H} \times \overline{E}) - \frac{\partial}{\partial t} (\tfrac{1}{2} \overline{H} \cdot \overline{H}) - \frac{\partial}{\partial t} (\tfrac{1}{2} \varepsilon \overline{E} \cdot \overline{E})$$

or

$$\overline{E} \cdot \overline{J} = \nabla \cdot (\overline{H} \times \overline{E}) - \frac{\partial}{\partial t} (\tfrac{1}{2} \overline{H} \cdot \overline{H} + \tfrac{1}{2} \varepsilon \overline{E} \cdot \overline{E}) \tag{15}$$

Notice that this equation has the desired form of eq.(4). Now, comparing eq.(3) with eq.(15),

$$\overline{E} \cdot \overline{J} = - \frac{\partial}{\partial t} (\tfrac{1}{2} \overline{H} \cdot \overline{H} + \tfrac{1}{2} \varepsilon \overline{E} \cdot \overline{E}) + \nabla \cdot (\overline{H} \times \overline{E})$$

$$\overline{E} \cdot \overline{J} = - \frac{\partial}{\partial t} u - \nabla \cdot \overline{S}$$

we conclude that

$$u = \tfrac{1}{2} \overline{H} \cdot \overline{H} + \tfrac{1}{2} \varepsilon \overline{E} \cdot \overline{E} \qquad (16)$$

and

$$\overline{S} = -\overline{H} \times \overline{E} \qquad (17)$$

Eq.(16) expresses u, the energy density, in terms of the electric and magnetic fields. $\overline{S}$, the energy flow vector of the electromagnetic field, is also expressed in terms of the electric and magnetic fields.

● **PROBLEM 11-36**

The Maxwell equations for a dielectric material in which there are no extra charges other than those bound in the atoms are

$$\nabla \cdot \overline{E} = - \frac{\nabla \cdot \overline{P}}{\varepsilon_0} \qquad (1)$$

$$\nabla \times \overline{E} = - \frac{\partial \overline{H}}{\partial t} \qquad (2)$$

$$c^2 \nabla \times \overline{H} = \frac{\partial}{\partial t} \left(\frac{1}{\varepsilon_0} \overline{P} + \overline{E} \right) \qquad (3)$$

$$\nabla \cdot \overline{H} = 0 \qquad (4)$$

where the polarization $\overline{P}$ is a function of position and time.

The D'Alembertian is an operator defined as

$$\frac{\partial^2}{\partial x^2} + \frac{\partial^2}{\partial y^2} + \frac{\partial^2}{\partial z^2} - \frac{1}{c^2} \frac{\partial^2}{\partial t^2} = \nabla^2 - \frac{1}{c^2} \frac{\partial^2}{\partial t^2} \qquad (5)$$

Express the D'Alembertian of $\overline{E}$ in terms of the polarization vector $\overline{P}$.

Solution: Begin by taking the curl of eq.(2)

$$\nabla \times (\nabla \times \overline{E}) = -\nabla \times \frac{\partial \overline{H}}{\partial t} = - \frac{\partial}{\partial t} \left(\nabla \times \overline{H} \right) \qquad (6)$$

Now, use the vector identity:

$$\nabla \times (\nabla \times \overline{E}) = \nabla(\nabla \cdot \overline{E}) - \nabla^2 \overline{E} \qquad (7)$$

Substitute eq.(7) into eq.(6) to obtain

501

$$\nabla(\nabla \cdot \overline{E}) - \nabla^2 \overline{E} = - \frac{\partial}{\partial t}\left(\nabla \times \overline{H}\right) \qquad (8)$$

From eq.(3) we have

$$\nabla \times \overline{H} = \frac{1}{c^2} \frac{\partial}{\partial t}\left(\frac{1}{\varepsilon_0} \overline{P} + \overline{E}\right) \qquad (9)$$

Substituting eq.(9) into eq.(8) and bringing the $\frac{1}{c^2}$ term inside, results in

$$\nabla(\nabla \cdot \overline{E}) - \nabla^2 \overline{E} = - \frac{\partial^2}{\partial t^2}\left(\frac{1}{\varepsilon_0 c^2} \overline{P} + \frac{1}{c^2} \overline{E}\right)$$

$$= - \frac{1}{\varepsilon_0 c^2} \frac{\partial^2 \overline{P}}{\partial t^2} - \frac{1}{c^2} \frac{\partial^2 \overline{E}}{\partial t^2} \qquad (10)$$

From eq.(1), obtain

$$\nabla(\nabla \cdot \overline{E}) = \nabla\left(-\frac{\nabla \cdot \overline{P}}{\varepsilon_0}\right) = - \frac{1}{\varepsilon_0} \nabla(\nabla \cdot \overline{P}) \qquad (11)$$

Substituting eq.(11) into eq.(10) and transposing terms finally gives

$$\nabla^2 \overline{E} - \frac{1}{c^2} \frac{\partial^2 \overline{E}}{\partial t^2} = - \frac{1}{\varepsilon_0} \nabla(\nabla \cdot \overline{P}) + \frac{1}{\varepsilon_0 c^2} \frac{\partial^2 \overline{P}}{\partial t^2} \qquad (12)$$

The left-hand side of eq.(12) is the D'Alembertian of $\overline{E}$.

● PROBLEM 11-37

Consider the diffusion of neutrons in graphite. Since graphite does not absorb slow neutrons, these relatively slow neutrons travel in a straight line before being scattered by a graphite nucleus. If these neutrons are in a particular location of a large block, then after some time they will diffuse to other locations. Derive the neutron diffusion equation. The diffusion constant λ is given by

$$\lambda = \frac{1}{3} \ell v \qquad (1)$$

where v is the mean velocity and ℓ the mean free path between the scatterings.

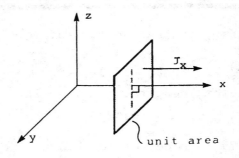

unit area

502

Solution: Let N be the number of neutrons per unit volume, where N is a function of position and time

$$N = N(x,y,z,t) \tag{2}$$

The number of neutrons in a volume ΔV is thus

$$N \cdot \Delta V \tag{3}$$

We will now define the flow vector $\bar{J}$ as that vector which describes the flow of neutrons.

The x-component of $\bar{J}$, J_x, is the net number of neutrons that pass, per unit time, through a unit area perpendicular to the x-axis, as shown in Fig. 1. Therefore, J_x is proportional to $\frac{\partial N}{\partial x}$ with the constant of proportionality $-\lambda$; thus

$$J_x = -\lambda \frac{\partial N}{\partial x} \tag{4}$$

where $\lambda = \frac{1}{3} \ell v$.

From eq.(4), we conclude that the vector equation for $\bar{J}$ can be written as

$$\bar{J} = -\lambda \nabla N \tag{5}$$

If ds is any surface element, then $\bar{J} \cdot \bar{n}$ ds represents the rate at which neutrons flow through ds ($\bar{n}$ is a unit normal vector). The net flow out of a volume element dV is then

$$\nabla \cdot \bar{J} \, dV \tag{6}$$

Note that the number of neutrons in dV will decrease by $-\frac{\partial N}{\partial t}$. If the neutrons are created within the volume, say, at the rate R neutrons per unit time per unit volume, then using eq.(6), we can write

$$\nabla \cdot \bar{J} = R - \frac{\partial N}{\partial t} \tag{7}$$

Substituting eq.(5) into eq.(7) leads to

$$\nabla \cdot (-\lambda \nabla N) = R - \frac{\partial N}{\partial t} \tag{8}$$

which is the neutron diffusion equation. In the static case, that is, where $\frac{\partial N}{\partial t} = 0$, eq.(8) reduces to

$$\nabla \cdot (-\lambda \nabla N) = R \tag{9}$$

CHAPTER 12

ORDINARY INTREGRALS OF VECTORS AND LINE INTEGRALS

INTRODUCTION

Chapter 12, along with the upcoming chapters, considers the most important, most practical and possibly most difficult topic of vector calculus - integration.

One can look at integration as a process of finding a function given its corresponding derivative, or, as in the case of definite integrals, as a process of finding the limit of a sum.

In this chapter, we begin with the concept of the indefinite and definite integral of a vector function. We then discuss some basic applications of vector integration by considering basic topics in mechanics such as kinematics, angular momentum, Kepler's laws and the concept of a central force field.

We then consider the parametric representation and the orientation of curves. This gives us the foundation for introducing the all-important concept of the line integral, which leads directly to the definition of work and the circulation of a vector field.

A large part of this chapter is concerned with a particular case of vector fields - conservative fields.

Conservative vector fields play a crucial role in vast physical applications. Fortunately for the physicists, many actual physical fields are conservative: for knowing that a field is conservative greatly simplifies otherwise complicated calculations, and makes the laws which govern the field much more compact and easier to deal with. Conservative fields are so important that we have, in addition, devoted a whole chapter to the topic - Chapter 18.

The upcoming chapters begin where Chapter 12 left off, and we move from the concept of the single integral of a vector field to line integrals, surface integrals, volume integrals and so on. It is important to always keep in mind that regardless of how complex the given integral is, it is always derived from the simple definition of the integral of a scalar function.

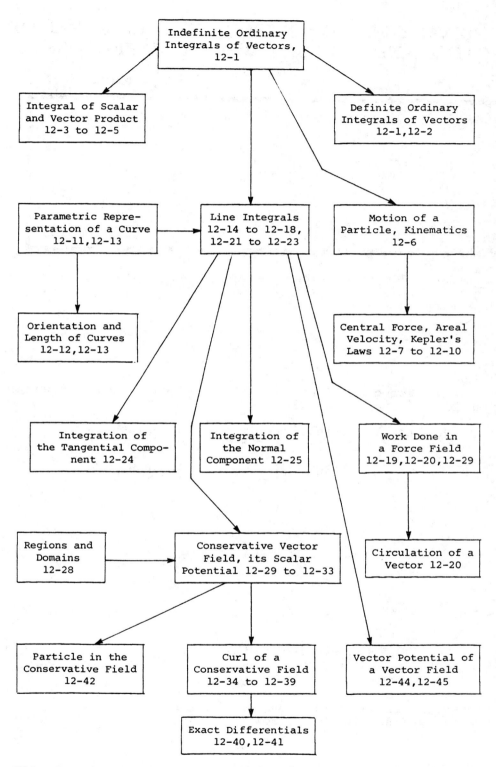

This chart is provided to facilitate rapid understanding of the inter-relationships of the topics and subject matter in this chapter. Also shown are the problem numbers associated with the subject matter.

ORDINARY VECTOR INTEGRATION, INTEGRAL OF SCALAR AND VECTOR PRODUCT OF VECTORS

Find the following integrals

1.
$$\int \overline{r}(u)du \tag{1}$$

2.
$$\int_{2}^{3} \overline{r}(u)du \tag{2}$$

where
$$\overline{r}(u) = (u^2+1)\overline{i} + 2\overline{j} - u^3\overline{k} \tag{3}$$

Solution: First, consider the following definitions regarding ordinary integrals of vectors. Let $\overline{r}(u)$ be a vector field depending on the parameter u such that

$$\overline{r}(u) = r_1(u)\overline{i} + r_2(u)\overline{j} + r_3(u)\overline{k} \tag{4}$$

where the component functions $r_1(u)$, $r_2(u)$, $r_3(u)$ are continuous functions.

The indefinite integral of $\overline{r}(u)$ is defined as

$$\int \overline{r}(u)du = \overline{i}\int r_1(u)du + \overline{j}\int r_2(u)du + \overline{k}\int r_3(u)du \tag{5}$$

If a vector $\overline{s}(u)$ exists such that

$$\overline{r}(u) = \frac{d}{du}\left[\overline{s}(u)\right], \tag{6}$$

then we can write

$$\int \overline{r}(u)du = \int \frac{d}{du}\left[\overline{s}(u)\right]du = \overline{s}(u)+\overline{c} \tag{7}$$

where $\overline{c}$ is an arbitrary constant vector. The definite integral is defined in the following manner:

$$\int_{\alpha}^{\beta} \overline{r}(u)du = \int_{\alpha}^{\beta} \frac{d}{du}\left[\overline{s}(u)\right]du = \left[\overline{s}(u)+\overline{c}\right]\Big|_{\alpha}^{\beta} = \overline{s}(\beta)-\overline{s}(\alpha) \tag{8}$$

It is assumed that $\bar{r}(u)$ is defined and continuous in the interval $u = \alpha$, $u = \beta$.

1. Substituting eq.(3) into eq.(5) yields

$$\int \bar{r}(u)du = \bar{i}\int(u^2+1)du + \bar{j}\int 2du - \bar{k}\int u^3 du$$

$$= \bar{i}\left(\frac{u^3}{3}+u+c_1\right) + \bar{j}(2u+c_2)- \bar{k}\left(\frac{u^4}{4}-c_3\right) \qquad (9)$$

or, we can alternatively write

$$\bar{s}(u)+\bar{c} = \bar{i}\left(\frac{u^3}{3}+u\right) + \bar{j}\,2u -\bar{k}\,\frac{u^4}{4} + \bar{i}c_1+\bar{j}c_2+\bar{k}c_3 \qquad (10)$$

It could be easily verified that

$$\frac{d}{du}\left[\bar{s}(u)\right] = \bar{r}(u) \qquad (11)$$

Notice that in order to evaluate an ordinary integral of a vector field, we have to evaluate the ordinary integrals of its respective components. From this, it is clear that ordinary integrals of vectors are basically the same as ordinary integrals.

2. To find the integral

$$\int_2^3 \bar{r}(u)du$$

we shall use eq.(8) and the indefinite integral of $\bar{r}(u)$ given by eq.(10).

$$\int_2^3 \bar{r}(u)du = \int_2^3 \frac{d}{du}\left[\bar{s}(u)\right]du$$

$$= \bar{i}\left(\frac{u^3}{3}+u\right) + \bar{j}\,2u - \bar{k}\,\frac{u^4}{4} \,\Big|_2^3 \qquad (12)$$

$$= \bar{i}(9+3-\frac{8}{3}-2) + \bar{j}(6-4) - \bar{k}(\frac{81}{4}-4)$$

$$= \frac{22}{3}\,\bar{i} + 2\bar{j} - \frac{65}{4}\,\bar{k}$$

Evaluate the following integrals

1.
$$\int_0^{\frac{\pi}{2}} (2\cos u\, \bar{i} + \sin u\, \bar{k})du \qquad (1)$$

2.
$$\int_0^1 (e^x\, \bar{i} + \frac{1}{x}\, \bar{j} - x^3\bar{k})dx \qquad (2)$$

<u>Solution</u>: 1. From the definition of the integral of a vector, we have

$$\int_0^{\frac{\pi}{2}} (2\cos u\, \bar{i} + \sin u\, \bar{k})du$$

$$= \bar{i}\int_0^{\frac{\pi}{2}} 2\cos u\, du + \bar{k}\int_0^{\frac{\pi}{2}} \sin u\, du \qquad (3)$$

$$= \bar{i}(2\sin u)\Big|_0^{\frac{\pi}{2}} + \bar{k}(-\cos u)\Big|_0^{\frac{\pi}{2}}$$

$$= 2\bar{i} + \bar{k}$$

2. To solve this problem, recall the following integration formulas

$$\int e^x dx = e^x + c \qquad (4)$$

$$\int \frac{1}{x}\, dx = \ln|x| + c \qquad (5)$$

Directly from the definition of the integral of a vector, obtain

$$\int_0^1 (e^x\, \bar{i} + \frac{1}{x}\, \bar{j} - x^3\bar{k})dx$$

$$= \bar{i}\int_0^1 e^x dx + \bar{j}\int_0^1 \frac{1}{x}\, dx - \bar{k}\int_0^1 x^3 dx \qquad (6)$$

$$= \bar{i}(e^x)\Big|_0^1 + \bar{j}(\ln|x|)\Big|_0^1 - \bar{k}\left(\frac{x^4}{4}\right)\Big|_0^1$$

$$= \bar{i}(e-1) + \bar{j}(\ln 1 - \ln 0) - \bar{k}\frac{1}{4}$$

Notice that this integral cannot be evaluated, since $\ln 0 = -\infty$. Indeed, it can be seen, from eq.(2), that the second component $\frac{1}{x}\bar{j}$ is not continuous in the interval [0,1], leading us to conclude that the integral in eq.(2) does not exist.

Evaluate the following integrals

1. $\int_0^3 \overline{a} \cdot \overline{b} \, dt$ (1)

2. $\int_0^2 \overline{a} \times \overline{b} \, dt$ (2)

where

$$\overline{a} = t^2\overline{i} + (t+1)\overline{j} - t^3\overline{k} \qquad (3)$$

$$\overline{b} = 2\overline{i} - t\overline{j} + t^2\overline{k} \qquad (4)$$

Solution: 1. Notice that we have to evaluate the definite integral of a scalar product of two vectors $\overline{a}$ and $\overline{b}$ (which, in this case, are given by eqs.(3) and (4)). Note that since the scalar product of any two vectors yields a scalar function, the integral in eq.(1) may be evaluated by actually carrying out the dot product of the two vectors and then integrating the resulting scalar function.

Doing this, obtain, from the definition of the scalar product, the following:

$$\overline{a} \cdot \overline{b} = (t^2, \ t+1, \ -t^3) \cdot (2, \ -t, \ t^2)$$
$$= 2t^2 - t^2 - t - t^5 = -t^5 + t^2 - t \qquad (5)$$

Substituting eq.(5) into (1) results in

$$\int_0^3 \overline{a} \cdot \overline{b} \, dt = \int_0^3 (-t^5 + t^2 - t) dt$$

$$= -\frac{t^6}{6} + \frac{t^3}{3} - \frac{t^2}{2} \Bigg|_0^3 \qquad (6)$$

$$= -\frac{3^6}{6} + \frac{3^3}{3} - \frac{3^2}{2} = -117$$

2. To evaluate integral (2), first determine the vector product of $\overline{a}$ and $\overline{b}$ and then integrate the resulting vector. Doing this, we obtain

$$\overline{a} \times \overline{b} = (t^2, \ t+1, \ -t^3) \times (2, \ -t, \ t^2)$$
$$= (t^3 + t^2 - t^4, \ -2t^3 - t^4, \ -t^3 - 2t - 2) \qquad (7)$$

Substituting eq.(7) into (2) leads to

$$\int_0^2 \overline{a} \times \overline{b} \, dt =$$

$$\int_0^2 \left[\bar{i}(-t^4+t^3+t^2)+\bar{j}(-t^4-2t^3)+\bar{k}(-t^3-2t-2) \right] dt$$

$$= \left[\bar{i} \left(-\frac{t^5}{5}+\frac{t^4}{4}+\frac{t^3}{3} \right) + \bar{j} \left(-\frac{t^5}{5}-\frac{t^4}{2} \right) + \bar{k} \left(-\frac{t^4}{4}-t^2-2t \right) \right] \Bigg|_0^2 \qquad (8)$$

$$= \bar{i} \left(-\frac{32}{5}+4+\frac{8}{3} \right) + \bar{j} \left(-\frac{32}{5}-8 \right) + \bar{k}(-4-4-4)$$

$$= \frac{4}{15} \bar{i} - \frac{72}{5} \bar{j} - 12\bar{k}$$

Notice that the definite integral of the vector product of two vectors is a vector while the definite integral of the dot product of two vectors is a scalar.

● **PROBLEM 12-4**

Evaluate the integral

$$\int_2^4 \bar{a} \times \frac{d^2\bar{a}}{dt^2} \, dt \qquad (1)$$

if

$$\bar{a}(4) = (6,7,3), \qquad \frac{d\bar{a}}{dt}\bigg|_{t=4} = (1,1,1) \qquad (2)$$

$$\bar{a}(2) = (3,1,1), \qquad \frac{d\bar{a}}{dt}\bigg|_{t=2} = (0,0,0)$$

Solution: The value of the vector $\bar{a}$ and its time derivative is given only at the points $t=2$ and $t=4$. To evaluate the integral (1), express $\bar{a} \times \frac{d^2\bar{a}}{dt^2}$ as a time derivative of some vector function, $\bar{f}(t)$

$$\bar{a} \times \frac{d^2\bar{a}}{dt^2} = \frac{d}{dt}(\bar{f}(t)) \qquad (3)$$

It is now required to find $\bar{f}(t)$. Assume that $\bar{f}(t)$ can be expressed as

$$\bar{f}(t) = \bar{b} \times \bar{c} \qquad (4)$$

where $\bar{b}$ and $\bar{c}$ are unknown vector functions. Differentiating eq.(4) results in

$$\frac{d\bar{f}}{dt} = \bar{b} \times \frac{d\bar{c}}{dt} + \frac{d\bar{b}}{dt} \times \bar{c} \qquad (5)$$

Now, notice that if we let $\bar{c} = \frac{d\bar{b}}{dt}$, then the second term of the right-hand side of eq.(5) would equal zero. Therefore, if we arbitrarily let

510

$$\overline{b} = \overline{a} \quad \text{and} \quad \overline{c} = \frac{d\overline{b}}{dt} = \frac{d\overline{a}}{dt}, \qquad (6)$$

then eq.(3) becomes

$$\overline{a} \times \frac{d^2\overline{a}}{dt^2} = \frac{d}{dt}\left(\overline{a} \times \frac{d\overline{a}}{dt}\right) \qquad (7)$$

Now, substituting eq.(7) into eq.(1) results in

$$\int_2^4 \overline{a} \times \frac{d^2\overline{a}}{dt^2}\, dt = \int_2^4 \frac{d}{dt}\left(\overline{a} \times \frac{d\overline{a}}{dt}\right)dt$$

$$= \overline{a} \times \frac{d\overline{a}}{dt}\Big|_2^4 = \overline{a}(4) \times \frac{d\overline{a}(4)}{dt} - \overline{a}(2) \times \frac{d\overline{a}(2)}{dt}$$

$$\qquad (8)$$

$$= (6,7,3)\times(1,1,1)-(3,1,1)\times(0,0,0)$$

$$= (4,-3,-1) = 4\overline{i} - 3\overline{j} - \overline{k}$$

• **PROBLEM 12-5**

Evaluate the integral

$$\int_2^3 \overline{a} \cdot \frac{d\overline{a}}{dt}\, dt \qquad (1)$$

if vector $\overline{a}$ is such that

$$|\overline{a}| = \text{const} \qquad (2)$$

<u>Solution</u>: First, try to express $\overline{a} \cdot \frac{d\overline{a}}{dt}$ in a more convenient form. Do this by differentiating the scalar product $\overline{a} \cdot \overline{a}$,

$$\frac{d}{dt}(\overline{a} \cdot \overline{a}) = \overline{a} \cdot \frac{d\overline{a}}{dt} + \frac{d\overline{a}}{dt} \cdot \overline{a} = 2\overline{a} \cdot \frac{d\overline{a}}{dt} \qquad (3)$$

or

$$\overline{a} \cdot \frac{d\overline{a}}{dt} = \frac{1}{2}\frac{d}{dt}(\overline{a} \cdot \overline{a}) \qquad (4)$$

Substituting eq.(4) into (1) leads to

$$\int_2^3 \overline{a} \cdot \frac{d\overline{a}}{dt}\, dt = \frac{1}{2}\int_2^3 \frac{d}{dt}(\overline{a} \cdot \overline{a})dt$$

$$\qquad (5)$$

$$= \frac{1}{2}\left[\overline{a} \cdot \overline{a}\ \Big|_2^3\right]$$

Notice that we are not yet able to evaluate eq.(5) -- since vector $\overline{a}$ is not known. Note however, that since the magnitude of vector $\overline{a}$ is constant, we may write

$$|\overline{a}| = \sqrt{\overline{a} \cdot \overline{a}} = \text{const} \qquad (6)$$

511

and
$$\overline{a} \cdot \overline{a} = \text{const} \tag{7}$$
and therefore,
$$\overline{a} \cdot \overline{a} \Big|_2^3 = \overline{a}(3) \cdot \overline{a}(3) - \overline{a}(2) \cdot \overline{a}(2) = 0$$
Thus
$$\int_2^3 \overline{a} \cdot \frac{d\overline{a}}{dt} \, dt = 0 \tag{8}$$

KINEMATICS, CENTRAL FORCE, ANGULAR MOMENTUM, AERIAL VELOCITY AND KEPLER'S LAWS

● **PROBLEM 12-6**

A particle is moving in space with the acceleration

$$\overline{a} = t^2\overline{i} + \sin t \, \overline{j} - t^3\overline{k} \tag{1}$$

where the parameter t is time. Find the velocity and the position of the particle at any time t. Assume that at t=0 the velocity and displacement are zero.

Solution: First, recall the basic definitions of kinematics. The position of a particle is the vector function
$$\overline{r} = \overline{r}(t) \tag{2}$$
The velocity of the particle is defined as
$$\overline{v} = \frac{d\overline{r}}{dt} \tag{3}$$
and the acceleration is defined as
$$\overline{a} = \frac{d\overline{v}}{dt} \tag{4}$$
Substituting eq.(3) into eq.(4) leads to
$$\overline{a} = \frac{d}{dt}\left(\frac{d\overline{r}}{dt}\right) = \frac{d^2\overline{r}}{dt^2} \tag{5}$$
Now, to find the velocity of the particle whose acceleration is given by eq.(1), we must integrate eq.(4):
$$\overline{v} = \int \overline{a} \, dt \tag{6}$$
For $\overline{a}$ given by eq.(1), we have
$$\overline{v} = \int \left[t^2\overline{i} + \sin t \, \overline{j} - t^3\overline{k}\right] dt$$
$$= \frac{t^3}{3}\overline{i} - \cos t \, \overline{j} - \frac{t^4}{4}\overline{k} + \overline{c}_1 \tag{7}$$

where $\overline{c}_1$ is a constant vector of integration. $\overline{c}_1$ can be found by applying the initial conditions, namely, that at t=0 the velocity of the particle is zero. Thus, from eq.(7) obtain

$$\bar{v}\Big|_{t=0} = \bar{0} = -\cos o\,\bar{j} + \bar{c}_1$$

and therefore   (8)

$$\bar{c}_1 = \bar{j}$$

Eq.(7) then becomes

$$\bar{v} = \frac{t^3}{3}\,\bar{i} + (1 - \cos t\,)\bar{j} - \frac{t^4}{4}\,\bar{k} \qquad (9)$$

Next, to find the displacement vector $\bar{r}$, integrate eq.(9)

$$\bar{r} = \int \bar{v}\,dt = \int \left[\frac{t^3}{3}\,\bar{i} + (1 - \cos t\,)\bar{j} - \frac{t^4}{4}\,\bar{k}\right]dt$$

$$= \frac{t^4}{12}\,\bar{i} + (t - \sin t)\,\bar{j} - \frac{t^5}{20}\,\bar{k} + \bar{c}_2 \qquad (10)$$

Now, from the initial condition $\bar{r}\Big|_{t=0} = \bar{0}$, we can determine the constant $\bar{c}_2$.

Since

$$\bar{r}\Big|_{t=0} = \bar{0} = 0\bar{i} + 0\bar{j} - 0\bar{k} + \bar{c}_2\,,$$

we obtain

$$\bar{c}_2 = \bar{0}. \qquad (11)$$

Therefore, the displacement vector is

$$\bar{r} = \frac{t^4}{12}\,\bar{i} + (t - \sin t)\bar{j} - \frac{t^5}{20}\,\bar{k} \qquad (12)$$

Now, as a check, note that differentiating vector $\bar{r}$ twice should, as eq.(5) indicates, leave us with vector $\bar{a}$ as given by eq.(1). Indeed,

$$\frac{d^2\bar{r}}{dt^2} = \frac{d}{dt}\left\{\frac{d}{dt}\left[\frac{t^4}{12}\,\bar{i} + (t - \sin t)\bar{j} - \frac{t^5}{20}\,\bar{k}\right]\right\}$$

$$= \frac{d}{dt}\left[\frac{t^3}{3}\,\bar{i} + (1 - \cos t\,)\bar{j} - \frac{t^4}{4}\,\bar{k}\right] \qquad (13)$$

$$= t^2\bar{i} + \sin t\,\bar{j} - t^3\bar{k}$$

● **PROBLEM 12-7**

Consider the motion of a particle under the influence of a central force.

A central force is a force which is directed toward or away from a fixed point O and whose magnitude is dependent only upon the distance r from point O. A central force may be generally represented by

$$F_c = f(r)\,\frac{\bar{r}}{|\bar{r}|}$$

The angular momentum of a particle is defined as

$$\overline{H} = \overline{r} \times m\overline{v} \qquad (1)$$

and the aerial velocity is given by

$$\overline{h} = \frac{1}{2} \overline{r} \times \overline{v} \qquad (2)$$

Show that a particle moving under a central force field has a constant angular momentum and aerial velocity.

Also, discuss the cases for which

$$f(r) > 0$$

and

$$f(r) < 0.$$

<u>Solution</u>: From Newton's second law, $m\overline{a} = \overline{F}_c$, we obtain

$$m \frac{d^2 \overline{r}}{dt^2} = f(r) \frac{\overline{r}}{|\overline{r}|} \qquad (3)$$

Now, multiplying eq.(3) vectorially by $\overline{r}$ gives

$$\overline{r} \times \left(m \frac{d^2\overline{r}}{dt^2} \right) = \overline{r} \times \left(f(r) \frac{\overline{r}}{|\overline{r}|} \right) \qquad (4)$$

$$= \frac{f(r)}{|\overline{r}|} (\overline{r} \times \overline{r})$$

$$= \overline{0}$$

since $\overline{r} \times \overline{r} = \overline{0}$.

Thus,

$$\overline{r} \times m \frac{d^2\overline{r}}{dt^2} = \overline{0}$$

or

$$m\left(\overline{r} \times \frac{d^2\overline{r}}{dt^2} \right) = \overline{0} \qquad (5)$$

Now, notice that

$$\left(\overline{r} \times \frac{d^2\overline{r}}{dt^2} \right) = \frac{d}{dt}\left(\overline{r} \times \frac{d\overline{r}}{dt} \right) \qquad (6)$$

since

$$\frac{d}{dt}\left(\overline{r} \times \frac{d\overline{r}}{dt} \right) = \frac{d\overline{r}}{dt} \times \frac{d\overline{r}}{dt} + \overline{r} \times \frac{d^2\overline{r}}{dt^2}$$

$$= \overline{r} \times \frac{d^2\overline{r}}{dt^2}$$

Thus, eq.(5) may be written as

$$m \frac{d}{dt}\left(\overline{r} \times \frac{d\overline{r}}{dt} \right) = \frac{d}{dt}\left(\overline{r} \times m \frac{d\overline{r}}{dt} \right) = \overline{0} \qquad (7)$$

Integrating eq.(7) yields

$$\int \frac{d}{dt}\left(\bar{r} \times m \frac{d\bar{r}}{dt}\right)dt = \bar{r} \times m \frac{d\bar{r}}{dt} = \bar{c} \qquad (8)$$

where $\bar{c}$ is a constant vector. Now, since

$$\bar{r} \times m \frac{d\bar{r}}{dt} = \bar{r} \times m \bar{v} = \bar{H} = \bar{c}$$

we see that a particle travelling under a central force field has a constant angular momentum.

Also, since the mass m of the particle is a constant, we see that

$$\frac{1}{2}(\bar{r} \times \bar{v}) = \frac{1}{2}\frac{1}{m}\bar{c} = \overline{\text{const.}}$$

the aerial velocity is also a constant for a particle under the influence of a central force field.

Now, consider eq.(3) for the case f(r)<0. Notice that for this case the acceleration $\frac{d^2\bar{r}}{dt^2}$ is in a direction opposite to that of $\bar{r}$, from which we conclude that the force is directed toward the origin O – indicating that the particle would be attracted toward O.

Now, if f(r)>0, then the acceleration is directed in the direction of $\bar{r}$ and consequently the particle experiences a repulsive force.

The gravitational force of the earth is an example of a force field for which

$$f(r)<0.$$

● **PROBLEM 12-8**

Find the geometrical interpretation of the results of Problem 12-7, which state that under the influence of a central force, a particle has a constant aerial velocity.

Apply the results to planetary motion.

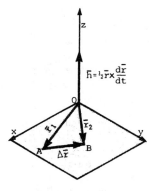

Fig. 1

Solution: From Problem 12-7, obtain the following equation of motion for a particle moving under the influence of a central force:

$$m \frac{d^2 \overline{r}}{dt^2} = f(r) \frac{\overline{r}}{|\overline{r}|} \tag{1}$$

Note that for this motion, we have the following condition

$$\overline{r} \times \overline{v} = \text{const} \tag{2}$$

Now, refer to Fig. 1, which illustrates the path of a particle subject to a central force field. If the position vector of the particle at time $t=t_1$ is given by $\overline{r}_1$, where point A is the endpoint of vector $\overline{r}_1$, and at time $t=t_2$ is given by $\overline{r}_2$, such that B is the endpoint of $\overline{r}_2$, then we can arbitrarily place points A and B on the x-y plane so that the particle moves from A to B in the time Δt. Now, note that during the time interval Δt, vector $\overline{r}$ sweeps out an area approximately equal to half of the area enclosed by the parrallelogram formed by vectors $\overline{r}_1$ and $\Delta \overline{r}$; thus

$$\text{area} = \frac{1}{2} \overline{r} \times \Delta \overline{r} \tag{3}$$

From eq.(3), we readily conclude that the area swept out by $\overline{r}$, per unit time, is approximately $\frac{1}{2} \overline{r} \times \frac{\Delta \overline{r}}{\Delta t}$.

Therefore, the instantaneous rate of change of area is given by

$$\lim_{\Delta t \to o} \frac{1}{2} \overline{r} \times \frac{\Delta \overline{r}}{\Delta t} = \frac{1}{2} \overline{r} \times \overline{v} \tag{4}$$

where $\overline{v}$ is the velocity of the particle. Now, from Problem 12-7, we have

$$\overline{h} = \frac{1}{2} \overline{r} \times \overline{v} = \text{const} \tag{5}$$

But, since

$$\overline{h} \cdot \overline{r} = \frac{1}{2}(\overline{r} \times \overline{v}) \cdot \overline{r} = 0$$

we conclude that vectors $\overline{h}$ and $\overline{r}$ are perpendicular, and therefore the particle travels in a plane perpendicular to $\overline{h}$, as shown in Fig. 1.

Now, as far as the motion of planets is concerned, we should note that Newton's law of gravitation governs all planetary motion. Newton's gravitational law states that any two masses m and M are attracted toward each other with a force given by

$$\overline{F} = -G \frac{mM}{r^2} \frac{\overline{r}}{|\overline{r}|} \tag{6}$$

Now, let M represent the mass of the sun and m denote the mass of some planet. If a coordinate system is chosen in such a way that the sun is at the origin 0 of the system, then the equation of motion for the planet may be expressed by

$$m \frac{d^2\overline{r}}{dt^2} = -G \frac{mM}{r^2} \frac{\overline{r}}{|\overline{r}|} \qquad (7)$$

or

$$\frac{d^2\overline{r}}{dt^2} = -G \frac{M}{r^2} \frac{\overline{r}}{|\overline{r}|} \qquad (8)$$

and, since the planet is subject to a central force (since $\overline{F}$ is parallel to vector $\overline{r}$), we conclude that the position vector of the planet, as was previously shown for any particle travelling in a central force field, sweeps out equal areas in equal intervals of time.

The above law is one of Kepler's three laws describing planetary motion and is illustrated in Fig. 2.

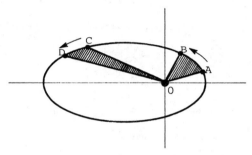

Fig. 2

Note that if the planet moves from A to B in a time interval t_{AB}, and if the planet moves from C to D in a time interval t_{CD}, then if $t_{AB} = t_{CD}$, we conclude, from the above law, that the shaded areas are equal.

$$\text{area DCO} = \text{area BAO} \qquad (9)$$

● **PROBLEM** 12-9

If the motion of a planet revolving around the sun is described by the equations

$$\frac{d^2\overline{r}}{dt^2} = -G \frac{M}{r^2} \frac{\overline{r}}{|\overline{r}|} \qquad (1)$$

and

$$\frac{1}{2} \overline{r} \times \frac{d\overline{r}}{dt} = \overline{h} = \text{const.} \qquad (2)$$

then show that the trajectory of the planet is an ellipse with the sun at one focus.

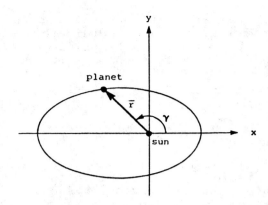

Solution: Begin by introducing a vector $\bar{u}$ such that

$$\bar{u} = \frac{\bar{r}}{|\bar{r}|} \tag{3}$$

or

$$\bar{r} = |\bar{r}|\bar{u} \tag{4}$$

Differentiating eq.(4) with respect to time results in

$$\frac{d\bar{r}}{dt} = \bar{v} = r\frac{d\bar{u}}{dt} + \frac{dr}{dt}\bar{u} \tag{5}$$

where

$$|\bar{r}| = r$$

Next, let vector $\bar{H}$ denote:

$$\bar{H} = 2\bar{h} = \bar{r} \times \bar{v} \tag{6}$$

Substituting eq.(5) into eq.(6) leads to

$$\bar{H} = \bar{r} \times \bar{v} = r\bar{u} \times \left(r\frac{d\bar{u}}{dt} + \frac{dr}{dt}\bar{u} \right) = r^2\bar{u} \times \frac{d\bar{u}}{dt} \tag{7}$$

At this point we can utilize eq.(1) by taking the vector product of eq.(1) with vector $\bar{H}$; therefore

$$\frac{d^2\bar{r}}{dt^2} \times \bar{H} = \frac{d\bar{v}}{dt} \times \bar{H} = \frac{-GM}{r^2}\bar{u} \times \bar{H} \tag{8}$$

Substituting eq.(7) into the right-hand side of eq.(8) yields

$$\frac{d\bar{v}}{dt} \times \bar{H} = \frac{-GM}{r^2}\bar{u} \times \left(r^2\bar{u} \times \frac{d\bar{u}}{dt} \right)$$

$$= -GM\left[\left(\bar{u} \cdot \frac{d\bar{u}}{dt} \right)\bar{u} - (\bar{u} \cdot \bar{u})\frac{d\bar{u}}{dt} \right] \tag{9}$$

$$= GM\frac{d\bar{u}}{dt}$$

Here we used an identity involving the vector triple product (see Problem 3-28) as well as the fact that

$$\bar{u} \cdot \frac{d\bar{u}}{dt} = 0$$

and
$$\overline{u} \cdot \overline{u} = 1$$

Now, since $\overline{H}$ is a constant vector, we can write

$$\frac{d\overline{v}}{dt} \times \overline{H} = \frac{d}{dt}(\overline{v} \times \overline{H}) \tag{10}$$

Combining eqs.(9) and (10) gives

$$\frac{d}{dt}(\overline{v} \times \overline{H}) = GM\frac{d\overline{u}}{dt} \tag{11}$$

Integrating eq.(11) results in

$$\overline{v} \times \overline{H} = GM\overline{u} + \overline{a} \tag{12}$$

where $\overline{a}$ is an arbitrary constant vector with magnitude a. Now, taking the dot product of eq. (12) with $\overline{r}$ leads to

$$\overline{r} \cdot (\overline{v} \times \overline{H}) = GM \, \overline{r} \cdot \overline{u} + \overline{r} \cdot \overline{a}$$
$$= GM \, r + r \, \overline{u} \cdot \overline{a} = GM \, r + ra \, \cos\theta \tag{13}$$

where θ represents the angle between vectors $\overline{u}$ and $\overline{a}$.

Next, since
$$\overline{r} \cdot (\overline{v} \times \overline{H}) = (\overline{r} \times \overline{v}) \cdot \overline{H} = \overline{H} \cdot \overline{H} = H^2,$$

eq.(13) becomes,
$$H^2 = GM \, r + ra \, \cos\theta \tag{14}$$
or

$$r = \frac{H^2}{GM + a\cos\theta} = \frac{\dfrac{H^2}{GM}}{1 + \dfrac{a}{GM}\cos\theta} \tag{15}$$

Now, from analytic geometry, the polar equation of a conic section with focus at the origin is given by

$$r = \frac{b}{1 + \varepsilon\cos\theta} \tag{16}$$

where b is some constant and ε denotes the eccentricity. Therefore, eq.(15) describes a conic section with eccentricity

$$\varepsilon = \frac{a}{GM}$$

Since the eccentricity is greater than or equal to one for open curves ($\varepsilon=1$ for a parabola and $\varepsilon>1$ for a hyperbola), and less than one for an ellipse, we conclude, since orbits are closed curves, that the orbit of a planet about the sun is an ellipse. This is known as Kepler's second law of planetary motion.

Problems 12-8 and 12-9 proved two of Kepler's laws of planetary motion.

Kepler's third law states that the squares of the periods of planets in their motion around the sun are proportional to the cubes of the major axes of their elliptical trajectories.

If the trajectory of a particle is given by the equation

$$\bar{r} = \alpha \cos\omega t \ \bar{i} + \beta \sin\omega t \ \bar{j} \qquad (1)$$

where α, β, ω are constants, determine its areal velocity.

Solution: The areal velocity of a particle is given by

$$\bar{h} = \frac{1}{2} \ \bar{r} \times \bar{v} \qquad (2)$$

From eq.(1), differentiating with respect to t, the velocity of the particle is found to be

$$\bar{v} = \frac{d\bar{r}}{dt} = -\alpha\omega \sin\omega t \ \bar{i} + \beta\omega \cos\omega t \ \bar{j} \qquad (3)$$

Taking the vector product of $\bar{r}$ and $\bar{v}$, the areal velocity is determined to be

$$\bar{h} = \frac{1}{2} \ \bar{r} \times \bar{v} = \frac{1}{2}(\alpha\cos\omega t\bar{i}+\beta\sin\omega t\bar{j})\times(-\alpha\omega\sin\omega t\bar{i}+\beta\omega\cos\omega t\bar{j})$$

$$= \frac{1}{2}\left[\alpha\beta\omega\cos^2\omega t\bar{k} + \alpha\beta\omega\sin^2\omega t\bar{k}\right] = \qquad (4)$$

$$= \frac{1}{2} \ \alpha\beta\omega\bar{k}$$

PARAMETRIC REPRESENTATION, ORIENTATION AND LENGTH OF CURVES

Show that the arc represented parametrically by

$$x = \cos t$$
$$y = \sin t \qquad 0 \leq t \leq 2\pi \qquad (1)$$
$$z = 0$$

is smooth. Also determine if the arc is closed and define its orientation.

Solution: An arc is said to be smooth if its parametrization $\bar{r} = \bar{r}(t)$, $t_1 \leq t \leq t_2$ satisfies the following conditions:

1. For all values of t such that $t_1 \leq t \leq t_2$, $\frac{d\bar{r}}{dt}$ exists and is a continuous function of t.

2. If $t_a \neq t_b$ then $\bar{r}(t_a) \neq \bar{r}(t_b)$

3. $\frac{d\bar{r}}{dt} \neq 0$ for all values of t, $t_1 \leq t \leq t_2$.

Now, for the curve described by eq.(1),

$$\bar{r}(t) = (\cos t, \sin t, 0) \qquad (2)$$

and

$$\frac{d\bar{r}}{dt} = (-\sin t, \cos t, 0) \qquad (3)$$

Thus, $\frac{d\bar{r}}{dt}$ exists and is continuous, fulfilling condition 1. Condition 2 is fulfilled as well. For $0 \leq t \leq 2\pi$, $\frac{d\bar{r}}{dt} \neq 0$, thus, the arc with the parametric equations of eq.(1) is smooth.

Now, since an arc is said to be closed if $\bar{r}(t_a) = \bar{r}(t_b)$ for $t_a \leq t \leq t_b$, we conclude that the arc in question is closed, since for $t_a = 0$ and $t_b = 2\pi$, $\bar{r}(0) = \bar{r}(2\pi)$.

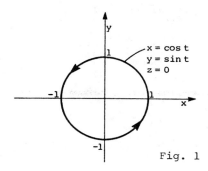

x = cos t
y = sin t
z = 0

Fig. 1

The arc is a circle of unit radius lying in the xy plane. Note that if at t=0 a point on the arc lies on the x-axis, then as t increases from 0 to 2π this point moves counter-clockwise around the circle, as shown in Fig. 1. A different orientation is also possible. Indeed, consider the parametrization

$$x = \cos t$$

$$y = -\sin t \qquad (5)$$

$$z = 0$$

Though this parametrization gives us the same curve, note that a point on the arc initially lying on the x-axis will move in a clockwise direction (opposite to that of the previous parametrization) as t increases from 0 to 2π (see Fig. 2).

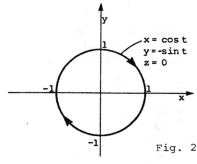

x = cos t
y = -sin t
z = 0

Fig. 2

The same curve can be represented non-parametrically by the equation

$$x^2 + y^2 = 1$$

$$z = 0$$

This representation does not, however, define the orientation of the curve.

● **PROBLEM** 12-12

1. Find the length of the curve

$$y = \cos h\, x \qquad\qquad (1)$$

between x=1 and x=0.

2. Find the circumference of a circle of radius r.

3. Find the length of the curve

$$y = x^{\frac{2}{3}} \qquad\qquad (2)$$

between x=-1 and x=4.

Solution: In general, when a curve is given by the equation

$$y = y(x) \quad \text{for} \quad a \le x \le b \qquad\qquad (3)$$

its length is

$$\int_a^b \sqrt{1 + \left(\frac{dy}{dx}\right)^2}\; dx \qquad \text{(see Fig. 1)} \qquad (4)$$

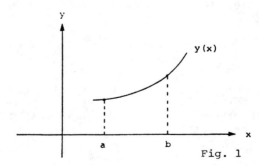

Fig. 1

Often, it is more convenient to express x as a single-valued function of y;

$$x = x(y) \quad c \le y \le d \qquad\qquad (5)$$

The formula for the length is then

$$\int_c^d \sqrt{1 + \left(\frac{dx}{dy}\right)^2}\; dy \qquad\qquad (6)$$

(see Fig. 2).

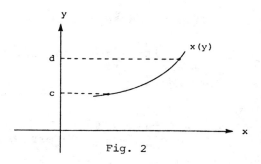

Fig. 2

Now, for a curve represented in the parametrical form

$$x = x(t), \qquad y = y(t)$$

the length of the curve is given by

$$\int_{t_1}^{t_2} \sqrt{\left(\frac{dx}{dt}\right)^2 + \left(\frac{dy}{dt}\right)^2}\ dt \qquad (7)$$

1. Here, the curve is given in the form

$$y = y(x) = \cos h\,x \qquad (8)$$

Therefore, eq.(4) will be used to find its length between the points x=1 and x=0.

The hyperbolic cosine and hyperbolic sine functions are defined as

$$\cos h\,x = \frac{e^x + e^{-x}}{2}$$
$$\sin h\,x = \frac{e^x - e^{-x}}{2} \qquad (9)$$

The following are some basic rules for hyperbolic functions.

$$\cos h^2 x - \sin h^2 x = 1 \qquad (10)$$
$$\frac{d}{dx}\cos h\,x = \sin h\,x \qquad (11)$$
$$\frac{d}{dx}\sin h\,x = \cos h\,x \qquad (12)$$

Now, from eq.(4), we have

$$\int_0^1 \sqrt{1 + \left(\frac{d}{dx}\cos h\,x\right)^2}\ dx = \int_0^1 \sqrt{1 + \sin h^2 x}\ dx \qquad (13)$$

$$= \int_0^1 \sqrt{\cos h^2 x}\ dx = \int_0^1 \cos h\,x\,d\,x$$

$$= \sin h\,x \Big|_0^1 = \frac{e^x - e^{-x}}{2}\Big|_0^1$$

$$= \frac{e - e^{-1}}{2} - \frac{e^0 - e^0}{2} = \frac{e - e^{-1}}{2}$$

523

2. The circle of radius r can be represented by the equation

$$x^2 + y^2 = r^2 \qquad (14)$$

For our purposes however, it is more convenient to represent the circle in the parametric form

$$x = r \cos \phi$$
$$\qquad (15)$$
$$y = r \sin \phi$$

where the central angle ϕ varies from 0 to 2π. From eq.(7), the circumference of the circle may be expressed as

$$c = \int_0^{2\pi} \sqrt{\left(\frac{dx}{d\phi}\right)^2 + \left(\frac{dy}{d\phi}\right)^2} \, d\phi \qquad (16)$$

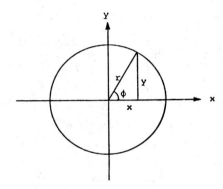

Differentiating eq.(15) results in

$$\frac{dx}{d\phi} = -r \sin \phi$$
$$\qquad (17)$$
$$\frac{dy}{d\phi} = r \cos \phi$$

Substituting eq.(17) into eq.(16) leads to

$$c = \int_0^{2\pi} \sqrt{r^2 \sin^2 \phi + r^2 \cos^2 \phi} \, d\phi = r \int_0^{2\pi} d\phi$$
$$\qquad (18)$$
$$= r \left(\phi \Big|_0^{2\pi} \right) = 2\pi r$$

3. The equation of the curve is

$$y = x^{2/3} \qquad (19)$$

and thus,

$$\frac{dy}{dx} = \frac{2}{3} x^{-\frac{1}{3}} \qquad (20)$$

Now, note that at x=0, $\frac{dy}{dx}$ is infinite and therefore eq. (4) cannot be used, since the point x=0 lies within the limits of integration x=-1 and x=4. A different procedure will now be followed.

Express x as a function of y

$$x = \pm y^{\frac{3}{2}} \qquad (21)$$

The function is shown in Fig. 3. The derivative of x with respect to y is

$$\frac{dx}{dy} = \pm 3/2 \, y^{\frac{1}{2}}$$

and the differential dx is then

$$dx = \pm \frac{3}{2} \, y^{\frac{1}{2}} \, dy$$

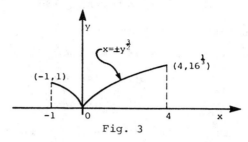

Fig. 3

The differential of arc length ds is then

$$ds = \sqrt{dx^2 + dy^2} = \sqrt{\tfrac{9}{4}y \, dy^2 + dy^2} = \sqrt{\tfrac{9}{4}y + 1} \; dy \qquad (22)$$

Now, if we let L_1 denote the length of the curve between the point (-1,1) and the origin, and L_2 denote the length of the curve between the origin and the point $(4, 16^{\frac{1}{3}})$, then the total length of the curve is

$$L = L_1 + L_2$$

$$= \int_0^1 \sqrt{\tfrac{9}{4}\, y + 1} \; dy + \int_0^{16^{\frac{1}{3}}} \sqrt{\tfrac{9}{4}\, y + 1} \; dy$$

$$= \frac{8}{27}\left[(\tfrac{9}{4}y + 1)^{\frac{3}{2}} \Big|_0^1 \right] + \frac{8}{27}\left[(\tfrac{9}{4}y + 1)^{\frac{3}{2}} \Big|_0^{16^{\frac{1}{3}}} \right]$$

$$= \frac{8}{27}\left[(\tfrac{13}{4})^{\frac{3}{2}} - 1 \right] + \frac{8}{27}\left[(\tfrac{9}{4}(16)^{\frac{1}{3}} + 1)^{\frac{3}{2}} - 1 \right]$$

$$= 6.247$$

● **PROBLEM 12-13**

1. Find the arc length between the points (0,0,1) and (1,0,1) of a helix winding about the x axis. The helix is given by the equation

$$y = \sin 2\pi x$$
$$z = \cos 2\pi x \qquad (1)$$

2. Reparametrize the following curve in terms of arc length.

$$\bar{r}(t) = (3 \cos t)\, \bar{i} + (3 \sin t)\, \bar{j} \qquad (2)$$

$$0 \leq t \leq 2\pi$$

<u>Solution</u>: 1.   Begin by writing the expression for a length element ds.   We have

$$ds^2 = dx^2 + dy^2 + dz^2 \tag{3}$$

From eq.(1), the differentials dy and dz are determined to be

$$dy = (2\pi \cos 2\pi x)dx \tag{4}$$

$$dz = (-2\pi \sin 2\pi x)dx \tag{5}$$

Substituting eqs.(4) and (5) in eq.(3) results in

$$ds^2 = dx^2 + (2\pi \cos 2\pi x\, dx)^2 + (-2\pi \sin 2\pi x\, dx)^2$$

$$= dx^2 + 4\pi^2 dx^2(\cos^2 2\pi x + \sin^2 2\pi x) \tag{6}$$

$$= (1 + 4\pi^2)dx^2$$

Now, the arc length of the helix is given by

$$\int ds = \int_0^1 \sqrt{1+4\pi^2}\ dx = \sqrt{1+4\pi^2}$$

Note that if the curve were given in the parametrical form,

$$x = x(t)$$

$$y = y(t) \tag{7}$$

$$z = z(t)$$

then its length would be

$$\int_a^b \sqrt{\left(\frac{dx}{dt}\right)^2 + \left(\frac{dy}{dt}\right)^2 + \left(\frac{dz}{dt}\right)^2}\ dt \tag{8}$$

$$= \int_a^b \left|\frac{d\overline{r}}{dt}\right| dt$$

2.   For $t_1=0$, the arc length for the curve given by eq.(2) is given by

$$s = \int_0^t \left|\frac{d\overline{r}}{dt}\right| dt = \int_0^t \sqrt{(-3\sin t)^2+(3\cos t)^2}\, dt \tag{9}$$

$$= \int_0^t \sqrt{9}\ dt = 3t$$

Notice that we can now replace the parameter t with the new parameter s, since $t = \frac{s}{3}$.   Eq.(2) can therefore be written as

$$\overline{r}(s) = \left(3\cos\frac{s}{3}\right)\overline{i} + \left(3\sin\frac{s}{3}\right)\overline{j} \tag{10}$$

where $0 \le s \le 6\pi$

LINE INTEGRALS, WORK DONE IN A FORCE FIELD

Using the definition of the integral as the limit of a sum, evaluate

$$\int_C \overline{F} \cdot d\overline{r} \tag{1}$$

where C is the curve

$$y = x^2 \tag{2}$$

lying in the xy plane which extends from (0,0,0) to (1,1,0). The vector field $\overline{F}$ is given by

$$\overline{F} = y\overline{i} + x^2 y^2 \overline{k} \tag{3}$$

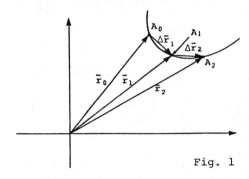

Fig. 1

Solution: First, consider the general case, where C is some smooth curve. C is partitioned by n+1 points A_0, $A_1 \ldots A_n$ which have the corresponding position vectors $\overline{r}_0$, $\overline{r}_1 \ldots \overline{r}_n$. Now, define the vectors $\Delta\overline{r}_1$, $\Delta\overline{r}_2, \ldots \Delta\overline{r}_n$ as

$$\Delta\overline{r}_k = \overline{r}_k - \overline{r}_{k-1} \quad \text{for} \quad k=1, \ldots n \tag{4}$$

(see Fig. 1).

The length of the curve C can be considered as the limit

$$\lim_{n \to \infty} \sum_{k=1}^{n} |\Delta\overline{r}_k|$$

where the partitions are made in such a way that the largest length $|\Delta\overline{r}_k|$ tends to zero, $\lim\limits_{k \to \infty} \max\limits_k |\Delta\overline{r}_k| = 0$.

If the curve is parametrized by

$$\overline{r} = \overline{r}(t); \quad a \le t \le b \tag{5}$$

then the interval [a,b] is partitioned in the manner

$$a = t_0 < t_1 < t_2 < \ldots < t_n = b, \tag{6}$$

527

and the corresponding points are then
$$\overline{r}_k = \overline{r}(t_k) \tag{7}$$
Now, note that we can write
$$\frac{\Delta \overline{r}_k}{\Delta t} \approx \frac{d\overline{r}}{dt}$$
or
$$\Delta \overline{r}_k \approx \frac{d\overline{r}}{dt} \Delta t \tag{8}$$
as Δt tends to zero.

Therefore,

$$\int_C |d\overline{r}| \equiv \lim_{n \to \infty} \sum_{k=1}^{n} |\Delta \overline{r}_k| = \lim_{n \to \infty} \left| \frac{d\overline{r}}{dt} \Delta t_k \right| = \int_a^b \left| \frac{d\overline{r}}{dt} \right| dt \tag{9}$$

Now, if there exists a continuous vector field $\overline{F}$ in a region containing a smooth oriented curve C, then the foregoing method can be used to define the line integral. If $\overline{F}_k$ denotes the value of $\overline{F}$ at the point A_k, then we define the line integral $\int_C \overline{F} \cdot d\overline{r}$ as the limit of the sum

$$\int_C \overline{F} \cdot d\overline{r} = \lim_{n \to \infty} \sum_{k=1}^{n} \overline{F}_k \cdot \Delta \overline{r}_k \tag{10}$$

It can be shown that the above limit is independent of the particular division of the curve C, as long as the maximum value of $|\Delta \overline{r}_k|$ tends to zero.

Now consider the curve $y = x^2$ from the point $(0,0,0)$ to the point $(1,1,0)$, as shown in Fig. 2.

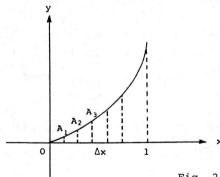

Fig. 2

Let us take
$$\Delta x = \frac{1}{n} \tag{11}$$
The dividing points are then
$$A_k = (x_k, y_k, z_k) = \left(\frac{k}{n}, \left(\frac{k}{n} \right)^2, 0 \right)$$
$$= \left(\frac{k}{n}, \frac{k^2}{n^2}, 0 \right), \tag{12}$$

528

and the vectors $\Delta \overline{r}_k$ are

$$\Delta \overline{r}_k = A_k - A_{k-1} = \left[\frac{k}{n}, \frac{k^2}{n^2}, 0\right] - \left[\frac{k-1}{n}, \frac{(k-1)^2}{n^2}, 0\right]$$

$$= \frac{1}{n}\overline{i} + \left[\frac{k^2}{n^2} - \frac{(k-1)^2}{n^2}\right]\overline{j} + 0\overline{k} \tag{13}$$

$$= \frac{1}{n}\overline{i} + \frac{2k-1}{n^2}\overline{j}$$

Since $\overline{F}$ is given by eq.(3), the corresponding values of $\overline{F}_k$ are found to be

$$\overline{F}_k = \overline{F}(\overline{r}_k) = y_k\overline{i} + x_k^2 y_k^2 \overline{k}$$

$$= \frac{k^2}{n^2}\overline{i} + \left(\frac{k}{n}\right)^2 \frac{k^4}{n^4}\overline{k} = \frac{k^2}{n^2}\overline{i} + \frac{k^6}{n^6}\overline{k} \tag{14}$$

We can then write

$$\sum_{k=1}^{n} \overline{F}_k \cdot \Delta\overline{r}_k = \sum_{k=1}^{n} \left(\frac{k^2}{n^2}, 0, \frac{k^6}{n^6}\right) \cdot \left(\frac{1}{n}, \frac{k^2}{n^2} - \frac{(k-1)^2}{n^2}, 0\right)$$

$$= \sum_{k=1}^{n} \frac{k^2}{n^3} = \frac{1}{n^3} \sum_{k=1}^{n} k^2 \tag{15}$$

It could be easily verified that

$$\sum_{k=1}^{n} k^2 = \frac{1}{6} n(n+1)(2n+1) \tag{16}$$

Substituting eq.(16) into eq.(15) yields

$$\sum_{k=1}^{n} \overline{F}_k \cdot \Delta\overline{r}_k = \frac{1}{n^3} \frac{1}{6} n(n+1)(2n+1)$$

$$= \frac{1}{6n^2} (n+1)(2n+1) = \frac{1}{6}\left(1+\frac{1}{n}\right)\left(2+\frac{1}{n}\right) \tag{17}$$

Now, from eqs.(10) and (17), we finally obtain

$$\int_C \overline{F} \cdot d\overline{r} = \lim_{n\to\infty} \frac{1}{6}\left(1+\frac{1}{n}\right)\left(2+\frac{1}{n}\right) = \frac{1}{3} \tag{18}$$

Using the foregoing definition is a tedious, laborious solution route and, as far as practical purposes are concerned, more direct methods are usually used when evaluating line integrals.

● **PROBLEM 12-15**

If vector field $\overline{F}$ is given by

$$\overline{F} = xy\overline{i} + x^2\overline{j} + (x-z)\overline{k}, \tag{1}$$

evaluate the line integral

$$\int_C \overline{F} \cdot d\overline{r} \tag{2}$$

from (0,0,0) to (1,2,4) along

1. the line segment joining these two points

2. the curve given parametrically by

$$x = t^2, \quad y = 2t^3, \quad z = 4t \qquad (3)$$

Solution: 1. Begin by writing the parametric equations of the line passing through the points (0,0,0) and (1,2,4). We have,
$$x = t, \quad y = 2t, \quad z = 4t \qquad (4)$$

and for this line segment, t is restricted to
$$0 \le t \le 1 \qquad (5)$$

Now, note that the integral can be expressed as

$$\int_C \overline{F} \cdot d\overline{r} = \int_C \left[xy\overline{i} + x^2\overline{j} + (x-z)\overline{k} \right] \cdot \left[dx\overline{i} + dy\overline{j} + dz\overline{k} \right] \qquad (6)$$

$$= \int_C xy\,dx + x^2\,dy + (x-z)\,dz$$

Differentiating eq.(4) gives
$$dx = dt$$
$$dy = 2dt \qquad (7)$$
$$dz = 4dt$$

Substituting eq.(7) and eq.(4) into eq.(6) results in

$$\int_C \overline{F} \cdot d\overline{r} = \int_0^1 2t^2\,dt + 2t^2\,dt + (t-4t)4\,dt$$

$$= \int_0^1 (4t^2 - 12t)\,dt = \left(\frac{4}{3} t^3 - 6t^2 \right)\Big|_0^1 \qquad (8)$$

$$= \frac{4}{3} - 6 = -\frac{14}{3}$$

At this point, it should be noted that in order to evaluate a line integral we need to know not only the parametric equations of the respective curve, but the orientation as well. In this example, the orientation of the line segment was from the point (0,0,0) to the point (1,2,4).

2. From eq.(3), the differentials dx, dy, dz are found to be
$$dx = 2t\,dt$$
$$dy = 6t^2\,dt \qquad (9)$$
$$dz = 4\,dt$$

Substituting eq.(9) and eq.(2) into the expression (2), we obtain

$$\int_C \overline{F} \cdot d\overline{r} = \int_C \left[xy\overline{i} + x^2\overline{j} + (x-z)\overline{k} \right] \cdot \left[dx\overline{i} + dy\overline{j} + dz\overline{k} \right]$$

$$= \int_C xy\,dx + x^2\,dy + (x-z)\,dz$$

$$= \int_0^1 (t^2)(2t^3)2t\,dt + (t^4)6t^2\,dt + (t^2-4t)4\,dt$$

$$= \int_0^1 (4t^6 + 6t^6 + 4t^2 - 16t)\,dt \qquad (10)$$

$$= \int_0^1 (10t^6 + 4t^2 - 16t)\,dt$$

$$= \left(\frac{10t^7}{7} + \frac{4t^3}{3} - 8t^2 \right) \Bigg|_0^1$$

$$= \frac{10}{7} + \frac{4}{3} - 8 = -\frac{110}{21}$$

● **PROBLEM** 12-16

If $\quad \overline{F} = (x^2+y^2)\overline{i} - 3xz\overline{j} + y^3\,\overline{k}$ $\qquad\qquad$ (1)

compute the line integral

$$\int_C \overline{F} \cdot d\overline{r} \qquad\qquad (2)$$

from (0,0,0) to (1,1,1) along the following paths:

1. the line segment joining (0,0,0) and (1,1,1)

2. the path shown in Fig. 1

3. the curve given by

$$x = t, \quad y = t^2, \quad z = t^3 \qquad\qquad (3)$$

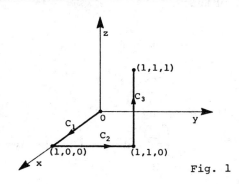

Fig. 1

531

Solution: 1. The straight line passing through the points (0,0,0) and (1,1,1) can be expressed in the parametrical form

$$x = t$$

$$y = t \tag{4}$$

$$z = t$$

The differentials are then

$$dx = dt$$

$$dy = dt \tag{5}$$

$$dz = dt$$

The line integral can then be computed as follows

$$\int_c \overline{F} \cdot d\overline{r} = \int_c (x^2 + y^2) dx - 3xz dy + y^3 dz$$

$$= \int_0^1 2t^2 dt - 3t^2 dt + t^3 dt = \int_0^1 (-t^2 + t^3) dt \tag{6}$$

$$= \left(-\frac{t^3}{3} + \frac{t^4}{4} \right) \Bigg|_{t=0}^{t=1} = -\frac{1}{3} + \frac{1}{4} = -\frac{1}{12}$$

2. In this case, we will compute the line integrals along each of the line segments c_1, c_2 and c_3 and then take their sum in order to compute the line integral of the total path.

First, for path c_1, which stretches from (0,0,0) to (1,0,0), note that y=0 and z=0 and therefore dy=dz=0. Now, since x varies from 0 to 1, the line integral becomes

$$\int_{c_1} \overline{F} \cdot d\overline{r} = \int_{c_1} (x^2 + y^2) dx = \int_0^1 x^2 dx \tag{7}$$

$$= \frac{x^3}{3} \Bigg|_0^1 = \frac{1}{3}$$

Now, along the path c_2 (which stretches from (1,0,0) to (1,1,0)), obtain

$$x = 1$$

and

$$z = 0$$

therefore $dx = dz = 0$

y varies from 0 to 1. The line integral for this line segment is

$$\int_{c_2} \overline{F} \cdot d\overline{r} = \int_{c_2} -3xz \, dy = 0 \tag{8}$$

Along the path c_3, $x=1$ and $y=1$. Thus
$$dx = dy = 0 \qquad (9)$$
and z varies from 0 to 1. Therefore,
$$\int_{c_3} \overline{F} \cdot d\overline{r} = \int_{c_3} y^3 dz = \int_0^1 dz = z\Big|_0^1 = 1 \qquad (10)$$
The total line integral is given by
$$\int_c \overline{F} \cdot d\overline{r} = \int_{c_1} \overline{F} \cdot d\overline{r} + \int_{c_2} \overline{F} \cdot d\overline{r} + \int_{c_3} \overline{F} \cdot d\overline{r}$$
$$= \frac{1}{3} + 0 + 1 = \frac{4}{3} \qquad (11)$$

3. In this case the line integral is computed along the curve
$$x = t, \quad y = t^2, \quad z = t^3 \qquad (12)$$
from the point $(0,0,0)$ to the point $(1,1,1)$. The parameter t varies from $t=0$ to $t=1$ for this path. The differentials are found to be
$$dx = dt, \quad dy = 2tdt, \quad dz = 3t^2dt \qquad (13)$$

The line integral is then

$$\int_c \overline{F} \cdot d\overline{r} = \int_c (x^2+y^2)dx - 3xzdy + y^3dz$$

$$= \int_0^1 (t^2+t^4)dt - 3tt^3 2tdt + t^6 3t^2dt$$

$$= \int_0^1 (t^2+t^4-6t^5+3t^8)dt \qquad (14)$$

$$= \left(\frac{t^3}{3} + \frac{t^5}{5} - t^6 + \frac{t^9}{3}\right)\Big|_0^1 = \frac{1}{3} + \frac{1}{5} - 1 + \frac{1}{3}$$

$$= -\frac{2}{15}$$

● **PROBLEM 12-17**

Evaluate the line integral from $(-1,0)$ to $(1,0)$ in the xy-plane of the vector field
$$\overline{F} = y\overline{i} + x\overline{j} \qquad (1)$$

along 1. the x axis

2. the semicircle $y = \sqrt{1-x^2}$

3. the semicircle $y = -\sqrt{1-x^2}$

<u>Solution</u>: 1. Along the x axis, y = 0, hence dy = 0 and the line integral is

$$\int_C \overline{F} \cdot d\overline{r} = \int_C (y\overline{i} + x\overline{j}) \cdot (dx\overline{i} + dy\overline{j}) \qquad (2)$$

$$= \int_C y \ dx + x \ dy = 0$$

Since, again y = 0 and dy = 0.

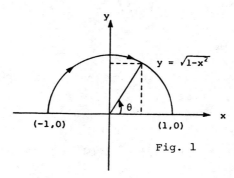

Fig. 1

2. The semicircle is shown in Fig. 1. A convenient parameter is the polar coordinate θ. The radius of the circle is one, r = 1 and for points (x,y) on the semicircle, we have

$$x = \cos \theta$$
$$y = \sin \theta \qquad (3)$$

Note that the parameter θ changes from π at (-1,0) to 0 at (1,0). The differentials are

$$dx = -\sin \theta \ d\theta$$
$$dy = \cos \theta \ d\theta \qquad (4)$$

The line integral along the semicircle is then

$$\int_C \overline{F} \cdot d\overline{r} = \int_C y dx + x dy$$

$$= \int_\pi^0 -\sin^2\theta \ d\theta + \cos^2\theta d\theta$$

$$= \int_\pi^0 (\cos^2\theta - \sin^2\theta) d\theta$$

$$= \int_\pi^0 \cos 2\theta \ d\theta = \left. \frac{\sin 2\theta}{2} \right|_\pi^0 \qquad (5)$$

$$= 0$$

3. The semicircle $y = -\sqrt{1-x^2}$ is shown in Fig. 2. We can parametrize this curve as follows

$$x = \cos \theta$$

$$y = -\sin \theta \qquad (6)$$

534

where the parameter θ varies from π to 0.

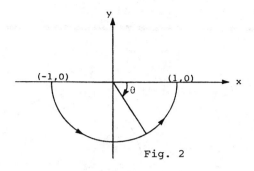

Fig. 2

The line integral for this curve is given by

$$\int_C \overline{F} \cdot d\overline{r} = \int_C y\,dx + x\,dy \qquad (7)$$

The differentials dx and dy are evaluated from eq.(6)

$$dx = -\sin\theta\ d\theta$$
$$dy = -\cos\theta\ d\theta \qquad (8)$$

Substituting eq.(8) and eq.(6) into eq.(7) gives

$$\int_C \overline{F} \cdot d\overline{r} = \int_\pi^0 \sin^2\theta\,d\theta - \int_\pi^0 \cos^2\theta\,d\theta$$

$$= \int_\pi^0 (\sin^2\theta - \cos^2\theta)\,d\theta = \int_0^\pi \cos 2\theta\,d\theta \qquad (9)$$

$$= \left. \frac{\sin 2\theta}{2} \right|_0^\pi = 0$$

● **PROBLEM 12-18**

Using the following procedures, evaluate the integral

$$\int_C (y^3 - x^3)\,dy \qquad (1)$$

where C is the semicircle

$$y = \sqrt{1-x^2} \qquad (2)$$

from the point (1,0) to (-1,0).

1. Using the parametric representation of a semicircle, namely

$$x = \cos\theta\ ,\quad y = \sin\theta\ ,\quad 0 \le \theta \le \pi \qquad (3)$$

535

2. Using x as the parameter

3. Using y as the parameter

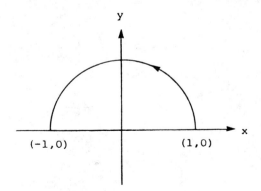

y

$(-1,0)$ $(1,0)$ x

<u>Solution</u>: 1. From eq.(3), the differential dy is found to be

$$dy = \cos\theta \, d\theta \qquad (4)$$

The integral in eq.(1) then becomes

$$\int_C (y^3 - x^3)dy = \int_0^\pi (\sin^3\theta - \cos^3\theta)\cos\theta d\theta$$

$$= \int_0^\pi \sin^3\theta\cos\theta d\theta - \int_0^\pi \cos^4\theta d\theta \qquad (5)$$

$$= \frac{1}{4}\sin^4\theta \Big|_0^\pi - \left(\frac{1}{32}\sin4\theta + \frac{1}{4}\sin2\theta + \frac{3}{8}\theta\right)\Big|_0^\pi$$

$$= -\frac{3}{8}\pi$$

The above integral formula may be obtained by direct substitution along with the half-angle formulas; or by referring to any standard table of integrals.

2. Using x as a parameter, the equation of the semicircle may be written as

$$x = x$$
$$y = \sqrt{1-x^2} \qquad (6)$$

The differential dy is then

$$dy = \frac{-x}{\sqrt{1-x^2}} \, dx \qquad (7)$$

The integral then becomes

$$\int_C (y^3 - x^3)dy = \int_1^{-1} \left[(1-x^2)^{\frac{3}{2}} - x^3\right] \frac{-xdx}{\sqrt{1-x^2}} \qquad (8)$$

Now, to find the integral given in eq.(8), substitute

$$x = \cos\theta \qquad (9)$$

and

$$dx = -\sin\theta \, d\theta \qquad \text{into eq.(8).}$$

536

Notice that as x changes from 1 to -1, the angle θ has to change from 0 to π, and since $\sin\theta = \sqrt{1-\cos^2\theta}$ for this range of θ, eq.(8) becomes

$$\int_c (y^3-x^3)dy = \int_0^\pi \left[(1-\cos^2\theta)^{\frac{3}{2}}-\cos^3\theta\right]\frac{(-\cos\theta)(-\sin\theta)}{\sqrt{1-\cos^2\theta}}\,d\theta$$

$$= \int_0^\pi \left[\sin^3\theta-\cos^3\theta\right]\frac{\cos\theta\sin\theta}{\sin\theta}\,d\theta \qquad (10)$$

$$= \int_0^\pi (\sin^3\theta-\cos^3\theta)\cos\theta\,d\theta$$

Notice that this is the same exact integral obtained in part (1) of this problem (see eq.(5)).

Thus,

$$\int_c (y^3-x^3)dy = -\frac{3\pi}{8} \qquad (11)$$

3. Now, parametrize the semicircle using y as the parameter. Since y changes from zero to one and then back to zero, the integral has to be split into two parts -- one from (1,0) to (0,1) and the other from (0,1) to (1,0). The semicircle is represented as

$$\begin{array}{ll} y = y & \\ & 0\le y\le 1 \\ x = \sqrt{1-y^2} & \end{array} \qquad (12)$$

for the part of the semicircle ranging from (1,0) to (0,1). For the part ranging from (0,1) to (-1,0), we have

$$\begin{array}{l} y = y \\ \\ x = -\sqrt{1-y^2} \end{array} \qquad (13)$$

as y changes from 1 to 0. Integral (1) becomes

$$\int_c (y^3-x^3)dy = \int_0^1 (y^3-x^3)dy + \int_1^0 (y^3-x^3)dy \qquad (14)$$

For the first part, the differentials are

$$dx = \frac{-ydy}{\sqrt{1-y^2}} \qquad (15)$$

and for the second part,

$$dx = \frac{ydy}{\sqrt{1-y^2}} \qquad (16)$$

Therefore, we obtain

$$\int_c (y^3-x^3)dy = \int_0^1 \left[y^3-(1-y^2)^{\frac{3}{2}}\right]dy + \int_1^0 \left[y^3+(1-y^2)^{\frac{3}{2}}\right]dy$$

$$= \int_0^1 y^3dy + \int_1^0 y^3dy - \int_0^1 (1-y^2)^{\frac{3}{2}}dy + \int_1^0 (1-y^2)^{\frac{3}{2}}dy \qquad (17)$$

Now, since in general

$$\int_a^b = -\int_b^a ,$$

537

eq.(17) becomes

$$\int_C (y^3-x^3)dy = -2 \int_0^1 (1-y^2)^{\frac{3}{2}}dy$$

Finally, substituting
$$y = \sin \theta \tag{18}$$

we obtain

$$\int_C (y^3-x^3)dy = -2 \int_0^{\frac{\pi}{2}} \cos^4\theta d\theta = -\frac{3\pi}{8} \tag{19}$$

Note that the value of the given line integral, as our results indicate, does not depend on the particular parametrization of the given curve.

Also, note that in the case where y is the parameter, it was unnecessary to calculate the differentials given by eqs. (15) and (16).

• **PROBLEM 12-19**

Find the work done by the force field

$$\overline{F} = x^2\overline{i} + 2xy\overline{j} + yz^2\overline{k} \tag{1}$$

in moving a particle along the curve

$$x = t^2, \quad y = t^2+1, \quad z = t^3 \tag{2}$$

from t = 0 to t = 2.

Solution: The work W done by a force $\overline{F}$ in moving a particle from an initial point to some final point of an oriented curve C is given by

$$W = \int_C \overline{F} \cdot d\overline{r} \tag{3}$$

From eq.(2), the differentials are found to be

$$dx = 2t \, dt$$
$$dy = 2t \, dt \tag{4}$$
$$dz = 3t^2 dt$$

Substituting eq.(1) and eq.(4) into eq.(3) results in

$$W = \int_C \overline{F} \cdot d\overline{r} = \int_C \left[x^2\overline{i}+2xy\overline{j}+yz^2\overline{k}\right] \cdot \left[dx\overline{i}+dy\overline{j}+dz\overline{k}\right]$$

$$= \int_C x^2 dx + 2xy dy + yz^2 dz \tag{5}$$

$$= \int_0^2 t^4 2t dt + 2t^2(t^2+1)2t dt + (t^2+1)t^6 3t^2 dt$$

$$= \int_0^2 \left[2t^5 + 4t^5 + 4t^3 + 3t^{10} + 3t^8 \right] dt$$

$$= \int_0^2 \left[3t^{10} + 3t^8 + 6t^5 + 4t^3 \right] dt$$

$$= \left(3 \frac{t^{11}}{11} + \frac{t^9}{3} + t^6 + t^4 \right) \Big|_0^2$$

$$= \frac{3}{11} 2^{11} + \frac{1}{3} 2^9 + 2^6 + 2^4$$

$$= 809$$

● **PROBLEM** 12-20

A particle moves around a circle C in the xy plane. If the center of the circle is at the origin, and if it has a radius of 4, then determine the work done in moving the particle once around the circle in the positive direction if the force field is given by

$$\bar{F} = (3x + 2y - z)\bar{i} + (x - y)\bar{j} + z^2\bar{k} \qquad (1)$$

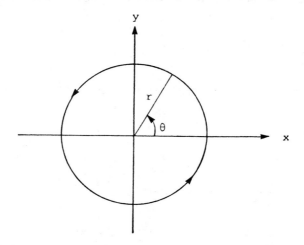

Solution: A closed curve can be traversed in two directions: the counterclockwise direction, called the positive direction, and the clockwise direction, called the negative direction. The circle C is shown in the figure with the positive direction indicated.

The work done in moving the particle around the circle is

$$W = \oint_C \bar{F} \cdot d\bar{r} = \oint_C (3x+2y)dx + (x-y)dy \qquad (2)$$

Note that z=0 and dz=0 since the circle lies in the xy plane. Also, notice that since the curve is closed, that is its initial and final points coincide, we use the notation

$$\oint_C \overline{F} \cdot d\overline{r} \tag{3}$$

The line integral of $\overline{F}$ around a closed curve C is called the circulation of $\overline{F}$ about C.

Now, since the parametric equations of the circle are
$$x = 4\cos\theta \tag{4}$$
$$y = 4\sin\theta ,$$

where θ varies from 0 to 2π, the differentials are found to be
$$dx = -4 \sin\theta d\theta \tag{5}$$
$$dy = 4 \cos\theta d\theta$$

Substituting eq.(4) and eq.(5) into eq.(2) results in

$$W = \oint \overline{F} \cdot d\overline{r} =$$

$$\int_0^{2\pi} -(12\cos\theta+8\sin\theta)4\sin\theta d\theta + (4\cos\theta - 4\sin\theta)4\cos\theta d\theta$$

$$= \int_0^{2\pi} (-32\sin^2\theta+16\cos^2\theta-64\cos\theta\sin\theta)d\theta \tag{6}$$

$$= 16 \int_0^{2\pi} (\cos^2\theta-2\sin^2\theta-4\cos\theta\sin\theta)d\theta$$

Now, applying these fundamental identities
$$\cos^2\theta = \tfrac{1}{2} (1+\cos2\theta)$$

$$\sin^2\theta = \tfrac{1}{2} (1-\cos2\theta)$$

$$\sin2\theta = 2\sin\theta\cos\theta$$

to the above integral, results in

$$W = \oint \overline{F} \cdot d\overline{r} = 16 \int_0^{2\pi} (\tfrac{1}{2} + \tfrac{1}{2}\cos2\theta-1+\cos2\theta-2\sin2\theta)d\theta \tag{7}$$

$$= 16 \int_0^{2\pi} (-\tfrac{1}{2} + \tfrac{3}{2} \cos2\theta-2\sin2\theta)d\theta$$

$$= 8 \int_0^{2\pi} (-1 + 3\cos2\theta-4\sin2\theta)d\theta$$

$$= 8 (-\theta + \tfrac{3}{2} \sin2\theta+2\cos2\theta) \Big|_0^{2\pi}$$

$$= -16\pi$$

A closed curve is shown in the figure.

Evaluate $\int_C \overline{F} \cdot d\overline{r}$ around the curve in the direction indicated.

$$\overline{F} = (2x+y)\overline{i} + (x-y)\overline{j} \tag{1}$$

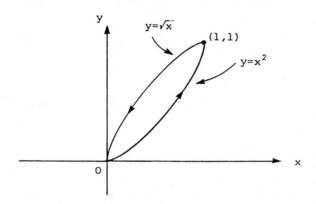

Solution: To find the total line integral of the given curve, first calculate the line integral for the curve $y = x^2$ from the point $(0,0)$ to the point $(1,1)$. Then calculate the line integral for the curve $y = \sqrt{x}$ from $(1,1)$ to $(0,0)$ and add the two results.

We have

$$\int_C \overline{F} \cdot d\overline{r} = \int_C (2x+y)dx + (x-y)dy \tag{2}$$

Now, for the first path, x can be considered as the parameter

$$x = x, \quad y = x^2 \tag{3}$$

where x changes from 0 to 1. The differentials are

$$dx \quad and \quad dy = 2xdx \tag{4}$$

The integral along this path is

$$\int_0^1 (2x+x^2)dx + (x-x^2)2xdx$$

$$= \int_0^1 \left[2x+3x^2-2x^3\right]dx = \left(-\frac{x^4}{2} +x^3+x^2\right)\Big|_0^1 \tag{5}$$

$$= -\frac{1}{2} + 1 + 1 = \frac{3}{2}$$

The second part of the curve is given by $y = \sqrt{x}$ or

$$y^2 = x \tag{6}$$

Here, y can be considered as the parameter

$$y = y \quad x = y^2$$

The differentials are

$$dy \quad \text{and} \quad dx = 2ydy \tag{7}$$

where y changes from 1 to 0. Therefore,

$$\int_1^0 (2y^2+y)2ydy + (y^2-y)dy$$

$$= \int_1^0 \left[4y^3+3y^2-y\right]dy = \left(y^4+y^3-\frac{y^2}{2}\right)\Big|_1^0 \tag{8}$$

$$= -\frac{3}{2}$$

The total integral is the sum of the integrals given by eqs.(5) and (8)

$$\int_c \overline{F} \cdot d\overline{r} = \frac{3}{2} - \frac{3}{2} = 0 \tag{9}$$

Note that the value of the line integral does not depend on the particular type of parametrization of the curve. Whenever possible, however, the student should choose the parametrization that is most convenient for integrating.

● **PROBLEM 12-22**

If $\quad \overline{F} = (2x+y)\overline{i} + (x-y^2)\overline{j}$ $\qquad$ (1)

evaluate

$$\oint_c \overline{F} \cdot d\overline{r}$$

around the square shown in the figure if we proceed in

1. the positive direction

2. the negative direction.

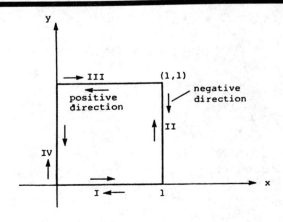

<u>Solution:</u>   The line integral around the square is given by

$$\oint_c \overline{F} \cdot d\overline{r} = \oint_c (2x+y)dx + (x-y^2)dy \qquad (2)$$

First we will evaluate this integral in the positive (counter-clockwise) direction.

1.   For segment I, we have

$$y = 0, \quad \text{and hence} \quad dy = 0$$

while x changes from 0 to 1.   Therefore, the integral over this part of the path is

$$\int_0^1 2x dx = x^2 \Big|_0^1 = 1 \qquad (3)$$

For segment II,

$$x = 1, \quad \text{hence} \quad dx = 0 \quad \text{and}$$

y changes from 0 to 1.   The integral over this part of the path is then

$$\int_0^1 (1-y^2)dy = y - \frac{y^3}{3} \Big|_0^1 = 1 - \frac{1}{3} = \frac{2}{3} \qquad (4)$$

For segment III, we have

$$y = 1 \quad \text{hence} \quad dy = 0 \quad \text{and}$$

x changes from 1 to 0.   Therefore, the integral over this segment is

$$\int_1^0 (2x+1)dx = x^2+x \Big|_1^0 = -2 \qquad (5)$$

For segment IV we have

$$x = 0 \quad \text{hence} \quad dx = 0 \quad \text{and}$$

y changes from 1 to 0; consequently, the integral over this segment is given by

$$\int_1^0 - y^2 dy = \frac{-y^3}{3} \Big|_1^0 = \frac{1}{3} \qquad (6)$$

Now, adding the integrals obtained for each of the above four segments gives us the total line integral over the square when proceeding in the positive direction.
     Therefore,

$$\int_c \overline{F} \cdot d\overline{r} = 1 + \frac{2}{3} - 2 + \frac{1}{3} = 0 \qquad (7)$$

2.   For this case, start at point (1,0) and proceed in the negative direction around the square.   For each of the corresponding segments, one obtains

I $$\int_1^0 2x dx = x^2 \Big|_1^0 = -1 \qquad (8)$$

$$\text{II} \qquad \int_1^0 (1-y^2)dy = -\frac{2}{3} \tag{9}$$

$$\text{III} \qquad \int_0^1 (2x+1)dx = 2 \tag{10}$$

$$\text{IV} \qquad \int_0^1 -y^2 dy = -\frac{1}{3} \tag{11}$$

Therefore, the line integral over the square when proceeding in the negative direction is found to be

$$\oint_C \overline{F} \cdot d\overline{r} = -1 - \frac{2}{3} + 2 - \frac{1}{3} = 0 \tag{12}$$

Notice that proceeding in either the negative or positive direction around the square results in a line integral equal to zero.

In general however, we have that over any curve C,

$$\begin{bmatrix} \text{line integral in the} \\ \text{positive direction} \end{bmatrix} = - \begin{bmatrix} \text{line integral in the} \\ \text{negative direction} \end{bmatrix}$$

● **PROBLEM 12-23**

Evaluate the following line integrals

1. $\oint_C (x^2-y^2)ds$ where c is the circle $x^2+y^2=9$.

2. $\int_C^{(1,1)}_{(0,0)} xds$ where c is the line x=y.

Solution: Arc length s is defined for a smooth or piecewise smooth curve C as the distance traversed from the initial point t_o to a general point t

$$s = \int_{t_o}^t \sqrt{\left(\frac{dx}{dt}\right)^2 + \left(\frac{dy}{dt}\right)^2} \, dt \tag{1}$$

Consider the integral

$$\int_C f(x,y)ds \tag{2}$$

where f(x,y) is continuous on c. Using the parametric form

$$x = x(t) \qquad y = y(t), \tag{3}$$

the above integral can be evaluated as

$$\int_C f(x,y)ds = \int_{t_o}^{t_1} f(x(t),y(t))\sqrt{\left(\frac{dx}{dt}\right)^2 + \left(\frac{dy}{dt}\right)^2} \, dt \qquad (4)$$

1. In parametrical form, the circle $x^2+y^2 = 9$ can be represented as

$$x = 3 \cos \theta$$
$$y = 3 \sin \theta \qquad (5)$$

where the parameter θ changes from 0 to 2π.

Now, since

$$\frac{dx}{d\theta} = -3 \sin \theta \qquad (6)$$

and

$$\frac{dy}{d\theta} = 3 \cos \theta, \qquad (7)$$

the line integral may be found by substituting eqs.(5), (6) and (7) into the formula of eq.(4) with θ of course, as the parameter. Doing this, results in

$$\oint (x^2-y^2)ds = \int_0^{2\pi} (9\cos^2\theta - 9\sin^2\theta) \sqrt{(-3\sin\theta)^2 + (3\cos\theta)^2} \, d\theta$$

$$= \int_0^{2\pi} (9\cos^2\theta - 9\sin^2\theta)3d\theta$$

$$= 27 \int_0^{2\pi} (\cos^2\theta - \sin^2\theta)d\theta = 27 \int_0^{2\pi} \cos2\theta d\theta$$

$$= 27 \left[\frac{\sin 2\theta}{2} \,\Big|_0^{2\pi}\right] = 0 \qquad (8)$$

2. Now, if x is used as the parameter, formula (4) becomes

$$\int_C f(x,y)ds = \int_a^b f[x,y(x)] \sqrt{1 + \left(\frac{dy}{dx}\right)^2} \, dx \qquad (9)$$

For the line $y = x$, we have

$$\frac{dy}{dx} = 1 \qquad (10)$$

Therefore, expression (9) becomes

$$\int_{(0,0)}^{(1,1)} x ds = \int_0^1 x\sqrt{2} \, dx = \sqrt{2} \, \frac{x^2}{2} \,\Big|_0^1$$

$$= \frac{\sqrt{2}}{2} \qquad (11)$$

One could easily prove the following relationship between line intergals:

$$\int_c F_1 dx + F_2 dy = \int_c (F_1 \cos\alpha + F_2 \sin\alpha) ds \qquad (12)$$

Here α represents the angle between the positive x-axis and a tangent vector in the direction of increasing s.

INTEGRATION OF TANGENTIAL AND NORMAL COMPONENTS OF A VECTOR, KINETIC AND POTENTIAL ENERGY, REGIONS AND DOMAINS

● **PROBLEM 12-24**

Evaluate $\quad \int_c F_T \ ds \quad$ for

$$\overline{F} = (x^2+y^2)\overline{i} + 2xy\,\overline{j} \qquad (1)$$

along the following paths

1. on the line y=x from (0,0) to (1,1)

2. on the line x=y^2 from (0,0) to (1,1).

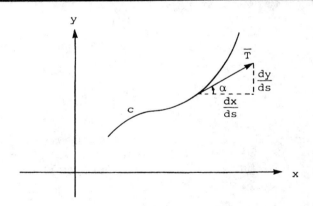

Solution: Observe that F_T denotes the tangential component of $\overline{F}$, that is, the component of $\overline{F}$ in the direction of the unit tangent vector $\overline{T}$, in the direction of increasing s.

$\overline{T}$ has the components

$$\overline{T} = \frac{dx}{ds}\,\overline{i} + \frac{dy}{ds}\,\overline{j} = \cos\alpha\overline{i} + \sin\alpha\overline{j} \qquad (2)$$

as shown in the figure.

Notice that F_T can be expressed as

$$F_T = \overline{F} \cdot \overline{T} = (F_1\overline{i}+F_2\overline{j}) \cdot (\cos\alpha\overline{i}+\sin\alpha\overline{j})$$

$$= F_1 \cos\alpha + F_2 \sin\alpha \qquad (3)$$

and therefore, the integral may be expressed as

$$\int_C F_T ds = \int_C (F_1 \cos\alpha + F_2 \sin\alpha) ds = \int_C F_1 dx + F_2 dy \qquad (4)$$

Now, substituting eq.(1) into eq.(4) results in

$$\int_C F_T ds = \int_C (x^2 + y^2) dx + 2xy \, dy \qquad (5)$$

Next, use x as the parameter. Since $y = x$, then $dy = dx$ while x changes from 0 to 1.

Therefore, for the path $y = x$, the line integral is found to be

$$\int_C F_T ds = \int_0^1 (x^2 + x^2) dx + 2x^2 dx = 4 \int_0^1 x^2 dx \qquad (6)$$

$$= 4 \left(\frac{x^3}{3} \bigg|_0^1 \right) = \frac{4}{3}$$

2.   For this case, use y as the parameter. Since $x = y^2$, $dx = 2y \, dy$. Consequently, for this path, the line integral becomes

$$\int_C F_T ds = \int_0^1 (y^4 + y^2) 2y \, dy + 2y^3 dy \qquad (7)$$

$$= 2 \int_0^1 [y^5 + 2y^3] dy = 2 \left(\frac{y^6}{6} + \frac{y^4}{2} \right) \bigg|_0^1 = \frac{4}{3}$$

● **PROBLEM 12-25**

Evaluate $\int_C F_n ds$ from the point $(0,0)$ to $(1,4)$ for the vector field

$$\overline{F} = e^x \overline{i} + e^{3x} \overline{j} \qquad (1)$$

along the paths

1. $y = 4x$

2. $y = x^2 + 3x$ $\qquad (2)$

Solution: Consider a differentiable curve C which lies in the x-y plane. Let $\overline{T}$ be the unit tangent vector and $\overline{n}$ the unit normal vector, perpendicular to $\overline{T}$, as shown in the figure.

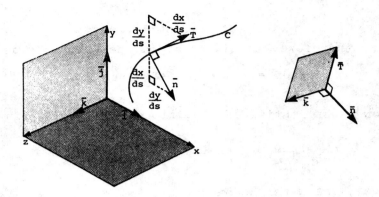

Since the curve C lies in the x-y plane, both vectors $\bar{n}$ and $\bar{T}$ lie in the x-y plane as well.

Now, note that the term F_n represents the component of vector $\bar{F}$ in the direction of vector $\bar{n}$, and therefore

$$F_n = \bar{F} \cdot \bar{n}$$

Since $\bar{F}$ is given, we now need to find $\bar{n}$. To find $\bar{n}$, note that $\bar{n}$ is perpendicular to the plane of vector $\bar{k}$ and $\bar{T}$, and therefore

$$\bar{n} = \bar{T} \times \bar{k} = \left(\frac{dx}{ds}\bar{i} + \frac{dy}{ds}\bar{j}\right) \times \bar{k} = \frac{dy}{ds}\bar{i} - \frac{dx}{ds}\bar{j} \tag{3}$$

F_n is then calculated to be

$$F_n = \bar{F} \cdot \bar{n} = (F_1\bar{i} + F_2\bar{j}) \cdot \left(\frac{dy}{ds}\bar{i} - \frac{dx}{ds}\bar{j}\right)$$

$$= F_1\frac{dy}{ds} - F_2\frac{dx}{ds} \tag{4}$$

and the line integral becomes

$$\int_C F_n ds = \int_C \left(F_1\frac{dy}{ds} - F_2\frac{dx}{ds}\right) ds = \int_C -F_2 dx + F_1 dy \tag{5}$$

Substituting eq.(1) into eq.(5) leads to

$$\int_C F_n ds = \int_C -e^{3x} dx + e^x dy \tag{6}$$

1. For the line y=4x, x can be used as the parameter. Thus

$$dy = 4\,dx \tag{7}$$

Note that x changes from 0 to 1.

The integral in eq.(6) then becomes

$$\int_C F_n ds = \int_0^1 -e^{3x} dx + e^x 4dx = \int_0^1 (4e^x - e^{3x})dx$$

$$= \left(4e^x - \frac{1}{3}e^{3x}\right)\Big|_0^1 \tag{8}$$

$$= 4e - \frac{1}{3} e^3 - 4 + \frac{1}{3}$$

$$= .51$$

2. For the curve $y = x^2+3x$, x will again be used as the parameter, thus

$$dy = 2xdx + 3dx = (2x+3)dx \qquad (9)$$

Now, since x changes from 0 to 1, eq.(6) becomes

$$\int_C F_n ds = \int_0^1 -e^{3x} dx + e^x(2x+3)dx$$

$$= \int_0^1 (2xe^x + 3e^x - e^{3x})dx \qquad (10)$$

$$= \left[2e^x(x-1) + 3e^x - \frac{1}{3} e^{3x} \right] \Bigg|_0^1$$

$$= (3e - \frac{1}{3} e^3) - (-2 + 3 - \frac{1}{3})$$

$$= .79$$

● **PROBLEM** 12-26

1. Consider the motion of a particle in a force field $\overline{F}$. Apply Newton's Second Law and show that the work done equals the gain in kinetic energy.

2. Consider the motion of a particle in the gravitational field near the earth's surface. Show that the work done by the gravitational force on a particle is equal to the difference of potential energies of the particle.

Solution: 1. Let $\overline{r}$ be the position vector of a particle of mass m moving along a curve C. Newton's Second Law states that

$$\overline{F} = m \frac{d\overline{v}}{dt} = m \frac{d^2\overline{r}}{dt^2} \qquad (1)$$

where $\overline{F}$ is the applied force.

Since the motion of the particle takes place in the interval of time $t = t_0$ to $t = t_1$, the work done is

$$\int_C \overline{F} \cdot d\overline{r} = \int_{t_0}^{t_1} \left(\overline{F} \cdot \frac{d\overline{r}}{dt} \right) dt = \int_{t_0}^{t_1} \left(m\frac{d\overline{v}}{dt} \cdot \overline{v} \right) dt$$

$$= \int_{t_0}^{t_1} \frac{d}{dt} \left(\frac{1}{2} m\overline{v} \cdot \overline{v} \right) dt = \int_{t_0}^{t_1} \frac{d}{dt} \left(\frac{1}{2} mv^2 \right) dt \qquad (2)$$

549

$$= \frac{1}{2} mv^2 \left.\right|_{t=t_0}^{t=t_1} = E_{k_{t_1}} - E_{k_{t_0}}$$

where the kinetic energy of a particle is defined as

$$E_k = \frac{1}{2} mv^2 \qquad (3)$$

2. We can represent the gravitational force near the earth's surface by

$$\overline{F}_g = -mg\overline{k} \qquad (4)$$

Note that the z axis points upwards. The particle moves from the point (x_1, y_1, z_1) to the point (x_2, y_2, z_2) along the curve C, as shown in the figure.

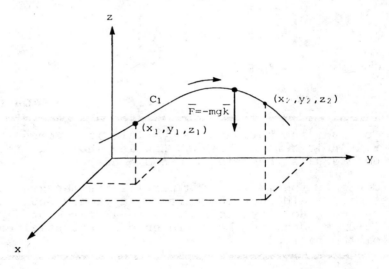

The potential energy of a particle in the gravitational field is defined as

$$E_p = mgh \qquad (5)$$

In our coordinate system $h = z$; thus the work done in moving the particle along the curve C is

$$\int_c \overline{F} \cdot d\overline{r} = \int_c F_1 dx + F_2 dy + F_3 dz$$

$$= \int_{z_1}^{z_2} F_3 dz = -mg \int_{z_1}^{z_2} dz = mgz_1 - mgz_2 \qquad (6)$$

$$= E_p(1) - E_p(2)$$

550

Consider the motion of a particle in the earth's gravitational field, whose potential is

$$\phi = - \frac{kMm}{r} \qquad (1)$$

Show that the work done by the gravitational force

$$\overline{F} = - \frac{kMm}{r^2} \; \frac{\overline{r}}{r} \qquad (2)$$

in bringing the particle from an infinite distance to its present position along the ray through the earth's center, is equal to the negative of the potential.

Solution: Choose the coordinate system in such a way that the ray through the earth's center is the z axis.

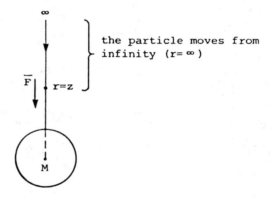

The gravitational potential is then

$$\phi = - \frac{kMm}{z} \qquad (3)$$

and the gravitational force is then

$$\overline{F} = \left(0, \; 0, \; - \frac{kMm}{z^2}\right) \qquad (4)$$

The work done is

$$
\begin{aligned}
\int_C \overline{F} \cdot d\overline{r} &= \int_C F_1 dx + F_2 dy + F_3 dz \\
&= \int F_3 dz = \int_{z=\infty}^{z=r} - \frac{kMm}{z^2} \, dz \\
&= -kMm(-z^{-1}) \Big|_{z=\infty}^{z=r} = -kMm\left(-\frac{1}{r}\right) \\
&= \frac{kMm}{r} = -\phi
\end{aligned}
\qquad (5)
$$

Note that this method enables us to compute the gravitational potential of the earth.

Determine which of the following regions is a domain.
If it is a domain, determine whether or not it is simply
connected.

1. The region D consisting of all points (x,y,z) for
    which $x \geq 0$.

2. The region defining a magnetic field due to a steady
    current flowing along the y axis.

3. The set of all points in the interior of a torus.

4. The set of all points (x,y,z) such that

    $$1 < x^2 + y^2 + z^2 < 9$$

Solution: First, we will repeat some basic definitions.

   Consider a set of points D in the three-dimensional
space. Let a point P belong to D, $P \in D$. We define an ε
neighborhood of P, such that $\varepsilon > 0$, as the set of all points
whose distance from P is less than ε.

   In the plane, an ε neighborhood of P consists of all
points in the interior of a circle of radius ε and center at
P.
   In the three-dimensional space, an ε neighborhood of P
is the interior of a sphere. We say that P is an interior
point of D if it is possible to find an ε neighborhood of P
that lies completely within D. For the circle (see Fig. 1)

$$x^2 + y^2 \leq 1$$

the interior points are all points inside the circle, i.e.
points for which $x^2 + y^2 < 1$. A region is said to be open
if every point in the region is an interior point of the
region.

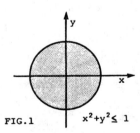

FIG.1 $x^2 + y^2 \leq 1$

   An open region D is said to be connected if, given any
two points A and B in D, there can be found a smooth curve in
D that joins A and B. The region consisting of the two sets
shown in Fig. 2 is not connected, since we cannot join A to
B by a smooth curve that lies completely within the region.
The region consisting of all points in the shaded area of
Fig. 3 is connected.

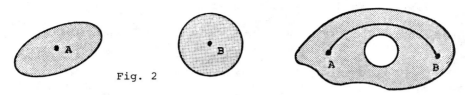

Fig. 2

Fig. 3

A region that is both open and connected is called a domain. Therefore,

1. is open and connected, hence it is a domain

2. The magnetic field is defined everywhere except the y-axis. Thus the region consists of all points for which
$$x^2 + z^2 > 0$$
This region is open and connected, thus it is a domain.

3. The interior of a torus (Fig. 4) is an open set and it is connected. It is therefore a domain.

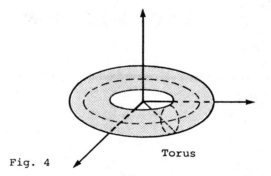

Fig. 4

Torus

4. Here we have two concentric spheres of radii 1 and 3. The region consists of all points outside the inner sphere but inside the outer sphere. It is open and connected and thus it is a domain.

Now, we will define a simply-connected domain. A domain is said to be simply-connected if every closed curve lying in the domain can be continuously shrunk to a point in the domain without any part of the curve passing through regions outside the domain. This simply means that the region in consideration cannot have any "holes" within it. We therefore see that the region of Fig. 5 indicated by a shaded area is not simply-connected. Therefore, for the given regions

Fig. 5

1. This domain is simply-connected.

2. This domain, as explained in Fig. 6, is not simply-connected.

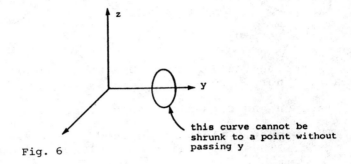

Fig. 6

this curve cannot be shrunk to a point without passing y

3. Not simply-connected.

4. Not simply-connected.

CONSERVATIVE VECTOR FIELDS, SCALAR POTENTIAL

● **PROBLEM** 12-29

Consider a force Field $\overline{F}$ such that

$$\overline{F} = \nabla\phi \qquad (1)$$

where ϕ is a single-valued function with continuous partial derivatives. Show that the work done in moving a particle from a point (x_1, y_1, z_1) to a point (x_2, y_2, z_2) is independent of the path joining the two points.

Solution: We have to show that the work done by the force field $\overline{F} = \nabla\phi$ in moving a particle from point $P_1(x_1, y_1, z_1)$ to $P_2(x_2, y_2, z_2)$ depends only on the position, or the coordinates, of the two points and not on the particular path taken in going from P_1 to P_2.

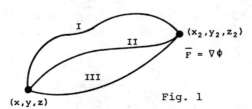

Fig. 1

For example, Fig. 1 illustrates three different paths taken in getting from point $P_1(x_1, y_1, z_1)$ to $P_2(x_2, y_2, z_2)$. To say that the work done in moving the particle from P_1 to P_2 is independant of path is equivalent to saying that

$$W_1 = W_2 = W_3$$

Now, in general, the work done by a force field $\overline{F}$ is given by

$$W = \int_{P_1}^{P_2} \overline{F} \cdot d\overline{r}$$

For $\overline{F}$ given by eq.(1), we have

$$W = \int_{P_1}^{P_2} \nabla\phi \cdot d\overline{r} \qquad (2)$$

$$= \int_{P_1}^{P_2} \left(\frac{\partial\phi}{\partial x} \overline{i} + \frac{\partial\phi}{\partial y} \overline{j} + \frac{\partial\phi}{\partial z} \overline{k} \right) \cdot (dx\overline{i} + dy\overline{j} + dz\overline{k})$$

$$= \int_{P_1}^{P_2} \frac{\partial\phi}{\partial x} dx + \frac{\partial\phi}{\partial y} dy + \frac{\partial\phi}{\partial z} dz$$

$$= \int_{P_1}^{P_2} d\phi = \phi \Big|_{P_1}^{P_2} = \phi(P_2) - \phi(P_1) = \phi(x_2,y_2,z_2) - \phi(x_1,y_1,z_1)$$

Therefore, for $\overline{F} = \nabla\phi$,

$$W = \int_{P_1}^{P_2} \overline{F} \cdot d\overline{r} = \phi(x_2,y_2,z_2) - \phi(x_1,y_1,z_1) \qquad (3)$$

Eq.(3) indicates that the work done by $\overline{F} = \nabla\phi$ in moving a particle from an initial point P_1 to a final point P_2 is equal to the value of the function ϕ at the final point P_2 minus the value of ϕ at the point P_1. In other words, the work done, for $\overline{F} = \nabla\phi$, is solely dependent on the endpoints of the path taken in getting from P_1 to P_2 and not on the path itself.

☛ **PROBLEM 12-30**

Consider a vector field $\overline{F}$ such that the line integral

$$\int_C \overline{F} \cdot d\overline{r} \qquad (1)$$

is independent of the path C joining any two points. Show that there exists a function ϕ such that

$$\overline{F} = \nabla\phi \qquad (2)$$

<u>Solution</u>: If the line integral $\int_C \overline{F} \cdot d\overline{r}$ is independent of the path C joining any two points, which we may take as (x_1, y_1, z_1) and (x,y,z), then the function

$$\phi(x,y,z) = \int_{(x_1,y_1,z_1)}^{(x,y,z)} \overline{F} \cdot d\overline{r} = \int_{(x_1,y_1,z_1)}^{(x,y,z)} F_1 dx + F_2 dy + F_3 dz \qquad (3)$$

is independent of the path joining points (x_1, y_1, z_1) and (x,y,z). Thus, we can write that

$$\phi(x+\Delta x, y, z) - \phi(x, y, z)$$

$$= \int_{(x_1,y_1,z_1)}^{(x+\Delta x, y, z)} \overline{F} \cdot d\overline{r} - \int_{(x_1,y_1,z_1)}^{(x,y,z)} \overline{F} \cdot d\overline{r}$$

$$= \int_{(x,y,z)}^{(x_1,y_1,z_1)} \overline{F} \cdot d\overline{r} + \int_{(x_1,y_1,z_1)}^{(x+\Delta x, y, z)} \overline{F} \cdot d\overline{r} \qquad (4)$$

$$= \int_{(x,y,z)}^{(x+\Delta x, y, z)} \overline{F} \cdot d\overline{r} = \int_{(x,y,z)}^{(x+\Delta x, y, z)} F_1 dx + F_2 dy + F_3 dz$$

By hypothesis the last integral is independent of the path joining the points $(x+\Delta x, y, z)$ and (x,y,z), and we can therefore choose the path to be a straight line joining these points - so that

$$dy = dz = 0 \qquad (5)$$

and

$$\frac{\phi(x+\Delta x, y, z) - \phi(x,y,z)}{\Delta x} = \frac{1}{\Delta x} \int_{(x,y,z)}^{(x+\Delta x, y, z)} F_1 dx \qquad (6)$$

Taking the limit as $\Delta x \rightarrow 0$ of both sides of eq.(6) leads to

$$\frac{\partial \phi}{\partial x} = F_1 \qquad (7)$$

In a similar manner, we can show that

$$\frac{\partial \phi}{\partial y} = F_2 \quad \text{and} \quad \frac{\partial \phi}{\partial z} = F_3 \qquad (8)$$

Thus

$$\overline{F} = F_1 \overline{i} + F_2 \overline{j} + F_3 \overline{k} = \nabla \phi \qquad (9)$$

Vector field $\overline{F}$, such that $\int_{A_1}^{A_2} \overline{F} \cdot d\overline{r}$ is independent of the path C joining A_1 and A_2, is called a conservative field. The results of Problem 12-24 and 12-25 can be written as

$$\begin{pmatrix} \text{vector field } \bar{F} \\ \text{is conservative} \end{pmatrix} \quad \overset{\text{if and only if}}{\Longleftrightarrow} \quad \begin{pmatrix} \text{there exists} \\ \phi \text{ such that} \\ \bar{F} = \nabla\phi \end{pmatrix}$$

We can prove the above theorem by using vectors. If the line integral is independent of the path, then

$$\phi(x,y,z) = \int_{(x_1,y_1,z_1)}^{(x,y,z)} \bar{F} \cdot d\bar{r} = \int_{(x_1,y_1,z_1)}^{(x,y,z)} \bar{F} \cdot \frac{d\bar{r}}{ds} \, ds \quad (10)$$

Differentiating eq.(10) results in

$$\frac{d\phi}{ds} = \bar{F} \cdot \frac{d\bar{r}}{ds} \quad (11)$$

The left-hand side of eq.(11) is equal to

$$\frac{d\phi}{ds} = \nabla\phi \cdot \frac{d\bar{r}}{ds} \quad (12)$$

Combining eqs.(11) and (12) leads to

$$(\nabla\phi - \bar{F}) \cdot \frac{d\bar{r}}{ds} = 0 \quad (13)$$

Now, since eq.(13) holds true for any $\frac{d\bar{r}}{ds}$, we conclude that

$$\bar{F} = \nabla\phi \quad (14)$$

● **PROBLEM 12-31**

Show that the vector field

$$\bar{F} = xy\bar{i} + x^2y\bar{j} \quad (1)$$

is not conservative.

Solution: A vector field $\bar{F}$ is said to be conservative in a domain D (see Problem 12-28) if there exists some scalar field ϕ defined in D such that

$$\bar{F} = \nabla\phi \quad (2)$$

ϕ is called a potential for $\bar{F}$. Now, consider the following fundamental theorem:

A vector field $\bar{F}$, continuous in a domain D is conservative if and only if the line integral of the tangential component of $\bar{F}$ along every regular curve in D depends only on the endpoints of the curve. We have then,

$$\int_C \bar{F} \cdot d\bar{r} = \phi(A) - \phi(B) \quad (3)$$

where A and B are the terminal and initial points of the curve C respectively. To show that the vector field given by eq.(1) is not conservative, compute the line integral of $\overline{F}$ along two different paths, both of which have (0,0) and (1,1) as the initial and final points respectively.

As the first path, choose the line segment $y = x$ joining points (0,0) and (1,1). For this path,

$$dx = dy \qquad (4)$$

and the line integral is

$$\int_C \overline{F} \cdot d\overline{r} = \int_C xydx + x^2ydy$$

$$= \int_0^1 (x^2 + x^3)dx = \left(\frac{x^3}{3} + \frac{x^4}{4}\right)\Bigg|_0^1 \qquad (5)$$

$$= \frac{1}{3} + \frac{1}{4} = \frac{7}{12}$$

Note that x changes from 0 to 1.

Now, take the second path along the curve

$$y = x^2 \qquad (6)$$

so that

$$dy = 2xdx$$

The line integral for this path is

$$\int_C \overline{F} \cdot d\overline{r} = \int_C xydx + x^2ydy = \int_0^1 xx^2dx + x^2x^2 2xdx$$

$$\qquad (7)$$

$$= \int_0^1 (x^3 + 2x^5)dx = \left(\frac{x^4}{4} + \frac{x^6}{3}\right)\Bigg|_0^1 = \frac{1}{4} + \frac{1}{3} = \frac{7}{12}$$

Note that both integrals along the first and second paths are equal. Thus, we have yet to prove that the field $\overline{F}$ is not conservative. We will now try a third path -- the path shown in the figure.

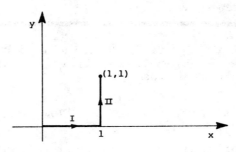

Along the first segment I, $y = 0$ and therefore the integral is

$$(8)$$

$$\int_{C_I} \overline{F} \cdot d\overline{r} = \int_{C_I} xydx + x^2ydy = 0 \qquad (9)$$

Along the second segment II,

$$x = 1 \quad \text{and} \quad dx = 0 \tag{10}$$

as y changes from 0 to 1. Therefore,

$$\int_{C_{II}} \overline{F} \cdot d\overline{r} = \int_0^1 ydy = \frac{y^2}{2} \bigg|_0^1 = \frac{1}{2} \tag{11}$$

and the line integral for the curve consisting of segments I and II is

$$\int_C \overline{F} \cdot d\overline{r} = \frac{1}{2}$$

This time we were fortunate -- for we obtained different values for the line integrals along two different paths with the same initial and terminal points; which leads us to conclude that the force field given by eq.(1) is not conservative.

Note that this is not the most efficient method of determining whether a given field is not conservative (or conservative). Also note that we can, by coincidence, obtain equal line integrals for different paths even though the corresponding force field is not conservative (as exemplified by the two particular paths chosen in this problem). A more efficient method of determining whether a force field is conservative or not will be discussed later in the book.

● **PROBLEM 12-32**

Evaluate the line integral

$$\int_C \overline{F} \cdot d\overline{r} \tag{1}$$

where

$$\overline{F} = \cos h\, x\overline{i} + 6yz^2\overline{j} + 6y^2z\overline{k} \tag{2}$$

between the points $(0,0,0)$ and $(2,4,2)$ along the curve given by the parametric equations

$$x = t^2 + 1$$

$$y = 3t^2 + \sqrt{t} \tag{3}$$

$$z = t^3 + t$$

Solution: Before proceeding with the standard procedure of directly computing the line integral, which was the procedure in previous examples, note that if $\overline{F}$, as given by eq.(2), were conservative, then we could use the fact that the line integral is independent of path, and

$$\int_{P_1}^{P_2} \overline{F} \cdot d\overline{r} = \phi(P_2) - \phi(P_1) \tag{4}$$

559

where
$$\overline{F} = \nabla\phi = \text{grad } \phi$$

Consequently, if we can find a potential ϕ for $\overline{F}$ (as given by eq.(2)), then we could use eq.(4) to determine the value of the line integral for $P_1 = (0,0,0)$ and $P_2 = (2,4,2)$. If a function ϕ is not obtainable, then we would have to resort to the actual lengthy calculation of finding the line integral along the curve given by eq.(3).

Assuming ϕ does exist, we obtain, from
$$\overline{F} = \nabla\phi, \tag{5}$$
the following
$$\cosh x = \frac{\partial\phi}{\partial x} \tag{6}$$

$$6yz^2 = \frac{\partial\phi}{\partial y} \tag{7}$$

$$6y^2z = \frac{\partial\phi}{\partial z} \tag{8}$$

Integrating eq.(6) leads to
$$\phi(x,y,z) = \sinh x + \psi(y,z) \tag{9}$$

and since $\sinh x$ is a function of x only, differentiating ϕ with respect to y gives
$$\frac{\partial\phi}{\partial y} = \frac{\partial\psi}{\partial y} \tag{10}$$

Substituting eq.(7) into eq.(10) yields
$$6yz^2 = \frac{\partial\psi}{\partial y}$$

Now, integrating gives
$$\psi(y,z) = 3y^2z^2 + \zeta(z) \tag{11}$$

From eq.(8) we conclude that
$$\zeta(z) = 0$$

Thus, the potential of $\overline{F}$ is found to be
$$\phi(x,y,z) = \sinh x + 3y^2z^2 \tag{12}$$

and the line integral is therefore
$$\int_C \overline{F} \cdot d\overline{r} = \phi(2,4,2) - \phi(0,0,0) \tag{13}$$

Now, since
$$\sinh x = \frac{e^x - e^{-x}}{2} \tag{14}$$

we have
$$\phi(2,4,2) - \phi(0,0,0) = \sinh 2 + 3\cdot16\cdot4$$
$$= \frac{e^2 - e^{-2}}{2} + 192 \tag{15}$$

The same result can be obtained by integrating $\overline{F}$ along the
path given by eq.(3).

Prove the following theorem

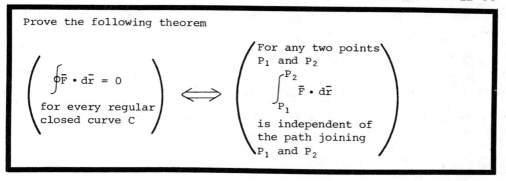

$$\left(\begin{array}{l} \oint \overline{F} \cdot d\overline{r} = 0 \\[10pt] \text{for every regular} \\ \text{closed curve } C \end{array}\right) \iff \left(\begin{array}{l} \text{For any two points} \\ P_1 \text{ and } P_2 \\ \displaystyle\int_{P_1}^{P_2} \overline{F} \cdot d\overline{r} \\ \text{is independent of} \\ \text{the path joining} \\ P_1 \text{ and } P_2 \end{array}\right)$$

<u>Solution</u>: The symbol ⇔ means "if and only if". To prove
the above theorem, it must be proven that

1. if the left-hand side is true, that implies that the
    right-hand side is true;

2. if the right-hand side is true, that implies that the
    left-hand side is true.

1. For the first part of the theorem, begin by assuming that

$$\oint_C \overline{F} \cdot d\overline{r} = 0 \tag{1}$$

for any closed curve, and let P_1 and P_2 be any two points in
the domain.

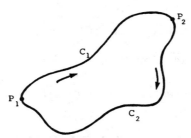

New let C_1 and C_2 be any two arbitrary paths joining points
P_1 and P_2. As indicated by (1), it must be shown that the
line integral is independent of the path of integration.

Now, note that

$$\oint_{C_1+C_2} \overline{F} \cdot d\overline{r} = \int_{C_1} \overline{F} \cdot d\overline{r} + \int_{C_2} \overline{F} \cdot d\overline{r}$$
$$\qquad\qquad \underset{\substack{\text{from } P_1 \\ \text{to } P_2}}{} \qquad \underset{\substack{\text{from } P_2 \\ \text{to } P_1}}{}$$

$$= \int_{C_1} \overline{F} \cdot d\overline{r} - \int_{C_2} \overline{F} \cdot d\overline{r} = 0 \qquad (2)$$

from P_1 from P_1

to P_2 to P_2

Thus,

$$\int_{C_1} \overline{F} \cdot d\overline{r} = \int_{C_2} \overline{F} \cdot d\overline{r} \qquad (3)$$

and this completes the first part of the proof.

2. Now, to see if the converse is true, assume that

$$\int_{P_1}^{P_2} \overline{F} \cdot d\overline{r} \qquad (4)$$

is independent of the path of integration.

Now, take any closed path containing the two points P_1 and P_2. Then we can write

$$\oint_{C_1+C_2} \overline{F} \cdot d\overline{r} = \int_{C_1} \overline{F} \cdot d\overline{r} + \int_{C_2} \overline{F} \cdot d\overline{r}$$

from P_1 from P_2

to P_2 to P_1

$$(5)$$

$$= \int_{C_1} \overline{F} \cdot d\overline{r} - \int_{C_2} \overline{F} \cdot d\overline{r} = 0$$

from P_1 from P_1

to P_2 to P_2

Since, by hypothesis, both integrals

$$\int_{C_1} \overline{F} \cdot d\overline{r} \quad \text{and} \quad \int_{C_2} \overline{F} \cdot d\overline{r}$$

are equal. This completes the proof of the theorem.

CURL OF A CONSERVATIVE FIELD

● PROBLEM 12-34

Show that a vector field $\overline{F}$ is conservative if and only if

$$\text{curl } \overline{F} = \overline{0} \qquad (1)$$

where the domain D of $\overline{F}$ is simply connected.

Solution: First, we will assume that the vector field $\overline{F}$ is conservative and then subsequently show that curl $\overline{F} = \overline{0}$ for such a field.

From Problem 12-30, we know that if a vector field $\overline{F}$ is conservative, then there exists a scalar field ϕ such that

$$\overline{F} = \nabla\phi \tag{2}$$

Taking the curl of both sides of eq.(2) leads to

$$\text{curl } \overline{F} = \nabla \times \overline{F} = \nabla \times (\nabla\phi) = \overline{0} \tag{3}$$

Since, for any scalar function f

$$\text{curl grad } f = \overline{0}. \tag{4}$$

Therefore, we see that if $\overline{F}$ is conservative, then

$$\text{curl } \overline{F} = \overline{0}.$$

Now, we will check to see if the converse is true -- that is, if curl $\overline{F} = 0$, then $\overline{F}$ is conservative.

To show this, obtain
$$\text{curl } \overline{F} = \left(\frac{\partial F_3}{\partial y} - \frac{\partial F_2}{\partial z}, \frac{\partial F_1}{\partial z} - \frac{\partial F_3}{\partial x}, \frac{\partial F_2}{\partial x} - \frac{\partial F_1}{\partial y} \right) = \overline{0} \tag{5}$$

or

$$\frac{\partial F_3}{\partial y} = \frac{\partial F_2}{\partial z}$$

$$\frac{\partial F_1}{\partial z} = \frac{\partial F_3}{\partial x} \tag{6}$$

$$\frac{\partial F_2}{\partial x} = \frac{\partial F_1}{\partial y}$$

Now, consider the line integral from (x_0, y_0, z_0) to (x, y, z) along a path C,

$$\int_C \overline{F} \cdot d\overline{r} = \int_C F_1(x,y,z)dx + F_2(x,y,z)dy + F_3(x,y,z)dz \tag{7}$$

We define a scalar function $\phi(x,y,z)$ such that

$$\phi(x,y,z) = \int_C \overline{F} \cdot d\overline{r} \tag{8}$$

and let the path C consist of the line segments

from (x_0, y_0, z_0) to (x, y_0, z_0)

from (x, y_0, z_0) to (x, y, z_0)

from (x, y, z_0) to (x, y, z)

The line integral in eq.(7) becomes

$$\phi(x,y,z) = \int_{x_0}^{x} F_1(x, y_0, z_0)dx + \int_{y_0}^{y} F_2(x, y, z_0)dy$$

$$+ \int_{z_0}^{z} F_3(x, y, z)dz \tag{9}$$

Differentiating eq.(9) with respect to z results in

$$\frac{\partial \phi}{\partial z} = F_3(x,y,z) \tag{10}$$

Differentiating eq.(9) with respect to y gives

$$\begin{aligned}
\frac{\partial \phi}{\partial y} &= F_2(x,y,z_0) + \int_{z_0}^{z} \frac{\partial F_3}{\partial y}(x,y,z)dz \\
&= F_2(x,y,z_0) + \int_{z_0}^{z} \frac{\partial F_2}{\partial z}(x,y,z)dz \\
&= F_2(x,y,z_0) + F_2(x,y,z) \Big|_{z_0}^{z} \\
&= F_2(x,y,z_0) + F_2(x,y,z) - F_2(x,y,z_0) = F_2(x,y,z)
\end{aligned} \tag{11}$$

Finally, differentiating eq.(9) with respect to x and using eq.(6) gives

$$\begin{aligned}
\frac{\partial \phi}{\partial x} &= F_1(x,y_0,z_0) + \int_{y_0}^{y} \frac{\partial F_2}{\partial x}(x,y,z_0)dy + \int_{z_0}^{z} \frac{\partial F_3}{\partial x}(x,y,z)dz \\
&= F_1(x,y_0,z_0) + \int_{y_0}^{y} \frac{\partial F_1}{\partial y}(x,y,z_0)dy + \int_{z_0}^{z} \frac{\partial F_1}{\partial x}(x,y,z)dz \\
&= F_1(x,y_0,z_0) + F_1(x,y,z_0) \Big|_{y_0}^{y} + F_1(x,y,z) \Big|_{z_0}^{z} \\
&= F_1(x,y,z)
\end{aligned} \tag{12}$$

Thus proving that

$$\overline{F} = F_1 \overline{i} + F_2 \overline{j} + F_3 \overline{k} = \frac{\partial \phi}{\partial x} \overline{i} + \frac{\partial \phi}{\partial y} \overline{j} + \frac{\partial \phi}{\partial z} \overline{k} \tag{13}$$

or

$$\overline{F} = \nabla \phi,$$

from which we conclude that $\overline{F}$ is conservative.

Therefore, a necessary and sufficient condition for a vector field $\overline{F}$ to be conservative is that $\nabla \times \overline{F} = \overline{0}$.

● **PROBLEM 12-35**

Using the curl $\overline{F}$ criterion, determine if the vector field

$$\overline{F} = x^2 y \overline{i} + yx \overline{j} + z^2 \overline{k} \tag{1}$$

is conservative.

Solution: We will use the following theorem to determine whether the given vector field $\overline{F}$ is conservative.

Theorem

A vector field $\overline{F}$, defined in a simply-connected domain D and having continuous partial derivatives, is conservative if and only if curl $\overline{F} = \overline{0}$, throughout D.

For the most part, it is usually assumed that $\overline{F}$ is defined over a simply-connected domain and we consequently neglect to mention it.

Before proceeding, for purposes of clarity, it would be wise to list all the necessary conditions for a vector field $\overline{F}$ to be conservative.

A vector field $\overline{F}$ is conservative if and only if $\overline{F}$ possesses any one of the following properties:

I. curl $\overline{F} = \overline{0}$

II. Its integral along any regular curve from a point A to a point B is independent of the path.

III. It is the gradient of a scalar function,

$\overline{F} = \text{grad } \phi$.

IV. It's integral around any regular closed curve is zero.

Note that any one of the above properties implies the other three properties. Hence, a vector field satisfying any one of the above properties also satisfies all of the properties.

Thus, to determine if the vector field given by eq.(1) is conservative, it is sufficient to check if it possesses any one of the above properties.

Let us take $\overline{F}$ as given by eq.(1) and compute curl $\overline{F}$ to obtain

$$\nabla \times \overline{F} = \left(\frac{\partial}{\partial x}, \ \frac{\partial}{\partial y}, \ \frac{\partial}{\partial z} \right) \times (x^2 y, \ xy, \ z^2) \tag{2}$$

$$= \left(\frac{\partial}{\partial y} z^2 - \frac{\partial}{\partial z} xy, \ \frac{\partial}{\partial z} x^2 y - \frac{\partial}{\partial x} z^2, \ \frac{\partial}{\partial x} xy - \frac{\partial}{\partial y} x^2 y \right)$$

$$= (0, \ 0, \ y - x^2)$$

Since $$\text{curl } \overline{F} \neq \overline{0}, \tag{3}$$

it is concluded that the given vector field is not conservative.

● **PROBLEM** 12-36

Find the path C between the points (2,1,3) and (4,2,7) for which the line integral

$$\int_c \overline{F} \cdot d\overline{r} \tag{1}$$

where $$\overline{F} = e^x y \overline{i} + (e^x + 2yz^2)\overline{j} + 2y^2 z \overline{k},$$

reaches its minimum value.

Solution: Before starting to look for the required path $\dot{C}$, first check the value of curl $\overline{F}$.

$$\text{curl } \overline{F} = \nabla \times \overline{F} = \left[\frac{\partial}{\partial y} 2y^2z - \frac{\partial}{\partial z}(e^x + 2yz^2), \ \frac{\partial}{\partial z} e^x y - \frac{\partial}{\partial x} 2y^2z, \right.$$

$$\left. \frac{\partial}{\partial x}(e^x + 2yz^2) - \frac{\partial}{\partial y} e^x y \right] \tag{2}$$

$$= (4yz - 4yz, \ 0, \ e^x - e^x) = \overline{0}$$

Since curl $\overline{F} = \overline{0}$, it is concluded that the given vector field $\overline{F}$ is conservative; therefore, the value of the line integral does not depend on the path C -- which is equivalent saying that the line integral is the same for all paths joining the points $(2,1,3)$ and $(4,2,7)$.

Consequently, there is no particular path C for which the line integral has a minimum value, since indeed, it has a constant value between the given endpoints.

To find the actual value of the line integral, note that since $\overline{F}$ is conservative, we have

$$\int_C \overline{F} \cdot d\overline{r} = \int_C \nabla\phi \cdot d\overline{r} = \int_C d\phi = \phi(B) - \phi(A) \tag{3}$$

Now, to find ϕ, use eq.(9) of Problem 12-34. This gives

$$\phi(x,y,z) = \int_{x_0}^{x} F_1(x,y_0,z_0)dx + \int_{y_0}^{y} F_2(x,y,z_0)dy$$

$$+ \int_{z_0}^{z} F_3(x,y,z)dz$$

$$= \int_{x_0}^{x} y_0 e^x dx + \int_{y_0}^{y} (e^x + 2yz_0^2)dy + \int_{z_0}^{z} 2y^2z\,dz$$

$$= y_0 e^x \Big|_{x_0}^{x} + (e^x y + y^2 z_0^2) \Big|_{y_0}^{y} + y^2 z^2 \Big|_{z_0}^{z} \tag{4}$$

$$= y_0 e^x - y_0 e^{x_0} + e^x y - e^x y_0 + y^2 z_0^2 - y_0^2 z_0^2 + y^2 z^2 - y^2 z_0^2$$

$$= ye^x + y^2 z^2 + (-y_0 e^{x_0} - y_0^2 z_0^2)$$

$$= ye^x + y^2 z^2 + const$$

Having $\phi(x,y,z)$, we can now find the value of the line integral:

$$\int_C \overline{F} \cdot d\overline{r} = \phi(B) - \phi(A) = \phi(4,2,7,) - \phi(2,1,3,)$$

$$= 2e^4 + 196 - (e^2 + 9) = 2e^4 - e^2 + 187 \tag{5}$$

Thus the value of the line integral $\int_C \overline{F} \cdot d\overline{r}$ between the points $(2,1,3)$ and $(4,2,7)$ is the same for all paths and is equal to $2e^4 - e^2 + 187$.

1. Determine whether the vector field

$$\overline{F} = r\,\overline{r} \qquad (1)$$

is conservative and evaluate $\oint_c \overline{F} \cdot d\overline{r}$ along any simple closed curve.

2. Determine whether the vector field

$$\overline{F} = r^2\overline{r} \qquad (2)$$

is conservative. If it is, then determine its scalar potential.

__Solution__: 1. To find out if the vector field $\overline{F} = r\,\overline{r}$ is conservative, use the curl $\overline{F}$ criterion.

For curl $\overline{F}$, obtain

$$\nabla \times \overline{F} = \left(\frac{\partial}{\partial x},\ \frac{\partial}{\partial y},\ \frac{\partial}{\partial z}\right) \times \left[x\sqrt{x^2+y^2+z^2},\ y\sqrt{x^2+y^2+z^2},\ z\sqrt{x^2+y^2+z^2}\right]$$

$$(3)$$

$$= \left(\frac{\partial}{\partial y}z\sqrt{x^2+y^2+z^2} - \frac{\partial}{\partial z}y\sqrt{x^2+y^2+z^2},\ \frac{\partial}{\partial z}x\sqrt{x^2+y^2+z^2} - \frac{\partial}{\partial x}z\sqrt{x^2+y^2+z^2},\right.$$

$$\left.\frac{\partial}{\partial x}y\sqrt{x^2+y^2+z^2} - \frac{\partial}{\partial y}x\sqrt{x^2+y^2+z^2}\right)$$

$$= (0,0,0) = \overline{0}$$

Since curl $\overline{F} = 0$, it is concluded that $\overline{F}$ is a conservative vector field, and consequently a scalar function ϕ (the scalar potential of $\overline{F}$) exists such that

$$\overline{F} = \nabla\phi \qquad (4)$$

or

$$\frac{\partial\phi}{\partial x} = x\sqrt{x^2+y^2+z^2} \qquad (5)$$

$$\frac{\partial\phi}{\partial y} = y\sqrt{x^2+y^2+z^2} \qquad (6)$$

$$\frac{\partial\phi}{\partial z} = z\sqrt{x^2+y^2+z^2} \qquad (7)$$

Now, to find ϕ, integrate eq.(5)

$$\phi(x,y,z) = \frac{1}{3}(x^2+y^2+z^2)^{\frac{3}{2}} + f(y,z) \qquad (8)$$

Partially differentiating eq.(8) with respect to y gives

$$\frac{\partial\phi}{\partial y} = y\sqrt{x^2+y^2+z^2} + \frac{\partial f}{\partial y} \qquad (9)$$

Comparing eq.(6) with eq.(9) results in

$$\frac{\partial f}{\partial y} = 0 \qquad (10)$$

or

$$f = f(z)$$

Taking the partial derivative of eq.(8) with respect to z gives

$$\frac{\partial \phi}{\partial z} = z(x^2 + y^2 + z^2) + \frac{\partial f}{\partial z} \tag{11}$$

Comparing eq.(7) with eq.(11) leads to

$$\frac{\partial f}{\partial z} = 0 \tag{12}$$

or
$$f = \text{const}$$

Thus.
$$\phi(x,y,z) = \frac{1}{3}(x^2 + y^2 + z^2)^{\frac{3}{2}} + \text{const}$$

$$= \frac{r^3}{3} + \text{const} \tag{13}$$

Now, since $\overline{F} = r \, \overline{r}$ is a conservative field, its line integral along any closed curve is equal to zero.

$$\int_C \overline{F} \cdot d\overline{r} = 0 \tag{14}$$

2. As in Part I, proceed by evaluating curl $\overline{F}$.

$$\text{curl } \overline{F} = \nabla \times \overline{F} = \left(\frac{\partial}{\partial x}, \frac{\partial}{\partial y}, \frac{\partial}{\partial z}\right) \times \left[x(x^2 + y^2 + z^2), y(x^2 + y^2 + z^2),\right.$$

$$\left. z(x^2 + y^2 + z^2)\right]$$

$$= \left[\frac{\partial}{\partial y}z(x^2 + y^2 + z^2) - \frac{\partial}{\partial z}y(x^2 + y^2 + z^2), \frac{\partial}{\partial z}x(x^2 + y^2 + z^2) - \frac{\partial}{\partial x}z(x^2 + y^2 + z^2),\right.$$

$$\left. \frac{\partial}{\partial x}y(x^2 + y^2 + z^2) - \frac{\partial}{\partial y}x(x^2 + y^2 + z^2)\right]$$

$$= (z2y - y2z, \; x2z - z2x, \; y2x - x2y) = \overline{0} \tag{15}$$

Thus, the vector field $\overline{F} = r^2\overline{r}$ is conservative, and we may write

$$\overline{F} = \nabla \phi \tag{16}$$

or
$$\frac{\partial \phi}{\partial x} = x(x^2 + y^2 + z^2) \tag{17}$$

$$\frac{\partial \phi}{\partial y} = y(x^2 + y^2 + z^2) \tag{18}$$

$$\frac{\partial \phi}{\partial z} = z(x^2 + y^2 + z^2) \tag{19}$$

Integrating eq.(17) results in

$$\phi(x,y,z) = \frac{(x^2 + y^2 + z^2)^2}{4} + f(y,z) \tag{20}$$

Substituting eq.(20) into eqs.(18) and (19) leads to

$$\phi(x,y,z) = \frac{(x^2 + y^2 + z^2)^2}{4} + \text{const}$$

$$\tag{21}$$

$$= \frac{r^4}{4} + \text{const}$$

Show that the vector field $\overline{F}$

$$\overline{F} = e^x \overline{i} + z^2 \overline{j} + 2yz\overline{k} \tag{1}$$

is conservative and find its scalar potential.

Solution: From Problem 12-34, it is known that a vector field $\overline{F}$ is conservative if, and only if

$$\nabla \times \overline{F} = \overline{0}. \tag{2}$$

The curl of $\overline{F}$ given by eq.(1) is, using the matrix form of the cross product,

$$\nabla \times \overline{F} = \begin{vmatrix} \overline{i} & \overline{j} & \overline{k} \\ \dfrac{\partial}{\partial x} & \dfrac{\partial}{\partial y} & \dfrac{\partial}{\partial z} \\ e^x & z^2 & 2yz \end{vmatrix} \tag{3}$$

$$= (2z-2z)\overline{i} + (0+0)\overline{j} + (0+0)\overline{k} = \overline{0}$$

Thus, the vector field given by eq.(1) is conservative.

Now we must find the scalar potential ϕ such that

$$\overline{F} = \nabla\phi, \tag{4}$$

or

$$\frac{\partial\phi}{\partial x} = e^x \tag{5}$$

$$\frac{\partial\phi}{\partial y} = z^2 \tag{6}$$

$$\frac{\partial\phi}{\partial z} = 2yz \tag{7}$$

Integrating eq.(5) results in

$$\phi(x,y,z) = e^x + f(y,z) \tag{8}$$

Substituting eq.(8) into eq.(6) gives

$$\frac{\partial f}{\partial y} = z^2 \tag{9}$$

Integrating eq.(9) leads to

$$f(y,z) = z^2y + g(z) \tag{10}$$

Substituting eq.(10) into eq.(7) gives

$$\frac{\partial\phi}{\partial z} = \frac{\partial f}{\partial z} = 2yz + \frac{\partial g}{\partial z} = 2yz \tag{11}$$

Thus, since $\dfrac{\partial g(z)}{\partial z} = 0$, $g(z) =$ const and therefore

$$\phi(x,y,z) = e^X + z^2y + \text{const} \qquad (12)$$

The above procedure is usually the method used when determining the scalar potential of a given vector field.

Another method that may be used, however, is by taking the dot product of

$$\overline{F} = \nabla\phi$$

with vector $d\overline{r}$ to give

$$\overline{F} \cdot d\overline{r} = \nabla\phi \cdot d\overline{r}$$

$$= \frac{\partial\phi}{\partial x} dx + \frac{\partial\phi}{\partial y} dy + \frac{\partial\phi}{\partial z} dz = d\phi \qquad (13)$$

For $\overline{F}$ as given by eq.(1), one obtains

$$d\phi = e^X dx + z^2 dy + 2yz dz$$

$$= d(e^X) + d(yz^2) = d(e^X + yz^2) \qquad (14)$$

and thus

$$\phi(x,y,z) = e^X + yz^2 + \text{const} \qquad (15)$$

Finally, there is a third method of finding $\phi(x,y,z)$ - the method described in Problem 12-34.

Since $\overline{F}$ is conservative, the integral $\int_C \overline{F} \cdot d\overline{r}$ is independent of the path C joining (x_0,y_0,z_0) and (x,y,z). Therefore

$$\phi(x,y,z) = \int_C \overline{F} \cdot d\overline{r} \qquad (16)$$

$$= \int_{x_0}^{x} e^X dx + \int_{y_0}^{y} z_0^2 dy + \int_{z_0}^{z} 2yz\, dz$$

$$= e^X \Big|_{x_0}^{x} + z_0^2 y \Big|_{y_0}^{y} + yz^2 \Big|_{z_0}^{z}$$

$$= e^X - e^{X_0} + z_0^2 y - z_0^2 y_0 + yz^2 - yz_0^2$$

$$= e^X + yz^2 + (-e^{X_0} - z_0^2 y_0) = e^X + yz^2 + \text{const}$$

● **PROBLEM 12-39**

Consider the following vector field

$$\overline{F} = \frac{-y\overline{i} + x\overline{j}}{x^2 + y^2} \qquad (1)$$

Determine whether this field is conservative.

<u>Solution</u>: The usual procedure followed in determining whether a given vector field $\overline{F}$ is conservative is to first determine if curl $\overline{F}$ is equal to zero. For $\overline{F}$ given by eq.(1), we have

$$\nabla \times \overline{F} = \left(\frac{\partial}{\partial x}, \frac{\partial}{\partial y}, \frac{\partial}{\partial z}\right) \times \left(\frac{-y}{x^2+y^2}, \frac{x}{x^2+y^2}, 0\right)$$

$$= \left[0, 0, \frac{\partial}{\partial x}\left(\frac{x}{x^2+y^2}\right) - \frac{\partial}{\partial y}\left(\frac{-y}{x^2+y^2}\right)\right] \quad (2)$$

$$= (0, 0, 0)$$

$$= \overline{0}$$

Now, since curl $\overline{F} = \overline{0}$, it seems that the curl $\overline{F}$ criterion is satisfied and we would ordinarily conclude that $\overline{F}$ is conservative. Note, however, that a fundamental requirement for any vector field to be conservative is that the domain over which the field exists must be simply connected (see Problem 12-35). Since the given field

$$\overline{F} = \frac{-y\overline{i}+x\overline{j}}{x^2+y^2}$$

is undefined when $x=y=0$ (along the z axis) we conclude that the domain of $\overline{F}$ is not simply connected, and consequently, $\overline{F}$ is not a conservative vector field. Note that the curl $\overline{F}$ criterion holds true only for a vector field defined over a simply connected domain -- thus, though curl $\overline{F}$ may equal zero, the criterion cannot be used if the domain is not simply connected (if $\overline{F}$ is not defined on some point in the domain).

To verify that $\overline{F}$ is not conservative, compute $\oint \overline{F} \cdot d\overline{r}$

around some closed curve C and determine whether or not the integral is equal to zero. If the integral is not equal to zero, then we would conclude that $\overline{F}$ is not conservative, since for a conservative field,

$$\oint_C \overline{F} \cdot d\overline{r} = 0.$$

Now, for the closed curve C, let us choose a circle of radius r which is centered at the origin. We have

$$x = r \cos\theta$$
$$\qquad\qquad\qquad\qquad (4)$$
$$y = r \sin\theta$$

and the differentials are

$$dx = -r \sin\theta d\theta$$
$$\qquad\qquad\qquad\qquad (5)$$
$$dy = r \cos\theta d\theta$$

The line integral around the circle is then

$$\overline{F} \cdot d\overline{r} = \oint \frac{-y}{x^2+y^2} dx + \frac{x}{x^2+y^2} dy$$

$$= \oint \frac{r\sin\theta}{r^2} r\sin\theta d\theta + \frac{r\cos\theta}{r^2} r\cos\theta d\theta \quad (6)$$

$$= \int_0^{2\pi} (\sin^2\theta+\cos^2\theta)d\theta = \int_0^{2\pi} d\theta = \theta \Big|_0^{2\pi}$$

$$= 2\pi$$

Notice that since

$$\oint \overline{F} \cdot d\overline{r} \neq 0,$$

we have verified that

$$\overline{F} = \frac{-y\overline{i} + x\overline{j}}{x^2+y^2}$$

is not a conservative field.

EXACT DIFFERENTIALS, PARTICLE IN THE CONSERVATIVE FIELD AND VECTOR POTENTIAL

● PROBLEM 12-40

An exact differential of a function $\phi(x,y,z)$ is

$$d\phi = \frac{\partial \phi}{\partial x} dx + \frac{\partial \phi}{\partial y} dy + \frac{\partial \phi}{\partial z} dz \qquad (1)$$

1. Let

$$\overline{F} = F_1\overline{i} + F_2\overline{j} + F_3\overline{k} \qquad (2)$$

Show that a necessary and sufficient condition that $F_1 dx + F_2 dy + F_3 dz$ be an exact differential is that $\nabla \times \overline{F} = \overline{0}$.

2. Find ϕ such that

$$(2xy+y^3\cos z)dx + (x^2+3xy^2\cos z)dy - xy^3\sin z\,dz \qquad (3)$$

is an exact differential of ϕ.

Solution: First, assume that $F_1 dx + F_2 dy + F_3 dz$ is an exact differential. Then,

$$F_1 dx + F_2 dy + F_3 dz = d\phi = \frac{\partial \phi}{\partial x} dx + \frac{\partial \phi}{\partial y} dy + \frac{\partial \phi}{\partial z} dz \qquad (4)$$

from which we obtain

$$F_1 = \frac{\partial \phi}{\partial x}, \qquad F_2 = \frac{\partial \phi}{\partial y}, \qquad F_3 = \frac{\partial \phi}{\partial z} \qquad (5)$$

and

$$\overline{F} = \nabla\phi. \qquad (6)$$

Now, obtain

$$\nabla \times \overline{F} = \nabla \times (\nabla\phi) = \overline{0} \qquad (7)$$

which completes the first part of the proof, in other words, if

$$\overline{F} = F_1\overline{i} + F_2\overline{j} + F_3\overline{k}$$

then

$$F_1 dx + F_2 dy + F_3 dz$$

is a differential if $\nabla \times \overline{F} = \overline{0}$.

Now, to show that the converse is true, start with curl $\overline{F} = \overline{0}$. If curl $\overline{F} = \overline{0}$, then there exists a scalar function ϕ such that

$$\overline{F} = \nabla\phi \tag{8}$$

and we may write

$$\overline{F} \cdot d\overline{r} = \nabla\phi \cdot d\overline{r} = \frac{\partial\phi}{\partial x}dx + \frac{\partial\phi}{\partial y}dy + \frac{\partial\phi}{\partial z}dz = d\phi \tag{9}$$

or

$$F_1 dx + F_2 dy + F_3 dz = d\phi \tag{10}$$

Therefore, if $\nabla \times \overline{F} = \overline{0}$, where

$$\overline{F} = F_1\overline{i} + F_2\overline{j} + F_3\overline{k},$$

then

$$F_1 dx + F_2 dy + F_3 dz$$

is an exact differential

2. Before searching for a scalar function ϕ we should verify that eq.(3) represents an exact differential. Eq.(3) would be an exact differential only if

$$\nabla \times \overline{F} = \overline{0} \tag{11}$$

for $\overline{F}$ given by

$$\overline{F} = (2xy + y^3\cos z)\overline{i} + (x^2+3xy^2\cos z)\overline{j} - xy^3\sin z\overline{k} \tag{12}$$

Since,

$$\nabla \times \overline{F} = \left[\frac{\partial}{\partial y}(-xy^3\sin z) - \frac{\partial}{\partial z}(x^2+3xy^2\cos z)\right]\overline{i}$$

$$+ \left[\frac{\partial}{\partial z}(2xy+y^3\cos z) - \frac{\partial}{\partial x}(-xy^3\sin z)\right]\overline{j}$$

$$+ \left[\frac{\partial}{\partial x}(x^2+3xy^2\cos z) - \frac{\partial}{\partial y}(2xy+y^3\cos z)\right]\overline{k}$$

$$= (-3xy^2\sin z + 3xy^2\sin z)\overline{i} + (-y^3\sin z + y^3\sin z)\overline{j}$$

$$+ (2x+3y^2\cos z-2x-3y^2\cos z)\overline{k}$$

$$= \overline{0}$$

eq.(3) does indeed represent an exact differential.

Now, obtain

$$\frac{\partial\phi}{\partial x} = 2xy + y^3\cos z \tag{13}$$

$$\frac{\partial\phi}{\partial y} = x^3 + 3xy^2\cos z \tag{14}$$

$$\frac{\partial\phi}{\partial z} = -xy^3\sin z \tag{15}$$

Integrating eq.(13) results in

$$\phi(x,y,z) = x^2y + xy^3\cos z + f(y,z) \tag{16}$$

Substituting eq.(16) into eq.(14) and integrating the result gives

$$x^2 + 3xy^2\cos z + \frac{\partial f}{\partial y} = x^2 + 3xy^2\cos z \qquad (17)$$

and

$$f(y,z) = \text{const} \qquad (18)$$

Thus

$$\phi(x,y,z) = x^2y + xy^3\cos z + \text{const} \qquad (19)$$

● **PROBLEM 12-41**

Which of the following expressions is an exact differential?

1. $(x^2+y)dx + z^3dy + dz$ (1)

2. $(2xy+e^xz^2)dx + x^2dy + 2ze^xdz$ (2)

Solution: From Problem 12-40, we know that a necessary and sufficient condition for $F_1dx + F_2dy + F_3dz$ to be an exact differential is that

$$\nabla \times \overline{F} = \overline{0} \qquad (3)$$

1. For expression (1),

$$\overline{F} = (x^2+y)\overline{i} + z^3\overline{j} + \overline{k}$$

and therefore,

$$\nabla \times \overline{F} = \left(\frac{\partial}{\partial x}, \frac{\partial}{\partial y}, \frac{\partial}{\partial z}\right) \times (x^2+y, z^3, 1)$$

$$= (-3z^2, 0, -1) \neq \overline{0} \qquad (4)$$

Thus, expression (1) is not an exact differential.

2. For expression (2), obtain

$$\text{curl } \overline{F} = \nabla \times \overline{F}$$

$$= \left(\frac{\partial}{\partial x}, \frac{\partial}{\partial y}, \frac{\partial}{\partial z}\right) \times (2xy + e^xz^2, x^2, 2ze^x) \qquad (5)$$

$$= (0, 2ze^x-2ze^x, 2x-2x) = \overline{0}$$

Thus, eq.(2) is an exact differential.

● **PROBLEM 12-42**

The principle of conservation of energy is one of the basic laws of physics. Show that in the conservative field $\overline{F}$ the total energy of a particle is constant.

Solution: Since the field is conservative, a scalar potential ϕ exists such that

$$\overline{F} = -\nabla\phi \qquad (1)$$

The minus sign is used for convenience.

Now, consider two points of the field, A and B. Let v_A and v_B be the magnitudes of the velocities of the particles at A and B, respectively.

We have

$$\overline{F} = m\overline{a} = m \frac{d^2\overline{r}}{dt^2} \tag{2}$$

Then

$$\overline{F} \cdot \frac{d\overline{r}}{dt} = m \frac{d^2\overline{r}}{dt^2} \cdot \frac{d\overline{r}}{dt}$$

Now, note that

$$\frac{d^2\overline{r}}{dt^2} \cdot \frac{d\overline{r}}{dt} = \frac{1}{2} \frac{d}{dt} (v^2)$$

since

$$\frac{1}{2} \frac{d}{dt} v^2 = \frac{1}{2} \frac{d}{dt} \left| \frac{d\overline{r}}{dt} \right|^2 = \frac{1}{2} \frac{d}{dt} \left(\frac{d\overline{r}}{dt} \cdot \frac{d\overline{r}}{dt} \right)$$

$$= \frac{1}{2} \left(\frac{d^2\overline{r}}{dt^2} \cdot \frac{d\overline{r}}{dt} + \frac{d\overline{r}}{dt} \cdot \frac{d^2\overline{r}}{dt^2} \right)$$

$$= \frac{d^2\overline{r}}{dt^2} \cdot \frac{d\overline{r}}{dt}$$

Therefore,

$$\overline{F} \cdot \frac{d\overline{r}}{dt} = m \frac{d}{dt} \frac{1}{2} v^2 = \frac{d}{dt} \left[\frac{1}{2} mv^2 \right] \tag{3}$$

and

$$\int_A^B \overline{F} \cdot d\overline{r} = \int_A^B d(\tfrac{1}{2}mv^2) = \frac{1}{2} mv^2 \Big|_A^B = \frac{1}{2} mv_B^2 - \frac{1}{2} mv_A^2 \tag{4}$$

On the other hand, since

$$\overline{F} = -\nabla\phi \tag{5}$$

we have

$$\int_A^B \overline{F} \cdot d\overline{r} = -\int_A^B \nabla\phi \cdot d\overline{r} = -\int_A^B d\phi$$

$$\tag{6}$$

$$= -\phi \Big|_A^B = \phi(A) - \phi(B)$$

Combining eqs.(4) and (6) results in

$$\int_A^B \overline{F} \cdot d\overline{r} = \frac{1}{2} mv_B^2 - \frac{1}{2} mv_A^2 = \phi(A) - \phi(B)$$

or

$$\frac{1}{2} mv_B^2 + \phi(B) = \frac{1}{2} mv_A^2 + \phi(A) \tag{7}$$

Now, note that the term $\frac{1}{2} mv^2$ represents the kinetic energy, usually denoted "KE" or "T", while ϕ represents the potential energy - usually denoted "PE" or "V". Thus, what eq.(7) indicates is that the total energy of a particle under the influence of a conservative force is a constant,

$$\frac{1}{2} mv^2 + \phi = \text{const.}$$

Evaluate the following integrals

1. $\int_C \phi d\overline{r}$ (1)

2. $\int_C \overline{F} \cdot d\overline{r}$ (2)

3. $\int_C \overline{F} \times d\overline{r}$ (3)

where C is the curve

$$x = 2t, \quad y = 3t, \quad z = t^3 \tag{4}$$

between $t = 0$ and $t = 1$, and

$$\phi(x,y,z) = 2x^2yz \tag{5}$$

$$\overline{F} = x^2\overline{i} + y\overline{j} + zy\overline{k} \tag{6}$$

Solution: 1. For the curve given by eq.(4), we have
$$\phi(x,y,z) = 2x^2yz = 2(2t)^2\,3t\,t^3 = 24t^6 \tag{7}$$
and
$$\overline{r} = x\overline{i} + y\overline{j} + z\overline{k} = 2t\overline{i} + 3t\overline{j} + t^3\overline{k} \tag{8}$$
The line segment $d\overline{r}$ is
$$d\overline{r} = 2\overline{i}dt + 3\overline{j}dt + 3t^2\overline{k}dt$$
$$= (2\overline{i} + 3\overline{j} + 3t^2\overline{k})dt \tag{9}$$

The integral (1) is

$$\int_C \phi d\overline{r} = \int_{t=0}^{t=1} 24t^6(2\overline{i} + 3\overline{j} + 3t^2\overline{k})dt$$

$$= \overline{i}\int_0^1 48t^6dt + \overline{j}\int_0^1 72t^6dt + \overline{k}\int_0^1 72t^8dt$$

$$= \overline{i}\,48\frac{t^7}{7}\Big|_0^1 + \overline{j}\,72\frac{t^7}{7}\Big|_0^1 + \overline{k}\,72\frac{t^9}{9}\Big|_0^1$$

$$= \frac{48}{7}\overline{i} + \frac{72}{7}\overline{j} + \frac{72}{9}\overline{k} \tag{10}$$

2. Along the curve C, $\overline{F}$ may be written as

$$\overline{F} = x^2\overline{i} + y\overline{j} + zy\overline{k} = 4t^2\overline{i} + 3t\overline{j} + 3t^4\overline{k} \tag{11}$$

and

$$\int_C \overline{F} \cdot d\overline{r} = \int_0^1 (4t^2\overline{i}+3t\overline{j}+3t^4\overline{k})\cdot(2\overline{i}+3\overline{j}+3t^2\overline{k})dt$$

$$= \int_0^1 (8t^2+9t+9t^6)dt = \left(8\frac{t^3}{3}+9\frac{t^2}{2}+9\frac{t^7}{7}\right)\Bigg|_0^1$$

$$= \frac{8}{3} + \frac{9}{2} + \frac{9}{7}$$

3. First, find an expression for the vector $\overline{F} \times d\overline{r}$ along the curve C:

$$\overline{F} \times d\overline{r} = (4t^2\overline{i} + 3t\overline{j} + 3t^4\overline{k})\times(2\overline{i} + 3\overline{j} + 3t^2\overline{k})dt$$

$$= \begin{vmatrix} \overline{i} & \overline{j} & \overline{k} \\ 4t^2 & 3t & 3t^4 \\ 2 & 3 & 3t^2 \end{vmatrix} dt \qquad (12)$$

$$= \left[\overline{i}(9t^3-9t^4)+\overline{j}(-6t^4)+\overline{k}(12t^2-6t)\right]dt$$

We have

$$\int_C \overline{F} \times d\overline{r} = \overline{i} \int_0^1 (9t^3-9t^4)dt+\overline{j} \int_0^1 (-6t^4)dt+\overline{k} \int_0^1 (12t^2-6t)dt$$

$$= \overline{i}\left(9\frac{t^4}{4} - 9\frac{t^5}{5}\right)\Bigg|_0^1 + \overline{j}\left(-6\frac{t^5}{5}\right)\Bigg|_0^1 \qquad (13)$$

$$+ \overline{k}\left(12\frac{t^3}{3} - 6\frac{t^2}{2}\right)\Bigg|_0^1 = \frac{9}{20}\overline{i} - \frac{6}{5}\overline{j} + \overline{k}$$

● **PROBLEM 12-44**

What vector fields have a scalar potential?

What vector fields have a vector potential?

Find a vector potential for the field

$$\overline{F} = y\overline{k} \qquad (1)$$

Solution: A scalar potential of any vector field $\overline{F}$ is a scalar field ϕ such that

$$\overline{F} = \nabla\phi \qquad (2)$$

The following theorem states the necessary and sufficient conditions for a vector field $\overline{F}$ to have a scalar potential.

Theorem

A vector field $\overline{F}$ defined and continuously differentiable in a simply connected domain P has a scalar potential if, and only if, curl $\overline{F} = \overline{0}$ throughout the domain P.

This theorem has an important practical aspect. It indicates that before starting to search for the scalar potential of a vector field, we should first determine if curl $\overline{F} = \overline{0}$, that is, we should first check if a scalar potential does indeed exist.

Before giving the conditions that determine whether a vector potential exists for a given vector field, the definition of a star-shaped domain should be given.

A domain P is called a star-shaped domain when it has a point A $\in$ P such that if B is any other point in P, then the entire line segment AB lies in the domain.

By definition, a star-shaped domain is simply connected. Examples of star-shaped domains are shown in Fig. 1.

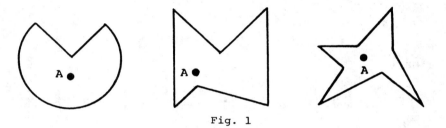

Fig. 1

An example of a domain that is not star-shaped is given in Fig. 2. Note how the line segment AB does not lie completely within the domain.

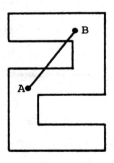

Fig. 2

The following theorem gives the necessary and sufficient conditions for a vector field to have a vector potential.

Theorem

A vector field $\overline{F}$, defined and continuously differentiable in a star-shaped domain P, has a vector potential $\overline{G}$, $\overline{F} = $ curl $\overline{G}$ throughout P if, and only if div $\overline{F} = 0$.

Let P be a star-shaped domain with respect to A (Fig. 3).

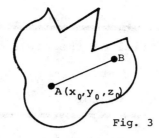

Fig. 3

Let $\overline{r}_0 = (x_0, y_0, z_0)$ be the coordinates of A and $\overline{r}_1 = (x_1, y_1, z_1)$ be the coordinates of B. The straight-line segment from A to B may be parametricized in the following manner:

$$\overline{r}(t) = \overline{r}_0 + t(\overline{r}_1 - \overline{r}_0), \quad 0 \le t \le 1 \qquad (3)$$

Now, we will evaluate the integral

$$\overline{G}(x,y,z) = \int_A^B t\, \overline{F} \times d\overline{r} \qquad (4)$$

Applying eq.(3) to integral (4) gives

$$\overline{G}(x,y,z) = \int_0^1 t\, F \times \frac{d\overline{r}}{dt}\, dt \qquad (5)$$

Point A is the origin of the system, A(0,0,0). We now parametrize the straight-line segment from (0,0,0) to (x_1, y_1, z_1),

$$\overline{r}(t) = t\overline{r}_1 \qquad (6)$$

where

$$\overline{r}_1 = (x_1, y_1, z_1). \qquad (7)$$

From eq.(7), it is evident that

$$\frac{d\overline{r}}{dt} = \overline{r}_1$$

Thus,

$$\overline{G}(x_1, y_1, z_1) = \int_0^1 t\overline{F} \times \frac{d\overline{r}}{dt}\, dt = \int_0^1 t t y_1 \overline{k} \times \overline{r}_1\, dt$$

$$= y_1\, \overline{k} \times \overline{r}_1 \int_0^1 t^2\, dt = \frac{1}{3}\, y_1\, \overline{k} \times \overline{r}_1$$

$$= \left[-\frac{1}{3}\, y_1^2,\ \frac{1}{3}\, x_1 y_1,\ 0 \right] \qquad (8)$$

and therefore, the vector potential of $\overline{F} = y\overline{k}$ is

$$\overline{G}(x,y,z) = \left(-\frac{1}{3}\, y^2,\ \frac{1}{3}\, xy,\ 0 \right) \qquad (9)$$

$$= -\frac{1}{3}\, y^2 \overline{i} + \frac{1}{3}\, xy \overline{j}$$

Find a vector potential of the field

$$\overline{F} = \overline{\omega} \times \overline{r} \qquad (1)$$

where $\overline{\omega}$ is a constant vector.

Solution: First, verify that $\overline{F}$ does indeed have a vector potential by evaluating div $\overline{F}$. Since

$$\overline{F} = \overline{\omega} \times \overline{r} = (\omega_2 z - \omega_3 y, \; \omega_3 x - \omega_1 z, \; \omega_1 y - \omega_2 x)$$

we have

$$\text{div } \overline{F} = \left(\frac{\partial}{\partial x}, \frac{\partial}{\partial y}, \frac{\partial}{\partial z}\right) \cdot (\omega_2 z - \omega_3 y, \; \omega_3 x - \omega_1 z, \; \omega_1 y - \omega_2 x) = 0 \qquad (2)$$

Thus, $\overline{F} = \overline{\omega} \times \overline{r}$ has a vector potential.

Now, we will use eq.(4) of Problem 12-44. Let A be the origin of the coordinate system. We parametrize the straight-line segment from $(0,0,0)$ to (x,y,z)

$$\overline{r}(t) = t\overline{r}_1 \qquad (3)$$

where

$$\overline{r}_1 = (x, y, z) \qquad (4)$$

The vector potential of $\overline{F} = \overline{\omega} \times \overline{r}$ can be evaluated as follows:

$$\overline{G}(x,y,z) = \int_0^1 t \, \overline{F} \times \frac{d\overline{r}}{dt} \, dt = \int_0^1 t(\overline{\omega} \times t\overline{r}_1) \times \overline{r}_1 dt$$

$$= (\overline{\omega} \times \overline{r}_1) \times \overline{r}_1 \int_0^1 t^2 dt = \frac{1}{3}(\overline{\omega} \times \overline{r}_1) \times \overline{r}_1 \qquad (5)$$

One could easily verify that

$$\overline{G}(x,y,z) = \frac{1}{3}(\overline{\omega} \times \overline{r}) \times \overline{r} \qquad (6)$$

is the vector potential of

$$\overline{F} = \overline{\omega} \times \overline{r}. \qquad (7)$$

Note that we omitted the index 1 in $\overline{r}_1$.

From previous problems, it was learned that conservative (or irrotational) vector fields (that is fields for which curl $\overline{F} = \overline{0}$) can be derived from a scalar potential ϕ, as in $\overline{F} = \text{grad } \phi$. We also found that solenoidal fields (i.e. fields for which div $\overline{F}=0$) can be derived from a vector potential $\overline{G}$, $\overline{F} = \text{curl } \overline{G}$.

It is possible to prove that:

An arbitrary vector field $\overline{F}$ can be represented as, under certain circumstances, a sum of an irrotational vector field and a solenoidal vector field:

$$\overline{F} = \overline{F}_{ir} + \overline{F}_{sol} \tag{8}$$

This statement is known as the Fundamental Theorem of Vector Analysis. We can write this theorem as:

An arbitrary vector field $\overline{F}$, under appropriate circumstances, can be expressed as a gradient of some scalar field plus the curl of some other vector field,

$$\overline{F} = \text{grad } \phi + \text{curl } \overline{G} \tag{9}$$

The proof of this theorem is quite complex and will not be presented here.

CHAPTER 13

DOUBLE INTEGRALS

INTRODUCTION

Double integrals, which are a particular case of multiple integrals, occur in various branches of physics and pure and applied mathematics.

This chapter deals almost exclusively with double integrals, and its main purpose is to form an adequate foundation for the study of surface integrals.

Though this chapter is not concerned with surface integrals in itself, certain basic concepts concerning the concept of a surface, and how a surface may be described, are considered. Indeed, the first few problems in the chapter introduce the concepts of smooth and piecewise smooth surfaces, and how a surface is characterized by its normal vector. It is interesting to note that a normal vector to a surface gives us a description of the surface in the same manner that a tangent vector describes a curve.

It is assumed, of course, that the student is familiar with the concept of the definite integral of a function of one variable as the limit of a sum. This approach can be extended to integrals of functions of two or more variables. The interval of integration for single integrals becomes a definite region in the plane for double integrals.

A large part of the chapter deals with the actual evaluation of double integrals through the use of iterated integrals.

The chapter closes with some basic physical applications which should help the student understand the practical aspects of double integrals.

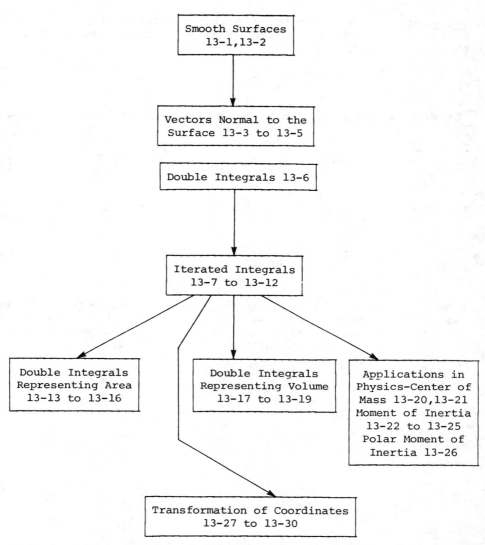

This chart is provided to facilitate rapid understanding of the inter-
relationships of the topics and subject matter in this chapter. Also
shown are the problem numbers associated with the subject matter.

SMOOTH SURFACES, ORIENTATION AND VECTORS NORMAL TO A SURFACE

● PROBLEM 13-1

A surface is given by the equation

$$x^2+y^2+z^2 = 9 \tag{1}$$

Determine whether this surface is smooth. Determine
whether a cube is a smooth surface or piecewise-smooth
surface. Also, define the consistent orientation of
the cube.

Solution: We will begin with the definition of the normal vector to a surface. Let a surface be described by the equation

$$f(x,y,z) = 0 \qquad (2)$$

The normal vector to this surface at a point (x,y,z) is given by

$$\overline{N} = \text{grad } f(x,y,z) \equiv \left(\frac{\partial f}{\partial x}, \frac{\partial f}{\partial y}, \frac{\partial f}{\partial z}\right) \qquad (3)$$

and the unit normal to the surface is given by

$$\overline{n} = \frac{\overline{N}}{|\overline{N}|} = \frac{\text{grad } f}{|\text{grad } f|} \qquad (4)$$

A surface S is said to be smooth if at every point of S we can choose a unit normal vector $\overline{n}$ in such a way that $\overline{n}$ varies continuously on S. Also, at every point of a smooth surface S there exist two unit normal vectors, $\overline{n}$ and $-\overline{n}$.

Now, for the surface described by eq.(1),

$$f(x,y,z) = x^2+y^2+z^2-9 = 0 \qquad (5)$$

and the normal vector is

$$\overline{N} = \text{grad } f(x,y,z) = (2x,2y,2z) \qquad (6)$$

The unit normal vector $\overline{n}$ is then

$$\overline{n} = \frac{\text{grad } f}{|\text{grad } f|} = \frac{(2x,2y,2z)}{\sqrt{(2x)^2+(2y)^2+(2z)^2}} = \frac{2(x,y,z)}{2\sqrt{x^2+y^2+z^2}} = \left(\frac{x}{3}, \frac{y}{3}, \frac{z}{3}\right) \qquad (7)$$

since from eq.(5)

$$\sqrt{x^2+y^2+z^2} = 3$$

The other unit normal vector to the surface is

$$\overline{n}_1 = \frac{-\text{grad } f}{|\text{grad } f|} = \left(\frac{-x}{3}, \frac{-y}{3}, \frac{-z}{3}\right) \qquad (8)$$

Notice that $\bar{n}$ varies continuously on the surface

$$x^2+y^2+z^2-9 = 0$$

and therefore, the surface is smooth. Notice that since we can define two unit normal vectors to a smooth surface, there are two possibilities of choosing the orientation of the surface.

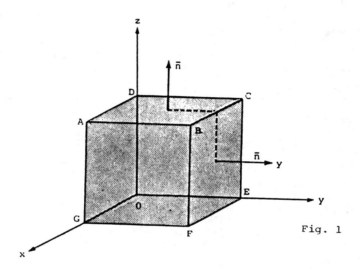

Fig. 1

Now, consider the cube shown in Fig. 1. Notice that the unit normal vector does not vary continuously on this surface.

Indeed, as $\bar{n}$ moves along the dotted line, its direction changes discontinuously at the point where it crosses the edge BC, and therefore the cube is not a smooth surface. Intuitively, a smooth surface has no "corners".

Now, a surface is said to be piecewise-smooth if it consists of a finite number of smooth surfaces joined together. A cube consists of six smooth surfaces joined together, thus it is piecewise-smooth. Consider a surface S bounded by a regular closed curve C, as shown in Fig. 2.

The unit normal field $\bar{n}$ is chosen as shown. A positive direction along C is defined as follows:

An observer on the positive side of a surface, that is on the side on which $\bar{n}$ emerges, walks along the boundary in the positive direction when he always has the surface to his left. In Fig. 2, the observer moves in the positive direction.

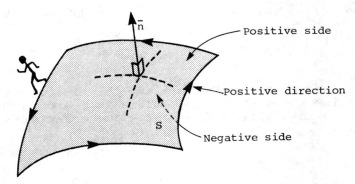

Fig. 2 Observer walks in the positive direction
when he keeps the surface to his left.

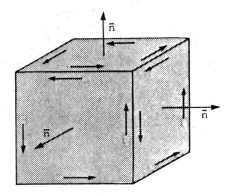

Fig. 3

A piecewise-smooth surface is consistently oriented when
along every edge that is shared by two smooth surfaces, the
positive direction on the edge relative to one smooth surface is opposite to the positive direction relative to the
other surface. Fig. 3 shows a cube consistently oriented.

● **PROBLEM 13-2**

Show that the surface of the Möbius strip is piecewise-
smooth. Is it possible to find the consistent orientation of the smooth parts of the strip?

Solution: Let us actually construct the Möbius strip. Take
a strip of paper, as shown in Fig. 1 and twist it so that
points A and B fall on A' and B' respectively. The Möbius
strip is of particular interest because it is a one-sided or

586

non-orientable surface. Indeed, if we attempted to color just one side of the surface we would soon find the whole thing completely colored.

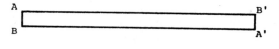

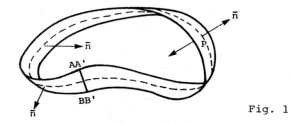

Fig. 1

If $\bar{n}$ is the unit normal vector at a point P, then as $\bar{n}$ moves around the strip its original direction is reversed by the time it reaches P again (see Fig. 1).

Since the Möbius strip may be divided into a number of smooth parts, we see that the strip is piecewise-smooth.

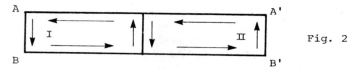

Fig. 2

Now, consider again the strip ABA'B' and let us divide the strip into parts I and II as shown in Fig. 2. If we arbitrarily select the direction shown for part I of the strip, then since we want the surface to be consistently oriented, the direction for part II must be as shown. Putting the strip together, that is A to A' and B to B', we see that the requirement of consistent orientation is not fulfilled along the line A'B' (or AB).

It is easy to verify that we will obtain the same result for any number of parts.

● **PROBLEM 13-3**

1. Compute the vector normal to the surface given in the parametric form

    $$x = (u+v)^2$$

    $$y = uv \qquad\qquad (1)$$

    $$z = v^3$$

2. Write the equation of the plane tangent to this surface at the point corresponding to $u = 2$, $v = 1$.

Solution: 1. We will begin with the definition of a regu-

lar surface element. Any part of a surface represented by
the equations

$$x = x(u,v) \quad y = y(u,v) \quad z = z(u,v) \tag{2}$$

or, in vector notation

$$\bar{r} = \bar{r}(u,v), \tag{3}$$

in such a way that to distinct ordered pairs (u,v) there
correspond distinct points (x,y,z) is called a regular surface element.

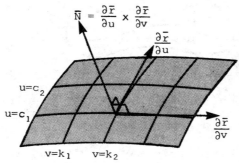

Fig. 1

For a fixed value of u, as v varies, the position vector
$\bar{r}(u,v)$ traces out a curve lying in the surface, as shown in
the figure. Likewise, for a fixed value of v, as u varies,
$\bar{r}(u,v)$ traces another curve lying on the surface.

Note that $\frac{\partial \bar{r}}{\partial v}$, the partial derivative of $\bar{r}$ with respect to v when holding u fixed, represents a vector tangent
to the curve u = constant. By the same token, $\frac{\partial \bar{r}}{\partial u}$ (v held
fixed) represents a vector tangent to the curve v = constant.
It is assumed that these derivatives exist, are continuous
and are non-zero and non-parallel at every point on the surface.

Notice that $\frac{\partial \bar{r}}{\partial u}$ and $\frac{\partial \bar{r}}{\partial v}$ are tangent to curves in the
surface, and therefore they are tangent to the surface it-
self. From this, it is concluded that

$$\bar{N} = \frac{\partial \bar{r}}{\partial u} \times \frac{\partial \bar{r}}{\partial v} \tag{4}$$

is a vector normal to the surface (see Fig. 1).

Now, to determine the normal vector to the surface given
by eqs.(1), we have

$$\bar{r} = (u+v)^2\bar{i} + uv\bar{j} + v^3\bar{k} \tag{5}$$

and therefore

$$\frac{\partial \bar{r}}{\partial u} = (2u + 2v, \ v, \ 0) \tag{6}$$

$$\frac{\partial \bar{r}}{\partial v} = (2v + 2u, \ u, \ 3v^2) \tag{7}$$

The normal vector is then

$$\bar{N} = \frac{\partial \bar{r}}{\partial u} \times \frac{\partial \bar{r}}{\partial v} = (2u+2v, \ v, \ 0) \times (2u+2v, \ u, \ 3v^2)$$

$$= (3v^3, \ -6uv^2 - 6v^3, \ 2u^2 - 2v^2)$$

or

$$\bar{N} = 3v^3 \bar{i} - (6uv^2 + 6v^3)\bar{j} + (2u^2 - 2v^2)\bar{k} \tag{8}$$

2. The equation of the plane may be expressed as

$$(\bar{r} - \bar{r}_0) \cdot \bar{N} = 0 \tag{9}$$

where $\bar{r}_0$ and $\bar{N}$ are the position vector and normal vector of the plane evaluated at the point in question.

Since,

$$\bar{r} = (u+v)^2 \bar{i} + uv\bar{j} + v^3 \bar{k},$$

at the point $u = 2$, $v = 1$, we have

$$\bar{r}_0 = (2+1)^2 \bar{i} + 2(1)\bar{j} + (1)^3 \bar{k} = 9\bar{i} + 2\bar{j} + \bar{k} \tag{10}$$

and, for $\bar{N}$ as given by eq.(8), we have, at the point $u = 2$, $v = 1$,

$$\bar{N} = 3(1)^3 \bar{i} - \left[6(2)(1)^2 + 6(1)^3\right]\bar{j} + \left[2(2)^2 - 2(1)^2\right]\bar{k}$$

$$= 3\bar{i} - 18\bar{j} + 6\bar{k} \tag{11}$$

Now, substituting eqs.(5), (10) and (11) into eq.(9) yields ·

$$((u+v)^2 - 9, \ uv-2, \ v^3-1) \cdot (3, \ -18, \ 6) = 0$$

or

$$(x-9, \ y-2, \ z-1) \cdot (3, \ -18, \ 6) = 0$$

$$3(x-9) - 18(y-2) + 6(z-1) = 0 \tag{12}$$

Eq.(12) gives the non-parametric equation of the plane tangent to the given surface at the point $u = 2$, $v = 1$.

● **PROBLEM 13-4**

A surface is given in the parametric form

$$x = 2u, \qquad y = uv, \qquad z = uv^2 \tag{1}$$

Evaluate the normal vector $\bar{N}$ to the surface at the point corresponding to $u=1$, $v=2$.

Also, find the equation of the surface in the non-parametric form
$$f(x,y,z) = 0$$

and again determine the normal vector to this surface at the same point as above.

589

Solution: There are two ways of computing the normal vector to a surface.

When a surface is given in the parametric form

$$x = x(u,v) \qquad y = y(u,v) \qquad z = z(u,v)$$

the normal vector to the surface is given by (see Problem 13-3)

$$\bar{N} = \frac{\partial \bar{r}}{\partial u} \times \frac{\partial \bar{r}}{\partial v} \tag{2}$$

where

$$\bar{r} = x(u,v)\bar{i} + y(u,v)\bar{j} + z(u,v)\bar{k}.$$

Now, when the surface is given in the non-parametric form

$$f(x,y,z) = 0,$$

the normal vector to the surface is

$$\bar{N} = \text{grad } f \equiv \nabla f.$$

Now, since the surface at hand (eq.(1)) is given in the parametric form, the normal vector may be obtained from eq.(2).

For $\bar{r}$, we have

$$\bar{r} = 2u\bar{i} + uv\bar{j} + uv^2\bar{k}, \tag{3}$$

therefore

$$\frac{\partial \bar{r}}{\partial u} = 2\bar{i} + v\bar{j} + v^2\bar{k} = (2, v, v^2) \tag{4}$$

and

$$\frac{\partial \bar{r}}{\partial v} = u\bar{j} + 2uv\bar{k} = (0, u, 2uv) \tag{5}$$

Hence,

$$\bar{N} = \frac{\partial \bar{r}}{\partial u} \times \frac{\partial \bar{r}}{\partial v} = (2,v,v^2) \times (0,u,2uv)$$

$$= (2uv^2 - v^2u, \ 0-4uv, \ 2u-0)$$

or

$$\bar{N} = v^2u\bar{i} - 4uv\bar{j} + 2u\bar{k} \tag{6}$$

At the point $u=1$, $v=2$, the normal vector to the surface is

$$\bar{N} = (2)^2(1)\bar{i} - 4(1)(2)\bar{j} + 2(1)\bar{k}$$

$$= 4\bar{i} - 8\bar{j} + 2\bar{k} = (4, -8, 2) \tag{7}$$

Now, to find the non-parametric form of the given surface, use eq.(1).

$$x = 2u \text{ gives } u = \frac{x}{2}$$

and, since $y = uv$,

$$v = \frac{y}{u} = \frac{2y}{x}$$

and

$$z = uv^2 = \frac{x}{2}\left(\frac{2y}{x}\right)^2 = \frac{2y^2}{x} \qquad (8)$$

Thus, from eq.(8) we have

$$xz = 2y^2$$

or

$$f(x,y,z) = xz - 2y^2 = 0 \qquad (9)$$

The normal vector at any point of the surface is then

$$\overline{N} = \text{grad } f = \nabla f$$

$$= \nabla(xz - 2y^2)$$

$$= z\overline{i} - 4y\overline{j} + x\overline{k} \qquad (10)$$

Now, the coordinates of the point corresponding to u=1, v=2 are

$$x = 2u = 2$$

$$y = uv = 2 \qquad (11)$$

$$z = uv^2 = 4$$

From eqs.(10) and (11), the normal vector to the given surface at the point x=1, y=2, z=4 is then

$$\overline{N} = 4\overline{i} - 8\overline{j} + 4\overline{k}$$

$$= (4, -8, 4) \qquad (12)$$

which is the same result obtained in eq.(7). Note that eqs. (6) and (10) are the same vectors. Indeed, substituting eq.(1) into eq.(7) yields eq.(10).

● **PROBLEM 13-5**

A surface is given by

$$x = u \qquad y = v^2 \qquad z = uv \qquad (1)$$

1. Find the unit normal vector at the point corresponding to u = 2, v = 1.

2. Write the equation of the surface in the form f(x,y,z) = 0 and again find the unit normal vector at the point u = 2, v = 1.

Solution: 1. Note that the surface is given in the parametric form. Thus, the normal vector at any point on the surface is given by

$$\overline{N} = \frac{\partial \overline{r}}{\partial u} \times \frac{\partial \overline{r}}{\partial v}$$

Now, for $\bar{r}$, we have

$$\bar{r} = x\bar{i} + y\bar{j} + z\bar{k}$$
$$= (u, v^2, uv) \tag{2}$$

and therefore

$$\frac{\partial\bar{r}}{\partial u} = \bar{i} + v\bar{k} = (1,0,v) \tag{3}$$

$$\frac{\partial\bar{r}}{\partial v} = 2v\bar{j} + u\bar{k} = (0,2v,u) \tag{4}$$

Thus, for $\bar{N}$ we obtain

$$\bar{N} = \frac{\partial\bar{r}}{\partial u} \times \frac{\partial\bar{r}}{\partial v}$$

$$= (1,0,v) \times (0,2v,u)$$

$$= (0-2v^2, 0-u, 2v-0)$$

$$= -2v^2\bar{i} - u\bar{j} + 2v\bar{k} \tag{5}$$

At the point $u = 2$, $v = 1$

$$\bar{N} = -2(1)^2\bar{i} - 2\bar{j} + 2(1)\bar{k}$$

$$= (-2, -2, 2) \tag{6}$$

Hence, the unit normal vector at this point is

$$\bar{n} = \frac{(-2,-2,2)}{\sqrt{(-2)^2+(-2)^2+2^2}} = \left(\frac{-2}{\sqrt{12}}, \frac{-2}{\sqrt{12}}, \frac{2}{\sqrt{12}}\right) = \left[\frac{-1}{\sqrt{3}}, \frac{-1}{\sqrt{3}}, \frac{1}{\sqrt{3}}\right] \tag{7}$$

2. To obtain an equation of the surface in the form of $f(x,y,z) = 0$, take the given parametric representation of the surface,

$$x = u, \qquad y = v^2, \qquad z = uv$$

and note that

$$u^2v^2 - (uv)^2 = 0 \tag{8}$$

Now, since $u^2 = x^2$, $v^2 = y$ and $z = uv$, we have

$$f(x,y,z) = x^2y - z^2 = 0 \tag{9}$$

which is the desired form.
Note that eq.(1) and eq.(9) represent the same surface.

Now, since we have the surface in the form $f(x,y,z)=0$, the normal vector to the surface is

$$\bar{N} = \text{grad } f = \text{grad}[x^2y-z^2]$$

$$= (2xy, x^2, -2z) \tag{10}$$

592

To evaluate grad f at the point u = 2, v = 1, note that

$$x = u = 2, \quad y = v^2 = 1, \quad z = uv = 2$$

and consequently,

$$\text{grad } f = 2(2)(1)\overline{i} + 2^2\overline{j} + (-2)(2)\overline{k}$$

$$= 4\overline{i} + 4\overline{j} - 4\overline{k}$$

$$= (4, 4, -4)$$

Therefore, at the point $\overline{r} = (2,1,2)$, the unit normal vector is

$$\overline{n} = \frac{\text{grad } f}{|\text{grad } f|} = \frac{(4,4,-4)}{\sqrt{4^2+4^2+(-4)^2}} \tag{11}$$

$$= \left(\frac{1}{\sqrt{3}}, \frac{1}{\sqrt{3}}, \frac{-1}{\sqrt{3}}\right)$$

Note that at any given point of the surface $f(x,y,z) = 0$ there are two unit normal vectors given by

$$\overline{n} = \frac{\text{grad } f}{|\text{grad } f|} \quad \text{and} \quad -\overline{n} = \frac{-\text{grad } f}{|\text{grad } f|} \tag{12}$$

Thus, from eq.(11), we obtain

$$-\overline{n} = \left(\frac{-1}{\sqrt{3}}, \frac{-1}{\sqrt{3}}, \frac{1}{\sqrt{3}}\right) \tag{13}$$

Notice that both methods used lead to the same result, as would be expected.

DEFINITION OF DOUBLE INTEGRAL, ITERATED INTEGRALS

● **PROBLEM** 13-6

Using the definition of the double integral, evaluate

$$\iint_D f(x,y) \, dxdy \tag{1}$$

where

$$f(x,y) = xy \tag{2}$$

and D is the subset of the xy plane such that $0 \le x \le 1$ and $0 \le y \le 1$.

Solution: We will first briefly outline the definition of the double integral

$$\iint_D f(x,y) \, dxdy$$

The function f(x,y) is defined over a closed region D of the xy plane. It is assumed that D is bounded, that is, that D can be enclosed in a circle of finite radius. We subdivide the region D into n rectangles by drawing parallel lines to the x and y axes, as shown in Fig. 1.

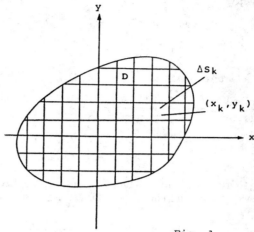

Fig. 1

The rectangles are then numbered from 1 to n and we then denote the area of the k-th rectangle by ΔS_k. Let (x_k, y_k) be an arbitrary point in the k-th rectangle. We form the sum

$$\sum_{k=1}^{n} f(x_k, y_k) \Delta S_k \tag{3}$$

If this sum approaches a unique limit as n tends to infinity and the maximum diagonal of the rectangles approaches 0, then we can define the double integral as

$$\iint_D f(x,y)dxdy = \lim_{\substack{n \to \infty \\ \max \Delta S_k \to 0}} \sum_{k=1}^{n} f(x_k, y_k) \Delta S_k \tag{4}$$

There are some additional conditions that must be satisfied. For instance, the function f(x,y) must be continuous over D. Also, we must be able to subdivide D into a finite number of subsets, each of which is described by the inequalities.

$$x_1(y) \le x \le x_2(y), \quad y_1 \le y \le y_2 \tag{5}$$

or

$$y_1(x) \le y \le y_2(x), \quad x_1 \le x \le x_2 \tag{6}$$

where the functions $x_1(y)$, $x_2(y)$, $y_1(x)$, $y_2(x)$ are all continuous. Eq.(5) is illustrated in Fig. 2.

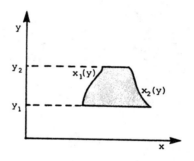

Fig. 2

Now, to evaluate the integral

$$\iint\limits_{D} xy \; dxdy$$

where D is given by

$$0 \leq x \leq 1, \quad 0 \leq y \leq 1,$$

subdivide the region D, as shown in Fig. 3.   As a next step, we divide the segments along the x and y axes into n equal parts.   The squares are then numbered from 1 to n^2, in the manner shown in Fig. 3.

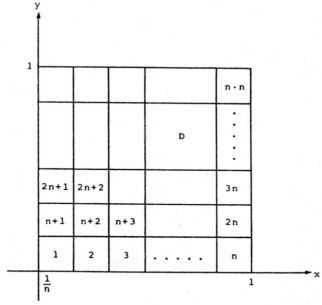

Fig. 3

Now, since $f(x,y) = yx$, for the first row of the squares, the value of the function is

$$f_1(x_1,y_1) = \frac{1}{n} \cdot \frac{1}{n}, \quad f_2(x_2,y_2) = \frac{1}{n} \cdot \frac{2}{n} \ldots f_n(x_n,y_n) = \frac{1}{n} \cdot \frac{n}{n} \quad (8)$$

Note that we take the maximum value of $f(x,y)$ in the squares.

For the second row

$$f_{n+1}(x_{n+1},y_{n+1}) = \frac{1}{n} \cdot \frac{2}{n}, \quad f_{n+2}(x_{n+2},y_{n+2}) = \frac{2}{n} \cdot \frac{2}{n} \ldots f_{2n}(x_{2n},y_{2n})$$

(9)

$$= \frac{n}{n} \cdot \frac{2}{n}$$

and for the n-th row

$$f_{(n-1)n+1}\left(x_{(n-1)n+1},y_{(n-1)n+1}\right) = \frac{1}{n} \cdot \frac{n}{n} \ldots f_{n^2}(x_{n^2},y_{n^2})$$

(10)

$$= \frac{n}{n} \cdot \frac{n}{n}$$

In this case the areas of all the squares are equal

$$\Delta S_1 = \Delta S_2 = \ldots = \Delta S_{n^2} = \frac{1}{n} \cdot \frac{1}{n}$$

(11)

The sum in eq.(4) can be written as

$$\sum_{k=1}^{n^2} f(x_k,y_k)\Delta S_k = \frac{1}{n^2} \sum_{k=1}^{n^2} f(x_k,y_k)$$

(12)

Now, let us add the values of $f(x_k,y_k)$ for each row

1st Row

$$\frac{1}{n} \cdot \frac{1}{n} + \frac{1}{n} \cdot \frac{2}{n} + \frac{1}{n} \cdot \frac{3}{n} + \ldots + \frac{1}{n} \cdot \frac{n}{n} = \frac{1}{n^2}(1+2+\ldots+n)$$

(13)

$$= \frac{1}{n^2} \frac{n(n+1)}{2}$$

2nd Row

$$\frac{2}{n} \cdot \frac{1}{n} + \frac{2}{n} \cdot \frac{2}{n} + \frac{2}{n} \cdot \frac{3}{n} + \ldots + \frac{2}{n} \cdot \frac{n}{n} = \frac{2}{n^2} \frac{n(n+1)}{2}$$

(14)

For the k-th row

$$\frac{k}{n} \cdot \frac{1}{n} + \frac{k}{n} \cdot \frac{2}{n} + \ldots + \frac{k}{n} \cdot \frac{n}{n} = \frac{k}{n^2} \frac{n(n+1)}{2}$$

(15)

For the n^2 row

$$\frac{n}{n} \cdot \frac{1}{n} + \frac{n}{n} \cdot \frac{2}{n} + \ldots + \frac{n}{n} \cdot \frac{n}{n} = \frac{n}{n^2} \frac{n(n+1)}{2}$$

(16)

Adding all the rows results in

$$\frac{1}{n^2} \frac{n(n+1)}{2} + \frac{2}{n^2} \frac{n(n+1)}{2} + \ldots + \frac{n}{n^2} \frac{n(n+1)}{2}$$

$$= \frac{1}{n^2} \frac{n(n+1)}{2}(1+2+\ldots+n) = \frac{1}{n^2} \frac{n(n+1)}{2} \cdot \frac{n(n+1)}{2}$$

(17)

$$= \frac{(n+1)^2}{4}$$

Substituting eq.(17) into eq.(12) yields

$$\sum_{k=1}^{n} f(x_k,y_k)\Delta S_k = \frac{1}{n^2} \cdot \frac{(n+1)^2}{4} \qquad (18)$$

From eq.(4) we evaluate the integral

$$\iint_D xydxdy = \lim_{n\to\infty} \frac{1}{n^2} \frac{(n+1)^2}{4}$$

$$= \lim_{n\to\infty} \left(\frac{n^2}{4n^2} + \frac{n}{2n^2} + \frac{1}{4n^2}\right) = \frac{1}{4} \qquad (19)$$

In practical applications, more direct methods of evaluating double integrals are used. This problem was merely designed to illustrate how the definition of the double integral can be used as a means of solution.

● **PROBLEM 13-7**

By reducing the double integral to the iterated integral, evaluate

$$\iint_D (x^2+y^2)dxdy \qquad (1)$$

where D is a quarter-circle such that

$$0 \le x \le 1 \quad \text{and} \quad 0 \le y \le 1.$$

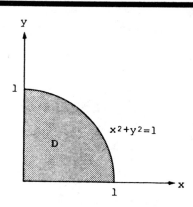

Solution: The following theorem illustrates the method of evaluating double integrals known as the reduction to an iterated integral.
Theorem
   Let D be a closed region lying in the xy plane described by the inequalities

$$x_1(y) \le x \le x_2(y) \qquad (2)$$

$$y_1 \le y \le y_2 \qquad (3)$$

If $f(x,y)$ is a continuous function defined in D, then for $y_1 \leq y \leq y_2$

$$\int_{x_1(y)}^{x_2(y)} f(x,y)dx \qquad (4)$$

is a continuous function of y and

$$\iint_D f(x,y)dxdy = \int_{y_1}^{y_2} \int_{x_1(y)}^{x_2(y)} f(x,y)dxdy \qquad (5)$$

The expression on the right side of eq.(5) is called an iterated (double) integral. In the case where region D is described by the inequalities

$$y_1(x) \leq y \leq y_2(x) \qquad (6)$$

$$x_1 \leq x \leq x_2, \qquad (7)$$

the double integral is expressed as

$$\iint_D f(x,y)dxdy = \int_{x_1}^{x_2} \int_{y_1(x)}^{y_2(x)} f(x,y)dydx \qquad (8)$$

Now, to return to the problem at hand, notice that region D, as shown in the figure, can be described by the inequalities

$$0 \leq x \leq 1 \qquad (9)$$

$$0 \leq y \leq \sqrt{1-x^2} \qquad (10)$$

and therefore, we can use eq.(9) as a means of evaluation.

For the function $f(x,y) = x^2+y^2$, we have

$$\iint_D (x^2+y^2)dxdy = \int_{x_1}^{x_2} \int_{y_1(x)}^{y_2(x)} (x^2+y^2)dydx$$

$$= \int_0^1 \int_0^{\sqrt{1-x^2}} (x^2+y^2)dydx$$

$$= \int_0^1 \left[\int_0^{\sqrt{1-x^2}} (x^2+y^2)dy \right] dx \qquad (11)$$

$$= \int_0^1 \left[\left(x^2 y + \frac{y^3}{3} \right) \Big|_0^{\sqrt{1-x^2}} \right] dx = \int_0^1 \left[x^2\sqrt{1-x^2} + \frac{1}{3}(1-x^2)^{\frac{3}{2}} \right] dx$$

Now, to solve this integral, use the method of trigonometric substitution.

Substituting $x = \sin\alpha$ yields

$$\int_0^1 \left[x^2 \sqrt{1-x^2} + \frac{1}{3}(1-x^2)^{\frac{3}{2}} \right] dx$$

$$= \int_0^{\frac{\pi}{2}} \left[\sin^2\alpha\cos\alpha + \frac{1}{3}\cos^3\alpha \right] \cos\alpha\, d\alpha$$

$$= \int_0^{\frac{\pi}{2}} \sin^2\alpha\cos^2\alpha\, d\alpha + \int_0^{\frac{\pi}{2}} \frac{1}{3}\cos^4\alpha\, d\alpha$$

$$= \left[\frac{\alpha}{8} - \frac{1}{32}\sin 4\alpha \right] \Big|_0^{\frac{\pi}{2}} + \frac{1}{3}\left[\frac{3}{8}\alpha + \frac{1}{4}\sin 2\alpha + \frac{1}{32}\sin 4\alpha \right] \Big|_0^{\frac{\pi}{2}} \quad (12)$$

$$= \frac{\pi}{8}$$

The above results of eq.(12) may be obtained through the use of a table of integrals.

● **PROBLEM 13-8**

Evaluate the double integral

$$\iint_D (x^3 + y^2)\, dy\, dx \qquad (1)$$

where D is the shaded area shown in the figure.

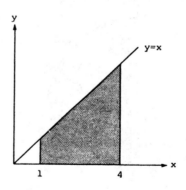

Solution: The region D can be described by the inequalities
$$0 \le y \le x$$
$$1 \le x \le 4 \qquad (2)$$

Thus the integral in eq.(1) becomes

$$\iint_D (x^3 + y^2)\, dy\, dx = \int_1^4 \int_0^x (x^3 + y^2)\, dy\, dx \qquad (3)$$

599

We will first evaluate the inner integral.

$$\int_0^x (x^3+y^2)\,dy = \left(x^3 y + \frac{y^3}{3}\right)\Bigg|_0^x = x^4 + \frac{x^3}{3} \tag{4}$$

Substituting eq.(4) into eq.(3) yields

$$\iint_D (x^3+y^2)\,dy\,dx = \int_1^4 \left(x^4 + \frac{x^3}{3}\right)\,dx \tag{5}$$

$$= \left(\frac{x^5}{5} + \frac{x^4}{12}\right)\Bigg|_1^4 = 225.85$$

• PROBLEM 13-9

Evaluate the double integral

$$\iint_D x^2\,dy\,dx \tag{1}$$

where D is a quarter circle of radius a.

Evaluate the same integral by reversing the order of integration.

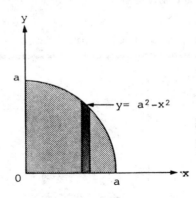

Solution: For the order of integration as in eq.(1), the region D shown in the figure can be described by the inequalities

$$0 \le y \le \sqrt{a^2-x^2}$$
$$0 \le x \le a \tag{2}$$

The integral in eq.(1) can then be written as

$$\iint_D x^2\,dy\,dx = \int_{x=0}^a \int_{y=0}^{\sqrt{a^2-x^2}} x^2\,dy\,dx \tag{3}$$

600

$$= \int_0^a \left[x^2 y \;\Big|\;^{\sqrt{a^2-x^2}}_{y=0} \right] dx = \int_0^a x^2 \sqrt{a^2-x^2}\; dx$$

From a table of integrals, the last integral of eq.(3) is found to be

$$\int x^2 \sqrt{a^2-x^2}\; dx = \frac{x}{8}(2x^2-a^2)\sqrt{a^2-x^2} + \frac{a^4}{8} \text{ arc sin } \frac{x}{a} + C \qquad (4)$$

Applying eq.(4) to eq.(3) results in

$$\int_0^a x^2 \sqrt{a^2-x^2}\; dx = \left[\frac{x}{8}(2x^2-a^2)\sqrt{a^2-x^2} + \frac{a^4}{8} \text{ arc sin } \frac{x}{a} \right] \Big|^a_{x=0}$$

$$\qquad (5)$$

$$= \frac{a^4}{8} \text{ arc sin} 1 = \frac{a^4}{8} \cdot \frac{\pi}{2} = \frac{\pi a^4}{16}$$

For the reverse order of integration, we first integrate with respect to x and then with respect to y. In such a case, the region D is described as

$$0 \le x \le \sqrt{a^2-y^2}$$

$$0 \le y \le a \qquad (6)$$

The double integral then becomes

$$\iint_D x^2 dxdy = \int_{y=0}^a \int_{x=0}^{\sqrt{a^2-y^2}} x^2 dxdy$$

$$= \int_0^a \left[\frac{x^3}{3} \;\Big|\;^{\sqrt{a^2-y^2}}_{x=0} \right] dx = \frac{1}{3} \int_0^a (a^2-y^2)^{\frac{3}{2}} dy \qquad (7)$$

From the following formula

$$\int (a^2-y^2)^{\frac{3}{2}} dy = \frac{y}{8}(5a^2-2y^2)\sqrt{a^2-y^2} + \frac{3}{8} a^4 \text{arc sin } \frac{y}{a} + C$$

we obtain

$$\frac{1}{3} \int_0^a (a^2-y^2)^{\frac{3}{2}} dy = \frac{1}{3} \left[\frac{y}{8}(5a^2-2y^2)\sqrt{a^2-y^2} + \frac{3}{8} a^4 \text{arc sin } \frac{y}{a} \right] \Big|^a_{y=0}$$

$$= \frac{1}{3} \left[\frac{3}{8} a^4 \text{arc sin } 1 \right] = \frac{\pi a^4}{16}$$

Notice that the same result is obtained for both orders of integration, as would be expected.

For both orders of integration, dxdy and dydx, evaluate
the double integral of the function

$$f(x,y) = x \qquad (1)$$

over the shaded area shown in the figure.

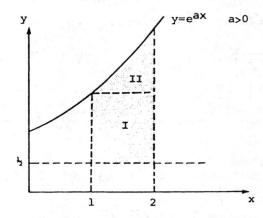

Solution: For the order of integration dydx, the region of
integration can be described by the inequalities

$$\frac{1}{2} \le y \le e^{ax}$$

$$1 \le x \le 2 \qquad (2)$$

The double integral of the function $f(x,y) = x$ is then

$$\iint\limits_{D} f(x,y)dydx = \int_{x=1}^{2} \int_{y=\frac{1}{2}}^{e^{ax}} x\, dydx$$

$$= \int_{1}^{2} \left[xy\right]\Big|_{y=\frac{1}{2}}^{e^{ax}} dx = \int_{1}^{2} \left(xe^{ax} - \frac{x}{2}\right) dx \qquad (3)$$

Now, to find the value of the integral in eq.(3), use the
following formula

$$\int xe^{ax}\, dx = \frac{e^{ax}}{a^2}(ax-1) + C \qquad (4)$$

From eq.(3), we obtain

$$\int_{1}^{2} \left(xe^{ax} - \frac{x}{2}\right)dx = \left[\frac{e^{ax}}{a^2}(ax-1) - \frac{x^2}{4}\right]\Big|_{x=1}^{2}$$

$$= \frac{2e^{2a}}{a} - \frac{e^{2a}}{a^2} - \frac{e^a}{a} + \frac{e^a}{a^2} - \frac{3}{4} \qquad (5)$$

602

$$= e^{2a}\left(\frac{2}{a} - \frac{1}{a^2}\right) + e^a\left(\frac{1}{a^2} - \frac{1}{a}\right) - \frac{3}{4}$$

Now we shall evaluate the integral for the dxdy order of integration. In this case, the region of integration consists of regions I and II shown in the figure. The integral can be written as

$$\iint_D f(x,y)dxdy = \iint_I f(x,y)dxdy + \iint_{II} f(x,y)dxdy \qquad (6)$$

Now region I can be described by the inequalities

$$1 \le x \le 2$$
$$\frac{1}{2} \le y \le e^a \qquad (7)$$

Since $y = e^{ax}$, we have that $x = \frac{\ln y}{a}$, thus, region II can be described by

$$\frac{\ln y}{a} \le x \le 2$$
$$e^a \le y \le e^{2a} \qquad (8)$$

Therefore we obtain

$$\iint_I xdxdy + \iint_{II} xdxdy$$

$$= \int_{y=\frac{1}{2}}^{e^a} \int_{x=1}^{2} xdxdy + \int_{e^a}^{e^{2a}} \int_{x=\frac{\ln y}{a}}^{2} xdxdy$$

$$= \frac{3}{2}\int_{\frac{1}{2}}^{e^a} dy + \int_{e^a}^{e^{2a}}\left[2 - \frac{(\ln y)^2}{2a^2}\right]dy \qquad (9)$$

Now, using the formula

$$\int(\ln y)^2 dy = y(\ln y)^2 - 2y\ln y + 2y \qquad (10)$$

we obtain

$$\iint_D xdxdy = \frac{3}{2}\left[e^a - \frac{1}{2}\right] + 2\left[e^{2a} - e^a\right]$$

$$- \frac{1}{2a^2}\int_{e^a}^{e^{2a}} [\ln y]^2 dy \qquad (11)$$

$$= \frac{2e^{2a}}{a} - \frac{e^{2a}}{a^2} + \frac{e^a}{a^2} - \frac{e^a}{a} - \frac{3}{4}$$

$$= e^{2a} \left(\frac{2}{a} - \frac{1}{a^2} \right) + e^a \left(\frac{1}{a^2} - \frac{1}{a} \right) - \frac{3}{4}$$

1. By changing the order of integration, reduce the double integral

$$\int_{u=0}^{x} \int_{t=0}^{u} e^{p(x-t)} f(t)\,dt\,du \qquad (1)$$

to a single integral.

2. Using the relation

$$\int_{a}^{b} e^{-xy}\,dy = \frac{e^{-ax} - e^{-bx}}{x} \qquad (2)$$

evaluate the integral

$$\int_{0}^{\infty} \frac{e^{-ax} - e^{-bx}}{x}\,dx \qquad (3)$$

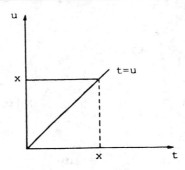

<u>Solution</u>: 1. From eq.(1), we see that the region of integration is

$$0 \le t \le u$$
$$0 \le u \le x \qquad (4)$$

as shown in the figure.

Now, changing the order of integration in integral (1) yields

$$\int_{u=0}^{x} \int_{y=0}^{u} e^{p(x-t)} f(t)\,dt\,du = \int_{t=0}^{x} \int_{u=t}^{x} e^{p(x-t)} f(t)\,du\,dt \qquad (5)$$

$$= \int_{0}^{x} e^{p(x-t)} f(t)(x-t)\,dt$$

2. To evaluate the given integral, substitute eq.(2) into eq.(3) to obtain

$$\int_0^\infty \frac{e^{-ax} - e^{-bx}}{x} \, dx = \int_{x=0}^\infty \int_{y=a}^b e^{-xy} \, dy \, dx$$

$$= \int_{y=a}^b \int_{x=0}^\infty e^{-xy} \, dx \, dy = \int_{y=a}^b \left[\frac{e^{-xy}}{-y} \right] \Big|_0^\infty dy$$

$$= \int_a^b \frac{1}{y} \, dy = \ln y \Big|_a^b = \ln \frac{b}{a}$$

● PROBLEM 13-12

The curve called the witch of Agnesi is described by the equation

$$y = \frac{8a^3}{x^2 + 4a^2} \qquad (1)$$

and shown in the figure.

Evaluate the integral

$$\iint_D x \, dy \, dx \qquad (2)$$

where D is the shaded area shown.

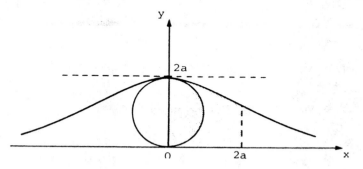

Solution: From the figure, we see that for any fixed x, y changes from $y = 0$ to $y = \frac{8a^3}{x^2 + 4a^2}$. The region D can be described by the inequalities

$$0 \le y \le \frac{8a^3}{x^2 + 4a^2}$$

$$0 \le x \le 2a \qquad (3)$$

The integral in eq.(2) can then be written

605

$$\int_{x=0}^{2a} \int_{y=0}^{\frac{8a^3}{x^2+4a^2}} x \, dy \, dx$$

$$= \int_{x=0}^{2a} \left[xy \right] \Bigg|_{y=0}^{\frac{8a^3}{x^2+4a^2}} dx \qquad (4)$$

$$= \int_{0}^{2a} \frac{8a^3 x}{x^2+4a^2} \, dx$$

Now, to calculate the above integral, use the following form-ula, which may be obtained from any table of integrals,

$$\int \frac{x \, dx}{a^2+x^2} = \frac{1}{2} \ln(a^2+x^2) + C, \qquad (5)$$

Therefore,

$$\int_{0}^{2a} \frac{8a^3 x}{x^2+4a^2} \, dx = 8a^3 \left[\frac{1}{2} \ln(x^2+4a^2) \right] \Bigg|_{x=0}^{2a}$$

$$= 4a^3 \left[\ln 8a^2 - \ln 4a^2 \right] \qquad (6)$$

$$= 4a^3 \ln 2$$

DOUBLE INTEGRALS REPRESENTING AREA

● **PROBLEM** 13-13

Using double integrals, evaluate:

1. The area of the triangle S with vertices $(0,0)$, $(1,1)$, $(1,0)$.

2. The volume between the surface

$$z = x^3 + y^3 \qquad (1)$$

and the triangle S on the xy plane whose vertices are $(0,0,0)$, $(1,1,0)$, $(1,0,0)$.

Solution: 1. First, notice that if we take $f(x,y)=1$, then the double integral may be expressed as

$$\iint_{D} f(x,y) \, dx \, dy = \iint_{D} dx \, dy = A \qquad (2)$$

where A is the area of region D.

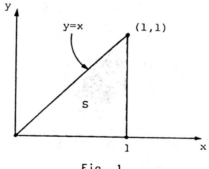

Fig. 1

The triangle S, shown in Fig. 1, can be described by the inequalities

$$0 \le y \le x$$
$$0 \le x \le 1 \tag{3}$$

The integral in eq.(2) can then be written

$$\iint\limits_{D} dxdy = \int_0^1 \int_0^x dydx$$

$$= \int_0^1 \left[y \Big|_0^x \right] dx = \int_0^1 xdx = \frac{1}{2} \tag{4}$$

2. Let $f(x,y)=z$ be the general equation of a surface. The
    volume between the surface $z=f(x,y)$ and the xy plane is
    given by

$$V = \iint\limits_{D} f(x,y)dxdy \tag{6}$$

where D is some general region lying in the xy plane, as
shown in Fig. 2. Volumes above the xy plane are considered positive, while volumes below the xy plane are considered negative.

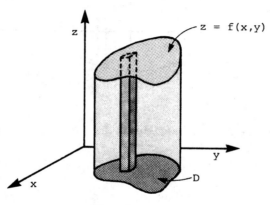

Fig. 2

607

In this case, the function $z=f(x,y)$ is given by

$$z = x^3 + y^3 \qquad (7)$$

The region D can be described by the inequalities

$$0 \le y \le x$$
$$\qquad (8)$$
$$0 \le x \le 1$$

Substituting eq.(7) and eq.(8) into eq.(6) results in

$$V = \iint_D f(x,y)dxdy$$

$$= \int_0^1 \int_0^x (x^3+y^3)dydx = \int_0^1 \left[\left(x^3 y + \frac{y^4}{4}\right) \Big|_0^x \right] dx \qquad (9)$$

$$= \int_0^1 \left(x^4 + \frac{1}{4} x^4\right) dx = \frac{5}{4} \int_0^1 x^4 dx$$

$$= \left(\frac{5}{4} \frac{x^5}{5}\right) \Big|_0^1 = \frac{1}{4}$$

● **PROBLEM 13-14**

Find the area of the ellipse

$$\frac{x^2}{a^2} + \frac{y^2}{b^2} = 1 \qquad (1)$$

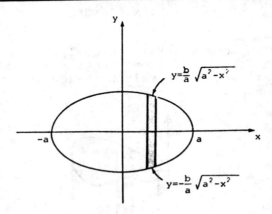

Solution: The area of a region D lying in the xy plane is given by

$$A = \iint_D dydx \qquad (2)$$

Now, to find the area of the ellipse, first note that for fixed values of x, y changes from

608

$$y = \frac{-b}{a} \sqrt{a^2 - x^2}$$

to

$$y = \frac{b}{a} \sqrt{a^2 - x^2}$$

x varies from x = -a to x = a (see Fig. 1).

Therefore, the ellipse D may be described by

$$-\frac{b}{a} \sqrt{a^2 - x^2} \le y \le \frac{b}{a} \sqrt{a^2 - x^2}$$

$$\tag{3}$$

$$-a \le x \le a$$

and the area may then be expressed as

$$A = \iint_D dy\,dx$$

$$= \int_{x=-a}^{a} \int_{y=-\frac{b}{a}\sqrt{a^2-x^2}}^{\frac{b}{a}\sqrt{a^2-x^2}} dy\,dx$$

$$= \frac{2b}{a} \int_{-a}^{a} \sqrt{a^2-x^2}\,dx \tag{4}$$

Now, using the formula

$$\int \sqrt{a^2-x^2}\,dx = \frac{x}{2}\sqrt{a^2-x^2} + \frac{a^2}{2}\sin^{-1}\frac{x}{a} + c$$

integral (4) becomes

$$\frac{2b}{a} \int_{-a}^{a} \sqrt{a^2-x^2}\,dx$$

$$= \frac{2b}{a} \left[\frac{x}{2}\sqrt{a^2-x^2} + \frac{a^2}{2}\sin^{-1}\frac{x}{a} \right]\Big|_{-a}^{a}$$

$$= \frac{2b}{a} \left[\frac{a^2}{2}\sin^{-1}1 - \frac{a^2}{2}\sin^{-1}(-1) \right]$$

$$= \frac{2b}{a} \left[\frac{a^2}{2}\frac{\pi}{2} - \frac{a^2}{2}\left(\frac{-\pi}{2}\right) \right]$$

$$= \pi ab$$

● **PROBLEM 13-15**

Evaluate the area of the region bounded by

$$y^2 = x$$

and

$$\tag{1}$$

$$y^2 = 6 - x$$

<u>Solution</u>: The region bounded by the curves $y^2 = x$ and $y^2 = 6 - x$ is shown in the figure.

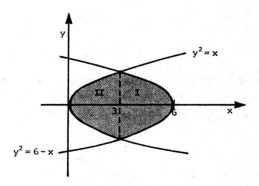

The area of this region is given by

$$A = \iint_D dy\,dx \qquad (2)$$

Now, note that in this case it is easier to integrate with respect to x first and then with respect to y.

Indeed, if we follow the dydx order of integration, then the region of integration would consist of regions I and II (shown in the figure), which are described by the inequalities

$$\left.\begin{array}{c} -\sqrt{x} \le y \le \sqrt{x} \\[2mm] 0 \le y \le 3 \end{array}\right\} \ \text{II} \qquad (3)$$

$$\left.\begin{array}{c} -\sqrt{6-x} \le y \le \sqrt{6-x} \\[2mm] 3 \le x \le 6 \end{array}\right\} \ \text{I} \qquad (4)$$

However, if we follow the dxdy order of integration, we deal with a simpler region of integration, namely

$$\begin{array}{c} y^2 \le x \le 6-y^2 \\[2mm] -\sqrt{3} \le y \le \sqrt{3} \end{array} \qquad (5)$$

Thus,

$$A = \iint_D dx\,dy = \int_{y=-\sqrt{3}}^{\sqrt{3}} \int_{x=y^2}^{6-y^2} dx\,dy$$

$$= \int_{-\sqrt{3}}^{\sqrt{3}} \left[x \Big|_{x=y^2}^{6-y^2} \right] dy = \int_{-\sqrt{3}}^{\sqrt{3}} (6-2y^2)\,dy$$

$$\qquad (6)$$

$$= \left(6y - \frac{2}{3}y^3\right) \Big|_{y=-\sqrt{3}}^{\sqrt{3}} = 8\sqrt{3}$$

Sketch the region whose area is given by

$$A = \int_{-1}^{1+\sqrt{6}} \int_{x^2+1}^{2x+6} dy\,dx \qquad (1)$$

and evaluate this area.

Solution: In the integral in eq.(1), we first integrate with respect to y. The limits of integration are from $y=x^2+1$ to $y=2x+6$. Thus the region is bounded by the curve $y=x^2+1$ and the line $y=2x+6$, as shown in the figure.

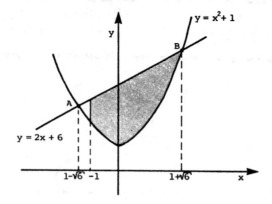

Now, let us find the points of intersection A and B. We have

$$x^2+1 = 2x+6$$

or

$$x^2-2x-5 = 0 \qquad (2)$$

and

$$x_1 = 1-\sqrt{6}, \quad x_2 = 1+\sqrt{6} \qquad (3)$$

Now, in eq.(1), the limits of integration with respect to x are from $x=-1$ to $x=1+\sqrt{6}$.

We therefore see that the integral in eq.(1) does not represent the area of the whole region bounded by $y=x^2+1$ and $y=2x+6$.

Instead the region represented by the integral in eq.(1) is bounded by

$$x = -1, \quad y = 2x+6 \quad \text{and} \quad y = x^2+1, \qquad (4)$$

as shown in the figure. The area of the region is

$$A = \int_{-1}^{1+\sqrt{6}} \int_{x^2+1}^{2x+6} dy\,dx$$

$$= \int_{-1}^{1+\sqrt{6}} \left[2x+6-x^2-1 \right] dx = \int_{-1}^{1+\sqrt{6}} (-x^2+2x+5)dx$$

$$= \left(-\frac{x^3}{3} + x^2 + 5x \right) \Big|_{x=-1}^{1+\sqrt{6}} \tag{5}$$

$$= 4\sqrt{6} + \frac{13}{3}$$

DOUBLE INTEGRALS REPRESENTING VOLUME

● PROBLEM 13-17

Evaluate the volume of the solid bounded by z=xy (for z ≥0) over the region in the first quadrant bounded by y=0, y²=x and y²=6-x.

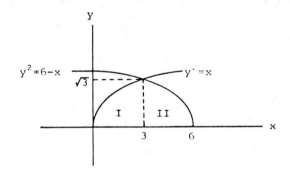

Solution: If z=f(x,y) represents a surface, then the volume bounded by the surface and the region D in the xy plane is given by

$$V = \iint_D f(x,y)dxdy \tag{1}$$

The volume above the xy plane is positive and volume below is negative.

In our case, we have

$$f(x,y) = xy \tag{2}$$

The region D of the xy plane bounded by y=0, y²=x and y²=6-x is shown in the figure.

Now, if we integrate first with respect to y and then with respect to x, then the region D has to be divided into the two regions:

$$\left. \begin{array}{c} 0 \le y \le \sqrt{x} \\[2ex] 0 \le x \le 3 \end{array} \right\} \quad I \tag{3}$$

$$\left.\begin{array}{l} 0 \le y \le \sqrt{6-x} \\ 3 \le x \le 6 \end{array}\right\} II \qquad (4)$$

and the volume is

$$V = \iint_D xy \ dy \ dx = \iint_I xy \ dy \ dx + \iint_{II} xy \ dy \ dx$$

$$= \int_{x=0}^{3} \int_{y=0}^{\sqrt{x}} xy\,dy\,dx + \int_{x=3}^{6} \int_{y=0}^{\sqrt{6-x}} xy\,dy\,dx \qquad (5)$$

$$= \int_0^3 \frac{x^2}{2} \ dx + \int_3^6 \frac{x}{2}(6-x)dx = \frac{27}{2}$$

Note that it would have been easier to integrate first with respect to x and then with respect to y. Indeed, for this case the region D is

$$y^2 \le x \le 6-y^2$$
$$0 \le y \le \sqrt{3} \qquad (6)$$

and the volume is

$$V = \iint_D xy \ dx \ dy = \int_{y=0}^{\sqrt{3}} \int_{x=y^2}^{6-y^2} xy \ dx \ dy$$

$$= \int_0^{\sqrt{3}} \frac{y}{2}(36-12y^2)dy = \left(9y^2 - \frac{3}{2}y^4\right)\Bigg|_0^{\sqrt{3}} \qquad (7)$$

$$= \frac{27}{2}$$

Both procedures do of course lead to the same result.

The sequence of integration is important, especially when calculations are complicated and long. Without mentioning it explicitly, we have frequently used the following theorem.

Theorem I

Let D be a subset of R^n, $D \subset R^n$ such that the iterated integral

$$\overbrace{\int \ldots \ldots \int}^{n \ times}_{D} f \ dx_1 dx_2 \ldots dx_n \qquad (8)$$

exists over D, if furthermore the multiple integral exists

$$\int_D f \ dV \qquad (9)$$

then the two integrals are equal

$$\int\ldots\ldots\int_D f \ dx_1 dx_2 \ldots dx_n = \int_D f \ dV \qquad (10)$$

A direct consequence of Theorem I is Theorem II.

<u>Theorem II</u>

If $\int_D f \ dV$ exists, and iterated integrals exist for some orders of integration, then all of these integrals are equal.

For n=2, if both integrals

$$\iint_D f \ dxdy \quad \text{and} \quad \iint_D f dydx \quad \text{exist then}$$

$$\iint_D f \ dxdy = \iint_D f \ dydx \qquad (11)$$

● **PROBLEM 13-18**

Find the volume of the solid bounded by the paraboloid $x^2 + y^2 = 5z$, the xy-plane and the cylinder $x^2 + y^2 = 9$.

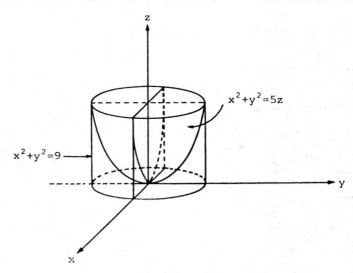

<u>Solution</u>: The solid is shown in the figure.

Now, the volume of the solid is given by

$$V = \iint_D f(x,y)dydx \qquad (1)$$

where $f(x,y) = z$ represents the equation of the surface and D represents the corresponding region in the xy-plane.

In our case

$$z = \frac{x^2+y^2}{5} \qquad (2)$$

and region D is a circle of radius 3

$$x^2 + y^2 = 9 \qquad (3)$$

Now, it just so happens that in this case, it is much simpler to compute the volume by first transforming eq.(1) into polar coordinates.

$$V = \iint_D \frac{x^2+y^2}{5} \, dydx = \int_{\theta=0}^{2\pi} \int_{r=0}^{3} r \cdot \frac{r^2}{5} \, drd\theta$$

$$= \int_0^{2\pi} \left[\frac{r^4}{20} \right] \Big|_0^3 \, d\theta = \frac{81\pi}{10} \qquad (4)$$

Note that the region D in the xy-plane is the projection of the intersection of the cylinder $x^2 + y^2 = 9$ with the paraboloid $x^2 + y^2 = 5z$.

● **PROBLEM 13-19**

Find the volume of the solid bounded above by $x^2+y^2+z-10 = 0$, below by the xy-plane, and laterally by the cylinder $x^2+y^2 = 9$.

<u>Solution</u>: The volume of the solid is given by

$$V = \iint_D f(x,y)dxdy \qquad (1)$$

We have $x^2+y^2+z-10 = 0$, thus

$$f(x,y) = z = 10 - x^2 - y^2$$

The region of integration D is described by the inequalities

$$-\sqrt{9-x^2} \le y \le \sqrt{9-x^2}$$

$$-3 \le x \le 3$$

Integral in eq.(1) becomes

$$V = \int_{x=-3}^{3} \int_{y=-\sqrt{9-x^2}}^{\sqrt{9-x^2}} (10-x^2-y^2)dydx$$

$$= \int_{-3}^{3} \left[10y-x^2y - \frac{y^3}{3} \right] \Bigg|_{y=-\sqrt{9-x^2}}^{\sqrt{9-x^2}} dx = \int_{-3}^{3} (14 - \frac{4}{3}x^2)\sqrt{9-x^2} \, dx$$

615

$$= 14 \int_{-3}^{3} \sqrt{9-x^2} \, dx - \frac{4}{3} \int_{-3}^{3} x^2 \sqrt{9-x^2} \, dx$$

We will now use the formulas

$$\int \sqrt{a^2-x^2} \, dx = \frac{x}{2}\sqrt{a^2-x^2} + \frac{a^2}{2} \text{ arc sin } \frac{x}{a} + C$$

$$\int x^2 \sqrt{a^2-x^2} \, dx = \frac{x}{8}(2x^2-a^2)\sqrt{a^2-x^2} + \frac{a^4}{8} \text{ arc sin } \frac{x}{a} + C$$

to obtain

$$\int_{-3}^{3} \sqrt{9-x^2} \, dx = \frac{9}{2} \text{ arc sin } 1 - \frac{9}{2} \text{ arc sin } -1 = \frac{9}{2}\pi$$

$$\int_{-3}^{3} x^2\sqrt{9-x^2} \, dx = \frac{81}{8} \text{ arc sin } 1 - \frac{81}{8} \text{ arc sin } -1 = \frac{81}{8}\pi$$

Thus,

$$V = 14 \cdot \frac{9}{2}\pi - \frac{4}{3}\left(\frac{81}{8}\pi\right) = \frac{99}{2}\pi$$

CENTER OF MASS AND MOMENTS OF INERTIA

● PROBLEM 13-20

Find the mass and the coordinates of the center of mass of the thin plate P shown in the figure.

The density of the plate is given by

$$\rho(x,y) = \alpha x^2 + y^4 \qquad (1)$$

where α is a positive constant.

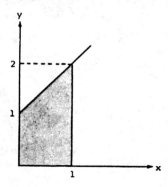

Solution: Since density is mass per unit area, the total mass of the plate is given by

$$M = \iint_P \rho(x,y)dxdy \qquad (2)$$

The region P can be described by the inequalities

$$0 \le x \le 1 \qquad (3)$$

$$0 \le y \le x+1 \qquad (4)$$

Substituting eq.(1) into eq.(2) and applying eqs.(3) and (4) results in

$$M = \iint_P \rho(x,y)dxdy = \int_0^1 \int_0^{x+1} (\alpha x^2 + y^4)dydx$$

$$= \int_0^1 \left[\alpha x^2 y + \frac{y^5}{5}\right]\Big|_0^{x+1} dx = \int_0^1 \left[\alpha x^2(x+1) + \frac{(x+1)^5}{5}\right] dx$$

$$= \int_0^1 \left(\alpha x^3 + \alpha x^2 + \frac{(x+1)^5}{5}\right) dx$$

$$= \left[\alpha \frac{x^4}{4} + \alpha \frac{x^3}{3} + \frac{(x+1)^6}{30}\right]\Big|_0^1 \qquad (5)$$

$$= \frac{\alpha}{4} + \frac{\alpha}{3} + \frac{2^6}{30} - \frac{1}{30} = \frac{7\alpha}{12} + \frac{2^6-1}{30} = \frac{7}{12}\alpha + \frac{21}{10}$$

The coordinates of the center of mass (x_M, y_M) are given by the equations

$$x_M = \frac{1}{M} \iint_P x\,\rho(x,y)dxdy \qquad (6)$$

$$y_M = \frac{1}{M} \iint_P y\,\rho(x,y)dxdy \qquad (7)$$

From eq.(6), we obtain

$$x_M = \frac{1}{M} \iint_P (\alpha x^3 + y^4 x)dxdy$$

$$= \frac{1}{M} \int_0^1 \int_0^{x+1} (\alpha x^3 + y^4 x)dydx$$

$$= \frac{1}{M} \int_0^1 \left[\alpha x^3 y + x\frac{y^5}{5}\right]\Big|_0^{x+1} dx$$

$$= \frac{1}{M} \int_0^1 \left[\alpha x^3(x+1) + x\frac{(x+1)^5}{5}\right] dx = \frac{1}{M} \int_0^1 \left[\alpha x^4 + \alpha x^3 + x\frac{(x+1)^5}{5}\right] dx$$

617

$$= \frac{1}{M} \left[\alpha \frac{x^5}{5} + \alpha \frac{x^4}{4} + \frac{x}{30} (x+1)^6 - \frac{(x+1)^7}{5 \cdot 42} \right] \Big|_0^1 \qquad (8)$$

$$= \frac{1}{M} \left[\frac{\alpha}{5} + \frac{\alpha}{4} + \frac{2^6}{30} - \frac{2^7}{5 \cdot 42} + \frac{1}{5 \cdot 42} \right]$$

$$= \frac{1}{M} \left(\frac{9}{20} \alpha + \frac{32}{15} - \frac{127}{210} \right)$$

For the y coordinate we obtain

$$y_M = \frac{1}{M} \iint_P y\rho(x,y)dxdy = \frac{1}{M} \int_0^1 \int_0^{x+1} (\alpha x^2 y + y^5)dydx$$

$$= \frac{1}{M} \int_0^1 \left[\alpha x^2 \frac{y^2}{2} + \frac{y^6}{6} \right] \Big|_0^{x+1} dx$$

$$= \frac{1}{M} \int_0^1 \left[\alpha x^2 \frac{(x+1)^2}{2} + \frac{(x+1)^6}{6} \right] dx$$

$$= \frac{1}{M} \int_0^1 \left[\frac{\alpha x^4}{2} + \alpha x^3 + \frac{\alpha x^2}{2} + \frac{(x+1)^6}{6} \right] dx$$

$$= \frac{1}{M} \left[\frac{\alpha x^5}{10} + \frac{\alpha x^4}{4} + \frac{\alpha x^3}{6} + \frac{(x+1)^7}{42} \right] \Big|_0^1 \qquad (9)$$

$$= \frac{1}{M} \left[\frac{\alpha}{10} + \frac{\alpha}{4} + \frac{\alpha}{6} + \frac{2^7}{42} - \frac{1}{42} \right]$$

M, the total mass of the plate, is given by eq. (5).

● **PROBLEM 13-21**

Find the centroid of the region D bounded by $y^2=3x$ and
y=2x, where the density is uniformly 1.

Solution: If $\rho(x,y)$ is the density of a region D, then the
centroid, or center of mass (x_M, y_M) can be obtained from

$$x_M = \frac{1}{M} \iint_D x\rho(x,y)dxdy \qquad (1)$$

$$y_M = \frac{1}{M} \iint_D y\rho(x,y)dxdy \qquad (2)$$

where M represents the mass, which is given by

$$M = \iint_D \rho(x,y)dxdy \qquad (3)$$

618

Now, for this problem, the region D is bounded by $y^2=3x$ and $y=2x$, as shown in the figure.

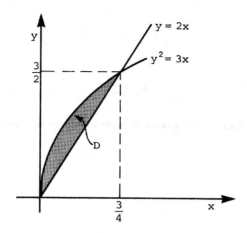

From eq.(3), the mass M of the region D is, since $\rho(x,y)=1$,

$$M = \int_{x=0}^{\frac{3}{4}} \int_{y=2x}^{\sqrt{3x}} dy\,dx = \int_{0}^{\frac{3}{4}} (y) \Big|_{2x}^{\sqrt{3x}} dx$$

$$= \int_{0}^{\frac{3}{4}} (\sqrt{3x} - 2x)dx = \left(\frac{2\sqrt{3}}{3} x^{\frac{3}{2}} - x^2\right)\Big|_{0}^{\frac{3}{4}} = \frac{3}{16}$$

From eq.(1), we have

$$x_M = \frac{16}{3} \int_{x=0}^{\frac{3}{4}} \int_{y=2x}^{\sqrt{3x}} x\,dy\,dx$$

$$= \frac{16}{3} \int_{0}^{\frac{3}{4}} [xy]\Big|_{y=2x}^{\sqrt{3x}} dx \qquad (4)$$

$$= \frac{16}{3} \int_{0}^{\frac{3}{4}} (\sqrt{3}\, x^{\frac{3}{2}} - 2x^2)dx = \frac{16}{3}\left[\frac{2\sqrt{3}}{5} x^{\frac{5}{2}} - \frac{2}{3} x^3\right]\Big|_{0}^{\frac{3}{4}} = \frac{3}{10}$$

From eq.(2), y_M is found to be

$$y_M = \frac{16}{3} \int_{x=0}^{\frac{3}{4}} \int_{y=2x}^{\sqrt{3x}} y\,dy\,dx$$

$$= \frac{16}{3} \int_{0}^{\frac{3}{4}} \frac{1}{2}(3x - 4x^2)dx = \frac{3}{4} \qquad (5)$$

Thus, the centroid of the region is

$$(x_M, y_M) = \left(\frac{3}{10}, \frac{3}{4}\right) \qquad (6)$$

619

Consider the thin plate P shown in the figure, whose density is given by

$$\rho(x,y) = \alpha e^x + y^2 \qquad (1)$$

where α is a positive constant.

Find the moments of inertia of this plate about the x and y axes.

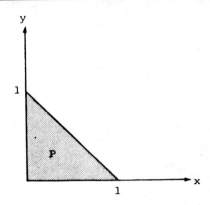

Solution: The moments of inertia of the thin plate about the x and y axes are given by the equations

$$I_x = \iint_P y^2 \rho(x,y) dxdy \qquad (2)$$

$$I_y = \iint_P x^2 \rho(x,y) dxdy \qquad (3)$$

In this case, the region P can be described by the inequalities

$$0 \le x \le 1$$
$$0 \le y \le -x+1 \qquad (4)$$

Substituting eq.(1) and eq.(4) into eq.(2) results in

$$I_x = \iint_P y^2(\alpha e^x + y^2) dxdy$$

$$= \int_0^1 \int_0^{-x+1} (\alpha y^2 e^x + y^4) dydx = \int_0^1 \left[\left(\alpha e^x \frac{y^3}{3} + \frac{y^5}{5} \right) \Big|_0^{-x+1} \right] dx$$

$$= \int_0^1 \left[\frac{\alpha e^x}{3}(-x+1)^3 + \frac{1}{5}(-x+1)^5 \right] dx \qquad (5)$$

$$= \left\{ \frac{\alpha}{3} \left[e^x(-x+1)^3 + 3e^x(-x+1)^2 + 6e^x(-x+1) + 6e^x \right] + \frac{(-x+1)^6}{30} \right\} \Big|_0^1$$

$$= \frac{\alpha}{3} \left[6e - 16 \right] - \frac{1}{30}$$

To evaluate the moment of inertia about the y axis, we substitute eq.(1) and eq.(4) into eq.(3) and obtain

$$I_y = \iint\limits_P x^2 (\alpha e^x + y^2) dx dy$$

$$= \int_0^1 \int_0^{-x+1} (\alpha x^2 e^x + x^2 y^2) dy dx$$

$$= \int_0^1 \left[\left(\alpha x^2 e^x y + x^2 \frac{y^3}{3} \right) \Big|_0^{-x+1} \right] dx$$

$$= \int_0^1 \left[\alpha x^2 (-x+1) e^x + x^2 \frac{(-x+1)^3}{3} \right] dx \qquad (6)$$

$$= \int_0^1 \left[\alpha x^2 e^x - \alpha x^3 e^x + \frac{1}{3} x^2 - x^3 + x^4 - \frac{1}{3} x^5 \right] dx$$

$$= \alpha \left[x^2 e^x - 2xe^x + 2e^x \right] \Big|_0^1 - \alpha \left[x^3 e^x - 3x^2 e^x + 6xe^x - 6e^x \right] \Big|_0^1$$

$$+ \left[\frac{x^3}{9} - \frac{x^4}{4} + \frac{x^5}{5} - \frac{x^6}{18} \right] \Big|_0^1$$

$$= \alpha(e-2) - \alpha(-2e+6) + \left(\frac{1}{9} - \frac{1}{4} + \frac{1}{5} - \frac{1}{18} \right)$$

$$= 3\alpha e - 8\alpha + \frac{1}{18} - \frac{1}{20} = \alpha(3e-8) + \frac{1}{180}$$

Taking the approximation of e,

$$e \approx 2.71 \qquad (7)$$

we finally obtain

$$I_x = 0.086\alpha + 0.033 \qquad (8)$$

$$I_y = 0.13\alpha + 0.0055 \qquad (9)$$

● **PROBLEM 13-23**

Find the moments of inertia I_x and I_y of a thin plate of density 1 bounded by x=0, x=1, y=0 and the curve $y = a \cosh \left(\frac{x}{a} \right)$.

Solution: The curve

$$y = a \cosh\left(\frac{x}{a}\right) = \frac{a}{2}\left(e^{\frac{x}{a}} + e^{-\frac{x}{a}}\right) \tag{1}$$

is called a catenary from the Latin word catena, meaning chain. The thin plate bounded by x=0, x=1, y=0 and $y = \frac{a}{2}\left(e^{\frac{x}{a}} + e^{-\frac{x}{a}}\right)$ is shown in the figure.

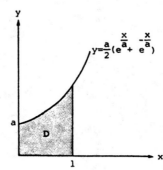

Since the density $\rho(x,y)$ of the plate is 1, the moments of inertia are given by

$$I_x = \iint_D y^2 \, dy \, dx \tag{2}$$

$$I_y = \iint_D x^2 \, dy \, dx \tag{3}$$

The plate D is described by

$$0 \le y \le \frac{a}{2}\left(e^{\frac{x}{a}} + e^{-\frac{x}{a}}\right)$$

$$0 \le x \le 1 \tag{4}$$

From eq.(2) we determine I_x.

$$I_x = \iint_D y^2 \, dy \, dx = \int_{x=0}^{1} \int_{y=0}^{\frac{a}{2}\left(e^{\frac{x}{a}} + e^{-\frac{x}{a}}\right)} y^2 \, dy \, dx$$

$$= \int_0^1 \frac{a}{6}\left[e^{\frac{x}{a}} + e^{-\frac{x}{a}}\right]^3 dx \tag{5}$$

$$= \frac{a}{6}\left[\frac{1}{3} ae^{\left(\frac{3x}{a}\right)} - \frac{1}{3} ae^{\left(\frac{-3x}{a}\right)} + 3\,ae^{\frac{x}{a}} - 3\,ae^{-\frac{x}{a}}\right]\Bigg|_0^1$$

$$= \frac{a^2}{6}\left[\frac{1}{3} e^{\frac{3}{a}} - \frac{1}{3} e^{\left(\frac{-3}{a}\right)} + 3\, e^{\frac{1}{a}} - 3\, e^{\left(\frac{-1}{a}\right)}\right]$$

From eq.(3), we have

$$I_y = \iint_D x^2 \, dy \, dx = \int_{x=0}^{1} \int_{y=0}^{\frac{a}{2}\left(e^{\frac{x}{a}} + e^{-\frac{x}{a}}\right)} x^2 \, dy \, dx$$

$$= \frac{a}{2} \int_0^1 \left(x^2 \, e^{\frac{x}{a}} + x^2 \, e^{-\frac{x}{a}}\right) \, dx \tag{6}$$

To evaluate the last integral in eq.(6), note that

$$\int x \, e^x dx = x \, e^x - e^x \tag{7}$$

$$\int x^2 e^x dx = x^2 e^x - 2 \int x e^x dx = x^2 e^x - 2xe^x + 2e^x \tag{8}$$

Now, if we substitute $x=at$, we obtain

$$\int x^2 e^{\frac{x}{a}} dx = a^3 \int t^2 e^t dt = a^3 \left[t^2 e^t - 2te^t + 2e^t \right]$$

$$= ax^2 e^{\frac{x}{a}} - 2a^2 xe^{\frac{x}{a}} + 2a^3 e^{\frac{x}{a}} \tag{9}$$

Replacing a by -a in eq.(9), we obtain

$$\int x^2 e^{-\frac{x}{a}} dx = -ax^2 e^{\left(-\frac{x}{a}\right)} - 2a^2 xe^{\left(-\frac{x}{a}\right)} - 2a^3 e^{\left(-\frac{x}{a}\right)} \tag{10}$$

Substituting eqs.(9) and (10) into eq.(6) results in

$$I_y = \frac{a}{2} \left[ax^2 e^{\frac{x}{a}} - 2a^2 xe^{\frac{x}{a}} + 2a^3 e^{\frac{x}{a}} \right.$$

$$\left. - ax^2 e^{\left(-\frac{x}{a}\right)} - 2a^2 xe^{\left(-\frac{x}{a}\right)} - 2a^3 e^{\left(-\frac{x}{a}\right)} \right] \Bigg|_0^1 \tag{11}$$

$$= \frac{a^2}{2} (2a^2 - 2a + 1) \left(e^{\frac{1}{a}} - e^{\left(-\frac{1}{a}\right)} \right)$$

● **PROBLEM 13-24**

A thin plate of uniform density covers the region of the xy plane bounded by

$$y = x^2$$
$$y = x+6 \tag{1}$$

Find the moment of inertia I_y about the y-axis and the radius of gyration with respect to the y-axis.

<u>Solution</u>: The plate is shown in the figure.

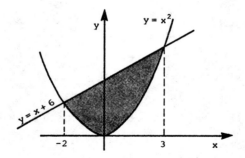

The moment of inertia I_y is given by

$$I_y = \iint_D x^2 \rho(x,y) \, dy \, dx \qquad (2)$$

Since the density is uniform, we have

$$\rho(x,y) = \text{const} = \rho$$

Thus

$$I_y = \rho \int_{x=-2}^{3} \int_{y=x^2}^{x+6} x^2 \, dy \, dx$$

$$= \rho \int_{-2}^{3} \left[\left(x^2 [y] \right) \Big|_{y=x^2}^{x+6} \right] dx = \rho \int_{-2}^{3} (6x^2 + x^3 - x^4) \, dx \qquad (3)$$

$$= \rho \left(2x^3 + \frac{x^4}{4} - \frac{x^5}{5} \right) \Bigg|_{-2}^{3} = \frac{125\rho}{4}$$

The radius of gyration with respect to the y-axis, R_y, is given by

$$I_y = M R_y^2 \qquad (4)$$

or

$$R_y = \sqrt{\frac{I_y}{M}} \qquad (5)$$

R_y is defined as that distance from the y-axis at which the total mass M could be concentrated so as to give the same moment of inertia I_y. The mass M is equal to

$$M = \int_{x=-1}^{2} \int_{y=x}^{x+6} \rho(x,y) \, dy \, dx = \rho \int_{-1}^{2} (x+6-x^2) \, dx$$

$$= \rho \left(\frac{x^2}{2} + 6x - \frac{1}{3} x^3 \right) \Bigg|_{-1}^{2} \qquad (6)$$

624

$$= \frac{33}{2} \rho$$

The radius of gyration is thus

$$R_y = \sqrt{\frac{I_y}{M}} = \sqrt{\frac{125\rho}{4} \left(\frac{2}{33\rho}\right)} = \sqrt{\frac{125}{66}} \qquad (7)$$

● **PROBLEM 13-25**

Consider a thin plate of unit density which is in the form of a cardioid. The equation of the cardioid in polar coordinates is given by

$$r = a(1 - \cos\theta) \qquad (1)$$

Find the moment of inertia about the y-axis of this plate.

Solution: The plate is shown in the figure.

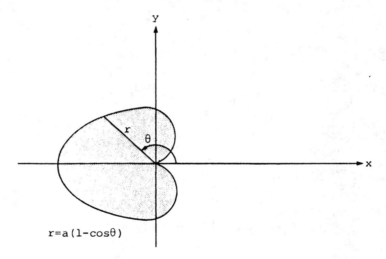

$r = a(1-\cos\theta)$

Since the density of the plate is 1, its moment of inertia about the y-axis is

$$I_y = \iint_D x^2 \, dy \, dx \qquad (2)$$

It is easier to carry out all the calculations in polar co-ordinates. We shall integrate first with respect to r then with respect to θ. Note that for any θ between 0 and 2π, r varies from 0 to $a(1-\cos\theta)$.

Thus,

$$0 \le r \le a(1-\cos\theta)$$

$$0 \le \theta \le 2\pi \qquad (3)$$

In polar coordinates integral (2) becomes

$$I_y = \iint_D (r\cos\theta)^2 r \, dr d\theta \tag{4}$$

Now, since

$$x = r\cos\theta, \tag{5}$$

we have

$$I_y = \int_{\theta=0}^{2\pi} \int_{r=0}^{a(1-\cos\theta)} r^3 \cos^2\theta \, dr d\theta$$

$$= \int_0^{2\pi} \frac{a^4}{4} \cos^2\theta (1-\cos\theta)^4 d\theta \tag{6}$$

$$= \frac{a^4}{4} \int_0^{2\pi} \left[\cos^6\theta - 4\cos^5\theta + 6\cos^4\theta - 4\cos^3\theta + \cos^2\theta \right] d\theta$$

Now we will use the following reduction formula,

$$\int_0^{2\pi} \cos^n\theta \, d\theta = \left. \frac{\cos^{n-1}\theta \sin\theta}{n} \right|_{\theta=0}^{2\pi} + \frac{n-1}{n} \int_0^{2\pi} \cos^{n-2}\theta \, d\theta \tag{7}$$

Since $\sin 0 = \sin 2\pi = 0$, eq.(7) becomes

$$\int_0^{2\pi} \cos^n\theta \, d\theta = \frac{n-1}{n} \int_0^{2\pi} \cos^{n-2}\theta \, d\theta \tag{8}$$

Therefore,

$$\int_0^{2\pi} \cos^2\theta \, d\theta = \frac{1}{2} \int_0^{2\pi} d\theta = \pi \tag{9}$$

$$\int_0^{2\pi} \cos^3\theta \, d\theta = \frac{2}{3} \int_0^{2\pi} \cos\theta \, d\theta = 0 \tag{10}$$

$$\int_0^{2\pi} \cos^4\theta \, d\theta = \frac{3}{4} \int_0^{2\pi} \cos^2\theta \, d\theta = \frac{3\pi}{4} \tag{11}$$

$$\int_0^{2\pi} \cos^5\theta \, d\theta = 0 \tag{12}$$

$$\int_0^{2\pi} \cos^6\theta \, d\theta = \frac{5}{6} \int_0^{2\pi} \cos^4\theta \, d\theta = \frac{5\pi}{8} \tag{13}$$

Substituting eqs.(9) through (13) into eq.(6) results in

$$I_y = \frac{a^4}{4} \left[\frac{5}{8}\pi + \frac{9\pi}{2} + \pi \right] = \frac{49}{32} a^4 \pi \tag{14}$$

1. Find the polar moment of inertia about an axis through 0 perpendicular to the xy-plane, for a thin plate of density 1 bounded by x=0, y=3x, y=6.

2. Show that the polar moment of inertia I_0 about an axis through 0 perpendicular to the xy-plane is equal to

$$I_0 = I_x + I_y \tag{1}$$

for any area in the xy-plane.

Solution: The polar moment of inertia about an axis through 0 perpendicular to the xy-plane is given by

$$I_0 = \iint_D r^2 \rho(x,y)dxdy \tag{2}$$

where $\rho(x,y)$ is the density and r,

$$r = \sqrt{x^2+y^2} \tag{3}$$

is the distance from the origin.

1. The plate is shown in the figure.

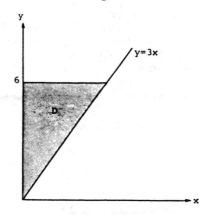

From eq.(2) we find

$$I_0 = \iint_D r^2 \rho(x,y)dydx = \int_{x=0}^{2} \int_{y=3x}^{6} (x^2+y^2)dydx$$

$$= \int_{0}^{2} \left[x^2y + \frac{y^3}{3} \right] \Bigg|_{y=3x}^{6} dx = \int_{0}^{2} [72+6x^2-12x^3]dx$$

$$= [72x+2x^3-3x^4] \Bigg|_{x=0}^{2} = 112 \tag{4}$$

2. The polar moment of inertia I_0 about an axis through 0 perpendicular to the xy-plane is equal to

$$I_0 = \iint_D r^2 \rho(x,y)dxdy$$

$$= \iint_D (x^2+y^2)\rho(x,y)dxdy \qquad (5)$$

$$= \iint_D x^2 \rho(x,y)dxdy + \iint_D y^2 \rho(x,y)dxdy$$

$$= I_y + I_x$$

This holds true for any area in the xy-plane.

TRANSFORMATION OF COORDINATES

● PROBLEM 13-27

Let
$$x = 2u-v$$
$$y = u+2v \qquad (1)$$

be a transformation from the xy-plane to the uv-plane. Consider the region D of the xy-plane, $0 \le x \le 2$, $0 \le y \le 2$, whose area is S=4. Region D is transformed by eq.(1) into a region D' of the uv-plane whose area is S'. Find the relationship between S, S' and the Jacobian of the transformation given in eq.(1).

Solution: The region D is shown in Fig. 1.

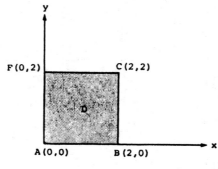

Fig. 1

D is bounded by

$$x=0, \quad x=2, \quad y=0 \quad \text{and} \quad y=2 \qquad (2)$$

Under the given transformation,

$$x = 2u-v$$

$$y = u+2v$$

we get

$$x=0 \rightarrow 2u=v$$

$$x=2 \rightarrow 2+v=2u \tag{3}$$

$$y=0 \rightarrow u=-2v$$

$$y=2 \rightarrow 2-2v=u$$

The points A,B,C,F are transformed as follows

$$A(0,0) \rightarrow A'(0,0)$$

$$B(2,0) \rightarrow B'\left(\frac{4}{5}, -\frac{2}{5}\right)$$

$$C(2,2) \rightarrow C'\left(\frac{6}{5}, \frac{2}{5}\right) \tag{4}$$

$$F(0,2) \rightarrow F'\left(\frac{2}{5}, \frac{4}{5}\right)$$

The region D' is shown in Fig. 2.

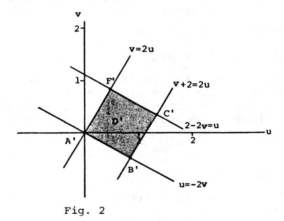

Fig. 2

Note that D' is rectangular. Indeed, the vectors $\overline{A'F'}$ and $\overline{A'B'}$ are orthogonal. Their scalar product is

$$\overline{A'F'} \cdot \overline{A'B'} = \left(\frac{2}{5}, \frac{4}{5}\right) \cdot \left(\frac{4}{5}, -\frac{2}{5}\right) = 0 \tag{5}$$

The area S' of the region D' is

$$|\overline{A'F'}| \cdot |\overline{A'B'}| = \sqrt{\frac{4}{25} + \frac{16}{25}} \cdot \sqrt{\frac{16}{25} + \frac{4}{25}} = \frac{20}{25} = \frac{4}{5} \tag{6}$$

Thus,

$$S' = \frac{4}{5} \tag{7}$$

The Jacobian of transformation (1) is

$$\frac{\partial(x,y)}{\partial(u,v)} = \begin{vmatrix} \dfrac{\partial x}{\partial u} & \dfrac{\partial y}{\partial u} \\[2mm] \dfrac{\partial x}{\partial v} & \dfrac{\partial y}{\partial v} \end{vmatrix} = \begin{vmatrix} 2 & 1 \\ -1 & 2 \end{vmatrix} = 5 \qquad (8)$$

We see that

$$S = \frac{\partial(x,y)}{\partial(u,v)}\, S \qquad (9)$$

since

$$4 = 5 \cdot \frac{4}{5}$$

● **PROBLEM** 13-28

By transforming into polar coordinates, evaluate the integral

$$\int_{x=0}^{a} \int_{y=0}^{\sqrt{a^2-x^2}} (x^2+y^2)\,dy\,dx \qquad (1)$$

Solution: We will not give here a rigorous treatment of the problem of changing the variables in a double integral. Instead, we will only cite the results. Consider the transformation of the x,y coordinates into u,v coordinates.

$$x = f(u,v)$$
$$y = g(u,v) \qquad (2)$$

Eq.(2) may be interpreted as the mapping of a region D of the xy-plane into a region G of the uv-plane. Under some restrictions on the functions f and g, the following formula for changing from xy-coordinates to uv-coordinates holds

$$\iint_D F(x,y)\,dx\,dy = \iint_G F[f(u,v),g(u,v)]\,\frac{\partial(x,y)}{\partial(u,v)}\,du\,dv \qquad (3)$$

Here $\frac{\partial(x,y)}{\partial(u,v)}$ denotes the Jacobian of the transformation,

$$\frac{\partial(x,y)}{\partial(u,v)} = \begin{vmatrix} \dfrac{\partial x}{\partial u} & \dfrac{\partial x}{\partial v} \\[2mm] \dfrac{\partial y}{\partial u} & \dfrac{\partial y}{\partial v} \end{vmatrix} \qquad (4)$$

For the polar coordinates, we have

$$x = r\cos\theta$$
$$y = r\sin\theta \qquad (5)$$

Thus,

$$\frac{\partial(x,y)}{\partial(r,\theta)} = \begin{vmatrix} \cos\theta & -r\sin\theta \\ \sin\theta & r\cos\theta \end{vmatrix} = r(\cos^2\theta+\sin^2\theta) = r \qquad (6)$$

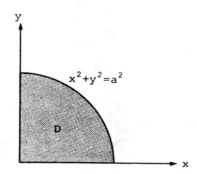

Eq.(3) becomes

$$\iint_D F(x,y)dxdy = \iint_G F(r\cos\theta, r\sin\theta)r\ drd\theta \qquad (7)$$

Applying eq.(7) to eq.(1) and noting that $x^2+y^2 = r^2$ yields

$$\int_{x=0}^{a}\int_{y=0}^{\sqrt{a^2-x^2}}(x^2+y^2)dydx = \int_{\theta=0}^{\frac{\pi}{2}}\int_{r=0}^{a} r^2 r\ drd\theta \qquad (8)$$

The region of integration is shown in the figure.

Note that since D is a quarter circle, we have

$$0 \le r \le a$$
$$0 \le \theta \le \frac{\pi}{2} \qquad (9)$$

From eq.(8) we compute

$$\int_{\theta=0}^{\frac{\pi}{2}}\int_{r=0}^{a} r^3 drd\theta = \int_{0}^{\frac{\pi}{2}}\frac{a^4}{4}\ d\theta = \frac{\pi a^4}{8} \qquad (10)$$

● **PROBLEM 13-29**

Find the total area enclosed by the lemniscate of Bernoulli, sometimes called the two-leaved rose.

$$(x^2+y^2)^2 = a^2(x^2-y^2) \qquad (1)$$

Solution: From eq.(1), it is clear that it will be easier to compute the area using polar coordinates.

We have,
$$x = r\ \cos\theta$$
$$y = r\ \sin\theta \qquad (2)$$

Eq.(1) becomes

$$(r^2\cos^2\theta + r^2\sin^2\theta)^2 = a^2(r^2\cos^2\theta - r^2\sin^2\theta) \qquad (3)$$

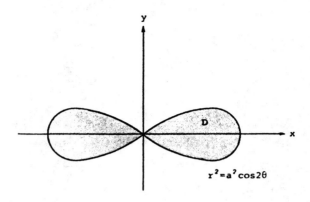

$$r^2 = a^2 \cos 2\theta$$

Since

$$\cos^2\theta - \sin^2\theta = \cos 2\theta \qquad (4)$$

we obtain

$$r^2 = a^2 \cos 2\theta \qquad (5)$$

The lemniscate is shown in the figure.

Note that the total area S is equal to

$$S = 4D \qquad (6)$$

where D represents the area of the region in the first quadrant, as indicated in the figure.

Note that for

$$\theta = 0, \qquad r = a \qquad (7)$$
$$\theta = \frac{\pi}{4}, \qquad r = 0$$

and for

$$\frac{\pi}{4} \le \theta \le \frac{\pi}{2}, \qquad r = 0.$$

The area D is represented by the double integral

$$D = \int_{\theta=0}^{\frac{\pi}{4}} \int_{r=0}^{r=a\sqrt{\cos 2\theta}} r \, dr d\theta \qquad (8)$$

$$= \int_0^{\frac{\pi}{4}} \left[\frac{r^2}{2} \Big|_{r=0}^{a\sqrt{\cos 2\theta}} \right] d\theta = \frac{a^2}{2} \int_0^{\frac{\pi}{4}} \cos 2\theta d\theta = \frac{a^2}{4}$$

Thus, the total area of the lemniscate is

$$S = 4D = 4 \left(\frac{a^2}{4} \right) = a^2 \qquad (9)$$

● **PROBLEM 13-30**

Transform the integral

$$\iint_S (x+y) dx dy \qquad (1)$$

where S is the parallelogram shown in Fig. 1 into an integral over a rectangle R and evaluate its value.

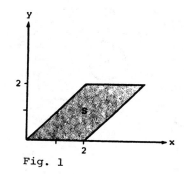

Fig. 1

Solution: Let us first define the transformation T which transforms the parallelogram S into a rectangle R, shown in Fig. 2. The transformation is given by

$$\begin{pmatrix} x \\ y \end{pmatrix} \xrightarrow{T} T\begin{pmatrix} u \\ v \end{pmatrix} = \begin{pmatrix} u+v \\ v \end{pmatrix} \qquad (2)$$

from which we obtain

$$x = u+v$$
$$y = v \qquad (3)$$

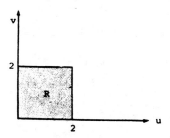

Fig. 2

Before proceeding, we shall quote here the theorem of the n-dimensional change of variables.

Theorem

Let S^n and R^n be n-dimensional spaces and $T : S^n \rightarrow R^n$ be a continuously differentiable transformation.

Let $A \subseteq S^n$, such that its boundary consists of a finite number of smooth sets.

It is assumed that

1. T is one-to-one on A

2. the Jacobian determinant of T, denoted det T' is different from zero on A.

If the function f is bounded and continuous on T(A), then

$$\int_{T(A)} f \, dV = \int_A (f \circ T) |\det T'| \, dV \qquad (4)$$

633

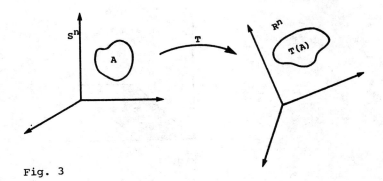

Fig. 3

In the next chapters we will show how this theorem functions for the three-dimensional spaces.

Now, getting back to the problem at hand, note that we are dealing with the two-dimensional space in this case.

From eq.(2) (or eq.(3)), the Jacobian determinant of T is found to be

$$\det T' = \begin{vmatrix} \dfrac{\partial x}{\partial u} & \dfrac{\partial x}{\partial v} \\[2mm] \dfrac{\partial y}{\partial u} & \dfrac{\partial y}{\partial v} \end{vmatrix} = \begin{vmatrix} 1 & 1 \\ 0 & 1 \end{vmatrix} = 1 \tag{5}$$

Applying the change-of-variables theorem results in

$$\iint\limits_{S} (x+y)\,dxdy = \iint\limits_{R} \Big((u+v)+v\Big)\,dudv$$

$$= \int_{0}^{2} \int_{0}^{2} \Big(u+v+v\Big)\,dudv = \int_{0}^{2} \left[\frac{u^2}{2} + 2uv\right] \Bigg|_{u=0}^{2} dv \tag{6}$$

$$= \int_{0}^{2} (4v+2)\,dv = (2v^2+2v) \Bigg|_{0}^{2}$$

$$= 12$$

CHAPTER 14

SURFACE INTEGRALS OF VECTORS, FLUX

INTRODUCTION

Chapter 14 deals with the surface integral of a vector field.

The basic elements of a surface integral are a vector field and an oriented smooth (or piecewise-smooth) surface, and the end result is a scalar.

The surface integral of a vector field $\overline{F}$ over a surface S is called the flux of $\overline{F}$ through S.

Flux is a fundamental concept of vector analysis. It has vast applications in the physical sciences. In particular, the concept of flux is most significant in electromagnetic theory and fluid dynamics (see Chapter 15).

Since, of course, a surface integral involves integration over a surface, it is crucial that the student understand the different methods of representing and characterizing surfaces. For this purpose, the first few problems of the chapter (as well as the first few problems of Chapter 13) discuss the various ways in which we define and characterize a surface.

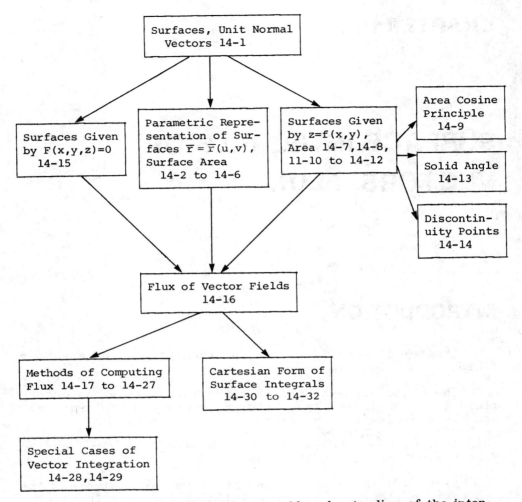

This chart is provided to facilitate rapid understanding of the inter-relationships of the topics and subject matter in this chapter. Also shown are the problem numbers associated with the subject matter.

SURFACES, UNIT NORMAL VECTOR, AND PARAMETRIC REPRESENTATION OF A SURFACE

● **PROBLEM 14-1**

1. Describe the various methods of defining a surface S. How do you find the unit normal vector $\bar{n}$?

2. Find the surface area of

$$z = \sqrt{x^2+y^2} \tag{1}$$

over the region D bounded by

$$0 \le x \le 4$$
$$1 \le y \le 6 \tag{2}$$

Solution: 1. A surface S may be given by:

a. An implicit function $f(x,y,z)=0$

b. An explicit function $f(x,y)=z$

c. A position vector $\bar{r}(u,v)$

d. A parametric set of two variables

$$x = \phi_1(u,v)$$
$$y = \phi_2(u,v) \qquad\qquad (3)$$
$$z = \phi_3(u,v)$$

At every point of a smooth surface there are two choices for the unit normal vector $\bar{n}$.

a. $\bar{n} = \pm \dfrac{\nabla f}{|\nabla f|}$ where $f(x,y,z)=0$ $\qquad\qquad (4)$

b. $\bar{n} = \pm \dfrac{-\left(\frac{\partial f}{\partial x}\right)\bar{i} - \left(\frac{\partial f}{\partial y}\right)\bar{j} + \bar{k}}{\sqrt{\left(\frac{\partial f}{\partial x}\right)^2 + \left(\frac{\partial f}{\partial y}\right)^2 + 1}}$ $\qquad\qquad (5)$

c. $\bar{n} = \pm \dfrac{\frac{\partial \bar{r}}{\partial u} \times \frac{\partial \bar{r}}{\partial v}}{\left|\frac{\partial \bar{r}}{\partial u} \times \frac{\partial \bar{r}}{\partial v}\right|}$ where $\dfrac{\partial \bar{r}}{\partial u} \times \dfrac{\partial \bar{r}}{\partial v} \neq \bar{0}$ $\qquad (6)$

d. For the parametric set of two variables

$$\bar{\Phi} = (\phi_1, \phi_2, \phi_3)$$

and

$$\bar{n} = \pm \dfrac{\frac{\partial \bar{\Phi}}{\partial u} \times \frac{\partial \bar{\Phi}}{\partial v}}{\left|\frac{\partial \bar{\Phi}}{\partial u} \times \frac{\partial \bar{\Phi}}{\partial v}\right|} \quad \text{where} \quad \left|\dfrac{\partial \bar{\Phi}}{\partial u} \times \dfrac{\partial \bar{\Phi}}{\partial v}\right| \neq 0 \qquad (7)$$

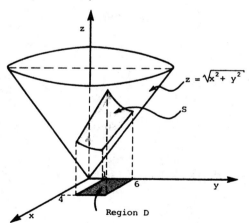

$z = \sqrt{x^2 + y^2}$

S

Region D

2. When a surface is given in the form of (b), that is $f(x,y)=z$, the surface area of the surface over a region D is given by

$$S = \iint_D \sqrt{\left(\frac{\partial z}{\partial x}\right)^2 + \left(\frac{\partial z}{\partial y}\right)^2 + 1} \; dxdy$$

In this case,

$$z = \sqrt{x^2+y^2}, \qquad\qquad (8)$$

thus the area of the surface over the region given by (2) is given by

$$S = \iint_D \sqrt{\left(\frac{\partial z}{\partial x}\right)^2 + \left(\frac{\partial z}{\partial y}\right)^2 + 1} \; dxdy$$

(9)

$$= \iint_D \sqrt{\frac{x^2}{x^2+y^2} + \frac{y^2}{x^2+y^2} + 1} \; dxdy = \int_{y=1}^6 \int_{x=0}^4 \sqrt{2} \; dxdy$$

$$= 20\sqrt{2}$$

The area of the surface is illustrated in the figure.

● **PROBLEM 14-2**

Find the surface area of the surface defined by the equations

$$x = \cos u$$

$$y = \sin u$$ (1)

$$z = v$$

for $0 \le u \le 2\pi$ and $0 \le v \le 1$.

<u>Solution</u>: First, consider a regular surface element described by the equation

$$\bar{r} = \bar{r}(u,v)$$ (2)

The surface area of a regular surface element is given by

$$S = \iint \left| \frac{\partial \bar{r}}{\partial u} \times \frac{\partial \bar{r}}{\partial v} \right| \; dudv$$ (3)

We often introduce the vector $d\bar{S}$

$$d\bar{S} = \frac{\partial \bar{r}}{\partial u} \, du \times \frac{\partial \bar{r}}{\partial v} \, dv$$

or

$$d\bar{S} = \left(\frac{\partial \bar{r}}{\partial u} \times \frac{\partial \bar{r}}{\partial v} \right) \; dudv$$ (4)

Note that $d\bar{S}$ is a vector normal to the surface, its magnitude $|d\bar{S}| = dS$ is the element of area.

Integral (3) can be written

$$S = \iint \left| \frac{\partial \bar{r}}{\partial u} \times \frac{\partial \bar{r}}{\partial v} \right| \; dudv = \iint |d\bar{S}|$$

$$= \iint dS = \iint \bar{n} \cdot d\bar{S}$$ (5)

where $\bar{n}$ is a unit normal vector in the direction of $d\bar{S}$.

Now, since

638

$$\bar{r} = (\cos u, \sin u, v)$$

the tangent vectors $\dfrac{\partial \bar{r}}{\partial u}$ and $\dfrac{\partial \bar{r}}{\partial v}$ are

$$\frac{\partial \bar{r}}{\partial u} = (-\sin u, \cos u, 0) \qquad (6)$$

$$\frac{\partial \bar{r}}{\partial v} = (0,0,1) \qquad (7)$$

Their vector product is

$$\frac{\partial \bar{r}}{\partial u} \times \frac{\partial \bar{r}}{\partial v} = (-\sin u, \cos u, 0) \times (0,0,1)$$

$$= (\cos u, \sin u, 0) \qquad (8)$$

Substituting eq.(8) into eq.(4) results in

$$d\bar{S} = (\cos u, \sin u, 0)dudv \qquad (9)$$

The area of the surface is given by eq.(5), thus

$$S = \iint |d\bar{S}| = \int_0^1 \int_0^{2\pi} \sqrt{\cos^2 u + \sin^2 u} \; dudv$$

$$= \int_0^1 \left[u \; \Big|_0^{2\pi} \right] dv \qquad (10)$$

$$= 2\pi$$

● **PROBLEM 14-3**

Find the area of the section of the surface

$$x = v^2 \qquad y = uv \qquad z = \tfrac{1}{2}u^2 \qquad (1)$$

bounded by the curves

$$u = 0, \qquad u = 1, \qquad v = 0 \quad \text{and} \quad v = 2 \qquad (2)$$

Solution: The surface area is given by

$$S = \iint |d\bar{S}| \qquad (3)$$

where

$$d\bar{S} = \frac{\partial \bar{r}}{\partial u} du \times \frac{\partial \bar{r}}{\partial v} dv = \left(\frac{\partial \bar{r}}{\partial u} \times \frac{\partial \bar{r}}{\partial v} \right) dudv \qquad (4)$$

Since, in this case

$$\bar{r} = (v^2, uv, \tfrac{1}{2}u^2)$$

we obtain

$$\frac{\partial \bar{r}}{\partial u} = (0, v, u) \qquad (5)$$

and

$$\frac{\partial \bar{r}}{\partial v} = (2v, u, 0) \qquad (6)$$

The vector product is

639

$$\frac{\partial \overline{r}}{\partial u} \times \frac{\partial \overline{r}}{\partial v} = (0,v,u) \times (2v,u,0) \qquad (7)$$

$$= (-u^2, 2uv, -2v^2)$$

Thus, $d\overline{S}$ is

$$d\overline{S} = (-u^2, 2uv, -2v^2)dudv \qquad (8)$$

and the magnitude of $d\overline{S}$ is

$$|d\overline{S}| = \sqrt{u^4 + 4u^2v^2 + 4v^4}\ dudv = \sqrt{(u^2 + 2v^2)^2}dudv$$
$$= (u^2 + 2v^2)dudv \qquad (9)$$

Substituting eq.(9) into eq.(3) results in

$$S = \int_0^1 \int_0^2 (u^2 + 2v^2)dvdu \qquad (10)$$

$$= \int_0^1 \left[u^2v + \frac{2}{3}v^3 \right] \Bigg|_0^2 du = \int_0^1 \left(2u^2 + \frac{16}{3} \right) du$$

$$= \left(\frac{2}{3}u^3 + \frac{16}{3}u \right) \Bigg|_0^1 = \frac{18}{3}$$

● **PROBLEM 14-4**

Parametrize a sphere of radius a using its longitude and latitude angles β and φ and compute its surface area.

Solution: The sphere is shown in the figure.

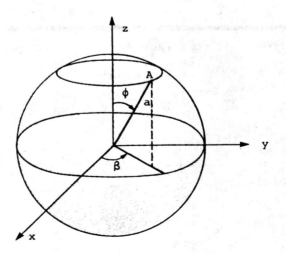

The coordinates of point A on the sphere are
$$x = a\ \sin\phi\ \cos\beta$$

640

$$y = a \sin\phi \sin\beta \tag{1}$$

$$z = a \cos\phi$$

$$0 \leq \beta \leq 2\pi, \quad 0 \leq \phi \leq \pi \tag{2}$$

To evaluate the area, we will use the formula

$$S = \iint \left| d\bar{S} \right| \tag{3}$$

where

$$d\bar{S} = \frac{\partial \bar{r}}{\partial u} du \times \frac{\partial \bar{r}}{\partial v} dv = \left(\frac{\partial \bar{r}}{\partial u} \times \frac{\partial \bar{r}}{\partial v} \right) du dv \tag{4}$$

(see Problem 14-2).

The position vector $\bar{r}$ is

$$\bar{r} = a \sin\phi \cos\beta \, \bar{i} + a \sin\phi \sin\beta \, \bar{j} + a \cos\phi \, \bar{k} \tag{5}$$

Differentiating eq.(5) with respect to ϕ gives

$$\frac{\partial \bar{r}}{\partial \phi} = a \cos\phi \cos\beta \, \bar{i} + a \cos\phi \sin\beta \, \bar{j} - a \sin\phi \, \bar{k}, \tag{6}$$

and with respect to β

$$\frac{\partial \bar{r}}{\partial \beta} = -a \sin\phi \sin\beta \, \bar{i} + a \sin\phi \cos\beta \, \bar{j} \tag{7}$$

The vector product of $\dfrac{\partial \bar{r}}{\partial \phi}$ and $\dfrac{\partial \bar{r}}{\partial \beta}$ is

$$\frac{\partial \bar{r}}{\partial \phi} \times \frac{\partial \bar{r}}{\partial \beta} = \begin{vmatrix} \bar{i} & \bar{j} & \bar{k} \\ a\cos\phi\cos\beta & a\cos\phi\sin\beta & -a\sin\phi \\ -a\sin\phi\sin\beta & a\sin\phi\cos\beta & 0 \end{vmatrix}$$

$$= a^2 \sin^2\phi \cos\beta \, \bar{i} + a^2 \sin^2\phi \sin\beta \, \bar{j} + a^2 \sin\phi \cos\phi \, \bar{k} \tag{8}$$

The magnitude of the vector $\dfrac{\partial \bar{r}}{\partial \phi} \times \dfrac{\partial \bar{r}}{\partial \beta}$ is

$$\left| \frac{\partial \bar{r}}{\partial \phi} \times \frac{\partial \bar{r}}{\partial \beta} \right| = \sqrt{a^4 \sin^4\phi(\cos^2\beta + \sin^2\beta) + a^4 \sin^2\phi \cos^2\phi}$$

$$= a^2 \sin\phi \sqrt{\sin^2\phi + \cos^2\phi} = a^2 \sin\phi \tag{9}$$

Thus

$$dS = a^2 \sin\phi \, d\phi \, d\beta \tag{10}$$

The area of the sphere is given by

$$S = \int_0^{2\pi} \int_0^{\pi} a^2 \sin\phi \, d\phi \, d\beta$$

$$= a^2 \int_0^{2\pi} \left(-\cos\phi \right) \Big|_0^{\pi} \, d\beta = 2a^2 \int_0^{2\pi} d\beta = 4\pi a^2 \tag{11}$$

A surface is described by the equation

$$\bar{r} = \bar{r}(u,v) \tag{1}$$

In differential geometry, in the theory of surfaces, we often use the quantities

$$K_1 = \left|\frac{\partial \bar{r}}{\partial u}\right|^2 \tag{2}$$

$$K_2 = \frac{\partial \bar{r}}{\partial u} \cdot \frac{\partial \bar{r}}{\partial v} \tag{3}$$

$$K_3 = \left|\frac{\partial \bar{r}}{\partial v}\right|^2 \tag{4}$$

which establish the Second Fundamental Form. Show that

$$dS = \sqrt{K_1 K_3 - K_2^2} \; dudv \tag{5}$$

Solution: Let us repeat the definition of $d\bar{S}$

$$d\bar{S} = \frac{\partial \bar{r}}{\partial u} \times \frac{\partial \bar{r}}{\partial v} \; dudv \tag{6}$$

The magnitude of $d\bar{S}$ is

$$dS = \left|\frac{\partial \bar{r}}{\partial u} \times \frac{\partial \bar{r}}{\partial v}\right| \; dudv \tag{7}$$

Therefore, it is required to prove the following equality

$$\sqrt{K_1 K_3 - K_2^2} \overset{?}{=} \left|\frac{\partial \bar{r}}{\partial u} \times \frac{\partial \bar{r}}{\partial v}\right| \tag{8}$$

where K_1, K_2 and K_3 are defined by eqs.(2), (3), (4). We have

$$\frac{\partial \bar{r}}{\partial u} = \left(\frac{\partial x}{\partial u}, \; \frac{\partial y}{\partial u}, \; \frac{\partial z}{\partial u}\right) \tag{9}$$

$$\frac{\partial \bar{r}}{\partial v} = \left(\frac{\partial x}{\partial v}, \; \frac{\partial y}{\partial v}, \; \frac{\partial z}{\partial v}\right) \tag{10}$$

The vector product is

$$\frac{\partial \bar{r}}{\partial u} \times \frac{\partial \bar{r}}{\partial v} = \left(\frac{\partial y}{\partial u}\frac{\partial z}{\partial v} - \frac{\partial z}{\partial u}\frac{\partial y}{\partial v}, \; \frac{\partial z}{\partial u}\frac{\partial x}{\partial v} - \frac{\partial x}{\partial u}\frac{\partial z}{\partial v}, \; \frac{\partial x}{\partial u}\frac{\partial y}{\partial v} - \frac{\partial y}{\partial u}\frac{\partial x}{\partial v}\right) \tag{11}$$

The magnitude of $\frac{\partial \bar{r}}{\partial u} \times \frac{\partial \bar{r}}{\partial v}$ is

$$\left|\frac{\partial \bar{r}}{\partial u} \times \frac{\partial \bar{r}}{\partial v}\right| = \sqrt{\left(\frac{\partial y}{\partial u}\frac{\partial z}{\partial v} - \frac{\partial z}{\partial u}\frac{\partial y}{\partial v}\right)^2 + \left(\frac{\partial z}{\partial u}\frac{\partial x}{\partial v} - \frac{\partial x}{\partial u}\frac{\partial z}{\partial v}\right)^2 + \left(\frac{\partial x}{\partial u}\frac{\partial y}{\partial v} - \frac{\partial y}{\partial u}\frac{\partial x}{\partial v}\right)^2} \tag{12}$$

The left-hand side of eq.(8) is equal to

$$\sqrt{K_1 K_3 - K_2{}^2} = \left\{ \left[\left(\frac{\partial x}{\partial u}\right)^2 + \left(\frac{\partial y}{\partial u}\right)^2 + \left(\frac{\partial z}{\partial u}\right)^2 \right] \left[\left(\frac{\partial x}{\partial v}\right)^2 + \left(\frac{\partial y}{\partial v}\right)^2 + \left(\frac{\partial z}{\partial v}\right)^2 \right] \right.$$
$$\left. - \left[\frac{\partial x}{\partial u} \frac{\partial x}{\partial v} + \frac{\partial y}{\partial u} \frac{\partial y}{\partial v} + \frac{\partial z}{\partial u} \frac{\partial z}{\partial v} \right]^2 \right\}^{\frac{1}{2}} \qquad (13)$$

It is easy to show that the right-hand side of eq.(12) is equal to the right-hand side of eq.(13). That completes the proof of eq.(5).

● **PROBLEM 14-6**

A surface S is described by the parametric equation

$$\overline{r}(u,v) = (u, v, u^2+v^2) \qquad (1)$$

for $1 \leq u^2+v^2 \leq 9$

If the density ρ at each point of the surface is proportional to the distance from the axis of symmetry of S,

$$\rho(x,y,z) = \rho(\overline{r}(u,v)) = \alpha\sqrt{u^2+v^2} \qquad (2)$$

where $\alpha > 0$ is a constant, find the area and the mass of the surface S.

Solution: The surface S is shown in the figure.

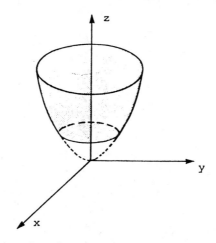

The surface is the graph of
$$z = x^2+y^2 \quad \text{for} \quad 1 \leq x^2+y^2 \leq 9$$
From eq.(1), we obtain
$$\frac{\partial \overline{r}}{\partial u} = (1,0,2u)$$
$$\frac{\partial \overline{r}}{\partial v} = (0,1,2v) \qquad (3)$$
and

$$\frac{\partial \overline{r}}{\partial u} \times \frac{\partial \overline{r}}{\partial v} = (1,0,2u) \times (0,1,2v) = (-2u,-2v,1) \qquad (4)$$

Thus,

$$dS = \left| \frac{d\overline{r}}{du} \times \frac{d\overline{r}}{dv} \right| \, dudv$$

$$= \sqrt{4u^2+4v^2+1} \; dudv \qquad (5)$$

and the area of S is given by

$$S = \iint ds = \iint\limits_{1 \le u^2 + v^2 \le 9} \sqrt{4u^2+4v^2+1} \; dudv$$

or, transforming into polar coordinates,

$$S = \int_0^{2\pi} \int_1^3 \sqrt{4r^2+1} \; r \, dr d\theta \qquad (6)$$

Now, using the following formula,

$$\int x\sqrt{x^2+a^2} \; dx = \frac{1}{3}\sqrt{(x^2+a^2)^3} \qquad (7)$$

integral (6) becomes

$$\int_0^{2} \int_1^3 \sqrt{4r^2+1} \; r dr d\theta = 4\pi \int_1^3 \sqrt{r^2+\frac{1}{4}} \; r dr$$

$$= \frac{4}{3}\pi\left[\sqrt{\left(\frac{37}{4}\right)^3} - \sqrt{\left(\frac{5}{4}\right)^3} \right] = \frac{\pi}{6}\left(37^{\frac{3}{2}} - 5^{\frac{3}{2}}\right) \qquad (8)$$

The total mass of the surface S is given by

$$M = \iint \rho dS \qquad (9)$$

Substituting eqs.(2) and (5) into eq.(8) yields

$$M = \iint\limits_{1 \le u^2 + v^2 \le 9} \alpha\sqrt{u^2+v^2} \; \sqrt{4u^2+4v^2+1} \; dudv \qquad (10)$$

Transforming to polar coordinates yields

$$M = \alpha \int_0^{2\pi} \int_1^3 r^2\sqrt{4r^2+1} \; dr d\theta \qquad (11)$$

Note that α is a constant.

Now, from the formula

$$\int x^2 \sqrt{x^2+a^2} \; dx = \frac{x}{4}\sqrt{(x^2+a^2)^3} - \frac{a^2}{8} x\sqrt{x^2+a^2} - \frac{a^4}{8} \log(x+\sqrt{x^2+a^2}) \qquad (12)$$

integral (11) becomes, after first integrating with respect to θ,

$$M = 4\alpha\pi \int_1^3 \sqrt{r^2 + \frac{1}{4}} \; r^2 dr$$

$$= \frac{\alpha\pi}{2} \left[27\left(\frac{3}{8}\right)\sqrt{37} - \frac{9\sqrt{5}}{8} + \frac{1}{4} \log \frac{2+\sqrt{5}}{6+\sqrt{37}} \right] \tag{13}$$

SURFACES GIVEN BY Z=F(X, Y)

● **PROBLEM** 14-7

Consider the surface S given by the equation
$$z = \frac{x^2}{2} + 3y \tag{1}$$
The projection T of the surface element on the xy plane is bounded by

$$0 \le x \le 1$$
$$0 \le y \le 1 \tag{2}$$

Find the surface area of this surface element.

Solution: Note that in this case the surface is described in the form

$$z = f(x,y) \tag{3}$$

We will now derive the expression for the area of a surface element for the general case where the projection on the xy plane is bounded by the curves

$$y_1(x) \le y \le y_2(x)$$
$$a \le x \le b \tag{4}$$

as shown in the figure.

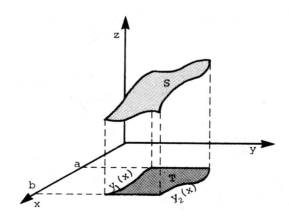

Now, as given in problem 14-2, we know that

$$dS = \left| \frac{\partial \overline{r}}{\partial u} \times \frac{\partial \overline{r}}{\partial v} \right| dudv \tag{5}$$

If we let the x and y be used as parameters,

$$u = x, \quad y = v \tag{6}$$

then since $\quad \overline{r} = (x,y,z)$
we have

$$\frac{\partial \overline{r}}{\partial u} = \frac{\partial \overline{r}}{\partial x} = \left(1, \ 0, \ \frac{\partial f}{\partial x}\right) = \overline{i} + \left(\frac{\partial f}{\partial x}\right)\overline{k} \tag{7}$$

$$\frac{\partial \overline{r}}{\partial v} = \frac{\partial \overline{r}}{\partial y} = \left(0, \ 1, \ \frac{\partial f}{\partial y}\right) = \overline{j} + \left(\frac{\partial f}{\partial y}\right)\overline{k} \tag{8}$$

The vector product is

$$\frac{\partial \overline{r}}{\partial x} \times \frac{\partial \overline{r}}{\partial y} = \left(1, \ 0, \ \frac{\partial f}{\partial x}\right) \times \left(0, \ 1, \ \frac{\partial f}{\partial y}\right) = \left(-\frac{\partial f}{\partial x}, \ -\frac{\partial f}{\partial y}, \ 1\right)$$

$$= -\frac{\partial f}{\partial x}\overline{i} - \frac{\partial f}{\partial y}\overline{j} + \overline{k} \tag{9}$$

and its magnitude

$$\left| \frac{\partial \overline{r}}{\partial x} \times \frac{\partial \overline{r}}{\partial y} \right| = \sqrt{1 + \left(\frac{\partial f}{\partial x}\right)^2 + \left(\frac{\partial f}{\partial y}\right)^2} \tag{10}$$

Now, substituting eq.(10) into eq.(5) yields

$$dS = \sqrt{1 + \left(\frac{\partial f}{\partial x}\right)^2 + \left(\frac{\partial f}{\partial y}\right)^2} \ dydx$$

and finally

$$S = \iint dS = \int_a^b \int_{y_1(x)}^{y_2(x)} \sqrt{1 + \left(\frac{\partial f}{\partial x}\right)^2 + \left(\frac{\partial f}{\partial y}\right)^2} \ dydx \tag{11}$$

Now, in this case we are given

$$z = f(x,y) = \frac{x^2}{2} + 3y$$

and thus

$$\frac{\partial f}{\partial x} = x \qquad \frac{\partial f}{\partial y} = 3 \tag{12}$$

Thus,

$$S = \int_0^1 \int_0^1 \sqrt{1+x^2+9} \ dydx = \int_0^1 \sqrt{10+x^2} \ dx \tag{13}$$

$$= \left[\frac{x}{2}\sqrt{x^2+10} + 5 \ \log(x+\sqrt{x^2+10})\right]\Big|_0^1$$

$$= \frac{1}{2}\sqrt{11} + 5 \ \log \frac{1+\sqrt{11}}{\sqrt{10}}$$

A surface is given by the equation

$$z = f(x,y) \qquad (1)$$

such that the angle α between $d\overline{S}$ and $\overline{k}$ is constant. The projection of this surface on the xy plane is given by the inequalities

$$x_0 \leq x \leq x_1, \qquad y_0(x) \leq y \leq y_1(x) \qquad (2)$$

where the functions $y_0(x)$ and $y_1(x)$ are such that

$$\frac{d}{dx} Y_0(x) = y_0(x) \qquad (3)$$

$$\frac{d}{dx} Y_1(x) = y_1(x) \qquad (4)$$

Evaluate the area of this surface.

Solution: For a surface given in the form

$$z = f(x,y),$$

the surface area is given by

$$S = \int_{x_0}^{x_1} \int_{y_0(x)}^{y_1(x)} \sqrt{1 + \left(\frac{\partial f}{\partial x}\right)^2 + \left(\frac{\partial f}{\partial y}\right)^2} \, dydx \qquad (5)$$

In this case we are told that the angle α between $d\overline{S}$ and $\overline{k}$ is a constant. The scalar product of $d\overline{S}$ and $\overline{k}$ is

$$d\overline{S} \cdot \overline{k} = |d\overline{S}||\overline{k}|\cos\alpha = |d\overline{S}|\cos\alpha \qquad (6)$$

Taking the absolute value results in

$$|\cos\alpha| = \frac{|d\overline{S} \cdot \overline{k}|}{|d\overline{S}|} \qquad (7)$$

The vector $d\overline{S}$ is defined as

$$d\overline{S} = \frac{\partial \overline{r}}{\partial x} \times \frac{\partial \overline{r}}{\partial y} \, dxdy \qquad (8)$$

From eq.(9) of Problem 14-7, we have

$$\frac{\partial \overline{r}}{\partial x} \times \frac{\partial \overline{r}}{\partial y} = -\frac{\partial f}{\partial x} \overline{i} - \frac{\partial f}{\partial y} \overline{j} + \overline{k}$$

and thus

$$d\overline{S} = \left[- \frac{\partial f}{\partial x} \overline{i} - \frac{\partial f}{\partial y} \overline{j} + \overline{k}\right] dxdy \qquad (9)$$

$$|d\overline{S}| = dS = \sqrt{1+\left(\frac{\partial f}{\partial x}\right)^2 + \left(\frac{\partial f}{\partial y}\right)^2}\ |dx|\,|dy| \tag{10}$$

Also,

$$d\overline{S} \cdot \overline{k} = \left[\left(-\frac{\partial f}{\partial x}\overline{i} - \frac{\partial f}{\partial y}\overline{j} + \overline{k}\right) \cdot \overline{k}\right] dxdy \tag{11}$$

$$= dxdy$$

and

$$|d\overline{S} \cdot \overline{k}| = |dx|\,|dy| \tag{12}$$

Now, substituting eq.(10) and eq.(12) into eq.(7) results in

$$|\cos\alpha| = \frac{1}{\sqrt{1+\left(\frac{\partial f}{\partial x}\right)^2 + \left(\frac{\partial f}{\partial y}\right)^2}} \tag{13}$$

Eq.(5) becomes

$$S = \int_{x_0}^{x_1}\int_{y_0(x)}^{y_1(x)} \frac{dydx}{|\cos\alpha|} \tag{14}$$

Now, since the problem states that α is a constant, we conclude that $\cos\alpha$ = constant and we obtain

$$S = \frac{1}{|\cos\alpha|} \int_{x_0}^{x_1} \left[y_0(x)-y_1(x)\right] dx \tag{15}$$

Applying eqs.(3) and (4) gives us

$$S = \frac{1}{|\cos\alpha|} \left[Y_0(x)-Y_1(x)\right]\ \Big|_{x_0}^{x_1} \tag{16}$$

$$= \frac{1}{|\cos\alpha|} \left[Y_0(x_1)-Y_1(x_1)-Y_0(x_0)+Y_1(x_0)\right]$$

Eq.(14) is the area cosine principle in the integral form. This principle will be discussed in Problem 14-9.

● **PROBLEM 14-9**

1. Using the area cosine principle, find the area of the ellipse shown in Fig. 1.

2. Find the area of the cone shown in Fig. 2.

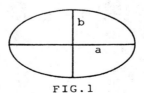

FIG.1

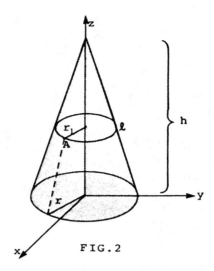

FIG.2

Solution: 1. The area cosine principle states that if we look at a plane area S whose normal makes an acute angle with the line of sight, then the area we appear to see is S cosα.

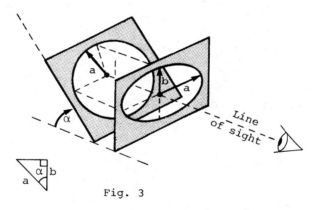

Fig. 3

Instead of an ellipse, we can assume that we see a circle of radius a at an angle α, where α is such that the distance a appears to be b (see Fig. 3). Thus,

$$\cos\alpha = \frac{b}{a} \tag{1}$$

It is concluded that the area of the ellipse is

$$S\cos\alpha = \pi a^2 \cdot \frac{b}{a} = \pi ab \tag{2}$$

2. To find the equation describing the surface of the cone, let us take any point A on the cone. We have,

$$x^2 + y^2 = r_1^2$$

and

$$\frac{r_1}{r} = \frac{h-z}{h} \tag{3}$$

or

$$x^2 + y^2 - \frac{r^2}{h^2}(h-z)^2 = 0 \qquad (4)$$

We will now apply the area cosine principle to determine the surface of the cone.

Now, looking at the cone along the z axis, we see a circle of radius r. A normal to the cone is

$$\nabla\left[x^2+y^2-\frac{r^2}{h^2}(h-z)^2\right] = \left(2x,\ 2y,\ \frac{2r^2}{h^2}(h-z)\right) \qquad (5)$$

The angle α which the normal makes with the z axis is

$$\cos\alpha = \frac{\nabla\left[x^2+y^2-\frac{r^2}{h^2}(h-z)^2\right]\cdot\overline{k}}{\left|\nabla\left[x^2+y^2-\frac{r^2}{h^2}(h-z)^2\right]\right|} = \frac{\frac{2r^2}{h^2}(h-z)}{\sqrt{4x^2+4y^2+\frac{4r^4}{h^4}(h-z)^2}}$$

$$= \frac{r}{\sqrt{h^2+r^2}} \qquad (6)$$

Since the projection of the cone on the xy plane is a circle of radius r, we have

$$S = \iint \frac{dy\,dx}{\cos\alpha} = \int_{-r}^{r}\int_{-\sqrt{r^2-x^2}}^{\sqrt{r^2-x^2}} \frac{\sqrt{h^2+r^2}}{r}\,dy\,dx$$

$$= \frac{\sqrt{h^2+r^2}}{r}\int_{-r}^{r} 2\sqrt{r^2-x^2}\,dx \qquad (7)$$

Since

$$\int\sqrt{r^2-x^2}\,dx = \frac{x}{2}\sqrt{r^2-x^2} + \frac{r^2}{2}\ \text{arc sin}\ \frac{x}{r} \qquad (8)$$

eq.(7) becomes

$$S = \frac{2\sqrt{h^2+r^2}}{r}\left[\frac{x}{2}\sqrt{r^2-x^2} + \frac{r^2}{2}\text{arc sin}\ \frac{x}{r}\right]\Bigg|_{x=-r}^{x=r}$$

$$= \frac{\sqrt{h^2+r^2}}{r}\left[r^2\text{arc sin}\ 1 - r^2\text{arc sin}\ (-1)\right] \qquad (9)$$

$$= \frac{\sqrt{h^2+r^2}}{r}\ \pi r^2 = \pi r \ell$$

● **PROBLEM 14-10**

Find the surface area of the plane

$$x + 2y + 4z = 16 \qquad (1)$$

cut off by   x=0,   y=0   and

$$x^2+y^2 = 9 \qquad (2)$$

as shown in Fig. 1(a).

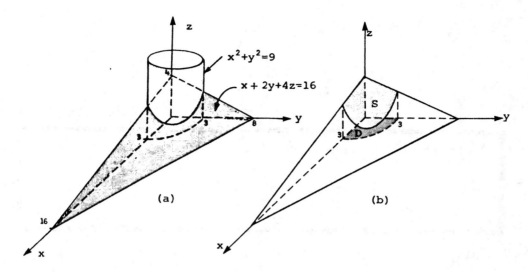

(a) (b)

Solution: Let S be a surface given by

$$z = f(x,y) \qquad (3)$$

and D the projection of S on the xy plane. The surface area of S is given by

$$\iint\limits_{D} \sqrt{\left(\frac{\partial f}{\partial x}\right)^2 + \left(\frac{\partial f}{\partial y}\right)^2 + 1} \; dxdy \qquad (4)$$

From eq.(1) we find

$$z = 4 - \frac{y}{2} - \frac{x}{4} \qquad (5)$$

Surface S is shown in Fig. 1(b).

The projection D of the surface S on the xy plane is a quarter circle of radius 3.

Now, since

$$\frac{\partial f}{\partial x} = -\frac{1}{4} \qquad \frac{\partial f}{\partial y} = -\frac{1}{2}$$

the area of the surface is

$$\iint\limits_{D} \sqrt{1 + \left(-\frac{1}{4}\right)^2 + \left(-\frac{1}{2}\right)^2} \; dxdy$$

$$= \iint\limits_{D} \sqrt{\frac{21}{16}} \; dxdy = \frac{\sqrt{21}}{4} \iint\limits_{D} dxdy = \frac{\sqrt{21}}{4} \int_0^3 \int_0^{\sqrt{9-y^2}} dxdy$$

$$= \frac{\sqrt{21}}{4} \int_0^3 \sqrt{9-y^2} \; dy \qquad (6)$$

651

$$= \frac{\sqrt{21}}{4} \left[\frac{y}{2} \sqrt{9-y^2} + \frac{9}{2} \sin^{-1} \frac{y}{3} \right] \Big|_0^3$$

$$= \frac{9\sqrt{21}}{16} \pi$$

Evaluate the surface area of the region common to the intersecting cylinders

$$x^2 + z^2 = a^2 \qquad (1)$$

$$x^2 + y^2 = a^2 \qquad (2)$$

Solution: The region is shown in the figure.

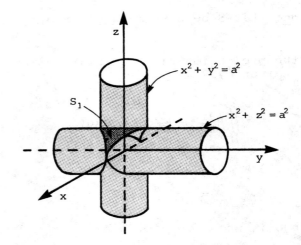

Its surface consists of four elements of equal area. One element S_1 is shown in the figure by the shaded area. The projection of S_1 on the xy plane is a circle of radius a.

Consider the surface of the cylinder

$$x^2 + z^2 = a^2 \qquad (3)$$

Eq.(3) can be written

$$z = \sqrt{a^2 - x^2} \qquad (4)$$

Let T be the projection of surface S on the xy plane. If the equation of the surface is

$$z = f(x,y) \qquad (5)$$

then the surface area S is given by

$$\iint_T \sqrt{1 + \left(\frac{\partial f}{\partial x}\right)^2 + \left(\frac{\partial f}{\partial y}\right)^2} \, dxdy \qquad (6)$$

Substituting eq.(4) into eq.(6) results in

$$\iint_T \frac{a}{\sqrt{a^2-x^2}} \, dxdy \qquad (7)$$

Since the projection of S_1 on the xy plane is a circle of radius a, we have

$$\int_{-a}^{a} \int_{-\sqrt{a^2-x^2}}^{\sqrt{a^2-x^2}} \frac{a}{\sqrt{a^2-x^2}} \, dydx$$

$$= \int_{-a}^{a} \left(\frac{a}{\sqrt{a^2-x^2}}\right) \left(2\sqrt{a^2-x^2}\right) dx \qquad (8)$$

$$= 2a \int_{-a}^{a} dx = 4a^2$$

Since the total area consists of four areas $4a^2$, we have

$$S = 4S_1 = 4 \cdot 4a^2 = 16a^2 \qquad (9)$$

● **PROBLEM 14-12**

1. Evaluate the integral

$$\iint_D \sqrt{x^2+y^2} \, dxdy \qquad (1)$$

over the region D in the xy plane bounded by $x^2+y^2 = 25$.

Solution: It is easier to solve this problem in polar coordinates. We have

$$x = \rho \cos \alpha$$
$$y = \rho \sin \alpha \qquad (2)$$

Thus

$$\sqrt{x^2+y^2} = \rho \qquad (3)$$

The integral in eq.(1) can be written

$$\iint_D \sqrt{x^2+y^2} \, dxdy = \iint_D \rho\rho \, d\rho \, d\alpha \qquad (4)$$

$$= \int_0^{2\pi} \int_0^5 \rho^2 \, d\rho \, d\alpha = \int_0^{2\pi} \frac{125}{3} d\alpha = \frac{250\pi}{3}$$

Compute the solid angle determined by the cone

$$x^2+y^2 \leq 5z^2, \quad z \geq 0 \tag{1}$$

<u>Solution</u>: We shall first give the definition of the solid angle.

Consider a sphere of unit radius r=1, and a solid cone with vertex at the origin as shown in the figure.

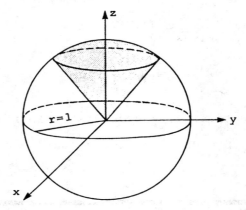

We define the solid angle as the area of the intersection of the solid cone with the unit sphere.

To compute the solid angle, we have to find the area of the intersection of the cone

$$x^2+y^2 \leq 5z^2, \quad z \geq 0 \tag{2}$$

and the sphere

$$x^2+y^2+z^2 = 1 \tag{3}$$

The intersection is the part of the sphere bounded by the cone

$$\left.\begin{array}{r} x^2+y^2+z^2 = 1 \\ x^2+y^2 = 5z^2 \end{array}\right\} \rightarrow 6z^2 = 1 \tag{4}$$

Thus,

$$z = \frac{1}{\sqrt{6}} \tag{5}$$

and

$$x^2+y^2 = \frac{5}{6} \tag{6}$$

The projection of the intersection on the xy plane is a disk D_{xy} such that

$$x^2+y^2 \leq \frac{5}{6} \tag{7}$$

Now, we will find the surface area in the first octant and multiply by 4, since the intersection is symmetric with respect to the z-axis.

For a surface given in the form

$$f(x,y,z) = 0,$$

the surface area is given by

$$S = \iint\limits_{D_{xy}} \frac{\sqrt{\left(\frac{\partial f}{\partial x}\right)^2 + \left(\frac{\partial f}{\partial y}\right)^2 + \left(\frac{\partial f}{\partial z}\right)^2}}{\left|\frac{\partial f}{\partial z}\right|} \, dxdy \qquad (8)$$

Here

$$f(x,y,z) = x^2+y^2+z^2-1 = 0 \qquad (9)$$

and

$$\frac{\partial f}{\partial x} = 2x, \quad \frac{\partial f}{\partial y} = 2y, \quad \frac{\partial f}{\partial z} = 2z \qquad (10)$$

Thus,

$$S = \iint\limits_{D_{xy}} \frac{\sqrt{4x^2+4y^2+4z^2}}{|2z|} \, dxdy = \iint\limits_{D_{xy}} \frac{1}{z} \, dxdy$$

$$\qquad (11)$$

$$= \iint\limits_{D_{xy}} \frac{1}{\sqrt{1-x^2-y^2}} \, dxdy$$

Using a polar transformation and integrating in the first octant, we obtain

$$S = 4 \int_0^{\frac{\pi}{2}} \int_0^{\sqrt{\frac{5}{6}}} \frac{1}{\sqrt{1-r^2}} \, r \, drd\theta$$

$$= 4 \int_0^{\frac{\pi}{2}} \left[-\sqrt{1-r^2}\right] \Big|_{r=0}^{\sqrt{\frac{5}{6}}} d\theta \qquad (12)$$

$$= 4 \cdot \frac{\pi}{2} \left[-\sqrt{1 - \frac{5}{6}} + 1\right] = 2\pi \left(1 - \frac{1}{\sqrt{6}}\right)$$

● **PROBLEM 14-14**

Find the volume bounded by the surface

$$z = -\log(x^2+y^2) \qquad (1)$$

and the xy plane.

<u>Solution</u>: The function $z = -\log(x^2+y^2)$ is shown in the figure.

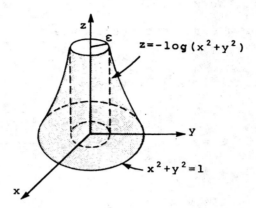

Note that the function $-\log(x^2+y^2)$ becomes unbounded at the point $(0,0)$. The projection of $z = -\log(x^2+y^2)$ on the xy plane is the disk D

$$x^2+y^2 \le 1 \tag{2}$$

Since z is unbounded at $(0,0)$, we cut out from D a small disk of radius ε. The remaining part of D we denote D_ε. The volume integral is

$$\iint_{D_\varepsilon} -\log(x^2+y^2)dxdy = \int_0^{2\pi}\int_\varepsilon^1 (-\log r^2)rdrd\theta$$

$$= -2\pi\left[r^2\log r - \frac{1}{2} r^2\right]\Big|_{r=\varepsilon}^1 \tag{3}$$

$$= \pi + 2\pi\varepsilon^2\log\varepsilon - \pi\varepsilon^2$$

Let us find the limit of the integral as $\varepsilon \to 0$.

$$\lim_{\varepsilon\to 0}\left[\pi + 2\pi\varepsilon^2\log\varepsilon - \pi\varepsilon^2\right] = \pi \tag{4}$$

Thus,

$$\iint_D -\log(x^2+y^2)dxdy = \lim_{\varepsilon\to 0}\iint_{D_\varepsilon} -\log(x^2+y^2)dxdy \tag{5}$$

$$= \pi$$

Note that we integrated an unbounded function $z = -\log(x^2+y^2)$. Indeed, at the point $(0,0)$ the function has an infinite discontinuity.

● **PROBLEM 14-15**

Derive the expression for the surface area of a surface given in the form

$$F(x,y,z) = 0. \tag{1}$$

Solution: Let $d\overline{S}$ be a vector normal to the surface, whose magnitude

$$dS = |d\overline{S}| \qquad (2)$$

is the element of area.

The surface area is

$$\iint_S dS = \iint_S |d\overline{S}| \qquad (3)$$

Let $\overline{n}$ be the unit normal vector to the surface S. We have

$$d\overline{S} = \frac{\overline{n}}{|\overline{n}\cdot\overline{k}|}\, dxdy \qquad (4)$$

Eq.(3) becomes

$$\iint_S dS = \iint_T \frac{|\overline{n}|}{|\overline{n}\cdot\overline{k}|}\, dxdy = \iint_T \frac{dxdy}{|\overline{n}\cdot\overline{k}|} \qquad (5)$$

Taking the gradient of $F(x,y,z)$ gives us the vector normal to the surface S

$$\overline{N} = \frac{\partial F}{\partial x}\,\overline{i} + \frac{\partial F}{\partial y}\,\overline{j} + \frac{\partial F}{\partial z}\,\overline{k} \qquad (6)$$

The unit normal vector is

$$\overline{n} = \frac{\overline{N}}{|\overline{N}|} = \frac{\frac{\partial F}{\partial x}\overline{i} + \frac{\partial F}{\partial y}\overline{j} + \frac{\partial F}{\partial z}\overline{k}}{\sqrt{\left(\frac{\partial F}{\partial x}\right)^2 + \left(\frac{\partial F}{\partial y}\right)^2 + \left(\frac{\partial F}{\partial z}\right)^2}} \qquad (7)$$

We have

$$\overline{n}\cdot\overline{k} = \frac{\frac{\partial F}{\partial z}}{\sqrt{\left(\frac{\partial F}{\partial x}\right)^2 + \left(\frac{\partial F}{\partial y}\right)^2 + \left(\frac{\partial F}{\partial z}\right)^2}} \qquad (8)$$

Substituting eq.(8) into eq.(5) results in

$$\iint_S dS = \iint_T \frac{\sqrt{\left(\frac{\partial F}{\partial x}\right)^2 + \left(\frac{\partial F}{\partial y}\right)^2 + \left(\frac{\partial F}{\partial z}\right)^2}}{\left|\frac{\partial F}{\partial z}\right|}\, dxdy \qquad (9)$$

where T is the projection of S on the xy plane.

FLUX OF A VECTOR FIELD

• PROBLEM 14-16

Define the flux of a vector field $\overline{F}$ through a surface S. Consider the cases where the surface S is given in the parametric form

$$\overline{r} = \overline{r}(u,v) \qquad (1)$$

and by the equation

$$z = f(x,y) \qquad (2)$$

Solution: The flux of $\overline{F}$ through a surface S is defined as

$$\iint_S \overline{F} \cdot d\overline{S} \qquad (3)$$

Since

$$d\overline{S} = \overline{n} \, dS \qquad (4)$$

we have

$$\iint_S \overline{F} \cdot d\overline{S} = \iint_S \overline{F} \cdot \overline{n} \, dS \qquad (5)$$

Let us subdivide the area S into N elements of area ΔS_k, $k=1,2,\ldots,N$, and choose arbitrarily the points $P_1, P_2, \ldots P_N$ such that $P_1 \in \Delta S_1$, $P_2 \in \Delta S_2, \ldots, P_N \in \Delta S_N$. $P_1 \in \Delta S_1$ means P_1 belongs to ΔS_1. The coordinates of the points $P_1, P_2, \ldots P_N$ are (x_1, y_1, z_1), $(x_2, y_2, z_2), \ldots, (x_N, y_N, z_N)$. We define

$$\overline{F}(x_i, y_i, z_i) = \overline{F}_i \qquad (6)$$

Let $\overline{n}_i$ be the positive unit normal to ΔS_i at P_i.

We form the sum

$$\sum_{i=1}^{N} \overline{F}_i \cdot \overline{n}_i \, \Delta S_i \qquad (7)$$

Taking the limit of expression (7) as $N \to \infty$ in such a way that the maximum dimension of the areas $\Delta S_1, \Delta S_2, \ldots, \Delta S_N$ tends to zero, we define the integral

$$\iint_S \overline{F} \cdot \overline{n} \, dS = \lim_{\substack{N \to \infty \\ \max \Delta S_i \to 0}} \sum_{i=1}^{N} \overline{F}_i \cdot \overline{n}_i \, \Delta S_i \qquad (8)$$

as the flux of F through the surface S.

When the surface is given in the parametric form $\overline{r} = \overline{r}(u,v)$, the surface element $d\overline{S}$ is given by

$$d\overline{S} = \frac{\partial \overline{r}}{\partial u} \times \frac{\partial \overline{r}}{\partial v} \, du \, dv \qquad (9)$$

(see Problem 14-2), and the flux of $\overline{F}$ becomes

$$\iint_S \overline{F} \cdot \frac{\partial \overline{r}}{\partial u} \times \frac{\partial \overline{r}}{\partial v} \, du \, dv \qquad (10)$$

For the surface given by

$$z = f(x,y) \qquad (11)$$

the flux is

$$\iint \overline{F} \cdot \overline{n} \; \frac{dxdy}{|\cos\alpha|} \qquad (12)$$

In both cases we integrate over the projected area of S onto the xy plane.

● **PROBLEM 14-17**

Compute the flux of the vector field

$$\overline{F} = \frac{x}{\sqrt{2}} \; \overline{i} + \frac{y}{\sqrt{2}} \; \overline{j} + \frac{z}{\sqrt{2}} \; \overline{k} \qquad (1)$$

across the surface S given by

$$x^2 + y^2 + z^2 = 9 \qquad (2)$$

Solution: The surface is illustrated in the figure.

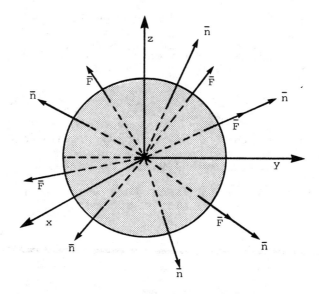

The normal vector to the surface S is

$$\overline{N} = grad(x^2 + y^2 + z^2) = 2x\overline{i} + 2y\overline{j} + 2z\overline{k} \qquad (3)$$

and the unit normal vector is

$$\overline{n} = \frac{\overline{N}}{|\overline{N}|} = \frac{1}{2\sqrt{x^2+y^2+z^2}} \; (2x\overline{i} + 2y\overline{j} + 2z\overline{k})$$

$$= \frac{1}{3} \; (x\overline{i} + y\overline{j} + z\overline{k}) \qquad (4)$$

since $x^2 + y^2 + z^2 = 9$.

Now, notice that

$$\overline{F} = \beta \overline{n}$$

where

$$\beta = \frac{3}{\sqrt{2}} \ .$$

Note that both vectors $\overline{n}$ and $\overline{F}$ point directly away from the origin.

Now, note that

$$\overline{F} \cdot \overline{n} = |\overline{F}||\overline{n}| \cos \alpha$$

$$= \sqrt{\frac{1}{2}(x^2+y^2+z^2)} \ \cos \ 0 \qquad (5)$$

$$= \sqrt{\frac{1}{2}(9)} \ \cos \ 0$$

$$= \frac{3}{\sqrt{2}}$$

The flux of $\overline{F}$ across the surface S is thus

$$\iint_S \overline{F} \cdot d\overline{S} = \iint_S \overline{F} \cdot \overline{n} \ dS = \iint_S \frac{3}{\sqrt{2}} \ dS$$

$$= \frac{3}{\sqrt{2}} \iint_S dS = \frac{3}{\sqrt{2}}(4\pi r^2) = \frac{3}{\sqrt{2}} \ 4\pi 9 = \frac{108}{\sqrt{2}} \ \pi \qquad (6)$$

Note that in this case, $\iint_S dS$ represented the total surface area of a sphere, which is $4\pi r^2$.

Also, note that since $\overline{F} \cdot \overline{n}$ is a constant over the entire surface, no integration is necessary.

● **PROBLEM 14-18**

A surface is given by

$$x = u^2+v^2 \qquad y = uv \qquad z = u \qquad (1)$$

$$0 \le u \le 1 \qquad 0 \le v \le 1$$

Compute the flux of the vector field

$$\overline{F} = z\overline{i} + zy\overline{k} \qquad (2)$$

across this surface.

Solution: The flux across a surface is given by

$$\text{flux across a surface} = \iint \overline{F} \cdot d\overline{S}$$

660

For a surface given in parametric form (as is the case with eq.(1)) the flux is

$$\iint \overline{F} \cdot d\overline{S} = \iint \overline{F} \cdot \frac{\partial \overline{r}}{\partial u} \times \frac{\partial \overline{r}}{\partial v} \, dudv \qquad (3)$$

(see Problem 14-16).

From eq.(1), the position vector is

$$\overline{r} = (u^2 + v^2, \ uv, \ u) \qquad (4)$$

Thus

$$\frac{\partial \overline{r}}{\partial u} = (2u, \ v, \ 1)$$

$$\frac{\partial \overline{r}}{\partial v} = (2v, \ u, \ 0) \qquad (5)$$

and

$$\overline{F} = z\overline{i} + zy\overline{k} = (u, \ 0, \ u^2 v) \qquad (6)$$

We have

$$\overline{F} \cdot \frac{\partial \overline{r}}{\partial u} \times \frac{\partial \overline{r}}{\partial v} = \begin{vmatrix} u & 0 & u^2 v \\ 2u & v & 1 \\ 2v & u & 0 \end{vmatrix} = -u^2 + 2u^4 v - 2u^2 v^3 \qquad (7)$$

Substituting eq.(7) into eq.(3) results in

$$\iint \overline{F} \cdot \frac{\partial \overline{r}}{\partial u} \ \frac{\partial \overline{r}}{\partial v} \, dudv = \int_{v=0}^{1} \int_{u=0}^{1} (-u^2 + 2u^4 v - 2u^2 v^3) dudv$$

$$= \int_0^1 \left(-\frac{1}{3} + \frac{2}{5} v - \frac{2}{3} v^3 \right) dv = -\frac{1}{3} + \frac{1}{5} - \frac{1}{6} = -\frac{3}{10} \qquad (8)$$

● **PROBLEM 14-19**

Compute

$$\iint_S \overline{F} \cdot d\overline{S} \qquad (1)$$

where S is the surface of the cube shown in the figure and

$$\overline{F} = x\overline{i} + y\overline{j} + z\overline{k} \qquad (2)$$

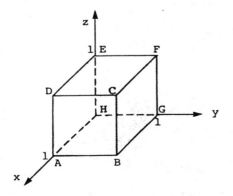

Solution: As a procedure, we will compute the flux of $\overline{F}$ for each of the six individual faces and then subsequently add up the results.

From the figure, we see that the unit normal to the face ABCD is

$$\overline{n} = \overline{i} \qquad (3)$$

Thus

$$\overline{F} \cdot \overline{n} = (x\overline{i} + y\overline{j} + z\overline{k}) \cdot \overline{i} = x = 1 \qquad (4)$$

The integral over this face is

$$\iint \overline{F} \cdot d\overline{S} = \iint \overline{F} \cdot \overline{n} \; dS = \iint dS = 1 \qquad (5)$$

since the surface area of this face is, of course, 1.

For the face EFGH, we have

$$\overline{n} = -\overline{i} \qquad (6)$$

and

$$\overline{F} \cdot \overline{n} = -x = 0$$

since x=0 for all points on this face.

The integral for face EFGH is thus

$$\iint \overline{F} \cdot d\overline{S} = 0 \qquad (7)$$

For the face BCFG, we have

$$\overline{n} = \overline{j} \qquad (8)$$

and

$$\overline{F} \cdot \overline{n} = y = 1$$

Thus,

$$\iint \overline{F} \cdot d\overline{S} = \iint dS = 1 \qquad (9)$$

For the face ADEH

$$\overline{n} = -\overline{j}$$

and

$$\overline{F} \cdot \overline{n} = -y = 0$$

Therefore,

$$\iint \overline{F} \cdot d\overline{S} = 0 \qquad (10)$$

For the face CDEF,

$$\overline{n} = \overline{k}$$

$$\overline{F} \cdot \overline{n} = z = 1$$

and

$$\iint \overline{F} \cdot d\overline{S} = 1 \qquad (11)$$

Finally, for the face ABGH, we have

$$\overline{n} = -\overline{k}$$

$$\overline{F} \cdot \overline{n} = -z = 0 \quad \text{and} \quad \iint \overline{F} \cdot d\overline{S} = 0 \qquad (12)$$

Summing the results yields

$$\iint \overline{F} \cdot d\overline{S} = 1 + 1 + 1 = 3 \qquad (13)$$

Note that in computing the integral (1) we took $\overline{n}$ to be the outward normal. This is the usual convention for closed surfaces.

● **PROBLEM 14-20**

Evaluate the integral

$$\iint_S \overline{F} \cdot \overline{n} \, dS \qquad (1)$$

over the triangle with vertices (1,0,0), (0,2,0), (0,0,3). The vector field $\overline{F}$ is

$$\overline{F} = xy\overline{i} + y^2\overline{j} + zy\overline{k} \qquad (2)$$

Solution: The flux through a surface is given by

$$\iint_S \overline{F} \cdot d\overline{S} = \iint_S \overline{F} \cdot \overline{n} \, dS = \iint \frac{\overline{F} \cdot \overline{n}}{|\cos \alpha|}$$

In this case, the surface is the plane shown in the figure.

Since we need the unit normal vector $\overline{n}$ to compute the integral, we must first find the equation of the plane which passes through the points (1,0,0), (0,2,0), (0,0,3). The general equation of a plane is

$$Ax + By + Cz = D \qquad (3)$$

where A, B, C, D are constant coefficients.

Now, since the plane passes through the point (1,0,0), we have

$$A = D \qquad (4)$$

For the point (0,2,0) we have

$$2B = A \qquad (5)$$

For the point (0,0,3) we have

$$3C = A \qquad (6)$$

Eq.(3) becomes

$$Ax + \frac{A}{2}y + \frac{A}{3}z = A \qquad (7)$$

or

$$6x + 3y + 2z = 6 \tag{8}$$

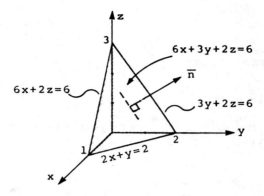

The triangle (or plane) is oriented in such way that its positive side is directed away from the origin.

Now, the unit normal vector is given by

$$\bar{n} = \frac{\bar{N}}{|\bar{N}|} = \frac{\text{grad } f}{|\text{grad } f|} \equiv \frac{\nabla f}{|\nabla f|}$$

where

$$f = f(x,y,z) = 0$$

From eq.(8), we may write

$$f(x,y,z) = 6x + 3y + 2z - 6 = 0$$

Thus,

$$\nabla(6x+3y+2z-6) = 6\bar{i} + 3\bar{j} + 2\bar{k} \tag{9}$$

and

$$\bar{n} = \frac{6}{7}\bar{i} + \frac{3}{7}\bar{j} + \frac{2}{7}\bar{k} \tag{10}$$

We have

$$\cos \alpha = \bar{n} \cdot \bar{k} = \frac{2}{7} \tag{11}$$

and

$$\bar{F} \cdot \bar{n} = \frac{6}{7}xy + \frac{3}{7}y^2 + \frac{2}{7}zy \tag{12}$$

Integral (1) becomes

$$\iint\limits_{S} \bar{F} \cdot \bar{n} \; dS' = \iint \frac{\bar{F} \cdot \bar{n}}{|\cos\alpha|} \; dxdy$$

$$= \int_0^1 \int_0^{2-2x} \frac{7}{2}\left(\frac{6}{7}xy + \frac{3}{7}y^2 + \frac{2}{7}zy\right) dydx \tag{13}$$

$$= \int_0^1 \int_0^{2-2x} \left(3xy + \frac{3}{2}y^2 + zy\right) dydx$$

On the surface S we have

$$z = 3 - 3x - \frac{3}{2}y$$

and

$$zy = 3y - 3xy - \frac{3}{2}y^2 \tag{14}$$

664

Substituting eq.(14) into eq.(13) results in

$$\iint_S \overline{F} \cdot \overline{n} \, dS = \int_0^1 \int_0^{2-2x} \left(3xy + \frac{3}{2}y^2 + 3y - 3xy - \frac{3}{2}y^2\right) dy\,dx$$

$$= \int_0^1 \int_0^{2-2x} 3y \, dy\,dx = \int_0^1 \left[\frac{3}{2} y^2\right] \Bigg|_0^{2-2x} dx \qquad (15)$$

$$= \int_0^1 (6x^2 - 12x + 6)\,dx = \left[6 \frac{x^3}{3} - 12 \frac{x^2}{2} + 6x\right] \Bigg|_0^1 = 2 - 6 + 6 = 2$$

● **PROBLEM 14-21**

The projection of a surface S on the xy plane is T. Show that if $\overline{F}$ is a vector field, then

$$\iint_S \overline{F} \cdot \overline{n} \, dS = \iint_T \frac{\overline{F} \cdot \overline{n}}{|\overline{n} \cdot \overline{k}|} \, dx\,dy \qquad (1)$$

where $\overline{k} = (0,0,1)$.

The surfaces S and T are shown in the figure.

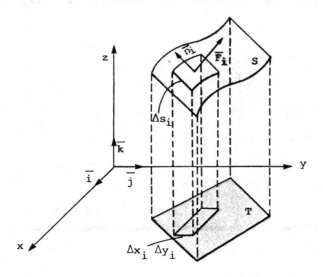

Solution: Using the results of Problem 14-16, we can express the left-hand side of eq. (1) as the limit

$$\iint_S \overline{F} \cdot \overline{n} \, dS = \lim_{\substack{N \to \infty \\ \max \Delta S_i \to 0}} \sum_{i=1}^{N} \overline{F}_i \cdot \overline{n}_i \, \Delta S_i \qquad (2)$$

The projection of ΔS_i on the xy plane is $|\overline{n}_i \cdot \overline{k}| \Delta S_i$. Both

665

vectors $\bar{n}_i$ and $\bar{k}$ are unit vectors and $\bar{n}_i \cdot \bar{k} = \cos \alpha$, where α is the angle between ΔS_i and its projection on the xy plane. Neglecting the infinitesimals of order higher than $\Delta x_i \Delta y_i$. we can write

$$\Delta x_i \Delta y_i = |\bar{n}_i \cdot \bar{k}| \Delta S_i \qquad (3)$$

or
$$\Delta S_i = \frac{\Delta x_i \Delta y_i}{|\bar{n}_i \cdot \bar{k}|} \qquad (4)$$

Substituting eq.(4) into the sum in eq.(2) gives

$$\sum_{i=1}^{N} \bar{F}_i \cdot \bar{n}_i \, \Delta S_i = \sum_{i=1}^{N} \frac{\bar{F}_i \cdot \bar{n}_i}{|\bar{n}_i \cdot \bar{k}|} \Delta x_i \Delta y_i \qquad (5)$$

Taking the limit of this sum as $N \to \infty$ in such a way that max $\Delta x_i \to 0$ and max $\Delta y_i \to 0$, we obtain

$$\lim_{\substack{N \to \infty \\ \max \Delta x_i \to 0 \\ \max \Delta y_i \to 0}} \sum_{i=1}^{N} \frac{\bar{F}_i \cdot \bar{n}_i}{|\bar{n}_i \cdot \bar{k}|} \Delta x_i \Delta y_i = \iint_T \frac{\bar{F} \cdot \bar{n}}{|\bar{n} \cdot \bar{k}|} \, dxdy \qquad (6)$$

In eq.(6), we applied the fundamental theorem of integral calculus.

That completes the proof of eq.(1).

Note that since
$$\bar{n} \cdot \bar{k} = \cos \alpha$$

and
$$|\bar{n} \cdot \bar{k}| = |\cos \alpha| \qquad (7)$$

eq.(1) can be written

$$\iint_S \bar{F} \cdot \bar{n} \, dS = \iint_T \frac{\bar{F} \cdot \bar{n}}{|\cos \alpha|} \, dxdy, \qquad (8)$$

which is eq.(12) of Problem 14-16.

● **PROBLEM 14-22**

Evaluate the integral

$$\iint_S \bar{F} \cdot \bar{n} \, dS \qquad (1)$$

where
$$\bar{F} = 12y\bar{i} + 2x\bar{j} - 3\bar{k} \qquad (2)$$

and S is the plane

$$x + 2y + 8z = 12 \qquad (3)$$

$$x \geq 0, \quad y \geq 0, \quad z \geq 0$$

Solution: Let us find the projection of the surface S on the xy plane and then use the formula

$$\iint_S \overline{F} \cdot \overline{n} \ dS = \iint_T \frac{\overline{F} \cdot \overline{n}}{|\overline{n} \cdot \overline{k}|} \ dxdy \tag{4}$$

(see Problem 14-21). The surface S and its projection on the xy plane are shown in the figure.

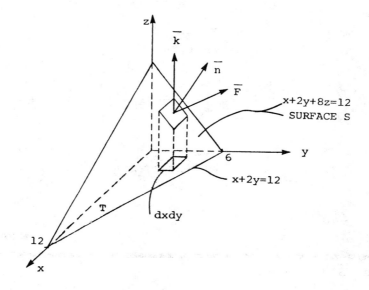

The vector perpendicular to the surface $f(x,y,z)=0$ is given by

$$\text{grad } f$$

Thus, a unit normal to the surface is $\overline{n} = \dfrac{\text{grad } f}{|\text{grad } f|}$.

From eq.(3), obtain

$$\text{grad } f = \overline{i} + 2\overline{j} + 8\overline{k}$$

and

$$\overline{n} = \frac{(1,2,8)}{\sqrt{1+2^2+8^2}} = \frac{1}{\sqrt{69}} \overline{i} + \frac{2}{\sqrt{69}} \overline{j} + \frac{8}{\sqrt{69}} \overline{k} \tag{5}$$

The scalar product of $\overline{n}$ and $\overline{k}$ is

$$\overline{n} \cdot \overline{k} = \frac{8}{\sqrt{69}} \tag{6}$$

The scalar product of $\overline{F}$ and $\overline{n}$ is

$$\overline{F} \cdot \overline{n} = (12y\overline{i} + 2x\overline{j} - 3\overline{k}) \cdot \left[\frac{1}{\sqrt{69}} \overline{i} + \frac{2}{\sqrt{69}} \overline{j} + \frac{8}{\sqrt{69}} \overline{k} \right]$$

$$= \frac{12y+4x-24}{\sqrt{69}} \tag{7}$$

667

Substituting eqs.(6) and (7) into eq.(4) results in

$$\iint_T \frac{\overline{F} \cdot \overline{n}}{|\overline{n} \cdot \overline{k}|} \, dxdy = \iint_T \left(\frac{3}{2}y + \frac{x}{2} - 3\right) \, dxdy \qquad (8)$$

We now have to evaluate the double integral over T. The limits are

$$0 \le y \le \frac{12-x}{2}$$
$$0 \le x \le 12 \qquad (9)$$

Thus, eq.(8) can be written

$$\int_0^{12} \int_0^{6-\frac{x}{2}} \left(\frac{3}{2}y + \frac{x}{2} - 3\right) dydx = \int_0^{12} \left[\frac{3}{4}y^2 + \frac{xy}{2} - 3y\right] \Bigg|_{y=0}^{y=6-\frac{x}{2}} dx$$

$$= \int_0^{12} \left[-\frac{1}{16}x^2 + 9\right] dx = \left[-\frac{1}{16}\frac{x^3}{3} + 9x\right] \Bigg|_{x=0}^{x=12} \qquad (10)$$

$$= 72$$

● **PROBLEM 14-23**

Let S be the surface

$$y^2 = 5x \qquad (1)$$

in the first octant bounded by the planes x=3 and z=4.

   Evaluate

$$\iint_S \overline{F} \cdot \overline{n} \, dS \qquad (2)$$

where

$$\overline{F} = 3y\overline{i} + 2z\overline{j} + x^2yz\overline{k} \qquad (3)$$

Solution: The surface S is shown in the figure.

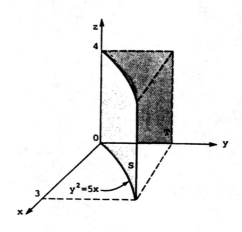

Let T be the projection of S on the zy plane. Integral (2) can be written

$$\iint_S \overline{F} \cdot \overline{n} \ dS = \iint_T \frac{\overline{F} \cdot \overline{n}}{|\overline{n} \cdot \overline{i}|} \ dzdy \qquad (4)$$

The vector normal to the surface

$$y^2 = 5x \qquad (5)$$

is

$$\nabla(5x-y^2) = 5\overline{i} - 2y\overline{j} \qquad (6)$$

Thus, the unit normal to S is

$$\overline{n} = \frac{5}{\sqrt{25+4y^2}} \ \overline{i} - \frac{2y}{\sqrt{25+4y^2}} \ \overline{j} \qquad (7)$$

The scalar product $\overline{F} \cdot \overline{n}$ is

$$\overline{F} \cdot \overline{n} = (3y\overline{i}+2z\overline{j}+x^2yz\overline{k}) \cdot \left[\frac{5}{\sqrt{25+4y^2}} \ \overline{i} - \frac{2y}{\sqrt{25+4y^2}} \ \overline{j} \right]$$

$$\qquad (8)$$

$$= \frac{15y}{\sqrt{25+4y^2}} - \frac{4zy}{\sqrt{25+4y^2}}$$

and

$$\overline{n} \cdot \overline{i} = \frac{5}{\sqrt{25+4y^2}} \qquad (9)$$

Substituting eqs.(8) and (9) into eq.(4) results in

$$\iint_T \frac{15y-4zy}{\sqrt{25+4y^2}} \left(\frac{\sqrt{25+4y^2}}{5} \right) \ dzdy \qquad (10)$$

$$= \iint_T \left(3y - \frac{4}{5}\right)zy \ dzdy$$

Since the surface S is bounded by the plane x=3, we have $y = \sqrt{5x} = \sqrt{15}$. Thus integral (10) becomes

$$\int_{y=0}^{\sqrt{15}} \int_{z=0}^{4} \left(3y - \frac{4}{5} \ zy\right) dzdy = \int_{y=0}^{\sqrt{15}} \left[3yz - \frac{2}{5} \ z^2 \ y \right] \Bigg|_{z=0}^{4} \ dy$$

$$\qquad (11)$$

$$= \int_{0}^{\sqrt{15}} \left(12y - \frac{32}{5} \ y\right) dy = \left(6y^2 - \frac{16}{5} \ y^2\right) \Bigg|_{0}^{\sqrt{15}}$$

$$= 6 \cdot 15 - \frac{16}{5} \cdot 15 = 42$$

● PROBLEM 14-24

Evaluate

$$\iint_S \overline{F} \cdot \overline{n} \ dS \qquad (1)$$

where S is the surface of the tetrahedron with vertices

$$(1,0,0), \quad (0,1,0), \quad (0,0,1) \text{ and}$$

$$\overline{F} = x^2\overline{i} - xy\overline{j} + y^2z^2\overline{k} \tag{2}$$

Solution: The tetrahedron is shown in the figure.

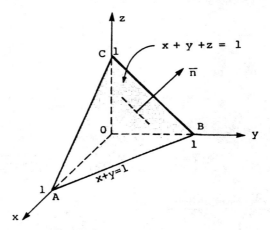

We will now evaluate the integral for each face of the tetra-hedron and then add up the results.

The equation of the face ABC is

$$x + y + z = 1 \tag{3}$$

The unit vector normal to the face ABC is

$$\overline{n} = \frac{1}{\sqrt{3}}\,\overline{i} + \frac{1}{\sqrt{3}}\,\overline{j} + \frac{1}{\sqrt{3}}\,\overline{k} \tag{4}$$

We have

$$\overline{F} \cdot \overline{n} = \frac{x^2}{\sqrt{3}} - \frac{xy}{\sqrt{3}} + \frac{y^2z^2}{\sqrt{3}} \tag{5}$$

and

$$\cos\,\alpha = \overline{n} \cdot \overline{k} = \frac{1}{\sqrt{3}} \tag{6}$$

$$\iint\limits_{ABC} \overline{F} \cdot \overline{n}\ dS = \iint \frac{\overline{F} \cdot \overline{n}}{|\cos\alpha|}\ dxdy$$

$$= \int_{x=0}^{1} \int_{y=0}^{1-x} \sqrt{3}\left(\frac{x^2}{\sqrt{3}} - \frac{xy}{\sqrt{3}} + \frac{y^2z^2}{\sqrt{3}}\right)dydx$$

$$= \int_{x=0}^{1} \int_{y=0}^{1-x} (x^2 - xy + y^2z^2)dydx \tag{7}$$

On the face ABC we have

$$z = 1 - x - y \tag{8}$$

670

and

$$\iint \overline{F} \cdot \overline{n} \ dS = \int_{x=0}^{1} \int_{y=0}^{1-x} \left[2x^2 + xy + y^2 - 2x - 2y + 1 \right] dydx$$

$$= \int_{x=0}^{1} \left[2x^2 y + x \frac{y^2}{2} + \frac{y^3}{3} - 2xy - y^2 + y \right] \Bigg|_{y=0}^{y=1-x} dx$$

$$= \int_{0}^{1} \left(-\frac{11}{6} x^3 + 3x^2 - \frac{3}{2} x + \frac{1}{3} \right) dx \qquad (9)$$

$$= \left(-\frac{11}{6} \frac{x^4}{4} + x^3 - \frac{3}{4} x^2 + \frac{1}{3} x \right) \Bigg|_{0}^{1} = \frac{1}{8}$$

For the face AOC we have
$$\overline{n} = -j \qquad (10)$$

$$\overline{F} \cdot \overline{n} = (x^2 \overline{i}) \cdot (-\overline{j}) = 0 \qquad (11)$$

Thus

$$\iint_{AOC} \overline{F} \cdot \overline{n} \ dS = 0 \qquad (12)$$

For the face COB we have
$$n = -i \qquad (13)$$

$$\overline{F} \cdot \overline{n} = (y^2 z^2 \overline{k}) \cdot (-\overline{i}) = 0 \qquad (14)$$

and

$$\iint_{COB} \overline{F} \cdot \overline{n} \ dS = 0 \qquad (15)$$

For the face AOB we have
$$\overline{n} = -\overline{k}$$

$$\overline{F} \cdot \overline{n} = (x^2 \overline{i} - xy \overline{j}) \cdot (-\overline{k}) = 0 \qquad (16)$$

and

$$\iint_{AOB} \overline{F} \cdot \overline{n} \ dS = 0 \qquad (17)$$

The total integral is thus

$$\iint_{S} \overline{F} \cdot \overline{n} \ dS = \frac{1}{8} \qquad (18)$$

● **PROBLEM 14-25**

Compute
$$\iint_{S} \overline{F} \cdot \overline{n} \ dS \qquad (1)$$

where
$$\overline{F} = z\overline{i} + 2x\overline{j} - 4x^2 z\overline{k} \qquad (2)$$

and S is the surface of the cylinder
$$x^2 + y^2 = 25 \qquad (3)$$

in the first octant between the planes z=0 and z=3.

671

Solution: The part of the cylinder in the first octant is shown in the figure.

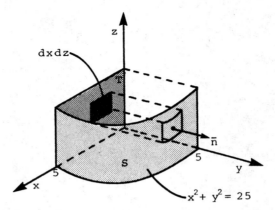

To evaluate the integral

$$\iint_S \overline{F} \cdot \overline{n} \, dS$$

Let us project S on the xz plane so that we can use the formula

$$\iint_S \overline{F} \cdot \overline{n} \, dS = \iint_T \frac{\overline{F} \cdot \overline{n}}{|\overline{n} \cdot \overline{j}|} \, dxdz \qquad (4)$$

Taking the gradient of $x^2 + y^2$ we find

$$\nabla(x^2 + y^2) = 2x\overline{i} + 2y\overline{j} \qquad (5)$$

Thus, the unit normal vector is

$$\overline{n} = \frac{2x}{\sqrt{4x^2 + 4y^2}} \, \overline{i} + \frac{2y}{\sqrt{4x^2 + 4y^2}} \, \overline{j} = \frac{x}{5} \, \overline{i} + \frac{y}{5} \, \overline{j} \qquad (6)$$

and

$$\overline{F} \cdot \overline{n} = \frac{xz}{5} + \frac{2xy}{5} \qquad (7)$$

$$\overline{n} \cdot \overline{j} = \frac{y}{5} \qquad (8)$$

Substituting eqs.(7) and (8) into eq.(4) results in

$$\iint_T \frac{\overline{F} \cdot \overline{n}}{|\overline{n} \cdot \overline{j}|} \, dxdz = \int_{z=0}^{3} \int_{x=0}^{5} \left(\frac{xz + 2xy}{y} \right) \, dxdz$$

$$= \int_{z=0}^{3} \int_{x=0}^{5} \left(\frac{xz}{\sqrt{25 - x^2}} + 2x \right) \, dxdz \qquad (9)$$

In eq.(9) we substituted

$$y = \sqrt{25 - x^2} \qquad (10)$$

Now, using the formula

$$\int \frac{t}{\sqrt{a^2 - t^2}} \, dt = -\sqrt{a^2 - t^2} \qquad (11)$$

672

we evaluate integral (9)

$$\int_{z=0}^{3} \int_{x=0}^{5} \left(\frac{xz}{\sqrt{25-x^2}} + 2x\right) dxdz = \int_{z=0}^{3} \left[-z\sqrt{25-x^2} + x^2\right] \Bigg|_{x=0}^{5} dz$$

$$= \int_{z=0}^{3} \left[5z+25\right] dz = \left(\frac{5z^2}{2} + 25z\right) \Bigg|_{0}^{3} = \frac{195}{2} \qquad (12)$$

● **PROBLEM 14-26**

Consider the surface S given in the parametric form

$$x = 2u+v \qquad y = u^2 \qquad z = u-v \qquad (1)$$

$$0 \leq u \leq 1 \qquad 0 \leq v \leq 1$$

Evaluate the flux of the vector field

$$\overline{F} = \overline{i} + y^2\overline{j} \qquad (2)$$

across this surface.

Solution: The surface S is given in the parametric form

$$\overline{r} = \overline{r}(u,v) \qquad (3)$$

Therefore, to evaluate the flux we can use eq.(10) of Problem 14-16,

$$\text{Flux of } \overline{F} \text{ across } S = \iint_S \overline{F} \cdot \frac{\partial \overline{r}}{\partial u} \times \frac{\partial \overline{r}}{\partial v} \, dudv \qquad (4)$$

We have

$$\frac{\partial \overline{r}}{\partial u} = (2, \ 2u, \ 1) \qquad (5)$$

$$\frac{\partial \overline{r}}{\partial v} = (1, \ 0, \ -1) \qquad (6)$$

and the vector product is

$$\frac{\partial \overline{r}}{\partial u} \times \frac{\partial \overline{r}}{\partial v} = (2,2u,1) \times (1,0,-1) = (-2u,3,-2u) \qquad (7)$$

$$= -2u\overline{i} + 3\overline{j} - 2u\overline{k}$$

Thus,

$$\overline{F} \cdot \frac{\partial \overline{r}}{\partial u} \times \frac{\partial \overline{r}}{\partial v} = (\overline{i}+u^4\overline{j}) \cdot (2u\overline{i}+3\overline{j}-2u\overline{k})$$

$$= 2u + 3u^4 \qquad (8)$$

In eq.(8) we substituted

$$y^2 = u^4$$

Integral (4) becomes

$$\iint_S \overline{F} \cdot \overline{n} \, dS = \iint_S \overline{F} \cdot \frac{\partial \overline{r}}{\partial u} \times \frac{\partial \overline{r}}{\partial v} \, du \, dv$$

$$= \int_0^1 \int_0^1 (2u + 3u^4) \, du \, dv = \int_0^1 \left(u^2 + \frac{3}{5} u^5\right)\bigg|_0^1 \, dv$$

$$= \int_0^1 \frac{8}{5} \, dv = \frac{8}{5} v \bigg|_0^1 = \frac{8}{5} \tag{9}$$

● **PROBLEM 14-27**

Evaluate the integral

$$\iint_S \overline{F} \cdot \overline{n} \, dS \tag{1}$$

where

$$\overline{F} = x\overline{i} + y\overline{j} + z\overline{k} \tag{2}$$

and S is the surface

$$\cos u\overline{i} + \sin u\overline{j} + v\overline{k} \tag{3}$$

$0 \le u \le 2\pi$ and $0 \le v \le 1$.

Solution: Since the surface S is given in the parametric form, we may use the following

$$\iint_S \overline{F} \cdot \overline{n} \, dS = \iint_{S_{uv}} \overline{F} \cdot \frac{\partial \overline{r}}{\partial u} \times \frac{\partial \overline{r}}{\partial v} \, du \, dv \tag{4}$$

In this case

$$\overline{r} = \cos u\overline{i} + \sin u\overline{j} + v\overline{k}$$

and

$$\frac{\partial \overline{r}}{\partial u} = -\sin u\overline{i} + \cos u\overline{j} = (-\sin u, \cos u, 0)$$

$$\frac{\partial \overline{r}}{\partial v} = \overline{k} = (0,0,1)$$

Thus,

$$\frac{\partial \overline{r}}{\partial u} \times \frac{\partial \overline{r}}{\partial v} = (-\sin u, \cos u, 0) \times (0,0,1)$$

$$= \cos u\overline{i} + \sin u\overline{j}$$

Now, since

$$\overline{F} = x\overline{i} + y\overline{j} + z\overline{k}$$

$$= \cos u\overline{i} + \sin u\overline{j} + v\overline{k},$$

we obtain

$$\overline{F} \cdot \left(\frac{\partial \overline{r}}{\partial u} \times \frac{\partial \overline{r}}{\partial v}\right) = (\cos u, \sin u, v) \cdot (\cos u, \sin u, 0)$$

$$= \cos^2 u + \sin^2 u = 1$$

Integral (4) thus becomes

$$\iint \overline{F} \cdot \overline{n} \; dS = \iint \overline{F} \cdot \frac{\partial \overline{r}}{\partial u} \times \frac{\partial \overline{r}}{\partial v} \; dudv$$

$$= \int_0^{2\pi} \int_0^1 dudv = 2\pi$$

SPECIAL CASES OF VECTOR INTEGRATION, CARTESIAN FORM OF SURFACE INTEGRALS

● **PROBLEM** 14-28

Evaluate the integral

$$\iint_S f \; \overline{n} \; dS \tag{1}$$

where $\qquad\qquad f(x,y,z) = 2x^3yz \tag{2}$

and S is the surface of the part of the cylinder

$$x^2 + y^2 = 9$$

$$0 \le z \le 4 \tag{3}$$

$$y \ge 0$$

as shown in the figure.

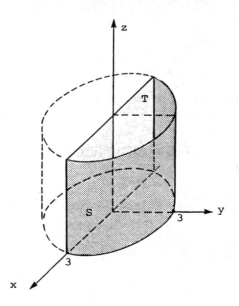

Solution: Let T be the projection of S on the xz plane. Integral (1) can be written as

$$\iint_S f\,\bar{n}\,dS = \iint_T f\,\bar{n}\,\frac{dxdz}{|\bar{n}\cdot\bar{j}|} \tag{4}$$

The unit normal vector $\bar{n}$ is given by

$$\bar{n} = \frac{\bar{N}}{|\bar{N}|} = \frac{\text{grad } F}{|\text{grad } F|} = \frac{\Delta F}{|\Delta F|}$$

where $F = F(x,y,z)=0$ represents the surface.

In this case, from (3) we conclude that

$$F(x,y,z) = x^2+y^2-9 = 0$$

and

$$\bar{n} = \frac{\text{grad }(x^2+y^2-9)}{|\text{grad }(x^2+y^2-9)|}$$

$$= \frac{2x}{\sqrt{4x^2+4y^2}}\,\bar{i} + \frac{2y}{\sqrt{4x^2+4y^2}}\,\bar{j} = \frac{x}{3}\,\bar{i} + \frac{y}{3}\,\bar{k} \tag{5}$$

since from eq.(3), $x^2+y^2=9$. We have,

$$\bar{n}\cdot\bar{j} = \frac{y}{3} \tag{6}$$

Substituting eqs.(2), (5) and (6) into eq.(4) yields

$$\iint_T 2x^3yz\left[\frac{x}{3}\,\bar{i} + \frac{y}{3}\,\bar{j}\right]\frac{3}{y}\,dxdz \tag{7}$$

$$= \int_{z=0}^{4}\int_{x=-3}^{3} 2x^3z(x\bar{i}+y\bar{j})dxdz$$

From eq.(3), we have

$$y = \sqrt{9-x^2} \tag{8}$$

Now, we can evaluate integral (7)

$$\int_{z=0}^{4}\int_{x=-3}^{3} 2x^3z(x\bar{i} + \sqrt{9-x^2}\,\bar{j})dxdz$$

$$= \int_{z=0}^{4}\left[\frac{2}{5}zx^5\bar{i} + 2z\left(-\frac{1}{5}x^2 - \frac{6}{5}\right)\sqrt{(9-x^2)^3}\,\bar{j}\right]\Big|_{x=-3}^{3}\,dz$$

$$= \int_{z=0}^{4}\frac{4}{5}\,3^5z\bar{i}\,dz = 194.4\,\frac{z^2}{2}\bar{i}\,\Big|_{z=0}^{4} \tag{9}$$

$$= 1555\,\bar{i}$$

Integrating eq.(9) we used the following formula

$$\int x^3 \sqrt{a^2-x^2} \ dx \ = \ \left(-\frac{1}{5} \ x^2 \ - \ \frac{2}{15} \ a^2\right) \sqrt{(a^2-x^2)^3} \tag{10}$$

● **PROBLEM 14-29**

Evaluate the integral

$$\iint\limits_{S} \text{rot} \ \overline{F} \cdot \overline{n} \ dS \tag{1}$$

where

$$\overline{F} \ = \ y^2 \overline{i} \ + \ 2xy \overline{j} \ + \ xy \overline{k} \tag{2}$$

and S is the surface of the part of the sphere

$$x^2+y^2+z^2 \ = \ 4 \tag{3}$$

$$z \geq 0$$

<u>Solution</u>: Begin by evaluating the rotation of the vector field F.

$$\nabla \times \overline{F} \ = \ \begin{vmatrix} \overline{i} & \overline{j} & \overline{k} \\ \frac{\partial}{\partial x} & \frac{\partial}{\partial y} & \frac{\partial}{\partial z} \\ y^2 & 2xy & xy \end{vmatrix} = \ x\overline{i} - y\overline{j} + (2y-2y)\overline{k} \tag{4}$$

$$= \ x\overline{i} \ - \ y\overline{j}$$

A vector normal to the sphere is

$$\nabla(x^2+y^2+z^2) \ = \ 2x\overline{i} \ + \ 2y\overline{j} \ + \ 2z\overline{k} \tag{5}$$

Thus, the unit normal is

$$\overline{n} \ = \ \frac{2x\overline{i}+2y\overline{j}+2z\overline{k}}{\sqrt{4x^2+4y^2+4z^2}} \ = \ \frac{x}{2} \ \overline{i} \ + \ \frac{y}{2} \ \overline{j} \ + \ \frac{z}{2} \ \overline{k} \tag{6}$$

since $x^2+y^2+z^2 \ = \ 4$.

T is the projection of S on the xy plane, as shown in the figure.

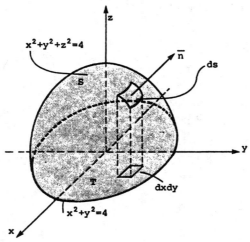

677

Integral (1) can be written

$$\iint_S (\nabla \times \overline{F}) \cdot \overline{n}\ dS = \iint_T \frac{(\nabla \times \overline{F}) \cdot \overline{n}}{|\overline{n} \cdot \overline{k}|}\ dxdy$$

$$= \iint_T (x\overline{i} - y\overline{j}) \cdot \left(\frac{x}{2}\overline{i} + \frac{y}{2}\overline{j} + \frac{z}{2}\overline{k} \right) \frac{dxdy}{\frac{z}{2}}$$

(7)

$$= \iint_T \frac{x^2 - y^2}{z}\ dxdy = \int_{x=-2}^{2} \int_{y=-\sqrt{4-x^2}}^{\sqrt{4-x^2}} \frac{x^2 - y^2}{\sqrt{4-x^2-y^2}}\ dydx$$

Here we used

$$z = \sqrt{4-x^2-y^2} \tag{8}$$

Let us transform integral (7) to polar coordinates (ρ, α)

$$x = \rho \cos \alpha$$
$$y = \rho \sin \alpha \tag{9}$$

From eq.(9) we have

$$dydx = \rho\, d\rho d\alpha \tag{10}$$

Integral (7) becomes

$$\int_{\alpha=0}^{2\pi} \int_{\rho=0}^{2} \frac{\rho^2 \cos^2\alpha - \rho^2 \sin^2\alpha}{\sqrt{4-\rho^2}}\ \rho d\rho d\alpha$$

$$= \int_{\alpha=0}^{2\pi} \int_{\rho=0}^{2} \frac{\rho^3}{\sqrt{4-\rho^2}} \left[\cos^2\alpha - \sin^2\alpha \right] d\rho d\alpha$$

$$= \int_{\alpha=0}^{2\pi} (\cos^2\alpha - \sin^2\alpha) \left[-\frac{2}{3}(4-\rho^2)^{\frac{3}{2}} - \rho^2(4-\rho^2)^{\frac{1}{2}} - \frac{1}{3}\sqrt{4-\rho^2}(\rho^2+8) \right] \Bigg|_{\rho=0}^{2} d\alpha$$

$$= \frac{32}{3} \int_{\alpha=0}^{2\pi} (\cos^2\alpha - \sin^2\alpha) d\alpha = \frac{32}{3} \int_{\alpha=0}^{2\pi} (1-2\sin^2\alpha) d\alpha$$

$$= \frac{32}{3} \alpha \Bigg|_0^{2\pi} - \frac{64}{3} \int_{\alpha=0}^{2\pi} \sin^2\alpha d\alpha$$

$$= \frac{32}{3} 2\pi - \frac{64}{3} \left[\frac{1}{2}\alpha - \frac{1}{4} \sin 2\alpha \right] \Bigg|_{\alpha=0}^{\alpha=2\pi} \tag{11}$$

$$= \frac{64}{3}\pi - \frac{64}{3}\pi = 0$$

In eq.(11) we used the formula

$$\int \frac{x^3 dx}{\sqrt{a^2-x^2}} = -\frac{2}{3}(a^2-x^2)^{\frac{3}{2}}-x^2(a^2-x^2)^{\frac{1}{2}}-\frac{1}{3}(a^2-x^2)^{\frac{1}{2}}(x^2+2a^2) \quad (12)$$

● **PROBLEM 14-30**

Evaluate the integral

$$\iint\limits_{S} xdydz + ydzdx + zdxdy \qquad (1)$$

where S is
$$x = 2u+v; \qquad y = u+2v; \qquad z = 2-v \qquad (2)$$

$$0 \leq u \leq 1; \qquad 0 \leq v \leq 1 \qquad (3)$$

Solution: If the vector field $\bar{F}$ is
$$\bar{F} = P\bar{i} + Q\bar{j} + R\bar{k} \qquad (4)$$
then the surface integral can be expressed in the cartesian form

$$\iint\limits_{S} \bar{F} \cdot \bar{n}\ dS = \iint\limits_{S} Pdydz + Qdxdz + Rdxdy \qquad (5)$$

The surface S is given by
$$\bar{r} = \bar{r}(u,v) = \left[x(u,v),\ y(u,v),\ z(u,v) \right] \qquad (6)$$

The integral in eq.(5) can be transformed into

$$\iint\limits_{S} \bar{F} \cdot \bar{n}\ dS = \iint\limits_{S}(P\bar{i} + Q\bar{j} + R\bar{k}) \cdot \bar{n}\ dS$$

$$= \pm \iint\limits_{D_{uv}} (P\bar{i}+Q\bar{j}+R\bar{k}) \cdot \frac{\frac{\partial \bar{r}}{\partial u} \times \frac{\partial \bar{r}}{\partial v}}{\left| \frac{\partial \bar{r}}{\partial u} \times \frac{\partial \bar{r}}{\partial v} \right|} \left| \frac{\partial \bar{r}}{\partial u} \times \frac{\partial \bar{r}}{\partial v} \right| dudv$$

$$= \pm \iint\limits_{D_{uv}} \begin{vmatrix} P & Q & R \\ \frac{\partial x}{\partial u} & \frac{\partial y}{\partial u} & \frac{\partial z}{\partial u} \\ \frac{\partial x}{\partial v} & \frac{\partial y}{\partial v} & \frac{\partial z}{\partial v} \end{vmatrix} dudv \qquad (7)$$

In eq.(7) the sign + or - is determined by the unit normal vector $\bar{n}$.

The determinant in eq.(7) can be written in the form

$$\pm \iint\limits_{D_{uv}} \left[P \begin{vmatrix} \frac{\partial y}{\partial u} & \frac{\partial z}{\partial u} \\ \frac{\partial y}{\partial v} & \frac{\partial z}{\partial v} \end{vmatrix} + Q \begin{vmatrix} \frac{\partial z}{\partial u} & \frac{\partial x}{\partial u} \\ \frac{\partial z}{\partial v} & \frac{\partial x}{\partial v} \end{vmatrix} + R \begin{vmatrix} \frac{\partial x}{\partial u} & \frac{\partial y}{\partial u} \\ \frac{\partial x}{\partial v} & \frac{\partial y}{\partial v} \end{vmatrix} \right] dudv$$

$$= \pm \iint\limits_{D_{uv}} \left[P \frac{\partial(y,z)}{\partial(u,v)} + Q \frac{\partial(z,x)}{\partial(u,v)} + R \frac{\partial(x,y)}{\partial(u,v)} \right] dudv \qquad (8)$$

From eq.(1), we conclude that

$$P = x, \qquad Q = y, \qquad R = z \qquad (9)$$

We have

$$\frac{\partial(y,z)}{\partial(u,v)} = \begin{vmatrix} 1 & 0 \\ 2 & -1 \end{vmatrix} = -1 \qquad (10)$$

$$\frac{\partial(z,x)}{\partial(u,v)} = \begin{vmatrix} 0 & 2 \\ -1 & 1 \end{vmatrix} = 2 \qquad (11)$$

$$\frac{\partial(x,y)}{\partial(u,v)} = \begin{vmatrix} 2 & 1 \\ 1 & 2 \end{vmatrix} = 3 \qquad (12)$$

Substituting eqs.(10)-(12) into eq.(8) results in

$$\iint\limits_{D_{uv}} (-x + 2y + 3z)dudv$$

$$= \iint\limits_{D_{uv}} (-2u - v + 2u + 4v + 6 - 3v)dudv \qquad (13)$$

$$= \int_0^1 \int_0^1 6 \; dudv = 6$$

● **PROBLEM 14-31**

If a vector field $\overline{F}$ is given by

$$\overline{F} = P\overline{i} + Q\overline{j} + R\overline{k}, \qquad (1)$$

a surface S is given by

$$f(x,y,z) = 0, \qquad (2)$$

and the projection of S on the xy plane is D_{xy}, then reduce the surface integral

$$\iint\limits_{S} \overline{F} \cdot \overline{n} \; dS = \iint\limits_{S} Pdydz + Qdxdz + Rdxdy \qquad (3)$$

to an integral over D_{xy}.

Solution: Substituting eq.(1) into eq.(3) results in

680

$$\iint_S \overline{F} \cdot \overline{n} \ dS = \iint_S (P\overline{i} + Q\overline{j} + R\overline{k}) \cdot \overline{n} \ dS \qquad (4)$$

The unit normal to the surface is

$$\overline{n} = \frac{\nabla f}{|\nabla f|} \qquad (5)$$

From eq.(4), we obtain

$$\iint_S \overline{F} \cdot \overline{n} \ dS = \pm \iint_{D_{xy}} (P\overline{i} + Q\overline{j} + R\overline{k}) \cdot \frac{\nabla f}{|\nabla f|} \quad \frac{|\nabla f|}{|\nabla f \cdot \overline{k}|} \ dxdy \qquad (6)$$

Since

$$\nabla f \cdot \overline{k} = \left(\frac{\partial f}{\partial x}, \ \frac{\partial f}{\partial y}, \ \frac{\partial f}{\partial z}\right) \cdot (0,0,1) = \frac{\partial f}{\partial z} \qquad (7)$$

eq.(7) can be written

$$\iint_S \overline{F} \cdot \overline{n} \ dS = \pm \iint_{D_{xy}} \frac{P \frac{\partial f}{\partial x} + Q \frac{\partial f}{\partial y} + R \frac{\partial f}{\partial z}}{\left|\frac{\partial f}{\partial z}\right|} \ dxdy \qquad (8)$$

The sign + or - is determined by the unit normal $\overline{n}$.

● **PROBLEM 14-32**

Evaluate the integral

$$\iint_S dxdy + dzdx + dydz \qquad (1)$$

where S is

$$z = \sqrt{1-x^2-y^2} \qquad (2)$$

over the disk $\qquad x^2+y^2 \leq 1 \qquad (3)$

Solution: Integral (1) is the cartesian form of the surface integral. In general, if

$$\overline{F} = P\overline{i} + Q\overline{j} + R\overline{k} \qquad (4)$$

then the integral can be written

$$\iint_S \overline{F} \cdot \overline{n} \ dS = \iint_S Pdydz + Qdxdz + Rdxdy \qquad (5)$$

Depending on the form of the equation for the surface, we use the appropriate formulas for $\overline{n}$ and dS.

For a surface given by

$$z = f(x,y),$$

as is the case in this problem, the unit normal vector is given by

681

$$\bar{n} = \frac{-\left(\frac{\partial z}{\partial x}\right)\bar{i} - \left(\frac{\partial z}{\partial y}\right)\bar{j} + \bar{k}}{\sqrt{1 + \left(\frac{\partial z}{\partial x}\right)^2 + \left(\frac{\partial z}{\partial y}\right)^2}} \tag{6}$$

and

$$dS = \sqrt{1 + \left(\frac{\partial z}{\partial x}\right)^2 + \left(\frac{\partial z}{\partial y}\right)^2}\ \ dxdy \tag{7}$$

Thus, substituting eqs.(6), (7) and (4) into the left-hand side of eq.(5) leads to

$$\iint\limits_{S}\bar{F}\cdot\bar{n}\ dS = \iint\limits_{S}(P\bar{i}+Q\bar{j}+R\bar{k})\cdot\bar{n}\ dS$$

$$= \pm\iint\limits_{D_{xy}}(P\bar{i}+Q\bar{j}+R\bar{k})\cdot\frac{-\left(\frac{\partial z}{\partial x}\right)\bar{i} - \left(\frac{\partial z}{\partial y}\right)\bar{j} + \bar{k}}{\sqrt{1 + \left(\frac{\partial z}{\partial x}\right)^2 + \left(\frac{\partial z}{\partial y}\right)^2}}\sqrt{1 + \left(\frac{\partial z}{\partial x}\right)^2 + \left(\frac{\partial z}{\partial y}\right)^2}\ dxdy$$

$$= \pm\iint\limits_{D_{xy}}\left(-P\ \frac{\partial z}{\partial x} - Q\ \frac{\partial z}{\partial y} + R\right)\ dxdy \tag{8}$$

The sign + or - is determined by the unit normal vector $\bar{n}$.

For the surface given by eq.(2) we have

$$\frac{\partial z}{\partial x} = \frac{-x}{\sqrt{1-x^2-y^2}}\ ;\qquad \frac{\partial z}{\partial y} = \frac{-y}{\sqrt{1-x^2-y^2}} \tag{9}$$

From eqs.(1) and (5) we see that

$$P = Q = R = 1 \tag{10}$$

Thus

$$\iint\limits_{D_{xy}}\left(\frac{x}{\sqrt{1-x^2-y^2}} + \frac{y}{\sqrt{1-x^2-y^2}} + 1\right)\ dxdy \tag{11}$$

Transforming into polar coordinates yields

$$\int_0^{2\pi}\int_0^1\left(\frac{r\cos\theta}{\sqrt{1-r^2}} + \frac{r\sin\theta}{\sqrt{1-r^2}} + 1\right)\ r\ drd\theta$$

$$= \int_0^{2\pi}\int_0^1\frac{r^2\cos\theta}{\sqrt{1-r^2}}\ drd\theta + \int_0^{2\pi}\int_0^1\frac{r^2\sin\theta}{\sqrt{1-r^2}}\ drd\theta \tag{12}$$

$$+ \int_0^{2\pi}\int_0^1 r\ drd\theta = \pi$$

CHAPTER 15

SURFACE INTEGRALS AND FLUX
IN PHYSICAL APPLICATIONS

INTRODUCTION

Chapter 15 introduces only a few of the vast physical applications of the surface integrals (or flux) of vector fields.

The chapter considers applications in fluid dynamics, heat flow and electrostatics.

One thing that this chapter hopes to point out is that the same mathematical concept, the flux of a vector field, may be used to describe and define various different physical quantities. Indeed, the flow of fluid, the flow of heat, the flow of an electrical field, from a mathematical point are all defined and calculated using the concept of flux.

If the student finds certain equations or notions too difficult, he should refer to Chapter 14 and review the basic definitions of the surface integral and flux.

FLUX OF A FLUID FLOW

● **PROBLEM 15-1**

The speed and direction of a fluid flow are described by the continuous vector field

$$\overline{v} = \overline{v}(x,y,z) \tag{1}$$

Using a surface integral, define the flux, that is, the rate of flow per unit area per unit time across a smooth surface S.

Solution: Let us assume that S is a perfectly flat surface and that $\overline{v}$ is a constant field. In such a case, the flux is equal to

$$F = \bar{v} \cdot \bar{n}\, S \tag{2}$$

where $\bar{n}$ is a unit normal to S. Also, for such a case, the flux is equal to the volume of a tube of fluid, as shown in Fig. 1.

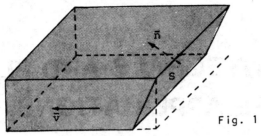

Fig. 1

Let us consider now a more general case of a regular surface S, and assume that S is given in the parametric form

$$\bar{r} = \bar{r}(u,v) \tag{3}$$

where $\bar{r}$ is a position vector of a point of the surface S. S can be partitioned along the coordinate curves u=const and v=const. For sufficiently small segments S_k, the vector field $\bar{v}$ is constant within each segment (see Fig. 2).

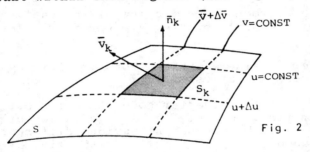

Fig. 2

The flux across S_k is

$$F_k = \bar{v}_k \cdot \bar{n}_k\, S_k \tag{4}$$

The normal vector to S_k is given by

$$\frac{\partial \bar{r}}{\partial u} \times \frac{\partial \bar{r}}{\partial v} \tag{5}$$

and the unit normal is

$$\bar{n}_k = \frac{\dfrac{\partial \bar{r}}{\partial u}(u_k,v_k) \times \dfrac{\partial \bar{r}}{\partial v}(u_k,v_k)}{\left| \dfrac{\partial \bar{r}}{\partial u}(u_k,v_k) \times \dfrac{\partial \bar{r}}{\partial v}(u_k,v_k) \right|} \tag{6}$$

The area S_k is given approximately by

$$S_k = \left| \frac{\partial \bar{r}}{\partial u}(u_k,v_k) \times \frac{\partial \bar{r}}{\partial v}(u_k,v_k) \right| \Delta u \Delta v \tag{7}$$

The approximate flux across S_k is thus

$$F_k = \bar{v}_k \cdot \bar{n}_k\, S_k = \bar{v}\left(\bar{r}(u_k,v_k)\right) \cdot \left[\frac{\partial \bar{r}}{\partial u}(u_k,v_k) \times \frac{\partial \bar{r}}{\partial v}(u_k,v_k) \right] \Delta u \Delta v$$

Note that u_k and v_k are the values of parameters for S_k. For the whole surface S, subdivided into N segments, the total flux is

$$F = \sum_{k=1}^{N} F_k = \sum_{k=1}^{N} \bar{v}\left(\bar{r}(u_k, v_k)\right) \cdot \left[\frac{\partial \bar{r}}{\partial u}(u_k, v_k) \times \frac{\partial \bar{r}}{\partial v}(u_k, v_k)\right] \Delta u \Delta v$$

If $\bar{v}$ is continuous on S and $\bar{r} = \bar{r}(u,v)$ is continuously differentiable, then

$$\lim_{\substack{\max(S_k) \to 0 \\ N \to \infty}} \sum_{k=1}^{N} = \iint \bar{v}\left(\bar{r}(u,v)\right) \cdot \left[\frac{\partial \bar{r}}{\partial u} \times \frac{\partial \bar{r}}{\partial v}\right] dudv$$

$$= \iint_S \bar{v} \cdot \bar{n} \, dS = \iint_S \bar{v} \cdot d\bar{S}$$

Thus, the flux of $\bar{v}$ across the surface S is

$$F = \iint_S \bar{v} \cdot \bar{n} \, dS$$

● **PROBLEM** 15-2

A fluid flows outward from the origin, its flow described by

$$\bar{v} = \frac{x}{x^2+y^2+z^2} \bar{i} + \frac{y}{x^2+y^2+z^2} \bar{j} + \frac{z}{x^2+y^2+z^2} \bar{k} \qquad (1)$$

Find the flux of $\bar{v}$ across a sphere S_a of radius a and center at the origin.

Solution: The flux of $\bar{v}$ across the sphere S_a is given by

$$\iint_{S_a} \bar{v} \cdot d\bar{S} = \iint_{S_a} \frac{xdydz + ydxdz + zdxdy}{x^2+y^2+z^2} \qquad (2)$$

Since on the sphere S_a

$$x^2+y^2+z^2 = a^2 \qquad (3)$$

eq.(2) can be written

$$\iint_{S_a} \bar{v} \cdot d\bar{S} = \frac{1}{a^2} \iint_{S_a} (xdydz + ydxdz + zdxdy) \qquad (4)$$

The sphere S_a can be parametrized in terms of the parameters a, ϕ and θ,

$$x = a\sin\phi\cos\theta$$

$$y = a\sin\phi\sin\theta \qquad (5)$$

$$z = a\cos\phi$$

where $0 \leq \phi \leq \pi$ and $0 \leq \theta \leq 2\pi$ $\qquad\qquad$ (6)

We can use the change of variables theorem to obtain

$$\iint\limits_{S_a} \bar{v} \cdot d\bar{S} = \frac{1}{a^2} \iint\limits_{x^2+y^2+z^2=a^2} (xdydz + ydxdz + zdxdy)$$

$$= \frac{1}{a^2} \int_0^{2\pi} \int_0^\pi \left[a\sin\phi\cos\theta \left|\frac{\partial(y,z)}{\partial(\phi,\theta)}\right| + a\sin\phi\sin\theta \left|\frac{\partial(x,z)}{\partial(\phi,\theta)}\right| \right.$$

$$\left. + a\cos\phi \left|\frac{\partial(x,y)}{\partial(\phi,\theta)}\right| \right] d\phi d\theta \qquad (7)$$

From eq.(5), we find

$$\frac{\partial(y,z)}{\partial(\phi,\theta)} = a^2\sin^2\phi\cos\theta$$

$$\frac{\partial(z,x)}{\partial(\phi,\theta)} = a^2\sin^2\phi\sin\theta \qquad\qquad (8)$$

$$\frac{\partial(x,y)}{\partial(\phi,\theta)} = a^2\sin\phi\cos\phi$$

Substituting eq.(8) into eq.(7) results in

$$\iint\limits_{S_a} \bar{v} \cdot d\bar{S} = a \int_0^{2\pi} \int_0^\pi (\sin^3\phi\cos^2\theta + \sin^3\phi\sin^2\theta + \sin\phi\cos^2\phi)d\phi d\theta$$

$$= a \int_0^{2\pi} \int_0^\pi \sin\phi d\phi d\theta = 4\pi a$$

● **PROBLEM 15-3**

Consider the vortex flow of a fluid, where the fluid rotates with an angular velocity $\bar{\omega}$ about the z-axis. Where should a unit square S lying on the yz-plane be located if there is to be a minimum amount of fluid crossing the square per unit time?

Solution: Let us assume that the angular velocity vector points in the positive z-direction. We may then write

$$\bar{\omega} = (0,0,\omega) \qquad\qquad (1)$$

Since

$$\bar{v} = \bar{\omega} \times \bar{r} \qquad\qquad (2)$$

we have $\qquad\qquad \bar{v} = (0,0,\omega) \times (x,y,z) \qquad\qquad (3)$

$$= -\omega y\bar{i} + \omega x\bar{j}$$

Now, since $\bar{v}$ does not depend on z, we can position the square S in such way that one of its sides is on the y-axis, as shown in the figure.

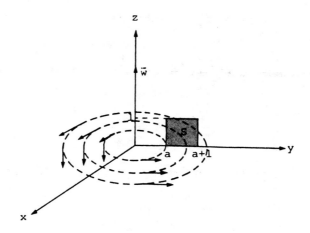

Now, if we let M denote the amount of fluid passing through the unit square S, then

$$M = \iint_S \rho \overline{v} \cdot \overline{n} \, dS \tag{4}$$

where ρ is the density of the fluid. Since in this case

$$\overline{n} = \overline{i}$$

we have

$$\overline{v} \cdot \overline{n} = (-\omega y \overline{i} + \omega x \overline{j}) \cdot \overline{i} = -\omega y \tag{5}$$

and thus

$$M = \iint_S \rho \overline{v} \cdot \overline{n} \, dS = -\int_0^1 \int_a^{a+1} \rho \omega y \, dy \, dz$$

$$\tag{6}$$

$$= -\rho \omega \int_0^1 \frac{y^2}{2} \Big|_{y=a}^{a+1} dz = -\rho \omega \frac{(2a+1)}{2}$$

Now, notice that for $a = -\frac{1}{2}$, we obtain

$$M = -\rho \omega \left[\frac{2(-\frac{1}{2})+1}{2} \right] = 0 \tag{7}$$

Thus, we see that M reaches its minimum value of 0 for $a = -\frac{1}{2}$.

HEAT FLOW

● **PROBLEM 15-4**

The temperature at a point (x,y,z) of a region $D \subset R^3$ is given by the continuously differentiable function

$$T = T(x,y,z) = x^2 + y^2 \tag{1}$$

Find the total rate of flow of heat across the cylindrical surface given by

$$x^2+y^2 = 1 \qquad |z| \le 1 \qquad (2)$$

<u>Solution</u>: In general, the total rate of heat flow is given by

$$\iint\limits_{S} (\nabla T) \cdot \bar{n} \ dS \qquad (3)$$

where ∇T is the temperature gradient. For the cylindrical surface, we may write

$$\iint\limits_{S} (\nabla T) \cdot \bar{n} \ dS = \iint\limits_{I} (\nabla T) \cdot \bar{n} \ dS \qquad (4)$$

$$+ \iint\limits_{II} (\nabla T) \cdot \bar{n} \ dS + \iint\limits_{III} (\nabla T) \cdot \bar{n} \ dS$$

where surface I denotes the top of the cylinder, surface II the bottom of the cylinder and surface III the side of the cylinder, as shown in the figure.

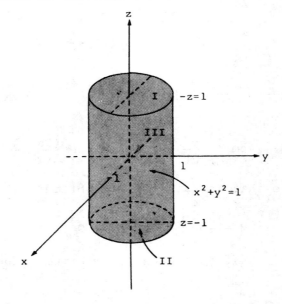

Now, since

$$T(x,y,z) = x^2+y^2$$

the temperature gradient ∇T is

$$\nabla T = 2x\bar{i} + 2y\bar{j} \qquad (5)$$

The unit vector normal to surface I is

$$\bar{n} = \bar{k}$$

Thus

688

$$(\nabla T) \cdot \overline{n} = (2x, 2y, 0) \cdot (0, 0, 1) = 0 \qquad (6)$$

and

$$\iint_{I} (\nabla T) \cdot \overline{n} \, dS = 0 \qquad (7)$$

The unit normal to surface II is

$$\overline{n} = -\overline{k}$$

and

$$(\nabla T) \cdot \overline{n} = (2x, 2y, 0) \cdot (0, 0, -1) = 0 \qquad (8)$$

Thus

$$\iint_{II} (\nabla T) \cdot \overline{n} \, dS = 0 \qquad (9)$$

The unit normal to surface III is

$$(10)$$

$$n = \frac{\text{grad}(x^2+y^2-1)}{|\text{grad}(x^2+y^2-1)|} = \left(\frac{2x}{\sqrt{4x^2+4y^2}}, \frac{2y}{\sqrt{4x^2+4y^2}}, 0 \right) = (x, y, 0)$$

since $x^2+y^2=1$.

The rate of flow of heat across the side of the cylinder is thus

$$\iint_{III} (\nabla T) \cdot \overline{n} \, dS = \iint_{III} (2x, 2y, 0) \cdot (x, y, 0) dS$$

$$(11)$$

$$= \iint_{III} 2(x^2+y^2) dS = 2 \iint_{III} dS = 2 \cdot 4\pi = 8\pi$$

Note that $\iint_{III} dS$ is nothing more than the surface area of the side, given by $2\pi(1)(1) = 4\pi$.

Thus, for the temperature function given by eq.(1), the total rate of flow of heat across the cylindrical surface is

$$\iint_{S} (\nabla T) \cdot \overline{n} \, dS = 8\pi \qquad (12)$$

● PROBLEM 15-5

Consider a rod made of a homogeneous material whose co-efficient of thermal conductivity is κ. Its temperature distribution is

$$T(x,y,z) = \frac{\alpha}{z^2} + \beta x \qquad (1)$$

where α and β are positive constants.

Find the total number of calories per second flowing across the surface S shown in the figure.

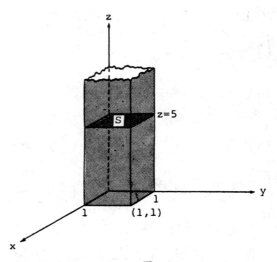

Solution: Let us define vector $\bar{h}$

$$\bar{h} = -\kappa \, \nabla T \tag{2}$$

which at each point in space (or in the region where $T(x,y,z)$ is defined) gives the direction in which the heat is flowing. The magnitude of $\bar{h}$ gives the rate of heat flow per unit area across an area perpendicular to $\bar{h}$.

The minus sign in the equation accounts for the fact that the temperature gradient points in the direction of maximum rate of increase of temperature while heat flows in the direction of decreasing temperature, opposite to that of the temperature gradient. The total number of calories per second flowing across the surface S is given by

$$H = \iint\limits_{S} (-\kappa \nabla T) \cdot \bar{n} \; dS \tag{3}$$

Now, from eq.(1), we have

$$\nabla T = \nabla \left(\frac{\alpha}{z^2} + \beta x \right) = \beta \bar{i} - 2\alpha z^{-3} \bar{k} \tag{4}$$

Substituting eq.(4) into eq.(3) results in

$$H = \iint\limits_{S} (-\kappa \beta \bar{i} + 2\kappa \alpha z^{-3} \bar{k}) \cdot \bar{k} \; dS$$

$$\tag{5}$$

$$= \int_0^1 \int_0^1 (2\kappa \alpha z^{-3}) \, dx \, dy = 2\kappa \alpha z^{-3}$$

$$= \frac{2\kappa \alpha}{5^3} = 0.016 \kappa \alpha$$

Here, the unit normal to the surface S is

$$\bar{n} = \bar{k} \tag{6}$$

A hollow sphere of inner radius a and outer radius b is made of a homogeneous material. The inner temperature is T_a and the outer temperature is T_b. Find the steady-state temperature as a function of r, where r is the distance from the center and $a \le r \le b$.

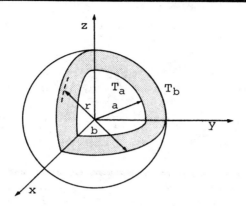

Solution: Since the distribution of temperature is symmetrical, we have

$$|\nabla T| = -\frac{dT}{dr} \tag{1}$$

We assume that the inside of the sphere is hotter than the outside. Let S represent the sphere shown in the figure. We have

$$H = \iint_S (-\kappa \nabla T) \cdot \overline{n}\ dS = \iint_S -\kappa \frac{dT}{dr}\ dS \tag{2}$$

$$= -\kappa \frac{dT}{dr}\ 4\pi r^2$$

Since H is constant, we may write

$$H \frac{dr}{r^2} = -4\pi\kappa\ dT \tag{3}$$

Now, integrating eq.(3) from r=a to r yields

$$H \int_a^r \frac{dr}{r^2} = -4\pi\kappa \int_{T_a}^T dT$$

$$H \left(-\frac{1}{r} + \frac{1}{a}\right) = -4\pi\kappa(T-T_a)$$

Solving for T yields

$$T = \left[-H\left(-\frac{1}{r} + \frac{1}{a}\right) + 4\pi\kappa T_a\right]\frac{1}{4\pi\kappa} \tag{4}$$

Now, to find H, apply the boundary condition $T=T_b$ at $r=b$. Doing this yields

$$T_b = \left[-H \left(-\frac{1}{b} + \frac{1}{a} \right) + 4\pi\kappa T_a \right] \frac{1}{4\pi\kappa}$$

and thus

$$H = \frac{-4\pi\kappa(T_b - T_a)}{\left(\frac{1}{a} - \frac{1}{b} \right)} \tag{5}$$

Finally, for the temperature distribution, we obtain

$$T = T_a + (T_b - T_a) \left[\frac{\frac{1}{a} - \frac{1}{r}}{\frac{1}{a} - \frac{1}{b}} \right] \tag{6}$$

Notice that this equation does, of course, satisfy the boundary conditions.

● **PROBLEM** 15-7

Consider a cylindrical steampipe surrounded by a cylindrical heat insulator as shown in the figure.

The radius of the pipe is a and the radius of the insulator is b. The temperatures of the inner and outer surfaces of the insulator are T_a and T_b, respectively.

Assuming that the temperature distribution is symmetrical, find the temperature T inside the insulator as a function of r.

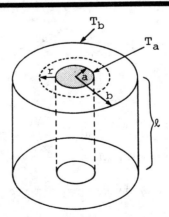

Solution: We shall consider a section of the insulator of length ℓ. The distribution of the temperature within the insulator is symmetrical, thus

$$|\nabla T| = -\frac{dT}{dr} \tag{1}$$

Since the pipe is hotter than the surroundings, $\frac{dT}{dr}$ is negative. ∇T is directed radially toward the center of the pipe.

Let S be a cylinder of radius r and length ℓ within the insulator. The quantity of heat flowing per unit time across S is

$$H = \iint (-\kappa \nabla T) \cdot \bar{n} \, dS \tag{2}$$

Since the direction of $\bar{n}$ is outward, we have

$$(-\kappa \nabla T) \cdot \bar{n} = -\kappa \frac{dT}{dr} \tag{3}$$

Integral (2) becomes

$$H = \iint_S -\kappa \frac{dT}{dr} \, dS = -\kappa \frac{dT}{dr} \iint_S dS \tag{4}$$

$$= -\kappa \frac{dT}{dr} \, 2\pi r \ell$$

Since H is independent of r, we have

$$H = -\kappa \frac{dT}{dr} \, 2\pi r \ell$$

or

$$H \frac{dr}{r} = -2\pi \ell \kappa \, dT \tag{5}$$

Integrating eq.(5) results in

$$H \int_a^b \frac{dr}{r} = -2\pi \ell \kappa \int_{T_a}^{T_b} dT \tag{6}$$

$$H \left[\ln r \right] \Big|_a^b = H \ln \frac{b}{a} = -2\pi \ell \kappa (T_b - T_a) \tag{7}$$

$$H = \frac{2\pi \ell \kappa (T_a - T_b)}{\ln \frac{b}{a}} \tag{8}$$

Integrating again eq.(5) and substituting H from eq.(8) results in

$$H \int_a^r \frac{dr}{r} = -2\pi \ell \kappa \int_{T_a}^{T_r} dT \tag{9}$$

$$H \ln \frac{r}{a} = -2\pi \ell \kappa (T_r - T_a) \tag{10}$$

$$T_r = T_a - (T_a - T_b) \frac{\ln\left(\frac{r}{a}\right)}{\ln\left(\frac{b}{a}\right)} \tag{11}$$

Note that the temperature T_r does not depend on the thermal conductivity κ.

ELECTRIC FIELD, GAUSS' LAW AND ELECTROSTATIC POTENTIAL

The Newtonian potential function is

$$\phi(x,y,z) = \frac{1}{\sqrt{x^2+y^2+z^2}} \qquad (1)$$

The gradient of ϕ is the force field $\overline{F}$ of a charged particle at the origin

$$\overline{F} = grad\ \phi \qquad (2)$$

Show that the flux of $\overline{F}$ across a sphere of radius a whose center is at the origin is independent of a.

Solution: The flux of a vector field $\overline{F}$ across a smooth surface S is given by

$$\iint_S \overline{F} \cdot \overline{n}\ dS$$

where $\overline{n}$, the unit normal vector to the surface, is given by

$$\overline{n} = \frac{grad\ f}{|grad\ f|}$$

when the surface is described in the form $f(x,y,z) = 0$.

Since in this case, the surface is a sphere of radius a with center at the origin, we may write

$$x^2+y^2+z^2 = a^2$$

or

$$f(x,y,z) = x^2+y^2+z^2-a^2 = 0.$$

Now, the vector field $\overline{F}$ may be obtained from eqs.(1) and (2):

$$\overline{F} = grad\ \phi$$

$$= grad\left[\frac{1}{\sqrt{x^2+y^2+z^2}}\right]$$

$$= \left[\frac{-x}{(x^2+y^2+z^2)^{\frac{3}{2}}},\ \frac{-y}{(x^2+y^2+z^2)^{\frac{3}{2}}},\ \frac{-z}{(x^2+y^2+z^2)^{\frac{3}{2}}}\right]$$

$$= \left(\frac{-x}{a^3},\ \frac{-y}{a^3},\ \frac{-z}{a^3}\right)$$

The unit normal vector is

$$n = \frac{grad\ f}{|grad\ f|}$$

694

$$= \left[\frac{x}{\sqrt{x^2+y^2+z^2}}, \quad \frac{y}{\sqrt{x^2+y^2+z^2}}, \quad \frac{z}{\sqrt{x^2+y^2+z^2}} \right]$$

$$= \left(\frac{x}{a}, \frac{y}{a}, \frac{z}{a} \right)$$

Thus, the flux is

$$\iint_S \overline{F} \cdot \overline{n} \ dS = \iint_S \left(\frac{-x}{a^3}, \frac{-y}{a^3}, \frac{-z}{a^3} \right) \cdot \left(\frac{x}{a}, \frac{y}{a}, \frac{z}{a} \right) \ dS$$

$$= \iint_S - \frac{1}{a^2} \ dS = - \frac{1}{a^2} \iint_S dS = - \frac{1}{a} 4\pi a^2 = -4\pi$$

We see that the flux of $\overline{F}$ across the sphere S is independent of a.

For a single charge q located at the origin, the electrostatic potential $\phi(x,y,z)$ is given by

$$\phi(x,y,z) = \frac{q}{r} \tag{1}$$

where $\qquad r = \sqrt{x^2+y^2+z^2}$

In eq.(1) we omitted the coefficient $\frac{1}{4\pi\varepsilon_0}$ since it does not affect our reasoning.

The electric field $\overline{E}$ is given by

$$\overline{E} = -\nabla\phi \tag{2}$$

Consider a charge of density σ distributed uniformly over the surface of a sphere of radius r_1.

The potential at the point A is given by

$$\phi(x_0,y_0,z_0) = \iint_S \frac{\sigma dS}{\sqrt{(x-x_0)^2+(y-y_0)^2+(z-z_0)^2}} \tag{3}$$

where the integral is calculated over the surface of the sphere.

Find the potential at the points for which

1. $\sqrt{x_0^2+y_0^2+z_0^2} < r_1$ $\qquad\qquad\qquad$ (4)

2. $\sqrt{x_0^2+y_0^2+z_0^2} > r_1$ $\qquad\qquad\qquad$ (5)

Solution: 1. Let $\overline{E}$ be the electric field inside the sphere. Since there is no charge inside the sphere, by Gauss' law and symmetry, we have

$$\overline{E} = \overline{0}. \tag{6}$$

Since

$$\overline{E} = -\nabla\phi = 0$$

we conclude that the potential ϕ is a constant within the sphere.

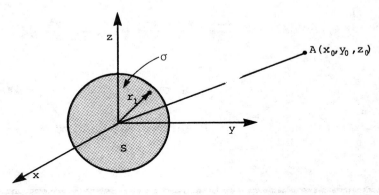

Now, if we consider the center of the sphere, we obtain

$$\phi(0,0,0) = \iint_S \frac{\sigma dS}{\sqrt{x^2+y^2+z^2}} = \frac{\sigma}{r_1} 4\pi r_1^2 = 4\pi \sigma r_1 \tag{7}$$

2. Now, to evaluate the potential outside the sphere, let us note that by Gauss' law and symmetry, the electric field outside the sphere is the same as the electric field due to a point charge $4\pi r_1^2 \sigma$ located at the center.

Thus

$$\phi(x_0, y_0, z_0) = \frac{q}{r_0} = \frac{4\pi r_1^2 \sigma}{r_0} \tag{8}$$

● **PROBLEM** 15-10

Use Gauss' law to determine the magnitude and direction of the electric field vector $\overline{E}$ due to a point charge of magnitude q.

Solution: Consider an electrostatic field $\overline{E}$ defined in a region of space. Let S be a closed surface in that region. Gauss' law states that

$$\iint_S \overline{E} \cdot \overline{n} \, dS = \frac{q}{\varepsilon_0} \tag{1}$$

where q is the total charge enclosed by the surface and ε_0 is a constant depending on the system of units we use.

The surface integral in eq.(1) is called the flux across S. Consider a point charge of magnitude q, as shown in Fig 1.

696

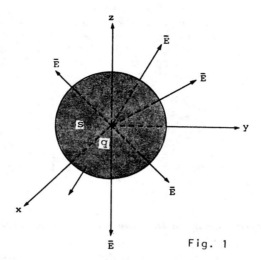

Fig. 1

Let us choose the closed surface S to be a sphere of radius r with q at its center. Since q is a point charge, the electric field is symmetrical and $\overline{E}$ is normal to S. Thus, $\overline{E} \cdot \overline{n}$ has a constant value over the surface S. The magnitude $|\overline{E}|$ is constant over the surface of the sphere S. Integral (1) becomes

$$\iint\limits_{S} \overline{E} \cdot \overline{n} \ dS = \overline{E} \cdot \overline{n} \iint\limits_{S} dS = 4\pi r^2 \ \overline{E} \cdot \overline{n} \tag{2}$$

since $\iint dS$ represents the total surface area $(4\pi r^2)$ of a sphere.

Now, from Gauss' law, we have

$$4\pi r^2 \ \overline{E} \cdot \overline{n} = \frac{q}{\varepsilon_0} \tag{3}$$

or

$$\overline{E} \cdot \overline{n} = \frac{q}{4\pi r^2 \varepsilon_0} \tag{4}$$

From eq.(4) we conclude that if the charge q is positive, then
$$|\overline{E}| = \frac{q}{4\pi r^2 \varepsilon_0} \tag{5}$$

and $\overline{E}$ is directed away from q. If the charge q is negative, then $\overline{E}$ is directed towards q.

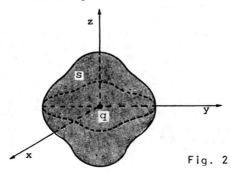

Fig. 2

697

Now, notice that we have evaluated the electric field of a point charge by selecting a sphere as the enclosing surface. If we would have chosen any other surface, the integration would have been quite complicated. Indeed, let us consider any other surface S (see Fig. 2). We can again apply Gauss' law

$$\iint\limits_{S} \overline{E} \cdot \overline{n} \; dS = \frac{q}{\varepsilon_0}$$

but now the dot product $\overline{E} \cdot \overline{n}$ does not have a constant value and thus it cannot be brought outside the integral, causing complications in the integration.

● PROBLEM 15-11

Consider an infinitely long thin wire carrying a charge of density β. Determine the magnitude of the electric field of this wire.

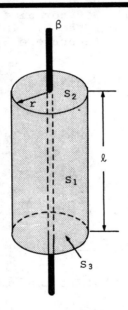

Solution: We shall use Gauss' law,

$$\iint\limits_{S} \overline{E} \cdot \overline{n} \; dS = \frac{q}{\varepsilon_0}$$

as a means of solution.   The problem now is to select a surface such that $\overline{E} \cdot \overline{n}$ is a constant over that surface.   Let us consider an infinite cylinder of radius r concentric with the wire, as shown in the figure.

Since the cylinder encloses the wire, we can apply Gauss' law.   Let us take into consideration a part of the cylinder of length ℓ.   Note that the electric field vector $\overline{E}$ caused by the charged wire is perpendicular to the side surface of the cylinder.

The total surface, or just surface, may be thought of as consisting of parts S_1, S_2 and S_3, as shown in the figure.

We may write

$$\iint_S \overline{E} \cdot \overline{n} \, dS = \iint_{S_1} \overline{E} \cdot \overline{n} \, dS + \iint_{S_2} \overline{E} \cdot \overline{n} \, dS + \iint_{S_3} \overline{E} \cdot \overline{n} \, dS$$

Now, we should note that for surfaces S_2 and S_3, the electric field vector is perpendicular to the normal vector, and thus

$$\overline{E} \cdot \overline{n} = 0$$

and

$$\iint_{S_2} \overline{E} \cdot \overline{n} \, dS = 0 \qquad \iint_{S_3} \overline{E} \cdot \overline{n} \, dS = 0 \qquad (1)$$

The surface of the cylinder consists of the part S_1 over which $\overline{E} \cdot \overline{n}$ is constant and two parts S_2 and S_3 for which $\overline{E}$ and $\overline{n}$ are perpendicular and their scalar product $\overline{E} \cdot \overline{n} = 0$.

Eq.(1) becomes

$$\iint_S \overline{E} \cdot \overline{n} \, dS = \iint_{S_1} \overline{E} \cdot \overline{n} \, dS + \iint_{S_2} \overline{E} \cdot \overline{n} \, dS + \iint_{S_3} \overline{E} \cdot \overline{n} \, dS$$

$$= \iint_{S_1} \overline{E} \cdot \overline{n} \, dS = \overline{E} \cdot \overline{n} \iint_{S_1} dS = \overline{E} \cdot \overline{n}(2\pi r \ell) \qquad (2)$$

$$= \frac{q}{\varepsilon_0}$$

Since the density of the charge is β, we have

$$q = \beta \ell \qquad (3)$$

and

$$\overline{E} \cdot \overline{n}(2\pi r \ell) = \frac{\beta \ell}{\varepsilon_0}$$

$$|\overline{E}| = \frac{\beta}{2\pi r \varepsilon_0} \qquad (4)$$

● **PROBLEM 15-12**

Determine the magnitude of the electric field $\overline{E}$ of an infinite plate carrying a charge of density α.

Solution: Since the charged plate is infinite, the electric vector $\overline{E}$ at any point in space will be perpendicular to the plate. Consider a surface S shown in the figure.

S_1 and S_2 are parallel to the plate and the other four sides of the surface S are perpendicular to the plate. The charge within S is

$$q = \alpha S_1 \qquad (1)$$

For both S_1 and S_2 we have

$$\overline{E} \cdot \overline{n} = const \tag{2}$$

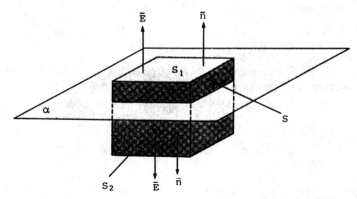

Let us assume that S_1 and S_2 are located at a distance r from the plate. Note that the four sides perpendicular to the plate do not contribute to the surface integral, since for these four sides the normal vector and the electric field vector are perpendicular to each other (and thus $\overline{E} \cdot \overline{n} = 0$). Thus

$$\iint_S \overline{E} \cdot \overline{n} \ dS = \overline{E} \cdot \overline{n} \iint_S dS = 2S_1\overline{E} \cdot \overline{n} \tag{3}$$

Applying Gauss' law and eq.(4), we obtain

$$2S_1\overline{E} \cdot \overline{n} = \frac{q}{\varepsilon_0} = \frac{\alpha S_1}{\varepsilon_0}$$

$$\overline{E} \cdot \overline{n} = \frac{\alpha}{2\varepsilon_0} \tag{4}$$

For positive α, $\overline{E}$ is in the same direction as $\overline{n}$ and

$$|\overline{E}| = \frac{\alpha}{2\varepsilon_0}$$

● **PROBLEM 15-13**

Evaluate the following integrals

1. $$\iint_S \frac{dS}{\sqrt{(x-2)^2+y^2+(z-1)^2}} \tag{1}$$

where S is the sphere

$$x^2+y^2+z^2 = 25 \tag{2}$$

2. $$\iint_S \frac{dS}{\sqrt{(x+1)^2+(y-1)^2+(z-2)^2}} \tag{3}$$

where S is the sphere

$$x^2+y^2+z^2 = 1 \tag{4}$$

Solution: 1. This problem could be solved by regarding integral (1) as a potential function. In general, the potential at a point $A(x_0, y_0, z_0)$ is given by

$$\phi(x_0, y_0, z_0) = \iint\limits_{S} \frac{\sigma dS}{\sqrt{(x-x_0)^2+(y-y_0)^2+(z-z_0)^2}} \qquad (5)$$

where the integral is calculated over the surface of a sphere. σ represents the charge density, where the charge is distributed over the surface of the sphere.

In this case, we see that point A is the point $(2,0,1)$ and that $\sigma=1$. Now, since

$$r_A = \sqrt{2^2+1^2} = \sqrt{5} \qquad (6)$$

which is less than 5, we conclude that point A is located inside the sphere given by eq.(2).

It is known that the potential inside a sphere is constant and equal to

$$\phi(x_0, y_0, z_0) = 4\pi r_1 \sigma \qquad (7)$$

where r_1 represents the radius of the sphere. Since in this case $r_1 = 5$ and $\sigma=1$, we determine that

$$\phi = 20\pi \qquad (8)$$

and

$$\iint\limits_{\substack{S \\ x+y+z=25}} \frac{dS}{\sqrt{(x-2)^2+y^2+(z-1)^2}} = 20\pi \qquad (9)$$

2. Here again we shall interpret integral (3) as the potential at the point

$$A = (-1, 1, 2) \qquad (10)$$

which is a point outside the sphere $x^2+y^2+z^2 = 1$.

The potential outside the sphere is given by

$$\phi(x_0, y_0, z_0) = \frac{4\pi\sigma r_1^2}{r_0} \qquad (11)$$

We have

$$\sigma = 1, \quad r_1 = 1, \quad \text{and } r_0 = \sqrt{1+1+4} = \sqrt{6} \qquad (12)$$

Thus

$$\iint\limits_{\substack{S \\ x^2+y^2+z^2=1}} \frac{dS}{\sqrt{(x+1)^2+(y-1)^2+(z-2)^2}} = \frac{4\pi}{\sqrt{6}} \qquad (13)$$

The sphere S is given by the equation

$$x^2+y^2+z^2 = 16 \tag{1}$$

Evaluate the following integrals by interpreting them as potentials.

1. $$\iint_S \frac{dS}{\sqrt{(x+1)^2+(y-2)^2+z^2}} \tag{2}$$

2. $$\iint_S \frac{dS}{\sqrt{(x-1)^2+(y-1)^2+(z+10)^2}} \tag{3}$$

3. $$\iint_S \frac{dS}{\sqrt{(x+\alpha)^2+(y+1)^2+z^2}} \tag{4}$$

where α is a constant parameter.

Solution: The potential function is given by

$$\phi(x_0,y_0,z_0) = \iint_S \frac{\sigma dS}{\sqrt{(x-x_0)^2+(y-y_0)^2+(z-z_0)^2}}$$

where the integral is calculated over the surface of a sphere and σ denotes the charge density. For points interior to a sphere of radius r_1, the potential is

$$\phi(x_0,y_0,z_0) = \iint_S \frac{\sigma dS}{\sqrt{(x-x_0)^2+(y-y_0)^2+(z-z_0)^2}} = 4\pi r_1 \sigma$$

where

$$x_0^2 + y_0^2 + z_0^2 < r_1^2$$

For points outside the sphere, we have

$$\phi(x_0,y_0,z_0) = \iint_S \frac{\sigma dS}{\sqrt{(x-x_0)^2+(y-y_0)^2+(z-z_0)^2}} = 4\pi \frac{r_1^2}{r_0} \sigma$$

where

$$r_0 = \sqrt{x_0^2+y_0^2+z_0^2}$$
and
$$r_0 > r_1$$

In this case, the radius of the sphere is $r_1 = 4$

1. For this integral, the coordinates of point A are $(-1,2,0)$
and
$$r_0 = \sqrt{x_0^2+y_0^2+z_0^2} = \sqrt{1+4} = \sqrt{5}$$

Recognizing that $\sigma=1$ and that the point $A=(-1,2,0)$ is inside the sphere of radius $r_1 = 4$, we conclude that

$$\iint_S \frac{dS}{\sqrt{(x+1)^2+(y-2)^2+z^2}} = 4\pi r_1 \sigma = 16\pi$$

2. Here, point A is located outside the sphere. Since

$$A = (1,1,-10)$$

and

$$r_0 = \sqrt{1+1+100} = \sqrt{102} > 4.$$

We thus obtain

$$\iint_S \frac{dS}{\sqrt{(x-1)^2+(y-1)^2+(z+10)^2}} = \frac{4\pi r_1^2}{r_0}\sigma = \frac{64\pi}{\sqrt{102}}$$

3. The coordinates of A are

$$A = (-\alpha,-1,0)$$

For the point A located inside the sphere

$$\sqrt{\alpha^2+1} < 4$$

$$\alpha^2 < 15$$

$$|\alpha| < \sqrt{15}$$

and the integral is equal to

$$\iint_S \frac{dS}{\sqrt{(x+\alpha)^2+(y+1)^2+z^2}} = 16\pi$$

For the points outside the sphere

$$|\alpha| > \sqrt{15}$$

and

$$\iint_S \frac{dS}{\sqrt{(x+\alpha)^2+(y+1)^2+z^2}} = \frac{64\pi}{\sqrt{\alpha^2+1}}$$

CHAPTER 16

VOLUME INTEGRALS

INTRODUCTION

The volume integral of a function is defined through the familiar Riemann sum construction.

In this chapter we consider the volume integral of a vector field. The methods of evaluating the volume integral of a vector field are basically the same as for regular (scalar) functions.

We also consider, though briefly, multiple integrals.

Numerous applications of triple integrals are also given. Mass, center of gravity (centroid), volume of a region are among the problems dealing with integration of scalar fields. Moment of inertia, electrostatic potential, Gauss' law among others are some of the problems dealing directly or indirectly with vector fields.

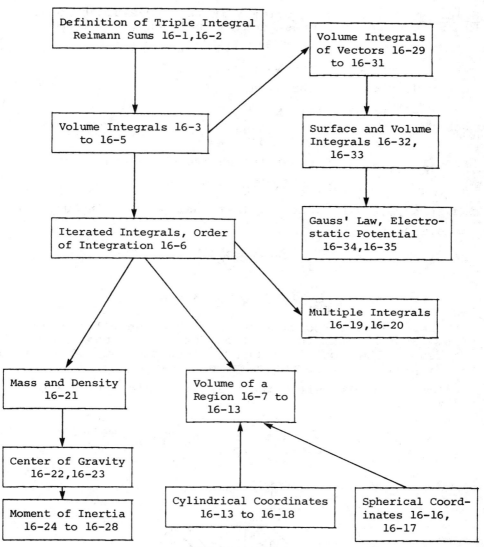

This chart is provided to facilitate rapid understanding of the inter-relationships of the topics and subject matter in this chapter. Also shown are the problem numbers associated with the subject matter.

DEFINITION OF TRIPLE INTEGRAL, RIEMANN SUMS, ITERATED INTEGRALS

● PROBLEM 16-1

Using the Riemann sum evaluate the integral

$$\iiint_K f(x,y,z) \, dxdydz \qquad (1)$$

where $f(x,y,z) = x^P$, $P \geq 0$ $\qquad (2)$
and K is the three-dimensional cube

$$0 \leq x \leq 1, \quad 0 \leq y \leq 1, \quad 0 \leq z \leq 1 \qquad (3)$$

Solution: Consider a region V in the three-dimensional space R^3 and a function f whose domain includes V

$$f(x,y,z) : W \to R^3 \tag{4}$$

where $$V \subset W$$

We divide V into N subregions

$$\Delta V_1, \ \Delta V_2, \ldots, \Delta V_N \tag{5}$$

such that

$$\Delta V_1 \cup \Delta V_2 \cup \ldots \cup \Delta V_N \supset V \tag{6}$$

Let (x_K, y_K, z_K) be a point in the kth subregion

$$(x_K, y_K, z_K) \in \Delta V_K \tag{7}$$

and $f(x_K, y_K, z_K)$ the value of f at that point. The Riemann sum is defined as

$$F = \sum_{K=1}^{N} f(x_K, y_K, z_K) \Delta V_K$$

$$= \sum_{K=1}^{N} f(x_K, y_K, z_K) \Delta x \Delta y \Delta z \tag{8}$$

There are some conditions on V which we will not discuss here. Suppose that the function $f(x,y,z)$ is continuous throughout V and on its boundary, then the sum (8) has a limit as $\Delta V_1, \Delta V_2, \ldots \Delta V_N$ approaches zero.

This limit is called the Riemann triple integral of $f(x,y,z)$ over V.

$$\iiint_V f(x,y,z) dV = \lim_{\substack{N \to \infty \\ \max\{\Delta V_1, \ldots, \Delta V_N\} \to 0}} \sum_{K=1}^{N} f(x_K, y_K, z_K) \Delta V_K \tag{9}$$

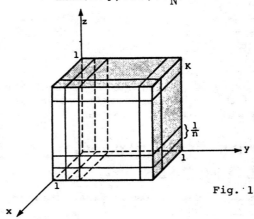

Fig. 1

We shall divide the cube K (as given by (3)) into n^3 cubes as shown in Fig. 1. We draw n-1 planes parallel to the xy-plane and obtain n slices. Then, we draw n-1 planes parallel to the yz-plane and obtain n^2 columns. Finally, we draw n-1 planes parallel to the xz-plane and obtain n^3 cubes. Each cube has dimension $\frac{1}{n}$ by $\frac{1}{n}$ by $\frac{1}{n}$ and since there are n^3 cubes,

the volume of each cube is $\frac{1}{n^3}$. The triple integral over K
will be evaluated from eq.(9). Let us now consider the lowest
slice of the cube K (see Fig. 2), which consists of n^2 cubes.
Consider the first row of cubes. The value of the function

$f(x,y,z) = x^P$ for the first cube is $\left(\frac{1}{n}\right)^P$, for the second cube
$\left(\frac{2}{n}\right)^P$,...,for the nth cube $\left(\frac{n}{n}\right)^P$.

The contribution of the first row to the total sum (as
given in eq.(9)) is

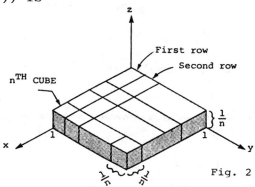

z

First row

Second row

n^{TH} CUBE

$\frac{1}{n}$

x

1

1

y

$\frac{1}{n}$ $\frac{1}{n}$

Fig. 2

$$\left(\frac{1}{n}\right)^P \cdot \frac{1}{n^3} + \left(\frac{2}{n}\right)^P \cdot \frac{1}{n^3} + \left(\frac{3}{n}\right)^P \cdot \frac{1}{n^3} + \ldots + \left(\frac{n}{n}\right)^P \frac{1}{n^3}$$

$$= \frac{1}{n}\left(\frac{1^P + 2^P + 3^P + \ldots + n^P}{n^P}\right) \tag{10}$$

Now, note that since $f(x,y,z) = x^P$ is a continuous function, and since the cubes become small for large n, any value
of $f(x,y,z)$ within the small cube may be chosen to make up
the sum in eq. (10). For each of the rows shown in Fig. 2,
the value given by eq. (10) is the same, thus the total contribution of the slice is

$$n \cdot \frac{1}{n^3}\left(\frac{1^P + 2^P + 3^P + \ldots + n^P}{n^P}\right) = \frac{1}{n^2}\left(\frac{1^P + 2^P + \ldots + n^P}{n^P}\right) \tag{11}$$

The cube K consists of n slices. Each slice gives the same
value as in eq.(11). The Riemann sum for the cube K and
function $f(x,y,z) = x^P$ is

$$S = n \, \frac{1}{n^2}\left(\frac{1^P + 2^P + \ldots + n^P}{n^P}\right) = \frac{1^P + 2^P + \ldots + n^P}{n^{P+1}} \tag{12}$$

The volume integral is defined as

$$\iiint\limits_K x^P \, dV = \lim_{n \to \infty} \frac{1^P + 2^P + \ldots + n^P}{n^{P+1}} \tag{13}$$

To evaluate the right side of eq.(13), we shall use the following theorem.

Theorem

If $f(x)$ is continuous for $0 \le x \le 1$, then

707

$$\lim_{n \to \infty} \frac{1}{n} \left[f\left(\frac{1}{n}\right) + f\left(\frac{2}{n}\right) + \ldots + f\left(\frac{n-1}{n}\right) + f\left(\frac{n}{n}\right) \right] = \int_0^1 f(x)dx \qquad (14)$$

Now, for $f(x) = x^P$, the left-hand side of eq.(14) becomes

$$\lim_{n \to \infty} \frac{1}{n} \left[\left(\frac{1}{n}\right)^P + \left(\frac{2}{n}\right)^P + \ldots + \left(\frac{n}{n}\right)^P \right] = \int_0^1 x^P dx = \left. \frac{x^{P+1}}{P+1} \right|_{x=0}^{1}$$

$$= \frac{1}{P+1} \qquad (15)$$

Substitution of eq.(15) into eq.(13) yields

$$\iiint_K x^P dV = \frac{1}{P+1} \qquad (16)$$

Fortunately, there are simpler methods of evaluating triple integrals.

● **PROBLEM 16-2**

Using the definition of the volume integral evaluate the volume integral of

$$f(x,y,z) = x^2y \qquad (1)$$

over the cube bounded by the coordinate planes and the planes x=1, y=1, z=1.

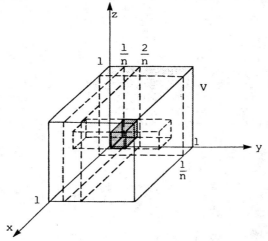

Solution: The volume integral is defined through the use of a partition construction. Let f(x,y,z) be a function defined within and on the boundary of a domain V. We assume that V is bounded. The domain V has to be subdivided into subdomains $\delta V_1, \delta V_2, \ldots \delta V_n$. We will not discuss here the various methods of subdividing a domain. Let us select a point (x_i, y_i, z_i) in each subdomain δV_i. The volume integral of f over V is defined as

$$\iiint_V f(x,y,z)dV = \lim_{n \to \infty} \sum_{i=1}^{N} f(x_i, y_i, z_i)\delta V_i \qquad (2)$$

708

where the limit is taken as the dimensions of each δV_i tend to zero. For the definition (2) to define the volume integral in an unambiguous way, it is necessary that the limit does not depend on the particular manner of subdivision. For functions continuous within and on the boundary of V, the limit is independent of subdivision. We often write

$$\iiint_V f(x,y,z)dV = \iiint_V f(x,y,z)dxdydz \tag{3}$$

To find the integral

$$\iiint_V x^2y \; dxdydz \tag{4}$$

let us subdivide the cube V into cubes by passing planes through the cube which are parallel to the coordinate planes (see the figure).

We draw n-1 planes parallel to the xy-plane, n-1 planes parallel to the xz-plane, and n-1 planes parallel to the zy-plane. The planes are drawn in such a way that they divide the cube V into n^3 equal cubes. The volume of each cube is $\frac{1}{n^3}$.

Let us number the cubes in such way that to every cube there correspond three integers

$$(i,j,k) \quad i,j,k = 1,\ldots n \tag{5}$$

The maximum value of the x coordinate in this cube is $\frac{i}{n}$, the maximum value of the y coordinate is $\frac{j}{n}$ and the maximum value of the z coordinate is $\frac{k}{n}$. The maximum value of the function

$$f(x,y,z) = x^2y \tag{6}$$

for this cube is

$$f_{(i,j,k)} (x,y,z) = x^2y = \left(\frac{i}{n}\right)^2 \cdot \frac{j}{n} = \frac{i^2j}{n^3} \tag{7}$$

As stated before, the volume of each cube is

$$\delta V_{(i,j,k)} = \frac{1}{n^3} \tag{8}$$

Definition (2) becomes

$$\iiint_V f(x,y,z)dV = \lim_{n\to\infty} \sum_{k=1}^{n} \sum_{j=1}^{n} \sum_{i=1}^{n} f_{(i,j,k)}(x,y,z)\delta V_{(i,j,k)} \tag{9}$$

Let us find the sum

$$\sum_{i=1}^{n} f_{(i,j,k)}(x,y,z)\delta V_{(i,j,k)} = \sum_{i=1}^{n} \frac{i^2j}{n^3} \cdot \frac{1}{n^3} \tag{10}$$

It is easy to verify the formula

$$1^2 + 2^2 + \ldots + n^2 = \frac{n(n+1)(2n+1)}{6} \tag{11}$$

709

Eq.(10) becomes

$$\sum_{i=1}^{n} \frac{i^2 j}{n^6} = \frac{j}{n^6} \sum_{i=1}^{n} i^2 = \frac{j}{n^6} \frac{n(n+1)(2n+1)}{6} \qquad (12)$$

Taking the sum of (12) with respect to j results in

$$\sum_{j=1}^{n} \frac{j}{n^6} n(n+1)(2n+1) = \frac{n(n+1)}{2} \frac{n(n+1)(2n+1)}{6n^6} \qquad (13)$$

Here we used

$$1 + 2 + \ldots + n = \frac{n(n+1)}{2} \qquad (14)$$

Taking the sum of (13) with respect to k gives

$$\sum_{k=1}^{n} \frac{n(n+1)}{2} \frac{n(n+1)(2n+1)}{6n^6} = \frac{n^2(n+1)n(n+1)(2n+1)}{2 \cdot 6n^6} \qquad (15)$$

Substituting eq.(15) into eq.(9) results in

$$\iiint_{V} x^2 y \ dV = \lim_{n \to \infty} \frac{n^2(n+1)n(n+1)(2n+1)}{2 \cdot 6n^6} = \frac{1}{6} \qquad (16)$$

In the following problems, we will show less time-consuming methods of evaluating volume integrals.

This problem in particular is solved through more direct methods in Problem 16-3.

● **PROBLEM 16-3**

1. Evaluate the volume integral

$$\iiint_{V} x^2 y \ dV \qquad (1)$$

where V is the closed region bounded by the coordinate planes and x=1, y=1, z=1.

2. Evaluate the volume integral of

$$\phi(x,y,z) = xz + yz \qquad (2)$$

over the closed region V bounded by the coordinate planes and

$$x=2, \quad y=3, \quad z=-x + 4 \qquad (3)$$

Solution: 1. V is a cube bounded by the planes x=0, x=1, y=0, y=1, z=0, z=1. Thus, we integrate from x=0 to x=1, from y=0 to y=1, from z=0 to z=1. Eq.(1) can be written

$$\iiint\limits_{V} x^2 y \ dV = \int_{x=0}^{1} \int_{y=0}^{1} \int_{z=0}^{1} x^2 y \ dz\,dy\,dx$$

$$= \int_{x=0}^{1} \int_{y=0}^{1} x^2 y \ dy\,dx \tag{4}$$

$$= \int_{x=0}^{1} \frac{1}{2} x^2 \, dx = \frac{1}{6}$$

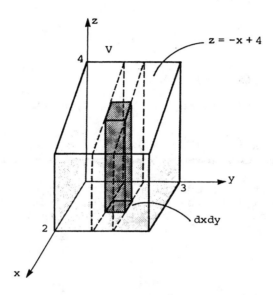

2. The region V is shown in the figure. It is required to find the volume integral

$$\iiint\limits_{V}(xz+yz)dz\,dy\,dx \tag{5}$$

Consider a point (x,y,z) inside the region V. Letting x and y be fixed, we can vary z from z=0 to z=-x+4 to obtain a column, as shown in the figure. Holding y fixed and varying x from x=0 to x=2, we obtain a slice, as shown. Adding the slices from y=0 to y=3 gives us the volume integral over the region V. Thus,

$$\iiint\limits_{V}(xz+yz)dV = \int_{y=0}^{3} \int_{x=0}^{2} \int_{z=0}^{-x+4}(xz+yz)dz\,dx\,dy$$

$$= \int_{y=0}^{3} \int_{x=0}^{2} \left[(x+y)\ \frac{z^2}{2} \right] \Bigg|_{z=0}^{-x+4} dx\,dy$$

$$= \int_{y=0}^{3} \int_{x=0}^{2} \left[\frac{1}{2} x^3 - 4x^2 + 8x + \frac{1}{2} x^2 y - 4xy + 8y \right] dx\,dy \tag{6}$$

711

$$= \int_{y=0}^{3} \left(\frac{22}{3} + \frac{28}{3} y \right) dy = \left[\frac{22}{3} y + \frac{28}{3} \frac{y^2}{2} \right] \Bigg|_{y=0}^{3}$$

$$= 64$$

● PROBLEM 16-4

Evaluate the integral

$$\iiint_V \phi \, dV \qquad\qquad (1)$$

where

$$\phi(x,y,z) = 4xy^2 \qquad\qquad (2)$$

and V is the closed region bounded by the coordinate planes and

$$x + 3y + 2z = 6 \qquad\qquad (3)$$

<u>Solution</u>: The procedure of evaluation of the volume integral is very similar to the one applied to the surface integrals. The closed region V is shown in the figure.

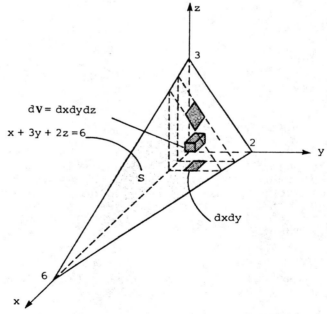

Keeping x and y constant, we integrate from z=0 to $z = 3 - \frac{3}{2} y - \frac{1}{2} x$. Next, keeping x constant we integrate with respect to y from y=0 to $y = 2 - \frac{1}{3} x$. Finally we integrate with respect to x from x=0 to x=6. Thus, the volume integral (1) can be written

$$\iiint_V \phi dV = \int_{x=0}^{6} \int_{y=0}^{2-\frac{1}{3}x} \int_{z=0}^{3-\frac{3}{2}y-\frac{1}{2}x} 4xy^2 dz dy dx$$

$$= \int_{x=0}^{6} \int_{y=0}^{2-\frac{1}{3}x} 4xy^2 \left[3 - \frac{3}{2}y - \frac{1}{2}x \right] dy dx \qquad (4)$$

$$= \int_{x=0}^{6} \int_{y=0}^{2-\frac{1}{3}x} \left[12xy^2 - 6xy^3 - 2x^2y^2 \right] dy dx$$

$$= \int_{x=0}^{6} \left[12x \frac{y^3}{3} - 6x \frac{y^4}{4} - 2x^2 \frac{y^3}{3} \right]_{y=0}^{2-\frac{1}{3}x} dx$$

$$= \int_{0}^{6} \frac{x}{2}\left(2 - \frac{1}{3}x\right)^4 dx$$

To evaluate the last integral, let us note that

$$\int x\left(2 - \frac{1}{3}x\right)^4 dx = \int x \left[-\frac{3}{5}\left(2 - \frac{1}{3}x\right)^5 \right] dx$$

$$= x\left[-\frac{3}{5}\left(2 - \frac{1}{3}x\right)^5 \right] + \frac{3}{5} \int \left(2 - \frac{1}{3}x\right)^5 dx \qquad (5)$$

$$= -\frac{3}{5}x\left(2 - \frac{1}{3}x\right)^5 - \frac{3}{10}\left(2 - \frac{1}{3}x\right)^6$$

Substituting eq.(5) into eq.(4) results in

$$\int_{x=0}^{6} \frac{x}{2}\left(2 - \frac{1}{3}x\right)^4 dx = \frac{1}{2}\left[-\frac{3}{5}x\left(2 - \frac{1}{3}x\right)^5 - \frac{3}{10}\left(2 - \frac{1}{3}x\right)^6 \right]_{x=0}^{6}$$

$$= \frac{3}{10} \cdot \frac{1}{2} \cdot 2^6 = \frac{3 \cdot 16}{5} = \frac{48}{5} \qquad (6)$$

● **PROBLEM 16-5**

Find the volume integral of $\phi(x,y,z) = x$ over the sphere

$$x^2+y^2+z^2 = 1 \qquad (1)$$

<u>Solution</u>: We shall first establish the limits of integration. The sphere is shown in the figure.
Now, for x and y fixed, z traces out a column from $z=-(1-x^2-y^2)^{\frac{1}{2}}$ to $z=(1-x^2-y^2)^{\frac{1}{2}}$, as shown in the figure. We can move the column in the x-direction from $x=-(1-y^2)^{\frac{1}{2}}$ to $x=(1-y^2)^{\frac{1}{2}}$. Finally, y changes from y=-1 to y=1.
The integral can be written as

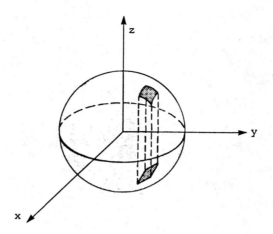

$$\int_{y=-1}^{1} \int_{x=-(1-y^2)^{\frac{1}{2}}}^{(1-y^2)^{\frac{1}{2}}} \int_{z=-(1-x^2-y^2)^{\frac{1}{2}}}^{(1-x^2-y^2)^{\frac{1}{2}}} x \, dz \, dx \, dy$$

$$= \int_{y=-1}^{1} \int_{x=-(1-y^2)^{\frac{1}{2}}}^{(1-y^2)^{\frac{1}{2}}} 2x(1-x^2-y^2)^{\frac{1}{2}} \, dx \, dy \qquad (2)$$

It is easy to verify the following formula

$$\int x\sqrt{a^2-x^2} \, dx = -\frac{1}{3}(a^2-x^2)^{\frac{3}{2}} \qquad (3)$$

Substituting eq.(3) into eq.(2) results in

$$-\int_{y=-1}^{1} \left[\frac{2}{3}(1-x^2-y^2)^{\frac{3}{2}}\right]\Bigg|_{x=-(1-y^2)^{\frac{1}{2}}}^{(1-y^2)^{\frac{1}{2}}} dy = \int_{y=-1}^{1} 0 \, dy = 0 \qquad (4)$$

It is possible to reach this answer without any calculations. Indeed, let the integral over the half of the sphere with positive x > 0 be P, then the integral over the other half with negative x ≤ 0 is -P, because of the symmetry of the sphere and the function $\phi(x,y,z) = x$. Thus, the total integral is P + (-P) = 0.

● **PROBLEM 16-6**

Find the volume integral of

$$\phi(x,y,z) = x + y \qquad (1)$$

over the volume bounded by the coordinate planes and

$$2x + y + 4z = 8 \qquad (2)$$

Show that the volume integral can be iterated in any order.

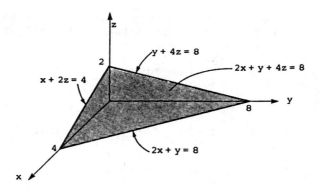

Solution: The figure shows the region of integration.

If we fix x and y, then z changes from z=0 to $z=2-\frac{1}{2}x-\frac{1}{4}y$. The volume integral is thus

$$\int_{x=0}^{4}\int_{y=0}^{8-2x}\int_{z=0}^{2-\frac{1}{2}x-\frac{1}{4}y}(x+y)\,dz\,dy\,dz \tag{3}$$

$$=\int_{x=0}^{4}\int_{y=0}^{8-2x}(x+y)(2-\tfrac{1}{2}x-\tfrac{1}{4}y)\,dy\,dx$$

$$=\int_{x=0}^{4}\int_{y=0}^{8-2x}(2x-\tfrac{1}{2}x^2-\tfrac{3}{4}xy+2y-\tfrac{1}{4}y^2)\,dy\,dx$$

$$=\int_{x=0}^{4}(8-2x)\left(-\frac{1}{12}x^2-\frac{1}{3}x+\frac{8}{3}\right)\,dx$$

$$=\int_{x=0}^{4}\left[\frac{1}{6}x^3-8x+\frac{8\cdot 8}{3}\right]\,dx = 32$$

Let us fix x and z, then y changes from y=0 to y=8−2x−4z.

The volume integral can be written as

$$\int_{z=0}^{2}\int_{x=0}^{4-2z}\int_{y=0}^{8-2x-4z}(x+y)\,dy\,dx\,dz$$

$$=\int_{z=0}^{2}\int_{x=0}^{4-2z}(32-32z-8x+4xz+8z^2)\,dx\,dz \tag{4}$$

$$=\int_{z=0}^{2}(4-2z)(16-16z+4z^2)\,dz$$

$$=8\int_{z=0}^{2}(2-z)(4-4z+z^2)\,dz = 32$$

We see that the answer is the same as in eq.(3).

Finally, let us fix z and y. The coordinate x changes from x=0 to x=4-½y-2z. The volume integral can be written

$$\int_{z=0}^{2} \int_{y=0}^{8-4z} \int_{x=0}^{4-\frac{1}{2}y-2z} (x+y)\,dx\,dy\,dz$$

(5)

$$= \int_{z=0}^{2} \int_{y=0}^{8-4z} (2z^2 - 8z - zy + 2y - \frac{3}{8}y^2 + 8)\,dy\,dz$$

$$= \int_{z=0}^{2} (2z^2y - 8zy - \frac{1}{2}zy^2 + y^2 - \frac{1}{8}y^3 + 8y)\,\Big|_{y=0}^{8-4z}\,dz$$

$$= 8\int_{z=0}^{2} (2-z)^3\,dz = 8\left[-\frac{(2-z)^4}{4}\right]\Big|_{z=0}^{2} = 32$$

Again, we obtain the same result. This problem illustrates that volume integrals can be iterated in any order.

It should be noted that certain orders of integration lead to integrals which are easier to evaluate.

VOLUME OF A REGION

● **PROBLEM 16-7**

Find the volume of the region of space bounded by the planes x=0, y=0, z=0, z=3-2x+y and the surface y=1-x².

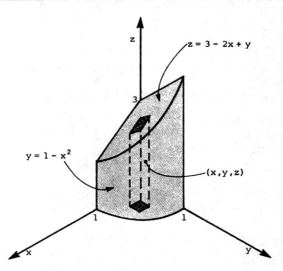

Solution: The region is shown in the figure. The volume integral is given by

$$\iiint_V \phi(x,y,z)\,dV$$

(1)

716

Taking $\phi(x,y,z) \equiv 1$, that is $\phi(x,y,z)$ identically equal to unity, we obtain the expression for the volume of the region V.

$$\text{Volume of V} = \iiint\limits_V dxdydz = \iiint\limits_V dV \qquad (2)$$

where $dV = dx \, dy \, dz$.

Let us now find the limits of integration. Taking an arbitrary point (x,y,z) inside the region and fixing x and y, we find that z can change from $z=0$ to $z=3-2x+y$. By the same token, for fixed values of x the coordinate y can vary from $y=0$ to $y=1-x^2$. Finally, we find that x changes from $x=0$ to $x=1$. The volume integral (2) can thus be written

$$\int_{x=0}^{1} \int_{y=0}^{1-x^2} \int_{z=0}^{3-2x+y} dz \, dy \, dx$$

$$= \int_{x=0}^{1} \int_{y=0}^{1-x^2} (3 - 2x + y) dy \, dx \qquad (3)$$

$$= \int_{0}^{1} \left[3y - 2xy + \frac{y^2}{2} \right] \Bigg|_{y=0}^{1-x^2} dx$$

$$= \int_{0}^{1} \left[\frac{1}{2} x^4 + 2x^3 - 4x^2 - 2x + \frac{7}{2} \right] dx$$

$$= \left[\frac{x^5}{10} + \frac{x^4}{2} - \frac{4}{3} x^3 - x^2 + \frac{7}{2} x \right] \Bigg|_{x=0}^{1}$$

$$= \frac{53}{30}$$

● **PROBLEM 16-8**

Find the volume of a sphere of radius r.

Solution: The equation of a sphere of radius r is

$$x^2 + y^2 + z^2 = r^2 \qquad (1)$$

The sphere is shown in the figure.

Let us take an arbitrary point (x,y,z) inside the sphere. If we fix x and y, the coordinate z can change from $z = -\sqrt{r^2-x^2-y^2}$ to $z = \sqrt{r^2-x^2-y^2}$. Then, for fixed values of x, y can change from $y = -\sqrt{r^2-x^2}$ to $y = \sqrt{r^2-x^2}$. Thus, the volume of the sphere of radius r can be written as the triple integral

$$\int_{-r}^{r} \int_{-\sqrt{r^2-x^2}}^{\sqrt{r^2-x^2}} \int_{-\sqrt{r^2-x^2-y^2}}^{\sqrt{r^2-x^2-y^2}} dz \, dy \, dx \qquad (2)$$

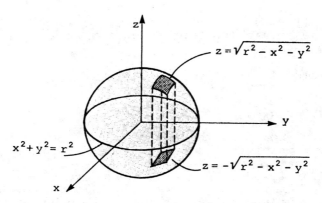

$$z = \sqrt{r^2 - x^2 - y^2}$$

$$x^2 + y^2 = r^2$$

$$z = -\sqrt{r^2 - x^2 - y^2}$$

$$= 2 \int_{-r}^{r} \int_{-\sqrt{r^2-x^2}}^{\sqrt{r^2-x^2}} \sqrt{r^2-x^2-y^2} \; dy dx$$

We shall now use the formula

$$\int \sqrt{a^2-y^2} \; dy = \frac{y}{2} \sqrt{a^2-y^2} + \frac{a^2}{2} \text{ arc sin } \frac{y}{a} \tag{3}$$

to find the integral in eq.(2).

$$2 \int_{-r}^{r} \int_{-\sqrt{r^2-x^2}}^{\sqrt{r^2-x^2}} \sqrt{r^2-x^2-y^2} \; dy dx$$

$$= 2 \int_{-r}^{r} \left[\frac{y}{2} \sqrt{r^2-x^2-y^2} + \frac{r^2-x^2}{2} \text{ arc sin } \frac{y}{\sqrt{r^2-x^2}} \right] \Bigg|_{y=-\sqrt{r^2-x^2}}^{y=\sqrt{r^2-x^2}} dx \tag{4}$$

$$= 2 \int_{-r}^{r} \left[\frac{r^2-x^2}{2} \text{ arc sin } 1 - \frac{r^2-x^2}{2} \text{ arc sin } (-1) \right] dx$$

Since

$$\text{arc sin } 1 = \frac{\pi}{2}, \quad \text{arc sin}(-1) = -\frac{\pi}{2} \tag{5}$$

the integral in eq.(4) can be written

$$2 \int_{-r}^{r} \frac{\pi}{2} (r^2-x^2) dx = \pi \left[r^2 x - \frac{x^3}{3} \right] \Bigg|_{x=-r}^{r} \tag{6}$$

$$= \frac{4}{3} \pi r^3$$

● **PROBLEM 16-9**

Find the volume of the region common to the two inter-secting cylinders

$$x^2 + y^2 = a^2$$

$$x^2 + z^2 = a^2 \tag{1}$$

<u>Solution</u>: The two cylinders are shown in the figure.

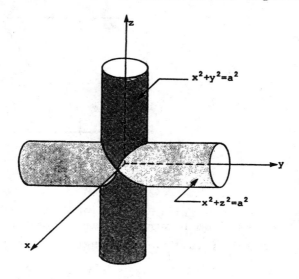

Let us take an arbitrary point (x,y,z) inside the region, which is common to both cylinders. Taking the x and <u>y co-</u> <u>ordinates</u> fixed, we see that z can change from $z = -\sqrt{a^2-x^2}$ to $z = \sqrt{a^2-x^2}$. The integral expressing the volume of the region can then be written as

$$\int_{x=-a}^{a} \int_{y=-\sqrt{a^2-x^2}}^{\sqrt{a^2-x^2}} \int_{z=-\sqrt{a^2-x^2}}^{\sqrt{a^2-x^2}} dz\ dy\ dx$$

$$= 2 \int_{x=-a}^{a} \int_{y=-\sqrt{a^2-x^2}}^{\sqrt{a^2-x^2}} \sqrt{a^2-x^2}\ dy dx \qquad (2)$$

$$= 2 \int_{-a}^{a} \sqrt{a^2-x^2}\ (y)\ \Big|_{y=-\sqrt{a^2-x^2}}^{\sqrt{a^2-x^2}}\ dx$$

$$= 4 \int_{-a}^{a} (a^2-x^2) dx = 4 \left[a^2 x - \frac{x^3}{3} \right] \Big|_{x=-a}^{a}$$

$$= \frac{16}{3}\ a^3$$

● **PROBLEM 16-10**

Sketch the region whose volume is given by the triple integral

$$\int_{y=0}^{3} \int_{x=\frac{-1-\sqrt{33}}{4}}^{\frac{-1+\sqrt{33}}{4}} \int_{z=x^2}^{-\frac{1}{2}x+2} dz\ dx\ dy \qquad (1)$$

Find the volume of this region.

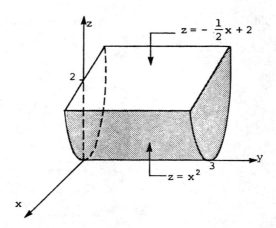

$$z = -\frac{1}{2}x + 2$$

$$z = x^2$$

Solution: From the integral, we see that z changes from $z=x^2$ to $z=-\frac{1}{2}x+2$. Both surfaces are shown in the figure.

These two surfaces intersect each other at the lines such that

$$z = x^2 = -\frac{1}{2}x + 2 \tag{2}$$

Thus,

$$x^2 + \frac{1}{2}x - 2 = 0$$

and

$$x_1 = \frac{-1+\sqrt{33}}{4}, \qquad x_2 = \frac{-1-\sqrt{33}}{4} \tag{3}$$

We see that x_1 and x_2 in eq.(3) are the integration limits of the integral in eq.(1). Now we can sketch the region whose volume is represented by the integral in eq.(1).

To find the volume of the region, we have to evaluate integral (1).

$$\int_{y=0}^{3} \int_{x=\frac{-1-\sqrt{33}}{4}}^{\frac{-1+\sqrt{33}}{4}} \int_{z=x^2}^{-\frac{1}{2}x+2} dz\ dx\ dy \tag{4}$$

$$= \int_{y=0}^{3} \int_{x=\frac{-1-\sqrt{33}}{4}}^{\frac{-1+\sqrt{33}}{4}} (-x^2 - \frac{1}{2}x + 2)dxdy$$

$$= \int_{y=0}^{3} \left[-\frac{x^3}{3} - \frac{x^2}{4} + 2x \right] \Bigg|_{x=\frac{-1-\sqrt{33}}{4}}^{\frac{-1+\sqrt{33}}{4}} dy$$

$$= \int_{y=0}^{3} \left[-\frac{1}{3}\left(\frac{-1+\sqrt{33}}{4}\right)^3 - \frac{1}{4}\left(\frac{-1+\sqrt{33}}{4}\right)^2 + 2\left(\frac{-1+\sqrt{33}}{4}\right) + \frac{1}{3}\left(\frac{-1-\sqrt{33}}{4}\right)^3 \right.$$

$$\left. + \frac{1}{4}\left(\frac{-1-\sqrt{33}}{4}\right)^2 - 2\left(\frac{-1-\sqrt{33}}{4}\right) \right] dy$$

$$= \frac{11\sqrt{33}}{16} \int_{y=0}^{3} dy = \frac{33\sqrt{33}}{16}$$

Find the volume of the region enclosed by the two surfaces

$$z = x^2 + 4y^2 \qquad (1)$$

$$z = 9 - 2x^2 - 2y^2 \qquad (2)$$

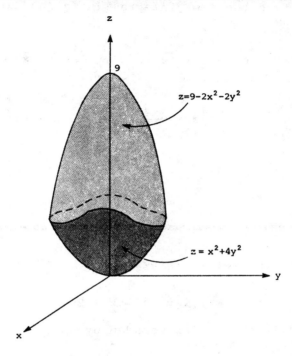

Solution: Both surfaces are shown in the figure. They intersect along the curve

$$3 = x^2 + 2y^2 \qquad (3)$$

The coordinate z varies from $z = x^2 + 4y^2$ to $z = 9 - 2x^2 - 2y^2$. From
eq.(3), we see that for fixed values of x, y changes
from $y = -\sqrt{\frac{3-x^2}{2}}$ to $y = \sqrt{\frac{3-x^2}{2}}$. Also, x varies from $-\sqrt{3}$ to
$\sqrt{3}$.

The volume of the region between both surfaces is given by

$$\int_{x=-\sqrt{3}}^{\sqrt{3}} \int_{y=-\sqrt{\frac{3-x^2}{2}}}^{\sqrt{\frac{3-x^2}{2}}} \int_{z=x^2+4y^2}^{9-2x^2-2y^2} dz\, dy\, dx$$

$$= \int_{x=-\sqrt{3}}^{\sqrt{3}} \int_{y=-\sqrt{\frac{3-x^2}{2}}}^{\sqrt{\frac{3-x^2}{2}}} (9 - 3x^2 - 6y^2)\, dy\, dx$$

$$= \int_{-\sqrt{3}}^{\sqrt{3}} \left[9y - 3x^2y - 2y^3 \right] \Biggr|_{y \,=\, -\sqrt{\frac{3-x^2}{2}}}^{\sqrt{\frac{3-x^2}{2}}} dx \tag{4}$$

$$= \int_{-\sqrt{3}}^{\sqrt{3}} \frac{4}{\sqrt{2}} (3-x^2)^{\frac{3}{2}} \, dx$$

To find the last integral in eq.(4), we will use the following formula

$$\int (a^2-x^2)^{\frac{3}{2}} dx = \frac{1}{4}\left[x\sqrt{(a^2-x^2)^3} + \frac{3a^2x}{2}\sqrt{a^2-x^2} + \frac{3a^4}{2} \text{arc sin} \frac{x}{|a|} \right]$$

Thus

$$\frac{4}{\sqrt{2}} \int_{-\sqrt{3}}^{\sqrt{3}} (3-x^2)^{\frac{3}{2}} dx = \frac{4}{\sqrt{2}} \cdot \frac{3 \cdot 9}{2} \cdot \frac{1}{4} \text{ arc sin } \frac{x}{\sqrt{3}} \Biggr|_{x=-\sqrt{3}}^{\sqrt{3}}$$

$$= \frac{27}{2\sqrt{2}} \pi$$

• PROBLEM 16-12

Evaluate the volume integral $\iiint_V f \, dV$ of the function

$$f(x,y,z) = x + 2y \tag{1}$$

where V is the region bounded by the cylinder $z = 5-x^2$, the coordinate planes and $y = 3$.

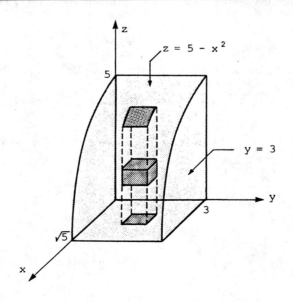

Solution : Let us establish the limits of integration. The point (x,y,z) is an arbitrary point inside the region V. Taking x and y to be fixed, we see that z can change from $z=0$ to $z=5-x^2$. The coordinate x can change from $x=0$ to $x=\sqrt{5}$ and y from $y=0$ to $y=3$ as shown in the figure.

Thus, the volume integral can be written as

$$\int_{x=0}^{\sqrt{5}} \int_{y=0}^{3} \int_{z=0}^{5-x^2} (x + 2y)dz\ dy\ dx$$

$$= \int_{x=0}^{\sqrt{5}} \int_{y=0}^{3} [\ xz + 2yz\ ] \Big|_{z=0}^{5-x^2} dy\ dx \qquad (2)$$

$$= \int_{x=0}^{\sqrt{5}} \int_{y=0}^{3} [\ x(5-x^2) + 2y(5-x^2)\ ]\ dydx$$

$$= \int_{0}^{\sqrt{5}} (15x - 3x^3 + 45 - 9x^2)dx = \frac{75}{4} + 30\sqrt{5}$$

TRIPLE INTEGRATION IN CYLINDRICAL AND SPHERICAL COORDINATES

● **PROBLEM 16-13**

Find the volume of the region bounded by the surfaces

$$x^2+y^2 = z^2, \quad z = h \qquad (1)$$

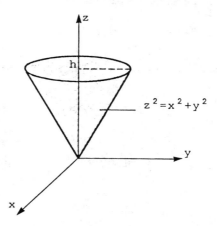

Solution: The region bounded by the surfaces given in eq.(1) is shown in the figure.

Note that the equation $x^2+y^2 = z^2$ describes a cone. Using the standard procedure, let us establish the limits of integration. Taking an arbitrary point (x,y,z) inside the region

723

and fixing x and y, we find that z can change from $z=\sqrt{x^2+y^2}$ to z=h. The coordinate x changes from $x=-\sqrt{h^2-y^2}$ to $x=\sqrt{h^2-y^2}$ and y changes from y=-h to y=h.

Thus, the volume integral can be written

$$\iiint_V dV = \int_{y=-h}^{h} \int_{x=-\sqrt{h^2-y^2}}^{\sqrt{h^2-y^2}} \int_{z=\sqrt{x^2+y^2}}^{h} dz\, dx\, dy$$

$$= \int_{y=-h}^{h} \int_{x=-\sqrt{h^2-y^2}}^{\sqrt{h^2-y^2}} \left[h - \sqrt{x^2+y^2}\right] dx\, dy \tag{2}$$

This integral leads to rather complicated calculations.

Changing the order of integration would not lessen the difficulty. This integral could be solved much more easily if we would transform into the cylindrical coordinates (ρ, ϕ, z).

We have,

$$x = \rho \cos \phi$$

$$y = \rho \sin \phi \tag{3}$$

$$z = z$$

The volume element is

$$dV = \rho\, d\rho\, d\phi\, dz \tag{4}$$

The limits of integration are

for ρ from 0 to h,

for ϕ from 0 to 2π

for z from z=ρ to z=h

Thus, the volume integral can be expressed as

$$\int_{\phi=0}^{2\pi} \int_{\rho=0}^{h} \int_{z=\rho}^{h} \rho\, dz\, d\rho\, d\phi$$

$$= \int_{\phi=0}^{2\pi} \int_{\rho=0}^{h} \rho(h-\rho)\, d\rho\, d\phi = \int_{0}^{2\pi} \left(h\frac{\rho^2}{2} - \frac{\rho^3}{3}\right) \Bigg|_{\rho=0}^{h} d\phi \tag{5}$$

$$= \int_{0}^{2\pi} \frac{h^3}{6}\, d\phi = \frac{1}{3}\pi h^3$$

This problem illustrates that it is worthwhile to spend some time on selecting the appropriate system of coordinates. All systems of coordinates do, of course, lead to the same result.

Using cylindrical coordinates, find the volume of the cylinder $x^2+y^2 = a^2$ inside the sphere $x^2+y^2+z^2 = 4a^2$.

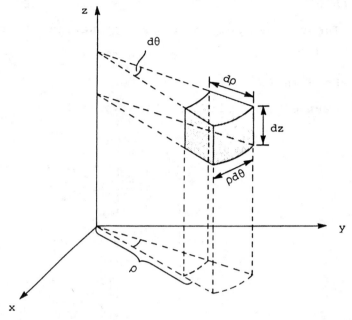

Fig. 1

Solution: The cylindrical transformation is given by

$$x = \rho \cos \theta$$
$$y = \rho \sin \theta \qquad (1)$$
$$z = z$$

The Jacobian of the transformation is

$$J = \frac{\partial(x,y,z)}{\partial(\rho,\theta,z)} = \begin{vmatrix} \cos\theta & -\rho\sin\theta & 0 \\ \sin\theta & \rho\cos\theta & 0 \\ 0 & 0 & 1 \end{vmatrix} = \rho \qquad (2)$$

The change of variables formula is

$$\iiint\limits_{D_{xyz}} f(x,y,z)\,dx\,dy\,dz = \iiint\limits_{D_{\rho\theta z}} F(\rho,\theta,z) \left| \frac{\partial(x,y,z)}{\partial(\rho,\theta,z)} \right| d\rho\,d\theta\,dz \qquad (3)$$

where

$$F(\rho,\theta,z) = f(x(\rho,\theta,z),y(\rho,\theta,z),z(\rho,\theta,z)) \qquad (4)$$

Eq.(3) can be written

725

$$\iiint\limits_{D_{xyz}} f(x,y,z)dxdydz = \iiint\limits_{D_{\rho\theta z}} f(\rho\cos\theta, \rho\sin\theta, z)\rho \; d\rho \; d\theta \; dz \qquad (5)$$

To find the volume, $f(x,y,z) = 1$ should be substituted into eq.(5).

The volume element in the cylindrical coordinates is

$$dV = \rho \; d\rho \; d\theta \; dz \qquad (6)$$

as shown in Fig. 1.

The part of the cylinder is shown in Fig. 2.

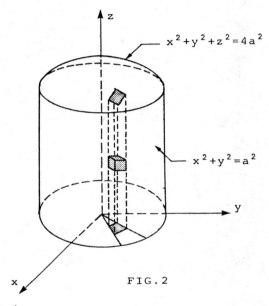

FIG.2

The volume integral is

$$V = \int_{-a}^{a} \int_{y=-\sqrt{a^2-x^2}}^{\sqrt{a^2-x^2}} \int_{z=-\sqrt{4a^2-x^2-y^2}}^{\sqrt{4a^2-x^2-y^2}} dz \; dy \; dx$$

$$= 8 \int_{0}^{a} \int_{0}^{\sqrt{a^2-x^2}} \int_{0}^{\sqrt{4a^2-x^2-y^2}} dz \; dy \; dx \qquad (7)$$

In the cylindrical coordinates, eq.(7) becomes

$$V = 8 \int_{0}^{\frac{\pi}{2}} \int_{0}^{a} \int_{0}^{\sqrt{4a^2-\rho^2}} \rho \; dz d\rho d\theta \qquad (8)$$

$$= 8 \cdot \frac{\pi}{2} \int_{0}^{a} \rho\sqrt{4a^2-\rho^2} \; d\rho = \frac{4}{3} \pi a^3 (8-3\sqrt{3})$$

Here we used the identity

$$\int x\sqrt{b^2-x^2}\ dx = -\frac{1}{3}\ \sqrt{(b^2-x^2)^3} \qquad (9)$$

Consider the closed region bounded by the surfaces

$$z = e^{-x^2-y^2}, \quad z = 0, \quad x^2+y^2 = 1 \qquad (1)$$

1. Express the volume of this region as a triple integral in Cartesian coordinates.

2. Find the volume of this region using cylindrical coordinates.

<u>Solution</u>: The region is shown in the figure.

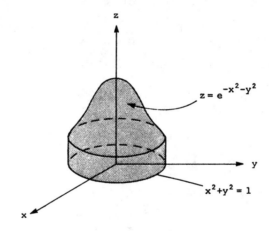

1. Let us first establish the limits of integration. For x and y fixed, z can change from z=0 to z=$e^{-x^2-y^2}$. For x fixed, y can change from y=$-\sqrt{1-x^2}$ to y=$\sqrt{1-x^2}$. Finally, x can change from x=-1 to x=1. The volume is given by the triple integral

$$\iiint dV = \int_{x=-1}^{1} \int_{y=-\sqrt{1-x^2}}^{\sqrt{1-x^2}} \int_{z=0}^{e^{-x^2-y^2}} dz\ dy\ dx \qquad (2)$$

2. In the cylindrical coordinates, we have

$$dV = \rho\ d\rho d\phi dz \qquad (3)$$

Note that z changes from z=0 to z=$e^{-x^2-y^2} = e^{-\rho^2}$, ρ from ρ=0 to ρ=1 and ϕ from ϕ=0 to ϕ=2π.

The volume of the region is

$$\iiint dV = \int_{\phi=0}^{2\pi} \int_{\rho=0}^{1} \int_{z=0}^{e^{-\rho^2}} \rho\ dz\ d\rho\ d\phi$$

$$= \int_{\phi=0}^{2\pi} \int_{\rho=0}^{1} \rho \, e^{-\rho^2} \, d\rho \, d\phi \qquad (4)$$

$$= \int_{\phi=0}^{2\pi} \left[-\frac{e^{-\rho^2}}{2} \right] \Bigg|_{\rho=0}^{1} d\phi = \left(\frac{1}{2} - \frac{e^{-1}}{2} \right) \int_{0}^{2\pi} d\phi$$

$$= \pi(1-e^{-1})$$

● **PROBLEM 16-16**

Compute the Jacobian of the spherical transformation.
Using spherical coordinates, find the volume of a sphere
of radius a.

Solution: The transformation to spherical coordinates is defined by

$$x = \rho \sin\phi \cos\theta \qquad 0 < \rho < \infty$$
$$y = \rho \sin\phi \sin\theta \qquad 0 < \phi < \pi \qquad (1)$$
$$z = \rho \cos\phi \qquad 0 \leq \theta < 2\pi$$

The volume element dV is

$$dV = \rho^2 \sin\phi \, d\rho d\phi d\theta, \qquad (2)$$

as shown in the figure.

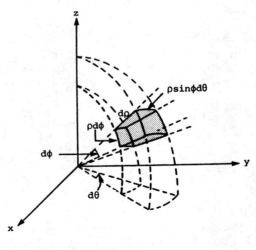

$$dV = (\rho\sin\phi d\theta)(\rho d\phi) d\rho$$
$$= \rho^2 \sin\phi d\rho d\phi d\theta$$

Now, from eq.(1), we may determine the Jacobian of transformation for the spherical coordinates

728

$$J = \frac{\partial(x,y,z)}{\partial(\rho,\phi,\theta)} = \begin{vmatrix} \frac{\partial x}{\partial \rho} & \frac{\partial x}{\partial \phi} & \frac{\partial x}{\partial \theta} \\ \frac{\partial y}{\partial \rho} & \frac{\partial y}{\partial \phi} & \frac{\partial y}{\partial \theta} \\ \frac{\partial z}{\partial \rho} & \frac{\partial z}{\partial \phi} & \frac{\partial z}{\partial \theta} \end{vmatrix}$$

$$= \begin{vmatrix} \sin\phi\cos\theta & \rho\cos\phi\cos\theta & -\rho\sin\phi\sin\theta \\ \sin\phi\sin\theta & \rho\cos\phi\sin\theta & \rho\sin\phi\cos\theta \\ \cos\phi & -\rho\sin\phi & 0 \end{vmatrix} \quad (3)$$

$$= \rho^2\sin\phi$$

Under the transformation to spherical coordinates, a triple integral becomes

$$\iiint\limits_{D_{xyz}} f(x,y,z)dxdydz = \iiint\limits_{D_{\rho\phi\theta}} F(\rho,\phi,\theta)\rho^2\sin\phi d\rho d\phi d\theta \quad (4)$$

where

$$F(\rho,\phi,\theta) = f(x(\rho,\phi,\theta),y(\rho,\phi,\theta),z(\rho,\phi,\theta)) \quad (5)$$

$$= f(\rho\sin\phi\cos\theta,\ \rho\sin\phi\sin\theta,\ \rho\cos\phi)$$

For the volume, function f becomes

$$f(x,y,z) \equiv 1 \quad (6)$$

The volume of a sphere of radius a is

$$V = \iiint\limits_{D_{xyz}} dxdydz = \iiint\limits_{D_{\rho\phi\theta}} \rho^2\sin\phi d\rho d\phi d\theta$$

$$= \int_0^{2\pi} \int_0^\pi \int_0^a \rho^2\sin\phi d\rho d\phi d\theta = \frac{a^3}{3}\int_0^{2\pi}\int_0^\pi \sin\phi d\phi d\theta$$

$$= \frac{4}{3}\pi a^3 \quad (7)$$

● **PROBLEM 16-17**

Find the volume of a sphere of radius r with a cut out cone of angle α, as shown in the figure.

Solution: In this problem there is symmetry with respect to a point (the origin of the system). It is convenient to use in such cases the spherical coordinates. They are related to the Cartesian coordinates by the equations

$$x = \rho\sin\phi\cos\theta$$
$$y = \rho\sin\phi\sin\theta \quad (1)$$
$$z = \rho\cos\phi$$

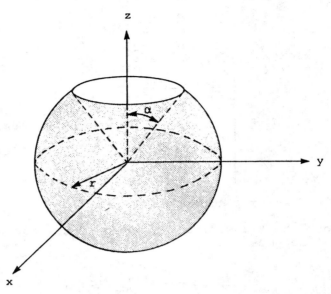

It is easy to verify that the volume element in spherical co-ordinates is given by

$$dV = \rho^2 \sin\phi \, d\rho d\phi d\theta \qquad (2)$$

For the limits of integration, we have that ρ changes from $\rho=0$ to $\rho=r$, ϕ changes from α to π, and θ changes from 0 to 2π. Thus, the volume is given by

$$\iiint dV = \int_{\theta=0}^{2\pi} \int_{\phi=\alpha}^{\pi} \int_{\rho=0}^{r} \rho^2 \sin\phi \, d\rho d\phi d\theta$$

$$= \int_{\theta=0}^{2\pi} \int_{\phi=\alpha}^{2\pi} \frac{r^3}{3} \sin\phi \, d\phi d\theta$$

$$= 2\pi \frac{r^3}{3} (\cos\alpha + 1) \qquad (3)$$

Let us verify our results by considering certain values for α. When $\alpha=0$, no cone is present, and eq.(3) should give us the volume of a sphere:

$$V = 2\pi \frac{r^3}{3} (\cos 0 + 1) = \frac{4\pi r^3}{3} \qquad (4)$$

For $\alpha=\pi$, we notice that the sphere vanishes, and we should obtain zero volume:

$$V = 2\pi \frac{r^3}{3} (\cos \pi + 1) = 0 \qquad (5)$$

● **PROBLEM 16-18**

Consider two coaxial cylinders of height h and radii r_1 and r_2. Find the volume integral of the function $f(x,y,z) = x^2+y^2$ over the volume contained between the two cylinders.

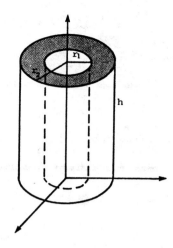

<u>Solution</u>: The cylinders are shown in the figure.
All computations will be performed in cylindrical coordinates:

$$x = \rho \cos\phi$$
$$y = \rho \sin\phi \qquad\qquad (1)$$
$$z = z$$

where $0 \le z \le h$.

The function f becomes

$$\begin{aligned}
f &= x^2 + y^2 \\
&= (\rho\cos\phi)^2 + (\rho\sin\phi)^2 \\
&= \rho^2(\cos^2\phi + \sin^2\phi) \qquad\qquad (2)\\
&= \rho^2
\end{aligned}$$

or

$$f(\rho,\phi,z) = \rho^2$$

The volume element is given by

$$dV = \rho\, d\rho d\phi dz \qquad\qquad (3)$$

Thus, the volume integral of $f(\rho,\phi,z)$ is

$$\begin{aligned}
\iiint &f(\rho,\phi,z)dV \\
&= \int_{z=0}^{h} \int_{\phi=0}^{2\pi} \int_{\rho=r_1}^{r_2} \rho^2 \rho\, d\rho d\phi dz \\
&= \int_{z=0}^{h} \int_{\phi=0}^{2\pi} \frac{\rho^4}{4} \Bigg|_{r_1}^{r_2} d\phi dz \\
&= \pi h \left[\frac{r_2^4}{2} - \frac{r_1^4}{2} \right] \qquad\qquad (4)
\end{aligned}$$

MULTIPLE INTEGRALS, MASS AND DENSITY, CENTER OF GRAVITY

● PROBLEM 16-19

Evaluate the n-fold iterated integral

$$\int_0^1 dx_1 \int_0^{x_1} dx_2 \int_0^{x_2} dx_3 \ldots \int_0^{x_{n-1}} dx_n \qquad (1)$$

Solution: In multiple integration, the following notational convention is often used

$$\int_{x=a}^b \int_{y=c}^d f(x,y) dy dx = \int_a^b dx \int_c^d f(x,y) dy \qquad (2)$$

This notation makes clear which variable goes with which integral sign. Consider a region in n-dimensional Euclidean space defined by the inequalities

$$0 \le x_n \le x_{n-1} \le \cdots \le x_2 \le x_1 \le 1 \qquad (3)$$

Integral (1) represents the volume of this region. For n-1, eq.(1) becomes

$$\int_0^1 dx_1 = 1 \qquad (4)$$

which is the length of the unit interval $0 \le x_1 \le 1$.

For n=2

$$\int_0^1 dx_1 \int_0^{x_1} dx_2 = \int_0^1 x_1 dx_1 = \frac{x_1^2}{2} \Big|_0^1 = \frac{1}{2} \qquad (5)$$

The region of integration is

$$0 \le x_2 \le x_1 \le 1 \qquad (6)$$

For n=3

$$\int_0^1 dx_1 \int_0^{x_1} dx_2 \int_0^{x_2} dx_3 = \int_0^1 dx_1 \frac{x_1^2}{2} = \frac{x_1^3}{2 \cdot 3} \Big|_0^1 = \frac{1}{6} \quad (7)$$

The region of integration is

$$0 \le x_3 \le x_2 \le x_1 \le 1 \qquad (8)$$

The integral in eq.(1) can be evaluated step by step

$$\int_0^1 dx_1 \int_0^{x_1} dx_2 \int_0^{x_2} dx_3 \ldots \int_0^{x_{n-1}} dx_n$$

$$= \int_0^1 dx_1 \int_0^{x_1} dx_2 \ldots \int_0^{x_{n-2}} x_{n-1} \, dx_{n-1} \qquad (9)$$

$$= \int_0^1 dx_1 \int_0^{x_1} dx_2 \ldots \int_0^{x_{n-3}} \frac{x_{n-2}^2}{2} \, dx_{n-2}$$

$$= \int_0^1 dx_1 \int_0^{x_1} dx_2 \ldots \int_0^{x_{n-4}} \frac{x_{n-3}^3}{2 \cdot 3} \, dx_{n-3}$$

$$= \ldots = \int_0^1 \frac{x_1^{n-1}}{(n-1)!} \, dx_1 = \frac{1}{n!}$$

● **PROBLEM** 16-20

The function $f(x_1, x_2, \ldots, x_n)$ is defined on the n-dimensional unit cube

$$f(x_1, x_2, \ldots, x_n) = x_1 x_2 \ldots x_n \qquad (1)$$

Evaluate the integral

$$I_n = \int_0^1 dx_1 \int_0^1 dx_2 \ldots \int_0^1 dx_{n-1} \int_0^1 f(x_1, x_2, \ldots, x_n) dx_n \qquad (2)$$

<u>Solution</u>: The n-dimensional unit cube is described by

$$0 \le x_1 \le 1, \quad 0 \le x_2 \le 1, \ldots, 0 \le x_n \le 1 \qquad (3)$$

Substitution of eq.(1) into eq.(2) transforms the integral to

$$\int_0^1 dx_1 \int_0^1 dx_2 \ldots \int_0^1 dx_{n-1} \int_0^1 x_1 x_2 \ldots x_n \, dx_n$$

$$= \int_0^1 dx_1 \int_0^1 dx_2 \ldots \int_0^1 (x_1 x_2 \ldots x_{n-1}) dx_{n-1} \int_0^1 x_n \, dx_n \qquad (4)$$

$$= \frac{1}{2} \int_0^1 dx_1 \int_0^1 dx_2 \ldots \int_0^1 (x_1 x_2 \ldots x_{n-1}) \, dx_{n-1} = I_n$$

From eq.(4), we see that

$$I_n = \frac{1}{2} I_{n-1} \qquad (5)$$

Let us note that

$$I_1 = \int_0^1 x_1 dx_1 = \frac{1}{2} \qquad (6)$$

Combining eq.(6) and eq.(5), one obtains

$$I_n = \frac{1}{2} I_{n-1} = \frac{1}{2^n} \tag{7}$$

● **PROBLEM** 16-21

Find the total mass M of the cylinder shown in the figure. The density δ is given by

$$\delta(x,y,z) = \alpha(x^2+y^2) + \beta e^{-z} \tag{1}$$

where α and β are positive constants.

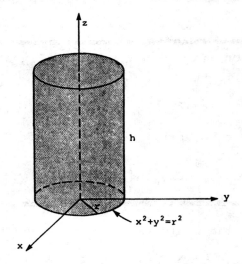

Solution: The mass M is given by the triple integral

$$M = \iiint_V \delta \; dV \tag{2}$$

where $\delta=\delta(x,y,z)$ is the mass density. In our case, the limits of integration for z are from z=0 to z=h. Taking x fixed, we see that y varies from $y=-\sqrt{r^2-x^2}$ to $y=\sqrt{r^2-x^2}$. Finally, x changes from x=-r to x=r. Eq.(2) for the cylinder of density δ becomes

$$M = \int_{x=-r}^{r} \int_{y=-\sqrt{r^2-x^2}}^{\sqrt{r^2-x^2}} \int_0^h \left[\alpha(x^2+y^2)+\beta e^{-z}\right] dzdydx \tag{3}$$

It is much more convenient to operate in the cylindrical coordinates (ρ,ϕ,z).

Since

$$x^2+y^2 = \rho^2$$

in cylindrical coordinates, the density becomes

$$\delta(\rho,\phi,z) = \alpha\rho^2 + \beta e^{-z} \tag{4}$$

734

and the mass is given by

$$M = \int_{\phi=0}^{2\pi} \int_{\rho=0}^{r} \int_{z=0}^{h} \left[\alpha\rho^2 + \beta e^{-z} \right] dz \, \rho \, d\rho d\phi$$

$$= \int_{\phi=0}^{2\pi} \int_{\rho=0}^{r} (\alpha\rho^3 h - \beta\rho e^{-h} + \beta\rho) d\rho d\phi$$

$$= 2\pi \left[\frac{\alpha h}{4} \rho^4 - \beta e^{-h} \frac{\rho^2}{2} + \beta \frac{\rho^2}{2} \right] \Bigg|_{\rho=0}^{r} \tag{5}$$

$$= \frac{\pi\alpha h}{2} r^4 - \pi\beta e^{-h} r^2 + \pi\beta r^2 = \frac{\pi\alpha h}{2} r^4 + \pi\beta r^2 (1-e^{-h})$$

● **PROBLEM 16-22**

Find the center of gravity of a homogeneous solid hemi-sphere of radius r.

Solution: The hemisphere is shown in the figure.

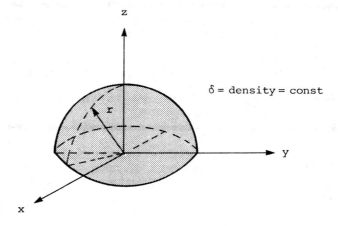

δ = density = const

For a homogeneous solid hemisphere, the density δ is a constant.

The mass of the solid is given by

$$M = \iiint_V \delta \, dV \tag{1}$$

The coordinates of the center of gravity, (or center of mass), $(\bar{x}, \bar{y}, \bar{z})$ are given by

$$\bar{x} = \frac{\iiint x\delta dV}{\iiint \delta dV} \tag{2}$$

735

$$\bar{y} = \frac{\iiint y\delta dV}{\iiint \delta dV} \tag{3}$$

$$\bar{z} = \frac{\iiint z\delta dV}{\iiint \delta dV} \tag{4}$$

By symmetry, for a homogeneous hemisphere $\bar{x} = \bar{y} = 0$.

To find $\bar{z}$, we shall perform the integration in cylindrical coordinates. The coordinate z changes from z=0 to $z=\sqrt{r^2-\rho^2}$. Thus,

$$\bar{z} = \frac{\iiint z \, dV}{\iiint dV} = \frac{\int_{\phi=0}^{2\pi} \int_{\rho=0}^{r} \int_{z=0}^{\sqrt{r^2-\rho^2}} z \, dz \rho \, d\rho \, d\phi}{\frac{2}{3}\pi r^3} \tag{5}$$

$$= \frac{3r}{8}$$

● PROBLEM 16-23

Consider an "ice-cream cone" made of a homogeneous material, that is a material of constant density, $\delta = $ const.

Geometrically, an "ice-cream cone" can be represented by the volume bounded above by a sphere of radius r and below by a cone of angle α, as shown in the figure. Find the center of mass of this volume.

Solution: Since the cone is symmetrical with respect to a point, it is most convenient to use spherical coordinates. Let $(\bar{x},\bar{y},\bar{z})$ denote the coordinates of the center of gravity. We have,

$$\bar{x} = \frac{\iiint x \, \delta dV}{\iiint dV} \quad , \quad \bar{y} = \frac{\iiint y \, \delta \, dV}{\iiint dV} \quad , \quad \bar{z} = \frac{\iiint z \, \delta \, dV}{\iiint dV} \tag{1)-(3}$$

By symmetry, it is concluded that $\bar{x} = \bar{y} = 0$.

Since the material is homogeneous, eq.(3) becomes

$$\bar{z} = \frac{\iiint z dV}{\iiint dV} \tag{4}$$

In the spherical coordinates, we have

$$dV = \rho^2 \sin\phi \, d\rho \, d\phi \, d\theta \tag{5}$$

$$z = \rho \cos \phi \tag{6}$$

From the figure, we see that ρ changes from $\rho=0$ to $\rho=r$, ϕ changes from $\phi=0$ to $\phi=\alpha$ and θ changes from $\theta=0$ to $\theta=2\pi$. Sub-

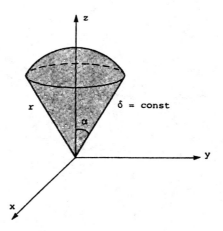

δ = const

stituting eqs.(5) and (6) into eq.(4) results in

$$\overline{z} = \frac{\displaystyle\int_{\theta=0}^{2\pi}\int_{\phi=0}^{\alpha}\int_{\rho=0}^{r}\rho\cos\phi\rho^2\sin\phi d\rho d\phi d\theta}{\displaystyle\int_{\theta=0}^{2\pi}\int_{\phi=0}^{\alpha}\int_{\rho=0}^{r}\rho^2\sin\phi d\rho d\phi d\theta}$$

$$= \frac{\dfrac{r^4}{4}\,2\pi\displaystyle\int_0^\alpha\cos\phi\sin\phi d\phi}{\dfrac{r^3}{3}\,2\pi\displaystyle\int_0^\alpha\sin\phi d\phi}$$

$$= \frac{\dfrac{r^4\pi}{8}[-\cos2\phi]\Big|_{\phi=0}^{\alpha}}{\dfrac{2\pi r^3}{3}[-\cos\phi]\Big|_{\phi=0}^{\alpha}} = \frac{3}{16}r\left(\frac{1-\cos2\alpha}{1-\cos\alpha}\right) \qquad (7)$$

It is interesting to note that when $\alpha = \dfrac{\pi}{2}$, the cone becomes a hemisphere, and from eq.(7), we obtain

$$\overline{z} = \frac{3}{16}r\left(\frac{1-\cos\pi}{1-\cos\dfrac{\pi}{2}}\right) = \frac{3}{8}r$$

This agrees with the result obtained in Problem 16-22.

MOMENT OF INERTIA

● **PROBLEM 16-24**

Find the moments of inertia I_x, I_y, I_z of a mass M distributed over the region V shown in the figure and having constant density δ.

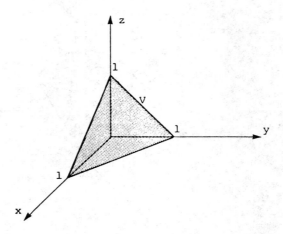

Solution: From the figure, we conclude that the region V is bounded by the coordinate planes x=0, y=0, z=0 and the plane

$$x + y + z = 1 \qquad (1)$$

The moments of inertia with respect to the axes x, y and z are given by

$$I_x = \iiint (y^2+z^2)\delta dV \qquad (2)$$

$$I_y = \iiint (x^2+z^2)\delta dV \qquad (3)$$

$$I_z = \iiint (x^2+y^2)\delta dV \qquad (4)$$

From the figure, we obtain the limits of integration:

z changes from z=0 to z=1-x-y

y changes from y=0 to 1-x

x changes from x=0 to x=1.

Eq.(2) can be written

$$I_x = \iiint (y^2+z^2)\delta dV = \int_{x=0}^{1} \int_{y=0}^{1-x} \int_{z=0}^{1-x-y} (y^2+z^2)\delta dz dy dx$$

$$= \delta \int_{x=0}^{1} \int_{y=0}^{1-x} \left[y^2 z + \frac{z^3}{3} \right] \Bigg|_{z=0}^{1-x-y} dy dx \qquad (5)$$

$$= \delta \int_{x=0}^{1} \int_{y=0}^{1-x} (-2y^3+4y^2-4xy^2+6xy-3x^2y-3y+3x^2-3x-x^3+1) dy dx$$

$$= \delta \int_{0}^{1} \left[-\frac{y^4}{2}+\frac{4}{3}y^3-\frac{4}{3}xy^3+3xy^2-\frac{3}{2}x^2y^2-\frac{3}{2}y^2+3x^2y-3xy-x^3y+y \right] \Bigg|_{y=0}^{1-x} dx$$

$$= \delta \int_0^1 \left[\frac{5}{6}(1-x)^4 - \frac{3}{2}(1-x)^2(x^2+1) + (1-x)(1-x^3) \right] dx$$

$$= \delta \int_0^1 \frac{1}{3}(1-x)^4 dx = \frac{1}{3} \delta \left. \frac{(x-1)^5}{5} \right|_{x=0}^{1}$$

$$= \frac{1}{15} \delta$$

By symmetry, it is concluded that all moments of inertia are equal. Thus,

$$I_x = I_y = I_z = \frac{1}{15} \delta \qquad (6)$$

● **PROBLEM 16-25**

Consider a homogeneous solid structure of density $\delta=$const bounded by the xy plane and bounded above by the sphere

$$x^2+y^2+z^2 = r^2 \qquad (1)$$

and by the cylinder

$$\rho = r \cos \theta \qquad (2)$$

Find its moment of inertia with respect to the z-axis.

Solution: Let us note that the orthogonal projection of the cylinder $\rho=r\cos\theta$ on the xy plane is the circle $\rho=r\cos\theta$, as shown in Fig. 1.

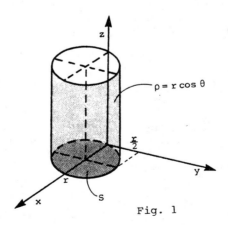

Fig. 1

In cylindrical coordinates, the area S of the projection of the cylinder on the xy plane is

$$S = \int_{-\frac{\pi}{2}}^{\frac{\pi}{2}} \int_0^{r\cos\theta} \rho d\rho d\theta = \int_{-\frac{\pi}{2}}^{\frac{\pi}{2}} \frac{r^2\cos^2\theta}{2} d\theta \qquad (3)$$

739

$$= \frac{1}{2} \cdot \frac{r^2}{2} \left[\theta + \frac{\sin 2\theta}{2} \right] \Bigg|_{\theta = -\frac{\pi}{2}}^{\frac{\pi}{2}} = \frac{\pi r^2}{4}$$

Now, for this problem, it is required to find the moment of inertia I_z of the structure bounded above by the sphere $x^2 + y^2 + z^2 = r^2$, as shown in Fig. 2.

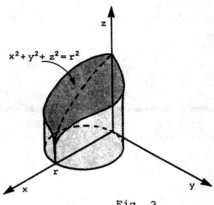

$$x^2 + y^2 + z^2 = r^2$$

Fig. 2

We see that when we integrate with respect to z, the lower limit is z=0 and the upper limit is

$$z = \sqrt{r^2 - x^2 - y^2} = \sqrt{r^2 - \rho^2} \qquad (4)$$

The moment I_z is given by

$$I_z = \delta \iiint (x^2 + y^2) dV \qquad (5)$$

In cylindrical coordinates, we have

$$x^2 + y^2 = \rho^2 \qquad (6)$$

$$dV = \rho \, d\rho \, dz \, d\theta \qquad (7)$$

Eq.(5) can be written

$$I_z = \int_{-\frac{\pi}{2}}^{\frac{\pi}{2}} \int_0^{r\cos\theta} \int_0^{\sqrt{r^2 - \rho^2}} \rho^2 \cdot \rho \, dz \, d\rho \, d\theta \qquad (8)$$

$$= \int_{-\frac{\pi}{2}}^{\frac{\pi}{2}} \int_0^{r\cos\theta} \rho^3 \sqrt{r^2 - \rho^2} \, d\rho \, d\theta$$

To evaluate the last integral, use the formula

$$\int x^3 \sqrt{a^2 - x^2} \, dx = \frac{1}{5} (a^2 - x^2)^{\frac{5}{2}} - \frac{a^2}{3} (a^2 - x^2)^{\frac{3}{2}} \qquad (9)$$

740

to obtain

$$I_z = \int_{-\frac{\pi}{2}}^{\frac{\pi}{2}} \left[\frac{1}{5} (r^2-\rho^2)^{\frac{5}{2}} - \frac{r^2}{3} (r^2-\rho^2)^{\frac{3}{2}} \right] \Bigg|_{\rho=0}^{r\cos\theta} d\theta$$

$$= \frac{r^5}{15} \int_{-\frac{\pi}{2}}^{\frac{\pi}{2}} (3\sin^5\theta - 5\sin^3\theta + 2) d\theta$$

$$= \frac{2r^5}{15} \left(\pi - \frac{26}{15} \right)$$

● **PROBLEM 16-26**

Consider a sphere of radius a and mass m. Find its
moment of inertia with respect to a tangent line.

Solution: Let us choose the system of coordinates in such a
way that the z axis is tangent to the sphere and the center
of the sphere has coordinates (a,0,0), as shown in the figure.

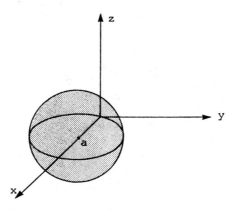

We assume that the sphere is homogeneous and its mass density
is ρ. The moment of inertia with respect to the z axis is

$$I = \iiint_V (x^2+y^2)\rho dV \qquad (1)$$

The sphere is described by the equation

$$(x-a)^2 + y^2 + z^2 = a^2 \qquad (2)$$

Now, for the limits of integration, we see that:

z changes from $z = -\sqrt{a^2-(x-a)^2-y^2}$ to $z = \sqrt{a^2-(x-a)^2-y^2}$

y changes from $y = -\sqrt{a^2-(x-a)^2}$ to $y = \sqrt{a^2-(x-a)^2}$

·x changes from x = 0   to   x = 2a.

741

The integral in eq.(1) can thus be written

$$I = \int_{x=0}^{2a} \int_{y=-\sqrt{a^2-(x-a)^2}}^{\sqrt{a^2-(x-a)^2}} \int_{z=-\sqrt{a^2-(x-a)^2-y^2}}^{\sqrt{a^2-(x-a)^2-y^2}} (x^2+y^2)\rho\,dzdydx$$

$$= 2\rho \int_{x=0}^{2a} \int_{y=-\sqrt{a^2-(x-a)^2}}^{\sqrt{a^2-(x-a)^2}} (x^2+y^2)\sqrt{a^2-(x-a)^2-y^2}\,dydx \qquad (3)$$

To evaluate integral (3), use the following equations

$$\int \sqrt{\alpha^2-y^2}\,dy = \frac{1}{2}\left[y\sqrt{\alpha^2-y^2} + \alpha^2 \text{arc sin} \frac{y}{|\alpha|} \right] \qquad (4)$$

$$\int y^2\sqrt{\alpha^2-y^2}\,dy = -\frac{y}{4}\sqrt{(\alpha^2-y^2)^3} + \frac{\alpha^2}{8}(y\sqrt{\alpha^2-y^2} + \alpha^2 \text{arc sin} \frac{y}{|\alpha|}) \quad (5)$$

Eq.(3) becomes

$$2\rho \int_{x=0}^{2a} \int_{y=-\sqrt{a^2-(x-a)^2}}^{\sqrt{a^2-(x-a)^2}} \left[x^2\sqrt{a^2-(x-a)^2-y^2} + y^2\sqrt{a^2-(x-a)^2-y^2} \right] dy\,dx$$

$$\qquad (6)$$

$$= \rho\pi \int_0^{2a} (-x^4+2x^3a)dx + \frac{\rho\pi}{4} \int_0^{2a} \left[2xa-x^2 \right]^2 dx$$

$$= \rho\pi a^5 \frac{8}{5} + \rho\pi a^5 \left[\frac{8}{3} - 4 + \frac{8}{5} \right] = \frac{28}{15} \rho\pi a^5$$

The mass of the sphere is

$$m = \frac{4}{3} \pi a^3 \rho \qquad (7)$$

The moment of inertia is

$$I = \frac{28}{15} \rho\pi a^5 = \frac{7}{5} ma^2 \qquad (8)$$

● **PROBLEM 16-27**

Let I_p be the moment of inertia of a solid V about an arbitrary line p

$$I_p = \iiint_V d^2 \delta(x,y,z)dxdydz \qquad (1)$$

where d is the distance from a general point of the solid to the line p and δ is the density of the solid. Show that

$$I_p = I_{\bar{p}} + Ms^2 \qquad (2)$$

where $\bar{p}$ is a line passing through the center of mass parallel to p, S is the distance between p and $\bar{p}$, and M is the mass of the solid.

Solution: Let us establish two coordinate systems $(\bar{x}, \bar{y}, \bar{z})$ and (x, y, z) in such way that $\bar{p}$ is the $\bar{z}$ axis and $\bar{y}$ and y overlap (see the figure).

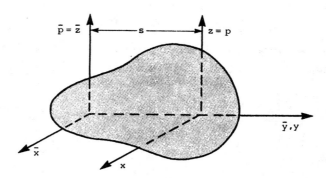

The center of mass is on the $\bar{z}$ axis. The transformation from (x, y, z) to $(\bar{x}, \bar{y}, \bar{z})$ is given by

$$x = \bar{x}$$
$$y = \bar{y} - s \qquad (3)$$
$$z = \bar{z}$$

The moment of inertia I_p can be expressed as

$$I_p = \iiint_V d^2 \delta(x,y,z)dxdydz = \iiint_V (x^2+y^2)\delta dxdydz$$

$$= \iiint_V [\bar{x}^2 + (\bar{y}-s)^2]\delta\, d\bar{x}d\bar{y}d\bar{z} \qquad (4)$$

$$= \iiint_V (\bar{x}^2+\bar{y}^2)\delta d\bar{x}d\bar{y}d\bar{z} - 2s \iiint_V \bar{y}\, \delta d\bar{x}d\bar{y}d\bar{z}$$

$$+ s^2 \iiint_V \delta d\bar{x}d\bar{y}d\bar{z}$$

The mass is given by

$$M = \iiint_V \delta(x,y,z)dxdydz \qquad (5)$$

The position of the center of mass with respect to the $\bar{y}$ axis is

$$0 = \bar{y} = \frac{1}{M} \iiint_V \bar{y}\, \delta\, d\bar{x}d\bar{y}d\bar{z} \qquad (6)$$

Substitution of eq.(5) and (6) into eq.(4) leads to

$$I_p = \iiint_V (\bar{x}^2 + \bar{y}^2)\, \delta d\bar{x}d\bar{y}d\bar{z} + Ms^2$$

(7)

$$= I_{\bar{p}} + Ms^2$$

which completes the proof.

● **PROBLEM 16-28**

Let p be a line through the origin 0, whose direction cosines are α, β, γ. Show that

$$I_p = I_x \alpha^2 + I_y \beta^2 + I_z \gamma^2 - 2I_{xy}\alpha\beta - 2I_{xz}\alpha\gamma - 2I_{yz}\beta\gamma$$

(1)

where I_p is the moment of inertia about p, and

$$I_{xy} = \iiint xy\delta(x,y,z)\, dxdydz$$

(2)

$$I_{xz} = \iiint xz\delta(x,y,z)\, dxdydz$$

$$I_{yz} = \iiint yz\delta(x,y,z)\, dxdydz$$

represent the products of inertia.

The ellipsoid

$$I_x x^2 + I_y y^2 + I_z z^2 - 2I_{xy}xy - 2I_{xz}xz - 2I_{yz}yz = 1$$

(3)

is called the ellipsoid of inertia.

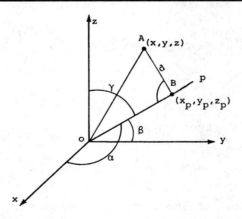

Solution: The direction cosines of the line p are α, β and γ. Let (x_p, y_p, z_p) be an arbitrary point on p as shown in the figure.

744

The following identities hold

$$\frac{x_p}{\sqrt{x_p^2 + y_p^2 + z_p^2}} = \alpha \;\; ; \;\; \frac{y_p}{\sqrt{x_p^2 + y_p^2 + z_p^2}} = \beta \;\; ; \;\; \frac{z_p}{\sqrt{x_p^2 + y_p^2 + z_p^2}} = \gamma \qquad (4)$$

From eq.(4) we obtain

$$\alpha^2 + \beta^2 + \gamma^2 = 1 \qquad (5)$$

and

$$x_p^2 = \frac{\alpha^2 y_p^2 + \alpha^2 z_p^2}{1 - \alpha^2} \qquad (6)$$

Substituting eq.(6) into

$$\frac{y_p}{\sqrt{x_p^2 + y_p^2 + z_p^2}} = \beta$$

yields

$$y_p^2 = \beta^2 \left[\frac{\alpha^2 y_p^2 + \alpha^2 z_p^2}{1 - \alpha^2} + y_p^2 + z_p^2 \right] \qquad (7)$$

After some simple transformations, eq.(7) can be transformed to

$$\beta^2 (y_p^2 + z_p^2) = y_p^2 (1 - \alpha^2) \qquad (8)$$

Since

$$1 = \alpha^2 + \beta^2 + \gamma^2 \qquad (9)$$

eq.(8) becomes

$$\beta^2 z_p^2 = \gamma^2 y_p^2 \qquad (10)$$

All three equations can be obtained in the same manner

$$\beta^2 x_p^2 = \alpha^2 y_p^2 \qquad (11)$$

$$\gamma^2 x_p^2 = \alpha^2 z_p^2 \qquad (12)$$

$$\beta^2 z_p^2 = \gamma^2 y_p^2 \qquad (13)$$

The distance between the point (x,y,z) and the point (x_p, y_p, z_p) on the line p is

$$d = \sqrt{(x - x_p)^2 + (y - y_p)^2 + (z - z_p)^2} \qquad (14)$$

From the figure,

$$(OA)^2 = d^2 + (OB)^2 \qquad (15)$$

Thus

$$x^2 + y^2 + z^2 = (x - x_p)^2 + (y - y_p)^2 + (z - z_p)^2 + x_p^2 + y_p^2 + z_p^2 \qquad (16)$$

or

$$x_p^2 + y_p^2 + z_p^2 = xx_p + yy_p + zz_p \qquad (17)$$

Substituting eqs.(11) and (12) into eq.(17) yields

$$x_p + \frac{\beta^2}{\alpha^2} x_p + \frac{\gamma^2}{\alpha^2} x_p = x + y \frac{\beta}{\alpha} + z \frac{\gamma}{\alpha} \tag{18}$$

or

$$x_p = \alpha^2 x + \alpha\beta y + \alpha\gamma z \tag{19}$$

From eq.(14), we find

$$d^2 = (x-x_p)^2 + (y-y_p)^2 + (z-z_p)^2 \tag{20}$$

$$= x^2+y^2+z^2 + x_p^2+y_p^2+z_p^2 - 2(xx_p+yy_p+zz_p)$$

Now, substituting eqs.(11), (12), (13) and (19) into eq.(20) gives us

$$d^2 = x^2+y^2+z^2 + \frac{1}{\alpha^2} (\alpha^2 x+\alpha\beta y+\gamma\alpha z)^2$$

$$-2(\alpha^2 x+\alpha\beta y+\alpha\gamma z)\left(x+y \frac{\beta}{\alpha} +z \frac{\gamma}{\alpha}\right) \tag{21}$$

$$= x^2+y^2+z^2 + [\alpha^2 x+\alpha\beta y+\alpha\gamma z][-x - \frac{\beta}{\alpha} y - \frac{\gamma}{\alpha} z]$$

$$= x^2(\beta^2+\gamma^2) + y^2(\alpha^2+\gamma^2) + z^2(\alpha^2+\beta^2) - 2\alpha\beta\, xy - 2\alpha\gamma xz - 2\beta\gamma yz$$

The moment of inertia I_p of a body about p is

$$I_p = \iiint d^2 \delta(x,y,z)dxdydz \tag{22}$$

Substitution of eq.(21) into eq.(22) leads to

$$I_p = \iiint \alpha^2(y^2+z^2)\delta\ dxdydz + \iiint \beta^2(x^2+z^2)\delta\ dxdydz$$

$$+ \iiint \gamma^2(x^2+y^2)\delta\ dxdydz - 2\alpha\beta\iiint xy\delta dxdydz$$

$$-2\alpha\gamma \iiint xz\delta dxdydz - 2\beta\gamma \iiint yz\delta dxdydz \tag{23}$$

$$= \alpha^2 I_x + \beta^2 I_y + \gamma^2 I_z - 2\alpha\beta I_{xy} - 2\alpha\gamma I_{xz} - 2\beta\gamma I_{yz}$$

VOLUME INTEGRALS OF VECTORS, SURFACE AND VOLUME INTEGRAL RELATIONSHIP, GAUSS' LAW AND ELECTROSTATIC POTENTIAL

● **PROBLEM 16-29**

Evaluate the integral

$$\iiint_V \overline{F}\ dV \tag{1}$$

where

$$\overline{F} = xz\overline{i} - x^2\overline{j} + y\overline{k} \qquad (2)$$

and V is the region bounded by the surfaces

$$x = 0, \quad y = 0, \quad y = 5, \quad z = x^2, \quad z = 9$$

<u>Solution</u>: Notice that in this case we have to evaluate the volume integral of a vector field. The calculations are basically the same as for volume integrals of scalar fields. Let $\overline{G}$ be a vector field

$$\overline{G} = f(x,y,z)\overline{i} + g(x,y,z)\overline{j} + h(x,y,z)\overline{k} \qquad (3)$$

The volume integral of $\overline{G}$ can be written as

$$\iiint_V \overline{G}\ dV = \iiint_V [f\,\overline{i} + g\,\overline{j} + h\,\overline{k}]\ dV$$

$$= \overline{i}\ \iiint_V f(x,y,z)dV + \overline{j}\ \iiint_V g(x,y,z)dV + \overline{k}\ \iiint_V h(x,y,z)dV \qquad (4)$$

Let us sketch the region of integration and take an arbitrary point (x,y,z) inside this region.

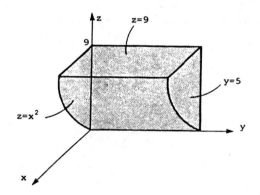

Taking x and y fixed, we see that z can change from $z=x^2$ to $z=9$. The y coordinate can change from $y=0$ to $y=5$ and the x coordinate from $x=0$ to $x=3$. The integral (1) can be written

$$\iiint_V \overline{F}dV = \int_{x=0}^{3} \int_{y=0}^{5} \int_{z=x^2}^{9} (xz\overline{i} - x^2\overline{j} + y\overline{k})dzdydx$$

$$= \int_{x=0}^{3} \int_{y=0}^{5} \left[x\,\frac{z^2}{2}\,\overline{i} - x^2z\overline{j} + yz\overline{k} \right] \Bigg|_{z=x^2}^{9} dydx$$

$$\qquad (5)$$

$$= \int_{x=0}^{3} \int_{y=0}^{5} \left[\frac{81}{2}x\overline{i} - 9x^2\overline{j} + 9y\overline{k} - \frac{x^5}{2}\overline{i} + x^4\overline{j} - yx^2\overline{k} \right] dydx$$

$$= \int_0^3 \left[\frac{81}{2}xy\overline{i} - 9x^2y\overline{j} + \frac{9}{2}y^2\overline{k} - \frac{x^5}{2}y\overline{i} + x^4y\overline{j} - \frac{1}{2}y^2x^2\overline{k} \right] \Bigg|_{y=0}^{5} dx$$

$$= \int_0^3 \left[\frac{81 \cdot 5}{2} x\overline{i} - 45x^2\overline{j} + \frac{9 \cdot 25}{2}\overline{k} - \frac{5}{2}x^5\overline{i} + 5x^4\overline{j} - \frac{25}{2}x^2\overline{k} \right] dx$$

$$= \left[\frac{81 \cdot 5}{2 \cdot 2} x^2\overline{i} - \frac{45}{3}x^3\overline{j} + \frac{9 \cdot 25}{2}x\overline{k} - \frac{5}{2}\frac{x^6}{6}\overline{i} + x^5\overline{j} - \frac{25}{2}\frac{x^3}{3}\overline{k} \right] \Bigg|_{x=0}^{3}$$

$$= \left(\frac{81 \cdot 5 \cdot 9}{4} - \frac{5}{2}\frac{3^6}{6} \right)\overline{i} + (3^5 - 45 \cdot 9)\overline{j} + \left(\frac{27 \cdot 25}{2} - \frac{25 \cdot 9}{2} \right)\overline{k}$$

$$= 607.5\overline{i} - 162\overline{j} + 225\overline{k}$$

● **PROBLEM 16-30**

Find the value of the volume integral

$$\iiint_V \overline{F}\ dV \tag{1}$$

where $\qquad\qquad \overline{F} = ye^z\overline{i} + x^2\overline{j} + za^2\overline{k}$ $\qquad\qquad$ (2)

and V is the region bounded by the surfaces

$$z = 0, \quad z = 2, \quad x^2 + y^2 = a^2 \tag{3}$$

Solution: The region V is shown in the figure.

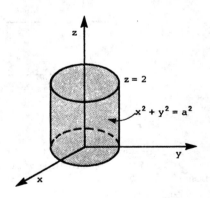

For any fixed x and y, z changes from z=0 to z=2. For fixed values of y, x changes from $-\sqrt{a^2-y^2}$ to $\sqrt{a^2-y^2}$. Integral (1) becomes

$$\iiint_V \overline{F}\ dV = \int_0^2 \int_{-a}^{1} \int_{-\sqrt{a^2-y^2}}^{\sqrt{a^2-y^2}} (ye^z\overline{i} + x^2\overline{j} + za^2\overline{k})\,dxdydz \tag{4}$$

or

$$\iiint_V \overline{F}\ dV = \int_0^2 dz \int_{-a}^{a} dy \int_{-\sqrt{a^2-y^2}}^{\sqrt{a^2-y^2}} (ye^z\overline{i} + x^2\overline{j} + za^2\overline{k})\,dx \tag{5}$$

In eq.(5) we used the commonly used notation convention discussed in Problem 16-19.

748

Now, performing the integration,

$$\iiint_V \overline{F}\, dV = \int_0^2 dz \int_{-a}^a \left[xye^z\overline{i} + \frac{x^3}{3}\overline{j} + xza^z\overline{k} \right] \Bigg|_{x=-\sqrt{a^2-y^2}}^{\sqrt{a^2-y^2}} dy$$

$$= 2\int_0^2 dz \int_{-a}^a \left[y\sqrt{a^2-y^2}\, e^z\overline{i} + \frac{1}{3}(a^2-y^2)\sqrt{a^2-y^2}\,\overline{j} + \sqrt{a^2-y^2}za^z\overline{k} \right] dy \quad (6)$$

The following formulas are useful in evaluating integral (6).

$$\int \sqrt{a^2-x^2}\, dx = \frac{1}{2}\left[x\sqrt{a^2-x^2} + a^2 \arcsin \frac{x}{|a|} \right] \quad (7)$$

$$\int x\sqrt{a^2-x^2}\, dx = -\frac{1}{3}\sqrt{(a^2-x^2)^3} \quad (8)$$

$$\int x^2\sqrt{a^2-x^2}\, dx = -\frac{x}{4}\sqrt{(a^2-x^2)^3} + \frac{a^2}{8}\left(x\sqrt{a^2-x^2}+a^2\arcsin\frac{x}{|a|}\right) \quad (9)$$

Substituting eqs.(7), (8), (9) into eq.(6) leads to

$$2\int_0^2 \Bigg[-\frac{1}{3}e^z\sqrt{(a^2-y^2)^3}\,\overline{i} + \frac{1}{6}a^2\left(y\sqrt{a^2-y^2} + a^2\arcsin\frac{y}{|a|}\right)\overline{j}$$

$$+ \frac{y}{12}\sqrt{(a^2-y^2)^3}\,\overline{j} - \frac{a^2}{24}\left(y\sqrt{a^2-y^2} + a^2\arcsin\frac{y}{|a|}\right)\overline{j} \quad (10)$$

$$+ \frac{1}{2}za^z\left(y\sqrt{a^2-y^2} + a^2\arcsin\frac{y}{|a|}\right)\overline{k} \, \Bigg|_{y=-a}^{a}\Bigg] dz$$

$$= 2\int_0^2 \left(\frac{\pi}{8}a^4\overline{j} + \frac{\pi}{2}a^2za^z\overline{k} \right) dz$$

Now, since

$$a^z = e^{z\ln a},$$

we can use the formula

$$\int xe^{ax}dx = \frac{e^{ax}}{a^2}(ax-1)$$

Eq.(10) becomes

$$2\int_0^2 \left(\frac{\pi}{8}a^4\overline{j} + \frac{\pi}{2}a^2ze^{z\ln a}\overline{k} \right) dz$$

$$= \frac{\pi}{4}a^4z \Bigg|_0^2 \overline{j} + \pi a^2\frac{e^{z\ln a}}{(\ln a)^2}(z\ln a-1) \Bigg|_0^2 \overline{k}$$

$$= \frac{\pi}{2}a^4\overline{j} + \frac{\pi a^2 e^{2\ln a}}{(\ln a)^2}(2\ln a - 1)\overline{k} + \frac{\pi a^2}{(\ln a)^2}\overline{k} \quad (13)$$

749

Evaluate the integrals

1. $$\iiint_V \text{div } \overline{F} \, dV \qquad\qquad (1)$$

2. $$\iiint_V \text{curl } \overline{F} \, dV \qquad\qquad (2)$$

where
$$\overline{F} = (x^2-z)\overline{i} + 2xy\overline{j} - 2x\overline{k} \qquad\qquad (3)$$

and V is the closed region bounded by the planes x=0, y=0, z=0 and 2x + 2y + z = 6.

Solution: As a procedure, we will simply calculate div $\overline{F}$ and curl $\overline{F}$ and perform the required integration.

1. For div $\overline{F}$, we obtain

$$\text{div } \overline{F} = \nabla \cdot \overline{F} = \left(\frac{\partial}{\partial x}, \frac{\partial}{\partial y}, \frac{\partial}{\partial z}\right) \cdot (x^2-z, \; 2xy, \; -2x)$$

$$= 2x + 2x = 4x \qquad\qquad (4)$$

Thus, the volume integral is

$$\int_{x=0}^{3} \int_{y=0}^{3-x} \int_{z=0}^{6-2x-2y} 4x \, dz \, dy \, dx$$

$$= \int_{x=0}^{3} \int_{y=0}^{3-x} 4x(6-2x-2y) dy \, dx$$

$$= 8 \int_{0}^{3} \left[3xy - x^2 y - \frac{x}{2} y^2 \right] \Bigg|_{y=0}^{3-x} dx \qquad\qquad (5)$$

$$= 8 \int_{0}^{3} \left(\frac{x^3}{2} - 3x^2 + \frac{9x}{2} \right) dx = 8 \left[\frac{x^4}{8} - x^3 + \frac{9x^2}{4} \right] \Bigg|_{x=0}^{3}$$

$$= 27$$

2. For curl $\overline{F}$, we obtain

$$\text{curl } \overline{F} = \left(\frac{\partial}{\partial x}, \frac{\partial}{\partial y}, \frac{\partial}{\partial z}\right) \times (x^2-z, \; 2xy, \; -2x)$$

$$= \overline{j} + 2y\,\overline{k} \qquad\qquad (6)$$

The volume integral is

$$\iiint_V \text{curl } \overline{F} \, dV = \int_{x=0}^{3} \int_{y=0}^{3-x} \int_{z=0}^{6-2x-2y} (\overline{j}+2y\overline{k}) dz dy dz$$

$$= \int_{x=0}^{3} \int_{y=0}^{3-x} (\overline{j}z+2yz\overline{k}) \Bigg|_{z=0}^{6-2x-2y} dydx \qquad (7)$$

$$= \int_{x=0}^{3} \int_{y=0}^{3-x} \left[\overline{j}(6-2x-2y)+\overline{k}(12y-4xy-4y^{2}) \right] dydx$$

$$= \int_{0}^{3} \left[(9-6x+x^{2})\overline{j} + \left(-\frac{2x^{3}}{3}+6x^{2}-18x+18 \right)\overline{k} \right] dx$$

$$= 9\overline{j} + \frac{27}{2} \overline{k}$$

● **PROBLEM 16-32**

Let V be the cube bounded by the surfaces x=0, x=1, y=0, y=1, z=0, z=1.

Let $\overline{F}(x,y,z)$ be the vector field

$$\overline{F}(x,y,z) = 2x\overline{i} + y\overline{j} + z^{2}\overline{k} \qquad (1)$$

1. Compute

$$\iint_{S} \overline{F} \cdot d\overline{S} \qquad (2)$$

where S is the surface of the cube.

2. Compute

$$\iiint_{V} \text{div } \overline{F} \ dV \qquad (3)$$

3. Compare the results of parts 1 and 2.

Can we reach any general conclusion?

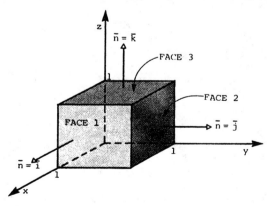

<u>Solution</u>: The cube is shown in the figure.
1. To evaluate the surface integral (2), we will evaluate

$$\iint_{S} \overline{F} \cdot d\overline{S} = \iint \overline{F} \cdot \overline{n} \ dS$$

751

for each of the six individual faces and subsequently sum the results.

For face (1) of the cube, the unit outer normal vector is $\bar{n} = \bar{i}$, so that

$$\bar{F} \cdot \bar{n} = (2x\bar{i} + y\bar{j} + z^2\bar{k}) \cdot \bar{i} = 2x = 2$$

since x=1 for this face.

Thus,

$$\iint \bar{F} \cdot \bar{n} \ dS = 2 \iint dS = 2 \tag{5}$$

for face (1).

For the face opposite to face (1), we have

$$\bar{n} = -\bar{i}, \quad \text{so} \quad \bar{F} \cdot \bar{n} = -2x = 0 \tag{6}$$

and

$$\iint \bar{F} \cdot \bar{n} \ dS = 0$$

For face (2), we have

$$\bar{n} = \bar{j}, \quad \text{so} \quad \bar{F} \cdot \bar{n} = y = 1 \quad \text{and}$$

$$\iint \bar{F} \cdot \bar{n} \ dS = \iint dS = 1 \tag{7}$$

For the face opposite to face (2),

$$\bar{n} = -\bar{j}, \quad \text{so} \quad \bar{F} \cdot \bar{n} = -y = 0 \quad \text{and}$$

$$\iint \bar{F} \cdot \bar{n} \ dS = 0 \tag{8}$$

For the face (3) we have

$$\bar{n} = \bar{k}, \quad \text{so} \quad \bar{F} \cdot \bar{n} = z^2 = 1 \quad \text{and}$$

$$\iint \bar{F} \cdot \bar{n} \ dS = \iint dS = 1 \tag{9}$$

For the face opposite to face (3), we have

$$\bar{n} = -\bar{k}, \quad \text{so} \quad \bar{F} \cdot \bar{n} = -z^2 = 0 \quad \text{and}$$

$$\iint \bar{F} \cdot \bar{n} \ dS = 0 \tag{10}$$

Adding the results for all the faces of the cube results in

$$\iint_S \bar{F} \cdot \bar{n} \ dS = 2 + 1 + 1 = 4 \tag{11}$$

2. To evaluate the volume integral (3), we will first evaluate div $\bar{F}$

$$\text{div } \bar{F} = 2 + 1 + 2z = 3 + 2z \tag{12}$$

The volume integral is

$$\iiint\limits_V \text{div } \overline{F} \text{ dV} = \int_{x=0}^{1} \int_{y=0}^{1} \int_{z=0}^{1} (3+2z)dzdydx$$

$$= \int_{x=0}^{1} \int_{y=0}^{1} 4 \text{ dy dx} = 4 \tag{13}$$

3. For the cube shown in the figure and the vector field $\overline{F}$ given in eq.(1), we conclude, from eqs.(11) and (13), that

$$\iint\limits_S \overline{F} \cdot d\overline{S} = \iiint\limits_V \text{div } \overline{F} \text{ dV} \tag{14}$$

Later on it will be shown that eq.(14) is true for any bounded domain and any vector field.

• **PROBLEM 16-33**

1. Let V be a domain of volume v and S the boundary of this domain. Evaluate the integral

$$\iint\limits_S \overline{F} \cdot d\overline{S} \tag{1}$$

where

$$\overline{F}(x,y,z) = e^y \overline{i} + xz \overline{j} + 3z\overline{k} \tag{2}$$

2. Evaluate the integral

$$\iint\limits_S \overline{F} \cdot d\overline{S} \tag{3}$$

where

$$\overline{F}(x,y,z) = y^2\overline{i} + 2z\overline{j} + \sin x \, \overline{k} \tag{4}$$

and S is given by the equation

$$x^2 + y^2 + z^2 = 9 \tag{5}$$

Solution: 1. Notice that integral (1) cannot be evaluated directly since we do not know the form, or equation, of the surface at hand. The integral may be computed however, by using the identity

$$\iint\limits_S \overline{F} \cdot d\overline{S} = \iiint\limits_V \text{div } \overline{F} \text{ dV} \tag{6}$$

We can evaluate the surface integral (2) by evaluating the above volume integral.

Now, for div $\overline{F}$, we obtain

$$\text{div } \overline{F} = \left(\frac{\partial}{\partial x} \overline{i} + \frac{\partial}{\partial y} \overline{j} + \frac{\partial}{\partial z} \overline{k} \right) \cdot (e^y\overline{i} + xz\overline{j} + 3z\overline{k})$$

753

$$= \frac{\partial}{\partial x} (e^y) + \frac{\partial}{\partial y} (xz) + \frac{\partial}{\partial z} (3z) \qquad (7)$$

$$= 3$$

Thus, the volume integral in eq.(6) becomes

$$\iiint_V \text{div } \overline{F} \text{ } dV = 3 \iiint_V dV = 3v \qquad (8)$$

The surface integral is therefore

$$\iint_S \overline{F} \cdot d\overline{S} = 3v \qquad (9)$$

2. In this case, we do have the equation of the surface, and we can evaluate

$$\iint_S \overline{F} \cdot d\overline{S} = \iint_S \overline{F} \cdot \overline{n} \text{ } dS$$

by determining the unit normal vector $\overline{n}$, taking the dot product with $\overline{F}$ and then integrating. There is however, a simpler, faster way of evaluating this integral.

Let us again consider the identity

$$\iint_S \overline{F} \cdot d\overline{S} = \iiint_V \text{div } \overline{F} \text{ } dV$$

If we evaluate div $\overline{F}$, we obtain

$$\text{div } \overline{F} = \left[\frac{\partial}{\partial x} \overline{i} + \frac{\partial}{\partial y} \overline{j} + \frac{\partial}{\partial z} \overline{k} \right] \cdot \left[y^2 \overline{i} + 2z\overline{j} + \sin x\overline{k} \right]$$

$$= \frac{\partial}{\partial x} (y^2) + \frac{\partial}{\partial y} (2z) + \frac{\partial}{\partial z} (\sin x)$$

$$= 0$$

Thus,
$$\iiint_V \text{div } \overline{F} \text{ } dV = 0$$

and
$$\iint_S \overline{F} \cdot d\overline{S} = \iiint_V \text{div } \overline{F} \text{ } dV = 0$$

● **PROBLEM 16-34**

Evaluate the integral

$$\iiint_V \frac{dxdydz}{\sqrt{(x-2)^2+(y+4)^2+z^2}} \qquad (1)$$

where V is the interior of the sphere

$$x^2+y^2+z^2 = 4 \qquad\qquad (2)$$

Use Gauss' law and interpret integral (1) as a potential.

Solution: First, let us note that the potential at a point B is given by

$$\phi(B) = \iiint\limits_{V} \frac{\sigma \; dxdydz}{\sqrt{(x-a)^2+(y-b)^2+(z-c)^2}} \qquad (3)$$

Here, v represents the volume enclosed by a sphere, σ denotes the charge density (the charge is distributed throughout the volume) and (x_0,y_0,z_0) denotes the coordinates of point B.

Noticing that integral (1) is nothing more than the potential at the point B(2,-4,0) with charge density $\sigma=1$, we have

$$\phi(B) = \iiint\limits_{V} \frac{dxdydz}{\sqrt{(x-2)^2+(y+4)^2+z^2}}$$

Here, the volume is enclosed by the sphere

$$x^2+y^2+z^2 = 4$$

which is of radius 2.

Now, if there is a point charge q at a point A, then the potential at a point B is

$$\phi(B) = \frac{q}{r_1} \qquad\qquad (4)$$

where r_1 is the distance between points A and B (see the figure).

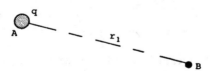

From Gauss' law, we could verify that the potential at a point B due to a uniformly charged sphere is the same as the potential due to a point charge located at the center of the sphere whose charge is equal to that of the sphere.

Since the total charge enclosed by the sphere is nothing more than

$$q = V\sigma = \frac{4}{3}\pi r^3\sigma = \frac{4}{3}\pi(2)^3(1) = \frac{32}{3}\pi \qquad (5)$$

we conclude, from eq.(4), that the potential at B is

$$\phi = \iiint\limits_{V} \frac{dxdydz}{\sqrt{(x-2)^2+(y+4)^2+z^2}} = \frac{q}{r_1} = \frac{32\pi}{\sqrt{2^2+4^2}} = \frac{32}{3\sqrt{20}}\pi$$

Note that r_1 is the distance from point B to the center of the sphere.

Consider a region of space V bounded by a surface S. This region contains an electric charge of density $\rho(x,y,z)$. The total charge in this region is

$$q = \iiint_V \rho(x,y,z)dV \qquad (1)$$

Gauss' law of electrostatics states that

$$\iint_S \bar{E} \cdot d\bar{S} = \frac{q}{\varepsilon_0} \qquad (2)$$

where ε_0 is constant and $\bar{E}$ is the electrostatic field.

What is the relationship between the divergence of $\bar{E}$ and the charge density ρ?

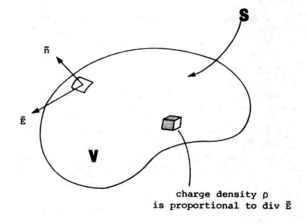

charge density ρ
is proportional to div $\bar{E}$

<u>Solution</u>: The total electric charge in the region V is

$$q = \iiint_V \rho(x,y,z)dV \qquad (3)$$

Combining eq.(3) with eq.(2), we have

$$\iint_S \bar{E} \cdot d\bar{S} = \frac{q}{\varepsilon_0} = \frac{1}{\varepsilon_0} \iiint_V \rho(x,y,z)dV \qquad (4)$$

Now, the following identity relates the surface integral to the volume integral

$$\iint_S \bar{E} \cdot d\bar{S} = \iiint_V \text{div } \bar{E} \, dV \qquad (5)$$

Here, V is the region bounded by the surface S.

Combining eqs.(4) and (5) results in

$$\iint_S \overline{E} \cdot d\overline{S} = \iiint_V \text{div } \overline{E} \, dV = \frac{1}{\varepsilon_0} \iiint_V \rho(x,y,z)dV \qquad (6)$$

Thus, we obtain

$$\text{div } \overline{E} = \frac{1}{\varepsilon_0} \rho \, , \qquad (7)$$

which is one of Maxwell's equations. It relates the divergence of the electric field vector $\overline{E}$ to the charge density ρ.

We often use

$$\varepsilon_0 = \frac{1}{4\pi k} \qquad (8)$$

Eq.(7) becomes

$$\text{div } \overline{E} = 4\pi k \rho \qquad (9)$$

CHAPTER 17

GREEN'S THEOREM IN THE PLANE

INTRODUCTION

By far, the most important, and probably most interesting part of vector analysis consists of the three theorems known as Green's theorem, Stokes' theorem and Gauss' theorem, also called the divergence theorem. To some extent, everything that is covered in this book up to now may be regarded as a lengthy preliminary to the heart of the book - the three fundamental theorems.

It is customary, convenient and logical to first introduce Green's theorem, since it provides a good base for the other two theorems. Indeed, in a way, Gauss' theorem and Stokes' theorem can be regarded as an extension of Green's theorem. Green's theorem states that if F_1 and F_2 are continuously differentiable functions defined on a domain D, and if R is a region contained in D, then

$$\iint\limits_{R} \left(\frac{\partial F_2}{\partial x} - \frac{\partial F_1}{\partial y} \right) dxdy = \oint\limits_{C} F_1 dx + F_2 dy$$

Here, C is the boundary of R. Note that Green's theorem enables us to evaluate a double integral over a region by actually computing a single line integral over the boundary of the region.

Green's theorem, named after the English mathematical physicist George Green (1793-1841), has numerous physical applications - particularly in theoretical physics. Some of these applications are presented in this chapter.

It should be noted that the theorems of Green, Stokes and Gauss are highly useful. Indeed, what might appear to be a difficult problem may, with the use of the proper theorem, be reduced to a simple exercise.

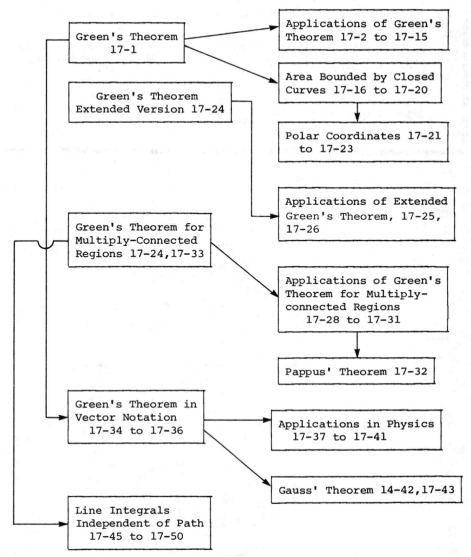

This chart is provided to facilitate rapid understanding of the inter-relationships of the topics and subject matter in this chapter. Also shown are the problem numbers associated with the subject matter.

GREEN'S THEOREM, APPLICATIONS AND VERIFICATION OF GREEN'S THEOREM

● PROBLEM 17-1

Let D be a domain of the xy-plane and let C be a piece-wise smooth simple closed curve in D whose interior is in D. R is the closed region bounded by C such that R can be described by both forms

$$a \leq x \leq b, \ f_1(x) \leq y \leq f_2(x) \qquad (1)$$
$$c \leq y \leq d, \ g_1(y) \leq x \leq g_2(y), \qquad (2)$$

as shown in Fig. 1. Prove Green's theorem for R.

<u>Green's Theorem</u>

If $P(x,y)$ and $Q(x,y)$ are defined and are continuous functions having continuous first partial derivatives in D, then

$$\oint_C Pdx + Qdy = \iint_R \left(\frac{\partial Q}{\partial x} - \frac{\partial P}{\partial y}\right) dxdy \tag{3}$$

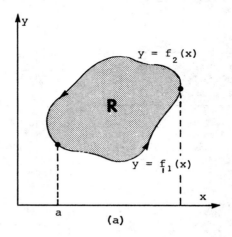

(a)

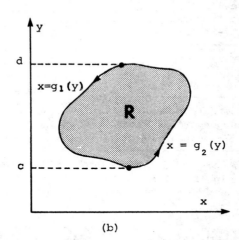

(b)

<u>Solution</u>: The right-hand side of the double integral of eq. (3) may be written in the iterated form

$$\iint_R \frac{\partial P}{\partial y} dxdy = \int_a^b dx \int_{f_1(x)}^{f_2(x)} \frac{\partial P}{\partial y} dy \tag{4}$$

where region R is described by the inequality in eq.(1) (see Fig. 1(a)).

Integration of eq.(4) leads to

$$\int_a^b dx \int_{f_1(x)}^{f_2(x)} \frac{\partial P}{\partial y} dy = \int_a^b \left[P(x,f_2(x)) - P(x,f_1(x)) \right] dx$$

$$= -\int_b^a P(x,f_2(x))dx - \int_a^b P(x,f_1(x))dx$$

$$= - \oint_C P(x,y)dx$$

Thus,

$$\iint_R \frac{\partial P}{\partial y} dxdy = - \oint_C P(x,y)dx \tag{5}$$

Now, if region R is described by the inequality in eq.(2) (see Fig. 1(b)), then we may write

$$\iint_R \frac{\partial Q}{\partial x} dxdy = \int_c^d dy \int_{g_1(y)}^{g_2(y)} \frac{\partial Q}{\partial x} dx$$

$$= \int_c^d \left[Q(g_2(y),y) - Q(g_1(y),y) \right] dy$$

$$= \int_c^d Q(g_2(y),y)dy + \int_d^c Q(g_1(y),y)dy$$

$$= \oint_C Q(x,y)dy$$

Thus,

$$\iint_R \frac{\partial Q}{\partial x} dxdy = \oint_C Q(x,y)dy \tag{6}$$

Adding the two double integrals in eqs.(5) and (6) results in

$$\oint_C Pdx + Qdy = \iint_R \left(\frac{\partial Q}{\partial x} - \frac{\partial P}{\partial y} \right) dxdy \tag{7}$$

which completes the proof.

Let us note that we proved Green's theorem for special regions R in the plane, described by eqs.(1) and (2). Here C is a closed curve such that any straight line parallel to the coordinate axes cuts C in at most two points.

Let

$$P(x,y) = x^2y^3 + y \cos x \qquad (1)$$

$$Q(x,y) = x^3y^2 + \sin x$$

and let C be the circle

$$x^2 + y^2 = 1 \qquad (2)$$

Evaluate the integral

$$\oint_C Pdx + Qdy \qquad (3)$$

Solution: Since the functions P and Q are continuous and have continuous first partial derivatives, and since the curve C is closed, we could use Green's theorem,

$$\oint_C Pdx + Qdy = \iint_R \left(\frac{\partial Q}{\partial x} - \frac{\partial P}{\partial y} \right) dxdy \qquad (4)$$

as a means of solution.

In this case, the closed curve C is a unit circle $x^2 + y^2 = 1$, and region R is the interior of the circle (see the figure).

Now, we have, from (1),

$$\frac{\partial Q}{\partial x} = 3x^2y^2 + \cos x , \quad \frac{\partial P}{\partial y} = 3x^2y^2 + \cos x \qquad (5)$$

Thus, applying Green's theorem, we obtain

$$\oint_C Pdx + Qdy = \oint_{x^2+y^2=1} (x^2y^3+y\cos x)dx + (x^3y^2+\sin x)dy$$

$$= \iint_R \left(\frac{\partial Q}{\partial x} - \frac{\partial P}{\partial y} \right) dxdy \qquad (6)$$

$$= \iint_R (3x^2y^2 + \cos x - 3x^2y^2 - \cos x)dxdy = 0$$

Note that Green's theorem was extremely useful in solving this problem. Indeed, rather than going through the tedious work of solving the line integral

$$\oint Pdx+Qdy = \oint_{x^2+y^2=1} (x^2y^3+y\cos x)dx + (x^3y^2+\sin x)dx$$

we were able to obtain a simple, fast result.

It is not always advantageous, however, to use Green's theorem as a means of solution. Whenever the assumptions of the theorem are fulfilled, then the equality does hold,

$$\oint Pdx+Qdy = \iint_R \left(\frac{\partial Q}{\partial x} - \frac{\partial P}{\partial y}\right) dxdy$$

Before going through any calculations, however, we should decide which side of the equation is simplest to compute.

In this problem, since

$$\frac{\partial Q}{\partial x} - \frac{\partial P}{\partial y} = 0$$

it was clearly more advantageous to evaluate

$$\iint_R \left(\frac{\partial Q}{\partial x} - \frac{\partial P}{\partial y}\right) dxdy.$$

● **PROBLEM** 17-3

Verify Green's theorem in the plane for

$$\oint_C (x^2y + y)dx + y^2dy \qquad (1)$$

where C is the closed curve shown in the figure.

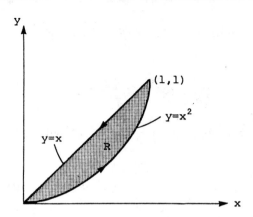

Solution: Before attempting to verify the theorem, we must first check if the conditions, or assumptions, of the theorem are satisfied (see Problem 17-1). We have:

C is a piecewise smooth curve (since it consists of two smooth curves).

Any straight line parallel to the coordinate axes cuts C in at most two points.

Functions $P = x^2y+y$ and $Q = y^2$ are continuous in R and have continuous first partial derivatives.

From the above, we conclude that Green's theorem,

$$\oint_C Pdx + Qdy = \iint_R \left(\frac{\partial Q}{\partial x} - \frac{\partial P}{\partial y}\right) dxdy \tag{2}$$

is applicable.

Now, to verify theorem (2), we will evaluate both sides of the equation and subsequently show that they are equal.

For the line integral

$$\oint_C Pdx + Qdy = \oint_C (x^2y+y)dx + y^2dy$$

(from here on we will elect not to include the arrow indicating the positive direction), we have that the line integral along $y = x^2$ equals

$$\int_{y=x^2} Pdx + Qdy = \int_{y=x^2} (x^4+x^2)dx + x^4 2xdx$$

$$= \int_0^1 (2x^5+x^4+x^2)dx = \frac{13}{15} \tag{3}$$

and along $y = x$,

$$\int_{y=x} Pdx + Qdy = \int_{y=x} (x^3+x)dx + x^2dx = \int_1^0 (x^3+x^2+x)dx$$

$$= -\frac{13}{12} \tag{4}$$

Thus,

$$\oint_C (x^2y+y)dx + y^2dy = \frac{13}{15} - \frac{13}{12} = \frac{-39}{180} \tag{5}$$

Now, since

$$\frac{\partial P}{\partial y} = x^2 + 1, \quad \frac{\partial Q}{\partial x} = 0,$$

we obtain

$$\iint_R \left(\frac{\partial Q}{\partial x} - \frac{\partial P}{\partial y}\right) dxdy = \iint_R (-x^2 - 1)dxdy$$

$$= \int_0^1 dx \int_{x^2}^x (-x^2-1)dy = \int_0^1 (x^4-x^3+x^2-x)dx \tag{6}$$

$$= \frac{1}{5} - \frac{1}{4} + \frac{1}{3} - \frac{1}{2} = \frac{-39}{140}$$

and the theorem is verified.

Verify Green's theorem in the plane for

$$\oint_C (4x^3+2y^2)dx + (4xy+e^y)dy \qquad (1)$$

where C is the boundary of the region between $y = x^2$ and $y = \sqrt{x}$.

<u>Solution</u>: The region R is shown in Fig. 1.

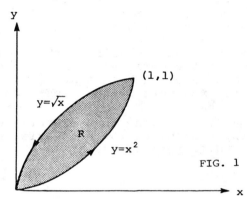

FIG. 1

Now, since both functions

$$P(x,y) = 4x^3 + 2y^2$$
$$Q(x,y) = 4xy + e^y$$

are continuous and have continuous first partial derivatives, and since any straight line parallel to the coordinate axes cuts the smooth curve C in at most two points, we see that the conditions for Green's theorem are satisfied.

Now, to verify the theorem, let us first evaluate the integral

$$\iint_R \left(\frac{\partial Q}{\partial x} - \frac{\partial P}{\partial y}\right) dxdy \qquad (2)$$

Since

$$\frac{\partial Q}{\partial x} = \frac{\partial}{\partial x} (4xy + e^y) = 4y \qquad (3)$$

and

$$\frac{\partial P}{\partial y} = \frac{\partial}{\partial y} (4x^3 + 2y^2) = 4y \qquad (4)$$

integral (2) equals

$$\iint_R \left(\frac{\partial Q}{\partial x} - \frac{\partial P}{\partial y}\right) dxdy = 0 \qquad (5)$$

Next, we evaluate the line integral

$$\oint (4x^3+2y^2)dx + (4xy+e^y)dy$$

$$= \int_{y=x^2} (4x^3+2x^4)\,dx + (4x^3+e^{x^2})2x\,dx$$

$$+ \int_{y=\sqrt{x}} (4x^3+2x)\,dx + (4x\sqrt{x}+e^{\sqrt{x}})\,\frac{dx}{2\sqrt{x}} \tag{6}$$

$$= \int_0^1 (10x^4+4x^3+2xe^{x^2})\,dx + \int_1^0 \left(4x^3+4x+\frac{e^{\sqrt{x}}}{2\sqrt{x}}\right)dx$$

$$= (2x^5+x^4+e^{x^2}) \Big|_{x=0}^{1} + (x^4+2x^2+e^{\sqrt{x}}) \Big|_{x=1}^{0} = 0$$

Thus, the theorem is verified.

Thus far we have been dealing with Green's theorem in the plane in its most restricted form. The region R bounded by the curve C has to be such that any straight line parallel to the coordinate axes cuts C in at most two points, see Fig. 2.

Note that region R_1 meets the requirements, while R_2 doesn't. The straight line p parallel to the y-axis intersects the curve C_2 at four different points.

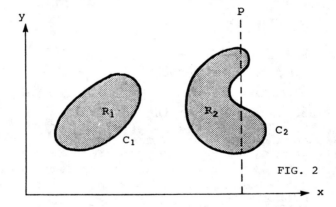

FIG. 2

What is the relationship between the above requirement and the requirement that the region R be a convex set?

A convex set may be defined as a set such that for any two points in the set, the line segment joining these two points must also belong to the set.

● **PROBLEM** 17-5

Using Green's theorem, evaluate the integral

$$\oint_C ay\,dx + bx\,dy \tag{1}$$

along any closed curve C.

Solution: Let us first assume that C is such that any straight line parallel to the coordinate axes cuts C in at most two points.

Since both functions

$$P(x,y) = ay$$

$$Q(x,y) = bx$$

are continuous and have continuous first partial derivatives, Green's theorem is applicable. Thus,

$$\oint_C aydx + bxdy = \iint_R (b - a)dxdy$$

$$= (b - a)\iint_R dxdy \qquad (2)$$

Now, since $\iint_R dxdy$ represents the area S enclosed by C (the area of the region), we have

$$\oint_C aydx + bxdy = (b - a) \cdot S \qquad (3)$$

● **PROBLEM 17-6**

Evaluate the integral

$$\oint_C (6x+2y)dx + (5x-3y)dy \qquad (1)$$

where C is the ellipse

$$9x^2 + y^2 = 9 \qquad (2)$$

traversed in the positive direction.

Solution: Obviously, both functions $P(x,y) = 6x+2y$ and $Q(x,y) = 5x-3y$ are continuous. The curve C represented by eq. (2) meets the requirements of Green's theorem. Therefore, to evaluate integral (1) we can apply Green's theorem.

$$\oint_C (6x+2y)dx + (5x-3y)dy$$

$$= \iint_R \left[\frac{\partial}{\partial x} (5x-3y) - \frac{\partial}{\partial y} (6x+2y) \right] dxdy \qquad (3)$$

$$= \iint_R (5-2)dxdy = 3 \iint_R dxdy$$

The integral $\iint\limits_{R} dxdy$ represents the area of the ellipse. Its semi-axes are $a = 1$, $b = 3$. The area of the ellipse is

$$A = \pi \, ab = 3\pi \tag{4}$$

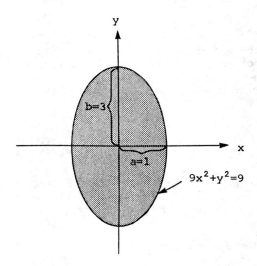

The value of integral (1) is thus

$$\oint\limits_{C} (6x+2y)dx + (5x-3y)dy$$

$$= 3 \iint\limits_{R} dxdy = 3(3\pi) = 9\pi \tag{5}$$

● **PROBLEM 17-7**

Evaluate the integral

$$\oint\limits_{C} (3x+4y)dx + (x-3y)dy \tag{1}$$

where C is a circle of radius a.

Solution: Both functions in integral (1) are continuous and have continuous first partial derivatives.
     Also, the curve C meets the assumptions of Green's theorem. Thus, integral (1), which is a line integral, can be transformed into a double integral.

$$\oint\limits_{C} (3x+4y)dx + (x-3y)dy$$

$$= \iint\limits_{R} (1 - 4)dxdy = -3 \iint\limits_{R} dxdy \tag{2}$$

768

Here $\iint\limits_R$ dxdy is the area of the circle C. Thus

$$\iint\limits_R dxdy = \pi a^2 \qquad (3)$$

and

$$\oint\limits_C (3x+4y)dx + (x-3y)dy = -3\pi a^2 \qquad (4)$$

Note that the value of integral (1) does not depend on the position of the center of the circle C.

● **PROBLEM** 17-8

Let C be a circle of radius three with center at the origin of the xy-plane. Evaluate the integral

$$\oint\limits_C (2x^2+y^2)dx + (2xy^2+5y^2)dy \qquad (1)$$

<u>Solution</u>: Since the functions

$$P(x,y) = 2x^2 + y^2$$
$$Q(x,y) = 2xy^2 + 5y^2 \qquad (2)$$

are continuous and have continuous first partial derivatives within the region R bounded by C, we conclude that Green's theorem is applicable.

Integral (1) becomes

$$\oint\limits_C (2x^2+y^2)dx + (2xy^2+5y^2)dy$$

$$= \iint\limits_R \left[\frac{\partial}{\partial x} (2xy^2+5y^2) - \frac{\partial}{\partial y} (2x^2+y^2) \right] dxdy$$

$$= \iint\limits_R (2y^2 - 2y)dxdy \qquad (3)$$

Transforming into polar coordinates,

$$x = r \cos\theta$$
$$y = r \sin\theta \qquad (4)$$

integral (3) becomes

$$\iint\limits_R (2y^2-2y)dxdy = \int_0^{2\pi}\int_0^3 (2r^2\sin^2\theta - 2r\sin\theta)drd\theta$$

769

$$= \int_0^{2\pi} \left(\frac{2}{3} r^3 \sin^2\theta - r^2\sin\theta \right) \Bigg|_{r=0}^{3} d\theta \qquad (5)$$

$$= \int_0^{2\pi} (18 \sin^2\theta - 9 \sin\theta)d\theta$$

Since $\int \sin^2\theta d\theta = \frac{\theta}{2} - \frac{1}{4} \sin 2\theta,$ (6)

integral (5) becomes

$$\int_0^{2\pi} (18 \sin^2\theta - 9 \sin\theta)d\theta$$

$$= 18 \left[\frac{\theta}{2} - \frac{1}{4} \sin2\theta \right] \Bigg|_{\theta=0}^{2\pi} + 9 \cos\theta \Bigg|_{\theta=0}^{2\pi} \qquad (7)$$

$$= 18\pi$$

● **PROBLEM 17-9**

Evaluate the integral

$$\oint_C (x^2+y^2)dx + (2xy+3)dy \qquad (1)$$

where C is the boundary of the region defined by

$$y^2 = 2x \quad \text{and} \quad x = 8 \qquad (2)$$

1. directly from (1)
2. using Green's theorem.

Solution: 1. The region R bounded by $y^2 = 2x$ and $x = 8$ is shown in the figure.

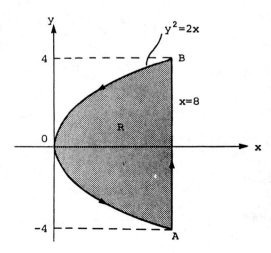

The line integral from A to B is equal to

$$\int_A^B (x^2+y^2)dx + (2xy+3)dy = \int_{-4}^4 (16y+3)dy = 24 \qquad (3)$$

From B to 0 and from 0 to A,

$$\int_B^0 (x^2+y^2)dx + (2xy+3)dy + \int_0^A (x^2+y^2)dx + (2xy+3)dy$$

$$= \int_8^0 (x^2+2x)dx + (2x\sqrt{2x}+3) \cdot \frac{\sqrt{2}}{2\sqrt{x}} dx \qquad (4)$$

$$+ \int_0^8 (x^2+2x)dx + (-2x\sqrt{2x}+3) \cdot \frac{-\sqrt{2}}{2\sqrt{x}} dx$$

$$= -\int_0^8 \frac{3\sqrt{2}}{\sqrt{x}} dx = -24$$

Thus, summing up eqs.(3) and (4) results in

$$\oint (x^2+y^2)dx + (2xy+3)dy = 24-24 = 0 \qquad (5)$$

2. The assumptions of Green's theorem are fulfilled. We have,

$$\oint_C (x^2+y^2)dx + (2xy+3)dy$$

$$= \iint_R (2y-2y)dxdy = 0 \qquad (6)$$

Notice that both methods do, of course, lead to the same result. The application of Green's theorem significantly reduces calculations.

● **PROBLEM** 17-10

Evaluate the integral

$$\int_{(0,0)}^{(\pi,2)} (2x^2+3y^2)dx + (6xy+4y^2)dy \qquad (1)$$

along the cycloid

$$x = \theta - \sin\theta$$
$$y = 1 - \cos\theta \qquad (2)$$

Solution: The above line integral (1) could be solved directly (though extremely tediously) by transforming integral (1) into polar coordinate form through the use of eqs. (2).

Green's theorem, however, provides a simpler, less complicated solution route.

It is required to evaluate integral (1) along the portion OB of the cycloid (see the figure).

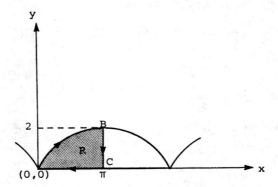

By constructing lines BC and CO, we obtain the region R bounded by curve OBC, as shown. Applying Green's theorem yields

$$\int_{OCBO} (2x^2+3y^2)dx + (6xy+4y^2)dy$$

$$= \iint_R \left(\frac{\partial}{\partial x} \left[6xy+4y^2 \right] - \frac{\partial}{\partial y} \left[2x^2+3y^2 \right] \right) dxdy$$

$$= \iint_R (6y - 6y)dxdy = 0 \qquad (3)$$

Notice that the counterclockwise direction is always the positive direction, and that is why we evaluated the integral along OCBO. Since we want to evaluate the integral along the cycloid (along portion OB to be exact), we must proceed in the clockwise direction OBCO (the negative direction) as shown in the figure. However, it is obvious that since

$$\oint_{OCBO} = - \oint_{OBCO}$$

we conclude (from (3)) that

$$\oint_{OBCO} = 0 \qquad (4)$$

Now, since

$$\int_{OBCO} = \int_O^B + \int_B^C + \int_C^O \qquad (5)$$

we obtain, from (4), that

$$0 = \int_0^B + \int_B^C + \int_C^0$$

Now, since the line integral along paths BC and CO are easily calculable, we obtain

$$\int_B^C (2x^2+3y^2)dx + (6xy+4y^2)dy$$

$$= \int_2^0 (6\pi y+4y^2)dy = -\left[3\pi y^2 + \frac{4}{3}y^3\right]\Big|_0^2 = -12\pi - \frac{32}{3} \qquad (6)$$

and

$$\int_C^0 (2x^2+3y^2)dx + (6xy+4y^2)dy$$

$$= \int_\pi^0 2x^2 dx = -\frac{2}{3}x^3\Big|_0^\pi = -\frac{2}{3}\pi^3 \qquad (7)$$

Thus, from (5), we obtain

$$\int_{0(0,0)}^{B(\pi,2)} (2x^2+3y^2)dx + (6xy+4y^2)dy = -12\pi - \frac{32}{3} + \frac{2}{3}\pi^3$$

● **PROBLEM 17-11**

Evaluate the integral

$$\oint_C (\sin x + 3y^2)dx + e^y dy \qquad (1)$$

where C is the square with vertices (1,1), (1,-1), (-1,-1), (-1,1).

Solution: From Green's theorem, we obtain

$$\oint_C (\sin x + 3y^2)dx + e^y dy = -\iint_R 6y\,dxdy \qquad (2)$$

$$= -\int_{-1}^1 dx \int_{-1}^1 6y\,dy = -\int_{-1}^1 (1-1)dx = 0$$

There is a faster method of evaluating the integral

$$-\iint_R 6y\,dxdy.$$

Recall that the center of mass $(\bar{x},\bar{y})$ of a thin plate of unit density is

$$\bar{x} = \frac{1}{M} \iint_R x \; dxdy \qquad (3)$$

$$\bar{y} = \frac{1}{M} \iint_R y \; dxdy \qquad (4)$$

where M is the total mass of R.

In our case, the center of mass of the square is $\bar{x} = 0$, $\bar{y} = 0$. Thus

$$-\iint_R 6y \; dxdy = -6M\bar{y} = 0 \qquad (5)$$

● **PROBLEM 17-12**

Evaluate the integral

$$\oint e^x \sin y \; dx + \sin x \cos y \; dy \qquad (1)$$

around the rectangle having vertices $(0,0)$, $(\pi,0)$, (π,π), $(0,\pi)$.

Solution: The rectangle is shown in the figure.

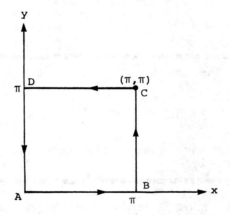

Application of Green's Theorem to integral (1) results in

$$\oint e^x \sin y \; dx + \sin x \cos y \; dy = \iint (\cos x \cos y - e^x \cos y) dx dy$$

$$= \int_0^\pi \int_0^\pi (\cos x \cos y - e^x \cos y) dx dy = \int_0^\pi \int_0^\pi (\cos x - e^x) \cos y \, dx dy$$

$$= \int_0^\pi (\cos x - e^x) \left[\sin y \Big|_0^\pi \right] dx = 0 \qquad (2)$$

In this case, the line integral is also easy to evaluate.

$$\oint e^x \sin y \; dx + \sin x \cos y \; dy = \int_A^B e^x \sin y \; dx$$

774

$$+ \int_{B}^{C} \sin x \ \cos y \, dy + \int_{C}^{D} e^{x} \sin y \, dx + \int_{D}^{A} \sin x \ \cos y \, dy \qquad (3)$$

$$= 0 + 0 + 0 + 0 = 0$$

● **PROBLEM 17-13**

Evaluate the integral

$$\oint (4x^2 + 3\sin y) dx + (3x\cos y + 4x) dy \qquad (1)$$

around the parallelogram having vertices (0,0), (4,0), (5,2) and (1,2).

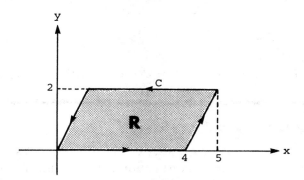

Solution: Both functions
$$P = (4x^2 + 3\sin y) \qquad Q = (3x\cos y + 4x)$$

are continuous and have continuous first partial derivatives.
Therefore, we can use Green's theorem,

$$\oint_{C} P dx + Q dy = \iint_{R} \left(\frac{\partial Q}{\partial x} - \frac{\partial P}{\partial y} \right) dx dy$$

as a means of solution.
Applying the theorem, we obtain

$$\oint (4x^2 + 3\sin y) dx + (3x\cos y + 4x) dy$$

$$= \iint_{R} \left[\frac{\partial}{\partial x} (3x\cos y + 4x) - \frac{\partial}{\partial y} (4x^2 + 3\sin y) \right] dx dy$$

$$= \iint_{R} (3\cos y + 4 - 3\cos y) dx dy$$

$$= 4 \iint_{R} dx dy \qquad (2)$$

Now, notice that the integral $\iint_{R} dx dy$ is nothing more than the area of the parallelogram, which is

$$\iint_R dxdy = 4 \times 2 = 8 \tag{3}$$

Therefore,

$$\oint (4x^2+3\sin y)dx + (3x\cos y+4x)dy$$

$$= 4 \cdot 8 = 32 \tag{4}$$

● **PROBLEM 17-14**

Evaluate

$$\oint e^x \sin y\, dx + (e^x\cos y+3x)dy \tag{1}$$

around the rectangle with vertices (0,0), (1,0), (1,e), (0,e).

Solution: Since both functions

$$P(x,y) = e^x\sin y, \quad Q(x,y) = e^x\cos y + 3x$$

are continuous and have continuous first partial derivatives, we can apply Green's theorem,

$$\oint_C Pdx + Qdy = \iint_R \left(\frac{\partial Q}{\partial x} - \frac{\partial P}{\partial y}\right) dxdy.$$

In this case,

$$\frac{\partial P}{\partial y} = e^x\cos y \quad \frac{\partial Q}{\partial x} = e^x\cos y + 3$$

Thus,

$$\oint e^x\sin y\, dx + (e^x\cos y + 3x)dy$$

$$= \iint_R (e^x\cos y + 3 - e^x\cos y)dxdy \tag{2}$$

$$= \iint_R 3dxdy$$

The area of the rectangle is

$$A = \iint_R dxdy = e \tag{3}$$

Thus,

$$\oint e^x\sin y\, dx + (e^x\cos y + 3x)dy = 3e \tag{4}$$

In this chapter, we have used the notation

$$\oint_C P\,dx + Q\,dy \tag{5}$$

The arrow in integral (5) indicates one of two possible directions. The counterclockwise arrow refers to a counterclockwise direction on C. This is termed the positive direction. The clockwise direction is called the negative direction. For simplicity, whenever the direction is positive we neglect writing the arrow, thus

$$\oint_C F\,dx + G\,dy = \oint_C F\,dx + G\,dy \tag{6}$$

● **PROBLEM 17-15**

Why is Green's theorem not applicable to the integral

$$\oint_C \frac{y}{x^2+y^2}\,dx - \frac{x}{x^2+y^2}\,dy \tag{1}$$

where C is the ellipse $x^2 + 4y^2 = 4$? $\tag{2}$

Solution: Green's theorem deals with functions which are defined, are continuous and have continuous first partial derivatives in some domain D.

Both functions $\dfrac{y}{x^2+y^2}$ and $\dfrac{-x}{x^2+y^2}$ are not continuous at the origin. The origin is located within the ellipse C

$$x^2 + 4y^2 = 4 \tag{3}$$

Thus, both functions are not continuous within the closed region bounded by C, and we conclude that Green's theorem is not applicable. In this case, thoughtless application of Green's theorem would have led to an incorrect answer.

AREA BOUNDED BY A CLOSED CURVE, POLAR COORDINATES

● **PROBLEM 17-16**

Show by Green's theorem that the area bounded by a simple closed curve C is given by

1. area $= \oint_C x\,dy = -\oint y\,dx$ $\tag{1}$

2. area $= \dfrac{1}{2}\oint x\,dy - y\,dx$ $\tag{2}$

Solution: 1. Let C be a simple closed curve and D a region in the xy-plane bounded by C. The area of D is given by

$$\iint_D dxdy \qquad (3)$$

Applying Green's theorem to eq.(3) results in

$$\iint_D dxdy = \iint_D \left(\frac{\partial Q}{\partial x} - \frac{\partial P}{\partial y}\right) dxdy$$

$$= \oint_C Pdx + Qdy \qquad (4)$$

Further, let us assume that Q = 0. In this case

$$\frac{\partial P}{\partial y} = -1 \qquad (5)$$

and

$$P = -y \qquad (6)$$

From eqs.(4) and (6), we obtain

$$\text{area of D} = \iint_D dxdy = - \oint_C ydx \qquad (7)$$

If, on the other hand, P = 0, then

$$\frac{\partial Q}{\partial x} = 1 \qquad (8)$$

and

$$Q = x$$

Thus, eq.(4) becomes

$$\text{area of D} = \iint_D dxdy = \oint_C xdy \qquad (9)$$

2. Adding eqs.(7) and (9) results in

$$\text{area of D} = \frac{1}{2} \oint_C xdy - ydx \qquad (10)$$

● PROBLEM 17-17

Compute the area of the ellipse

$$x = a \cos\theta$$

$$y = b \sin\theta \qquad (1)$$

Solution: An expression for the area of a region bounded by a simple closed curve C is

$$\text{area} = \oint_C xdy \qquad (2)$$

or

$$\text{area} = \frac{1}{2} \oint_C x dy - y dx \qquad (3)$$

The above results are directly obtainable from Green's theorem (see Problem 17-12).

Let us use both eqs.(2) and (3) as a means of solution. From (1), the differentials are

$$dx = -a \sin\theta d\theta \qquad (4)$$

$$dy = b \cos\theta \, d\theta \qquad (5)$$

Thus, using eq.(2), we obtain

$$\text{area} = A = \oint_C x dy = \int_0^{2\pi} a \cos\theta \, b \cos\theta d\theta$$

$$= ab \int_0^{2\pi} \cos^2\theta d\theta = ab \left[\frac{\theta}{2} + \frac{1}{4} \sin2\theta \right] \Big|_{\theta=0}^{2\pi} \qquad (6)$$

$$= \pi ab$$

We can verify our result by using eq.(3),

$$\text{area} = A = \frac{1}{2} \oint_C x dy - y dx$$

$$= \frac{1}{2} \int_0^{2\pi} a\cos\theta \, b\cos\theta d\theta + b\sin\theta \, a\sin\theta d\theta \qquad (7)$$

$$= \frac{1}{2} \int_0^{2\pi} ab(\cos^2\theta + \sin^2\theta) d\theta = \pi ab$$

● PROBLEM 17-18

Find the area bounded by one arch of the cycloid

$$x = a(\theta - \sin\theta), \quad a > 0$$

$$y = a(1 - \cos\theta) \qquad (1)$$

and the x-axis.

Solution: The cycloid is shown in the figure.

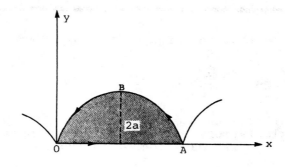

The area is given by

$$\text{area} = \frac{1}{2} \oint x \, dy - y \, dx \qquad (2)$$

(see Problem 17-16, eq.(2)).

From eq.(2), we have

$$dx = a(1 - \cos\theta)d\theta \qquad (3)$$
$$dy = a \sin\theta \, d\theta \qquad (4)$$

Integral (2) is evaluated along OA and ABO. Since for OA, $y = 0$ and $dy = 0$, we have

$$\frac{1}{2} \int_{OA} x \, dy - y \, dx = 0 \qquad (5)$$

Thus, the integral around the boundary is equal to

$$\text{area} = \frac{1}{2} \oint x \, dy - y \, dx$$

$$= \frac{1}{2} \int_{ABO} x \, dy - y \, dx$$

$$= \frac{1}{2} \int_{2\pi}^{0} \left[a(\theta - \sin\theta)a\sin\theta - a(1 - \cos\theta)a(1 - \cos\theta) \right] d\theta$$

$$= \frac{1}{2} a^2 \int_{2\pi}^{0} \left[\theta\sin\theta + 2\cos\theta - 2 \right] d\theta \qquad (6)$$

$$= \frac{1}{2} a^2 \left[-\theta\cos\theta + \sin\theta + 2\sin\theta - 2\theta \right] \Bigg|_{\theta = 2\pi}^{0}$$

$$= \frac{1}{2} a^2 [6\pi] = 3\pi a^2$$

● **PROBLEM 17-19**

The curve called the folium of Descartes is given by the equation

$$x^3 + y^3 = 3axy, \quad a > 0 \qquad (1)$$

and shown in the figure.

Find the area of the loop.

Solution: To find the area of the loop, we shall use the formula

$$\text{area} = \frac{1}{2} \oint x \, dy - y \, dx \qquad (2)$$

Direct substitution of eq.(1) into eq.(2) would lead to complicated calculations. To avoid these complications, let us find the parametric equation of the curve. For

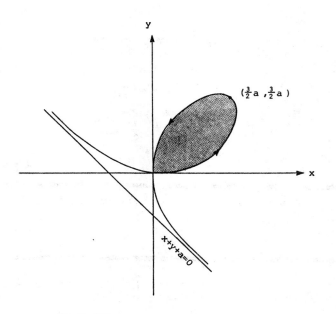

$$y = px \tag{3}$$

we obtain

$$x^3 + p^3x^3 = 3apx^2 \tag{4}$$

Thus

$$x = \frac{3ap}{1+p^3} \tag{5}$$

Note that the loop starts at the point

$$x = 0, \quad p = 0$$

or

$$x = 0, \quad y = 0 \tag{6}$$

For $p = 1$, it reaches the point

$$x = \frac{3}{2}\,a, \quad y = \frac{3}{2}\,a \tag{7}$$

Then, as $p \to \infty$,

$$x = 0, \quad y = 0 \tag{8}$$

Thus, the parameter p changes from $p = 0$ to ∞.
    Eq.(2) becomes

$$\frac{1}{2} \oint x\,dy - y\,dx = \frac{1}{2} \oint x(x\,dp + p\,dx) - px\,dx$$

$$= \frac{1}{2} \oint x^2 dp \tag{9}$$

since

$$dy = pdx + xdp \tag{10}$$

Substituting eq.(5) into eq.(9) results in

$$\frac{1}{2} \oint x^2 dp = \frac{1}{2} \int_0^\infty \frac{9a^2p^2}{(1+p^3)^2}\,dp \tag{11}$$

781

$$= \frac{9}{2} a^2 \int_0^\infty \frac{p^2}{(1+p^3)^2} \, dp$$

Now, making the substitution

$$z = 1 + p^3, \quad dz = 3p^2 dp \qquad (12)$$

we obtain

$$\frac{9}{2} a^2 \int_0^\infty \frac{p^2}{(1+p^3)^2} \, dp = \frac{9}{2} a^2 \int_1^\infty \frac{dz}{3z^2} = \frac{3}{2} a^2 \qquad (13)$$

● **PROBLEM** 17-20

Find the area bounded by the hypocycloid of four cusps

$$x^{\frac{2}{3}} + y^{\frac{2}{3}} = a^{\frac{2}{3}}, \quad a > 0 \qquad (1)$$

Solution: Let us first find the parametric equation of the curve. From eq.(1), we can guess that this equation is of the form

$$x = a \cos^n \theta$$
$$y = a \sin^n \theta \qquad (2)$$

To find n, let us substitute eq.(2) into eq.(1),

Thus $\qquad a^{\frac{2}{3}} (\cos^n \theta)^{\frac{2}{3}} + a^{\frac{2}{3}} (\sin^n \theta)^{\frac{2}{3}} = a^{\frac{2}{3}} \qquad (3)$

and $\qquad \cos^{\frac{2n}{3}} \theta + \sin^{\frac{2n}{3}} \theta = 1 \qquad (4)$

$$n = 3$$

The hypocycloid, whose parametric equation is

$$x = a \cos^3 \theta$$
$$y = a \sin^3 \theta \qquad (5)$$

is shown in the figure.

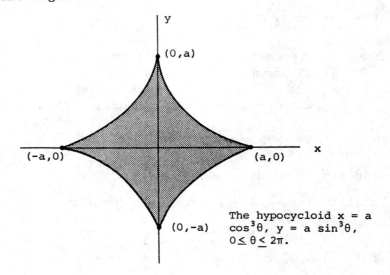

The hypocycloid $x = a \cos^3 \theta$, $y = a \sin^3 \theta$, $0 \leq \theta \leq 2\pi$.

782

Differentiation of eq.(5) yields

$$dx = -3a \cos^2\theta \sin\theta d\theta$$
$$dy = 3a \sin^2\theta \cos\theta d\theta \qquad (6)$$

Substituting eq.(5) and eq.(6) into

$$\frac{1}{2} \oint x \, dy - y \, dx \qquad (7)$$

results in

$$\frac{1}{2} \oint x dy - y dx = \frac{1}{2} \int_0^{2\pi} 3a^2(\sin^2\theta\cos^4\theta + \sin^4\theta\cos^2\theta)d\theta$$

$$\qquad (8)$$

$$= \frac{3}{2} a^2 \int_0^{2\pi} \sin^2\theta \cos^2\theta d\theta$$

From the basic identity

$$\sin2\theta = 2 \sin\theta\cos\theta \qquad (9)$$

we obtain

$$\frac{3}{2} a^2 \int_0^{2\pi} \sin^2\theta\cos^2\theta d\theta = \frac{3}{8} a^2 \int_0^{2\pi} \sin^2 2\theta d\theta \qquad (10)$$

Since

$$\int \sin^2 2\theta d\theta = \frac{1}{2} \theta - \frac{1}{8} \sin4\theta \qquad (11)$$

eq.(10) becomes

$$\frac{3}{8} a^2 \int_0^{2\pi} \sin^2 2\theta d\theta = \frac{3}{8} \pi a^2 \qquad (12)$$

● **PROBLEM 17-21**

Find the value of the expression

$$x \, dy - y \, dx \qquad (1)$$

in polar coordinates (ρ,θ).

<u>Solution</u>: The polar coordinates of a point (x,y) are

$$x = \rho \cos \theta$$
$$y = \rho \sin \theta$$

Thus

$$dx = \cos\theta d\rho - \rho \sin\theta d\theta$$
$$dy = \sin\theta d\rho + \rho \cos\theta d\theta \qquad (3)$$

Substitution of eq.(2) and (3) into eq.(1) gives $\qquad (2)$

783

$$xdy - ydx = \rho \cos\theta(\sin\theta d\rho + \rho\cos\theta d\theta) - \rho\sin\theta(\cos\theta d\rho - \rho\sin\theta d\theta)$$

$$= \rho^2 d\theta \qquad (4)$$

The integral expressing the area becomes

$$\frac{1}{2} \oint_C x \, dy - y \, dx = \frac{1}{2} \oint \rho^2 d\theta \qquad (5)$$

● **PROBLEM 17-22**

Find the area of a loop of the four-leaved rose

$$\rho = a \sin 2\theta \qquad (1)$$

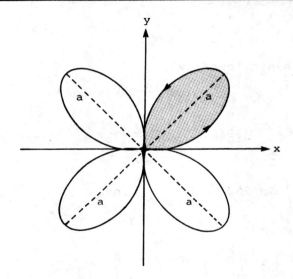

Solution: To evaluate the area of the loop, we shall use eq.(5) of Problem 17-21,

$$\text{area} = \frac{1}{2} \oint \rho^2 d\theta \qquad (2)$$

For the first loop of the rose, the angle θ changes from 0 to $\frac{\pi}{2}$, therefore

$$\text{area} = \frac{1}{2} \int_0^{\frac{\pi}{2}} \rho^2 d\theta = \frac{1}{2} \int_0^{\frac{\pi}{2}} a^2 \sin^2 2\theta d\theta$$

$$= \frac{a^2}{2} \int_0^{\frac{\pi}{2}} \sin^2 2\theta d\theta \qquad (3)$$

Using the formula

$$\int \sin^2 2\theta d\theta = \frac{1}{2} \theta - \frac{1}{8} \sin 4\theta \qquad (4)$$

we evaluate the integral in eq.(3),

$$\frac{a^2}{2} \int_0^{\frac{\pi}{2}} \sin^2 2\theta \, d\theta = \frac{a^2}{2} \left[\frac{1}{2} \theta - \frac{1}{8} \sin 4\theta \right] \Bigg|_{\theta=0}^{\frac{\pi}{2}}$$

$$= \frac{\pi a^2}{8} \tag{5}$$

● **PROBLEM 17-23**

The lemniscate of Bernoulli, whose equation is

$$(x^2 + y^2)^2 = a^2 (x^2 - y^2) \tag{1}$$

is shown in the figure.

Verify that its parametric equation is

$$\rho^2 = a^2 \cos 2\theta \tag{2}$$

and find the area of both loops of the lemniscate.

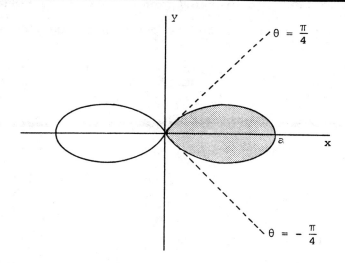

Solution: The transformation from rectangular coordinates to polar coordinates is given by

$$x = \rho \cos\theta$$
$$y = \rho \sin\theta \tag{3}$$

Substituting the above into eq.(1) results in

$$(\rho^2 \cos^2\theta + \rho^2 \sin^2\theta)^2 = a^2 (\rho^2 \cos^2\theta - \rho^2 \sin^2\theta)$$

or

$$\rho^2 = a^2 (\cos^2\theta - \sin^2\theta) = a^2 \cos 2\theta \tag{4}$$

Now, in Problem 17-21 we derived the expression for the area in polar form,

$$\text{area} = \frac{1}{2} \oint \rho^2 d\theta \qquad (5)$$

For the right-hand loop, the angle θ changes from $\theta = -\frac{\pi}{4}$ to $\theta = \frac{\pi}{4}$. Thus,

$$\text{area} = \frac{1}{2} \int_{-\frac{\pi}{4}}^{\frac{\pi}{4}} \rho^2 d\theta = \frac{1}{2} \int_{-\frac{\pi}{4}}^{\frac{\pi}{4}} a^2 \cos 2\theta \, d\theta$$

$$\qquad (6)$$

$$= \frac{a^2}{2} \left[\frac{\sin 2\theta}{2} \Bigg|_{\theta = -\frac{\pi}{4}}^{\frac{\pi}{4}} \right] = \frac{a^2}{2}$$

Thus, the area of both loops is a^2.

GREEN'S THEOREM (EXTENDED VERSION)

● **PROBLEM 17-24**

In Problem 17-1, we proved Green's theorem for the special type of region R bounded by a curve C such that any straight line parallel to the coordinate axes cuts C in at most two points.

Prove Green's theorem for a region R which is not itself of this type, but can be decomposed into a finite number of such regions: R_1, R_2, ... ,R_n by suitable arcs and lines.

Solution: Consider region R shown in the figure.

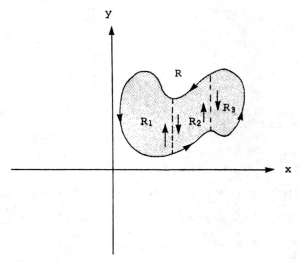

R can be decomposed into three regions R_1, R_2, R_3. To each of these regions R_1, R_2, R_3, Green's theorem can be applied,

786

as proved in Problem 17-1. Let us assume, in general, that R consists of regions $R_1, R_2, \ldots, R_n$ and let $C_1, C_2, \ldots, C_n$ be the corresponding boundaries. Each region meets the assumptions of Green's theorem. Thus

$$\oint_{C_i} Pdx + Qdy = \iint_{R_i} \left(\frac{\partial Q}{\partial x} - \frac{\partial P}{\partial y} \right) dxdy \qquad (1)$$

for $i = 1, 2, \ldots, n$.

Adding, we obtain

$$\oint_{C_1} (Pdx + Qdy) + \oint_{C_2} (Pdx + Qdy) + \ldots + \oint_{C_n} (Pdx + Qdy)$$

$$= \iint_{R_1} \left(\frac{\partial Q}{\partial x} - \frac{\partial P}{\partial y} \right) dxdy + \iint_{R_2} \left(\frac{\partial Q}{\partial x} - \frac{\partial P}{\partial y} \right) dxdy + \ldots + \iint_{R_n} \left(\frac{\partial Q}{\partial x} - \frac{\partial P}{\partial y} \right) dxdy \qquad (2)$$

The sum of the integrals on the left is

$$\oint_C Pdx + Qdy \qquad (3)$$

The integrals along the added lines are taken once in each direction, thus they cancel each other. The integrals on the right add up to

$$\iint_R \left(\frac{\partial Q}{\partial x} - \frac{\partial P}{\partial y} \right) dxdy \qquad (4)$$

Hence, we obtain

$$\oint_C Pdx + Qdy = \iint_R \left(\frac{\partial Q}{\partial x} - \frac{\partial P}{\partial y} \right) dxdy \qquad (5)$$

That completes the proof. The theorem in this form covers all regions that can be found in practical problems.

● **PROBLEM** 17-25

Evaluate the line integral

$$\oint_C (x+\sin y)dx + \cos y \, dy \qquad (1)$$

where C is the triangle shown in the figure. Verify your results by using Green's theorem.

Solution: Let us directly evaluate the line integral by evaluating the integral for each of the line segments and subsequently adding up the results.

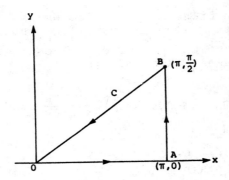

Along OA, $y = 0$, $dy = 0$ thus

$$\int_{OA} (x+\sin y)dx + \cos y\, dy = \int_0^{\pi} x\, dx = \frac{\pi^2}{2} \qquad (2)$$

Along AB, $dx = 0$

$$\int_{AB} \cos y\, dy = \int_0^{\frac{\pi}{2}} \cos y\, dy = 1 \qquad (3)$$

Along BO, we have

$$y = \frac{1}{2}\, x \quad \text{and} \quad dy = \frac{1}{2}\, dx, \qquad (4)$$

thus

$$\int_{\frac{\pi}{2}}^{0} (2y+\sin y)2dy + \cos y\, dy = \left[2y^2 - 2\cos y + \sin y \right]\Bigg|_{y=\frac{\pi}{2}}^{0}$$

$$\qquad (5)$$

$$= -3 - \frac{\pi^2}{2}$$

The integral along C is

$$\oint_C (x+\sin y)dx + \cos y\, dy = \frac{\pi^2}{2} + 1 - 3 - \frac{\pi^2}{2} = -2 \qquad (6)$$

Let us now verify our result by using Green's theorem. We have

$$\oint (x+\sin y)dx + \cos y\, dy$$

$$= \iint_R \left[\frac{\partial}{\partial x}(\cos y) - \frac{\partial}{\partial y}(x+\sin y) \right] dx\, dy$$

$$= -\iint_R \cos y\, dx\, dy = - \int_{x=0}^{\pi} \int_{y=0}^{\frac{x}{2}} \cos y\, dy\, dx$$

$$\qquad (7)$$

$$= -\int_0^{\pi} \sin \frac{x}{2}\, dx = -2$$

Notice that in this case there do exist lines parallel to the coordinate axes (lines OA and OB) which meet C at an infinite number of points. Green's theorem does still hold

for this type of region. In general, Green's theorem is
valid for boundaries C consisting of a finite number of
straight line segments.

● **PROBLEM** 17-26

Utilizing line integrals, derive the equation for the
area of a triangle.

Solution: For simplicity, we shall locate the triangle in
such a way that one of its sides is on the x-axis. The
area of a region in the xy-plane is

$$S = \iint_B dxdy \qquad (1)$$

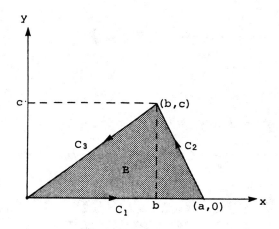

Green's theorem is

$$\oint_C Pdx + Qdy = \iint_B \left(\frac{\partial Q}{\partial x} - \frac{\partial P}{\partial y} \right) dxdy \qquad (2)$$

where C is a closed curve and is the boundary of B, oriented
in the positive direction (counterclockwise). If P = 0 and
Q = x, then eq.(2) becomes

$$\oint_C xdy = \iint_B dxdy = S = \text{area of B} \qquad (3)$$

Thus, the area of the triangle is

$$\oint_C xdy = \int_{C_1} xdy + \int_{C_2} xdy + \int_{C_3} xdy \qquad (4)$$

Along C_1, y = 0 and dy = 0, thus

$$\int_{C_1} xdy = 0 \qquad (5)$$

In the parametric form, C_2 may be expressed as

$$x = a + t(b-a)$$
$$\qquad\qquad 0 \le t \le 1 \qquad\qquad (6)$$
$$y = tc$$

Thus,

$$\int_{C_2} x\,dy = \int_0^1 \left[a+t(b-a)\right] c\,dt \qquad\qquad (7)$$

$$= c \left[at + \frac{t^2}{2}(b-a)\right]\Bigg|_{t=0}^{1} = \frac{c}{2}(b+a)$$

To evaluate $\int_{C_3} x\,dy$, we will use the parametric equation of C_3,

Thus,

$$x = b - tb$$
$$\qquad\qquad\qquad\qquad (8)$$
$$y = c - tc$$

$$\int_{C_3} x\,dy = -c\int_0^1 (b-tb)\,dt = -c\left[bt - \frac{t^2}{2}b\right]\Bigg|_{t=0}^{1} \qquad (9)$$

$$= \frac{-bc}{2}$$

From eq.(4), we obtain

$$\text{Area} = \oint_C x\,dy = 0 + \frac{c}{2}(b+a) - \frac{cb}{2} = \frac{ac}{2} \qquad (10)$$

Fortunately, there are simpler ways of deriving this formula.

GREEN'S THEOREM FOR MULTIPLY-CONNECTED REGIONS AND ITS APPLICATIONS

● PROBLEM 17-27

So far we've proven Green's theorem for simply-connected regions. That is, regions such that every closed curve in the region can be shrunk to a point without leaving the region. Prove Green's theorem for a multiply-connected region.

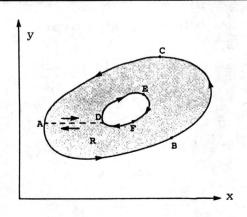

Solution: It is easy to show that the shaded region R is multiply-connected. Consider a curve surrounding DFE. This curve cannot be shrunk to a point without leaving region R. The boundary of R (ABC and DFE) is to be traversed in the positive direction, that is, the point moving in this direction has the region on its left. The positive direction is indicated by the arrows. Note that for the ABC boundary, the positive direction is counterclockwise, while for DEF, the positive direction is clockwise. Let us draw a line AD connecting both boundaries. The region R, which was multiply-connected, becomes the region ADEFDABCA, which is simply-connected. Thus, Green's theorem for this region is valid.

$$\iint\limits_{R} \left(\frac{\partial Q}{\partial x} - \frac{\partial P}{\partial y} \right) dxdy = \int\limits_{\substack{ADEF \\ DABCA}} Pdx + Qdy \tag{1}$$

The integral on the right is equal to

$$\int\limits_{AD} + \int\limits_{DEFD} + \int\limits_{DA} + \int\limits_{ABCA} \tag{2}$$

Since

$$\int\limits_{AD} = - \int\limits_{DA} \tag{3}$$

eq.(1) becomes

$$\iint\limits_{R} \left(\frac{\partial Q}{\partial x} - \frac{\partial P}{\partial y} \right) dxdy = \int\limits_{ABCA} Pdx+Qdy + \int\limits_{DEFD} Pdx+Qdy \tag{4}$$

If C denotes the boundary of R, then the right side of eq.(4) becomes

$$\oint\limits_{C} Pdx + Qdy = \iint\limits_{R} \left(\frac{\partial Q}{\partial x} - \frac{\partial P}{\partial y} \right) dxdy \tag{5}$$

The boundary of R is traversed in the positive direction.

● **PROBLEM 17-28**

Verify Green's theorem in the plane for

$$\oint\limits_{C} (x^2+xy)dx - x^2ydy \tag{1}$$

where C is the boundary of the shaded region shown in the figure.

Solution: First, we shall evaluate integral (1) along the boundary C of the shaded region.

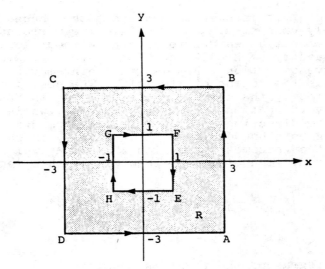

Along AB

$$-\int_{-3}^{3} 9y\,dy = -\frac{9}{2}\,y^2\,\bigg|_{-3}^{3} = 0 \tag{2}$$

along BC

$$\int_{3}^{-3} (x^2+3x)\,dx = \left(\frac{x^3}{3}+\frac{3x^2}{2}\right)\bigg|_{3}^{-3} = -9 - 9 = -18 \tag{3}$$

along CD

$$\int_{3}^{-3} 9y\,dy = -\frac{9}{2}\,y^2\,\bigg|_{3}^{-3} = 0 \tag{4}$$

along DA

$$\int_{-3}^{3} (x^2-3x)\,dx = \left(\frac{x^3}{3}-\frac{3}{2}\,x^2\right)\bigg|_{-3}^{3} = 18 \tag{5}$$

along GF

$$\int_{-1}^{1} (x^2+x)\,dx = \left(\frac{x^3}{3}+\frac{x^2}{2}\right)\bigg|_{-1}^{1} = \frac{2}{3} \tag{6}$$

along FE

$$\int_{1}^{-1} y\,dy = -\frac{y^2}{2}\,\bigg|_{1}^{-1} = 0 \tag{7}$$

along EH

$$\int_{1}^{-1} (x^2-x)\,dx = \left(\frac{x^3}{3}-\frac{x^2}{2}\right)\bigg|_{1}^{-1} = -\frac{2}{3} \tag{8}$$

along HG

$$-\int_{-1}^{1} y\,dy = -\frac{y^2}{2}\,\bigg|_{-1}^{1} = 0 \tag{9}$$

Thus, the total integral equals

$$\oint_{C} (x^2+xy)\,dx - x^2 y\,dy = -18 + 18 + \frac{2}{3} - \frac{2}{3} = 0 \tag{10}$$

Applying Green's theorem, we obtain

$$\oint_C (x^2+xy)dx - x^2ydy = \iint_R (-2xy-x)dxdy \qquad (11)$$

where the integral on the right side is taken over the shaded area. We have

$$\iint_R (-2xy-x)dxdy = \iint_{ABCD} (-2xy-x)dxdy - \iint_{EFGH} (-2xy-x)dxdy \qquad (12)$$

where

$$\iint_{ABCD} (-2xy-x)dydx = \int_{x=-3}^{3} \int_{y=-3}^{3} (-2xy-x)dydx$$

$$= \int_{-3}^{3} (-6x)dx = 0 \qquad (13)$$

In the same way, we find

$$\iint_{EFGH} (-2xy-x)dxdy = 0 \qquad (14)$$

Thus

$$\iint_R (-2xy-x)dxdy = 0 \qquad (15)$$

Eq.(10) and eq.(15) lead to the same results. Green's theorem has been verified for a multiply-connected region R.

● **PROBLEM** 17-29

Verify Green's theorem in the plane for

$$\oint_C (3x-2y)dx + (x-4y)dy \qquad (1)$$

where C is the boundary of the multiply-connected region R enclosed by the circles $x^2+y^2 = 16$ and $x^2+y^2 = 1$.

Solution: Green's theorem states that

$$\oint_C (3x-2y)dx + (x-4y)dy = \iint_R (1+2)dxdy \qquad (2)$$

since $\qquad \frac{\partial}{\partial x} (x-4y) - \frac{\partial}{\partial y} (3x-2y) = 1 + 2 \qquad (3)$

Thus, the integral on the right side of eq.(2) is

$$\iint_R 3dxdy = 3\int_{\rho=1}^{4} \int_{\theta=0}^{2\pi} \rho d\rho d\theta = 45\pi \qquad (4)$$

We shall check if the line integral in eq.(2) leads to the same result.

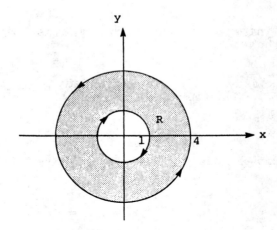

In polar coordinates,
$$x = \rho \cos\theta$$
$$y = \rho \sin\theta \qquad (5)$$

For the circle, $\rho = $ const, thus
$$dx = -\rho \sin\theta d\theta$$
$$dy = \rho \cos\theta d\theta \qquad (6)$$

For $x^2 + y^2 = 16$, integral (1) is equal to

$$\oint (3x-2y)dx + (x-4y)dy$$

$$= \int_0^{2\pi} (3\rho\cos\theta - 2\rho\sin\theta)(-\rho\sin\theta)d\theta + (\rho\cos\theta - 4\rho\sin\theta)\rho\cos\theta d\theta$$

$$= 16 \int_0^{2\pi} (-3\cos\theta\sin\theta + 2\sin^2\theta + \cos^2\theta - 4\sin\theta\cos\theta)d\theta \qquad (7)$$

$$= 16 \int_0^{2\pi} (-7\sin\theta\cos\theta + \sin^2\theta + 1)d\theta$$

Using the identities
$$\sin 2\theta = 2\sin\theta\cos\theta$$
$$\sin^2\theta = \frac{1-\cos 2\theta}{2} \qquad (8)$$

we find

$$16 \int_0^{2\pi} (-7\sin\theta\cos\theta + \sin^2\theta + 1)d\theta$$

$$= 16 \int_0^{2\pi} \left(-\frac{7}{2}\sin 2\theta + \frac{3}{2} - \frac{\cos 2\theta}{2} \right) d\theta \qquad (9)$$

794

$$= 16 \left[\frac{7}{2} \frac{\cos 2\theta}{2} + \frac{3}{2} \theta - \frac{\sin 2\theta}{4} \right] \Bigg|_{\theta=0}^{2\pi} = 48\pi$$

For the circle $x^2 + y^2 = 1$,

$$\oint (3x-2y)dx + (x-4y)dy$$

$$= \int_0^{-2\pi} (-7\sin\theta\cos\theta + \sin^2\theta + 1)d\theta \qquad (10)$$

$$= \left[\frac{7}{2} \frac{\cos 2\theta}{2} + \frac{3}{2} \theta - \frac{\sin 2\theta}{4} \right] \Bigg|_0^{-2\pi} = -3\pi$$

Thus, the total integral along the boundaries is

$$\oint_C (3x-2y)dx + (x-4y)dy = 48\pi - 3\pi = 45\pi \qquad (11)$$

This result is in agreement with eq.(4).

● **PROBLEM** 17-30

Evaluate the integral

$$\oint_C \frac{-ydx}{x^2+y^2} + \frac{xdy}{x^2+y^2} \qquad (1)$$

over the path C shown in the figure.

C consists of C_1, C_2 and C_3.

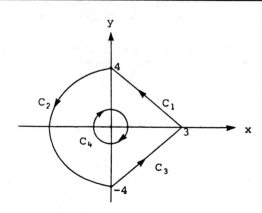

Solution: The path C consists of three curves, C_1, C_2, C_3. The origin $(0,0)$ is located in the region R enclosed by C. The function in eq.(1) is not defined at the origin.

Both partial derivatives are equal,

$$\frac{\partial Q}{\partial x} - \frac{\partial P}{\partial y} = \frac{(x^2+y^2)-2x^2+(x^2+y^2)-2y^2}{(x^2+y^2)^2} = 0 \tag{2}$$

Thus, if we integrate along any path which does not encircle the origin, then by Green's theorem

$$\oint_C Pdx+Qdy = \iint_R \left(\frac{\partial Q}{\partial x} - \frac{\partial P}{\partial y}\right) dxdy = \iint_R 0dxdy = 0 \tag{3}$$

the integral equals zero.

Integral (1) can be evaluated directly as a sum of integrals along C_1, C_2 and C_3:

$$\oint_C = \int_{C_1} + \int_{C_2} + \int_{C_3} \tag{4}$$

This, however, leads to complicated calculations. In order to apply Green's theorem, we have to exclude (0,0) from the region of integration. To achieve this, let us draw a small circle C_4 around the origin. For this circle the positive direction is clockwise. If R' is the region between the circle C_4 and the path C, then R' does not include the origin and

$$\int_C Pdx+Qdy + \oint_{C_4} Pdx+Qdy = \iint_{R'} \left(\frac{\partial Q}{\partial x} - \frac{\partial P}{\partial y}\right) dxdy = 0 \tag{5}$$

Thus,

$$\oint_C Pdx+Qdy = - \oint_{C_4} Pdx+Qdy = \oint_{C_4} Pdx+Qdy \tag{6}$$

The last integral is evaluated in the counterclockwise direction.

From eq.(6), we conclude that the line integral (1) is the same for any path enclosing the origin. To simplify the calculations, let us take C_4 to be a unit circle $x^2 + y^2 = 1$ parametrized by

$$x = \cos\theta$$
$$\qquad\qquad 0 \le \theta \le 2\pi \tag{7}$$
$$y = \sin\theta$$

$$dx = -\sin\theta d\theta$$

$$dy = \cos\theta d\theta$$

Thus, $$\oint_C \frac{-ydx+xdy}{x^2+y^2} = \int_0^{2\pi} \sin^2\theta d\theta + \cos^2\theta d\theta$$

796

$$= \int_0^{2\pi} d\theta = 2\pi \qquad (8)$$

Thus, for all curves enclosing the origin, integral (1) equals 2π.

● **PROBLEM 17-31**

Evaluate

$$\oint_C \frac{-x^2 y\,dx + x^3 dy}{(x^2+y^2)^2} = \oint_C \overline{F} \cdot d\overline{r} \qquad (1)$$

around the ellipse $4x^2 + y^2 = 1$. $\qquad (2)$

<u>Solution</u>: It is possible, even though cumbersome, to evaluate integral (1) directly.

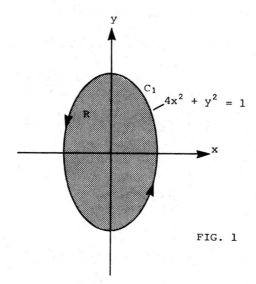

FIG. 1

Application of Green's provides a shortcut.

Notice, however, that the function

$$\overline{F} = \left(\frac{-x^2 y}{(x^2+y^2)^2} , \frac{x^3}{(x^2+y^2)^2} \right) \qquad (3)$$

is undefined at the origin. This causes a slight complication, since Green's theorem is not directly applicable because the region of integration R enclosed by the ellipse (Fig. 1) includes the origin. We can work around this problem, however, by eliminating the point $(0,0)$ from our region of integration. By drawing a small circle C_2 around the origin, we obtain a new region R' (Fig. 2) to which Green's theorem is now applicable. Note that we are now dealing with a multiply-connected region. Also note that the positive direction for C_2 is clockwise.

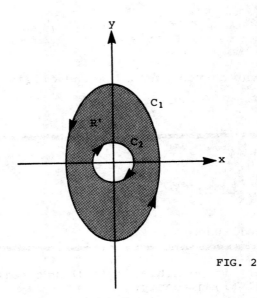

FIG. 2

The partial derivatives are

$$\frac{\partial P}{\partial y} = \frac{\partial}{\partial y}\left(\frac{-x^2y}{(x^2+y^2)^2}\right) = \frac{-x^2(x^2+y^2)^2+4x^2y^2(x^2+y^2)}{(x^2+y^2)^4}$$

$$= \frac{-x^4+3x^2y^2}{(x^2+y^2)^3} \tag{4}$$

$$\frac{\partial Q}{\partial x} = \frac{\partial}{\partial x}\left(\frac{x^3}{(x^2+y^2)^2}\right) = \frac{3x^2(x^2+y^2)^2-4x^4(x^2+y^2)}{(x^2+y^2)^4}$$

$$= \frac{-x^4+3x^2y^2}{(x^2+y^2)^3} \tag{5}$$

Thus

$$\frac{\partial Q}{\partial x} - \frac{\partial P}{\partial y} = 0 \tag{6}$$

Green's theorem leads to

$$\oint_{C_1}\frac{-x^2y\,dx+x^3\,dy}{(x^2+y^2)^2} + \oint_{C_2}\frac{-x^2y\,dx+x^3\,dy}{(x^2+y^2)^2}$$

$$= \iint_{R'} 0 \, dx\,dy = 0 \tag{7}$$

From eq.(7), we conclude that

$$\oint_{C_1}\frac{-x^2y\,dx+x^3\,dy}{(x^2+y^2)^2} = - \oint_{C_2}\frac{-x^2y\,dx+x^3\,dy}{(x^2+y^2)^2}$$

$$= \int_{\substack{C_2\\ccw}}\frac{-x^2y\,dx+x^3\,dy}{(x^2+y^2)^2} \tag{8}$$

where the "ccw" stands for the counterclockwise direction. Eq.(8) tells us that the integral around the ellipse has the same value as the integral around the circle C_2 (or any other closed curve enclosing the origin $(0,0)$).

For convenience, we will replace the ellipse with the circle $x^2+y^2 = 1$, whose parametric equations are

$$x = \cos\theta$$
$$0 \leq \theta \leq 2\pi \qquad (9)$$
Thus,
$$y = \sin\theta$$

$$\int_0^{2\pi} \frac{\cos^2\theta\sin^2\theta d\theta + \cos^4\theta d\theta}{(\sin^2\theta + \cos^2\theta)^2} = \int_0^{2\pi} \cos^2\theta d\theta \qquad (10)$$

Since

$$\cos^2\theta = \frac{1 + \cos2\theta}{2} \qquad (11)$$

eq.(10) becomes

$$\int_0^{2\pi} \left(\frac{1}{2} + \frac{\cos2\theta}{2}\right) d\theta = \pi \qquad (12)$$

Thus,

$$\oint_{C_1} \frac{-x^2y dx + x^3 dy}{(x^2+y^2)^2} = \pi \qquad (13)$$

where C_1 is the ellipse $4x^2+y^2 = 1$.

● **PROBLEM** 17-32

Prove the theorem of Pappus, using Green's theorem.

Pappus Theorem

Let B be a region located entirely on one side of the x-axis. If B is revolved about the x-axis, then the volume V of the solid that is generated is

$$V = 2\pi S y_c \qquad (1)$$

where S is the area of B and (x_c, y_c) is the centroid of B.

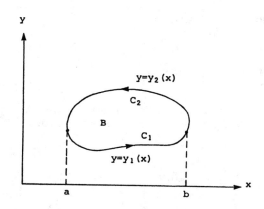

799

Solution: Let B be a bounded closed region in the xy-plane whose boundary consists of a finite number of simple, sectionally smooth curves that do not intersect each other.

For simplicity, we assume that the boundary of B consists of two curves, C_1 and C_2, as shown in the figure. When B is revolved about the x-axis, the volume of the generated solid is equal to the volume generated by revolving the upper curve, $y = y_2(x)$, minus the volume generated by revolving the lower curve, $y = y_1(x)$.

Now, in general, the volume generated by revolving a curve $y = y(x)$ about the x-axis is given by

$$V = \int_{x_1}^{x_2} \pi[y(x)]^2 dx$$

Thus, for our case, we have

$$V = \int_a^b \pi(y_2(x))^2 dx - \int_a^b \pi(y_1(x))^2 dx \qquad (2)$$

$$= -\pi \left[\int_a^b (y_1(x))^2 dx + \int_b^a (y_2(x))^2 dx \right]$$

If C denotes the boundary of B, then

$$V = -\pi \left[\int_{C_1} y^2 dx + \int_{C_2} y^2 dx \right] = -\pi \oint_C y^2 dx \qquad (3)$$

Note that the integral (3) is evaluated in the counterclockwise (positive) direction.
Now, applying Green's theorem results in
$$P = -\pi y^2 \ , \quad Q = 0 \qquad (4)$$

$$V = -\pi \oint_C y^2 dx = \iint_B 2\pi y \, dx \, dy = 2\pi \iint_B y \, dx \, dy \qquad (5)$$

Now, note that the centroid (x_c, y_c) of a thin sheet (lamina) lying in the xy-plane is given by

$$Mx_c = \iint_B x\rho \, dx \, dy \qquad (6)$$

$$My_c = \iint_B y\rho \, dx \, dy \qquad (7)$$

where M is the total mass of the lamina and ρ is its density. If we consider a uniform lamina (constant density), then we may write

$$x_c = \frac{\rho}{M} \iint_B x \, dx \, dy \qquad (8)$$

800

$$y_c = \frac{\rho}{M} \iint_B y\,dxdy \qquad (9)$$

Now, since the mass of a uniform lamina is given by

$$M = \rho S \qquad (10)$$

where S is the surface area, we conclude that

$$y_c = \frac{\rho}{M} \iint_B y\,dxdy = \frac{1}{S} \iint_B y\,dxdy$$

or

$$\iint_B y\,dxdy = S y_c \qquad (11)$$

Substituting eq.(11) into eq.(5) yields

$$V = 2\pi S y_c \qquad (12)$$

That completes the proof of Pappus' theorem.

● **PROBLEM 17-33**

Consider a multiply-connected region R bounded by the simple closed curves C_1, C_2, C_3, C_4 and C_5 shown in the figure.

Prove Green's theorem for this region by constructing additional lines and converting it into a simply-connected region.

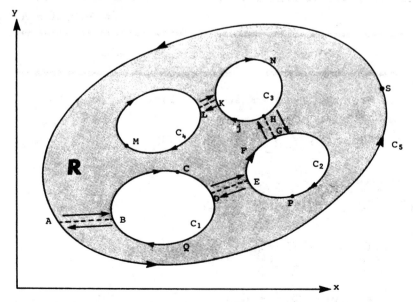

Solution: Drawing the lines AB, DE, GH and KL, we obtain a region which is simply-connected. Thus, Green's theorem can be applied. The integral over the boundary of the region is equal to

$$\int_{AB} + \int_{BCD} + \int_{DE} + \int_{EFG} + \int_{GH} + \int_{HJK} + \int_{KL} + \int_{LML} + \int_{LK}$$

$$+ \int_{KNH} + \int_{HG} + \int_{GPE} + \int_{ED} + \int_{DQB} + \int_{BA} + \int_{ASA} \tag{1}$$

The following integrals cancel out in pairs: integrals along AB and BA, DE and ED, GH and HG, KL and LK. Thus eq.(1) becomes

$$\int_{BCD} + \int_{DQB} + \int_{EFG} + \int_{GPE} + \int_{HJK} + \int_{KNH} + \int_{LML} + \int_{ASA} \tag{2}$$

$$= \int_{C_1} + \int_{C_2} + \int_{C_3} + \int_{C_4} + \int_{C_5} = \oint_{C}$$

where C is the boundary of R, consisting of C_1, C_2, C_3, C_4 and C_5. Thus, Green's theorem for a multiply-connected region R is proved,

$$\oint_{C} Pdx + Qdy = \iint_{R}\left(\frac{\partial Q}{\partial x} - \frac{\partial P}{\partial y}\right) dxdy \tag{3}$$

GREEN'S THEOREM IN VECTOR NOTATION

● **PROBLEM 17-34**

Express Green's theorem in the plane in vector notation.

Solution: Green's theorem in the plane is given by

$$\oint_{C} Pdx+Qdy = \iint_{R}\left(\frac{\partial Q}{\partial x} - \frac{\partial P}{\partial y}\right) dxdy \tag{1}$$

Let us denote

$$\bar{a} = P\bar{i} + Q\bar{j} \tag{2}$$

Then

$$Pdx+Qdy = (P\bar{i}+Q\bar{j}) \cdot (dx\bar{i}+dy\bar{j})$$

$$= \bar{a} \cdot d\bar{r} \tag{3}$$

where

$$d\bar{r} = dx\bar{i} + dy\bar{j} \tag{4}$$

Now, note that from the definition of rotation,

$$\text{curl } \bar{a} = \nabla \times \bar{a} = \begin{vmatrix} \bar{i} & \bar{j} & \bar{k} \\ \frac{\partial}{\partial x} & \frac{\partial}{\partial y} & \frac{\partial}{\partial z} \\ P & Q & O \end{vmatrix}$$

$$= -\frac{\partial Q}{\partial z}\bar{i} + \frac{\partial P}{\partial z}\bar{j} + \left(\frac{\partial Q}{\partial x} - \frac{\partial P}{\partial y}\right)\bar{k} \qquad (5)$$

From eq:(5), the following relationship can be obtained:

$$(\nabla \times \bar{a}) \cdot \bar{k} = \frac{\partial Q}{\partial x} - \frac{\partial P}{\partial y} \qquad (6)$$

From eqs.(3) and (6), we conclude that Green's theorem can be written in the vector form

$$\oint_{C} \bar{a} \cdot d\bar{r} = \iint_{R} (\nabla \times \bar{a}) \cdot \bar{k}\ dR \qquad (7)$$

where   dR = dxdy.

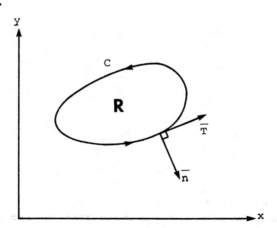

Green's theorem can also be expressed in another vector form.

Let $\bar{T}$ be the unit tangent vector to a closed curve C.

Since

$$\bar{T} = \frac{d\bar{r}}{ds} \qquad (8)$$

we may write

$$Pdx + Qdy = \bar{a} \cdot d\bar{r} = \bar{a} \cdot \frac{d\bar{r}}{ds}\ ds = \bar{a} \cdot \bar{T}\ ds \qquad (9)$$

Now, since the curve C lies in the xy-plane, we obtain

$$\bar{T} = \bar{k} \times \bar{n} \qquad (10)$$

where $\bar{n}$ is, of course, the unit normal vector to C.

Eq.(9) can be written

$$Pdx + Qdy = \bar{a} \cdot \bar{T}\ ds = \bar{a} \cdot (\bar{k} \times \bar{n})ds$$

$$= (\bar{a} \times \bar{k}) \cdot \bar{n}\ ds \qquad (11)$$

Now, if we introduce a vector $\bar{b}$ such that

$$\bar{b} = \bar{a} \times \bar{k} \qquad (12)$$

then

$$\bar{b} = (P\bar{i} + Q\bar{j}) \times \bar{k} = Q\bar{i} - P\bar{j} \qquad (13)$$

and

$$\frac{\partial Q}{\partial x} - \frac{\partial P}{\partial y} = \nabla \cdot \bar{b} \qquad (14)$$

Green's theorem in the plane can now be written

$$\oint_C \bar{b} \cdot \bar{n}\,ds = \iint_R \nabla \cdot \bar{b} \; dxdy \qquad (15)$$

● **PROBLEM 17-35**

Evaluate by Green's theorem

1. $\oint_C u_T\,ds$, where

$$\bar{u} = \operatorname{grad}(x^2 y^2 + e^x + e^y) \qquad (1)$$

and C is the circle $x^2 + y^2 = 1$.

2. $\oint_C u_n\,ds$, where

$$\bar{u} = x\sin y\,\bar{i} + (x^2 + \cos y)\bar{j} \qquad (2)$$

and C is the circle $x^2 + y^2 = 1$.

Solution: 1. First, notice that from Problem 17-26, eq.(7) we may write Green's theorem in the vector form

$$\oint_C \bar{a} \cdot d\bar{r} = \iint_R (\nabla \times \bar{a}) \cdot \bar{k} \; dxdy$$

or, since $\bar{T} = \dfrac{d\bar{r}}{ds}$,

$$\oint_C \bar{a} \cdot \bar{T}\,ds = \iint_R (\nabla \times \bar{a}) \cdot \bar{k} \; dxdy$$

we have

$$\bar{a} \cdot \bar{T} = a_T$$
$$(\nabla \times \bar{a}) \cdot \bar{k} = (\nabla \times \bar{a})_z$$

so that Green's theorem may be given by

$$\oint_C a_T ds = \iint_R (\nabla \times \bar{a})_z \, dxdy$$

In our case, we can let vector $\bar{u}$ be vector $\bar{a}$, and, since

$$\bar{u} = \text{grad}(x^2 y^2 + e^x + e^y)$$

$$= (2xy^2 + e^x)\bar{i} + (2yx^2 + e^y)\bar{j}$$

and

$$(\nabla \times \bar{u})_z = \frac{\partial}{\partial x}(2yx^2 + e^y) - \frac{\partial}{\partial y}(2xy^2 + e^x)$$

$$= 4xy - 4xy = 0$$

we obtain

$$u_T ds = \iint_R (\nabla \times \bar{u})_z dxdy = \iint 0 \, dxdy = 0$$

2. From Problem 17-26, eq.(15), we find that another vector form of Green's theorem is

$$\oint_C \bar{b} \cdot \bar{n} \, ds = \iint_R \nabla \cdot \bar{b} \, dxdy$$

If we let vector $\bar{u}$ be vector $\bar{b}$, then

$$\oint_C u_n ds = \iint_R \text{div } \bar{u} \, dxdy$$

since

$$\bar{u} \cdot \bar{n} = u_n$$

and

$$\nabla \cdot \bar{u} = \text{div } \bar{u}$$

Now, for div $\bar{u}$, we have, from eq.(2),

$$\text{div } \bar{u} = \frac{\partial}{\partial x}(x \sin y) + \frac{\partial}{\partial y}(x^2 + \cos y)\bar{j}$$

$$= \sin y - \sin y = 0$$

Thus,

$$\oint_C u_n ds = \iint_R \text{div } \bar{u} \, dxdy = \iint 0 \, dxdy = 0$$

● **PROBLEM 17-36**

If

$$\bar{r} = x\bar{i} + y\bar{j} \qquad (1)$$

is the position vector of an arbitrary point (x,y), show that

$$\text{area enclosed by } C = \frac{1}{2}\oint_C r_n \, ds \qquad (2)$$

where $\bar{n}$ is the outer normal to C.

Solution: In Problem 17-12, we showed that

$$\text{area bounded by } C = \frac{1}{2} \oint x \, dy - y \, dx \tag{3}$$

where C is a simple closed curve.

It can be easily verified that for any vector $\bar{u} = P\bar{i} + Q\bar{j}$,

$$\oint_C \bar{u} \cdot \bar{n} \, ds = \oint_C u_n \, ds = \oint_C \left(P \frac{dy}{ds} - Q \frac{dx}{ds} \right) ds$$

$$\tag{4}$$

$$= \oint_C -Q dx + P dy$$

Thus, for the vector

$$\bar{r} = x\bar{i} + y\bar{j}, \tag{5}$$

we have

$$\oint_C \bar{r} \cdot \bar{n} \, ds = \oint_C r_n \, ds = \oint_C x \, dy - y \, dx$$

$$\tag{6}$$

$$= \text{two times the area enclosed by C.}$$

We can reach the same result by applying eq.(15) of Problem 17-26.

$$\oint_C \bar{r} \cdot \bar{n} \, ds = \oint_C r_n \, ds = \iint_R \text{div } \bar{r} \, dx dy$$

$$\tag{7}$$

$$= 2 \iint_R dx dy$$

where

$$\iint_R dx dy = \text{area enclosed by C.} \tag{8}$$

APPLICATIONS IN PHYSICS-FORCE FIELD, FLOW, CIRCULATION AND GAUSS' THEOREM

● PROBLEM 17-37

Green's theorem can be expressed in the vector form

$$\oint_C \bar{a} \cdot d\bar{r} = \iint_R (\nabla \times \bar{a}) \cdot \bar{k} \, dx dy \tag{1}$$

Find the physical interpretation of this statement if $\bar{a}$ is the force field acting on a particle.

Solution: If vector $\bar{a}$ denotes the force field acting on a particle, then

$$\oint_C \overline{a} \cdot d\overline{r}$$

represents the work done in moving the particle around a closed path C.

Let us now repeat some basic facts discussed in previous chapters.

A continuously differentiable vector field $\overline{a}$ is said to be conservative in a domain R if there exists some scalar field ϕ defined in R such that

$$\overline{a} = \text{grad } \phi$$

Moreover, a continuously differentiable vector field $\overline{a}$ defined in a domain R is conservative if and only if it possesses any of the following properties:

1. curl $\overline{a} = \overline{0}$ in R

2. $\overline{a} = \text{grad } \phi$

3. Integral of $\overline{a}$ around any closed curve is zero.

4. Integral of $\overline{a}$ along any regular curve from A to B is independent of path.

Thus, if curl $\overline{a} = \overline{0}$ or $\overline{a} = \text{grad}\phi$, then we conclude that the integral around any closed path is zero. We also conclude that the work done in moving a particle from one point in a plane to another point in the plane is independent of the path in the plane joining these two points (from condition 4).

On the other hand, if the integral around any closed path is zero (or the integral is independent of path), then we conclude that curl $\overline{a} = \overline{0}$.

Now, note that in the plane, we may write vector field $\overline{a}$ as

$$\overline{a} = P\overline{i} + Q\overline{j}$$

and the condition curl $\overline{a} = \overline{0}$ gives us

$$\frac{\partial Q}{\partial x} - \frac{\partial P}{\partial y} = 0$$

or

$$\frac{\partial P}{\partial y} = \frac{\partial Q}{\partial x} .$$

Notice that when curl $\overline{a} = \overline{0}$, that is, when vector $\overline{a}$ is conservative, Green's theorem gives

$$\oint_C \overline{a} \cdot d\overline{r} = \iint_R (\nabla \times \overline{a}) \cdot \overline{k} \, dxdy$$

$$= \iint_R (0)dxdy = 0$$

which is in agreement with the foregoing discussion.

Consider the motion of a particle in a plane perpendicular to the surface of the earth. The particle moves in the gravitational field

$$\overline{F}(x,y) = (0,mg) \tag{1}$$

where m is the mass of the particle and g is the gravitational acceleration.

Show that the amount of work required to move the particle from a point A to a point B depends only on the position of points A and B. Also, show that the work required to move the particle along any closed curve is zero.

Solution: It is already known that if $\overline{F}$ is the force field and C is a simple closed curve, then

$$\oint_C \overline{F} \cdot \overline{T} \, ds = \iint_R curl \, \overline{F} \, dxdy \tag{2}$$

This is one of the vector forms of Green's theorem (see Problem 17-34). The line integral represents the work done in moving a particle around a closed curve C in the counter-clockwise (positive) direction under the influence of $\overline{F}$.

In this case, $\overline{F}$ is the gravitational field

$$\overline{F} = (0, \, mg) \tag{3}$$

Thus,

$$curl \, \overline{F} = \left[\frac{\partial(mg)}{\partial x} - \frac{\partial 0}{\partial y} \right] \overline{k} = \overline{0} \tag{4}$$

By combining eqs.(2) and (4), we conclude that

$$\oint_C \overline{F} \cdot \overline{T} \, ds = 0 \tag{5}$$

That is, the work done in moving a particle around a closed curve is zero. Consider two arbitrary paths connecting A and B.

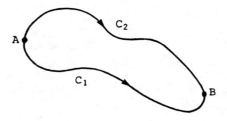

Let L_1 denote the work done in moving the particle from A to B along path C_1, and L_2 denote the work done in moving the particle from A to B along path C_2 (see the figure).

From eq.(5), we conclude that

$$L_1 + (-L_2) = 0 \tag{6}$$

since C_1 and C_2 form a closed curve. Thus,

$$L_1 = L_2 \tag{7}$$

and we conclude that the work required to move the particle from A to B is independent of path and is dependent only on the position of points A and B.

In general, for any field

$$\overline{F} = (f_1, f_2) \tag{8}$$

such that

$$\frac{\partial F_2}{\partial x} = \frac{\partial F_1}{\partial y} \tag{9}$$

the work done in moving the particle along any closed curve in the plane is equal to zero.

● **PROBLEM 17-39**

Let C be a regular closed curve enclosing region $B \subset R^2$, and $\overline{F}$ be a continuously differentiable vector field defined on a region containing B and C. Define the circulation of $\overline{F}$ around C. What conclusions can you draw after applying Green's theorem?

Solution: We can assume that C has a smooth parametrization

$$\overline{p}(t) = (p_1(t), p_2(t)), \quad a \le t \le b \tag{1}$$

The unit tangent to C is

$$\overline{T}(t) = \frac{\overline{p}'(t)}{|\overline{p}'(t)|} = \left[\frac{p_1'(t)}{|\overline{p}'(t)|}, \frac{p_2'(t)}{|\overline{p}'(t)|} \right] \tag{2}$$

Here

$$p_i'(t) = \frac{dp_i(t)}{dt} \tag{3}$$

and

$$\overline{p}'(t) = \frac{d\overline{p}(t)}{dt} \tag{4}$$

The unit normal vector is given by

$$\overline{n}(t) = \left[\frac{p_2'(t)}{|\overline{p}'(t)|}, \frac{-p_1'(t)}{|\overline{p}'(t)|} \right] \tag{5}$$

The circulation of $\overline{F}$ around C is defined as

$$\oint_C F_1 dx_1 + F_2 dx_2 \tag{6}$$

The line integral in eq.(6) can be written in the form

$$\oint_C F_1 dx_1 + F_2 dx_2 = \int_a^b \overline{F}(\overline{p}(t)) \cdot \overline{T}(t) |\overline{p}'(t)| dt$$

(7)

$$= \oint_C \overline{F} \cdot \overline{T} \ ds$$

From the definition of curl, we obtain

$$\text{curl } \overline{F} = \frac{\partial F_2}{\partial x_1} - \frac{\partial F_1}{\partial x_2}$$

(8)

Thus, Green's theorem can be written as

$$\oint_C \overline{F} \cdot \overline{T} \ ds = \iint_B \text{curl } \overline{F} \ dx_1 dx_2$$

(9)

Eq.(9) is sometimes called Stoke's Theorem. If $\overline{F}$ represents the force field, then the line integral represents the work done in moving a particle around C in the positive (counterclockwise) direction.

In particular, if curl $\overline{F} = \overline{0}$ in B, then the work is zero for every smooth path contained in B.

Thus, if curl $\overline{F} = \overline{0}$ everywhere in B, then the circulation of $\overline{F}$ around every smooth closed curve in B is zero.

A field $\overline{F}$ such that curl $\overline{F} = \overline{0}$ is called an irrotational field.

● **PROBLEM** 17-40

Consider the flow through a region S of the $x_1 x_2$-plane. Using Green's theorem, show that the rate of flow out of S is equal to the integral over S of the divergence of the flow.

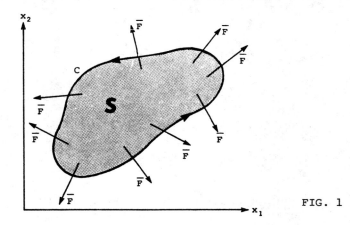

FIG. 1

Solution: Let $\overline{F}$ be the velocity field of flow

$$\overline{F}(x,y) = (f_1(x,y), \ f_2(x,y))$$

(1)

810

The rate of flow out of S is the amount of substance that
flows out of S per unit time.

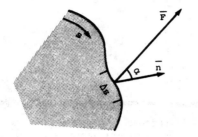

FIG. 2

Let $\bar{n}$ be the unit normal vector to S and let s denote
the arclength parameter (taken along the boundary curve C,
of surface S). The amount of substance that flows out of an
element Δs is

$$|\bar{F}|\Delta s \ \cos\alpha = \bar{F} \cdot \bar{n} \ \Delta s \qquad (2)$$

as shown in Fig. 2.

Taking the limit $\Delta s \to 0$ and integrating over S,

$$\lim_{\Delta s \to 0} \sum \bar{F} \cdot \bar{n} \ \Delta s = \int_{s_0}^{s_1} \bar{F} \cdot \bar{n} \ ds \qquad (3)$$

Now, if the curve is parametrized by

$$\begin{aligned} x &= x(s) \\ y &= y(s) \end{aligned} \qquad (4)$$

then the unit normal vector is

$$\bar{n} = \left(\frac{dy}{ds} \ , \ -\frac{dx}{ds}\right) \qquad (5)$$

Integral (3) then becomes

$$\int_{s_0}^{s_1} (f_1,f_2) \cdot \left(\frac{dy}{ds} \ , \ -\frac{dx}{ds}\right) ds$$

$$= \int_{s_0}^{s_1} f_1\left(\frac{dy}{ds} - f_2 \ \frac{dx}{ds}\right) ds = \oint_C -f_2(x,y)dx + f_1(x,y)dy \qquad (6)$$

Thus,

$$\begin{array}{l} \text{the rate of flow} \\ \text{out of S} \end{array} = \oint_C -f_2 dx + f_1 dy \qquad (7)$$

Now, applying Green's theorem, we may write

$$\oint_C -f_2 dx + f_1 dy = \iint_S \left(\frac{\partial f_1}{\partial x} + \frac{\partial f_2}{\partial y}\right) dx dy$$

Thus,

$$\text{Rate of flow} = \iint_S \left(\frac{\partial f_1}{\partial x} + \frac{\partial f_2}{\partial y}\right) \, dxdy$$

(8)

$$= \iint_S \text{div } \overline{F} \, dxdy$$

● **PROBLEM** 17-41

Consider the flow $\overline{F}$ defined in a region B such that the divergence of $\overline{F}$ is zero everywhere in B. Show that the rate of flow across every closed path in B is zero.

Solution: Region B is shown in the figure.

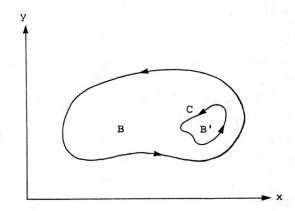

Let C be an arbitrary closed curve in B.
The rate of flow across C is

$$\oint_C -f_2(x,y)dx + f_1(x,y)dy$$

(1)

where

$$\overline{F} = (f_1(x,y), \ f_2(x,y))$$

(2)

We are told that at every point in B, the flow $\overline{F}$ has zero divergence,

$$\text{div } \overline{F} = \frac{\partial f_1}{\partial x} + \frac{\partial f_2}{\partial y} = 0$$

(3)

or

$$\frac{\partial f_1}{\partial x} = -\frac{\partial f_2}{\partial y}$$

(4)

Let us apply Green's theorem to region B' enclosed by curve C.

$$\oint_C -f_2(x,y)dx + f_1(x,y)dy = \iint_B \left(\frac{\partial f_1}{\partial x} + \frac{\partial f_2}{\partial y}\right) \, dxdy$$

$$= \iint_B 0 \ dxdy = 0 \tag{5}$$

Hence the rate of flow across any closed path in B is zero.

● **PROBLEM 17-42**

Write Green's theorem in the form called Gauss' theorem.

<u>Solution</u>: Let B be a region whose boundary is a smooth closed curve C.

Curve C has a smooth parametrization

$$\bar{p}(t) = (p_1(t), p_2(t)) \quad a \leq t \leq b \tag{1}$$

The unit normal vector $\bar{n}$ is

$$\bar{n}(t) = \left[\frac{p_2'(t)}{|\bar{p}'(t)|}, \frac{-p_1'(t)}{|\bar{p}'(t)|} \right] \tag{2}$$

Here, the prime denotes differentiation with respect to t,

$$p_1'(t) = \frac{dp_1(t)}{dt} \tag{3}$$

Applying Green's theorem to the pair of functions $\bar{F} = (-F_2, F_1)$, we find

$$\oint_C -F_2 dx_1 + F_1 dx_2 = \int_a^b \bar{F}(\bar{p}(t)) \cdot \bar{n}(t) |\bar{p}'(t)| dt$$

$$= \oint_C \bar{F} \cdot \bar{n} \ ds = \iint_B \left(\frac{\partial F_1}{\partial x_1} + \frac{\partial F_2}{\partial x_2} \right) dx_1 dx_2 \tag{4}$$

Since

$$\frac{\partial F_1}{\partial x_1} + \frac{\partial F_2}{\partial x_2} = \text{div} \ \bar{F} \tag{5}$$

eq.(4) becomes

$$\oint_C \bar{F} \cdot \bar{n} \ ds = \iint_B \text{div} \ \bar{F} \ dx_1 dx_2 \tag{6}$$

Green's theorem in this form is called Gauss' theorem.

If we describe a fluid flow where $\bar{F} = \bar{v}$ represents the velocity field, then

$$\oint_C \bar{v} \cdot \bar{n} \ ds = \iint_B \text{div} \ \bar{v} \ dx_1 dx_2 \tag{7}$$

The line integral in eq.(7) represents the total flow, or flux ϕ of $\bar{v}$ across C in the outward direction.

813

$$\phi = \oint_C \overline{v} \cdot \overline{n} \ ds \qquad (8)$$

Gauss' theorem states that the flux across C is equal to the integral of the divergence of $\overline{v}$ over the region enclosed by C. If div $\overline{v}$ is positive in B, then the flux ϕ (defined as the outward flow) will be positive. If div $\overline{v} = 0$ throughout B, then $\overline{v}$ is said to represent an incompressible flow.

● **PROBLEM 17-43**

Derive Gauss' theorem for the vector field $\overline{F}$ such that

$$\overline{F} = \text{grad } f \qquad (1)$$

where f is a real-valued function. Assume that all the necessary partial derivatives exist and are continuous.

Solution: If $\overline{F}$ is a vector field such that

$$\overline{F} = (F_1, F_2) \qquad (2)$$

then

$$\text{div } \overline{F} = \frac{\partial F_1}{\partial x_1} + \frac{\partial F_2}{\partial x_2} \qquad (3)$$

Green's theorem written in the form

$$\oint_C \overline{F} \cdot \overline{n} \ ds = \iint_B \text{div } \overline{F} \ dx_1 dx_2 \qquad (4)$$

is called Gauss' theorem.

For $\overline{F}$ given by

$$\overline{F} = \text{grad } f = \left(\frac{\partial f}{\partial x_1}, \frac{\partial f}{\partial x_2} \right) \qquad (5)$$

the divergence of $\overline{F}$ is

$$\text{div } \overline{F} = \frac{\partial F_1}{\partial x_1} + \frac{\partial F_2}{\partial x_2} = \frac{\partial^2 f}{\partial x_1^2} + \frac{\partial^2 f}{\partial x_2^2} = \Delta f \qquad (6)$$

where

$$\Delta \equiv \frac{\partial^2}{\partial x_1^2} + \frac{\partial^2}{\partial x_2^2} \qquad (7)$$

is the Laplacian operator.

Substituting eq.(6) into eq.(4),

$$\oint_C \nabla f \cdot \overline{n} \ ds = \iint_B \Delta f \ dx_1 dx_2 \qquad (8)$$

If f is a harmonic function in the region B, that is,

$$\Delta f(x_1, x_2) \equiv 0 \quad \text{for all } (x_1, x_2) \ \varepsilon \ B, \qquad (9)$$

then the integral of grad $f \cdot \overline{n}$ around the curve C which encloses B is zero.

CAUCHY-RIEMANN EQUATIONS, LINE INTEGRALS INDEPENDENT OF PATH

● PROBLEM 17-44

The Cauchy-Riemann equations

$$\frac{\partial u}{\partial x} = \frac{\partial v}{\partial y} \quad , \quad \frac{\partial u}{\partial y} = -\frac{\partial v}{\partial x} \tag{1}$$

frequently appear in the theory of functions of a complex variable. These equations can be written in the vector form

$$\text{div } \overline{v} = 0, \quad \text{curl } \overline{v} = \overline{0} \tag{2}$$

Indeed, if

$$\overline{v} = u\overline{i} - v\overline{j} \tag{3}$$

then

$$\text{div } \overline{v} = \frac{\partial u}{\partial x} - \frac{\partial v}{\partial y} = 0 \tag{4}$$

and

$$\text{curl } \overline{v} = \left(-\frac{\partial v}{\partial x} - \frac{\partial u}{\partial y}\right)\overline{k} = \overline{0}$$

Show that if $u(x,y)$ and $v(x,y)$ are the real and imaginary parts, respectively, of the complex-valued functions

1. e^{x+iy}

2. $(x+iy)^2$

then the vector field

$$\overline{F}(x,y) = (v(x,y), u(x,y)) \tag{5}$$

is irrotational and incompressible (solenoidal).

Solution: 1. From the Euler formula

$$e^{i\theta} = \cos\theta + i\sin\theta \tag{6}$$

we have

$$e^{x+iy} = e^x e^{iy} = e^x(\cos y + i\sin y)$$
$$= e^x \cos y + i e^x \sin y \tag{7}$$

Thus

$$u(x,y) = e^x \cos y$$

and

$$v(x,y) = e^x \sin y \tag{8}$$

The vector field

$$\overline{F}(x,y) = (e^x \sin y, \ e^x \cos y) \tag{9}$$

is irrotational, since

$$\text{curl } \overline{F} = \left[\frac{\partial F_2}{\partial x} - \frac{\partial F_1}{\partial y} \right] \overline{k} = \left[e^x \cos y - e^x \cos y \right] \overline{k} = \overline{0} \tag{10}$$

and incompressible, since

$$\text{div } \overline{F} = \frac{\partial F_1}{\partial x} + \frac{\partial F_2}{\partial y} = e^x \sin y - e^x \sin y = 0 \tag{11}$$

2. In this case, we have

$$(x+iy)^2 = x^2 - y^2 + 2xyi \tag{12}$$

Thus

$$u(x,y) = x^2 - y^2$$
$$v(x,y) = 2xy \tag{13}$$

and

$$\overline{F} = (2xy, \ x^2 - y^2) \tag{14}$$

Now, since

$$\text{curl } \overline{F} = \left[\frac{\partial}{\partial x}(x^2 - y^2) - \frac{\partial}{\partial y} \right] \overline{k} = \overline{0} \tag{15}$$

and

$$\text{div } \overline{F} = \frac{\partial}{\partial x}(2xy) + \frac{\partial}{\partial y}(x^2 - y^2) = 0 \tag{16}$$

we conclude that the vector field $\overline{F}$ given by eq.(14) is irrotational and incompressible.

● **PROBLEM 17-45**

Evaluate

$$\int_{(0,0)}^{(4,1)} (12x^3 - 2y^3)dx - 6xy^2 dy \tag{1}$$

along the curve

$$x^3 - 3xy^2 = 52y^3 \tag{2}$$

Solution: This integral can be evaluated directly from the definition of the line integral. There is a simpler method, however.

Let

$$P(x,y) = 12x^3 - 2y^3 \tag{3}$$

$$Q(x,y) = -6xy^2 \tag{4}$$

Since

$$\frac{\partial P}{\partial y} = \frac{\partial Q}{\partial x} = -6y^2, \tag{5}$$

both derivatives are equal, and it follows that the integral is independent of the path. Therefore, we can use any path joining points (0,0) and (4,1). The simplest path consists of the two line segments shown in the figure.

Along the line from (0,0) to (4,0), $y = 0$ and $dy = 0$, thus

$$\int_0^4 12x^3 dx = 3x^4 \Big|_0^4 = 768 \tag{6}$$

Along the straight line from (4,0) to (4,1), we have $x = 4$ and $dx = 0$. Therefore,

$$-\int_0^1 24y^2 dy = -8y^3 \Big|_0^1 = -8 \tag{7}$$

Thus, the total value of the line integral is

$$\int_{(0,0)}^{(4,1)} (12x^3 - 2y^3) dx - 6xy^2 dy = 768 - 8 = 760 \tag{8}$$

There is still another method of evaluating integral (1).

Since

$$\frac{\partial P}{\partial y} = \frac{\partial Q}{\partial x} \tag{9}$$

the expression $(12x^3 - 2y^3)dx - 6xy^2 dy$ is an exact differential of some function $f(x,y)$, and we may write

$$df = \frac{\partial f}{\partial x} dx + \frac{\partial f}{\partial y} dy \tag{10}$$

$$= (12x^3 - 2y^3)dx - 6xy^2 dy$$

Since

$$\frac{\partial f}{\partial x} = 12x^3 - 2y^3$$

$$\frac{\partial f}{\partial y} = -6xy^2$$

we easily obtain that

$$f(x,y) = 3x^4 - 2xy^3 \tag{11}$$

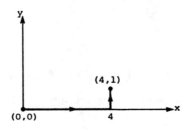

Thus, integral (1) can be written as

$$\int_{(0,0)}^{(4,1)} (12x^3 - 2y^3)dx - 6xy^2 dy = \int_{(0,0)}^{(4,1)} d(3x^4 - 2xy^3) \tag{12}$$

$$= 3x^4 - 2xy^3 \left. \right|_{(0,0)}^{(4,1)} = 760$$

● **PROBLEM** 17-46

Show that

$$\oint_C \overline{r} \cdot d\overline{r} = 0 \tag{1}$$

where

$$\overline{r} = x\overline{i} + y\overline{j} \tag{2}$$

and C is any closed curve.

Solution: Integral (1) can be evaluated directly from eq. (7) of Problem 17-34, which is a vector form of Green's theorem.

Substituting

$$\overline{a} = \overline{r} \tag{3}$$

we obtain

$$\oint_C \overline{r} \cdot d\overline{r} = \iint_R (\nabla \times \overline{r})_z \, dxdy \tag{4}$$

Note the notation

$$(\nabla \times \overline{r})_z = (\nabla \times \overline{r}) \cdot \overline{k}$$

From the definition of curl,

$$(\nabla \times \overline{r})_z = \frac{\partial}{\partial x}(y) - \frac{\partial}{\partial y}(x) = 0 \tag{5}$$

Thus

$$\oint_C \overline{r} \cdot d\overline{r} = 0 \tag{6}$$

along any closed curve.

● **PROBLEM** 17-47

Evaluate

$$\int_{(1,0)}^{(-1,0)} \frac{ydx-xdy}{x^2+y^2} \tag{1}$$

along

1. The semicircle shown in Fig. 1.

2. The path consisting of the straight line segments shown in Fig. 2.

Although $\frac{\partial Q}{\partial y} = \frac{\partial P}{\partial x}$, the line integral is not independent of the path joining (1,0) and (-1,0).

Explain this apparent discrepancy.

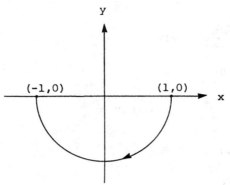

Fig. 1

Solution: 1. The semicircle can be parametrized by

$$x = \cos t \quad -\pi \le t \le 0 \tag{2}$$

$$y = \sin t$$

Thus

$$dx = -\sin t \, dt \tag{3}$$

$$dy = \cos t \, dt$$

Integral (1) can be evaluated as follows:

$$\int_{(1,0)}^{(-1,0)} \frac{ydx-xdy}{x^2+y^2} = \int_0^{-\pi} \frac{-\sin^2 t dt - \cos^2 t dt}{\sin^2 t + \cos^2 t} \tag{4}$$

$$= -\int_0^{-\pi} dt = \pi$$

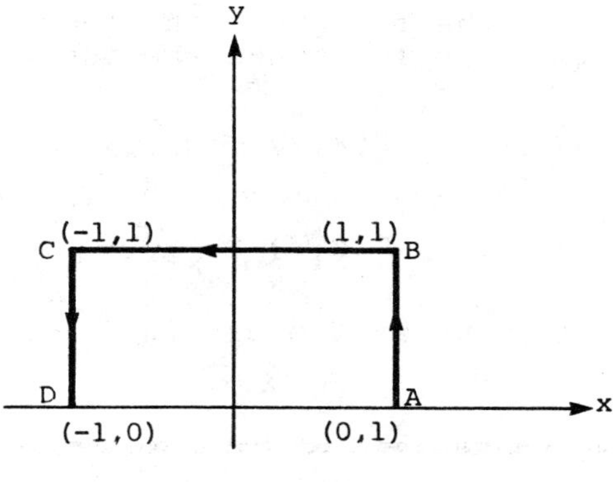

Fig. 2

2. We shall calculate integral (1) along each of the line segments and subsequently add up the results. Along AB, x = 1 and dx = 0, thus the line integral reduces to

$$\int_0^1 \frac{-dy}{1+y^2} \tag{5}$$

819

Since

$$\frac{dx}{1+x^2} = arc\ tan\ x \tag{6}$$

integral (5) becomes

$$\int_0^1 \frac{-dy}{1+y^2} = -arc\ tan\ y \ \bigg|_0^1 = -\frac{\pi}{4} \tag{7}$$

Along BC, y = 1 and dy = 0, thus

$$\int_1^{-1} \frac{dx}{1+x^2} = arc\ tan\ x \ \bigg|_1^{-1} = -\frac{\pi}{4} - \frac{\pi}{4} = -\frac{\pi}{2} \tag{8}$$

Along CD, x = -1, dx = 0, thus

$$\int_1^0 \frac{dy}{1+y^2} = arc\ tan\ y \ \bigg|_1^0 = -\frac{\pi}{4} \tag{9}$$

Integral (1) evaluated along ABCD equals

$$\int_{(1,0)}^{(-1,0)} \frac{ydx-xdy}{x^2+y^2} = -\frac{\pi}{4} - \frac{\pi}{2} - \frac{\pi}{4} = -\pi \tag{10}$$

Since eqs.(10) and (4) are not equal, we have shown that the value of integral (1) is not independent of path but rather does depend on the path of integration even though the partial derivatives are equal,

$$\frac{\partial Q}{\partial y} = \frac{\partial P}{\partial x}$$

This is due to the fact that the theorem on conservative fields does not apply, since the functions

$$P(x,y) = \frac{y}{x^2+y^2}$$

$$Q(x,y) = \frac{-x}{x^2+y^2}$$

are not continuous at the origin.

● **PROBLEM 17-48**

Let P(x,y) and Q(x,y) be two functions such that P, Q, $\frac{\partial Q}{\partial x}$, $\frac{\partial P}{\partial y}$ are continuous and

$$\frac{\partial Q}{\partial x} = \frac{\partial P}{\partial y} \tag{1}$$

except at the points (-2,0), (0,0) and (2,0).

Let

$$C_1 : x^2+y^2 = 16 \qquad C_2 : (x+2)^2+y^2 = 1$$

$$C_3 : x^2+y^2 = \frac{1}{4} \qquad C_4 : (x-2)^2+y^2 = 1$$

Furthermore, let

$$\oint_{C_n} Pdx + Qdy = A_n \qquad (2)$$

for $n = 1,2,3,4$.

1. Evaluate A_2 if $A_1 = 10$, $A_3 = -4$ and $A_4 = 3$.

2. Evaluate A_1 if $A_2 = 3$, $A_3 = 4$ and $A_4 = -7$.

<u>Solution</u>: 1. Consider the shaded region R shown in the figure.

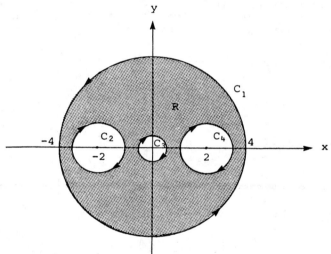

In R, the functions P and Q are continuous and have continuous derivatives. Thus, Green's theorem can be applied to yield

$$\oint_{C} Pdx + Qdy = \iint_{R} \left(\frac{\partial Q}{\partial x} - \frac{\partial P}{\partial y} \right) dxdy$$

$$= \iint_{R} 0 \; dxdy = 0 \qquad (3)$$

Note that $\frac{\partial Q}{\partial x} = \frac{\partial P}{\partial y}$ except at the points which do not belong to R. The positive direction is indicated by the arrows. The integral in eq.(3) is taken over the boundary of R consisting of C_1, C_2, C_3 and C_4.

$$\int_{C_1} + \int_{C_2} + \int_{C_3} + \int_{C_4} = 0 \qquad (4)$$

821

The last three integrals in eq.(4) are calculated for the clockwise direction. Therefore,

$$A_1 - A_2 - A_3 - A_4 = 0 \tag{5}$$
$$10 - A_2 + 4 - 3 = 0$$
$$A_2 = 11 \quad \text{or} \quad \oint_{C_2} Pdx + Qdy = 11 \tag{6}$$

2. Substituting the numerical values into eq.(5) results in

$$A_1 - 3 - 4 + 7 = 0 \tag{7}$$

and

$$A_1 = 0 \quad \text{or}$$
$$\oint_{C_1} Pdx + Qdy = 0 \tag{8}$$

● PROBLEM 17-49

Let C be a simple closed curve and R a region bounded by this curve, and let P(x,y) and Q(x,y) be continuous and have continuous derivatives everywhere in R.

Prove that around every closed curve C

$$\oint_C Pdx + Qdy = 0 \tag{1}$$

if and only if

$$\frac{\partial P}{\partial y} = \frac{\partial Q}{\partial x} \tag{2}$$

Solution: First, we shall prove that

$$\left(\oint_C Pdx + Qdy = 0 \right) \Leftarrow \left(\frac{\partial P}{\partial y} = \frac{\partial Q}{\partial x} \right) \tag{3}$$

The sign ⇒ means "implies that". Since P and Q are continuous and have continuous first partial derivatives, we can apply Green's theorem,

$$\oint_C Pdx + Qdy = \iint_R \left(\frac{\partial Q}{\partial x} - \frac{\partial P}{\partial y} \right) dxdy \tag{4}$$

If $\frac{\partial Q}{\partial x} - \frac{\partial P}{\partial y} = 0$ in R, then

$$\oint_C Pdx + Qdy = 0 \tag{5}$$

Now, we shall prove the theorem in the opposite direction,

$$\left(\oint_C Pdx + Qdy = 0 \right) \Rightarrow \left(\frac{\partial P}{\partial y} = \frac{\partial Q}{\partial x} \right) \tag{6}$$

Let us assume that

$$\frac{\partial Q}{\partial x} - \frac{\partial P}{\partial y} > 0 \tag{7}$$

at some point A in R. From the continuity of the derivatives, we conclude that there exists some region D surrounding A such that

$$\frac{\partial Q}{\partial x} - \frac{\partial P}{\partial y} > 0 \tag{8}$$

everywhere in region D.

If M is the boundary of D, then

$$\oint_M Pdx + Qdy = \iint_D \left(\frac{\partial Q}{\partial x} - \frac{\partial P}{\partial y} \right) dxdy > 0 \tag{9}$$

However, this contradicts the assumption that

$$\oint_C Pdx + Qdy = 0 \tag{10}$$

around every closed curve.

By the same token, we can show that the assumption

$$\frac{\partial Q}{\partial x} - \frac{\partial P}{\partial y} < 0 \tag{11}$$

also leads to a contradiction. Thus

$$\frac{\partial Q}{\partial x} = \frac{\partial P}{\partial y} \tag{12}$$

everywhere in the region R.

● **PROBLEM 17-50**

Consider vector field

$$\bar{a} = \frac{-y\bar{i} + x\bar{j}}{x^2 + y^2} \text{.} \tag{1}$$

Evaluate curl $\bar{a}$ and then

$$\oint_C \bar{a} \cdot d\bar{r} \tag{2}$$

around any closed curve C.

<u>Solution</u>: From the definition of curl,

823

$$\text{curl } \overline{a} = \begin{vmatrix} \overline{i} & \overline{j} & \overline{k} \\ \dfrac{\partial}{\partial x} & \dfrac{\partial}{\partial y} & \dfrac{\partial}{\partial z} \\ \dfrac{-y}{x^2+y^2} & \dfrac{x}{x^2+y^2} & 0 \end{vmatrix} = (0,0,0) \qquad (3)$$

everywhere in the xy-plane except the origin (0,0).

From eq.(1)

$$\oint_C \overline{a} \cdot d\overline{r} = \oint_C \frac{-ydx+xdy}{x^2+y^2} \qquad (4)$$

In polar coordinates (ρ,θ),

$$x = \rho \cos\theta \ , \quad dx = -\rho\sin\theta d\theta + \cos\theta d\rho \qquad (5)$$
$$y = \rho \sin\theta \quad\quad dy = \rho \cos\theta d\theta + \sin\theta d\rho$$

Thus

$$\frac{-ydx+xdy}{x^2+y^2} = d\left(\arctan \frac{y}{x}\right) = d\theta \qquad (6)$$

Consider now the two curves, ABCA which surrounds the origin (0,0) (0,0), and DEFD, which does not surround the origin.

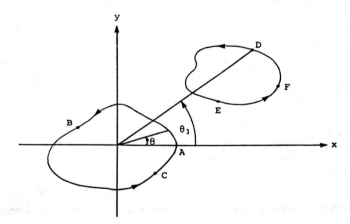

For ABCA

$$\int_{ABCA} \overline{a} \cdot d\overline{r} = \int_0^{2\pi} d\theta = 2\pi \qquad (7)$$

For the curve DEFD, the angle θ changes from $\theta = \theta_1$ to $\theta = \theta_1$, thus

$$\int_{DEFD} \overline{a} \cdot d\overline{r} = \int_{\theta_1}^{\theta_1} d\theta = 0 \qquad (8)$$

Even though curl $\overline{a} = \overline{0}$, we still obtained different values for different curves. The reason for this is that the functions $\dfrac{-y}{x^2+y^2}$ and $\dfrac{x}{x^2+y^2}$ are not continuous and do not have continuous derivatives throughout any region containing (0,0).

TRANSFORMATION OF COORDINATES

Consider a regular closed curve C and a region R bounded by C. Let P(x,y) and Q(x,y) be continuous functions with continuous partial derivatives. Green's theorem can be applied to this situation,

$$\oint_C P dx + Q dy = \iint_R \left(\frac{\partial Q}{\partial x} - \frac{\partial P}{\partial y} \right) dx dy \qquad (1)$$

Let us now interchange functions P and Q as well as co-ordinates x and y. Derive Green's theorem for the new situation and discuss the results.

Solution: The curve C and region R are shown in the figure.

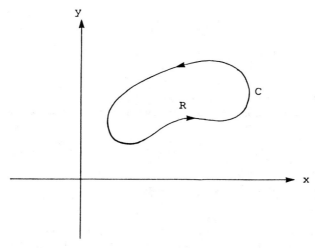

In eq.(1) the line integral is computed along the curve C in the positive direction, which is the counterclockwise direction. Interchanging functions P and Q and coordinates x and y transforms eq.(1) into

$$\oint_C Q dy + P dx = \iint_R \left(\frac{\partial P}{\partial y} - \frac{\partial Q}{\partial x} \right) dx dy \qquad (2)$$

The left side of eq.(2) is the same as the left side of eq. (1), but the right side has the opposite sign. In inter-changing the coordinates, we changed the orientation of the curve. In eq.(2) the integral $\oint_{-C} Q dy + P dx$ is evaluated in

825

the negative direction. Thus, the integral on the right side has the opposite sign.

In general,

$$\oint_C \bar{a} \cdot d\bar{r} = -\oint_{-C} \bar{a} \cdot d\bar{r} \tag{3}$$

where C and -C indicate opposite directions.

● **PROBLEM** 17-52

Let C be a simple closed curve and R a region bounded by this curve. The transformation of coordinates (x,y) is given by

$$x = x(u,v)$$
$$y = y(u,v) \tag{1}$$

Show that the area of R is given by

$$\iint_R \left| \frac{\partial(x,y)}{\partial(u,v)} \right| \, du\,dv \tag{2}$$

where

$$\frac{\partial(x,y)}{\partial(u,v)} = \begin{vmatrix} \dfrac{\partial x}{\partial u} & \dfrac{\partial y}{\partial u} \\[2mm] \dfrac{\partial x}{\partial v} & \dfrac{\partial y}{\partial v} \end{vmatrix} \tag{3}$$

is the Jacobian of the transformation.

Solution: If C is a simple closed curve and R is the region bounded by this curve, then the area A of the region is given by

$$A = \frac{1}{2} \oint_C x\,dy - y\,dx \tag{4}$$

Let us transform integral (4) to the coordinates (u,v). The differentials dx and dy can be evaluated from eq. (1),

$$dx = \frac{\partial x}{\partial u}\,du + \frac{\partial x}{\partial v}\,dv$$
$$dy = \frac{\partial y}{\partial u}\,du + \frac{\partial y}{\partial v}\,dv \tag{5}$$

Eq.(4) becomes

$$A = \frac{1}{2} \oint_C x\,dy - y\,dx$$

$$= \frac{1}{2} \oint_C \left[x \frac{\partial y}{\partial u} - y \frac{\partial x}{\partial u} \right] du + \left[x \frac{\partial y}{\partial v} - y \frac{\partial x}{\partial v} \right] dv \tag{6}$$

826

If all the functions in eq.(6) are continuous and have continuous partial derivatives, then we can apply Green's theorem to obtain

$$A = \frac{1}{2} \iint_R \left(\frac{\partial}{\partial u}\left[x\,\frac{\partial y}{\partial v} - y\,\frac{\partial x}{\partial v} \right] - \frac{\partial}{\partial v}\left[x\,\frac{\partial y}{\partial u} - y\,\frac{\partial x}{\partial u} \right] \right) du\,dv$$

$$= \frac{1}{2} \iint_R \left[\frac{\partial x}{\partial u}\,\frac{\partial y}{\partial v} + x\,\frac{\partial^2 y}{\partial u \partial v} - \frac{\partial y}{\partial u}\,\frac{\partial x}{\partial v} - y\,\frac{\partial^2 x}{\partial u \partial v} - \frac{\partial x}{\partial v}\,\frac{\partial y}{\partial u} \right.$$

$$\left. - x\,\frac{\partial^2 y}{\partial v \partial u} + \frac{\partial y}{\partial v}\,\frac{\partial x}{\partial u} + y\,\frac{\partial^2 x}{\partial v \partial u} \right] du\,dv \qquad (7)$$

$$= \iint_R \left[\frac{\partial x}{\partial u}\,\frac{\partial y}{\partial v} - \frac{\partial x}{\partial v}\,\frac{\partial y}{\partial u} \right] du\,dv$$

In eq.(7) we used the fact that

$$\frac{\partial^2 y}{\partial u \partial v} = \frac{\partial^2 y}{\partial v \partial u}$$

$$\frac{\partial^2 x}{\partial u \partial v} = \frac{\partial^2 x}{\partial v \partial u} \qquad (8)$$

since all the partial derivatives are continuous.

Now, since the Jacobian is

$$\frac{\partial(x,y)}{\partial(u,v)} = \begin{vmatrix} \dfrac{\partial x}{\partial u} & \dfrac{\partial y}{\partial u} \\[2ex] \dfrac{\partial x}{\partial v} & \dfrac{\partial y}{\partial v} \end{vmatrix} = \frac{\partial x}{\partial u}\,\frac{\partial y}{\partial v} - \frac{\partial x}{\partial v}\,\frac{\partial y}{\partial u} \qquad (9)$$

we conclude from (7) and (9) that

$$A = \iint_R \left| \frac{\partial(x,y)}{\partial(u,v)} \right| du\,dv.$$

CHAPTER 18

CONSERVATIVE VECTOR FIELDS

INTRODUCTION

Among all vector fields considered, conservative vector fields deserve special attention. The reason for this is that conservative fields, aside from having pleasant mathematical properties, are frequently encountered in physics in the form of gravitational fields, electrostatic fields and magnetic fields, among others.

The most important feature of conservative fields is that the line integral evaluated along a path from a point A to a point B is independent of the path that joins the two points. This leads directly to the statement that the line integral of a conservative field computed along any closed curve is zero. Often, either of these two properties are used as a definition of a conservative vector field.

Another interesting property of a conservative field is that such fields can be expressed as the gradient of a scalar field, called the potential function,

$$\overline{F} = \text{grad } f = \nabla f$$

This leads directly to the necessary condition that the curl, or rotation of a conservative field be zero,

$$\text{curl } \overline{F} = \overline{0}$$

This last condition has vast mathematical implications. A practical aspect of this is that if we wish to determine if a vector field $\overline{F}$ is conservative, then it is sufficient to evaluate its curl. If it turns out to be conservative, then it has, as mentioned before, a scalar potential $f(x,y,z)$ such that

$$\overline{F} = \text{grad } f$$

Thus, instead of having three functions $F_1(x,y,z)$, $F_2(x,y,z)$, $F_3(x,y,z)$ necessary to describe the physical field $\overline{F}$, it is enough to give one function $f(x,y,z)$ such that grad $f = \overline{F}$.

One important thing to keep in mind is that the poten-

tial function of a conservative field is not uniquely defined. Indeed, one can always add an arbitrary constant to
f(x,y,z) to obtain a new potential whose gradient is also $\overline{F}$.
However, in physics, certain boundary conditions are imposed
on the potential to ensure its uniqueness. A perfect example
of this is the condition that the potential due to gravitation, or the potential function of an electric field tend to
zero at infinity.

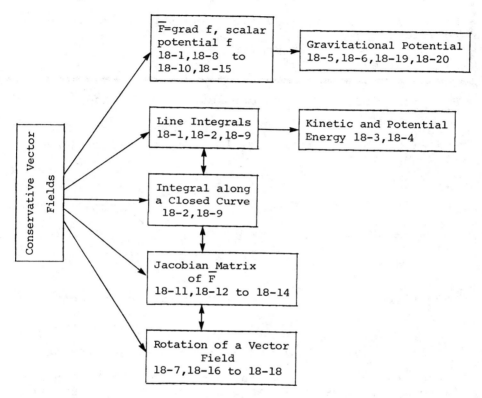

This chart is provided to facilitate rapid understanding of the inter-
relationships of the topics and subject matter in this chapter. Also
shown are the problem numbers associated with the subject matter.

● **PROBLEM** 18-1

A vector field $\overline{F}$ for which there exists a real-valued
function f such that

$$\overline{F} = \text{grad } f = \nabla f \tag{1}$$

is called a conservative field or gradient field. The
function f is called the potential of $\overline{F}$.

Prove the theorem:

Let $\overline{F}$ be a continuous vector field defined in a poly-
gonally connected open set B in the n-dimensional
Cartesian space, $B \subset R^n$. If the line integral

$$\int_C \overline{F} \cdot d\overline{x} \tag{2}$$

is independent of the piecewise smooth path C from $\overline{x}_0$ to $\overline{x}$ in B, then the function $f(\overline{x})$

$$f(\overline{x}) = \int_{\overline{x}_0}^{\overline{x}} \overline{F} \cdot d\overline{x} \tag{3}$$

is continuously differentiable and throughout B the relationship

$$\overline{F} = \text{grad } f$$

is satisfied.

Solution: Since B is an open subset of R^n and

$$\overline{x} = (x_1, x_2, \ldots, x_n) \tag{4}$$

and $\overline{x} \in B$, there exists a ball $K(\overline{x}, \delta)$ of radius δ and center at $\overline{x}$ such that

$$K(\overline{x}, \delta) \subset B \tag{5}$$

For all real numbers $|\alpha| < \delta$ and for any unit vector $\overline{u}$

$$\overline{x} + \alpha \overline{u} \in B$$

The line integral $\int_C \overline{F} \cdot d\overline{x}$ is independent of the path, therefore, we can choose any piecewise smooth path C from $\overline{x}_0$ to $\overline{x}$, lying in B and extend it to $\overline{x} + \alpha \overline{u}$, by a linear segment. Now, we shall show that the function $f(\overline{x})$ defined by (3) is continuously differentiable.

$$f(\overline{x} + \alpha\overline{u}) - f(\overline{x}) = \int_{\overline{x}_0}^{\overline{x}+\alpha\overline{u}} \overline{F} \cdot d\overline{x} - \int_{\overline{x}_0}^{\overline{x}} \overline{F} \cdot d\overline{x}$$

$$\tag{6}$$

$$= \int_{\overline{x}}^{\overline{x}+\alpha\overline{u}} \overline{F} \cdot d\overline{x} = \int_0^\alpha \overline{F}(\overline{x}+\beta\overline{u}) \cdot \overline{u} \, d\beta$$

If $\overline{u} = \overline{e}_k$ is the base vector in R^n, we obtain

$$\frac{\partial f}{\partial x_k}(\overline{x}) = \lim_{\alpha \to 0} \frac{f(\overline{x}+\alpha\overline{e}_k) - f(\overline{x})}{\alpha}$$

$$= \lim_{\alpha \to 0} \frac{1}{\alpha} \int_0^\alpha \overline{F}(\overline{x}+\beta\overline{e}_k) \cdot \overline{e}_k \, d\beta$$

$$= \frac{d}{d\alpha} \int_0^\alpha F(\overline{x}+\beta\overline{e}_k) \cdot \overline{e}_k \, d\beta \bigg|_{\alpha=0}$$

$$= \overline{F}(\overline{x}) \cdot \overline{e}_k = F_k(\overline{x}) \qquad (7)$$

Here, F_K indicates the kth component of F.

Since F is continuous, so are the partial derivatives $\frac{\partial f}{\partial x_k} = F_k$, and thus f is continuously differentiable in B. From eq.(7), we conclude that

$$\overline{F}(\overline{x}) = \text{grad } f(\overline{x}) = \nabla f(\overline{x}) \qquad (8)$$

where

$$\nabla \equiv \left(\frac{\partial}{\partial x_1}, \frac{\partial}{\partial x_2}, \ldots, \frac{\partial}{\partial x_n} \right) \qquad (9)$$

● **PROBLEM 18-2**

Show that if $\overline{F}$ is a continuous vector field defined in a region B of R^n, then the following two conditions are equivalent:

1. The line integral

$$\int_C \overline{F} \cdot d\overline{x} \qquad (1)$$

is independent of the piecewise smooth path C from $\overline{x}_0$ to $\overline{x}$ in B.

2. For every piecewise smooth closed curve E

$$\oint_E \overline{F} \cdot d\overline{x} = 0 \qquad (2)$$

Solution: First, we shall show that if condition 1 holds, then condition 2 holds as well. Indeed, let us take any closed piecewise smooth curve E in B and two arbitrary points $\overline{x}_0$ and $\overline{x}_1$ on E.

Since the line integral is independent of the path, we may write

$$\int_{\overline{x}_0}^{\overline{x}_1} \overline{F} \cdot d\overline{x} = \int_{\overline{x}_0}^{\overline{x}_1} \overline{F} \cdot d\overline{x} = - \int_{\overline{x}_1}^{\overline{x}_0} \overline{F} \cdot d\overline{x} \qquad (3)$$

along I   along II   along II

$$\int_{\overline{x}_0}^{\overline{x}_1} \overline{F} \cdot d\overline{x} + \int_{\overline{x}_1}^{\overline{x}_0} \overline{F} \cdot d\overline{x} = \oint_E \overline{F} \cdot d\overline{x} = 0 \qquad (4)$$

along I   along II

which verifies that condition 2 holds if condition 1 holds.

Now, we shall show that if condition 2 holds, then condition 1 holds as well.

Let $\overline{x}_0$ and $\overline{x}_1$ be any two points in B and C_1 and C_2 any two piecewise smooth curves in B.

From condition 2, we have

$$\oint_{C_1 \cup C_2} \overline{F} \cdot d\overline{x} = 0 \tag{5}$$

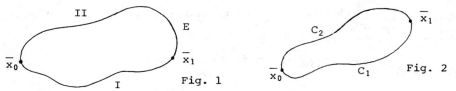

Fig. 1

Fig. 2

or

$$\int_{\overline{x}_0}^{\overline{x}_1} \overline{F} \cdot d\overline{x} + \int_{\overline{x}_1}^{\overline{x}_0} \overline{F} \cdot d\overline{x} = 0 \tag{6}$$

along C_1 along C_2

Thus

$$\int_{\overline{x}_0}^{\overline{x}_1} \overline{F} \cdot d\overline{x} = \int_{\overline{x}_0}^{\overline{x}_1} \overline{F} \cdot d\overline{x} \tag{7}$$

along C_1 along C_2

and condition 1 holds.

● **PROBLEM 18-3**

Consider a continuous force field $\overline{F}$ in the three-dimensional space R^3, such that the work done in moving a particle from one point to another under the influence of $\overline{F}$ is independent of the path between the two points. The work done in moving the particle from $\overline{r}_1$ to $\overline{r}_2$ is

$$L_{\overline{r}_1 \overline{r}_2} = \int_{\overline{r}_1}^{\overline{r}_2} \overline{F} \cdot d\overline{r} \tag{1}$$

Derive the formula for the kinetic energy of the particle and show that its total energy, kinetic plus potential, is constant.

Solution: The velocity and the acceleration vectors of the particle are

$$\overline{v}(t) = \frac{d\overline{r}}{dt} \qquad \overline{a}(t) = \frac{d\overline{v}}{dt} = \frac{d^2\overline{r}}{dt} \tag{2}$$

Newton's second law states that

$$\overline{F} = m\overline{a} \tag{3}$$

Thus

$$L_{\overline{r}_1 \overline{r}_2} = \int_{t_1}^{t_2} m\overline{a}(t) \cdot \overline{v}(t)dt \tag{4}$$

where $\overline{r}_1 = \overline{r}(t_1)$ and $\overline{r}_2 = \overline{r}(t_2)$.

Since

$$\bar{a}(t) = \frac{d\bar{v}}{dt}$$

and

$$\frac{d}{dt}(v^2(t)) = 2\bar{v}(t) \cdot \frac{d\bar{v}}{dt} = 2\bar{v}(t) \cdot \bar{a}(t) \qquad (5)$$

eq.(4) becomes

$$L_{\bar{r}_1\bar{r}_2} = \frac{m}{2}\int_{t_1}^{t_2} \frac{d}{dt}(v^2(t))dt$$

$$= \frac{m}{2}\left[v^2(t_2) - v^2(t_1)\right] = E(t_2) - E(t_1) \qquad (6)$$

The term

$$E = \frac{mv^2}{2} \qquad (7)$$

is, of course, the kinetic energy of the particle. Consider the scaler function

$$u(\bar{r}) = -\int_{\bar{r}_0}^{\bar{r}} \bar{F} \cdot d\bar{r} \qquad (8)$$

where $\bar{r}_0$ is a fixed point in R^3. Since the integral is independent of the path, we may write

$$L_{\bar{r}_1\bar{r}_2} = \int_{\bar{r}_1}^{\bar{r}_2} \bar{F} \cdot d\bar{r} = \int_{\bar{r}_1}^{\bar{r}_0} \bar{F} \cdot d\bar{r} + \int_{\bar{r}_0}^{\bar{r}_2} \bar{F} \cdot d\bar{r}$$

$$= \int_{\bar{r}_0}^{\bar{r}_2} \bar{F} \cdot d\bar{r} - \int_{\bar{r}_0}^{\bar{r}_1} \bar{F} \cdot d\bar{r} = -u(\bar{r}_2) + u(\bar{r}_1) \qquad (9)$$

Comparing eqs.(6) and (9), results in

$$\frac{mv^2(t_2)}{2} + u(\bar{r}_2) = \frac{mv^2(t_1)}{2} + u(\bar{r}_1) \qquad (10)$$

which tells us that the total energy of the particle is constant along the path.

Note that in the definition of potential energy (eq. (8)) the point $\bar{r}_0$ was arbitrarily chosen as the point for which potential energy is zero.

● **PROBLEM 18-4**

Consider the motion of a particle of mass m in the earth's gravitational field represented by

$$\bar{F}(x,y,z) = (0,0,-g) \qquad (1)$$

Find the potential function u(x,y,z) such that

$$u(0,0,0) = 0 \qquad (2)$$

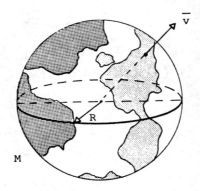

Solution: The potential function at a point $\bar{r}$ is defined by

$$u(\bar{r}) = - \int_{r_0}^{\bar{r}} \bar{F} \cdot d\bar{r} \qquad (3)$$

Substituting eq.(1) into eq.(3) results in

$$u(\bar{r}) = - \int_{r_0}^{\bar{r}} (0,0,-g) \cdot (dx,dy,dz)$$

$$= - \int_{r_0}^{\bar{r}} -gdz = g \int_{r_0}^{\bar{r}} dz = g(z-z_0) \qquad (4)$$

If we choose the point $\bar{r}_0$ such that

$$\bar{r}_0 = (0,0,0)$$

then

$$u(\bar{r}) = gz \qquad (5)$$

Note that the potential function $u(\bar{r})$ is zero for all the points with $z = 0$, that is, points on the earth's surface.

● **PROBLEM** 18-5

Express the gravitational force in terms of the gravitational potential.

What are the equipotential surfaces due to the gravitational field of a point mass i.e., a concentrated mass whose dimensions we neglect?

Solution: The gravitational force on a mass m due to a mass M located at the origin in R^3 is, according to Newton's law of gravitation, given by

$$\bar{F} = - \frac{GMm}{r^3} \bar{r} \qquad (1)$$

where G is the universal gravitational constant, $\bar{r} = x\bar{i} + y\bar{j} + z\bar{k}$, and $r = |\bar{r}| = \sqrt{x^2+y^2+z^2}$ is the distance of mass m from the origin.

Now, the gravitational potential function is

$$\phi = -\frac{GMm}{r} \qquad (2)$$

Now, let us calculate $\nabla\phi$.

$$\nabla\phi = \left[\frac{\partial}{\partial x}\,\overline{i} + \frac{\partial}{\partial y}\,\overline{j} + \frac{\partial}{\partial z}\,\overline{k}\right]\left(\frac{-GMm}{r}\right)$$

$$= -GMm\left[\frac{\partial}{\partial x}\,\frac{1}{\sqrt{x^2+y^2+z^2}}\,\overline{i} + \frac{\partial}{\partial y}\,\frac{1}{\sqrt{x^2+y^2+z^2}}\,\overline{j}\right.$$

$$\left. +\frac{\partial}{\partial z}\,\frac{1}{\sqrt{x^2+y^2+z^2}}\,\overline{k}\right]$$

$$= GMm\left[(x^2+y^2+z^2)^{-\frac{3}{2}}x\overline{i} + (x^2+y^2+z^2)^{-\frac{3}{2}}y\overline{j}\right.$$

$$\left. + (x^2+y^2+z^2)^{-\frac{3}{2}}z\overline{k}\right]$$

$$= \frac{GMm}{(\sqrt{x^2+y^2+z^2})^3}\left[x\overline{i} + y\overline{j} + z\overline{k}\right]$$

$$= \frac{GMm}{r^3}\,\overline{r}$$

Thus,

$$\nabla\phi = \frac{GMm}{r^3}\,\overline{r} \qquad (3)$$

From eqs.(3) and (1), we conclude that

$$\overline{F} = -\nabla\phi$$

that is, the gravitational force $\overline{F}$ is the negative of the gradient of the gravitational potential function ϕ.

Now, the surfaces for which a given potential function is constant are called equipotential surfaces. If we consider mass M to be point mass (concentrated mass with negligible dimensions), then the equipotential surfaces are those surfaces for which $r = $ constant. Thus, the equipotential surfaces are concentric spheres.

● **PROBLEM 18-6**

Using the conservation of energy principle,determine the initial velocity needed by a mass m in order that it may leave the earth's gravitational field.

Solution: First, note that at the surface of the earth, we take potential energy to be zero. Thus, the mass m has only kinetic energy at the surface of the earth.

On the other hand, as the distance from the earth's surface tends to infinity ∞, the total energy becomes potential.

Now, the gravitational force on a body of mass m at a distance r from the center of the earth is given by

$$\overline{F} = -G \frac{Mm}{r^3} \overline{r} \qquad (1)$$

where G is the gravitational constant and M denotes the mass of the earth.

This force is related to the gravitational potential function (the potential energy)

$$\phi = - \frac{GMm}{r} \qquad (2)$$

by

$$\overline{F} = -\nabla\phi. \qquad (3)$$

Now, from the conservation of energy principle, we conclude that the total energy at the earth's surface (all kinetic) is equal to the total energy (all potential) at infinity. Thus,

$$\frac{1}{2} mv^2 = \phi_{r\to\infty} \qquad (4)$$

Here, v represents the velocity that mass m must attain in order to leave the earth's surface.

Now, since work is the negative of potential, we may write

$$\frac{1}{2} mv^2 = -\lim_{R_1\to\infty} \int_R^{R_1} \overline{F} \cdot d\overline{r} \qquad (5)$$

Here, the term

$$\lim_{R_1\to\infty} \int_R^{R_1} \overline{F} \cdot d\overline{r}$$

represents the work done in going from the surface of the earth to infinity.

Substituting eq.(3) into eq.(5) yields

$$\frac{1}{2} mv^2 = -\lim_{R_1\to\infty} \int_R^{R_1} -\nabla\phi \cdot d\overline{r} = \lim_{R_1\to\infty} \int_R^{R_1} \nabla\phi \cdot d\overline{r} \qquad (6)$$

Now, since

$$\nabla\phi \cdot d\overline{r} = \left(\frac{\partial\phi}{\partial x}, \frac{\partial\phi}{\partial y}, \frac{\partial\phi}{\partial z} \right) \cdot (dx, dy, dz)$$

$$= \frac{\partial\phi}{\partial x} dx + \frac{\partial\phi}{\partial y} dy + \frac{\partial\phi}{\partial z} dz \qquad (7)$$

$$= d\phi$$

we obtain

$$\frac{1}{2} mv^2 = \lim_{R_1\to\infty} \int_R^{R_1} \nabla\phi \cdot d\overline{r} = \lim_{R_1\to\infty} \int_R^{R_1} d\phi$$

836

$$= \lim_{R_1 \to \infty} \left[\frac{-GMm}{r} \right]_{R}^{R_1}$$

$$= \lim_{R_1 \to \infty} \left[\frac{-GMm}{R_1} + \frac{GMm}{R} \right] \qquad (8)$$

$$= \frac{GMm}{R}$$

Thus,

$$v^2 = \frac{2GM}{R}$$

or

$$v = \sqrt{\frac{2GM}{R}} \qquad (9)$$

For

$$G = 9.97 \times 10^{-8} \frac{\text{dyne}}{\text{gm}^2 \text{cm}^2}$$

$$M = 6.1 \times 10^{27} \text{ gm}$$

$$R = 6.37 \times 10^8 \text{ cm}$$

we obtain

$$v = \sqrt{\frac{2GM}{R}} = 1.13 \times 10^6 \frac{\text{cm}}{\text{sec}} \ .$$

● **PROBLEM** 18-7

1. Show that a necessary and sufficient condition for

$$F_1 dx + F_2 dy + F_3 dz \qquad (1)$$

    to be an exact differential is that

$$\text{curl } \overline{F} = \overline{0} \qquad (2)$$

    where $\overline{F} = (F_1, F_2, F_3)$.

2. Show that

$$2xy^2 dx + (2x^2 y + 3y^2 \sin z) dy + y^3 \cos z\, dz \qquad (3)$$

    is an exact differential of $\phi(x,y,z)$ and determine $\phi(x,y,z)$.

Solution: Assuming that

$$F_1 dx + F_2 dy + F_3 dz = \frac{\partial \phi}{\partial x} dx + \frac{\partial \phi}{\partial y} dy + \frac{\partial \phi}{\partial z} dz = d\phi \qquad (4)$$

is an exact differential, we obtain

$$F_1 = \frac{\partial \phi}{\partial x} \ ; \quad F_2 = \frac{\partial \phi}{\partial y} \ ; \quad F_3 = \frac{\partial \phi}{\partial z} \qquad (5)$$

Therefore

$$\overline{F} = F_1 \overline{i} + F_2 \overline{j} + F_3 \overline{k} = \frac{\partial \phi}{\partial x} \overline{i} + \frac{\partial \phi}{\partial y} \overline{j} + \frac{\partial \phi}{\partial z} \overline{k} = \nabla \phi \qquad (6)$$

From the identity
$$\text{curl grad } f = 0 \tag{7}$$
we get
$$\text{curl } \overline{F} = \text{curl grad } \phi = \overline{0} \tag{8}$$
Conversely, if
$$\text{curl } \overline{F} = \overline{0} \tag{9}$$
then there exists ϕ, such that
$$\overline{F} = \text{grad } \phi \tag{10}$$
From eq.(10),
$$\overline{F} \cdot d\overline{r} = \nabla\phi \cdot d\overline{r} = d\phi \tag{11}$$
and
$$F_1 dx + F_2 dy + F_3 dz = d\phi \tag{12}$$
This is an exact differential.

2. From eq.(3), we conclude that
$$\overline{F} = 2xy^2\overline{i} + (2x^2y + 3y^2\sin z)\overline{j} + y^3\cos z\overline{k} \tag{13}$$
curl $\overline{F}$ is equal to

$$\nabla \times \overline{F} = \left[\frac{\partial}{\partial y} (y^3\cos z) - \frac{\partial}{\partial z} (2x^2y + 3y^2\sin z) \right] \overline{i}$$

$$+ \left[\frac{\partial}{\partial z} (2xy^2) - \frac{\partial}{\partial x} (y^3\cos z) \right] \overline{j}$$

$$+ \left[\frac{\partial}{\partial x} (2x^2y + 3y^2\sin z) - \frac{\partial}{\partial y} (2xy^2) \right] \overline{k}$$

$$= (3y^2\cos z - 3y^2\cos z)\overline{i} + (4xy - 4xy)\overline{k}$$

$$= \overline{0}$$

Thus, eq.(3) represents an exact differential
$$2xy^2 dx + (2x^2y + 3y^2\sin z)dy + y^3\cos z dz = d\phi \tag{14}$$
and
$$\frac{\partial\phi}{\partial x} = 2xy^2 \tag{15}$$

$$\frac{\partial\phi}{\partial y} = 2x^2y + 3y^2\sin z \tag{16}$$

$$\frac{\partial\phi}{\partial z} = y^3\cos z \tag{17}$$

Integrating eq.(15) results in
$$\phi(x,y,z) = x^2y^2 + f(y,z) \tag{18}$$
Differentiating with respect to y and comparing with eq.(16) we obtain
$$\frac{\partial\phi}{\partial y} = 2x^2y + \frac{\partial f}{\partial y} = 2x^2y + 3y^2\sin z$$
Thus,

$$\frac{\partial f}{\partial y} = 3y^2\sin z$$

and

$$f(y,z) = y^3\sin z + g(z) \qquad (19)$$

Substituting eq.(19) into eq.(18) gives

$$\phi(x,y,z) = x^2y^2 + y^3\sin z + g(z)$$

Differentiating with respect to z and comparing with eq.(17) yields

$$\frac{\partial \phi}{\partial z} = y^3\cos z + \frac{dg}{dz} = y^3\cos z \qquad (20)$$

or

$$\frac{dg}{dz} = 0 \quad \text{and} \quad g = \text{const.}$$

Therefore, the required function is

$$\phi(x,y,z) = x^2y^2 + y^3\sin z + \text{const.} \qquad (21)$$

● **PROBLEM** 18-8

Show that if $\overline{F}$ and $\overline{G}$ are conservative fields defined on the same domain B, then $\overline{F} + \overline{G}$ and $a\overline{F}$ (a is a constant) are also conservative fields.

<u>Solution</u>: Since $\overline{F}$ and $\overline{G}$ are conservative fields, they have potential functions f and g such that

$$\overline{F} = \nabla f \qquad (1)$$

$$\overline{G} = \nabla g \qquad (2)$$

It is easy to show that f + g is a potential function of the vector field $\overline{F} + \overline{G}$.

$$\overline{F} + \overline{G} = \nabla f + \nabla g = \nabla(f+g) \qquad (3)$$

Since $\overline{F}$ is a conservative vector field $\overline{F} = \nabla f$, $a\overline{F}$ is also a conservative vector field. Indeed

$$a\overline{F} = a\nabla f = \nabla(af) \qquad (4)$$

The potential function of $a\overline{F}$ is af.

It is worthwhile to mention that the vector space of conservative fields defined on B has infinite dimension.

● **PROBLEM** 18-9

Let $\overline{F}$ be a continuous vector field defined in an open set B of R^n. What is the relationship between these statements:

1. For every piecewise smooth curve C in B

$$\oint_C \overline{F} \cdot d\overline{x} = 0 \tag{1}$$

where $\quad \overline{x} = (x_1, x_2, \ldots, x_n)$.

2. The line integral of $\overline{F}$ over a path from $\overline{x}_0$ to $\overline{x}_1$ is independent of the piecewise smooth curve C from $\overline{x}_0$ to $\overline{x}_1$

$$\int_{\overline{x}_0}^{\overline{x}_1} \overline{F} \cdot d\overline{x} \tag{2}$$

3. A continuously differentiable function f exists such that

$$\overline{F} = \nabla f = \left(\frac{\partial f}{\partial x_1}, \frac{\partial f}{\partial x_2}, \ldots, \frac{\partial f}{\partial x_n} \right) \tag{3}$$

Solution: From Problem 18-1, we conclude that conditions 2 and 3 are equivalent.

From Problem 18-2, we see that the conditions 1 and 2 are also equivalent.

Thus, all three conditions are equivalent, and any one of these conditions guarantees that the vector field is conservative.

● **PROBLEM** 18-10

Show that

$$\overline{F} = (6xy^2+z)\overline{i} + (6x^2y+3y^2)\overline{j} + x\overline{k} \tag{1}$$

is conservative and find its potential function.

Solution: The potential function of $\overline{F}$ is that function ϕ such that

$$\overline{F} = \text{grad } \phi \tag{2}$$

From eqs.(1) and (2), we obtain

$$\frac{\partial \phi}{\partial x} = 6xy^2 + z \tag{3}$$

$$\frac{\partial \phi}{\partial y} = 6x^2y + 3y^2 \tag{4}$$

$$\frac{\partial \phi}{\partial z} = x \tag{5}$$

Integration of eq.(3) gives

$$\phi(x,y,z) = 3x^2y^2 + zx + f(y,z) \tag{6}$$

Differentiating eq.(6) we find

$$\frac{\partial \phi}{\partial y} = 6x^2y + \frac{\partial f}{\partial y} \tag{7}$$

From eqs. (4) and (7), we obtain

$$\frac{\partial f}{\partial y} = 3y^2 \tag{8}$$

Thus

$$f(y,z) = y^3 + g(z) \tag{9}$$

Substituting eq.(9) into eq.(6) results in

$$\phi(x,y,z) = 3x^2y^2 + zx + y^3 + g(z) \tag{10}$$

Differentiating eq.(10) with respect to z gives

$$\frac{\partial \phi}{\partial z} = x + \frac{dg}{dz} \tag{11}$$

Finally, comparing eqs.(5) and (11), we obtain

$$g = \text{const.} \tag{12}$$

Therefore

$$\phi(x,y,z) = 3x^2y^2 + y^3 + zx + \text{const.} \tag{13}$$

It is easy to verify that

$$\overline{F} = \text{grad } \phi \tag{14}$$

● **PROBLEM 18-11**

Prove the theorem:

If $\overline{F}: R^n \rightarrow R^n$ is a continuously differentiable con-servative vector field, then the Jacobian matrix of $\overline{F}$ is symmetric.

Solution: Vector field $\overline{F}$ is an n-dimensional vector field defined on R^n

$$\overline{F} = (F_1, F_2, \ldots, F_n) \tag{1}$$

Note that

$$F_i = F_i(x_1, x_2, \ldots, x_n) \tag{2}$$

for $i = 1, 2, \ldots, n$.

$\overline{F}$ is a conservative field, hence there is some function $f = f(x_1, x_2, \ldots, x_n)$ such that

$$\overline{F} = \nabla f = \left(\frac{\partial f}{\partial x_1}, \frac{\partial f}{\partial x_2}, \ldots, \frac{\partial f}{\partial x_n} \right) \tag{3}$$

and

841

$$F_i = \frac{\partial f}{\partial x_i} \tag{4}$$

Differentiating eq.(4) with respect to x_k yields

$$\frac{\partial F_i}{\partial x_k} = \frac{\partial^2 f}{\partial x_k \partial x_i} = \frac{\partial^2 f}{\partial x_i \partial x_k} = \frac{\partial F_k}{\partial x_i} \tag{5}$$

Note that $\dfrac{\partial F_i}{\partial x_k}$ and $\dfrac{\partial F_k}{\partial x_i}$ are the entries in the $n \times n$

Jacobian matrix. From eq.(5), we conclude that the matrix is symmetric.

The converse of this theorem is not true, as will be shown in the proceeding problem.

● **PROBLEM 18-12**

Determine which of the following vector fields are conservative:

1. $\overline{F}(x,y) = (x - 2y, \ x + 2y)$ (1)

2. $\overline{G}(x,y,z) = (x,z,x)$ (2)

3. $\overline{H}(x,y) = \left(\dfrac{-y}{x^2+y^2}, \ \dfrac{x}{x^2+y^2} \right); \ x^2+y^2 > 0$ (3)

Solution: First, note that if a vector field

$$\overline{F} = (F_1, F_2, \ldots, F_n)$$

where

$$F_i = F_i(x_1, x_2, \ldots, x_n)$$

for $i = 1,2,\ldots,n$ is conservative, then the Jacobian matrix must be symmetric.

Note however, that the converse is not true. If a vector field exists such that its Jacobian matrix is symmetric, this does not insure that the vector field is conservative.

1. Let us find the Jacobian matrix of $\overline{F}$

$$F' = \begin{vmatrix} \dfrac{\partial F_1}{\partial x} & \dfrac{\partial F_1}{\partial y} \\ \dfrac{\partial F_2}{\partial x} & \dfrac{\partial F_2}{\partial y} \end{vmatrix} = \begin{vmatrix} 1 & -2 \\ 1 & 2 \end{vmatrix} \tag{4}$$

Matrix F' is not symmetric, therefore $\overline{F}$ is not a conservative vector field.

2. The Jacobian matrix of $\overline{G}$ is

$$G' = \begin{vmatrix} 1 & 0 & 0 \\ 0 & 0 & 1 \\ 1 & 0 & 0 \end{vmatrix} \qquad (5)$$

G' is not symmetric, thus $\overline{G}$ is not a conservative vector field.

3. From eq.(3), we have

$$\frac{\partial}{\partial y}\left(\frac{-y}{x^2+y^2}\right) = \frac{\partial}{\partial x}\left(\frac{x}{x^2+y^2}\right) \qquad (6)$$

The Jacobian matric of $\overline{H}$ is symmetric, but that does not guarantee that $\overline{H}$ is conservative. As a matter of fact it is not. There is no continuously differentiable function f such that

$$\overline{H} = \text{grad } f \qquad (7)$$

For $x > 0$, the function

$$f(x,y) = \text{arc tan } \frac{y}{x} \qquad (8)$$

satisfies

$$\overline{H} = \text{grad } f$$

But f cannot be extended to be a single-valued solution of $\overline{H} = \text{grad } f$ in the entire plane except the origin.

● **PROBLEM 18-13**

Let B be an open coordinate rectangle in R^n, that is, the set of points $\overline{x}$ such that

$$B = \left\{\overline{x} : a_i < x_i < b_i, \ i = 1,2,\ldots,n\right\} \qquad (1)$$

and let $\overline{x}_0$ and $\overline{x}_1$ be any points in B. Furthermore, let K be the set of all paths from $\overline{x}_0$ to $\overline{x}_i$ such that each path consists of a sequence of line segments parallel to the coordinate axes and such that each coordinate variable varies on at most one line segment.

How many elements has the set K?

Solution: Let us first analyze the three-dimensional case shown in the figure.
Each path consists of three line segments and can be described by a sequence of coordinate directions, only one of which varies at a time.
  For example, the path $\overline{x}_0 DE \overline{x}_1$ corresponds to x_3, x_1, x_2, From the figure, we conclude that for R^3, the set K consists of six elements.

  In the more general case of the n-dimensional space R^n, we can move from some point $\overline{x}_0$ in any of n directions. If we take one direction, then we are left with n-1 directions

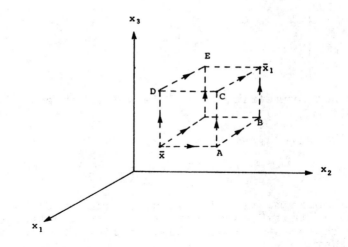

to which we can move, since one direction has already been taken. If we choose another direction, then we are left with n-2 directions. If we continue this, then for the last segment of the path, we will be left with one direction.

● **PROBLEM 18-14**

Prove the theorem:

Let B be an open rectangle in R^n and $\overline{F}$ a continuously differentiable vector field defined on B.

If the Jacobian matrix of $\overline{F}$ is symmetric on B, then $\overline{F}$ is a conservative field.

(Hint: Pick a fixed point $\overline{x}_1$ in B and any other $\overline{x}_2$ in B and consider the paths described in Problem 18-13).

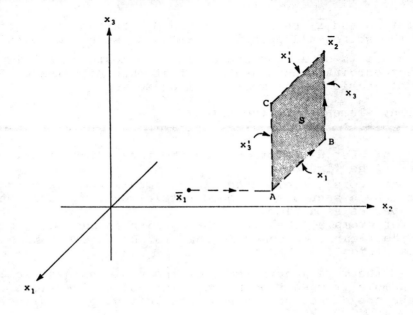

<u>Solution</u>: Consider paths from $\bar{x}_1$ to $\bar{x}_2$ each consisting of a sequence of line segments parallel to the axes and such that each coordinate variable changes on at most one such segment. (This procedure was described in Problem 18-13.)

The three-dimensional case is shown in the figure. Let K be the set of all such paths from $\bar{x}_1$ to $\bar{x}_2$ and let $C_1, C_2 \ldots$ be its elements.

We shall show that the function

$$f(\bar{x}) = \int_{C_i} \bar{F} \cdot d\bar{x} \tag{1}$$

where $C_i \, \varepsilon K$, is the same for all elements of K.

Let us take two paths C_m and C_ℓ. The path C_m can be altered step by step into C_ℓ.

C_m can be described by the sequence of coordinate directions

$$x_{m_1}, \; x_{m_2}, \ldots, x_{m_n} \tag{2}$$

and C_ℓ by

$$x_{\ell_1}, \; x_{\ell_2}, \ldots, x_{\ell_n} \tag{3}$$

We can change sequence (2) into (3) by successively interchanging adjacent variables in pairs. Each interchange replaces a pair (x_p, x_q) by another pair $(x_{p'}, x_{q'})$ lying in the same two-dimensional plane.

To get a clearer picture of what's going on, refer to the figure. The path $\bar{x}_1$ AB $\bar{x}_2$ corresponds to x_2, x_1, x_3 and the path $\bar{x}_1$ AC $\bar{x}_2$ corresponds to x_2, x_3, x_1.

Each replacement leaves the value of integral (1) invariant. Indeed, consider a closed path consisting of the segments x_p and x_q and then $x_{q'}$ and $x_{p'}$. The only variables that change along this path are x_p and x_q. Thus, the line integral can be written

$$\oint \bar{F} \cdot d\bar{x} = \oint F_p \, dx_p + F_q \, dx_q \tag{4}$$

Now, applying Green's theorem, we obtain

$$\oint \bar{F} \cdot d\bar{x} = \int_S \int \left(\frac{\partial F_q}{\partial x_p} - \frac{\partial F_p}{\partial x_q} \right) dx_p \, dx_q = 0 \tag{5}$$

since it is assumed that the Jacobian matrix is symmetric, that is

$$\frac{\partial F_i}{\partial x_k} = \frac{\partial F_k}{\partial x_i} \tag{6}$$

845

Thus, the change of path leaves the integral invariant.

Point $\bar{x}_2$ can be approached along any direction in such a way that only an arbitrary coordinate will vary.

Thus, for the ith coordinate, we have

$$F_i(\bar{x}) = \frac{\partial f}{\partial x_i}(\bar{x}) \tag{7}$$

(see Problem 18-1).

Since eq.(7) is true for all coordinates, we have

$$\bar{F}(\bar{x}) = \nabla f(\bar{x}) \tag{8}$$

Thus, $\bar{F}(\bar{x})$ is a conservative vector field.

● **PROBLEM 18-15**

In Problem 18-12, we showed that the vector field

$$\bar{F}(x,y) = \left(\frac{-y}{x^2+y^2} , \frac{x}{x^2+y^2} \right) \tag{1}$$

is not conservative in the plane. Find the potential function $f(x,y)$ of $\bar{F}$ for the half-plane $x > 0$.

Solution: A potential function $f(x,y)$ can be evaluated from the line integral

$$f(x,y) = \int_{(1,0)}^{(x,y)} \bar{F} \cdot d\bar{r} = \int_{(1,0)}^{(x,y)} \frac{-ydx}{x^2+y^2} + \frac{xdy}{x^2+y^2} \tag{2}$$

The path of integration is any piecewise smooth curve from (1,0) to (x,y).

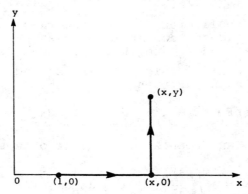

For simplicity, let us take the curve shown in the figure. Along the segment from (1,0) to (x,0), $y = 0$ and $dy = 0$. Along the segment from (x,0) to (x,y), we have that $dx = 0$. Thus,

$$f(x,y) = \int_0^y \frac{xdy}{x^2+y^2} = \arctan \frac{y}{x} + C \tag{3}$$

where C is some constant.

The potential function given by eq.(3) is the most general potential of $\overline{F}$ in the plane x > 0.
Thus,

$$\nabla f(x,y) = \overline{F}(x,y) \; ; \quad x > 0 \tag{4}$$

● **PROBLEM** 18-16

Prove the theorem:

A vector field $\overline{F}$ defined and continuously differentiable in all space is conservative if, and only if,

$$\nabla \times \overline{F} = \overline{0} \tag{1}$$

throughout the whole space.

Solution: Let us rewrite this theorem using logical notation. Note that $\overline{F}$ is defined and continuously differentiable in all space. The theorem may be written as

$$\left(\begin{array}{l}\overline{F} \text{ is a conservative} \\ \text{vector field}\end{array}\right) <=> (\nabla \times \overline{F} = \overline{0})$$

The sign <=> means "if and only if".

The sign A⇒B means "if A then B". We have to prove the theorem in both directions. Let us prove the theorem in the direction ⇒ .

$$\left(\begin{array}{l}\overline{F} \text{ is a conservative} \\ \text{vector field}\end{array}\right) => (\nabla \times \overline{F} = \overline{0})$$

This proof is trivial because $\overline{F}$ is conservative, and we may thus write $\overline{F}$ = grad f and curl grad f = $\overline{0}$.

To prove the theorem in this direction <=,

$$\begin{array}{l}\overline{F} \text{ is a conservative} \\ \text{vector field}\end{array} <= (\nabla \times \overline{F} = \overline{0})$$

we have to show that if $\nabla \times \overline{F} = \overline{0}$ then f exists such that $\overline{F} = \nabla f$. Let us define f as a line integral of $\overline{F}$ from (0,0,0) to (x,y,z) along the line segments:

a. from (0,0,0) to (x,0,0) along the x-axis

b. from (x,0,0) to (x,y,0) parallel to the y-axis

c. from (x,y,0) to (x,y,z) parallel to the z-axis

(see the figure).

Now, we can define a scalar function f(x,y,z) as

$$f(x,y,z) = \int_0^x F_1(t,0,0)dt + \int_0^y F_2(x,t,0)dt + \int_0^z F_3(x,y,t)dt \tag{2}$$

The function f(x,y,z) is defined along a specific path.

We will now show that

$$\overline{F} = \nabla f \qquad (3)$$

The z-component is

$$\frac{\partial f}{\partial z} = \lim_{\Delta z \to o} \frac{f(x,y,z+\Delta z) - f(x,y,z)}{\Delta z}$$

$$= \lim_{\Delta z \to o} \frac{\int_z^{z+\Delta z} F_3(x,y,t)dt}{\Delta t} = F_3(x,y,z) \qquad (4)$$

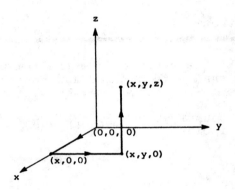

The y-component is

$$\frac{\partial f}{\partial y} = \lim_{\Delta y \to o} \frac{f(x,y+\Delta y,z) - f(x,y,z)}{\Delta y}$$

$$= \lim_{\Delta y \to o} \frac{1}{\Delta y}\left[\int_0^{y+\Delta y} F_2(x,t,0)dt + \int_0^z F_3(x,y+\Delta y,t)dt \right.$$

$$\left. - \int_0^y F_2(x,t,0)dt - \int_0^z F_3(x,y,t)dt \right]$$

$$= \lim_{\Delta y \to o} \frac{\int_y^{y+\Delta y} F_2(x,t,0)dt}{\Delta y} + \lim_{\Delta y \to o} \frac{\int_0^z \left[F_3(x,y+\Delta y,t)-F_3(x,y,t) \right] dt}{\Delta y}$$

$$= F_2(x,y,0) + \int_0^z \frac{\partial F_3(x,y,t)}{\partial y} dt \qquad (5)$$

Since

$$\nabla \times \overline{F} = \overline{0} \qquad (6)$$

we have

$$\frac{\partial F_1}{\partial y} = \frac{\partial F_2}{\partial x} \;\; ; \;\; \frac{\partial F_2}{\partial z} = \frac{\partial F_3}{\partial y} \;\; ; \;\; \frac{\partial F_1}{\partial z} = \frac{\partial F_3}{\partial x} \qquad (7)$$

and eq.(5) becomes

848

$$\frac{\partial f}{\partial y} = F_2(x,y,0) + \int_0^z \frac{\partial F_2(x,y,t)}{\partial t} dt$$

$$= F_2(x,y,0) + F_2(x,y,z) - F_2(x,y,0) = F_2(x,y,z) \tag{8}$$

Finally, for the x-component

$$\frac{\partial f}{\partial x} = \lim_{\Delta x \to 0} \frac{f(x+\Delta x, y, z) - f(x,y,z)}{\Delta x}$$

$$= F_1(x,0,0) + \int_0^y \frac{\partial F_2(x,t,0)}{\partial x} dt + \int_0^z \frac{\partial F_3(x,y,t)}{\partial x} dt$$

$$= F_1(x,0,0) + \int_0^y \frac{\partial F_1(x,t,0)}{\partial t} dt + \int_0^z \frac{\partial F_1(x,y,t)}{\partial t} dt$$

$$= F_1(x,0,0) + F_1(x,y,0) - F_1(x,0,0) + F_1(x,y,z)$$

$$- F(x,y,0)$$

$$= F_1(x,y,z). \tag{9}$$

Thus

$$\nabla f = \overline{F} \tag{10}$$

and that completes the proof.

● **PROBLEM 18-17**

Show that

$$\overline{F} = (y^2\cos x+1)\overline{i} + (2y \sin x+3y^2z)\overline{j} + y^3\overline{k} \tag{1}$$

is conservative. Using the method described in Problem 18-16, find a scalar potential of $\overline{F}$.

Check the answer by integrating $\overline{F}$ along the straight line segment from $(0,0,0)$ to (x,y,z).

Solution: From eq.(1), we evaluate

$$\text{curl } \overline{F} = \left[\frac{\partial}{\partial y}(y^3) - \frac{\partial}{\partial z}(2y\sin x+3y^2z)\right]\overline{i}$$

$$+ \left[\frac{\partial}{\partial z}(y^2\cos x+1) - \frac{\partial}{\partial x}(y^3)\right]\overline{j}$$

$$+ \left[\frac{\partial}{\partial x}(2y\sin x+3y^2z) - \frac{\partial}{\partial y}(y^2\cos x+1)\right]\overline{k} \tag{2}$$

$$= (3y^2-3y^2)\overline{i} + (0-0)\overline{j} + (2y\cos x-2y\cos x)\overline{k}$$

$$= \overline{0}$$

Hence, the vector field $\overline{F}$ is conservative.

The scalar potential is

$$f(x,y,z) = \int_0^x F_1(t,0,0)dt + \int_0^y F_2(x,t,0)dt + \int_0^z F_3(x,y,t)dt$$

$$(3)$$

$$= \int_0^x dt + \int_0^y 2t\ sinxdt + \int_0^z y^3dt$$

$$= x + y^2sinx + zy^3$$

Now, we shall compute $f(x,y,z)$ by integrating $\overline{F}$ along the straight line segment from $(0,0,0)$ to (x,y,z). In parametric form, the line segment is

$$\overline{r}(t) = tx\overline{i} + ty\overline{j} + tz\overline{k} \qquad 0 \le t \le 1 \qquad (4)$$

We have

$$f(x,y,z) = \int_0^1 \overline{F} \cdot d\overline{r}\ dt$$

$$= \int_0^1 \left[(t^2y^2costx+1)\overline{i} + (2ytsintx+3t^3y^2z)\overline{j} + t^3y^3\overline{k}\right]$$

$$\cdot \left[tx\overline{i}+ty\overline{j}+tz\overline{k}\right] dt \qquad (5)$$

$$= \int_0^1 \left[t^3xy^2costx+tx+2t^2y^2sintx+3t^4y^3z+t^4y^3z\right] dt$$

$$= x + y^2sinx + zy^3$$

● **PROBLEM 18-18**

Determine if the following vector field $\overline{F}$ is conservative and find its potential which has the value 7 at the origin.

$$\overline{F}(x,y,z) = (1+2xy^2+e^y)\overline{i} + (2x^2y+xe^y)\overline{j} + 3z^2\overline{k} \qquad (1)$$

Solution: First, let us check if the vector field $\overline{F}$ is conservative. Since $\overline{F}$ is defined everywhere in R^3 and is continuously differentiable, it is enough to evaluate curl $\overline{F}$.

$$curl\ \overline{F} = \nabla \times \overline{F} = \left(\frac{\partial F_3}{\partial y} - \frac{\partial F_2}{\partial z}\right)\overline{i} + \left(\frac{\partial F_1}{\partial z} - \frac{\partial F_3}{\partial x}\right)\overline{j} + \left(\frac{\partial F_2}{\partial x} - \frac{\partial F_1}{\partial y}\right)\overline{k}$$

$$(2)$$

$$= 0\overline{i} + 0\overline{j} + (4xy + e^y - 4xy - e^y)\overline{k} = \overline{0}$$

Hence, the vector field $\overline{F}$ is conservative. Using the method described in Problem 18-16, we shall compute the potential function

$$f(x,y,z) = \int_0^x F_1(t,0,0)dt + \int_0^y F_2(x,t,0)dt$$

$$+ \int_0^z F_3(x,y,t)dt = \int_0^x dt + \int_0^y (2tx^2 + xet)dt$$

$$+ \int_0^z 3t^2 dt = t \Big|_0^x + \left[t^2x^2 + xe^t \right] \Big|_0^y + t^3 \Big|_0^z \tag{3}$$

$$= x + x^2y^2 + xe^y + z^3 + C$$

where C is a constant.

Since the value of the potential at the origin is 7, we conclude that

$$f(0,0,0) = C = 7 \tag{4}$$

Thus, the potential function of the vector field $\overline{F}$ is

$$f(x,y,z) = x + x^2y^2 + xe^y + z^3 + 7 \tag{5}$$

● **PROBLEM** 18-19

Show that the scalar field

$$\phi = - \frac{1}{|\overline{r}|} \tag{1}$$

defined everywhere in R^3 except at the origin is a potential function of the vector field

$$\overline{F} = \frac{\overline{r}}{|\overline{r}|^3} \tag{2}$$

where $\overline{r} = x\overline{i} + y\overline{j} + z\overline{k}$ (3)

and $|\overline{r}| = \sqrt{x^2+y^2+z^2}$ (4)

Solution: The scalar field ϕ is a potential function of $\overline{F}$ if

$$\overline{F} = \nabla\phi = \frac{\partial\phi}{\partial x}\overline{i} + \frac{\partial\phi}{\partial y}\overline{j} + \frac{\partial\phi}{\partial z}\overline{k} \tag{5}$$

For the partial derivatives of ϕ, we obtain

$$\frac{\partial\phi}{\partial x} = \frac{\partial}{\partial x}\left[\frac{-1}{|\overline{r}|} \right] = \frac{\partial}{\partial x}\left[\frac{-1}{\sqrt{x^2+y^2+z^2}} \right] \tag{6}$$

$$= \frac{x}{(x^2+y^2+z^2)^{3/2}} = \frac{x}{|\overline{r}|^3}$$

$$\frac{\partial\phi}{\partial y} = \frac{\partial}{\partial y}\left[\frac{-1}{\sqrt{x^2+y^2+z^2}} \right] = \frac{y}{|\overline{r}|^3} \tag{7}$$

$$\frac{\partial\phi}{\partial z} = \frac{\partial}{\partial z}\left[\frac{-1}{\sqrt{x^2+y^2+z^2}} \right] = \frac{z}{|\overline{r}|^3} \tag{8}$$

851

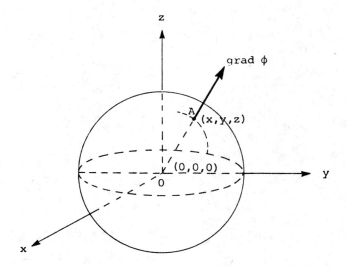

Hence

$$\nabla\phi = \frac{x}{|\overline{r}|^3}\,\overline{i} + \frac{y}{|\overline{r}|^3}\,\overline{j} + \frac{z}{|\overline{r}|^3}\,\overline{k}$$

$$= \frac{1}{|\overline{r}|^3}\,(x\overline{i}+y\overline{j}+z\overline{k}) = \frac{\overline{r}}{|\overline{r}|^3} \qquad (9)$$

and thus
$$\overline{F} = \nabla\phi \qquad (10)$$

The scalar potential ϕ of a gravitational field plays an important role in physics. In general, the scalar potential is given by

$$\phi(\overline{x}) = -\sum_{bodies} \frac{m_i{}^A}{|\overline{x}-\overline{x}_i|} \qquad (11)$$

where i is an index labeling the bodies, $\overline{x}_i$ is the position vector of the ith body and $m_i{}^A$ is a constant associated with the ith body called its active gravitational mass.

In studying gravitational radiation in Newtonian theory, we often examine the gravitational potential ϕ which satisfies Poisson's equation

$$\nabla^2\phi = 4\pi k\rho \qquad (12)$$

where k is a constant and ρ is the mass density.

In general relativity, the gravitational potential satisfies the equation

$$\Box\phi = 4\pi k\rho \qquad (13)$$

where $\qquad \Box =: \nabla^2 - \frac{\partial^2}{\partial t^2}$ is the D'Alembertian operator.

A force field is defined by

$$\overline{F} = \frac{x\overline{i} + y\overline{j} + z\overline{k}}{(x^2+y^2+z^2)^{\frac{3}{2}}} \tag{1}$$

everywhere in R^3 except the origin. What is the work done by the force on the particle which is moved from (2,1,4) to (6,0,3) along a straight line?

How does the work change when any other path is taken?

Solution: Using the results of Problem 18-19, we see that the vector field given by eq.(1) has the scalar potential

$$\phi(x,y,z) = - \frac{1}{\sqrt{x^2+y^2+z^2}} \tag{2}$$

Hence, the vector field $\overline{F}$ is conservative and the line integral

$$\int_{\overline{r}_1}^{\overline{r}_2} \overline{F} \cdot d\overline{r} \tag{3}$$

is independent of the path, and we may write

$$\int_{\overline{r}_1}^{\overline{r}_2} \overline{F} \cdot d\overline{r} = \phi(\overline{r}_2) - \phi(\overline{r}_1) \tag{4}$$

we have

$$\phi(\overline{r}_2) = \phi(6,0,3) = - \frac{1}{\sqrt{36+9}} = - \frac{1}{\sqrt{45}} \tag{5}$$

$$\phi(\overline{r}_1) = \phi(2,1,4) = - \frac{1}{\sqrt{4+1+16}} = - \frac{1}{\sqrt{21}} \tag{6}$$

Substituting eqs.(5) and (6) into eq.(4) results in

$$\int_{\overline{r}_1}^{\overline{r}_2} \overline{F} \cdot d\overline{r} = \frac{1}{\sqrt{21}} - \frac{1}{\sqrt{45}} = \frac{\sqrt{21}}{21} - \frac{\sqrt{45}}{45} = 0.691 \tag{7}$$

CHAPTER 19

THE DIVERGENCE THEOREM

INTRODUCTION

The divergence theorem, also called Gauss' theorem (particularly in older books) establishes a pertinent relationship between an integral over a volume to an integral over the surface which binds the volume.

As pointed out in Chapter 17, Green's theorem can be written in the vector form

$$\oint_C \overline{F} \cdot \overline{n} \ ds = \iint_D \operatorname{div} \overline{F} \ dxdy \tag{1}$$

The above relationship in its two-dimensional form has a three-dimensional counterpart. Indeed, in R^3, we have

$$\iint_R \overline{F} \cdot \overline{n} \ dS = \iiint_V \operatorname{div} \overline{F} \ dV \tag{2}$$

Note the simila ities between eqs.(1) and (2).

In its crudest form, the divergence theorem can be formulated as follows: the total divergence within a bounded domain is equal to the net flux emerging from the domain.

A few problems in the chapter are devoted to basic identities, among them Green's first and second identities.

An important section of the chapter illustrates the numerous applications of the divergence theorem in physics with special emphasis on electromagnetism.

It is interesting to note that the necessity to mathematically describe various physical phenomena gave rise to many of the integral theorems of vector analysis.

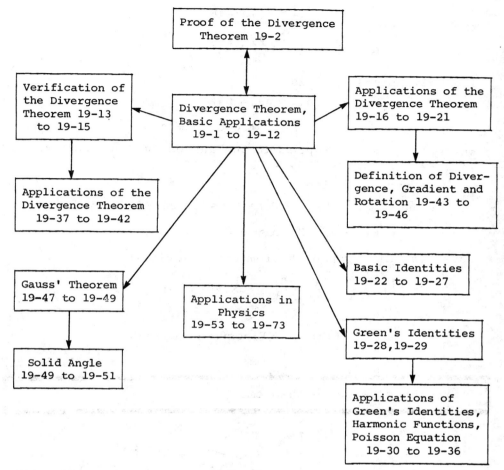

This chart is provided to facilitate rapid understanding of the inter-relationships of the topics and subject matter in this chapter. Also shown are the problem numbers associated with the subject matter.

DIVERGENCE THEOREM, BASIC APPLICATIONS

● **PROBLEM** 19-1

State the divergence theorem and write it in rectangular form.

<u>Solution</u>: The divergence theorem states that if

$\overline{F} = F_1\overline{i} + F_2\overline{j} + F_3\overline{k}$ is a continuously differentiable vector field in a region D in space and if S is an oriented surface in space which is the boundary of the bounded closed region D, and if $\overline{n}$ is an outer normal to S, then

$$\iiint_D \text{div } \overline{F} \, dV = \iint_S \overline{F} \cdot \overline{n} \, dS \qquad (1)$$

Now, to write the divergence theorem in rectangular form, note that since

$$\overline{F} = F_1\overline{i} + F_2\overline{j} + F_3\overline{k} \qquad (2)$$

then

$$\text{div } \overline{F} = \frac{\partial F_1}{\partial x} + \frac{\partial F_2}{\partial y} + \frac{\partial F_3}{\partial z} \qquad (3)$$

The unit normal to S is

$$\overline{n} = n_1\overline{i} + n_2\overline{j} + n_3\overline{k} \qquad (4)$$

$$= \cos\alpha\ \overline{i} + \cos\beta\ \overline{j} + \cos\gamma\ \overline{k}$$

where α, β, and γ represent the angles that $\overline{n}$ makes with the $\overline{i}$, $\overline{j}$, and $\overline{k}$ directions, respectively.

We may now write

$$\overline{F} \cdot \overline{n} = (F_1\overline{i} + F_2\overline{j} + F_3\overline{k}) \cdot (\cos\alpha\overline{i} + \cos\beta\overline{j} + \cos\gamma\overline{k})$$
$$= F_1\cos\alpha + F_2\cos\beta + F_3\cos\gamma \qquad (5)$$

Thus, the divergence theorem can be written as

$$\iiint_D \frac{\partial F_1}{\partial x} + \frac{\partial F_2}{\partial y} + \frac{\partial F_3}{\partial z}\ dxdydz$$

$$= \iint_S (F_1\cos\alpha + F_2\cos\beta + F_3\cos\gamma)dS \qquad (6)$$

● **PROBLEM 19-2**

Prove the divergence theorem.

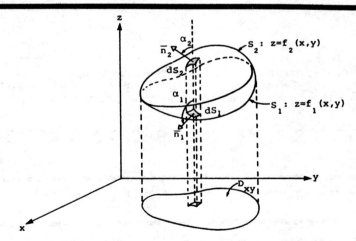

Solution: Divergence Theorem: Let $\overline{F} = F_1\overline{i} + F_2\overline{j} + F_3\overline{k}$ be a continuous vector field in a domain D of space, having continuous derivatives in D. Let S be a piecewise smooth surface in D which forms the complete boundary of a bounded closed region V in D. Furthermore, let $\overline{n}$ be the unit outer-normal vector to S. Then,

$$\iiint_V \text{div } \overline{F}\ dV = \iint_S \overline{F} \cdot \overline{n}\ dS \qquad (1)$$

Let us prove the theorem for the special case of a closed

surface S such that any line parallel to the coordinate axes cuts S in at most two points (*). Let the equations of the lower and upper parts of the surface be $S_1: z = f_1(x,y)$ and $S_2: z = f_2(x,y)$ respectively (see the figure).

D_{xy} is the projection of S on the xy-plane.

$$\iiint_V \frac{\partial F_3}{\partial z} \, dV = \iiint_V \frac{\partial F_3}{\partial z} \, dz\,dy\,dx$$

$$\iint_{D_{xy}} \left[\int_{z=f_1(x,y)}^{f_2(x,y)} \frac{\partial F_3}{\partial z} \, dz \right] dy\,dx \qquad (2)$$

$$= \iint_{D_{xy}} F_3(x,y,z) \Big|_{z=f_1(x,y)}^{f_2(x,y)} dy\,dx$$

$$= \iint_{D_{xy}} \Big[F_3(x,y,f_2) - F_3(x,y,f_1) \Big] dy\,dx$$

Notice that for the lower part S_1,

$$dy\,dx = -\cos\alpha_1 dS_1 = -\overline{k} \cdot \overline{n}_1 \, dS_1 \qquad (3)$$

since the normal $\overline{n}_1$ to S_1 makes an obtuse angle α_1 with $\overline{k}$, as shown in the figure.

For S_2,

$$dy\,dx = \cos\alpha_2 dS_2 = \overline{k} \cdot \overline{n}_2 \, dS_2 \qquad (4)$$

and α_2 is an acute angle.

Hence,

$$\iint_{D_{xy}} F_3(x,y,f_2)\,dy\,dx = \iint_{S_2} F_3 \, \overline{k} \cdot \overline{n}_2 \, dS_2 \qquad (5)$$

$$\iint_{D_{xy}} F_3(x,y,f_1)\,dy\,dx = - \iint_{S_1} F_3 \, \overline{k} \cdot \overline{n}_1 \, dS_1 \qquad (6)$$

From eqs.(5) and (6) we obtain

$$\iint_{D_{xy}} F_3(x,y,f_2)\,dy\,dx - \iint_{D_{xy}} F_3(x,y,f_1)\,dy\,dx$$

$$\qquad (7)$$

$$= \iint_{S_2} F_3\overline{k} \cdot \overline{n}_2 \, dS_2 + \iint_{S_1} F_3 \, \overline{k} \cdot \overline{n}_1 dS_1 = \iint_S F_3\overline{k} \cdot \overline{n} \, dS$$

Therefore

$$\iiint_V \frac{\partial F_3}{\partial z} \, dV = \iint_S F_3 \, \overline{k} \cdot \overline{n} \, dS \qquad (8)$$

Similarly, by projecting S on the other coordinate planes, we obtain

$$\iiint\limits_{V} \frac{\partial F_1}{\partial x} \, dV = \iint\limits_{S} F_1 \bar{i} \cdot \bar{n} \, dS \qquad (9)$$

$$\iiint\limits_{V} \frac{\partial F_2}{\partial y} \, dV = \iint\limits_{S} F_2 \bar{j} \cdot \bar{n} \, dS \qquad (10)$$

Adding eqs.(8), (9) and (10) results in

$$\iiint\limits_{V} \left(\frac{\partial F_1}{\partial x} + \frac{\partial F_2}{\partial y} + \frac{\partial F_3}{\partial z} \right) \, dV = \iiint\limits_{V} \text{div } \bar{F} \, dV$$

$$= \iint\limits_{S} (F_1 \bar{i} + F_2 \bar{j} + F_3 \bar{k}) \cdot \bar{n} dS = \iint\limits_{S} \bar{F} \cdot \bar{n} \, dS \qquad (11)$$

The divergence theorem can be extended to any region V which can be cut up into a finite number of pieces of type (*) by means of piecewise smooth surfaces. This extension can be established by adding the result for each part separately and observing that the surface integrals over the cutting surfaces cancel in pairs. This result can be extended even further by a limit process in the potential theory.

● **PROBLEM 19-3**

Evaluate

$$\iint\limits_{S} \bar{F} \cdot \bar{n} \, dS \qquad (1)$$

where

$$\bar{F} = (x^2 + xz)\bar{i} + 2y^2 \bar{j} - \frac{z^2}{2} \bar{k} \qquad (2)$$

and S is the surface of the cube bounded by

$$x = 0, \ x = 1, \ y = 0, \ y = 1, \ z = 0, \ z = 1. \qquad (3)$$

Solution: The above surface integral may be evaluated by calculating the surface integral of each of the six individual faces of the unit cube.

It is much simpler, and much faster, however, to use the divergence theorem

$$\iint\limits_{S} \bar{F} \cdot \bar{n} \, dS = \iiint\limits_{V} \text{div } \bar{F} \, dV \qquad (4)$$

as a means of solution by evaluating the above volume integral.

Since in this case,

$$\bar{F} = (x^2 + xz)\bar{i} + 2y^2 \bar{j} - \frac{z^2}{2} \bar{k}$$

we obtain

$$\text{div } \bar{F} = \frac{\partial}{\partial x} (x^2 + xz) + \frac{\partial}{\partial y} (2y^2) + \frac{\partial}{\partial z} \left(-\frac{z^2}{2} \right)$$

$$= 2x + z + 4y - z \tag{5}$$
$$= 2x + 4y$$

The volume integral is equal to

$$\iiint\limits_{V} \text{div } \overline{F} \ dv = \iiint\limits_{V} (2x+4y) dV$$

$$= \int_0^1 \int_0^1 \int_0^1 (2x+4y) dx dy dz \tag{6}$$

$$= \int_0^1 \int_0^1 (2x+4y) dx dy = \int_0^1 (x^2+4xy) \ \Big|_{x=0}^{1} \ dy$$

$$= \int_0^1 (4y+1) dy = (2y^2+y) \ \Big|_0^1 = 3$$

Thus,

$$\iint\limits_{S} \overline{F} \cdot \overline{n} \ dS = 3 \tag{7}$$

● **PROBLEM 19-4**

Evaluate

$$\iint\limits_{S} \overline{F} \cdot \overline{n} \ dS \tag{1}$$

where

$$\overline{F} = x^2 y^2 \overline{i} + yz^2 \overline{j} + e^z \overline{k} \tag{2}$$

and S is the surface of the parallelepiped bounded by

$$x = 0, \ y = 0, \ z = 0, \ x = 1, \ y = 2, \ z = 3. \tag{3}$$

Solution:
Rather than going through the tedious task of directly evaluating the above surface integral, we will use the divergence theorem

$$\iint\limits_{S} \overline{F} \cdot \overline{n} \ dS = \iiint\limits_{V} \text{div } \overline{F} \ dV \tag{4}$$

as a means of solution by evaluating the volume integral.

Here, the surface is the parallelepiped shown in the figure.

From eq.(2), we obtain

$$\text{div } \overline{F} = \frac{\partial}{\partial x} (x^2 y^2) + \frac{\partial}{\partial y} (yz^2) + \frac{\partial}{\partial z} (e^z)$$

$$= 2xy^2 + z^2 + e^z \tag{5}$$

859

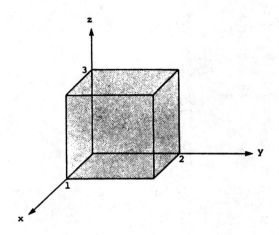

The volume integral is equal to

$$\iiint_V \text{div } \overline{F} \, dV = \int_{z=0}^{3} \int_{y=0}^{2} \int_{x=0}^{1} (2xy^2+z^2+e^z)dxdydz$$

$$= \int_{z=0}^{3} \int_{y=0}^{2} \left[x^2y^2 + xz^2 + xe^z\right] \Big|_0^1 \, dydz \qquad (6)$$

$$= \int_0^3 \int_0^2 (y^2+z^2+e^z)dydz = \int_0^3 \left[\frac{y^3}{3} + z^2y + e^zy\right] \Big|_{y=0}^{2} dz$$

$$= \int_0^3 \left(\frac{8}{3} + 2z^2 + 2e^z\right) dz = \left(\frac{8}{3}z + \frac{2}{3}z^3 + 2e^z\right) \Big|_0^3$$

$$= 24 + 2e^3$$

Thus,

$$\iint_S \overline{F} \cdot \overline{n} \, dS = 24 + 2e^3$$

● **PROBLEM 19-5**

Evaluate

$$\iint_S \overline{F} \cdot \overline{n} \, dS \qquad (1)$$

where

$$\overline{F} = x^2y\overline{i} + xy^3\overline{j} + z^2\overline{k} \qquad (2)$$

and S is the surface of the region bounded by x = 0,
y = 0, z = 0, y = 2, and 2x + z = 4.

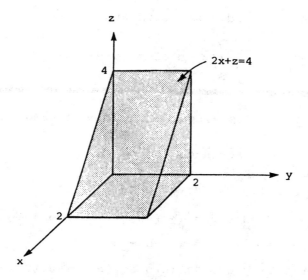

Solution: The surface integral may be evaluated by using the divergence theorem

$$\iint_S \overline{F} \cdot \overline{n} \; dS = \iiint_V \text{div } \overline{F} \; dV \tag{3}$$

From eq.(2),

$$\text{div } \overline{F} = 2xy + 3xy^2 + 2z \tag{4}$$

The region V is shown in the figure.

The volume integral is equal to

$$\iiint_V \text{div } \overline{F} \; dV = \int_{y=0}^{2} \int_{x=0}^{2} \int_{z=0}^{4-2x} (2xy+3xy^2+2z)dzdxdy$$

$$= \int_0^2 \int_0^2 (8xy - 4x^2y + 12xy^2 - 6x^2y^2 + 16 - 16x + 4x^2)dxdy$$

$$= \int_0^2 \left. (4x^2y - \frac{4}{3}x^3y + 6x^2y^2 - 2x^3y^2 + 16x - 8x^2 + \frac{4}{3}x^3) \right|_{x=0}^{2} dy$$

$$= \int_0^2 \left(3y^2 + \frac{16}{3}y + \frac{32}{3} \right) dy = \frac{160}{3} \tag{5}$$

Thus, by means of the divergence theorem, we obtain

$$\iint_S \overline{F} \cdot \overline{n} \; dS = \frac{160}{3}$$

● PROBLEM 19-6

Show that if S is any closed surface enclosing a volume V and

$$\overline{F} = ax\overline{i} + by\overline{j} + cz\overline{k} \tag{1}$$

where a, b and c are constants, then

$$\iint_S \overline{F} \cdot \overline{n} \ dS = (a+b+c)V \qquad (2)$$

Solution: Applying the divergence theorem, we obtain

$$\iint_S \overline{F} \cdot \overline{n} \ dS = \iiint_V \text{div} \ \overline{F} \ dV \qquad (3)$$

From eq.(1), the divergence of $\overline{F}$ is

$$\text{div} \ \overline{F} = \frac{\partial}{\partial x} \ (ax) + \frac{\partial}{\partial y} \ (by) + \frac{\partial}{\partial z} \ (cz)$$

$$= a + b + c \qquad (4)$$

Substituting eq.(4) into eq.(3) results in

$$\iint_S \overline{F} \cdot \overline{n} \ dS = \iiint_V (a+b+c) dV \qquad (5)$$

$$= (a+b+c) \iiint_V dV = (a+b+c)V$$

● **PROBLEM 19-7**

Use the divergence theorem to evaluate

$$\iint_S \overline{F} \cdot \overline{n} \ dS \qquad (1)$$

where $\overline{F}$ is the vector field

$$\overline{F} = 2xy\overline{i} + (yz+x^2)\overline{j} + xy\overline{k} \qquad (2)$$

and S is the boundary of the region

$$x^2 + y^2 \leq z, \quad 0 \leq z \leq 1 \qquad (3)$$

Solution: The divergence theorem states that

$$\iint_S \overline{F} \cdot \overline{n} \ dS = \iiint_V \text{div} \ \overline{F} \ dV \qquad (4)$$

The divergence of $\overline{F}$ is

$$\text{div} \ \overline{F} = \frac{\partial}{\partial x} \ (2xy) + \frac{\partial}{\partial y} \ (yz+x^2) + \frac{\partial}{\partial z} \ (xy)$$

$$= 2y + z \qquad (5)$$

862

Therefore

$$\iint_S \overline{F} \cdot \overline{n} \, dS = \iiint_V (2y+z) \, dx \, dy \, dz \qquad (6)$$

The volume integral is

$$\iiint_V (2y+z) \, dx \, dy$$

$$= \int_{z=0}^{1} \int_{y=-\sqrt{z}}^{\sqrt{z}} \int_{x=-\sqrt{z-y^2}}^{\sqrt{z-y^2}} (2y+z) \, dx \, dy \, dz$$

For simplicity, we will work in the cylindrical coordinates

$$x = r \cos\theta$$
$$y = r \sin\theta \qquad (7)$$
$$z = z$$

so that the volume integral becomes

$$\iiint_V \text{div} \, \overline{F} \, dV = \int_{z=0}^{1} \int_{\theta=0}^{2\pi} \int_{r=0}^{\sqrt{z}} (2r\sin\theta + z) r \, dr \, d\theta \, dz \qquad (8)$$

$$= \int_0^1 \int_0^{2\pi} \left[\left(\frac{2}{3} r^3 \sin\theta + z \frac{r^2}{2} \right) \Big|_{r=0}^{\sqrt{3}} \right] d\theta \, dz$$

$$= \int_0^1 \int_0^{2\pi} \left[\frac{2}{3} z^{3/2} \sin\theta + \frac{z^2}{2} \right] d\theta \, dz$$

$$= \int_0^1 \left(-\frac{2}{3} z^{3/2} \cos\theta + \frac{z^2}{2} \theta \right) \Big|_{\theta=0}^{2\pi} dz$$

$$= \int_0^1 \pi z^2 \, dz = \frac{\pi z^3}{3} \Big|_0^1 = \frac{\pi}{3}$$

Thus, by means of the divergence theorem, we conclude that

$$\iint_S \overline{F} \cdot \overline{n} \, dS = \frac{\pi}{3} \qquad (9)$$

● **PROBLEM 19-8**

Evaluate the integral

$$\iint_S \overline{F} \cdot \overline{n} \, dS \qquad (1)$$

where

$$\overline{F} = (2x+y)\overline{i} + y^2\overline{j} + z^2\overline{k} \qquad (2)$$

and S is a unit sphere with center at the origin.

863

Solution: We will evaluate the surface integral by using the divergence theorem

$$\iint_S \overline{F} \cdot \overline{n} \, dS = \iiint_V div \, \overline{F} \, dV \qquad (3)$$

For div $\overline{F}$, we have

$$div \, \overline{F} = \frac{\partial}{\partial x}(2x+y) + \frac{\partial}{\partial y}(y^2) + \frac{\partial}{\partial z}(z^2) \qquad (4)$$

$$= 2 + 2y + 2z$$

Hence,

$$\iint_S \overline{F} \cdot \overline{n} \, dS = \iiint_V (2+2y+2z) dxdydz \qquad (5)$$

Now, to evaluate the volume integral, it is easier to carry out the integration in spherical coordinates.

$$x = r \, sin\phi cos\theta \qquad 0 \le \theta \le 2\pi$$

$$y = r \, sin\phi sin\theta \qquad 0 \le \phi \le \pi \qquad (6)$$

$$z = r \, cos\phi$$

Recalling that the volume element dV is given by

$$dV = dxdydz$$

$$= r^2 sin\phi drd\theta d\phi$$

in spherical coordinates, the volume integral becomes

$$\iiint_V (2+2y+2z) dxdydz$$

$$= \int_0^\pi \int_0^{2\pi} \int_0^1 (2+2rsin\phi sin\theta+2rcos\phi) r^2 sin\phi drd\theta d\phi$$

$$= \int_0^\pi \int_0^{2\pi} \int_0^1 (2r^2 sin\phi+2r^3 sin^2\phi sin\theta+2r^3 sin\phi cos\phi) drd\theta d\phi$$

$$= \int_0^\pi \int_0^{2\pi} \left[\frac{2}{3} sin\phi+\frac{1}{2} sin^2\phi sin\theta +\frac{1}{2}sin\phi cos\phi\right] d\theta d\phi$$

$$\qquad\qquad (7)$$

$$= \int_0^\pi \left[\frac{2}{3} \theta sin\phi + \frac{1}{2} \theta sin\phi cos\phi - \frac{1}{2} sin^2\phi cos\theta\right]\Big|_{\theta=0}^{2\pi} d\phi$$

$$= \int_0^\pi \left[\frac{4\pi}{3} sin\phi + \pi sin\phi cos\phi\right] d\phi$$

$$= \frac{4\pi}{3}(-cos\phi)\Big|_0^\pi + \pi \frac{sin^2\phi}{2}\Big|_0^\pi = \frac{8\pi}{3}$$

Thus, by means of the divergence theorem, we conclude that

$$\iint_S \overline{F} \cdot \overline{n} \, dS = \frac{8\pi}{3}$$

Use the divergence theorem to evaluate the integral

$$\iint_S \overline{F} \cdot \overline{n} \, dS \qquad (1)$$

where

$$\overline{F} = x\overline{i} + y\overline{j} + z\overline{k} \qquad (2)$$

and S is a sphere of radius a with the center at the origin of the coordinate system.

Solution: From the divergence theorem,

$$\iint_S \overline{F} \cdot \overline{n} \, dS = \iiint_V \text{div } \overline{F} \, dV \qquad (3)$$

it is evident that we could find the value of the surface integral by actually evaluating the above volume integral.

Now, since div $\overline{F}$ = 1 + 1 + 1 = 3, we obtain

$$\iint_S \overline{F} \cdot \overline{n} \, dS = \iiint_V 3 \, dV = 3 \iiint_V dV \qquad (4)$$

Since the surface at hand is a sphere of radius a, we conclude that

$$\iiint_V dV = \frac{4}{3}\pi a^3 \qquad (5)$$

since the above integral represents the total volume of the sphere.

Thus, substituting eq.(5) into eq.(4) yields

$$\iint_S \overline{F} \cdot \overline{n} \, dS = 3 \cdot \frac{4}{3}\pi a^3 = 4\pi a^3$$

Notice that in this case the location of the center of the sphere does not affect the value of the surface integral.

Let S be the surface

$$x^2+y^2+z^2 = 1 \qquad (1)$$

and let f be the function

$$f(x,y,z) = x^2+y^2+z^2 \qquad (2)$$

Compute the integral

$$\iint_S \text{grad } f \cdot \overline{n} \, dS \qquad (3)$$

Solution: Since S is a smooth boundary of a closed region in R^3, and since ∇f is continuous and has continuous derivatives, we can apply the divergence theorem

$$\iint_S \overline{F} \cdot \overline{n} \ dS = \iiint_V \text{div } \overline{F} \ dV \tag{4}$$

In this case, $\overline{F} = \text{grad } f$.

We have,
$$\text{div } \overline{F} = \text{div grad } f = \frac{\partial^2 f}{\partial x^2} + \frac{\partial^2 f}{\partial y^2} + \frac{\partial^2 f}{\partial z^2} \tag{5}$$

$$= 2 + 2 + 2 = 6$$

Hence,
$$\iint_S \nabla f \cdot \overline{n} \ dS = 6 \iiint_V dV \tag{6}$$

Now, since the integral $\iiint_V dV$ is nothing more than the volume of the unit sphere $x^2 + y^2 + z^2 = 1$, we have

$$\iiint_V dV = \frac{4}{3} \pi(1)^3 = \frac{4}{3} \pi$$

Thus,
$$\iint_S \text{grad } f \cdot \overline{n} \ dS = \iint_S \nabla f \cdot \overline{n} \ dS = 6 \cdot \frac{4}{3} \pi = 8\pi$$

● **PROBLEM 19-11**

Evaluate the integral

$$\iint_S \overline{F} \cdot \overline{n} \ dS \tag{1}$$

where

$$\overline{F} = (3x+yz)\overline{i} + (y-e^z)\overline{j} + (3z+2)\overline{k} \tag{2}$$

and S is the hemisphere

$$x^2 + y^2 + z^2 = 1, \quad z \geq 0 \tag{3}$$

Solution: Attempting to evaluate the given surface integral over the hemisphere shown in the figure is a complicated, tedious task. As was done in the previous problems in this chapter, we would like to use the divergence theorem

$$\iint_S \overline{F} \cdot \overline{n} \ dS = \iiint_V \text{div } \overline{F} \ dV$$

as a means of evaluating the surface integral by actually evaluating the volume integral.

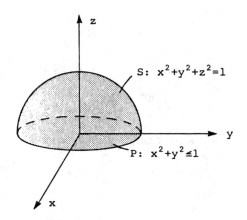

S: $x^2+y^2+z^2=1$

P: $x^2+y^2 \leq 1$

The problem here is that the surface is not a closed surface, and therefore the divergence theorem is not directly applicable.

However, we can form a closed surface by considering the surface that consists of the hemisphere S and the surface P, whose equation is $x^2 + y^2 \leq 1$ (see the figure).

Since this surface is closed, we can now apply the divergence theorem

$$\iint_{SUP} \overline{F} \cdot \overline{n}\ dS = \iiint_V div\ \overline{F}\ dV \tag{4}$$

The surface integral may be written as

$$\iint_{SUP} \overline{F} \cdot \overline{n}\ dS = \iint_S \overline{F} \cdot \overline{n}\ dS + \iint_P \overline{F} \cdot \overline{n}\ dP \tag{5}$$

Since

$$div\ \overline{F} = 3 + 1 + 3 = 7 \tag{6}$$

the volume integral is equal to

$$\iiint_V div\ \overline{F}\ dV = 7 \iiint_V dV \tag{7}$$

The volume of a hemisphere of radius one is

$$\iiint_V dV = \frac{1}{2} \cdot \frac{4}{3} \pi (1)^3 = \frac{2}{3} \pi \tag{8}$$

Hence,

$$\iint_S \overline{F} \cdot \overline{n}\ dS + \iint_P \overline{F} \cdot \overline{n}\ dP = 7 \cdot \frac{2}{3} \pi = \frac{14}{3} \pi \tag{9}$$

The outer unit normal vector to P is $-\overline{k}$, therefore

$$\iint_P \overline{F} \cdot (-\overline{k}) dP = \iint_P \left[(3x+yz)\overline{i}+(y-e^z)\overline{j}+(3z+2)\overline{k} \right] \cdot (-\overline{k}) dP \tag{10}$$

867

$$= - \iint\limits_{P} 2dP$$

The surface area of a unit circle is

$$\iint\limits_{P} dP = \pi \tag{11}$$

From eqs.(9) and (11), we obtain

$$\iint\limits_{S} \overline{F} \cdot \overline{n} \ dS = \frac{14}{3} \pi + 2\pi = \frac{20}{3} \pi \tag{12}$$

● **PROBLEM 19-12**

Evaluate

$$\iint\limits_{S} \overline{F} \cdot \overline{n} \ dS \tag{1}$$

where

$$\overline{F} = (2x+y)\overline{i} + (x^2+y)\overline{j} + 3z\overline{k} \tag{2}$$

and S is the part of the cylinder

$$x^2 + y^2 = 4 \tag{3}$$

between the surfaces z = 0 and z = 5.

Solution: Since the surface S is not closed, the divergence theorem cannot be applied directly.

Consider instead the closed surface consisting of the surface S and the bottom S_1 and the top S_2 of the cylinder, that is, two circles of radius 2.

Applying the divergence theorem, we obtain

$$\iint\limits_{S} \overline{F} \cdot \overline{n} \ dS + \iint\limits_{S_1} \overline{F} \cdot \overline{n} \ dS + \iint\limits_{S_2} \overline{F} \cdot \overline{n} \ ds$$

$$= \iiint\limits_{V} \text{div} \ \overline{F} \ dV \tag{4}$$

Since

$$\text{div} \ \overline{F} = 2 + 1 + 3 = 6 \tag{5}$$

the volume integral is equal to

$$\iiint\limits_{V} \text{div} \ \overline{F} \ dV = 6 \iiint\limits_{V} dV \tag{6}$$

The triple integral represents the volume of the cylinder, which is

$$\iiint_V \text{div } \overline{F} \text{ } dV = 6 \cdot 5 \cdot \pi \cdot 4 = 120\pi \tag{7}$$

The unit normal to the bottom S_1 is $-\overline{k}$, hence

$$\iint_{S_1} \overline{F} \cdot \overline{n} \text{ } dS = \iint_{S_1} \left[(2x+y)\overline{i} + (x^2+y)\overline{j} \right] \cdot (-\overline{k}) dS = 0 \tag{8}$$

The unit normal to the top S_2 is $\overline{k}$. For $z = 5$, we obtain

$$\iint_{S_2} \overline{F} \cdot \overline{n} \text{ } dS = \iint_{S_2} \left[(2x+y)\overline{i} + (x^2+y)\overline{j} + 15\overline{k} \right] \cdot \overline{k} \text{ } dS$$

$$= 15 \iint_{S_2} dS = 15 \cdot \pi \cdot 4 = 60\pi \tag{9}$$

Substituting eqs.(7), (8) and (9) into eq.(4) results in

$$\iint_S \overline{F} \cdot \overline{n} \text{ } dS = 120\pi - 60\pi = 60\pi \tag{10}$$

VERIFICATION OF THE DIVERGENCE THEOREM

● **PROBLEM 19-13**

Verify the divergence theorem for

$$\overline{F} = z\overline{k} \tag{1}$$

and the region V

$$V = \{(x,y,z)\varepsilon \text{ } R^3; \text{ } a \le x \le b; \text{ } c \le y \le d; \text{ } e \le z \le f\} \tag{2}$$

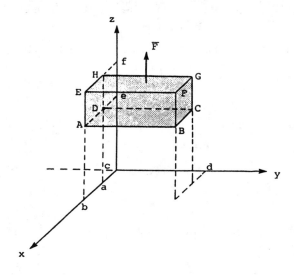

Solution: The divergence theorem states that

$$\iiint\limits_V \text{div } \overline{F} \, dV = \iint\limits_S \overline{F} \cdot \overline{n} \, dS \tag{3}$$

We will now verify the divergence theorem by first evaluating the volume integral and then subsequently evaluating the surface integral.

To evaluate the volume integral, first note that from eq.(1), we obtain

$$\text{div } \overline{F} = 1 \tag{4}$$

Hence,

$$\iiint\limits_V \text{div } \overline{F} \, dV = \iiint\limits_V dV = (b-a)(d-c)(f-e) \tag{5}$$

Note that the triple integral $\iiint\limits_V dV$ is the volume of the

parallelepiped (see the figure).

Before evaluating the surface integral, note that the surface S consists of six rectangles as shown in the figure.

Since

$$\overline{F} \cdot \overline{n} = |\overline{F}||\overline{n}| \cos \alpha \tag{6}$$

where α is the angle between $\overline{F}$ and $\overline{n}$ and

$$\overline{F} = 0\overline{i} + 0\overline{j} + z\overline{k}, \tag{7}$$

we conclude that the surface integral $\iint \overline{F} \cdot \overline{n} \, dS$ is equal to zero for all the faces except ABCD and EFGH.

Hence,

$$\iint\limits_S \overline{F} \cdot \overline{n} \, dS = \iint\limits_{ABCD} \overline{F} \cdot \overline{n} \, dS + \iint\limits_{EFGH} \overline{F} \cdot \overline{n} \, dS \tag{8}$$

For face ABCD, the value of the vector field $\overline{F}$ is constant

$$\overline{F} = e\overline{k} \tag{9}$$

and the unit outer normal vector is $-\overline{k}$. Thus

$$\iint\limits_{ABCD} e\overline{k} \cdot (-\overline{k}) dS = -e \iint\limits_{ABCD} dS \tag{10}$$

The double integral $\iint\limits_{ABCD} dS$ represents the surface area of ABCD,

hence,

$$\iint\limits_{ABCD} dS = (b-a)(d-c) \tag{11}$$

and thus,

$$\iint\limits_{ABCD} \overline{F} \cdot \overline{n} \, dS = -e(b-a)(d-c) \tag{12}$$

870

The unit normal to EFGH is $\bar{k}$ and

$$\iint\limits_{EFGH} \bar{F} \cdot \bar{n} \ dS = \iint\limits_{EFGH} f\bar{k} \cdot \bar{k} \ dS = f(b-a)(d-c) \qquad (13)$$

Substituting eq.(12) and (13) into eq.(8) results in

$$\iint\limits_{S} \bar{F} \cdot \bar{n} \ dS = f(b-a)(d-c) - e(b-a)(d-c)$$

$$= (b-a)(d-c)(f-e) \qquad (14)$$

That verifies the divergence theorem.

● **PROBLEM** 19-14

Verify the divergence theorem for

$$\bar{F} = 2x^2\bar{i} - 3y\bar{j} + z^2\bar{k} \qquad (1)$$

where S is the region bounded by

$$x^2+y^2 = 9$$

$$z = 0 \qquad (2)$$

$$z = 2$$

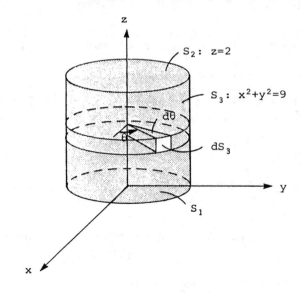

Solution: We have to show that

$$\iiint\limits_{V} \text{div } \bar{F} \ dV = \iint\limits_{S} \bar{F} \cdot \bar{n} \ dS \qquad (3)$$

The region V is shown in the figure.

871

From eq.(1), we obtain
$$\text{div } \overline{F} = 4x - 3 + 2z \tag{4}$$

The volume integral in eq.(3) is equal to

$$\iiint\limits_{V} \text{div } \overline{F} \, dV = \int_{z=0}^{2} \int_{x=-3}^{3} \int_{y=-\sqrt{9-x^2}}^{\sqrt{9-x^2}} (4x-3+2z) \, dy \, dx \, dz \tag{5}$$

$$= 2 \int_{z=0}^{2} \int_{x=-3}^{3} \left[4x\sqrt{9-x^2} - 3\sqrt{9-x^2} + 2z\sqrt{9-x^2} \right] dx \, dz$$

Since

$$\int x\sqrt{a^2-x^2} \, dx = -\frac{1}{3}\sqrt{(a^2-x^2)^3} \tag{6}$$

$$\int \sqrt{a^2-x^2} \, dx = \frac{x}{2}\sqrt{a^2-x^2} + \frac{a^2}{2} \text{ arc sin } \frac{x}{|a|}$$

integral (5) is equal to

$$2\int_{0}^{2} \left\{ 4\left[-\frac{1}{3}\sqrt{(9-x^2)^3} \right]\Big|_{-3}^{3} + (2z-3)\left[\frac{x}{2}\sqrt{9-x^2} + \frac{9}{2} \text{ arcsin} \frac{x}{3} \right]\Big|_{-3}^{3} \right\} dz$$

$$= 2\int_{0}^{2} (2z-3) \cdot \frac{9}{2} \pi \, dz = 9\pi\left[z^2-3z \right]\Big|_{0}^{2} = -18\pi$$

The surface S of the cylinder consists of three parts: the base $S_1(z=0)$, the top $S_2(z=2)$ and the side $S_3(x^2+y^2=9)$.

On $S_1(z=0)$, we have

$$\iint\limits_{S_1} \overline{F} \cdot \overline{n} \, dS = \iint\limits_{S_1} \left[2x^2\overline{i} - 3y\overline{j} \right] \cdot (-\overline{k}) dS = 0 \tag{8}$$

On $S_2(z=2)$, we have

$$\iint\limits_{S_2} \left[2x^2\overline{i} - 3y\overline{j} + 4\overline{k} \right] \cdot \overline{k} \, dS = 4 \iint\limits_{S_2} dS = 36\pi \tag{9}$$

On the side S_3, the perpendicular to $x^2+y^2=9$ is

$$\nabla(x^2+y^2) = 2x\overline{i} + 2y\overline{j} \tag{10}$$

Hence, the unit normal vector is

$$\overline{n} = \frac{2x\overline{i} + 2y\overline{j}}{\sqrt{4x^2+4y^2}} = \frac{x}{3}\overline{i} + \frac{y}{3}\overline{j} \tag{11}$$

and the surface integral can be written

$$\iint\limits_{S_3} \overline{F} \cdot \overline{n} \, dS = \iint\limits_{S_3} \left[2x^2\overline{i} - 3y\overline{j} + z^2\overline{k} \right] \cdot \left[\frac{x}{3}\overline{i} + \frac{y}{3}\overline{j} \right] dS$$

$$= \iint\limits_{S_3} \left(\frac{2}{3} x^3 - y^2 \right) dS \qquad (12)$$

From the figure, we have
$$x = 3 \cos\theta$$

$$y = 3 \sin\theta \qquad (13)$$

$$dS = 3 \, d\theta dz$$

and
$$\iint\limits_{S_3} \overline{F} \cdot \overline{n} \, dS = \int_{\theta=0}^{2\pi} \int_{z=0}^{2} 3 \left[18\cos^3\theta - 9\sin^2\theta \right] d\theta dz$$

$$= \int_0^{2\pi} 6(18\cos^3\theta - 9\sin^2\theta) d\theta \qquad (14)$$

Since
$$\int \sin^2 x dx = \frac{x}{2} - \frac{1}{4} \sin 2x$$

$$\int \cos^3 x dx = \frac{1}{3} (\sin x)(\cos^3 x + 2) \qquad (15)$$

integral (14) becomes
$$6 \cdot 18 \left[\frac{1}{3} (\sin x)(\cos^2 x + 2) \right] \Big|_0^{2\pi} - 6 \cdot 9 \left[\frac{x}{2} - \frac{1}{4} \sin 2x \right] \Big|_0^{2\pi}$$

$$= -54\pi \qquad (16)$$

The total surface integral is thus equal to
$$\iint\limits_{S} \overline{F} \cdot \overline{n} \, dS = 0 + 36\pi - 54\pi = -18\pi \qquad (17)$$

which verifies eq.(3).

● **PROBLEM 19-15**

Verify the divergence theorem for
$$\overline{F} = z\overline{i} + x\overline{j} - 3y^2 z\overline{k} \qquad (1)$$

taken over the region in the first octant bounded by
$$x^2 + y^2 = 9 \quad \text{and} \quad z = 4 \qquad (2)$$

Solution: The region V is shown in the figure.

We have to show that

$$\iiint\limits_{V} \text{div} \, \overline{F} \, dV = \iint\limits_{S} \overline{F} \cdot \overline{n} \, dS \qquad (3)$$

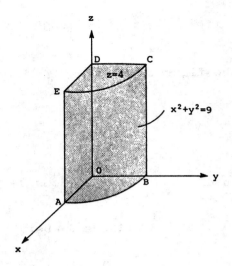

Since

$$\text{div } \overline{F} = -3y^2 \tag{4}$$

the volume integral is equal to

$$\iiint\limits_{V} \text{div } F \; dV = \int_{z=0}^{4} \int_{x=0}^{3} \int_{y=0}^{\sqrt{9-x^2}} (-3y^2) dy dx dz$$

$$= \int_{z=0}^{4} \int_{x=0}^{3} \left[-y^3 \right]_{y=0}^{\sqrt{9-x^2}} dx dz$$

$$= \int_{z=0}^{4} \int_{x=0}^{3} -(9-x^2)^{\frac{3}{2}} dx dz \tag{5}$$

To evaluate the last integral, we shall use the formula
$$\tag{6}$$

$$\int \sqrt{(a^2-x^2)^3} \; dx = \frac{1}{4}\left[x\sqrt{(a^2-x^2)^3} + \frac{3a^2 x}{2}\sqrt{a^2-x^2} + \frac{3a^4}{2} \text{ arcsin} \frac{x}{|a|}\right]$$

We have

$$-\frac{1}{4} \int_{z=0}^{4} \left[x\sqrt{(9-x^2)^3} + \frac{27x}{2}\sqrt{9-x^2} + \frac{3\cdot 81}{2} \text{ arc sin} \frac{x}{|3|}\right]\Bigg|_{x=0}^{3} dz$$

$$= -\frac{1}{4} \int_{0}^{4} \frac{3\cdot 81}{2} \cdot \frac{\pi}{2} \; dz = -\frac{3\cdot 81}{4} \pi = -60.75\pi$$

Thus,

$$\iiint\limits_{V} \text{div } \overline{F} \; dV = -60.75\pi \tag{7}$$

Now, to evaluate the surface integral, we shall evaluate the integral over each of the five surfaces which enclose the quarter cylinder.

For AODE, $y = 0$ and $\bar{n} = -\bar{j}$, so that

$$\iint\limits_{AODE} (z\bar{i}+x\bar{j})\cdot(-j)dS = \int_{z=0}^{4} \int_{x=0}^{3} -xdxdz$$

$$= \int_{z=0}^{4} -\frac{9}{2}\ dz = -18 \tag{8}$$

For OBCD, $x = 0$ and $\bar{n} = -\bar{i}$, thus

$$\iint\limits_{OBCD} (z\bar{i}-3y^2z\bar{k})\cdot(-\bar{i})dS = \int_{z=0}^{4} \int_{y=0}^{3} -zdydz \tag{9}$$

$$= -24$$

For ABO, $z = 0$ and $\bar{n} = -\bar{k}$, so that

$$\iint\limits_{ABO} (x\bar{j})\cdot(-\bar{k})dS = 0 \tag{10}$$

For ECD, $z = 4$ and $\bar{n} = \bar{k}$, thus

$$\iint\limits_{ECD} (4\bar{i}+x\bar{j}-12y^2\bar{k}) \cdot \bar{k}\ dS$$

$$= \int_{x=0}^{3} \int_{y=0}^{\sqrt{9-x^2}} \left(-12y^2\right)dydz = \int_{x=0}^{3} -4\sqrt{(9-x^2)^3}\ dx \tag{11}$$

Applying eq.(6) we find

$$-4 \int_{x=0}^{3} \sqrt{(9-x^2)^3}\ dx = -\frac{3\cdot81}{4}\ \pi = -60.75\pi \tag{12}$$

For ABCE, the unit normal is

$$\bar{n} = \frac{x}{3}\ \bar{i} + \frac{y}{3}\ \bar{j} \tag{13}$$

and

$$\iint\limits_{\substack{ABCE}} \bar{F}\cdot\bar{n}\ dS = \iint\limits_{\substack{\text{projection of} \\ \text{ABCE on xz plane}}} \bar{F}\cdot\bar{n}\ \frac{dxdz}{|\bar{n}\cdot\bar{j}|} \tag{14}$$

We have,

$$\bar{F}\cdot\bar{n} = (z\bar{i} + x\bar{j} - 3y^2z\bar{k})\cdot\left[\frac{x}{3}\ \bar{i} + \frac{y}{3}\ \bar{j}\right]$$

$$= \frac{zx}{3}\ \bar{i} + \frac{xy}{3}\ \bar{j} \tag{15}$$

and

$$\bar{n}\cdot\bar{j} = \frac{y}{3} \tag{16}$$

875

Thus,

$$\iint\limits_{ABCE} \overline{F} \cdot \overline{n} \; dS = \int_{z=0}^{4} \int_{x=0}^{3} \left(\frac{zx+xy}{y} \right) dxdz$$

$$= \int_{z=0}^{4} \int_{x=0}^{3} \left[\frac{zx}{\sqrt{9-x^2}} + x \right] dxdz$$

$$= \int_{z=0}^{4} \left[-z\sqrt{9-x^2} + \frac{x^2}{2} \right] \Big|_{x=0}^{3} dz = \int_{z=0}^{4} \left(3z + \frac{9}{2} \right) dz \tag{17}$$

$$= 3 \cdot 8 + 9 \cdot 2 = 24 + 18$$

Thus, the total surface integral is equal to

$$-18 - 24 - 60.75\pi + 18 + 24 = -60.75\pi \tag{18}$$

which agrees with (7).

BASIC APPLICATIONS OF THE DIVERGENCE THEOREM

● PROBLEM 19-16

Evaluate

$$\iint\limits_{S} x^2 dydz + y^2 dxdz + z^2 dxdy \tag{1}$$

where S is the surface of the cube

$$0 \le x \le 1, \quad 0 \le y \le 1, \quad 0 \le z \le 1.$$

Solution: The divergence theorem

$$\iiint\limits_{V} \text{div} \; \overline{F} \; dV = \iint\limits_{S} \overline{F} \cdot \overline{n} \; dS \tag{2}$$

can be written in the form

$$\iiint\limits_{V} \left(\frac{\partial F_1}{\partial x} + \frac{\partial F_2}{\partial y} + \frac{\partial F_3}{\partial z} \right) dxdydz = \iint\limits_{S} F_1 dydz + F_2 dxdz + F_3 dxdy \tag{3}$$

Comparing eqs.(3) and (1), we find

$$\overline{F} = x^2 \overline{i} + y^2 \overline{j} + z^2 \overline{k} \tag{4}$$

Thus,

$$\text{div} \; \overline{F} = 2x + 2y + 2z \tag{5}$$

Substituting eq.(5) into eq.(3) results in

$$\iiint_V \text{div } \overline{F} \, dV = 2 \iiint_V (x+y+z) \, dV$$

$$= 2 \int_{z=0}^{1} \int_{y=0}^{1} \int_{x=0}^{1} (x+y+z) \, dx \, dy \, dz$$

$$= 2 \int_0^1 \int_0^1 \left[\frac{x^2}{2} + xy + xz \right]\Bigg|_{x=0}^{1} dy \, dz$$

$$= 2 \int_0^1 \int_0^1 \left[y+z+\frac{1}{2} \right] dy \, dz = 2 \int_0^1 \left[\frac{y^2}{2} + zy + \frac{1}{2}y \right]\Bigg|_{y=0}^{1} dz$$

(6)

$$= 2 \int_0^1 (z+1) \, dz = 3$$

Thus,

$$\iint_S x^2 \, dy \, dz + y^2 \, dx \, dz + z^2 \, dx \, dy = 3$$

● **PROBLEM 19-17**

Let $\underline{S}$ be the boundary surface of a region D in space and let $\overline{n}$ be its outer normal. Prove the formulas

$$V = \iint_S x \, dy \, dz = \iint_S y \, dz \, dx = \iint_S z \, dx \, dy$$

(1)

$$= \frac{1}{3} \iint_S x \, dy \, dz + y \, dz \, dx + z \, dx \, dy$$

where V is the volume of D.

Solution: Let $\overline{F}$ be an arbitrary continuously differentiable vector function. The divergence theorem states that

$$\iiint_D \left(\frac{\partial F_1}{\partial x} + \frac{\partial F_2}{\partial y} + \frac{\partial F_3}{\partial z} \right) dx \, dy \, dz = \iint_S F_1 \, dy \, dz + F_2 \, dx \, dz + F_3 \, dx \, dy$$

(2)

Assuming that $\overline{F}$ is such that

$$\text{div } \overline{F} = 1$$

(3)

we obtain, from eq.(2),

$$\iiint_D dx \, dy \, dz = \iint_S F_1 \, dy \, dz + F_2 \, dx \, dz + F_3 \, dx \, dy$$

(4)

877

The volume of the region D is given by the triple integral

$$V = \iiint_D dx\,dy\,dz \tag{5}$$

Combining eq.(4) and eq.(5) we obtain

$$V = \iint_S F_1 dy\,dz + F_2 dx\,dz + F_3 dx\,dy \tag{6}$$

where

$$\frac{\partial F_1}{\partial x} + \frac{\partial F_2}{\partial y} + \frac{\partial F_3}{\partial z} = 1 \tag{7}$$

Suppose

$$\overline{F} = x\overline{i} + 0\overline{j} + 0\overline{k} \tag{8}$$

then

$$\text{div } \overline{F} = 1$$

and eq.(6) becomes

$$V = \iint_S x\,dy\,dz \tag{9}$$

For $\overline{F} = y\overline{j}$, we obtain

$$\text{div } \overline{F} = 1$$

and

$$V = \iint_S y\,dx\,dz \tag{10}$$

For $\overline{F} = z\overline{k}$, div $\overline{F} = 1$ and

$$V = \iint_S z\,dx\,dy \tag{11}$$

Adding eq.(9), (10) and (11) we obtain

$$V = \frac{1}{3} \iint_S x\,dy\,dz + y\,dx\,dz + z\,dx\,dy \tag{12}$$

● **PROBLEM 19-18**

Using the results of Problem 19-17, find the volume of a sphere of radius a.

Solution: To find the volume, we shall use the formula

$$V = \iint_S x\,dy\,dz \tag{1}$$

which was proven in problem 19-17. The equation of a sphere of radius a is

$$x^2 + y^2 + z^2 = a^2 \tag{2}$$

The center of the sphere is the origin of the coordinate system.

From eq.(2)

$$x = \sqrt{a^2 - y^2 - z^2} \qquad (3)$$

If the integration in eq.(1) is taken over the first octant, then

$$V = 8 \iint_{S(\text{First octant})} x \, dy \, dz \qquad (4)$$

$$= 8 \int_{z=0}^{a} \int_{y=0}^{\sqrt{a^2-z^2}} \sqrt{(a^2-z^2)-y^2} \, dy \, dz$$

Using the formula

$$\int \sqrt{a^2-x^2} \, dx = \frac{1}{2}\left[x\sqrt{a^2-x^2} + a^2 \text{arc sin} \frac{x}{|a|} \right] \qquad (5)$$

we can evaluate integral (4).

$$V = 8 \int_{z=0}^{a} \frac{1}{2}\left[y\sqrt{a^2-z^2-y^2} + (a^2-z^2)\text{arc sin} \frac{y}{\sqrt{a^2-z^2}} \right] \Bigg|_{y=0}^{\sqrt{a^2-z^2}} dz$$

$$\qquad (6)$$

$$= 4 \int_{0}^{a} \frac{\pi}{2} (a^2-z^2) dz = \frac{4}{3} \pi a^3$$

● **PROBLEM 19-19**

Find the volume of the ellipsoid

$$\frac{x^2}{a^2} + \frac{y^2}{b^2} + \frac{z^2}{c^2} = 1 \qquad (1)$$

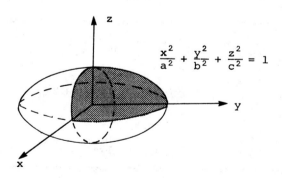

$$\frac{x^2}{a^2} + \frac{y^2}{b^2} + \frac{z^2}{c^2} = 1$$

<u>Solution</u>: From the divergence theorem, it is easy to show that the volume of a region D in space having S as its boundary surface may be given by

$$V = \iint_{S} z \, dx \, dy$$

879

Now, in this case, it is required to evaluate the volume of the ellipsoid

$$\frac{x^2}{a^2} + \frac{y^2}{b^2} + \frac{z^2}{c^2} = 1$$

Because of symmetry, we can evaluate the volume of the portion of the ellipsoid lying in the first octant (see the figure) which is an eighth of the total volume.

Thus,

$$V = 8 \iint_S z \, dx \, dy$$

Now, from eq.(1), we find

$$z = c\sqrt{1 - \frac{x^2}{a^2} - \frac{y^2}{b^2}}$$

Therefore, the total volume of the solid is

$$V = 8 \iint_S z \, dx \, dy = 8 \int_{y=0}^{b} \int_{x=0}^{a\sqrt{1-\frac{y^2}{b^2}}} c\sqrt{1 - \frac{x^2}{a^2} - \frac{y^2}{b^2}} \, dx \, dy$$

$$= \frac{8c}{a} \int_{y=0}^{b} \frac{1}{2}\left[x\sqrt{a^2 - \frac{y^2 a^2}{b^2} - x^2} + \left(a^2 - \frac{y^2 a^2}{b^2}\right) \arcsin \frac{x}{\sqrt{a^2 - \frac{y^2 a^2}{b^2}}} \right] \Bigg|_{x=0}^{a\sqrt{1-\frac{y^2}{b^2}}} \, dy$$

$$= \frac{4c}{a} \int_{y=0}^{b} \frac{\pi}{2}\left(a^2 - \frac{y^2 a^2}{b^2}\right) dy = \frac{2c\pi}{a}\left[a^2 y - \frac{a^2}{b^2}\frac{y^3}{3}\right] \Bigg|_{y=0}^{b}$$

$$= \frac{4}{3}\pi abc$$

● **PROBLEM 19-20**

Let S be the boundary surface of a region D in space and let $\underline{n}$ be its outer normal. Prove that

$$\iint_S x^2 dy dz + 2xy dz dx + 2xz dx dy = 6V\overline{x} \qquad (1)$$

where V is the volume of D and $(\overline{x}, \overline{y}, \overline{z})$ is the centroid of D. Assume that the mass density $\rho(x,y,z) = 1$.

Solution: Recall that if $\rho(x,y,z)$ represents the density of a solid D, then the mass of the solid is given by

$$M = \iiint_D \rho(x,y,z) dx dy dz \qquad (2)$$

Also, recall that

$$\bar{x} = \frac{1}{M} \iiint_D x\rho(x,y,z)dxdydz \qquad (3)$$

$$\bar{y} = \frac{1}{M} \iiint_D y\rho(x,y,z)dxdydz \qquad (4)$$

$$\bar{z} = \frac{1}{M} \iiint_D z\rho(x,y,z)dxdydz \qquad (5)$$

where $(\bar{x},\bar{y},\bar{z})$ is the center of mass, or centroid, of D.

Now, notice that when $\rho(x,y,z) = 1$, the mass of the solid is

$$M = \iiint_D dxdydz = V \qquad (6)$$

That is, when the solid is homogeneous and of unit density, the mass of the body is equal to its volume.

Also, for such a case, we have, from eq.(3),

$$\bar{x} = \frac{1}{M} \iiint_D xdxdydz = \frac{1}{V} \iiint_D xdxdydz \qquad (7)$$

Now, notice that the divergence theorem can be written in the form

$$\iint_S F_1 dydz + F_2 dxdz + F_3 dxdy$$

$$= \iiint_V \left(\frac{\partial F_1}{\partial x} + \frac{\partial F_2}{\partial y} + \frac{\partial F_3}{\partial z} \right) dxdydz \qquad (8)$$

Applying this theorem to eq.(1), we obtain

$$\iint_S x^2 dydz + 2xydzdx + 2xzdxdy$$

$$= \iiint_D (2x+2y+2z)dxdydz$$

$$= 6 \iiint_D xdxdydz \qquad (9)$$

But, from eq.(7),

$$\iiint_D xdxdydz = V\bar{x}$$

Therefore,

$$\iint_S x^2 dydz + 2xydzdx + 2xzdxdy = 6V\bar{x}$$

Evaluate

$$\iint_S \bar{r} \cdot \bar{n} \; dS \qquad (1)$$

where S is

1. the surface of the cube bounded by $x = -3$, $y = -3$, $z = -3$, $x = 0$, $y = 0$, and $z = 0$;

2. a sphere of radius 3;

3. the surface of the region bounded by the paraboloid $z = 4-(x^2+y^2)$ and the xy plane.

Solution: Applying the divergence theorem to the vector $\bar{r} = x\bar{i} + y\bar{j} + z\bar{k}$, we obtain

$$\iint_S \bar{r} \cdot \bar{n} \; dS = \iiint_V \text{div } \bar{r} \; dV$$

$$= \iiint_V (1+1+1) dV$$

$$= 3 \iiint_V dV$$

Now, notice that the integral $\iiint_V dV$ represents the volume of the region at hand.

1. In this case, the region is a cube whose volume is $3 \cdot 3 \cdot 3 = 27$, thus,

$$\iint_S \bar{r} \cdot \bar{n} \; dS = 3 \iiint_V dV = 3 \cdot 27 = 81$$

2. The volume of a sphere of radius 3 is

$$\iiint_V dV = \frac{4}{3} \pi (3)^3 = 36\pi$$

Thus,

$$\iint_S \bar{r} \cdot \bar{n} \; dS = 3 \cdot 36\pi = 108\pi$$

3. The volume bounded by the paraboloid is 8π, thus

$$\iint_S \bar{r} \cdot \bar{n} \; dS = 3 \cdot 8\pi = 24\pi$$

BASIC IDENTITIES, GREEN'S FIRST AND SECOND IDENTITIES

Let ψ be a continuously differentiable function

$$\psi = \psi(x,y,z) \tag{1}$$

Prove that

$$\iiint_V \nabla\psi \; dV = \iint_S \psi\bar{n} \; dS \tag{2}$$

Solution: Let $\quad \bar{F} = \psi\bar{a} \tag{3}$
where $\bar{a}$ is a constant vector.

From the divergence theorem, we may write

$$\iiint_V \nabla \cdot (\psi\bar{a}) dV = \iint_S (\psi\bar{a}) \cdot \bar{n} \; dS \tag{4}$$

Since $\bar{a}$ is a constant vector, we may write

and
$$\nabla \cdot (\psi\bar{a}) = \nabla\psi \cdot \bar{a} = \bar{a} \cdot \nabla\psi \tag{5}$$

$$(\psi\bar{a}) \cdot \bar{n} = \bar{a} \cdot (\psi\bar{n}) \tag{6}$$

Eq.(4) becomes

$$\iiint_V \bar{a} \cdot \nabla\psi \; dV = \iint_S \bar{a} \cdot (\psi\bar{n}) dS \tag{7}$$

Since $\bar{a}$ is a constant vector, we can take $\bar{a}$ outside of the integrals.

$$\bar{a} \cdot \iiint_V \nabla\psi dV = \bar{a} \cdot \iint_S \psi\bar{n} \; dS \tag{8}$$

Since $\bar{a}$ is an arbitrary constant vector,

$$\iiint_V \nabla\psi dV = \iint_S \psi\bar{n} \; dS \tag{9}$$

Let $\bar{F}$ be a continuously differentiable vector field.
Prove that

$$\iiint_V \nabla \times \bar{F} \; dV = \iint_S \bar{n} \times \bar{F} \; dS \tag{1}$$

Solution: Let $\bar{a}$ be a constant vector. The divergence theorem can be applied to the vector $\bar{F} \times \bar{a}$.

$$\quad (2)$$

$$\iiint_V \nabla \cdot (\overline{F} \times \overline{a}) dV = \iint_S (\overline{F} \times \overline{a}) \cdot \overline{n} \, dS \quad (3)$$

Since $\overline{a}$ is a constant vector,

$$\nabla \cdot (\overline{F} \times \overline{a}) = \overline{a} \cdot (\nabla \times \overline{F}) - \overline{F} \cdot (\nabla \times \overline{a}) = \overline{a} \cdot (\nabla \times \overline{F}) \quad (4)$$

since $\nabla \times \overline{a} = \overline{0}$.

We also have,

$$(\overline{F} \times \overline{a}) \cdot \overline{n} = \overline{F} \cdot (\overline{a} \times \overline{n}) = (\overline{a} \times \overline{n}) \cdot \overline{F} = \overline{a} \cdot (\overline{n} \times \overline{F}) \quad (5)$$

Substituting eqs.(4) and (5) into eq.(3) results in

$$\iiint_V \overline{a} \cdot (\nabla \times \overline{F}) dV = \iint_S \overline{a} \cdot (\overline{n} \times \overline{F}) dS \quad (6)$$

Since $\overline{a}$ is an arbitrary constant vector, eq.(6) can be written in the form

$$\overline{a} \cdot \int_V \nabla \times \overline{F} \, dV = \overline{a} \cdot \int_S \overline{n} \times \overline{F} \, dS \quad (7)$$

which leads to

$$\iiint_V \nabla \times \overline{F} \, dV = \iint_S \overline{n} \times \overline{F} \, dS \quad (8)$$

● **PROBLEM 19-24**

Show that if $\overline{F}$ is a vector that is always normal to a given closed surface S, then

$$\iiint_V \text{curl} \ \overline{F} \ dV = \overline{0} \quad (1)$$

where V is the region bounded by S.

Solution: Let $\overline{a}$ be an arbitrary constant vector. The divergence theorem for the vector field $\overline{F} \times \overline{a}$ states that

$$\iiint_V \nabla \cdot (\overline{F} \times \overline{a}) dV = \iint_S (\overline{F} \times \overline{a}) \cdot \overline{n} \, dS \quad (2)$$

Since $\overline{a}$ is constant

$$\nabla \cdot (\overline{F} \times \overline{a}) = \overline{a} \cdot (\nabla \times \overline{F}) \quad (3)$$

Furthermore,

$$(\overline{F} \times \overline{a}) \cdot \overline{n} = \overline{a} \cdot (\overline{n} \times \overline{F}) \quad (4)$$

Eq.(2) becomes

$$\iiint_V \overline{a} \cdot (\nabla \times \overline{F})dV = \iint_S \overline{a} \cdot (\overline{n} \times \overline{F})dS \qquad (5)$$

$\overline{F}$ is normal to S, and $\overline{n}$ is normal to S, thus
$$\overline{n} \times \overline{F} = \overline{0} \qquad (6)$$
and therefore
$$\iiint_V \overline{a} \cdot (\nabla \times \overline{F})dV = 0 \qquad (7)$$

Since $\overline{a}$ is an arbitrary constant vector,
$$\iiint_V \text{curl } \overline{F} \ dV = \overline{0} \qquad (8)$$

● **PROBLEM 19-25**

Prove that if $\qquad \overline{H} = \nabla \times \overline{A}$ $\qquad (1)$

then $\qquad \iint_S \overline{H} \cdot \overline{n} \ dS = 0 \qquad (2)$

for any closed surface S.

Solution: Let us apply the divergence theorem to $\overline{H}$
$$\iiint_V \nabla \cdot \overline{H} \ dV = \iint_S \overline{H} \cdot \overline{n} \ dS \qquad (3)$$

Since, for any vector $\overline{F}$
$$\text{div curl } \overline{F} = \nabla \cdot (\nabla \times \overline{F}) = 0 \qquad (4)$$
then substituting eq.(1) into eq.(3) results in
$$\iiint_V \nabla \cdot \overline{H} \ dV = \iiint_V \nabla \cdot (\nabla \times \overline{H})dV = \iiint_V 0 \ dV$$
$$= 0 = \iint_S \overline{H} \cdot \overline{n} \ dS \qquad (5)$$

● **PROBLEM 19-26**

Show that
$$\iint_S \phi\overline{F} \cdot \overline{n} \ dS = \iiint_V \overline{F} \cdot \nabla\phi dV + \iiint_V \phi\nabla \cdot \overline{F} \ dV \qquad (1)$$

where ϕ is a differentiable scalar function.

Solution: Applying the divergence theorem to the vector function $\phi\overline{F}$, we obtain

$$\iiint_V div(\phi\overline{F})dV = \iint_S \phi\overline{F} \cdot \overline{n} \, dS \tag{2}$$

We have

$$div(\phi\overline{F}) = \frac{\partial}{\partial x}(\phi F_1) + \frac{\partial}{\partial y}(\phi F_2) + \frac{\partial}{\partial z}(\phi F_3)$$

$$= \phi\frac{\partial F_1}{\partial x} + F_1\frac{\partial \phi}{\partial x} + \phi\frac{\partial F_2}{\partial y} + F_2\frac{\partial \phi}{\partial y} + \phi\frac{\partial F_3}{\partial z} + F_3\frac{\partial \phi}{\partial z}$$

$$= \phi\left(\frac{\partial F_1}{\partial x} + \frac{\partial F_2}{\partial y} + \frac{\partial F_3}{\partial z}\right) + F_1\frac{\partial \phi}{\partial x} + F_2\frac{\partial \phi}{\partial y} + F_3\frac{\partial \phi}{\partial z} \tag{3}$$

$$= \phi \, div \, \overline{F} + \overline{F} \cdot grad\phi = \phi\nabla \cdot \overline{F} + \overline{F} \cdot \nabla\phi$$

Substituting eq.(3) into eq.(2) results in

$$\iiint_V div(\phi\overline{F})dV = \iiint_V (\phi\nabla \cdot \overline{F} + \overline{F} \cdot \nabla\phi)dV$$

$$= \iiint_V \phi\nabla \cdot \overline{F} \, dV + \iiint_V \overline{F} \cdot \nabla\phi \, dV \tag{4}$$

Thus, from (2) and (4), we obtain

$$\iiint_S \phi\overline{F} \cdot \overline{n} \, dS = \iiint_V \overline{F} \cdot \nabla\phi dV + \iiint_V \phi\nabla \cdot \overline{F} \, dV$$

● **PROBLEM** 19-27

Show that if D is a region bounded by a surface S, then

$$\iiint_D \left[a\nabla^2\phi + b\nabla^2\psi\right]dV = a\iint_S \nabla\phi \cdot \overline{n}dS + b\iint_S \nabla\psi \cdot \overline{n}dS \tag{1}$$

where a and b are constant and $\phi = \phi(x,y,z)$, $\psi = \psi(x,y,z)$ are continuously differentiable at least twice.

Solution: Eq.(1) involves integrals taken over a region D and over its bounding surface S. In such case, chances are that the divergence theorem,

$$\iint_S \overline{F} \cdot \overline{n} \, dS = \iiint_D div \, \overline{F} \, dV$$

can be utilized.

886

We now wish to find the vector function $\bar{F}$.

The right-hand side of eq.(1) can be written as

$$a \iint_S \nabla\phi \cdot \bar{n} \; dS + b \iint_S \nabla\psi \cdot \bar{n} \; dS$$

$$= \iint_S \left[a\nabla\phi + b\nabla\psi \right] \cdot \bar{n} \; dS \tag{2}$$

From eq.(2), we can guess that

$$\bar{F} = a\nabla\phi + b\nabla\psi \tag{3}$$

Now, let us actually apply the divergence theorem to the vector function $\bar{F}$

$$\iiint_D \text{div } \bar{F} \; dV = \iiint_D \nabla \cdot \left[a\nabla\phi + b\nabla\psi \right] dV$$

$$= \iiint_D \left[a\nabla \cdot \nabla\phi + b\nabla \cdot \nabla\psi \right] dV$$

$$= \iiint_D \left[a\nabla^2\phi + b\nabla^2\psi \right] dV \tag{4}$$

$$= \iint_S \left[a\nabla\phi + b\nabla\psi \right] \cdot \bar{n} \; dS$$

$$= a \iint_S \nabla\phi \cdot \bar{n} \; dS + b \iint_S \nabla\psi \cdot \bar{n} \; dS$$

● **PROBLEM 19-28**

Prove Green's first identity

$$\iiint_D \left[\phi\nabla^2\psi + (\nabla\phi) \cdot (\nabla\psi) \right] dV = \iint_S \phi\nabla\psi \cdot \bar{n} \; dS \tag{1}$$

We assume that $\phi = \phi(x,y,z)$ and $\psi = \psi(x,y,z)$ have continuous derivatives of the second order at least.

Solution: Let us apply the divergence theorem to
$$\bar{F} = \phi\nabla\psi \tag{2}$$
Then

$$\iiint_D \nabla \cdot (\phi\nabla\psi) dV = \iint_S (\phi\nabla\psi) \cdot \bar{n} \; dS \tag{3}$$

Using the identity

887

$$\nabla \cdot (\phi \nabla \psi) = \phi(\nabla \cdot \nabla \psi) + (\nabla \phi) \cdot (\nabla \psi)$$

$$= \phi \nabla^2 \psi + (\nabla \phi) \cdot (\nabla \psi) \qquad (4)$$

we can transform eq.(3) to

$$\iiint_D \nabla \cdot (\phi \nabla \psi) dV = \iiint_D \left[\phi \nabla^2 \psi + (\nabla \phi) \cdot (\nabla \psi) \right] dV$$

$$= \iint_S (\phi \nabla \psi) \cdot \overline{n} \, dS \qquad (5)$$

which completes the proof of Green's first identity.

● **PROBLEM** 19-29

Prove Green's second identity, also known as the symmetrical identity.

$$\iiint_D (\phi \nabla^2 \psi - \psi \nabla^2 \phi) dV = \iint_S (\phi \nabla \psi - \psi \nabla \phi) \cdot \overline{n} \, dS \qquad (1)$$

Here, $\phi = \phi(x,y,z)$ and $\psi = \psi(x,y,z)$ have continuous derivatives of the second order.

<u>Solution</u>: Let us recall Green's first identity.

$$\iiint_D \left[\phi \nabla^2 \psi + (\nabla \phi) \cdot (\nabla \psi) \right] dV = \iint_S \phi \nabla \psi \cdot \overline{n} \, dS \qquad (2)$$

Interchanging ϕ and ψ in eq.(2), we obtain

$$\iiint_D \left[\psi \nabla^2 \phi + (\nabla \psi) \cdot (\nabla \phi) \right] dV = \iint_S \psi \nabla \phi \cdot \overline{n} \, dS \qquad (3)$$

Now, subtracting eq.(3) from eq.(2) results in

$$\iiint_D \left[\phi \nabla^2 \psi - \psi \nabla^2 \phi \right] dV = \iint_S \left[\phi \nabla \psi - \psi \nabla \phi \right] \cdot \overline{n} \, dS \qquad (4)$$

That completes the proof of Green's second identity.

APPLICATIONS OF GREEN'S IDENTITIES, HARMONIC FUNCTIONS

● **PROBLEM** 19-30

Show that Green's first and second identities can be written

$$\iiint_D \left[\phi \nabla^2 \psi + \nabla\phi \cdot \nabla\psi \right] dV = \iint_S \phi \, \frac{\partial \psi}{\partial n} \, dS \qquad (1)$$

$$\iiint_D \left[\phi \nabla^2 \psi - \psi \nabla^2 \phi \right] dV = \iint_S \left(\phi \, \frac{\partial \psi}{\partial n} - \psi \, \frac{\partial \phi}{\partial n} \right) dS \qquad (2)$$

Solution: Often, a partial derivative notation is used for the directional derivative.

For example, if $\overline{n}$ is a unit normal vector to a surface S described by a function f, then we write

$$\frac{\partial f}{\partial n} \equiv \nabla f \cdot \overline{n} \equiv \nabla_n f$$

In eq.(1) of Problem 19-28, we derived Green's first identity

$$\iiint_D \left[\phi \nabla^2 \psi + (\nabla\phi) \cdot (\nabla\psi) \right] dV = \iint_S \phi \nabla\psi \cdot \overline{n} \, dS$$

Noting that

$$\nabla\psi \cdot \overline{n} = \frac{\partial \psi}{\partial n},$$

we may write Green's first identity as

$$\iiint_D \left[\phi \nabla^2 \psi + (\nabla\phi) \cdot (\nabla\psi) \right] dV = \iint_S \phi \, \frac{\partial \psi}{\partial n} \, dS$$

Green's second identity, as derived in Problem 19-29, is

$$\iiint_V (\phi \nabla^2 \psi - \psi \nabla^2 \phi) dV = \iint_S (\phi \nabla\psi - \psi \nabla\phi) \cdot \overline{n} \, dS$$

Since we may write

$$(\phi \nabla\psi - \psi \nabla\phi) \cdot \overline{n} = \phi \nabla\psi \cdot \overline{n} - \psi \nabla\phi \cdot \overline{n}$$

$$= \phi \, \frac{\partial \psi}{\partial n} - \psi \, \frac{\partial \phi}{\partial n}$$

Green's second identity becomes

$$\iiint_V (\phi \nabla^2 \psi - \psi \nabla^2 \phi) dV = \iint_S \left(\phi \, \frac{\partial \psi}{\partial n} - \psi \, \frac{\partial \phi}{\partial n} \right) dS$$

● **PROBLEM 19-31**

Let S be the boundary surface of a region D. If ϕ is harmonic in a domain R containing D, then show that

1. $\iint_S \dfrac{\partial \phi}{\partial n} \, dS = 0$
$\qquad\qquad\qquad\qquad\qquad\qquad\qquad (1)$

889

2. $$\iint\limits_{S} \phi \, \frac{\partial \phi}{\partial n} \, dS = \iiint\limits_{D} |\nabla \phi|^2 \, dV \qquad (2)$$

Solution: First, note that if $\phi = \phi(x,y,z)$ has continuous second derivatives in a domain D and

$$\nabla^2 \phi = 0 \qquad (3)$$

in D, then ϕ is said to be harmonic in D.

1. We shall use Green's first identity

$$\iiint\limits_{D} \left[f \nabla^2 g + \nabla f \cdot \nabla g \right] dV = \iint\limits_{S} f \, \frac{\partial g}{\partial n} \, dS \qquad (4)$$

Let us substitute $g = \phi$ and $f = 1$ into the above identity to obtain

$$\iiint\limits_{D} \nabla^2 \phi \, dV = \iint\limits_{S} \frac{\partial \phi}{\partial n} \, dS \qquad (5)$$

Note that $\nabla f = 0$.

Now, since we are told that ϕ is harmonic, we obtain, from (5)

$$\iint\limits_{S} \frac{\partial \phi}{\partial n} \, dS = 0 \qquad (6)$$

which is the required result.

2. To prove eq.(2), substitute $f = \phi$ and $g = \phi$ $\qquad (7)$
    into Green's first identity to obtain

$$\iiint\limits_{D} \left[\phi \cdot 0 + \nabla \phi \cdot \nabla \phi \right] dV = \iint\limits_{S} \phi \, \frac{\partial \phi}{\partial n} \, dS \qquad (8)$$

or $\quad \displaystyle\iiint\limits_{D} |\nabla \phi|^2 \, dV = \iint\limits_{S} \phi \, \frac{\partial \phi}{\partial n} \, dS \qquad (9)$

Note that $\qquad \nabla \phi \cdot \nabla \phi = |\nabla \phi|^2.$ $\qquad (10)$

● **PROBLEM** 19-32

Let S be the boundary surface of a region D. Let $\phi(x,y,z)$ be a function defined and continuous, with continuous first and second derivatives, in a domain R containing D.

Prove the following relation:
If ϕ is harmonic in R and $\phi \equiv 0$ on S, then $\phi \equiv 0$ in D.

Solution: Since $\phi(x,y,z)$ is harmonic in R, we can use eq. (2) of Problem 19-31.

$$\iint_S \phi \frac{\partial \phi}{\partial n} \, dS = \iiint_D |\nabla \phi|^2 \, dV \tag{1}$$

Since $\phi \equiv 0$ on S, eq.(1) becomes

$$\iiint_D |\nabla \phi|^2 \, dV = 0 \tag{2}$$

Now, a basic property of triple integrals is that if a function $f(x,y,z)$ is continuous in a bounded closed region D and

$$\iiint_D \left[f(x,y,z)\right]^2 dxdydz = 0 \tag{3}$$

then $f(x,y,z) \equiv 0$ in D. $\tag{4}$

By virtue of this property we conclude, from eq.(2), that

$$\nabla \phi \equiv 0 \quad \text{in D.} \tag{5}$$

Therefore $\phi = a$ $\tag{6}$

where a is a constant.

Since $\phi \equiv 0$ on S and ϕ is continuous in R, we conclude that

$$\phi \equiv 0 \quad \text{in D.} \tag{7}$$

● **PROBLEM 19-33**

Let S be the boundary surface of a region D. Let $\phi(x,y,z)$ and $\psi(x,y,z)$ be functions defined and continuous, with continuous first and second derivatives in a domain R containing D.

Prove that

1.   if ϕ and ψ are harmonic in R and $\phi \equiv \psi$ on S, then $\phi \equiv \psi$ in D;

2.   if ϕ is harmonic in R and $\frac{\partial \phi}{\partial n} = 0$ on S, then ϕ is constant in D.

Solution: 1. Consider the function $\phi - \psi$. Since ϕ and ψ are harmonic in R, $\phi - \psi$ is also harmonic in R. Since $\phi \equiv \psi$ on S, $\phi - \psi \equiv 0$ on S. We can apply the relation proven in Problem 19-32 to the function $\phi - \psi$.

$\phi - \psi$ is harmonic in R and $\phi - \psi \equiv 0$ on S, therefore

$$\phi - \psi \equiv 0 \quad \text{in D.}$$

Hence, $\phi \equiv \psi$ in D.

2. Since ϕ is harmonic in R, we can utilize eq.(2) of Problem 19-31.

$$\iint_S \phi \frac{\partial \phi}{\partial n}\, dS = \iiint_D |\nabla \phi|^2\, dV \qquad (1)$$

But, $\frac{\partial \phi}{\partial n} = 0$ on S, therefore

$$\iiint_D |\nabla \phi|^2\, dV = 0 \qquad (2)$$

Since $\nabla \phi$ is continuous, we can conclude from eq.(2) that

$$\nabla \phi \equiv 0 \quad \text{in D}$$

and $\qquad \phi = \text{const} \quad$ in D. $\qquad (3)$

● **PROBLEM 19-34**

Let S be the boundary surface of a region D, and let $\phi(x,y,z)$ and $\psi(x,y,z)$ be functions defined and continuous with continuous first and second derivatives in a domain R containing D.

Prove that

1. if ϕ and ψ are harmonic in R and

$$\frac{\partial \phi}{\partial n} = \frac{\partial \psi}{\partial n} \quad \text{on S} \qquad (1)$$

then $\qquad \phi = \psi + \text{const} \quad$ in D. $\qquad (2)$

2. if ϕ and ψ are harmonic in R, and

$$\frac{\partial \phi}{\partial n} = -\phi + f(x,y,z) \quad \text{on S} \qquad (3)$$

$$\frac{\partial \psi}{\partial n} = -\psi + f(x,y,z) \quad \text{on S} \qquad (4)$$

then $\qquad \phi \equiv \psi$ in D. $\qquad (5)$

Solution: 1. Consider the function $\phi - \psi$. Since ϕ and ψ are harmonic, $\phi - \psi$ is also harmonic. From eq.(1), we obtain

$$\frac{\partial}{\partial n}(\phi - \psi) \equiv 0 \quad \text{on S} \qquad (6)$$

Now, we can use property 2 of Problem 19-33, which states that:

If $\phi - \psi$ is harmonic in R and $\frac{\partial}{\partial n}(\phi - \psi) = 0$ on S, then $\phi - \psi$ is constant in D.

Hence, $\qquad \phi = \psi + \text{const} \quad$ in D. $\qquad (7)$

2.   Since ϕ and ψ are harmonic in R, $\phi - \psi$ is also harmonic in R.

Now, subtracting eq.(4) from eq.(3) results in

$$\frac{\partial}{\partial n} (\phi - \psi) = -(\phi - \psi) \tag{8}$$

In Problem 19-31, we proved the following relationship for harmonic functions

$$\iint_S \phi \frac{\partial \phi}{\partial n} \, dS = \iiint_D |\nabla \phi|^2 \, dV \tag{9}$$

Utilizing the fact that $\phi - \psi$ is harmonic and eq.(8), we obtain, from eq.(9)

$$\iint_S (\phi - \psi) \frac{\partial}{\partial n} (\phi - \psi) dS = - \iint_S (\phi - \psi)^2 dS$$

$$= \iiint_D |\nabla(\phi - \psi)|^2 \, dV \tag{10}$$

From eq.(10), we conclude that since

$$\iiint_D |\nabla(\phi - \psi)|^2 \, dV \geq 0$$

and $\tag{11}$

$$\iint_S (\phi - \psi)^2 \, dS \geq 0$$

then

$$\iint_S (\phi - \psi)^2 \, dS = 0 \tag{12}$$

Therefore $\phi \equiv \psi$ on S. $\tag{13}$

In Problem 19-33 we proved that:

If ϕ and ψ are harmonic in R and $\phi \equiv \psi$ on S, then $\phi \equiv \psi$ in D. That completes the proof of property 2.

● **PROBLEM** 19-35

Let S be the boundary surface of a region D.

Let $\phi(x,y,z)$ and $\psi(x,y,z)$ be functions defined and continuous, with continuous first and second derivatives in a domain R containing D.   Prove that:

1.   if ϕ and ψ are harmonic in R, then

$$\iint_S \left(\phi \frac{\partial \psi}{\partial n} - \psi \frac{\partial \phi}{\partial n} \right) dS = 0 \tag{1}$$

2. if ϕ and ψ satisfy the equations

$$\nabla^2\phi = f\phi, \quad \nabla^2\psi = f\psi; \quad f = f(x,y,z) \qquad (2)$$

in D, then

$$\iint_S \left(\phi \frac{\partial\psi}{\partial n} - \psi \frac{\partial\phi}{\partial n}\right) dS = 0 \qquad (3)$$

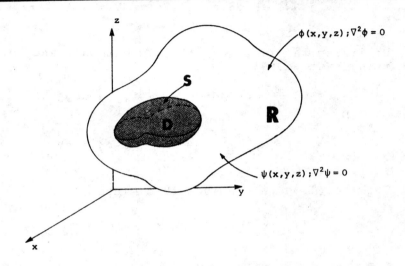

Solution: First note that Green's second identity states that

$$\iint_S \left(\phi \frac{\partial\psi}{\partial n} - \psi \frac{\partial\phi}{\partial n}\right) dS = \iiint_V \left[\phi\nabla^2\psi - \psi\nabla^2\phi\right] dV \qquad (4)$$

1. Since both functions are harmonic in R

$$\nabla^2\phi = 0$$
$$\nabla^2\psi = 0 \qquad (5)$$

we obtain, from eq.(4)

$$\iint_S \left(\phi \frac{\partial\psi}{\partial n} - \psi \frac{\partial\phi}{\partial n}\right) dS = 0 \qquad (6)$$

2. Substituting eq.(2) into eq.(4), we find

$$\iint_S \left(\phi \frac{\partial\psi}{\partial n} - \psi \frac{\partial\phi}{\partial n}\right) dS = \iiint_V \left[\phi\nabla^2\psi - \psi\nabla^2\phi\right] dV$$

$$= \iiint_V \left[\phi f\psi - \psi f\phi\right] dV = \iiint_V 0 \, dV = 0 \qquad (7)$$

Notice that in setting $f = 0$ in property 2, we obtain property 1.

S, D and R are as described in Problem 19-35. $\phi(x,y,z)$ and $\psi(x,y,z)$ are functions defined and continuous, with continuous first and second derivatives in R.

ϕ and ψ satisfy the same Poisson equation in D, that is

$$\nabla^2 \phi = -4\pi f \qquad (1)$$

$$\nabla^2 \psi = -4\pi f \qquad (2)$$

Prove that if

$$\phi \equiv \psi \text{ on S}, \qquad (3)$$

then

$$\phi \equiv \psi \text{ in D}.$$

Solution: Subtracting eq.(2) from eq.(1) results in

$$\nabla^2 \phi - \nabla^2 \psi = 0 \qquad (5)$$

or

$$\nabla^2 (\phi-\psi) = 0$$

Therefore the function $\phi - \psi$ is harmonic. Since $\phi \equiv \psi$ on S, then $\phi - \psi = 0$ on S. $\qquad (6)$

In Problem 19-32 we proved that if ϕ is harmonic and $\phi \equiv 0$ on S, then $\phi \equiv 0$ in D.

Therefore $\qquad \phi - \psi \equiv 0 \text{ in D}$

and $\qquad\qquad \phi \equiv \psi \text{ in D}. \qquad (7)$

FURTHER APPLICATIONS OF THE DIVERGENCE THEOREM

Let D be a region bounded by a closed surface S and $\bar{n}$ be the unit outer normal to S. Prove that for any closed surface S

$$\iint_S \bar{n} \, dS = \bar{0} \qquad (1)$$

Solution: Let $\bar{F}$ be an arbitrary continuously differentiable vector field. The divergence theorem states that

$$\iiint_V \text{div } \bar{F} \, dV = \iint_S \bar{F} \cdot \bar{n} \, dS \qquad (2)$$

In Problem 19-22, by using the divergence theorem we proved

that if $\phi(x,y,z)$ is a continuously differentiable function, then

$$\iiint_D \nabla\phi \, dV = \iint_S \phi\bar{n} \, dS \qquad (3)$$

The function $\phi(x,y,z) = a$, where a is constant, is continuously differentiable, thus from eq.(3), we obtain

$$\iiint_D \nabla\phi \, dV = \bar{0} = \iint_S a\bar{n} \, dS = a \iint_S \bar{n} \, dS \qquad (4)$$

Note that for $\phi(x,y,z) = a$, $\nabla\phi = \bar{0}$. $\qquad (5)$

We have proven that

$$\iint_S \bar{n} \, dS = \bar{0} \qquad (6)$$

for any closed surface S.

● **PROBLEM** 19-38

Show that for any closed surface S,

$$\iint_S \bar{r} \times \bar{n} \, dS = \bar{0} \qquad (1)$$

Solution: Let us check if any of the previously proved equations can be used in this problem. The divergence theorem cannot be directly applied since the surface integral $\iint_S \bar{F} \cdot \bar{n} \, dS$ contains a scalar function and in eq.(1), we integrate $\bar{r} \times \bar{n}$, which is a vector.

In Problem 19-23⹁ it was proven that if $\bar{F}$ is a continuously differentiable vector field, then

$$\iiint_D \nabla \times \bar{F} \, dV = \iint_S \bar{n} \times \bar{F} \, dS \qquad (2)$$

For $\bar{F} = \bar{r}$, eq.(2) yields

$$\iint_S \bar{r} \times \bar{n} \, dS = - \iiint_D \nabla \times \bar{r} \, dV \qquad (3)$$

But

$$\nabla \times \bar{r} = \left[\frac{\partial}{\partial x}, \frac{\partial}{\partial y}, \frac{\partial}{\partial z}\right] \times (x,y,z) = (0,0,0) \qquad (4)$$

Thus, from eqs.(3) and (4), we deduce that

$$\iint_S \bar{r} \times \bar{n} \, dS = \bar{0}$$

Let S be a closed surface and D be a region bounded by S. Show that

$$\iiint_D \text{div } \bar{n} \, dV = A \qquad (1)$$

where $\bar{n}$ is the unit outer normal to S and A is the area of S.

Solution: Eq.(1) is a triple integral of the divergence of the vector field $\bar{n}$. The triple integral of the divergence of a vector field also occurs in the divergence theorem.

$$\iiint_D \text{div } \bar{F} \, dV = \iint_S \bar{F} \cdot \bar{n} \, dS \qquad (2)$$

Substituting $\bar{F} = \bar{n}$ in eq.(2), we obtain

$$\iiint_D \text{div } \bar{n} \, dV = \iint_S \bar{n} \cdot \bar{n} \, dS = \iint_S dS = A \qquad (3)$$

Note that $\bar{n} \cdot \bar{n} = |\bar{n}| = 1$ because $\bar{n}$ is a unit vector. Also, note that $\iint_S dS$ represents the area of S.

Let S be the boundary surface of a region D, with outer unit normal $\bar{n}$. Show that

$$\iiint_D \frac{1}{r^2} \, dV = \iint_S \frac{\bar{r} \cdot \bar{n}}{r^2} \, dS \qquad (1)$$

Solution: Eq.(1) combines a volume and a surface integral, therefore, we will use the divergence theorem in order to prove eq.(1).

$$\iiint_D \text{div } \bar{F} \, dV = \iint_S \bar{F} \cdot \bar{n} \, dS \qquad (2)$$

Now, note that $\bar{r} = x\bar{i} + y\bar{j} + z\bar{k}$ and $r^2 = x^2 + y^2 + z^2$.

Let

$$\bar{F} = \frac{\bar{r}}{r^2} \qquad (3)$$

The divergence of $\frac{\bar{r}}{r^2}$ is equal to

$$\text{div } \frac{\bar{r}}{r^2} = \left(\frac{\partial}{\partial x}, \frac{\partial}{\partial y}, \frac{\partial}{\partial z} \right) \cdot \left(\frac{x}{x^2+y^2+z^2}, \frac{y}{x^2+y^2+z^2}, \frac{z}{x^2+y^2+z^2} \right)$$

$$= \frac{y^2+z^2-x^2+x^2+z^2-y^2+x^2+y^2-z^2}{(x^2+y^2+z^2)^2} = \frac{1}{x^2+y^2+z^2} = \frac{1}{r^2} \quad (4)$$

Thus,

$$\iiint_D \operatorname{div} \frac{\overline{r}}{r^2} \, dV = \iiint_D \frac{1}{r^2} \, dV = \iint_S \frac{\overline{r} \cdot \overline{n}}{r^2} \, dS$$

● **PROBLEM 19-41**

Let S be the closed boundary of a region D. If

$$\iiint_D r^3 \, dV = p \quad (1)$$

evaluate the integral

$$\iint_S r^3 \, \overline{r} \cdot \overline{n} \, dS \quad (2)$$

Solution: It is required to compute the surface integral of a function in the situation where the volume integral of some other function is given.

Applying the divergence theorem to eq.(2), we obtain

$$\iint_S r^3 \, \overline{r} \cdot \overline{n} \, dS = \iiint_D \operatorname{div}(r^3 \overline{r}) dV \quad (3)$$

We have

$$\operatorname{div}(r^3 \overline{r}) = \left(\frac{\partial}{\partial x}, \frac{\partial}{\partial y}, \frac{\partial}{\partial z} \right) \cdot \left[x(x^2+y^2+z^2)^{\frac{3}{2}}, y(x^2+y^2+z^2)^{\frac{3}{2}}, z(x^2+y^2+z^2)^{\frac{3}{2}} \right]$$

$$= 3(x^2+y^2+z^2)^{\frac{3}{2}} + (x^2+y^2+z^2)^{\frac{1}{2}}(3x^2+3y^2+3z^2) \quad (4)$$

$$= 3r^3 + 3r^3 = 6r^3$$

Substituting eq.(4) into eq.(3) results in

$$\iint_S r^3 \, \overline{r} \cdot \overline{n} \, dS = \iiint_D 6r^3 \, dV = 6 \iiint_D r^3 \, dV$$

$$(5)$$

$$= 6p$$

● **PROBLEM 19-42**

Let S be the closed boundary of a region D. Prove that

1. $$\iiint_D 5r^3 \overline{r} \, dV = \iint_S r^5 \overline{n} \, dS \quad (1)$$

$$2. \quad \iiint\limits_{D} n \; r^{n-2} \; \overline{r} \; dV = \iint\limits_{S} r^n \; \overline{n} \; dS \qquad (2)$$

Solution: 1. Eq.(1) involves the volume integral of the vector function $5r^3\overline{r}$ and the surface integral of the vector function $r^5\overline{n}$. The divergence theorem cannot be directly applied.

In Problem 19-22, it was proven that if ϕ is a continuously differentiable function, then

$$\iiint\limits_{D} \nabla\phi \; dV = \iint\limits_{S} \phi\overline{n} \; dS \qquad (3)$$

If $\qquad \phi = r^5 \qquad (4)$

then

$$\nabla\phi = \nabla r^5 = \nabla(x^2+y^2+z^2)^{\frac{5}{2}} = 5r^3\overline{r} \qquad (5)$$

Substituting eq.(4) and eq.(5) into eq.(3), we obtain

$$\iiint\limits_{D} 5r^3\overline{r} \; dV = \iint\limits_{S} r^5\overline{n} \; dS \qquad (6)$$

2. First, let us evaluate ∇r^n,

We have

$$\nabla r^n = \nabla(x^2+y^2+z^2)^{\frac{n}{2}}$$

$$= \overline{i} \; \frac{\partial}{\partial x}\left[(x^2+y^2+z^2)^{\frac{n}{2}}\right] + \overline{j} \; \frac{\partial}{\partial y}\left[(x^2+y^2+z^2)^{\frac{n}{2}}\right] + \overline{k} \; \frac{\partial}{\partial z}\left[(x^2+y^2+z^2)^{\frac{n}{2}}\right]$$

$$(7)$$

$$= n(x^2+y^2+z^2)^{\frac{n}{2}-1}(x\overline{i}+y\overline{j}+z\overline{k}) = nr^{n-2} \; \overline{r}$$

From eqs.(3) and (7), we obtain

$$\iiint\limits_{D} nr^{n-2} \; \overline{r} \; dV = \iint\limits_{S} r^n \; \overline{n} \; dS \qquad (8)$$

DEFINITION OF DIVERGENCE, GRADIENT AND ROTATION

● **PROBLEM** 19-43

Let div $\overline{F}$ denote the divergence of a vector field $\overline{F}$ at a point P. Show that

$$\text{div } \overline{F} = \lim_{\Delta V \to 0} \frac{1}{\Delta V} \iint\limits_{\Delta S} \overline{F} \cdot \overline{n} \; dS \qquad (1)$$

where ΔV is the volume bounded by the surface ΔS. The limit is obtained by shrinking ΔV to the point P.

Solution: By the divergence theorem,

$$\iiint_{\Delta D} \text{div } \overline{F} \, dV = \iint_{\Delta S} \overline{F} \cdot \overline{n} \, dS \qquad (2)$$

The mean value theorem for integrals asserts that

$$\iiint_{\Delta D} f(x,y,z) dV = f(x_p, y_p, z_p) \Delta V \qquad (3)$$

where (x_p, y_p, z_p) is a point of ΔD and ΔV is the volume of ΔD. The function $f(x,y,z)$ is continuous in ΔD.

Applying the mean value theorem, we obtain

$$\iiint_{\Delta D} \text{div } \overline{F} \, dV = \left[\text{div } \overline{F}\right]\Big|_P \Delta V \qquad (4)$$

where P is a point in ΔD.

From eqs.(4) and (2) we obtain

$$\left[\text{div } \overline{F}\right]\Big|_P = \frac{\iint_{\Delta S} \overline{F} \cdot \overline{n} \, dS}{\Delta V} \qquad (5)$$

Taking the limit as $\Delta V \to 0$ in such a way that P always belongs to ΔV, $P \varepsilon \Delta V$, we obtain

$$\text{div } \overline{F} = \lim_{\Delta V \to 0} \frac{1}{\Delta V} \iint_{\Delta S} \overline{F} \cdot \overline{n} \, dS \qquad (6)$$

Here, div $\overline{F}$ is evaluated at the point P. Eq.(6) is often used as the definition of divergence. It is of fundamental significance because it gives us a definition of the divergence in a manner that is independent of any coordinate system.

All the properties of divergence, including the divergence theorem, may be derived from eq.(6).

Since the integral

$$\iint_S \overline{F} \cdot \overline{n} \, dS$$

represents the flux of the vector field $\overline{F}$ across ΔS, we conclude that the right-hand side of eq.(6),

$$\frac{1}{\Delta V} \iint_{\Delta S} \overline{F} \cdot \overline{n} \, dS$$

represents the flux per unit volume of the vector field $\overline{F}$ across the surface ΔS.

If div $\overline{F}$ is negative in the neighborhood of P, then the flux is an inflow and P is called a sink. On the other hand, if div $\overline{F} > 0$ in the neighborhood of P, then P is said to be a source.

If in the neighborhood of P there are no sinks or sources, that is div $\overline{F} = 0$, then $\overline{F}$ is called a solenoidal vector field.

● **PROBLEM** 19-44

Using the results of Problem 19-43, show that at any point P

$$\nabla \phi = \lim_{\Delta V \to 0} \frac{1}{\Delta V} \iint_{\Delta S} \phi \ \overline{n} \ dS \qquad (1)$$

where ΔV is the volume of the region ΔD enclosed by ΔS. The limit is obtained by shrinking ΔD to the point P.

Solution: We shall use the identity proven in Problem 19-22, namely

$$\iiint_{\Delta D} \nabla \phi \ dV = \iint_{\Delta S} \phi \overline{n} \ dS \qquad (2)$$

or

$$\iiint_{\Delta D} \nabla \phi \cdot \overline{i} \ dV = \iint_{\Delta S} \phi \overline{n} \cdot \overline{i} \ dS \qquad (3)$$

Applying the mean value theorem for integrals, we obtain

$$\left[\nabla \phi \cdot \overline{i} \right] \Big|_A = \frac{1}{\Delta V} \iiint_{\Delta D} \nabla \phi \cdot \overline{i} \ dV = \frac{1}{\Delta V} \iint_{\Delta S} \phi \overline{n} \cdot \overline{i} \ dS \qquad (4)$$

where A is a point in ΔD.

Taking the limit as $\Delta V \to 0$ in such a way that P is always an element of $\Delta D, P \ \varepsilon \ \Delta D$, we find

$$\nabla \phi \cdot \overline{i} = \lim_{\Delta V \to 0} \frac{1}{\Delta V} \iint_{\Delta S} \phi \overline{n} \cdot \overline{i} \ dS \qquad (5)$$

In a similar manner, we evaluate the two remaining integrals

$$\nabla \phi \cdot \overline{j} = \lim_{\Delta V \to 0} \frac{1}{\Delta V} \iint_{\Delta S} \phi \overline{n} \cdot \overline{j} \ dS \qquad (6)$$

$$\nabla \phi \cdot \overline{k} = \lim_{\Delta V \to 0} \frac{1}{\Delta V} \iint_{\Delta S} \phi \overline{n} \cdot \overline{k} \ dS \qquad (7)$$

Since

$$\nabla \phi = (\nabla \phi \cdot \overline{i}) \overline{i} + (\nabla \phi \cdot \overline{j}) \overline{j} + (\nabla \phi \cdot \overline{k}) \overline{k} \qquad (8)$$

and

$$\overline{n} = (\overline{n} \cdot \overline{i}) \overline{i} + (\overline{n} \cdot \overline{j}) \overline{j} + (\overline{n} \cdot \overline{k}) \overline{k} \qquad (9)$$

we multiply eqs.(5), (6) and (7) by $\overline{i}$, $\overline{j}$ and $\overline{k}$ respectively and add the results

$$(\nabla\phi \cdot \overline{i})\overline{i} + (\nabla\phi \cdot \overline{j})\overline{j} + (\nabla\phi \cdot \overline{k})\overline{k} = \nabla\phi$$

(10)

$$= \lim_{\Delta V \to 0} \frac{1}{\Delta V} \iint_{\Delta S} \phi\left[(\overline{n} \cdot \overline{i})\overline{i} + (\overline{n} \cdot \overline{j})\overline{j} + (\overline{n} \cdot \overline{k})\overline{k}\right] dS$$

Thus,

$$\nabla\phi = \lim_{\Delta V \to 0} \frac{1}{\Delta V} \iint_{\Delta S} \phi\overline{n} \ dS$$

(11)

Eq.(11) can be used as a definition of the gradient. Notice that this definition is independent of the coordinate system.

● **PROBLEM** 19-45

Show that at any point P

$$\nabla \times \overline{F} = \lim_{\Delta V \to 0} \frac{1}{\Delta V} \iint_{\Delta S} \overline{n} \times \overline{F} \ dS$$

(1)

where ΔV is the volume of the region ΔD enclosed by the surface ΔS. The limit is evaluated in such a way that the point P always belongs to ΔD.

Solution: The following identity was proven in Problem 19-23,

$$\iiint_{\Delta D} \nabla \times \overline{F} \ dV = \iint_{\Delta S} \overline{n} \times \overline{F} \ dS$$

(2)

Eq.(2) can be written for the x-component

$$\iiint_{\Delta D} (\nabla \times \overline{F}) \cdot \overline{i} \ dV = \iint_{\Delta S} (\overline{n} \times \overline{F}) \cdot \overline{i} \ dS$$

(3)

Applying the law of the mean for integrals we obtain

$$\left[(\nabla \times \overline{F}) \cdot \overline{i}\right]\Big|_A = \frac{1}{\Delta V} \iint_{\Delta S} (\overline{n} \times \overline{F}) \cdot \overline{i} \ dS$$

(4)

Taking the limit as the volume ΔV of the region ΔD tends to zero in such a way that ΔD shrinks to point P and $P \ \varepsilon \ \Delta D$, we obtain

$$(\nabla \times \overline{F}) \cdot \overline{i} = \lim_{\Delta V \to 0} \frac{1}{\Delta V} \iint_{\Delta S} (\overline{n} \times \overline{F}) \cdot \overline{i} \ dS$$

(5)

In the same manner, we find

$$(\nabla \times \overline{F}) \cdot \overline{j} = \lim_{\Delta V \to 0} \frac{1}{\Delta V} \iint_{\Delta S} (\overline{n} \times \overline{F}) \cdot \overline{j} \ dS$$

(6)

$$(\nabla \times \overline{F}) \cdot \overline{k} = \lim_{\Delta V \to 0} \frac{1}{\Delta V} \iint_{\Delta S} (\overline{n} \times \overline{F}) \cdot \overline{k} \, dS \qquad (7)$$

Multiplying eqs.(5), (6) and (7) by $\overline{i}$, $\overline{j}$, $\overline{k}$ respectively, and adding, we find

$$\nabla \times \overline{F} = \lim_{\Delta V \to 0} \frac{1}{\Delta V} \iint_{\Delta S} \overline{n} \times \overline{F} \, dS \qquad (8)$$

● **PROBLEM 19-46**

The following equation defines an operator

$$\nabla o \equiv \lim_{\Delta V \to 0} \frac{1}{\Delta V} \iint_{\Delta S} d\overline{S} o \qquad (1)$$

The symbol o indicates either ordinary multiplication, a dot product or a cross product.

Show that both operators on the left-hand side and the right-hand side of eq.(1) are equivalent.

<u>Solution</u>: If o indicates ordinary multiplication, then the operator ∇o acts on a scalar field $\phi(x,y,z)$ and we obtain

$$\nabla o \, \phi = \lim_{\Delta V \to 0} \frac{1}{\Delta V} \iint_{\Delta S} d\overline{S} o \phi$$

$$= \lim_{\Delta V \to 0} \frac{1}{\Delta V} \iint_{\Delta S} \overline{n} \phi \, o \, dS \qquad (2)$$

or

$$\nabla \phi = \lim_{\Delta V \to 0} \iint_{\Delta S} \overline{n} \phi \, dS \qquad (3)$$

In Problem 19-44, we proved that eq.(3) holds true; therefore, we have shown that both operators are equivalent under multiplication.

Now, if o indicates a dot product, then ∇o acts on a vector field.

$$\nabla o \, \overline{F} = \lim_{\Delta V \to 0} \frac{1}{\Delta V} \iint_{\Delta S} d\overline{S} \circ \overline{F} \qquad (4)$$

or

$$\nabla \cdot \overline{F} = \text{div } \overline{F} = \lim_{\Delta V \to 0} \frac{1}{\Delta V} \iint_{\Delta S} d\overline{S} \cdot \overline{F}$$

$$= \lim_{\Delta V \to 0} \frac{1}{\Delta V} \iint_{\Delta S} \overline{n} \cdot \overline{F} \, dS \tag{5}$$

In Problem 19-43, we proved eq.(5), thus, we see that both operators are equivalent under the dot product.

Finally, if o is the cross product, then ∇o acts on a vector field and we obtain

$$\nabla \text{o} \, \overline{F} = \lim_{\Delta V \to 0} \frac{1}{\Delta V} \iint_{\Delta S} d\overline{S} \text{ o } \overline{F} \tag{6}$$

or

$$\nabla \times \overline{F} = \lim_{\Delta V \to 0} \frac{1}{\Delta V} \iint_{\Delta S} \overline{n} \times \overline{F} \, dS \tag{7}$$

Eq.(7) is proven in Problem 19-45; therefore we have established the operator equivalence.

GAUSS' THEOREM, SOLID ANGLE DIVERGENCE OF N-DIMENSIONAL SPACE

● **PROBLEM 19-47**

Let D be a region enclosed by a surface S.

Let $\qquad \overline{r} = x\overline{i} + y\overline{j} + z\overline{k}$ (1)

denote the position vector of some point (x,y,z).

Prove that

$$\iint_S \frac{\overline{r} \cdot \overline{n}}{r^3} \, dS = \begin{cases} 0 & \text{if the origin lies} \\ & \text{outside S} \\ \\ 4\pi & \text{if the origin lies} \\ & \text{inside S} \end{cases} \tag{2}$$

Eq.(2) is known as Gauss' theorem.

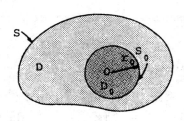

Solution: 1. By the divergence theorem, we have

$$\iint_S \frac{\overline{r} \cdot \overline{n}}{r^3} \, dS = \iiint_D \nabla \cdot \frac{\overline{r}}{r^3} \, dV \tag{3}$$

To evaluate div $\frac{\overline{r}}{r^3}$ we shall use the identities

$$\nabla \cdot (f\overline{F}) = \overline{F} \cdot \nabla f + f \nabla \cdot \overline{F} \tag{4}$$

$$\nabla r^n = n r^{n-2} \overline{r} \tag{5}$$

For $\nabla \cdot \frac{\overline{r}}{r^3}$, we now obtain, applying identity (4),

$$\nabla \cdot \left(\frac{\overline{r}}{r^3} \right) = \nabla \cdot (r^{-3}\overline{r}) = \overline{r} \cdot \nabla r^{-3} + r^{-3} \nabla \cdot \overline{r}$$

Now, applying identity (5) yields

$$\begin{aligned} \nabla \cdot \left(\frac{\overline{r}}{r^3} \right) &= \overline{r} \cdot \nabla r^{-3} + r^{-3} \nabla \cdot \overline{r} \\ &= -3r^{-5} \overline{r} \cdot \overline{r} + 3r^{-3} \\ &= -3r^{-5} r^2 + 3r^{-3} = 0 \end{aligned} \tag{6}$$

and therefore

$$\iint_S \frac{\overline{r} \cdot \overline{n}}{r^3} \, dS = \iiint_D \nabla \cdot \frac{\overline{r}}{r^3} \, dV = 0 \tag{7}$$

Note that the above holds true only for $r \neq 0$; that is, the surface integral is equal to zero for a surface that does not enclose the origin. Or, equivalently, div $\frac{\overline{r}}{r^3}$ is equal to zero everywhere exept the origin.

2. If the origin 0 is inside S we surround 0 by a small sphere S_0 of radius r_0.

We integrate over the region bounded by S and S_0. By the divergence theorem

$$\begin{aligned} \iint_{S \cup S_0} \frac{\overline{r} \cdot \overline{n}}{r^3} \, dS &= \iint_S \frac{\overline{r} \cdot \overline{n}}{r^3} \, dS + \iint_{S_0} \frac{\overline{r} \cdot \overline{n}}{r^3} \, dS \\ &= \iiint_{D-D_0} \nabla \cdot \frac{\overline{r}}{r^3} \, dV = 0 \end{aligned} \tag{8}$$

since the origin does not lie inside $D - D_0$.

From eq.(8), we obtain

$$\iint_S \frac{\overline{r} \cdot \overline{n}}{r^3} \, dS = - \iint_{S_0} \frac{\overline{r} \cdot \overline{n}}{r^3} \, dS \tag{9}$$

905

we have,

$$\iint_{S_0} \frac{\overline{r} \cdot \overline{n}}{r^3} \, dS = \iint_{S_0} \frac{\overline{r}}{r_0^3} \cdot \left(-\frac{\overline{r}}{r_0}\right) dS$$

(10)

$$= - \iint_{S_0} \frac{r_0^2}{r_0^4} \, dS = -\frac{1}{r_0^2} \iint_{S_0} dS = -\frac{1}{r_0^2}(4\pi r_0^2) = -4\pi$$

Therefore,

$$\iint_{S} \frac{\overline{r} \cdot \overline{n}}{r^3} \, dS = 4\pi$$

(11)

• **PROBLEM** 19-48

Let S be a closed surface and D a region bounded by this surface. Let $\overline{r}$ be the position vector of any point relative to the origin 0 and let $f = f(x,y,z)$ be a function with continuous derivatives of at least the second order.

Prove that

$$\iiint_{D} \frac{\nabla^2 f}{r} \, dV + A = \iint_{S} \left[\frac{1}{r} \nabla f - f \nabla\left(\frac{1}{r}\right)\right] \cdot \overline{n} \, dS$$

(1)

where

$$A = \begin{cases} 0 & \text{if the origin is outside S} \\ 4\pi f_0 & \text{if the origin is inside S} \end{cases}$$

(2)

$$f(0,0,0) = f_0$$

(3)

Solution: To the right-hand side of eq.(1) we shall apply the divergence theorem,

$$\iint_{S} \left[\frac{1}{r} \nabla f - f \nabla\left(\frac{1}{r}\right)\right] \cdot \overline{n} \, dS = \iiint_{D} \nabla \cdot \left[\frac{1}{r} \nabla f - f \nabla\left(\frac{1}{r}\right)\right] dV$$

(4)

$$= \iiint_{D} \left[\nabla \cdot \left(\frac{1}{r} \nabla f\right) - \nabla \cdot \left(f \nabla\left(\frac{1}{r}\right)\right)\right] dV$$

We can simplify the volume integral - eq.(4) - by using the identities

$$\nabla \cdot (f\overline{F}) = \overline{F} \cdot \nabla f + f \nabla \cdot \overline{F}$$

(5)

$$\nabla r^n = n r^{n-2} \overline{r}$$

(6)

906

$$\iiint_D \left[\nabla f \cdot \nabla\left(\frac{1}{r}\right) + \frac{1}{r}\ \nabla^2 f - \nabla\left(\frac{1}{r}\right) \cdot \nabla f - f\nabla^2\left(\frac{1}{r}\right) \right] dV$$

$$= \iiint_D \left[\frac{1}{r}\ \nabla^2 f - f\ \nabla \cdot \nabla \frac{1}{r} \right] dV \tag{7}$$

$$= \iiint_D \frac{\nabla^2 f}{r}\ dV + \iiint_D f\ \nabla \cdot \frac{\overline{r}}{r^3}\ dV$$

Since $\nabla \cdot \dfrac{\overline{r}}{r^3} = 0$ everywhere except the origin, the value of the integral $\iiint_D f\nabla \cdot \dfrac{\overline{r}}{r^3}\, dv$ is zero where the origin lies outside of S. Thus,

$$\iiint_D \frac{\nabla^2 f}{r}\ dV + A = \iint_S \left[\frac{1}{r}\ \nabla f - f\nabla\left(\frac{1}{r}\right) \right] \cdot \overline{n}\ dS \tag{8}$$

and A = 0 if the origin lies outside of S.

Consider the situation where 0 lies inside S.

Since $\nabla \cdot \dfrac{\overline{r}}{r^3} = 0$ everywhere except the origin, we can write

$$\iiint_D f\ \nabla \cdot \frac{\overline{r}}{r^3}\ dV = f(0,0,0) \iiint_D \nabla \cdot \frac{\overline{r}}{r^3}\ dV$$

$$= f_0 \iiint_D \nabla \cdot \frac{\overline{r}}{r^3}\ dV \tag{9}$$

Using the results of Problem 19-47, we obtain

$$f_0 \iiint_D \nabla \cdot \frac{\overline{r}}{r^3}\ dV = f_0 \iint_S \frac{\overline{r} \cdot \overline{n}}{r^3}\ dS = 4\pi f_0 \tag{10}$$

Therefore $A = 4\pi f_0$ if the origin lies inside S.

● **PROBLEM** 19-49

Let S be a closed surface and let $\overline{r}$ denote the position vector of any point (x,y,z) measured from an origin 0. Consider an element dS of surface area which is cut out by a cone C.

$d\Omega$ is the area of that part of a sphere of radius r and center at 0 which is cut out by the cone C.

We define the solid angle subtended by dS at 0 as

$$d\omega = \frac{d\Omega}{r^2} \tag{1}$$

Using the definition of the solid angle, give the geometrical interpretation of Gauss' theorem (see Problem 19-48).

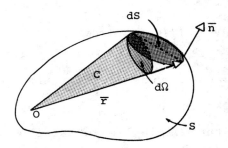

Fig. 1.

Solution: Let $\bar{n}$ be the unit normal to dS directed outward and let α be the angle between $\bar{n}$ and $\bar{r}$. By the definition of the scalar product, we may write

$$\cos \alpha = \frac{\bar{n} \cdot \bar{r}}{r} \tag{2}$$

From Fig. 1

$$d\Omega = \pm dS \cos\alpha = \pm \frac{\bar{n} \cdot \bar{r}}{r} dS \tag{3}$$

Substituting eq.(3) into eq.(1) we obtain

$$d\omega = \pm \frac{\bar{n} \cdot \bar{r}}{r^3} dS \tag{4}$$

The choice of the sign + or - depends on the angle α.

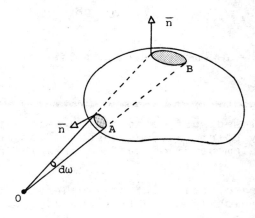

Fig. 2.

908

Let S be an oval shaped surface, that is, let S be such that any line that crosses S pierces S in at most two points.

Let us now consider the case where the origin 0 lies outside of S. In such case, we see that at point A (see Fig. 2), we may write

$$d\omega = \frac{\overline{n} \cdot \overline{r}}{r^3} \qquad (5)$$

and at the corresponding point B,

$$-d\omega = \frac{\overline{n} \cdot \overline{r}}{r^3} \qquad (6)$$

Since the contributions to the solid angle cancel out, the integration over these two elements of surface A and B yields zero.

Therefore, the integration over S gives zero.

$$\iint_S \frac{\overline{n} \cdot \overline{r}}{r^3} \, dS = 0 \qquad (7)$$

which is in agreement with Gauss' theorem.

The case when 0 lies inside S is shown in Fig. 3.

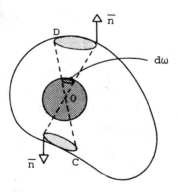

Fig. 3.

Here, the contributions at C and D add together. Indeed, at C we have

$$d\omega = \frac{\overline{n} \cdot \overline{r}}{r^3} \, dS \qquad (8)$$

and at D

$$d\omega = \frac{\overline{n} \cdot \overline{r}}{r^3} \, dS \qquad (9)$$

Since in this case the total solid angle is equal to the area of a unit sphere, we obtain

$$\iint_S \frac{\overline{n} \cdot \overline{r}}{r^3} \, dS = 4\pi \qquad (10)$$

909

It is easy to apply the above reasoning to a surface S such that a line may cross S at more than two points. One has to remember that for the origin O outside S, the solid angles subtended at O cancel out in pairs.

● PROBLEM 19-50

Show that the solid angle is given by

$$\Omega = \iint_S \frac{\cos \phi}{r^2} \, dS \tag{1}$$

$$\Omega = \iint_S \frac{\overline{n} \cdot \overline{OP}}{r^3} \, dS \tag{2}$$

where r is the distance OP and $\overline{n}$ is the unit normal to S at P. The angle ϕ between $\overline{OP}$ and $\overline{n}$ is acute.

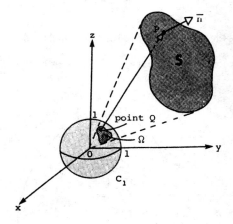

Fig. 1.

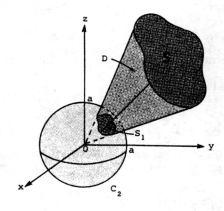

Fig. 2.

Solution: Let us first define the solid angle Ω. Let S be a surface element and 0 a fixed point not on S. S is such that any ray from 0 pierces S in at most one point. Let C_1 be the unit sphere with center at 0. As a point P varies over S, so does the point Q in which the ray $\overline{OP}$ intersects the unit sphere C_1. All the points Q cover a certain portion of the surface of C_1, as shown in Fig. 1. The area Ω of this portion is defined to be the solid angle subtended by S at 0.

Let C_2 be a sphere with radius a and center 0. C_2 is small enough so that S lies entirely outside C_2. All the rays joining the points on S with the point 0 cut out a surface S_1 from C_2, as shown in Fig. 2.

We shall apply the divergence theorem to the function

$$\overline{F} = \frac{\overline{OP}}{r^3} = \left\{ \frac{x}{(x^2+y^2+z^2)^{\frac{3}{2}}}, \ \frac{y}{(x^2+y^2+z^2)^{\frac{3}{2}}}, \ \frac{z}{(x^2+y^2+z^2)^{\frac{3}{2}}} \right\} \tag{3}$$

It is easy to evaluate

$$\text{div } \overline{F} = \text{div } \frac{\overline{OP}}{r^3} = 0 \tag{4}$$

We have

$$\tag{5}$$

$$\iiint_D \text{div } \overline{F} \, dV = 0 = \iint_{S_1} \overline{F} \cdot \overline{n} \, dS + \iint_S \overline{F} \cdot \overline{n} \, dS + \iint_{\text{cone}} \overline{F} \cdot \overline{n} \, dS$$

where $\overline{n}$ is the outer normal. Since $\overline{F}$ has the same direction as $\overline{OP}$, we have that on the cone,

$$\iint_{\text{cone}} \overline{F} \cdot \overline{n} \, dS = 0 \tag{6}$$

From eqs.(5) and (6) it follows that

$$\iint_{S_1} \overline{F} \cdot \overline{n} \, dS + \iint_S \overline{F} \cdot \overline{n} \, dS = 0 \tag{7}$$

or

$$\iint_{S_1} \frac{\overline{OP} \cdot \overline{n}}{r^3} \, dS + \iint_S \frac{\overline{OP} \cdot \overline{n}}{r^3} \, dS = 0 \tag{8}$$

Now, since it is required to show that

$$\iint_S \frac{\overline{OP} \cdot \overline{n}}{r^3} \, dS = \Omega,$$

we see, from eq.(8), that we must show that

$$\iint_{S_1} \overline{F} \cdot \overline{n} \, dS = -\Omega \tag{9}$$

911

Now, since $r = a$ on S_1, and $F = \dfrac{\overline{OP}}{r^3}$, we have

$$\overline{F} \cdot \overline{n} = \frac{-1}{a^2} \tag{10}$$

The minus sign is due to the fact that $\overline{F}$ and $\overline{n}$ point in the opposite directions. Integral (9) becomes

$$-\frac{1}{a^2} \iint\limits_{S_1} dS = -\frac{1}{a^2} \cdot \text{area of } S_1 \tag{11}$$

For the unit sphere, $a = 1$ and the area of S_1 is equal to Ω.

In general

$$\frac{1}{a^2} \cdot (\text{area of } S_1) = \Omega \tag{12}$$

● **PROBLEM 19-51**

Let D be a region enclosed by a surface S, and let $P(x,y,z)$ denote any point on S.

If point A is any fixed point in space, then show that the volume of D is given by

$$V = \frac{1}{3} \iint\limits_{S} r \, \cos\alpha \, dS \tag{1}$$

where r is the distance AP and α is the angle between AP and the outer unit normal vector to S at P, as shown in Fig. 1.

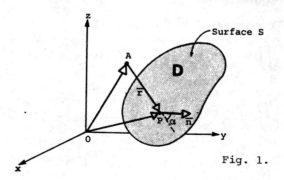

Fig. 1.

Solution: Before we use the divergence theorem

$$\iiint\limits_{D} \text{div } \overline{F} \, dV = \iint\limits_{S} \overline{F} \cdot \overline{n} \, dS \tag{2}$$

as an aid, let us first refer to Fig. 1.

Notice that $\overline{r} = \overline{AP}$, and, from the definition of the dot product,

$$\overline{r} \cdot \overline{n} = |\overline{r}||\overline{n}|\cos\alpha = r\cos\alpha \qquad (3)$$

Here, of course, $|\overline{r}| = r$ and $|\overline{n}| = 1$.

Now, let the fixed point A have coordinates $A(a,b,c)$, where a, b and c are constants.

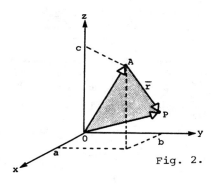

Fig. 2.

Then, referring to Fig. 2, we may write

$$\overline{OA} + \overline{r} = \overline{OP} \qquad (4)$$

or

$$\overline{r} = \overline{OP} - \overline{OA}$$

$$= x\overline{i} + y\overline{j} + z\overline{k} - \left[a\overline{i} + b\overline{j} + c\overline{k}\right] \qquad (5)$$

$$= (x-a)\overline{i} + (y-b)\overline{j} + (z-c)\overline{k}$$

Now, if we let $\overline{F} = \overline{r}$ in the divergence theorem, then

$$\iiint_D \mathrm{div}\ \overline{r}\ dV = \iint_S \overline{r} \cdot \overline{n}\ dS \qquad (6)$$

Substituting eqs.(5) and (3) into (6) yields

$$\iiint_D \mathrm{div}\left[(x-a)\overline{i} + (y-b)\overline{j} + (z-c)\overline{k}\right] dV = \iint_S r\cos\alpha\ dS \qquad (7)$$

or

$$\iiint_D \left[1+1+1\right] dV = \iint_S r\cos\alpha\ dS \qquad (8)$$

and

$$3\iiint_D dV = \iint_S r\cos\alpha\ dS \qquad (9)$$

Since $\iiint_D dV$ represents the volume of the region D, we conclude from eq.(9), that

$$V = \frac{1}{3} \iint_S r \cos\alpha \, dS$$

which is the required result.

● PROBLEM 19-52

Let $A = \begin{bmatrix} a_{ij} \end{bmatrix}$ be a square matrix, where $i,j = 1,2,\ldots,n$. The trace of a square matrix A is defined as

$$\text{Tr } A = \sum_{i=1}^{n} a_{ii} \tag{1}$$

If
$$F : R^n \rightarrow R^n \tag{2}$$

is a differentiable vector field, then we define div F to be the function given by

$$\text{div } F(x_1,\ldots,x_n) = \text{Tr } F'(x_1,\ldots,x_n) \tag{3}$$

Show that for two- and three-dimensional cases, eq.(3) leads to the well-known, previously defined divergence.

Solution: Consider the two-dimensional case
$$\bar{F} : R^2 \rightarrow R^2 \tag{4}$$

The matrix F' is defined as follows:

$$\bar{F}' = \begin{bmatrix} \dfrac{\partial f_1}{\partial x_1} & \dfrac{\partial f_2}{\partial x_1} \\[2mm] \dfrac{\partial f_1}{\partial x_2} & \dfrac{\partial f_2}{\partial x_2} \end{bmatrix} \tag{5}$$

where
$$\bar{F} = (f_1, f_2). \tag{6}$$

From eq.(3), we obtain
$$\text{div } F = \text{Tr } \bar{F}' = \frac{\partial f_1}{\partial x_1} + \frac{\partial f_2}{\partial x_2} = \text{div } \bar{F} \tag{7}$$

Eq.(7) is the previously given definition of divergence in two-dimensional space.

For three-dimensional space,
$$\bar{F} : R^3 \rightarrow R^3 \tag{8}$$

914

and the matrix $\overline{F}'$ is

$$\overline{F}' = \begin{bmatrix} \dfrac{\partial f_1}{\partial x_1} & \dfrac{\partial f_2}{\partial x_1} & \dfrac{\partial f_3}{\partial x_1} \\[2mm] \dfrac{\partial f_1}{\partial x_2} & \dfrac{\partial f_2}{\partial x_2} & \dfrac{\partial f_3}{\partial x_2} \\[2mm] \dfrac{\partial f_1}{\partial x_3} & \dfrac{\partial f_2}{\partial x_3} & \dfrac{\partial f_3}{\partial x_3} \end{bmatrix} \qquad (9)$$

where $\qquad \overline{F} = (f_1, f_2, f_3).$ $\qquad (10)$

From eq.(3), we have

$$\text{div } F = \text{Tr } F' = \frac{\partial f_1}{\partial x_1} + \frac{\partial f_2}{\partial x_2} + \frac{\partial f_3}{\partial x_3} = \text{div } \overline{F} \qquad (11)$$

Again we obtained the divergence of $\overline{F}$ as previously defined.

● **PROBLEM** 19-53

If D is a region bounded by a surface S, and $\overline{n}$ is the unit outer normal to S, then show that

$$I_z = \frac{1}{4} \iint\limits_{S} (x^2+y^2)(x\overline{i}+y\overline{j}) \cdot \overline{n} \ dS \qquad (1)$$

where I_z is the moment of inertia of D about the z-axis.

Solution: We assume that the body is homogeneous and of unit density.

For such a case, the moment of inertia of D about the z-axis is given by

$$I_z = \iiint\limits_{D} (x^2+y^2) dV \qquad (2)$$

It is now required to show that integral (2) and integral (1) are equivalent. Let us apply the divergence theorem

$$\iint\limits_{S} \overline{F} \cdot \overline{n} \ dS = \iiint\limits_{D} \text{div } \overline{F} \ dV$$

to integral (1).

Noting that in this case,

$$\overline{F} = (x^2+y^2)\left[x\overline{i}+y\overline{j}\right] ,$$

we obtain

915

$$I_z = \frac{1}{4} \iint\limits_S (x^2+y^2)(x\overline{i}+y\overline{j}) \cdot \overline{n} \; dS$$

$$= \frac{1}{4} \iiint\limits_D \text{div} \left[(x^2+y^2)(x\overline{i}+y\overline{j}) \right] dV$$

$$= \frac{1}{4} \iiint\limits_D \left[\frac{\partial}{\partial x} (x^3+xy^2) + \frac{\partial}{\partial y} (yx^2+y^3) \right] dV \qquad (3)$$

$$= \frac{1}{4} \iiint\limits_D \left[3x^2+y^2+x^2+3y^2 \right] dV$$

$$= \frac{1}{4} \iiint\limits_D 4(x^2+y^2) dV$$

$$= \iiint\limits_D (x^2+y^2) dV$$

That completes the proof.

● **PROBLEM** 19-54

By considering the flow of fluid through an arbitrary closed surface S, demonstrate the physical significance of the divergence theorem.

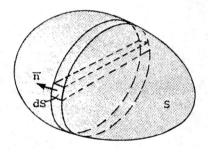

Solution: Let S be an arbitrary closed surface and let $\overline{v}$ be the velocity of the fluid.

The volume of fluid crossing dS in Δt seconds is equal to the volume contained in a cylinder of base dS and slant height $\overline{v}\Delta t$, that is $(\overline{v}\Delta t) \cdot \overline{n} \; dS$. Therefore, the volume of fluid crossing dS per second is $\overline{v} \cdot \overline{n} \; dS$, and the total volume of fluid crossing the closed surface S per second is

$$\iint_S \bar{v} \cdot \bar{n} \, dS \qquad (1)$$

On the other hand, the volume of fluid emerging from a volume element dV per second is

$$\text{div } \bar{v} \, dV \qquad (2)$$

Thus, the total volume of fluid per second emerging from all volume elements enclosed by S is

$$\iiint_V \text{div } \bar{v} \, dV \qquad (3)$$

Comparing eq.(1) and eq.(3), we obtain

$$\iint_S \bar{v} \cdot \bar{n} \, dS = \iiint_V \text{div } \bar{v} \, dV \qquad (4)$$

Eq.(4) is, of course, the well-known divergence theorem.

● **PROBLEM 19-55**

The motion of a fluid is described by the density of the fluid

$$\rho = \rho(x,y,z,t) \qquad (1)$$

and its velocity

$$\bar{v} = \bar{v}(x,y,z,t) \qquad (2)$$

Derive the equation of continuity

$$\frac{\partial \rho}{\partial t} + \nabla \cdot (\rho \bar{v}) = 0 \qquad (3)$$

assuming there are no sinks or sources.

Solution: Let S be a closed surface enclosing a region D of volume V.

The mass M of the fluid within S is given by

$$M = \iiint_D \rho \, dV \qquad (4)$$

The mass of fluid in the region D increases at the rate

$$\frac{\partial M}{\partial t} = \frac{\partial}{\partial t} \iiint_D \rho \, dV = \iiint_D \frac{\partial \rho}{\partial t} \, dV \qquad (5)$$

917

On the other hand, the mass of fluid entering D per unit time is

$$- \iint_S \rho \bar{v} \cdot \bar{n} \ dS \tag{6}$$

Since there are no sinks or sources, the rate of mass entering the region D must equal the rate of increase of mass in D.

Therefore
$$\iiint_D \frac{\partial \rho}{\partial t} \ dV = - \iint_S \rho \bar{v} \cdot \bar{n} \ dS \tag{7}$$

Now, applying the divergence theorem to the right side of eq.(7) yields

$$- \iint_S \rho \bar{v} \cdot \bar{n} \ dS = - \iiint_D \nabla \cdot (\rho \bar{v}) dV \tag{8}$$

Substituting eq.(8) into eq.(7) yields

$$\iiint_D \frac{\partial \rho}{\partial t} \ dV = - \iiint_D \nabla \cdot (\rho \bar{v}) dV$$

Thus,
$$\iiint_D \frac{\partial \rho}{\partial t} \ dV + \iiint_D \nabla \cdot (\rho \bar{v}) dV = 0$$

or

$$\iiint_D \left[\frac{\partial \rho}{\partial t} + \nabla \cdot (\rho \bar{v}) \right] \ dV = 0$$

Now, since the region D is arbitrary and the integrand is assumed to be continuous, it follows that

$$\frac{\partial \rho}{\partial t} + \nabla \cdot \rho \bar{v} = 0 \tag{9}$$

Eq.(9) can be written

$$\frac{\partial \rho}{\partial t} + \nabla \rho \cdot \bar{v} + \rho \nabla \cdot \bar{v} = 0 \tag{10}$$

or

$$\frac{\partial \rho}{\partial t} + \text{grad } \rho \cdot \bar{v} + \rho \ \text{div } \bar{v} = 0 \tag{11}$$

If ρ = constant, the fluid is said to be incompressible, and $\nabla \cdot \bar{v}$ = div $\bar{v}$ = 0, that is, $\bar{v}$ is solenoidal.

Often, we use the Stokes total derivative, defined as

$$\frac{D}{Dt} \equiv \frac{\partial}{\partial t} + \frac{dx}{dt} \frac{\partial}{\partial x} + \frac{dy}{dt} \frac{\partial}{\partial y} + \frac{dz}{dt} \frac{\partial}{\partial z} \tag{12}$$

918

so that we may write

$$\frac{D\rho}{Dt} = \frac{\partial \rho}{\partial t} + \nabla \rho \cdot \overline{v} \tag{13}$$

$\frac{D\rho}{Dt}$ describes the rate of change of ρ as one considers one particular particle of fluid in motion.

For an incompressible fluid

$$\frac{D\rho}{Dt} = 0 \quad \text{and} \quad \nabla \cdot \overline{v} = 0 \tag{14}$$

If also, $\qquad\qquad \nabla \times \overline{v} = \overline{0} \tag{15}$

then the flow is called irrotational.

In such case, $\overline{v}$ can be expressed as

$$\overline{v} = \text{grad } \phi \tag{16}$$

and ϕ is the velocity potential. If the flow is both incompressible and irrotational, that is

$$\nabla \cdot \overline{v} = 0$$
and $\tag{17}$
$$\nabla \times \overline{v} = 0,$$

then ϕ satisfies the equation

$$\text{div grad}\phi = \nabla \cdot \nabla \phi = 0 \tag{18}$$

That is, ϕ satisfies Laplace's equation,

$$\nabla^2 \phi = \frac{\partial^2 \phi}{\partial x^2} + \frac{\partial^2 \phi}{\partial y^2} + \frac{\partial^2 \phi}{\partial z^2} = 0 \tag{19}$$

and ϕ is a harmonic function.

● **PROBLEM 19-56**

Consider an irrotational, incompressible flow in a three-dimensional domain whose projection on the xy-plane is D. The z-component of velocity is zero and the x and y components of velocity do not depend on z. Let the velocity vector $\overline{v}$ be

$$\overline{v} = f\overline{i} - g\overline{j} \tag{1}$$

Show that:

1. f and g satisfy the Cauchy-Riemann equations

$$\frac{\partial f}{\partial x} = \frac{\partial g}{\partial y} \tag{2}$$

$$\frac{\partial f}{\partial y} = -\frac{\partial g}{\partial x} \quad \text{in D} \tag{3}$$

2. f and g are harmonic in D.

<u>Solution</u>: 1. The flow is two-dimensional

$$\overline{v} = (f, -g, 0) \tag{4}$$

We have

$$\frac{\partial f}{\partial z} = \frac{\partial g}{\partial z} = 0 \tag{5}$$

It is incompressible, thus

$$\text{div } \overline{v} = \frac{\partial f}{\partial x} + \frac{\partial (-g)}{\partial y} = 0 \tag{6}$$

and

$$\frac{\partial f}{\partial x} = \frac{\partial g}{\partial y} \tag{7}$$

To prove eq.(3), let us utilize the fact that the flow is irrotational. We have,

$$\text{curl } \overline{v} = \left(\frac{\partial}{\partial x}, \frac{\partial}{\partial y}, \frac{\partial}{\partial z}\right) \times (f, -g, 0)$$

$$= \left(0, 0, -\frac{\partial g}{\partial x} - \frac{\partial f}{\partial y}\right) = \overline{0} \tag{8}$$

Hence $\qquad \dfrac{\partial f}{\partial y} = -\dfrac{\partial g}{\partial x} \tag{9}$

Thus, f and g satisfy the Cauchy-Riemann equations.

2. A function f is said to be harmonic if it satisfies Laplace's equation

$$\nabla^2 f = 0$$

In the two-dimensional case, we have

$$\frac{\partial^2 f}{\partial x^2} + \frac{\partial^2 f}{\partial y^2} = 0 \tag{10}$$

To show that f is harmonic for this problem, let us take the first of the Cauchy-Riemann equations,

$$\frac{\partial f}{\partial x} = \frac{\partial g}{\partial y} \tag{11}$$

and differentiate it with respect to x to obtain

$$\frac{\partial^2 f}{\partial x^2} = \frac{\partial^2 g}{\partial x \partial y} \tag{12}$$

From the other Cauchy-Riemann equation

$$\frac{\partial f}{\partial y} = -\frac{\partial g}{\partial x}, \tag{13}$$

we obtain

$$\frac{\partial^2 f}{\partial y^2} = -\frac{\partial g}{\partial y \partial x} \tag{14}$$

Now, since we assume that g (and f as well) has continuous partial derivatives of the second order, we conclude, from eqs.(12) and (14), that

$$\frac{\partial^2 f}{\partial x^2} + \frac{\partial^2 f}{\partial y^2} = \frac{\partial g}{\partial x \partial y} - \frac{\partial g}{\partial y \partial x} = 0 \qquad (15)$$

since

$$\frac{\partial g}{\partial y \partial x} = \frac{\partial g}{\partial x \partial y}.$$

Thus, we have shown that f is harmonic.

Now, to show that g is harmonic, obtain from (11),

$$\frac{\partial^2 g}{\partial y^2} = \frac{\partial f}{\partial y \partial x} \qquad (16)$$

and from (13)

$$\frac{\partial^2 g}{\partial x^2} = - \frac{\partial f}{\partial x \partial y} \qquad (17)$$

Thus,

$$\frac{\partial^2 g}{\partial x^2} + \frac{\partial^2 g}{\partial y^2} = \frac{\partial f}{\partial y \partial x} - \frac{\partial f}{\partial x \partial y} = 0 \qquad (18)$$

and therefore g is harmonic.

Two functions f and g which satisfy the Cauchy-Riemann equations and which satisfy Laplace's equation are called harmonic conjugates.

● **PROBLEM 19-57**

A fluid flows with velocity

$$\overline{v} = f\overline{i} - g\overline{j} \qquad (1)$$

in a three-dimensional domain whose projection on the xy-plane is D.

If the flow is incompressible and irrotational, then show that

1. Both integrals,

$$\int fdx - gdy$$

    and

$$\int gdx + fdy$$

    are independent of the path of integration in D.

2. A vector

$$\overline{\omega} = \phi\overline{i} - \psi\overline{j}$$

    exists in D such that

$$\frac{\partial \phi}{\partial x} = \frac{\partial \psi}{\partial y} = f \qquad (2)$$

$$\frac{\partial \phi}{\partial y} = - \frac{\partial \psi}{\partial x} = -g \qquad (3)$$

Solution: 1. Let us repeat the basic properties of conservative vector fields. A continuously differentiable vector field $\overline{F}$ defined in a domain D is conservative if, and only if, it has any one (and therefore all) of the properties:

a. it is the gradient of a scalar function

b. curl $\overline{F}$ = $\overline{0}$

c. its integral around any regular closed curve is zero

d. its integral along any regular curve from a point A to a point B is independent of the path in going from A to B.

In hydrodynamics, we use the term irrotational instead of conservative.

Since the flow $\overline{v}$ = $f\overline{i}$ - $g\overline{j}$ is irrotational, then

$$\text{curl } \overline{v} = \overline{0} \tag{4}$$

and by condition d, we conclude that the line integral

$$\int \overline{v} \cdot d\overline{r} = \int (f\overline{i}-g\overline{j}) \cdot (dx\overline{i}+dy\overline{j}) = \int fdx - gdy \tag{5}$$

is independent of path.

Now, consider the vector field

$$\overline{u} = g\overline{i} + f\overline{j} \tag{6}$$

Its curl is

$$\text{curl } \overline{u} = \left(0, \ 0, \ \frac{\partial f}{\partial x} - \frac{\partial g}{\partial y}\right) \tag{7}$$

Now, note that since $\overline{v}$ is incompressible, we have

$$\text{div } \overline{v} = 0 = \frac{\partial f}{\partial x} + \frac{\partial (-g)}{\partial y}$$

and therefore

$$\frac{\partial f}{\partial x} = \frac{\partial g}{\partial y} \tag{8}$$

Thus, from eqs.(7) and (8), we conclude that

$$\text{curl } \overline{u} = \overline{0} \tag{9}$$

and therefore $\overline{u}$, as well as $\overline{v}$, are irrotational and consequently, the line integral

$$\int \overline{u} \cdot d\overline{r} = \int (g\overline{i}+f\overline{j}) \cdot (dx\overline{i}+dy\overline{j})$$

$$= \int gdx + fdy \tag{10}$$

is independent of path.

2. Again, the velocity field is irrotational
$$\text{curl } \bar{v} = \bar{0}. \tag{11}$$

Therefore by condition(a), a scalar function ϕ exists such that
$$\bar{v} = \text{grad } \phi \tag{12}$$

or, since $\bar{v} = f\bar{i} - g\bar{j}$,

$$f = \frac{\partial \phi}{\partial x}$$

$$-g = \frac{\partial \phi}{\partial y} \tag{13}$$

Now, since the vector field $\bar{u} = g\bar{i} + f\bar{j}$ is also irrotational (see eq.(9)), we conclude that a scalar function ψ also exists such that
$$\bar{u} = \text{grad } \psi \tag{14}$$

or
$$g = \frac{\partial \psi}{\partial x}$$

$$f = \frac{\partial \psi}{\partial y} \tag{15}$$

Therefore, we conclude that there exists some vector field
$$\bar{\omega} = \phi\bar{i} - \psi\bar{j}$$
whose components satisfy the conditions (2) and (3).

● **PROBLEM** 19-58

Consider the flow described in Problem 19-56 and the vector field
$$\bar{\omega} = \phi\bar{i} - \psi\bar{j} \tag{1}$$
described in Problem 19-57.

The function ϕ is the velocity potential and ψ is the stream function.

Show that:

1. curl $\bar{\omega} = 0$ and div $\bar{\omega} = 0$ in D;

2. ϕ and ψ are harmonic in D;

3. $\bar{v} = \text{grad } \phi$

where $\bar{v} = f\bar{i} - g\bar{j}$.

Solution: 1.   In Problem 19-57,we proved that

$$\frac{\partial \phi}{\partial x} = \frac{\partial \psi}{\partial y} = f \tag{2}$$

923

$$\frac{\partial \phi}{\partial y} = - \frac{\partial \psi}{\partial x} = -g \qquad (3)$$

Thus,

$$\text{div } \bar{\omega} = \nabla \cdot (\phi \bar{i} - \psi \bar{j}) = \frac{\partial \phi}{\partial x} - \frac{\partial \psi}{\partial y} = f - f = 0 \qquad (4)$$

and

$$\text{curl } \bar{\omega} = \left(\frac{\partial}{\partial x}, \frac{\partial}{\partial y}, \frac{\partial}{\partial z} \right) \times (\phi, -\psi, 0)$$

$$= \left(0, 0, -\frac{\partial \psi}{\partial x} - \frac{\partial \phi}{\partial y} \right) = \bar{0} \qquad (5)$$

2.   Differentiating eq.(2) with respect to x gives

$$\frac{\partial^2 \phi}{\partial x^2} = \frac{\partial^2 \psi}{\partial x \partial y} \qquad (6)$$

Differentiating eq.(3) with respect to y yields

$$\frac{\partial^2 \phi}{\partial y^2} = - \frac{\partial^2 \psi}{\partial y \partial x} \qquad (7)$$

Adding eqs.(6) and (7) results in

$$\frac{\partial^2 \phi}{\partial x^2} + \frac{\partial^2 \phi}{\partial y^2} = 0 \text{ in D.} \qquad (8)$$

Thus, ϕ is harmonic in D.

Differentiating eq.(2) with respect to y gives

$$\frac{\partial^2 \phi}{\partial y \partial x} = \frac{\partial^2 \psi}{\partial y^2} \qquad (9)$$

Differentiating eq.(3) with respect to x yields

$$\frac{\partial^2 \phi}{\partial x \partial y} = - \frac{\partial^2 \psi}{\partial x^2} \qquad (10)$$

Subtracting eq.(10) from eq.(9) gives

$$\frac{\partial^2 \psi}{\partial x^2} + \frac{\partial^2 \psi}{\partial y^2} = 0 \quad \text{in D.} \qquad (11)$$

We therefore see that ψ, as well as ϕ, is harmonic in D.

3.   Since the flow of the fluid

$$\bar{v} = f\bar{i} - g\bar{j} \qquad (12)$$

is irrotational,

$$\text{curl } \bar{v} = \bar{0} \qquad (13)$$

and therefore there exists a scalar function ϕ such that

$$\bar{v} = \text{grad } \phi \qquad (14)$$

924

Considering the momentum of a body D, derive the equation of motion

$$\frac{\partial}{\partial t} \iiint_D \rho \bar{u}\, dV = \iiint_D \rho \bar{G}\, dV + \iint_S \bar{P}\, dS - \iint_S \rho \bar{u}(\bar{u} \cdot d\bar{S}) \qquad (1)$$

where $\dot{\rho}$ is the density, $\bar{G}$ is the body force per unit mass, $\bar{P}$ is the surface force per unit area and $\bar{u} = \bar{u}(x_1, x_2, x_3, t)$.

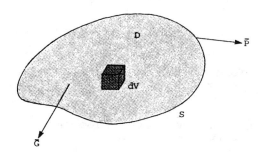

Solution: Let us take an element of the body whose density is ρ and whose volume is dV. We shall consider the momentum in a fixed region of space D.

By Newton's second law,

$$\rho \frac{d\bar{u}}{dt}\, dV = \rho \bar{G}\, dV + \bar{T} \qquad (2)$$

where $\bar{T}$ is the stress force exerted by the surrounding material.

Now, note that if we integrate over the entire volume of body D, all the stress forces, except those on the boundary S of D, cancel out by the law of action and reaction.

Hence,

$$\iiint_D \rho \frac{d\bar{u}}{dt}\, dV = \iiint_D \rho \bar{G}\, dV + \iint_S \bar{P}\, dS \qquad (3)$$

The total derivative $\frac{d\bar{u}}{dt}$ in the volume integral can be written as

$$\iiint_D \rho \frac{d\bar{u}}{dt}\, dV = \iiint_D \left[\rho \frac{\partial \bar{u}}{\partial t} + \rho(\bar{u} \cdot \nabla)\bar{u} \right] dV$$

$$= \iiint_D \left[\rho \frac{\partial \bar{u}}{\partial t} + \rho u_i \frac{\partial \bar{u}}{\partial x_i} \right] dV \qquad (4)$$

In eq.(4), we used the Einstein convention, i.e.

$$u_i \frac{\partial \bar{u}}{\partial x_i} = u_1 \frac{\partial \bar{u}}{\partial x_1} + u_2 \frac{\partial \bar{u}}{\partial x_2} + u_3 \frac{\partial \bar{u}}{\partial x_3} \tag{5}$$

We sum over the range of the repeated index. The equation of continuity

$$\frac{\partial \rho}{\partial t} + \frac{\partial (\rho u_i)}{\partial x_i} = 0 \tag{6}$$

multiplied by $\bar{u}$

$$\bar{u} \frac{\partial \rho}{\partial t} + \bar{u} \frac{\partial (\rho u_i)}{\partial x_i} = 0 \tag{7}$$

and added to the integrand of eq.(4) leads to

$$\iiint_D \rho \frac{d\bar{u}}{dt} dV = \iiint_D \left[\frac{\partial (\rho \bar{u})}{\partial t} + \frac{\partial}{\partial x_i} (\rho u_i \bar{u}) \right] dV \tag{8}$$

Applying the divergence theorem to the volume integral in eq.(8) results in

$$\iiint_D \frac{\partial}{\partial x_i} (\rho u_i \bar{u}) dV = \iint_S \rho \bar{u} (\bar{u} \cdot \bar{n}) dS \tag{9}$$

where $\bar{n}$ is the unit outer normal to the boundary S.

Since the volume is fixed, the limits of integration in eq.(8) are fixed and we can interchange integration and differentiation.

$$\iiint_D \frac{\partial (\rho \bar{u})}{\partial t} dV = \frac{\partial}{\partial t} \iiint_D \rho \bar{u} dV \tag{10}$$

From eq.(3), we obtain

$$\frac{\partial}{\partial t} \iiint_D \rho \bar{u} dV = \iiint_D \rho \bar{G} dV + \iint_S \bar{P} dS - \iint_S \rho \bar{u} (\bar{u} \cdot \bar{n}) dS \tag{11}$$

which is the desired result.

● **PROBLEM 19-60**

Determine the force exerted by a jet stream impinging on a flat plate. The area of the jet is α and the speed of the jet stream is v.

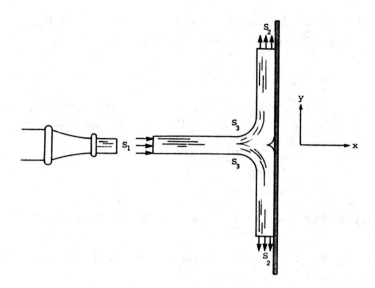

Solution: We shall take the control volume shown in the figure and apply eq.(1) of Problem 19-59.

$$\frac{\partial}{\partial t} \iiint_D \rho \bar{u}dV = \iiint_D \rho \bar{G}dV + \iint_S \bar{P}dS - \iint_S \rho \bar{u}(\bar{u}\cdot\bar{n})dS \qquad (1)$$

Since the total momentum is constant within the control volume, we write

$$\frac{\partial}{\partial t} \iiint_D \rho \bar{u}dV = \bar{0} \qquad (2)$$

The body forces can be neglected

$$\iiint_D \rho \bar{G}dV = \bar{0} \qquad (3)$$

Eq.(1) reduces to

$$\iint_S \bar{P}dS - \iint_S \rho \bar{u}(\bar{u}\cdot\bar{n})dS = \bar{0} \qquad (4)$$

At the surfaces S_3 of the jet, $|\bar{P}|$ is the normal stress or atmospheric pressure p_{at}.

At S_1, in the fluid, the pressure gradient is zero. That we conclude from Euler's equation, since the fluid velocity is constant in time and space and external body forces are neglected. At S_2 in the fluid,

$$\frac{\partial p}{\partial x} = 0, \quad \text{because} \quad u = 0.$$

Since the pressure at the wall of the jet is p_{at}, the pressure in the fluid at S_1 and S_2 must also be p_{at}. We obtain

$$\iint_S \overline{P}\, dS = - \iint_S (p_{at} + p)\overline{n}\, dS \tag{5}$$

Note that $p = 0$ everywhere except at the plate and also note that $\overline{n}$ is the unit outer normal to the control surface.

Since over any closed surface

$$\iint_S \overline{n}\, dS = \overline{0} \tag{6}$$

The only contribution to the surface integral is from the excess pressure p at the plate.

Let F_x be the total force in the x-direction that the plate exerts on the fluid.

From eq.(5), we obtain

$$F_x - \iint_{S_1} \rho v(-v)\, dS = 0 \tag{7}$$

or

$$F_x + \iint_{S_1} \rho v^2\, dS = 0$$

$$F_x + \rho v^2 \iint_{S_1} dS = F_x + \rho v^2 \alpha = 0 \tag{8}$$

Therefore,

$$F_x = -\rho v^2 \alpha \tag{9}$$

and the force that the jet stream exerts on the wall is

$$-F_x = \rho v^2 \alpha \tag{10}$$

● **PROBLEM** 19-61

Let B be a solid whose temperature is described by

$$T = T(x,y,z,t) \tag{1}$$

Derive the fundamental equation of heat conduction

$$c\rho \frac{\partial T}{\partial t} - k \text{ div grad } T = 0 \tag{2}$$

where c is the specific heat of the solid, ρ is the density and k is the thermal conductivity.

Solution: If heat is being conducted in a solid B, then the flow of heat is represented by a vector $\bar{u}$, such that the flux integral

$$\iint_S \bar{u} \cdot \bar{n} \, dS \tag{3}$$

for each oriented surface S contained in B represents the number of calories crossing S per unit time.

The basic law of thermal conduction postulates that

$$\bar{u} = -k \text{ grad } T \tag{4}$$

If D is a closed region in the solid B and S is the boundary of D, then by the divergence theorem, we may write

$$\iint_S \bar{u} \cdot \bar{n} \, dS = \iiint_D \text{div } \bar{u} \, dV \tag{5}$$

Therefore, the total amount of heat entering D is

$$-\iint_S \bar{u} \cdot \bar{n} \, dS = \iiint_D k \text{ div grad } T \, dV \tag{6}$$

Now, the rate at which heat is being absorbed per unit mass is

$$c \frac{\partial T}{\partial t} \tag{7}$$

where c is the specific heat.

For the region D, the heat is being received at the rate

$$\iiint_D c\rho \frac{\partial T}{\partial t} \, dV \tag{8}$$

It follows from eqs.(6) and (8) that

$$\iiint_D k \text{ div grad } T \, dV = \iiint_D c\rho \frac{\partial T}{\partial t} \, dV$$

or

$$\iiint_D (c\rho \frac{\partial T}{\partial t} - k \text{ div grad } T) dV = 0 \tag{9}$$

Now, since eq.(9) holds for any arbitrary region D in the solid B, and since the integrand is assumed to be continuous, we conclude that

$$c\rho \frac{\partial T}{\partial t} - k \text{ div grad } T = 0 \tag{10}$$

Eq.(10) is the fundamental equation of heat conduction.

Now, in the case where the body is in temperature equilibrium, that is, the temperature does not vary with time, we have

$$\frac{\partial T}{\partial t} = 0 \qquad (11)$$

and from eq.(10) we obtain

$$\text{div grad } T = \nabla^2 T = 0 \qquad (12)$$

which indicates that T is harmonic.

● **PROBLEM** 19-62

Determine the temperature distribution in a solid whose boundaries are two parallel planes which are a units apart. The temperatures of the planes are T_1 and T_2.

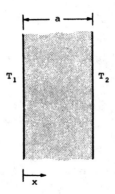

Solution: To find the temperature distribution, we shall use the fundamental equation of heat conduction (see Problem 19-61)

$$c\rho \frac{\partial T}{\partial t} - k\nabla^2 T = 0. \qquad (1)$$

Now, since the temperatures of the planes are constant, we have

$$\frac{\partial T}{\partial t} = 0 \qquad (2)$$

and eq.(1) reduces to

$$\nabla^2 T = 0 \qquad (3)$$

Now let us note that from symmetry, we conclude that the temperature function is independent of y and z and is a function of x alone, T = T(x). Thus, eq.(3) reduces to

$$\frac{\partial^2 T(x)}{\partial x^2} = 0 \qquad (4)$$

Integrating twice yields

$$T(x) = \alpha x + \beta \qquad (5)$$

where α and β are constants which we will now determine from the boundary conditions.

Since at $x = 0$, $T(0) = T_1$, and since at $x = a$, $T(a) = T_2$ (see the figure), α and β are found to be

$$\beta = T_1 \qquad (6)$$

$$\alpha = \frac{T_2 - T_1}{a} \qquad (7)$$

and the temperature distribution is thus

$$T(x) = \frac{T_2 - T_1}{a} x + T_1 \qquad (8)$$

● **PROBLEM** 19-63

Experiments indicate that for each type of gas there is an equation of state

$$f(P, V, T) = 0 \qquad (1)$$

where the parameters P, V and T are, of course, the pressure, volume and temperature of the gas, respectively.

For an ideal gas, eq.(1) takes the form

$$\frac{PV}{T} = R \qquad (2)$$

where R is a constant and one mole of gas is used.

Furthermore, for each gas, there is associated a scalar function U, the internal energy, which is a function of the state. Since the internal energy is a function of the state, we may write

$$U = U(P, V) \qquad (3)$$

For an ideal gas, eq.(3) takes the form

$$U = c_v \frac{PV}{R} = c_v T \qquad (4)$$

where c_v is a constant called the specific heat at constant volume.

1. Using P-V coordinates, describe a process that a gas may go through.

2. Show that the amount of heat introduced in a particular process is

$$Q(t_1) - Q(0) = \int_0^{t_1} \left(\frac{dU}{dt} + P \frac{dV}{dt} \right) dt \qquad (5)$$

931

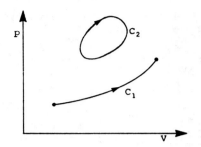

Solution: 1. Since a process is a succession of changes in the state, p, V, T and U become functions of time t.

The state of a gas at a time t can be represented by a point (p,V). The process that the gas goes through is characterized by a curve C, with t as the parameter. The figure shown shows two arbitrary processes described by the curves C_2 and C_1.

2. By the use of the first law of thermodynamics, we can measure the amount of heat Q that is received by the gas in going through a particular process.

The first law of thermodynamics may be written

$$\frac{dQ}{dt} = \frac{dU}{dt} + P \frac{dV}{dt} \tag{6}$$

Now, if the gas goes through a process that begins at time t = 0 and ends at time t = t_1, then the total heat absorbed by the gas is found by integrating eq.(6).

Thus,
$$Q(t_1) - Q(0) = \int_0^{t_1} \left[\frac{dU}{dt} + P \frac{dV}{dt} \right] dt \tag{7}$$

● **PROBLEM 19-64**

The total internal energy U of a gas has continuous second derivatives, hence

$$\frac{\partial^2 U}{\partial V \partial p} = \frac{\partial^2 U}{\partial p \partial V} \tag{1}$$

Show that the amount of heat, Q, received by a gas during a process is dependent on the path between the initial and final states.

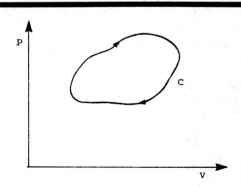

Solution: The amount of heat received by a gas during a particular process is given by

$$Q(t_1) - Q(t_0) = \int_{t_0}^{t_1} \left(\frac{dU}{dt} + p \frac{dV}{dt} \right) dt \qquad (2)$$

(see Problem 19-63).

Since U is a function of p and V,

$$U = U(p,V) \qquad (3)$$

we have

$$dU = \left(\frac{\partial U}{\partial p} \right)_V dp + \left(\frac{\partial U}{\partial V} \right)_p dV \qquad (4)$$

The expression $\left(\frac{\partial U}{\partial P} \right)_V$ indicates that we differentiate U with respect to P while holding V constant.

Now, eq.(2) can be written as the line integral

$$Q(t_1) - Q(t_0) = \int_{t_0}^{t_1} \left\{ \left(\frac{\partial U}{\partial p} \right)_V \frac{dp}{dt} + \left[\left(\frac{\partial U}{\partial V} \right)_p + p \right] \frac{dV}{dt} \right\} dt$$

$$= \int_C \left(\frac{\partial U}{\partial p} \right)_V dp + \left[\left(\frac{\partial U}{\partial V} \right)_p + p \right] dV \qquad (5)$$

Here, C represents the path taken in going from the initial state at time t_0 to the final state at time t_1.

Now, from eq.(4), we see that integral (5) can be written in the more compact form

$$Q(t_1) - Q(t_0) = \int_C dU + pdV \qquad (6)$$

For integral (5) to be independent of the path C, we must have that

$$\frac{\partial}{\partial p} \left[\left(\frac{\partial U}{\partial V} \right)_p + p \right] = \frac{\partial}{\partial V} \left[\left(\frac{\partial U}{\partial p} \right)_V \right] \qquad (7)$$

or

$$\frac{\partial^2 U}{\partial p \partial V} + 1 = \frac{\partial^2 U}{\partial V \partial p} \qquad (8)$$

Because of eq.(1), this is impossible, therefore the heat received by the gas is dependent on the path.

For a simple closed path C, the heat received is

$$\oint_C dU + pdV = \oint_C pdV \qquad (9)$$

A simple closed path C represents a process.

Determine whether the heat introduced during this process is positive or negative. What is the physical
interpretation of the area enclosed by the curve C?

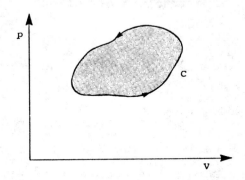

Solution: From Problem 19-64, we know that the heat received by the gas during a process is given by

$$\oint_C dU + pdV \tag{1}$$

Since U is a given function of p and V

$$\oint_C dU = 0 \tag{2}$$

Thus, the heat introduced is equal to

$$\oint_C pdV \tag{3}$$

Integral (3) represents the area enclosed by the curve C.
   Thus, for a counterclockwise cycle as shown in the figure, the heat introduced is negative. There is a heat loss
equal to the area enclosed by the curve C. On the other

hand, the integral $\int_C pdV$ represents the mechanical work

done by the gas on the surrounding environment.
   We therefore see that the heat loss equals the work done
on the gas during the process represented by the curve C,
and thus, the total energy is constant.

Experiments show that the integral

$$\int \frac{1}{T} dU + \frac{p}{T} dV \tag{1}$$

is independent of path.

Based on this information, define the scalar function S, called the entropy. What is the most significant property of the entropy of a closed system?

Solution: Since integral (1) is independent of path, a scalar function S exists such that

$$dS = \frac{1}{T} dU + \frac{p}{T} dV \qquad (2)$$

or

$$dS = \frac{1}{T} \frac{\partial U}{\partial p} dp + \frac{1}{T}\left(\frac{\partial U}{\partial V} + p\right) dV \qquad (3)$$

S is called the entropy of the system. In eq.(2), U and V are independent variables, therefore

$$\left(\frac{\partial S}{\partial U}\right)_V = \frac{1}{T}, \quad \left(\frac{\partial S}{\partial V}\right)_u = \frac{p}{T} \qquad (4)$$

and

$$\frac{\partial^2 S}{\partial V \partial U} = \frac{\partial}{\partial V}\left(\frac{1}{T}\right) = \frac{\partial}{\partial U}\left(\frac{p}{T}\right) = \frac{\partial^2 S}{\partial U \partial V} \qquad (5)$$

From eq.(5) we obtain

$$-\frac{1}{T^2} \frac{\partial T}{\partial V} + \frac{T \frac{\partial p}{\partial U} - p \frac{\partial T}{\partial U}}{T^2} = 0 \qquad (6)$$

or

$$\frac{\partial T}{\partial V} + T \frac{\partial p}{\partial U} - p \frac{\partial T}{\partial U} = 0 \qquad (7)$$

Now, the second law of thermodynamics states that the entropy S exists and for any closed system

$$\frac{dS}{dt} \geq 0 \qquad (8)$$

That is, the entropy of a closed system can never decrease.

● **PROBLEM** 19-67

On the basis of the laws of thermodynamics, show that the line integral

$$\int S\ dT + p\ dV \qquad (1)$$

is independent of the path in the TV plane.

Solution: The independent variables in eq.(1) are T and V.

In order to prove that integral (1) is independent of path, we have to prove that

$$\frac{\partial S}{\partial V} = \frac{\partial p}{\partial T} \tag{2}$$

where

$$S = S(T,V) \tag{3}$$

$$p = p(T,V)$$

As explained in Problem 19-66, it is already known that the line integral

$$\int \frac{1}{T} \, dU + \frac{p}{T} \, dV \tag{4}$$

is independent of path.

Now, for the entropy S of the system, we have

$$dS = \frac{1}{T} \, dU + \frac{p}{T} \, dV \tag{5}$$

Now, in terms of the T, V variables, we may write

$$dU = \frac{\partial U}{\partial T} \, dT + \frac{\partial U}{\partial V} \, dV \tag{6}$$

so that

$$dS = \frac{1}{T} \frac{\partial U}{\partial T} \, dT + \left[\frac{1}{T} \frac{\partial U}{\partial V} + \frac{p}{T} \right] dV \tag{7}$$

On the other hand, dS is equal to

$$dS = \frac{\partial S}{\partial T} \, dT + \frac{\partial S}{\partial V} \, dV \tag{8}$$

From eqs.(7) and (8) we obtain

$$\frac{\partial S}{\partial T} = \frac{1}{T} \frac{\partial U}{\partial T} \tag{9}$$

$$\frac{\partial S}{\partial V} = \frac{1}{T} \frac{\partial U}{\partial V} + \frac{p}{T} \tag{10}$$

Differentiating eq.(9) with respect to V and eq.(10) with respect to T results in

$$\frac{\partial^2 S}{\partial V \partial T} = \frac{1}{T} \frac{\partial^2 U}{\partial V \partial T} \tag{11}$$

$$\frac{\partial^2 S}{\partial T \partial V} = \frac{1}{T} \frac{\partial^2 U}{\partial T \partial V} - \frac{1}{T^2} \frac{\partial U}{\partial V} - \frac{p}{T^2} + \frac{1}{T} \frac{\partial p}{\partial T} \tag{12}$$

We assume that S and U have continuous partial derivatives, therefore

$$\frac{\partial^2 S}{\partial T \partial V} = \frac{\partial^2 S}{\partial V \partial T} \tag{13}$$

$$\frac{\partial^2 U}{\partial T \partial V} = \frac{\partial^2 U}{\partial V \partial T} \tag{14}$$

Subtracting eq.(11) from (12) gives

$$-\frac{1}{T}\frac{\partial U}{\partial V} - \frac{p}{T} + \frac{\partial p}{\partial T} = 0 \qquad (15)$$

Substituting eq.(10) into eq.(15) results in

$$\frac{\partial S}{\partial V} = \frac{\partial p}{\partial T} \qquad (16)$$

which is eq.(2).

● **PROBLEM** 19-68

An electromagnetic field is characterized by the electric field intensity $\overline{E}$ and the magnetic field intensity $\overline{H}$.

Vectors $\overline{E}$ and $\overline{H}$ are, generally, functions of time.

In the absence of conductors, $\overline{E}$ and $\overline{H}$ satisfy Maxwell's equations

$$\begin{aligned} \text{div } \overline{E} &= 4\pi\rho \\ \text{curl } \overline{E} &= -\frac{1}{c}\frac{\partial \overline{H}}{\partial t} \\ \text{div } \overline{H} &= 0 \\ \text{curl } \overline{H} &= \frac{1}{c}\frac{\partial \overline{E}}{\partial t} \end{aligned} \qquad (1)$$

Here, ρ is the charge density and c is the speed of light (a constant).

Define the electrostatic potential ϕ and show that in a domain which is free of charge, ϕ is a harmonic function.

Solution: Consider the electrostatic case, that is when

$$\frac{\partial \overline{E}}{\partial t} = \overline{0} \quad \text{and} \quad \overline{H} = \overline{0}. \qquad (2)$$

For this case, Maxwell's equations become

$$\text{div } \overline{E} = 4\pi\rho \qquad (3)$$

$$\text{Curl } \overline{E} = \overline{0} \qquad (4)$$

Now, from eq.(4), we conclude that a function ϕ exists in a simply connected domain such that

$$\overline{E} = -\text{grad } \phi \qquad (5)$$

ϕ is the electrostatic potential.

From eqs.(5) and (3), we see that ϕ satisfies the

Poisson equation

$$\text{div grad } \phi = \nabla^2 \phi = -4\pi\rho \tag{6}$$

In a domain free of charge, $\rho = 0$, and thus

$$\nabla^2 \phi = 0 \tag{7}$$

which indicates that ϕ is a harmonic function.

● **PROBLEM** 19-69

A wire occupies the line segment extending from $(0,-a)$ to $(0,a)$ in the xy-plane. If the charge density ρ is constant, then show that the electrostatic potential ϕ due to the wire at a point (x_0,y_0) of the xy-plane is

$$\phi(x_0,y_0) = \rho \log \frac{\sqrt{x_0^2+(c-y_0)^2} + c-y_0}{\sqrt{x_0^2+(c+y_0)^2} - c-y_0} + \alpha \tag{1}$$

where α is an arbitrary constant.

Furthermore, show that if α is such that

$$\phi(1,0) = 0 \tag{2}$$

then

$$\lim_{a\to\infty} \phi(x_0,y_0) = -2\rho \log|x_0| \tag{3}$$

Solution: For any given charge distribution the function ϕ can be computed by Coulomb's Law. For a point charge e at the origin

$$\phi = \frac{e}{r} + \alpha \tag{4}$$

where α is constant and $r = \sqrt{x^2+y^2+z^2}$.

For a charge distributed along a wire C

$$\phi(x_0,y_0,z_0) = \int_C \frac{\rho dS}{r} + \alpha \tag{5}$$

where α is a constant,

$$r = \sqrt{(x-x_0)^2 + (y-y_0)^2 + (z-z_0)^2} \tag{6}$$

and ρ is the density, i.e. charge per unit length.

For a wire occupying the line segment from $(0,-a)$ to $(0,a)$, eq.(5) becomes

$$\phi(x_0,y_0) = \int_{-a}^{a} \frac{\rho dy}{\sqrt{x_0^2+(y-y_0)^2}} + \alpha \tag{7}$$

Using the formula

$$\int \frac{dy}{\sqrt{y^2+a^2}} = \log|y+\sqrt{y^2+a^2}| + C \tag{8}$$

938

we evaluate integral (7)

$$\phi(x_0,y_0) = \int_{-a}^{a} \frac{\rho dy}{\sqrt{x_0^2+(y-y_0)^2}} + \alpha$$

$$= \rho \int_{-a-y_0}^{a-y_0} \frac{dz}{\sqrt{x^2+z^2}} + \alpha$$

$$= \rho \left[\log|z| + \sqrt{x_0^2+z^2}| \right] \Bigg|_{z=-a-y_0}^{a-y_0} + \alpha$$

$$= \rho \log \frac{\sqrt{(a-y_0)^2 + x_0^2} + a-y_0}{\sqrt{(a+y_0)^2+x_0^2}-a-y_0} + \alpha \qquad (9)$$

Since

$$\phi(1,0) = 0 \qquad (10)$$

we obtain

$$\alpha = -\rho \log \frac{\sqrt{a^2+1}+a}{\sqrt{a^2+1}-a} \qquad (11)$$

From eqs.(9), (10) and (11) we obtain

$$\lim_{a\to\infty} \phi(x_0,y_0) = -2\rho\log|x_0| \qquad (12)$$

● **PROBLEM** 19-70

Consider a closed surface S enclosing the point charges $q_1, q_2, \ldots, q_m$.

The total charge Q is

$$Q = \sum_{i=1}^{m} q_i \qquad (1)$$

The potential $\phi(x,y,z)$ at any point on the surface is given by

$$\phi(x,y,z) = \sum_{i=1}^{m} \frac{q_i}{r_i} \qquad (2)$$

where $\bar{r}_1, \bar{r}_2, \ldots, \bar{r}_m$ are the position vectors of the charges $q_1, q_2, \ldots, q_m$ with respect to the point (x,y,z).

Prove that

$$\iint_S \bar{E} \cdot \bar{n} \, dS = 4\pi Q \qquad (3)$$

where

$$\bar{E} = -\nabla \phi \qquad (4)$$

Solution: Let us substitute eq.(2) into eq.(4) to obtain

$$\overline{E} = -\nabla\phi = -\nabla\left[\sum_{i=1}^{m} \frac{q_i}{r_i}\right] = -\sum_{i=1}^{m} q_i \nabla\left(\frac{1}{r_i}\right) \qquad (5)$$

Here we used the fact that

$$\nabla(\Sigma f_i) = \Sigma \nabla f_i$$

and

$$\nabla cf = c\nabla f \qquad (c \text{ is a constant})$$

Now, using the equation

$$\nabla r^n = nr^{n-2}\overline{r} \qquad (6)$$

we find

$$\nabla\left(\frac{1}{r_i}\right) = \nabla(r_i^{-1}) = -\frac{1}{r_i^3}\overline{r}_i \qquad (7)$$

The surface integral can now be written in the form

$$\iint_S \overline{E}\cdot\overline{n}\ dS = -\iint_S \sum_{i=1}^{m} q_i \nabla\left(\frac{1}{r_i}\right)\cdot\overline{n}\ dS$$

$$= \iint_S \sum_{i=1}^{m} q_i \frac{\overline{r}_i}{r_i^3}\cdot\overline{n}\ dS \qquad (8)$$

We shall apply now Gauss' theorem, which states that:

If S is a closed surface and $\overline{r}$ is the position vector of any point (x,y,z), then

$$\iint_S \frac{\overline{r}\cdot\overline{n}}{r^3}\ dS = \begin{cases} 0 & \text{if the origin lies outside S} \\ 4\pi & \text{if the origin lies inside S} \end{cases} \qquad (9)$$

Eq.(8) becomes

$$\iint_S \sum_{i=1}^{m} q_i \frac{\overline{r}_i}{r_i^3}\cdot\overline{n}\ dS = 4\pi\sum_{i=1}^{m} q_i = 4\pi Q \qquad (10)$$

● **PROBLEM** 19-71

From Maxwell's equations, show that the total magnetic flux through a closed surface is zero.

Solution: Maxwell's equations in Gaussian units are

$$\text{curl } \overline{E} = -\frac{1}{c}\frac{\partial\overline{B}}{\partial t} \qquad (1)$$

$$\text{div } \overline{D} = 4\pi\rho \qquad (2)$$

$$\text{curl } \overline{H} = \frac{1}{c}\frac{\partial\overline{D}}{\partial t} + \frac{4\pi}{c}\,\overline{j} \qquad (3)$$

$$\text{div } \overline{B} = 0 \qquad (4)$$

Now, the total magnetic flux through a closed surface is given by the surface integral

$$\iint_S \overline{B}\cdot\overline{n}\ dS \qquad (5)$$

Applying the divergence theorem to eq.(5) yields

$$\iint_S \overline{B}\cdot\overline{n}\ dS = \iiint_D \text{div } \overline{B}\ dV \qquad (6)$$

But, from eq.(4), div $\overline{B}$ = 0, therefore from eq.(6) we obtain

$$\iint_S \overline{B}\cdot\overline{n}\ dS = 0$$

which is the required result.

● **PROBLEM 19-72**

Maxwell's equations in Gaussian units are

$$\text{curl } \overline{E} = -\frac{1}{c}\frac{\partial\overline{B}}{\partial t} \qquad (1)$$

$$\text{div } \overline{D} = 4\pi\rho \qquad (2)$$

$$\text{curl } \overline{H} = \frac{1}{c}\frac{\partial\overline{D}}{\partial t} + \frac{4\pi}{c}\,\overline{j} \qquad (3)$$

$$\text{div } \overline{B} = 0 \qquad (4)$$

Here, $\overline{E}$ represents the electric field, $\overline{H}$ denotes the magnetic field, $\overline{B}$ is the magnetic induction, $\overline{j}$ is the electric current, c is the speed of light, ρ is the charge density and the term

$$\frac{1}{4\pi}\,\overline{D}$$

is the displacement current.

With the exception of equation (3), these laws were completely derived from the experimental results of Faraday and Oersted, among others.

Originally, eq.(3) did not contain the term $\frac{1}{c}\frac{\partial\overline{D}}{\partial t}$. Indeed, experimental results solely led to the equation

$$\text{curl } \overline{H} = \frac{4\pi}{c} \overline{j} \tag{5}$$

Mathematical considerations, however, lead Maxwell to the conclusion that the term

$$\frac{1}{c} \frac{\partial \overline{D}}{\partial t}$$

should be added to eq.(5).

The divergence of the left-hand side of eq.(5) is identically zero, whereas the divergence of the right-hand side is not.

Verify this fact by considering the flux of electric current through an arbitrary area and assuming that charge is conserved.

<u>Solution</u>: First, note that for any vector field $\overline{A}$, we have

$$\text{div curl } \overline{A} \equiv \overline{0}$$

Thus, for eq.(5), we have

$$\text{div curl } \overline{H} = 0$$

and this would indicate that the divergence of $\overline{j}$ must always be zero.

We will now show that this is not true.

The flux of electric current through an arbitrary area is given by

$$\iint_S \overline{j} \cdot \overline{n} \, dS \tag{6}$$

By the divergence theorem, eq.(6) is equal to

$$\iint_S \overline{j} \cdot \overline{n} \, dS = \iiint_D \text{div } \overline{j} \, dV \tag{7}$$

If Q is the total charge inside the volume V,

$$Q = \iiint_D \rho \, dV \tag{8}$$

then assuming the conservation of charge, we get

$$\iiint_D \text{div } \overline{j} \, dV = -\frac{\partial Q}{\partial t} \tag{9}$$

where D is a region of volume V bounded by a surface S.

Substituting eq.(8) into eq.(9) yields

$$\iiint\limits_{D} \text{div } \bar{\jmath} \ dV = -\frac{\partial}{\partial t} \iiint\limits_{D} \rho \ dV$$

$$= -\iiint\limits_{D} \frac{\partial \rho}{\partial t} \ dV \qquad (10)$$

or

$$\iiint\limits_{D} \left(\text{div } \bar{\jmath} + \frac{\partial \rho}{\partial t} \right) dV = 0$$

Since eq.(10) is independent of the region D, the integrand is equal to zero,

$$\text{div } \bar{\jmath} + \frac{\partial \rho}{\partial t} = 0 \qquad (11)$$

Thus, we see that the divergence of $\bar{\jmath}$ is not necessarily equal to zero. As a consequence, eq.(5), a product of experimental ventures, must be modified.

● **PROBLEM 19-73**

Repeat Maxwell's reasoning.

He had $\qquad \text{div } \bar{D} = 4\pi\rho \qquad (1)$

which, he assumed was valid, and

$$\text{curl } \bar{H} = \frac{4\pi}{c} \bar{\jmath} \qquad (2)$$

obtained from experimental results which, form the mathematical point of view, was not correct (see Problem 19-71).

Using $\qquad \text{div } \bar{\jmath} + \frac{\partial \rho}{\partial t} = 0 \qquad (3)$

modify eq.(2).

Solution: As discussed in Problem 19-71, taking the divergence of eq.(2),

$$\text{div curl } \bar{H} = 0 = \frac{4\pi}{c} \text{ div } \bar{\jmath}$$

leads us to the incorrect conclusion that the divergence of $\bar{\jmath}$ is always zero.

As derived in Problem 19-71, it was found that the divergence of $\bar{\jmath}$ is not necessarily zero, but instead is related to the rate of change of charge density, as given by eq.(3).

943

Thus, it is evident that eq.(2) must be modified.

Now, from eq.(1), we obtain

$$\rho = \frac{1}{4\pi} \operatorname{div} \overline{D} \tag{4}$$

and it follows that

$$\frac{\partial \rho}{\partial t} = \frac{1}{4\pi} \operatorname{div} \frac{\partial \overline{D}}{\partial t} \tag{5}$$

Substituting eq.(5) into eq.(3) results in

$$\operatorname{div} \overline{j} + \frac{1}{4\pi} \operatorname{div} \frac{\partial \overline{D}}{\partial t} = \operatorname{div}\left(\overline{j} + \frac{1}{4\pi} \frac{\partial \overline{D}}{\partial t}\right) = 0 \tag{6}$$

This indicates that the divergence of $\overline{j}$ is not necessarily zero, but the divergence of the term

is always zero. $\overline{j} + \frac{1}{4\pi} \frac{\partial \overline{D}}{\partial t}$

In this case, mathematics turned out to be more important than physical experiments, and Maxwell hypothesized that

In this case, mathematics turned out to be

$$\operatorname{curl} \overline{H} = \frac{4\pi}{c}\left(\overline{j} + \frac{1}{4\pi} \frac{\partial \overline{D}}{\partial t}\right) \tag{7}$$

The divergence of both sides is now equal to zero.

Later, in his experiments, Hertz confirmed the existence of the displacement current $\frac{1}{4\pi} \frac{\partial \overline{D}}{\partial t}$.

CHAPTER 20

STOKES' THEOREM

INTRODUCTION

The last of the fundamental integral theorems discussed in this book is Stokes' theorem, named after G.G. Stokes (1819-1903) – an English mathematician contemporary of the mathematical physicist George Green. The theorem first appeared as a problem in a Cambridge examination paper in 1854 and it has since played a significant role in the mathematical formulation of physical theories in electromagmagnetics and fluid dynamics among others.

In Chapter 17, it is shown that Green's theorem can be written in the form

$$\iint_D (\text{curl } \overline{F})_z \, dxdy = \oint_C \overline{F} \cdot d\overline{r}$$

This implies that for any planar surface S bounded by a simple closed plane curve C, we may write

$$\iint_S \text{curl } \overline{F} \cdot d\overline{S} = \oint_C \overline{F} \cdot d\overline{r}$$

This equation can be generalized further by replacing a planar surface S by an arbitrary, smooth orientable surface whose boundary is a simple closed curve C, not necessarily a plane curve. In this form, the equation is known as Stokes' theorem.

As usual, whenever possible, applications in physics are given. In particular, the irrotational vector fields, i.e. fields with the property

$$\oint_C \overline{F} \cdot d\overline{r} = 0 \tag{1}$$

play an important role. The term irrotational arises from a physical interpretation of $\overline{F}$ as a velocity field in a fluid. The condition curl $\overline{F} = \overline{0}$ (which leads to property (1)) is a mathematical formulation of the fact that the particles of the fluid have no rotational tendencies, or no rotational velocity.

Solendoidal fields, that is, fields such that div $\overline{F} = 0$ are also briefly discussed in the chapter.

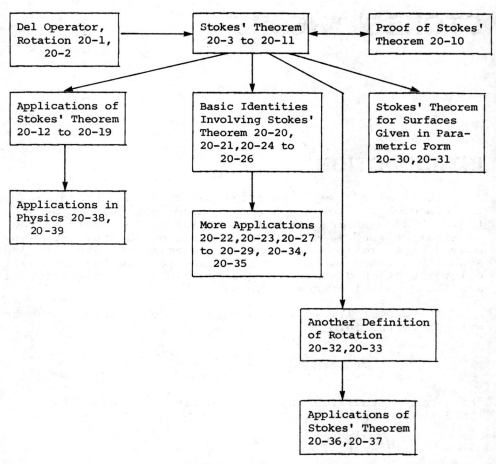

This chart is provided to facilitate rapid understanding of the inter-relationships of the topics and subject matter in this chapter. Also shown are the problem numbers associated with the subject matter.

DEL OPERATOR, ROTATION OF A VECTOR FUNCTION

● **PROBLEM** 20-1

1. Using the del operator,

$$\nabla = \frac{\partial}{\partial x}\,\overline{i} + \frac{\partial}{\partial y}\,\overline{j} + \frac{\partial}{\partial z}\,\overline{k} \qquad (1)$$

define the curl of the vector function

$$\overline{F} = F_1\overline{i} + F_2\overline{j} + F_3\overline{k} \qquad (2)$$

2. Find curl $\overline{f}$ where

$$\overline{f} = x^2y\overline{i} + y^2z^2\overline{j} + \sin x\overline{k} \qquad (3)$$

Solution: 1. The curl of a vector function $\overline{F}$ is defined as the cross product of the del operator and the vector function,

$$\text{curl } \overline{F} = \nabla \times \overline{F} = \left(\frac{\partial}{\partial x}\overline{i} + \frac{\partial}{\partial y}\overline{j} + \frac{\partial}{\partial z}\overline{k}\right) \times \ (F_1\overline{i} + F_2\overline{j} + F_3\overline{k})$$

$$= \begin{vmatrix} \overline{i} & \overline{j} & \overline{k} \\ \frac{\partial}{\partial x} & \frac{\partial}{\partial y} & \frac{\partial}{\partial z} \\ F_1 & F_2 & F_3 \end{vmatrix} \qquad (4)$$

Expanding the determinant by minors results in

$$\nabla \times \overline{F} = \left(\frac{\partial F_3}{\partial y} - \frac{\partial F_2}{\partial z}\right)\overline{i} + \left(\frac{\partial F_1}{\partial z} - \frac{\partial F_3}{\partial x}\right)\overline{j} + \left(\frac{\partial F_2}{\partial x} - \frac{\partial F_1}{\partial y}\right)\overline{k} \qquad (5)$$

2. To find curl $\overline{f}$, let us substitute eq.(3) into eq.(5), noting that

$$f_1 = x^2y$$

$$f_2 = y^2z^2 \qquad (6)$$

$$f_3 = \sin x$$

and

$$\frac{\partial f_3}{\partial y} = 0 \qquad \frac{\partial f_2}{\partial z} = 2y^2z$$

$$\frac{\partial f_1}{\partial z} = 0 \qquad \frac{\partial f_3}{\partial x} = \cos x \qquad (7)$$

$$\frac{\partial f_2}{\partial x} = 0 \qquad \frac{\partial f_1}{\partial y} = x^2$$

Thus,

$$\text{curl } \overline{f} = \nabla \times \overline{f} = -2y^2z\overline{i} - \cos x\overline{j} - x^2\overline{k} \qquad (8)$$

947

Show that if

$$\overline{F} = P(x,y,z)\overline{i} + Q(x,y,z)\overline{j} + R(x,y,z)\overline{k} \qquad (1)$$

then

$$\text{curl } \overline{F} = \overline{i} \times \overline{F}_x + \overline{j} \times \overline{F}_y + \overline{k} \times \overline{F}_z \qquad (2)$$

where

$$\overline{F}_x = \frac{\partial}{\partial x}\overline{F} = \overline{i}\,\frac{\partial P}{\partial x} + \overline{j}\,\frac{\partial Q}{\partial x} + \overline{k}\,\frac{\partial R}{\partial x} \qquad (3)$$

$$= \overline{i}\,P_x + \overline{j}\,Q_x + \overline{k}\,R_x$$

$$\overline{F}_y = \frac{\partial}{\partial y}\overline{F}, \quad \overline{F}_z = \frac{\partial}{\partial z}\overline{F}$$

<u>Solution</u>: From the definition of curl, we find

$$\text{curl } \overline{F} = \begin{vmatrix} \overline{i} & \overline{j} & \overline{k} \\ \dfrac{\partial}{\partial x} & \dfrac{\partial}{\partial y} & \dfrac{\partial}{\partial z} \\ P & Q & R \end{vmatrix}$$

$$= (R_y - Q_z)\overline{i} + (P_z - R_x)\overline{j} + (Q_x - P_y)\overline{k} \qquad (4)$$

On the other hand,

$$\overline{i} \times \overline{F}_x = \begin{vmatrix} \overline{i} & \overline{j} & \overline{k} \\ 1 & 0 & 0 \\ P_x & Q_x & R_x \end{vmatrix} = -R_x\overline{j} + Q_x\overline{k} \qquad (5)$$

$$\overline{j} \times \overline{F}_y = \begin{vmatrix} \overline{i} & \overline{j} & \overline{k} \\ 0 & 1 & 0 \\ P_y & Q_y & R_y \end{vmatrix} = R_y\overline{i} - P_y\overline{k} \qquad (6)$$

$$\overline{k} \times \overline{F}_z = \begin{vmatrix} \overline{i} & \overline{j} & \overline{k} \\ 0 & 0 & 1 \\ P_z & Q_z & R_z \end{vmatrix} = -Q_z\overline{i} + P_z\overline{j} \qquad (7)$$

Substituting eqs.(4), (5), (6) and (7) into eq.(2) results in

$$\text{curl } \overline{F} = \overline{i} \times \overline{F}_x + \overline{j} \times \overline{F}_y + \overline{k} \times \overline{F}_z \qquad (8)$$

STOKES' THEOREM, PROOF OF STOKES' THEOREM

● **PROBLEM** 20-3

Write Stokes' theorem in vector form and in terms of the components.

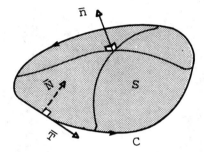

Solution: Let S denote an oriented surface and C an oriented boundary curve; that is, the positive normal to S and the positive direction around C are related by the right-hand rule, as shown in the figure.

Here $\overline{T}$ is the unit tangent vector to C, $\overline{N}$ is the inner normal to C and $\overline{n}$ is the outer normal to the surface S.

Stokes' Theorem

    If S is an oriented surface and C is an oriented closed boundary of S and $\overline{F}$ is a continuously differentiable vector field defined in S, then

$$\oint_C \overline{F} \cdot d\overline{r} = \iint_S \text{curl } \overline{F} \cdot \overline{n} \; dS \qquad (1)$$

In the component form,

$$\overline{F} = F_1 \overline{i} + F_2 \overline{j} + F_3 \overline{k} \qquad (2)$$

and

$$\overline{n} = \cos\alpha \, \overline{i} + \cos\beta \, \overline{j} + \cos\gamma \, \overline{k} \qquad (3)$$

curl $\overline{F}$ is

$$\nabla \times \overline{F} = \begin{vmatrix} \overline{i} & \overline{j} & \overline{k} \\ \dfrac{\partial}{\partial x} & \dfrac{\partial}{\partial y} & \dfrac{\partial}{\partial z} \\ F_1 & F_2 & F_3 \end{vmatrix} \qquad (4)$$

$$= \left(\frac{\partial F_3}{\partial y} - \frac{\partial F_2}{\partial z}\right)\overline{i} + \left(\frac{\partial F_1}{\partial z} - \frac{\partial F_3}{\partial x}\right)\overline{j} + \left(\frac{\partial F_2}{\partial x} - \frac{\partial F_1}{\partial y}\right)\overline{k}$$

Thus

$$\nabla \times \overline{F} \cdot \overline{n} = \left(\frac{\partial F_3}{\partial y} - \frac{\partial F_2}{\partial z}\right)\cos\alpha + \left(\frac{\partial F_1}{\partial z} - \frac{\partial F_3}{\partial x}\right)\cos\beta + \left(\frac{\partial F_2}{\partial x} - \frac{\partial F_1}{\partial y}\right)\cos\gamma \quad (5)$$

Now, since

$$\overline{F} \cdot d\overline{r} = F_1 dx + F_2 dy + F_3 dz, \qquad (6)$$

Stokes' theorem becomes

$$\oint_C F_1 dx + F_2 dy + F_3 dz = \iint_S \left[\left(\frac{\partial F_3}{\partial y} - \frac{\partial F_2}{\partial z}\right)\cos\alpha + \left(\frac{\partial F_1}{\partial z} - \frac{\partial F_3}{\partial x}\right)\cos\beta \right.$$

$$\left. + \left(\frac{\partial F_2}{\partial x} - \frac{\partial F_1}{\partial y}\right)\cos\gamma\right] dS \quad (7)$$

● **PROBLEM 20-4**

Let S be a piecewise smooth surface and let

$$\overline{F} = F_1\overline{i} + F_2\overline{j} + F_3\overline{k}$$

be a continuously differentiable vector field. Consider three cases of a surface S given by

1. $z = f(x,y)$ (1)

2. $f(x,y,z) = 0$ (2)

3. $x = \phi_1(u,v)$

    $y = \phi_2(u,v)$ (3)

    $z = \phi_3(u,v)$

Find an expression for the integral

$$\iint_S \overline{F} \cdot \overline{n} \, dS \qquad (4)$$

for each of these cases.

Solution: 1. If the surface is given by

$$z = f(x,y)$$

then

$$\iint_S \overline{F} \cdot \overline{n}\, dS = \iint_{R_{xy}} \overline{F} \cdot \overline{n}\, \frac{1}{|\overline{n}\cdot\overline{k}|}\, dxdy \tag{5}$$

$$= \pm \iint_{R_{xy}} (F_1\overline{i}+F_2\overline{j}+F_3\overline{k}) \cdot \frac{-\left(\frac{\partial z}{\partial x}\right)\overline{i}-\left(\frac{\partial z}{\partial y}\right)\overline{j}+\overline{k}}{\sqrt{\left(\frac{\partial z}{\partial x}\right)^2+\left(\frac{\partial z}{\partial y}\right)^2+1}}\, \sqrt{\left(\frac{\partial z}{\partial x}\right)^2+\left(\frac{\partial z}{\partial y}\right)^2+1}\, dxdy$$

$$= \pm \iint_{R_{xy}} \left[-F_1\frac{\partial z}{\partial x} - F_2\frac{\partial z}{\partial y} + F_3\right] dxdy$$

Here, the sign ± depends on the unit normal $\overline{n}$.

2. If S is given by $f(x,y,z) = 0$, then

$$\iint_S \overline{F} \cdot \overline{n}\, dS = \pm \iint_{R_{xy}} \overline{F} \cdot \frac{\nabla f}{|\nabla f|}\, \frac{|\nabla f|}{|\nabla f \cdot \overline{k}|}\, dxdy \tag{6}$$

$$= \pm \iint_{R_{xy}} \frac{F_1\frac{\partial f}{\partial x} + F_2\frac{\partial f}{\partial y} + F_3\frac{\partial f}{\partial z}}{\left|\frac{\partial f}{\partial z}\right|}\, dxdy$$

3. If S is given by the parametric equations, then

$$\iint_S \overline{F} \cdot \overline{n}\, dS = \pm \iint_{R_{uv}} \overline{F} \cdot \frac{\overline{\phi}_u \times \overline{\phi}_v}{|\overline{\phi}_u \times \overline{\phi}_v|}\, |\overline{\phi}_u \times \overline{\phi}_v|\, dudv$$

$$= \pm \iint_{R_{uv}} \begin{vmatrix} F_1 & F_2 & F_3 \\ \frac{\partial \phi_1}{\partial u} & \frac{\partial \phi_2}{\partial u} & \frac{\partial \phi_3}{\partial u} \\ \frac{\partial \phi_1}{\partial v} & \frac{\partial \phi_2}{\partial v} & \frac{\partial \phi_3}{\partial v} \end{vmatrix} dudv \tag{7}$$

$$= \pm \iint_{R_{uv}} \left[F_1\frac{\partial(\phi_2,\phi_3)}{\partial(u,v)} + F_2\frac{\partial(\phi_3,\phi_1)}{\partial(u,v)} + F_3\frac{\partial(\phi_1,\phi_2)}{\partial(u,v)}\right] dudv$$

951

Verify Stokes' theorem for

$$\overline{F} = 4y\overline{i} - 4x\overline{j} + 3\overline{k} \qquad (1)$$

where S is a disk of radius one lying on the plane z=1 and C is its boundary.

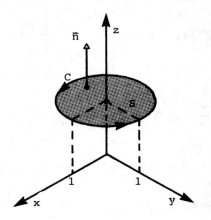

Solution: The surface S is shown in the figure. Note that the boundary C of S is a circle of radius one.

Stokes' theorem states that

$$\iint_S \text{curl } \overline{F} \cdot \overline{n} \, dS = \oint_C \overline{F} \cdot d\overline{r} \qquad (2)$$

We will now verify Stokes' theorem by evaluating both sides of the theorem.

To evaluate the surface integral, note that from the definition of curl, we obtain

$$\text{curl } \overline{F} = \nabla \times \overline{F} = \left(\frac{\partial}{\partial x}, \ \frac{\partial}{\partial y}, \ \frac{\partial}{\partial z} \right) \times (4y, \ -4x, \ 3)$$

$$= (0, \ 0, \ -8) = -8\overline{k} \qquad (3)$$

Since $\overline{n} \cdot \overline{k} = 1$, the surface integral of eq.(2) is equal to

$$\iint_S \text{curl } \overline{F} \cdot \overline{n} \, dS = -8 \iint_S \overline{k} \cdot \overline{n} \, dS = -8 \iint_S dS \qquad (4)$$

Now, since the area of a circle of radius 1 is π, eq.(4) yields

$$\iint_S \text{curl } \overline{F} \cdot \overline{n} \, dS = -8\pi \qquad (5)$$

To evaluate the line integral of eq.(2), we shall use the polar coordinates

$$x = \cos t$$
$$y = \sin t, \quad 0 \le t \le 2\pi \tag{6}$$

for the circle of radius one. The differentials dx, dy and the vector field $\overline{F}$ become

$$dx = -\sin t\, dt$$
$$dy = \cos t\, dt \tag{7}$$

$$\overline{F} = (4\sin t, -4\cos t, 3) \tag{8}$$

The line integral is equal to

$$\oint_C \overline{F} \cdot d\overline{r} = \int_0^{2\pi} 4\sin t(-\sin t)dt - 4\cos t \cos t\, dt$$

$$= \int_0^{2\pi} -4(\sin^2 t + \cos^2 t)dt$$

$$= -4 \int_0^{2\pi} dt = -8\pi \tag{9}$$

That completes the verification of Stokes' theorem.

● **PROBLEM** 20-6

Verify Stokes' theorem for

$$\overline{F} = \left(\frac{z^4}{4} + x^3\right)\overline{i} + 4x\overline{j} + (xz^3+z^2)\overline{k} \tag{1}$$

where S is the upper half surface of the sphere $x^2+y^2+z^2 = 1$ and C is its boundary directed counterclockwise.

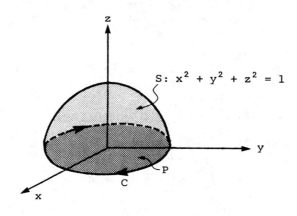

S: $x^2 + y^2 + z^2 = 1$

Solution: It is easy to check that all the assumptions of Stokes' theorem are fulfilled. Thus

$$\iint_S \text{curl } \overline{F} \cdot \overline{n} \, dS = \oint_C \overline{F} \cdot d\overline{r} \tag{2}$$

For the surface integral, first note that the curl of $\overline{F}$ is

$$\text{curl } \overline{F} = \nabla \times \overline{F} = \left(\frac{\partial}{\partial x}, \frac{\partial}{\partial y}, \frac{\partial}{\partial z}\right) \times \left(\frac{z^4}{4} + x^3, 4x, xz^3 + z^2\right)$$
$$= (0, 0, 4) = 4\overline{k} \tag{3}$$

and thus

$$\iint_S \nabla \times \overline{F} \cdot \overline{n} \, dS = 4 \iint_S \overline{k} \cdot \overline{n} \, dS = 4 \iint_P \overline{k} \cdot \overline{n} \, \frac{dxdy}{|\overline{n} \cdot \overline{k}|} \tag{4}$$

Here, P is the projection of S on the xy-plane, as shown in the figure.

Now, the surface S of the sphere may be written as

$$f(x,y,z) = x^2 + y^2 + z^2 - 1 = 0$$

so that

$$\overline{n} = \frac{\nabla f}{|\nabla f|} = \frac{2x\overline{i} + 2y\overline{j} + 2z\overline{k}}{2\sqrt{x^2+y^2+z^2}}$$
$$= x\overline{i} + y\overline{j} + z\overline{k} \tag{5}$$

since $\quad x^2 + y^2 + z^2 = 1$.

Integral (4) now becomes

$$\iint_S \nabla \times \overline{F} \cdot \overline{n} \, dS = 4 \iint_P \overline{k} \cdot \overline{n} \, \frac{dxdy}{|\overline{n} \cdot \overline{k}|}$$

$$= 4 \iint_P \overline{k} \cdot (x\overline{i} + y\overline{j} + z\overline{k}) \, \frac{dxdy}{|(x\overline{i} + y\overline{j} + z\overline{k}) \cdot \overline{k}|}$$

$$= 4 \iint_P z \, \frac{dxdy}{z} = 4 \iint_P dxdy \tag{6}$$

Now, since P is a disk of radius 1, its area is π.

Thus, from (6), we obtain

$$\iint_S \nabla \times \overline{F} \cdot \overline{n} \, dS = 4\pi \tag{7}$$

Now, to evaluate the line integral, let us first note that the boundary C of S is the circle $x^2+y^2=1$, as shown in the figure. Its parametric equations are

$$x = \cos t$$
$$0 \leq t \leq 2\pi \tag{8}$$
$$y = \sin t$$

Since $z = 0$ for the xy-plane, we have

$$\overline{F} = x^3\overline{i} + 4x\overline{j} = \cos^3 t\,\overline{i} + 4\cos t\,\overline{j} \tag{9}$$

The line integral is

$$\oint_C \overline{F} \cdot d\overline{r} = \int_0^{2\pi} \cos^3 t(-\sin t)dt + 4\cos t \cos t\, dt$$
$$= \int_0^{2\pi} \left[4\cos^2 t - \cos^3 t \sin t \right] dt \tag{10}$$

Now, since

$$\int \cos^2 t\, dt = \frac{1}{2}t + \frac{1}{4}\sin 2t$$

and

$$\int \sin t \cos^3 t\, dt = -\frac{\cos^4 t}{4} \tag{11}$$

integral (10) now becomes

$$\oint_C \overline{F} \cdot d\overline{r} = \left[2t + \sin 2t + \frac{\cos^4 t}{4} \right] \Bigg|_{t=0}^{2\pi} \tag{12}$$
$$= 4\pi$$

The results obtained in eqs.(7) and (12) are equal. Therefore, Stokes' theorem has been verified for this case.

● **PROBLEM 20-7**

Verify Stokes' theorem for

$$\overline{F} = \left(x^3 + \frac{yz^2}{2}, \ \frac{xz^2}{2} + y^2, \ xyz \right) \tag{1}$$

where S is the surface of the cube $x = 0$, $y = 0$, $z = 0$, $x = 3$, $y = 3$ and $z = 3$ above the xy-plane.

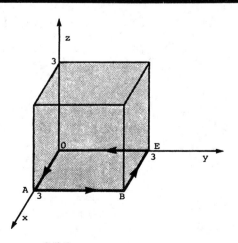

Solution: The surface S is shown in the figure.

It is required to show that

$$\iint_S \text{curl } \overline{F} \cdot \overline{n} \, dS = \oint_C \overline{F} \cdot d\overline{r} \tag{2}$$

Before proceeding to evaluate the surface integral, it should be noted that the surface in consideration is that surface that lies above the xy-plane, and in light of this, the surface integral will be evaluated over all of the faces of the cube except the face lying on the xy-plane.

Now, for curl $\overline{F}$, we have

$$\text{curl } \overline{F} = \left(\frac{\partial}{\partial x}, \frac{\partial}{\partial y}, \frac{\partial}{\partial z}\right) \times \left(x^3 + \frac{yz^2}{2}, \frac{xz^2}{2} + y^2, xyz\right)$$

$$= (0,0,0) = \overline{0} \tag{3}$$

Since curl $\overline{F} = \overline{0}$ everywhere in S,

$$\iint_S \text{curl } \overline{F} \cdot \overline{n} \, dS = 0 \tag{4}$$

and in this case, we were fortunate, for it is not necessary to evaluate the surface integral over any of the faces of the cube.

We now proceed to evaluate the line integral

$$\oint_C \overline{F} \cdot d\overline{r}, \tag{5}$$

where C is the square OABE.

Along OA, integral (5) becomes

$$\int_{OA} \overline{F} \cdot d\overline{r} = \int_0^3 x^3 dx = \left.\frac{x^4}{4}\right|_0^3 = \frac{81}{4} \tag{6}$$

Note that for the xy-plane, z=0 and $\overline{F}$ given by eq.(1) is

$$\overline{F} = (x^3, y^2, 0). \tag{7}$$

Along AB,

$$\int_0^3 y^2 dy = \left.\frac{y^3}{3}\right|_0^3 = \frac{27}{3} \tag{8}$$

Along BE,

$$\int_3^0 x^3 dx = \left.\frac{x^4}{4}\right|_3^0 = -\frac{81}{4} \tag{9}$$

and along EO,

$$\int_3^0 y^2\,dy = \frac{y^3}{3}\bigg|_3^0 = -\frac{27}{3} \qquad (10)$$

Summing up integrals (6), (8), (9) and (10) results in

$$\oint_C \overline{F} \cdot d\overline{r} = \frac{81}{4} + \frac{27}{3} - \frac{81}{4} - \frac{27}{3} = 0 \qquad (11)$$

That verifies Stokes' theorem for this case.

● **PROBLEM 20-8**

Verify Stokes' theorem for

$$\overline{F} = (x+2y)\overline{i} + 3z\overline{j} + yz\overline{k} \qquad (1)$$

where S is the surface of the cube $x = 0$, $y = 0$, $z = 0$, $x = 1$, $y = 1$, $z = 1$ above the xy-plane.

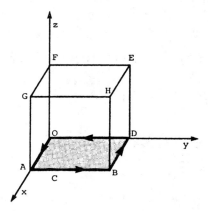

Solution: The cube is shown in the figure.

It is required to show that

$$\iint_S \nabla \times \overline{F} \cdot \overline{n}\,dS = \oint_C \overline{F} \cdot d\overline{r} \qquad (2)$$

We will now evaluate the surface integral.

The curl of $\overline{F}$ is

$$\nabla \times \overline{F} = \left(\frac{\partial}{\partial x}, \frac{\partial}{\partial y}, \frac{\partial}{\partial z}\right) \times (x+2y, 3z, yz) = (z-3, 0, -2) \qquad (3)$$

For the face OAGF, the surface integral is

$$\iint_{OAGF} \left[(z-3)\overline{i} - 2\overline{k}\right] \cdot (-\overline{j})\,dS = 0 \qquad (4)$$

957

For the face ABHG,

$$\iint\limits_{ABHG} (z-3)\overline{i} \cdot \overline{i}\ dS = \int_0^1 \int_0^1 (z-3)dydz = -\frac{5}{2} \tag{5}$$

and for BDEH

$$\iint\limits_{BDEH} 0 \cdot \overline{j}\ dS = 0 \tag{6}$$

For the face ODEF we obtain

$$\iint\limits_{ODEF} (z-3)\overline{i} \cdot (-\overline{i})dS = \int_0^1 \int_0^1 (3-z)dydz = \frac{5}{2} \tag{7}$$

and for EFGH,

$$\iint\limits_{EFGH} -2\overline{k} \cdot \overline{k}\ dS = -2 \iint\limits_{EFGH} dS = -2 \tag{8}$$

Adding eqs.(4) through (10) gives us the total surface integral

$$\iint\limits_{S} \nabla \times \overline{F} \cdot \overline{n}\ dS = -\frac{5}{2} + \frac{5}{2} - 2 = -2 \tag{9}$$

Note that in evaluating the surface integral, we did not consider the face OABD, since we are considering the surface above the xy-plane.

Now, let us evaluate the line integral along the contour C lying in the xy-plane.

Since z=0 in the xy-plane, the vector field $\overline{F}$ reduces to

$$\overline{F} = (x+2y)\overline{i} \tag{10}$$

We have

$$\int\limits_{OA} \overline{F} \cdot d\overline{r} = \int_0^1 x\ dx = \frac{1}{2} \tag{11}$$

$$\int\limits_{AB} \overline{F} \cdot d\overline{r} = 0 \tag{12}$$

$$\int\limits_{BD} \overline{F} \cdot d\overline{r} = \int_1^0 (x+2)dx = -\frac{5}{2} \tag{13}$$

$$\int\limits_{DO} \overline{F} \cdot d\overline{r} = 0 \tag{14}$$

958

Adding eqs.(11) through (14) gives us

$$\oint_C \overline{F} \cdot d\overline{r} = \frac{1}{2} - \frac{5}{2} = -2 \qquad (15)$$

Eqs.(9) and (15) give the same result; thus, we have veri-fied Stokes' theorem for this case.

● **PROBLEM 20-9**

Verify Stokes' theorem for

$$\overline{F} = xz\overline{i} + y\overline{j} + y^2x\overline{k} \qquad (1)$$

where S is the surface bounded by $y = 0$, $z = 0$ and $4x + y + 2z = 4$ above the zy-plane.

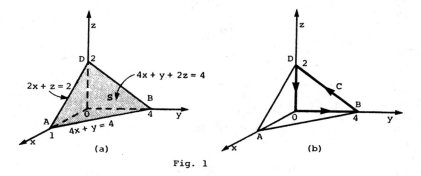

Fig. 1

Solution: The surface S is shown in Fig. 1(a).

Stokes' theorem states that

$$\iint_S \nabla \times \overline{F} \cdot \overline{n} \, dS = \oint_C \overline{F} \cdot d\overline{r} \qquad (2)$$

We will now evaluate the surface integral.

The curl of $\overline{F}$ is equal to

$$\nabla \times \overline{F} = \left(\frac{\partial}{\partial x}, \frac{\partial}{\partial y}, \frac{\partial}{\partial z}\right) \times (xz, y, y^2x) = 2xy\overline{i} + (x-y^2)\overline{j} \qquad (3)$$

Now, for the face ADO, we have

$$\iint_{ADO} \left[2xy\overline{i} + (x-y^2)\overline{j}\right] \cdot (-\overline{j})dS = \iint_{ADO} -x \, dS$$

$$= \int_{z=0}^{2} \int_{x=0}^{\frac{2-z}{2}} -xdxdz = -\frac{1}{8} \int_0^2 (4-4z+z^2)dz = -\frac{1}{3} \qquad (4)$$

For the face ABO, we obtain

959

$$\iint\limits_{ABO} \left[2xy\bar{i} + (x-y^2)\bar{j}\right] \cdot (-\bar{k})dS = 0 \tag{5}$$

To evaluate the surface integral over ABD, we shall first find the unit outer normal vector $\bar{n}$.

$$\bar{n} = \frac{grad\ f}{|grad\ f|} = \left(\frac{4}{\sqrt{21}}, \frac{1}{\sqrt{21}}, \frac{2}{\sqrt{21}}\right) \tag{6}$$

Here, $f(x,y,z) = 4x + y + 2z$.

We now have

$$\iint\limits_{ABD} \nabla \times \bar{F} \cdot \bar{n}\ dS = \iint\limits_{ABD} \frac{\sqrt{21}}{2}\left[2xy\ \frac{4}{\sqrt{21}} + (x-y^2)\ \frac{1}{\sqrt{21}}\right]dxdy$$

$$= \int_{x=0}^{1}\int_{y=0}^{4-4x}\left(4xy + \frac{x}{2} - \frac{y^2}{2}\right)dydx$$

$$= \int_{x=0}^{1}\left[2xy^2 + \frac{x}{2}y - \frac{1}{6}y^3\right]\bigg|_0^{4-4x}dx \tag{7}$$

$$= \int_{x=0}^{1}\left[\frac{4\cdot 32}{3}x^3 - 98x^2 + 66x - \frac{32}{3}\right]dx = \frac{1}{3}$$

Hence, the total surface integral is

$$\iint\limits_{S} \nabla \times \bar{F} \cdot \bar{n}\ dS = -\frac{1}{3} + 0 + \frac{1}{3} = 0 \tag{8}$$

Notice that we did not consider the face OBD when evaluating the surface integral. The reason for this is that we are considering the surface that lies above the yz-plane.

Now, to evaluate the line integral, we should first note that the border C is the contour lying in the yz-plane consisting of the three line segments OB, BD and DO as shown in Fig. 2(b).

Since we are dealing in the yz-plane, x=0, and therefore $\bar{F}$ reduces to

$$\bar{F} = y\bar{j}$$

The line integrals along each of the line segments are

$$\int_{DO} \bar{F} \cdot d\bar{r} = \int_{DO} \bar{0} \cdot d\bar{r} = 0 \tag{9}$$

$$\int_{OB} \bar{F} \cdot d\bar{r} = \int_0^4 y\ dy = \frac{y^2}{2}\bigg|_0^4 = 8 \tag{10}$$

960

$$\int_{BD} \overline{F} \cdot d\overline{r} = \int_{BD} y\overline{j} \cdot (dy\overline{i} + dz\overline{k}) = \int_{4}^{0} y \, dy = -8 \qquad (11)$$

Summing up eqs.(9), (10) and (11) gives us the total line integral

$$\oint_{C} \overline{F} \cdot d\overline{r} = 0 + 8 - 8 = 0 \qquad (12)$$

From eqs.(8) and (12), we see that Stokes' theorem has been verified.

● **PROBLEM** 20-10

A surface S, given by

$$z = f(x,y), \qquad (1)$$

is an oriented surface and has C as its boundary.

Prove Stokes' theorem for S and C.

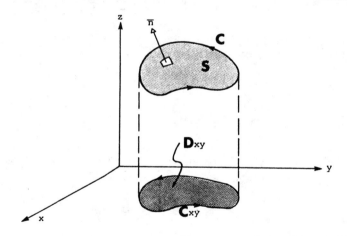

<u>Solution</u>:   Stokes' theorem states that:

If S is an oriented surface with C as its oriented closed boundary and $\overline{F}$ is a continuously differentiable vector field defined in the region S, then

$$\oint_{C} \overline{F} \cdot d\overline{r} = \iint_{S} \text{curl } \overline{F} \cdot \overline{n} \, dS \qquad (2)$$

where

$$\overline{F} = F_1\overline{i} + F_2\overline{j} + F_3\overline{k} \qquad (3)$$

$$d\overline{r} = dx\overline{i} + dy\overline{j} + dz\overline{k} \qquad (4)$$

and $\overline{n}$ is an outer normal vector to S.

961

It is required to show that

$$\oint_C \overline{F} \cdot d\overline{r} = \iint_S \nabla \times \overline{F} \cdot \overline{n} \ dS$$

$$= \iint_S \nabla \times (F_1 \overline{i} + F_2 \overline{j} + F_3 \overline{k}) \cdot \overline{n} \ dS \tag{5}$$

Consider

$$\iint_S \left[\nabla \times (F_1 \overline{i}) \right] \cdot \overline{n} \ dS \tag{6}$$

We have

$$\nabla \times (F_1 \ \overline{i}) = \begin{vmatrix} \overline{i} & \overline{j} & \overline{k} \\ \dfrac{\partial}{\partial x} & \dfrac{\partial}{\partial y} & \dfrac{\partial}{\partial z} \\ F_1 & 0 & 0 \end{vmatrix} = \dfrac{\partial F_1}{\partial z} \overline{j} - \dfrac{\partial F_1}{\partial y} \overline{k} \tag{7}$$

and

$$\nabla \times (F_1 \overline{i}) \cdot \overline{n} \ dS = \left(\dfrac{\partial F_1}{\partial z} \overline{n} \cdot \overline{j} - \dfrac{\partial F_1}{\partial y} \overline{n} \cdot \overline{k} \right) dS \tag{8}$$

Now, since $z = f(x,y)$ is the equation of S, then the position vector $\overline{r}$ of any point on S is

$$\overline{r} = x\overline{i} + y\overline{j} + f(x,y)\overline{k} \tag{9}$$

and

$$\dfrac{\partial \overline{r}}{\partial y} = \overline{j} + \dfrac{\partial f(x,y)}{\partial y} \overline{k} = \overline{j} + \dfrac{\partial z}{\partial y} \overline{k} \tag{10}$$

Now, notice that $\dfrac{\partial \overline{r}}{\partial y}$ is a vector tangent to S and thus perpendicular to $\overline{n}$, so that

$$\overline{n} \cdot \dfrac{\partial \overline{r}}{\partial y} = \overline{n} \cdot \overline{j} + \dfrac{\partial z}{\partial y} \overline{n} \cdot \overline{k} = 0 \tag{11}$$

from which we obtain

$$\overline{n} \cdot \overline{j} = - \dfrac{\partial z}{\partial y} \overline{n} \cdot \overline{k} \tag{12}$$

Substituting eq.(12) into eq.(8) results in

$$\nabla \times (F_1 \overline{i}) \cdot \overline{n} dS = \left(\dfrac{\partial F_1}{\partial z} \left(-\dfrac{\partial z}{\partial y} \right) \overline{n} \cdot \overline{k} - \dfrac{\partial F_1}{\partial y} \overline{n} \cdot \overline{k} \right)$$

$$= - \left(\dfrac{\partial F_1}{\partial y} + \dfrac{\partial F_1}{\partial z} \dfrac{\partial z}{\partial y} \right) \overline{n} \cdot \overline{k} \ dS \tag{13}$$

Again, utilizing the fact that S is given by $z = f(x,y)$, we note that on the surface S we may write

$$F_1(x,y,z) = F_1(x,y,f(x,y)) = G(x,y) \tag{14}$$

962

Now, noting that

$$\frac{\partial G}{\partial y} = \frac{\partial F_1}{\partial y} + \frac{\partial F_1}{\partial z} \frac{\partial z}{\partial y} \tag{15}$$

we see that eq.(13) may be written as

$$\nabla \times (F_1 \bar{i}) \cdot \bar{n} \, dS = -\frac{\partial F_1}{\partial y} \, \bar{n} \cdot \bar{k} \, dS \tag{16}$$

Now, in general, we have that if D_{xy} is the projection of S on the xy-plane, then

$$\iint_S \bar{F} \cdot \bar{n} \, dS = \iint_{D_{xy}} \bar{F} \cdot \bar{n} \, \frac{dxdy}{|\bar{n} \cdot \bar{k}|} \tag{17}$$

From eqs.(13) and (17), we obtain

$$\iint_S \nabla \times (F_1 \bar{i}) \cdot \bar{n} \, dS = - \iint_{D_{xy}} \frac{\partial F_1}{\partial y} \, dxdy \tag{18}$$

Green's theorem in the plane states that

$$\oint_{C_{xy}} Pdx + Qdy = \iint_{D_{xy}} \left(\frac{\partial Q}{\partial x} - \frac{\partial P}{\partial y} \right) dxdy \tag{19}$$

If $\frac{\partial Q}{\partial x} = 0$, then applying eq.(19) to eq.(18) results in

$$-\iint_{D_{xy}} \frac{\partial F_1}{\partial y} \, dxdy = \oint_{C_{xy}} F_1 dx \tag{20}$$

Note that here, C_{xy} represents the boundary curve of region D_{xy}; whereas the C is Stokes' theorem (eq.(2)) denotes the boundary curve of surface S. Note however, that for each point (x,y) of the curve C_{xy}, the value of F_1 is the same as for the corresponding point (x,y,z) of C. Also, since dx is the same for both curves, we conclude that

$$\oint_{C_{xy}} F_1 dx = \oint_C F_1 dx \tag{21}$$

Finally, from eqs.(18), (20) and (21), we obtain

$$\iint_S \nabla \times (F_1 \bar{i}) \cdot \bar{n} \, dS = \oint_C F_1 dx \tag{22}$$

In the same manner, it can be shown that

$$\iint_S \nabla \times (F_2 \bar{j}) \cdot \bar{n} \, dS = \oint_C F_2 dy \tag{23}$$

$$\iint_S \nabla \times (F_3 \overline{k}) \cdot \overline{n} \, dS = \oint_C F_3 dz \qquad (24)$$

Adding eqs.(22), (23) and (24) results in

$$\iint_S \nabla \times \overline{F} \cdot \overline{n} \, dS = \oint_C F_1 dx + F_2 dy + F_3 dz$$

$$\qquad (25)$$

$$= \oint_C \overline{F} \cdot d\overline{r}$$

which is Stokes' theorem.

● **PROBLEM 20-11**

Write Stokes' theorem in the cartesian form.

Solution: In Problem 20-10, we showed that

$$\oint_C F_1(x,y,z)dx = \iint_{D_{xy}} \left(- \frac{\partial F_1}{\partial y} - \frac{\partial F_1}{\partial z} \frac{\partial z}{\partial y} \right) dxdy \qquad (1)$$

On the other hand, we have

$$\iint_{D_{xy}} \left(-F_1 \frac{\partial z}{\partial x} - F_2 \frac{\partial z}{\partial y} + F_3 \right) dxdy = \iint_S F_1 dydz + F_2 dxdz + F_3 dxdy \qquad (2)$$

Setting in eq.(2)

$$\frac{\partial z}{\partial x} = 0, \quad F_3 = - \frac{\partial F_1}{\partial y} , \quad F_2 = - \frac{\partial F_1}{\partial z} \qquad (3)$$

we obtain, from eqs.(1) and (2),

$$\oint_C F_1(x,y,z)dx = \iint_S \frac{\partial F_1}{\partial z} dzdx - \frac{\partial F_1}{\partial y} dxdy \qquad (4)$$

Similarly, we find

$$\oint_C F_2(x,y,z)dy = \iint_S \frac{\partial F_2}{\partial x} dxdy - \frac{\partial F_2}{\partial z} dydz \qquad (5)$$

$$\oint_C F_3(x,y,z)dz = \iint_S \frac{\partial F_3}{\partial y} dydz - \frac{\partial F_3}{\partial x} dzdx \qquad (6)$$

Adding eqs.(4), (5) and (6), we obtain Stokes' theorem in the cartesian form

$$\oint_C F_1 dx + F_2 dy + F_3 dz = \iint_S \left[\frac{\partial F_3}{\partial y} - \frac{\partial F_2}{\partial z}\right] dydz + \left[\frac{\partial F_1}{\partial z} - \frac{\partial F_3}{\partial x}\right] dzdx$$

$$+ \left[\frac{\partial F_2}{\partial x} - \frac{\partial F_1}{\partial y}\right] dxdy \qquad (7)$$

APPLICATIONS OF STOKES' THEOREM

● **PROBLEM** 20-12

Evaluate by Stokes' theorem

$$\oint_C (2xy^2 + \sin z)dx + 2x^2 y dy + x\cos z dz \qquad (1)$$

around the curve

$$x = \cos t, \quad y = \sin t, \quad z = \sin t \qquad (2)$$
$$0 \le t \le 2\pi$$

directed with increasing t.

Solution: Since the surface defined by eq.(2) is piecewise smooth and the vector field

$$\overline{F} = (2xy^2 + \sin z)\overline{i} + 2x^2 y\overline{j} + x\cos z\overline{k}$$

is continuously differentiable, we can apply Stokes' theorem. Thus,

$$\oint_C (2xy^2 + \sin z)dx + 2x^2 y dy + x\cos z dz$$

$$\oint_C \overline{F} \cdot d\overline{r} = \iint_S \text{curl } \overline{F} \cdot \overline{n} \ dS \qquad (3)$$

Let us now evaluate the surface integral. For curl $\overline{F}$, we have

$$\text{curl } \overline{F} = \nabla \times \overline{F} = \left(\frac{\partial}{\partial x}, \frac{\partial}{\partial y}, \frac{\partial}{\partial z}\right) \times (2xy^2 + \sin z, 2x^2 y, x\cos z)$$

$$= (0, \ \cos z - \cos z, \ 4xy - 4xy) = \overline{0} \qquad (4)$$

From eqs.(4) and (3), we obtain

$$\oint_C (2xy^2 + \sin z)dx + 2x^2 y dy + x\cos z dz = 0 \qquad (5)$$

Evaluate

$$\iint_S \nabla \times \overline{\mathbf{F}} \cdot n \ dS \qquad (1)$$

where

$$\overline{F} = (x^2+y+2)\overline{i} + 2xy\overline{j} - (3xyz+z^3)\overline{k} \qquad (2)$$

and S is the surface of the hemisphere

$$x^2 + y^2 + z^2 = 9 \qquad (3)$$

above the xy-plane.

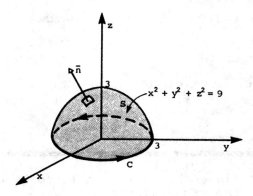

Solution: The surface S is shown in the figure.

Now, note that we have a choice to make. We can either evaluate the surface integral directly, or, since $\overline{F}$ is continuously differentiable and S is a piecewise smooth surface, we can apply Stokes' theorem

$$\iint_S \nabla \times \overline{F} \cdot \overline{n} \ dS = \oint_C \overline{F} \cdot d\overline{r} \qquad (4)$$

and determine the value of the surface integral by evaluating the corresponding line integral.

In this case, if we were to evaluate the surface integral directly, we would first have to find curl $\overline{F}$, then the unit normal vector to S, then the scalar product of curl $\overline{F}$ and $\overline{n}$, then finally integrate.

It is obviously easier to evaluate

$$\oint_C \overline{F} \cdot d\overline{r}. \qquad (5)$$

To evaluate this line integral, let us introduce the polar coorindates and write the circle $C: x^2+y^2 = 9$, which

966

lies on the xy-plane, as

$$x = 3 \cos t$$
$$y = 3 \sin t \qquad (6)$$

so that

$$dx = -3 \sin t \, dt$$
$$dy = 3 \cos t \, dt \qquad (7)$$

The vector field $\overline{F}$ becomes

$$\overline{F} = (x^2 + y + 2)\overline{i} + 2xy\overline{j} \qquad (8)$$
$$= (9\cos^2 t + 3\sin t + 2)\overline{i} + 18 \sin t \cos t \, \overline{j}$$

Note that since the curve C lies on the xy-plane, $z = 0$.

The line integral is equal to

$$\oint_C \overline{F} \cdot d\overline{r} = \int_0^{2\pi} \left[9\cos^2 t + 3\sin t + 2 \right](-3\sin t)dt + 18\sin t\cos t \cdot (3\cos t) \, dt$$

$$= \int_0^{2\pi} (27\cos^2 t\sin t - 9\sin^2 t - 6\sin t)dt \qquad (9)$$

$$= 27\left(-\frac{\cos^3 t}{3} \Big|_0^{2\pi} \right) - 9\left(\frac{t}{2} - \frac{1}{4} \sin 2t \right)\Big|_0^{2\pi} - 6(-\cos t)\Big|_0^{2\pi}$$

$$= -9\pi$$

Thus,

$$\iint_S \nabla \times \overline{F} \cdot \overline{n} \, dS = -9\pi$$

● **PROBLEM 20-14**

Evaluate the surface integral

$$\iint_S (\text{curl } \overline{F}) \cdot \overline{n} \, dS \qquad (1)$$

where

$$\overline{F} = (x^2 + y + 2)\overline{i} + 2xy\overline{j} + 4ze^x\overline{k} \qquad (2)$$

and S is the paraboloid

$$z = 9 - (x^2 + y^2) \qquad (3)$$

above the xy-plane.

Use the results of Problem 20-13.

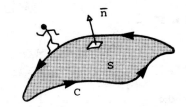

Fig. 1. A boundary curve C
traversed in the positive
direction.

Solution: Here, the surface S is piecewise smooth and the
vector field $\overline{F}$ is continuously differentiable; therefore,
Stokes' theorem is applicable

$$\iint_S \nabla \times \overline{F} \cdot \overline{n} \; dS = \oint_C \overline{F} \cdot d\overline{r} \qquad (4)$$

We see that we can determine the value of the surface integral by actually evaluating the line integral

$$\oint_C \overline{F} \cdot d\overline{r}$$

Before proceeding, it should be noted that the curve C is
traversed in the positive direction. That is, C is traversed in the direction such that an observer walking along the
boundary C of a surface S keeps the surface S to his left
while having his head pointing in the direction of the positive (outward) normal vector to S, as shown in Fig. 1. As a
further illustration, figures two and three show two surfaces (both of which are paraboloids) with their boundary
curves.

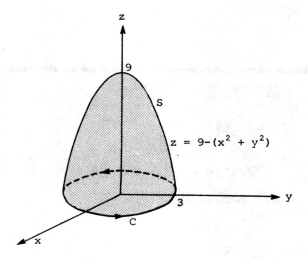

Fig. 2.

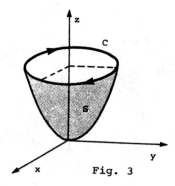

Fig. 3

Now, in our case; the surface at hand is that of Fig. 2, and the boundary curve C is the circle

$$x^2+y^2 = 9$$

which may be parametrized by

$$x = 3 \cos t$$

$$y = 3 \sin t$$

Since the circle lies in the xy-plane, $z = 0$ and the vector field $\overline{F}$ (eq.(2)) reduces to

$$\overline{F} = (x^2+y+2)\overline{i} + 2xy\overline{j}$$

$$= (9\cos^2 t+3\sin t+2)\overline{i} + 18\cos t\sin t\overline{j}$$

The line integral may be written as

$$\oint_C \overline{F} \cdot d\overline{r} = \int_0^{2\pi} \Big[(9\cos^2 t+3\sin t+2)(-3\sin t)$$
$$+(18\sin t\cos t)3\cos t\Big] dt \qquad (5)$$

This integral has been evaluated in Problem 20-13, eq.(9).
Hence,

$$\iint_S \overline{F} \cdot \overline{n} \ dS = \int_C \overline{F} \cdot d\overline{r} = -9\pi$$

● **PROBLEM 20-15**

Evaluate the surface integral

$$\iint_S (\text{curl } \overline{F}) \cdot \overline{n} \ dS \qquad (1)$$

where $\overline{F} = 3y\overline{i} - xz\overline{j} + yz^2\overline{k}$ $\qquad (2)$

and S is the surface

$$x^2+y^2 = 2z \qquad (3)$$

bounded by $z = 2$.

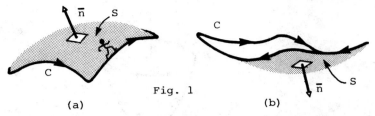

Fig. 1

(a)   (b)

Two surfaces and their corresponding boundary curves
traversed in the positive direction.

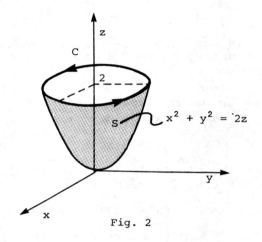

Fig. 2

<u>Solution</u>:   Since $\overline{F}$ is continuously differentiable and S is a
piecewise smooth surface, we can apply Stokes' theorem.

$$\iint_S (\text{curl } \overline{F}) \cdot \overline{n} \, dS = \oint_C \overline{F} \cdot d\overline{r} \qquad (4)$$

We will now determine the value of the surface integral by
evaluating the line integral

$$\oint_C \overline{F} \cdot d\overline{r} \qquad (5)$$

It is important to note that C, the boundary curve of S,
is traversed in the positive direction.   That is, C is traversed in the direction such that an observer walking along C
always keeps the surface S to his left while having his head
pointed in the direction of the positive (outward) normal
vector to S (see Fig. 1).

In our case, the surface S is the paraboloid shown in
Fig. 2.   Notice that C is the circle

$$x^2 + y^2 = 4, \quad z = 2 \qquad (6)$$

which may be parametrized by

$$x = 2 \cos \theta$$

$$y = 2 \sin \theta \tag{7}$$

$$z = 2$$

From eq.(7), we obtain

$$dx = -2\sin\theta \, d\theta$$

$$dy = 2\cos\theta \, d\theta \tag{8}$$

$$dz = 0$$

so that

$$d\bar{r} = -2\sin\theta \, d\theta \, \bar{i} + 2\cos\theta \, d\theta \, \bar{j} \tag{9}$$

Now, note that in traversing C in the positive direction, the angle θ goes from $\theta = 2\pi$ to $\theta = 0$.

Also, note that the vector field $\bar{F}$ becomes

$$\bar{F} = 3y\bar{i} - xz\bar{j} + yz^2\bar{k}$$

$$= 3(2\sin\theta)\bar{i} - 2\cos\theta(2)\bar{j} + (2\sin\theta)(2)^2\bar{k} \tag{10}$$

$$= 6\sin\theta\bar{i} - 4\cos\theta\bar{j} + 8\sin\theta\bar{k}$$

From eqs.(7), (9) and (10), we evaluate the line integral

$$\oint_C \bar{F} \cdot d\bar{r} = \int_{\theta=2\pi}^{0} \left[6\sin\theta\bar{i} - 4\cos\theta\bar{j} + 8\sin\theta\bar{k} \right]$$

$$\cdot \left[-2\sin\theta\bar{i} + 2\cos\theta\bar{j} \right] d\theta$$

$$= \int_{2\pi}^{0} \left[-12\sin^2\theta - 8\cos^2\theta \right] d\theta$$

$$= \int_{0}^{2\pi} (12\sin^2\theta + 8\cos^2\theta) d\theta$$

$$= \int_{0}^{2\pi} \left[12\left[\frac{1}{2}(1-\cos2\theta)\right] + 8\left[\frac{1}{2}(1+\cos2\theta)\right] \right] d\theta$$

$$= \int_{0}^{2\pi} (10 - 2\cos2\theta) d\theta$$

$$= (10\theta - \sin2\theta) \Big|_{0}^{2\pi}$$

$$= 20\pi$$

● **PROBLEM 20-16**

For the vector field

$$\bar{F} = \frac{-y}{x^2+y^2}\bar{i} + \frac{x}{x^2+y^2}\bar{j} \tag{1}$$

and the surface

$$x^2+y^2+z^2 = 1, \quad z \geq 0,$$ (2)

evaluate the surface integral

$$\iint_S (\text{curl } \overline{F}) \cdot \overline{n} \, dS$$ (3)

and the line integral

$$\oint_C \overline{F} \cdot d\overline{r}$$ (4)

where C is the boundary of S.

Are the results compatible with Stokes' theorem?

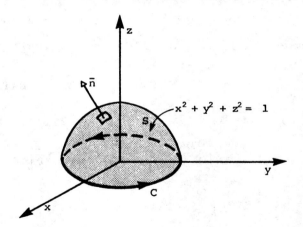

Solution: To evaluate the surface integral, let us first evaluate curl $\overline{F}$

We have

$$\text{curl } \overline{F} = \left(\frac{\partial}{\partial x}, \frac{\partial}{\partial y}, \frac{\partial}{\partial z}\right) \times \left(\frac{-y}{x^2+y^2}, \frac{x}{x^2+y^2}, 0\right)$$ (5)

$$= (0,0,0) = \overline{0}$$

Thus,

$$\iint_S (\text{curl } \overline{F}) \cdot \overline{n} \, dS = \iint_S \overline{0} \cdot \overline{n} \, dS = 0$$ (6)

Now, to evaluate the line integral, note that S is a unit hemisphere (see the figure) and the boundary curve C is the circle

$$x^2+y^2 = 1, \quad z=0$$ (7)

which may be parametrized by

$$x = \cos \theta$$

$$y = \sin \theta \qquad (8)$$

$$z = 0$$

We have,

$$dx = -\sin\theta d\theta$$

$$dy = \cos\theta d\theta$$

$$dz = 0$$

The parameter θ changes from $\theta = 0$ to $\theta = 2\pi$ so that the line integral is

$$\oint_C \overline{F} \cdot d\overline{r} = \oint_C \frac{-y}{x^2+y^2} dx + \frac{x}{x^2+y^2} dy$$

$$= \int_0^{2\pi} (-\sin\theta)(-\sin\theta d\theta) + \cos\theta(\cos\theta d\theta)$$

$$= \int_0^{2\pi} (\sin^2\theta + \cos^2\theta)d\theta$$

$$= \int_0^{2\pi} d\theta = 2\pi \qquad (9)$$

Now, Stokes' theorem states that

$$\iint_S (\text{curl } \overline{F}) \cdot \overline{n} \, dS = \oint_C \overline{F} \cdot d\overline{r} \qquad (10)$$

However, from eqs.(6) and (9), we see that

$$\iint_S (\text{curl } \overline{F}) \cdot \overline{n} \, dS \neq \oint_C \overline{F} \cdot d\overline{r} \qquad (11)$$

which seems to contradict Stokes' theorem.

Notice however, that the curve C includes the origin (0,0,0) and the vector field

$$\overline{F} = \left[\frac{-y}{x^2+y^2}, \frac{x}{x^2+y^2}, 0 \right]$$

is not continuously differentiable throughout any region including (0,0,0).

Since Stokes' theorem assumes that $\overline{F}$ has continuous partial derivatives in a region of space including S (and thus C), we see that the theorem is not applicable to this problem and, therefore, no contradiction exists.

Consider the vector field

$$\overline{F} = \frac{-y}{x^2+y^2}\,\overline{i} + \frac{x}{x^2+y^2}\,\overline{j} + z\overline{k} \qquad (1)$$

and the torus D obtained by rotating the circle

$$(x-2)^2 + z^2 = 1, \quad y = 0 \qquad (2)$$

about the z-axis.

Show that in D

$$\text{curl } \overline{F} = \overline{0} \qquad (3)$$

but

$$\oint_C \overline{F} \cdot d\overline{r} \neq 0 \qquad (4)$$

where C is the circle

$$x^2+y^2 = 4, \quad z = 0. \qquad (5)$$

What are the possible values of the integral

$$\int_{(2,0,0)}^{(0,2,0)} \overline{F} \cdot d\overline{r} \qquad (6)$$

along a path in D?

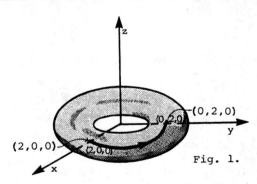

Fig. 1.

Solution: Let us first show that curl $\overline{F} = \overline{0}$. We have

$$\text{curl } \overline{F} = \left(\frac{\partial}{\partial x}, \frac{\partial}{\partial y}, \frac{\partial}{\partial z}\right) \times \left(\frac{-y}{x^2+y^2}, \frac{x}{x^2+y^2}, z\right)$$

$$= \left\{0, 0, \frac{\partial}{\partial x}\left(\frac{x}{x^2+y^2}\right) - \frac{\partial}{\partial y}\left(\frac{-y}{x^2+y^2}\right)\right\} \qquad (7)$$

$$= \left\{0, 0, \frac{x^2+y^2-2x^2+x^2+y^2-2y^2}{x^2+y^2}\right\} = (0,0,0) = \overline{0}$$

974

Let us now evaluate the line integral

$$\oint_C \overline{F} \cdot d\overline{r}$$

Here, C is the circle $x^2 + y^2 = 4$, which may be parametrized by

$$x = 2\cos\theta$$
$$0 \le \theta \le 2\pi \qquad (8)$$
$$y = 2\sin\theta$$

Thus,

$$dx = -2\sin\theta\, d\theta$$
$$\qquad (9)$$
$$dy = 2\cos\theta\, d\theta$$

so that

$$d\overline{r} = dx\,\overline{i} + dy\,\overline{j}$$

$$= -2\sin\theta\, d\theta\,\overline{i} + 2\cos\theta\, d\theta\,\overline{j} \qquad (10)$$

Now, since C lies on the xy-plane, $z = 0$ and the vector field $\overline{F}$ reduces to

$$\overline{F} = \frac{-y}{x^2 + y^2}\,\overline{i} + \frac{x}{x^2 + y^2}\,\overline{j}$$

$$= -\frac{1}{2}\sin\theta\,\overline{i} + \frac{1}{2}\cos\theta\,\overline{j} \qquad (11)$$

The line integral is thus,

$$\oint_C \overline{F} \cdot d\overline{r} = \int_0^{2\pi} \left[-\frac{1}{2}\sin\theta\,\overline{i} + \frac{1}{2}\cos\theta\,\overline{j} \right] \cdot \left[-2\sin\theta\,\overline{i} + 2\cos\theta\,\overline{j} \right] d\theta$$

$$= \int_0^{2\pi} (\sin^2\theta + \cos^2\theta)\, d\theta \qquad (12)$$

$$= \int_0^{2\pi} d\theta = 2\pi$$

Now, before we evaluate the integral

$$\int_{(2,0,0)}^{(0,2,0)} \overline{F} \cdot d\overline{r} \qquad (13)$$

let us note that the domain is doubly connected, as shown in Fig. 1. We have

$$\qquad (14)$$

$$\int_{(2,0,0)}^{(0,2,0)} \overline{F} \cdot d\overline{r} = \int_{(2,0,0)}^{(0,2,0)} d\theta = \begin{array}{l} \text{total increase in} \\ \theta \text{ between } (2,0,0) \\ \text{and } (0,2,0) \end{array}$$

Hence,

$$\int_{(2,0,0)}^{(0,2,0)} \overline{F} \cdot d\overline{r} = \frac{\pi}{2} \pm 2n\pi \qquad (15)$$

975

The path shown in Fig. 1 (for n = 0) yields

$$\int_{(2,0,0)}^{(0,2,0)} \overline{F} \cdot d\overline{r} = \frac{\pi}{2} \qquad (16)$$

● **PROBLEM 20-18**

Evaluate the integral

$$\iint_S \text{curl } \overline{F} \cdot \overline{n} \ dS \qquad (1)$$

where

$$\overline{F} = yz\overline{i} + (2x+y-1)\overline{j} + (x^2+2z)\overline{k} \qquad (2)$$

and S is the surface of intersection of the cylinders

$$x^2+y^2 = a^2$$
$$x^2+z^2 = a^2 \qquad (3)$$

which is contained in the first octant.

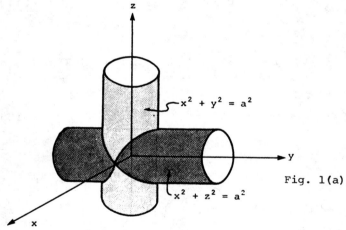

x² + y² = a²

x² + z² = a²

Fig. 1(a)

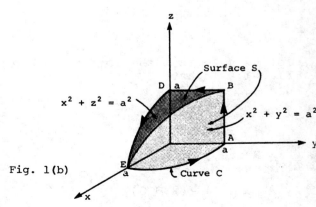

Surface S

x² + z² = a²

x² + y² = a²

Curve C

Fig. 1(b)

Solution: The value of the surface integral can be found through the use of Stokes' theorem

$$\iint_S \text{curl } \overline{F} \cdot \overline{n} \, dS = \oint_C \overline{F} \cdot d\overline{r} \tag{4}$$

Before evaluating the line integral, let us note that the intersection of the cylinders is the surface shown in Fig. 1(b). The closed curve C, which is the boundary curve of S, consists of the curves AB, BD, DE and EA as shown.

We may write

$$\oint_C \overline{F} \cdot d\overline{r} = \int_A^B \overline{F} \cdot d\overline{r} + \int_B^D \overline{F} \cdot d\overline{r} + \int_D^E \overline{F} \cdot d\overline{r} + \int_E^A \overline{F} \cdot d\overline{r} \tag{5}$$

Evaluating each of the integrals separately, we obtain:

For AB, $y = a$, $x = 0$, and $dy = dx = 0$, thus

$$\overline{F} = yz\overline{i} + (2x+y-1)\overline{j} + (x^2+2z)\overline{k}$$

$$= az\overline{i} + (a-1)\overline{j} + 2z\overline{k}$$

$$d\overline{r} = dx\overline{i} + dy\overline{j} + dz\overline{k}$$

$$= dz\overline{k}$$

Therefore

$$\int_A^B \overline{F} \cdot d\overline{r} = \int_{z=0}^a (az\overline{i} + (a-1)\overline{j} + 2z\overline{k}) \cdot dz\overline{k}$$

$$= \int_0^a 2z \, dz = a^2 \tag{6}$$

For BD, $z = a$, $x = 0$ and $dz = dx = 0$, thus

$$\overline{F} = ay\overline{i} + (y-1)\overline{j} + 2a\overline{k}$$

and

$$\int_B^D \overline{F} \cdot d\overline{r} = \int_B^D F_1 \, dx + F_2 \, dy + F_3 \, dz$$

$$= \int_0^a (y-1) dy = \left(\frac{y^2}{2} - y\right)\Big|_a^0 \tag{7}$$

$$= a - \frac{a^2}{2}$$

For DE, $x^2 = a^2 - z^2$, $y = 0$ and $dy = 0$, thus

$$\int_D^E \overline{F} \cdot d\overline{r} = \int_D^E F_1 \, dx + F_2 \, dy + F_3 \, dz$$

977

$$= \int_a^0 (x^2+2z)dz = \int_a^0 (a^2-z^2+2z)dz$$

$$= \left[a^2z - \frac{z^3}{3} + z^2\right]\Big|_a^0 = -\frac{2}{3} a^3 - a^2 \qquad (8)$$

For <u>EA</u>, $x^2 = a^2-y^2$, $z = 0$, and $dz = 0$, thus

$$\int_E^{A.} \overline{F} \cdot d\overline{r} = \int_0^a (2x+y-1)dy$$

$$= \int_0^a (2\sqrt{a^2-y^2} + y - 1)dy \qquad (9)$$

$$= \left[y\sqrt{a^2-y^2} + a^2\sin^{-1} \frac{y}{a} + \frac{y^2}{2} - y\right]\Big|_0^a$$

$$= \frac{a^2}{2} (\pi+1) - a$$

Adding (6), (7), (8) and (9) results in

$$\oint_C \overline{F} \cdot d\overline{r} = a^2 + a - \frac{a^2}{2} - \frac{2}{3} a^3 - a^2 + \frac{a^2}{2} \pi + \frac{a^2}{2} - a$$

$$= \frac{a^2}{2} \pi - \frac{2}{3} a^3 \qquad (10)$$

Thus, from Stokes' theorem, we conclude that

$$\iint_S \text{curl } \overline{F} \cdot \overline{n} \ dS = \frac{a^2}{2} \pi - \frac{2}{3} a^3 \qquad (11)$$

● **PROBLEM** 20-19

Let S be a cylinder having an unspecified smooth border and an orientation as shown in the figure. Evaluate the integral

$$\oint_C \overline{F} \cdot d\overline{r} \qquad (1)$$

where C is the border of S and

$$\overline{F} = y^2\overline{i} + 3x^2\overline{j} + z^2\overline{k} \qquad (2)$$

is a continuously differentiable vector field.

<u>Solution</u>: In general, Stokes' theorem can be extended to an arbitrary oriented surface S whose boundary curve C consists of n distinct simple closed curves $C_1, C_2, \ldots, C_n$.

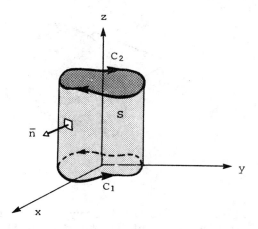

In our case, the boundary C consists of curves C_1 and C_2 as shown in the figure. Thus, Stokes' theorem can be written as

$$\oint_C \overline{F} \cdot d\overline{r} = \oint_{C_1} \overline{F} \cdot d\overline{r} + \oint_{C_2} \overline{F} \cdot d\overline{r}$$

$$= \iint_S (\text{curl } \overline{F}) \cdot \overline{n} \, dS \qquad (3)$$

Let us now evaluate the surface integral. From eq.(2), we obtain

$$\text{curl } \overline{F} = \left[\frac{\partial}{\partial x}, \frac{\partial}{\partial y}, \frac{\partial}{\partial z} \right] \times (y^2, 3x^2, z^2)$$

$$= (0, 0, 6x-2y) = (6x-2y)\overline{k} \qquad (4)$$

Now, since $\overline{n}$ is parallel to the xy-plane,

$$\overline{n} \cdot \overline{k} = 0 \qquad (5)$$

and thus

$$\oint_C \overline{F} \cdot d\overline{r} = \iint_S (\text{curl } \overline{F}) \cdot \overline{n} \, dS = \iint_S (6x-2y)\overline{k} \cdot \overline{n} \, dS = 0 \qquad (6)$$

BASIC IDENTITIES INVOLVING STOKES' THEOREM, FURTHER APPLICATIONS

● **PROBLEM** 20-20

Prove that

$$\iint_S \nabla \times \overline{F} \cdot \overline{n} \, dS = 0 \qquad (1)$$

where $\overline{F}$ is a continuously differentiable vector field and S is any closed regular surface.

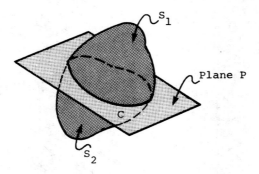

Fig. 1

Solution: Let P be an arbitrary plane that cuts the surface S into two parts, S_1 and S_2, as shown in Fig. 1. The closed curve C formed by the intersection of the plane with S lies on the plane P and is the boundary curve of surfaces S_1 and S_2.

$$C \subset P, \quad C \subset S_1, \quad C \subset S_2 \tag{2}$$

Stokes' theorem can be applied to both surfaces S_1 and S_2. Thus,

$$\iint_{S_1} \nabla \times \overline{F} \cdot \overline{n} \; dS = \oint_C \overline{F} \cdot d\overline{r} \tag{3}$$

and

$$\iint_{S_2} \nabla \times \overline{F} \cdot \overline{n} \; dS = \oint_C \overline{F} \cdot d\overline{r} \tag{4}$$

Now, it is important to note that for the surface S_2, the boundary curve C is traversed in the positive direction, which is oppositive to the positive direction for the boundary curve of surface S_1 (refer to Fig. 2). This accounts for the directions of the arrows in eqs.(3) and (4).

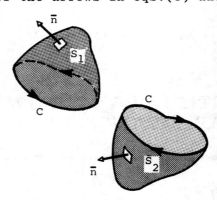

Now, since in general

$$\oint_C \overline{F} \cdot d\overline{r} = - \oint_C \overline{F} \cdot d\overline{r} \tag{5}$$

980

or

$$\oint_{-C} \overline{F} \cdot d\overline{r} + \oint_{C} \overline{F} \cdot d\overline{r} = 0 \qquad (6)$$

we conclude that for the "total" surface S,

$$\iint_{S} \nabla \times \overline{F} \cdot \overline{n} \, dS = \iint_{S_1} \nabla \times \overline{F} \cdot \overline{n} \, dS + \iint_{S_2} \nabla \times \overline{F} \cdot \overline{n} \, dS$$

$$= \oint_{C} \overline{F} \cdot d\overline{r} + \oint_{C} \overline{F} \cdot d\overline{r} = 0 \qquad (7)$$

which is the desired result.

● **PROBLEM 20-21**

Can you obtain the results of Problem 20-20 without any calculations?

Hint: Imagine that S is the surface of a bag with a draw-string.

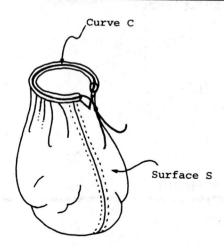

Curve C

Surface S

Solution: In Problem 20-20, it was proven that for a closed surface S and a continuously differentiable vector field $\overline{F}$,

$$\iint_{S} \text{curl } \overline{F} \cdot \overline{n} \, dS = 0 \qquad (1)$$

Let us now see if we can come to this conclusion without any calculations.

Consider the bag shown in the figure.

Let S be the surface of the bag, and let the curve C (the boundary curve of S) be the opening, which of course, can be adjusted by pulling the draw string.

981

Now, if we let $\overline{F}$ be a continuously differentiable vector field, then Stokes' theorem is applicable,

$$\iint_S \text{curl } \overline{F} \cdot \overline{n} \ dS = \oint_C \overline{F} \cdot d\overline{r} \tag{2}$$

Now, by pulling the draw string, we slowly close the bag, and thus, the boundary curve C becomes zero, while at the same time, the surface S becomes a closed surface.

Hence,

$$\iint_S \text{curl } \overline{F} \cdot \overline{n} \ dS = \oint_{C=0} \overline{F} \cdot d\overline{r} = 0 \tag{3}$$

which is the required result.

Often, the term curl $\overline{F} \cdot \overline{n}$ is referred to as the normal component of the vector curl $\overline{F}$. We see that eq.(3) tells us that the surface integral of the normal component of curl $\overline{F}$ over a closed surface is zero.

● **PROBLEM** 20-22

Evaluate the integral

$$\iint_S \text{curl } \overline{F} \cdot \overline{n} \ dS \tag{1}$$

over the hemisphere

$$x^2+y^2+z^2 = 1, \quad z \geq 0. \tag{2}$$

where

$$\overline{F} = -y^3\overline{i} + (x^3+z)\overline{j} + z^3\overline{k} \tag{3}$$

Use the results of Problem 20-20.

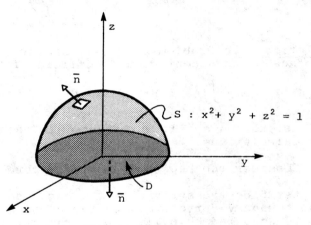

Fig. 1

982

Solution: The surface S is the hemisphere

$$x^2+y^2+z^2 = 1, \quad z \geq 0.$$

Let us consider the closed surface S' which consists of the hemisphere S and the disk D, as shown in Fig. 1.

We have,

$$\iint_{S'} \text{curl } \overline{F} \cdot \overline{n} \ dS = \iint_{S} \text{curl } \overline{F} \cdot \overline{n} \ dS + \iint_{D} \text{curl } \overline{F} \cdot \overline{n} \ dS \quad (4)$$

Now, since S' is a closed surface, we have that

$$\iint_{S'} \text{curl } \overline{F} \cdot \overline{n} \ dS = 0 \quad (5)$$

as proven in Problem 20-20.

Thus, from (5) and (4) we obtain

$$\iint_{S} \text{curl } \overline{F} \cdot \overline{n} \ dS = - \iint_{D} \text{curl } \overline{F} \cdot \overline{n} \ dS \quad (6)$$

From eq.(3), we get

$$\text{curl } \overline{F} = \left(\frac{\partial}{\partial x}, \frac{\partial}{\partial y}, \frac{\partial}{\partial z}\right) \times (-y^3, x^3+z, z^3)$$

$$= (-1, 0, 3x^2+3y^2) = -\overline{i} + (3x^2+3y^2)\overline{k} \quad (7)$$

The outer unit normal vector to D is $\overline{n} = -\overline{k}$. From eqs.(6) and (7), we obtain

$$\iint_{S} \text{curl } \overline{F} \cdot \overline{n} \ dS = - \iint_{D} \left[-\overline{i} + (3x^2+3y^2)\overline{k}\right] \cdot \left[-\overline{k}\right] dS$$

$$= 3 \iint_{D} (x^2+y^2) dS \quad (8)$$

Transforming to polar coordinates,

$$x = \rho \cos \alpha$$
$$y = \rho \sin \alpha \quad (9)$$

we obtain

$$3 \iint_{D} (x^2+y^2) dxdy = 3 \iint_{D} \rho^3 \ d\rho d\alpha$$

$$(10)$$

$$= 3 \int_{\alpha=0}^{2\pi} \int_{\rho=0}^{1} \rho^3 \ d\rho d\alpha = \frac{3}{2} \pi$$

Thus,

$$\iint_{S} \text{curl } \overline{F} \cdot \overline{n} \ dS = \frac{3}{2} \pi \quad (11)$$

983

Given the vector field

$$\overline{F} = (e^x + y^2)\overline{i} - ye^x\overline{j} + (x^2+y^2)\overline{k} \tag{1}$$

find

$$\iint\limits_S \overline{F} \cdot \overline{n} \, dS \tag{2}$$

where S is the sphere

$$(x+3)^2 + (y-1)^2 + z^2 = 4. \tag{3}$$

<u>Solution</u>: The standard procedure for evaluating integral (2) is to find an expression for the unit normal vector $\overline{n}$ of the surface S, then taking the dot product of $\overline{n}$ with the given $\overline{F}$, and then integrating.

Following this procedure, however, would result in lengthy, cumbersome calculations.

Fortunately, there is a faster, less cumbersome way of determining integral (2).

Let us observe that $\overline{F}$ is a solenoidal field, that is, a field such that div $\overline{F} = 0$.

Indeed,

$$\text{div } \overline{F} = \frac{\partial}{\partial x}(e^x + y^2) + \frac{\partial}{\partial y}(-ye^x) + \frac{\partial}{\partial z}(x^2+y^2)$$

$$= e^x - e^x = 0 \tag{4}$$

Consider the following theorem:

<u>Theorem</u>

Let $\overline{F}$ be a continuously differentiable vector field in a spherical (star-shaped) domain D. Then $\overline{F}$ is solenoidal if, and only if, there is a vector field $\overline{G}$ such that

$$\overline{F} = \text{curl } \overline{G} \tag{5}$$

throughout D.

Since $\overline{F}$ given by eq.(1) is solenoidal and S (a sphere) is a spherical domain, we conclude that a vector field $\overline{G}$ exists such that

$$\overline{F} = \text{curl } \overline{G} \tag{6}$$

Thus, integral (2) can be written in the form

$$\iint\limits_S \overline{F} \cdot \overline{n} \, dS = \iint\limits_S \text{curl } \overline{G} \cdot \overline{n} \, dS \tag{7}$$

Now, as proven in Problem 20-20, we have that for any regular closed surface S (in this case, a sphere) and any continuously differentiable vector field $\overline{G}$,

$$\iint_S \text{curl } \overline{G} \cdot \overline{n} \ dS = 0 \tag{8}$$

Thus, from (7) and (8), we conclude that

$$\iint_S \overline{F} \cdot \overline{n} \ dS = 0 \tag{9}$$

● **PROBLEM** 20-24

Prove the identity

$$\oint_C d\overline{r} \times \overline{F} = \iint_S (\overline{n} \times \nabla) \times \overline{F} \ dS \tag{1}$$

with C and S as in Stokes' theorem.

Solution: First, note that Stokes' theorem is

$$\oint_C \overline{A} \cdot d\overline{r} = \iint_S \nabla \times \overline{A} \cdot \overline{n} \ dS \tag{2}$$

where $\overline{A}$ is a continuously differentiable vector field, and C is the boundary curve of the surface S.

Now, to prove identity (1), let us introduce a vector field $\overline{F}$ and a constant vector $\overline{c}$ such that

$$\overline{A} = \overline{F} \times \overline{c} \tag{3}$$

Substituting this into (2) yields

$$\oint_C d\overline{r} \cdot (\overline{F} \times \overline{c}) = \iint_S \left[\nabla \times (\overline{F} \times \overline{c}) \right] \cdot \overline{n} \ dS \tag{4}$$

Now, using the identity

$$\overline{a} \cdot (\overline{b} \times \overline{c}) = (\overline{a} \times \overline{b}) \cdot \overline{c} \tag{5}$$

we may write the line integral as

$$\oint_C d\overline{r} \cdot (\overline{F} \times \overline{c}) = \oint_C \overline{c} \cdot (d\overline{r} \times \overline{F}) = \overline{c} \cdot \oint_C d\overline{r} \times \overline{F} \tag{6}$$

Note that $\overline{c}$ is a constant vector.

985

Now, using the identity

$$\nabla \times (\bar{a} \times \bar{b}) = (\bar{b} \cdot \nabla)\bar{a} - \bar{b}(\nabla \cdot \bar{a}) - (\bar{a} \cdot \nabla)\bar{b} + \bar{a}(\nabla \cdot \bar{b}) \tag{7}$$

and noting the fact that $\nabla \cdot \bar{c} = 0$ (since $\bar{c}$ is a constant vector), we transform the surface integral of eq.(4).

$$\iint_S \left[\nabla \times (\bar{F} \times \bar{c}) \right] \cdot \bar{n} \; dS = \iint_S \left[(\bar{c} \cdot \nabla)\bar{F} - \bar{c}(\nabla \cdot \bar{F}) \right] \cdot \bar{n} \; dS$$

$$= \iint_S \left[(\bar{c} \cdot \nabla)\bar{F} \right] \cdot \bar{n} \; dS - \iint_S \left[\bar{c}(\nabla \cdot \bar{F}) \right] \cdot \bar{n} \; dS \tag{8}$$

$$= \iint_S \bar{c} \cdot \left[\nabla(\bar{F} \cdot \bar{n}) \right] dS - \iint_S \bar{c} \cdot \left[\bar{n}(\nabla \cdot \bar{F}) \right] dS$$

Finally, substituting eqs.(6) and (8) into eq.(4) results in

$$\bar{c} \cdot \oint_C d\bar{r} \times \bar{F} = \iint_S \bar{c} \cdot \left[\nabla(\bar{F} \cdot \bar{n}) \right] dS - \iint_S \bar{c} \cdot \left[\bar{n}(\nabla \cdot \bar{F}) \right] dS$$

$$= \bar{c} \cdot \iint_S \left[\nabla(\bar{F} \cdot \bar{n}) - \bar{n}(\nabla \cdot \bar{F}) \right] dS \tag{9}$$

$$= \bar{c} \cdot \iint_S (\bar{n} \times \nabla) \times \bar{F} \; dS$$

Now, obviously, for any constant vector $\bar{c}$,

$$\bar{c} \cdot \bar{B} = \bar{c} \cdot \bar{D}$$

if and only if

$$\bar{B} = \bar{D}.$$

Therefore, we conclude from eq.(9) that

$$\oint_C d\bar{r} \times \bar{F} = \iint_S (\bar{n} \times \nabla) \times \bar{F} \; dS \tag{10}$$

● **PROBLEM 20-25**

Prove the identity

$$\oint_C \phi \; d\bar{r} = \iint_S d\bar{S} \times \nabla\phi \tag{1}$$

with C and S as in Stokes' theorem.

Solution: Stokes' theorem states that

$$\oint_C \overline{F} \cdot d\overline{r} = \iint_S \nabla \times \overline{F} \cdot \overline{n} \ dS \tag{2}$$

If we let

$$\overline{F} = \overline{a}\phi$$

where $\overline{a}$ is an arbitrary constant vector and ϕ is a scalar function, then

$$\oint_C (\phi\overline{a}) \cdot d\overline{r} = \iint_S \left[\nabla \times (\phi\overline{a})\right] \cdot \overline{n} \ dS \tag{3}$$

Now, the line integral can be written in the form

$$\oint_C \phi\overline{a} \cdot d\overline{r} = \overline{a} \cdot \oint_C \phi \ d\overline{r} \tag{4}$$

since $\overline{a}$ is a constant vector,

$$\nabla \times (\phi\overline{a}) = (\nabla\phi) \times \overline{a} \tag{5}$$

and the surface integral becomes

$$\iint_S \left[\nabla \times (\phi\overline{a})\right] \cdot \overline{n} \ dS = \iint_S \left[(\nabla\phi) \times \overline{a}\right] \cdot \overline{n} \ dS \tag{6}$$

Furthermore, using the identity

$$\overline{a} \cdot (\overline{b} \times \overline{c}) = \overline{c} \cdot (\overline{a} \times \overline{b}) \tag{7}$$

we can transform the surface integral in eq.(6) to

$$\iint_S \left[\nabla\phi \times \overline{a}\right] \cdot \overline{n} \ dS = \iint_S \overline{a} \cdot \left[\overline{n} \times \nabla\phi\right] dS$$

$$= \overline{a} \cdot \iint_S \overline{n} \times \nabla\phi \ dS \tag{8}$$

Substituting eqs.(4) and (8) into eq.(3) results in

$$\overline{a} \cdot \oint_C \phi \ d\overline{r} = \overline{a} \cdot \iint_S \overline{n} \times \nabla\phi \ dS$$

$$= \overline{a} \cdot \iint_S d\overline{S} \times \nabla\phi \tag{9}$$

Note that $d\overline{S} = \overline{n} \ dS$.

Since $\overline{a}$ is an arbitrary constant vector, we conclude from eq.(9) that

$$\oint_C \phi \ d\overline{r} = \iint_S d\overline{S} \times \nabla\phi \tag{10}$$

• PROBLEM 20-26

Prove the identity

$$\oint_C \phi\nabla\psi \cdot d\overline{r} = \iint_S \nabla\phi \times \nabla\psi \cdot \overline{n}\, dS \tag{1}$$

with C and S as in Stokes' theorem.

Solution: Applying Stokes' theorem to C and S and the vector field $\phi\nabla\psi$, we find

$$\oint_C \phi\nabla\psi \cdot d\overline{r} = \iint_S \text{curl}(\phi\nabla\psi) \cdot \overline{n}\, dS \tag{2}$$

Now, using the identity

$$\nabla \times (\phi\overline{F}) = \phi\nabla \times \overline{F} + \nabla\phi \times \overline{F} \tag{3}$$

we may write

$$\text{curl}(\phi\nabla\psi) = \phi\nabla \times \nabla\psi + \nabla\phi \times \nabla\psi \tag{4}$$

Since

$$\nabla \times \nabla\psi = \text{curl grad}\psi = 0 \tag{5}$$

identically, eq.(4) becomes

$$\nabla \times (\phi\nabla\psi) = \nabla\phi \times \nabla\psi \tag{6}$$

Substituting eq.(6) into eq.(2) results in

$$\oint_C \phi\nabla\psi \cdot d\overline{r} = \iint_S \nabla\phi \times \nabla\psi \cdot \overline{n}\, dS \tag{7}$$

which is the desired result.

• PROBLEM 20-27

Let C be a simple closed plane curve in space (see the figure) whose unit normal vector is

$$\overline{n} = a\overline{i} + b\overline{j} + c\overline{k} \tag{1}$$

Show that the area enclosed by C is equal to

$$\frac{1}{2} \oint_C (bz-cy)dx + (cx-az)dy + (ay-bx)dz \tag{2}$$

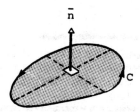

Fig. 1.

Solution: To show that integral (2) represents the area of a planar surface, notice that if

$$\overline{F} = (bz-cy)\overline{i} + (cx-az)\overline{j} + (ay-bx)\overline{k}$$

then integral (2) may be written as

$$\frac{1}{2} \oint_C \overline{F} \cdot d\overline{r} \qquad (3)$$

where $d\overline{r} = dx\overline{i} + dy\overline{j} + dz\overline{k}$, of course.

Now, since $\overline{F}$ is continuously differentiable and the surface S bounded by the curve C is smooth, we can apply Stokes' theorem to integral (2).

$$\frac{1}{2} \oint_C \overline{F} \cdot d\overline{r} = \frac{1}{2} \iint_S \text{curl } \overline{F} \cdot \overline{n} \, dS \qquad (4)$$

Since

$$\text{curl } \overline{F} = \left(\frac{\partial}{\partial x}, \frac{\partial}{\partial y}, \frac{\partial}{\partial z}\right) \times (bz - cy, \ cx - az, \ ay - bx)$$

$$= (2a, \ 2b, \ 2c) \qquad (5)$$

we have

$$\text{curl } \overline{F} \cdot \overline{n} = (2a, \ 2b, \ 2c) \cdot (a,b,c)$$

$$= 2(a^2+b^2+c^2)$$

$$= 2 \ |\overline{n}|^2 \qquad (6)$$

$$= 2$$

since $\overline{n}$ is a unit vector.

Now, from eqs.(6) and (4) we see that integral (2) may be written as

$$\frac{1}{2} \oint_C (bz-cy)dx + (cx-az)dy + (ay-bx)dz$$

$$= \frac{1}{2} \oint_C \overline{F} \cdot d\overline{r} = \frac{1}{2} \iint_S 2 \ dS = \iint_S dS$$

The integral $\iint_S dS$ represents the area of the plane surface S enclosed by the curve C.

Let $\overline{F}$ be a continuously differentiable vector field defined on a smooth surface S such that curl $\overline{F}$ is tangent
to S everywhere on S. Prove that the integral of $\overline{F}$
around the border of S is zero.

Solution: Since $\overline{F}$ is a continuously differentiable vector
field and S is a smooth surface, we can apply Stokes' theorem
to $\overline{F}$.

$$\oint_C \overline{F} \cdot d\overline{r} = \iint_S (\text{curl } \overline{F}) \cdot \overline{n} \, dS \qquad (1)$$

At each point of S, the vector curl $\overline{F}$ is tangent to S, therefore

$$(\text{curl } \overline{F}) \cdot \overline{n} = 0 \qquad (2)$$

From eqs.(1) and (2) we conclude that

$$\oint_C \overline{F} \cdot d\overline{r} = 0 \qquad (3)$$

Let $\overline{F}$ be a continuously differentiable vector field such
that

$$\overline{F} = f(x,y)\overline{i} + g(x,y)\overline{j} \qquad (1)$$

Show that Stokes' theorem applied to a planar surface in
the xy-plane yields Green's theorem.

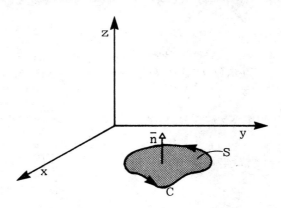

Solution: Consider the planar surface S lying in the xy-
plane whose border is the curve C shown in the figure.

Stokes' theorem for S, C and the vector field $\overline{F}$ is

990

$$\oint_C \overline{F} \cdot d\overline{r} = \iint_S \text{curl } \overline{F} \cdot \overline{n} \ dS \qquad (2)$$

Now, notice that since

$$\overline{F} \cdot d\overline{r} = \left[f(x,y)\overline{i} + g(x,y)\overline{j} \right] \cdot \left[dx\overline{i} + dy\overline{j} + dz\overline{k} \right]$$
$$= fdx + gdy \qquad (3)$$

the line integral may be written as

$$\oint_C \overline{F} \cdot d\overline{r} = \oint_C fdx + gdy \qquad (4)$$

Now, since

$$\text{curl } \overline{F} = \left[\frac{\partial}{\partial x}, \frac{\partial}{\partial y}, \frac{\partial}{\partial z} \right] \times \left[f(x,y), g(x,y), 0 \right]$$

$$= \left[0, \ 0, \ \frac{\partial g}{\partial x} - \frac{\partial f}{\partial y} \right] \qquad (5)$$

$$= \left(\frac{\partial g}{\partial x} - \frac{\partial f}{\partial y} \right) \overline{k}$$

and

$$\overline{n} = \overline{k} \qquad (6)$$

as shown in the figure, we have

$$\text{curl } \overline{F} \cdot \overline{n} = \left(\frac{\partial g}{\partial x} - \frac{\partial f}{\partial y} \right) \overline{k} \cdot \overline{k}$$

$$= \frac{\partial g}{\partial x} - \frac{\partial f}{\partial y} \qquad (7)$$

so that we may write the surface integral as

$$\iint_S \text{curl } \overline{F} \cdot \overline{n} \ dS = \iint_S \left(\frac{\partial g}{\partial x} - \frac{\partial f}{\partial y} \right) dS$$

$$= \iint_S \left(\frac{\partial g}{\partial x} - \frac{\partial f}{\partial y} \right) dxdy \qquad (8)$$

Note that for a planar surface in the xy-plane, dS = dxdy.

Substituting eqs.(4) and (8) into (2) gives us

$$\oint_C f \ dx + g \ dy = \iint_S \left(\frac{\partial g}{\partial x} - \frac{\partial f}{\partial y} \right) dxdy$$

which is the well-known Green's theorem.

STOKES' THEOREM FOR SURFACES GIVEN IN PARAMETRIC FORM

Stokes' theorem has been proved for a surface S given by $z = f(x,y)$. Using vector concepts, prove Stokes' theorem for the surface S given by the parametric equations

$$x = f_1(u,v) \qquad (1)$$

$$y = f_2(u,v) \qquad (2)$$

$$z = f_3(u,v) \qquad (3)$$

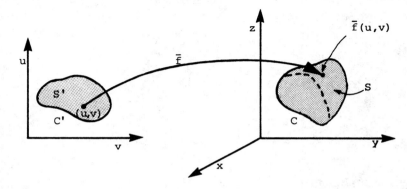

Solution: Eqs.(1), (2) and (3) can be written in the form

$$\overline{r} = \overline{f}(u,v) \qquad (4)$$

Let S' be a region in the uv-plane such that there is a one-to-one correspondence between the points of S' and S.

The unit normal to S is

$$\overline{n} = \pm \frac{\frac{\partial \overline{f}}{\partial u} \times \frac{\partial \overline{f}}{\partial v}}{\left| \frac{\partial \overline{f}}{\partial u} \times \frac{\partial \overline{f}}{\partial v} \right|} \quad , \quad \left| \frac{\partial \overline{f}}{\partial u} \times \frac{\partial \overline{f}}{\partial v} \right| \neq 0 \qquad (5)$$

where the sign is chosen so that the vectors $\frac{\partial \overline{f}}{\partial u}$, $\frac{\partial \overline{f}}{\partial v}$, and $\overline{n}$ form a positive triple.

We can replace

$$\overline{n} \; dS \qquad (6)$$

by

$$\left(\frac{\partial \overline{f}}{\partial u} \times \frac{\partial \overline{f}}{\partial v} \right) du\,dv \qquad (7)$$

Hence,

$$\iint_S \text{curl } \overline{F} \cdot \overline{n} \; dS = \iint_{S'} \text{curl } \overline{F} \cdot \left(\frac{\partial \overline{f}}{\partial u} \times \frac{\partial \overline{f}}{\partial v} \right) du\,dv. \qquad (8)$$

Since the image of the boundary curve C of the surface S is C', then the line integral

$$\oint_C \overline{F} \cdot d\overline{r} \tag{9}$$

can be determined by the line integral

$$\oint_{C'} \overline{F} \cdot \left[\frac{\partial \overline{f}}{\partial u} \, du + \frac{\partial \overline{f}}{\partial v} \, dv \right] \tag{10}$$

where $\qquad \overline{r} = \overline{f}(u,v) \quad$ and

$$d\overline{r} = \frac{\partial \overline{f}}{\partial u} \, du + \frac{\partial \overline{f}}{\partial v} \, dv \tag{11}$$

Using Green's theorem in the uv-plane, we will now show that

$$\iint_{S'} \text{curl } \overline{F} \cdot \left(\frac{\partial \overline{f}}{\partial u} \times \frac{\partial \overline{f}}{\partial v} \right) du \, dv$$

$$\tag{12}$$

$$= \oint_{C'} \overline{F} \cdot \left[\frac{\partial \overline{f}}{\partial u} \, du + \frac{\partial \overline{f}}{\partial v} \, dv \right]$$

In order to simplify the integrand $\text{curl } \overline{F} \cdot \left(\frac{\partial \overline{f}}{\partial u} \times \frac{\partial \overline{f}}{\partial v} \right)$, we have to perform some tedious calculations. Note that

$$\text{curl } \overline{F} \cdot \left(\frac{\partial \overline{f}}{\partial u} \times \frac{\partial \overline{f}}{\partial v} \right)$$

$$\tag{13}$$

$$= \left(\frac{\partial \overline{f}}{\partial u} \times \frac{\partial \overline{f}}{\partial v} \right) \cdot \left(\overline{i} \times \frac{\partial \overline{F}}{\partial x} + \overline{j} \times \frac{\partial \overline{F}}{\partial y} + \overline{k} \times \frac{\partial \overline{F}}{\partial z} \right)$$

Using the identity

$$(\overline{a} \times \overline{b}) \cdot (\overline{c} \times \overline{d}) = (\overline{a} \cdot \overline{c})(\overline{b} \cdot \overline{d}) - (\overline{a} \cdot \overline{d})(\overline{b} \cdot \overline{c}) \tag{14}$$

we obtain

$$\text{curl } \overline{F} \cdot \left(\frac{\partial \overline{f}}{\partial u} \times \frac{\partial \overline{f}}{\partial v} \right) = \left[\left(\frac{\partial \overline{f}}{\partial u} \cdot \overline{i} \right) \left(\frac{\partial \overline{f}}{\partial v} \cdot \frac{\partial \overline{F}}{\partial x} \right) - \left(\frac{\partial \overline{f}}{\partial u} \cdot \frac{\partial \overline{F}}{\partial x} \right) \left(\frac{\partial \overline{f}}{\partial v} \cdot \overline{i} \right) \right]$$

$$+ \left[\left(\frac{\partial \overline{f}}{\partial u} \cdot \overline{j} \right) \left(\frac{\partial \overline{f}}{\partial v} \cdot \frac{\partial \overline{F}}{\partial y} \right) - \left(\frac{\partial \overline{f}}{\partial u} \cdot \frac{\partial \overline{F}}{\partial y} \right) \left(\frac{\partial \overline{f}}{\partial v} \cdot \overline{j} \right) \right]$$

$$+ \left[\left(\frac{\partial \overline{f}}{\partial u} \cdot \overline{k} \right) \left(\frac{\partial \overline{f}}{\partial v} \cdot \frac{\partial \overline{F}}{\partial z} \right) - \left(\frac{\partial \overline{f}}{\partial u} \cdot \frac{\partial \overline{F}}{\partial z} \right) \left(\frac{\partial \overline{f}}{\partial v} \cdot \overline{k} \right) \right] \tag{15}$$

Since

$$\frac{\partial \overline{f}}{\partial u} \cdot \overline{i} = \frac{\partial f_1}{\partial u} \,, \quad \frac{\partial \overline{f}}{\partial u} \cdot \overline{j} = \frac{\partial f_2}{\partial u} \,, \quad \frac{\partial \overline{f}}{\partial u} \cdot \overline{k} = \frac{\partial f_3}{\partial u}$$

993

and
$$\frac{\partial \overline{f}}{\partial v} \cdot \overline{i} = \frac{\partial f_1}{\partial v} \ , \quad \frac{\partial \overline{f}}{\partial v} \cdot \overline{j} = \frac{\partial f_2}{\partial v} \ , \quad \frac{\partial \overline{f}}{\partial v} \cdot \overline{k} = \frac{\partial f_3}{\partial v} \tag{16}$$

eq.(15) becomes

$$\text{curl } \overline{F} \cdot \left(\frac{\partial \overline{f}}{\partial u} \times \frac{\partial \overline{f}}{\partial v} \right) = \frac{\partial f_1}{\partial u} \frac{\partial \overline{f}}{\partial v} \cdot \frac{\partial \overline{F}}{\partial x} - \frac{\partial f_1}{\partial v} \frac{\partial \overline{f}}{\partial u} \cdot \frac{\partial \overline{F}}{\partial x}$$

$$+ \frac{\partial f_2}{\partial u} \frac{\partial \overline{f}}{\partial v} \cdot \frac{\partial \overline{F}}{\partial y} - \frac{\partial f_2}{\partial v} \frac{\partial \overline{f}}{\partial u} \cdot \frac{\partial \overline{F}}{\partial y} + \frac{\partial f_3}{\partial u} \frac{\partial \overline{f}}{\partial v} \cdot \frac{\partial \overline{F}}{\partial z} - \frac{\partial f_3}{\partial v} \frac{\partial \overline{f}}{\partial u} \cdot \frac{\partial \overline{F}}{\partial z} \tag{17}$$

$$= \frac{\partial \overline{f}}{\partial v} \cdot \frac{\partial \overline{F}}{\partial u} - \frac{\partial \overline{f}}{\partial u} \cdot \frac{\partial \overline{F}}{\partial v} = \frac{\partial}{\partial u} \left(\frac{\partial \overline{f}}{\partial v} \cdot \overline{F} \right) - \frac{\partial}{\partial v} \left(\frac{\partial \overline{f}}{\partial u} \cdot \overline{F} \right)$$

The surface integral in eq.(12) can be written

$$\iint\limits_{S'} \text{curl } \overline{F} \cdot \left(\frac{\partial \overline{f}}{\partial u} \times \frac{\partial \overline{f}}{\partial v} \right) dudv = \iint\limits_{S'} \left[\frac{\partial}{\partial u} \left(\frac{\partial \overline{f}}{\partial v} \cdot \overline{F} \right) - \frac{\partial}{\partial v} \left(\frac{\partial \overline{f}}{\partial u} \cdot \overline{F} \right) \right] dudv$$

$$\tag{18}$$

By Green's theorem

$$\iint\limits_{S'} \text{curl } \overline{F} \cdot \left(\frac{\partial \overline{f}}{\partial u} \times \frac{\partial \overline{f}}{\partial v} \right) dudv = \oint\limits_{C'} \left(\frac{\partial \overline{f}}{\partial u} \cdot \overline{F} \right) du + \left(\frac{\partial \overline{f}}{\partial v} \cdot \overline{F} \right) dv$$

$$\tag{19}$$

$$= \oint\limits_{C'} \overline{F} \cdot \left[\frac{\partial \overline{f}}{\partial u} \, du + \frac{\partial \overline{f}}{\partial v} \, dv \right]$$

That completes the proof.

● **PROBLEM 20-31**

The surface S given by

$$\frac{y}{x} = \text{Tan } z \tag{1}$$

is parametrized by the equations

$$x = u \cos v$$
$$y = u \sin v \tag{2}$$
$$z = v$$

where $0 \le u \le 1$, $0 \le v \le \frac{\pi}{2}$

Evaluate the integral

$$\oint\limits_{C} \overline{F} \cdot d\overline{r} \tag{3}$$

where C is the border of S and

$$\overline{F} = z\overline{i} + x\overline{j} + y\overline{k} \tag{4}$$

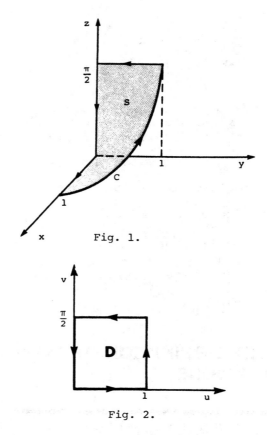

Fig. 1.

Fig. 2.

Solution: Since S is a smooth surface in R^3 and $\overline{F}$ is a continuously differentiable vector field defined on S, Stokes' theorem is applicable.

$$\oint_C \overline{F} \cdot d\overline{r} = \iint_S \text{curl } \overline{F} \cdot \overline{n} \, dS$$

It is easier to evaluate the surface integral than the line integral. The surface S and its border C are shown in Fig.1.

The domain of the parametrization given by eq.(2) is shown in Fig. 2.

The surface integral may be written as

$$\iint_S \text{curl } \overline{F} \cdot \overline{n} \, ds = \iint_D \left[\frac{\partial(y,z)}{\partial(u,v)} + \frac{\partial(z,x)}{\partial(u,v)} + \frac{\partial(x,y)}{\partial(u,v)} \right] dudv$$

From eqs.(2), we obtain

$$\frac{\partial(y,z)}{\partial(u,v)} = \begin{vmatrix} \dfrac{\partial y}{\partial u} & \dfrac{\partial z}{\partial u} \\[2mm] \dfrac{\partial y}{\partial v} & \dfrac{\partial z}{\partial v} \end{vmatrix} = \begin{vmatrix} \sin v & 0 \\ u\cos v & 1 \end{vmatrix} = \sin v$$

995

$$\frac{\partial(z,x)}{\partial(u,v)} = \begin{vmatrix} \dfrac{\partial z}{\partial u} & \dfrac{\partial x}{\partial u} \\[2mm] \dfrac{\partial z}{\partial v} & \dfrac{\partial x}{\partial v} \end{vmatrix} = \begin{vmatrix} 0 & \cos v \\ 1 & -u\sin v \end{vmatrix} = -\cos v$$

$$\frac{\partial(x,y)}{\partial(u,v)} = \begin{vmatrix} \cos v & \sin v \\ -u\sin v & u\cos v \end{vmatrix}$$

$$= u\cos^2 v + u\sin^2 v = u$$

The surface integral is thus equal to

$$\iint\limits_{S} \text{curl } \overline{F} \cdot \overline{n} \ dS$$

$$= \int_{u=0}^{1} \int_{v=0}^{\frac{\pi}{2}} (\sin v - \cos v + u) dv du$$

$$= \frac{\pi}{4}$$

ANOTHER DEFINITION OF ROTATION, FURTHER APPLICATIONS

● **PROBLEM 20-32**

The surface ΔS and its border C are shown in Fig. 1.

The point P belongs to ΔS and is not on the curve C. Show that P,

$$(\text{curl } \overline{F}) \cdot \overline{n} = \lim_{\Delta S \to 0} \frac{1}{\Delta S} \oint_{C} \overline{F} \cdot d\overline{r} \qquad (1)$$

where $\overline{F}$ is any continuously differentiable vector field defined on ΔS, $\overline{n}$ is the unit normal vector to ΔS at the point P and the limit is taken in such a way that ΔS shrinks to P.

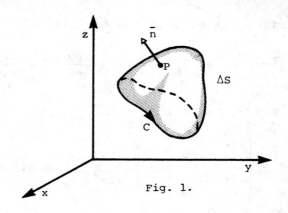

Fig. 1.

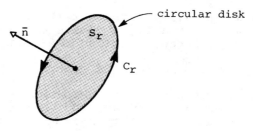

Fig. 2

Solution: By Stokes' theorem we obtain

$$\iint_{\Delta S} (\operatorname{curl} \overline{F}) \cdot \overline{n} \ dS = \oint_C \overline{F} \cdot d\overline{r} \tag{2}$$

Let point P have coordinates (x_a, y_a, z_a).

Applying the mean value theorem for integrals, we find

$$\iint_{\Delta S} (\operatorname{curl} \overline{F}) \cdot \overline{n} \ dS = \operatorname{curl} \overline{F} \Big|_{(x_a, y_a, z_a)} \cdot \overline{n} \ \Delta S \tag{3}$$

where ΔS is the area of the surface ΔS. From eqs.(2) and (3) we get

$$\operatorname{curl} \overline{F} \Big|_{(x_a, y_a, z_a)} \cdot \overline{n} = \frac{1}{\Delta S} \oint_C \overline{F} \cdot d\overline{r} \tag{4}$$

Taking the limit as $\Delta S \to 0$ while noting that P always belongs to ΔS, we find

$$(\operatorname{curl} \overline{F}) \cdot \overline{n} = \lim_{\Delta S \to 0} \frac{1}{\Delta S} \oint_C \overline{F} \cdot d\overline{r} \tag{5}$$

We see that similar to the manner in which the divergence
theorem gives a new interpretation of divergence, the Stokes'
theorem gives us a new interpretation of the curl of a vector field.

Let S_r be a circular disk in space of radius r and center
(x_A, y_A, z_A) bounded by the circle C_r, as shown in Fig. 2.

We have

$$(\operatorname{curl} \overline{F}) \cdot \overline{n} = \lim_{r \to 0} \frac{1}{S_r} \oint_{C_r} \overline{F} \cdot d\overline{r} \tag{6}$$

In the case of a fluid flow with velocity $\overline{v}$, the integral

$\oint_{C_r} \overline{v} \cdot d\overline{r}$, often referred to as the circulation around C_r,
is a measure of the extent of rotation that the fluid flow
exhibits around the circle C_r in the given direction.

From eq.(6), we see that the curl is equal to the circulation per unit area, and this might explain why we often call the curl the rotation of a vector,

$$\text{curl } \overline{F} \equiv \text{rot } \overline{F}.$$

It is interesting to note that eq.(6) is independent of the coordinate system at hand. Thus, it provides a general definition of curl that is independent of the particular coordinate system.

● **PROBLEM** 20-33

curl $\overline{F}$ is defined by the limiting process

$$(\text{curl } \overline{F}) \cdot \overline{n} = \lim_{\Delta S \to 0} \frac{1}{\Delta S} \oint_C \overline{F} \cdot d\overline{r} \qquad (1)$$

Find the z-component of curl $\overline{F}$.

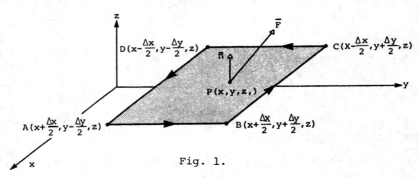

Fig. 1.

Solution: Let ABCD be a rectangle parallel to the xy-plane, as shown in Fig. 1.

We have

$$\oint_{ABCD} \overline{F} \ d\overline{r} = \int_{AB} \overline{F} \ d\overline{r} + \int_{BC} \overline{F} \ d\overline{r} + \int_{CD} \overline{F} \ d\overline{r} + \int_{DA} \overline{F} \ d\overline{r} \qquad (2)$$

Now, let $\overline{F} = F_1\overline{i} + F_2\overline{j} + F_3\overline{k}.$

Neglecting the terms of order higher than $\Delta x \Delta y$, we obtain

$$\int_{AB} \overline{F} \cdot d\overline{r} = \left[F_2 + \frac{1}{2} \frac{\partial F_2}{\partial x} \Delta x \right] \Delta y \qquad (3)$$

$$\int_{BC} \overline{F} \cdot d\overline{r} = -\left[F_1 + \frac{1}{2} \frac{\partial F_1}{\partial y} \Delta y \right] \Delta x \qquad (4)$$

$$\int_{CD} \overline{F} \cdot d\overline{r} = -\left[F_2 - \frac{1}{2} \frac{\partial F_2}{\partial x} \Delta x \right] \Delta y \qquad (5)$$

998

$$\int_{DA} \overline{F} \cdot d\overline{r} = \left[F_1 - \frac{1}{2} \frac{\partial F_1}{\partial y} \Delta y \right] \Delta x \qquad (6)$$

Adding eqs.(3) thru (6) results in

$$\oint_{ABCD} \overline{F} \cdot d\overline{r} = \left(\frac{\partial F_2}{\partial x} - \frac{\partial F_1}{\partial y} \right) \Delta x \Delta y \qquad (7)$$

Now, note that since $\Delta S = \Delta x \Delta y$, we obtain from eqs.(1) and (7),

$$(curl\ \overline{F}) \cdot \overline{k} = (curl\ \overline{F})_z$$

$$= \lim_{\Delta S \to 0} \frac{1}{\Delta S} \oint_{ABCD} \overline{F} \cdot d\overline{r}$$

$$= \lim_{\substack{\Delta x \to 0 \\ \Delta y \to 0}} \left(\frac{\partial F_2}{\partial x} - \frac{\partial F_1}{\partial y} \right) \frac{\Delta x \Delta y}{\Delta x \Delta y} = \frac{\partial F_2}{\partial x} - \frac{\partial F_1}{\partial y} \qquad (8)$$

In the same manner, we can determine the x and y components of curl $\overline{F}$.

● **PROBLEM 20-34**

By applying the divergence theorem and the results of Problem 20-20, derive the identity

$$div\ curl\ \overline{F} = 0 \qquad (1)$$

Solution: In Problem 20-20, we proved that

$$\iint_S curl\ \overline{F} \cdot \overline{n}\ dS = 0 \qquad (2)$$

for any regular closed surface S and any continuously differentiable vector field $\overline{F}$.

The divergence theorem states that

$$\iiint_V div\ \overline{F}\ dV = \iint_S \overline{F} \cdot \overline{n}\ dS \qquad (3)$$

In eq.(3), let us replace $\overline{F}$ by curl $\overline{F}$, then

$$\iiint_V div\ curl\ \overline{F}\ dV = \iint_S curl\ \overline{F} \cdot \overline{n}\ dS \qquad (4)$$

From eqs.(2) and (4), we conclude that the volume integral of the divergence of curl $\overline{F}$ over a domain V is zero

$$\iiint_V \text{div curl } \overline{F} \, dV = 0 \qquad (5)$$

Since eq.(5) is true for any regular closed surface S, we obtain

$$\text{div curl } \overline{F} = 0 \qquad (6)$$

● **PROBLEM 20-35**

Let S be a surface with boundary C and let $\overline{F}$ be a continuously differentiable vector field such that

$$\overline{F} = \text{grad } f \qquad (1)$$

Evaluate the integral

$$\iint_S \text{curl grad } f \cdot \overline{n} \, dS \qquad (2)$$

What is the value of curl grad $f \cdot \overline{n}$ and curl grad f for any unit normal vector $\overline{n}$ and any point in space?

Solution: Let us apply the Stokes' theorem to C, S and the vector field grad $f = \overline{F}$

$$\oint_C \overline{F} \cdot d\overline{r} = \iint_S \text{curl } \overline{F} \cdot \overline{n} \, dS \qquad (3)$$

or

$$\oint_C \text{grad } f \cdot d\overline{r} = \iint_S \text{curl grad } f \cdot \overline{n} \, dS \qquad (4)$$

Now, since $\overline{F} = \text{grad } f$, we conclude that $\overline{F}$ is conservative, and therefore

$$\oint_C \overline{F} \cdot d\overline{r} = 0 \qquad (5)$$

Thus, from eqs.(5) and (4) we obtain

$$\iint_S \text{curl grad } f \cdot \overline{n} \, dS = 0 \qquad (6)$$

Since eq.(6) is true for any surface S in space, we can write

$$\text{curl grad } f \cdot \overline{n} = 0 \qquad (7)$$

Since the above result is independent of the direction of $\overline{n}$, we have

$$\text{curl grad } f = \overline{0} \qquad (8)$$

for any continuously differentiable scalar function f.

Given the vector field

$$\overline{F} = 4y\overline{i} - 3x\overline{j} + (2z^2+1)\overline{k} \qquad (1)$$

find curl $\overline{F}$ and the surface integral of the normal component of curl $\overline{F}$ over the open hemisphere $x^2+y^2+z^2 = 9$ above the xy-plane.

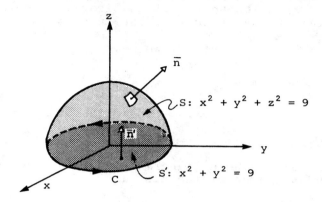

Solution: The normal component of the vector curl $\overline{F}$ is the component of that vector that is directed along the unit normal vector $\overline{n}$ of the surface at hand.

Thus,
normal component of curl $\overline{F} =$ curl $\overline{F} \cdot \overline{n}$

It is required to find the surface integral

$$\iint_S \text{curl } \overline{F} \cdot \overline{n} \, dS \qquad (2)$$

Certainly, we could evaluate this integral by computing curl $\overline{F}$, finding an expression for $\overline{n}$, taking the dot product of the two and then integrating over the hemisphere.

Through the use of Stokes' theorem, however, we could evaluate this integral in a simpler, though less direct, fashion.

Consider two surfaces: the hemisphere S, $x^2+y^2+z^2 = 9$, $z \geq 0$ and the disk S', $x^2+y^2 \leq 9$, $z=0$, which lies on the xy-plane, as shown in Fig. 1.

It is important to note that S and S' have the same boundary curve C.

Let us now apply Stokes' theorem to both S and S',

$$\iint_S \text{curl } \overline{F} \cdot \overline{n} \, dS = \oint_C \overline{F} \cdot d\overline{r} \qquad (3)$$

1001

$$\iint\limits_{S'} \text{curl } \overline{F} \cdot \overline{n}' \, dS = \oint\limits_{C} \overline{F} \cdot d\overline{r} \tag{4}$$

From eqs.(3) and (4) we see that

$$\iint\limits_{S} \text{curl } \overline{F} \cdot \overline{n} \, dS = \iint\limits_{S'} \text{curl } \overline{F} \cdot \overline{n}' \, dS \tag{5}$$

From the above, it is clear that we could evaluate integral (2) by evaluating the integral over the disk S'

Now, for curl $\overline{F}$, we have

$$\text{curl } \overline{F} = \nabla \times \overline{F} = \left(\frac{\partial}{\partial x}, \frac{\partial}{\partial y}, \frac{\partial}{\partial z}\right) \times (4y, -3x, 2z^2+1)$$

$$= (0,0,-3-4) \tag{6}$$

$$= -7\overline{k}$$

Since the unit normal vector to the disk S' is $\overline{n}' = \overline{k}$, and the area of the disk is $3^2\pi = 9\pi$, we obtain

$$\iint\limits_{S'} \text{curl } \overline{F} \cdot \overline{n}' \, dS = \iint\limits_{S'} (-7\overline{k}) \cdot \overline{k} \, dS$$

$$\tag{7}$$

$$= -7 \iint\limits_{S'} dS = -7(9\pi) = -63\pi$$

Hence,

$$\iint\limits_{S} \text{curl } \overline{F} \cdot \overline{n} \, dS = -63\pi \tag{8}$$

● **PROBLEM 20-37**

A vector field $\overline{F}$ is such that

$$\text{curl } \overline{F} = \sin x \, \overline{i} + x^2\overline{j} + 5\overline{k} \tag{1}$$

On the basis of inspection, determine, with minimal calculations, the surface integral of the normal component of curl $\overline{F}$ over

1. the open hemisphere

$$x^2+y^2+z^2 = 4; \quad z \geq 0 \tag{2}$$

2. the sphere

$$x^2+y^2+z^2 = 4 \tag{3}$$

Solution: 1. The open hemisphere, $x^2+y^2+z^2 = 4$ $z \geq 0$, and the disk $x^2+y^2 = 4$ lying on the xy-plane have the same boundary curve.

Therefore, the surface integral $\iint\limits_{S} \text{curl } \overline{F} \cdot \overline{n} \, dS$ is the same for both surfaces. In the case of the disk, curl $\overline{F} \cdot \overline{n} = 5$, since $\overline{n} = \overline{k}$. Thus, the surface integral of the normal component of curl $\overline{F}$ over the disk is equal to five times the area of the disk. Since the area of a disk of radius two is $2^2 \pi = 4\pi$, we conclude that the integral is equal to 20π.

2. The surface integral of the normal component of curl $\overline{F}$ over any closed surface is always zero. Hence, since a sphere is a closed surface, the value of the surface integral is zero.

APPLICATIONS IN ELECTROMAGNETICS

● **PROBLEM** 20-38

Show that the line integral of the tangential component of the magnetic field intensity vector $\overline{H}$ around a closed loop C is proportional to the total current I passing through any surface S having C as its boundary.

That is, show that

$$\oint_C \overline{H} \cdot d\overline{r} = \mu_o I \qquad (1)$$

Apply Maxwell's law of electromagnetism, which states that, in the absence of a time-varying electric field,

$$\text{curl } \overline{H} = \mu_o \overline{J} \qquad (2)$$

where $\overline{J}$ denotes the electric current density.

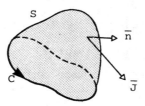

Solution: Let S be any surface bounded by a closed loop C. To the vector field $\overline{H}$ we can apply Stokes' theorem

$$\oint_C \overline{H} \cdot d\overline{r} = \iint_S \text{curl } \overline{H} \cdot \overline{n} \, dS \qquad (3)$$

Substituting eq.(2) into eq.(3) results in

$$\oint_C \overline{H} \cdot d\overline{r} = \iint_S \mu_o \overline{J} \cdot \overline{n} \, dS \qquad (4)$$

The total current passing across surface S can be written as

$$I = \iint_S \overline{J} \cdot \overline{n} \, dS \qquad (5)$$

Substituting eq.(5) into eq.(4) gives us

$$\oint_C \overline{H} \cdot d\overline{r} = \mu_o I$$

which is the desired result.

● **PROBLEM 20-39**

Faraday's law of electromagnetic induction states that

$$\oint_C \overline{E} \cdot d\overline{r} = - \frac{1}{c} \frac{\partial}{\partial t} \iint_S \overline{H} \cdot \overline{n} \, dS \qquad (1)$$

in Guassian units.

Here, S is any surface bounded by the curve C. Show that

$$\text{curl } \overline{E} = - \frac{1}{c} \frac{\partial \overline{H}}{\partial t} \qquad (2)$$

Solution: By Stokes' theorem, we have

$$\oint_C \overline{E} \cdot d\overline{r} = \iint_S \text{curl } \overline{E} \cdot \overline{n} \, dS \qquad (3)$$

Now, assuming that the vector field $\overline{H}(\overline{r}, t)$ is continuous and has a continuous time derivative, $\frac{\partial \overline{H}}{\partial t}$, we can apply Leibnitz's rule to the surface integral in eq.(1).

$$- \frac{1}{c} \frac{\partial}{\partial t} \iint_S \overline{H} \cdot \overline{n} \, dS = - \frac{1}{c} \iint_S \frac{\partial \overline{H}}{\partial t} \cdot \overline{n} \, dS \qquad (4)$$

From eqs.(1), (3) and (4), we obtain

$$\iint_S \text{curl } \overline{E} \cdot \overline{n} \, dS = \iint_S - \frac{1}{c} \frac{\partial \overline{H}}{\partial t} \cdot \overline{n} \, dS \qquad (5)$$

Since eq.(5) is true for any surface S, we can write

$$\text{curl } \bar{E} = -\frac{1}{c}\frac{\partial \bar{H}}{\partial t} \tag{6}$$

Eq.(6) is one of Maxwell's equations.

● **PROBLEM 20-40**

By using Stokes' theorem and Maxwell's equations, show that

1. $$\oint_C \bar{E} \cdot d\bar{r} = -\frac{1}{c}\frac{\partial}{\partial t}\iint_S \bar{B} \cdot \bar{n} \, dS \tag{1}$$

which is Faraday's law of electromagnetic induction.

2. $$\oint_C \bar{H} \cdot d\bar{r} = \frac{4\pi}{c}\iint_S \bar{j} \cdot \bar{n} \, dS \tag{2}$$

which is Oersted's law $\left(\text{neglect the displacement current } \frac{1}{4\pi}\frac{\partial \bar{D}}{\partial t}\right)$.

<u>Solution</u>: Maxwell's equations in Guassian units are

$$\text{curl } \bar{E} = -\frac{1}{c}\frac{\partial \bar{B}}{\partial t} \tag{3}$$

$$\text{div } \bar{D} = 4\pi\rho \tag{4}$$

$$\text{curl } \bar{H} = \frac{1}{c}\frac{\partial \bar{D}}{\partial t} + \frac{4\pi}{c}\bar{j} \tag{5}$$

$$\text{div } \bar{B} = 0 \tag{6}$$

1. Let us apply Stokes' theorem to the vector field $\bar{E}$,

$$\oint_C \bar{E} \cdot d\bar{r} = \iint_S \text{curl } \bar{E} \cdot \bar{n} \, dS \tag{7}$$

Substituting eq.(3) into (7) yields

$$\oint_C \bar{E} \cdot d\bar{r} = \iint_S -\frac{1}{c}\frac{\partial \bar{B}}{\partial t} \cdot \bar{n} \, dS \tag{8}$$

or

$$\oint_C \bar{E} \cdot d\bar{r} = -\frac{1}{c}\frac{\partial}{\partial t}\iint_S \bar{B} \cdot \bar{n} \, dS \tag{9}$$

which is Faraday's law.

2. Applying Stokes' theorem to the vector field $\bar{H}$, we obtain

$$\oint_C \bar{H} \cdot d\bar{r} = \iint_S \text{curl } \bar{H} \cdot \bar{n} \, dS \qquad (10)$$

Now, substituting eq.(5) into (10) gives

$$\oint_C \bar{H} \cdot d\bar{r} = \iint_S \left[\frac{1}{c} \frac{\partial \bar{D}}{\partial t} + \frac{4\pi}{c} \bar{j} \right] \cdot \bar{n} \, dS \qquad (11)$$

If we neglect the displacement current $\frac{1}{c} \frac{\partial D}{\partial t}$, eq.(11) becomes

$$\oint_C \bar{H} \cdot d\bar{r} = \frac{4\pi}{c} \iint_S \bar{j} \cdot \bar{n} \, dS$$

which is the required result.

IRROTATIONAL FIELDS

● PROBLEM 20-41

Determine if the vector field

$$\bar{F} = e^y \bar{i} - e^x \bar{j} + z^2 \bar{k} \qquad (1)$$

is irrotational.

Solution: A vector field $\bar{F}$ is said to be irrotational (conservative) in a domain D if there exists some scalar function $f(x,y,z)$ defined in D such that

$$\bar{F} = \text{grad } f \qquad (2)$$

The scalar function $f(x,y,z)$ is called the potential of $\bar{F}$.

Now, a continuously differentiable vector field $\bar{F}$, defined in a domain D is conservative if and only if it possesses any (and hence all) of the following conditions:

1. it is the gradient of a scalar field
2. its integral along any regular path from P to Q is independent of the path
3. its integral around any regular closed curve is zero.

If the domain D is simply-connected, then we can add one more condition:

4. curl $\bar{F} = \bar{0}$ throughout D.

The following theorem is useful in the study of irrotational vector fields.

Theorem

Let $\overline{F}$ be a vector field in a domain D such that $\overline{F}$ has continuous partial derivatives in D. If

$$\int \overline{F} \cdot d\overline{r} \tag{3}$$

is independent of the path in D, then

$$\text{curl } \overline{F} = \overline{0} \tag{4}$$

in D. Conversely, if D is simply-connected and curl $\overline{F} = \overline{0}$, then $\int \overline{F} \cdot d\overline{r}$ is independent of the path in D.

For the vector field $\overline{F}$ given by eq.(1), we obtain

$$\text{curl } \overline{F} = \left(\frac{\partial}{\partial x}, \frac{\partial}{\partial y}, \frac{\partial}{\partial z} \right) \times (e^y, -e^x, z^2) \tag{5}$$

$$= (0, 0, -e^x - e^y) \neq \overline{0}$$

Since the domain D is simply-connected and curl $\overline{F} \neq \overline{0}$, we conclude that $\overline{F}$ is not irrotational.

● **PROBLEM 20-42**

Prove that a necessary and sufficient condition that

$$\oint_C \overline{F} \cdot d\overline{r} = 0 \tag{1}$$

for every closed curve C is that

$$\text{curl } \overline{F} = \overline{0} \tag{2}$$

identically. Assume that $\overline{F}$ is continuously differentiable.

Solution: First, we will show that condition (2) is sufficient. Suppose

$$\nabla \times \overline{F} = \overline{0}. \tag{3}$$

Then by Stokes' theorem

$$\iint_S \nabla \times \overline{F} \cdot \overline{n} \, dS = \oint_C \overline{F} \cdot d\overline{r} \tag{4}$$

Since $\nabla \times \overline{F} = \overline{0}$ identically,

$$\oint_C \overline{F} \cdot d\overline{r} = 0. \tag{5}$$

1007

Let us now show that the condition (2) is necessary. Suppose

$$\oint_C \overline{F} \cdot d\overline{r} = 0 \qquad (6)$$

around every closed curve C and curl $\overline{F} \neq \overline{0}$ at some point A. Since $\nabla \times \overline{F}$ is continuous, there exists a region D, having A as an interior point, $A \in D$, such that

$$\nabla \times \overline{F} \neq \overline{0} \qquad (7)$$

in D.

Now, let S be a surface in the region D, $S \subset D$, such that the normal vector $\overline{n}$ to S at each point is in the direction of $\nabla \times \overline{F}$, that is,

$$\overline{n} = t\nabla \times \overline{F}, \quad t > 0. \qquad (8)$$

If C is the boundary of S, then by Stokes' theorem

$$\oint_C \overline{F} \cdot \overline{n} = \iint_S \nabla \times \overline{F} \cdot \overline{n} \; dS = \frac{1}{t} \iint_S \overline{n} \cdot \overline{n} \; dS > 0 \qquad (9)$$

However, this contradicts the assumption that $\oint_C \overline{F} \cdot d\overline{r} = 0.$

Hence, $\qquad \nabla \times \overline{F} = \overline{0}. \qquad (10)$

Notice that $\nabla \times \overline{F} = \overline{0}$ is also a necessary and sufficient condition for a line integral

$$\int_{A_1}^{A_2} \overline{F} \cdot d\overline{r}$$

to be independent of the path joining points A_1 and A_2 (see the chapter on conservative vector fields).

Note that the above theorem is true for vector fields defined on simply-connected domains.

● **PROBLEM 20-43**

Consider the vector field

$$\overline{F} = \frac{-y\overline{i} + x\overline{j}}{x^2 + y^2} + 0\overline{k} \qquad (1)$$

defined in the three-dimensional space R^3. Verify that curl $\overline{F} = \overline{0}$. Compute

$$\oint_C \overline{F} \cdot d\overline{r} \qquad (2)$$

where C is a circle of radius r, centered at the origin, located in the xy-plane.

Explain the results.

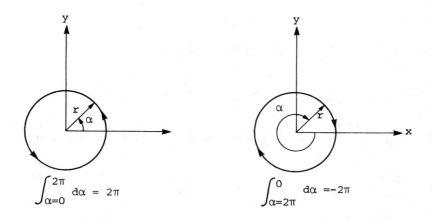

$$\int_{\alpha=0}^{2\pi} d\alpha = 2\pi \qquad\qquad \int_{\alpha=2\pi}^{0} d\alpha = -2\pi$$

Fig. 1.   Two different orientations of a circle of radius r.

<u>Solution</u>: Let us first calculate curl $\overline{F}$. We have

$$\text{curl } \overline{F} = \left(\frac{\partial}{\partial x}, \frac{\partial}{\partial y}, \frac{\partial}{\partial z}\right) \times \left(\frac{-y}{x^2+y^2}, \frac{x}{x^2+y^2}, 0\right)$$

$$= \left(0, 0, \frac{\partial}{\partial x}\left(\frac{x}{x^2+y^2}\right) - \frac{\partial}{\partial y}\left(\frac{-y}{x^2+y^2}\right)\right) \qquad (3)$$

$$= \left(0, 0, \frac{-x^2+y^2}{(x^2+y^2)^2} + \frac{-y^2+x^2}{(x^2+y^2)^2}\right)$$

$$= (0,0,0) = \overline{0}$$

Since curl $\overline{F} = \overline{0}$, it would seem that $\overline{F}$ is a conservative vector field and therefore,

$$\oint_C \overline{F} \cdot d\overline{r} = 0$$

where C is any closed curve.

Now, since in our case C is a circle of radius r lying on the xy-plane, we would ordinarily conclude that

$$\oint_C \overline{F} \cdot d\overline{r} = 0 \qquad (4)$$

since the circle is, of course, a closed curve.

Let us now actually evaluate the line integral.

The circle of radius r may be parametrized by

$$x = r \cos \alpha$$

$$y = r \sin \alpha$$

1009

Thus,

$$\oint_C \overline{F} \cdot d\overline{r} = \oint \frac{-y}{x^2+y^2} \, dx + \frac{x}{x^2+y^2} \, dy$$

$$= \int \frac{r^2 \sin^2 \alpha + r^2 \cos^2 \alpha}{r^2} \, d\alpha = \int d\alpha \qquad (5)$$

We see that depending on the direction, or orientation of the circle, we get

$$\oint_C \overline{F} \cdot d\overline{r} = \oint_C d\alpha = \pm 2\pi \qquad (6)$$

(see Fig. 1).

From eqs.(6) and (4), there seems to be a contradiction. There is no contradiction however, because the vector field $\overline{F}$ is not defined on the z-axis, where $x^2+y^2 = 0$. Thus, the domain of $\overline{F}$ is not simply-connected, and therefore, we cannot apply the curl $\overline{F} = \overline{0}$ criterion. The vector field $\overline{F}$ is not conservative, and therefore, the result of eq.(4) is incorrect.

We have

$$\oint_C \overline{F} \cdot d\overline{r} = \pm 2\pi \quad \text{where } C : x^2+y^2 = r^2, \ z = 0.$$

● **PROBLEM 20-44**

Let $\overline{F}$ be the gradient field of the Newtonian potential

$$f(x,y,z) = \frac{1}{\sqrt{x^2+y^2+z^2}} \qquad (1)$$

That is, $\qquad \overline{F} = \text{grad } f.$ $\qquad\qquad\qquad (2)$

Show that near each point of the domain of $\overline{F}$, the circulation of $\overline{F}$ is zero.

Solution: The value of the line integral

$$\oint_C \overline{F} \cdot d\overline{r} \qquad (3)$$

is called the circulation of $\overline{F}$ around C. It measures the strength of the field tangential to C.

We see from (1) and (2) that $\overline{F}$ is defined everywhere in R^3 except the origin. Thus, the domain of $\overline{F}$ is simply-connected. Since $\overline{F}$ is a gradient field, we get

$$\text{curl } \overline{F} = \text{curl grad } f = \overline{0} \qquad (4)$$

The vector field $\overline{F}$ is continuously differentiable in its domain.

1010

Thus, for every piecewise smooth curve lying in D (that is, curves which do not pass through the origin), we have

$$\oint_C \overline{F} \cdot d\overline{r} = 0 \tag{5}$$

SOLENOIDAL FIELDS

● **PROBLEM** 20-45

Determine if the following vector field is solenoidal. If it is solenoidal, find its vector potential.

$$\overline{F} = (y+1)\overline{i} + 3y\overline{j} - 3z\overline{k} \tag{1}$$

Solution: A vector field $\overline{F}$ satisfying the condition

$$\text{div } \overline{F} = 0 \tag{2}$$

is called a solenoidal field.

For the field given by eq.(1), we obtain

$$\text{div } \overline{F} = \left(\frac{\partial}{\partial x}, \frac{\partial}{\partial y}, \frac{\partial}{\partial z}\right) \cdot (y+1, 3y, -3z)$$

$$= 3 - 3 = 0. \tag{3}$$

Thus, $\overline{F}$ is solenoidal.

In suitable domains, the solenoidal fields are fields of the form curl $\overline{v}$, provided the fields are continuously differentiable. The following theorem is useful in that respect.

Theorem

Let $\overline{F}$ be a continuously differentiable vector field in a spherical domain D. If div $\overline{F} = 0$ in D, then a vector field $\overline{v}$ in D can be found such that

$$\overline{F} = \text{curl } \overline{v} \quad \text{in D.} \tag{4}$$

The field $\overline{v}$, called the vector potential of $\overline{F}$, is not unique. To find $\overline{v}$, we shall use the formula

$$\overline{v}(x,y,z) = \int_0^1 t\overline{F}(xt,yt,zt) \times (x\overline{i}+y\overline{j}+z\overline{k})dt \tag{5}$$

Substituting eq.(1) into eq.(5) results in

$$\overline{v}(x,y,z) = \int_0^1 t\left[ty+1, \ 3yt, \ -3zt\right] \times \left[x,y,z\right]dt$$

$$= \int_0^1 \left[6yzt^2, -3xzt^2 - t\overset{2}{y}z - zt, t^2y^2 + yt - 3xyt^2 \right] dt$$

$$= 2yz\bar{i} - \left(xz + \frac{1}{3}zy + \frac{z}{2} \right)\bar{j} + \left(\frac{1}{3}y^2 + \frac{y}{2} - xy \right)\bar{k} \qquad (6)$$

It is easy to verify that

$$\bar{F} = \text{curl } \bar{v} \qquad (7)$$

where $\bar{F}$ is given by eq.(1) and $\bar{v}$ is given by eq.(6).

● PROBLEM 20-46

Show that if $\bar{v}$ is one solution of the equation

$$\text{curl } \bar{v} = \bar{F} \qquad (1)$$

for a given vector field $\bar{F}$ in a simply-connected domain D, then all solutions are given by

$$\bar{v} + \text{grad } f \qquad (2)$$

where f is an arbitrary differentiable scalar function in D.

Also, for the vector field

$$\bar{F} = (x^2y^2 - x^2z^2)\bar{i} + (2xyz^2 + x^3y)\bar{j} - (x^3z + 2y^2xz)\bar{k} \qquad (3)$$

find all vectors $\bar{v}$ such that curl $\bar{v} = \bar{F}$.

Solution: Assume that $\bar{v}$ is a solution of the equation

$$\text{curl } \bar{v} = \bar{F}$$

Replacing $\bar{v}$ by $\bar{v}$ + grad f we get

$$\text{curl } (\bar{v} + \text{grad } f) = \text{curl } \bar{v} + \text{curl grad } f$$
$$= \text{curl } \bar{v} = \bar{F} \qquad (4)$$

Here, we used the identity

$$\text{curl grad } f = \bar{0}. \qquad (5)$$

Now, to find the vector potential of the vector field given by (3), we shall use the formula

$$\bar{v}(x,y,z) = \int_0^1 t \, \bar{F}(xt,yt,zt) \times (x\bar{i} + y\bar{j} + z\bar{k})dt \qquad (6)$$

Let us note that if the vector field $\bar{F}$ is homogeneous of degree n, that is

$$\bar{F}(xt,yt,zt) = t^n \, \bar{F}(x,y,t) \qquad (7)$$

1012

then the formula (6) can be simplified to

$$\bar{v}(x,y,z) = \int_0^1 t^{n+1} \bar{F}(x,y,z) \times (x\bar{i}+y\bar{j}+z\bar{k})dt$$

$$= \frac{1}{n+2} \bar{F} \times \bar{r}$$

(8)

The vector field $\bar{F}$ given by eq.(3) is homogeneous of degree 4, thus.

$$\bar{v} = \frac{1}{6} \bar{F} \times \bar{r} = \frac{1}{6} (x^2y^2-x^2z^2, \ 2xyz^2+x^3y, -x^3z-2xy^2z) \times (x,y,z)$$

$$= \frac{1}{6}\left[2xyz^3 + 2x^3yz + 2xy^3z, \ -x^4z-3x^2y^2z+x^2z^3, \right.$$

$$\left. x^2y^3-3x^2yz^2-x^4y \right]$$

(9)

Hence, in the most general form, the vector potential of $\bar{F}$ given by eq.(3) is $\bar{v}$ + grad f, where $\bar{v}$ is given by eq.(9) and f is any arbitrary differentiable scalar function.

● **PROBLEM 20-47**

Let f(x,y,z) and g(x,y,z) be continuously differentiable scalar fields defined in a domain D. Show that the vector field $\bar{F}$ such that

$$\bar{F} = \nabla f \times \nabla g$$

(1)

is solenoidal in D.

Solution: To show that $\bar{F}$ is solenoidal, we must prove that

$$\nabla \cdot \bar{F} = 0$$

(2)

everywhere in D.

From eq.(1), we have

$$\nabla \cdot \bar{F} = \nabla \cdot (\nabla f \times \nabla g)$$

(3)

Now, using the identity

$$\nabla \cdot (\bar{a} \times \bar{b}) = \bar{b} \cdot (\nabla \times \bar{a}) - \bar{a} \cdot (\nabla \times \bar{b})$$

eq.(3) becomes

$$\nabla \cdot \bar{F} = \nabla \cdot (\nabla f \times \nabla g) = \nabla g \cdot (\nabla \times \nabla f) - \nabla f \cdot (\nabla \times \nabla g)$$

But,

$$\nabla \times \nabla f = \text{curl grad } f = \bar{0}$$

$$\nabla \times \nabla g = \text{curl grad } g = \bar{0}$$

thus,

$$\nabla \cdot \bar{F} = \bar{0}$$

and therefore the vector field given by

$$\overline{F} = \nabla f \times \nabla g$$

is solenoidal.

It can be shown that in a suitably restricted domain, every solenoidal vector has a representation of the form $\nabla f \times \nabla g$.

CHAPTER 21

CYLINDRICAL AND SPHERICAL COORDINATES

INTRODUCTION

The cylindrical and spherical coordinate systems are two special cases of the general curvilinear coordinate systems.

The cylindrical and spherical systems can be regarded as a three-dimensional extension of the two-dimensional polar coordinate system. As is the case in two-dimensional space R^2, where the application of polar coordinates often allows us to express relationships in a more convenient form, the cylindrical and spherical systems prove quite useful in three-dimensional space R^3. Indeed, a seemingly complex equation (especially one with some kind of spherical symmetry) can often times be reduced and greatly simplified by transforming to such systems.

It should be noted that the variety of possible coordinate systems in R^3 is, of course, much greater than in R^2. Of all the coordinate systems in R^3, the cylindrical and spherical systems, with the exception of the Cartesian coordinate system, of course, have proven most useful.

The chapter attempts to illustrate how the various vector relationships are expressed in the cylindrical and spherical systems. A few examples of fundamental physical equations expressed in coordinate systems other than Cartesian are also given.

The transformation of coordinate systems, which is discussed in greater detail in Chapter 22 (Curvilinear Coordinates) play an important role in modern physics and is a fundamental concept of tensor analysis.

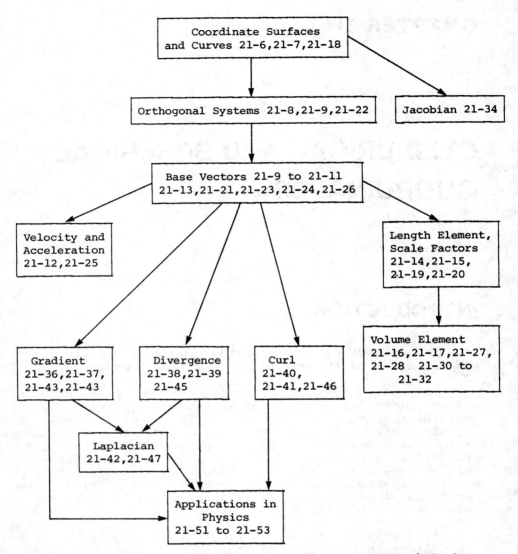

This chart is provided to facilitate rapid understanding of the inter-relationships of the topics and subject matter in this chapter. Also shown are the problem numbers associated with the subject matter.

POLAR COORDINATES

● **PROBLEM** 21-1

A curve is described by the equation

$$1 - \cos\theta = r \qquad (1)$$

in polar coordinates. Plot the graph of this curve.

Solution: Consider a Cartesian coordinate system in the plane. Each point of the plane can be described by a pair of coordinates. There is a one-to-one correspondence be-

tween all the points of the plane and all the ordered pairs
(x,y), where x ∈ R', y ∈ R'. That is, for every point A of
the plane, there exists one and only one ordered pair (x,y)

$$A \longleftrightarrow (x,y).$$ (2)

The converse is also true, for every ordered pair (x,y)
there exists one and only one corresponding point of the
plane.   The numbers x and y are, of course, the Cartesian
coordinates of the point.

    There are other methods of describing the points of the
plane.   One of them is the polar coordinate system.

    Let O be the origin of a polar coordinate system, as
shown in Fig. 1, and let the plane be covered by a network
of concentric circles, whose center is O.

    Let θ be the angle between the positive half of the x-
axis and OA.   Point A is located on a circle whose radius is
r.   We see that the pair (r,θ) describes the location of the
point A.   For r ≥ 0 and, 0 ≤ θ < 2π, this relationship is one-
to-one

$$A \longleftrightarrow (r,\theta).$$ (3)

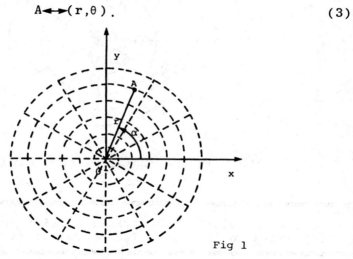

Fig 1

From Fig. 1, we see that

$$x = r \cos\theta$$
$$y = r \sin\theta$$ (4)

    Let us now plot the graph of the curve

$$1 - \cos\theta = r$$

by considering certain values of θ and computing the corresponding values of r.   The results are shown in the table.

θ	r
0°	0
30°	$1 - \frac{\sqrt{3}}{2} = 0.1339$
60°	$\frac{1}{2}$
90°	1
120°	$1\frac{1}{2}$

$$150^0 \qquad 1 + \frac{\sqrt{3}}{2} = 1.8660$$

$$180^0 \qquad 2$$

$$210^0 \qquad 1 + \frac{\sqrt{3}}{2}$$

$$240^0 \qquad 1\tfrac{1}{2}$$

$$270^0 \qquad 1$$

$$300^0 \qquad 1 - \frac{\sqrt{3}}{2}$$

$$330^0 \qquad \tfrac{1}{2}$$

$$360^0 \qquad 0$$

Using the results in the table, we can now plot the graph.

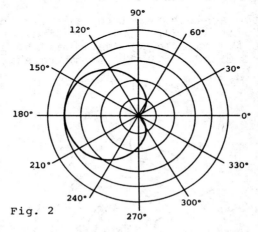

Fig. 2

The curve shown in Fig. 2 is called a cardioid.

● **PROBLEM 21-2**

Find the Jacobian of the transformation from the polar coordinates to the Cartesian coordinates.

Solution: The transformation from the polar to Cartesian (rectangular) coordinates is

$$x = r \cos\theta$$
$$y = r \sin\theta \qquad (1)$$

The Jacobian is

$$\frac{\partial(x,y)}{\partial(r,\theta)} = \begin{vmatrix} \frac{\partial x}{\partial r} & \frac{\partial x}{\partial \theta} \\ \\ \frac{\partial y}{\partial r} & \frac{\partial y}{\partial \theta} \end{vmatrix} \qquad (2)$$

From eqs.(1), we obtain

$$\frac{\partial x}{\partial r} = \cos\theta \qquad \frac{\partial x}{\partial \theta} = - r\sin\theta$$

$$\frac{\partial y}{\partial r} = \sin\theta \qquad \frac{\partial y}{\partial \theta} = r\cos\theta$$

Thus, the Jacobian of the transformation is

1018

$$\frac{\partial(x,y)}{\partial(r,\theta)} = \begin{vmatrix} \cos\theta & -r\sin\theta \\ \sin\theta & r\cos\theta \end{vmatrix}$$

$$= r(\cos^2\theta + \sin^2\theta) = r$$

● **PROBLEM 21-3**

Evaluate the improper integral

$$I = \int_0^\infty e^{-x^2} dx \qquad (1)$$

by finding the value of I^2. Use polar coordinates.

<u>Solution</u>: From eq.(1), we obtain for I^2

$$I^2 = \left(\int_0^\infty e^{-x^2} dx\right)\left(\int_0^\infty e^{-y^2} dy\right)$$

$$= \int_0^\infty \int_0^\infty e^{-(x^2+y^2)} dxdy \qquad (2)$$

In polar coordinates, we have

$$x = r\cos\theta$$
$$y = r\sin\theta \qquad (3)$$

In general, any double integral can be transformed from the Cartesian to the polar coordinates by

$$\iint f(x,y)dxdy = \iint f(r,\theta)rdrd\theta \qquad (4)$$

Now, the limits of integration for r are from $r = 0$ to $r = \infty$, and for θ, the limits are from $\theta = 0$ to $\theta = \frac{\pi}{2}$.

Eq.(2) can now be written

$$I^2 = \int_0^\infty \int_0^\infty e^{-(x^2+y^2)} dxdy$$

$$= \int_0^{\frac{\pi}{2}} \int_0^\infty e^{-r^2} rdrd\theta \qquad (5)$$

$$= \int_0^{\frac{\pi}{2}} \left[-\frac{e^{-r^2}}{2}\right]\Big|_0^\infty d\theta$$

$$= \frac{1}{2}\int_0^{\frac{\pi}{2}} \left[-\left(\frac{1}{e^\infty}\right)^2 + 1\right]d\theta = \frac{1}{2}\int_0^{\frac{\pi}{2}} d\theta = \frac{\pi}{4}$$

Thus,

$$I = \sqrt{I^2} = \int_0^\infty e^{-x^2} dx = \frac{\sqrt{\pi}}{2} \qquad (6)$$

1019

Note that since x changes from $x = 0$ to $x = \infty$, and y from $y = 0$ to $y = \infty$, the angle θ changes from $\theta = 0$ to $\theta = \dfrac{\pi}{2}$.

COORDINATE SURFACES AND CURVES, ORTHOGONAL SYSTEMS

● PROBLEM 21-4

Define, for the most general case, the transformation of coordinates and the curvilinear coordinate system.

Solution: Let the rectangular coordinates (x,y,z) of any point be expressed as functions of (u_1, u_2, u_3), that is

$$x = x(u_1, u_2, u_3)$$

$$y = y(u_1, u_2, u_3) \tag{1}$$

$$z = z(u_1, u_2, u_3)$$

Furthermore, let us assume that eq.(1) can be solved, that is

$$u_1 = u_1(x, y, z)$$

$$u_2 = u_2(x, y, z) \tag{2}$$

$$u_3 = u_3(x, y, z)$$

We see that eq.(1) (or eq.(2)) defines a one-to-one transformation.

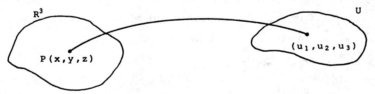

In practice, the one-to-one assumption may not hold true for certain points. These points require a special handling.

The sets of equations (1) and (2) define a transformation of coordinates. For any point P with rectangular coordinates (x,y,z), we can find, by applying eq.(2), a unique set of coordinates (u_1, u_2, u_3) which are called the curvilinear coordinates.

● PROBLEM 21-5

Define the coordinate surfaces and the coordinate curves of the curvilinear coordinate system. Make an appropriate drawing.

Solution: The curvilinear coordinate system is defined by

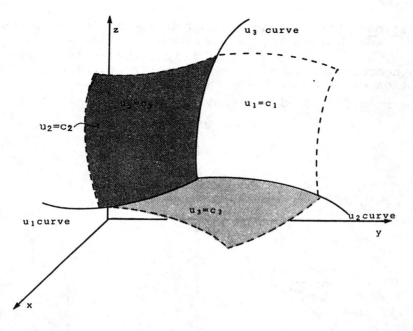

$$x = x(u_1, u_2, u_3), \quad y = y(u_1, u_2, u_3), \quad z = z(u_1, u_2, u_3) \qquad (1)$$

$$u_1 = u_1(x,y,z), \quad u_2 = u_2(x,y,z), \quad u_3 = u_3(x,y,z) \qquad (2)$$

The surfaces $u_1 = c_1 = $ const, $u_2 = c_2 = $ const, $u_3 = c_3 = $ const are called coordinate surfaces. Each pair of these surfaces intersect in curves called coordinate curves, as shown in Fig. 1.

In a curvilinear coordinate system, the u_1, u_2, u_3 coordinate curves are analogous to the x, y, z coordinate axes of a Cartesian coordinate system.

● **PROBLEM** 21-6

Describe the cylindrical system of coordinates. Determine the coordinate surfaces and coordinate curves for this system.

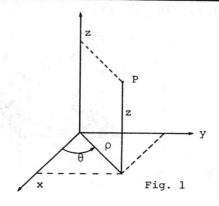

Fig. 1

<u>Solution</u>: The cylindrical coordinate system consists of three coordinates (ρ, θ, z), as shown in Fig. 1.

The coordinate z is the height above the xy-plane, while the coordinates ρ and θ are the polar coordinates of the projection of a point P on the xy-plane.

From Fig. 1, it is easy to see that

$$x = \rho \cos\theta$$

$$y = \rho \sin\theta \qquad\qquad (1)$$

$$z = z$$

Now, the coordinate surfaces are:

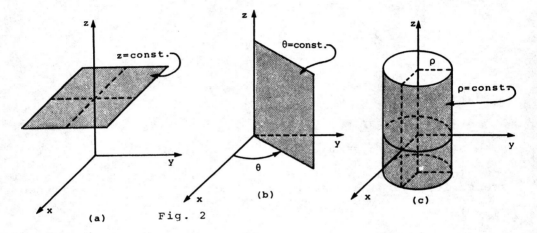

Fig. 2

$\rho = a_1 = \text{const.}$	cylinders coaxial with the z-axis (Fig. 2(c)).
$\theta = a_2 = \text{const.}$	half-planes extending out from the z-axis (Fig. 2(b)).
$z = a_3 = \text{const.}$	planes perpendicular to the z-axis (Fig. 2(a)).

The coordinate curves are formed by the intersections of the coordinate surfaces. The curve formed by the intersection of $\rho = a_1$ and $\theta = a_2$ is called the z-curve. Likewise, the curve formed by the intersection of $\rho = a_1$ and $z = a_3$ is called the θ-curve, and so on.

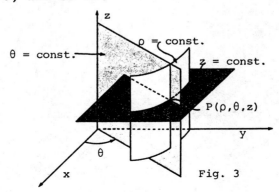

Fig. 3

Now, referring to Fig. 3, we see that the coordinate curves are:

Intersection of $\rho = a_1$ and $\theta = a_2$

The z-curve is a straight line parallel to the z-axis.

Intersection of $\rho = a_1$ and $z = a_3$

The θ-curve is a circle lying on a plane parallel to the xy-plane.

Intersection of $\theta = a_2$ and $z = a_3$

The ρ-curve is a straight line lying on a plane parallel to the xy-plane.

● PROBLEM 21-7

Determine the transformation from rectangular to· cylindrical coordinates.

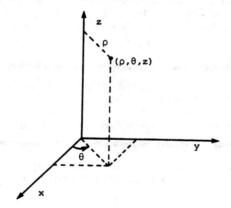

Solution: First, note that the transformation from cylindrical to rectangular coordinates is given by

$$x = \rho \cos\theta$$

$$y = \rho \sin\theta \tag{1}$$

$$z = z$$

We now wish to find the inverse transformation, that is, the transformation from rectangular to cylindrical coordinates.

From the first two equations, we obtain

$$x^2 + y^2 = \rho^2(\cos^2\theta + \sin^2\theta) = \rho^2 \tag{2}$$

Hence, since ρ is positive

$$\rho = \sqrt{x^2 + y^2} \tag{3}$$

Dividing the first two equations in (1), we find

$$\frac{y}{x} = \frac{\rho \sin\theta}{\rho \cos\theta} = \tan\theta \qquad (4)$$

Thus,

$$\theta = \text{arc } \tan \frac{y}{x} \qquad (5)$$

or

$$\theta = \text{arc } \sin \frac{y}{\sqrt{x^2+y^2}} = \text{arc } \cos \frac{x}{\sqrt{x^2+y^2}} \qquad (6)$$

Note that the value of θ extends from $\theta = 0$ to $\theta = 2\pi$. Also, note that on the z-axis, the value of θ is undefined.

The transformation from rectangular to cylindrical coordinates is

$$\rho = \sqrt{x^2+y^2}$$

$$\theta = \text{arc } \tan \frac{y}{x} \qquad (7)$$

$$z = z$$

Notice that with the exception of points lying on the z-axis, equations (1) and (7) define a one-to-one correspondence between the two coordinate systems.

● **PROBLEM** 21-8

Describe what is meant by a curvilinear coordinate system that is orthogonal.

Define the tangent vectors to the coordinate curves.

Solution: A curvilinear coordinate system is said to be orthogonal when the coordinate surfaces intersect at right angles.

Before we get a clearer picture of what this means, let us introduce the concept of the tangent vector to a coordinate curve.

Consider the position vector

$$\bar{r} = x\bar{i} + y\bar{j} + z\bar{k} \qquad (1)$$

of a point P in space.

Since

$$x = x(u_1, u_2, u_3)$$

$$y = y(u_1, u_2, u_3) \qquad (2)$$

$$z = z(u_1, u_2, u_3)$$

we may write $\bar{r}$ as a function of the curvilinear coordinates

$$\bar{r} = x(u_1, u_2, u_3)\bar{i} + y(u_1, u_2, u_3)\bar{j} + z(u_1, u_2, u_3)\bar{k}, \qquad (3)$$

or just simply

$$\bar{r} = \bar{r}(u_1, u_2, u_3).\tag{4}$$

Now, a tangent vector to the u_1 curve is $\dfrac{\partial \bar{r}}{\partial u_1}$. Then a unit tangent vector to the u_1 curve is

$$\bar{e}_1 = \frac{\dfrac{\partial \bar{r}}{\partial u_1}}{\left|\dfrac{\partial \bar{r}}{\partial u_1}\right|}\tag{5}$$

In the same manner, we obtain the unit tangent vectors to the u_2 and u_3 curves,

$$\bar{e}_2 = \frac{\dfrac{\partial \bar{r}}{\partial u_2}}{\left|\dfrac{\partial \bar{r}}{\partial u_2}\right|}\tag{6}$$

$$\bar{e}_3 = \frac{\dfrac{\partial \bar{r}}{\partial u_3}}{\left|\dfrac{\partial \bar{r}}{\partial u_3}\right|}\tag{7}$$

The unit tangent vectors $\bar{e}_1$, $\bar{e}_2$ and $\bar{e}_3$ at a point P are shown in Fig. 1.

Now, if the vectors $\bar{e}_1$, $\bar{e}_2$ and $\bar{e}_3$ are mutually perpendicular, then the u_1, u_2, u_3 curvilinear coordinate system is orthogonal (the coordinate surfaces would be mutually orthogonal).

It is clear then that a curvilinear coordinate system is orthogonal when

$$\bar{e}_1 \cdot \bar{e}_2 = 0$$
$$\bar{e}_2 \cdot \bar{e}_3 = 0\tag{8}$$

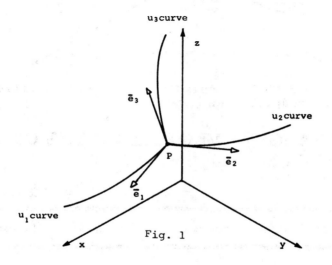

Fig. 1

$$\overline{e}_3 \cdot \overline{e}_1 = 0$$

It is interesting to note that when a curvilinear coordinate system is orthogonal, the unit tangent vectors are perpendicular to their respective coordinate surfaces. For example, in Fig. 2, if the coordinate system u_1, u_2, u_3 were orthogonal, then the vector $\overline{e}_2$ would be perpendicular to the surface $u_2 = $ const. Likewise, vectors $\overline{e}_1$ and $\overline{e}_3$ would be perpendicular to the surfaces $u_1 = $ const. and $u_3 = $ const., respectively. The vectors $\overline{e}_1$, $\overline{e}_2$ and $\overline{e}_3$ are directed toward increasing u_1, u_2, u_3, and for an orthogonal system $\overline{e}_1, \overline{e}_2, \overline{e}_3$ form a right-handed system of vectors, that is, $\overline{e}_3 = \overline{e}_1 \times \overline{e}_2$.

We often introduce the scale factors h_1, h_2 and h_3

$$h_1 = \left| \frac{\partial \overline{r}}{\partial u_1} \right|, \quad h_2 = \left| \frac{\partial \overline{r}}{\partial u_2} \right|, \quad h_3 = \left| \frac{\partial \overline{r}}{\partial u_3} \right|$$

so that

$$h_1 \overline{e}_1 = \frac{\partial \overline{r}}{\partial u_1}$$

$$h_2 \overline{e}_2 = \frac{\partial \overline{r}}{\partial u_2} \tag{9}$$

$$h_3 \overline{e}_3 = \frac{\partial \overline{r}}{\partial u_3}$$

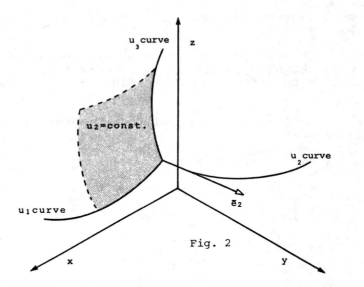

Fig. 2

For a more detailed analysis of general curvilinear coordinates, see chapter twenty-two.

THE UNIT TANGENT VECTORS OF THE CYLINDRICAL COORDINATE SYSTEM

● **PROBLEM** 21-9

Show that a cylindrical coordinate system is orthogonal.

Solution: In cylindrical coordinates, the position vector $\bar{r}$ is given by

$$\bar{r} = x\bar{i} + y\bar{j} + z\bar{k} = \rho\cos\theta\bar{i} + \rho\sin\theta\bar{j} + z\bar{k} \qquad (1)$$

Now, since the unit tangent vectors to the ρ, θ and z curves are

$$\frac{\partial\bar{r}}{\partial\rho}, \frac{\partial\bar{r}}{\partial\theta} \text{ and } \frac{\partial\bar{r}}{\partial z},$$

we obtain, from eq.(1)

$$\frac{\partial\bar{r}}{\partial\rho} = \cos\theta\bar{i} + \sin\theta\bar{j}$$

$$\frac{\partial\bar{r}}{\partial\theta} = -\rho\sin\theta\bar{i} + \rho\cos\theta\bar{j} \qquad (2)$$

$$\frac{\partial\bar{r}}{\partial z} = \bar{k}$$

The unit vectors in the respective directions are

$$\bar{e}_1 = \bar{e}_\rho = \frac{\frac{\partial\bar{r}}{\partial\rho}}{\left|\frac{\partial\bar{r}}{\partial\rho}\right|} = \frac{\cos\theta\bar{i} + \sin\theta\bar{j}}{\sqrt{\cos^2\theta+\sin^2\theta}} = \cos\theta\bar{i} + \sin\theta\bar{j} \qquad (3)$$

$$\bar{e}_2 = \bar{e}_\theta = \frac{\frac{\partial\bar{r}}{\partial\theta}}{\left|\frac{\partial\bar{r}}{\partial\theta}\right|} = \frac{-\rho\sin\theta\bar{i} + \rho\cos\theta\bar{j}}{\sqrt{\rho^2\sin^2\theta+\rho^2\cos^2\theta}} = -\sin\theta\bar{i} + \cos\theta\bar{j} \qquad (4)$$

$$\bar{e}_3 = \bar{e}_z = \frac{\frac{\partial\bar{r}}{\partial z}}{\left|\frac{\partial\bar{r}}{\partial z}\right|} = \bar{k} \qquad (5)$$

Then,

$$\bar{e}_1 \cdot \bar{e}_2 = (\cos\theta\bar{i}+\sin\theta\bar{j}) \cdot (-\sin\theta\bar{i}+\cos\theta\bar{j}) = 0$$

$$\bar{e}_1 \cdot \bar{e}_3 = (\cos\theta\bar{i}+\sin\theta\bar{j}) \cdot \bar{k} = 0 \qquad (6)$$

$$\bar{e}_2 \cdot \bar{e}_3 = (-\sin\theta\bar{i}+\cos\theta\bar{j}) \cdot \bar{k} = 0$$

Since $\bar{e}_1$, $\bar{e}_2$ and $\bar{e}_3$ are mutually perpendicular, the coordinate system is orthogonal.

● PROBLEM 21-10

Represent the vector

$$\bar{F} = 2y\bar{i} - 3x\bar{j} + xz\bar{k} \qquad (1)$$

in cylindrical coordinates.

<u>Solution:</u>   We have to find F_ρ, F_θ and F_z such that

$$\bar{F} = F_\rho \bar{e}_\rho + F_\theta \bar{e}_\theta + F_z \bar{e}_z \qquad (2)$$

The unit mutually perpendicular vectors are

$$\bar{e}_\rho = \cos\theta\bar{i} + \sin\theta\bar{j}$$

$$\bar{e}_\theta = -\sin\theta\bar{i} + \cos\theta\bar{j} \qquad (3)$$

$$\bar{e}_z = \bar{k}$$

From eq.(3), we can find

$$\bar{i} = \cos\theta\bar{e}_\rho - \sin\theta\bar{e}_\theta$$

$$\bar{j} = \sin\theta\bar{e}_\rho + \cos\theta\bar{e}_\theta \qquad (4)$$

$$\bar{k} = \bar{e}_z$$

Since

$$x = \rho\cos\theta$$

$$y = \rho\sin\theta \qquad (5)$$

$$z = z$$

vector $\bar{F}$ can be represented by

$$\bar{F} = 2\rho\sin\theta(\cos\theta\bar{e}_\rho - \sin\theta\bar{e}_\theta)$$

$$- 3\rho\cos\theta(\sin\theta\bar{e}_\rho + \cos\theta\bar{e}_\theta) + \rho\cos\theta z\bar{e}_z$$

$$= (2\rho\sin\theta\cos\theta - 3\rho\sin\theta\cos\theta)\bar{e}_\rho - (2\rho\sin^2\theta + 3\rho\cos^2\theta)\bar{e}_\theta$$

$$+ \rho\cos\theta z\ \bar{e}_z$$

$$= -\rho\sin\theta\cos\theta\bar{e}_\rho - (2\rho + \rho\cos^2\theta)\bar{e}_\theta + \rho\cos\theta z\ \bar{e}_z \qquad (6)$$

Hence

$$F_\rho = -\rho\sin\theta\cos\theta$$

$$F_\theta = -2\rho - \rho\cos^2\theta \qquad (7)$$

$$F_z = \rho\cos\theta z$$

● **PROBLEM 21-11**

Show that $$\dfrac{d\bar{e}_\rho}{dt} = \dfrac{d\theta}{dt}\ \bar{e}_\theta \qquad (1)$$

$$\dfrac{d\bar{e}_\theta}{dt} = -\dfrac{d\theta}{dt}\ \bar{e}_\rho \qquad (2)$$

Solution: Very often (especially in physics) differentiation with respect to time t is denoted by a dot, that is

$$\frac{dx}{dt} = \dot{x}$$

or

$$\frac{d\bar{e}_\rho}{dt} = \dot{\bar{e}}_\rho$$

etc.

We have

$$\bar{e}_\rho = \cos\theta\,\bar{i} + \sin\theta\,\bar{j}$$

$$\bar{e}_\theta = -\sin\theta\,\bar{i} + \cos\theta\,\bar{j} \tag{3}$$

Then,

$$\dot{\bar{e}}_\rho = (-\sin\theta)\dot{\theta}\,\bar{i} + (\cos\theta)\dot{\theta}\,\bar{j}$$

$$= (-\sin\theta\,\bar{i} + \cos\theta\,\bar{j})\dot{\theta} = \dot{\theta}\,\bar{e}_\theta \tag{4}$$

and

$$\dot{\bar{e}}_\theta = (-\cos\theta)\dot{\theta}\,\bar{i} - (\sin\theta)\dot{\theta}\,\bar{j}$$

$$= -(\cos\theta\,\bar{i} + \sin\theta\,\bar{j})\dot{\theta} = -\dot{\theta}\,\bar{e}_\rho \tag{5}$$

● **PROBLEM 21-12**

Express the velocity $\bar{v}$ and acceleration $\bar{a}$ of a particle
in cylindrical coordinates.

Solution: In rectangular coordinates, the position vector
of a particle is

$$\bar{r} = x\bar{i} + y\bar{j} + z\bar{k} \tag{1}$$

The velocity and acceleration vectors are defined as

$$\bar{v} = \frac{d\bar{r}}{dt} = \dot{\bar{r}} = \dot{x}\bar{i} + \dot{y}\bar{j} + \dot{z}\bar{k} \tag{2}$$

$$\bar{a} = \frac{d\bar{v}}{dt} = \frac{d^2\bar{r}}{dt} = \ddot{\bar{r}} = \ddot{x}\bar{i} + \ddot{y}\bar{j} + \ddot{z}\bar{k} \tag{3}$$

In cylindrical coordinates, the unit vectors are

$$\bar{e}_\theta = -\sin\theta\,\bar{i} + \cos\theta\,\bar{j} \tag{4}$$

$$\bar{e}_\rho = \cos\theta\,\bar{i} + \sin\theta\,\bar{j} \tag{5}$$

$$\bar{e}_z = \bar{k} \tag{6}$$

The position vector in cylindrical coordinates is

$$\bar{r} = x\bar{i} + y\bar{j} + z\bar{k} = (\rho\cos\theta)(\cos\theta\bar{e}_\rho - \sin\theta\bar{e}_\theta)$$

$$\tag{7}$$

$$+ (\rho\sin\theta)(\sin\theta\bar{e}_\rho + \cos\theta\bar{e}_\theta) + z\bar{e}_z$$

$$= \rho\bar{e}_\rho + z\bar{e}_z$$

Hence, the velocity vector becomes

$$\bar{v} = \frac{d\bar{r}}{dt} = \dot{\rho}\bar{e}_\rho + \rho\dot{\bar{e}}_\rho + \dot{z}\bar{e}_z = \dot{\rho}\bar{e}_\rho + \rho\dot{\theta}\bar{e}_\theta + \dot{z}\bar{e}_z \qquad (8)$$

and the acceleration vector is

$$\bar{a} = \frac{d^2\bar{r}}{dt} = \frac{d\bar{v}}{dt} = \frac{d}{dt}(\dot{\rho}\bar{e}_\rho + \rho\dot{\theta}\bar{e}_\theta + \dot{z}\bar{e}_z)$$

$$= \ddot{\rho}\bar{e}_\rho + \dot{\rho}\dot{\bar{e}}_\rho + \dot{\rho}\dot{\theta}\bar{e}_\theta + \rho\ddot{\theta}\bar{e}_\theta + \rho\dot{\theta}\dot{\bar{e}}_\theta + \ddot{z}\,\bar{e}_z$$

$$= \dot{\rho}\dot{\theta}\bar{e}_\theta + \ddot{\rho}\bar{e}_\rho + \rho\dot{\theta}(-\dot{\theta}\bar{e}_\rho) + \rho\ddot{\theta}\bar{e}_\theta + \dot{\rho}\dot{\theta}\bar{e}_\theta + \ddot{z}\,\bar{e}_z$$

$$= (\ddot{\rho} - \rho\dot{\theta}^2)\bar{e}_\rho + (\rho\ddot{\theta} + 2\dot{\rho}\dot{\theta})\bar{e}_\theta + \ddot{z}\,\bar{e}_z$$

• **PROBLEM 21-13**

Show on a drawing the directions of the vectors grad z, grad ρ, and grad θ. The unit vectors are

$$\bar{e}_\rho = \frac{\text{grad}\rho}{|\text{grad}\rho|} \qquad (1)$$

$$\bar{e}_\theta = \frac{\text{grad}\theta}{|\text{grad}\theta|} \qquad (2)$$

$$\bar{e}_z = \frac{\text{grad}z}{|\text{grad}z|} \qquad (3)$$

By using the identity

$$|\text{grad }f| = \frac{df}{ds} \qquad (4)$$

simplify equations (1) through (3).

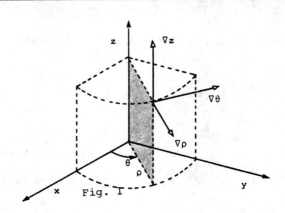

Fig. I

Solution: The vectors grad ρ, grad θ, and grad z are every-where tangent to their respective coordinate curves.

Since $|\text{grad } f| = \dfrac{df}{ds}$ (here s measures distance in the direction of grad f), along the coordinate curves of ρ

$$ds = |d\rho|$$

and

$$|\text{grad } \rho| = \frac{d\rho}{d\rho} = 1 \tag{5}$$

Along the coordinate curves of θ,

$$ds = \rho|d\theta| \tag{6}$$

and

$$|\text{grad } \theta| = \frac{d\theta}{\rho d\theta} = \frac{1}{\rho} \tag{7}$$

Finally, along the coordinate curves of z,

$$ds = |dz|$$

and

$$|\text{grad } z| = \frac{dz}{dz} = 1 \tag{8}$$

Eqs.(1), (2) and (3) can be written in the simplified form

$$\bar{e}_\rho = \text{grad } \rho \tag{9}$$

$$\bar{e}_\theta = \rho \text{ grad } \theta \tag{10}$$

$$\bar{e}_z = \text{grad } z \tag{11}$$

ELEMENT OF ARC LENGTH, VOLUME ELEMENT AND SCALE FACTORS OF THE CYLINDRICAL AND SPHERICAL COORDINATE SYSTEMS

● PROBLEM 21-14

Find the expression for the differential of arc length ds in cylindrical coordinates and determine the corresponding scale factors.

Solution: In general, we have

$$ds^2 = d\bar{r} \cdot d\bar{r} = |d\bar{r}|^2 \tag{1}$$

Let us now find an expression for the differential $d\bar{r}$. The position vector is

$$\bar{r} = x\bar{i} + y\bar{j} + z\bar{k}$$

$$= \rho\cos\theta\bar{i} + \rho\sin\theta\bar{j} + z\bar{k} \qquad (2)$$

Now, the differential $d\bar{r}$ may be written as

$$d\bar{r} = \frac{\partial\bar{r}}{\partial\rho}\,d\rho + \frac{\partial\bar{r}}{\partial\theta}\,d\theta + \frac{\partial\bar{r}}{\partial z}\,dz \qquad (3)$$

From eq.(2), we obtain

$$\frac{\partial\bar{r}}{\partial\rho} = \frac{\partial}{\partial\rho}(\rho\cos\theta\bar{i} + \rho\sin\theta\bar{j} + z\bar{k})$$

$$= \cos\theta\bar{i} + \sin\theta\bar{j} \qquad (4)$$

$$\frac{\partial\bar{r}}{\partial\theta} = \frac{\partial}{\partial\theta}(\rho\cos\theta\bar{i} + \rho\sin\theta\bar{j} + z\bar{k})$$

$$= -\rho\sin\theta\bar{i} + \rho\cos\theta\bar{j} \qquad (5)$$

$$\frac{\partial\bar{r}}{\partial z} = \frac{\partial}{\partial z}(\rho\cos\theta\bar{i} + \rho\sin\theta\bar{j} + z\bar{k}) = \bar{k} \qquad (6)$$

Substituting eqs.(4), (5) and (6) into eq.(3) yields

$$d\bar{r} = (\cos\theta\bar{i} + \sin\theta\bar{j})d\rho + (-\rho\sin\theta\bar{i} + \rho\cos\theta\bar{j})d\theta + \bar{k}\,dz$$

$$= (\cos\theta d\rho - \rho\sin\theta d\theta)\bar{i} + (\sin\theta d\rho + \rho\cos\theta d\theta)\bar{j} + dz\,\bar{k}$$

Substituting this into eq.(1) finally gives us

$$ds^2 = d\bar{r}\cdot d\bar{r} = |d\bar{r}|^2 = (\cos\theta d\rho - \rho\sin\theta d\theta)^2 + (\sin\theta d\rho + \rho\cos\theta d\theta)^2$$

$$+ dz^2$$

$$= (\cos^2\theta + \sin^2\theta)d\rho^2 + (\sin^2\theta + \cos^2\theta)\rho^2 d\theta^2$$

$$-2\rho\sin\theta\cos\theta d\rho d\theta + 2\rho\sin\theta\cos\theta d\rho d\theta + dz^2$$

$$= d\rho^2 + \rho^2 d\theta^2 + dz^2 \qquad (7)$$

Thus, the differential of arc length in cylindrical co-ordinates is

$$ds^2 = d\rho^2 + \rho^2 d\theta^2 + dz^2 \qquad (8)$$

or

$$ds = \sqrt{d\rho^2 + \rho^2 d\theta^2 + dz^2}$$

Note that, of course, $d\rho^2 = (d\rho)^2$, $dz^2 = (dz)^2$..., and so on.

Let us now determine the scale factors for the cylindrical coordinate system.

In general, if $\bar{r} = \bar{r}(u_1, u_2, u_3)$, then the scale factors are

$$h_1 = \left|\frac{\partial\bar{r}}{\partial u_1}\right| \qquad h_2 = \left|\frac{\partial\bar{r}}{\partial u_2}\right| \qquad h_3 = \left|\frac{\partial\bar{r}}{\partial u_3}\right| \qquad (10)$$

Note that the unit tangent vectors to the u_1, u_2 and u_3 curves are

$$\bar{e}_1 = \frac{\frac{\partial \bar{r}}{\partial u_1}}{\left|\frac{\partial \bar{r}}{\partial u_1}\right|} \qquad \bar{e}_2 = \frac{\frac{\partial \bar{r}}{\partial u_2}}{\left|\frac{\partial \bar{r}}{\partial u_2}\right|} \qquad \bar{e}_3 = \frac{\frac{\partial \bar{r}}{\partial u_3}}{\left|\frac{\partial \bar{r}}{\partial u_3}\right|}$$

so that we may write

$$\frac{\partial \bar{r}}{\partial u_1} = h_1 \bar{e}_1, \quad \frac{\partial \bar{r}}{\partial u_2} = h_2 \bar{e}_2, \quad \frac{\partial \bar{r}}{\partial u_3} = h_3 \bar{e}_3$$

Now, for the cylindrical coordinate system, we let $u_1 = \rho$, $u_2 = \theta$, $u_3 = z$.

From eqs.(4), (5) and (6) we obtain

$$h_1 = h_\rho = \left|\frac{\partial \bar{r}}{\partial \rho}\right| = \sqrt{\cos^2\theta + \sin^2\theta} = 1 \qquad (11)$$

$$h_2 = h_\theta = \left|\frac{\partial \bar{r}}{\partial \theta}\right| = \sqrt{(-\rho\sin\theta)^2 + (\rho\cos\theta)^2} = \rho \qquad (12)$$

$$h_3 = h_z = \left|\frac{\partial \bar{r}}{\partial z}\right| = 1 \qquad (13)$$

There is another method of determining arc length in cylindrical coordinates which is perhaps slightly clearer. Since we may write
$$ds^2 = dx^2 + dy^2 + dz^2$$
and since

$$x = \rho\cos\theta \qquad dx = -\rho\sin\theta d\theta + \cos\theta d\rho$$
$$y = \rho\sin\theta \qquad dy = \rho\cos\theta d\theta + \sin\theta d\rho$$
$$z = z \qquad dz = dz$$

we have
$$ds^2 = (-\rho\sin\theta d\theta + \cos\theta d\rho)^2 + (\rho\cos\theta d\theta + \sin\theta d\rho)^2 + dz^2$$

$$= d\rho^2 + \rho^2 d\theta^2 + dz^2 \qquad (14)$$

Also, since

$$ds^2 = \left|\frac{\partial \bar{r}}{\partial \rho}\right|^2 d\rho^2 + \left|\frac{\partial \bar{r}}{\partial \theta}\right|^2 d\theta^2 + \left|\frac{\partial \bar{r}}{\partial z}\right|^2 dz^2$$

$$= h_\rho^2 d\rho^2 + h_\theta^2 d\theta^2 + h_z^2 dz^2 \qquad (15)$$

we conclude (from eqs.(14) and (15)) that

$$h_\rho = 1, \quad h_\theta = \rho, \quad h_z = 1.$$

● **PROBLEM 21-15**

Compute the arc length along the helix

$$x = \sin t$$

$$y = \cos t \qquad (1)$$

$$z = t$$

for $\qquad 0 \le t \le 2\pi$

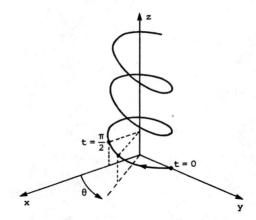

The helix $x = \sin t$, $y = \cos t$, $z = t$

Solution: It is easier to evaluate the arc length by trans-forming to the cylindrical coordinates. Since the rectangu-lar coordinates x, y and z are functions of t, the cylindri-cal coordinates ρ, θ and z will also be functions of t.

Now, we have

$$\rho^2 = x^2 + y^2 = \sin^2 t + \cos^2 t = 1 \qquad (1)$$

and

$$z = t \qquad (2)$$

By referring to the figure, we see that at t = 0, $\theta = \frac{\pi}{2}$ and at $\tau = \frac{\pi}{2}$, $\theta = 0$, so that θ varies with t by

$$\theta = \frac{\pi}{2} - t. \qquad (3)$$

Now, as obtained in problem 21-14, the differential of arc length in cylindrical coordinates is

$$ds = \sqrt{d\rho^2 + \rho^2 d\theta^2 + dz^2} \qquad (4)$$

Note that ρ, θ and z are functions of t, so that it is convenient for us to write

$$ds = \sqrt{\left(\frac{d\rho}{dt}\right)^2 + \rho^2\left(\frac{d\theta}{dt}\right)^2 + \left(\frac{dz}{dt}\right)^2} \; dt \qquad (5)$$

Notice that eqs. (4) and (5) are equivalent, since, of course,

$$ds = \sqrt{\left(\frac{d\rho}{dt}\right)^2 + \rho^2\left(\frac{d\theta}{dt}\right)^2 + \left(\frac{dz}{dt}\right)^2} \; dt$$

$$= \frac{1}{\sqrt{dt^2}} \; \sqrt{d\rho^2 + \rho^2 d\theta^2 + dz^2} \; dt$$

$$= \sqrt{d\rho^2 + \rho^2 d\theta^2 + dz^2}$$

The arc length is thus

$$s = \int_{s_0}^{s_1} ds = \int_{t_0}^{t_1} \sqrt{\left(\frac{d\rho}{dt}\right)^2 + \rho^2 \left(\frac{d\theta}{dt}\right)^2 + \left(\frac{dz}{dt}\right)^2}\ dt \qquad (6)$$

From eqs.(1) – (3), we obtain

$$\frac{d\rho}{dt} = 0 \qquad (7)$$

$$\frac{d\theta}{dt} = -1 \qquad (8)$$

$$\frac{dz}{dt} = 1 \qquad (9)$$

Substituting eqs.(7), (8), (9) and (1) into eq.(6) and noting that $t_0 = 0$ and $t_1 = 2\pi$, we find

$$s = \int_{t=0}^{2\pi} \sqrt{(0)^2 + (1)^2(-1)^2 + (1)^2}\ dt = \int_{t=0}^{2\pi} \sqrt{2}\ dt = 2\sqrt{2}\ \pi$$

● **PROBLEM 21-16**

Sketch a volume element in cylindrical coordinates and find the magnitudes of its edges.

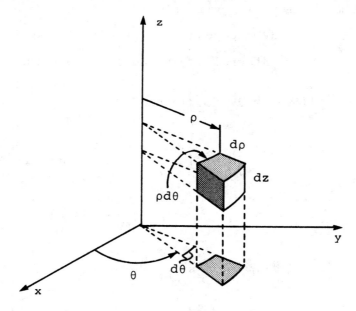

Solution: A volume element in cylindrical coordinates is shown in Fig. 1. The magnitudes of its edges are $\rho d\theta$, $d\rho$ and dz.

Therefore, the volume element is equal to

$$dV = (d\rho)(\rho d\theta)(dz) = \rho d\rho d\theta dz$$

1035

Evaluate the volume integral of the function

$$f(x,y,z) = x^2 + y^2 \tag{1}$$

over the volume contained between the two cylinders $\rho = 1$ and $\rho = 2$ and the two planes $z = 0$ and $z = 3$.

Solution: It is required to evaluate the volume integral

$$\iiint_V (x^2+y^2)dV$$

It is simpler to work in the cylindrical coordinates

$$x = \rho \cos \theta$$

$$y = \rho \sin \theta$$

$$z = z$$

Thus,
$$x^2 + y^2 = \rho^2(\cos^2\theta + \sin^2\theta) = \rho^2$$

The volume element in cylindrical coordinates is

$$dV = \rho d\rho d\theta dz$$

Thus the volume integral in cylindrical coordinates is

$$\iiint_V (x^2+y^2)dV = \iiint_V \rho^2 \rho d\rho d\theta dz$$

$$= \int_{z=0}^{3} \int_{\theta=0}^{2\pi} \int_{\rho=1}^{2} \rho^3 d\rho d\theta dz$$

$$= \frac{15}{4} \int_{z=0}^{3} \int_{\theta=0}^{2\pi} d\theta dz$$

$$= \frac{15\pi}{2} \int_{0}^{3} dz$$

$$= \frac{45\pi}{2}$$

● PROBLEM 21-18

Describe the spherical coordinates and the coordinate surfaces and coordinate curves for this system.

Solution: The spherical coordinates are (r,ϕ,θ), as shown in Fig. 1.

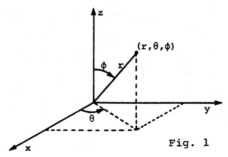

Fig. 1

Here, r is the distance of the point from the origin, θ is the same angle as in the cylindrical coordinate system and ϕ is the angle between the positive z-axis and the position vector $\bar{r}$. It is easy to see that

$$x = r \sin\phi\cos\theta$$
$$y = r \sin\phi\sin\theta \qquad\qquad (1)$$
$$z = r \cos\phi$$

The coordinate surfaces are:

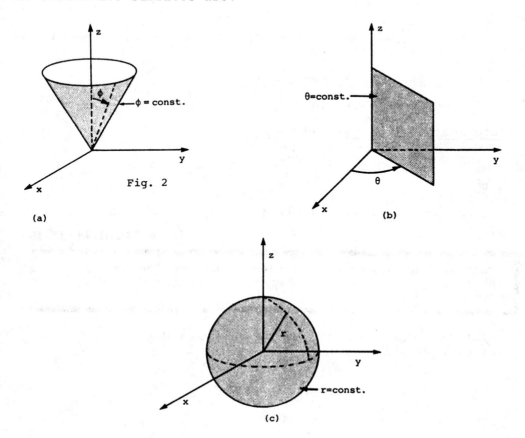

Fig. 2

(a)

(b)

(c)

$\underline{r_1 = a_1 = const}$ spheres with the center at the origin (Fig. 2(c))

$\underline{\phi = a_2 = const}$ cones with the vertex at the origin (Fig. 2(a))

$\underline{\theta = a_3 = const}$ planes (actually half-planes) through the z-axis (Fig. 2(b))

The coordinate surfaces for any set of constants a_1, a_2, a_3 are mutually orthogonal and therefore, the spherical coordinate system is orthogonal (we formally prove this in Problem 21-22).

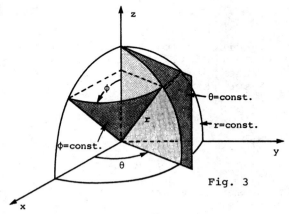

Fig. 3

Now, as can be seen from Fig. 3, we see that the coordinate curves are:

Intersection of $r = a_1$ and $\phi = a_2$

      θ curve is a circle

Intersection of $r = a_1$ and $\theta = a_3$

      ϕ curve is a semi-circle

Intersection of $\phi = a_2$ and $\theta = a_3$

      r curve is a line passing through the origin.

● **PROBLEM** 21-19

Evaluate the square of the element of arc length in spherical coordinates and determine the corresponding scale factors.

<u>Solution</u>: The spherical coordinates are described by the set of equations

$$x = r\,\sin\phi\cos\theta$$

$$y = r\,\sin\phi\sin\theta \qquad\qquad (1)$$

$$z = r\,\cos\phi$$

1038

Then

$$dx = -r\sin\phi\sin\theta d\theta + r\cos\phi\cos\theta d\phi + \sin\phi\cos\theta dr \qquad (2)$$

$$dy = r\sin\phi\cos\theta d\theta + r\cos\phi\sin\theta d\phi + \sin\phi\sin\theta dr$$

$$dz = -r\sin\phi d\phi + \cos\phi dr$$

Therefore

$$ds^2 = dx^2 + dy^2 + dz^2 = dr^2 + r^2 d\phi^2 + r^2\sin^2\phi d\theta^2 \qquad (3)$$

Now, since for any orthogonal curvilinear coordinate system,

$$ds^2 = h_1^2 \, du_1^2 + h_2^2 du_2^2 + h_3^2 du_3^2$$

we see that the scale factors for the spherical coordinates, $u_1 = r$, $u_2 = \phi$, $u_3 = \theta$ are

$$h_1 = h_r = 1, \quad h_2 = h_\phi = r, \quad h_3 = h_\theta = r\sin\phi \qquad (4)$$

● **PROBLEM 21-20**

Determine the transformation from rectangular to spherical coordinates.

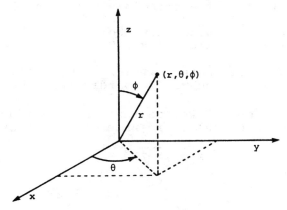

Solution: Given the spherical coordinates (r,ϕ,θ) we can obtain the rectangular coordinates through the transformation equations

$$x = r\sin\phi\cos\theta \qquad (1)$$

$$y = r\sin\phi\sin\theta \qquad (2)$$

$$z = r\cos\phi \qquad (3)$$

This can be easily seen by referring to the figure.
We now wish to find the inverse transformation – the transformation from rectangular to spherical coordinates. We have

$$x^2+y^2+z^2 = r^2\sin^2\phi\cos^2\theta + r^2\sin^2\phi\sin^2\theta + r^2\cos^2\phi$$

$$= r^2\sin^2\phi(\cos^2\theta+\sin^2\theta) + r^2\cos^2\phi$$

$$= r^2(\sin^2\phi+\cos^2\phi)$$

$$= r^2$$

so that

$$r = \sqrt{x^2+y^2+z^2} \tag{4}$$

This we could have easily obtained by simply referring to the figure.

Now, from eqs.(3) and (4), we obtain

$$\phi = \cos^{-1}\frac{z}{\sqrt{x^2+y^2+z^2}} \tag{5}$$

and from eqs.(1) and (2)

$$\text{Tan}\,\theta = \frac{y}{x} \qquad \theta = \text{Tan}^{-1}\frac{y}{x} \tag{6}$$

or

$$\theta = \sin^{-1}\frac{y}{\sqrt{x^2+y^2}} \tag{7}$$

or

$$\theta = \cos^{-1}\frac{x}{\sqrt{x^2+y^2}} \tag{8}$$

It is important to note here that in eq.(5) we restrict the angle ϕ to the principle value range, that is, $0 \le \phi \le \pi$.

It is not necessary, however, to restrict the angle θ to the principal value range, $0 \le \theta \le 2\pi$.

We should note that for $r = 0$, θ and ϕ are not defined. Therefore, in spherical coordinates, the origin must be excluded.

As a whole, we see that the transformation from rectangular to spherical coordinates is given by

$$r = \sqrt{x^2+y^2+z^2}$$

$$\phi = \cos^{-1}\frac{z}{\sqrt{x^2+y^2+z^2}} \qquad 0 \le \phi \le \pi$$

$$\theta = \text{Tan}^{-1}\frac{y}{x} \qquad 0 \le \theta \le 2\pi$$

THE UNIT TANGENT VECTORS OF THE SPHERICAL COORDINATE SYSTEM

● PROBLEM 21-21

Express the unit vectors $\bar{e}_r$, $\bar{e}_\phi$, and $\bar{e}_\theta$ of a spherical coordinate system in terms of $\bar{i}$, $\bar{j}$, and $\bar{k}$.

Solve for $\bar{i}$, $\bar{j}$, and $\bar{k}$ in terms of $\bar{e}_r$, $\bar{e}_\phi$, $\bar{e}_\theta$.

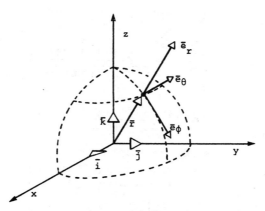

Solution: The spherical coordinates are related to the rectangular coordinates by

$$x = r \sin\phi\cos\theta$$

$$y = r \sin\phi\sin\theta \tag{1}$$

so that

$$z = r \cos\phi$$

$$\begin{aligned}
\bar{r} &= x\bar{i} + y\bar{j} + z\bar{k} \\
&= r\sin\phi\cos\theta\,\bar{i} + r\sin\phi\sin\theta\,\bar{j} + r\cos\phi\,\bar{k}
\end{aligned} \tag{2}$$

and

$$\frac{\partial \bar{r}}{\partial r} = \sin\phi\cos\theta\,\bar{i} + \sin\phi\sin\theta\,\bar{j} + \cos\phi\,\bar{k} \tag{3}$$

$$\frac{\partial \bar{r}}{\partial \phi} = r\cos\phi\cos\theta\,\bar{i} + r\cos\phi\sin\theta\,\bar{j} - r\sin\phi\,\bar{k} \tag{4}$$

$$\frac{\partial \bar{r}}{\partial \theta} = -r\sin\phi\sin\theta\,\bar{i} + r\sin\phi\cos\theta\,\bar{j} \tag{5}$$

Thus,

$$\bar{e}_r = \frac{\dfrac{\partial \bar{r}}{\partial r}}{\left|\dfrac{\partial \bar{r}}{\partial r}\right|} = \frac{\sin\phi\cos\theta\,\bar{i}+\sin\phi\sin\theta\,\bar{j}+\cos\phi\,\bar{k}}{\sqrt{(\sin^2\phi\cos^2\theta)+(\sin^2\phi\sin^2\theta)+\cos^2\phi}}$$

$$= \sin\phi\cos\theta\,\bar{i} + \sin\phi\sin\theta\,\bar{j} + \cos\phi\,\bar{k} \tag{6}$$

Note that

$$\begin{aligned}
\left|\frac{\partial \bar{r}}{\partial r}\right| &= \sqrt{(\sin^2\theta\cos^2\theta) + (\sin^2\phi\sin^2\theta) + \cos^2\phi} \\
&= \sqrt{\sin^2\phi(\cos^2\theta+\sin^2\theta) + \cos^2\phi} \\
&= \sqrt{\sin^2\phi+\cos^2\phi} \\
&= 1
\end{aligned}$$

Continuing, we obtain

$$\bar{e}_\phi = \frac{\dfrac{\partial \bar{r}}{\partial \phi}}{\left|\dfrac{\partial \bar{r}}{\partial \phi}\right|} = \frac{r\cos\phi\cos\theta\,\bar{i}+r\cos\phi\sin\theta\,\bar{j}-r\sin\phi\,\bar{k}}{\sqrt{(r^2\cos^2\phi\cos^2\theta)+r^2\cos^2\phi\sin^2\theta+r^2\sin^2\phi}} \tag{7}$$

1041

$$= \cos\phi\cos\theta\bar{i} + \cos\phi\sin\theta\bar{j} - \sin\phi\bar{k}$$

$$\bar{e}_\theta = \frac{\dfrac{\partial\bar{r}}{\partial\theta}}{\left|\dfrac{\partial\bar{r}}{\partial\theta}\right|} = \frac{-r\sin\phi\sin\theta\bar{i}+r\sin\phi\cos\theta\bar{j}}{\sqrt{r^2\sin^2\phi\sin^2\theta+r^2\sin^2\phi\cos^2\theta}}$$

$$= \frac{-r\sin\phi\sin\theta\bar{i}+r\sin\phi\cos\theta\bar{j}}{r\sin\phi} \tag{8}$$

$$= -\sin\theta\bar{i} + \cos\theta\bar{j}$$

At this point we should mention that for the spherical coordinate system, the scale factors are

$$h_r = \left|\frac{\partial\bar{r}}{\partial r}\right| = 1 \tag{9}$$

$$h_\phi = \left|\frac{\partial\bar{r}}{\partial\phi}\right| = r \tag{10}$$

$$h_\theta = \left|\frac{\partial\bar{r}}{\partial\theta}\right| = r\sin\phi \tag{11}$$

From eqs.(6), (7) and (8) we may solve for $\bar{i}$, $\bar{j}$ and $\bar{k}$ in terms of $\bar{e}_r$, $\bar{e}_\phi$ and $\bar{e}_\theta$.

$$\bar{i} = \sin\phi\cos\theta\bar{e}_r + \cos\phi\cos\theta\bar{e}_\phi - \sin\theta\bar{e}_\theta \tag{12}$$

$$\bar{j} = \sin\phi\sin\theta\bar{e}_r + \cos\phi\sin\theta\bar{e}_\phi + \cos\theta\bar{e}_\theta \tag{13}$$

$$\bar{k} = \cos\phi\bar{e}_r - \sin\phi\bar{e}_\phi \tag{14}$$

The unit tangent vectors $\bar{e}_r$, $\bar{e}_\phi$ and $\bar{e}_\theta$ are shown in the figure.

● PROBLEM 21-22

Show that a spherical coordinate system is orthogonal.

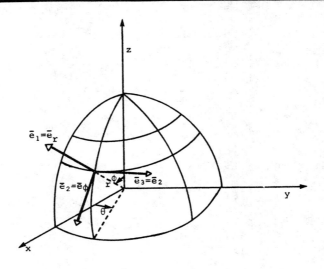

1042

Solution: In general, a curvilinear coordinate system u_1, u_2, u_3 is said to be orthogonal when the coordinate surfaces intersect at right angles. Mathematically, we can prove that such a system is orthogonal by simply showing that the corresponding unit tangent vectors

$$\bar{e}_1 = \frac{\frac{\partial \bar{r}}{\partial u_1}}{\left|\frac{\partial \bar{r}}{\partial u_1}\right|} \quad , \quad \bar{e}_2 = \frac{\frac{\partial \bar{r}}{\partial u_2}}{\left|\frac{\partial \bar{r}}{\partial u_2}\right|} \quad , \quad \bar{e}_3 = \frac{\frac{\partial \bar{r}}{\partial u_3}}{\left|\frac{\partial \bar{r}}{\partial u_3}\right|}$$

are mutually perpendicular.

Thus, a curvilinear coordinate system is orthogonal when

$$\bar{e}_1 \cdot \bar{e}_2 = 0$$
$$\bar{e}_2 \cdot \bar{e}_3 = 0 \tag{1}$$
$$\bar{e}_1 \cdot \bar{e}_3 = 0$$

For the special case of the spherical coordinate system, we may let $u_1 = r$, $u_2 = \phi$, $u_3 = \theta$, and

$$\bar{e}_1 = \bar{e}_r = \frac{\frac{\partial \bar{r}}{\partial r}}{\left|\frac{\partial \bar{r}}{\partial r}\right|} \quad , \quad \bar{e}_2 = \bar{e}_\phi = \frac{\frac{\partial \bar{r}}{\partial \phi}}{\left|\frac{\partial \bar{r}}{\partial \phi}\right|} \quad , \quad \bar{e}_3 = \bar{e}_\theta = \frac{\frac{\partial \bar{r}}{\partial \theta}}{\left|\frac{\partial \bar{r}}{\partial \theta}\right|}$$

The unit tangent vectors $\bar{e}_r$, $\bar{e}_\phi$ and $\bar{e}_\theta$ are shown in the figure.

Now, the spherical coordinates are related to the rectangular coordinates by

$$x = r\sin\phi\cos\theta$$
$$y = r\sin\phi\sin\theta \tag{2}$$
$$z = r\cos\phi$$

so that
$$\bar{r} = x\bar{i} + y\bar{j} + z\bar{k}$$
$$= r\sin\phi\cos\theta\bar{i} + r\sin\phi\sin\theta\bar{j} + r\cos\phi\bar{k}$$

and
$$\frac{\partial \bar{r}}{\partial r} = \sin\phi\cos\theta\bar{i} + \sin\phi\sin\theta\bar{j} + \cos\phi\bar{k} \tag{3}$$

$$\frac{\partial \bar{r}}{\partial \phi} = r\cos\phi\cos\theta\bar{i} + r\cos\phi\sin\theta\bar{j} - r\sin\phi\bar{k} \tag{4}$$

$$\frac{\partial \bar{r}}{\partial \theta} = -r\sin\phi\sin\theta\bar{i} + r\sin\phi\cos\theta\bar{j} \tag{5}$$

Thus,
$$\bar{e}_1 = \bar{e}_r = \frac{\frac{\partial \bar{r}}{\partial r}}{\left|\frac{\partial \bar{r}}{\partial r}\right|} = \frac{\sin\phi\cos\theta\bar{i} + \sin\phi\sin\theta\bar{j} + \cos\phi\bar{k}}{\sqrt{(\sin^2\phi\cos^2\theta) + (\sin^2\phi\sin^2\theta) + \cos^2\phi}}$$

$$= \sin\phi\cos\theta\bar{i} + \sin\phi\sin\theta\bar{j} + \cos\phi\bar{k} \tag{6}$$

$$\bar{e}_2 = \bar{e}_\phi = \frac{\frac{\partial \bar{r}}{\partial \phi}}{\left|\frac{\partial \bar{r}}{\partial \phi}\right|} = \cos\phi\cos\theta\bar{i} + \cos\phi\sin\theta\bar{j} - \sin\phi\bar{k} \qquad (7)$$

$$\bar{e}_3 = \bar{e}_\theta = \frac{\frac{\partial \bar{r}}{\partial \theta}}{\left|\frac{\partial \bar{r}}{\partial \theta}\right|} = -\sin\theta\bar{i} + \cos\theta\bar{j} \qquad (8)$$

Therefore, from eqs.(6), (7) and (8), we find

$$\bar{e}_r \cdot \bar{e}_\theta = -\sin\phi\sin\theta\cos\theta + \sin\phi\sin\theta\cos\theta = 0 \qquad (9)$$

$$\bar{e}_\phi \cdot \bar{e}_\theta = -\sin\theta\cos\phi\cos\theta + \sin\theta\cos\phi\cos\theta = 0 \qquad (10)$$

$$\bar{e}_r \cdot \bar{e}_\phi = \sin\phi\cos\phi\cos^2\theta + \sin\phi\cos\phi\sin^2\theta - \sin\phi\cos\phi$$

$$= (\sin^2\theta + \cos^2\theta)\sin\phi\cos\phi - \sin\phi\cos\phi \qquad (11)$$

$$= \sin\phi\cos\phi - \sin\phi\cos\phi = 0$$

From eqs.(9) through (11), we conclude that the spherical coordinate system is orthogonal. The vectors $\bar{e}_r$, $\bar{e}_\phi$, $\bar{e}_\theta$ form a right-handed system of vectors, as shown in the figure.

● **PROBLEM 21-23**

Represent the vector

$$\bar{F} = 3y\bar{i} - 2z\bar{j} + 2x\bar{k} \qquad (1)$$

in spherical coordinates.

Solution: The vectors $\bar{e}_r$, $\bar{e}_\phi$, and $\bar{e}_\theta$ form a system of mutually orthogonal unit vectors. Thus, they can be used as a base for the three-dimensional vector space.

$$\bar{F} = F_r\bar{e}_r + F_\phi\bar{e}_\phi + F_\theta\bar{e}_\theta \qquad (2)$$

Since the relationship between the spherical and rectangular coordinates is

$$x = r\sin\phi\cos\theta$$

$$y = r\sin\phi\sin\theta \qquad (3)$$

$$z = r\cos\phi$$

and since the unit vectors $\bar{i}$, $\bar{j}$ and $\bar{k}$ are related to $\bar{e}_r$, $\bar{e}_\phi$ and $\bar{e}_\theta$ by

$$\bar{i} = \sin\phi\cos\theta\bar{e}_r + \cos\phi\cos\theta\bar{e}_\phi - \sin\theta\bar{e}_\theta \qquad (4)$$

$$\bar{j} = \sin\phi\sin\theta\,\bar{e}_r + \cos\phi\sin\theta\,\bar{e}_\phi + \cos\theta\,\bar{e}_\theta \qquad (5)$$

$$\bar{k} = \cos\phi\,\bar{e}_r - \sin\phi\,\bar{e}_\phi \qquad (6)$$

we see that we may write

$$\bar{F} = 3y\bar{i} - 2z\bar{j} + 2x\bar{k}$$

$$= 3r\sin\phi\sin\theta(\sin\phi\cos\theta\,\bar{e}_r + \cos\phi\cos\theta\,\bar{e}_\phi - \sin\theta\,\bar{e}_\theta)$$

$$- 2r\cos\phi(\sin\phi\sin\theta\,\bar{e}_r + \cos\phi\sin\theta\,\bar{e}_\phi + \cos\theta\,\bar{e}_\theta)$$

$$+ 2r\sin\phi\cos\theta(\cos\phi\,\bar{e}_r - \sin\phi\,\bar{e}_\phi)$$

$$= \Big[3r\sin^2\phi\sin\theta\cos\theta - 2r\cos\phi\sin\phi\sin\theta$$
$$+ 2r\sin\phi\cos\phi\cos\theta\Big]\bar{e}_r$$

$$+ \Big[3r\sin\phi\sin\theta\cos\phi\cos\theta - 2r\cos^2\phi\sin\theta$$
$$- 2r\sin^2\phi\cos\theta\Big]\bar{e}_\phi \qquad (7)$$

$$- \Big[3r\sin\phi\sin^2\theta + 2r\cos\phi\cos\theta\Big]\bar{e}_\theta$$

By comparing eqs. (7) and (2) we can evaluate the coefficients F_r, F_ϕ, F_θ.

$$F_r = 3r\sin^2\phi\sin\theta\cos\theta - 2r\sin\phi\cos\phi\sin\theta + 2r\sin\phi\cos\phi\cos\theta \qquad (8)$$

$$F_\phi = 3r\sin\phi\cos\phi\sin\theta\cos\theta - 2r\cos^2\phi\sin\theta - 2r\sin^2\phi\cos\theta \qquad (9)$$

$$F_\theta = -3r\sin\phi\sin^2\theta - 2r\cos\phi\cos\theta \qquad (10)$$

● **PROBLEM 21-24**

Prove the relationships

$$\dot{\bar{e}}_r = \dot{\phi}\,\bar{e}_\phi + \sin\phi\,\dot{\theta}\,\bar{e}_\theta \qquad (1)$$

$$\dot{\bar{e}}_\phi = -\dot{\phi}\,\bar{e}_r + \cos\phi\,\dot{\theta}\,\bar{e}_\theta \qquad (2)$$

$$\dot{\bar{e}}_\theta = -\sin\phi\,\dot{\theta}\,\bar{e}_r - \cos\phi\,\dot{\theta}\,\bar{e}_\phi \qquad (3)$$

Solution: The vectors $\bar{e}_r$, $\bar{e}_\phi$, and $\bar{e}_\theta$ are given by

$$\bar{e}_r = \sin\phi\cos\theta\,\bar{i} + \sin\phi\sin\theta\,\bar{j} + \cos\phi\,\bar{k} \qquad (4)$$

$$\bar{e}_\phi = \cos\phi\cos\theta\,\bar{i} + \cos\phi\sin\theta\,\bar{j} - \sin\phi\,\bar{k} \qquad (5)$$

$$\bar{e}_\theta = -\sin\theta\,\bar{i} + \cos\theta\,\bar{j} \qquad (6)$$

Differentiating eq.(4) with respect to time we obtain

$$\dot{\bar{e}}_r = (\cos\phi\dot\phi\cos\theta - \sin\phi\sin\theta\dot\theta)\bar{i} + (\cos\phi\dot\phi\sin\theta + \sin\phi\cos\theta\dot\theta)\bar{j} - \sin\phi\dot\phi\bar{k}$$

$$= \dot\phi(\cos\phi\cos\theta\bar{i} + \cos\phi\sin\theta\bar{j} - \sin\phi\bar{k}) + \sin\phi\dot\theta(-\sin\theta\bar{i} + \cos\theta\bar{j})$$

$$= \dot\phi\ \bar{e}_\phi + \sin\phi\dot\theta\ \bar{e}_\theta \tag{7}$$

Differentiating eq.(5) with respect to time we find

$$\dot{\bar{e}}_\phi = (-\sin\phi\dot\phi\cos\theta - \cos\phi\sin\theta\dot\theta)\bar{i} + (-\sin\phi\dot\phi\sin\theta + \cos\phi\cos\theta\dot\theta)\bar{j}$$
$$- \cos\phi\dot\phi\bar{k}$$

$$= -\dot\phi(\sin\phi\cos\theta\bar{i} + \sin\phi\sin\theta\bar{j} + \cos\phi\bar{k}) + \cos\phi\dot\theta(-\sin\theta\bar{i} + \cos\theta\bar{j})$$

$$= -\dot\phi\bar{e}_r + \cos\phi\dot\theta\ \bar{e}_\theta \tag{8}$$

Now, differentiating eq.(6), we get

$$\dot{\bar{e}}_\theta = -\cos\theta\dot\theta\bar{i} - \sin\theta\dot\theta\bar{j} \tag{9}$$

$$= -\dot\theta(\cos\theta\bar{i} + \sin\theta\bar{j})$$

We may write

$$\cos\theta\bar{i} + \sin\theta\bar{j} = \sin\phi(\sin\phi\cos\theta\bar{i} + \sin\phi\sin\theta\bar{j} + \cos\phi\bar{k})$$

$$+ \cos\phi(\cos\phi\cos\theta\bar{i} + \cos\phi\sin\theta\bar{j} - \sin\phi\bar{k})$$

$$= \sin\phi\bar{e}_r + \cos\phi\bar{e}_\phi$$

so that eq.(9) can be written

$$\dot{\bar{e}}_\theta = -\dot\theta(\sin\phi\bar{e}_r + \cos\phi\bar{e}_\phi) \tag{10}$$

$$= -\sin\phi\dot\theta\ \bar{e}_r - \cos\phi\dot\theta\ \bar{e}_\phi$$

● **PROBLEM 21-25**

Express the velocity $\bar{v}$ and acceleration $\bar{a}$ of a particle in spherical coordinates.

Solution: The velocity of a particle is given by

$$\bar{v} = \frac{d\bar{r}}{dt} = \frac{d}{dt}(x\bar{i} + y\bar{j} + z\bar{k})$$

$$= \frac{d}{dt}(r\sin\phi\cos\theta)\bar{i} + \frac{d}{dt}(r\sin\phi\sin\theta)\bar{j} + \frac{d}{dt}(r\cos\phi)\bar{k} \tag{1}$$

Differentiating with respect to time and introducing vectors $\bar{e}_r$, $\bar{e}_\phi$ and $\bar{e}_\theta$, we obtain

$$\bar{v} = (\dot{r}\sin\phi\cos\theta + r\cos\phi\cos\theta\dot\phi - r\sin\phi\sin\theta\dot\theta)\bar{i}$$

$$+ (r\sin\phi\sin\theta + r\cos\phi\dot\phi\sin\theta + r\sin\phi\cos\theta\dot\theta)\bar{j}$$

$$+ (r\cos\phi - r\sin\phi\dot\phi)\bar{k} \qquad (2)$$

$$= \dot{r}\,\bar{e}_r + r\dot\phi\,\bar{e}_\phi + r\sin\phi\dot\theta\,\bar{e}_\theta$$

To express the acceleration $\bar{a}$ in spherical coordinates, let us note that

$$\bar{a} = \ddot{\bar{r}} = \dot{\bar{v}} = \ddot{r}\,\bar{e}_r + \dot{r}\,\dot{\bar{e}}_r + \dot{r}\dot\phi\,\bar{e}_\phi + r\ddot\phi\,\bar{e}_\phi$$

$$+ r\dot\phi\,\dot{\bar{e}}_\phi + \dot{r}\sin\phi\dot\theta\,\bar{e}_\theta + r\cos\phi\dot\phi\dot\theta\,\bar{e}_\theta \qquad (3)$$

$$+ r\sin\phi\ddot\theta\,\bar{e}_\theta + r\sin\phi\dot\theta\,\dot{\bar{e}}_\theta$$

Expressing the vectors $\dot{\bar{e}}_r$, $\dot{\bar{e}}_\phi$, and $\dot{\bar{e}}_\theta$ in terms of the vectors $\bar{e}_r$, $\bar{e}_\phi$ and $\bar{e}_\theta$, we find

$$\bar{a} = a_r\bar{e}_r + a_\phi\bar{e}_\phi + a_\theta\bar{e}_\theta \qquad (4)$$

where

$$a_r = \ddot{r} - r\dot\phi^2 - r\sin^2\phi\,\dot\theta^2 \qquad (5)$$

$$a_\phi = 2\dot{r}\dot\phi + r\ddot\phi - r\sin\phi\cos\phi\,\dot\theta^2 \qquad (6)$$

$$a_\theta = 2\dot{r}\dot\theta\sin\phi + 2r\dot\phi\dot\theta\cos\phi + r\sin\phi\,\ddot\theta \qquad (7)$$

● **PROBLEM 21-26**

For the system of spherical coordinates, evaluate the vectors $\bar{e}_r$, $\bar{e}_\phi$ and $\bar{e}_\theta$.

Solution: We define a set of unit vectors

$$\bar{e}_r = \frac{\text{grad } r}{|\text{grad } r|} \qquad (1)$$

$$\bar{e}_\phi = \frac{\text{grad } \phi}{|\text{grad } \phi|} \qquad (2)$$

$$\bar{e}_\theta = \frac{\text{grad } \theta}{|\text{grad } \theta|} \qquad (3)$$

These vectors are tangent to their respective coordinate curves and are also mutually orthogonal.

The vectors $\bar{e}_r$, $\bar{e}_\phi$, $\bar{e}_\theta$, in that order, form a right-handed system (see the figure of Problem 21-22). Since

$\left|\text{grad } f\right| = \dfrac{df}{ds}$ we can write eqs.(1)-(3) in a new form.

Along the coordinate curves of r, $\left|dr\right| = ds$ and

$$\bar{e}_r = \frac{\text{grad } r}{\dfrac{dr}{ds}} = \text{grad } r \tag{4}$$

The coordinate curves of ϕ are semicircles of radius r, and since $ds = \left|rd\phi\right|$, we obtain

$$\bar{e}_\phi = \frac{\text{grad } \phi}{\dfrac{d\phi}{ds}} = r \text{ grad } \phi \tag{5}$$

The coordinate curves of θ are circles of radius $r\sin\phi$, hence

$$ds = \left|r\sin\phi d\theta\right| \tag{6}$$

$$\bar{e}_\theta = \frac{\text{grad } \theta}{\dfrac{d\theta}{ds}} = r\sin\phi \text{grad}\theta \tag{7}$$

VOLUME ELEMENT IN SPHERICAL, CYLINDRICAL AND CURVILINEAR COORDINATES

● **PROBLEM** 21-27

Evaluate the element of arc length and the volume element in spherical coordinates.

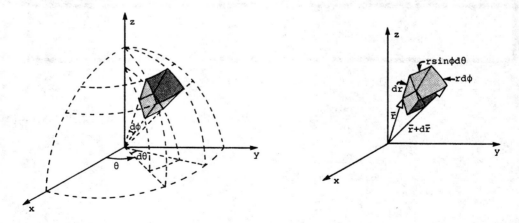

Solution: Let us note that the position vector in spherical coordinates is

$$\bar{r} = r \bar{e}_r \tag{1}$$

The displacement vector $d\bar{r}$ can be expressed as

$$d\bar{r} = \bar{e}_r dr + \bar{e}_\phi rd\phi + \bar{e}_\theta rsin\phi d\theta \tag{2}$$

(refer to Fig. 1).

Thus, the element of arc length in spherical coordinates is

$$ds = |d\bar{r}| = (d\bar{r} \cdot d\bar{r})^{\frac{1}{2}}$$

$$= (\bar{e}_r \cdot \bar{e}_r dr^2 + \bar{e}_\phi \cdot \bar{e}_\phi r^2 d\phi^2 + \bar{e}_\theta \cdot \bar{e}_\theta r^2 sin^2\phi d\theta^2)^{\frac{1}{2}}$$

$$= \sqrt{dr^2 + r^2 d\phi^2 + r^2 sin^2\phi d\theta^2} \tag{3}$$

Note that the vectors $\bar{e}_r$, $\bar{e}_\phi$ and $\bar{e}_\theta$ are unit vectors that are mutually orthogonal:

$$\bar{e}_r \cdot \bar{e}_r = \bar{e}_\phi \cdot \bar{e}_\phi = \bar{e}_\theta \cdot \bar{e}_\theta = 1 \tag{4}$$

$$\bar{e}_r \cdot \bar{e}_\phi = \bar{e}_r \cdot \bar{e}_\theta = \bar{e}_\phi \cdot \bar{e}_\theta = 0 \tag{5}$$

From Fig. 1 we see that the volume element in spherical coordinates is given by

$$dV = (dr)(rd\phi)(rsin\phi d\theta)$$

$$= r^2 sin\phi dr d\phi d\theta \tag{6}$$

● **PROBLEM** 21-28

Evaluate

$$\iiint (x^2+y^2+z^2)^{\frac{3}{2}} dxdydz \tag{1}$$

integrated over that part of a sphere of radius 3 for which $y > 0$ and $z > 0$.

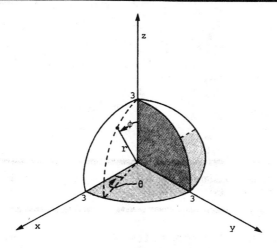

Solution: Whenever any sort of spherical symmetry exists, it is usually most convenient to work in spherical coordinates.

Just by simple inspection of integral (1), it is clear that spherical coordinates would be helpful, since

$$(x^2+y^2+z^2)^{\frac{3}{2}} = r^3 \tag{2}$$

Now, the volume element in spherical coordinates is
$$dV = dxdydz = r^2\sin\phi\, dr d\phi d\theta \tag{3}$$
Thus, the volume integral (1) may be written

$$\iiint_V r^3(r^2\sin\phi\, dr d\phi d\theta) = \iiint_V r^5\sin\phi\, dr d\phi d\theta$$

Now, we are dealing with a quarter of a sphere such that $y > 0$ and $z > 0$, as shown in Fig. 1.

The limits of integration are

$$r \quad \text{from} \quad r = 0 \quad \text{to} \quad 3$$

$$\phi \quad \text{from} \quad \phi = 0 \quad \text{to} \quad \frac{\pi}{2}$$

$$\theta \quad \text{from} \quad \theta = 0 \quad \text{to} \quad \pi$$

Thus, the volume integral is

$$\iiint (x^2+y^2+z^2)^{\frac{3}{2}}\, dxdydz = \int_{r=0}^{3}\int_{\theta=0}^{\pi}\int_{\phi=0}^{\frac{1}{2}\pi} r^5\sin\phi\, d\phi d\theta dr$$

$$= \int_{r=0}^{3}\int_{\theta=0}^{\pi} r^5\left[-\cos\phi\right]\Big|_0^{\frac{1}{2}\pi} d\theta dr$$

$$= \int_{r=0}^{3}\int_{\theta=0}^{\pi} r^5 d\theta dr$$

$$= \pi \int_{r=0}^{3} r^5 dr$$

$$= \pi \left.\frac{r^6}{6}\right|_0^3 = \frac{243}{2}\pi$$

● **PROBLEM 21-29**

Evaluate the volume element dV for an orthogonal curvilinear coordinate system.

Solution: Let the position vector of a point P be
$$\bar{r} = \bar{r}(u_1, u_2, u_3) \tag{1}$$

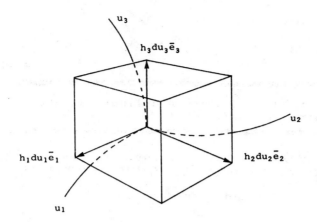

Then

$$d\overline{r} = \frac{\partial \overline{r}}{\partial u_1} du_1 + \frac{\partial \overline{r}}{\partial u_2} du_2 + \frac{\partial \overline{r}}{\partial u_3} du_3 \qquad (2)$$

Since

$$h_1\overline{e}_1 = \frac{\partial \overline{r}}{\partial u_1}, \quad h_2\overline{e}_2 = \frac{\partial \overline{r}}{\partial u_2}, \quad h_3\overline{e}_3 = \frac{\partial \overline{r}}{\partial u_3} \qquad (3)$$

eq.(2) can be written

$$d\overline{r} = h_1 du_1 \overline{e}_1 + h_2 du_2 \overline{e}_2 + h_3 du_3 \overline{e}_3 \qquad (4)$$

The differential of the arc length ds is evaluated from

$$ds^2 = d\overline{r} \cdot d\overline{r} \qquad (5)$$

For orthogonal systems

$$\overline{e}_1 \cdot \overline{e}_2 = \overline{e}_1 \cdot \overline{e}_3 = \overline{e}_2 \cdot \overline{e}_3 = 0 \qquad (6)$$

and

$$ds^2 = h_1^2 du_1^2 + h_2^2 du_2^2 + h_3^2 du_3^2 \qquad (7)$$

Now, let us note that along the u_1 curve, u_2 and u_3 are constant, and thus,

$$d\overline{r} = h_1 du_1 \overline{e}_1 \qquad (8)$$

along this curve.

Therefore, along the u_1 curve, the differential of arc length is

$$ds_1 = d\overline{r} \cdot d\overline{r} = |d\overline{r}| = h_1 du_1$$

Similarly, the differential of arc length along the u_2 and u_3 curves are $ds_2 = h_2 du_2$ and $ds_3 = h_3 du_3$, respectively. Consider the volume element shown in Fig. 1.

The volume of this parallelepiped is

$$dV = |(h_1 du_1 \overline{e}_1) \cdot (h_2 du_2 \overline{e}_2) \times (h_3 du_3 \overline{e}_3)|$$

$$= h_1 h_2 h_3 du_1 du_2 du_3 \qquad (9)$$

Note that

1051

$$|\overline{e}_1 \cdot \overline{e}_2 \times \overline{e}_3| = 1$$

since $$\overline{e}_2 \times \overline{e}_3 = \overline{e}_1$$

(10)

● **PROBLEM 21-30**

Find the volume element in cylindrical and in spherical coordinates.

Solution: In general, for any orthogonal curvilinear coordinate system u_1, u_2, u_3, the volume element is

$$dV = h_1 h_2 h_3 du_1 du_2 du_3$$

where

$$h_1 = \left|\frac{\partial \overline{r}}{\partial u_1}\right| \quad h_2 = \left|\frac{\partial \overline{r}}{\partial u_2}\right| \quad h_3 = \left|\frac{\partial \overline{r}}{\partial u_3}\right|$$

are the scale factors.

Both the cylindrical and the spherical coordinate systems are orthogonal.

For the cylindrical coordinate system,

$$u_1 = \rho \quad u_2 = \theta \quad u_3 = z$$

and, as determined in Problem 21-14 (eqs.(11) through (13)),

$$h_1 = h_\rho = \left|\frac{\partial \overline{r}}{\partial \rho}\right| = 1$$

$$h_2 = h_\theta = \left|\frac{\partial \overline{r}}{\partial \theta}\right| = \rho$$

$$h_3 = h_z = \left|\frac{\partial \overline{r}}{\partial z}\right| = 1$$

Therefore, the volume element in cylindrical coordinates is

$$dV = h_1 h_2 h_3 du_1 du_2 du_3$$

$$= h_\rho h_\theta h_z d\rho d\theta dz$$

$$= \rho d\rho d\theta dz$$

Now, for the spherical coordinate system,

$$u_1 = r \quad u_2 = \phi \quad u_3 = \theta$$

and, as determined in Problem 21-21 (eqs.(9) through (11)),

$$h_1 = h_r = \left|\frac{\partial \overline{r}}{\partial r}\right| = 1$$

$$h_2 = h_\phi = \left|\frac{\partial \overline{r}}{\partial \phi}\right| = r$$

$$h_3 = h_\theta = \left|\frac{\partial \overline{r}}{\partial \theta}\right| = r\sin\phi$$

Hence, the volume element in spherical coordinates is

$$dV = h_r h_\phi h_\theta dr d\phi d\theta$$

$$= r^2 \sin\phi dr d\phi d\theta$$

● **PROBLEM** 21-31

Evaluate the moment of inertia with respect to the origin of a sphere of radius a centered at the origin.

Assume that the sphere is of unit density.

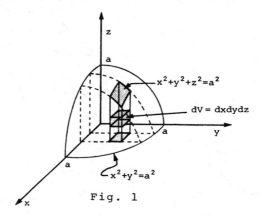

Fig. 1

Solution: In general, the moment of inertia I with respect to a point (chosen to be the origin) of a solid is

$$I = \iiint_V \rho (x^2 + y^2 + z^2) dx dy dz$$

Here $\bar{\rho} = \bar{\rho}(x,y,z)$ represents the density of the solid.

For our case, the solid is a sphere of unit density $\rho = 1$.

Thus, it is required to evaluate the volume integral

$$I = \iiint_V (x^2 + y^2 + z^2) dx dy dz \qquad (1)$$

Let us evaluate this integral in the first octant and then multiply the result by 8 (see Fig. 1).
We have

$$I = 8 \int_{x=0}^{a} \int_{y=0}^{\sqrt{a^2-x^2}} \int_{z=0}^{\sqrt{a^2-x^2-y^2}} (x^2 + y^2 + z^2) dz dy dx \qquad (2)$$

Carrying out the above integration is quite tedious. It is convenient to use spherical coordinates.

1053

Indeed, in spherical coordinates

$$x^2 + y^2 + z^2 = r^2 \qquad (3)$$

The volume element is

$$dV = dxdydz = r^2 \sin\phi \, dr d\theta d\phi \qquad (4)$$

as shown in Fig. 2.

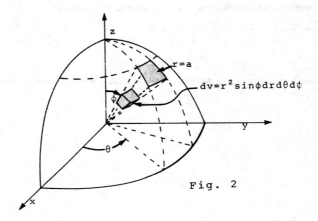

Fig. 2

We find,

$$I = 8 \int_{\theta=0}^{\frac{\pi}{2}} \int_{\phi=0}^{\frac{\pi}{2}} \int_{r=0}^{a} r^2 \cdot r^2 \sin\phi \, dr d\phi d\theta$$

$$= 8 \int_{\theta=0}^{\frac{\pi}{2}} \int_{\phi=0}^{\frac{\pi}{2}} \left[\frac{r^5}{5} \right] \Big|_{r=0}^{a} \sin\phi \, d\phi d\theta \qquad (5)$$

$$= \frac{8a^5}{5} \int_{\theta=0}^{\frac{\pi}{2}} (-\cos\phi) \Big|_{\phi=0}^{\frac{\pi}{2}} d\theta$$

$$= \frac{8a^5}{5} \int_{\theta=0}^{\frac{\pi}{2}} d\theta = \frac{4\pi a^5}{5}$$

It is interesting to note that in general, upon transforming a multiple integral from rectangular to orthogonal curvilinear coordinates, the volume element $dV = dxdydz$ is replaced by

$$\frac{\partial(x,y,z)}{\partial(u_1,u_2,u_3)} \, du_1 du_2 du_3 = h_1 h_2 h_3 du_1 du_2 du_3 \ .$$

That is,

$$\iiint_V f(x,y,z)dxdydz = \iiint_V g(u_1,u_2,u_3) \frac{\partial(x,y,z)}{\partial(u_1,u_2,u_3)} du_1 du_2 du_3$$

or

$$\iiint_V f(x,y,z)dxdydz = \iiint_V g(u_1,u_2,u_3) h_1 h_2 h_3 du_1 du_2 du_3$$

where
$$f(x(u_1,u_2,u_3),y(u_1,u_2,u_3),z(u_1,u_2,u_3)) = g(u_1,u_2,u_3)$$

● **PROBLEM** 21-32

Evaluate

$$\iiint_V \sqrt{x^2+y^2}\ dxdydz \qquad (1)$$

where V is the region bounded by the intersection of the surfaces
$$z = x^2+y^2$$
and
$$z = 4 - (x^2+y^2)$$

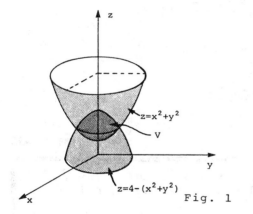

Fig. 1

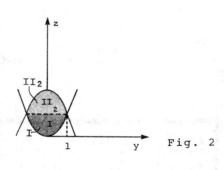

Fig. 2

Solution: The region V is shown in Fig. 1. It is easier to evaluate integral (1) in cylindrical coordinates.

In cylindrical coordinates,

$$\sqrt{x^2+y^2} = \rho^2 \qquad (2)$$
and
$$dV = \rho\, d\rho\, d\theta\, dz \qquad (3)$$

Now, let us refer to Fig. 2, which illustrates the projection of the solid V onto the yz-plane.

We may write

$$\iiint_V \sqrt{x^2+y^2}\ dxdydz = \iiint_V \rho^2\, d\rho\, d\theta\, dz$$

$$= \iiint_I \rho^2\, d\rho\, d\theta\, dz + \iiint_{II} \rho^2\, d\rho\, d\theta\, dz$$

$$= \int_{z=0}^{2} \int_{\theta=0}^{2\pi} \int_{\rho=0}^{\sqrt{z}} \rho^2\, d\rho\, d\theta\, dz$$

1055

$$+ \int_{z=2}^{4} \int_{\theta=0}^{2\pi} \int_{\rho=0}^{\sqrt{4-z}} \rho^2 \, d\rho \, d\theta \, dz \qquad (4)$$

$$= 2\pi \int_{z=0}^{2} \left[\frac{\rho^3}{3} \Big|_0^{\sqrt{z}} \right] dz + 2\pi \int_{z=2}^{4} \left[\frac{\rho^3}{3} \Big|_0^{\sqrt{4-z}} \right] dz$$

$$= \frac{2\pi}{3} \int_0^2 z^{\frac{3}{2}} \, dz + \frac{2\pi}{3} \int_2^4 (4-z)^{\frac{3}{2}} \, dz$$

To evaluate the last integral, we shall note that

$$\int (a+bz)^{\frac{h}{2}} \, dz = \frac{2(a+bz)^{\frac{2+n}{2}}}{b(2+n)} \qquad (5)$$

We obtain

$$\frac{2\pi}{3} \left[\frac{2z^{\frac{5}{2}}}{5} \Big|_0^2 \right] + \frac{2\pi}{3} \left[\frac{-2(4-z)^{\frac{5}{2}}}{5} \Big|_2^4 \right]$$

$$\qquad (6)$$

$$= \frac{32\sqrt{2}\pi}{15}$$

so that

$$\iiint_V \sqrt{x^2+y^2} \, dx\,dy\,dz = \frac{32\sqrt{2}}{15} \pi$$

● **PROBLEM** 21-33

Let (u_1, u_2, u_3) be a system of orthogonal curvilinear coordinates. Show that the Jacobian of the transformation $\bar{r} = \bar{r}(u_1, u_2, u_3)$ is

$$J\left(\frac{x,y,z}{u_1,u_2,u_3}\right) = \frac{\partial(x,y,z)}{\partial(u_1,u_2,u_3)} = h_1 h_2 h_3 \qquad (1)$$

Solution: By definition, the Jacobian is equal to

$$J\left(\frac{x,y,z}{u_1,u_2,u_3}\right) = \begin{vmatrix} \dfrac{\partial x}{\partial u_1} & \dfrac{\partial y}{\partial u_1} & \dfrac{\partial z}{\partial u_1} \\[2mm] \dfrac{\partial x}{\partial u_2} & \dfrac{\partial y}{\partial u_2} & \dfrac{\partial z}{\partial u_2} \\[2mm] \dfrac{\partial x}{\partial u_3} & \dfrac{\partial y}{\partial u_3} & \dfrac{\partial z}{\partial u_3} \end{vmatrix} \qquad (2)$$

On the other hand, the determinant in eq.(2) can be expressed in the form

$$\left(\frac{\partial x}{\partial u_1}\bar{i} + \frac{\partial y}{\partial u_1}\bar{j} + \frac{\partial z}{\partial u_1}\bar{k} \right) \cdot \left[\left(\frac{\partial x}{\partial u_2}\bar{i} + \frac{\partial y}{\partial u_2}\bar{j} + \frac{\partial z}{\partial u_2}\bar{k} \right) \cdot \left(\frac{\partial x}{\partial u_3}\bar{i} + \frac{\partial y}{\partial u_3}\bar{j} + \frac{\partial z}{\partial u_3}\bar{k} \right) \right]$$

$$= \frac{\partial \bar{r}}{\partial u_1} \cdot \frac{\partial \bar{r}}{\partial u_2} \times \frac{\partial \bar{r}}{\partial u_3} = h_1\bar{e}_1 \cdot h_2\bar{e}_2 \times h_3\bar{e}_3$$

1056

$$= h_1h_2h_3\overline{e}_1 \cdot \overline{e}_2 \times \overline{e}_3$$

$$= h_1h_2h_3$$

Note that $\overline{e}_1$, $\overline{e}_2$ and $\overline{e}_3$ are mutually orthogonal unit vectors that form a right-hand system of vectors and therefore $\overline{e}_1 \cdot \overline{e}_2 \times \overline{e}_3 = 1$.

Thus

$$J\left(\frac{x,y,z}{u_1,u_2,u_3}\right) = h_1h_2h_3 \tag{3}$$

Note that eq.(3) only holds true when u_1,u_2,u_3 is an orthogonal system. Also note that the Jacobian must be different from zero.

$$J\left(\frac{x,y,z}{u_1,u_2,u_3}\right) = h_1h_2h_3 \neq 0.$$

THE GRADIENT, DIVERGENCE, CURL, LAPLACIAN AND JACOBIAN IN CYLINDRICAL AND SPHERICAL COORDINATES

● PROBLEM 21-34

Evaluate the Jacobian

$$J\left(\frac{x,y,z}{u_1,u_2,u_3}\right)$$

of the transformation to

1. cylindrical coordinates

2. spherical coordinates.

Solution: In general, for a transformation
$$x = x(u_1,u_2,u_3)$$

$$y = y(u_1,u_2,u_3)$$

$$z = z(u_1,u_2,u_3)$$
the Jacobian is defined as

$$J\frac{(x,y,z)}{(u_1,u_2,u_3)} = \begin{vmatrix} \frac{\partial x}{\partial u_1} & \frac{\partial y}{\partial u_1} & \frac{\partial z}{\partial u_1} \\ \frac{\partial x}{\partial u_2} & \frac{\partial y}{\partial u_2} & \frac{\partial z}{\partial u_2} \\ \frac{\partial x}{\partial u_3} & \frac{\partial y}{\partial u_3} & \frac{\partial z}{\partial u_3} \end{vmatrix}$$

Here, u_1, u_2 and u_3 may represent a general curvilinear coordinate system.

If the curvilinear coordinate system is orthogonal, then the Jacobian may be given by

$$J \frac{(x,y,z)}{(u_1,u_2,u_3)} = h_1 h_2 h_3$$

Here, h_1, h_2 and h_3 are the scale factors (often called the metrical coefficients) of the u_1, u_2, u_3 coordinate system.

1. Since the cylindrical coordinate system

$$u_1 = \rho \qquad u_2 = \theta \qquad u_3 = z$$

is orthogonal, we may write the Jacobian as

$$J \frac{(x,y,z)}{(\rho,\theta,z)} = h_1 h_2 h_3$$

Now, the scale factors for the cylindrical coordinate system are

$$h_1 = h_\rho = 1 \qquad h_2 = h_\theta = \rho \qquad h_3 = h_z = 1$$

(see Problem 20-14).

Therefore

$$J \frac{(x,y,z)}{(\rho,\theta,z)} = (1)(\rho)(1) = \rho$$

2. For the spherical coordinates,

$$u_1 = r \qquad u_2 = \phi \qquad u_3 = \theta$$

the scale factors are

$$h_1 = h_r = 1 \qquad h_2 = h_\phi = r \qquad h_3 = h_\theta = r\sin\phi$$

The spherical coordinate system is, of course, orthogonal.
We may write

$$J \frac{(x,y,z)}{(r,\theta,\phi)} = h_1 h_2 h_3 = (1)(r)(r\sin\phi)$$

$$= r^2\sin\phi$$

● **PROBLEM** 21-35

Describe the system of parabolic cylindrical coordinates and evaluate the square of the element of arc length in this system.

Solution: The parabolic cylindrical coordinates (u,v,z) are defined by the system of equations

$$x = \frac{1}{2}(u^2 - v^2)$$

$$y = uv \qquad\qquad\qquad (1)$$

$$z = z$$

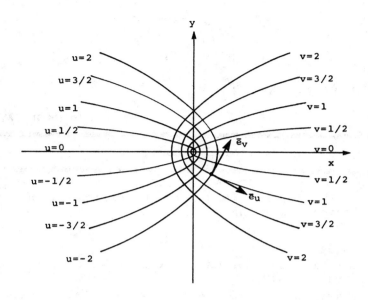

where

$$-\infty < u < \infty$$

$$v \geq 0$$

$$-\infty < z < \infty$$

Fig. 1 shows the traces of the coordinate surfaces on the xy-plane. Note that they are confocal parabolas with a common axis.

We now wish to find the square of the element of arc length, ds^2.

Since,

$$ds^2 = dx^2 + dy^2 + dz^2$$

we obtain, from eq.(1),

$$dx = \frac{\partial x}{\partial u} \, du + \frac{\partial x}{\partial v} \, dv$$

$$= u \, du - v \, dv$$

$$dy = \frac{\partial y}{\partial u} \, du + \frac{\partial y}{\partial v} \, dv$$

$$= u \, dv + v \, du$$

$$dz = dz$$

Hence,

$$ds^2 = dx^2 + dy^2 + dz^2$$

$$= (udu-vdv)^2 + (udv+vdu)^2 + dz^2$$

$$= (u^2+v^2)du^2 + (u^2+v^2)dv^2 + dz^2$$

Since,

$$ds^2 = h_1^2 \, du^2 + h_2^2 \, dv^2 + h_3 dz^2$$

we see that the scale factors for the parabolic cylindrical coordinates are

$$h_1 = h_u = \sqrt{u^2+v^2}$$

$$h_2 = h_v = \sqrt{u^2+v^2}$$

$$h_3 = h_z = 1$$

● **PROBLEM 21-36**

Express grad f in cylindrical coordinates.

Solution: The scalar field f may be expressed in terms of the cylindrical coordinates,

$$f = f(\rho,\theta,z) . \tag{1}$$

We now wish to express the vector ∇f in terms of cylincrical coordinates.

The base vectors to the (x,y,z) and (ρ,θ,z) coordinate systems are $\bar{i},\bar{j},\bar{k}$ and $\bar{e}_\rho,\bar{e}_\theta,\bar{e}_z$, respectively.

Let $\nabla f = \bar{a}$, where $\bar{a}$ is some arbitrary vector. For any vector $\bar{a}$, we may write

$$\bar{a} = a_1\bar{i} + a_2\bar{j} + a_3\bar{k} \tag{2}$$

or

$$\bar{a} = b_1\bar{e}_\rho + b_2\bar{e}_\theta + b_3\bar{e}_z \tag{3}$$

Let us scalar multiply eq.(3) by $\bar{e}_\rho$,

$$\bar{a} \cdot \bar{e}_\rho = b_1\bar{e}_\rho \cdot \bar{e}_\rho + b_2\bar{e}_\theta \cdot \bar{e}_\rho + b_3\bar{e}_z \cdot \bar{e}_\rho$$

$$= b_1\bar{e}_\rho \cdot \bar{e}_\rho = b_1 \tag{4}$$

Note that the vectors $\bar{e}_\rho$, $\bar{e}_\theta$ and $\bar{e}_z$ are mutually orthogonal unit vectors, and therefore,

$$\bar{e}_\theta \cdot \bar{e}_\rho = 0 \quad \bar{e}_z \cdot \bar{e}_\rho = 0 \quad \bar{e}_\theta \cdot \bar{e}_z = 0$$

In the same manner, we easily obtain

$$\bar{a} \cdot \bar{e}_\theta = b_2 \qquad \bar{a} \cdot \bar{e}_z = b_3$$

Hence, we may write vector $\bar{a}$ as

$$\bar{a} = (\bar{a} \cdot \bar{e}_\rho)\bar{e}_\rho + (\bar{e}_\theta \cdot \bar{a})\bar{e}_\theta + (\bar{e}_z \cdot \bar{a})\bar{e}_z \tag{5}$$

or

$$\nabla f = (\bar{e}_\rho \cdot \nabla f)\bar{e}_\rho + (\bar{e}_\theta \cdot \nabla f)\bar{e}_\theta + (\bar{e}_z \cdot \nabla f)\bar{e}_z \tag{6}$$

It is important to note that each of the coefficients of eq.(6) represents the rate of change of the function f with respect to the corresponding direction. That is, if s_1 denotes the arc length measured along the ρ-coordinate curve

1060

then the term $\quad \overline{e}_\rho \cdot \nabla f = \dfrac{\partial f}{\partial s_1} = \dfrac{\partial f}{\partial s}\Big|\theta, z=\text{const.}$ (7)

represents the rate of change of f along the ρ-coordinate curve (that curve for which θ and z are constant). Likewise we may write

$$\overline{e}_\theta \cdot \nabla f = \dfrac{\partial f}{\partial s_2} = \dfrac{\partial f}{\partial s}\Big|\rho, z=\text{const.}$$ (8)

$$\overline{e}_z \cdot \nabla f = \dfrac{\partial f}{s_3} = \dfrac{\partial f}{s}\Big|\theta, \rho=\text{const.}$$ (9)

Now, since the element of arc length in cylindrical coordinates is

$$ds = \sqrt{d\rho^2 + \rho^2 d\theta^2 + dz^2}$$ (10)

we see that along the ρ-curve (θ and z constant), we have ds = dρ (since dθ=dz=0).

Similarly, along the θ- and z-curves, ds = ρdθ and ds = dz, respectively.

We see that eqs.(7) through (9) may be written

$$\overline{e}_\rho \cdot \nabla f = \dfrac{\partial f}{\partial \rho}$$ (11)

$$\overline{e}_\theta \cdot \nabla f = \dfrac{\partial f}{\partial(\rho\theta)} = \dfrac{1}{\rho}\dfrac{\partial f}{\partial \theta}$$ (12)

$$\overline{e}_z \cdot \nabla f = \dfrac{\partial f}{\partial z}$$ (13)

Substituting eqs.(11) through (13) into eq.(6) results in

$$\nabla f = \text{grad } f = \dfrac{\partial f}{\partial \rho}\overline{e}_\rho + \dfrac{1}{\rho}\dfrac{\partial f}{\partial \theta}\overline{e}_\theta + \dfrac{\partial f}{\partial z}\overline{e}_z$$ (14)

Eq.(14) expresses grad f in terms of the cylindrical coordinates.

● **PROBLEM 21-37**

For the function

$$f(x,y,z) = \dfrac{z}{x^2+y^2} + e^z$$ (1)

compute grad f in cylindrical coordinates.

Solution: In cylindrical coordinates, the gradient of a function f is given by

$$\text{grad } f = \nabla f = \dfrac{\partial f}{\partial \rho}\overline{e}_\rho + \dfrac{1}{\rho}\dfrac{\partial f}{\partial \theta}\overline{e}_\theta + \dfrac{\partial f}{\partial z}\overline{e}_z$$ (2)

Here, f is expressed in terms of the cylindrical coordinates, $f = f(\rho, \theta, z)$.

To convert the function f given by eq.(1) into cylindrical coordinates, note that

$$x = \rho\cos\theta$$
$$y = \rho\sin\theta$$

so that
$$f(\rho, \theta, z) = \frac{z}{\rho^2\cos^2\theta + \rho^2\sin^2\theta} + e^z = \frac{z}{\rho^2} + e^z \qquad (3)$$

We have

$$\frac{\partial f}{\partial \rho} = -\frac{2z}{\rho^3} \qquad (4)$$

$$\frac{\partial f}{\partial \theta} = 0 \qquad (5)$$

$$\frac{\partial f}{\partial z} = e^z + \frac{1}{\rho^2} \qquad (6)$$

Hence,
$$\nabla f = \frac{\partial f}{\partial \rho}\bar{e}_\rho + \frac{1}{\rho}\frac{\partial f}{\partial \theta}\bar{e}_\theta + \frac{\partial f}{\partial z}\bar{e}_z$$

$$= \frac{-2z}{\rho^3}\bar{e}_\rho + \left(\frac{1}{\rho^2} + e^z\right)\bar{e}_z \qquad (7)$$

● **PROBLEM 21-38**

Find the expression for div $\bar{F}$ in cylindrical coordinates. Interpret div $\bar{F}$ as flux per unit volume out of a "box".

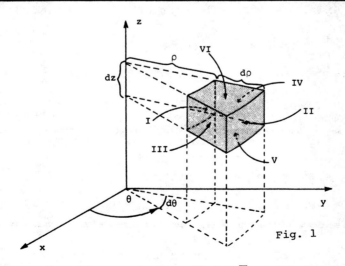

Fig. 1

<u>Solution</u>: Consider a vector field $\bar{F}$ given as a function of the cylindrical coordinates

$$\bar{F} = F_\rho(\rho, \theta, z)\bar{e}_\rho + F_\theta(\rho, \theta, z)\bar{e}_\theta + F_z(\rho, \theta, z)\bar{e}_z \qquad (1)$$

1062

We will now find the expression for div $\overline{F}$ in cylindrical coordinates. Note that in rectangular coordinates, of course

$$\text{div } \overline{F} = \frac{\partial F_x}{\partial x} + \frac{\partial F_y}{\partial y} + \frac{\partial F_z}{\partial z} \qquad (2)$$

To proceed in finding div $\overline{F}$ in cylindrical coordinates, let us consider the differential "box" shown in Fig. 1. The faces of the box are labeled I through VI, as shown. Let us consider faces I and II. The flux of $\overline{F}$ out of face I is equal to the component of $\overline{F}$ along the normal vector of the surface I times the surface area of face I. Since the normal vector to face I is $\overline{n} = -\overline{e}_\rho$, and since the area of face I is $(\rho d\theta)(dz)$, we see that the flux of $\overline{F}$ through face I is

$$(\overline{F} \cdot \overline{n}) \cdot (\text{area}) = (F_\rho \overline{e}_\rho + F_\theta \overline{e}_\theta + F_z \overline{e}_z) \cdot (-\overline{e}_\rho) \times (\rho d\theta dz)$$
$$\qquad (3)$$
$$= -F_\rho \rho d\theta dz$$

Note that for face I, the only component of $\overline{F}$ that contributes to the flux is F_ρ, since the other components F_θ and F_z are tangent to the face (see Fig. 2).

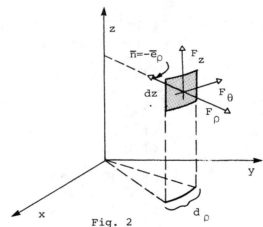

Fig. 2

Now, note that for face II, we have a different value of ρ (θ and z are the same as for face I). The noraml vector to face II is $\overline{n} = \overline{e}_\rho$. The flux of f through face II is

$$(F_\rho \rho d\theta dz)_{II} = (F_\rho \rho)_{II} d\theta dz \qquad (4)$$

The Roman numeral II under the bracket indicates that the bracketed expression is evaluated at face II. Now, the contribution of flux from faces I and II, in the limit, is given by

$$-(F_\rho \rho)_I d\theta dz + (F_\rho \rho)_{II} d\theta dz = \frac{\partial(\rho F_\rho)}{\partial \rho} d\rho d\theta dz \qquad (5)$$

For face III, $\overline{n} = -\overline{e}_\theta$ and its area is $d\rho dz$ (see Fig. 3).

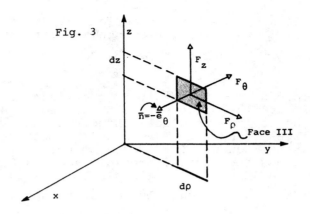

Fig. 3

Thus, the flux through face III is

$$\overline{F} \cdot \overline{n} \times (\text{area}) = \left[(F_\rho \overline{e}_\rho + F_\theta \overline{e}_\theta + F_z \overline{e}_z) \cdot (-\overline{e}_\theta) \right] d\rho dz \tag{6}$$

$$= -F_\theta d\rho dz$$

For face IV, the flux is

$$(F_\theta d\rho dz)_{IV} = (F_\theta)_{IV} d\rho dz \tag{7}$$

The total contribution from faces III and IV is

$$(F_\theta)_{IV} d\rho dz - (F_\theta)_{III} d\rho dz = \frac{\partial F_\theta}{\partial \theta} d\theta d\rho dz \tag{8}$$

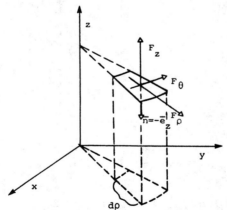

Fig. 4

Now, for face V $\overline{n} = -\overline{e}_z$ (see Fig. 4) and its area is $(\rho d\theta)(d\rho)$. Thus, the flux through face V is

$$\overline{F} \cdot \overline{n} \, \rho d\theta d\rho = -F_z \rho d\theta d\rho \tag{9}$$

and through face VI,

$$(F_z)_{VI} \rho d\theta d\rho \tag{10}$$

Thus, the flux contribution from faces V and VI is

$$(F_z)_{VI} \rho d\theta d\rho - (F_z)_V \rho d\theta d\rho = \frac{\partial F_z}{\partial z} \rho d\theta d\rho \qquad (11)$$

Note that faces V and VI are not rectangles. Indeed, one side is of length $\rho d\theta$ and the other is of length $(\rho + d\rho)d\theta$. In the limit $\rho + d\rho \to \rho$, so everything is taken care of.

By adding eqs.(5), (8) and (11), we obtain the total flux out of the box, or parallelpiped.

$$\frac{\partial(\rho F_\rho)}{\partial \rho} d\rho d\theta dz + \frac{\partial F_\theta}{\partial \theta} d\theta d\rho dz + \frac{\partial F_z}{\partial z} dz\rho d\theta d\rho \qquad (12)$$

Now, since the divergence of a vector field, div $\overline{F}$ may be interpreted as a measure of the flux per unit volume, we see that since

$$dV = \rho d\rho d\theta dz, \qquad (13)$$

then dividing eq.(12) by the volume gives

$$\text{div } \overline{F} = \frac{1}{\rho d\rho d\theta dz} \left[\frac{\partial(\rho F_\rho)}{\partial \rho} d\rho d\theta dz + \frac{\partial F_\theta}{\partial \theta} d\theta d\rho dz + \frac{\partial F_z}{\partial z} dz\rho d\theta d\rho \right]$$

$$= \frac{1}{\rho} \frac{\partial(\rho F_\rho)}{\partial \rho} + \frac{1}{\rho} \frac{\partial F_\theta}{\partial \theta} + \frac{\partial F_z}{\partial z} \qquad (14)$$

Or, since

$$\frac{1}{\rho} \frac{\partial(\rho F_\rho)}{\partial \rho} = \frac{1}{\rho} F_\rho + \frac{\partial F_\rho}{\partial \rho}$$

we may write

$$\text{div } \overline{F} = \frac{1}{\rho} F_\rho + \frac{\partial F_\rho}{\partial \rho} + \frac{1}{\rho} \frac{\partial F_\theta}{\partial \theta} + \frac{\partial F_z}{\partial z} \qquad (15)$$

Eq. (14) (or eq.(15)) gives the divergence of a vector field in cylindrical coordinates.

● **PROBLEM 21-39**

Compute the divergence of the vector field

$$\overline{F} = x^2y\overline{i} + 2yz\overline{j} + (x+z)\overline{k} \qquad (1)$$

in both the rectangular and cylindrical coordinates.

Solution: By definition, we have

$$\text{div } \overline{F} = \frac{\partial F_1}{\partial x} + \frac{\partial F_2}{\partial y} + \frac{\partial F_3}{\partial z}$$

$$= \frac{\partial}{\partial x}(x^2y) + \frac{\partial}{\partial y}(2yz) + \frac{\partial}{\partial z}(x+z) \qquad (2)$$

$$= 2xy + 2z + 1$$

Now, to evaluate div $\overline{F}$ in cylindrical coordinates, we must first express $\overline{F}$ in cylindrical coordinates.

We have,
$$x = \rho\cos\theta$$
$$y = \rho\sin\theta$$
$$\bar{i} = \cos\theta\bar{e}_\rho - \sin\theta\bar{e}_\theta \qquad \bar{j} = \sin\theta\bar{e}_\rho + \cos\theta\bar{e}_\theta \qquad \bar{k} = \bar{e}_z$$
so that $\bar{F}$ becomes
$$\bar{F} = (\rho\cos\theta)^2(\rho\sin\theta)(\cos\theta\bar{e}_\rho - \sin\theta\bar{e}_\theta) + 2(\rho\sin\theta)z(\sin\theta\bar{e}_\rho + \cos\theta\bar{e}_\theta)$$
$$+ (\rho\cos\theta + z)\bar{e}_z \tag{3}$$
$$= \bar{e}_\rho\left[\rho^3\cos^3\theta\sin\theta + 2\rho z\sin^2\theta\right] + \bar{e}_\theta\left[2\rho z\sin\theta\cos\theta - \rho^3\cos^2\theta\sin^2\theta\right]$$
$$+ \bar{e}_z\left[\rho\cos\theta + z\right]$$

Now, the divergence in cylindrical coordinates is
$$\text{div }\bar{F} = \frac{1}{\rho}\frac{\partial(\rho F_\rho)}{\partial\rho} + \frac{1}{\rho}\frac{\partial F_\theta}{\partial\theta} + \frac{\partial F_z}{\partial z} \tag{4}$$

Therefore,
$$\text{div }\bar{F} = \frac{1}{\rho}\frac{\partial}{\partial\rho}\left[\rho^4\cos^3\theta\sin\theta + 2\rho^2 z\sin^2\theta\right]$$
$$+ \frac{1}{\rho}\frac{\partial}{\partial\theta}\left[2\rho z\sin\theta\cos\theta - \rho^3\cos^2\theta\sin^2\theta\right] + \frac{\partial}{\partial z}\left[\rho\cos\theta + z\right]$$
$$= 4\rho^2\cos^3\theta\sin\theta + 4z\sin^2\theta + 2z\cos^2\theta - 2z\sin^2\theta$$
$$- 2\rho^2\cos^3\theta\sin\theta + 2\rho^2\sin^3\theta\cos\theta + 1$$
$$= 2\rho^2\cos^3\theta\sin\theta + 2\rho^2\sin^3\theta\cos\theta + 2z\sin^2\theta$$
$$+ 2z\cos^2\theta + 1 = 2\rho^2\sin\theta\cos\theta + 2z + 1 \tag{5}$$

Now, transforming eq.(5) back to rectangular coordinates gives
$$\text{div }\bar{F} = 2\rho^2\sin\theta\cos\theta + 2z + 1$$
$$= 2\rho^2\frac{x}{\rho}\frac{y}{\rho} + 2z + 1$$
$$= 2xy + 2z + 1 \tag{6}$$
which is the result obtained in eq.(2).

● **PROBLEM 21-40**

Employing the physical characterization of curl $\dot{\bar{F}}$ as swirl per unit area, express curl $\bar{F}$ in cylindrical coordinates.

<u>Solution</u>: Consider the vector field $\bar{F}$ given as a function of the cylindrical coordinates,
$$\bar{F} = F_\rho\bar{e}_\rho + F_\theta\bar{e}_\theta + F_z\bar{e}_z \tag{1}$$

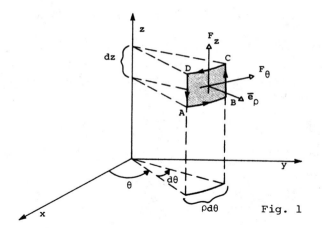

Fig. 1

It is required to find an expression for the curl of $\overline{F}$ in cylindrical coordinates.

Let us write curl $\overline{F}$ as

$$\text{curl } \overline{F} = A_\rho \overline{e}_\rho + A_\theta \overline{e}_\theta + A_z \overline{e}_z \tag{2}$$

Here, A_ρ, A_θ and A_z are the components of the vector curl $\overline{F}$ and they are, of course, what we wish to determine.

Now, to proceed, let us note that curl $\overline{F}$ may be interpreted as swirl (or circulation) per unit area.

Let us now determine A_ρ by considering the path ABCD shown in Fig. 1.

We may write

$$A_\rho = \frac{\text{swirl}}{\text{area}} = \frac{\oint \overline{F} \cdot d\overline{r}}{\text{area}} \tag{3}$$

Here, the integral $\oint \overline{F} \cdot d\overline{r}$ represents the line integral evaluated along the closed path ABCD.

To evaluate the line integral, we may write, using Fig. 1 as a guide,

$$\oint_{ABCD} \overline{F} \cdot d\overline{r} = \int_{AB} \overline{F} \cdot d\overline{r} + \int_{BC} \overline{F} \cdot d\overline{r} + \int_{CD} \overline{F} \cdot d\overline{r} + \int_{DA} \overline{F} \cdot d\overline{r}$$

$$= (F_\theta \rho d\theta)_{AB} + (F_z dz)_{BC} - (F_\theta \rho d\theta)_{CD} - (F_z dz)_{DA} \tag{4}$$

Notice that the components F_θ and F_z are the only components of $\overline{F}$ that contribute to the line integral along ABCD.

Now, note that for the paths AB and CD, ρ and $d\theta$ are the same, while z has changed. Thus, we may write

$$(F_\theta \rho d\theta)_{AB} - (F_\theta \rho d\theta)_{CD} = -\frac{\partial F_\theta}{\partial z} dz \rho d\theta \qquad (5)$$

For BC and DA, dz and ρ are unchanged, while θ has changed. Thus,

$$(F_z dz)_{BC} - (F_z dz)_{DA} = \frac{\partial F_z}{\partial \theta} d\theta dz \qquad (6)$$

From eqs.(5), (6) and (4), we see that the line integral is

$$\oint_{ABCD} \overline{F} \cdot dr = \frac{\partial F_z}{\partial \theta} d\theta dz - \frac{\partial F_\theta}{\partial z} \rho dz d\theta \qquad (7)$$

Since the area is $\rho d\theta dz$, we find

$$A_\rho = \frac{\oint \overline{F} \cdot d\overline{r}}{area} = \frac{1}{\rho d\theta dz} \left[\frac{\partial F_z}{\partial \theta} d\theta dz - \frac{\partial F_\theta}{\partial z} \rho dz d\theta \right]$$

$$= \frac{1}{\rho} \frac{\partial F_z}{\partial \theta} - \frac{\partial F_\theta}{\partial z} \qquad (8)$$

Let us now determine A_θ by considering the path EFGH shown in Fig. 2.

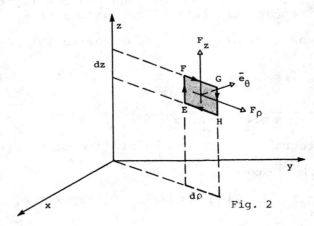

Fig. 2

We have,

$$\oint_{EFGH} \overline{F} \cdot d\overline{r} = \int_{EF} \overline{F} \cdot d\overline{r} + \int_{FG} \overline{F} \cdot d\overline{r} + \int_{GH} \overline{F} \cdot d\overline{r} + \int_{HE} \overline{F} \cdot d\overline{r}$$

$$= (F_z dz)_{EF} + (F_\rho d\rho)_{FG} - (F_z dz)_{GH} - (F_\rho d\rho)_{HE} \qquad (9)$$

Note that in this case, F_z and F_ρ are the components of $\overline{F}$ that contribute to the line integral.

Now, since for EF and GH θ and dz are the same while ρ

1068

has changed, we see that

$$(F_z dz)_{EF} - (F_z dz)_{GH} = -\frac{\partial F_z}{\partial \rho} d\rho dz \qquad (10)$$

For FG and HE, $d\rho$ and θ are the same while z has changed. Hence,

$$(F_\rho d\rho)_{FG} - (F_\rho d\rho)_{HE} = \frac{\partial F_\rho}{\partial z} dz d\rho \qquad (11)$$

It is clear that the line integral is

$$\oint_{EFGH} \overline{F} \cdot d\overline{r} = \frac{\partial F_\rho}{\partial z} d\rho dz - \frac{\partial F_z}{\partial \rho} d\rho dz \qquad (12)$$

and dividing by the area $d\rho dz$, we obtain

$$A_\theta = \frac{\partial F_\rho}{\partial z} - \frac{\partial F_z}{\partial \rho} \qquad (13)$$

Let us now finally obtain A_z by considering the path JKLM shown in Figure 3. Since for this case F_ρ and F_θ are the only components that contribute to the line integral, we see that

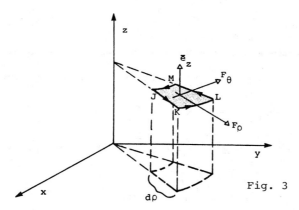

Fig. 3

$$\oint_{JKLM} \overline{F} \cdot d\overline{r} = \int_{JK} \overline{F} \cdot d\overline{r} + \int_{KL} \overline{F} \cdot d\overline{r} + \int_{LM} \overline{F} \cdot d\overline{r} + \int_{MJ} \overline{F} \cdot d\overline{r}$$

$$= (F_\rho d\rho)_{JK} + (F_\theta \rho d\theta)_{KL} - (F_\rho d\rho)_{LM} - (F_\theta \rho d\theta)_{MJ} \quad (14)$$

Now, note that for KL and MJ, $d\theta$ and z are the same while ρ has changed. Thus,

$$(F_\rho \rho d\theta)_{KL} - (F_\theta \rho d\theta)_{MJ} = \frac{\partial(\rho F_\theta)}{\partial \rho} d\rho d\theta \qquad (15)$$

For JK and LM, $d\rho$ and z are the same while θ has changed. Thus,

$$(F_\rho d\rho)_{JK} - (F_\rho d\rho)_{LM} = -\frac{\partial F_\rho}{\partial \theta} d\theta d\rho \qquad (16)$$

Substituting eqs.(16) and (15) into eq.(14) gives us

$$\oint_{JKLM} \overline{F} \cdot d\overline{r} = \frac{\partial(\rho F_\theta)}{\partial \rho} \, d\rho d\theta - \frac{\partial F_\rho}{\partial \theta} \, d\rho d\theta \qquad (17)$$

Finally, dividing eq.(17) by the area $\rho d\rho d\theta$ gives us

$$A_z = \frac{1}{\rho} \left[\frac{\partial(\rho F_\theta)}{\partial \rho} - \frac{\partial F_\rho}{\partial \theta} \right] \qquad (18)$$

Hence, substituting eqs.(8), (13) and (18) into eq.(2) gives us

$$\text{curl } \overline{F} = \left[\frac{1}{\rho} \frac{\partial F_z}{\partial \theta} - \frac{\partial F_\theta}{\partial z} \right] \overline{e}_\rho + \left[\frac{\partial F_\rho}{\partial z} - \frac{\partial F_z}{\partial \rho} \right] \overline{e}_\theta + \frac{1}{\rho} \left[\frac{\partial(\rho F_\theta)}{\partial \rho} - \frac{\partial F_\rho}{\partial \theta} \right] \overline{e}_z$$

which is the expression for curl $\overline{F}$ in cylindrical coordinates.

● **PROBLEM** 21-41

Evaluate the curl of the vector field

$$\overline{F} = x^2 y \overline{i} + 2yz \overline{j} + (x+z)\overline{k} \qquad (1)$$

in both the rectangular and cylindrical coordinate systems and compare the results.

<u>Solution</u>: Applying the definition of curl $\overline{F}$, we find

$$\text{curl } \overline{F} = \left(\frac{\partial}{\partial x}, \frac{\partial}{\partial y}, \frac{\partial}{\partial z} \right) \times (x^2 y, 2yz, x+z)$$

$$= \left[\frac{\partial}{\partial y}(x+z) - \frac{\partial}{\partial z}(2yz) \right] \overline{i} + \left[\frac{\partial}{\partial z}(x^2 y) - \frac{\partial}{\partial x}(x+z) \right] \overline{j}$$

$$+ \left[\frac{\partial}{\partial x}(2yz) - \frac{\partial}{\partial y}(x^2 y) \right] \overline{k}$$

$$= -2y \overline{i} - \overline{j} - x^2 \overline{k} \qquad (2)$$

We now wish to find curl $\overline{F}$ in cylindrical coordinates. Before we can do this, we must transform $\overline{F}$ into cylindrical coordinates.
We have $\quad x = \rho\cos\theta \quad y = \rho\sin\theta \quad z = z$

$$\overline{i} = \cos\theta\overline{e}_\rho - \sin\theta\overline{e}_\theta \quad \overline{j} = \sin\theta\overline{e}_\rho + \cos\theta\overline{e}_\theta \quad \overline{k} = \overline{e}_z$$

Thus, the vector field $\overline{F}$ expressed in cylindrical coordinates is

$$\overline{F} = (\rho\cos\theta)^2(\rho\sin\theta) \left[\cos\theta\overline{e}_\rho - \sin\theta\overline{e}_\theta \right]$$

$$+ 2(\rho\sin\theta)z \left[\sin\theta\overline{e}_\rho + \cos\theta\overline{e}_\theta \right] + (\rho\cos\theta + z)\overline{e}_z$$

$$= \bar{e}_\rho \left[\rho^3 \cos^3\theta \sin\theta + 2\rho z \sin^2\theta \right]$$
$$+ \bar{e}_\theta \left[2\rho z \sin\theta \cos\theta - \rho^3 \cos^2\theta \sin^2\theta \right] \qquad (3)$$
$$+ \bar{e}_z \left[\rho \cos\theta + z \right]$$

In cylindrical coordinates, curl $\bar{F}$ is

$$\text{curl } \bar{F} = \left[\frac{1}{\rho} \frac{\partial F_z}{\partial \theta} - \frac{\partial F_\theta}{\partial z} \right] \bar{e}_\rho + \left[\frac{\partial F_\rho}{\partial z} - \frac{\partial F_z}{\partial \rho} \right] \bar{e}_\theta + \frac{1}{\rho} \left[\frac{\partial (\rho F_\theta)}{\partial \rho} - \frac{\partial F_\rho}{\partial \theta} \right] \bar{e}_z$$

$$= \bar{e}_\rho \left[-\frac{1}{\rho} \rho \sin\theta - 2\rho \sin\theta \cos\theta \right] + \bar{e}_\theta (2\rho \sin^2\theta - \cos\theta) \qquad (4)$$
$$+ \bar{e}_z (-\rho^2 \cos^2\theta)$$

To compare the results let us express eq.(2) in cylindrical coordinates

$$\text{curl } \bar{F} = -2y\bar{i} - \bar{j} - x^2\bar{k}$$

$$= 2(\rho\sin\theta)(\cos\theta\bar{e}_\rho - \sin\theta\bar{e}_\theta) - \sin\theta\bar{e}_\rho$$
$$- \cos\theta\bar{e}_\theta - \rho^2\cos^2\theta\bar{e}_z$$

$$= \bar{e}_\rho (-2\rho\sin\theta\cos\theta - \sin\theta) + \bar{e}_\theta (2\rho\sin^2\theta - \cos\theta)$$
$$+ \bar{e}_z (-\rho^2\cos^2\theta) \qquad (5)$$

Eqs.(5) and (4) do, of course, agree with each other.

● **PROBLEM** 21-42

Express the Laplacian in polar and cylindrical coordinates.

Solution: Let us consider the two-dimensional Laplacian

$$\nabla^2 f = \frac{\partial^2 f}{\partial x^2} + \frac{\partial^2 f}{\partial y^2} \qquad (1)$$

We will now express the Laplacian in terms of the polar coordinates r and θ.

The polar coordinates are related to the rectangular coordinates by

$$x = r\cos\theta, \quad y = r\sin\theta \qquad (2)$$

Now, by the chain rule, we have

$$\frac{\partial f}{\partial x} = \frac{\partial f}{\partial r}\frac{\partial r}{\partial x} + \frac{\partial f}{\partial \theta}\frac{\partial \theta}{\partial x}$$

$$\frac{\partial f}{\partial y} = \frac{\partial f}{\partial r}\frac{\partial r}{\partial y} + \frac{\partial f}{\partial \theta}\frac{\partial \theta}{\partial y} \qquad (3)$$

To find $\frac{\partial r}{\partial x}$ and $\frac{\partial \theta}{\partial x}$, let us first find the differentials

1071

dr and dθ.

From eqs.(2), we have

$$dx = \frac{\partial x}{\partial r}\,dr + \frac{\partial x}{\partial \theta}\,d\theta$$

$$= \cos\theta dr - r\sin\theta d\theta \tag{4}$$

and

$$dy = \frac{\partial y}{\partial r}\,dr + \frac{\partial y}{\partial \theta}\,d\theta$$

$$= \sin\theta dr + r\cos\theta d\theta \tag{5}$$

Let us now solve eqs.(4) and (5) for dr and dθ.

$$dr = \frac{dx}{\cos\theta} + \frac{r\sin\theta}{\cos\theta}\,d\theta$$

$$= \frac{dx}{\cos\theta} + \frac{r\sin\theta}{\cos\theta}\left(\frac{dy}{r\cos\theta} - \frac{\sin\theta dr}{r\cos\theta}\right) \tag{6}$$

$$= \frac{dx}{\cos\theta} + \frac{\sin\theta dy}{\cos^2\theta} - \frac{\sin^2\theta dr}{\cos^2\theta}$$

Multiplying eq.(6) by $\cos^2\theta$ yields

$$\cos^2\theta dr = \cos\theta dx + \sin\theta dy - \sin^2\theta dr$$

or

$$(\cos^2\theta + \sin^2\theta)dr = \cos\theta dx + \sin\theta dy$$

$$dr = \cos\theta dx + \sin\theta dy \tag{7}$$

In a similar manner, we can obtain

$$d\theta = -\frac{\sin\theta}{r}\,dx + \frac{\cos\theta}{r}\,dy \tag{8}$$

From eqs.(7) and (8) we see that

$$\frac{\partial r}{\partial x} = \cos\theta \qquad \frac{\partial r}{\partial y} = \sin\theta \tag{9}$$

$$\frac{\partial \theta}{\partial x} = -\frac{\sin\theta}{r} \qquad \frac{\partial \theta}{\partial y} = \frac{\cos\theta}{r} \tag{10}$$

Eq.(3) can now be written in the form

$$\frac{\partial f}{\partial x} = \cos\theta \frac{\partial f}{\partial r} - \frac{\sin\theta}{r} \frac{\partial f}{\partial \theta} \tag{11}$$

$$\frac{\partial f}{\partial y} = \sin\theta \frac{\partial f}{\partial r} + \frac{\cos\theta}{r} \frac{\partial f}{\partial \theta} \tag{12}$$

Thus,

$$\frac{\partial^2 f}{\partial x^2} = \frac{\partial}{\partial x}\left(\frac{\partial f}{\partial x}\right) = \cos\theta \frac{\partial}{\partial r}\left(\frac{\partial f}{\partial x}\right) - \frac{\sin\theta}{r} \frac{\partial}{\partial \theta}\left(\frac{\partial f}{\partial x}\right)$$

$$= \cos\theta \frac{\partial}{\partial r}\left(\cos\theta \frac{\partial f}{\partial r} - \frac{\sin\theta}{r} \frac{\partial f}{\partial \theta}\right)$$

$$- \frac{\sin\theta}{r} \frac{\partial}{\partial\theta} \left(\cos\theta \frac{\partial f}{\partial r} - \frac{\sin\theta}{r} \frac{\partial f}{\partial\theta} \right)$$

$$= \cos^2\theta \frac{\partial^2 f}{\partial r^2} - \frac{2\sin\theta\cos\theta}{r} \frac{\partial^2 f}{\partial r \partial\theta} + \frac{\sin^2\theta}{r^2} \frac{\partial^2 f}{\partial\theta^2} \tag{13}$$

$$+ \frac{\sin^2\theta}{r} \frac{\partial f}{\partial r} + \frac{2\sin\theta\cos\theta}{r^2} \frac{\partial f}{\partial\theta}$$

Notice that $\frac{\partial}{\partial x}\left(\frac{\partial f}{\partial r}\right) = \frac{\partial}{\partial r}\left(\frac{\partial f}{\partial x}\right)$ and $\frac{\partial}{\partial x}\left(\frac{\partial f}{\partial\theta}\right) = \frac{\partial}{\partial\theta}\left(\frac{\partial f}{\partial x}\right)$ since the function f is assumed to be continuously differentiable to at least the second order.

Now, for $\frac{\partial^2 f}{\partial y^2}$, we obtain

$$\frac{\partial^2 f}{\partial y^2} = \frac{\partial}{\partial y}\left(\frac{\partial f}{\partial y}\right) = \sin\theta \frac{\partial}{\partial r}\left(\sin\theta \frac{\partial f}{\partial r} + \frac{\cos\theta}{r} \frac{\partial f}{\partial\theta}\right)$$

$$+ \frac{\cos\theta}{r} \frac{\partial}{\partial\theta}\left(\sin\theta \frac{\partial f}{\partial r} + \frac{\cos\theta}{r} \frac{\partial f}{\partial\theta}\right)$$

$$= \sin^2\theta \frac{\partial^2 f}{\partial r^2} + \frac{2\sin\theta\cos\theta}{r} \frac{\partial^2 f}{\partial r \partial\theta} + \frac{\cos^2\theta}{r^2} \frac{\partial^2 f}{\partial\theta^2} \tag{14}$$

$$+ \frac{\cos^2\theta}{r} \frac{\partial f}{\partial r} - \frac{2\sin\theta\cos\theta}{r^2} \frac{\partial f}{\partial\theta}$$

Adding eqs.(13) and (14) results in

$$\nabla^2 f = \frac{\partial^2 f}{\partial x^2} + \frac{\partial^2 f}{\partial y^2} = \frac{\partial^2 f}{\partial r^2} + \frac{1}{r^2} \frac{\partial^2 f}{\partial\theta^2} + \frac{1}{r} \frac{\partial f}{\partial r} \tag{15}$$

Now, for the three-dimensional system, we have

$$x = r\cos\theta, \quad y = r\sin\theta, \quad z = z$$

To find the Laplacian of f(x,y,z) in terms of r, θ, z, all we have to do is simply add the term $\frac{\partial^2 f}{\partial z^2}$ to eq.(15).

Thus, in cylindrical coordinates the Laplacian is given by

$$\nabla^2 f = \frac{\partial^2 f}{\partial r^2} + \frac{1}{r} \frac{\partial f}{\partial r} + \frac{1}{r^2} \frac{\partial^2 f}{\partial\theta^2} + \frac{\partial^2 f}{\partial z^2} \tag{16}$$

Notice that

$$\frac{1}{r} \frac{\partial}{\partial r}\left(r \frac{\partial f}{\partial r}\right) = \frac{\partial f}{\partial r} + \frac{1}{r^2} \frac{\partial f}{\partial r} \tag{17}$$

so that the Laplacian in cylindrical coordinates is also written

$$\nabla^2 f = \frac{1}{r} \frac{\partial}{\partial r}\left(r \frac{\partial f}{\partial r}\right) + \frac{1}{r^2} \frac{\partial^2 f}{\partial\theta^2} + \frac{\partial^2 f}{\partial z^2} \tag{18}$$

● **PROBLEM 21-43**

Find the expression for the gradient of f(r,φ,θ) in spherical coordinates.

Solution: The gradient of f can be expressed in the form

$$\nabla f = (\bar{e}_r \cdot \nabla f)\bar{e}_r + (\bar{e}_\phi \cdot \nabla f)\bar{e}_\phi + (\bar{e}_\theta \cdot \nabla f)\bar{e}_\theta \qquad (1)$$

The component of the gradient of $f(r,\phi,\theta)$ in the direction $\bar{e}_r$ is the rate of change of f with respect to distance along the r-coordinate curve.

Since
$$ds = \sqrt{dr^2 + r^2 d\phi^2 + r^2 \sin^2\phi\, d\theta^2} \qquad (2)$$

we obtain

$$\bar{e}_r \cdot \nabla f = \frac{\partial f}{\partial s}\Big|_{\phi,\theta=const} = \frac{\partial f}{\partial r} \qquad (3)$$

By the same token, we find

$$\bar{e}_\phi \cdot \nabla f = \frac{\partial f}{\partial s}\Big|_{r,\theta=const} = \frac{1}{r}\frac{\partial f}{\partial \phi} \qquad (4)$$

$$\bar{e}_\theta \cdot \nabla f = \frac{\partial f}{\partial s}\Big|_{r,\phi=const} = \frac{1}{r\sin\phi}\frac{\partial f}{\partial \theta} \qquad (5)$$

Thus, the expression for the gradient in spherical coordinates is

$$grad\ f(r,\phi,\theta) = \frac{\partial f}{\partial r}\bar{e}_r + \frac{1}{r}\frac{\partial f}{\partial \phi}\bar{e}_\phi + \frac{1}{r\sin\phi}\frac{\partial f}{\partial \theta}\bar{e}_\theta \qquad (6)$$

● **PROBLEM 21-44**

Evaluate
$$grad(x^2+y^2+z^2)^{\frac{n}{2}} \qquad (1)$$

Solution: It is easy to see that the function

$$(\sqrt{x^2+y^2+z^2})^n = r^n \qquad (2)$$

can be easily represented in spherical coordinates. The expression for the gradient in spherical coordinates is

$$grad\ f(r,\theta,\phi) = \frac{\partial f}{\partial r}\bar{e}_r + \frac{1}{r}\frac{\partial f}{\partial \phi}\bar{e}_\phi + \frac{1}{r\sin\theta}\frac{\partial f}{\partial \theta}\bar{e}_\theta \qquad (3)$$

For
$$f(r,\theta,\phi) = r^n \qquad (4)$$

we obtain

$$\nabla(r^n) = \frac{\partial}{\partial r}(r^n)\bar{e}_r + 0\,\bar{e}_\phi + 0\,\bar{e}_\theta \qquad (5)$$

$$= n\,r^{n-1}\,\bar{e}_r$$

By evaluating the total flux out of a "box", express the divergence of a vector field $\overline{F}$ in spherical coordinates.

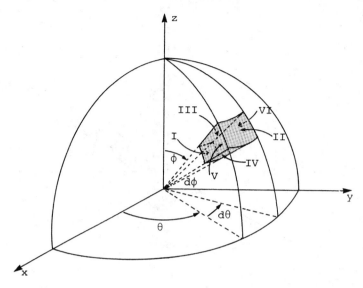

Solution: Consider a vector field $\overline{F}$ given in terms of the spherical coordinates

$$\overline{F}(r,\phi,\theta) = F_r\overline{e}_r + F_\phi\overline{e}_\phi + F_\theta\overline{e}_\theta \tag{1}$$

We will now determine an expression for div $\overline{F}$ by evaluating the total flux out of the infinitesimal parallelepiped shown in Fig. 1.

From Fig. 1 we see that the total flux out of all the faces of the parallelepiped is equal to

$$(F_r rsin\phi d\theta rd\phi)_{II} - (F_r rsin\phi d\theta rd\phi)_I + (F_\theta rd\phi dr)_{VI} - (F_\theta rd\phi dr)_V$$

$$+ (F_\phi rsin\phi d\theta dr)_{IV} - (F_\phi rsin\phi d\theta dr)_{III} \tag{2}$$

$$= \frac{\partial(r^2F_r)}{\partial r} drsin\phi d\theta d\phi + \frac{\partial F_\theta}{\partial\theta} d\theta rd\phi dr + \frac{\partial(F_\phi sin\phi)}{\partial\phi} d\phi rd\theta dr$$

Since the divergence may be interpreted as flux per unit volume, we see that dividing eq.(2) by the volume element

$$dV = r^2 sin\phi drd\phi d\theta \tag{3}$$

yields

$$\text{div } \overline{F} = \frac{1}{r^2}\frac{\partial(r^2F_r)}{\partial r} + \frac{1}{rsin\phi}\frac{\partial F_\theta}{\partial\theta} + \frac{1}{rsin\phi}\frac{\partial(sin\phi F_\phi)}{\partial\phi} \tag{4}$$

Eq.(4) gives the divergence of a vector field in spherical coordinates.

1075

Express the curl of a vector field in spherical coordinates.

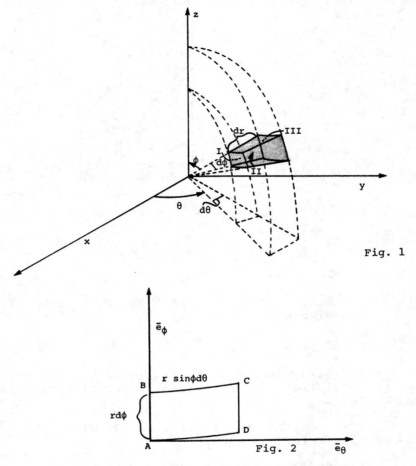

Fig. 1

Fig. 2

Solution: Consider the parallelepiped shown in Fig. 1.

Let us evaluate first the line integral around the properly-
oriented edge of Face I shown in Fig. 2.

$$(F_\phi rd\phi)_{AB} - (F_\phi rd\phi)_{CD} + (F_\theta r\sin\phi d\theta)_{BC}$$

$$- (F_\theta r\sin\phi d\theta)_{DA} = -\frac{\partial F_\phi}{\partial \theta} d\theta rd\phi + \frac{\partial (F_\theta \sin\phi)}{\partial \phi} d\phi rd\theta$$

(1)

The line integral around ABCD divided by the area
$r^2 \sin\phi d\phi d\theta$ yields the $\bar{e}_r$ component of curl $\bar{F}$

$$\bar{e}_r \cdot \text{curl } \bar{F} = \frac{1}{r\sin\phi}\left[\frac{\partial (F_\theta \sin\phi)}{\partial \phi} - \frac{\partial F_\phi}{\partial \theta}\right]$$

(2)

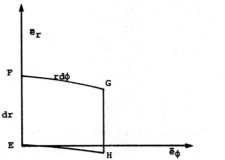

Fig. 3

The line integral around face II shown in Fig. 3 gives

$$(F_r dr)_{EF} - (F_r dr)_{GH} + (F_\phi rd\phi)_{FG} - (F_\phi rd\phi)_{HE}$$

$$= -\frac{\partial F_r}{\partial \phi} d\phi dr + \frac{\partial(rF_\phi)}{\partial r} drd\phi \qquad (3)$$

Dividing by the area of EFGH, $rd\phi dr$, we obtain the $\bar{e}_\theta$ component of curl $\bar{F}$

$$\bar{e}_\theta \cdot curl \ \bar{F} = \frac{1}{r}\left[\frac{\partial(rF_\phi)}{\partial r} - \frac{\partial F_r}{\partial \phi}\right] \qquad (4)$$

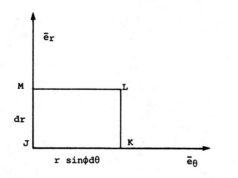

Fig. 4

The line integral around face III shown in Fig. 4 is

$$(F_\theta rsin\phi d\theta)_{JK} - (F_\theta rsin\phi d\theta)_{LM} + (F_r dr)_{KL} - (F_r dr)_{MJ}$$

$$= -\frac{\partial(rF_\theta)}{\partial r} sin\phi drd\theta + \frac{\partial F_r}{\partial \theta} d\theta dr \qquad (5)$$

Dividing by the area $rsin\phi d\theta dr$ we get the $\bar{e}_\phi$ component of
curl $\bar{F}$

$$\bar{e}_\phi \cdot curl \ \bar{F} = \frac{1}{rsin\phi}\left[\frac{\partial F_r}{\partial \theta} - \frac{\partial(rF_\theta)}{\partial r} sin\phi\right] \qquad (6)$$

In the matrix form we can write

$$\text{curl } \overline{F} = \frac{1}{r^2\sin\phi} \begin{vmatrix} \overline{e}_r & r\overline{e}_\phi & r\sin\phi\,\overline{e}_\theta \\[2mm] \dfrac{\partial}{\partial r} & \dfrac{\partial}{\partial \phi} & \dfrac{\partial}{\partial \theta} \\[2mm] F_r & rF_\phi & r\sin\phi F_\theta \end{vmatrix} \qquad (7)$$

● **PROBLEM 21-47**

Compute the Laplacian $\nabla^2 f$ in spherical coordinates.

Solution: Let $f = f(r,\phi,\theta)$ be a scalar field expressed in spherical coordinates. The Laplacian of f is

$$\nabla^2 f = \nabla \cdot (\nabla f) = \text{div grad } f \qquad (1)$$

Now, as derived in Problem 21-43, the gradient of a scalar field $f = f(r,\phi,\theta)$ in spherical coordinates is

$$\text{grad } f = \frac{\partial f}{\partial r} \overline{e}_r + \frac{1}{r} \frac{\partial f}{\partial \phi} \overline{e}_\phi + \frac{1}{r\sin\phi} \frac{\partial f}{\partial \theta} \overline{e}_\theta \qquad (2)$$

The divergence of a vector field $\overline{F}$ in spherical coordinates is

$$\text{div } \overline{F} = \frac{1}{r^2} \frac{\partial(r^2 F_r)}{\partial r} + \frac{1}{r\sin\phi} \frac{\partial F_\theta}{\partial \theta} + \frac{1}{r\sin\phi} \frac{\partial(\sin\phi F_\phi)}{\partial \phi} \qquad (3)$$

Substituting eqs.(2) and (3) into eq.(1) results in

$$\nabla^2 f = \text{div grad } f = \frac{1}{r^2} \frac{\partial}{\partial r}\left[r^2 \frac{\partial f}{\partial r}\right]$$

$$+ \frac{1}{r\sin\phi} \frac{\partial}{\partial \theta}\left(\frac{1}{r\sin\phi} \frac{\partial f}{\partial \theta}\right) + \frac{1}{r\sin\phi} \frac{\partial}{\partial \phi}\left(\frac{1}{r} \frac{\partial f}{\partial \phi} \sin\phi\right)$$

$$= \frac{1}{r^2} \frac{\partial}{\partial r}\left[r^2 \frac{\partial f}{\partial r}\right] + \frac{1}{r^2\sin\phi} \frac{\partial}{\partial \phi}\left(\sin\phi \frac{\partial f}{\partial \phi}\right) + \frac{1}{r^2\sin^2\phi} \frac{\partial^2 f}{\partial \theta^2} \qquad (4)$$

If in particular

$$\nabla^2 f = 0,$$

then f is said to satisfy Laplace's equation.

● **PROBLEM 21-48**

Show that if f is a function of r only, then

$$\nabla^2 f(r) = \frac{d^2 f}{dr^2} + \frac{2}{r} \frac{df}{dr} \qquad (1)$$

Solution: In general, if f is a function of the spherical coordinates $f = f(r,\phi,\theta)$ then the Laplacian of f is given by

$$\nabla^2 f = \frac{1}{r^2} \frac{\partial}{\partial r}\left(r^2 \frac{\partial f}{\partial r}\right) + \frac{1}{r^2 \sin\phi} \frac{\partial}{\partial \phi}\left(\sin\phi \frac{\partial f}{\partial \phi}\right) + \frac{1}{r^2 \sin^2\phi} \frac{\partial^2 f}{\partial \theta^2} \quad (2)$$

Now, since in our case f is a function of r only, eq.(2) reduces to

$$\nabla^2 f = \frac{1}{r^2} \frac{d}{dr}\left(r^2 \frac{df}{dr}\right)$$

$$= \frac{1}{r^2}\left[\left(\frac{d}{dr} r^2\right)\left(\frac{df}{dr}\right) + r^2 \frac{d^2 f}{dr^2}\right]$$

$$= \frac{1}{r^2}\left[2r \frac{df}{dr} + r^2 \frac{d^2 f}{dr^2}\right]$$

$$= \frac{2}{r} \frac{df}{dr} + r^2 \frac{d^2 f}{dr^2} \quad (3)$$

which is the required result. Notice that the partial derivative became an ordinary derivative since f is a function of r only.

● **PROBLEM 21-49**

1. For what value of n is

$$\text{div}(r^n \bar{e}_r) = 0? \quad (1)$$

2. Show that for all n,

$$\text{curl}(r^n \bar{e}_r) = \bar{0}. \quad (2)$$

Solution: 1. The expression for the divergence of a vector field

$$\bar{F} = F_r \bar{e}_r + F_\phi \bar{e}_\phi + F_\theta \bar{e}_\theta \quad (3)$$

in spherical coordinates is given by

$$\text{div } \bar{F} = \frac{1}{r^2} \frac{\partial(r^2 F_r)}{\partial r} + \frac{1}{r \sin\phi} \frac{\partial F_\theta}{\partial \theta} + \frac{1}{r \sin\phi} \frac{\partial(\sin\phi F_\phi)}{\partial \phi} \quad (4)$$

If we let the vector field $\bar{F}$ be

$$\bar{F} = r^n \bar{e}_r \quad (5)$$

then, of course $F_r = r^n$ and $F_\theta = F_\phi = 0$ so that we obtain from eq.(4),

$$\text{div } \bar{F} = \frac{1}{r^2} \frac{\partial}{\partial r}(r^2 r^n) = \frac{1}{r^2} \frac{\partial}{\partial r}(r^{2+n})$$

$$= \frac{2+n}{r^2} r^{1+n} \quad (6)$$

From eq.(6), it is clear that div $\bar{F} = 0$ for n = -2. Thus,

$$\text{div}(r^{-2}\overline{e}_r) = 0 \tag{7}$$

2. In general, for a vector field $\overline{F}$ given in the spherical coordinates

$$\overline{F} = F_r\overline{e}_r + F_\phi\overline{e}_\phi + F_\theta\overline{e}_\theta \tag{8}$$

the curl of $\overline{F}$ is given by

$$\text{curl } \overline{F} = \frac{1}{r^2\sin\phi} \begin{vmatrix} \overline{e}_r & r\overline{e}_\phi & r\sin\phi\,\overline{e}_\theta \\ \frac{\partial}{\partial r} & \frac{\partial}{\partial \phi} & \frac{\partial}{\partial \theta} \\ F_r & rF_\phi & r\sin\phi F_\theta \end{vmatrix} \tag{9}$$

Since in our case

$$\overline{F} = r^n\,\overline{e}_r,$$

we see that curl $\overline{F}$ is

$$\text{curl}(r^n\overline{e}_r) = \frac{1}{r^2\sin\phi} \begin{vmatrix} \overline{e}_r & r\overline{e}_\phi & r\sin\phi\,\overline{e}_\theta \\ \frac{\partial}{\partial r} & \frac{\partial}{\partial \phi} & \frac{\partial}{\partial \theta} \\ r^n & 0 & 0 \end{vmatrix}$$

$$= \frac{1}{r^2\sin\phi}\left[0\,\overline{e}_r + 0\,\overline{e}_\phi + 0\,\overline{e}_\theta\right]$$

$$= \overline{0}$$

This does, of course, hold true for all n.

● **PROBLEM 21-50**

Find a vector field $\overline{F} = F_r(r)\overline{e}_r$ such that

$$\nabla \cdot \overline{F} = r^n, \qquad n \geq 0 \tag{1}$$

Prove the formula

$$\iiint\limits_V r^n\,dV = \frac{1}{n+3} \iint\limits_S r^{n+1}\,\overline{e}_r \cdot \overline{n}dS \tag{2}$$

Solution: In general, if $\overline{F} = \overline{F}(r,\phi,\theta)$ is a vector field given as a function of the spherical coordinates, then the divergence of $\overline{F}$ is given by

$$\text{div } \overline{F} = \frac{1}{r^2}\frac{\partial(r^2F_r)}{\partial r} + \frac{1}{r\sin\phi}\frac{\partial F_\theta}{\partial \theta} + \frac{1}{r\sin\phi}\frac{\partial(\sin\phi F_\phi)}{\partial \phi}$$

Now, if $\overline{F} = F_r(r)\overline{e}_r$, then the divergence reduces to

$$\mathrm{div}(F_r \bar{e}_r) = \nabla \cdot (F_r \bar{e}_r) = \frac{1}{r^2} \frac{\partial}{\partial r} (r^2 F_r) \tag{3}$$

But, we are told that

$$\nabla \cdot \bar{F} = r^n, \qquad n \geq 0 \tag{4}$$

Thus, from eqs.(4) and (3) we obtain

$$\frac{1}{r^2} \frac{\partial}{\partial r} (r^2 F_r) = r^n$$

or

$$\frac{\partial}{\partial r} (r^2 F_r) = r^n r^2 = r^{n+2}$$

$$F_r \frac{\partial}{\partial r} r^2 + r^2 \frac{\partial}{\partial r} F_r = r^{n+2}$$

$$2rF_r + r^2 \frac{\partial}{\partial r} F_r = r^{n+2}$$

$$\frac{2}{r} F_r + \frac{\partial}{\partial r} F_r = r^n \tag{5}$$

The solution to the above differential equation is of the form

$$F_r = \frac{r^a}{b} . \tag{6}$$

Since

$$\frac{\partial}{\partial r} \left(r^2 \frac{r^a}{b} \right) = \frac{\partial}{\partial r} \left(\frac{r^{a+2}}{b} \right) = \frac{a+2}{b} r^{a+1} = r^{n+2}$$

we see that $a = n+1$ and $b = n+3$.

Thus,

$$F_r = \frac{r^{n+1}}{n+3} \tag{7}$$

and the required vector field is

$$\bar{F} = \frac{r^{n+1}}{n+3} \bar{e}_r \tag{8}$$

Now, to prove the formula of eq.(2), let us refer to the divergence theorem, which states that

$$\iiint_V \nabla \cdot F \, dV = \iint_S \bar{F} \cdot \bar{n} \, dS \tag{9}$$

Let us substitute

$$\bar{F} = \frac{r^{n+1}}{n+3} \bar{e}_r$$

into eq.(9) to obtain

$$\iiint_V \nabla \cdot \left(\frac{r^{n+1}}{n+3} \bar{e}_r \right) dV = \iiint_V r^n dV$$

1081

$$= \iint\limits_{S} \frac{r^{n+1}}{n+3} \, \overline{e}_r \cdot \overline{n} \, dS = \frac{1}{n+3} \iint\limits_{S} r^{n+1} \, \overline{e}_r \cdot dS$$

● **PROBLEM** 21-51

Express the heat equation

$$k\nabla^2 U = \frac{\partial U}{\partial t} \qquad (1)$$

in spherical coordinates.

Consider the case for which U is independent of

(1) r and t,

(2) φ and θ.

Solution: Let us assume that U is a function of the spherical coordinates, $u = u(r, \phi, \theta)$.

The Laplacian $\nabla^2 U$ in spherical coordinates is $\qquad (2)$

$$\nabla^2 U = \frac{1}{r^2} \frac{\partial}{\partial r}\left(r^2 \frac{\partial U}{\partial r}\right) + \frac{1}{r^2 \sin\phi} \frac{\partial}{\partial \phi}\left(\sin\phi \frac{\partial U}{\partial \phi}\right) + \frac{1}{r^2 \sin^2\phi} \frac{\partial^2 U}{\partial \theta^2}$$

Thus, the heat equation in spherical coordinates is

$$\frac{1}{k} \frac{\partial}{\partial t} U(r,\phi,\theta) = \frac{1}{r^2} \frac{\partial}{\partial r}\left(r^2 \frac{\partial U}{\partial r}\right)$$

$$+ \frac{1}{r^2 \sin\phi} \frac{\partial}{\partial \phi}\left(\sin\phi \frac{\partial U}{\partial \phi}\right) + \frac{1}{r^2 \sin^2\phi} \frac{\partial^2 U}{\partial \theta^2} \qquad (3)$$

1. Now, if U is independent of r and t, then

$$\frac{\partial U}{\partial t} = 0 \quad \text{and} \quad \frac{\partial U}{\partial r} = 0 \qquad (4)$$

so that eq.(3) reduces to

$$\frac{\partial}{\partial \phi}\left(\sin\phi \frac{\partial U}{\partial \phi}\right) + \frac{1}{\sin\phi} \frac{\partial^2 U}{\partial \theta^2} = 0 \qquad (5)$$

2. If U is independent of φ and θ, then

$$\frac{\partial U}{\partial \phi} = 0 \quad \text{and} \quad \frac{\partial U}{\partial \theta} = 0 \qquad (6)$$

so that eq.(3) reduces to

$$\frac{1}{k} \frac{\partial U}{\partial t} = \frac{1}{r^2} \frac{\partial}{\partial r}\left(r^2 \frac{\partial U}{\partial t}\right) \qquad (7)$$

Express Schrödinger's equation of quantum mechanics

$$\nabla^2\psi + \frac{8\pi^2 m}{h^2}(E - V)\psi = 0 \qquad (1)$$

in cylindrical coordinates where E, m, h are constants.

Consider the case where Schrodinger's function ϕ is independent of z and θ.

Solution: The function ψ is expressed in terms of the cylindrical coordinates

$$\psi = \psi(\rho,\theta,z) \qquad (2)$$

Now, the Laplacian of ψ is

$$\nabla^2\psi = \frac{1}{\rho}\frac{\rho}{\partial\rho}\left(\rho\frac{\partial\psi}{\partial\rho}\right) + \frac{1}{\rho^2}\frac{\partial^2\psi}{\partial\theta^2} + \frac{\partial^2\psi}{\partial z^2} \qquad (3)$$

Schrodinger's equation may thus be written in terms of the cylindrical coordinates as:

$$\frac{1}{\rho}\frac{\partial}{\partial\rho}\left(\rho\frac{\partial\psi}{\partial\rho}\right) + \frac{1}{\rho^2}\frac{\partial^2\psi}{\partial\theta^2} + \frac{\partial^2\psi}{\partial z^2} = \frac{8\pi^2 m}{h^2}\left[V(\rho,\theta,z) - E\right]\psi(\rho,\theta,z) \qquad (4)$$

If ψ is independent of z and θ, then

$$\frac{\partial\psi}{\partial z} = \frac{\partial\psi}{\partial\theta} = 0 \qquad (5)$$

and eq.(4) reduces to

$$\frac{1}{\rho}\frac{\partial}{\partial\rho}\left(\rho\frac{\partial\psi}{\partial\rho}\right) = \frac{8\pi^2 m}{h^2}\left[V(\rho,\theta,z) - E\right]\psi(\rho) \qquad (6)$$

Express Maxwell's equation

$$-\frac{1}{c}\frac{\partial\overline{H}}{\partial t} = \nabla \times \overline{E} \qquad (1)$$

in spherical coordinates.

Consider the case where $\overline{H}$ is constant and $\overline{E} = \overline{E}(r)$.

Solution: Both vectors $\overline{E}$ and $\overline{H}$ have to be expressed in terms of the spherical coordinates.

$$\overline{E} = E_r\overline{e}_r + E_\phi\overline{e}_\phi + E_\theta\overline{e}_\theta$$

$$\overline{H} = H_r\overline{e}_r + H_\phi\overline{e}_\phi + H_\theta\overline{e}_\theta \qquad (2)$$

Now, since the curl of a vector field in spherical coordinates is given by

$$\text{curl } \bar{E} = \nabla \times \bar{E} = \frac{1}{r^2 \sin\phi} \begin{vmatrix} \bar{e}_r & r\bar{e}_\phi & r\sin\phi\,\bar{e}_\theta \\ \frac{\partial}{\partial r} & \frac{\partial}{\partial \phi} & \frac{\partial}{\partial \theta} \\ E_r & rE_\phi & r\sin\phi E_\theta \end{vmatrix} \tag{3}$$

we see that Maxwell's equation in spherical coordinates is

$$\nabla \times \bar{E} = \frac{1}{r^2 \sin\phi} \begin{vmatrix} \bar{e}_r & r\bar{e}_\phi & r\sin\phi\,\bar{e}_\theta \\ \frac{\partial}{\partial r} & \frac{\partial}{\partial \phi} & \frac{\partial}{\partial \theta} \\ E_r & rE_\phi & r\sin\phi E_\theta \end{vmatrix}$$

$$= -\frac{1}{c}\frac{\partial H_r}{\partial t}\bar{e}_r - \frac{1}{c}\frac{\partial H_\phi}{\partial t}\bar{e}_\phi - \frac{1}{c}\frac{\partial H_\theta}{\partial t}\bar{e}_\theta \tag{4}$$

When the magnetic field vector $\bar{H}$ is constant, we have

$$\frac{\partial H_r}{\partial t} = \frac{\partial H_\phi}{\partial t} = \frac{\partial H_\theta}{\partial t} = 0 \tag{5}$$

Furthermore, if $\bar{E} = \bar{E}(r)$, that is, if the electric field vector is a function of r only, then

$$\frac{\partial \bar{E}}{\partial \phi} = \bar{0} \quad \text{and} \quad \frac{\partial \bar{E}}{\partial \theta} = \bar{0}$$

and eq.(4) becomes

$$\bar{e}_r \left[\frac{E_\theta \cos\phi}{r\sin\phi} \right] + \bar{e}_\theta \left[\frac{1}{r}\frac{\partial(rE_\phi)}{\partial r} \right] + \bar{e}_\phi \left[-\frac{1}{r}\frac{\partial(rE_\theta)}{\partial r} \right] = \bar{0} \tag{6}$$

● **PROBLEM** 21-54

Verify the divergence theorem for the vector field

$$\bar{F} = r^n \bar{e}_r \tag{1}$$

and the volume bounded by the unit upper hemisphere $r=1$, $0 \le \phi \le \frac{\pi}{2}$ and the plane $\phi = \frac{\pi}{2}$.

Solution: The divergence theorem states that

$$\iiint_V \text{div } \bar{F} \, dV = \iint_S \bar{F} \cdot \bar{n} \, dS \tag{2}$$

1084

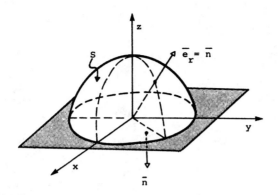

where S is a piecewise-smooth, closed, oriented surface and $\overline{F}$ is a continuously differentiable vector field.

We shall now verify the divergence theorem by evaluating both the volume integral and the surface integral. Let us first evaluate the volume integral. For div $\overline{F}$, we have

$$\text{div } \overline{F} = \nabla \cdot (r^n \overline{e}_r) = \frac{1}{r^2} \frac{\partial}{\partial r} (r^2 r^n)$$

$$= \frac{1}{r^2} \frac{\partial}{\partial r} (r^{n+2}) = \frac{n+2}{r^2} r^{n+1} = (n+2)r^{n-1} \qquad (3)$$

Now, the volume element in spherical coordinates is

$$dV = r^2 \sin\phi \, dr \, d\theta \, d\phi$$

The volume integral over the unit upper hemisphere (see Fig. 1) is thus,

$$\iiint_V \text{div } \overline{F} \cdot dV = \int_{\phi=0}^{\frac{\pi}{2}} \int_{\theta=0}^{2\pi} \int_{r=0}^{1} (n+2)r^{n-1} r^2 \sin\phi \, dr \, d\theta \, d\phi$$

$$= \int_{\phi=0}^{\frac{\pi}{2}} \int_{\theta=0}^{2\pi} \left[\frac{n+2}{n+2} r^{n+2} \right] \Bigg|_0^1 \sin\phi \, d\theta \, d\phi$$

$$= \int_{\phi=0}^{\frac{\pi}{2}} \int_{\theta=0}^{2\pi} \sin\phi \, d\theta \, d\phi$$

$$= \int_{\phi=0}^{\frac{\pi}{2}} \left(\theta \Bigg|_0^{2\pi} \right) \sin\phi \, d\phi = 2\pi \int_{\phi=0}^{\frac{\pi}{2}} \sin\phi \, d\phi$$

$$= 2\pi(-\cos\phi) \Bigg|_{\phi=0}^{\frac{\pi}{2}} = 2\pi \qquad (4)$$

Now, for the surface integral, we have

$$\iint_S \overline{F} \cdot \overline{n} \, dS = \iint_S (r^n \, \overline{e}_r) \cdot \overline{n} \, dS$$

$$= \iint_{\text{hemisphere}} r^n \, \overline{e}_r \cdot \overline{n} \, dS + \iint_{\text{circle}} r^n \, \overline{e}_r \cdot \overline{n} \, dS$$

$$= \iint_{\text{hemisphere}} r^n \, \overline{e}_r \cdot \overline{n} \, dS = \iint_{\text{hemisphere}} (1)^n dS$$

$$= \iint_{\text{hemisphere}} dS = 2\pi(1)^2 = 2\pi \qquad (5)$$

Note that the last integral represents the surface area of the unit hemisphere which is $2\pi r^2 = 2\pi$.

From eqs.(4) and (5) we see that the volume and surface integrals are equal in value. Thus, we have verified the divergence theorem for this case.

● **PROBLEM** 21-55

Verify Stokes' theorem for

$$\overline{F} = y\overline{i} \qquad (1)$$

and the hemisphere S described by

$$r = 1, \quad 0 \leq \phi \leq \frac{\pi}{2}, \quad 0 \leq \theta \leq 2\pi.$$

Use the spherical coordinates.

Solution: Stokes' theorem states that

$$\oint_C \overline{F} \cdot d\overline{r} = \iint_S \text{curl } \overline{F} \cdot d\overline{S} \qquad (2)$$

where S is a smooth oriented surface in space bounded by a piecewise smooth, closed curve C whose orientation is consistent with that of S. $\overline{F}$ is a continuously differentiable vector field. The vector field $\overline{F} = y\overline{i}$ expressed in spherical coordinates is

$$\overline{F} = r\sin^2\phi\sin\theta\cos\theta\overline{e}_r + r\sin\phi\cos\phi\sin\theta\cos\theta\overline{e}_\phi - r\sin\phi\sin^2\theta\overline{e}_\theta \qquad (3)$$

The length element is

$$d\overline{r} = \overline{e}_r dr + \overline{e}_\phi rd\phi + \overline{e}_\theta r\sin\phi d\theta \qquad (4)$$

1086

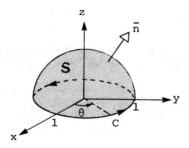

For the curve C, which is a circle of radius one (as shown in Fig. 1), we have

$$r = 1, \quad \phi = \frac{\pi}{2}, \quad 0 \leq \theta \leq 2\pi \tag{5}$$

$$d\overline{r} = \overline{e}_\theta d\theta \tag{6}$$

$$\overline{F} = \sin\theta\cos\theta\,\overline{e}_r - \sin^2\theta\,\overline{e}_\theta \tag{7}$$

The left-hand side of eq.(2) is equal to

$$\oint_C \overline{F} \cdot d\overline{r} = \int_{\theta=0}^{2\pi} (\sin\theta\cos\theta\,\overline{e}_r - \sin^2\theta\,\overline{e}_\theta) \cdot (\overline{e}_\theta d\theta)$$

$$= \int_0^{2\pi} -\sin^2\theta\,d\theta = -\pi \tag{8}$$

To compute the surface integral in eq.(2), we need to first determine curl $\overline{F}$.

$$\text{curl } \overline{F} = -\cos\phi\,\overline{e}_r + \sin\phi\,\overline{e}_\phi \tag{9}$$

The unit normal to the hemisphere is $\overline{n} = \overline{e}_r$. Thus

$$\iint_S \left[-\cos\phi\,\overline{e}_r + \sin\phi\,\overline{e}_\phi \right] \cdot \overline{e}_r \, \sin\phi\,d\phi\,d\theta$$

$$= \iint_S (-\sin\phi\cos\phi)\,d\phi\,d\theta$$

$$= \int_{\phi=0}^{\frac{\pi}{2}} \int_{\theta=0}^{2\pi} -\sin\phi\cos\phi\,d\phi\,d\theta \tag{10}$$

$$= \pi \left[\frac{\cos 2\phi}{2} \Big|_{\phi=0}^{\frac{\pi}{2}} \right] = -\pi$$

That completes the verification of eq.(2).

CHAPTER 22

CURVILINEAR COORDINATES

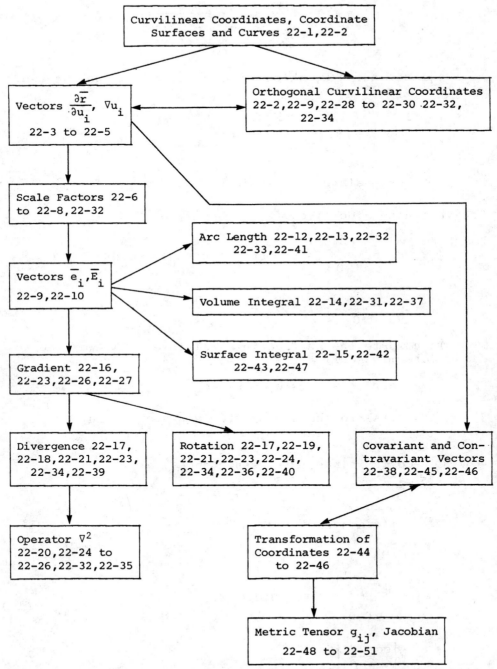

This chart is provided to facilitate rapid understanding of the inter-relationships of the topics and subject matter in this chapter. Also shown are the problem numbers associated with the subject matter.

COORDINATE SURFACES, COORDINATE CURVES, ORTHOGONAL COORDINATE SYSTEMS

Define the curvilinear coordinates. What conditions should be imposed on the transformation equations between the curvilinear coordinates and Cartesian coordinates?

Solution: Consider a region of space such that each point is specified by three numbers (u_1, u_2, u_3), which are called the curvilinear coordinates of a point.

The transformation equations between the curvilinear coordinates and the Cartesian coordinates are

$$x = x(u_1, u_2, u_3)$$

$$y = y(u_1, u_2, u_3) \tag{1}$$

$$z = z(u_1, u_2, u_3)$$

The functions (1) are single-valued functions of u_1, u_2, and u_3 and are assumed to be continuously differentiable. Furthermore, it is assumed that at every point the gradients of the functions are non-zero.

The set of eqs.(1) may be solved for u_1, u_2, u_3 in terms of x, y, z.

$$u_1 = u_1(x, y, z)$$

$$u_2 = u_2(x, y, z) \tag{2}$$

$$u_3 = u_3(x, y, z)$$

Here, u_1, u_2, u_3 are single-valued, continuously differentiable functions of x, y, and z.

The set of equations (1) and (2) define a one-to-one correspondence between each point (x, y, z) and the related set of values (u_1, u_2, u_3).

Let us consider, as an example, the set of equations

$$u_1 = x^2 + 1$$

$$u_2 = z - y \qquad (3)$$

$$u_3 = 2z - 2y$$

The set of eqs.(3) do not define a curvilinear coordinate system, since the functions u_1, u_2 and u_3 are not single-valued functions of x, y and z. Indeed, the points $(x,y,z) = (1,2,3)$ and $(x,y,z) = (-1,3,4)$ have identical curvilinear coordinates $(2,1,2)$.

● **PROBLEM** 22-2

Define the coordinate surfaces and coordinate curves. Find the normal vectors to these surfaces and define an orthogonal curvilinear coordinate system.

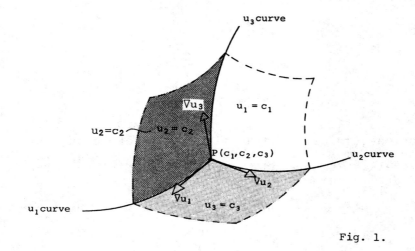

Fig. 1.

Solution: Consider a point P in the domain, having curvilinear coordinates (c_1, c_2, c_3). Three surfaces pass through this point

$$u_1(x,y,z) = c_1$$

$$u_2(x,y,z) = c_2 \qquad (1)$$

$$u_3(x,y,z) = c_3$$

as shown in Fig. 1.

These surfaces $u_1 = c_1$, $u_2 = c_2$, $u_3 = c_3$ are called the coordinate surfaces and they intersect pairwise in three curves, called the coordinate curves. On each of the coordinate curves, only one coordinate varies. The curve formed by the intersection of the coordinate surfaces $u_1 = c_1$ and $u_2 = c_2$ is called the u_3-curve, since only u_3 varies along this curve. Similarly, u_1 and u_2 vary along the u_1 and u_2 curves, respectively. For example, along the PA curve shown in the figure, only the u_3 coordinate varies (the other two remain constant).

The normal to the surface $u_i = c_i$ is the gradient

$$\nabla u_i = \frac{\partial u_i}{\partial x} \bar{i} + \frac{\partial u_i}{\partial y} \bar{j} + \frac{\partial u_i}{\partial z} \bar{k} \qquad (2)$$

Whenever the vectors $\nabla u_1, \nabla u_2, \nabla u_3$ are mutually orthogonal at every point, then u_1, u_2, u_3 is said to be an orthogonal curvilinear coordinate system.

● PROBLEM 22-3

Consider an orthogonal curvilinear coordinate system. The numbers u_i are ordered so that ∇u_1, ∇u_2, and ∇u_3 form a right-handed system.

Show that each gradient vector ∇u_i is parallel to the tangent vector $\frac{\partial \bar{r}}{\partial u_i}$ of the corresponding coordinate curve.

Solution: The normal vector to the surface $u_i = c_i$ is the gradient

$$\nabla u_i = \frac{\partial u_i}{\partial x} \bar{i} + \frac{\partial u_i}{\partial y} \bar{j} + \frac{\partial u_i}{\partial z} \bar{k} \qquad (1)$$

The vector

$$\frac{\partial \bar{r}}{\partial u_i} = \frac{\partial x}{\partial u_i} \bar{i} + \frac{\partial y}{\partial u_i} \bar{j} + \frac{\partial z}{\partial u_i} \bar{k} \qquad (2)$$

is tangent to the coordinate curve u_i.

Consider the coordinate curve u_1, which is formed by the intersection of the two surfaces $u_2 = c_2$ and $u_3 = c_3$. The vector tangent to u_1 is $\frac{\partial \bar{r}}{\partial u_1}$, and is also perpendicular to both surface normals ∇u_2 and ∇u_3. Now, since u_1, u_2, u_3 is an orthogonal system, ∇u_1 is also perpendicular to ∇u_2 and ∇u_3.

Thus, the vectors $\frac{\partial \bar{r}}{\partial u_1}$ and ∇u_1, both of which point in the direction of increasing u_1, are parallel.

Thus, $\frac{\partial \bar{r}}{\partial u_1}$ is parallel to ∇u_1.

1091

We conclude that when u_1, u_2, u_3 is an orthogonal system, any coordinate curve of u_i intersects the surface $u_i = c_i$ at right angles.

● PROBLEM 22-4

Show that if u_1, u_2, u_3 are general curvilinear coordinates, then $\nabla u_1, \nabla u_2, \nabla u_3$ and $\dfrac{\partial \overline{r}}{\partial u_1}, \dfrac{\partial \overline{r}}{\partial u_2}, \dfrac{\partial \overline{r}}{\partial u_3}$ are reciprocal systems of vectors.

<u>Solution</u>: We have to prove the identity

$$\frac{\partial \overline{r}}{\partial u_i} \cdot \nabla u_j = \delta_{ij} = \begin{cases} 1 & \text{if} \quad i = j \\ 0 & \text{if} \quad i \neq j \end{cases} \tag{1}$$

where $i, j = 1, 2, 3$.

The symbol δ_{ij} is called the Kronecker delta.

Applying the chain rule, we find

$$\frac{\partial \overline{r}}{\partial u_i} \cdot \nabla u_j = \left[\frac{\partial x}{\partial u_i} \overline{i} + \frac{\partial y}{\partial u_i} \overline{j} + \frac{\partial z}{\partial u_i} \overline{k} \right] \cdot \left[\frac{\partial u_j}{\partial x} \overline{i} + \frac{\partial u_j}{\partial y} \overline{j} + \frac{\partial u_j}{\partial z} \overline{k} \right]$$

$$= \frac{\partial x}{\partial u_i} \left(\frac{\partial u_j}{\partial x} \right) + \frac{\partial y}{\partial u_i} \left(\frac{\partial u_j}{\partial y} \right) + \frac{\partial z}{\partial u_i} \left(\frac{\partial u_j}{\partial z} \right)$$

$$= \frac{\partial u_j}{\partial u_i} = \begin{cases} 1 & \text{for} \quad j = i \\ 0 & \text{for} \quad j \neq i \end{cases} \tag{2}$$

● PROBLEM 22-5

Prove that

$$\left(\frac{\partial \overline{r}}{\partial u_1} \cdot \frac{\partial \overline{r}}{\partial u_2} \times \frac{\partial \overline{r}}{\partial u_3} \right) (\nabla u_1 \cdot \nabla u_2 \times \nabla u_3) = 1 \tag{1}$$

<u>Solution</u>: The vectors $\dfrac{\partial \overline{r}}{\partial u_1}, \dfrac{\partial \overline{r}}{\partial u_2}, \dfrac{\partial \overline{r}}{\partial u_3}$ and $\nabla u_1, \nabla u_2, \nabla u_3$ are reciprocal systems of vectors (see Problem 22-4).

Therefore, if

$$\frac{\partial \overline{r}}{\partial u_1} \cdot \frac{\partial \overline{r}}{\partial u_2} \times \frac{\partial \overline{r}}{\partial u_3} = a \tag{2}$$

then

$$\nabla u_1 \cdot \nabla u_2 \times \nabla u_3 = \frac{1}{a} \tag{3}$$

That proves eq.(1).

Another method of proving eq.(1) is by observing that

$$\nabla u_1 \cdot \nabla u_2 \times \nabla u_3 = \begin{vmatrix} \dfrac{\partial u_1}{\partial x} & \dfrac{\partial u_1}{\partial y} & \dfrac{\partial u_1}{\partial z} \\[2mm] \dfrac{\partial u_2}{\partial x} & \dfrac{\partial u_2}{\partial y} & \dfrac{\partial u_2}{\partial z} \\[2mm] \dfrac{\partial u_3}{\partial x} & \dfrac{\partial u_3}{\partial y} & \dfrac{\partial u_3}{\partial z} \end{vmatrix} = J\left(\dfrac{u_1,u_2,u_3}{x,y,z}\right) \qquad (4)$$

Therefore

$$J\left(\dfrac{u_1,u_2,u_3}{x,y,z}\right) J\left(\dfrac{x,y,z}{u_1,u_2,u_3}\right) = 1 \qquad (5)$$

UNIT TANGENT VECTORS AND SCALE FACTORS

● **PROBLEM** 22-6

Express the displacement vector $d\bar{r}$ in terms of the scale factors h_i.

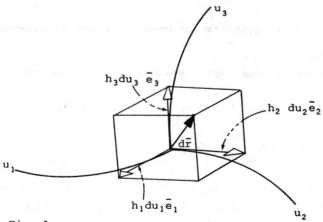

Fig. 1

Solution: The scale factor is defined as the rate at which arc length increases on the ith coordinate curve with respect to u_i.

If s_i denotes arc length on the ith coordinate curve, measured in the direction of increasing u_i, then

$$h_i = \frac{ds_i}{du_i} \qquad (1)$$

If the position vector $\bar{r}$ is given as a function of u_1, u_2, u_3, that is

$$\bar{r} = \bar{r}(u_1, u_2, u_3) \qquad (2)$$

then the arc length can be expressed as

$$ds = |d\bar{r}| = \left| \frac{\partial \bar{r}}{\partial u_1} du_1 + \frac{\partial \bar{r}}{\partial u_2} du_2 + \frac{\partial \bar{r}}{\partial u_3} du_3 \right| \qquad (3)$$

From eqs.(1) and (3) we conclude that

$$h_i = \left| \frac{\partial \bar{r}}{\partial u_i} \right| \qquad (4)$$

Defining the unit vectors

$$\bar{e}_1 = \frac{\frac{\partial \bar{r}}{\partial u_1}}{\left| \frac{\partial \bar{r}}{\partial u_1} \right|}, \qquad \bar{e}_2 = \frac{\frac{\partial \bar{r}}{\partial u_2}}{\left| \frac{\partial \bar{r}}{\partial u_2} \right|}, \qquad \bar{e}_3 = \frac{\frac{\partial \bar{r}}{\partial u_3}}{\left| \frac{\partial \bar{r}}{\partial u_3} \right|} \qquad (5)$$

we can express the displacement vector in terms of the scale factors by

$$d\bar{r} = h_1 du_1 \bar{e}_1 + h_2 du_2 \bar{e}_2 + h_3 du_3 \bar{e}_3 \qquad (6)$$

● **PROBLEM 22-7**

Express the scale factors h_1, h_2, h_3 in terms of the gradients $\nabla u_1, \nabla u_2, \nabla u_3$.

Solution: The scale factors are defined as

$$h_i = \frac{ds_i}{du_i} \qquad i = 1,2,3 \qquad (1)$$

Note that $|\nabla u_i|$ is the rate of change of u_i with respect to distance in the direction of ∇u_i. The direction of ∇u_i is the direction of the coordinate curve u_i.

s_i measures distance along the coordinate curve u_i. Therefore

$$|\nabla u_i| = \frac{du_i}{ds_i} = \frac{1}{h_i} \qquad (2)$$

and

$$h_1 = \frac{1}{|\nabla u_1|}, \qquad h_2 = \frac{1}{|\nabla u_2|}, \qquad h_3 = \frac{1}{|\nabla u_3|} \qquad (3)$$

Evaluate the scale factors for the paraboloidal system of coordinates.

Solution: The rectangular coordinates are related to the paraboloidal coordinates (u,v,ϕ) by

$$x = uv\cos\phi$$
$$y = uv\sin\phi \tag{1}$$
$$z = \frac{1}{2}(u^2 - v^2)$$

where $u \geq 0, \quad v \geq 0, \quad 0 \leq \phi \leq 2\pi.$

The scale factors are

$$h_u = \left|\frac{\partial \bar{r}}{\partial u}\right| = |(v\cos\phi, v\sin\phi, u)|$$
$$= \sqrt{v^2\cos^2\phi + v^2\sin^2\phi + u^2} = \sqrt{v^2 + u^2} \tag{2}$$

$$h_v = \left|\frac{\partial \bar{r}}{\partial v}\right| = |(u\cos\phi, u\sin\phi, -v)|$$
$$= \sqrt{u^2 + v^2} \tag{3}$$

$$h_\phi = \left|\frac{\partial \bar{r}}{\partial \phi}\right| = |(-uv\sin\phi, uv\cos\phi, 0)|$$
$$= uv \tag{4}$$

● **PROBLEM** 22-9

Show that for an orthogonal system of coordinates,

$$\bar{e}_i = \bar{E}_i \quad \text{where } i = 1,2,3 \tag{1}$$

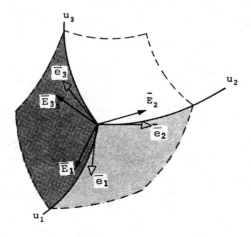

1095

Solution: A unit tangent vector to the curve u_i at a point P is

$$\bar{e}_i = \frac{\frac{\partial \bar{r}}{\partial u_i}}{\left| \frac{\partial \bar{r}}{\partial u_i} \right|} \tag{2}$$

A unit vector normal to the surface $u_i = c_i$ at P is

$$\bar{E}_i = \frac{\nabla u_i}{|\nabla u_i|} \tag{3}$$

At each point P of a curvilinear system, there exist, in general, two sets of vectors, $\bar{e}_1, \bar{e}_2, \bar{e}_3$, which are tangent to the coordinate curves, and $\bar{E}_1, \bar{E}_2, \bar{E}_3$, which are normal to the coordinate surfaces (as shown in Fig. 1).

We will now show that both sets are identical if and only if the curvilinear coordinate system is orthogonal.

In general, we can write

$$\nabla u_1 = g_1 \bar{e}_1 + g_2 \bar{e}_2 + g_3 \bar{e}_3 \tag{4}$$

Since

$$d\bar{r} = \frac{\partial \bar{r}}{\partial u_1} du_1 + \frac{\partial \bar{r}}{\partial u_2} du_2 + \frac{\partial \bar{r}}{\partial u_3} du_3 \tag{5}$$

$$= h_1 \bar{e}_1 du_1 + h_2 \bar{e}_2 du_2 + h_3 \bar{e}_3 du_3$$

we have

$$du_1 = \nabla u_1 \cdot d\bar{r} = h_1 g_1 du_1 + h_2 g_2 du_2 + h_3 g_3 du_3 \tag{6}$$

But,

$$du_1 = \frac{\partial u_1}{\partial u_1} du_1 = (1) du_1 = du_1 \tag{7}$$

From eqs.(6) and (7), we obtain

$$h_1 g_1 = 1, \quad h_2 g_2 = 0, \quad h_3 g_3 = 0 \tag{8}$$

or

$$g_2 = g_3 = 0$$

In eq.(5), we used the formula

$$\frac{\partial \bar{r}}{\partial u_i} = h_i \bar{e}_i \tag{9}$$

and in deriving eq.(6), we utilized the fact that $\bar{e}_1, \bar{e}_2, \bar{e}_3$ are mutually orthogonal unit vectors.

We have

$$\nabla u_1 = \frac{1}{h_1} \bar{e}_1 \tag{10}$$

Hence,

$$|\nabla u_1| = \frac{|\overline{e}_1|}{h_1} = h_1^{-1} \tag{11}$$

Finally

$$\overline{E}_1 = \frac{\nabla u_1}{|\nabla u_1|} = \frac{1}{h_1} \overline{e}_1 h_1 = \overline{e}_1 \tag{12}$$

In the same manner, we can show that

$$\overline{E}_2 = \overline{e}_2 \quad \text{and} \quad \overline{E}_3 = \overline{e}_3 \tag{13}$$

● **PROBLEM** 22-10

Prove the identities

$$\overline{e}_1 = h_2 h_3 \; \nabla u_2 \times \nabla u_3 \tag{1}$$

$$\overline{e}_2 = h_1 h_3 \; \nabla u_3 \times \nabla u_1 \tag{2}$$

$$\overline{e}_3 = h_1 h_2 \; \nabla u_1 \times \nabla u_2 \tag{3}$$

Solution: The set of vectors $\overline{e}_1, \overline{e}_2, \overline{e}_3$ form a right-handed orthogonal system.

From Problem 22-9, eq.(10), we have

$$\nabla u_1 = \frac{\overline{e}_1}{h_1}, \quad \nabla u_2 = \frac{\overline{e}_2}{h_2}, \quad \nabla u_3 = \frac{\overline{e}_3}{h_3} \tag{4,5,6}$$

Hence,

$$\overline{e}_1 = h_2 h_3 \; \nabla u_2 \times \nabla u_3 = h_2 h_3 \frac{\overline{e}_2}{h_2} \times \frac{\overline{e}_3}{h_3}$$

$$= \overline{e}_2 \times \overline{e}_3 \tag{7}$$

which is true, since $\overline{e}_1, \overline{e}_2, \overline{e}_3$ are mutually orthogonal and form a right-handed system.

In the same manner, we can prove eqs.(2) and (3).

● **PROBLEM** 22-11

Consider the curvilinear coordinate system

$$x = 2u_1 + u_2$$

$$y = u_1 - 2u_2 \tag{1}$$

$$z = u_3^2$$

defined for $z \geq 0$.

Compute the unit vectors $\bar{e}_i$ and the scale factors h_i.
Show that the system is orthogonal but not right-handed.

Solution: We shall first evaluate the vectors $\bar{e}_i$. We have,

$$\bar{r} = x\bar{i} + y\bar{j} + z\bar{k}$$

$$= (2u_1 + u_2)\bar{i} + (u_1 - 2u_2)\bar{j} + u_3^2\,\bar{k}$$

so that

$$\bar{e}_1 = \frac{\dfrac{\partial \bar{r}}{\partial u_1}}{\left|\dfrac{\partial \bar{r}}{\partial u_1}\right|} = \frac{2\bar{i} + \bar{j}}{\sqrt{5}} \qquad (2)$$

$$\bar{e}_2 = \frac{\dfrac{\partial \bar{r}}{\partial u_2}}{\left|\dfrac{\partial \bar{r}}{\partial u_2}\right|} = \frac{\bar{i} - 2\bar{j}}{\sqrt{5}} \qquad (3)$$

$$\bar{e}_3 = \frac{\dfrac{\partial \bar{r}}{\partial u_3}}{\left|\dfrac{\partial \bar{r}}{\partial u_3}\right|} = \frac{2u_3\bar{k}}{2u_3} = \bar{k} \qquad (4)$$

Now, let us note that

$$\bar{e}_1 \cdot \bar{e}_2 = \frac{1}{\sqrt{5}}(2\bar{i} + \bar{j}) \cdot \frac{1}{\sqrt{5}}(\bar{i} - 2\bar{j})$$

$$= \frac{2}{5} - \frac{2}{5} = 0$$

$$\bar{e}_2 \cdot \bar{e}_3 = \frac{1}{\sqrt{5}}(\bar{i} - 2\bar{j}) \cdot \bar{k} = 0$$

$$\bar{e}_3 \cdot \bar{e}_1 = \bar{k} \cdot \frac{1}{\sqrt{5}}(2\bar{i} + \bar{j}) = 0$$

Thus, the curvilinear coordinate system given by (1) is orthogonal.

Now, if an orthogonal coordinate system is right-handed, then

$$\bar{e}_1 = \bar{e}_2 \times \bar{e}_3 \qquad (5)$$

If it is left-handed, then

$$\bar{e}_1 = -\bar{e}_2 \times \bar{e}_3.$$

We have

$$\bar{e}_2 \times \bar{e}_3 = \frac{1}{\sqrt{5}} (\bar{i} - 2\bar{j}) \times \bar{k} = \frac{-2}{\sqrt{5}} \bar{i} - \frac{1}{\sqrt{5}} \bar{j} = -\bar{e}_1 \qquad (6)$$

From eq.(6), we see that the curvilinear coordinate system given by (1) is not right-handed, but rather, left-handed.

Now, the scale factors are defined as

$$h_i = \left| \frac{\partial \bar{r}}{\partial u_i} \right| \qquad (7)$$

It is easy to see that they are the denominators in the expressions for $\bar{e}_i$. Hence,

$$h_1 = \sqrt{5}, \qquad h_2 = \sqrt{5}, \qquad h_3 = 2u_3 \qquad (8)$$

ELEMENT OF ARC LENGTH, VOLUME ELEMENT

● **PROBLEM** 22-12

Derive the equation for the arc length along a curve C in orthogonal curvilinear coordinates.

<u>Solution</u>: From $\qquad \bar{r} = \bar{r}(u_1, u_2, u_3) \qquad (1)$

we get

$$d\bar{r} = \frac{\partial \bar{r}}{\partial u_1} du_1 + \frac{\partial \bar{r}}{\partial u_2} du_2 + \frac{\partial \bar{r}}{\partial u_3} du_3$$

$$= h_1 \bar{e}_1 du_1 + h_2 \bar{e}_2 du_2 + h_3 \bar{e}_3 du_3 \qquad (2)$$

The differential of arc length ds is evaluated from

$$ds^2 = d\bar{r} \cdot d\bar{r} \qquad (3)$$

For orthogonal systems

$$\bar{e}_1 \cdot \bar{e}_2 = \bar{e}_1 \cdot \bar{e}_3 = \bar{e}_2 \cdot \bar{e}_3 = 0 \qquad (4)$$

and eq.(3) becomes

$$ds^2 = h_1^2 du_1^2 + h_2^2 du_2^2 + h_3^2 du_3^2 \qquad (5)$$

so that

$$ds = \sqrt{h_1^2 du_1^2 + h_2^2 du_2^2 + h_3^2 du_3^2} \qquad (6)$$

The arc length along a curve C is given by the line integral

$$\int_C |d\overline{r}| = \int_C ds = \int_C \sqrt{h_1^2 du_1^2 + h_2^2 du_2^2 + h_3^2 du_3^2} \tag{7}$$

● **PROBLEM 22-13**

Derive the equation for the square of the element of arc length in general curvilinear coordinates. Define the fundamental quadratic form.

<u>Solution:</u> The displacement vector $d\overline{r}$ is

$$d\overline{r} = \frac{\partial \overline{r}}{\partial u_1} du_1 + \frac{\partial \overline{r}}{\partial u_2} du_2 + \frac{\partial \overline{r}}{\partial u_3} du_3$$

$$= \overline{g}_1 du_1 + \overline{g}_2 du_2 + \overline{g}_3 du_3 \tag{1}$$

We denote

$$\frac{\partial \overline{r}}{\partial u_i} = \overline{g}_i \tag{2}$$

Thus, the square of the element of arc length is

$$ds^2 = d\overline{r} \cdot d\overline{r} = (\overline{g}_1 du_1 + \overline{g}_2 du_2 + \overline{g}_3 du_3) \cdot (\overline{g}_1 du_1 + \overline{g}_2 du_2 + \overline{g}_3 du_3)$$

$$= \overline{g}_1 \cdot \overline{g}_1 du_1^2 + \overline{g}_1 \cdot \overline{g}_2 du_1 du_2 + \overline{g}_1 \cdot \overline{g}_3 du_1 du_3 + \overline{g}_2 \cdot \overline{g}_1 du_1 du_2$$

$$+ \overline{g}_2 \cdot \overline{g}_2 du_2^2 + \overline{g}_2 \cdot \overline{g}_3 du_2 du_3 + \overline{g}_3 \cdot \overline{g}_1 du_1 du_3 + \overline{g}_3 \cdot \overline{g}_2 du_2 du_3 \tag{3}$$

$$+ \overline{g}_3 \cdot \overline{g}_3 du_3^2$$

We define the fundamental quadratic form, or metric form,

$$g_{ij} = \overline{g}_i \cdot \overline{g}_j = \frac{\partial \overline{r}}{\partial u_i} \cdot \frac{\partial \overline{r}}{\partial u_j} \tag{4}$$

The elements g_{ij} are called metric coefficients. g_{ij} is symmetric, i.e.

$$g_{ij} = g_{ji}$$

as can be seen from the definition (eq.(4)).

If $g_{ij} = 0$ for $i \neq j$, then the coordinate system is orthogonal and

$$g_{11} = h_1^2, \quad g_{22} = h_2^2, \quad g_{33} = h_3^2 \tag{5}$$

Eq.(3) can be written in the form

$$ds^2 = \sum_{i=1}^{3} \sum_{j=1}^{3} g_{ij} du_i du_j \tag{6}$$

or, using the Einstein convention,

$$ds^2 = g_{ij} \, du_i du_j, \quad i,j = 1,2,3 \qquad (7)$$

Express the line integral of a continuous vector field $\overline{F}$ in general coordinates along a curve C.

Write the volume integral of a function $f(u_1, u_2, u_3)$.

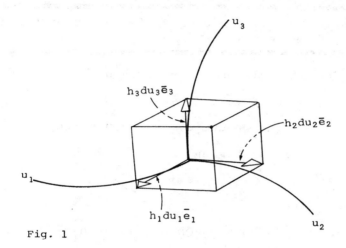

Fig. 1

Solution: Consider a continuous vector field $\overline{F}$ expressed in general coordinates

$$\overline{F} = F_1\overline{e}_1 + F_2\overline{e}_2 + F_3\overline{e}_3 \qquad (1)$$

The line integral of $\overline{F}$ along a curve C is

$$\int_C \overline{F} \cdot d\overline{r} = \int_C (F_1 h_1 du_1 + F_2 h_2 du_2 + F_3 h_3 du_3) \qquad (2)$$

The volume element for an orthogonal curvilinear coordinate system is shown in Fig. 1.

Note that since the displacement vector is given by

$$d\overline{r} = h_1 du_1 \overline{e}_1 + h_2 du_2 \overline{e}_2 + h_3 du_3 \overline{e}_3 \qquad (3)$$

Then, along a u_1 curve, u_2 and u_3 are constant and

$$d\overline{r} = h_1 du_1 \overline{e}_1 \qquad (4)$$

The volume element is

$$dV = |(h_1 du_1 \overline{e}_1) \cdot (h_2 du_2 \overline{e}_2) \times (h_3 du_3 \overline{e}_3)| \qquad (5)$$

1101

$$= h_1 h_2 h_3 \, du_1 du_2 du_3$$

since

$$|\bar{e}_1 \cdot \bar{e}_2 \times \bar{e}_3| = 1 \tag{6}$$

Thus, the volume integral is

$$\iiint\limits_V f(u_1, u_2, u_3) dV = \iiint\limits_V f(u_1, u_2, u_3) h_1 h_2 h_3 \, du_1 du_2 du_3 \tag{7}$$

● **PROBLEM** 22-15

Find expressions for the elements of area in orthogonal curvilinear coordinates.

Solution: The area elements are given by:

$$dA_1 = |(h_2 du_2 \bar{e}_2) \times (h_3 du_3 \bar{e}_3)|$$
$$= h_2 h_3 \, du_2 du_3 |\bar{e}_2 \times \bar{e}_3| = h_2 h_3 \, du_2 du_3, \tag{1}$$

since the system is orthogonal,

$$|\bar{e}_2 \times \bar{e}_3| = |\bar{e}_1| = 1. \tag{2}$$

Similarly, we find

$$dA_2 = |(h_1 du_1 \bar{e}_1) \times (h_3 du_3 \bar{e}_3)| = h_1 h_3 \, du_1 du_3 \tag{3}$$

and

$$dA_3 = |(h_1 du_1 \bar{e}_1) \times (h_2 du_2 \bar{e}_2)| = h_1 h_2 \, du_1 du_2 \tag{4}$$

THE GRADIENT, DIVERGENCE, CURL AND LAPLACIAN IN ORTHOGONAL COORDINATES

● **PROBLEM** 22-16

Derive an expression for grad f in orthogonal curvilinear coordinates.

Solution: Let
$$\nabla f = f_1 \bar{e}_1 + f_2 \bar{e}_2 + f_3 \bar{e}_3 \tag{1}$$

The functions f_1, f_2, f_3 are to be determined.

We have
$$df = \nabla f \cdot d\bar{r} \tag{2}$$

The differential df can be expressed

$$df = \frac{\partial f}{\partial u_1} du_1 + \frac{\partial f}{\partial u_2} du_2 + \frac{\partial f}{\partial u_3} du_3 \qquad (3)$$

On the other hand, $d\overline{r}$ equals

$$d\overline{r} = \frac{\partial \overline{r}}{\partial u_1} du_1 + \frac{\partial \overline{r}}{\partial u_2} du_2 + \frac{\partial \overline{r}}{\partial u_3} du_3$$
$$= h_1 \overline{e}_1 du_1 + h_2 \overline{e}_2 du_2 + h_3 \overline{e}_3 du_3 \qquad (4)$$

Substituting eqs.(1), (3), and eq.(4) into eq.(2) results in

$$\frac{\partial f}{\partial u_1} du_1 + \frac{\partial f}{\partial u_2} du_2 + \frac{\partial f}{\partial u_3} du_3 = f_1 h_1 du_1 + f_2 h_2 du_2 + f_3 h_3 du_3 \qquad (5)$$

Equating the coefficients, we find

$$f_1 = \frac{1}{h_1} \frac{\partial f}{\partial u_1}, \quad f_2 = \frac{1}{h_2} \frac{\partial f}{\partial u_2}, \quad f_3 = \frac{1}{h_3} \frac{\partial f}{\partial u_3} \qquad (6)$$

Hence,
$$\nabla f = \frac{\overline{e}_1}{h_1} \frac{\partial f}{\partial u_1} + \frac{\overline{e}_2}{h_2} \frac{\partial f}{\partial u_2} + \frac{\overline{e}_3}{h_3} \frac{\partial f}{\partial u_3} \qquad (7)$$

or, in the operator form,

$$\nabla = \frac{\overline{e}_1}{h_1} \frac{\partial}{\partial u_1} + \frac{\overline{e}_2}{h_2} \frac{\partial}{\partial u_2} + \frac{\overline{e}_3}{h_3} \frac{\partial}{\partial u_3} \qquad (8)$$

● **PROBLEM** 22-17

Let (u_1, u_2, u_3) be a system of orthogonal curvilinear co-ordinates. Show that

1. $\nabla \cdot (f_1 \overline{e}_1) = \frac{1}{h_1 h_2 h_3} \frac{\partial}{\partial u_1} (f_1 h_2 h_3)$ \qquad (1)

2. $\nabla \times (f_1 \overline{e}_1) = \frac{\overline{e}_2}{h_1 h_2} \frac{\partial}{\partial u_3} (f_1 h_1) - \frac{\overline{e}_3}{h_1 h_2} \frac{\partial}{\partial u_2} (f_1 h_1)$ \qquad (2)

Solution: 1. The vector $\overline{e}_1$ can be expressed in the form
$$\overline{e}_1 = h_2 h_3 \nabla u_2 \times \nabla u_3 \qquad (3)$$
Therefore,
$$\nabla \cdot (f_1 \overline{e}_1) = \nabla \cdot (f_1 h_2 h_3 \nabla u_2 \times \nabla u_3)$$
$$= \nabla(f_1 h_2 h_3) \cdot \nabla u_2 \times \nabla u_3 + f_1 h_2 h_3 \ \nabla \cdot (\nabla u_2 \times \nabla u_3)$$
$$= \nabla(f_1 h_2 h_3) \cdot \frac{\overline{e}_2}{h_2} \times \frac{\overline{e}_3}{h_3} + 0 = \nabla(f_1 h_2 h_3) \cdot \frac{\overline{e}_1}{h_2 h_3}$$
$$= \left[\frac{\overline{e}_1}{h_1} \frac{\partial}{\partial u_1}(f_1 h_2 h_3) + \frac{\overline{e}_2}{h_2} \frac{\partial}{\partial u_2}(f_1 h_2 h_3) \right.$$
$$\left. + \frac{\overline{e}_3}{h_3} \frac{\partial}{\partial u_3}(f_1 h_2 h_3) \right] \cdot \frac{\overline{e}_1}{h_2 h_3}$$

$$= \frac{1}{h_1 h_2 h_3} \frac{\partial}{\partial u_1} (f_1 h_2 h_3) \tag{4}$$

2. $\nabla \times (f_1 \bar{e}_1) = \nabla \times (f_1 h_1 \nabla u_1) = \nabla (f_1 h_1) \times \nabla u_1 + f_1 h_1 \nabla \times \nabla u_1$

$$= \nabla (f_1 h_1) \times \frac{\bar{e}_1}{h_1} + \bar{0}$$

$$= \left[\frac{\bar{e}_1}{h_1} \frac{\partial}{\partial u_1} (f_1 h_1) + \frac{\bar{e}_2}{h_2} \frac{\partial}{\partial u_2} (f_1 h_1) + \frac{\bar{e}_3}{h_3} \frac{\partial}{\partial u_3} (f_1 h_1) \right] \times \frac{\bar{e}_1}{h_1}$$

$$= \frac{\bar{e}_2}{h_1 h_3} \frac{\partial}{\partial u_3} (f_1 h_1) - \frac{\bar{e}_3}{h_1 h_2} \frac{\partial}{\partial u_2} (f_1 h_1) \tag{5}$$

● **PROBLEM** 22-18

Express div $\bar{F}$ in orthogonal curvilinear coordinates (u_1, u_2, u_3).

Solution: A vector $\bar{F}$ is expressed in curvilinear coordinates
by
$$\bar{F} = F_1 \bar{e}_1 + F_2 \bar{e}_2 + F_3 \bar{e}_3 \tag{1}$$

Applying eq.(1) of Problem 22-17 we obtain

div $\bar{F} = \nabla \cdot (F_1 \bar{e}_1 + F_2 \bar{e}_2 + F_3 \bar{e}_3)$

$$= \nabla \cdot (F_1 \bar{e}_1) + \nabla \cdot (F_2 \bar{e}_2) + \nabla \cdot (F_3 \bar{e}_3)$$

$$= \frac{1}{h_1 h_2 h_3} \left[\frac{\partial}{\partial u_1} (f_1 h_2 h_3) + \frac{\partial}{\partial u_2} (f_2 h_1 h_3) + \frac{\partial}{\partial u_3} (f_3 h_1 h_2) \right] \tag{2}$$

Here we used the property

$$\text{div}(\bar{a} + \bar{b}) = \text{div } \bar{a} + \text{div } \bar{b} \tag{3}$$

● **PROBLEM** 22-19

Express curl $\bar{F}$ in orthogonal curvilinear coordinates.

Solution: We have

curl $\bar{F} = \nabla \times (F_1 \bar{e}_1 + F_2 \bar{e}_2 + F_3 \bar{e}_3)$

$$= \nabla \times (F_1 \bar{e}_1) + \nabla \times (F_2 \bar{e}_2) + \nabla \times (F_3 \bar{e}_3)$$

$$= \frac{\bar{e}_2}{h_1 h_3} \frac{\partial}{\partial u_3} (F_1 h_1) - \frac{\bar{e}_3}{h_1 h_2} \frac{\partial}{\partial u_2} (F_1 h_1) + \frac{\bar{e}_3}{h_1 h_2} \frac{\partial}{\partial u_1} (F_2 h_2)$$

$$-\frac{\overline{e}_1}{h_2h_3}\frac{\partial}{\partial u_3}(F_2h_2) + \frac{\overline{e}_1}{h_2h_3}\frac{\partial}{\partial u_2}(F_3h_3) - \frac{\overline{e}_2}{h_1h_3}\frac{\partial}{\partial u_1}(F_3h_3)$$

$$= \frac{\overline{e}_1}{h_2h_3}\left[\frac{\partial}{\partial u_2}(F_3h_3) - \frac{\partial}{\partial u_3}(F_2h_2)\right]$$

$$+ \frac{\overline{e}_2}{h_1h_3}\left[\frac{\partial}{\partial u_3}(F_1h_1) - \frac{\partial}{\partial u_1}(F_3h_3)\right] \tag{1}$$

$$+ \frac{\overline{e}_3}{h_1h_2}\left[\frac{\partial}{\partial u_1}(F_2h_2) - \frac{\partial}{\partial u_2}(F_1h_1)\right]$$

Here we used eq.(2) of Problem 22-17 and the property

$$\text{curl}(\overline{a}+\overline{b}) = \text{curl } \overline{a} + \text{curl } \overline{b} \tag{2}$$

● **PROBLEM** 22-20

Express curl $\overline{F}$ in orthogonal curvilinear coordinates using the integral definition

$$(\text{curl } \overline{F}) \cdot \overline{n} = \lim_{\Delta s \to 0} \frac{\oint_C \overline{F} \cdot d\overline{r}}{\Delta s} \tag{1}$$

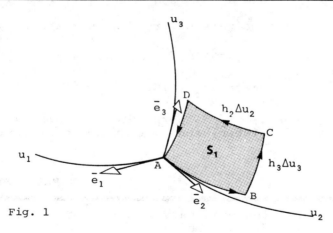

Fig. 1

Solution: We shall calculate $(\text{curl } \overline{F}) \cdot \overline{e}_1$. Let S_1 be a surface normal to $\overline{e}_1$ as shown in Fig. 1. C_1 is the boundary of S_1.

We have,

$$\oint_{C_1} \overline{F} \cdot d\overline{r} = \int_{AB} \overline{F} \cdot d\overline{r} + \int_{BC} \overline{F} \cdot d\overline{r} + \int_{CD} \overline{F} \cdot d\overline{r} + \int_{DA} \overline{F} \cdot d\overline{r} \tag{2}$$

For

$$\overline{F} = F_1\overline{e}_1 + F_2\overline{e}_2 + F_3\overline{e}_3 \tag{3}$$

1105

we have

$$\int_{AB} \overline{F} \cdot d\overline{r} = (\overline{F}|_P) \cdot (h_2 \Delta u_2 \overline{e}_2)$$

$$= (F_1\overline{e}_1 + F_2\overline{e}_2 + F_3\overline{e}_3) \cdot (h_2 \Delta u_2 \overline{e}_2) = F_2 h_2 \Delta u_2 \qquad (4)$$

where $\overline{F}|_P$ indicates the value of $\overline{F}$ at point P.

$$\int_{CD} \overline{F} \cdot d\overline{r} = -F_2 h_2 \Delta u_2 - \frac{\partial}{\partial u_3}(F_2 h_2 \Delta u_2)\Delta u_3 \qquad (5)$$

$$\int_{DA} \overline{F} \cdot d\overline{r} = -F_3 h_3 \Delta u_3 \qquad (6)$$

$$\int_{BC} \overline{F} \cdot d\overline{r} = F_3 h_3 \Delta u_3 + \frac{\partial}{\partial u_2}(F_3 h_3 \Delta u_3)\Delta u_2 \qquad (7)$$

Adding eqs.(4), (5), (6), and (7), we obtain

$$\oint_{C_1} \overline{F} \cdot d\overline{r} = \frac{\partial}{\partial u_2}(F_3 h_3 \Delta u_3)\Delta u_2 - \frac{\partial}{\partial u_3}(F_2 h_2 \Delta u_2)\Delta u_3$$

$$= \left[\frac{\partial}{\partial u_2}(F_3 h_3) - \frac{\partial}{\partial u_3}(F_2 h_2)\right]\Delta u_2 \Delta u_3 \qquad (8)$$

We neglected infinitesimals of order higher than $\Delta u_2 \Delta u_3$.

The area of S_1 is $A = h_2 h_3 \Delta u_2 \Delta u_3$, hence

$$(\text{curl } \overline{F}) \cdot \overline{e}_1 = \frac{1}{h_2 h_3}\left[\frac{\partial}{\partial u_2}(F_3 h_3) - \frac{\partial}{\partial u_3}(F_2 h_2)\right] \qquad (9)$$

Choosing the areas S_2 and S_3 perpendicular to $\overline{e}_2$ and $\overline{e}_3$, respectively, we find the $\overline{e}_2$ and $\overline{e}_3$ components of curl $\overline{F}$.

● **PROBLEM 22-21**

Express div $\overline{F}$ in orthogonal curvilinear coordinates using the integral definition

$$\text{div } \overline{F} = \lim_{\Delta V \to 0} \frac{\displaystyle\iint_{\Delta S} \overline{F} \cdot \overline{n} \, dS}{\Delta V} \qquad (1)$$

Solution: The volume element dV is shown in Fig. 1.

The edges of ΔV are $h_1 \Delta u_1$, $h_2 \Delta u_2$, and $h_3 \Delta u_3$. The vector $\overline{F}$ is expressed as a linear combination of $\overline{e}_1, \overline{e}_2, \overline{e}_3$.

1106

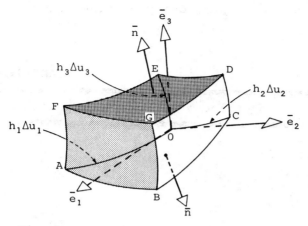

Fig. 1

$$\overline{F} = F_1\overline{e}_1 + F_2\overline{e}_2 + F_3\overline{e}_3 \qquad (2)$$

Let $\overline{n}$ be the outward unit normal to the surface ΔS of ΔV.

On the face CDEO, the surface integral is

$$\iint_{CDEO} \overline{F} \cdot \overline{n}\ dS = \iint_{CDEO} (F_1\overline{e}_1 + F_2\overline{e}_2 + F_3\overline{e}_3) \cdot (-\overline{e}_1)dS$$

$$= -F_1 h_2 h_3\ \Delta u_2 \Delta u_3 \qquad (3)$$

On face ABGF, the surface integral is

$$F_1 h_2 h_3 \Delta u_2 \Delta u_3 + \frac{\partial}{\partial u_1}(F_1 h_2 h_3 \Delta u_2 \Delta u_3)\Delta u_1 \qquad (4)$$

Note that infinitesimals of order higher than $\Delta u_1 \Delta u_2 \Delta u_3$ are neglected. The total contribution from the two faces CDEO and ABGF is

$$\frac{\partial}{\partial u_1}(F_1 h_2 h_3 \Delta u_2 \Delta u_3)\Delta u_1 = \frac{\partial}{\partial u_1}(F_1 h_2 h_3)\Delta u_1 \Delta u_2 \Delta u_3 \qquad (5)$$

In the same manner, we compute the contribution from the remaining four faces.

Adding up, we find the total contribution from all six faces of ΔV.

$$\left[\frac{\partial}{\partial u_1}(F_1 h_2 h_3) + \frac{\partial}{\partial u_2}(F_2 h_1 h_3) + \frac{\partial}{\partial u_3}(F_3 h_1 h_2)\right]\Delta u_1 \Delta u_2 \Delta u_3 \qquad (6)$$

Dividing (6) by the volume element

$$\Delta V = h_1 h_2 h_3\ \Delta u_1 \Delta u_2 \Delta u_3 \qquad (7)$$

we obtain

$$\text{div } \overline{F} = \frac{1}{h_1 h_2 h_3}\left[\frac{\partial}{\partial u_1}(F_1 h_2 h_3) + \frac{\partial}{\partial u_2}(F_2 h_1 h_3) + \frac{\partial}{\partial u_3}(F_3 h_1 h_2)\right] \qquad (8)$$

Compare eq.(8) with the previously obtained expression for div $\overline{F}$.

Express $\nabla^2 f$ in orthogonal curvilinear coordinates.

Solution: Note that

$$\nabla^2 f = \nabla \cdot \nabla f \qquad (1)$$

and the gradient of f is given by

$$\nabla f = \frac{\overline{e}_1}{h_1} \frac{\partial f}{\partial u_1} + \frac{\overline{e}_2}{h_2} \frac{\partial f}{\partial u_2} + \frac{\overline{e}_3}{h_3} \frac{\partial f}{\partial u_3} \qquad (2)$$

Applying the divergence of $\overline{F}$ expressed in curvilinear orthogonal coordinates

$$\text{div } \overline{F} = \frac{1}{h_1 h_2 h_3} \left[\frac{\partial}{\partial u_1}(F_1 h_2 h_3) + \frac{\partial}{\partial u_2}(F_2 h_1 h_3) + \frac{\partial}{\partial u_3}(F_3 h_1 h_2) \right] \qquad (3)$$

we obtain, from eq.(1)

$$\nabla^2 f = \nabla \cdot \left[\frac{\overline{e}_1}{h_1} \left(\frac{\partial f}{\partial u_1} \right) + \frac{\overline{e}_2}{h_2} \left(\frac{\partial f}{\partial u_2} \right) + \frac{\overline{e}_3}{h_3} \left(\frac{\partial f}{\partial u_3} \right) \right]$$

$$= \frac{1}{h_1 h_2 h_3} \left[\frac{\partial}{\partial u_1} \left(\frac{h_2 h_3}{h_1} \frac{\partial f}{\partial u_1} \right) + \frac{\partial}{\partial u_2} \left(\frac{h_1 h_3}{h_2} \frac{\partial f}{\partial u_2} \right) \right. \qquad (4)$$

$$\left. + \frac{\partial}{\partial u_3} \left(\frac{h_1 h_2}{h_3} \frac{\partial f}{\partial u_3} \right) \right]$$

Show that

$$\text{div curl } \overline{F} = 0 \qquad (1)$$

$$\text{curl grad } f = \overline{0} \qquad (2)$$

in any orthogonal curvilinear system.

Solution: Let $\overline{F}$ be a continuously differentiable vector field

$$\overline{F} = F_1 \overline{e}_1 + F_2 \overline{e}_2 + F_3 \overline{e}_3 \qquad (3)$$

The vector curl $\overline{F}$ is given by

$$\text{curl } \overline{F} = \frac{\overline{e}_1}{h_2 h_3} \left[\frac{\partial}{\partial u_2}(F_3 h_3) - \frac{\partial}{\partial u_3}(F_2 h_2) \right]$$

$$+ \frac{\bar{e}_2}{h_1 h_3}\left[\frac{\partial}{\partial u_3}(F_1 h_1) - \frac{\partial}{\partial u_1}(F_3 h_3)\right] \tag{4}$$

$$+ \frac{\bar{e}_3}{h_1 h_2}\left[\frac{\partial}{\partial u_1}(F_2 h_2) - \frac{\partial}{\partial u_2}(F_1 h_1)\right]$$

The divergence of a vector field is given by

$$\text{div } \bar{G} = \frac{1}{h_1 h_2 h_3}\left[\frac{\partial}{\partial u_1}(G_1 h_2 h_3) + \frac{\partial}{\partial u_2}(G_2 h_1 h_3) + \frac{\partial}{\partial u_3}(G_3 h_1 h_2)\right] \tag{5}$$

where

$$\bar{G} = G_1 \bar{e}_1 + G_2 \bar{e}_2 + G_3 \bar{e}_3 \tag{6}$$

From eqs.(4) and (5), we see that curl $\bar{F}$ may·be written as

$$\text{div curl } \bar{F} = \nabla \cdot \nabla \times \bar{F}$$

$$= \frac{1}{h_1 h_2 h_3}\left\{\frac{\partial}{\partial u_1}\left[\frac{\partial}{\partial u_2}(F_3 h_3) - \frac{\partial}{\partial u_3}(F_2 h_2)\right]\right.$$

$$+ \frac{\partial}{\partial u_2}\left[\frac{\partial}{\partial u_3}(F_1 h_1) - \frac{\partial}{\partial u_1}(F_3 h_3)\right] \tag{7}$$

$$+ \left.\frac{\partial}{\partial u_3}\left[\frac{\partial}{\partial u_1}(F_2 h_2) - \frac{\partial}{\partial u_2}(F_1 h_1)\right]\right\}$$

$$= \frac{1}{h_1 h_2 h_3}\left[\frac{\partial^2}{\partial u_1 \partial u_2}(F_3 h_3) - \frac{\partial^2}{\partial u_1 \partial u_3}(F_2 h_2) + \frac{\partial^2}{\partial u_2 \partial u_3}(F_1 h_1)\right.$$

$$\left. - \frac{\partial^2}{\partial u_2 \partial u_1}(F_3 h_3) + \frac{\partial^2}{\partial u_3 \partial u_1}(F_2 h_2) - \frac{\partial^2}{\partial u_3 \partial u_2}(F_1 h_1)\right]$$

$$= 0$$

To prove eq.(2), let us recall the expression for grad f. We have

$$\text{grad } f = \frac{\bar{e}_1}{h_1}\frac{\partial f}{\partial u_1} + \frac{\bar{e}_2}{h_2}\frac{\partial f}{\partial u_2} + \frac{\bar{e}_3}{h_3}\frac{\partial f}{\partial u_3} \tag{8}$$

We obtain

$$\text{curl grad } f = \nabla \times \nabla f$$

$$= \frac{\bar{e}_1}{h_2 h_3}\left[\frac{\partial}{\partial u_2}\left(\frac{\partial f}{\partial u_3}\right) - \frac{\partial}{\partial u_3}\left(\frac{\partial f}{\partial u_2}\right)\right]$$

$$+ \frac{\bar{e}_2}{h_1 h_3}\left[\frac{\partial}{\partial u_3}\left(\frac{\partial f}{\partial u_1}\right) - \frac{\partial}{\partial u_1}\left(\frac{\partial f}{\partial u_3}\right)\right] \tag{9}$$

$$+ \frac{\bar{e}_3}{h_1 h_2}\left[\frac{\partial}{\partial u_1}\left(\frac{\partial f}{\partial u_2}\right) - \frac{\partial}{\partial u_2}\left(\frac{\partial f}{\partial u_1}\right)\right]$$

$$= 0\bar{e}_1 + 0\bar{e}_2 + 0\bar{e}_3 = \bar{0}$$

Remember that if the second partial derivatives are continuous, then

$$\frac{\partial^2 f}{\partial u_i \partial u_j} = \frac{\partial^2 f}{\partial u_j \partial u_i} \tag{10}$$

SOME TYPES OF ORTHOGONAL COORDINATE SYSTEMS

● **PROBLEM** 22-24

Compute the element of arc length on a sphere of radius a.

Solution: Since we have to evaluate ds on a sphere, the most convenient coordinate system will be the spherical system (r,ϕ,θ). In general, the vector $\overline{dr}$ is given by

$$d\overline{r} = h_1\overline{e}_1 du_1 + h_2\overline{e}_2 du_2 + h_3\overline{e}_3 du_3 \tag{1}$$

Hence,

$$ds = \sqrt{d\overline{r} \cdot d\overline{r}} = \sqrt{h_1^2 du_1^2 + h_2^2 du_2^2 + h_3^2 du_3^2} \tag{2}$$

For the spherical coordinate system,

$$u_1 = r, \quad u_2 = \phi, \quad u_3 = \theta$$

$$h_r = 1, \quad h_\phi = r, \quad h_\theta = r\sin\phi \tag{3}$$

Therefore,

$$ds = \sqrt{dr^2 + r^2 d\phi^2 + r^2\sin^2\phi d\theta^2} \tag{4}$$

For a sphere $r = a$,

$$ds = a\sqrt{d\phi^2 + \sin^2\phi d\theta^2} \tag{5}$$

● **PROBLEM** 22-25

Express

1. grad f

2. div $\overline{F}$

3. curl $\overline{F}$

in cylindrical coordinates. Use the expressions for ∇f, $\nabla \cdot \overline{F}$ and $\nabla \times \overline{F}$ obtained for general curvilinear coordinates.

Solution: The cylindrical coordinates are described by

$$x = \rho\cos\phi, \quad y = \rho\sin\phi, \quad z = z \tag{1}$$

The scale factors are

$$h_\rho = 1, \quad h_\phi = \rho, \quad h_z = 1 \tag{2}$$

The gradient of f is

$$\nabla f = \frac{\overline{e}_1}{h_1} \frac{\partial f}{\partial u_1} + \frac{\overline{e}_2}{h_2} \frac{\partial f}{\partial u_2} + \frac{\overline{e}_3}{h_3} \frac{\partial f}{\partial u_3} \tag{3}$$

Substituting eq.(2) into eq.(3) we obtain, for cylindrical coordinates,

$$\nabla f = \overline{e}_\rho \frac{\partial f}{\partial \rho} + \frac{1}{\rho} \overline{e}_\phi \frac{\partial f}{\partial \phi} + \overline{e}_z \frac{\partial f}{\partial z} \tag{4}$$

The divergence of $\overline{F} = F_1\overline{e}_1 + F_2\overline{e}_2 + F_3\overline{e}_3$ is

$$\nabla \cdot \overline{F} = \frac{1}{h_1 h_2 h_3} \left[\frac{\partial}{\partial u_1}(F_1 h_2 h_3) + \frac{\partial}{\partial u_2}(F_2 h_1 h_3) + \frac{\partial}{\partial u_3}(F_3 h_1 h_2) \right] \tag{5}$$

Eq.(5) in cylindrical coordinates becomes

$$\nabla \cdot \overline{F} = \frac{1}{\rho} \left[\frac{\partial}{\partial \rho}(F_\rho \rho) + \frac{\partial F_\phi}{\partial \phi} + \frac{\partial}{\partial z}(F_z \rho) \right] \tag{6}$$

In general, the curl of $\overline{F}$ is

$$\nabla \times \overline{F} = \frac{1}{h_1 h_2 h_3} \begin{vmatrix} h_1\overline{e}_1 & h_2\overline{e}_2 & h_3\overline{e}_3 \\ \frac{\partial}{\partial u_1} & \frac{\partial}{\partial u_2} & \frac{\partial}{\partial u_3} \\ F_1 h_1 & F_2 h_2 & F_3 h_3 \end{vmatrix} \tag{7}$$

In cylindrical coordinates

$$\nabla \times \overline{F} = \frac{1}{\rho} \begin{vmatrix} \overline{e}_\rho & \rho\,\overline{e}_\phi & \overline{e}_z \\ \frac{\partial}{\partial \rho} & \frac{\partial}{\partial \phi} & \frac{\partial}{\partial z} \\ F_\rho & \rho F_\phi & F_z \end{vmatrix}$$

$$= \frac{1}{\rho} \left[\left(\frac{\partial F_z}{\partial \phi} - \frac{\partial}{\partial z}(\rho F_\phi) \right) \overline{e}_\rho + \left(\rho \frac{\partial F_\rho}{\partial z} - \rho \frac{\partial F_z}{\partial \rho} \right) \overline{e}_\phi \right.$$
$$\left. + \left(\frac{\partial}{\partial \rho}(\rho F_\phi) - \frac{\partial F_\rho}{\partial \phi} \right) \overline{e}_z \right] \tag{8}$$

● **PROBLEM** 22-26

Express $\nabla \times \overline{F}$ and $\nabla^2 f$ in spherical coordinates.

Solution: The spherical coordinates are
$$x = r\sin\phi\cos\theta$$
$$y = r\sin\phi\sin\theta$$
$$z = r\cos\phi \tag{1}$$

The scale factors are

$$h_r = 1, \quad h_\phi = r, \quad h_\theta = r\sin\phi \qquad (2)$$

The curl of $\overline{F}$ expressed in spherical coordinates is

$$\nabla \times \overline{F} = \frac{1}{h_1 h_2 h_3} \begin{vmatrix} h_1 \overline{e}_1 & h_2 \overline{e}_2 & h_3 \overline{e}_3 \\ \dfrac{\partial}{\partial u_1} & \dfrac{\partial}{\partial u_2} & \dfrac{\partial}{\partial u_3} \\ h_1 F_1 & h_2 F_2 & h_3 F_3 \end{vmatrix}$$

$$= \frac{1}{r^2\sin\phi} \begin{vmatrix} \overline{e}_r & r\overline{e}_\phi & r\sin\phi\,\overline{e}_\theta \\ \dfrac{\partial}{\partial r} & \dfrac{\partial}{\partial \phi} & \dfrac{\partial}{\partial \theta} \\ F_r & rF_\phi & r\sin\phi F_\theta \end{vmatrix} \qquad (3)$$

$$= \frac{1}{r^2\sin\phi} \left\{ \left[\frac{\partial}{\partial \phi}(r\sin\phi F_\theta) - \frac{\partial}{\partial \theta}(rF_\phi) \right]\overline{e}_r \right.$$

$$\left. + \left[\frac{\partial F_r}{\partial \theta} - \frac{\partial}{\partial r}(r\sin\phi F_\theta) \right]r\overline{e}_\phi + \left[\frac{\partial}{\partial r}(rF_\phi) - \frac{\partial F_r}{\partial \phi} \right]r\sin\phi\,\overline{e}_\theta \right\}$$

$\nabla^2 f$ in spherical coordinates is

$$\nabla^2 f = \frac{1}{h_1 h_2 h_3}\left[\frac{\partial}{\partial u_1}\left(\frac{h_2 h_3}{h_1}\frac{\partial f}{\partial u_1} \right) + \frac{\partial}{\partial u_2}\left(\frac{h_3 h_1}{h_2}\frac{\partial f}{\partial u_2} \right) + \frac{\partial}{\partial u_3}\left(\frac{h_1 h_2}{h_3}\frac{\partial f}{\partial u_3} \right) \right]$$

$$= \frac{1}{r^2\sin\phi}\left[\sin\phi\frac{\partial}{\partial r}\left(r^2\frac{\partial f}{\partial r} \right) + \frac{\partial}{\partial \phi}\left(\sin\phi\frac{\partial f}{\partial \phi} \right) + \frac{1}{\sin\phi}\frac{\partial^2 f}{\partial \theta^2} \right] \qquad (4)$$

● **PROBLEM 22-27**

Consider the system of parabolic cylindrical coordinates

$$x = \frac{1}{2}(u^2 - v^2)$$

$$y = uv$$

$$z = z$$

Express Laplace's equation in terms of these coordinates.

Solution: From eq.(1), we evaluate the scale factors

$$h_u = \left| \frac{\partial \overline{r}}{\partial u} \right| = |(u,v,0)| = \sqrt{u^2+v^2}$$

$$h_v = \left| \frac{\partial \overline{r}}{\partial v} \right| = |(-v,u,0)| = \sqrt{u^2+v^2} \qquad (2)$$

$$h_z = 1$$

Laplace's equation is

$$\nabla^2 f = 0 \qquad (3)$$

In parabolic cylindrical coordinates it becomes

$$\frac{1}{h_1 h_2 h_3} \left[\frac{\partial}{\partial u_1} \left(\frac{h_2 h_3}{h_1} \frac{\partial f}{\partial u_1} \right) + \frac{\partial}{\partial u_2} \left(\frac{h_1 h_3}{h_2} \frac{\partial f}{\partial u_2} \right) + \frac{\partial}{\partial u_3} \left(\frac{h_1 h_2}{h_3} \frac{\partial f}{\partial u_3} \right) \right]$$

$$= \frac{1}{u^2 + v^2} \left[\frac{\partial}{\partial u} \left(\frac{\partial f}{\partial u} \right) + \frac{\partial}{\partial v} \left(\frac{\partial f}{\partial v} \right) + \frac{\partial}{\partial z} \left((u^2 + v^2) \frac{\partial f}{\partial z} \right) \right] \qquad (4)$$

$$= \frac{1}{u^2 + v^2} \left[\frac{\partial^2 f}{\partial u^2} + \frac{\partial^2 f}{\partial v^2} \right] + \frac{\partial^2 f}{\partial z^2}$$

and

$$\frac{\partial^2 f}{\partial u^2} + \frac{\partial^2 f}{\partial v^2} + (u^2 + v^2) \frac{\partial^2 f}{\partial z^2} = 0 \qquad (5)$$

● **PROBLEM 22-28**

Write

1. ∇f (1)

2. $\dfrac{\partial^2 f}{\partial x^2} + \dfrac{\partial^2 f}{\partial y^2} = f$ (2)

in elliptic cylindrical coordinates (u,v,z).

Solution: Elliptic cylindrical coordinates are described by

$$x = a \cosh u \cos v$$

$$y = a \sinh u \sin v \qquad (3)$$

$$z = z$$

Note that

$$\cosh x = \frac{e^x + e^{-x}}{2}, \quad \sinh x = \frac{e^x - e^{-x}}{2} \qquad (4)$$

$$\frac{d}{dx} \cosh x = \sinh x, \quad \frac{d}{dx} \sinh x = \cosh x \qquad (5)$$

The scale factors are

$$h_u = \left| \frac{\partial \overline{r}}{\partial u} \right| = |(a \sinh u \cos v, \ a \cosh u \sin v, \ 0)|$$

$$= a \sqrt{\sinh^2 u \cos^2 v + \cosh^2 u \sin^2 v}$$

$$= a \sqrt{\sinh^2 u + \cosh^2 u \sin^2 v - \sinh^2 u \sin^2 v} \qquad (6)$$

$$= a \sqrt{\sinh^2 u + \sin^2 v}$$

We used the identity

$$\cosh^2 u - \sinh^2 u = 1. \tag{7}$$

$$h_v = \left| \frac{\partial \overline{r}}{\partial v} \right| = |(-a\cosh u \sin v,\ a\sinh u \cos v,\ 0)|$$

$$= a\sqrt{\cosh^2 u \sin^2 v + \sinh^2 u \cos^2 v} \tag{8}$$

$$= a\sqrt{\sinh^2 u + \sin^2 v}$$

$$h_z = 1$$

The gradient of f is

$$\nabla f = \frac{1}{a\sqrt{\sinh^2 u + \sin^2 v}} \left[\overline{e}_u \frac{\partial f}{\partial u} + \overline{e}_v \frac{\partial f}{\partial v} \right] + \overline{e}_z \frac{\partial f}{\partial z} \tag{10}$$

Eq.(2) can be written in the form

$$\frac{\partial^2 f}{\partial x^2} + \frac{\partial^2 f}{\partial y^2} = \nabla^2 f - \frac{\partial^2 f}{\partial z^2} = f \tag{11}$$

Eq.(11) in elliptic cylindrical coordinates becomes

$$\frac{1}{a^2(\sinh^2 u + \sin^2 v)} \left[\frac{\partial^2 f}{\partial u^2} + \frac{\partial^2 f}{\partial v^2} + a^2(\sinh^2 u + \sin^2 v)\frac{\partial^2 f}{\partial z^2} \right] - \frac{\partial^2 f}{\partial z^2}$$

$$= \frac{1}{a^2(\sinh^2 u + \sin^2 v)} \left[\frac{\partial^2 f}{\partial u^2} + \frac{\partial^2 f}{\partial v^2} \right] = f \tag{12}$$

● **PROBLEM 22-29**

For the orthogonal curvilinear coordinate system

$$x = 2u_1 + u_2$$

$$y = u_1 - 2u_2 \tag{1}$$

$$z = u_3^2$$

verify the expression for grad f where

$$f(u_1, u_2, u_3) = u_1 u_2^2 + u_3^2. \tag{2}$$

Express f in terms of the cartesian coordinates, apply the del operator and transform back to (u_1, u_2, u_3).

Solution: From eq.(1), we evaluate the scale factors

$$h_1 = \left| \frac{\partial \overline{r}}{\partial u_1} \right| = (2,1,0) = \sqrt{5} \tag{3}$$

$$h_2 = \left| \frac{\partial \overline{r}}{\partial u_2} \right| = (1,-2,0) = \sqrt{5}$$

1114

$$h_3 = \left| \frac{\partial \overline{r}}{\partial u_3} \right| = (0,0,2u_3) = 2u_3$$

The vectors $\overline{e}_1, \overline{e}_2, \overline{e}_3$ are

$$\overline{e}_1 = \frac{\dfrac{\partial \overline{r}}{\partial u_1}}{\left| \dfrac{\partial \overline{r}}{\partial u_1} \right|} = \frac{2\overline{i} + \overline{j}}{\sqrt{5}}$$

$$\overline{e}_2 = \frac{\dfrac{\partial \overline{r}}{\partial u_2}}{\left| \dfrac{\partial \overline{r}}{\partial u_2} \right|} = \frac{\overline{i} - 2\overline{j}}{\sqrt{5}} \qquad (4)$$

$$\overline{e}_3 \quad \frac{\dfrac{\partial \overline{r}}{\partial u_3}}{\left| \dfrac{\partial \overline{r}}{\partial u_3} \right|} = \overline{k}$$

Hence, grad f in (u_1, u_2, u_3) coordinates is

$$\nabla f = \frac{1}{h_1} \frac{\partial f}{\partial u_1} \overline{e}_1 + \frac{1}{h_2} \frac{\partial f}{\partial u_2} \overline{e}_2 + \frac{1}{h_3} \frac{\partial f}{\partial u_3} \overline{e}_3$$

$$= \frac{1}{\sqrt{5}} \cdot u_2^2 \overline{e}_1 + \frac{1}{\sqrt{5}} 2u_1 u_2 \overline{e}_2 + \frac{1}{2u_3} \cdot 2u_3 \overline{e}_3 \qquad (5)$$

$$= \frac{1}{\sqrt{5}} u_2^2 \overline{e}_1 + \frac{2}{\sqrt{5}} u_1 u_2 \overline{e}_2 + \overline{e}_3$$

To verify eq.(5) let us solve eq.(1) for u_1, u_2, u_3.

$$u_1 = \frac{y + 2x}{5}$$

$$u_2 = \frac{x - 2y}{5} \qquad (6)$$

$$u_3 = \sqrt{z}$$

Thus,

$$f = u_1 u_2^2 + u_3^2 = \frac{y + 2x}{5} \cdot \frac{(x - 2y)^2}{25} + z$$

$$= \frac{2x^3 + 4y^3 + 4xy^2 - 7x^2 y}{125} + z \qquad (7)$$

and grad f is equal to

$$\text{grad } f = \frac{6x^2 + 4y^2 - 14xy}{125} \overline{i} + \frac{12y^2 + 8xy - 7x^2}{125} \overline{j} + \overline{k} \qquad (8)$$

To compare eq.(5) and eq.(8) we shall transform the

former to (x,y,z) coordinates using eqs.(4) and (6).

$$\text{grad } f = \frac{1}{\sqrt{5}} u_2^2 \bar{e}_1 + \frac{2}{\sqrt{5}} u_1 u_2 \bar{e}_2 + \bar{e}_3$$

$$= \frac{1}{\sqrt{5}} \frac{(x-2y)^2}{25} \cdot \frac{2\bar{i}+\bar{j}}{\sqrt{5}} + \frac{2}{\sqrt{5}} \cdot \frac{y+2x}{5}\left(\frac{x-2y}{5}\right) \frac{\bar{i}-2\bar{j}}{\sqrt{5}} + \bar{k}$$

$$= \frac{2(x-2y)^2 + 2(y+2x)(x-2y)}{125} \bar{i} + \frac{(x-2y)^2 - 4(y+2x)(x-2y)}{125} \bar{j} + \bar{k}$$

$$= \frac{6x^2 + 4y^2 - 14xy}{125} \bar{i} + \frac{12y^2 + 8xy - 7x^2}{125} \bar{j} + \bar{k} \qquad (9)$$

which is the same as eq.(8).

TRANSFORMATION OF COORDINATES-ORTHOGONAL COORDINATE SYSTEMS

● **PROBLEM** 22-30

The plane transformation is given by

$$x = x(u,v)$$
$$y = y(u,v)$$
$$\qquad (1)$$

Under what conditions will the system (u,v) be orthogonal?

Solution: The transformation in eq.(1) transforms two-dimensional space into two-dimensional space.

First, we should evaluate vectors $\bar{e}_1$ and $\bar{e}_2$. To avoid confusion, let us denote them $\bar{e}_u$ and $\bar{e}_v$.

$$\bar{e}_u = \frac{\frac{\partial \bar{r}}{\partial u}}{\left|\frac{\partial \bar{r}}{\partial u}\right|} = \frac{\frac{\partial x}{\partial u}\bar{i} + \frac{\partial y}{\partial u}\bar{j}}{\sqrt{\left(\frac{\partial x}{\partial u}\right)^2 + \left(\frac{\partial y}{\partial u}\right)^2}} \qquad (2)$$

$$\bar{e}_v = \frac{\frac{\partial \bar{r}}{\partial v}}{\left|\frac{\partial \bar{r}}{\partial v}\right|} = \frac{\frac{\partial x}{\partial v}\bar{i} + \frac{\partial y}{\partial v}\bar{j}}{\sqrt{\left(\frac{\partial x}{\partial v}\right)^2 + \left(\frac{\partial y}{\partial v}\right)^2}} \qquad (3)$$

For the system to be orthogonal, the vectors $\bar{e}_u$ and $\bar{e}_v$ have to be orthogonal, that is

$$\bar{e}_u \cdot \bar{e}_v = 0 \qquad (4)$$

Hence,

$$\bar{e}_u \cdot \bar{e}_v = \frac{\dfrac{\partial x}{\partial u}\dfrac{\partial x}{\partial v} + \dfrac{\partial y}{\partial u}\dfrac{\partial y}{\partial v}}{\sqrt{\left(\dfrac{\partial x}{\partial u}\right)^2 + \left(\dfrac{\partial y}{\partial u}\right)^2}\sqrt{\left(\dfrac{\partial x}{\partial v}\right)^2 + \left(\dfrac{\partial y}{\partial v}\right)^2}} = 0 \tag{5}$$

Therefore, for the system to be orthogonal, the following condition has to be satisfied

$$\frac{\partial x}{\partial u}\frac{\partial x}{\partial v} + \frac{\partial y}{\partial u}\frac{\partial y}{\partial v} = 0 \tag{6}$$

● **PROBLEM 22-31**

If the transformation from (u_1, u_2, u_3) to (x, y, z) is given by

$$x = a_1 u_1 + a_2 u_2 + a_3 u_3$$

$$y = b_1 u_1 + b_2 u_2 + b_3 u_3$$

$$z = c_1 u_1 + c_2 u_2 + c_3 u_3$$

then under what conditions will the (u_1, u_2, u_3) system be orthogonal?

Solution: To determine if the system (u_1, u_2, u_3) is orthogonal, we should first evaluate the vectors $\bar{e}_1$, $\bar{e}_2$, and $\bar{e}_3$.

$$\bar{e}_1 = \frac{\dfrac{\partial \bar{r}}{\partial u_1}}{\left|\dfrac{\partial \bar{r}}{\partial u_1}\right|} = \frac{(a_1, b_1, c_1)}{\sqrt{a_1^2 + b_1^2 + c_1^2}} = \frac{a_1\bar{i} + b_1\bar{j} + c_1\bar{k}}{\sqrt{a_1^2 + b_1^2 + c_1^2}} \tag{2}$$

$$\bar{e}_2 = \frac{\dfrac{\partial \bar{r}}{\partial u_2}}{\left|\dfrac{\partial \bar{r}}{\partial u_2}\right|} = \frac{(a_2, b_2, c_2)}{\sqrt{a_2^2 + b_2^2 + c_2^2}} = \frac{a_2\bar{i} + b_2\bar{j} + c_2\bar{k}}{\sqrt{a_2^2 + b_2^2 + c_2^2}} \tag{3}$$

$$\bar{e}_3 = \frac{\dfrac{\partial \bar{r}}{\partial u_3}}{\left|\dfrac{\partial \bar{r}}{\partial u_3}\right|} = \frac{(a_3, b_3, c_3)}{\sqrt{a_3^2 + b_3^2 + c_3^2}} = \frac{a_3\bar{i} + b_3\bar{j} + c_3\bar{k}}{\sqrt{a_3^2 + b_3^2 + c_3^2}} \tag{4}$$

The system is orthogonal when

$$\bar{e}_1 \cdot \bar{e}_2 = \bar{e}_1 \cdot \bar{e}_3 = \bar{e}_2 \cdot \bar{e}_3 = 0 \tag{5}$$

The first equation leads to

$$\bar{e}_1 \cdot \bar{e}_2 = \frac{a_1 a_2 + b_1 b_2 + c_1 c_2}{A_{12}} = 0 \tag{6}$$

1117

The denominator A_{12} is immaterial.

$$\bar{e}_1 \cdot \bar{e}_3 = \frac{a_1 a_3 + b_1 b_3 + c_1 c_3}{A_{13}} = 0 \qquad (7)$$

$$\bar{e}_2 \cdot \bar{e}_3 = \frac{a_2 a_3 + b_2 b_3 + c_2 c_3}{A_{23}} = 0 \qquad (8)$$

The system is orthogonal when

$$a_1 a_2 + b_1 b_2 + c_1 c_2 = a_1 a_3 + b_1 b_3 + c_1 c_3$$
$$= a_2 a_3 + b_2 b_3 + c_2 c_3 = 0 \qquad (9)$$

The transformation matrix

$$A = \begin{bmatrix} a_1 & a_2 & a_3 \\ b_1 & b_2 & b_3 \\ c_1 & c_2 & c_3 \end{bmatrix} = \begin{bmatrix} \bar{v}_1, \bar{v}_2, \bar{v}_3 \end{bmatrix} \qquad (10)$$

consists of three orthogonal vectors

$$\bar{v}_1 = \begin{bmatrix} a_1 \\ b_1 \\ c_1 \end{bmatrix} \qquad \bar{v}_2 = \begin{bmatrix} a_2 \\ b_2 \\ c_2 \end{bmatrix} \qquad \bar{v}_3 = \begin{bmatrix} a_3 \\ b_3 \\ c_3 \end{bmatrix} \qquad (11)$$

● **PROBLEM 22-32**

Consider the system of curvilinear coordinates defined by the functions

$$u_1 = u_1(y)$$
$$u_2 = u_2(z) \qquad (1)$$
$$u_3 = u_3(x)$$

Show that this system is orthogonal. What other combinations of functions of the type $f(x)$, $g(y)$, $h(z)$ would lead to an orthogonal system?

Solution: For the system described by eq.(1), we shall find vectors $\bar{e}_1, \bar{e}_2, \bar{e}_3$.

$$\bar{e}_1 = \frac{\nabla u_1}{|\nabla u_1|} = \frac{\left(\frac{\partial u_1}{\partial x}, \frac{\partial u_1}{\partial y}, \frac{\partial u_1}{\partial z} \right)}{\sqrt{\left(\frac{\partial u_1}{\partial x}\right)^2 + \left(\frac{\partial u_1}{\partial y}\right)^2 + \left(\frac{\partial u_1}{\partial z}\right)^2}} = \frac{\left(0, \frac{\partial u_1}{\partial y}, 0 \right)}{\sqrt{\left(\frac{\partial u_1}{\partial y}\right)^2}} \qquad (2)$$

$$= \frac{\frac{\partial u_1}{\partial y} \bar{j}}{\frac{\partial u_1}{\partial y}} = \bar{j}$$

$$\bar{e}_2 = \frac{\nabla u_2}{|\nabla u_2|} = \frac{\left(0, \ 0, \ \frac{\partial u_2}{\partial z}\right)}{\sqrt{\left(\frac{\partial u_2}{\partial z}\right)^2}} = \bar{k} \qquad (3)$$

$$\bar{e}_3 = \frac{\nabla u_3}{|\nabla u_3|} = \frac{\left(\frac{\partial u_3}{\partial x}, \ 0, \ 0\right)}{\sqrt{\left(\frac{\partial u_3}{\partial x}\right)^2}} = \bar{i} \qquad (4)$$

Obviously, the system is orthogonal because

$$\bar{e}_1 \cdot \bar{e}_2 = \bar{e}_1 \cdot \bar{e}_3 = \bar{e}_2 \cdot \bar{e}_3 = 0 \qquad (5)$$

We see that as long as an independent variable x, y, or z appears exactly once in the system of type (1), then this system is orthogonal.

For example, if z appears two times

$$u_1 = u_1(y)$$

$$u_2 = u_2(z) \qquad (6)$$

$$u_3 = u_3(z)$$

then

$$\bar{e}_1 = \frac{\left(0, \ \frac{\partial u_1}{\partial y}, \ 0\right)}{\frac{\partial u_1}{\partial y}} = \bar{j}$$

$$\bar{e}_2 = \frac{\left(0, \ 0, \ \frac{\partial u_2}{\partial z}\right)}{\frac{\partial u_2}{\partial z}} = \bar{k} \qquad (7)$$

$$\bar{e}_3 = \frac{\left(0, \ 0, \ \frac{\partial u_3}{\partial z}\right)}{\frac{\partial u_3}{\partial z}} = \bar{k}$$

and system (6) is not orthogonal, since

$$\bar{e}_2 \cdot \bar{e}_3 = \bar{k} \cdot \bar{k} = 1 \neq 0 \qquad (8)$$

● **PROBLEM 22-33**

What is the volume element relative to the coordinate system

$$u_1 = e^x$$

$$u_2 = e^y \qquad (1)$$

$$u_3 = e^z$$

Solution: The volume element expressed in curvilinear co-ordinates (u_1, u_2, u_3) is

$$dV = h_1h_2h_3 \, du_1du_2du_3 \tag{2}$$

To evaluate the scale factors, we shall use the formula

$$h_i = \frac{1}{|\nabla u_i|} \tag{3}$$

Thus,
$$h_1 = \frac{1}{|\nabla u_1|} = \frac{1}{|(e^x,0,0)|} = \frac{1}{e^x} \tag{4}$$

$$h_2 = \frac{1}{|\nabla u_2|} = \frac{1}{|(0,e^y,0)|} = \frac{1}{e^y} \tag{5}$$

$$h_3 = \frac{1}{|\nabla u_3|} = \frac{1}{|(0,0,e^z)|} = \frac{1}{e^z} \tag{6}$$

Therefore, the volume element is

$$dV = \frac{1}{e^xe^ye^z} \, du_1du_2du_3 \tag{7}$$

$$= \frac{1}{u_1u_2u_3} \, du_1du_2du_3$$

● **PROBLEM** 22-34

Let
$$u_1 = 2x - y$$
$$u_2 = x + 2y \tag{1}$$
$$u_3 = 3z$$

1. Determine if the system (u_1,u_2,u_3) is orthogonal.

2. Find ds^2 and the scale factors h_1,h_2,h_3.

3. Express $\nabla^2 f$ in terms of u_1,u_2,u_3 where $f = u_2^2 + u_3$.

Solution: 1. From eq.(1), we can evaluate vectors

$\overline{E}_i = \dfrac{\nabla u_i}{|\nabla u_i|}$, check if they are orthogonal and hence determine if (u_1,u_2,u_3) is orthogonal.

$$\overline{E}_1 = \frac{\nabla u_1}{|\nabla u_1|} = \frac{(2,-1,0)}{\sqrt{5}} = \frac{2\overline{i} - \overline{j}}{\sqrt{5}} \tag{2}$$

$$\overline{E}_2 = \frac{\nabla u_2}{|\nabla u_2|} = \frac{(1,2,0)}{\sqrt{5}} = \frac{\overline{i} + 2\overline{j}}{\sqrt{5}} \tag{3}$$

$$\bar{E}_3 = \frac{\nabla u_3}{|\nabla u_3|} = \frac{(0,0,3)}{3} = \bar{k} \qquad (4)$$

The system is orthogonal because

$$\bar{E}_1 \cdot \bar{E}_2 = \bar{E}_1 \cdot \bar{E}_3 = \bar{E}_2 \cdot \bar{E}_3 = 0 \qquad (5)$$

2. Solving eq.(1) for x, y, and z we find

$$x = \frac{2u_1 + u_2}{5}$$

$$y = \frac{-u_1 + 2u_2}{5} \qquad (6)$$

$$z = \frac{u_3}{3}$$

Thus,

$$ds^2 = dx^2 + dy^2 + dz^2 = h_1^2 du_1^2 + h_2^2 du_2^2 + h_3^2 du_3^2$$
$$= \frac{1}{5} du_1^2 + \frac{1}{5} du_2^2 + \frac{1}{9} du_3^2 \qquad (7)$$

and

$$h_1 = \frac{1}{\sqrt{5}}, \qquad h_2 = \frac{1}{\sqrt{5}}, \qquad h_3 = \frac{1}{3} \qquad (8)$$

3. Having the scale factors we can evaluate $\nabla^2 f$.

$$\nabla^2 f = \frac{1}{h_1 h_2 h_3} \left[\frac{\partial}{\partial u_1} \left(\frac{h_2 h_3}{h_1} \frac{\partial f}{\partial u_1} \right) + \frac{\partial}{\partial u_2} \left(\frac{h_1 h_3}{h_2} \frac{\partial f}{\partial u_2} \right) + \frac{\partial}{\partial u_3} \left(\frac{h_1 h_2}{h_3} \frac{\partial f}{\partial u_3} \right) \right]$$

$$= 15 \left[\frac{\partial}{\partial u_2} \left(\frac{1}{3} 2u_2 \right) + \frac{\partial}{\partial u_3} \left(\frac{3}{5} \right) \right] \qquad (9)$$

$$= 15 \left(\frac{2}{3} \right) = 10$$

● **PROBLEM 22-35**

The transformation of coordinates is given by

$$u_1 = 2x + y$$

$$u_2 = x + y \qquad (1)$$

$$u_3 = 2z$$

Solve eq.(1) for x, y, and z.

What happens when you try to evaluate the scale factors from the expression for ds^2? Explain.

Solution: Solving eq.(1) for x,y,z we obtain

$$x = u_1 - u_2$$

$$y = -u_1 + 2u_2 \qquad (2)$$

$$z = \frac{u_3}{2}$$

The length element ds^2 is equal to

$$ds^2 = dx^2 + dy^2 + dz^2 = h_1^2 du_1^2 + h_2^2 du_2^2 + h_3^2 du_3^2 \qquad (3)$$

Thus, expressing ds^2 in terms of du_1, du_2, and du_3 we can find the scale factors

$$ds^2 = (du_1 - du_2)^2 + (-du_1 + 2du_2)^2 + \frac{1}{4} du_3^2$$

$$= du_1^2 - 2du_1 du_2 + du_2^2 + du_1^2 - 4du_1 du_2$$

$$+ 4du_2^2 + \frac{1}{4} du_3^2 = 2du_1^2 + 5du_2^2 + \frac{1}{4} du_3^2 - 6du_1 du_2 \qquad (4)$$

In eq.(4) the term $-6du_1 du_2$ appears. Therefore we cannot use eq.(3) to evaluate the scale factors.

The system described by eq.(1) is not orthogonal. That is why the term $-6du_1 du_2$ appears in the expression for ds^2.

● **PROBLEM** 22-36

1. Show that the transformation

$$x = 2u_1 u_2$$

$$y = u_2^2 - u_1^2 \qquad (1)$$

$$z = u_3$$

is orthogonal.

2. Evaluate the scale factors.

3. Evaluate div $\overline{F}$ and curl $\overline{F}$ where

$$\overline{F} = u_2 \overline{e}_1 + u_3 \overline{e}_2 + u_1 \overline{e}_3 \qquad (2)$$

Solution: We can start with the evaluation of the vectors

$$\overline{e}_i = \frac{\frac{\partial \overline{r}}{\partial u_i}}{\left| \frac{\partial \overline{r}}{\partial u_i} \right|} \qquad (3)$$

If $\overline{e}_1, \overline{e}_2, \overline{e}_3$ are orthogonal then (u_1, u_2, u_3) are orthogonal curvilinear coordinates. The scale factors are obtained from

$$\bar{e}_i = \frac{1}{h_i} \frac{\partial \bar{r}}{\partial u_i} \qquad (4)$$

We have,

$$\bar{e}_1 = \frac{\dfrac{\partial \bar{r}}{\partial u_1}}{\left| \dfrac{\partial \bar{r}}{\partial u_1} \right|} = \frac{(2u_2, -2u_1, 0)}{\sqrt{4u_1^2 + 4u_2^2}} = \frac{u_2\bar{i} - u_1\bar{j}}{\sqrt{u_1^2 + u_2^2}} \qquad (5)$$

$$\bar{e}_2 = \frac{\dfrac{\partial \bar{r}}{\partial u_2}}{\left| \dfrac{\partial \bar{r}}{\partial u_2} \right|} = \frac{(2u_1, 2u_2, 0)}{\sqrt{4u_1^2 + 4u_2^2}} = \frac{u_1\bar{i} + u_2\bar{j}}{\sqrt{u_1^2 + u_2^2}} \cdot \qquad (6)$$

$$\bar{e}_3 = \frac{\dfrac{\partial \bar{r}}{\partial u_3}}{\left| \dfrac{\partial \bar{r}}{\partial u_3} \right|} = \frac{(0, 0, 1)}{1} = \bar{k} \qquad (7)$$

Obviously

$$\bar{e}_1 \cdot \bar{e}_3 = \bar{e}_2 \cdot \bar{e}_3 = 0 \qquad (8)$$

and

$$e_1 \cdot e_2 = \frac{u_1 u_2 - u_1 u_2}{(u_1^2 + u_2^2)} = 0 \qquad (9)$$

Hence, the system is orthogonal.

The scale factors are

$$h_1 = 2\sqrt{u_1^2 + u_2^2}$$

$$h_2 = 2\sqrt{u_1^2 + u_2^2} \qquad (10)$$

$$h_3 = 1$$

Substituting eqs.(10) and (2) into the expression for divergence, we obtain

$$\text{div } \bar{F} = \frac{1}{4(u_1^2 + u_2^2)} \left[\frac{\partial}{\partial u_1}(2u_2 \sqrt{u_1^2 + u_2^2}) + \frac{\partial}{\partial u_2}(2u_3 \sqrt{u_1^2 + u_2^2}) \right.$$

$$\left. + \frac{\partial}{\partial u_3}(4u_1 (u_1^2 + u_2^2)) \right]$$

$$= \frac{u_2(u_1 + u_3)}{2(u_1^2 + u_2^2)^{\frac{3}{2}}} \qquad (11)$$

The curl of $\bar{F}$ is

$$\nabla \times \bar{F} = \frac{1}{4(u_1^2 + u_2^2)} \begin{vmatrix} 2\sqrt{u_1^2 + u_2^2}\ \bar{e}_1 & 2\sqrt{u_1^2 + u_2^2}\ \bar{e}_2 & \bar{e}_3 \\ \dfrac{\partial}{\partial u_1} & \dfrac{\partial}{\partial u_2} & \dfrac{\partial}{\partial u_3} \\ 2u_2 \sqrt{u_1^2 + u_2^2} & 2u_3 \sqrt{u_1^2 + u_2^2} & u_1 \end{vmatrix}$$

$$= -\bar{e}_1 - \frac{\bar{e}_2}{2\sqrt{u_1^2+u_2^2}} + \frac{\bar{e}_3}{2(u_1^2+u_2^2)}\left[\frac{u_1u_3-u_2^2}{\sqrt{u_1^2+u_2^2}} - \sqrt{u_1^2+u_2^2}\right] \quad (12)$$

For the following orthogonal coordinate system,

$$x = e^{u_3} \cos u_2$$

$$y = e^{u_3} \sin u_2 \qquad (1)$$

$$z = u_1$$

evaluate the scale factors and compute $\nabla^2 f$ where

$$f = u_1 u_2 u_3 . \qquad (2)$$

Solution: The arc length is

$$ds^2 = dx^2 + dy^2 + dz^2$$

$$= (e^{u_3} \cos u_2 \, du_3 - e^{u_3} \sin u_2 \, du_2)^2$$

$$+ (e^{u_3} \sin u_2 \, du_3 + e^{u_3} \cos u_2 \, du_2)^2 + du_1^2$$

$$= du_1^2 + du_2^2\left[e^{2u_3}\sin^2 u_2 + e^{2u_3}\cos^2 u_2\right] \qquad (3)$$

$$+ du_3^2\left[e^{2u_3}\cos^2 u_2 + e^{2u_3}\sin^2 u_2\right]$$

$$= du_1^2 + e^{2u_3}du_2^2 + e^{2u_3}du_3^2$$

The scale factors are

$$h_1 = 1, \quad h_2 = e^{u_3}, \quad h_3 = e^{u_3} \qquad (4)$$

Substituting the scale factors and eq.(2) into the expression for ∇^2 we find

$$\nabla^2 f = \frac{1}{h_1 h_2 h_3}\left[\frac{\partial}{\partial u_1}\left(\frac{h_2 h_3}{h_1}\frac{\partial f}{\partial u_1}\right) + \frac{\partial}{\partial u_2}\left(\frac{h_1 h_3}{h_2}\frac{\partial f}{\partial u_2}\right)\right.$$

$$\left. + \frac{\partial}{\partial u_3}\left(\frac{h_1 h_2}{h_3}\frac{\partial f}{\partial u_3}\right)\right] \qquad (5)$$

$$= \frac{1}{e^{2u_3}}\left[\frac{\partial}{\partial u_1}(u_2 u_3 \cdot e^{2u_3}) + \frac{\partial}{\partial u_2}(u_1 u_3) + \frac{\partial}{\partial u_3}(u_1 u_2)\right]$$

$$= 0$$

Determine if the coordinate system

$$u_1 = y$$

$$u_2 = x \qquad (1)$$

$$u_3 = z$$

is orthogonal. Evaluate curl $\overline{F}$ where

$$\overline{F} = -u_2\overline{e}_1 + u_1\overline{e}_2 \qquad (2)$$

Express $\overline{F}$ in (x,y,z) coordinates and again evaluate curl $\overline{F}$. Compare the results and explain the discrepancy.

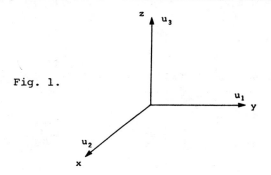

Fig. 1.

Solution: From eq.(1) vectors $\overline{e}_1,\overline{e}_2,\overline{e}_3$ can be evaluated

$$\overline{e}_1 = \frac{\frac{\partial \overline{r}}{\partial u_1}}{\left|\frac{\partial \overline{r}}{\partial u_1}\right|} = \overline{j}$$

$$\overline{e}_2 = \overline{i} \qquad (3)$$

$$\overline{e}_3 = \overline{k}$$

Since $\overline{e}_1 \cdot \overline{e}_2 = \overline{e}_1 \cdot \overline{e}_3 = \overline{e}_2 \cdot \overline{e}_3 = 0 \qquad (4)$

the system (u_1,u_2,u_3) is orthogonal. The scale factors are

$$h_1 = h_2 = h_3 = 1 \qquad (5)$$

The expression for curl $\overline{F}$ becomes

$$\text{curl } \overline{F} = \overline{e}_1\left[\frac{\partial F_3}{\partial u_2} - \frac{\partial F_2}{\partial u_3}\right] + \overline{e}_2\left[\frac{\partial F_1}{\partial u_3} - \frac{\partial F_3}{\partial u_1}\right] + \overline{e}_3\left[\frac{\partial F_2}{\partial u_1} - \frac{\partial F_1}{\partial u_2}\right] \qquad (6)$$

For $\overline{F} = -u_2\overline{e}_1 + u_1\overline{e}_2$,   we get

$$\text{curl } \overline{F} = \overline{e}_3(1+1) = 2\overline{e}_3 = 2\overline{k} \qquad (7)$$

Transforming vector $\overline{F}$ to cartesian coordinates (x,y,z) we find
$$\overline{F} = y\overline{i} - x\overline{j} \tag{8}$$

and evaluating curl $\overline{F}$ we find

$$\nabla \times \overline{F} = \left(\frac{\partial}{\partial x}, \frac{\partial}{\partial y}, \frac{\partial}{\partial z}\right) \times (y,-x,0) = (0,0,-1-1) = -2\overline{k} \tag{9}$$

Obviously the results, eqs.(7) and (9), are not equal. The system (u_1,u_2,u_3) shown in Fig. 1 is not right-handed.

Therefore, the standard formula for curl does not apply.

● PROBLEM 22-39

Let
$$x = \rho\cos\theta$$
$$y = \rho\sin\theta \tag{1}$$
$$z = z$$

Here, (ρ,θ,z) are the well-known cylindrical coordinates. The volume elements in Cartesian coordinates is

$$dV = dxdydz \tag{2}$$

while in cylindrical coordinates,

$$dV = \rho d\rho d\theta dz \tag{3}$$

Differentiate eq.(1) to obtain dx,dy,dz in terms of $d\rho,d\theta,dz$, then substitute into eq.(2). Did you get eq.(3)? Why not?

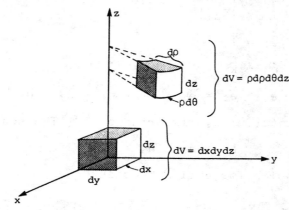

Solution: Differentiating eq.(1) yields
$$dx = \cos\theta d\rho - \rho\sin\theta d\theta$$
$$dy = \sin\theta d\rho + \rho\cos\theta d\phi$$
$$dz = dz \tag{4}$$

From the above, we obtain

dxdydz = $(\sin\theta\cos\theta d\rho^2 - \rho^2\sin\theta\cos\theta d\theta^2 + \rho\cos^2\theta d\rho d\theta - \rho\sin^2\theta d\rho d\theta)dz$

Obviously, the result is different from dV = $\rho d\rho d\theta dz$.

The volume element dxdydz in Cartesian coordinates is different from the volume element $\rho d\rho d\theta dz$ in cylindrical coordinates (see Fig. 1).

This example shows that not all the transformations from the Cartesian to a curvilinear coordinate system can be carried out "automatically".

CONTRAVARIANT AND COVARIANT COMPONENTS OF A VECTOR, METRIC COEFFICIENTS AND THE JACOBIAN OF A TRANSFORMATION

● **PROBLEM** 22-40

Let
$$x = u_1 - u_2$$
$$y = u_1 - 2u_3 \tag{1}$$
$$z = u_1 + u_3$$

Express the vector

$$\overline{F} = 2\overline{i} + \overline{j} + 3\overline{k} \tag{2}$$

in terms of its contravariant components and its covariant components.

Solution: Vector $\overline{F}$ can be expressed as a linear combination

$$\overline{F} = \alpha_1 \frac{\partial\overline{r}}{\partial u_1} + \alpha_2 \frac{\partial\overline{r}}{\partial u_2} + \alpha_3 \frac{\partial\overline{r}}{\partial u_3} \tag{3}$$

Here, $\frac{\partial\overline{r}}{\partial u_1}, \frac{\partial\overline{r}}{\partial u_2}, \frac{\partial\overline{r}}{\partial u_3}$ are called the unitary base vectors, and $\alpha_1, \alpha_2, \alpha_3$ are the contravariant components of $\overline{F}$. From eq.(1), we have
$$\frac{\partial\overline{r}}{\partial u_1} = (1,1,1) = \overline{i} + \overline{j} + \overline{k}$$

$$\frac{\partial\overline{r}}{\partial u_2} = (-1,0,0) = -\overline{i} \tag{4}$$

$$\frac{\partial\overline{r}}{\partial u_3} = (0,-2,1) = -2\overline{j} + \overline{k}$$

Substituting eq.(2) and eq.(4) into eq.(3) we obtain
$$(2,1,3) = \alpha_1(1,1,1) + \alpha_2(-1,0,0) + \alpha_3(0,-2,1) \tag{5}$$

The contravariant components of $\overline{F}$ are thus

$$\alpha_1 = \frac{7}{3} \qquad \alpha_2 = \frac{1}{3} \qquad \alpha_3 = \frac{2}{3} \tag{6}$$

Vector $\overline{F}$ can be represented as a linear combination

$$\overline{F} = \beta_1 \nabla u_1 + \beta_2 \nabla u_2 + \beta_3 \nabla u_3 \tag{7}$$

where $\beta_1, \beta_2, \beta_3$ are the covariant components of $\overline{F}$.

From eq.(1), we find

$$u_1 = \frac{y + 2z}{3}$$

$$u_2 = \frac{-3x + y + 2z}{3} \tag{8}$$

$$u_3 = \frac{-y + z}{3}$$

Hence,

$$\nabla u_1 = \left(0, \frac{1}{3}, \frac{2}{3} \right) = \frac{1}{3} \overline{j} + \frac{2}{3} \overline{k}$$

$$\nabla u_2 = \left(-1, \frac{1}{3}, \frac{2}{3} \right) = -\overline{i} + \frac{1}{3} \overline{j} + \frac{2}{3} \overline{k} \tag{9}$$

$$\nabla u_3 = \left(0, -\frac{1}{3}, \frac{1}{3} \right) = -\frac{1}{3} \overline{j} + \frac{1}{3} \overline{k}$$

Substituting eqs.(2) and (9) into eq.(7) results in

$$(2,1,3) = \beta_1 \left(0, \frac{1}{3}, \frac{2}{3} \right) + \beta_2 \left(-1, \frac{1}{3}, \frac{2}{3} \right) + \beta_3 \left(0, -\frac{1}{3}, \frac{1}{3} \right) \tag{10}$$

so that $\quad \beta_1 = 6, \qquad \beta_2 = -2, \qquad \beta_3 = 1$

Thus, the covariant components of $\overline{F}$ are
$$\beta_1 = 6, \qquad \beta_2 = -2, \qquad \beta_3 = 1.$$

● **PROBLEM** 22-41

The surface is given by (see Fig. 1)

$$\overline{r} = \overline{r}(u,v) \tag{1}$$

Show that the square of the element of arc length on this surface is

$$ds^2 = Edu^2 + 2Fdudv + Gdv^2 \tag{2}$$

Solution: Differentiating eq.(1), we find

$$d\overline{r} = \frac{\partial \overline{r}}{\partial u} du + \frac{\partial \overline{r}}{\partial v} dv \tag{3}$$

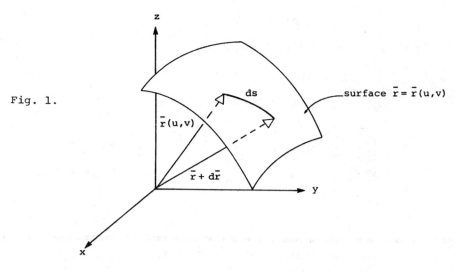

Fig. 1.

surface $\bar{r} = \bar{r}(u,v)$

ds

$\bar{r}(u,v)$

$\bar{r} + d\bar{r}$

Therefore,

$$ds^2 = d\bar{r} \cdot d\bar{r} = \left(\frac{\partial \bar{r}}{\partial u} du + \frac{\partial \bar{r}}{\partial v} dv \right) \cdot \left(\frac{\partial \bar{r}}{\partial u} du + \frac{\partial \bar{r}}{\partial v} dv \right)$$

$$= \frac{\partial \bar{r}}{\partial u} \cdot \frac{\partial \bar{r}}{\partial u} du^2 + 2 \frac{\partial \bar{r}}{\partial u} \cdot \frac{\partial \bar{r}}{\partial v} dudv + \frac{\partial \bar{r}}{\partial v} \cdot \frac{\partial \bar{r}}{\partial v} dv^2$$

$$= Edu^2 + 2Fdudv + Gdv^2 \tag{4}$$

where

$$E = \frac{\partial \bar{r}}{\partial u} \cdot \frac{\partial \bar{r}}{\partial u}$$

$$F = \frac{\partial \bar{r}}{\partial u} \cdot \frac{\partial \bar{r}}{\partial v} \tag{5}$$

$$G = \frac{\partial \bar{r}}{\partial v} \cdot \frac{\partial \bar{r}}{\partial v}$$

● **PROBLEM 22-42**

Express the element of surface area of the surface

$$\bar{r} = \bar{r}(u,v) \tag{1}$$

in terms of E, F, and G as defined in Problem 22-41.

Solution: The element of area is given by

$$dS = \left| \frac{\partial \bar{r}}{\partial u} \times \frac{\partial \bar{r}}{\partial v} \right| dudv$$

$$= \sqrt{\left(\frac{\partial \bar{r}}{\partial u} \times \frac{\partial \bar{r}}{\partial v} \right) \cdot \left(\frac{\partial \bar{r}}{\partial u} \times \frac{\partial \bar{r}}{\partial v} \right)} \, dudv \tag{2}$$

We now have to express the function under the square root sign in terms of E, F, and G.

Applying the identity

$$(\bar{a} \times \bar{b}) \cdot (\bar{a} \times \bar{b}) = (\bar{a} \cdot \bar{a})(\bar{b} \cdot \bar{b}) - (\bar{a} \cdot \bar{b})(\bar{a} \cdot \bar{b}), \qquad (3)$$

we get

$$dS = \sqrt{\left(\frac{\partial \bar{r}}{\partial u} \times \frac{\partial \bar{r}}{\partial v}\right) \cdot \left(\frac{\partial \bar{r}}{\partial u} \times \frac{\partial \bar{r}}{\partial v}\right)} \ dudv$$

$$= \sqrt{\left(\frac{\partial \bar{r}}{\partial u} \cdot \frac{\partial \bar{r}}{\partial u}\right)\left(\frac{\partial \bar{r}}{\partial v} \cdot \frac{\partial \bar{r}}{\partial v}\right) - \left(\frac{\partial \bar{r}}{\partial u} \cdot \frac{\partial \bar{r}}{\partial v}\right)\left(\frac{\partial \bar{r}}{\partial u} \cdot \frac{\partial \bar{r}}{\partial v}\right)} \ dudv$$

$$\qquad (4)$$

$$= \sqrt{EG - F^2} \ dudv$$

● **PROBLEM** 22-43

Using the results of Problem 22-42, find the surface area of a sphere of radius a.

Solution: We shall use the spherical coordinates

$$x = a\sin\phi\cos\theta$$

$$y = a\sin\phi\sin\theta \qquad (1)$$

$$z = a\cos\phi$$

Here a is the radius of the sphere, which, of course, is constant. The position vector of any point on the sphere is a function of ϕ and θ,

$$\bar{r} = \bar{r}(\phi, \theta) \qquad (2)$$

so that

$$\frac{\partial \bar{r}}{\partial \phi} = (a\cos\phi\cos\theta, \ a\cos\phi\sin\theta, \ -a\sin\phi) \qquad (3)$$

$$\frac{\partial \bar{r}}{\partial \theta} = (-a\sin\phi\sin\theta, \ a\sin\phi\cos\theta, \ 0) \qquad (4)$$

Substituting eqs.(3) and (4) into the expressions for E, G, and F, we obtain

$$E = \frac{\partial \bar{r}}{\partial \phi} \cdot \frac{\partial \bar{r}}{\partial \phi} = a^2$$

$$G = \frac{\partial \bar{r}}{\partial \theta} \cdot \frac{\partial \bar{r}}{\partial \theta} = a^2\sin^2\phi \qquad (5)$$

$$F = \frac{\partial \bar{r}}{\partial \phi} \cdot \frac{\partial \bar{r}}{\partial \theta} = 0$$

The surface area of a sphere is

$$\iint_S \sqrt{EG-F^2} \ d\phi d\theta = \int_{\theta=0}^{2\pi}\int_{\phi=0}^{\pi} \sqrt{a^4\sin^2\phi} \ d\phi d\theta$$

$$\qquad (6)$$

$$= 2\pi a^2 \int_0^\pi \sin\phi d\phi = 4\pi a^2$$

Two general curvilinear coordinate systems (u_1, u_2, u_3) and (v_1, v_2, v_3) are given.

Express $\dfrac{\partial \overline{r}}{\partial v_i}$ in terms of $\dfrac{\partial \overline{r}}{\partial u_i}$.

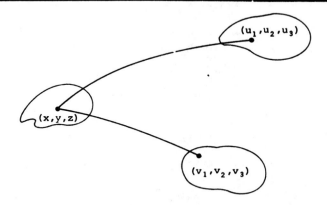

Solution: The transformation equations from a rectangular system (x,y,z) to (u_1, u_2, u_3) and to (v_1, v_2, v_3) are

$$x = x(u_1, u_2, u_3) \qquad x = x(v_1, v_2, v_3)$$
$$y = y(u_1, u_2, u_3) \qquad y = y(v_1, v_2, v_3) \tag{1}$$
$$z = z(u_1, u_2, u_3) \qquad z = z(v_1, v_2, v_3)$$

The transformations are one-to-one. There exists a direct transformation from (u_1, u_2, u_3) to (v_1, v_2, v_3), that is

$$u_1 = u_1(v_1, v_2, v_3)$$
$$u_2 = u_2(v_1, v_2, v_3) \tag{2}$$
$$u_3 = u_3(v_1, v_2, v_3)$$

The opposite transformation also exists and is one-to-one. Instead of writing eq.(2), we shall simply write

$$u_i = u_i(v_j) \quad i,j = 1,2,3 \tag{3}$$

From eq.(1) we get

$$d\overline{r} = \frac{\partial \overline{r}}{\partial u_1} \, du_1 + \frac{\partial \overline{r}}{\partial u_2} \, du_2 + \frac{\partial \overline{r}}{\partial u_3} \, du_3 \tag{4}$$

Using the Einstein convention, we can write eq.(4) as

$$d\overline{r} = \frac{\partial \overline{r}}{\partial u_i} \, du_i \tag{5}$$

Also,

$$d\overline{r} = \frac{\partial \overline{r}}{\partial v_j} \, dv_j \tag{6}$$

Comparing eqs.(5) and (6) we obtain

$$\frac{\partial \overline{r}}{\partial u_i} \, du_i = \frac{\partial \overline{r}}{\partial v_j} \, dv_j \tag{7}$$

From eq.(3), we have

$$du_i = \frac{\partial u_i}{\partial v_j} \, dv_j \qquad i,j = 1,2,3 \tag{8}$$

Substituting eq.(8) into eq.(7) and equating coefficients of dv_1, dv_2, dv_3 on both sides, we find

$$\frac{\partial \overline{r}}{\partial v_j} \, dv_j = \frac{\partial \overline{r}}{\partial u_i} \frac{\partial u_i}{\partial v_k} \, dv_k \tag{9}$$

$$\frac{\partial \overline{r}}{\partial v_j} = \frac{\partial \overline{r}}{\partial u_i} \frac{\partial u_i}{\partial v_j} \tag{10}$$

Eq.(10) represents three equations, namely

$$\frac{\partial \overline{r}}{\partial v_1} = \frac{\partial \overline{r}}{\partial u_1} \frac{\partial u_1}{\partial v_1} + \frac{\partial \overline{r}}{\partial u_2} \frac{\partial u_2}{\partial v_1} + \frac{\partial \overline{r}}{\partial u_3} \frac{\partial u_3}{\partial v_1} \tag{11}$$

$$\frac{\partial \overline{r}}{\partial v_2} = \frac{\partial \overline{r}}{\partial u_1} \frac{\partial u_1}{\partial v_2} + \frac{\partial \overline{r}}{\partial u_2} \frac{\partial u_2}{\partial v_2} + \frac{\partial \overline{r}}{\partial u_3} \frac{\partial u_3}{\partial v_2}$$

$$\frac{\partial \overline{r}}{\partial v_3} = \frac{\partial \overline{r}}{\partial u_1} \frac{\partial u_1}{\partial v_3} + \frac{\partial \overline{r}}{\partial u_2} \frac{\partial u_2}{\partial v_3} + \frac{\partial \overline{r}}{\partial u_3} \frac{\partial u_3}{\partial v_3}$$

● **PROBLEM 22-45**

Let $\overline{F}$ be a vector field defined with respect to the two general curvilinear coordinate systems (u_1, u_2, u_3) and (v_1, v_2, v_3).

Determine the relationship between the contravariant components of the vector in the two coordinate systems.

Solution: Let $\alpha_1, \alpha_2, \alpha_3$ be the contravariant components of $\overline{F}$ in the (u_1, u_2, u_3) coordinate system,

$$\overline{F} = \alpha_1 \frac{\partial \overline{r}}{\partial u_1} + \alpha_2 \frac{\partial \overline{r}}{\partial u_2} + \alpha_3 \frac{\partial \overline{r}}{\partial u_3} = \alpha_i \frac{\partial \overline{r}}{\partial u_i} \tag{1}$$

and let $\alpha_1', \alpha_2', \alpha_3'$ be the contravariant components of $\overline{F}$ in the (v_1, v_2, v_3) coordinate system,

$$\overline{F} = \alpha_1' \frac{\partial \overline{r}}{\partial v_1} + \alpha_2' \frac{\partial \overline{r}}{\partial v_2} + \alpha_3' \frac{\partial \overline{r}}{\partial v_3}$$

$$= \alpha_i' \frac{\partial \overline{r}}{\partial v_i} \tag{2}$$

1132

Thus,

$$\alpha_i \frac{\partial \overline{r}}{\partial u_i} = \alpha_k' \frac{\partial \overline{r}}{\partial v_k} \qquad i,k = 1,2,3 \tag{3}$$

Substituting eq.(10) of Problem 22-44, that is

$$\frac{\partial \overline{r}}{\partial v_j} = \frac{\partial \overline{r}}{\partial u_i} \frac{\partial u_i}{\partial v_j}$$

into eq.(3), we find

$$\alpha_i \frac{\partial \overline{r}}{\partial u_i} = \alpha_k' \frac{\partial \overline{r}}{\partial u_j} \frac{\partial u_j}{\partial v_k} \qquad i,j,k = 1,2,3 \tag{4}$$

Equating the coefficients in eq.(4) we obtain

$$\alpha_i = \alpha_k' \frac{\partial u_i}{\partial v_k} \tag{5}$$

Interchanging the coordinates results in

$$\alpha_i' = \alpha_j \frac{\partial v_i}{\partial u_j} \tag{6}$$

In general, we say that if three quantities $(\alpha_1, \alpha_2, \alpha_3)$ of a coordinate system (u_1, u_2, u_3) are related to three quantities $(\alpha_1', \alpha_2', \alpha_3')$ of another system (v_1, v_2, v_3) by the transformation equations (5) or (6), then $(\alpha_1, \alpha_2, \alpha_3)$ is a contravariant vector (sometimes called contravariant tensor of the first rank). This definition can be easily extended to the spaces of higher dimension.

● **PROBLEM 22-46**

Find the transformation laws for the covariant components of $\overline{F}$.

Solution: Consider two general curvilinear coordinate systems (u_1, u_2, u_3) and (v_1, v_2, v_3). In covariant components (see Problem 22-38) vector $\overline{F}$ can be represented as

$$\beta_1 \nabla u_1 + \beta_2 \nabla u_2 + \beta_3 \nabla u_3 = \beta_1' \nabla v_1 + \beta_2' \nabla v_2 + \beta_3' \nabla v_3 \tag{1}$$

where $(\beta_1, \beta_2, \beta_3)$ are the covariant components of $\overline{F}$ in the (u_1, u_2, u_3) system and $(\beta_1', \beta_2', \beta_3')$ are the covariant components of $\overline{F}$ in the (v_1, v_2, v_3) system.

Using the Einstein convention we can write eq.(1) in the form

$$\beta_i \nabla u_i = \beta_j' \nabla v_j \tag{2}$$

where $i,j = 1,2,3.$

Since,
$$u_i = u_i(v_j)$$

and   (3)

$$v_j = v_j(u_i)$$

we have

$$\frac{\partial v_j}{\partial x} = \frac{\partial v_j}{\partial u_1}\frac{\partial u_1}{\partial x} + \frac{\partial v_j}{\partial u_2}\frac{\partial u_2}{\partial x} + \frac{\partial v_j}{\partial u_3}\frac{\partial u_3}{\partial x}$$

(4)

$$= \frac{\partial v_j}{\partial u_k}\frac{\partial u_k}{\partial x} \qquad k = 1,2,3$$

Instead of using x, y, and z, let us introduce the notation

$$x = x_1$$

$$y = x_2$$ (5)

$$z = x_3$$

Therefore, (x_i) $i = 1,2,3$

indicates x, y, and z.

We can write equations similar to eq.(4) for $\frac{\partial v_j}{\partial y}$ and $\frac{\partial v_j}{\partial x}$.

In general

$$\frac{\partial v_j}{\partial x_\ell} = \frac{\partial v_j}{\partial u_k}\frac{\partial u_k}{\partial x_\ell}$$

(6)

Eq.(6) represents nine equations. We have

$$\beta_i \nabla u_i = \beta_j \frac{\partial u_j}{\partial x_1}\bar{i} + \beta_j \frac{\partial u_j}{\partial x_2}\bar{j} + \beta_j \frac{\partial u_j}{\partial x_3}\bar{k}$$

(7)

For the (v_1,v_2,v_3) system, we get

$$\beta'_j \nabla v_j = \beta'_j \frac{\partial v_j}{\partial x_1}\bar{i} + \beta'_j \frac{\partial v_j}{\partial x_2}\bar{j} + \beta'_j \frac{\partial v_j}{\partial x_3}\bar{k}$$

(8)

Equating the coefficients of $\bar{i}$, $\bar{j}$, and $\bar{k}$ in eqs.(7) and (8), we obtain

$$\beta_j \frac{\partial u_j}{\partial x_k} = \beta'_j \frac{\partial v_j}{\partial x_k}$$

(9)

Substituting eq.(6) into eq.(9) results in

$$\beta_j \frac{\partial u_j}{\partial x_k} = \beta'_j \frac{\partial v_j}{\partial u_i}\frac{\partial u_i}{\partial x_k}$$

(10)

Now, equating the coefficients of $\dfrac{\partial u_i}{\partial x_i}$ on each side gives us

$$\beta_j = \beta_i' \frac{\partial v_i}{\partial u_j} \tag{11}$$

where $\qquad i,j = 1,2,3.$

Multiplying eq.(11) by $\dfrac{\partial u_j}{\partial v_k}$, gives

$$\beta_j \frac{\partial u_j}{\partial v_k} = \beta_i' \frac{\partial v_i}{\partial u_j} \frac{\partial u_j}{\partial v_k} \tag{12}$$

If we recall that

$$\frac{\partial v_i}{\partial u_j} \frac{\partial u_j}{\partial v_k} = \delta_{ik} \tag{13}$$

where

$$\delta_{ik} = \begin{cases} 0 & \text{for} \quad i \neq k \\ 1 & \text{for} \quad i = k \end{cases} \tag{14}$$

we obtain

$$\beta_j \frac{\partial u_j}{\partial v_k} = \beta_i' \frac{\partial v_i}{\partial u_j} \frac{\partial u_j}{\partial v_k} = \beta_i' \delta_{ik} = \beta_k' \tag{15}$$

The laws of transformation for covariant components are

$$\beta_j = \beta_i' \frac{\partial v_i}{\partial u_j}$$
$$\beta_j' = \beta_i \frac{\partial u_i}{\partial v_j} \tag{16}$$

Eq.(16) can be used as a definition of a covariant vector.

If three quantities $(\beta_1, \beta_2, \beta_3)$ of a coordinate system (u_1, u_2, u_3) are related to $(\beta_1', \beta_2', \beta_3')$ of a system (v_1, v_2, v_3) by the transformation laws, eq.(16), then $\overline{\beta} = (\beta_1, \beta_2, \beta_3)$ is a covariant vector or a covariant tensor of the first rank.

● **PROBLEM 22-47**

The surface is described by

$$\overline{r} = \overline{r}(u,v) \tag{1}$$

Prove that a unit vector which is everywhere normal to the surface is given by

$$\overline{N} = \pm \frac{\dfrac{\partial \overline{r}}{\partial u} \times \dfrac{\partial \overline{r}}{\partial v}}{\sqrt{EG-F^2}} \tag{2}$$

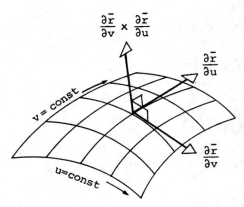

Fig. 1

Solution: The vector $\frac{\partial \overline{r}}{\partial u}$ is tangent to a curve with v=const and the vector $\frac{\partial \overline{r}}{\partial v}$ is tangent to a curve with u=const.

Therefore $\frac{\partial \overline{r}}{\partial u} \times \frac{\partial \overline{r}}{\partial v}$ is normal to the surface.

We have

$$E = \frac{\partial \overline{r}}{\partial u} \cdot \frac{\partial \overline{r}}{\partial u}$$

$$G = \frac{\partial \overline{r}}{\partial v} \cdot \frac{\partial \overline{r}}{\partial v} \tag{3}$$

$$F = \frac{\partial \overline{r}}{\partial u} \cdot \frac{\partial \overline{r}}{\partial v}$$

thus

$$\left| \frac{\partial \overline{r}}{\partial u} \times \frac{\partial \overline{r}}{\partial v} \right| = \sqrt{EG - F^2} \tag{4}$$

(see Problem 22-42).

Vector $\overline{N}$,

$$\overline{N} = \pm \frac{\frac{\partial \overline{r}}{\partial u} \times \frac{\partial \overline{r}}{\partial v}}{\sqrt{EG - F^2}} \tag{5}$$

is normal to $\overline{r} = \overline{r}(u,v)$ and it is a unit vector,

$$|\overline{N}| = \frac{\left| \frac{\partial \overline{r}}{\partial u} \times \frac{\partial \overline{r}}{\partial v} \right|}{\sqrt{EG - F^2}} = 1 \tag{6}$$

● **PROBLEM 22-48**

Prove that in general coordinates

$$g = \det(g_{ij}) = \left(\frac{\partial \overline{r}}{\partial u_1} \cdot \frac{\partial \overline{r}}{\partial u_2} \times \frac{\partial \overline{r}}{\partial u_3} \right)^2 \tag{1}$$

where

$$g_{ij} = \frac{\partial \overline{r}}{\partial u_i} \cdot \frac{\partial \overline{r}}{\partial u_j} \qquad i,j = 1,2,3. \qquad (2)$$

<u>Solution</u>: The coefficients g_{ij} were defined in Problem 22-13 as

$$g_{ij} = \frac{\partial \overline{r}}{\partial u_i} \cdot \frac{\partial \overline{r}}{\partial u_j}$$

We shall use the following identity

$$\overline{a} \cdot (\overline{b} \times \overline{c}) = \begin{vmatrix} a_1 & a_2 & a_3 \\ b_1 & b_2 & b_3 \\ c_1 & c_2 & c_3 \end{vmatrix} \qquad (3)$$

so that

$$\frac{\partial \overline{r}}{\partial u_1} \cdot \frac{\partial \overline{r}}{\partial u_2} \times \frac{\partial \overline{r}}{\partial u_3} = \begin{vmatrix} \frac{\partial x}{\partial u_1} & \frac{\partial y}{\partial u_1} & \frac{\partial z}{\partial u_1} \\ \frac{\partial x}{\partial u_2} & \frac{\partial y}{\partial u_2} & \frac{\partial z}{\partial u_2} \\ \frac{\partial x}{\partial u_3} & \frac{\partial y}{\partial u_3} & \frac{\partial z}{\partial u_3} \end{vmatrix} \qquad (4)$$

Remember that in multiplying the matrices, we multiply the row of the first matrix by the column of the second matrix.

We have

$$\left(\frac{\partial \overline{r}}{\partial u_1} \cdot \frac{\partial \overline{r}}{\partial u_2} \times \frac{\partial \overline{r}}{\partial u_3} \right)^2 = \begin{vmatrix} \frac{\partial x}{\partial u_1} & \frac{\partial y}{\partial u_1} & \frac{\partial z}{\partial u_1} \\ \frac{\partial x}{\partial u_2} & \frac{\partial y}{\partial u_2} & \frac{\partial z}{\partial u_2} \\ \frac{\partial x}{\partial u_3} & \frac{\partial y}{\partial u_3} & \frac{\partial z}{\partial u_3} \end{vmatrix} \begin{vmatrix} \frac{\partial x}{\partial u_1} & \frac{\partial x}{\partial u_2} & \frac{\partial x}{\partial u_3} \\ \frac{\partial y}{\partial u_1} & \frac{\partial y}{\partial u_2} & \frac{\partial y}{\partial u_3} \\ \frac{\partial z}{\partial u_1} & \frac{\partial z}{\partial u_2} & \frac{\partial z}{\partial u_3} \end{vmatrix} \qquad (5)$$

$$= \begin{vmatrix} g_{11} & g_{12} & g_{13} \\ g_{21} & g_{22} & g_{23} \\ g_{31} & g_{32} & g_{33} \end{vmatrix} = \det(g_{ij}) = g$$

For example, the element g_{23} was obtained by multiplying the second row of the first matrix by the third column of the second matrix:

$$\left(\frac{\partial x}{\partial u_2}, \frac{\partial y}{\partial u_2}, \frac{\partial z}{\partial u_2} \right) \cdot \left(\frac{\partial x}{\partial u_3}, \frac{\partial y}{\partial u_3}, \frac{\partial z}{\partial u_3} \right)$$

$$= \frac{\partial x}{\partial u_2} \frac{\partial x}{\partial u_3} + \frac{\partial y}{\partial u_2} \frac{\partial y}{\partial u_3} + \frac{\partial z}{\partial u_2} \frac{\partial z}{\partial u_3} \qquad (6)$$

$$= \frac{\partial \overline{r}}{\partial u_2} \cdot \frac{\partial \overline{r}}{\partial u_3} = g_{23}$$

1137

Show that the volume element in general coordinates (u_1, u_2, u_3) is

$$dV = \sqrt{g}\ du_1 du_2 du_3 \qquad (1)$$

Solution: In Problem 22-14, we have shown that the volume element is equal to

$$dV = |(h_1 du_1 \bar{e}_1) \cdot (h_2 du_2 \bar{e}_2) \times (h_3 du_3 \bar{e}_3)| \qquad (2)$$

Since

$$\frac{\partial \bar{r}}{\partial u_1} = h_1 \bar{e}_1$$

$$\frac{\partial \bar{r}}{\partial u_2} = h_2 \bar{e}_2 \qquad (3)$$

$$\frac{\partial \bar{r}}{\partial u_3} = h_3 \bar{e}_3$$

eq.(2) can be written in the form

$$dV = \left| \left(\frac{\partial \bar{r}}{\partial u_1} du_1 \right) \cdot \left(\frac{\partial \bar{r}}{\partial u_2} du_2 \times \frac{\partial \bar{r}}{\partial u_3} du_3 \right) \right|$$

$$\qquad (4)$$

$$= \left| \frac{\partial \bar{r}}{\partial u_1} \cdot \frac{\partial \bar{r}}{\partial u_2} \times \frac{\partial \bar{r}}{\partial u_3} \right| du_1 du_2 du_3$$

From Problem 22-48, we have

$$\sqrt{g} = \frac{\partial \bar{r}}{\partial u_1} \cdot \frac{\partial \bar{r}}{\partial u_2} \times \frac{\partial \bar{r}}{\partial u_3} \qquad (5)$$

Thus

$$dV = \sqrt{g}\ du_1 du_2 du_3 \qquad (6)$$

The system of equations

$$x = 3u - v$$
$$\qquad (1)$$
$$y = u + 3v$$

transforms points on the xy-plane to points on the uv-plane. Show that lines in the xy-plane correspond to lines in the uv-plane. What is the image of the square bounded by x = 0, x = 2, y = 0, y = 2 in the uv-plane? Find the area of the square and its image and relate it to the Jacobian of the transformation.

Solution: The equation of a line is

$$y = ax + b \tag{2}$$

Transforming eq.(2) to (u,v) coordinates we get

$$u + 3v = 3au - av + b$$

or

$$u = \frac{(3+a)}{2a} v + \frac{b}{2a} \tag{3}$$

which is the equation of a line.

From eq.(1), we see that (u,v) is an orthogonal system.

Solving eq.(1) for u and v we obtain

$$u = \frac{y + 3x}{10}$$
$$v = \frac{3y - x}{10} \tag{4}$$

The four points of the square are transformed into

$$(x,y) \longrightarrow (u,v)$$

(x,y)	(u,v)
(0,0)	(0,0)
(2,0)	$\left(\frac{3}{5}, -\frac{1}{5}\right)$
(2,2)	$\left(\frac{4}{5}, \frac{2}{5}\right)$
(0,2)	$\left(\frac{1}{5}, \frac{3}{5}\right)$

as shown in Fig. 1.

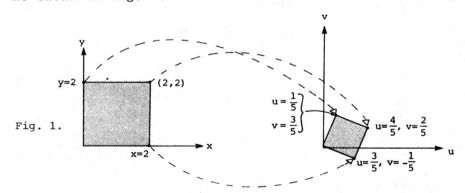

Fig. 1.

The area of the square in the (x,y) system is 2 · 2 = 4, and in the (u,v) system, the area is

$$\sqrt{\left(\frac{3}{5}\right)^2 + \left(\frac{1}{5}\right)^2} \sqrt{\left(\frac{3}{5}\right)^2 + \left(\frac{1}{5}\right)^2} = \frac{2}{5}$$

1139

The Jacobian of the transformation is

$$J = \frac{\partial(x,y)}{\partial(u,v)} = \begin{vmatrix} \dfrac{\partial x}{\partial u} & \dfrac{\partial y}{\partial u} \\ \dfrac{\partial x}{\partial v} & \dfrac{\partial y}{\partial v} \end{vmatrix} = \begin{vmatrix} 3 & 1 \\ -1 & 3 \end{vmatrix} = 10 \qquad (5)$$

Thus, $\qquad \dfrac{\text{Area in } (x,y)\text{coordinates}}{\text{Area in } (u,v)\text{coordinates}} = \dfrac{4}{\frac{2}{5}} = 10 = \text{Jacobian} \qquad (6)$

● **PROBLEM** 22-51

The transformation is given by

$$x = u_1 + u_2^2$$

$$y = u_1 + u_3 \qquad (1)$$

$$z = u_2^2 + u_2 u_3$$

Find g and the Jacobian. Verify that

$$J = \sqrt{g} \qquad (2)$$

<u>Solution</u>: Let us first find the Jacobian of the transformation.

We have

$$J = \frac{\partial(x,y,z)}{\partial(u_1,u_2,u_3)} = \begin{vmatrix} \dfrac{\partial x}{\partial u_1} & \dfrac{\partial y}{\partial u_1} & \dfrac{\partial z}{\partial u_1} \\ \dfrac{\partial x}{\partial u_2} & \dfrac{\partial y}{\partial u_2} & \dfrac{\partial z}{\partial u_2} \\ \dfrac{\partial x}{\partial u_3} & \dfrac{\partial y}{\partial u_3} & \dfrac{\partial z}{\partial u_3} \end{vmatrix}$$

$$= \begin{vmatrix} 1 & 1 & 0 \\ 2u_2 & 0 & 2u_2 + u_3 \\ 0 & 1 & u_2 \end{vmatrix}$$

$$= 2u_2^2 + 2u_2 + u_3 \qquad (3)$$

Now, g is defined as

$$g = \begin{vmatrix} g_{11} & g_{12} & g_{13} \\ g_{21} & g_{22} & g_{23} \\ g_{31} & g_{32} & g_{33} \end{vmatrix} \qquad (4)$$

1140

where

$$g_{ij} = \frac{\partial \bar{r}}{\partial u_i} \cdot \frac{\partial \bar{r}}{\partial u_j} \qquad (5)$$

We have

$$\frac{\partial \bar{r}}{\partial u_1} = (1,1,0)$$

$$\frac{\partial \bar{r}}{\partial u_2} = (2u_2,0,2u_2+u_3) \qquad (6)$$

$$\frac{\partial \bar{r}}{\partial u_3} = (0,1,u_2)$$

Thus,

$$g_{11} = \frac{\partial \bar{r}}{\partial u_1} \cdot \frac{\partial \bar{r}}{\partial u_1} = 2$$

$$g_{12} = 2u_2$$

$$g_{13} = 1 \qquad (7)$$

$$g_{22} = 8u_2^2 + 4u_2u_3 + u_3^2$$

$$g_{23} = 2u_2^2 + u_2u_3$$

$$g_{33} = 1 + u_2^2$$

Obviously

$$g_{12} = g_{21}, \quad g_{13} = g_{31}, \quad g_{32} = g_{23}. \qquad (8)$$

We have

$$g = \begin{vmatrix} 2 & 2u_2 & 1 \\ 2u_2 & 8u_2^2+4u_2u_3+u_3^2 & 2u_2^2+u_2u_3 \\ 1 & 2u_2^2+u_2u_3 & 1+u_2^2 \end{vmatrix}$$

$$= 2(1+u_2^2)(8u_2^2+4u_2u_3+u_3^2) + 2u_2(2u_2^2+u_2u_3)$$
$$+ 2u_2(2u_2^2+u_2u_3) - (8u_2^2+4u_2u_3+u_3^2)$$
$$- 2(2u_2^2+u_2u_3)(2u_2^2+u_2u_3) - \left[(1+u_2^2)2u_2\right]2u_2$$
$$= 4u_2^4 + 4u_2^2 + 8u_2^3 + 4u_2u_3 + 4u_2^2u_3 + u_3^2 \qquad (9)$$

Now, note that from eq.(3) we obtain

$$J^2 = (2u_2^2 + 2u_2 + u_3)^2$$

$$= 4u_2^4 + 8u_2^3 + 4u_2^2u_3 + 4u_2^2 + 4u_2u_3 + u_3^2 \qquad (10)$$

which is eq.(9).

Thus, we have verified that

$$J = \sqrt{g}.$$

CHAPTER 23

ADVANCED TOPICS

MATRIX METHODS IN VECTOR ANALYSIS

---

1. Define a matrix A whose elements are real numbers.

2. Write down the rows and columns of the matrix

$$\begin{pmatrix} 2 & 1 & 3 \\ 4 & 0 & 2 \end{pmatrix} \qquad (1)$$

Is this matrix a square matrix?

<u>Solution</u>: Let K be an arbitrary, but fixed field. A rectangular array of the form

$$\begin{pmatrix} a_{11} & a_{12} \cdots & a_{1n} \\ a_{21} & a_{22} \cdots & a_{2n} \\ \vdots & \vdots & \\ a_{m1} & a_{m2} \cdots & a_{mn} \end{pmatrix} \qquad (2)$$

where a_{ij} are scalars in K, is called a matrix over K. If K is the real field R, then we say that A is a matrix over R. A is denoted by

$$A = (a_{ij}) \qquad i = 1, \ldots m \qquad (3)$$
$$j = 1, \ldots n$$

When we want to address a single element of a matrix A, we use the notation a_{ij}, where i indicates the row number and j the column number.

2.   In eq.(2), the m horizontal n-tuples

$$(a_{11}, \quad a_{12}, \quad \ldots, \quad a_{1n})$$

$$(a_{21}, \quad a_{22}, \quad \ldots, \quad a_{2n}) \qquad (4)$$

$$\vdots$$

$$(a_{m1}, \quad a_{m2}, \quad \ldots, \quad a_{mn})$$

are the rows of the matrix.

   The n vertical m-tuples

$$\begin{pmatrix} a_{11} \\ a_{21} \\ \vdots \\ \\ a_{m1} \end{pmatrix} \quad \begin{pmatrix} a_{12} \\ a_{22} \\ \vdots \\ \\ a_{m2} \end{pmatrix} \cdots\cdots\cdots \begin{pmatrix} a_{1n} \\ a_{2n} \\ \vdots \\ \\ a_{mn} \end{pmatrix} \qquad (5)$$

are the columns of A.

   A matrix with m rows and n columns is called an m × n matrix.   The matrix in eq.(1) is a 2 × 3 matrix.   It has two rows,

$$(2 \ 1 \ 3) \quad \text{and} \quad (4 \ 0 \ 2), \qquad (6)$$

and three columns

$$\begin{pmatrix} 2 \\ 4 \end{pmatrix} \qquad \begin{pmatrix} 1 \\ 0 \end{pmatrix} \quad \text{and} \quad \begin{pmatrix} 3 \\ 2 \end{pmatrix}. \qquad (7)$$

   When the number of rows is equal to the number of columns, the matrix is called a square matrix.   Thus, matrix (1) is not a square matrix.   Remember that in a_{ij}, the index i refers to the ith row while j refers to the jth column.

   The following mnemonic rule can be helpful.

$a_{row \ column}$, $a_{Roman \ Catholic}$

● PROBLEM 23-2

1.   Construct a square matrix (a_{ij}) of order three where

$$a_{ij} = i^2 + j \qquad (1)$$

2.   Construct a 3 × 2 matrix where

$$b_{ij} = i^2 + j \qquad (2)$$

3. Are these matrices equal?

Solution: 1. We have

$$a_{11} = 1^2 + 1 = 2, \quad a_{21} = 4 + 1 = 5, \quad a_{31} = 10$$
$$a_{12} = 1^2 + 2 = 3, \quad a_{22} = 4 + 2 = 6, \quad a_{32} = 11 \qquad (3)$$
$$a_{13} = 1^2 + 3 = 4, \quad a_{23} = 4 + 3 = 7, \quad a_{33} = 12$$

Thus

$$A = \begin{pmatrix} 2 & 3 & 4 \\ 5 & 6 & 7 \\ 10 & 11 & 12 \end{pmatrix} \qquad (4)$$

2. Matrix $B = (b_{ij})$ given by eq.(2) is a 3×2 matrix. We have

$$b_{11} = 2 \quad b_{21} = 5 \quad b_{31} = 10$$
$$b_{12} = 3 \quad b_{22} = 6 \quad b_{32} = 11 \qquad (5)$$

Thus

$$B = \begin{pmatrix} 2 & 3 \\ 5 & 6 \\ 10 & 11 \end{pmatrix} \qquad (6)$$

3. Two matrices (a_{ij}) and (b_{ij}) are said to be equal if and only if they are of the same order, and $a_{ij} = b_{ij}$ for all pairs (i,j).

Since matrices A and B are not of the same order (A is a 3×3 matrix while B is a 3×2 matrix) we conclude that the two matrices are not equal.

● **PROBLEM 23-3**

Find

1. A + B

2. C + D

3. A + 3D

where

$$A = \begin{pmatrix} 2 & 1 & 4 \\ 0 & 1 & 1 \end{pmatrix} \qquad\qquad B = \begin{pmatrix} 1 & 0 & -1 \\ 0 & 1 & 1 \end{pmatrix}$$

$$C = \begin{pmatrix} 2 & 1 \\ 1 & 4 \end{pmatrix} \qquad\qquad D = \begin{pmatrix} 1 \\ 1 \end{pmatrix}$$

Solution: 1. The addition of two matrices $A = (a_{ij})$ and $B = (b_{ij})$ is defined if and only if the matrices are of the same order. The sum is defined as a matrix $A + B$ of that same order, whose elements are

$$A + B = (a_{ij} + b_{ij}). \qquad (1)$$

We have

$$A + B = \begin{pmatrix} 2+1 & 1+0 & 4-1 \\ 0+0 & 1+1 & 1+1 \end{pmatrix}$$

$$= \begin{pmatrix} 3 & 1 & 3 \\ 0 & 2 & 2 \end{pmatrix} \qquad (2)$$

2. The matrices C and D are of different orders, therefore $C + D$ is not defined.

3. The product of a real number k and a matrix $(a_{ij}) = A$ is a matrix (ka_{ij})

$$kA = (ka_{ij}). \qquad (3)$$

The matrices A and kA are of the same order.

We have

$$3B = 3\begin{pmatrix} 1 & 0 & -1 \\ 0 & 1 & 1 \end{pmatrix} = \begin{pmatrix} 3 & 0 & -3 \\ 0 & 3 & 3 \end{pmatrix} \qquad (4)$$

Thus

$$A + 3B = \begin{pmatrix} 2 & 1 & 4 \\ 0 & 1 & 1 \end{pmatrix} + \begin{pmatrix} 3 & 0 & -3 \\ 0 & 3 & 3 \end{pmatrix}$$

$$= \begin{pmatrix} 5 & 1 & 1 \\ 0 & 4 & 4 \end{pmatrix} \qquad (5)$$

kA is called the scalar multiple or the scalar product of a scalar k by the matrix A.

Prove that matrix addition is commutative, associative and distributive with respect to scalar multiplication.

<u>Solution</u>: Let A and B be two matrices of the same order

$$A = (a_{ij})$$
$$B = (b_{ij})$$
$$(1)$$

Since the addition of real numbers is commutative, we have

$$a_{ij} + b_{ij} = b_{ij} + a_{ij} \qquad (2)$$

for all pairs (i,j) so that

$$A + B = B + A \qquad (3)$$

Furthermore, let C = (c_{ij}) be a matrix of the same order as A and B.

Since the addition of real numbers is associative, we have

$$(a_{ij}+b_{ij}) + c_{ij} = a_{ij} + (b_{ij}+c_{ij}) \qquad (4)$$

for all pairs (i,j). Thus,

$$(A+B) + C = A + (B+C) \qquad (5)$$

Finally, we will show that

$$k(A+B) = kA + kB \qquad (6)$$
$$(k+q)A = kA + qA \qquad (7)$$

where k and q are arbitrary real numbers. We may write

$$k(a_{ij}+b_{ij}) = ka_{ij} + kb_{ij} \qquad (8)$$

for all pairs (i,j). This proves eq.(6). We have

$$(k+q)a_{ij} = ka_{ij} + qa_{ij} \qquad (9)$$

which proves eq.(7).

Find the products

   1.   AB

   2.   BA

   3.   CA

where

$$A = \begin{pmatrix} 2 & 1 \\ 3 & 1 \end{pmatrix} \qquad B = \begin{pmatrix} 1 & 2 & 1 \\ -1 & 0 & 2 \end{pmatrix}$$

$$(1)$$

$$C = (2 \quad 1)$$

Solution: In general, the product AB of two matrices A and B is defined only when the number of columns of the left factor A equals the number of rows of the right factor B. The product AB of two matrices A and B is a matrix C such that

$$c_{ij} = \sum_{k=1}^{s} a_{ik}b_{kj} \tag{2}$$

Note that c_{ij} is obtained by summing the products of the elements of the ith row of A and the corresponding elements of the jth column of B. Thus if

$$A = (a_{mk}) \qquad m = 1,. \ . \ . \ ., \ r$$
$$k = 1,. \ . \ . \ ., \ s$$

$$(3)$$

$$B = (b_{kn}) \qquad k = 1,. \ . \ . \ ., \ s$$
$$n = 1,. \ . \ . \ ., \ t$$

then

$$.C = AB$$

$$C = (c_{ij}) \qquad i = 1,. \ . \ . \ ., \ r$$
$$j = 1,. \ . \ . \ ., \ t$$

$$(4)$$

where

$$c_{ij} = \sum_{k=1}^{s} a_{ik}b_{kj} \tag{5}$$

1.   We have

$$AB = \begin{pmatrix} 2 & 1 \\ 3 & 1 \end{pmatrix}\begin{pmatrix} 1 & 2 & 1 \\ -1 & 0 & 2 \end{pmatrix}$$

1147

$$= \begin{pmatrix} 2 \cdot 1 + (1)(-1) & 2 \cdot 2 + 1 \cdot 0 & 2 \cdot 1 + 1 \cdot 2 \\ \\ 3 \cdot 1 + (1)(-1) & 3 \cdot 2 + 1 \cdot 0 & 3 \cdot 1 + 1 \cdot 2 \end{pmatrix} \qquad (6)$$

$$= \begin{pmatrix} 1 & 4 & 4 \\ 2 & 6 & 5 \end{pmatrix}$$

2. This product is not defined, because the number of columns of B is different from the number of rows of A $(3 \neq 2)$.

3.
$$CA = (2 \quad 1) \begin{pmatrix} 2 & 1 \\ 3 & 1 \end{pmatrix}$$

$$(2 \cdot 2 + 1 \cdot 3 \quad 2 \cdot 1 + 1 \cdot 1) = (7 \quad 3) \qquad (7)$$

● **PROBLEM 23-6**

Let
$$A = (2 \quad 3 \quad 1)$$
$$\qquad (1)$$

$$B = \begin{pmatrix} -1 \\ 2 \\ 0 \end{pmatrix}$$

Find the matrix products AB and BA, if they exist. Is matrix multiplication commutative?

Show that
$$CD \neq DC \qquad (2)$$

where
$$C = \begin{pmatrix} 2 & 1 \\ 0 & 1 \end{pmatrix} \qquad D = \begin{pmatrix} -1 & 3 \\ 1 & 2 \end{pmatrix} \qquad (3)$$

Solution: We have

$$AB = (2 \quad 3 \quad 1) \begin{pmatrix} -1 \\ 2 \\ 0 \end{pmatrix} = (-2+6) = (4) \qquad (4)$$

AB is a 1×1 matrix.

$$BA = \begin{pmatrix} -1 \\ 2 \\ 0 \end{pmatrix} (2 \quad 3 \quad 1) = \begin{pmatrix} -2 & -3 & -1 \\ 4 & 6 & 2 \\ 0 & 0 & 0 \end{pmatrix} \qquad (5)$$

Both matrices AB and BA exist, but

$$AB \neq BA. \qquad (6)$$

In general, matrix multiplication is not commutative.

We have

$$CD = \begin{pmatrix} 2 & 1 \\ 0 & 1 \end{pmatrix} \begin{pmatrix} -1 & 3 \\ 1 & 2 \end{pmatrix}$$

(7)

$$= \begin{pmatrix} -1 & 8 \\ 1 & 2 \end{pmatrix}$$

$$DC = \begin{pmatrix} -1 & 3 \\ 1 & 2 \end{pmatrix} \begin{pmatrix} 2 & 1 \\ 0 & 1 \end{pmatrix}$$

(8)

$$= \begin{pmatrix} -2 & 2 \\ 2 & 3 \end{pmatrix}$$

Thus,

$$CD \neq DC.$$

(9)

● **PROBLEM 23-7**

Prove that the multiplication of matrices is distributive with respect to addition.

Solution: Let $A = (a_{ij})$ and $B = (b_{ij})$ be matrices of order m by n, that is $i=1,. . .,m$, $j = 1,. . .,n$. Let $C = (c_{ij})$ be a matrix of order k by m. Then A+B, CA, CB and C(A+B) exist.

We have to prove that

$$C(A+B) = CA + CB$$

(1)

The elements of the ith row of C are

$$c_{i1}, c_{i2}, . . . , c_{im}$$

(2)

and the elements of the jth column of matrix (A+B) are

$$a_{1j}+b_{1j}, a_{2j}+b_{2j}, . . . , a_{mj}+b_{mj}$$

(3)

Hence, the ijth element of C(A+B) is

$$c_{i1}(a_{1j}+b_{1j}) + c_{i2}(a_{2j}+b_{2j}) +. . .+ c_{im}(a_{mj}+b_{mj})$$

(4)

Eq.(4) can be written in the form

$$(c_{i1}a_{1j}+c_{i2}a_{2j}+...+c_{im}a_{mj})+(c_{i1}b_{1j}+c_{i2}b_{2j}+...+c_{im}b_{mj})$$

(5)

1149

We see that (5) is the sum of the ijth elements of CA and CB, respectively. That proves

$$C(A+B) = CA + CB \qquad (6)$$

Eq.(6) represents the left-hand distributive property of matrix multiplication. Provided all necessary matrices exist, the right-hand distributive property

$$(A+B)C = AC + BC \qquad (7)$$

can be proven in the same manner as above.

● **PROBLEM 23-8**

Verify the associative property of matrix multiplication

$$A(BC) = (AB)C \qquad (1)$$

for

$$A = \begin{pmatrix} 0 & 1 \\ 1 & -1 \end{pmatrix} \qquad B = \begin{pmatrix} 2 & 1 \\ 0 & -1 \end{pmatrix} \qquad C = \begin{pmatrix} 3 & 1 \\ 1 & 0 \end{pmatrix} \qquad (2)$$

Prove the theorem: The multiplication of matrices is associative.

Solution: The left-hand side of eq.(1) is equal to

$$A(BC) = \begin{pmatrix} 0 & 1 \\ 1 & -1 \end{pmatrix} \left[\begin{pmatrix} 2 & 1 \\ 0 & -1 \end{pmatrix} \begin{pmatrix} 3 & 1 \\ 1 & 0 \end{pmatrix} \right]$$

$$\qquad (3)$$

$$= \begin{pmatrix} 0 & 1 \\ 1 & -1 \end{pmatrix} \begin{pmatrix} 7 & 2 \\ -1 & 0 \end{pmatrix} = \begin{pmatrix} -1 & 0 \\ 8 & 2 \end{pmatrix}$$

The right-hand side of eq.(1) is equal to

$$\left[\begin{pmatrix} 0 & 1 \\ 1 & -1 \end{pmatrix} \begin{pmatrix} 2 & 1 \\ 0 & -1 \end{pmatrix} \right] \begin{pmatrix} 3 & 1 \\ 1 & 0 \end{pmatrix}$$

$$\qquad (4)$$

$$= \begin{pmatrix} 0 & -1 \\ 2 & 2 \end{pmatrix} \begin{pmatrix} 3 & 1 \\ 1 & 0 \end{pmatrix} = \begin{pmatrix} -1 & 0 \\ 8 & 2 \end{pmatrix}$$

Thus, for the matrices given by eq.(2),

$$A(BC) = (AB)C \qquad (5)$$

To prove eq.(1) in general terms, we have to make sure that all necessary products exist.

Let $A = (a_{ij})$ be $k \times m$, $B = (b_{ij})$ be $m \times n$ and $C = (c_{ij})$ be $n \times p$. Then the products AB, BC, $A(BC)$, and $(AB)C$ exist. We shall evaluate the ijth element of $A(BC)$. The elements of the ith row of A are

$$a_{i1}, a_{i2}, \ldots, a_{im} \tag{6}$$

and the elements of the jth column of BC are

$$\begin{pmatrix} b_{11}c_{1j} + b_{12}c_{2j} + \ldots + b_{1n}c_{nj} \\ b_{21}c_{1j} + b_{22}c_{2j} + \ldots + b_{2n}c_{nj} \\ \vdots \\ b_{m1}c_{1j} + b_{m2}c_{2j} + \ldots + b_{mn}c_{nj} \end{pmatrix} \tag{7}$$

Thus, the ijth element of $A(BC)$ is

$$\begin{aligned} & a_{i1}(b_{11}c_{1j} + b_{12}c_{2j} + \ldots + b_{1n}c_{nj}) \\ + & a_{i2}(b_{21}c_{2j} + b_{22}c_{2j} + \ldots + b_{2n}c_{nj}) \\ + & \ldots + a_{im}(b_{m1}c_{1j} + b_{m2}c_{2j} + \ldots + b_{mn}c_{nj}) \end{aligned} \tag{8}$$

The expression in eq.(8) can be written in the form

$$\begin{aligned} & (a_{i1}b_{11} + a_{i2}b_{21} + \ldots + a_{im}b_{m1})c_{1j} \\ + & (a_{i1}b_{12} + a_{i2}b_{22} + \ldots + a_{im}b_{m2})c_{2j} \\ + & \ldots + (a_{i1}b_{1n} + a_{i2}b_{2n} + \ldots + a_{im}b_{mn})c_{nj} \end{aligned} \tag{9}$$

which represents the ijth element of $(AB)C$. Hence,

$$A(BC) = (AB)C \tag{10}$$

● **PROBLEM 23-9**

We define A^n as follows:

$$A^1 = A$$
$$A^2 = AA \tag{1}$$
$$A^n = A(A^{n-1})$$

where A is a square matrix and n is a positive integer. Discuss the property of A^n, where

$$A = \begin{pmatrix} 1 & 1 \\ 1 & 0 \end{pmatrix} \tag{2}$$

Solution: Let us first evaluate a few elements of the sequence $(A^1, A^2, A^3, A^4, \ldots)$.

We have,

$$A^1 = \begin{pmatrix} 1 & 1 \\ 1 & 0 \end{pmatrix}$$

$$A^2 = \begin{pmatrix} 1 & 1 \\ 1 & 0 \end{pmatrix} \begin{pmatrix} 1 & 1 \\ 1 & 0 \end{pmatrix} = \begin{pmatrix} 2 & 1 \\ 1 & 1 \end{pmatrix}$$

$$A^3 = \begin{pmatrix} 2 & 1 \\ 1 & 1 \end{pmatrix} \begin{pmatrix} 1 & 1 \\ 1 & 0 \end{pmatrix} = \begin{pmatrix} 3 & 2 \\ 2 & 1 \end{pmatrix} \tag{3}$$

$$A^4 = \begin{pmatrix} 3 & 2 \\ 2 & 1 \end{pmatrix} \begin{pmatrix} 1 & 1 \\ 1 & 0 \end{pmatrix} = \begin{pmatrix} 5 & 3 \\ 3 & 2 \end{pmatrix}$$

$$A^5 = \begin{pmatrix} 5 & 3 \\ 3 & 2 \end{pmatrix} \begin{pmatrix} 1 & 1 \\ 1 & 0 \end{pmatrix} = \begin{pmatrix} 8 & 5 \\ 5 & 3 \end{pmatrix}$$

Eq.(3) represents the first elements of an infinite sequence of 2×2 matrices. Consider a sequence of a_{11} elements

$$(1, 2, 3, 5, 8, \ldots) \tag{4}$$

Eq.(3) is a Fibonacci sequence, where each term is the sum of the two preceding terms.

Note that a_{12}, a_{21} and a_{22} also form Fibonacci sequences.

● **PROBLEM 23-10**

Two matrices A and B are said to anticommute with each other if

$$AB = -BA \tag{1}$$

In the study of electron spin in quantum mechanics, the Pauli spin matrices are useful.

$$\sigma_x = \begin{pmatrix} 0 & 1 \\ 1 & 0 \end{pmatrix} \qquad \sigma_y = \begin{pmatrix} 0 & -i \\ i & 0 \end{pmatrix} \qquad \sigma_z = \begin{pmatrix} 1 & 0 \\ 0 & -1 \end{pmatrix} \tag{2}$$

where $i^2 = -1$.

Show that the Pauli spin matrices anticommute with each other.

Note that in this problem we deal with matrices defined over the field of complex numbers.

Solution: Let us first check if the pair σ_x and σ_y is anti-commutative.

$$\sigma_x \sigma_y = \begin{pmatrix} 0 & 1 \\ 1 & 0 \end{pmatrix} \begin{pmatrix} 0 & -i \\ i & 0 \end{pmatrix} = \begin{pmatrix} i & 0 \\ 0 & -i \end{pmatrix}$$

$$(3)$$

$$\sigma_y \sigma_x = \begin{pmatrix} 0 & -i \\ i & 0 \end{pmatrix} \begin{pmatrix} 0 & 1 \\ 1 & 0 \end{pmatrix} = \begin{pmatrix} -i & 0 \\ 0 & i \end{pmatrix}$$

Hence

$$\sigma_x \sigma_y = -\sigma_y \sigma_x \tag{4}$$

$$\sigma_x \sigma_z = \begin{pmatrix} 0 & 1 \\ 1 & 0 \end{pmatrix} \begin{pmatrix} 1 & 0 \\ 0 & -1 \end{pmatrix} = \begin{pmatrix} 0 & -1 \\ 1 & 0 \end{pmatrix}$$

$$(5)$$

$$\sigma_z \sigma_x = \begin{pmatrix} 1 & 0 \\ 0 & -1 \end{pmatrix} \begin{pmatrix} 0 & 1 \\ 1 & 0 \end{pmatrix} = \begin{pmatrix} 0 & 1 \\ -1 & 0 \end{pmatrix}$$

Thus

$$\sigma_x \sigma_z = -\sigma_z \sigma_x \tag{6}$$

Finally

$$\sigma_y \sigma_z = \begin{pmatrix} 0 & -i \\ i & 0 \end{pmatrix} \begin{pmatrix} 1 & 0 \\ 0 & -1 \end{pmatrix} = \begin{pmatrix} 0 & i \\ i & 0 \end{pmatrix}$$

$$(7)$$

$$\sigma_z \sigma_y = \begin{pmatrix} 1 & 0 \\ 0 & -1 \end{pmatrix} \begin{pmatrix} 0 & -i \\ i & 0 \end{pmatrix} = \begin{pmatrix} 0 & -i \\ -i & 0 \end{pmatrix}$$

and

$$\sigma_y \sigma_z = -\sigma_z \sigma_y \tag{8}$$

Express the system of equations

$$x + 2y - 7z = 0$$

$$2x - y + z = 5 \qquad (1)$$

$$x + 3y + 2z = -1$$

as a matrix equation.

Solution: It is easy to verify that

$$\begin{bmatrix} 1 & 2 & -7 \\ 2 & -1 & 1 \\ 1 & 3 & 2 \end{bmatrix} \begin{bmatrix} x \\ y \\ z \end{bmatrix} = \begin{bmatrix} 0 \\ 5 \\ -1 \end{bmatrix} \qquad (2)$$

We can consider the rows of the matrix in eq.(2) to be vectors

$$\overline{a} = \overline{i} + 2\overline{j} - 7\overline{k}$$

$$\overline{b} = 2\overline{i} - \overline{j} + \overline{k} \qquad (3)$$

$$\overline{c} = \overline{i} + 3\overline{j} + 2\overline{k}$$

Then, eq.(2) can be written as follows:

$$\overline{a} \cdot \overline{r} = 0$$

$$\overline{b} \cdot \overline{r} = 5 \qquad (4)$$

$$\overline{c} \cdot \overline{r} = -1$$

where

$$\overline{r} = x\overline{i} + y\overline{j} + z\overline{k} \qquad (5)$$

From .eq.(4) we conclude that $\overline{r}$ is the position vector of a point lying simultaneously in three planes, whose normals are a, b, and c, respectively.

Prove the theorem:

If $A = (a_{ij})$ is an m × n matrix, then

$$I_{(m)}A = AI_{(n)} = A \qquad (1)$$

and $I_{(m)}$ and $I_{(n)}$ are the only matrices such that eq.(1) is true for any m × n matrix A.

<u>Solution</u>: A square matrix

$$I_{(n)} = (\delta_{ij}) \quad i=1,\ldots,n \quad j=1,\ldots,n \quad (2)$$

such that

$$\delta_{ij} = \begin{cases} 1 & \text{for} \quad i = j \\ 0 & \text{for} \quad i \neq j \end{cases} \quad (3)$$

is called an identity matrix, and will be denoted by $I_{(n)}$
First let us prove

$$I_{(m)}A = A \quad (4)$$

Since A is m × n we have

$$\begin{pmatrix} 1 & 0 & \cdots & 0 \\ 0 & 1 & \cdots & 0 \\ \vdots & & & \vdots \\ 0 & & \cdots & 1 \end{pmatrix} \begin{pmatrix} a_{11} & \cdots & a_{1n} \\ a_{21} & \cdots & a_{2n} \\ \vdots & & \vdots \\ a_{m1} & \cdots & a_{mn} \end{pmatrix}$$

$$(5)$$

$$= \begin{pmatrix} a_{11} & a_{12} & \cdots & a_{1n} \\ a_{21} & a_{22} & \cdots & a_{2n} \\ a_{m1} & a_{m2} & \cdots & a_{mn} \end{pmatrix} = A$$

There is only one matrix $I_{(m)}$ such that eq.(4) is true for all matrices A which are m × n.

Now, we shall prove

$$AI_{(n)} = A \quad (6)$$

$$\begin{pmatrix} a_{11} & a_{12} & \cdots & a_{1n} \\ a_{21} & & \cdots & a_{2n} \\ a_{m1} & & \cdots & a_{mn} \end{pmatrix} \begin{pmatrix} 1 & & \cdots & 0 \\ 0 & 1 & \cdots & 0 \\ \vdots & & & \vdots \\ 0 & & \cdots & 1 \end{pmatrix}$$

$$(7)$$

$$= \begin{pmatrix} a_{11} & \cdots & a_{1n} \\ \vdots & & \vdots \\ a_{m1} & \cdots & a_{mn} \end{pmatrix} = A$$

The elements a_{ij}, where i = j of a square matrix (a_{ij}), are called the diagonal elements. They are located on the main diagonal or principal diagonal.

A square matrix of the form

$$A = \begin{pmatrix} a_{11} & 0 & . & . & . & 0 \\ 0 & a_{22} & & ... & & 0 \\ \vdots & \vdots & & & & \vdots \\ 0 & 0 & & ..... & & a_{nn} \end{pmatrix} \qquad (8)$$

is called a diagonal matrix; that is, a diagonal matrix is a square matrix (a_{ij}) where $a_{ij} = 0$ for $i \neq j$ for all pairs (i,j).

Note that an identity matrix $I_{(n)}$ is a diagonal matrix.

● **PROBLEM** 23-13

The operation of interchanging the rows and columns of a given matrix is called "transposition". The matrix A^T obtained by transposing matrix A is called the transpose of A.

If $A = (a_{ij})$, then $A^T = (a_{ji})$

For example, if

$$A = \begin{pmatrix} 2 & 0 & -1 \\ 1 & 1 & 3 \end{pmatrix}$$

then   (1)

$$A^T = \begin{pmatrix} 2 & 1 \\ 0 & 1 \\ -1 & 3 \end{pmatrix}$$

1. Prove that the transposition operation is reflexive; that is

$$(A^T)^T = A \qquad (2)$$

2. Prove that the transpose of the product of two matrices is equal to the product of their transposes in reverse order, that is,

$$(AB)^T = B^T A^T \qquad (3)$$

Solution: 1. Let $A = (a_{ij})$

(4)

and

$$A^T = (b_{ij})$$

Then $a_{ij} = b_{ij}$ (5)

for all pairs (i,j).

The transpose of A^T is

$$(A^T)^T = (b_{ij})^T = (b_{ji}) = (a_{ij}) = A \qquad (6)$$

It is easy to show that

$$(A+B)^T = A^T + B^T$$
$$(A-B)^T = A^T - B^T \qquad (7)$$

2. Let $A = (a_{ij})$ be of order $k \times m$ and $B = (b_{ij})$ be of order $m \times n$. Then $C = AB = (c_{ij})$ and

$$c_{ij} = a_{i_1}b_{1j} + a_{i_2}b_{2j} + \ldots + a_{im}b_{mj}$$
$$= a_{ik}b_{kj} \qquad (8)$$

Since k is a repeated index in eq.(8), we sum over the range of k, that is, $k = 1,2,\ldots m$.

Note that c_{ij} is the element of the jth row and ith column of $(c_{ij})^-$; that is $(AB)^t$. The elements $b_{1j}, b_{2j}, \ldots,$ b_{mj} of the jth column of B are the elements of the jth row of B^T. The elements $a_{i_1}, a_{i_2}, \ldots, a_{im}$ of the ith row of A are the elements of the ith column of A^T. Thus, the (j,i) element of $B^T A^T$ is

$$b_{1j}a_{i_1} + b_{2j}a_{i_2} + \ldots + b_{mj}a_{im} = b_{kj}a_{ik} \qquad (9)$$

Hence

$$(AB)^T = B^T A^T \qquad (10)$$

● **PROBLEM 23-14**

1. Determine if the product of the matrices

$$A = \begin{pmatrix} 3 & -1 & 7 \\ 1 & 2 & 2 \\ 0 & 1 & 0 \end{pmatrix} \quad \text{and} \quad B = \begin{pmatrix} 3 & 1 & 0 \\ -1 & 2 & 1 \\ 7 & 2 & 0 \end{pmatrix} \qquad (1)$$

is symmetric.

2. Show that: The sum of any matrix and its transpose is a symmetric matrix, that is

$$(A+A^T)^T = A + A^T.$$

The difference of any matrix and its transpose is a skew-symmetric matrix, that is

$$(A-A^T)^T = A^T - A \qquad (2)$$

Solution: 1. It is easy to see from eq.(1) that

$$B = A^T \qquad (3)$$

We shall show that the product of any matrix and its transpose is a symmetric matrix, i.e.

$$(AA^T)^T = AA^T \qquad (4)$$

A matrix $A = (a_{ij})$ is called a symmetric matrix if and only if $a_{ij} = a_{ji}$ for all pairs (i,j). If A is a symmetric matrix then

$$A = A^T \qquad (5)$$

We have

$$(AA^T)^T = (A^T)^T A^T = AA^T \qquad (6)$$

Hence, the product of A and B given in eq.(1) is a symmetric matrix.

2. We have

$$(A+A^T)^T = A^T + (A^T)^T = A^T + A$$
$$= A + A^T \qquad (7)$$

Hence, $A + A^T$ is a symmetric matrix. A matrix $A = (a_{ij})$ is called a skew-symmetric or anti-symmetric matrix if and only if $a_{ij} = -a_{ji}$ for all pairs (i,j). For example, the matrix

$$\begin{pmatrix} 3 & -4 & 1 \\ 4 & 0 & 7 \\ -1 & -7 & 2 \end{pmatrix} \qquad (8)$$

is a skew-symmetric matrix. We have

$$(A-A^T)^T = A^T - (A^T)^T$$
$$= A^T - A = -(A-A^T) \qquad (9)$$

Notice that if A is a skew-symmetric matrix, then

$$A = -A^T \qquad (10)$$

1158

1. Write down all possible permutations of the set {1,2,3}.

2. What is the sign (sometimes called parity) of a permutation (2,4,1,3)?

Solution: 1. A one-to-one mapping of the set {1,2,...,n} onto itself is called a permutation. Usually the permutation is denoted by σ

$$\sigma = \begin{pmatrix} 1 & 2 \ldots n \\ k_1 & k_2 \ldots k_n \end{pmatrix} \tag{1}$$

Since σ is one-to-one and onto, the sequence $k_1, k_2, \ldots k_n$ is a rearrangement of the numbers $1, 2, \ldots, n$. The set consisting of n elements has n! permutations. For example, the set {1,2} has two permutations (1,2) and (2,1). Indeed 2! = 1 · 2 = 2.

The set {1,2,3} has

(1,2,3) (2,1,3) (2,3,1) (1,3,2) (3,1,2) (3,2,1) (2)

or 3! = 1 · 2 · 3 = 6 permutations.

An arbitrary permutation σ = $(k_1, k_2, \ldots, k_n)$ is even or odd depending on whether there is an even or odd number of pairs (i,k) for which:

i > k but i precedes k in σ. (3)

The sign or partiy of σ is defined by

$$\text{sgn } \sigma = \begin{cases} 1 & \text{for } \sigma \text{ even} \\ -1 & \text{for } \sigma \text{ odd} \end{cases} \tag{4}$$

To find the sign of (2,4,1,3) let us write down all pairs which satisfy (3).

(2,1) (4,1) (4,3)

There are three pairs, thus

$$\text{sgn}(2,4,1,3) = -1 \tag{5}$$

Directly from the definition of the determinant evaluate
the determinants of the following matrices.

1. $A = (a_{11})$ (1)

2. $B = \begin{pmatrix} a_{11} & a_{12} \\ a_{21} & a_{22} \end{pmatrix}$ (2)

3. $C = \begin{pmatrix} a_{11} & a_{12} & a_{13} \\ a_{21} & a_{22} & a_{23} \\ a_{31} & a_{32} & a_{33} \end{pmatrix}$ (3)

Solution: Let $A = (a_{ij})$ be a square matrix n × n.

The determinant of the n-square matrix $A = (a_{ij})$ is the
sum taken over all permutations $\sigma = (k_1 k_2 ... k_n)$.

$$\det A = \sum_{\sigma} (\mathrm{sgn}\,\sigma) a_{1k_1} a_{2k_2} \cdots a_{nk_n} \qquad (4)$$

The determinant of A is denoted by det A or $|A|$.

1. There is only one permutation of {1}. Hence

$$\det A = \mathrm{sgn}(1) a_{11} = a_{11} \qquad (5)$$

2. For {1,2} there are two permutations: (1,2) which is
even and (2,1) which is odd. Hence,

$$\begin{vmatrix} a_{11} & a_{12} \\ a_{21} & a_{22} \end{vmatrix} = a_{11}a_{22} - a_{12}a_{21} \qquad (6)$$

3. For {1,2,3} there are six permutations: (1,2,3),(2,3,1),
(3,1,2) which are even, and (3,2,1),(2,1,3),(1,3,2) which
are odd. Hence,

$$\begin{vmatrix} a_{11} & a_{12} & a_{13} \\ a_{21} & a_{22} & a_{23} \\ a_{31} & a_{32} & a_{33} \end{vmatrix} = a_{11}a_{22}a_{33} + a_{12}a_{23}a_{31}$$

$$+ a_{13}a_{21}a_{32} - a_{13}a_{22}a_{31} - a_{12}a_{21}a_{33} - a_{11}a_{23}a_{32} \qquad (7)$$

Prove the following basic properties of the determinant:

1. The determinant of a matrix A is equal to the deter-
    minant of its transpose.

$$|A| = |A^T|$$ (1)

2. If A has a row (or column) of zeros, then

$$|A| = 0$$ (2)

3. If every element of a row (column) of a determinant
    is multiplied by the factor k, then the value of the
    determinant is multiplied by k.

Solution: 1. Let us recall the definition of the determinant of a square matrix $A = (a_{ij})$ $i,j = 1,...n$.

$$\det A = \sum_{\sigma} (\text{sgn}\sigma) a_{1k_1} a_{2k_2} \cdots a_{nk_n}$$ (3)

Note that each term of $|A|$ contains one and only one element
from each row and each column of A, and every such product is
plus or minus some term of $|A|$.

For example, $a_{1k_1} a_{2k_2} \cdots a_{nk_n}$ is, except possibly for
sign, a term of $|A|$. This product can be written in the form
$a_{\ell_1 1} a_{\ell_2 2} \cdots a_{\ell_n n}$, by rearranging the factors so that the
second suffixes come into order $1,2,...n$. Both permutations
have the same sign,

$$\text{sgn}(k_1\ k_2 ... k_n) = \text{sgn}(\ell_1\ \ell_2 ... \ell_n)$$ (4)

It follows that the terms of $|A|$ are the terms of $|A^T|$, hence

$$|A| = |A^T|$$ (5)

2. If A has a row of zeros, then zero appears in every element of the sum in eq.(3). Therefore,

$$\det A = 0$$ (6)

3. If every element of a row of a determinant is multiplied
by k, then in every factor of the sum

$$|A| = \sum_{\sigma} (\text{sgn}\sigma) a_{1k_1} a_{2k_2} \cdots a_{nk_n},$$ (7)

one and only one a_{rs} has to be replaced by ka_{rs}. Thus the
value of the determinant has to be multiplied by k.

Compute the determinant of

$$A = \begin{pmatrix} 2 & 1 & 0 & 0 \\ 2 & -8 & -8 & -6 \\ 0 & 4 & 4 & 3 \\ 0 & 4 & 4 & 0 \end{pmatrix} \qquad (1)$$

Solution: It is rather difficult to evaluate the determinant of A directly from the definition.   To simplify the task, we shall apply this useful property of determinants.

The value of the determinant of A is not changed by adding a multiple of a row (column) of A to another row (column).   Now, we will add the third column multiplied by -1 to the second column

$$\begin{vmatrix} 2 & 1 & 0 & 0 \\ 2 & -8 & -3 & -6 \\ 0 & 4 & 4 & 3 \\ 0 & 4 & 4 & 0 \end{vmatrix} = \begin{vmatrix} 2 & 1 & 0 & 0 \\ 2 & 0 & -8 & -6 \\ 0 & 0 & 4 & 3 \\ 0 & 0 & 4 & 0 \end{vmatrix} \qquad (2)$$

Now we multiply the third row by 2 and add to the second row

$$\begin{vmatrix} 2 & 1 & 0 & 0 \\ 2 & 0 & -8 & -6 \\ 0 & 0 & 4 & 3 \\ 0 & 0 & 4 & 0 \end{vmatrix} = \begin{vmatrix} 2 & 1 & 0 & 0 \\ 2 & 0 & 0 & 0 \\ 0 & 0 & 4 & 3 \\ 0 & 0 & 4 & 0 \end{vmatrix} \qquad (3)$$

Finally we subtract the second row from the first row and subtract the fourth row from the third row

$$\begin{vmatrix} 2 & 1 & 0 & 0 \\ 2 & 0 & 0 & 0 \\ 0 & 0 & 4 & 3 \\ 0 & 0 & 4 & 0 \end{vmatrix} = \begin{vmatrix} 0 & 1 & 0 & 0 \\ 2 & 0 & 0 & 0 \\ 0 & 0 & 0 & 3 \\ 0 & 0 & 4 & 0 \end{vmatrix} \qquad (4)$$

In the sum

$$\det A = \sum_{\sigma}(\mathrm{sgn}\sigma)a_{1k_1}a_{2k_2}a_{3k_3}a_{4k_4} \qquad (5)$$

the only non-zero element is

$$\det A = \mathrm{sgn}(2,1,4,3)a_{12}a_{21}a_{34}a_{43}$$

$$= 1 \cdot 2 \cdot 3 \cdot 4 = 24 \qquad (6)$$

● **PROBLEM 23-19**

Show that

$$\begin{vmatrix} x & 0 & 0 & . & . & . & 0 & a_0 \\ -1 & x & 0 & . & . & . & 0 & a_1 \\ 0 & -1 & x & . & . & . & 0 & a_2 \\ . & . & & & & & . & . \\ . & . & & & & & . & . \\ . & . & & & & & . & . \\ 0 & 0 & 0 & . & . & . & x & a_{n-1} \\ 0 & 0 & 0 & . & . & .-1 & a_n \end{vmatrix} \qquad (1)$$

$$= a_n x^n + a_{n-1}x^{n-1} + \ldots + a_2 x^2 + a_1 x + a_0$$

Solution: We shall describe a useful method of evaluating determinants.

Let $\qquad A = (a_{ij}) \qquad i,j = 1,\ldots n \qquad (2)$

be an $n \times n$ matrix.

Let A_{ij} denote the $(n-1) \times (n-1)$ submatrix of the $n \times n$ matrix A obtained by deleting the ith row and the jth column of A. $|A_{ij}|$ is called the minor of element a_{ij} of A.

We have:

If A is a square matrix of order n, then

$$|A| = \sum_{j=1}^{n}(-1)^{i+j}a_{ij}|A_{ij}| \qquad (3)$$

$$|A| = \sum_{i=1}^{n}(-1)^{i+j}a_{ij}|A_{ij}| \qquad (4)$$

1163

Let us expand determinant (1) along the last column

$$(-1)^{n+1+1} a_0 \begin{vmatrix} -1 & x & 0 & . & . & . & 0 \\ 0 & -1 & x & . & . & . & 0 \\ 0 & 0 & -1 & . & . & . & . \\ . & . & & \ddots & & & . \\ . & . & & & -1 & x \\ 0 & 0 & . & . & . & . & -1 \end{vmatrix}$$

$$+(-1)^{n+1+2} a_1 \begin{vmatrix} x & 0 & 0 & . & . & . & 0 \\ 0 & -1 & x & . & . & . & 0 \\ 0 & 0 & -1 & . & . & . & 0 \\ . & . & & \ddots & & & . \\ . & . & & & & & . \\ 0 & 0 & . & . & . & . & -1 \end{vmatrix} + \ldots +$$

$$+(-1)^{n+1+n} a_{n-1} \begin{vmatrix} x & 0 & 0 & . & . & . & 0 \\ -1 & x & 0 & . & . & . & 0 \\ 0 & -1 & x & . & . & . & 0 \\ . & & & \ddots & & & . \\ . & & & & -1 & x & 0 \\ 0 & 0 & . & . & .0 & 0 & -1 \end{vmatrix} \qquad (5)$$

$$+(-1)^{n+1+n+1} a_n \begin{vmatrix} x & 0 & 0 & . & . & . & 0 \\ -1 & x & 0 & . & . & . & 0 \\ . & & \ddots & & & & . \\ . & & & & & & . \\ . & & & & & x & 0 \\ 0 & 0 & . & . & . & -1 & x \end{vmatrix}$$

$$= a_0 + a_1 x + \ldots + a_{n-1} x^{n-1} + a_n x^n$$

1164

Note that all determinants appearing in eq.(5) have all their elements above or below the diagonal equal to zero. In such cases the value of the determinant is obtained by multiplying all the elements on the diagonal. For example

$$\begin{vmatrix} a_1 & 0 & 0 \\ 3 & a_2 & 0 \\ 7 & 9 & a_3 \end{vmatrix} = a_1 a_2 a_3 \tag{6}$$

● **PROBLEM 23-20**

Show that

$$B = \begin{pmatrix} -\dfrac{1}{2} & \dfrac{1}{5} & -\dfrac{8}{5} \\ 0 & \dfrac{1}{5} & \dfrac{2}{5} \\ \dfrac{1}{2} & 0 & 1 \end{pmatrix} \tag{1}$$

is a right inverse of the matrix

$$A = \begin{pmatrix} 2 & -2 & 4 \\ 2 & 3 & 2 \\ -1 & 1 & -1 \end{pmatrix} \tag{2}$$

Solution: Given a square matrix A, we say R is a right inverse of A if

$$AR = I \tag{3}$$

To show that B is a right inverse of A we have to show that

$$AB = I$$

Indeed

$$\begin{pmatrix} 2 & -2 & 4 \\ 2 & 3 & 2 \\ -1 & 1 & -1 \end{pmatrix} \begin{pmatrix} -\dfrac{1}{2} & \dfrac{1}{5} & -\dfrac{8}{5} \\ 0 & \dfrac{1}{5} & \dfrac{2}{5} \\ \dfrac{1}{2} & 0 & 1 \end{pmatrix} = \begin{pmatrix} 1 & 0 & 0 \\ 0 & 1 & 0 \\ 0 & 0 & 1 \end{pmatrix} \tag{4}$$

Hence, B is a right inverse of A.

1165

Let A be a square matrix 3 × 3 and R its right inverse

$$AR = I \qquad (1)$$

Derive the equations for the relation between the rows of A and the columns of R.

Solution: If $\bar{a}$, $\bar{b}$ and $\bar{c}$ are the rows of A, then

$$A = \begin{pmatrix} \bar{a} \\ \bar{b} \\ \bar{c} \end{pmatrix} \qquad (2)$$

Let $\bar{d}$, $\bar{e}$ and $\bar{f}$ be the columns of R

$$R = (\bar{d}\ \bar{e}\ \bar{f}) \qquad (3)$$

Eq.(1) can be written

$$\begin{pmatrix} \bar{a} \\ \bar{b} \\ \bar{c} \end{pmatrix} (\bar{d}\ \bar{e}\ \bar{f}) = \begin{pmatrix} 1 & 0 & 0 \\ 0 & 1 & 0 \\ 0 & 0 & 1 \end{pmatrix} \qquad (4)$$

We have

$$\bar{a} \cdot \bar{d} = 1 \qquad \bar{b} \cdot \bar{e} = 1 \qquad \bar{c} \cdot \bar{f} = 1$$
$$\bar{a} \cdot \bar{e} = \bar{a} \cdot \bar{f} = \bar{b} \cdot \bar{d} = \bar{b} \cdot \bar{f} = \bar{c} \cdot \bar{d} = \bar{c} \cdot \bar{e} = 0 \qquad (5)$$

The two sets of vectors $\{\bar{a}, \bar{b}, \bar{c}\}$ and $\{\bar{d}, \bar{e}, \bar{f}\}$ satisfying eq.(5) are reciprocal. That is, one set of vectors is reciprocal, or dual, to the other set.

Derive the equations for the reciprocal vectors of the set $\{\bar{a}, \bar{b}, \bar{c}\}$.

Solution: The vectors $\{\bar{d}, \bar{e}, \bar{f}\}$ are reciprocal to $\{\bar{a}, \bar{b}, \bar{c}\}$ if

$$\bar{a} \cdot \bar{d} = \bar{b} \cdot \bar{e} = \bar{c} \cdot \bar{f} = 1$$
$$\bar{a} \cdot \bar{e} = \bar{a} \cdot \bar{f} = \bar{b} \cdot \bar{d} = \bar{b} \cdot \bar{f} = \bar{c} \cdot \bar{d} = \bar{c} \cdot \bar{e} = 0 \qquad (1)$$

From

$$\bar{d} \cdot \bar{b} = \bar{d} \cdot \bar{c} = 0$$

we conclude that $\bar{d}$ must be perpendicular to $\bar{b}$ and $\bar{c}$. Hence

$$\bar{d} = \alpha \bar{b} \times \bar{c} \qquad (2)$$

1166

From the equation

$$\overline{a} \cdot \overline{d} = 1, \tag{3}$$

we obtain α,

$$\overline{a} \cdot \overline{d} = \alpha \overline{a} \cdot \overline{b} \times \overline{c} = 1 \tag{4}$$

$$\alpha = \frac{1}{\overline{a} \cdot \overline{b} \times \overline{c}} = \frac{1}{[\overline{a}, \overline{b}, \overline{c}]} \tag{5}$$

We have for $\overline{d}$

$$\overline{d} = \frac{\overline{b} \times \overline{c}}{[\overline{a}, \overline{b}, \overline{c}]} \tag{6}$$

In the same manner, we find

$$\overline{e} = \frac{\overline{c} \times \overline{a}}{[\overline{a}, \overline{b}, \overline{c}]} \tag{7}$$

$$\overline{f} = \frac{\overline{a} \times \overline{b}}{[\overline{a}, \overline{b}, \overline{c}]} \tag{8}$$

It is assumed that

$$[\overline{a}, \overline{b}, \overline{c}] \neq 0 \tag{9}$$

that is, that the vectors $\overline{a}$, $\overline{b}$, and $\overline{c}$ are not coplanar.

If $\overline{a}$, $\overline{b}$ and $\overline{c}$ are coplanar, then $[\overline{a}, \overline{b}, \overline{c}] = 0$, and in such case, n^0 set of vectors $\overline{d}$, $\overline{e}$ and $\overline{f}$ exist such that eq. (1) holds true.

● **PROBLEM 23-23**

Show that the scalar triple product of the rows of a
3 × 3 matrix equals the scalar triple product of its
columns.

Solution: Let the matrix A be

$$
\begin{array}{cccc}
 & \overline{a} & \overline{b} & \overline{c} & \\
A = & \begin{pmatrix} a_{11} & a_{12} & a_{13} \\ a_{21} & a_{22} & a_{23} \\ a_{31} & a_{32} & a_{33} \end{pmatrix} & \begin{array}{c} \overline{d} \\ \overline{e} \\ \overline{f} \end{array}
\end{array} \tag{1}
$$

The rows and columns are denoted as shown in eq.(1).

1167

We have to prove that

$$\det A = \overline{a} \cdot \overline{b} \times \overline{c} = \overline{d} \cdot \overline{e} \times \overline{f}$$

or $\qquad\qquad\qquad\qquad\qquad\qquad\qquad\qquad\qquad\qquad\qquad\qquad$ (2)

$$\det A = [\overline{a}, \overline{b}, \overline{c}] = [\overline{d}, \overline{e}, \overline{f}]$$

We have

$[\overline{a}, \overline{b}, \overline{c}] = \overline{a} \cdot \overline{b} \times \overline{c}$

$= (a_{11}, a_{21}, a_{31}) \cdot (a_{12}, a_{22}, a_{32}) \times (a_{13}, a_{23}, a_{33})$ $\qquad$ (3)

$= (a_{11}, a_{21}, a_{31}) \cdot (a_{22}a_{33} - a_{32}a_{23}, a_{32}a_{13} - a_{12}a_{33}, a_{12}a_{23} - a_{22}a_{13})$

$= a_{11}(a_{22}a_{33} - a_{32}a_{23}) + a_{21}(a_{32}a_{13} - a_{12}a_{33}) + a_{31}(a_{12}a_{23} - a_{22}a_{13})$

$= a_{11}a_{22}a_{33} + a_{21}a_{32}a_{13} + a_{12}a_{31}a_{23} - a_{11}a_{32}a_{23}$

$\qquad\qquad - a_{12}a_{21}a_{33} - a_{13}a_{22}a_{31} = \det A$

That proves the first part of eq.(2).

Now, we have

$[\overline{d}, \overline{e}, \overline{f}] = \overline{d} \cdot \overline{e} \times \overline{f}$

$= (a_{11}, a_{12}, a_{13}) \cdot (a_{21}, a_{22}, a_{23}) \times (a_{31}, a_{32}, a_{33})$ $\qquad$ (4)

$= (a_{11}, a_{12}, a_{13}) \cdot (a_{22}a_{33} - a_{23}a_{32}, a_{23}a_{31} - a_{21}a_{33}, a_{21}a_{32} - a_{22}a_{31})$

$= a_{11}a_{22}a_{33} + a_{12}a_{23}a_{31} + a_{13}a_{21}a_{32} - a_{11}a_{23}a_{32}$

$\qquad\qquad - a_{12}a_{21}a_{33} - a_{13}a_{22}a_{31} = \det A$

● **PROBLEM 23-24**

Compute the right inverse of the matrix

$$A = \begin{pmatrix} 2 & 3 & 4 \\ 1 & 0 & 1 \\ -1 & 2 & -2 \end{pmatrix}$$ $\qquad$ (1)

Solution: Let us start with the formula for the right inverse of a matrix A. If $\overline{a}$, $\overline{b}$, $\overline{c}$ are the rows of A

$$A = \begin{pmatrix} \overline{a} \\ \overline{b} \\ \overline{c} \end{pmatrix}$$ $\qquad$ (2)

then the right inverse of A is

$$R = \frac{1}{[\overline{a}, \overline{b}, \overline{c}]} (\overline{b} \times \overline{c}, \ \overline{c} \times \overline{a}, \ \overline{a} \times \overline{b})$$

$$= \frac{1}{\det A} (\overline{b} \times \overline{c}, \ \overline{c} \times \overline{a}, \ \overline{a} \times \overline{b}) \tag{3}$$

See Problems 23-21 and 23-22. We have

$$\overline{a} = (2,3,4)$$
$$\overline{b} = (1,0,1) \tag{4}$$
$$\overline{c} = (-1,2,-2)$$

and

$$\det A = 7 \tag{5}$$

$$\overline{b} \times \overline{c} = (-2,1,2)$$
$$\overline{c} \times \overline{a} = (14,0,-7) \tag{6}$$
$$\overline{a} \times \overline{b} = (3,2,-3)$$

Substituting eqs.(5) and (6) into eq.(3), we obtain

$$R = \begin{pmatrix} -\frac{2}{7} & 2 & \frac{3}{7} \\ \frac{1}{7} & 0 & \frac{2}{7} \\ \frac{2}{7} & -1 & -\frac{3}{7} \end{pmatrix} \tag{7}$$

Indeed

$$\begin{pmatrix} 2 & 3 & 4 \\ 1 & 0 & 1 \\ -1 & 2 & -2 \end{pmatrix} \begin{pmatrix} -\frac{2}{7} & 2 & \frac{3}{7} \\ \frac{1}{7} & 0 & \frac{2}{7} \\ \frac{2}{7} & -1 & -\frac{3}{7} \end{pmatrix} = \begin{pmatrix} 1 & 0 & 0 \\ 0 & 1 & 0 \\ 0 & 0 & 1 \end{pmatrix} \tag{8}$$

● PROBLEM 23-25

1. Show that the right inverse R of the matrix A described in Problem 23-24 is also the left inverse.

2. Prove that the right inverse of a matrix is equal to the left inverse.

Solution: 1. Let us multiply R by A, then

$$
\begin{pmatrix} -\frac{2}{7} & 2 & \frac{3}{7} \\[2mm] \frac{1}{7} & 0 & \frac{2}{7} \\[2mm] \frac{2}{7} & -1 & -\frac{3}{7} \end{pmatrix}
\begin{pmatrix} 2 & 3 & 4 \\ 1 & 0 & 1 \\ -1 & 2 & -2 \end{pmatrix}
\tag{1}
$$

$$
= \begin{pmatrix} 1 & 0 & 0 \\ 0 & 1 & 0 \\ 0 & 0 & 1 \end{pmatrix}
$$

2. Let L be the left inverse of A,

$$
LA = I \tag{2}
$$

and let R be the right inverse,

$$
AR = I. \tag{3}
$$

Using the associative law, we obtain

$$
R = IR = (LA)R = L(AR) = LI = L \tag{4}
$$

Hence, the left and right inverses are equal.

● **PROBLEM 23-26**

Prove that if det $A \neq 0$, then the inverse of A exists and is unique.

Solution: Let us assume that matrix A has two inverse ma-trices A_1^{-1} and A_2^{-2}. Since

$$
A_1^{-1}A = I \quad \text{and}
$$
$$
A_2^{-1}A = I \tag{1}
$$

then

$$
A_1^{-1}A = A_2^{-1}A
$$
$$
(A_1^{-1}A)A_1^{-1} = (A_2^{-1}A)A_1^{-1} \tag{2}
$$

$$
A_1^{-1}(AA_1^{-1}) = A_2^{-1}(AA_1^{-1}) \tag{3}
$$
$$
A_1^{-1}I = A_2^{-1}I
$$

Hence

$$
A_1^{-1} = A_2^{-1} \tag{4}
$$

The inverse (if it exists) of a square matrix is unique.

If det A ≠ 0, then the inverse exists and is unique. We write

$$AA^{-1} = A^{-1}A = I \tag{5}$$

Derive the formula for the inverse of a square matrix
A = (a_{ij}) of any order.

Solution: The value of the determinant can be expressed in terms of its cofactors

$$\det A = \sum_{j=1}^{n} a_{ij}A_{ij} \quad \text{for} \quad i=1,\ldots,n \tag{1}$$

For any determinant of a matrix the sum of the products of the elements of any row and the cofactors of the corresponding elements of another row is zero.

$$\sum_{j=1}^{n} a_{kj}A_{ij} = 0 \quad \text{for} \quad k,i=1,2,\ldots n \tag{2}$$

$$\text{where} \quad k \neq i$$

Using the Kroenecker delta, we can express eqs.(1) and (2) as

$$\sum_{j=1}^{n} a_{kj}A_{ij} = \delta_{ki} \det A \quad \text{for} \quad k,i=1,\ldots,n \tag{3}$$

Eq.(3) represents n^2 equations, which can be written in the matrix form

$$(a_{ij})(A_{ij})^T = (\delta_{ij})\det A \tag{4}$$

For example, for n = 3, we get

$$\begin{pmatrix} a_{11} & a_{12} & a_{13} \\ a_{21} & a_{22} & a_{23} \\ a_{31} & a_{32} & a_{33} \end{pmatrix} \begin{pmatrix} A_{11} & A_{21} & A_{31} \\ A_{12} & A_{22} & A_{32} \\ A_{13} & A_{23} & A_{33} \end{pmatrix} = \begin{pmatrix} 1 & 0 & 0 \\ 0 & 1 & 0 \\ 0 & 0 & 1 \end{pmatrix} \det A \tag{5}$$

Since A = (a_{ij}) and (δ_{ij}) = I, we can write eq.(4) as

$$A(A_{ij})^T = I \det A \tag{6}$$

If   det A $\neq$ 0   then

$$A \frac{(A_{ij})^T}{\det A} = I \tag{7}$$

Hence, the matrix $\dfrac{(A_{ij})^T}{\det A}$ is the inverse of A

$$A^{-1} = \frac{1}{\det A} (A_{ij})^T \tag{8}$$

The inverse, if it exists, is the product of the reciprocal of the determinant of the matrix and the transpose of
the matrix of cofactors.

A necessary and sufficient condition for the inverse of
a matrix A to exist is that det A $\neq$ 0. A square matrix A is
said to be nonsingular if det A $\neq$ 0, and singular if

$$\det A = 0.$$

If A is not a square matrix, then it is possible for A to
have a left or a right inverse, but not both.

● **PROBLEM 23-28**

Applying the results of Problem 23-27, find the inverse
of the matrix

$$A = \begin{pmatrix} a & b \\ c & d \end{pmatrix} \tag{1}$$

Solution: The inverse of A is

$$A^{-1} = \frac{1}{\det A} (A_{ij})^T \tag{2}$$

The determinant of A is

$$\det A = ad - bc \tag{3}$$

The cofactors are

$$A_{11} = d$$
$$A_{12} = -c$$
$$A_{21} = -b \tag{4}$$
$$A_{22} = a$$

Thus,

$$(A_{ij})^T = \begin{pmatrix} d & -b \\ -c & a \end{pmatrix} \tag{5}$$

Hence, the inverse matrix of the matrix A given by eq.(1) is

$$A^{-1} = \begin{pmatrix} \dfrac{d}{ad - bc} & \dfrac{-b}{ad - bc} \\ \\ \dfrac{-c}{ad - bc} & \dfrac{a}{ad - bc} \end{pmatrix} \tag{6}$$

● **PROBLEM 23-29**

1. Show that the inverse of a product equals the product of the inverses in reverse order, i.e.,

$$(AB)^{-1} = B^{-1}A^{-1} \tag{1}$$

2. Prove that if AB = BA, then

$$A^{-1}B^{-1} = B^{-1}A^{-1} \tag{2}$$

Solution: 1. $(AB)^{-1}$ is an inverse of AB, thus

$$(AB)^{-1}(AB) = I \tag{3}$$

Multiplying eq.(3) by $B^{-1}A^{-1}$ we obtain

$$(AB)^{-1} \ AB \ B^{-1}A^{-1} = I \ B^{-1}A^{-1}$$

$$(AB)^{-1} \ A(BB^{-1})A^{-1} = (AB)^{-1} \ AIA^{-1} \tag{4}$$

$$= (AB)^{-1} \ AA^{-1} = (AB)^{-1}I = (AB)^{-1}$$

Therefore

$$(AB)^{-1} = B^{-1}A^{-1} \tag{5}$$

2. If $\qquad\qquad AB = BA \tag{6}$

then

$$(AB)^{-1} = (BA)^{-1} \tag{7}$$

and

$$B^{-1}A^{-1} = A^{-1}B^{-1} \tag{8}$$

Solve the system of equations

$$2x + y - 4z = 5$$

$$x - 2y - 5z = -\frac{13}{2} \qquad (1)$$

$$y + 2z = 4$$

by computing the inverse of the matrix of coefficients.

Solution: In the matrix form, eq.(1) can be written

$$\begin{pmatrix} 2 & 1 & -4 \\ 1 & -2 & -5 \\ 0 & 1 & 2 \end{pmatrix} \begin{pmatrix} x \\ y \\ z \end{pmatrix} = \begin{pmatrix} 5 \\ -\frac{13}{2} \\ 4 \end{pmatrix} \qquad (2)$$

Let

$$A = \begin{pmatrix} 2 & 1 & -4 \\ 1 & -2 & -5 \\ 0 & 1 & 2 \end{pmatrix}$$

The determinant of A is

$$\det A = -4 \qquad (3)$$

The inverse of A is

$$A^{-1} = \frac{1}{\det A} (A_{ij})^T = -\frac{1}{4} \begin{pmatrix} 1 & -6 & -13 \\ -2 & 4 & 6 \\ 1 & -2 & -5 \end{pmatrix}$$

$$\qquad (4)$$

$$= \begin{pmatrix} -\frac{1}{4} & \frac{3}{2} & \frac{13}{4} \\ \frac{1}{2} & -1 & -\frac{3}{2} \\ -\frac{1}{4} & \frac{1}{2} & \frac{5}{4} \end{pmatrix}$$

Multiplying both sides of eq.(2) by A^{-1} and remembering that

$$A^{-1}A = I,$$

we obtain

$$\begin{pmatrix} 1 & 0 & 0 \\ 0 & 1 & 0 \\ 0 & 0 & 1 \end{pmatrix} \begin{pmatrix} x \\ y \\ z \end{pmatrix} = \begin{pmatrix} -\frac{1}{4} & \frac{3}{2} & \frac{13}{4} \\ \frac{1}{2} & -1 & -\frac{3}{2} \\ -\frac{1}{4} & \frac{1}{2} & \frac{5}{4} \end{pmatrix} \begin{pmatrix} 5 \\ -\frac{13}{2} \\ 4 \end{pmatrix} = \begin{pmatrix} 2 \\ 3 \\ \frac{1}{2} \end{pmatrix}$$

(5)

Hence

$$x = 2$$

$$y = 3$$

$$z = \frac{1}{2}$$

(6)

● **PROBLEM 23-31**

Using matrix techniques derive a general formula for the solution of the system:

$$a_{11}x + a_{12}y + a_{13}z = \alpha$$

$$a_{21}x + a_{22}y + a_{23}z = \beta$$

$$a_{31}x + a_{32}y + a_{33}z = \gamma$$

(1)

Solution: Eq.(1) can be written in the form

$$\begin{pmatrix} a_{11} & a_{12} & a_{13} \\ a_{21} & a_{22} & a_{23} \\ a_{31} & a_{32} & a_{33} \end{pmatrix} \begin{pmatrix} x \\ y \\ z \end{pmatrix} = \begin{pmatrix} \alpha \\ \beta \\ \gamma \end{pmatrix}$$

(2)

Let

$$A = \begin{pmatrix} a_{11} & a_{12} & a_{13} \\ a_{21} & a_{22} & a_{23} \\ a_{31} & a_{32} & a_{33} \end{pmatrix}$$

where $\det A \neq 0$.

Let

$$\overline{a} = (a_{11}, a_{21}, a_{31})$$

$$\overline{b} = (a_{12}, a_{22}, a_{32})$$

$$\overline{c} = (a_{13}, a_{23}, a_{33})$$

(3)

1175

$\bar{a}$, $\bar{b}$, $\bar{c}$ are column vectors of A. The inverse of A is

$$A^{-1} = \frac{1}{[\bar{a}, \bar{b}, \bar{c}]} \begin{pmatrix} \bar{b} \times \bar{c} \\ \bar{c} \times \bar{a} \\ \bar{a} \times \bar{b} \end{pmatrix} \qquad (4)$$

We multiply eq.(2) by A^{-1}

$$A^{-1}A \begin{pmatrix} x \\ y \\ z \end{pmatrix} = I \begin{pmatrix} x \\ y \\ z \end{pmatrix} = \begin{pmatrix} x \\ y \\ z \end{pmatrix} = \frac{1}{[\bar{a}, \bar{b}, \bar{c}]} \begin{pmatrix} \bar{b} \times \bar{c} \\ \bar{c} \times \bar{a} \\ \bar{a} \times \bar{b} \end{pmatrix} \cdot \begin{pmatrix} \alpha \\ \beta \\ \gamma \end{pmatrix} \qquad (5)$$

The x component is

$$x = \frac{(\bar{b} \times \bar{c}) \cdot (\alpha \bar{i} + \beta \bar{j} + \gamma \bar{k})}{[\bar{a}, \bar{b}, \bar{c}]} \qquad (6)$$

or, in the matrix form

$$x = \frac{\begin{vmatrix} \alpha & : & : \\ \beta & \bar{b} & \bar{c} \\ \gamma & : & : \end{vmatrix}}{|\bar{a}, \bar{b}, \bar{c}|} = \frac{\begin{vmatrix} \alpha & a_{12} & a_{13} \\ \beta & a_{22} & a_{23} \\ \gamma & a_{32} & a_{33} \end{vmatrix}}{\begin{vmatrix} a_{11} & a_{12} & a_{13} \\ a_{21} & a_{22} & a_{23} \\ a_{31} & a_{32} & a_{33} \end{vmatrix}} \qquad (7)$$

In the same way we find y and z,

$$y = \frac{\begin{vmatrix} a_{11} & \alpha & a_{13} \\ a_{21} & \beta & a_{23} \\ a_{31} & \gamma & a_{33} \end{vmatrix}}{\begin{vmatrix} a_{11} & a_{12} & a_{13} \\ a_{21} & a_{22} & a_{23} \\ a_{31} & a_{32} & a_{33} \end{vmatrix}} \qquad (8)$$

$$z = \frac{\begin{vmatrix} a_{11} & a_{12} & \alpha \\ a_{21} & a_{22} & \beta \\ a_{31} & a_{32} & \gamma \end{vmatrix}}{\begin{vmatrix} a_{11} & a_{12} & a_{13} \\ a_{21} & a_{22} & a_{23} \\ a_{31} & a_{32} & a_{33} \end{vmatrix}} \qquad (9)$$

Formulas (7),(8), and (9) are called Cramer's rule.

● **PROBLEM 23-32**

An orthogonal matrix is a matrix whose inverse equals its transpose

$$0^{-1} = 0^T \qquad (1)$$

Show that if 0 is orthogonal and A is symmetric, then $0^{-1}AO$ is symmetric.

<u>Solution</u>: A symmetric matrix is such that

$$A = A^T \qquad (2)$$

Since multiplication of matrices is associative, we can write

$$(0^{-1}AO)^T = \left[0^{-1}(AO) \right]^T \qquad (3)$$

The transpose of a product is the product of the transposes in reverse order, thus

$$\left[0^{-1}(AO) \right]^T = (AO)^T (0^{-1})^T$$

$$= 0^T A^T (0^{-1})^T \qquad (4)$$

Since A is symmetric and 0 is orthogonal, we have

$$0^T A^T (0^{-1})^T = 0^{-1}AO \qquad (5)$$

Thus, we have proven that

$$0^{-1}AO = (0^{-1}AO)^T \qquad (6)$$

● **PROBLEM 23-33**

Let A be a 3 × 3 symmetric matrix. How many independent elements does A have?

How many independent elements does a 3 × 3 antisymmetric matrix have?

Answer the above questions for n × n matrices.

1177

Solution: In general, a 3×3 matrix A,

$$A = \begin{pmatrix} a_{11} & a_{12} & a_{13} \\ a_{21} & a_{22} & a_{23} \\ a_{31} & a_{32} & a_{33} \end{pmatrix} \tag{1}$$

has nine independent elements.   If A is symmetric, then

$$A = A^T$$

and

$$a_{12} = a_{21} \qquad a_{13} = a_{31} \qquad a_{23} = a_{32} \tag{2}$$

$$A = \begin{pmatrix} a_{11} & a_{12} & a_{13} \\ a_{12} & a_{22} & a_{23} \\ a_{13} & a_{23} & a_{33} \end{pmatrix} \tag{3}$$

A 3×3 symmetric matrix has six independent elements.

If A is antisymmetric, then

$$A = -A^T \tag{4}$$

and

$$a_{11} = -a_{11} \qquad a_{22} = -a_{22} \qquad a_{33} = -a_{33}$$

Therefore,
$$a_{11} = a_{22} = a_{33} = 0 \tag{5}$$

and
$$a_{12} = -a_{21} \qquad a_{13} = -a_{31} \qquad a_{23} = -a_{32} \tag{6}$$

$$A = \begin{pmatrix} 0 & a_{12} & a_{13} \\ -a_{12} & 0 & a_{23} \\ -a_{13} & -a_{23} & 0 \end{pmatrix} \tag{7}$$

Thus a 3×3 antisymmetric matrix has three independent elements.

In general, an $n \times n$ matrix has n^2 independent elements. If we are considering a symmetric matrix, then all the elements above (or below) and on the diagonal are independent. The number of elements of an $n \times n$ symmetric matrix is

$$s = n + \frac{n^2 - n}{2} = \frac{n^2 + n}{2} \tag{8}$$

For   n = 1   s = 1

        n = 2   s = 3   (9)

        n = 3   s = 6

If A is antisymmetric, then all the elements on the diagonal are equal to zero and the only independent elements are above (or below) the diagonal. Thus, an n × n antisymmetric matrix has

$$a = \frac{n^2 - n}{2}$$ (10)

independent elements.

For   n = 1   a = 0

            n = 2   a = 1   (11)

            n = 3   a = 3

LINEAR ORTHOGONAL TRANSFORMATIONS

TRANSFORMATION MATRIX, ROTATION, ORTHOGONAL TRANSFORMATION

● **PROBLEM** 23-34

Two right-handed coordinate systems (x,y,z) and (x',y',z') are given such that they have a common origin. Consider a point in space, whose position vector is

$$\bar{r} = x\bar{i} + y\bar{j} + z\bar{k} = x'\bar{i}' + y'\bar{j}' + z'\bar{k}'$$ (1)

where $\bar{i},\bar{j},\bar{k}$ and $\bar{i}',\bar{j}',\bar{k}'$ are the unit vectors in the (x,y,z) and (x',y',z') coordinate systems, respectively.

Express the x,y,z coordinates in terms of x',y',z' and determine the transformation matrix T

$$\bar{r} = T\bar{r}'$$ (2)

Solution: Scalar multiplying eq.(1) by $\bar{i}$ we obtain

$$x = x'\, i'\cdot \bar{i} + y'\, j'\cdot \bar{i} + z'\, k'\cdot \bar{i}$$ (3)

Multiplying by $\bar{j}$ and then $\bar{k}$ we get, respectively

$$y = x'\bar{i}' \cdot \bar{j} + y'\bar{j}' \cdot \bar{j} + z'\bar{k}' \cdot \bar{j}$$ (4)

$$z = x'\bar{i}' \cdot \bar{k} + y'\bar{j}' \cdot \bar{k} + z'\bar{k}' \cdot \bar{k}$$ (5)

Eqs.(3), (4), and (5) can be written

$$T \begin{pmatrix} x' \\ y' \\ z' \end{pmatrix} = \begin{pmatrix} x \\ y \\ z \end{pmatrix} \qquad (6)$$

where T is the transformation matrix

$$T = \begin{pmatrix} \overline{i}' \cdot \overline{i} & \overline{j}' \cdot \overline{i} & \overline{k}' \cdot \overline{i} \\ \overline{i}' \cdot \overline{j} & \overline{j}' \cdot \overline{j} & \overline{k}' \cdot \overline{j} \\ \overline{i}' \cdot \overline{k} & \overline{j}' \cdot \overline{k} & \overline{k}' \cdot \overline{k} \end{pmatrix} \qquad (7)$$

Note that the columns of T consist of the direction cosines of the vectors $\overline{i}', \overline{j}', \overline{k}'$ with respect to $\overline{i}, \overline{j}, \overline{k}$.

● **PROBLEM** 23-35

Consider an (x,y,z) coordinate system. If we rotate this coordinate system through an angle α about its own z-axis, we obtain a new coordinate system (x',y',z').

Compute the transformation matrix T.

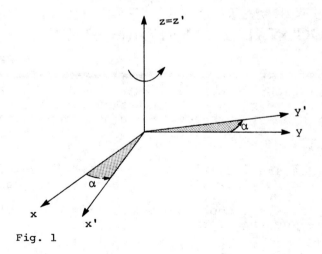

Fig. 1

<u>Solution</u>: The unit base vectors of the system x',y',z' are $\overline{i}', \overline{j}', \overline{k}'$. The angle between $\overline{i}'$ and $\overline{i}$ is α, while the angles between $\overline{i}'$ and $\overline{j}$ and $\overline{i}'$ and $\overline{k}$ are $\frac{\pi}{2} - \alpha$ and $\frac{\pi}{2}$, respectively.

We see that the direction cosines of $\overline{i}'$ are $\cos\alpha$, $\cos(\frac{\pi}{2} - \alpha)$ and zero.

The direction cosines of $\overline{j}'$ are $\cos(\frac{\pi}{2} + \alpha)$, $\cos\alpha$ and zero. For $\overline{k}'$, the direction cosines are 0, 0 and 1.

Hence, the transformation matrix T is

$$T = \begin{pmatrix} \cos\alpha & -\sin\alpha & 0 \\ \sin\alpha & \cos\alpha & 0 \\ 0 & 0 & 1 \end{pmatrix} \tag{1}$$

Note that det T = 1. This tells us that the transformation matrix is non-singular.

● **PROBLEM 23-36**

Consider the transformation of two cartesian coordinate systems as described in Problem 23-34. Show that the transformation matrix is orthogonal.

<u>Solution</u>: An orthogonal matrix is a matrix whose inverse equals its transpose, i.e.

$$0^{-1} = 0^T \tag{1}$$

Now, the transformation matrix T relates $\bar{r}$ and $\bar{r}'$,

$$\bar{r} = T\bar{r}' \tag{2}$$

Thus, the inverse of T can be evaluated from

$$\bar{r}' = T^{-1}\bar{r} \tag{3}$$

From

$$\bar{r} = x\bar{i} + y\bar{j} + z\bar{k} = x'\bar{i}' + y'\bar{j}' + z'\bar{k}' \tag{4}$$

we compute x',y',z' in terms of x,y,z. Multiplying eq.(4) by $\bar{i}',\bar{j}'$ and by $\bar{k}'$ we find

$$x' = x\bar{i} \cdot \bar{i}' + y\bar{j} \cdot \bar{i}' + z\bar{k} \cdot \bar{i}'$$

$$y' = x\bar{i} \cdot \bar{j}' + y\bar{j} \cdot \bar{j}' + z\bar{k} \cdot \bar{j}' \tag{5}$$

$$z' = x\bar{i} \cdot \bar{k}' + y\bar{j} \cdot \bar{k}' + z\bar{k} \cdot \bar{k}'$$

Eq.(5) can be written in the matrix form

$$\begin{pmatrix} x' \\ y' \\ z' \end{pmatrix} = \begin{pmatrix} \bar{i} \cdot \bar{i}' & \bar{j} \cdot \bar{i}' & \bar{k} \cdot \bar{i}' \\ \bar{i} \cdot \bar{j}' & \bar{j} \cdot \bar{j}' & \bar{k} \cdot \bar{j}' \\ \bar{i} \cdot \bar{k}' & \bar{j} \cdot \bar{k}' & \bar{k} \cdot \bar{k}' \end{pmatrix} \begin{pmatrix} x \\ y \\ z \end{pmatrix} \tag{6}$$

Hence,

$$T^{-1} = \begin{pmatrix} \bar{i} \cdot \bar{i}' & \bar{j} \cdot \bar{i}' & \bar{k} \cdot \bar{i}' \\ \bar{i} \cdot \bar{j}' & \bar{j} \cdot \bar{j}' & \bar{k} \cdot \bar{j}' \\ \bar{i} \cdot \bar{k}' & \bar{j} \cdot \bar{k}' & \bar{k} \cdot \bar{k}' \end{pmatrix} \tag{7}$$

In Problem 23-34, we evaluated matrix T.

$$T = \begin{pmatrix} \bar{i}' \cdot \bar{i} & \bar{j}' \cdot \bar{i} & \bar{k}' \cdot \bar{i} \\ \bar{i}' \cdot \bar{j} & \bar{j}' \cdot \bar{j} & \bar{k}' \cdot \bar{j} \\ \bar{i}' \cdot \bar{k} & \bar{j}' \cdot \bar{k} & \bar{k}' \cdot \bar{k} \end{pmatrix} \tag{8}$$

From eqs.(7) and (8), we conclude that

$$T^T = T^{-1} \tag{9}$$

Thus, the transformation matrix is orthogonal. That is why the transformations relating two cartesian coordinate systems having the same origin are called linear orthogonal transformations.

● **PROBLEM 23-37**

The transformation between two systems (x,y,z) and (x',y',z') is described by

$$\begin{pmatrix} x \\ y \\ z \end{pmatrix} = T \begin{pmatrix} x' \\ y' \\ z' \end{pmatrix} \tag{1}$$

It has been shown in Problem 23-36 that if both systems are cartesian, then the transformation matrix T is orthogonal. Suppose all we know about eq.(1) is that the old system (x,y,z) is cartesian and that T is an orthogonal matrix.

1. Show that the columns of T, interpreted as vectors expressed in the (x,y,z) system, point along x',y', and z' axes.

2. Show that the new axes are mutually orthogonal.

3. Prove that the distance of the point (x',y',z') from the origin is

$$\sqrt{x'^2 + y'^2 + z'^2}$$

From 1-3, we may conclude that the new system (x',y',z') is also a cartesian coordinate system.

Solution: 1. Consider the point

$$(x',y',z') = (1,0,0) \tag{2}$$

$$\begin{pmatrix} x \\ y \\ z \end{pmatrix} = \begin{pmatrix} a_{11} & a_{12} & a_{13} \\ a_{21} & a_{22} & a_{23} \\ a_{31} & a_{32} & a_{33} \end{pmatrix} \begin{pmatrix} 1 \\ 0 \\ 0 \end{pmatrix} = \begin{pmatrix} a_{11} \\ a_{21} \\ a_{31} \end{pmatrix} \qquad (3)$$

The transformation T in eq.(1) transforms the point (a_{11}, a_{21}, a_{31}) into $(1,0,0)$. In the same way, we can show that the point (a_{12}, a_{22}, a_{32}) is transformed to $(0,1,0)$ and the point (a_{13}, a_{23}, a_{33}) is transformed to $(0,0,1)$.

2. Matrix T is orthogonal, thus

$$T^T = T^{-1} \qquad (4)$$

Let the ith column of T be T_i. Since T is orthogonal, we have

$$TT^T = I \qquad (5)$$

Thus,

$$T_i \cdot T_i = 1 \qquad (6)$$

and

$$T_i \cdot T_j = 0 \quad \text{for } i \neq j. \qquad (7)$$

A square matrix T is orthogonal if and only if its columns (rows) are orthogonal.

Hence, the axes of the system (x', y', z') are mutually orthogonal.

3. Let us take the transpose of eq.(1).

$$(x, y, z) = (x', y', z')T^T \qquad (8)$$

Scalar multiplying eqs.(1) and (8), we obtain

$$(x, y, z) \cdot \begin{pmatrix} x \\ y \\ z \end{pmatrix} = (x', y', z')T^T T \begin{pmatrix} x' \\ y' \\ z' \end{pmatrix} \qquad (9)$$

Since T is orthogonal

$$T^T T = T^{-1} T = I \qquad (10)$$

Therefore,

$$(x^2 + y^2 + z^2)^{\frac{1}{2}} = (x'^2 + y'^2 + z'^2)^{\frac{1}{2}} \qquad (11)$$

Note that the new system (x',y',z') can be left-handed. For example, the transformation

$$
\begin{pmatrix} x \\ y \\ z \end{pmatrix} = \begin{pmatrix} 1 & 0 & 0 \\ 0 & 1 & 0 \\ 0 & 0 & -1 \end{pmatrix} \begin{pmatrix} x' \\ y' \\ z' \end{pmatrix} \tag{12}
$$

transforms (x,y,z) into a left-handed system (x',y',z').

TRANSFORMATION OF SCALAR AND VECTOR FIELDS, TRANSFORMATION OF GRAD f, DIV $\overline{F}$ AND PROPERTIES OF CURL $\overline{F}$

● **PROBLEM** 23-38

A scalar field f(x,y,z) is given in a cartesian coordinate system (x,y,z). This system is transformed to another cartesian system (x',y',z'). Derive the formula for the transformation of the scalar field

$$
f(x,y,z) \qquad \text{to} \qquad f'(x',y',z') \tag{1}
$$

Suppose that $\qquad$ f(x,y,z) = x² + 2xy $\qquad$ (2)

in the system (x,y,z). The linear orthogonal transformation described in Problem 23-35 is performed with $\alpha = \frac{\pi}{4}$. Compute the value of f at the point whose transformed coordinates are

$$
(x',y',z') = (1,-1,0) \tag{3}
$$

Solution: The function f represents a scalar field. It can, for example, be a temperature field. Obviously, the value of f at a given point is not changed by changing the coordinate system. The coordinates of the point, however, are changed.

Therefore, we have to express the original coordinates in terms of the transformed coordinates, and then apply the formula for f to the original coordinates.

$$
x = x(x',y',z')
$$
$$
y = y(x',y',z') \tag{4}
$$
$$
z = z'(x',y',z')
$$

Substituting eq.(4) into the original functional form for f

$$
f'(x',y',z') = f(x(x',y',z'),y(x',y',z'),z(x',y',z')) \tag{5}
$$

we obtain the formula for the transformation of the scalar field f.

Let $f(x,y,z) = x^2 + 2xy$, as in eq.(2). The transformation matrix is

$$\begin{pmatrix} x \\ y \\ z \end{pmatrix} = \begin{pmatrix} \cos\alpha & -\sin\alpha & 0 \\ \sin\alpha & \cos\alpha & 0 \\ 0 & 0 & 1 \end{pmatrix} \begin{pmatrix} x' \\ y' \\ z' \end{pmatrix} \qquad (6)$$

(see Problem 23-35).

$$x = x'\cos\alpha - y'\sin\alpha$$
$$y = x'\sin\alpha + y'\cos\alpha \qquad (7)$$
$$z = z'$$

For $\alpha = \frac{\pi}{4}$, and the point $(x',y',z') = (1,-1,0)$, we obtain

$$x = x'\frac{\sqrt{2}}{2} - y'\frac{\sqrt{2}}{2} = \sqrt{2}$$
$$y = \frac{\sqrt{2}}{2}x' + y'\frac{\sqrt{2}}{2} = 0 \qquad (8)$$
$$z = z' \qquad\qquad = 0$$

Hence, the value of the function f in the (x',y',z') system is
$$f'(x',y',z') = 2.$$

● **PROBLEM 23-39**

Derive the formula for the transformation of vector fields for linear orthogonal transformations.

Consider rotation through an angle α about the z-axis. The transformation matrix T is

$$T = \begin{bmatrix} \cos\alpha & -\sin\alpha & 0 \\ \sin\alpha & \cos\alpha & 0 \\ 0 & 0 & 1 \end{bmatrix} \qquad (1)$$

Express the vector field
$$\overline{F} = (x^2+y^2)\overline{i} + yz\overline{j} + \overline{k} \qquad (2)$$
in the new coordinate system (x',y',z').

Solution: An arbitrary vector field $\overline{F}$ has two representations

$$\overline{F} = F_1\overline{i} + F_2\overline{j} + F_3\overline{k} = F_1'\overline{i}' + F_2'\overline{j}' + F_3'\overline{k}' \qquad (3)$$

Taking the scalar products of eq.(3) with $\overline{i},\overline{j},\overline{k}$ we get

$$\begin{pmatrix} F_1 \\ F_2 \\ F_3 \end{pmatrix} = T \begin{pmatrix} F_1' \\ F_2' \\ F_3' \end{pmatrix} \qquad (4)$$

or

$$\begin{pmatrix} F_1' \\ F_2' \\ F_3' \end{pmatrix} = T^{-1} \begin{pmatrix} F_1 \\ F_2 \\ F_3 \end{pmatrix} \qquad (5)$$

The components of $\overline{F}$ transform like coordinates of a point.

Thus, if in the (x,y,z) system $\overline{F}$ is

$$\overline{F} = F_1(x,y,z)\overline{i} + F_2(x,y,z)\overline{j} + F_3(x,y,z)\overline{k} \qquad (6)$$

while in the (x',y',z') system

$$\overline{F}' = F_1'(x',y',z')\overline{i}' + F_2'(x',y',z')\overline{j}' + F_3'(x',y',z')\overline{k}'$$

then the components are related by

$$\begin{pmatrix} F_1'(x',y',z') \\ F_2'(x',y',z') \\ F_3'(x',y',z') \end{pmatrix} = T^{-1} \begin{pmatrix} F_1(x(x',y',z'),y(x',y',z'),z(x',y',z')) \\ F_2(x(x',y',z'),y(x',y',z'),z(x',y',z')) \\ F_3(x(x',y',z'),y(x',y',z'),z(x',y',z')) \end{pmatrix}$$

For the transformation given by eq.(1) and the vector field given in eq.(2), we have

$$\begin{pmatrix} F_1'(x',y',z') \\ F_2'(x',y',z') \\ F_3'(x',y',z') \end{pmatrix} = \begin{pmatrix} \cos\alpha & \sin\alpha & 0 \\ -\sin\alpha & \cos\alpha & 0 \\ 0 & 0 & 1 \end{pmatrix} \begin{pmatrix} (x'\cos\alpha - y'\sin\alpha)^2 + (x'\sin\alpha + y'\cos\alpha)^2 \\ x'\sin\alpha + y'\cos\alpha)z' \\ 1 \end{pmatrix}$$

$$= \begin{pmatrix} \cos\alpha & \sin\alpha & 0 \\ -\sin\alpha & \cos\alpha & 0 \\ 0 & 0 & 1 \end{pmatrix} \begin{pmatrix} x'^2 + y'^2 \\ x'z'\sin\alpha + y'z'\cos\alpha \\ 1 \end{pmatrix}$$

$$= \begin{pmatrix} x'^2\cos\alpha + y'^2\cos\alpha + x'z'\sin^2\alpha + y'z'\sin\alpha\cos\alpha \\ -x'^2\sin\alpha - y'^2\sin\alpha + x'z'\sin\alpha\cos\alpha + y'z'\cos^2\alpha \\ 1 \end{pmatrix}$$

and

$$\overline{F}' = (x'^2\cos\alpha + y'^2\cos\alpha + x'z'\sin^2\alpha + y'z'\sin\alpha\cos\alpha)\overline{i}'$$

$$+ (-x'^2\sin\alpha - y'^2\sin\alpha + x'z'\sin\alpha\cos\alpha + y'z'\cos^2\alpha)\overline{j}' + \overline{k}'$$

● **PROBLEM** 23-40

A linear orthogonal transformation is given

$$\begin{pmatrix} x \\ y \\ z \end{pmatrix} = T \begin{pmatrix} x' \\ y' \\ z' \end{pmatrix} \tag{1}$$

Derive the formula for the transformation of the vector field

grad f. (2)

<u>Solution</u>: The scalar function transforms according to

$$f'(x',y',z') = f(x(x',y',z'),y(x',y',z'),z(x',y',z')) \tag{3}$$

Hence,

$$\frac{\partial f'}{\partial x'} = \frac{\partial}{\partial x'}\left[f(x(x',y',z'),y(x',y',z'),z(x',y',z'))\right]$$

$$= \frac{\partial f}{\partial x}\frac{\partial x}{\partial x'} + \frac{\partial f}{\partial y}\frac{\partial y}{\partial x'} + \frac{\partial f}{\partial z}\frac{\partial z}{\partial x'} \tag{4}$$

From eqs.(3), (4) and (5) of Problem 23-34, we find

$$\frac{\partial x}{\partial x'} = \overline{i}'\cdot\overline{i} \qquad \frac{\partial x}{\partial y'} = \overline{j}'\cdot\overline{i} \qquad \frac{\partial x}{\partial z'} = \overline{k}'\cdot\overline{i} \tag{5}$$

$$\frac{\partial y}{\partial x'} = \overline{i}'\cdot\overline{j} \qquad \frac{\partial y}{\partial y'} = \overline{j}'\cdot\overline{j} \qquad \frac{\partial y}{\partial z'} = \overline{k}'\cdot\overline{j}$$

$$\frac{\partial z}{\partial x'} = \overline{i}'\cdot\overline{k} \qquad \frac{\partial z}{\partial y'} = \overline{j}'\cdot\overline{k} \qquad \frac{\partial z}{\partial z'} = \overline{k}'\cdot\overline{k}$$

Therefore, the transformation matrix T can be written in the form

$$T = \begin{pmatrix} \dfrac{\partial x}{\partial x'} & \dfrac{\partial x}{\partial y'} & \dfrac{\partial x}{\partial z'} \\[2mm] \dfrac{\partial y}{\partial x'} & \dfrac{\partial y}{\partial y'} & \dfrac{\partial y}{\partial z'} \\[2mm] \dfrac{\partial z}{\partial x'} & \dfrac{\partial z}{\partial y'} & \dfrac{\partial z}{\partial z'} \end{pmatrix} \qquad (6)$$

Thus, eq.(4) and similar equations for $\dfrac{\partial f'}{\partial y'}$ and $\dfrac{\partial f'}{\partial z'}$ can be written in the form

$$\left(\dfrac{\partial f'}{\partial x'}, \ \dfrac{\partial f'}{\partial y'}, \ \dfrac{\partial f'}{\partial z'} \right) = \left(\dfrac{\partial f}{\partial x}, \ \dfrac{\partial f}{\partial y}, \ \dfrac{\partial f}{\partial z} \right) T \ . \qquad (7)$$

Taking the transposes of eq.(7) we get

$$\begin{pmatrix} \dfrac{\partial f'}{\partial x'} \\[2mm] \dfrac{\partial f'}{\partial y'} \\[2mm] \dfrac{\partial f'}{\partial z'} \end{pmatrix} = T^{-1} \begin{pmatrix} \dfrac{\partial f}{\partial x} \\[2mm] \dfrac{\partial f}{\partial y} \\[2mm] \dfrac{\partial f}{\partial z} \end{pmatrix} \qquad (8)$$

Eq.(8) is a well known formula for the transformation of vector fields. Here, $\left(\dfrac{\partial f'}{\partial x'}, \dfrac{\partial f'}{\partial y'}, \dfrac{\partial f'}{\partial z'} \right)$ and $\left(\dfrac{\partial f}{\partial x}, \dfrac{\partial f}{\partial y}, \dfrac{\partial f}{\partial z} \right)$ describe the same vector field.

● **PROBLEM 23-41**

Derive the formula for the transformation of the divergence of an arbitrary vector field for a linear orthogonal transformation.

Solution: We have to find the relationship between $\nabla' \cdot \overline{F}'$ and $\nabla \cdot \overline{F}$, where

$$\nabla \cdot \overline{F} = \dfrac{\partial F_1}{\partial x} + \dfrac{\partial F_2}{\partial y} + \dfrac{\partial F_3}{\partial z}$$

and $\qquad (1)$

$$\nabla' \cdot \overline{F}' = \dfrac{\partial F_1'}{\partial x'} + \dfrac{\partial F_2'}{\partial y'} + \dfrac{\partial F_3'}{\partial z'}$$

Using the Einstein convention we can write eq.(1) in the form

$$\nabla \cdot \overline{F} = \dfrac{\partial F_i}{\partial x_i} \qquad x_1 = x, \ x_2 = y, \ x_3 = z$$

$$\qquad (2)$$

$$\nabla' \cdot \overline{F}' = \dfrac{\partial F_i'}{\partial x_i'}$$

The vector field transforms according to the rule (3)

$$\begin{pmatrix} F_1'\,(x',y',z') \\ F_2'\,(x',y',z') \\ F_3'\,(x',y',z') \end{pmatrix} = T^{-1} \begin{pmatrix} F_1(x(x',y',z'),y(x',y',z'),z(x',y',z')) \\ F_2(x(x',y',z'),y(x',y',z'),z(x',y',z')) \\ F_3(x(x',y',z'),y(x',y',z'),z(x',y',z')) \end{pmatrix}$$

In Problem 23-40, we showed that

$$T = \begin{pmatrix} \dfrac{\partial x}{\partial x'} & \dfrac{\partial x}{\partial y'} & \dfrac{\partial x}{\partial z'} \\[2mm] \dfrac{\partial y}{\partial x'} & \dfrac{\partial y}{\partial y'} & \dfrac{\partial y}{\partial z'} \\[2mm] \dfrac{\partial z}{\partial x'} & \dfrac{\partial z}{\partial y'} & \dfrac{\partial z}{\partial z'} \end{pmatrix} \tag{4}$$

We can write

$$T = \left(a_{ij} = \frac{\partial x_i}{\partial x_j'} \right) \tag{5}$$

Since T is orthogonal

$$T^T = T^{-1} \tag{6}$$

Eq.(3) can be written

$$F_i' = \frac{\partial x_k}{\partial x_i'} F_k \tag{7}$$

Taking the divergence of both sides we find

$$\nabla' \cdot \overline{F}' = \frac{\partial F_1'}{\partial x'} + \frac{\partial F_2'}{\partial y'} + \frac{\partial F_3'}{\partial z'} = \frac{\partial F_i'}{\partial x_i'} \tag{8}$$

$$= \frac{\partial x_k}{\partial x_i'} \frac{\partial}{\partial x_i'}\left[F_k(x_\ell(x_m')) \right] = \frac{\partial x_k}{\partial x_i'} \frac{\partial F_k}{\partial x_\ell} \frac{\partial x_\ell}{\partial x_i'}$$

$$= \frac{\partial x_k}{\partial x_i'} \frac{\partial x_\ell}{\partial x_i'} \frac{\partial F_k}{\partial x_\ell} = \delta_{k\ell} \frac{\partial F_k}{\partial x_\ell} = \frac{\partial F_k}{\partial x_\ell} = \nabla \cdot F$$

We conclude that both $\dfrac{\partial F_1}{\partial x} + \dfrac{\partial F_2}{\partial y} + \dfrac{\partial F_3}{\partial z}$ and $\dfrac{\partial F_1'}{\partial x'} + \dfrac{\partial F_2'}{\partial y'} + \dfrac{\partial F_3'}{\partial z'}$ represent the same scalar field expressed in different co-ordinates. We should have anticipated this result, because the divergence of a vector field can be defined without reference to any coordinate system.

Rotation through an angle α about the z-axis is described by the matrix

$$T = \begin{pmatrix} \cos\alpha & -\sin\alpha & 0 \\ \sin\alpha & \cos\alpha & 0 \\ 0 & 0 & 1 \end{pmatrix} \qquad (1)$$

(see Problem 23-39).

Show that curl $\overline{F}$ and curl'$\overline{F}'$ describe the same vector
field, where $\overline{F}$ is given by eq.(2) of Problem 23-39.

Solution: The vector field $\overline{F}$ is

$$\overline{F} = (x^2+y^2)\overline{i} + yz\overline{j} + \overline{k} \qquad (2)$$

and its curl is

$$\text{curl } \overline{F} = \left(\frac{\partial}{\partial x}, \frac{\partial}{\partial y}, \frac{\partial}{\partial z}\right) \times (x^2+y^2, yz, 1)$$
$$= (-y, 0, -2y) \qquad (3)$$

$\overline{F}$ is transformed into $\overline{F}'$ given by eq.(10) of Problem 23-39.
We shall compute the curl of $\overline{F}'$

$$\text{curl}'\overline{F}' = \left(\frac{\partial}{\partial x'}, \frac{\partial}{\partial y'}, \frac{\partial}{\partial z'}\right)$$

$$\times (x'^2\cos\alpha+y'^2\cos\alpha+x'z'\sin^2\alpha+y'z'\sin\alpha\cos\alpha,$$
$$-x'^2\sin\alpha-y'^2\sin\alpha+x'z'\sin\alpha\cos\alpha+y'z'\cos^2\alpha,1) \qquad (4)$$

$$= (-x'\sin\alpha\cos\alpha-y'\cos^2\alpha, x'\sin^2\alpha+y'\sin\alpha\cos\alpha,$$
$$-2x'\sin\alpha-2y'\cos\alpha)$$

Finally, we have to show that under transformation T
(eq.(1)), the vector field curl $\overline{F}$ (eq.(3)) transforms into
curl'$\overline{F}'$ (eq.(4)).   In general, we have

$$\overline{F}'(x',y',z') = T^{-1}\overline{F}(x(x',y',z'),y(x',y',z'),z(x',y',z')) \qquad (5)$$

Since

$$y = x'\sin\alpha + y'\cos\alpha \qquad (6)$$

we obtain

$$\begin{pmatrix} \cos\alpha & \sin\alpha & 0 \\ -\sin\alpha & \cos\alpha & 0 \\ 0 & 0 & 1 \end{pmatrix}\begin{pmatrix} -x'\sin\alpha - y'\cos\alpha \\ 0 \\ -2x'\sin\alpha - 2y'\cos\alpha \end{pmatrix}$$

$$= (-x'\sin\alpha\cos\alpha - y'\cos^2\alpha, x'\sin^2\alpha + y'\sin\alpha\cos\alpha, -2x'\sin\alpha - 2y'\cos\alpha) \quad (7)$$

which is the vector field curl'$\overline{F}$' given by eq.(4)

In this case, as in Problem 23-41, the result is obvious. Because of Stokes' theorem, the component of $\nabla \times \overline{F}$ in any direction is the swirl of a vector field $\overline{F}$ in that direction. This can be defined without reference to any coordinate system. Therefore, the vector field

$$\text{curl } \overline{F} = \begin{vmatrix} \overline{i} & \overline{j} & \overline{k} \\ \frac{\partial}{\partial x} & \frac{\partial}{\partial y} & \frac{\partial}{\partial z} \\ F_1 & F_2 & F_3 \end{vmatrix} \quad (8)$$

transforms to

$$\text{curl'}\overline{F}' = \begin{vmatrix} \overline{i}' & \overline{j}' & \overline{k}' \\ \frac{\partial}{\partial x'} & \frac{\partial}{\partial y'} & \frac{\partial}{\partial z'} \\ F_1' & F_2' & F_3' \end{vmatrix} \quad (9)$$

TRANSPORT THEOREM

FLUX THROUGH A MOVING SURFACE

● PROBLEM 23-43

Consider a vector field $\overline{F}$ that changes with time

$$\overline{F} = \overline{F}(\overline{r}, t) \quad (1)$$

and an oriented surface S that moves. Define the flux ϕ of $\overline{F}$ through S. Obviously, ϕ varies with time. What elements affect the value of $\phi(t)$?

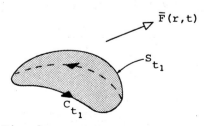

Fig. 1

Solution: At any given moment $t = t_1$, the vector field $\overline{F}$ is $\overline{F}(\overline{r}, t_1)$ and the surface S is located somewhere in space. If we denote the surface at the instant $t = t_1$ by S_{t_1} and the boundary curve of S_{t_1} by C_{t_1} (see Fig. 1), then the flux at this instant is

$$\phi(t=t_1) = \iint_{S_{t_1}} \overline{F}(\overline{r}, t_1) \cdot d\overline{S} \tag{2}$$

In general, we can write

$$\phi(t) = \iint_{S_t} \overline{F}(\overline{r}, t) \cdot d\overline{S} \tag{3}$$

Here, the change of $\phi(t)$ with respect to time is due to the changing vector field $\overline{F}(\overline{r}, t)$ and the motion of the surface S_{t_1}.

● PROBLEM 23-44

Consider a time varying vector field $\overline{F}(\overline{r}, t)$ and a moving surface S.

The flux of $\overline{F}$ through S varies with time, $\phi = \phi(t)$.

Using the definition of the derivative

$$\frac{df}{dt} = \lim_{\Delta t \to 0} \frac{f(t+\Delta t) - f(t)}{\Delta t} \tag{1}$$

define $\frac{d\phi}{dt}$.

Solution: Consider two instances, t_1 and t_2. The location of the surface S at time $t = t_1$ is S_{t_1}, and at $t = t_2$, the location of S is S_{t_2}. The time differential, or the time rate of change of ϕ, is given by

$$\frac{d\phi}{dt} = \lim_{\Delta t \to 0} \frac{\phi(t+\Delta t) - \phi(t)}{\Delta t} \tag{2}$$

Now, let $t_2 - t_1 = \Delta t$. Then

$$\frac{d\phi}{dt} = \lim_{t_2 \to t_1} \frac{\phi(t_2) - \phi(t_1)}{t_2 - t_1} \tag{3}$$

Substituting the definition of flux,

$$\phi(t) = \iint_{S_t} \overline{F}(\overline{r}, t) \cdot d\overline{S}$$

into eq.(3) yields

$$\frac{d\phi}{dt} = \lim_{t_2 \to t_1} \frac{1}{t_2 - t_1} \left[\iint_{S_{t_2}} \overline{F}(\overline{r}, t_2) \cdot d\overline{S} - \iint_{S_{t_1}} \overline{F}(\overline{r}, t_1) \cdot d\overline{S} \right] \quad (4)$$

FLUX TRANSPORT THEOREM

● **PROBLEM 23-45**

Let S_t be an expanding hemisphere described by

$$x^2 + y^2 + z^2 = v^2 t^2, \quad z \geq 0 \quad (1)$$

Verify the flux transport theorem for S_t and the vector fields

1. $\overline{F}(\overline{r}, t) = \overline{r}$ (2)

2. $\overline{F}(\overline{r}, t) = \overline{r}t$ (3)

<u>Solution</u>: Let $\phi(t)$ be the flux of $\overline{F}(\overline{r}, t)$ through S_t at time t

$$\phi(t) = \iint_{S_t} \overline{F}(\overline{r}, t) \cdot d\overline{S} \quad (4)$$

The flux transport theorem states that

$$\frac{d\phi}{dt} = \iint_{S_t} \left(\frac{\partial \overline{F}}{\partial t} + \overline{v} \; \text{div} \; \overline{F} \right) \cdot d\overline{S} + \oint_{C_t} \overline{F} \times \overline{v} \cdot d\overline{r} \quad (5)$$

1. The flux of the vector field $\overline{F}(\overline{r}, t) = \overline{r}$ through the hemisphere

$$x^2 + y^2 + z^2 = v^2 t^2, \quad z \geq 0 \quad \text{is}$$

$$\phi = \iint_{S_t} \overline{F} \cdot d\overline{S} = \iint_{S_t} \overline{r} \cdot \overline{n} \; dS$$

1193

$$= vt \iint_{S_t} dS = vt2\pi(vt)^2 = 2\pi v^3 t^3 \qquad (6)$$

Hence
$$\frac{d\phi}{dt} = 6\pi v^3 t^2 \qquad (7)$$

From eq.(5) we obtain

$$\frac{d\phi}{dt} = \iint_{S_t} \left(\overline{0} + 3v \, \frac{\overline{r}}{|\overline{r}|} \right) \cdot \overline{n} dS + \oint_{C_t} \overline{r} \times \frac{\overline{r}}{|\overline{r}|} \, v \cdot d\overline{r}$$

$$\qquad (8)$$

$$= \frac{3v}{|\overline{r}|} \iint_{S_t} \overline{r} \cdot \overline{n} \, dS = 3v \left[2\pi(vt)^2 \right] = 6\pi v^3 t^2$$

This result is the same as the one obtained in eq.(7).

2. The flux of $\overline{F}(\overline{r},t) = \overline{r}t$ is

$$\phi(\overline{r},t) = \iint_{S_t} \overline{F} \cdot d\overline{S} = \iint_{S_t} \overline{r}t \cdot \overline{n} dS$$

$$= t \iint_{S_t} |\overline{r}| dS = vt^2 2\pi(vt)^2 = 2\pi v^3 t^4 \qquad (9)$$

Thus,
$$\frac{d\phi}{dt} = 8\pi v^3 t^3 \qquad (10)$$

Now, we have

$$\frac{d\phi}{dt} = \iint_{S_t} \left[\overline{r} + 3tv \, \frac{\overline{r}}{|\overline{r}|} \right] \cdot d\overline{S} + \oint_{C_t} \overline{r}t \times v \, \frac{\overline{r}}{|\overline{r}|} \cdot d\overline{r}$$

$$= \iint_{S_t} \left(1 + 3t \, \frac{v}{|\overline{r}|} \right) \overline{r} \cdot \overline{n} dS = 4 \iint_{S_t} \overline{r} \cdot \overline{n} dS$$

$$\qquad (11)$$

$$= 4vt \iint_{S_t} dS = 8\pi v^3 t^3$$

which is the result in eq.(9).

Thus, we have verified the flux transport theorem for this case.

Verify the flux transport theorem for the vector field

$$\overline{F}(\overline{r},t) = xyz\overline{k} \qquad (1)$$

and the surface S_t, where S_t is a square with vertices (1,0,t), (1,1,t), (0,1,t), (0,0,t), as shown in the figure.

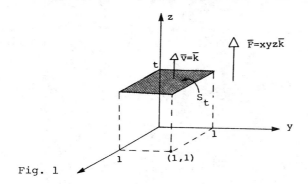

Fig. 1

<u>Solution</u>: The flux of $\overline{F}$ through S_t is

$$\phi = \iint_{S_t} \overline{F} \cdot d\overline{S} = \iint_{S_t} xyz\overline{k} \cdot \overline{n}dS$$

$$= t \int_0^1 \int_0^1 xy\,dxdy = \frac{t}{4} \qquad (2)$$

Hence,

$$\frac{d\phi}{dt} = \frac{1}{4} \qquad (3)$$

Applying the flux transport theorem, we arrive at

$$\frac{d\phi}{dt} = \iint_{S_t} \left(\frac{\partial \overline{F}}{\partial t} + \overline{v} \text{ div } \overline{F} \right) \cdot d\overline{S} + \oint_{C_t} \overline{F} \times \overline{v} \cdot d\overline{r}$$

$$= \iint_{S_t} xy\overline{k} \cdot \overline{n}d\overline{S} + \oint_{C_t} (xyz\overline{k}) \times \overline{k} \cdot d\overline{r} \qquad (4)$$

$$= \iint_{S_t} xy\,dS = \int_0^1 \int_0^1 xy\,dxdy = \frac{1}{4}$$

That verifies the flux transport theorem.

An oriented surface S_t, along with its properly oriented boundary curve C_t, moves through space. Fig. 1 shows the location of the surface at times t_1 and t_2.

The motion of the surface is described by a velocity field $\overline{v}(\overline{r},t)$. For sufficiently small $dt = t_2 - t_1$, a point on S_{t_1} is moved by $\overline{v}(\overline{r},t_1)dt$ to a point on S_{t_2}.

A variable vector field

$$\overline{F} = \overline{F}(\overline{r},t) \tag{1}$$

is given. The flux of $\overline{F}(\overline{r},t)$ through S_t at time t is

$$\phi(t) = \iint_{S_t} \overline{F}(\overline{r},t) \cdot d\overline{S} \tag{2}$$

Show that

$$\frac{d\phi}{dt} = \iint_{S_t} \left(\frac{\partial \overline{F}}{\partial t} + \overline{v} \ \mathrm{div} \ \overline{F} \right) \cdot d\overline{S} + \oint_{C_t} \overline{F} \times \overline{v} \cdot d\overline{r} \tag{3}$$

This formula is known as the flux transport theorem.

Hint: Apply the divergence theorem to the region V bounded by S_{t_1}, S_{t_2} and the side surface.

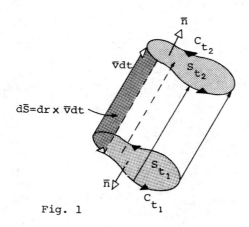

Fig. 1

Solution: We have

$$\frac{d\phi}{dt} = \lim_{t_2 \to t_1} \frac{\phi(t_2) - \phi(t_1)}{t_2 - t_1}$$

$$= \lim_{t_2 \to t_1} \frac{\iint_{S_{t_2}} \overline{F}(\overline{r}, t_2) \cdot d\overline{S} - \iint_{S_{t_1}} \overline{F}(\overline{r}, t_1) \cdot d\overline{S}}{t_2 - t_1} \tag{4}$$

Applying the divergence theorem at time t_1 we find

$$\iiint_V \text{div } \overline{F}(\overline{r}, t) dV = \iint_{S_{t_2}} \overline{F}(\overline{r}, t_1) \cdot d\overline{S}$$

$$- \iint_{S_{t_1}} \overline{F}(\overline{r}, t_1) \cdot d\overline{S} + \iint_{sides} \overline{F}(\overline{r}, t_1) \cdot d\overline{S} \tag{5}$$

Since,

$$\overline{F}(\overline{r}, t_2) \approx \overline{F}(\overline{r}, t_1) + \frac{\partial \overline{F}}{\partial t} dt \tag{6}$$

we have

$$\iint_{S_{t_2}} \overline{F}(\overline{r}, t_2) \cdot d\overline{S} - \iint_{S_{t_1}} \overline{F}(\overline{r}, t_1) \cdot d\overline{S}$$

$$= \iint_{S_{t_2}} \overline{F}(\overline{r}, t_1) \cdot d\overline{S} + \iint_{S_{t_2}} \frac{\partial \overline{F}}{\partial t} dt \cdot d\overline{S}$$

$$- \iint_{S_{t_2}} \overline{F}(\overline{r}, t_1) \cdot d\overline{S} + \iiint_V \text{div } \overline{F}(\overline{r}, t_1) dV - \iint_{sides} \overline{F}(\overline{r}, t_1) \cdot d\overline{S} \tag{7}$$

Note that on the sides, the surface element $d\overline{S}$ equals $d\overline{S} = d\overline{r} \times \overline{v} \, dt$; $d\overline{r}$ is taken along the boundary curve C_{t_1}. The volume element is

$$dV = d\overline{S} \cdot \overline{v} \, dt, \tag{8}$$

as shown in Fig. 2.

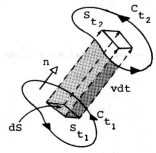

Fig. 2

Eq.(7) becomes

$$\iint\limits_{S_{t_2}} \overline{F}(\overline{r},t_2) \cdot d\overline{S} - \iint\limits_{S_{t_1}} \overline{F}(\overline{r},t_1) \cdot d\overline{S}$$

$$= dt \iint\limits_{S_{t_2}} \frac{\partial \overline{F}}{\partial t} \cdot d\overline{S} + dt \iint\limits_{S_{t_1}} (\text{div } \overline{F})\overline{v} \cdot d\overline{S} \qquad (9)$$

$$-dt \oint\limits_{C_{t_1}} \overline{F}(\overline{r},t_1) \cdot d\overline{r} \times \overline{v}$$

Dividing eq.(9) by dt (note that dt = $t_2 - t_1$) we obtain

$$\frac{d\phi}{dt} = \iint\limits_{S_t} \left(\frac{\partial \overline{F}}{\partial t} + \overline{v} \text{ div } \overline{F}\right) \cdot d\overline{S} + \oint\limits_{C_t} \overline{F} \times \overline{v} \cdot d\overline{r} \qquad (10)$$

If $\overline{F}$ does not depend on time $\left(\frac{\partial \overline{F}}{\partial t} = \overline{0}\right)$ and the surface does not move ($\overline{v} = 0$), we obtain

$$\frac{d\phi}{dt} = \iint\limits_{S_t} (\overline{0} + \overline{0} \text{ div } \overline{F}) \cdot d\overline{S} + \oint\limits_{C_t} \overline{F} \times \overline{0} \cdot d\overline{r} = 0 \qquad (11)$$

which indicates that the flux ϕ does not depend on time.

● **PROBLEM 23-48**

Consider a vector field

$$\overline{F} = \overline{F}(\overline{r}(u,v,t),t) \qquad (1)$$

where $\qquad \overline{r} = \overline{r}(u,v,t)$

Prove the identity

$$\frac{\partial \overline{F}}{\partial v} \cdot \overline{v} \times \frac{\partial \overline{r}}{\partial u} - \frac{\partial \overline{F}}{\partial u} \cdot \overline{v} \times \frac{\partial \overline{r}}{\partial v} = \left[(\nabla \cdot \overline{F})\overline{v} - (\overline{v} \cdot \nabla)\overline{F}\right] \cdot \left(\frac{\partial \overline{r}}{\partial u} \times \frac{\partial \overline{r}}{\partial v}\right) \qquad (2)$$

where $\qquad \overline{v} = \dfrac{\partial \overline{r}}{\partial t} \qquad (3)$

Solution: By the chain rule, we have

$$\frac{\partial \overline{F}}{\partial v} = \left(\frac{\partial \overline{r}}{\partial v} \cdot \nabla\right)\overline{F} \qquad (4)$$

and

$$\frac{\partial \overline{F}}{\partial u} = \left(\frac{\partial \overline{r}}{\partial u} \cdot \nabla\right)\overline{F} \qquad (5)$$

1198

We shall now apply tensor notation in this problem and use the Einstein convention.

The left-hand side of eq.(2) is

$$\frac{\partial \bar{F}}{\partial v} \cdot \bar{V} \times \frac{\partial \bar{r}}{\partial u} - \frac{\partial \bar{F}}{\partial u} \cdot \bar{V} \times \frac{\partial \bar{r}}{\partial v}$$

$$= \frac{\partial F_i}{\partial v} \left(\bar{V} \times \frac{\partial \bar{r}}{\partial u} \right)_i - \frac{\partial F_i}{\partial u} \left(\bar{V} \times \frac{\partial \bar{r}}{\partial v} \right)_i$$

$$= e_{ijk} \left(\frac{\partial F_i}{\partial v} \right) V_j \frac{\partial x_k}{\partial u} - e_{ijk} \left(\frac{\partial F_i}{\partial u} \right) V_j \frac{\partial x_k}{\partial v}$$

$$= e_{ijk} \left(\frac{\partial x_\ell}{\partial v} \frac{\partial F_i}{\partial x_\ell} \right) V_j \frac{\partial x_k}{\partial u} - e_{ijk} \left(\frac{\partial x_\ell}{\partial u} \frac{\partial F_i}{\partial x_\ell} \right) V_j \frac{\partial x_k}{\partial v}$$

$$= e_{ijk} V_j \frac{\partial F_i}{\partial x_\ell} \left(\frac{\partial x_\ell}{\partial v} \frac{\partial x_k}{\partial u} - \frac{\partial x_\ell}{\partial u} \frac{\partial x_k}{\partial v} \right)$$

$$= e_{ijk} V_j \frac{\partial F_i}{\partial x_\ell} \left(\delta_{\ell m} \delta_{kn} - \delta_{\ell n} \delta_{km} \right) \frac{\partial x_m}{\partial v} \frac{\partial x_n}{\partial u}$$

$$= e_{ijk} V_j \frac{\partial F_i}{\partial x_\ell} e_{\ell k r} e_{mnr} \frac{\partial x_m}{\partial v} \frac{\partial x_n}{\partial u}$$

$$= e_{ijk} e_{r\ell k} e_{mnr} V_j \frac{\partial x_m}{\partial v} \frac{\partial x_n}{\partial u} \frac{\partial F_i}{\partial x_\ell}$$

$$= \left(\delta_{ir}\delta_{j\ell} - \delta_{i\ell}\delta_{jr} \right) e_{mnr} V_j \frac{\partial x_m}{\partial v} \frac{\partial x_n}{\partial u} \frac{\partial F_i}{\partial x_\ell} \qquad (6)$$

$$= e_{mnr} \frac{\partial x_m}{\partial v} \frac{\partial x_n}{\partial u} V_\ell \frac{\partial F_r}{\partial x_\ell} - e_{mnj} \frac{\partial x_m}{\partial v} \frac{\partial x_n}{\partial u} V_j \frac{\partial F_\ell}{\partial x_\ell}$$

$$= -e_{rnm} V_\ell \left(\frac{\partial F_r}{\partial x_\ell} \right) \frac{\partial x_n}{\partial u} \frac{\partial x_m}{\partial v} + e_{jnm} \left(\frac{\partial F_\ell}{\partial x_\ell} \right) V_j \frac{\partial x_n}{\partial u} \frac{\partial x_m}{\partial v}$$

$$= -\left[(\bar{V} \cdot \nabla)\bar{F} \right]_r \left[\frac{\partial \bar{r}}{\partial u} \times \frac{\partial \bar{r}}{\partial v} \right]_r + \left[(\nabla \cdot \bar{F})\bar{V} \right]_j \left[\frac{\partial \bar{r}}{\partial u} \times \frac{\partial \bar{r}}{\partial v} \right]_j$$

$$= -\left[(\bar{V} \cdot \nabla)\bar{F} \right] \cdot \left(\frac{\partial \bar{r}}{\partial u} \times \frac{\partial \bar{r}}{\partial v} \right) + (\nabla \cdot \bar{F})\bar{V} \cdot \left(\frac{\partial \bar{r}}{\partial u} \times \frac{\partial \bar{r}}{\partial v} \right)$$

That proves identity (2).

It might seem that this problem does not belong in this section (on the Transport Theorem). However, as will be shown in the following problem, the above identity proves quite instrumental.

1199

Now, we are in a position to prove the flux transport theorem by use of the parametrization of a surface.

Consider a surface s_0 at time $t = 0$ such that s_0 is parametrized by

$$\bar{r} = \bar{r}_0(u,v) \tag{1}$$

where u,v range over a region Ω as shown in Fig. 1.

As time passes by, a point on s_0 traces out a curve called the trajectory

$$\bar{r} = \bar{r}(\bar{r}_0,t) \tag{2}$$

The position of a point depends on the (u,v) parameters and on time t,

$$\bar{r} = \bar{r}(u,v,t) \tag{3}$$

We define the velocity $\bar{v}$ of a point by

$$\bar{v} = \frac{\partial \bar{r}}{\partial t} \tag{4}$$

and the flux of $\bar{F}(\bar{r},t)$ through S_t as

$$\phi = \iint_{S_t} \bar{F} \cdot d\bar{S} = \iint_\Omega \bar{F}(\bar{r}(u,v,t),t) \cdot \frac{\partial \bar{r}}{\partial u} \times \frac{\partial \bar{r}}{\partial v}\, dudv \tag{5}$$

Since Ω is fixed and does not depend on time

$$\frac{d\phi}{dt} = \iint_\Omega \frac{d\bar{F}}{dt} \cdot \frac{\partial \bar{r}}{\partial u} \times \frac{\partial \bar{r}}{\partial v}\, dudv + \iint_\Omega \bar{F} \cdot \frac{\partial}{\partial t}\left(\frac{\partial \bar{r}}{\partial u} \times \frac{\partial \bar{r}}{\partial v}\right) dudv \tag{6}$$

Assume that the orientation of the surfaces S_t, Ω and their boundaries are consistent.

Prove the flux transport theorem.

Hint: Transform eq.(6) by applying the identity of Problem 23-48.

Solution: The time derivative of $\bar{F}$ is

$$\frac{d\bar{F}(\bar{r}(u,v,t),t)}{dt} = \frac{\partial \bar{F}}{\partial t} + \frac{\partial \bar{F}}{\partial x}\frac{\partial x}{\partial t} + \frac{\partial \bar{F}}{\partial y}\frac{\partial y}{\partial t} + \frac{\partial \bar{F}}{\partial z}\frac{\partial z}{\partial t}$$

$$\tag{7}$$

$$= \frac{\partial \bar{F}}{\partial t} + (\bar{v} \cdot \nabla)\bar{F}$$

Since

$$\frac{\partial}{\partial t}(\bar{a} \times \bar{b}) = \frac{\partial \bar{a}}{\partial t} \times \bar{b} + \bar{a} \times \frac{\partial \bar{b}}{\partial t} \tag{8}$$

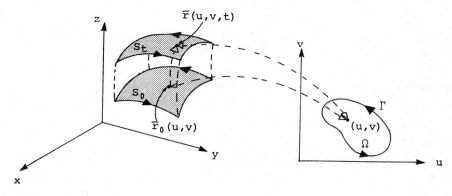

Fig. 1

we arrive at

$$\overline{F} \cdot \frac{\partial}{\partial t}\left(\frac{\partial \overline{r}}{\partial u} \times \frac{\partial \overline{r}}{\partial v}\right) = \overline{F} \cdot \left[\frac{\partial}{\partial u}\left(\frac{\partial \overline{r}}{\partial t} \times \frac{\partial \overline{r}}{\partial v}\right) - \frac{\partial}{\partial v}\left(\frac{\partial \overline{r}}{\partial t} \times \frac{\partial \overline{r}}{\partial u}\right)\right]$$

(9)

$$= \overline{F} \cdot \frac{\partial}{\partial u}\left(\overline{V} \times \frac{\partial \overline{r}}{\partial v}\right) - \overline{F} \cdot \frac{\partial}{\partial v}\left(\overline{V} \times \frac{\partial \overline{r}}{\partial u}\right)$$

$$= \frac{\partial}{\partial u}\left(\overline{F} \cdot \overline{V} \times \frac{\partial \overline{r}}{\partial v}\right) - \frac{\partial \overline{F}}{\partial u} \cdot \left(\overline{V} \times \frac{\partial \overline{r}}{\partial v}\right) - \frac{\partial}{\partial v}\left(\overline{F} \cdot \overline{V} \times \frac{\partial \overline{r}}{\partial u}\right)$$

$$+ \frac{\partial \overline{F}}{\partial v} \cdot \left(\overline{V} \times \frac{\partial \overline{r}}{\partial u}\right)$$

$$= \frac{\partial}{\partial u}\left(\overline{F} \cdot \overline{V} \times \frac{\partial \overline{r}}{\partial v}\right) - \frac{\partial}{\partial v}\left(\overline{F} \cdot \overline{V} \times \frac{\partial \overline{r}}{\partial u}\right)$$

$$+ \left[(\nabla \cdot \overline{F})\overline{V} - (\overline{V} \cdot \nabla)\overline{F}\right] \cdot \left(\frac{\partial \overline{r}}{\partial u} \times \frac{\partial \overline{r}}{\partial v}\right)$$

Note that we used the identity proven in Problem 23-48.

Substituting eqs.(7) and (9) into eq.(6) results in

$$\frac{d\phi}{dt} = \iint_{\Omega}\left[\frac{\partial \overline{F}}{\partial t} + (\overline{V} \cdot \nabla)\overline{F} + (\nabla \cdot \overline{F})\overline{V} - (\overline{V} \cdot \nabla)\overline{F}\right] \cdot \left(\frac{\partial \overline{r}}{\partial u} \times \frac{\partial \overline{r}}{\partial v}\right) du dv$$

(10)

$$+ \iint_{\Omega}\left[\frac{\partial}{\partial u}\left(\overline{F} \cdot \overline{V} \times \frac{\partial \overline{r}}{\partial v}\right) - \frac{\partial}{\partial v}\left(\overline{F} \cdot \overline{V} \times \frac{\partial \overline{r}}{\partial u}\right)\right] du dv$$

Since

$$\overline{a} \cdot \overline{b} \times \overline{c} = \overline{a} \times \overline{b} \cdot \overline{c}$$

(11)

eq.(10) becomes

$$\frac{d\phi}{dt} = \iint_{\Omega}\left[\frac{\partial \overline{F}}{\partial t} + (\nabla \cdot \overline{F})\overline{V}\right] \cdot \left(\frac{\partial \overline{r}}{\partial u} \times \frac{\partial \overline{r}}{\partial v}\right) du dv$$

$$+ \oint_{\Gamma} \left[\frac{\partial}{\partial u} \left(\overline{F} \times \overline{V} \cdot \frac{\partial \overline{r}}{\partial v} \right) - \frac{\partial}{\partial v} \left(\overline{F} \times \overline{V} \cdot \frac{\partial \overline{r}}{\partial u} \right) \right] dudv \qquad (12)$$

Applying Green's theorem and

$$d\overline{r} = \frac{\partial \overline{r}}{\partial u} du + \frac{\partial \overline{r}}{\partial v} dv \qquad (13)$$

$$d\overline{S} = \frac{\partial \overline{r}}{\partial u} \times \frac{\partial \overline{r}}{\partial v} dudv$$

we get

$$\frac{d\phi}{dt} = \iint_{\Omega} \left[\frac{\partial \overline{F}}{\partial t} + (\nabla \cdot \overline{F}) \overline{V} \right] \cdot \left(\frac{\partial \overline{r}}{\partial u} \times \frac{\partial \overline{r}}{\partial v} \right) dudv + \oint_{\Gamma} \left(\overline{F} \times \overline{V} \cdot \frac{\partial \overline{r}}{\partial u} du + \overline{F} \times \overline{V} \cdot \frac{\partial \overline{r}}{\partial v} dv \right)$$

$$\qquad (14)$$

$$= \iint_{S_t} \left[\frac{\partial \overline{F}}{\partial t} + (\nabla \cdot \overline{F}) \overline{V} \right] \cdot d\overline{S} + \oint_{C_t} \overline{F} \times \overline{V} \cdot d\overline{r}$$

which is the flux transport theorem.

• PROBLEM 23-50

In Problem 23-49, the velocity field $\overline{v}$ was defined on the surface S_t. Consider a situation where $\overline{v}$ is a continuously differentiable vector field defined in some region containing S_t. Modify the flux transport theorem by applying Stokes' theorem. Assume that $\overline{v}$ is a solenoidal field.

Solution: The flux transport theorem is

$$\frac{d\phi}{dt} = \iint_{S_t} \left[\frac{\partial \overline{F}}{\partial t} + (\nabla \cdot \overline{F}) \overline{v} \right] \cdot d\overline{S} + \oint_{C_t} \overline{F} \times \overline{v} \cdot d\overline{r} \qquad (1)$$

Since $\overline{v}$ is continuously differentiable and defined throughout some region containing S_t, Stokes' theorem can be applied

$$\frac{d\phi}{dt} = \iint_{S_t} \left[\frac{\partial \overline{F}}{\partial t} + (\nabla \cdot \overline{F}) \overline{v} + \nabla \times (\overline{F} \times \overline{v}) \right] \cdot d\overline{S} \qquad (2)$$

Applying the identity

$$\nabla \times (\overline{F} \times \overline{v}) = (\overline{v} \cdot \nabla) \overline{F} - (\overline{F} \cdot \nabla) \overline{v} + (\nabla \cdot \overline{v}) \overline{F} - (\nabla \cdot \overline{F}) \overline{v} \qquad (3)$$

1202

to eq.(2), we arrive at

$$\frac{d\phi}{dt} = \iint\limits_{S_t} \left[\frac{\partial \overline{F}}{\partial t} + (\overline{v} \cdot \nabla)\overline{F} - (\overline{F} \cdot \nabla)\overline{v} + (\nabla \cdot \overline{v})\overline{F} \right] \cdot d\overline{S} \qquad (4)$$

A vector field whose divergence is everywhere zero is called a solenoidal vector field. For solenoidal vector fields, div $\overline{v} = 0$ and eq.(4) reduces to

$$\frac{d\phi}{dt} = \iint\limits_{S_t} \left[\frac{\partial \overline{F}}{\partial t} + (\overline{v} \cdot \nabla)\overline{F} - (\overline{F} \cdot \nabla)\overline{v} \right] \cdot d\overline{S} \qquad (5)$$

REYNOLD'S TRANSPORT THEOREM, EULER'S EXPANSION FORMULA

● **PROBLEM** 23-51

Verify Reynold's transport theorem for the expanding sphere V_t

$$x^2 + y^2 + z^2 \leq (vt)^2 \qquad (1)$$

and the scalar fields

1. $f(\overline{r},t) = a$, where a is constant $\qquad (2)$

2. $f(\overline{r},t) = |\overline{r}|^2 t^2$ $\qquad (3)$

Solution: Let V_t denote the volume of integration at time t and let $f(\overline{r},t)$ be a continuously differentiable scalar field.

Reynold's transport theorem states that

$$\frac{d}{dt} \iiint\limits_{V_t} f dV = \iiint\limits_{V_t} \frac{\partial f}{\partial t} dV + \iint\limits_{S_t} f\overline{v} \cdot d\overline{S} \qquad (4)$$

1. For $f(\overline{r},t) = a$, we have

$$\frac{d}{dt} \iiint\limits_{V_t} a dV = a \frac{d}{dt} \iiint\limits_{V_t} dV = a \frac{d}{dt} \left(\frac{4}{3}\pi v^3 t^3 \right)$$

$$= 4\pi a v^3 t^2 \qquad (5)$$

$$\iiint\limits_{V_t} \frac{\partial f}{\partial t} dV + \iint\limits_{S_t} f\overline{v} \cdot d\overline{S} = \iint\limits_{S_t} av \frac{\overline{r}}{|\overline{r}|} \cdot \overline{n} dS$$

$$= av \iint\limits_{S_t} \frac{\overline{r}}{|\overline{r}|} \cdot \frac{\overline{r}}{|\overline{r}|} \, dS = av4\pi v^2 t^2 = 4\pi av^3 t^2$$

2. For $f(\overline{r}, t) = |\overline{r}|^2 t^2$ we have

$$\frac{d}{dt} \iiint\limits_{V_t} f \, dV = \frac{d}{dt} \iiint\limits_{V_t} |\overline{r}|^2 t^2 \, dV \tag{7}$$

Transforming to spherical coordinates leads to

$$\frac{d}{dt} \iiint\limits_{V_t} \rho^2 t^2 \, dV = \frac{d}{dt} \int_{\rho=0}^{vt} \int_{\phi=0}^{\pi} \int_{\theta=0}^{2\pi} t^2 \rho^4 \sin\phi \, d\rho \, d\phi \, d\theta$$

$$= \frac{d}{dt} \left[4\pi \int_{\rho=0}^{vt} t^2 \rho^4 \, d\rho \right] = \frac{d}{dt} \left(\frac{4}{5} \cdot \pi v^5 t^7 \right) \tag{8}$$

$$= \frac{28}{5} \pi v^5 t^6$$

The right-hand side of eq.(4) equals

$$\iiint\limits_{V_t} \frac{\partial f}{\partial t} \, dV + \iint\limits_{S_t} f\overline{v} \cdot d\overline{S}$$

$$= \iiint\limits_{V_t} 2t |\overline{r}|^2 \, dV + \iint\limits_{S_t} |\overline{r}|^2 t^2 \overline{v} \cdot \overline{n} \, dS$$

(9)

$$= 2t \left(\frac{4}{5} \pi v^5 t^5 \right) + \iint\limits_{S_t} v^2 t^4 v \, dS$$

$$= \frac{8}{5} \pi v^5 t^6 + 4\pi v^3 t^4 (vt)^2 = \frac{28}{5} \pi v^5 t^6$$

which is the same as in eq.(8).

● **PROBLEM** 23-52

In fluid mechanics, the equation of continuity

$$\frac{\partial \rho}{\partial t} + \text{div}(\rho \overline{v}) = 0 \tag{1}$$

expresses the law of conservation of mass. Here, $\overline{v}$ is the velocity field and ρ the density $\rho = \rho(\overline{r}, t)$. By applying Reynold's theorem, show that the mass of a specific portion of a moving fluid remains constant during the flow.

Solution: Reynold's theorem states that

$$\frac{d}{dt} \iiint_{V_t} f dV = \iiint_{V_t} \frac{\partial f}{\partial t} dV + \iint_{S_t} f \overline{v} \cdot d\overline{S} \qquad (2)$$

Setting $f = \rho$ and applying the divergence theorem, we obtain

$$\frac{d}{dt} \iiint_{V_t} \rho dV = \iiint_{V_t} \frac{\partial \rho}{\partial t} dV + \iiint_{V_t} div(\rho \overline{v}) dV \qquad (3)$$

At any time, the integral $\iiint_{V_t} \rho dV$ represents the mass of a specific portion of fluid. Substituting eq.(1) into eq.(3) we find

$$\frac{d}{dt} \iiint_{V_t} \rho dV = \iiint_{V_t} \left[\frac{\partial \rho}{\partial t} + div(\rho \overline{v}) \right] dV = 0 \qquad (4)$$

Hence,

$$\iiint_{V_t} \rho dV = constant \qquad (5)$$

● **PROBLEM** 23-53

Let $f(\overline{r}, t)$ be a continuously differentiable scalar field and let V_t be the volume of integration at time t.
Prove Reynold's transport theorem.

Hint: Since any continuous scalar field f can be expressed as the divergence of some vector field, substitute

$$f = div \; \overline{F} \qquad (1)$$

Solution: We have to compute

$$\frac{d}{dt} \iiint_{V_t} f(\overline{r}, t) dV \qquad (2)$$

Substituting eq.(1) and applying the divergence theorem results in

$$\iiint_{V_t} f dV = \iiint_{V_t} \nabla \cdot \overline{F} \; dV = \iint_{S_t} \overline{F} \cdot d\overline{S} \qquad (3)$$

The flux transport theorem for a closed surface S_t is

$$\frac{d}{dt} \iint_{S_t} \overline{F} \cdot d\overline{S} = \iint_{S_t} \left[\frac{\partial \overline{F}}{\partial t} + (\nabla \cdot \overline{F})\overline{v} \right] \cdot d\overline{S} \qquad (4)$$

Differentiating eq.(3) and substituting eq.(4) gives us

$$\frac{d}{dt} \iiint_{V_t} f dV = \frac{d}{dt} \iint_{S_t} \overline{F} \cdot d\overline{S} = \iint_{S_t} \frac{\partial \overline{F}}{\partial t} \cdot d\overline{S}$$

$$+ \iint_{S_t} (\nabla \cdot \overline{F})\overline{v} \cdot d\overline{S} = \iiint_{V_t} \nabla \cdot \frac{\partial \overline{F}}{\partial t} dV + \iint_{S_t} (\nabla \cdot \overline{F})\overline{v} \cdot d\overline{S} \qquad (5)$$

$$= \iiint_{V_t} \frac{\partial}{\partial t}(\nabla \cdot \overline{F}) dV + \iint_{S_t} (\nabla \cdot \overline{F})\overline{v} \cdot d\overline{S}$$

$$= \iiint_{V_t} \frac{\partial f}{\partial t} dV + \iint_{S_t} f\overline{v} \cdot d\overline{S}$$

● **PROBLEM** 23-54

At any time t, the volume can be defined as

$$V = \iiint_{V_t} dV \qquad (1)$$

By applying Reynold's transport theorem, prove Euler's expansion formula

$$\frac{d}{dt} \iiint_{V_t} dV = \iiint_{V_t} \nabla \cdot \overline{v} \, dV = \iint_{S_t} \overline{v} \cdot d\overline{S} \qquad (2)$$

Solution: Reynold's transport theorem states that

$$\frac{d}{dt} \iiint_{V_t} f dV = \iiint_{V_t} \left[\frac{\partial f}{\partial t} + \nabla \cdot (f\overline{v}) \right] dV \qquad (3)$$

$$= \iiint_{V_t} \frac{\partial f}{\partial t} dV + \iint_{S_t} f\overline{v} \cdot d\overline{S}$$

1206

Setting f ≡ 1 in eq.(3), we find

$$\frac{d}{dt} \iiint_{V_t} dV = \iiint_{V_t} \nabla \cdot \overline{v} \; dV = \iint_{S_t} \overline{v} \cdot d\overline{S} \qquad (4)$$

DIFFERENTIAL FORMS

DIFFERENTIAL ONE-FORM, EXTERIOR PRODUCT

● **PROBLEM** 23-55

Define a differential 1-form. Find the value of each of the following differential 1-forms:

1. $2dx_1 + 3dx_2$; acting on a vector $\overline{a} = (-1,-2)$

2. $3dx_1 + 2dx_2 + dx_3$; $\overline{a} = (1,1,-2)$

3. $dx_1 + 2dx_3$; $\overline{a} = (1,1,-2)$

4. $dx_1 + 2dx_2 + 3dx_3 + \ldots + ndx_n$; $\overline{a} = (1,2,3,\ldots,n)$

Solution: Let $\overline{x} \in R^n$ be an n-dimensional vector

$$\overline{x} = (x_1, x_2, \ldots, x_n) \qquad (1)$$

where $x_1, x_2, \ldots, x_n$ are real numbers. By dx_k, we denote the function that assigns to a vector $\overline{a} \in R^n$ its kth coordinate, i.e. $dx_k(\overline{a}) = a_k$. For example, if $\overline{a} = (2,1,6)$, then

$$dx_1(\overline{a}) = 2$$

$$dx_2(\overline{a}) = 1 \qquad (2)$$

$$dx_3(\overline{a}) = 6$$

We can form new functions taking linear combinations of dx_k with constant coefficients

$$\alpha_1 dx_1 + \alpha_2 dx_2 + \ldots + \alpha_n dx_n \qquad (3)$$

If $f_1, f_2, \ldots, f_n$ are real-valued functions defined in R^n (or a region D of R^n)

$$f_k : D \rightarrow R \qquad k = 1, 2, \ldots, n \qquad (4)$$

then for each $\bar{x} \in D$ we can form the linear combination

$$\omega_{\bar{x}} = f_1(\bar{x})dx_1 + \ldots + f_n(\bar{x})dx_n \qquad (5)$$

$\omega_{\bar{x}}$ acts on vector $\bar{a} \in R^n$ by

$$\omega_{\bar{x}}(\bar{a}) = f_1(\bar{x})dx_1(\bar{a}) + \ldots + f_n(\bar{x})dx_n(\bar{a}) \qquad (6)$$

$\omega_{\bar{x}}$ is called a differential 1-form.

We obtain

1. $2dx_1(-1,-2) + 3dx_2(-1,-2) = 2 \cdot (-1) + 3 \cdot (-2)$

$$= -2 - 6 = -8$$

2. $3dx_1(\bar{a}) + 2dx_2(\bar{a}) + dx_3(\bar{a}) = 3 + 2 - 2 = 3$

3. $dx_1(\bar{a}) + 2dx_3(\bar{a}) = 1 - 4 = -3$

4. $dx_1(\bar{a}) + 2dx_2(\bar{a}) + 3dx_3(\bar{a}) + \ldots + ndx_n(\bar{a})$

$$= 1 \cdot 1 + 2 \cdot 2 + 3 \cdot 3 + \ldots + n \cdot n$$

$$= 1^2 + 2^2 + \ldots + n^2 = \frac{n(n+1)(2n+1)}{6}$$

● **PROBLEM** 23-56

Let $f(x_1,x_2,x_3) \in R$ be a differentiable function. Show that $d_{\bar{x}}f$, the differential of f at $\bar{x}$ is a 1-form.

Solution: Let $\bar{a} \in R^3$

$$a = (a_1,a_2,a_3) \qquad (1)$$

$d_{\bar{x}}f$ acting on $\bar{a}$ can be written

$$d_{\bar{x}}f(\bar{a}) = \frac{\partial f}{\partial x_1}(\bar{x}) \, a_1 + \frac{\partial f}{\partial x_2}(\bar{x}) \, a_2 + \frac{\partial f}{\partial x_3}(\bar{x}) \, a_3 \qquad (2)$$

$$= \frac{\partial f}{\partial x_1}(\bar{x}) \, dx_1(\bar{a}) + \frac{\partial f}{\partial x_2}(\bar{x}) \, dx_2(\bar{a}) + \frac{\partial f}{\partial x_3}(\bar{x}) \, dx_3(\bar{a})$$

The coefficient functions are $\frac{\partial f}{\partial x_k}(\bar{x})$. Note that not every 1-form is the differential of a function.

1208

Find the value of the differential form

$$2dx_1 \wedge dx_2 \qquad\qquad (1)$$

acting on the vectors $(\bar{a},\bar{b})$ where

$$\bar{a} = (1,0,1) \qquad \bar{b} = (-2,3,1)$$

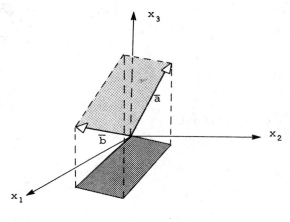

Fig. 1

Solution: We shall define the exterior product of basic 1-forms dx_1, dx_2, dx_3 in R^3.

The product $dx_1 \wedge dx_2$ is a function of an ordered pair of vectors

$$dx_1 \wedge dx_2(\bar{a},\bar{b}).$$

It is defined as

$$dx_1 \wedge dx_2(\bar{a},\bar{b}) = \det \begin{pmatrix} a_1 & b_1 \\ a_2 & b_2 \end{pmatrix}$$

$$(2)$$

$$= \det \begin{pmatrix} dx_1(\bar{a}) & dx_1(\bar{b}) \\ dx_2(\bar{a}) & dx_2(\bar{b}) \end{pmatrix}$$

Geometrically, $dx_1 \wedge dx_2(\bar{a},\bar{b})$ is the area of the parallelogram spanned by the projections of $\bar{a}$ and $\bar{b}$ onto the x_1x_2 plane.

We have

$$2dx_1 \wedge dx_2 = 2\det \begin{pmatrix} 1 & -2 \\ 0 & 3 \end{pmatrix} = 6 \qquad\qquad (3)$$

Evaluate the value of the differential form

$$dx_1 \wedge dx_2 + 3dx_2 \wedge dx_3 \; (\bar{a},\bar{b}) \tag{1}$$

where $\qquad \bar{a} = (1,1,0) \qquad \bar{b} = (-1,2,3)$

Solution: The exterior product of basic 1-forms is defined by

$$dx_i \wedge dx_j(\bar{a},\bar{b}) = \det \begin{pmatrix} dx_i(\bar{a}) & dx_i(\bar{b}) \\ dx_j(\bar{a}) & dx_j(\bar{b}) \end{pmatrix}. \tag{2}$$

Therefore,

$$dx_1 \wedge dx_2(\bar{a},\bar{b}) = \det \begin{pmatrix} dx_1(\bar{a}) & dx_1(\bar{b}) \\ dx_2(\bar{a}) & dx_2(\bar{b}) \end{pmatrix}$$

$$= \det \begin{pmatrix} 1 & -1 \\ 1 & 2 \end{pmatrix} = 2 + 1 = 3 \tag{3}$$

and

$$3dx_2 \wedge dx_3(\bar{a},\bar{b}) = 3\det \begin{pmatrix} dx_2(\bar{a}) & dx_2(\bar{b}) \\ dx_3(\bar{a}) & dx_3(\bar{b}) \end{pmatrix}$$

$$= 3\det \begin{pmatrix} 1 & 2 \\ 0 & 3 \end{pmatrix} = 9 \tag{4}$$

Hence,

$$dx_1 \wedge dx_2 + 3dx_2 \wedge dx_3(\bar{a},\bar{b}) = 3 + 9 = 12 \tag{5}$$

Prove the following properties of the exterior product

1. $\quad dx_i \wedge dx_i = 0 \tag{1}$

2. $\quad dx_i \wedge dx_j = -dx_j \wedge dx_i \tag{2}$

3. $\quad dx_i \wedge dx_j(\bar{a},\bar{b}) = -dx_j \wedge dx_i(\bar{b},\bar{a}) \tag{3}$

Solution: 1. Let $\quad \bar{a} = (a_1,a_2,a_3)$

$$\bar{b} = (b_1,b_2,b_3) \tag{4}$$

By definition

$$dx_i \wedge dx_j(\bar{a},\bar{b}) = \det \begin{pmatrix} dx_i(\bar{a}) & dx_i(\bar{b}) \\ dx_j(\bar{a}) & dx_j(\bar{b}) \end{pmatrix} \qquad (5)$$

Hence, for i = j,

$$ (6) $$

$$dx_i \wedge dx_i(\bar{a},\bar{b}) = \det \begin{pmatrix} dx_i(\bar{a}) & dx_j(\bar{b}) \\ dx_i(\bar{a}) & dx_j(\bar{b}) \end{pmatrix} = 0$$

2. $dx_i \wedge dx_j(\bar{a},\bar{b}) = \det \begin{pmatrix} a_i & b_i \\ a_j & b_j \end{pmatrix}$

$$ (7) $$

$$= a_i b_j - b_i a_j = -(b_i a_j - a_i b_j)$$

$$= -\det \begin{pmatrix} a_j & b_j \\ a_i & b_i \end{pmatrix} = -dx_j \wedge dx_i(\bar{a},\bar{b})$$

3. $dx_i \wedge dx_j(\bar{a},\bar{b}) = \det \begin{pmatrix} a_i & b_i \\ a_j & b_j \end{pmatrix}$ (8)

$$= -\det \begin{pmatrix} b_i & a_i \\ b_j & a_j \end{pmatrix} = -dx_i \wedge dx_j(\bar{b},\bar{a})$$

DIFFERENTIAL TWO-FORM, DIFFERENTIAL p-FORMS, ADDITION AND MULTIPLICATION OF FORMS

● **PROBLEM** 23-60

Define a differential 2-form.   Compute the value of the 2-form

$$\tau = 3dx_1 \wedge dx_2 - dx_3 \wedge dx_2 + 2dx_2 \wedge dx_3 \qquad (1)$$

acting on the ordered pair of vectors $(\bar{a},\bar{b})$ where

$$\bar{a} = (3,2,1)$$
$$\bar{b} = (-1,1,-1) \qquad (2)$$

Solution: Let $\overline{f} = (f_1, f_2, f_3)$ be a vector field defined in a region D of R^3.

For each $\overline{x} \in D$ we can form the linear combination

$$\tau_{\overline{x}} = f_1(\overline{x})dx_2 \wedge dx_3 + f_2(\overline{x})dx_3 \wedge dx_1 + f_3(\overline{x})dx_1 \wedge dx_2 \quad (3)$$

The function $\tau_{\overline{x}}$ acts on ordered pairs $(\overline{a}, \overline{b})$ of vectors in R^3. $\tau_{\overline{x}}$ is called a differential 2-form. Eq.(1) defines a 2-form with constant coefficients. That is why we used τ instead of $\tau_{\overline{x}}$.

$$\tau(\overline{a}, \overline{b}) = 3\det \begin{pmatrix} 3 & -1 \\ 2 & 1 \end{pmatrix} - dx_3 \wedge dx_2 + 2dx_2 \wedge dx_3$$

$$\quad (4)$$

$$= 3(3+2) + dx_2 \wedge dx_3 + 2dx_2 \wedge dx_3$$

$$= 15 + 3dx_2 \wedge dx_3$$

$$= 15 + 3 \det \begin{pmatrix} 2 & 1 \\ 1 & -1 \end{pmatrix} = 15 - 9 = 6$$

● **PROBLEM** 23-61

Multiply out and simplify the following products

1. $(3dx_1 + 2dx_2 - dx_3) \wedge dx_1$

2. $(dx_1 + dx_2) \wedge (dx_1 - dx_2)$

3. $(dx_1 + dx_2) \wedge (dx_1 + dx_2)$

4. $(x_1^2 dx_1 + x_1 dx_3) \wedge (\sin x_2 dx_2 - e^{x_1} dx_3)$

Solution: 1. $(3dx_1 + 2dx_2 - dx_3) \wedge dx_1$

$$= 3dx_1 \wedge dx_1 + 2dx_2 \wedge dx_1 - dx_3 \wedge dx_1$$

$$= 2dx_2 \wedge dx_1 - dx_3 \wedge dx_1$$

2. $(dx_1 + dx_2) \wedge (dx_1 - dx_2)$

$$= dx_1 \wedge dx_1 - dx_1 \wedge dx_2 + dx_2 \wedge dx_1$$

$$- dx_2 \wedge dx_2 = -dx_1 \wedge dx_2 - dx_1 \wedge dx_2$$

$$= -2dx_1 \wedge dx_2$$

1212

3. $(dx_1 + dx_2) \wedge (dx_1 + dx_2)$

$\quad = dx_1 \wedge dx_1 + dx_1 \wedge dx_2 + dx_2 \wedge dx_1 + dx_2 \wedge dx_2$

$\quad = dx_1 \wedge dx_2 - dx_1 \wedge dx_2 = 0$

4. $(x_1^2 dx_1 + x_1 dx_3) \wedge (sinx_2 dx_2 - e^{x_1} dx_3)$

$\quad = x_1^2 sinx_2 dx_1 \wedge dx_2 - x_1^2 e^{x_1} dx_1 \wedge dx_3$

$\quad + x_1 sinx_2 dx_3 \wedge dx_2$

● **PROBLEM 23-62**

Multiply out and evaluate

$\quad dx_1 \wedge (dx_1 \wedge dx_2 + dx_2 \wedge dx_3 + 2dx_1 \wedge dx_3)(\overline{a},\overline{b},\overline{c})$ (1)

where

$\quad\quad\quad\quad \overline{a} = (3,1,0)$

$\quad\quad\quad\quad \overline{b} = (2,-1,1)$ (2)

$\quad\quad\quad\quad \overline{c} = (5,1,1)$

Solution: The product of a 1-form and a 2-form yields a 3-form. If $\overline{a} = (a_1,a_2,a_3)$, $\overline{b} = (b_1,b_2,b_3)$ and $\overline{c} = (c_1,c_2,c_3)$ we define

$$dx_1 \wedge dx_2 \wedge dx_3(\overline{a},\overline{b},\overline{c}) = \det \begin{pmatrix} a_1 & b_1 & c_1 \\ a_2 & b_2 & c_2 \\ a_3 & b_3 & c_3 \end{pmatrix} \quad (3)$$

We have

$\quad dx_1 \wedge (dx_1 \wedge dx_2 + dx_2 \wedge dx_3 + 2dx_1 \wedge dx_3)(\overline{a},\overline{b},\overline{c})$

$\quad = dx_1 \wedge dx_2 \wedge dx_3(\overline{a},\overline{b},\overline{c})$ (4)

$$= \det \begin{pmatrix} 3 & 2 & 5 \\ 1 & -1 & 1 \\ 0 & 1 & 1 \end{pmatrix} = -3$$

Eq.(3) represents the volume of a 3-dimensional parallelepiped spanned by the vectors $\overline{a}$, $\overline{b}$, and $\overline{c}$.

1. If $\omega_{\bar{x}}$ is a one-form in a region D of R^n and $\bar{x}_0$ is a fixed point in D, $\bar{x}_0 \in D$, then $\omega_{\bar{x}}$ is a real-valued linear function on R^n.

2. If $\omega_{\bar{x}}$ is a real-valued linear function on R^n, then

$$\omega_{\bar{x}}(\bar{a}) = \sum_{i=1}^{n} f_i(\bar{x}_0)dx_i(\bar{a}) \tag{1}$$

for all $\bar{a} \in R^n$, $f_i(\bar{x}_0)$ are real numbers.

Prove the above statements.

Solution: 1. Since $\omega_{\bar{x}}$ is a one-form in $D \subset R^n$, it can be written

$$\omega_{\bar{x}} = f_1(\bar{x})dx_1 + \ldots + f_n(\bar{x})dx_n \tag{2}$$

For a fixed $\bar{x}_0 \in D$

$$\omega_{\bar{x}_0} = f_1(\bar{x}_0)dx_1 + \ldots + f_n(\bar{x}_0)dx_n \tag{3}$$

Let $\bar{a} \in R^n$, $\bar{b} \in R^n$, $\alpha \in R$, then

$$\omega_{\bar{x}_0}(\bar{a}) = f_1(\bar{x}_0)dx_1(\bar{a}) + \ldots + f_n(\bar{x}_0)dx_n(\bar{a})$$
$$= f_1(\bar{x}_0)a_1 + \ldots + f_n(\bar{x}_0)a_n \tag{4}$$

Since $f_1(\bar{x}_0),\ldots,f_n(\bar{x}_0)$ are real numbers, $\omega_{\bar{x}_0}$ is a real-valued function on R^n. $\omega_{\bar{x}_0}$ is a linear function because

$$\omega_{\bar{x}_0}(\bar{a}+\bar{b}) = f_1(\bar{x}_0)(a_1+b_1) + \ldots + f_n(\bar{x}_0)(a_n+b_n)$$
$$= f_1(\bar{x}_0)a_1 + \ldots + f_n(\bar{x}_0)a_n + f_1(\bar{x}_0)b_1$$
$$+ \ldots + f_n(\bar{x}_0)b_n \tag{5}$$
$$= \omega_{\bar{x}_0}(\bar{a}) + \omega_{\bar{x}_0}(\bar{b})$$
$$\omega_{\bar{x}_0}(\alpha\bar{a}) = f_1(\bar{x}_0)\alpha a_1 + \ldots + f_n(\bar{x}_0)\alpha a_n$$
$$= \alpha\left[f_1(\bar{x}_0)a_1 + \ldots + f_n(\bar{x}_0)a_n\right] \tag{6}$$
$$= \alpha\omega_{\bar{x}_0}(\bar{a})$$

2. $\omega_{\bar{x}_0}$ is a real-valued linear function on R^n. Any vector $\bar{a} \in R^n$ can be represented

$$\bar{a} = a_1 \bar{e}_1 + \ldots + a_n \bar{e}_n \tag{7}$$

Here $a_1, \ldots a_n$ are components of $\bar{a}$ and $\bar{e}_1, \ldots, \bar{e}_n$ are base vectors of R^n. Since $\omega_{\bar{x}_0}$ is a linear real-valued function

$$\begin{aligned}
\omega_{\bar{x}_0}(\bar{a}) &= \omega_{\bar{x}_0}(a_1 \bar{e}_1 + \ldots + a_n \bar{e}_n) \\
&= a_1 \omega_{\bar{x}_0}(\bar{e}_1) + \ldots + a_n \omega_{\bar{x}_0}(\bar{e}_n)
\end{aligned} \tag{8}$$

For a fixed $\bar{x}_0$, $\omega_{\bar{x}_0}(\bar{e}_1), \ldots, \omega_{\bar{x}_0}(\bar{e}_n)$ are real numbers.

Hence,

$$\omega_{\bar{x}_0}(\bar{a}) = f_1(\bar{x}_0)dx_1(\bar{a}) + \ldots + f_n(\bar{x}_0)dx_n(\bar{a}) \tag{9}$$

for all $\bar{a} \in R^n$.

● **PROBLEM** 23-64

Let ω, μ, ν be differential one-forms defined in a region D of R^n, and let f and g be real-valued functions defined in D.

1. Show that

$$f\omega + g\mu \tag{1}$$

is a one-form defined in D.

2. Show that

$$(f\omega + g\mu) \wedge \nu = f\omega \wedge \nu + g\mu \wedge \nu \tag{2}$$

Solution: 1. Both ω and μ are differential one-forms. For each $\bar{x} \in D$ we have

$$\omega_{\bar{x}} = f_1(\bar{x})dx_1 + \ldots + f_n(\bar{x})dx_n \tag{3}$$

$$\mu_{\bar{x}} = g_1(\bar{x})dx_1 + \ldots + g_n(\bar{x})dx_n \tag{4}$$

The linear combination is

$$f(\bar{x})\omega_{\bar{x}} + g(\bar{x})\mu_{\bar{x}}$$

$$= \left[f(\overline{x}) f_1(\overline{x}) + g(\overline{x}) g_1(\overline{x}) \right] dx_1 + \ldots + \left[f(\overline{x}) f_n(\overline{x}) + g(\overline{x}) g_n(\overline{x}) \right] dx_n$$

$$= \ell_1(\overline{x}) dx_1 + \ell_2(\overline{x}) dx_2 + \ldots + \ell_n(\overline{x}) dx_n \qquad (5)$$

where
$$\ell_k(\overline{x}) = f(\overline{x}) f_k(\overline{x}) + g(\overline{x}) g_k(\overline{x}) \qquad (6)$$

$$k = 1, 2, \ldots, n$$

Eq.(5) represents a differential one-form. Since all functions f, g, f_k, g_k are defined in D, this new one-form is also defined in D.

2. Both sides of eq.(2) consist of linear combinations of $dx_i \wedge dx_j$ where $i, j = 1, \ldots, n$, $i < j$.

On the left-hand side, the coefficient of $dx_i \wedge dx_j$ is

$$(ff_i + gg_i) h_j dx_i \wedge dx_j + (ff_j + gg_j) h_i dx_j \wedge dx_i$$

$$= \left[h_j (ff_i + gg_i) - h_i (ff_j + gg_j) \right] dx_i \wedge dx_j \qquad (7)$$

h_i are the coefficients of $\nu_{\overline{x}}$

$$\nu_{\overline{x}} = h_1(\overline{x}) dx_1 + \ldots + h_n(\overline{x}) dx_n \qquad (8)$$

On the other hand the coefficients of $dx_i \wedge dx_j$ on the right-hand side are

$$ff_i h_j dx_i \wedge dx_j + ff_j h_i dx_j \wedge dx_i + gg_i h_j dx_i \wedge dx_j$$

$$+ gg_j h_i dx_j \wedge dx_i \qquad (9)$$

$$= \left[ff_i h_j + gg_i h_j - ff_j h_i - gg_j h_i \right] dx_i \wedge dx_j$$

The coefficients are equal. That proves eq.(2).

● **PROBLEM** 23-65

Let ω be a real-valued function of pairs $(\overline{a}, \overline{b})$ of vectors $\overline{a}, \overline{b} \in R^3$ such that

$$\omega(\overline{a}, \overline{b}) = -\omega(\overline{b}, \overline{a}) \qquad (1)$$

ω is linear in both arguments.

Show that there exists a vector $\overline{c}_\omega \in R^3$ such that

$$\omega(\overline{a}, \overline{b}) = \det(\overline{a}, \overline{b}, \overline{c}_\omega) \qquad (2)$$

for all vectors $\overline{a}, \overline{b} \in R^3$.

<u>Solution:</u> Let $\bar{e}_1, \bar{e}_2, \bar{e}_3$ be the base vectors in R^3,

$$\bar{e}_1 = (1,0,0)$$
$$\bar{e}_2 = (0,1,0) \tag{3}$$
$$\bar{e}_3 = (0,0,1)$$

Then,

$$\bar{a} = a_1\bar{e}_1 + a_2\bar{e}_2 + a_3\bar{e}_3$$
$$\bar{b} = b_1\bar{e}_1 + b_2\bar{e}_2 + b_3\bar{e}_3 \tag{4}$$

Since $\omega(\bar{a},\bar{b})$ is linear in $\bar{a}$ and $\bar{b}$ and antisymmetric, we have

$$\begin{aligned}
\omega(\bar{a},\bar{b}) &= \omega(a_1\bar{e}_1 + a_2\bar{e}_2 + a_3\bar{e}_3, b_1\bar{e}_1 + b_2\bar{e}_2 + b_3\bar{e}_3) \\
&= a_1b_2\,\omega(\bar{e}_1,\bar{e}_2) + a_1b_3\omega(\bar{e}_1,\bar{e}_3) \\
&\quad + a_2b_1\omega(\bar{e}_2,\bar{e}_1) + a_2b_3\omega(\bar{e}_2,\bar{e}_3) \\
&\quad + a_3b_1\omega(\bar{e}_3,\bar{e}_1) + a_3b_2\omega(\bar{e}_3,\bar{e}_2) \\
&= (a_1b_2 - a_2b_1)\omega(\bar{e}_1,\bar{e}_2) + (a_1b_3 - a_3b_1)\omega(\bar{e}_1,\bar{e}_3) \\
&\quad + (a_2b_3 - a_3b_2)\omega(\bar{e}_2,\bar{e}_3)
\end{aligned} \tag{5}$$

We shall denote

$$\omega(\bar{e}_2,\bar{e}_3) = c_1$$
$$\omega(\bar{e}_3,\bar{e}_1) = c_2$$
$$\omega(\bar{e}_1,\bar{e}_2) = c_3$$

Hence, eq.(5) can be written in the form

$$\begin{aligned}
\omega(\bar{a},\bar{b}) &= (a_1b_2 - a_2b_1)c_3 + (a_3b_1 - a_1b_3)c_2 + (a_2b_3 - a_3b_2)c_1 \\
&= \det \begin{pmatrix} a_1 & b_1 & c_1 \\ a_2 & b_2 & c_2 \\ a_3 & b_3 & c_3 \end{pmatrix} \\
&= \det(\bar{a},\bar{b},\bar{c}_\omega)
\end{aligned} \tag{6}$$

We wrote $\bar{c}_\omega$ to indicate that $\bar{c}$ depends on ω.

Compute

$$2dx_1 \wedge dx_3 \wedge dx_4 + 3dx_1 \wedge dx_2 \wedge dx_4(\bar{a},\bar{b},\bar{c}) \quad (1)$$

where

$$\bar{a} = (0,1,0,2)$$
$$\bar{b} = (1,1,1,-1) \quad (2)$$
$$\bar{c} = (1,0,2,0)$$

Solution: We shall first give the definition of the basic p-form in R^n. Let $(a_1,a_2,\ldots,a_p)$ be an ordered set of vectors in R^n, where p 1. Then

$$dx_{i_1} \wedge dx_{i_2} \wedge \ldots \wedge dx_{i_p}(\bar{a}_1,\ldots,\bar{a}_p)$$
$$= \det\left[dx_{i_k}(\bar{a}_j)\right]_{\substack{k=1,\ldots,p \\ j=1,\ldots,0}} \quad (3)$$

Eq.(3) defines the basic p-forms in R^n.

In problem 23-58, we defined a differential two-form

$$dx_i \wedge dx_j(\bar{a},\bar{b}) = \det\begin{pmatrix} dx_i(\bar{a}) & dx_i(\bar{b}) \\ dx_j(\bar{a}) & dx_j(\bar{b}) \end{pmatrix} \quad (4)$$

Eq.(4) is a special case of eq.(3) for p = 2.

We shall evaluate the components of eq.(1)

$$dx_1 \wedge dx_3 \wedge dx_4(\bar{a},\bar{b},\bar{c}) = \det\begin{pmatrix} dx_1(\bar{a}) & dx_1(\bar{b}) & dx_1(\bar{c}) \\ dx_3(\bar{a}) & dx_3(\bar{b}) & dx_3(\bar{c}) \\ dx_4(\bar{a}) & dx_4(\bar{b}) & dx_4(\bar{c}) \end{pmatrix}$$

$$= \det\begin{pmatrix} 0 & 1 & 1 \\ 0 & 1 & 2 \\ 2 & -1 & 0 \end{pmatrix} = 2 \quad (5)$$

$$dx_1 \wedge dx_2 \wedge dx_4(\bar{a},\bar{b},\bar{c}) = \det\begin{pmatrix} dx_1(\bar{a}) & dx_1(\bar{b}) & dx_1(\bar{c}) \\ dx_2(\bar{a}) & dx_2(\bar{b}) & dx_2(\bar{c}) \\ dx_4(\bar{a}) & dx_4(\bar{b}) & dx_4(\bar{c}) \end{pmatrix}$$

$$= \begin{vmatrix} 0 & 1 & 1 \\ 1 & 1 & 0 \\ 2 & -1 & 0 \end{vmatrix} = -3 \qquad (6)$$

Hence,

$$2dx_1 \wedge dx_3 \wedge dx_4 + 3dx_1 \wedge dx_2 \wedge dx_4 (\bar{a}, \bar{b}, \bar{c})$$
$$= 2 \cdot 2 + 3 \cdot (-3) = -5 \qquad (7)$$

PROPERTIES OF p-FORMS, INTEGRALS OF ONE-FORMS AND p-FORMS

● PROBLEM 23-67

Consider the following theorems concerning determinants.

Theorem 1

    If two rows or two columns of a square matrix A are identical, then

$$\det A = 0.$$

Theorem 2

    If matrix B is obtained from a square matrix A by the interchange of two rows or two columns, then

$$\det A = -\det B \qquad (1)$$

Using the above, what properties of p-forms can we establish?

Write the general differential p-form.

Solution: If two rows of a square matrix A are identical, then $\det A = 0$. Therefore, if for some i_r and i_s, $i_r = i_s$, $r, s < p$, then

$$dx_{i_1} \wedge \ldots \wedge dx_{i_r} \wedge \ldots \wedge dx_{i_s} \wedge \ldots \wedge dx_{i_p} (\bar{a}_1, \ldots, \bar{a}_p)$$

$$= \det \left[dx_{i_k} (\bar{a}_j) \right]_{\substack{k=1,\ldots,p \\ j=1,\ldots,p}} = 0 \qquad (2)$$

A basic p-form with a repeated factor is zero.

By interchanging the rows, we can change the sign of the determinant. Therefore, the interchange of two factors in a basic p-form changes the sign of the form.

Using both properties, we can write the general p-form as

$$\omega^p = \sum_{i_1 < i_2 < \ldots < i_p} f_{i_1 \ldots i_p} dx_{i_1} \wedge \ldots \wedge dx_{i_p} \tag{3}$$

where $\quad 1 \le i_1 < i_2 \ldots < i_p \le n$

Let us note that if $p > n$, then ω^p is identically zero.

● **PROBLEM** 23-68

Consider a differential p-form ω^p and a differential q-form ω_q in R^n.

$$\omega^p = \sum_{i_1 < \ldots < i_p} f_{i_1 \ldots i_p} dx_{i_1} \wedge \ldots \wedge dx_{i_p} \tag{1}$$

$$\omega^q = \sum_{k_1 < \ldots < k_q} g_{k_1 \ldots k_q} dx_{k_1} \wedge \ldots \wedge dx_{k_q} \tag{2}$$

The exterior product $\omega^p \wedge \omega^q$ is defined by

$$\omega^p \wedge \omega^q = \sum f_{i_1 \ldots i_p} g_{k_1 \ldots k_q} dx_{i_1} \wedge \ldots \wedge dx_{ip} \wedge dx_{k_1} \wedge \ldots \wedge dx_{k_q} \tag{3}$$

Show that $\quad \omega^p \wedge \omega^q = (-1)^{pq} \omega^q \wedge \omega^p \tag{4}$

The interchange of two factors of a form changes its sign. A form with a repeated factor is zero. Based on this information, derive the formula for the number of terms in eq.(3).

Solution: In eq.(3), we have the term

$$dx_{i_1} \wedge \ldots \wedge dx_{i_p} \wedge dx_{k_1} \wedge \ldots \wedge dx_{k_q} \tag{5}$$

Making p interchanges with all the terms $dx_{i_1}, dx_{i_2}, \ldots dx_{i_p}$ and the term dx_{k_1}, we obtain

$$dx_{i_1} \wedge \ldots \wedge dx_{i_p} \wedge dx_{k_1} \wedge \ldots \wedge dx_{k_q}$$
$$\tag{6}$$
$$= (-1)^p dx_{k_1} \wedge dx_{i_1} \wedge \ldots \wedge dx_{i_p} \wedge dx_{k_2} \wedge \ldots \wedge dx_{k_q}$$

Performing the same operation on $dx_{k_2}, dx_{k_3}, \ldots, dx_{k_q}$, we obtain

$$dx_{i_1} \wedge \ldots \wedge dx_{i_p} \wedge dx_{k_1} \wedge \ldots \wedge dx_{k_q}$$

$$= (-1)^{pq} dx_{k_1} \wedge \ldots \wedge dx_{k_q} \wedge dx_{i_1} \wedge \ldots \wedge dx_{i_p} \qquad (7)$$

Thus,

$$\omega^p \wedge \omega^q = (-1)^{pq} \omega^q \wedge \omega^p \qquad (8)$$

Now, let us leave differential forms for a second to introduce a simple result from Probability. Consider taking m objects, or m numbers out of n numbers. The number of possibilities, or combinations is given by

$$\binom{n}{m} = \frac{n!}{m!(n-m)!} \qquad (9)$$

where, of course, $n! = n(n-1)(n-2) \ldots 3 \cdot 2 \cdot 1$.

Now, returning to eq.(3), we see that each term in the sum is one possibility and m = p+q. We conclude that

$$\binom{n}{p+q} \qquad (10)$$

is the number of terms in eq.(3)

● **PROBLEM** 23-69

Compute
$$\int_C \omega_{\overline{x}} \qquad (1)$$

where
$$\omega_{\overline{x}} = x_1^2 \, dx_1 + x_2^2 \, dx_2 + x_3^2 \, dx_3 \qquad (2)$$

and C is the helix parametrically described by

$$\overline{x}(t) = (\cos t, \sin t, t)$$
$$0 \leq t \leq 2\pi \qquad (3)$$

Solution: We shall define the integral of the one-form $\omega_{\overline{x}}$ over a curve C. Let $\omega_{\overline{x}}$ be a 1-form defined in $D \subset R^3$

$$\omega_{\overline{x}} = F_1(\overline{x}) dx_1 + F_2(\overline{x}) dx_2 + F_3(\overline{x}) dx_3 \qquad (4)$$

and let C be a differentiable curve lying in D given by $\overline{x} = \overline{x}(t)$, $a \le t \le b$. The vector tangent to C is

$$\overline{T}(t) = \frac{d\overline{x}}{dt} \tag{5}$$

The integral of the 1-form $\omega_{\overline{x}}$ over C is defined by

$$\int_C \omega_{\overline{x}} = \int_a^b \overline{F}(\overline{x}(t)) \cdot \frac{d\overline{x}}{dt}\, dt \tag{6}$$

Substituting eqs.(2) and (3) into eq.(6) results in

$$\int_C \omega_{\overline{x}} = \int_0^{2\pi} \left[x_1^2 \frac{dx_1}{dt} + x_2^2 \frac{dx_2}{dt} + x_3^2 \frac{dx_3}{dt} \right] dt$$

$$= \int_0^{2\pi} \left[\cos^2 t(-\sin t) + \sin^2 t \cos t + t^2 \right] dt$$

$$= \int_0^{2\pi} -\sin t \cos^2 t\, dt + \int_0^{2\pi} \sin^2 t \cos t\, dt + \int_0^{2\pi} t^2 dt$$

$$= 0 + 0 + \left. \frac{t^3}{3} \right|_0^{2\pi} = \frac{8\pi^3}{3} \tag{7}$$

● **PROBLEM 23-70**

Compute

$$\int_C \omega_{\overline{x}} \tag{1}$$

where

$$\omega_{\overline{x}} = (1 \cdot x_1)^3 dx_1 + (2x_2)^3 dx_2 + \ldots + (nx_n)^3 dx_n \tag{2}$$

and C is given by

$$\overline{x}(t) = (t, t, \ldots, t) \quad \text{for } 0 \le t \le 1 \tag{3}$$

Solution: Applying the definition of the integral of the one-form over C, we obtain

$$\int_C \omega_{\overline{x}} = \int_0^1 \left[F_1(\overline{x}(t)) \frac{dx_1}{dt} + F_2(\overline{x}(t)) \frac{dx_2}{dt} + \ldots + F_n(\overline{x}(t)) \frac{dx_n}{dt} \right] dt$$

$$= \int_0^1 \left[1^3 x_1^3 \frac{dx_1}{dt} + 2^3 x_2^3 \frac{dx_2}{dt} + \ldots + n^3 x_n^3 \frac{dx_n}{dt} \right] dt$$

$$= \int_0^1 \left[1^3 t^3 + 2^3 t^3 + \ldots + n^3 t^3 \right] dt \qquad (4)$$

$$= (1^3 + 2^3 + \ldots + n^3) \left. \frac{t^4}{4} \right|_0^1$$

$$= \frac{n^2(n+1)^2}{16}$$

● PROBLEM 23-71

Show that the definition of the integral of a p-form is in agreement with that of a one-form given in Problem 23-69.

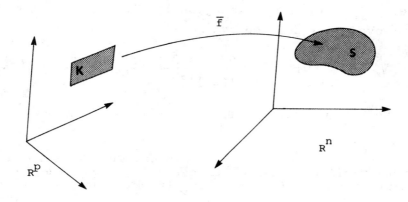

Fig. 1

Solution: First we shall define the integral of a different-ial p-form in R^n. Let ω^p be a differential p-form in R^n and let K be a closed bounded rectangle in R^p.

Furthermore, let $\bar{f} : R^p \to R^n$ be continuously different-iable on K.

S is the image of K, $S = \bar{f}(K)$.

If $\bar{u} \in K$, then $\bar{u}$ is

$$\bar{u} = (u_1, \ldots , u_p) \qquad (1)$$

and $\bar{f}(\bar{u}) \in S$ and

$$\bar{f}(\bar{u}) = (f_1(\bar{u}), \ldots , f_n(\bar{u})) \qquad (2)$$

We can apply ω^p at a point $\overline{f}(\overline{u})$ to the set of vectors

$$\frac{\partial \overline{f}}{\partial u_1}(\overline{u}), \quad \ldots, \quad \frac{\partial \overline{f}}{\partial u_p}(\overline{u}) \tag{3}$$

to obtain

$$\omega^p_{\overline{f}(\overline{u})}\left[\frac{\partial \overline{f}}{\partial u_1}(\overline{u}), \quad \ldots, \quad \frac{\partial \overline{f}}{\partial u_p}(\overline{u})\right] \tag{4}$$

If Ω is a grid over K with corner points $\overline{u}_1, \ldots, \overline{u}_\alpha$ and rectangles $K_1, \ldots, K_\alpha$, we can form the sum

$$\sum_{i=1}^{\alpha} \omega^p_{\overline{f}(\overline{u}_i)}\left[\frac{\partial \overline{f}}{\partial u_1}(\overline{u}_i), \ldots, \frac{\partial \overline{f}}{\partial u_p}(\overline{u}_i)\right] V(K_i) \tag{5}$$

Here, $V(K_i)$ is the p-dimensional volume of K_i. The integral of ω^p over S is defined by

$$\int_S \omega^p = \lim_{D(\Omega) \to 0} \sum_{i=1}^{\alpha} \omega^p_{\overline{f}(\overline{u}_i)}\left[\frac{\partial \overline{f}}{\partial u_1}(\overline{u}_i), \ldots, \frac{\partial \overline{f}}{\partial u_p}(\overline{u}_i)\right] V(K_i) \tag{6}$$

We assume that the limit exists in the Riemann sense.

If ω^p has continuous coefficient functions and g is continuously differentiable, then the function in eq.(4) is continuous on K. In this case, the Riemann integral exists and

$$\int_S \omega^p = \int_K \omega^p_{\overline{f}}\left[\frac{\partial \overline{f}}{\partial u_1}, \ldots, \frac{\partial \overline{f}}{\partial u_p}\right] dV \tag{7}$$

For $p = 1$ we have

$$K = [a,b] \ni t \to \overline{f}(t) \in S \subset R^n \tag{8}$$

$\overline{f}(t)$ is a curve in R^n.

If

$$\omega'_{\overline{x}} = F_1(\overline{x})dx_1 + \ldots + F_n(\overline{x})dx_n \tag{9}$$

then the definition given in eq.(7) reduces to

$$\int_S \omega'_{\overline{f}(t)} = \int_a^b \omega'_{\overline{f}(t)}\left[\frac{\partial \overline{f}}{\partial t}\right] dt$$

$$= \int_a^b \left[F_1(\overline{f}(t)) \frac{df_1}{dt} + \ldots + F_n(\overline{f}(t)) \frac{df_n}{dt} \right] dt \qquad (10)$$

which is eq.(6) of Problem 23-69. The definition given in eq.(7) can be extended to the more general regions other than closed bounded rectangles in R^p. Note that instead of writing

$$\overbrace{\int \cdots}^{p \text{ times}} \int_K \frac{\omega^p}{\overline{f}} \left(\frac{\partial \overline{f}}{\partial u_1}, \ldots, \frac{\partial \overline{f}}{\partial u_p} \right) dV$$

we use the shorter notation $\displaystyle\int_K \frac{\omega^p}{\overline{f}}$

● PROBLEM 23-72

Let ω^2 be a two-form

$$\frac{\omega^2}{x} = F_1(\overline{x}) dx_2 \wedge dx_3 + F_2(\overline{x}) dx_3 \wedge dx_1 + F_3(\overline{x}) dx_1 \wedge dx_2 \qquad (1)$$

with continuous coefficients in R^3. Let $\overline{f} : R^2 \rightarrow R^3$ be continuously differentiable on some closed bounded rectangle $K \subset R^2$. Derive the expression for

$$\int_S \omega^2 \qquad (2)$$

where
$$S = \overline{f}(K) \qquad (3)$$

Solution: Recall that

$$dx_i \wedge dx_j(\overline{a}, \overline{b}) = \det \begin{pmatrix} dx_i(\overline{a}) & dx_i(\overline{b}) \\ dx_j(\overline{a}) & dx_j(\overline{b}) \end{pmatrix} \qquad (4)$$

so that

$$\frac{\omega^2}{\overline{f}(\overline{u})} \left(\frac{\partial \overline{f}}{\partial u_1}, \frac{\partial \overline{f}}{\partial u_2} \right)$$

$$= F_1(\overline{f}(\overline{u})) \det \begin{pmatrix} dx_2\left(\frac{\partial \overline{f}}{\partial u_1}\right) & dx_2\left(\frac{\partial \overline{f}}{\partial u_2}\right) \\ dx_3\left(\frac{\partial \overline{f}}{\partial u_1}\right) & dx_3\left(\frac{\partial \overline{f}}{\partial u_2}\right) \end{pmatrix}$$

1225

$$+ F_2(\overline{f}(\overline{u}))\det \begin{pmatrix} dx_3\left(\dfrac{\partial\overline{f}}{\partial u_1}\right) & dx_3\left(\dfrac{\partial\overline{f}}{\partial u_2}\right) \\ dx_1\left(\dfrac{\partial\overline{f}}{\partial u_1}\right) & dx_1\left(\dfrac{\partial\overline{f}}{\partial u_2}\right) \end{pmatrix} \qquad (5)$$

$$+ F_3(\overline{f}(\overline{u}))\det \begin{pmatrix} dx_1\left(\dfrac{\partial\overline{f}}{\partial u_1}\right) & dx_1\left(\dfrac{\partial\overline{f}}{\partial u_2}\right) \\ dx_2\left(\dfrac{\partial\overline{f}}{\partial u_1}\right) & dx_2\left(\dfrac{\partial\overline{f}}{\partial u_2}\right) \end{pmatrix}$$

$$= F_1(\overline{f}(\overline{u}))\,\frac{\partial(f_2,f_3)}{\partial(u_1,u_2)} + F_2(\overline{f}(\overline{u}))\,\frac{\partial(f_3,f_1)}{\partial(u_1,u_2)}$$

$$+ F_3(\overline{f}(\overline{u}))\,\frac{\partial(f_1,f_2)}{\partial(u_1,u_2)}$$

Therefore, the integral $\displaystyle\int_S \omega^2$ is

$$\int_S \omega^2 = \int_S F_1 dx_2 \wedge dx_3 + F_2 dx_3 \wedge dx_1 + F_3 dx_1 \wedge dx_2$$

$$= \int_K \left[F_1(\overline{f}(u_1,u_2))\frac{\partial(f_2,f_3)}{\partial(u_1,u_2)} + F_2(\overline{f}(u_1,u_2))\frac{\partial(f_3,f_1)}{\partial(u_1,u_2)} \right.$$

$$\left. + F_3(\overline{f}(u_1,u_2))\frac{\partial(f_1,f_2)}{\partial(u_1,u_2)} \right] du_1 du_2 \qquad (6)$$

● **PROBLEM** 23-73

Compute $\qquad\qquad \displaystyle\int_S \omega^2 \qquad\qquad\qquad$ (1)

where
$$\omega^2 = -2dx_2 \wedge dx_1 + dx_1 \wedge dx_3 \qquad (2)$$

K is the subset of R^2, $K \subset R^2$ such that

$$K = \{(u_1,u_2) : 0 \le u_1 \le 1,\ 0 \le u_2 \le \pi\} \qquad (3)$$

and S is the image of K under

$$\overline{f}(u_1,u_2) = (u_1\cos u_2,\ u_1\sin u_2, u_2) \qquad (4)$$

Solution: To evaluate integral (1), we will use the results of Problem 23-71.

Hence,

$$\omega^2 = 0dx_2 \wedge dx_3 - dx_3 \wedge dx_1 + 2dx_1 \wedge dx_2 \tag{5}$$

and

$$F_1 = 0, \quad F_2 = -1, \quad F_3 = 2$$

The appropriate Jacobians are

$$\frac{\partial(f_2, f_3)}{\partial(u_1, u_2)} = \det \begin{pmatrix} \sin u_2, & u_1 \cos u_2 \\ 0 & 1 \end{pmatrix} = \sin u_2 \tag{6}$$

$$\frac{\partial(f_3, f_1)}{\partial(u_1, u_2)} = \det \begin{pmatrix} 0 & 1 \\ \cos u_2, & -u_1 \sin u_2 \end{pmatrix} = -\cos u_2 \tag{7}$$

$$\frac{\partial(f_1, f_2)}{\partial(u_1, u_2)} = \det \begin{pmatrix} \cos u_2, & -u_1 \sin u_2 \\ \sin u_2, & u_1 \cos u_2 \end{pmatrix} = u_1 \tag{8}$$

Consequently,

$$\int_S \omega^2 = \int_{u_2=0}^{\pi} \int_{u_1=0}^{1} \left[(-1)(-\cos u_2) + 2u_1 \right] du_1 du_2 \tag{9}$$

$$= \int_{u_2=0}^{\pi} (\cos u_2 + 1) du_2 = \pi$$

● **PROBLEM 23-74**

Consider ω^3, a differential three-form in R^3.

$$\omega_{\bar{x}}^3 = g(\bar{x}) dx_1 \wedge dx_2 \wedge dx_3 \tag{1}$$

Let $\bar{f}(\bar{x})$ be a differentiable function such that

$$\bar{f} : R^3 \to R^3 \tag{2}$$

Show that

$$\omega_{\bar{f}(\bar{u})}^3 \left(\frac{\partial \bar{f}}{\partial u_1}, \frac{\partial \bar{f}}{\partial u_2}, \frac{\partial \bar{f}}{\partial u_3} \right) = g(\bar{f}(\bar{u})) \frac{\partial(f_1, f_2, f_3)}{\partial(u_1, u_2, u_3)} \tag{3}$$

Compute

$$\int_S dx_1 \wedge dx_2 \wedge dx_3 \tag{4}$$

where S is the image of the three-dimensional rectangle

$$K = \{(u_1, u_2, u_3) : 0 \le u_1 \le 1, 0 \le u_2 \le 1, 0 \le u_3 \le 1\} \tag{5}$$

under

$$\bar{f}(u_1, u_2, u_3) = (u_1, u_2^2, u_3^3) \tag{6}$$

Solution: We have

$$\underset{\overline{f}(\overline{u})}{\overset{3}{\omega}} \left(\frac{\partial \overline{f}}{\partial u_1}, \frac{\partial \overline{f}}{\partial u_2}, \frac{\partial \overline{f}}{\partial u_3} \right)$$

$$= g(\overline{f}(\overline{u})) dx_1 \wedge dx_2 \wedge dx_3 \left(\frac{\partial \overline{f}}{\partial u_1}, \frac{\partial \overline{f}}{\partial u_2}, \frac{\partial \overline{f}}{\partial u_3} \right)$$

$$= g(\overline{f}(\overline{u})) \det \begin{vmatrix} \dfrac{\partial f_1}{\partial u_1} & \dfrac{\partial f_2}{\partial u_2} & \dfrac{\partial f_3}{\partial u_3} \\[2mm] \dfrac{\partial f_2}{\partial u_1} & \dfrac{\partial f_2}{\partial u_2} & \dfrac{\partial f_2}{\partial u_3} \\[2mm] \dfrac{\partial f_3}{\partial u_1} & \dfrac{\partial f_3}{\partial u_2} & \dfrac{\partial f_3}{\partial u_3} \end{vmatrix} \tag{7}$$

$$= g(\overline{f}(\overline{u})) \frac{\partial(f_1, f_2, f_3)}{\partial(u_1, u_2, u_3)}$$

To evaluate integral (4), let us first compute the Jacobian

$$\frac{\partial(f_1, f_2, f_3)}{\partial(u_1, u_2, u_3)} = \det \begin{pmatrix} 1 & 0 & 0 \\ 0 & 2u_2 & 0 \\ 0 & 0 & 3u_3^2 \end{pmatrix} = 6u_2 u_3^2 \tag{8}$$

We obtain

$$\int_S dx_1 \wedge dx_2 \wedge dx_3 = \int_K 6u_2 u_3^2 \, dV$$

$$= \int_{u_3=0}^{1} \int_{u_2=0}^{1} \int_{u_1=0}^{1} 6u_2 u_3^2 \, du_1 \, du_2 \, du_3 = 1 \tag{9}$$

EXTERIOR DERIVATIVE

EXTERIOR DIFFERENTIATION, BASIC IDENTITIES, CONSERVATIVE AND SOLENOIDAL FIELDS

● PROBLEM 23-75

Compute $d\omega$, where ω is:

$$\underset{(x_1, x_2, x_3)}{\overset{0}{\omega}} = x_1^2 x_2 + x_2 x_3^2$$

$$\omega^1_{(x_1,x_2)} = x_2{}^2 dx_1 + x_1 x_2 dx_2$$

$$\omega^2_{(x_1,x_2,x_3)} = x_1 x_2 dx_1 \wedge dx_2 + x_2{}^2 x_3 dx_2 \wedge dx_3$$

Solution: We shall define the operation of exterior differentiation. A 0-form is a real-valued function.

Hence,

$$\omega^0_{(x_1,\ldots,x_n)} = f(x_1,\ldots,x_n) \tag{1}$$

and

$$d\omega^0_{(x_1,\ldots,x_n)} = \frac{\partial f}{\partial x_1} dx_1 + \ldots + \frac{\partial f}{\partial x_n} dx_n \tag{2}$$

The exterior derivative of f (or 0-form as we call it) is a 1-form.

If $\quad \omega^1 = F_1 dx_1 + \ldots + F_n dx_n \tag{3}$

is a 1-form with differentiable coefficients $F_1,\ldots,F_n$ then

$$d\omega^1 = (dF_1) \wedge dx_1 + \ldots + (dF_n) \wedge dx_n \tag{4}$$

Note that $d\omega^1$ is a 2-form.

In the same manner, we can define the exterior derivatives of the differential forms of higher order. In general, if ω^p is a p-form, then $d\omega^p$ is the (p+1)-form obtained from ω^p by replacing each coefficient function of ω^p by the 1-form that is its exterior derivative. We obtain

$$d\omega^0 = d(x_1{}^2 x_2 + x_2 x_3{}^2)$$

$$= 2x_1 x_2 dx_1 + (x_1{}^2 + x_3{}^2) dx_2 + 2x_2 x_3 dx_3 \tag{5}$$

$$d\omega^1_{(x_1,x_2)} = d(x_2{}^2 dx_1 + x_1 x_2 dx_2)$$

$$= 2x_2 dx_2 \wedge dx_1 + x_2 dx_1 \wedge dx_2 + x_1 dx_2 \wedge dx_2 \tag{6}$$

$$= -x_2 dx_1 \wedge dx_2$$

$$d\omega^2_{(x_1,x_2,x_3)} = d(x_1 x_2 dx_1 \wedge dx_2 + x_2{}^2 x_3 dx_2 \wedge dx_3)$$

$$\tag{7}$$

$$= (x_2 dx_1 + x_1 dx_2) \wedge dx_1 \wedge dx_2$$

$$+ (2x_2 x_3 dx_2 + x_2^2 dx_3) \wedge dx_2 \wedge dx_3 = 0$$

Let f_1, f_2, f_3 be differentiable functions from R^3 to R, with the same domain. Show that

$$df_1 \wedge df_2 \wedge df_3 = \frac{\partial(f_1, f_2, f_3)}{\partial(x_1, x_2, x_3)} dx_1 \wedge dx_2 \wedge dx_3 \qquad (1)$$

Solution: Since each function is differentiable, we can compute their exterior derivatives

$$df_1 = \frac{\partial f_1}{\partial x_1} dx_1 + \frac{\partial f_1}{\partial x_2} dx_2 + \frac{\partial f_1}{\partial x_3} dx_3 \qquad (2)$$

$$df_2 = \frac{\partial f_2}{\partial x_1} dx_1 + \frac{\partial f_2}{\partial x_2} dx_2 + \frac{\partial f_2}{\partial x_3} dx_3 \qquad (3)$$

$$df_3 = \frac{\partial f_3}{\partial x_1} dx_1 + \frac{\partial f_3}{\partial x_2} dx_2 + \frac{\partial f_3}{\partial x_3} dx_3 \qquad (4)$$

Substituting eqs.(2), (3) and (4) into the differential form we obtain

$$df_1 \wedge df_2 \wedge df_3 = \left(\frac{\partial f_1}{\partial x_1} dx_1 + \frac{\partial f_1}{\partial x_2} dx_2 + \frac{\partial f_1}{\partial x_3} dx_3 \right)$$

$$\wedge \left(\frac{\partial f_2}{\partial x_1} dx_1 + \frac{\partial f_2}{\partial x_2} dx_2 + \frac{\partial f_2}{\partial x_3} dx_3 \right)$$

$$\wedge \left(\frac{\partial f_3}{\partial x_1} dx_1 + \frac{\partial f_3}{\partial x_2} dx_2 + \frac{\partial f_3}{\partial x_3} dx_3 \right)$$

$$= \left[\left(\frac{\partial f_1}{\partial x_1} \frac{\partial f_2}{\partial x_2} - \frac{\partial f_1}{\partial x_2} \frac{\partial f_2}{\partial x_1} \right) dx_1 \wedge dx_2 \right.$$

$$+ \left(\frac{\partial f_1}{\partial x_1} \cdot \frac{\partial f_2}{\partial x_3} - \frac{\partial f_1}{\partial x_3} \frac{\partial f_2}{\partial x_1} \right) dx_1 \wedge dx_3 + \left. \left(\frac{\partial f_1}{\partial x_2} \frac{\partial f_2}{\partial x_3} - \frac{\partial f_1}{\partial x_3} \frac{\partial f_2}{\partial x_2} \right) dx_2 \wedge dx_3 \right]$$

$$\wedge \left(\frac{\partial f_3}{\partial x_1} dx_1 + \frac{\partial f_3}{\partial x_2} dx_2 + \frac{\partial f_3}{\partial x_3} dx_3 \right)$$

$$= \left(\frac{\partial f_1}{\partial x_3} \frac{\partial f_2}{\partial x_1} \frac{\partial f_3}{\partial x_2} - \frac{\partial f_1}{\partial x_1} \frac{\partial f_2}{\partial x_3} \frac{\partial f_3}{\partial x_2} \right) dx_1 \wedge dx_2 \wedge dx_3$$

$$+ \left(\frac{\partial f_1}{\partial x_1} \frac{\partial f_2}{\partial x_2} \frac{\partial f_3}{\partial x_3} - \frac{\partial f_1}{\partial x_2} \frac{\partial f_2}{\partial x_1} \frac{\partial f_3}{\partial x_3} \right) dx_1 \wedge dx_2 \wedge dx_3$$

$$+ \left(\frac{\partial f_1}{\partial x_2} \frac{\partial f_2}{\partial x_3} \frac{\partial f_3}{\partial x_1} - \frac{\partial f_1}{\partial x_3} \frac{\partial f_2}{\partial x_2} \frac{\partial f_3}{\partial x_1} \right) dx_1 \wedge dx_2 \wedge dx_3$$

$$= \det \begin{vmatrix} \dfrac{\partial f_1}{\partial x_1} & \dfrac{\partial f_1}{\partial x_2} & \dfrac{\partial f_1}{\partial x_3} \\[2mm] \dfrac{\partial f_2}{\partial x_1} & \dfrac{\partial f_2}{\partial x_2} & \dfrac{\partial f_2}{\partial x_3} \\[2mm] \dfrac{\partial f_3}{\partial x_1} & \dfrac{\partial f_3}{\partial x_2} & \dfrac{\partial f_3}{\partial x_3} \end{vmatrix} dx_1 \wedge dx_2 \wedge dx_3$$

$$= \frac{\partial(f_1, f_2, f_3)}{\partial(x_1, x_2, x_3)} \, dx_1 \wedge dx_2 \wedge dx_3 \tag{5}$$

● **PROBLEM** 23-77

Prove the following:

If ω^0 is a zero-form in R^n (i.e. a function in R^n) twice continuously differentiable, then

$$d(d\omega^0) = 0. \tag{1}$$

Solution: Since ω^0 is a zero-form in R^n, we have

$$\omega_{\underline{x}}^0 = f(x_1, \ldots, x_n) \tag{2}$$

The exterior derivative of $\omega_{\underline{x}}^0$ is

$$d\omega_{\underline{x}}^0 = \frac{\partial f}{\partial x_1} \, dx_1 + \ldots + \frac{\partial f}{\partial x_n} \, dx_n \tag{3}$$

$d\omega_{\underline{x}}^0$ is a one-form.

$$d(d\omega^0) = \left[\frac{\partial^2 f}{\partial x_1 \partial x_1} \, dx_1 + \frac{\partial^2 f}{\partial x_2 \partial x_1} \, dx_2 + \ldots + \frac{\partial^2 f}{\partial x_n \partial x_1} \, dx_n \right] \wedge dx_1$$

$$+ \left[\frac{\partial^2 f}{\partial x_1 \partial x_2} \, dx_1 + \frac{\partial^2 f}{\partial x_2 \partial x_2} \, dx_2 + \ldots + \frac{\partial^2 f}{\partial x_n \partial x_2} \, dx_n \right] \tag{4}$$

$$+ \ldots + \left[\frac{\partial^2 f}{\partial x_1 x_n} \, dx_1 + \ldots + \frac{\partial^2 f}{\partial x_n \partial x_n} \, dx_n \right] \wedge dx_n$$

$$= \sum_{i,j=1}^{n} \frac{\partial^2 f}{\partial x_i \partial x_j} \, dx_i \wedge dx_j$$

Since f is twice continuously differentiable

$$\frac{\partial^2 f}{\partial x_i \partial x_j} = \frac{\partial^2 f}{\partial x_j \partial x_i} \tag{5}$$

On the other hand

$$dx_i \wedge dx_j = -dx_j \wedge dx_i \qquad (6)$$

Therefore

$$\frac{\partial^2 f}{\partial x_k \partial x_\ell} dx_k \wedge dx_\ell + \frac{\partial^2 f}{\partial x_\ell \partial x_k} dx_\ell \wedge dx_k$$

$$\qquad (7)$$

$$= \frac{\partial^2 f}{\partial x_k \partial x_\ell} (dx_k \wedge dx_\ell - dx_k \wedge dx_\ell) = 0$$

and

$$d(d\omega^0) = 0 \qquad (8)$$

● **PROBLEM** 23-78

Show that $\qquad d(d\omega^1) = 0 \qquad (1)$

where ω^1 is a one-form in R^n with twice continuously differentiable coefficients.

Solution: Consider ω^1, a one-form in R^n,

$$\underline{\omega^1} = F_1 dx_1 + \ldots + F_n dx_n \qquad (2)$$

The exterior derivative of ω^1 is

$$d\omega^1 = \left[\frac{\partial F_1}{\partial x_1} dx_1 + \ldots + \frac{\partial F_1}{\partial x_n} dx_n \right] \wedge dx_1$$

$$+ \left[\frac{\partial F_2}{\partial x_1} dx_1 + \ldots + \frac{\partial F_2}{\partial x_n} dx_n \right] \wedge dx_2 + \ldots$$

$$+ \left[\frac{\partial F_n}{\partial x_1} dx_1 + \ldots + \frac{\partial F_n}{\partial x_n} dx_n \right] \wedge dx_n$$

$$= \sum_{i,j=1}^{n} \frac{\partial F_j}{\partial x_i} dx_i \wedge dx_j \qquad (3)$$

For the next exterior derivative, we have

$$d(d\omega^1)$$

$$= \sum_{i,j=1}^{n} \left[\frac{\partial^2 F_j}{\partial x_1 \partial x_i} dx_1 + \frac{\partial^2 F_j}{\partial x_2 \partial x_i} dx_2 + \ldots + \frac{\partial^2 F_j}{\partial x_n \partial x_i} dx_n \right] \wedge dx_i \wedge dx_j$$

$$= \sum_{k,i,j=1}^{n} \frac{\partial^2 F_j}{\partial x_k \partial x_i} dx_k \wedge dx_i \wedge dx_j \qquad (4)$$

Since $F(\bar{x})$ is twice continuously differentiable

$$\frac{\partial^2 F_j}{\partial x_k \partial x_i} = \frac{\partial^2 F_j}{\partial x_i \partial x_k} \tag{5}$$

We have shown that

$$dx_k \wedge dx_i \wedge dx_j = -dx_i \wedge dx_k \wedge dx_j \tag{6}$$

Therefore,

$$\frac{\partial^2 F_j}{\partial x_k \partial x_i} dx_k \wedge dx_i \wedge dx_j + \frac{\partial^2 F_j}{\partial x_i \partial x_k} dx_i \wedge dx_k \wedge dx_j = 0 \tag{7}$$

and

$$d(d\omega^1) = 0 \tag{8}$$

In the same manner, we can show that if ω^p is a p-form with twice continuously differentiable coefficients, then

$$d(d\omega^p) = 0. \tag{9}$$

● PROBLEM 23-79

1. Show that $d(d\omega^0) = 0$ is equivalent to curl grad $f = \bar{0}$.

2. Show that $d(d\omega^1) = 0$ is equivalent to the relation div curl $\bar{f} = 0$.

Solution: 1. Let

$$\omega^0 = f(x_1, x_2, x_3) \tag{1}$$

Then,

$$d(d\omega^0) = \left(\frac{\partial^2 f}{\partial x_1 \partial x_2} - \frac{\partial^2 f}{\partial x_2 \partial x_1} \right) dx_1 \wedge dx_2$$

$$+ \left(\frac{\partial^2 f}{\partial x_3 \partial x_1} - \frac{\partial^2 f}{\partial x_1 \partial x_3} \right) dx_3 \wedge dx_1 + \left(\frac{\partial^2 f}{\partial x_2 \partial x_3} - \frac{\partial^2 f}{\partial x_3 \partial x_2} \right) dx_2 \wedge dx_3 \tag{2}$$

$$= 0$$

On the other hand,

$$\text{curl grad } f = \left(\frac{\partial}{\partial x_1}, \frac{\partial}{\partial x_2}, \frac{\partial}{\partial x_3} \right) \times \left(\frac{\partial f}{\partial x_1}, \frac{\partial f}{\partial x_2}, \frac{\partial f}{\partial x_3} \right)$$

$$= \left(\frac{\partial^2 f}{\partial x_2 \partial x_3} - \frac{\partial^2 f}{\partial x_3 \partial x_2}, \frac{\partial^2 f}{\partial x_3 \partial x_1} - \frac{\partial^2 f}{\partial x_1 \partial x_3}, \frac{\partial^2 f}{\partial x_1 \partial x_2} - \frac{\partial^2 f}{\partial x_2 \partial x_1} \right) = \bar{0} \tag{3}$$

The components of curl grad f are the coefficient functions of $d(d\omega^0)$. Thus, both conditions $d(d\omega^0) = 0$ and curl grad f = $\bar{0}$ are equivalent.

2. Consider a vector field $\bar{f}$

$$\bar{f} = (f_1, f_2, f_3) \tag{4}$$

and a differential one-form

$$\omega^1 = f_1 dx_1 + f_2 dx_2 + f_3 dx_3 \tag{5}$$

We have

$$d(d\omega^1) = \sum_{k,i,j=1}^{3} \frac{\partial^2 f_j}{\partial x_k \partial x_i} dx_k \wedge dx_i \wedge dx_j \tag{6}$$

$$= \left(\frac{\partial^2 f_3}{\partial x_1 \partial x_2} - \frac{\partial^2 f_2}{\partial x_1 \partial x_3} + \frac{\partial^2 f_1}{\partial x_2 \partial x_3} - \frac{\partial^2 f_3}{\partial x_2 \partial x_1} + \frac{\partial^2 f_2}{\partial x_3 \partial x_1} - \frac{\partial^2 f_1}{\partial x_3 \partial x_2} \right) dx_1 \wedge dx_2 \wedge dx_3$$

$$= 0$$

On the other hand

$$\text{div curl } \bar{f} = \frac{\partial^2 f_3}{\partial x_1 \partial x_2} - \frac{\partial^2 f_3}{\partial x_2 \partial x_1} + \frac{\partial^2 f_1}{\partial x_2 \partial x_3} - \frac{\partial^2 f_1}{\partial x_3 \partial x_2} + \frac{\partial^2 f_2}{\partial x_3 \partial x_1} - \frac{\partial^2 f_2}{\partial x_1 \partial x_3}$$

$$= 0 \tag{7}$$

Hence, both statements div curl $\bar{f} = 0$ and $d(d\omega^1) = 0$ are equivalent.

● **PROBLEM 23-80**

1. Find an example of a one-form in R^3 such that there is no zero-form ω^0 for which

$$d\omega^0 = \omega^1 \tag{1}$$

2. Is it possible that for a two-form ω^2 in R^3 a one-form ω^1 in R^3 such that

$$d\omega^1 = \omega^2 \tag{2}$$

does not exist?

Solution: 1. ω^1 is a one-form in R^3, hence

$$\omega^1 = F_1 dx_1 + F_2 dx_2 + F_3 dx_3 \tag{3}$$

We want to find $\omega^0 = f(x_1, x_2, x_3)$ such that

$$d\omega^0 = \frac{\partial f}{\partial x_1} dx_1 + \frac{\partial f}{\partial x_2} dx_2 + \frac{\partial f}{\partial x_3} dx_3$$

$$= F_1 dx_1 + F_2 dx_2 + F_3 dx_3$$

(4)

Having $\overline{F} = (F_1, F_2, F_3)$, we want to find f such that

$$\overline{F} = \text{grad } f \qquad (5)$$

It is not always possible to find such an f.

Eq.(5) is one of the properties of a conservative vector field.

A continuously differentiable vector field $\overline{F}$ is conservative if, and only if, it is the gradient of a scalar function.

An equivalent condition is

$$\text{curl } \overline{F} = \overline{0} \qquad (6)$$

Therefore, if curl $\overline{F} \neq \overline{0}$, then no scalar function would satisfy the condition grad $f = \overline{F}$.

For example, if

$$\overline{F} = (x_1 x_2, 0, 0) \qquad (7)$$

then

$$\text{curl } \overline{F} = (0, 0, -x\ ) \neq \overline{0} \qquad (8)$$

and f does not exist.

2. Let $\omega^2 = F_1 dx_2 \wedge dx_3 + F_2 dx_3 \wedge dx_1 + F_3 dx_1 \wedge dx_2$ (9)

We want to find ω^1 such that

$$d\omega^1 = \omega^2 \qquad (10)$$

Thus, if

$$\omega^1 = f_1 dx_1 + f_2 dx_2 + f_3 dx_3 \qquad (11)$$

then

$$d\omega^1 = \left(\frac{\partial f_3}{\partial x_2} - \frac{\partial f_2}{\partial x_3}\right) dx_2 \wedge dx_3 + \left(\frac{\partial f_1}{\partial x_3} - \frac{\partial f_3}{\partial x_1}\right) dx_3 \wedge dx_1$$

$$+ \left(\frac{\partial f_2}{\partial x_1} - \frac{\partial f_1}{\partial x_2}\right) dx_1 \wedge dx_2$$

(12)

Comparing the coefficient functions of ω^2 and $d\omega^1$, we get

$$\overline{F} = \text{curl } \overline{f} \tag{13}$$

The question can be phrased as follows: having a vector field $\overline{F} = (F_1, F_2, F_3)$ is it possible to find a vector field $\overline{f} = (f_1, f_2, f_3)$ such that $\overline{F} = \text{curl } \overline{f}$?

Remember solenoidal fields?

A vector field whose divergence is everywhere zero is called a solenoidal field.

Theorem

A vector field $\overline{F}$ continuously differentiable is solen-oidal if, and only if, there is a vector field $\overline{f}$ such that $\overline{F} = \text{curl } \overline{f}$. The vector field $\overline{f}$ is the vector potential of $\overline{F}$.

Therefore, if the coefficients of ω^2 in eq.(9) are such that

$$\text{div } \overline{F} = \frac{\partial F_1}{\partial x_1} + \frac{\partial F_2}{\partial x_2} + \frac{\partial F_3}{\partial x_3} \neq 0 \tag{14}$$

then $\overline{F}$ does not have a vector potential. Thus, a vector field $\overline{f}$ such that

$$\overline{F} = \text{curl } \overline{f} \tag{15}$$

does not exist.

GREEN'S THEOREM, STOKES' THEOREM, DIVERGENCE THEOREM, EXACT DIFFERENTIAL FORMS

● PROBLEM 23-81

Let D be a (p+1)-dimensional region and ∂D its p-dimen-sional boundary. We can state the general Stokes' form-ula using the exterior derivative

$$\int_D d\omega^p = \int_{\partial D} \omega^p \tag{1}$$

Taking a 1-form in R^2, derive Green's theorem from eq.(1).

Solution: We have

Thus,
$$\omega^1 = F_1 dx_1 + F_2 dx_2 \qquad (2)$$

$$d\omega^1 = \left(\frac{\partial F_1}{\partial x_1} dx_1 + \frac{\partial F_1}{\partial x_2} dx_2\right) \wedge dx_1 + \left(\frac{\partial F_2}{\partial x_1} dx_1 + \frac{\partial F_2}{\partial x_2} dx_2\right) \wedge dx_2$$

$$(3)$$

$$= \left(\frac{\partial F_2}{\partial x_1} - \frac{\partial F_1}{\partial x_2}\right) dx_1 \wedge dx_2$$

Substitution of eq.(2) and eq.(3) into eq.(1) leads to

$$\int_D \left(\frac{\partial F_2}{\partial x_1} - \frac{\partial F_1}{\partial x_2}\right) dx_1 \wedge dx_2 = \int_{\partial D} F_1 dx_1 + F_2 dx_2 \qquad (4)$$

Eq.(4) resembles Green's theorem

$$\iint_B \left(\frac{\partial F_2}{\partial x_1} - \frac{\partial F_1}{\partial x_2}\right) dx_1 dx_2 = \int_C F_1 dx_1 + F_2 dx_2 \qquad (5)$$

Thus, in our case, D stands for a suitable region in R^2 and ∂D is its counter-clockwise-oriented boundary curve. Note that the left-hand integral in eq.(4) is defined as an integral over a parametrized set, while the surface integral

$$\iint_B \left(\frac{\partial F_2}{\partial x_1} - \frac{\partial F_1}{\partial x_2}\right) dx_1 dx_2$$

in Green's theorem is evaluated over a set B without a parametrization. The difference is that parametrization of D may cover D more than once, while the surface integral in eq.(5) covers each part of B only once.

● **PROBLEM 23-82**

Taking a 1-form in R^3, derive the Stokes' formula from

$$\int_D d\omega^p = \int_{\partial D} \omega^p \qquad (1)$$

See Problem 23-81.

Solution: Let
$$\omega^1 = F_1 dx_1 + F_2 dx_2 + F_3 dx_3 \qquad (2)$$

The exterior derivative of ω^1 is

$$d\omega^1 = \left(\frac{\partial F_3}{\partial x_2} - \frac{\partial F_2}{\partial x_3}\right) dx_2 \wedge dx_3 + \left(\frac{\partial F_1}{\partial x_3} - \frac{\partial F_3}{\partial x_1}\right) dx_3 \wedge dx_1$$

$$+ \left(\frac{\partial F_2}{\partial x_1} - \frac{\partial F_1}{\partial x_2}\right) dx_1 \wedge dx_2 \tag{3}$$

The differential two-form $d\omega^1$ has, as coefficient functions, the components of curl $\overline{F}$ where $\overline{F} = (F_1, F_2, F_3)$.

Therefore, if D is a bounded surface and ∂D is the closed curve bounding the surface, then eq.(1) leads to Stokes' theorem.

$$\int_D \left[\left(\frac{\partial F_3}{\partial x_2} - \frac{\partial F_2}{\partial x_3}\right) dx_2 \wedge dx_3 + \left(\frac{\partial F_1}{\partial x_3} - \frac{\partial F_3}{\partial x_1}\right) dx_3 \wedge dx_1\right.$$

$$\left. + \left(\frac{\partial F_2}{\partial x_1} - \frac{\partial F_1}{\partial x_2}\right) dx_1 \wedge dx_2\right] = \int_{\partial D} F_1 dx_1 + F_2 dx_2 + F_3 dx_3 \tag{4}$$

● **PROBLEM** 23-83

Derive the divergence formula from

$$\int_D d\omega^p = \iint_{\partial D} \omega^p \tag{1}$$

Hint: Consider a differential two-form

$$\omega^2 = F_1 dx_2 \wedge dx_3 + F_2 dx_3 \wedge dx_1 + F_3 dx_1 \wedge dx_2 \tag{2}$$

Solution: Let us evaluate the exterior derivative of

$$d\omega^2 = \left(\frac{\partial F_1}{\partial x_1} + \frac{\partial F_2}{\partial x_2} + \frac{\partial F_3}{\partial x_3}\right) dx_1 \wedge dx_2 \wedge dx_3 \tag{3}$$

The coefficient function is the divergence of the vector field $\overline{F} = (F_1, F_2, F_3)$.

Substituting eqs.(2) and (3) into eq.(1) results in

$$\int_D \left(\frac{\partial F_1}{\partial x_1} + \frac{\partial F_2}{\partial x_2} + \frac{\partial F_3}{\partial x_3}\right) dx_1 \wedge dx_2 \wedge dx_3$$

$$= \int_{\partial D} F_1 dx_2 \wedge dx_3 + F_2 dx_3 \wedge dx_1 + F_3 dx_1 \wedge dx_2 \tag{4}$$

The divergence theorem states that

$$\iiint_D \left(\frac{\partial F_1}{\partial x_1} + \frac{\partial F_2}{\partial x_2} + \frac{\partial F_3}{\partial x_3} \right) dx_1\, dx_2\, dx_3$$

$$= \iint_{\partial D} F_1\, dx_2\, dx_3 + F_2\, dx_1\, dx_3 + F_3\, dx_1\, dx_2 \qquad (5)$$

The volume integral in eq.(5) is not identical with the integral of a three-form in eq.(4). For an explanation, see Problem 23-81. If $\overline{F}$ is a vector field in R^3, $\overline{F} = (F_1, F_2, F_3)$ and f a real-valued function, then we have the following correspondence.

if $\omega^0 \leftrightarrow f$,   then $d\omega^0 \leftrightarrow$ grad f

if $\omega^1 \leftrightarrow \overline{F}$,   then $d\omega^1 \leftrightarrow$ curl $\overline{F}$

if $\omega^2 \leftrightarrow \overline{F}$,   then $d\omega^2 \leftrightarrow$ div $\overline{F}$

(F_1, F_2, F_3) are coefficient functions of the differential form.

● **PROBLEM 23-84**

Show that $\qquad\qquad d\omega^2 = 0 \qquad\qquad\qquad$ (1)

where

$$\omega^2 = \frac{x_1}{(x_1^2 + x_2^2 + x_3^2)^{\frac{3}{2}}} dx_2 \wedge dx_3$$

$$(2)$$

$$+ \frac{x_2}{(x_1^2 + x_2^2 + x_3^2)^{\frac{3}{2}}} dx_3 \wedge dx_1$$

$$+ \frac{x_3}{(x_1^2 + x_2^2 + x_3^2)^{\frac{3}{2}}} dx_1 \wedge dx_2$$

Also, show that ω^2, given by eq.(2), is not exact. Hint: evaluate

$$\int_S \omega^2 \qquad\qquad\qquad (3)$$

where S is a unit sphere and show that

$$\int_S \omega^2 \neq 0.$$

Solution: Let us write eq.(2) in the form

$$\omega^2 = f_1 dx_2 \wedge dx_3 + f_2 dx_3 \wedge dx_1 + f_3 dx_1 \wedge dx_2 \qquad (4)$$

Hence,

$$d\omega^2 = \left[\frac{\partial f_1}{\partial x_1} + \frac{\partial f_2}{\partial x_2} + \frac{\partial f_3}{\partial x_3}\right] dx_1 \wedge dx_2 \wedge dx_3 \qquad (5)$$

We have

$$\frac{\partial f_1}{\partial x_1} = (x_1^2 + x_2^2 + x_3^2)^{-\frac{3}{2}} + \left[-\frac{3}{2}\right](2x_1^2)(x_1^2 + x_2^2 + x_3^2)^{-\frac{5}{2}} \qquad (6)$$

$$\frac{\partial f_2}{\partial x_2} = (x_1^2 + x_2^2 + x_3^2)^{-\frac{3}{2}} + \left[-\frac{3}{2}\right](2x_2^2)(x_1^2 + x_2^2 + x_3^2)^{-\frac{5}{2}} \qquad (7)$$

$$\frac{\partial f_3}{\partial x_3} = (x_1^2 + x_2^2 + x_3^2)^{-\frac{3}{2}} + \left[-\frac{3}{2}\right](2x_3^2)(x_1^2 + x_2^2 + x_3^2)^{-\frac{5}{2}} \qquad (8)$$

Adding equations (6) through (8) results in

$$\frac{\partial f_1}{\partial x_1} + \frac{\partial f_2}{\partial x_2} + \frac{\partial f_3}{\partial x_3} = 0 \qquad (8)$$

From eq.(5) we obtain

$$d\omega^2 = 0 \qquad (9)$$

To compute integral (3), we shall parametrize the unit sphere S as follows:

$$\begin{aligned} x_1 &= \sin\phi\cos\theta & 0 \le \phi \le \pi \\ x_2 &= \sin\phi\sin\theta & 0 \le \theta \le 2\pi \\ x_3 &= \cos\phi \end{aligned} \qquad (10)$$

Now, applying the results of Problem 23-72, we evaluate $\int_S \omega^2$.

We have,

$$\frac{\partial(x_1, x_2)}{\partial(\phi, \theta)} = \det\begin{pmatrix} \frac{\partial x_1}{\partial \phi} & \frac{\partial x_1}{\partial \theta} \\ \frac{\partial x_2}{\partial \phi} & \frac{\partial x_2}{\partial \theta} \end{pmatrix} = \det\begin{pmatrix} \cos\phi\cos\theta & -\sin\phi\sin\theta \\ \cos\phi\sin\theta & \sin\phi\cos\theta \end{pmatrix}$$

$$ (11)$$

$$= \sin\phi\cos\phi$$

$$\frac{\partial(x_3, x_1)}{\partial(\phi, \theta)} = \sin^2\phi\sin\theta$$

(12)

$$\frac{\partial(x_2, x_3)}{\partial(\phi, \theta)} = \sin^2\phi\cos\theta$$

Thus,

$$\int_S \omega^2 = \int_{\theta=0}^{2\pi} \int_{\phi=0}^{\pi} \left[(\sin\phi\cos\theta)(\sin^2\phi\cos\theta) \right.$$

$$+ (\sin\phi\sin\theta)(\sin^2\phi\sin\theta) + (\cos\phi)(\cos\phi\sin\phi) \Big] d\phi d\theta$$

$$= \int_{\theta=0}^{2\pi} \int_{\phi=0}^{\pi} \left[\sin^3\phi\cos^2\theta + \sin^3\phi\sin^2\theta + \cos^2\phi\sin\phi \right] d\phi d\theta$$

$$= \int_{\theta=0}^{2\pi} \int_{\phi=0}^{\pi} \sin\phi d\phi d\theta = 4\pi$$

INDEX

Numbers on this page refer to <u>PROBLEM NUMBERS</u>, not page numbers

Abelian group, 9-2, 9-3
Acceleration:
    angular, 5-43
    centripetal, 5-47
    normal component of, 5-27
    to 5-29
    of a particle, 5-19, 5-20,
    5-24, 5-26, 5-29, 5-47
    tangential component of,
    5-27 to 5-29
    vector, 5-19 to 5-21, 5-46
Additive inverse, 9-4, 9-5
Aerial velocity, 12-7, 12-8,
    12-10
Angular momentum, 5-35, 5-
    36, 12-7
    rate of change of, 5-33, 5-
    36, 12-7
Angular velocity, 5-22, 5-43,
    11-15
Annulus, 2-8
Arc:
    parametric representation,
    12-11
Arc length, 4-16, 12-13, 22-
    6, 22-37
    along a curve, 22-12
    differential of, 7-8
    element of, 21-27, 22-24
    square of an element of,
    21-19, 21-35, 22-13, 22-41

Area:
    cosine principal, 14-8, 14-
    9
    instantaneous rate of
    change, 12-8
Associative law, 23-4, 23-8
Auxiliary equation, 4-26, 4-27

Base vectors, 2-18 to 2-23,
    3-6, 3-12, 3-22, 8-20, 18-1
Biharmonic functions, 6-34
Binary operation, 9-1
Binomial expansion, 11-30
Binormal vector, 5-4 to 5-6,
    5-9, 5-11, 5-15
Boundary curve, 20-3, 20-5,
    20-10, 23-47
Cardioid, 13-25, 21-1
Cartesian coordinates:
    description of, 1-3, 21-1
Cartesian space, 18-1
Catenary, 13-23
Cauchy-Rieman equations,
    17-44, 19-56
Central force field, 12-7, 12-8
Centroid, 13-21
Chain rule, 7-14, 22-4

Change of variables:
    formula, 16-4
    theorem, 15-2
Characteristic vectors, 5-2 to
    5-8
Circular helix:
    parametric equations of, 4-5
Coefficient function, 23-79,
    23-80, 23-83
Cofactors, 10-12
Collinear vector, 1-14
Commutative:
    group, 9-2
    law, 23-4, 23-6
    operation, 9-3
    ring, 9-3, 9-4
Complex-valued functions, 17-
    17-44
Composite functions, 6-9 to
    6-11
Congruence, 9-2
Conic section, 5-40
    polar equation of, 12-9
Conservation of energy:
    principle of, 12-42, 18-6
Conservative fields, 18-1 to
    18-4
Constant vectors, 19-22 to 19-
    24
Continuity, 7-16
    definition of, 6-1
Continuity equation:
    for an electric charge, 11-33
    for an incompressible fluid,
    11-12
    for a fluid flow, 11-13, 11-
    14, 11-16, 11-19
Continuous function, 4-3, 4-7,
    6-1
Convex set, 17-4
Coordinate curves:
    definition of, 22-2
    of a curvilinear coordinate
    system, 21-5
    of the cylindrical coordinate
    system, 21-6
    of the spherical coordinate
    system, 21-18, 21-26

Coordinate surfaces:
    definition of, 22-2
    of a curvilinear coordinate
    system, 21-5
    of the cylindrical coordin-
    ate system, 21-6
    of the spherical coordinate
    system, 21-18
Coplanar vectors, 3-31, 3-32,
    3-47, 23-22
Coriolis acceleration, 5-47
Correspondence:
    one-to-one, 9-24, 9-25
Coulomb's law, 11-29, 19-69
Cramer's rule, 23-31
Cross product (see vector
    product)
Curl, 8-3, 8-18, 8-22, 8-28,
    8-35, 17-50, 22-19, 22-20
    of a gradient field, 8-8,
    23-79
    of a vector, 11-8, 11-9, 11-
    15
    of a vector field, 8-1, 8-9,
    11-3, 11-4, 11-8, 12-34 to
    12-36, 12-38, 12-41, 20-1,
    20-2, 20-8, 20-9, 20-32
Curvature, 5-2, 5-4, 5-5, 5-
    8, 5-9, 5-13, 5-29
    radius of, 5-2, 5-4, 5-10,
    5-12, 5-26, 5-30
Curves:
    in space, 4-3, 5-1, 7-7
    length of, 12-12, 12-14
    parametric equation of, 4-
    3 to 4-5, 17-19, 17-20, 17-
    23, 17-26, 17-30, 17-31
    piecewise-smooth, 17-1, 17-
    3, 18-1, 18-2, 18-9, 18-15
    plane, 5-11, 5-17
Curvilinear coordinates:
    definition of, 21-4, 22-1
    general, 22-4, 22-13, 22-14,
    22-44, 22-48
    orthogonal, 21-8, 21-19, 21-
    29, 22-2, 22-3, 22-9, 22-11,
    22-15 to 22-17, 22-29, 22-37
Cylinders:

coaxial, 16-18
intersection of, 20-18
Cylindrical coordinates, 5-24,
19-7, 22-25, 22-39
curl of a vector field in,
21-40, 21-41
description of, 21-6
differential of arc length in,
21-14, 21-15
divergence of a vector field
in, 21-38, 31-39
gradient in, 21-36, 21-37
scalar field in, 21-36
vector field in, 21-38
vectors in, 21-10, 21-12,
21-13, 21-36
volume element in, 21-16,
21-17, 21-30
volume integrals in, 21-17,
21-32

D'Alembertian operator, 11-36,
18-19
Definite integral, 12-1
of a scalar product, 12-3
Del operator, 7-10, 7-16, 7-
22, 8-36, 10-20, 11-5, 11-
22
definition of, 8-6
usage of, 20-1
Derivatives, 4-11, 4-15
of higher order, 4-19
of ordinary functions, 4-9
of vector functions, 4-8
Determinants, 2-17, 3-34, 10-
11, 10-12
expansion of, 10-11
multiplication theorem, 9-34
of a matrix, 23-16 to 23-19,
23-27
Differential equations:
vector solution to, 4-26
4-27
Differential form:

integrals of, 23-69 to 23-72
one-form, 23-55 to 23-57,
23-62 to 23-64
p-form, 23-66 to 23-68
three-form, 23-62, 23-74
two-form, 23-60 to 23-62
zero form, 23-75, 23-77

Differential geometry, 5-2
Differential operators of scalar and vector fields, 8-39
Differentiation:
exterior, 23-75 to 23-80,
23-84
operation, 9-28
of a scalar product, 12-5
of vector functions, 4-8,
4-9, 4-12 to 4-14, 4-23
Dipole, 2-23, 11-30
Direction cosines, 2-11, 3-3,
6-29
Directional derivative, 6-29 to
6-32
Displacement vector, 11-11
Divergence, 8-6, 8-18, 8-28,
8-35
of a function, 7-31
of a gradient, 7-18, 7-20,
7-24
of a vector field, 7-16 to
7-20, 7-23, 7-28, 7-30, 8-
10, 8-14, 8-16, 8-30, 10-
20, 11-1, 11-2, 11-11, 11-
16, 11-17, 19-6, 19-7, 22-
18, 22-23
of a vector product, 8-22,
8-26, 11-9
of the curl of a vector,
8-8, 23-79
Divergence theorem, 19-1 to
19-72
definition of, 19-43, 19-52
physical significance of,
19-54
proof of, 19-2
rectangular form of, 19-1
verification of, 19-13 to
19-15, 21-54

Domain, 12-28
    simply connected, 12-28, 12-34
    spherical, 10-23
Dot product (see scalar product)
Double integral, 13-6 to 13-19
    definition of, 13-6
    use of to evaluate area, 13-13 to 13-16
    use of to evaluate volume, 13-13, 13-17 to 13-19
Dummy index, 10-3, 10-12
Dummy variable, 10-5
Dyadic, 8-36 to 8-38

e-system, 10-10
Einstein convention, 10-3, 23-41, 23-48
Elastic-isotropic materials, 11-11
Elasticity, 11-11
Electric charges, 2-23
Electric field, 15-9, 15-11
Electromagnetic induction:
    Faraday's law, 20-39, 20-40
Electromagnetics, 11-26 to 11-37, 19-68
Electrostatic field, 15-10
Electrostatic potential, 15-9
    of a unit charge, 11-6
Ellipse, 11-7
    equation of, 9-13
Ellipsoid of inertia, 16-28
Elliptic cylindrical coordinates, 22-28
Entropy:
    definition of, 19-66
Euclidean space, 1-3, 4-4
Euler:
    equation of, 19-60
    expansion formula of, 23-54
    formula of, 17-44

theorem of for homogeneous functions, 8-34
Exact differential of a function, 12-40, 12-41, 18-7
Explicit function, 14-1
Exterior product:
    of one-forms, 23-57 to 23-59
    of p-forms, 23-68

Fibonacci sequence, 23-9
First law of thermodynamics, 19-63
First order systems, 10-1, 10-5, 10-6
Fluid flow, 20-32
    incompressible, 11-16, 11-17, 11-19, 11-21, 11-22
Flux, 11-1, 11-2
    of a fluid flow, 15-1, 15-2
    of a force field, 15-8
    of a vector field, 14-16 to 14-20, 14-26, 19-43
    through a moving surface, 23-43
Flux transport theorem, 23-47, 23-50
    proof of, 23-49
    verification of, 23-45, 23-46
Folium of Descartes:
    area of, 17-19
Force density, 11-11
Force field:
    constant, 3-14
    continuous, 18-3
Four-leaved rose:
    area of, 17-22
Frenet formulas, 5-2, 5-3, 5-5, 5-8 to 5-14
Function space, 9-7
Functional dependence, 7-15
Functionally related functions, 7-14, 7-15
Fundamental lemma, 6-4, 6-6

Gauss:
    law of, 15-10, 16-34, 16-35
    theorem of, 17-42, 17-43,
    19-47, 19-70
Gradient operator, 11-23
    definition of, 8-1
    properties of, 6-20 to 6-25
Gravitational field, 3-14, 6-14,
    11-5
Gravitational force, 2-3, 5-40
Green's first identity, 19-30,
    19-31
    proof of, 19-28
Green's second identity, 19-30,
    19-35
    proof of, 19-29
Green's theorem, 17-1 to 17-
    36, 20-10, 20-29
    applications of, 17-1 to 17-
    23
    for a multiply-connected
    region, 17-27 to 17-31, 17-
    33
    in vector notation, 17-34 to
    17-36, 17-38
    proof of, 17-1, 17-33
    verification of, 17-3, 17-4,
    17-28, 17-29
Gradient, 7-11, 7-12, 7-18, 7-
    24, 7-31, 8-3, 8-4, 19-57
    computation of, 6-28
    definition of, 6-23, 19-45
    field, 18-1
    of a scalar function, 6-16
    to 6-20, 7-10, 7-29, 8-7,
    8-15, 8-16, 8-30, 8-36, 10-
    20, 11-5,
    of a vector function, 22-16,
    22-25
    of the divergence of a vec-
    tor, 7-26, 7-29
    vector, 6-31
Group:
    definiton of, 9-2
    finite, 9-2
    infinite, 9-2
Gyration:
    radius of, 13-24

Harmonic conjugate, 19-56
Harmonic functions, 6-34, 11-
    6, 17-43, 19-31 to 19-36,
    19-56, 19-58, 19-61, 19-68
Heat equation, 19-61
    in spherical coordinates,
    21-51
Heat flow, 11-24, 11-25
    across a surface, 15-4; 15-
    5
Helix:
    arc length of, 12-13
    circular, 5-8
Hemisphere:
    open, 20-37
    surface of, 20-13, 20-16,
    20-22, 20-36
Hodograph, 5-37
Hydrostatics, 11-18
Hyperbolic:
    cosine, 12-12
    sine, 12-12
Hypocycloid:
    area of, 17-20

Identities:
    basic, 3-28, 3-31 to 3-35
    involving the characteris-
    tic vectors, 5-14 to 5-17
    involving the gradient, di-
    vergence, and curl, 7-23
    to 7-27, 8-18 to 8-26, 8-
    28 to 8-35, 8-39, 10-21, 10-
    23, 20-24 to 20-26, 22-10
    symmetrical, 19-29
Implicit function, 14-1
Incompressible fluid, 17-42,
    19-55, 19-56
Indical notation, 10-1
Integral of a vector, 12-2, 12-
    4
    indefinite, 12-1
Integration:
    operation, 9-28

order of, 13-9 to 13-11, 13-15, 13-17

Invariance of distances, 9-14, 9-17, 9-18

Inverse of a function, 9-7

Inviscid fluid, 11-19

Irrotational:
  field, 11-8, 11-11, 17-39, 17-44, 19-57
  flow, 19-55 to 19-57

Iterated integral, 13-7, 13-17, 17-1
  n-fold, 16-19

Jacobian, 13-27, 13-28, 13-30, 17-52
  determinant, 6-11
  of a transformation, 16-14, 16-16, 21-2, 21-33, 21-34, 22-50, 22-51

Kepler's laws, 12-8, 12-9

Kinematics:
  basic definitions of, 12-6

Kinetic energy, 12-26, 18-3
  conservation of, 5-41, 5-42

Kronecker delta, 3-9, 9-33, 9-34, 10-3, 10-21, 22-4, 23-27

Lagrange identity, 3-34

Lamina, 17-32

Laplace's equation, 7-20, 8-14, 8-35, 11-29, 19-55, 19-56, 22-27

Laplacian, ∇^2, 6-33, 7-18, 7-20, 7-23, 7-27, 8-14, 10-22, 11-6, 17-43
  in cylindrical coordinates, 21-42
  in orthogonal curvilinear coordinates, 22-22
  in polar coordinates, 21-47
  in spherical coordinates, 21-47, 21-48, 21-51

Law of cosines, 1-23, 3-7, 3-15

Law of sines, 1-23, 3-19

Left-handed coordinate system, 1-4, 22-11

Leibnitz's rule, 20-39

Lemniscate of Bernoulli, 13-29, area of, 17-23

L'Hôpital's rule, 5-1, 7-1

Light:
  reflection of, 11-7

Limiting position, 4-9, 5-1

Line:
  equation of, 3-39, 3-40, 22-50
  parallel to a vector, 3-39
  parametric equation of, 12-15
  perpendicular to a plane, 3-40
  through a point, 3-40

Line integral, 12-14 to 12-23, 12-36, 17-3, 20-6 to 20-9, 20-13 to 20-18, 20-43
  along a closed curve, 12-20, 12-21, 12-37, 17-4, 17-7, 17-9, 17-12

  independent of path, 17-45 to 17-47, 18-1 to 18-3, 18-9, 18-20, 19-57, 19-67

Linear combination:
  of base vectors, 7-3, 7-9
  of vectors, 3-30, 9-15, 9-29

Linear independence, 9-9, 9-26, 9-29

Linearly independent solutions,

4-26, 4-27

Locus of a point, 2-8, 2-9, 2-13

Lorentz force, 11-31, 11-35

Magic square, 9-6

Magnetic field, 12-28

Magnitude of an electric field:
    of a long thin wire, 15-11
    of an infinite plate, 15-12

Mapping:
    definition of, 9-1
    many-to-one, 9-1
    of a set, 9-1
    one-to-one, 9-1

Mass:
    center of, 5-34

Matrices:
    addition of, 23-3, 23-4
    linear combination of, 9-9
    products of, 23-3, 23-5 to 23-8

Matrix:
    anticommutative, 23-10
    anti-symmetric, 23-14, 23-33
    definition of, 23-1
    diagonal, 23-12
    equation of, 23-11
    identity, 23-12
    independent elements of, 23-33
    inverse of, 23-20, 23-21, 23-26 to 23-28, 23-30
    Jacobian, 18-11, 18-12, 18-14
    left inverse of, 23-25
    $m \times n$, 23-1, 23-12
    orthogonal, 23-32, 23-36, 23-37
    right inverse of, 23-21, 23-24, 23-25
    symmetric, 23-14, 23-32
    transformation, 23-34 to

23-40
    transpose of, 23-13

Maxwell's equations, 7-16, 11-27 to 11-29, 11-31 to 11-36, 16-35, 19-68, 19-71, 19-73,
    in spherical coordinates, 21-53

Maxwell's law of electromagnetism, 20-38

Mean value theorem for integrals, 19-43 to 19-45, 20-32

Metric coefficients, 21-34, 22-13

Möbius strip, 13-2

Modulus operation, 9-4

Moment of inertia, 13-22 to 13-25, 19-53
    about an arbitrary point, 16-27, 16-28
    about a coordinate axis, 16-24, 16-25
    of a sphere, 16-26
    polar, 13-26

Momentum:
    conservation of, 5-42
    linear, 5-33

Motion of a particle, 12-7

n-tuples, 23-1

Nabla operator (see Del operator)

Neutron diffusion equation, 11-37

Newtonian potential function, 15-8

Newton's:
    law of gravitation, 12-8, 18-5
    second law, 5-31 to 5-33, 5-36, 11-19, 12-7, 12-26, 18-3, 19-59
    third law, 5-34, 5-36

Non-parametric form of a surface, 13-4

Normal component of a vector:
    integration of, 12-25
Normal plane, 5-7
Null vector, 3-4

Oersted's law, 20-40
Open coordinate rectangle,
    18-13, 18-14
Operators, 8-21, 8-24, 8-31,
    8-32, 19-46
Ordinary functions, 4-11
Orthogonality of a system:
    conditions for, 22-31, 22-
    32, 22-38
Osculating plane, 5-7

Pappus:
    theorem of, 17-32
Parabolic cylindrical coordin-
    ates, 22-27
    description of, 21-35
Paraboloid, 13-18, 20-14, 20-
    15
Parallelepiped, 3-27, 11-12
Parallelogram:
    area of, 3-24
    method, 1-19, 1-22
Partial derivative, 6-2, 6-3,
    6-10, 7-5, 7-6, 7-27
    geometrical interpretation
    of, 6-2
    identities of, 7-10
    of functions, 7-1
    of vector functions, 7-1 to
    7-4
Particles:
    collision of, 4-4, 5-41, 5-
    42
    velocity of, 5-18 to 5-20,
    5-24, 5-47

Partition construction, 16-2
Permutations, 3-26, 23-15
Pfaff problem, 6-7
Plane:
    equation of, 3-41 to 3-43
    perpendicular to a vector,
    3-42, 3-43
    tangent to a sphere, 3-44
Planetary motion, 12-8, 12-9
Poisson's equation, 11-29, 18-
    19, 19-36, 19-69
Polar coordinates, 5-23, 5-35,
    13-8, 13-25, 13-28, 13-29,
    14-12, 14-29, 14-32, 17-18,
    17-21, 17-23, 17-50, 21-1,
    21-3
Polyhedron, 3-25
Position vector, 2-23, 3-12, 3-
    39, 5-5, 5-12, 5-18, 5-22,
    5-23, 5-32, 9-11, 14-1, 14-
    18, 19-47, 19-70
    in cylindrical coordinates,
    21-9
    in spherical coordinates,
    21-27
    of a fixed point in space,
    7-12
Potential:
    energy, 12-26
    function, 9-8, 18-1, 18-4,
    18-5, 18-8, 18-10, 18-15,
    18-18, 18-19
    of a sphere, 15-13, 15-14
Pythagorean theorem, 2-2

Quadratic form:
    definition of fundamental,
    22-13

Rate of change, 5-2

Rationals:
    set of, 9-4
Real numbers:
    set of, 9-4
Reciprocal vectors, 3-36 to 3-38, 23-22
Rectifying plane, 5-7
Reynold's number, 11-22
Reynold's transport theorem:
    application of, 23-52, 23-54
    proof of, 23-53
    verification of, 23-51
Riemann sum, 16-1
Right-handed coordinate system, 1-4, 2-19, 3-16, 9-34
Rigid body:
    planar motion of, 5-45
Rotation, 8-17, 17-34
    angle of, 9-18
    of axes, 9-18
    of a rigid body, 5-43, 5-44
Rotation of a vector (see curl)

Scalar quantity, 1-1
Scalar:
    field, 6-12, 6-13, 6-15 to 6-20, 7-23, 7-29, 8-13, 8-39, 11-23, 18-19
    potential, 8-11, 8-13, 8-27, 11-29, 11-30, 11-34, 12-38, 12-44, 18-17, 18-19, 18-20
    triple product, 3-26, 3-31, 3-32, 23-23
Scalar product, 3-1 to 3-16, 5-16, 10-16, 10-19
    commutative law for, 3-2
    definition, 3-3
    of base vectors, 3-9
Scale factors, 22-26, 22-28,
    definition of, 22-6
    evaluation of, 22-8, 22-34, to 22-37
    in terms of gradients, 22-7

of curvilinear coordinates, 21-8, 21-30
of cylindrical coordinate, 21-14, 21-34
of parabolic cylindrical coordinates, 21-35
of spherical coordinates, 21-21, 21-30, 21-34
Schrödinger's equation of quantum mechanics, 21-52
Second fundamental form, 14-5
Second law of thermodynamics, 19-66
Second order systems, 10-1, 10-6, 10-7, 10-9
    skew-symmetric, 10-7, 10-8
    sum of, 10-8
    symmetric, 10-7, 10-8
Semi-magic square, 9-6
Set, 9-1
Shear strain, 11-20
Shear stress, 11-20
Sink field, 11-14
Solenoid, 7-29
Solenoidal vector field, 7-31, 8-14, 11-11, 20-23
Solid angle, 14-13
Space:
    four-dimensional, 9-9, 9-29
    three dimensional, 2-17, 2-22, 3-9, 3-15
    two dimensional, 3-9
Space curve, 5-1 to 5-5, 5-9, 5-11 to 5-13, 5-15, 5-16
    parametric form of, 5-1, 5-9, 5-10, 5-17, 5-19
Span set, 9-10
Speed:
    of a particle, 5-18, 5-22, 5-23, 5-29, 5-44
    of a travelling wave, 11-11
Sphere, 3-44 to 3-46
    equation of, 3-45, 3-46, 9-12
    hollow, 15-6
    parametric form, 15-2

surface area of, 22-43
total mass of, 16-21
Spherical coordinates, 19-8,
  21-18, 22-24, 22-26, 23-51
  curl of a vector field in,
  21-46, 21-49, 21-53
  description of, 21-18
  divergence of a vector field
  in, 21-45, 21-47, 21-49,
  21-50
  element of arc length in,
  21-27
  element of volume in, 21-27
  21-54
  gradient of a function in,
  21-43, 21-44
  use of in volume integrals,
  21-28, 21-30, 21-31
Square array, 7-16
Square matrix, 19-52, 23-1,
  23-2, 23-9, 23-12, 23-17
  inverse of, 23-26 to 23-28
  nonsingular, 23-27
  singular, 23-27
Stokes' derivative, 11-13, 19-55
Stokes' theorem, 17-39, 23-42,
  23-50
  applications of, 20-12 to 20-
  19, 20-20 to 20-28, 20-30
  to 20-47
  derivation of, 23-82
  for surfaces in parametric
  form, 20-30, 20-31
  in cartesian form, 20-11
  in component form, 20-3
  in vector form, 20-3
  proof of, 20-10
  verification of, 20-5 to 20-
  9, 20-29, 21-55
Summation convention, 10-3,
  10-5, 10-14
Superposition:
  principle of, 11-29, 11-30
Surface:
  area, 14-1 to 14-4, 14-6 to
  14-8, 14-10, 14-11, 14-13,
  14-15
  element, 14-2, 19-50

parametric form of, 13-3 to
  13-5, 14-16, 14-26, 14-27
piecewise-smooth, 13-1, 13-
2
  tension, 11-10
Surface integral, 14-30, 14-31,
  16-32, 16-33
  cartesian form of, 14-30,
  14-32
  evaluation of, 20-5 to 20-9,
  20-14 to 20-18, 20-38
Surfaces, 14-1
  equipotential, 18-5
  intersecting, 6-27, 6-28
  isotimic, 6-33
  smooth, 13-1

Tangent plane, 6-26
Taylor's formula, 11-18
Temperature gradient, 15-4,
  15-6, 15-7
Tensor notation, 10-16 to 10-
  19, 10-22, 10-23, 23-48
Tetrahedron, 3-25
Third order systems, 10-1,
  10-2, 10-8, 10-10
  skew-symmetric, 10-8
Time derivative operator, 5-46
Torque, 11-20
Torsion, 5-2, 5-4, 5-5, 5-9,
  5-11, 5-16, 5-17
  radius of, 5-4
Torus, 12-28, 20-17
Total derivative, 19-59
Total differential, 6-4 to 6-6
  definition of, 6-5
Trajectory of a particle, 5-22,
  5-38, 5-39, 12-10
Transformation:
  equations, 9-12, 9-14, 9-17,
  9-33, 9-34, 9-37, 22-1, 22-
  35, 22-50
  identity, 9-20
  inverse, 9-16, 9-25, 9-35,

21-7, 21-20
laws, 22-46
linear, 9-19 to 9-24, 9-26
to 9-28, 9-30 to 9-32
linear orthogonal, 23-36,
23-39, 23-40
non-linear, 9-21
of coordinates, 5-32, 13-
27, 13-28, 13-30
one-to-one, 9-25, 9-27
onto, 9-25, 9-27
orthogonal, 13-27, 22-36
plane, 7-14, 22-30
product, 9-23
Translation of axes, 9-13, 9-14
Transposition, 23-13
Triadic, 8-36
Triangle:
area of, 3-24, 17-26
Trigonometric substitution,
13-7
Triple integral, 16-10, 16-15,
16-21
Two-dimensional operator, 11-
10

Unit cube:
n-dimensional, 16-20
Unit dyads, 8-36, 8-37
Unit normal, 13-1
vector, 5-5, 5-26, 13-5,
14-1, 14-2, 14-15, 14-20,
14-24, 14-32, 17-34, 17-
39, 22-9, 22-21, 22-47
Unit tangent:
to an ellipse, 11-7
vector, 5-4, 5-5, 5-9 to 5-
13, 5-26, 17-34, 17-39, 21-
8, 22-9
Unit vectors, 2-1, 2-4, 2-5,
3-6, 3-11, 6-31, 7-7, 7-11,
7-12, 8-30, 8-31, 11-7, 22-
40
mutually orthogonal, 5-2,

7-11

Vectors:
addition of, 1-17, 1-19
analytical operations on, 1-
17, 1-19 to 1-21
components of, 1-18, 3-20,
7-3, 7-23, 7-28, 7-30, 8-
2, 8-6, 8-23 to 8-25, 8-29,
8-31, 8-33, 11-1, 11-12
constant, 4-19, 7-23
definition of, 1-1
direction of, 2-6
graphical addition of, 1-8,
1-9
graphical construction of,
1-9, 1-13, 1-19
graphical representation of,
1-5 to 1-7, 2-10
graphical subtraction of,
1-9
laws of addition on, 1-10
laws of subtraction of, 1-
10
linear combination of, 2-12,
2-15, 2-16, 2-21, 2-22
linear dependence of, 2-14,
2-17
linearly dependent set of,
9-27
magnitude of, 2-1 to 2-7,
3-8, 7-12, 11-15
moment of, 3-47
multiplication of, 3-30
n-dimensional, 2-1, 2-12
non-collinear, 1-14
non-coplanar, 1-15
normal to a surface, 7-7,
7-11, 13-1, 13-3 to 13-5,
14-15, 14-17
operations, 1-16
orthogonal, 3-36, 9-17, 13-
27
perpendicular to a plane,

3-11
perpendicular to a surface, 7-11
principal normal, 5-4, 5-6 5-9
projection of a, 3-6
representation of, 1-1
subtraction, 1-17, 1-19
sum of, 1-10, 2-5
tangent to a curve, 4-10, 5-1, 5-2, 5-6, 7-7, 21-8
three-dimensional, 2-4, 2-15, 2-16
two-dimensional, 2-2, 2-15, 2-16
velocity, 4-17, 5-19 to 5-23, 5-25, 11-9
Vector fields, 6-12 to 6-14, 6-31, 7-10, 8-9, 8-10, 8-12, 8-39, 11-1 to 11-4, 11-11 to 11-16, 11-19, 11-23, 18-11, 18-12, 18-18, 18-19
algebraic operations on, 8-39
conservative, 8-11, 8-12, 12-30, 12-34, 12-37, 12-38, 12-42, 18-1 to 18-20, 20-41
continuously differentiable, 20-4, 20-14, 20-16, 20-17, 20-19, 20-20, 20-23, 20-24, 20-27 to 20-29, 20-31, 20-32, 20-35 to 20-37, 20-42, 22-14, 22-45
solenoidal, 17-44, 19-43, 20-45, 20-47
time varying, 23-43, 23-44
vector potential of, 12-44, 12-45
Vector potential, 11-32, 11-34, 20-45, 20-46
Vector product, 3-16 to 3-25, 5-16, 7-7, 7-23, 7-29, 10-16, 10-19, 12-3
component form of, 3-23
determinant form of, 3-21, 3-23, 3-26
distributive law for, 3-22
Vector space, 9-5 to 9-10, 9-

28
axioms, 9-5 to 9-10
three dimensional, 9-28
Vector triangle:
construction of, 1-8
Vector triple product, 3-26, 3-28, 12-9
Velocity:
of a fluid, 11-12, 11-16
of a particle, 12-6
relative, 5-41
Viscosity, 11-21
coefficient of, 11-20
Volume, 14-14
of a region, 16-7, 16-10, 16-11, 16-13
of a sphere, 16-8, 16-16, 16-17
Volume element:
in cylindrical coordinates, 21-16, 21-17, 21-30
in general coordinates, 22-49
in spherical coordinates, 21-27, 21-54
relative to a coordinate system, 22-33
Volume integral, 16-2 to 16-18, 16-29 to 16-32, 16-34, 16-35, 22-14
iteration of, 16-6
Vortex field, 11-8
Vortex flow of a fluid, 15-3
Vorticity, 11-19, 11-21

Wave equation, 11-11
Witch of Agnesi:
curve of, 13-12
Work, 3-13, 3-14, 12-19, 12-20, 12-26, 12-29

Zero-order system:
definition of, 10-1, 10-5
Zero transformation, 9-20
Zero vector, 1-10

HANDBOOK of
**MATHEMATICAL,
SCIENTIFIC, &
ENGINEERING**
FORMULAS, FUNCTIONS,
GRAPHS, TABLES,
& TRANSFORMS

RESEARCH & EDUCATION ASSOCIATION

A particularly useful reference for those in math, science, engineering and other technical fields. Includes the most-often used formulas, tables, transforms, functions, and graphs which are needed as tools in solving problems. The entire field of special functions is also covered. A large amount of scientific data which is often of interest to scientists and engineers has been included.

Available at your local bookstore or order directly from us by sending in coupon below.

REA's **Problem Solvers**

The "PROBLEM SOLVERS" are comprehensive supplemental text-books designed to save time in finding solutions to problems. Each "PROBLEM SOLVER" is the first of its kind ever produced in its field. It is the product of a massive effort to illustrate almost any imaginable problem in exceptional depth, detail, and clarity. Each problem is worked out in detail with a step-by-step solution, and the problems are arranged in order of complexity from elementary to advanced. Each book is fully indexed for locating problems rapidly.

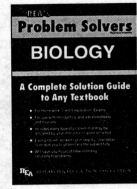

ADVANCED CALCULUS	HEAT TRANSFER
ALGEBRA & TRIGONOMETRY	LINEAR ALGEBRA
AUTOMATIC CONTROL	MACHINE DESIGN
SYSTEMS/ROBOTICS	MATHEMATICS for ENGINEERS
BIOLOGY	MECHANICS
BUSINESS, ACCOUNTING, & FINANCE	NUMERICAL ANALYSIS
CALCULUS	OPERATIONS RESEARCH
CHEMISTRY	OPTICS
COMPLEX VARIABLES	ORGANIC CHEMISTRY
COMPUTER SCIENCE	PHYSICAL CHEMISTRY
DIFFERENTIAL EQUATIONS	PHYSICS
ECONOMICS	PRE-CALCULUS
ELECTRICAL MACHINES	PSYCHOLOGY
ELECTRIC CIRCUITS	STATISTICS
ELECTROMAGNETICS	STRENGTH OF MATERIALS &
ELECTRONIC COMMUNICATIONS	MECHANICS OF SOLIDS
ELECTRONICS	TECHNICAL DESIGN GRAPHICS
FINITE & DISCRETE MATH	THERMODYNAMICS
FLUID MECHANICS/DYNAMICS	TOPOLOGY
GENETICS	TRANSPORT PHENOMENA
GEOMETRY	VECTOR ANALYSIS

*If you would like more information about any of these books,
complete the coupon below and return it to us or visit your local bookstore.*

RESEARCH & EDUCATION ASSOCIATION
61 Ethel Road W. • Piscataway, New Jersey 08854
Phone: (908) 819-8880

Please send me more information about your Problem Solver Books

Name _____

Address _____

City _____ State _____ Zip _____